W9-CIJ-439

Instructor's Annotated Edition

ESPACES

Rendez-vous avec le monde francophone

Cherie Mitschke
Southwestern University

Cheryl Tano
Emmanuel College and Tufts University

Valérie Thiers-Thiam
Borough of Manhattan Community College

Boston, Massachusetts

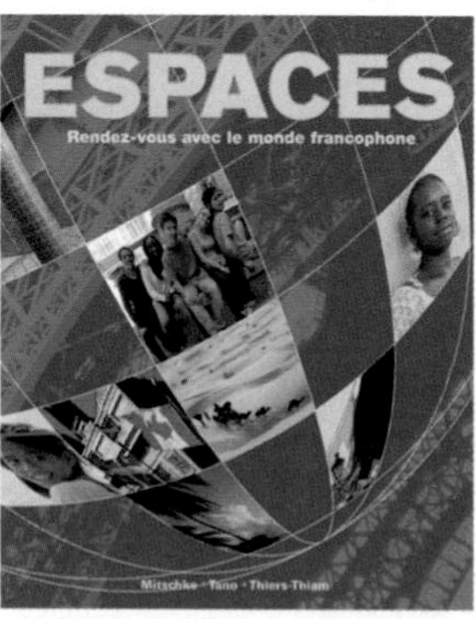

The **ESPACES** cover celebrates the diversity of the French-speaking world that you will find throughout the text and its ancillaries. Cover photos include images of (top left) a doorway in Telouet, Morocco; (middle far left) a Tahitian girl; (middle left) the flags of Quebec and Canada in Hull, Quebec; (middle right) the Sahara Desert, Algeria; (middle far right) a Senegalese woman; (bottom left) flags in Geneva, Switzerland.

Publisher: José Blanco
Senior Vice President, General Manager: Janet Dracksdorf
Vice President & Editorial Director: Denise St. Jean
Director of Art & Design: Linda Jurras
Director of Production & Manufacturing: Lisa Flanagan Perrier
Project Managers & Editors: Sharon Alexander, Marta Minnetyan
Contributing Writers: Sharon Alexander, Myriam Arcangeli, Séverine Champeny, Julie Cormier, Virginia Dosher, Rachel Dziallo, Ruthie Ford, Lynne Lipkind, Patricia Ménard, Marta Minnetyan
Design Manager: Polo Barrera
Designers: Andrea Golden, Deborah Rodman
Photo Researcher & Art Buyer: Linde Gee
Production: Oscar Diez, Mauricio Henao, María Eugenia Castaño
Manufacturing Coordinator: Gustavo Cinci
Senior Vice President, Operations: Tom Delano
Executive Marketing Manager: Ben Rivera

Student Text ISBN-13: 978-1-59334-836-6
ISBN-10: 1-59334-836-3
Instructor's Annotated Edition ISBN-13: 978-1-59334-833-5
ISBN-10: 1-59334-833-9

1 2 3 4 5 6 7 8 9 VH 10 09 08 07 06

Instructor's Annotated Edition

Table of Contents

The ESPACES Story

Vista Higher Learning, the publisher of **ESPACES**, was founded with one mission: to raise the teaching of modern languages to a higher level. In fall 2000, we published **VISTAS**, our first program for the introductory Spanish market. Developed with care and the involvement of hundreds of students and instructors, **VISTAS**, as well as the other introductory and intermediate Spanish programs we subsequently published, found wide acceptance and acclaim.

Responding to the request of many French instructors who have seen **VISTAS**, we built a team of professionals with French teaching, writing, and editing expertise to develop a new and innovative introductory French program. Throughout the process, we questioned everything about the way current textbooks support the teaching of French.

The result is **ESPACES: Rendez-vous avec le monde francophone**. It has been crafted with the same dedication as our Spanish programs, built completely around the diverse needs of students and instructors.

We welcome you and your students to **ESPACES**, and we hope that it finds a special place in your classroom. Please contact us with your questions, comments, and reactions.

Vista Higher Learning

31 St. James Avenue

Boston, MA 02116-4104

TOLLFREE: 800-618-7375

TELEPHONE: 617-426-4910

FAX: 617-426-5209

www.vistahigherlearning.com

Getting to Know ESPACES

Vibrant and original, **ESPACES** takes a fresh, student-friendly approach to introductory French aimed at making students' learning and instructors' teaching easier, more enjoyable, and more successful. At the same time, **ESPACES** takes a communicative approach to language learning. It develops students' speaking, listening, reading, and writing skills so that they will be able to express their own ideas and interact with others meaningfully and for real-life purposes. It emphasizes frequently used vocabulary, and it presents grammar as a tool for effective communication. In addition, because cultural knowledge is an integral part of both language learning and successful communication, **ESPACES** introduces students to the everyday lives of French speakers, as well as the areas and countries of the French-speaking world.

Whereas other introductory college French programs are based on many of these same pedagogical principles, **ESPACES** offers several additional features that make it truly different.

- **ESPACES** incorporates interior design—page layout, use of colors, typefaces, and other graphic elements—as an integral part of the learning process. To enhance learning and make navigation easy, lesson sections are color-coded and appear either completely on one page or on spreads of two facing pages. The textbook pages themselves are also visually dramatic, with an array of photos, drawings, realia, charts, graphs, diagrams, and word lists, all designed for both instructional impact and visual appeal.
- **ESPACES** integrates video with the student textbook in a distinct, more cohesive way up-front in each lesson's **Roman-photo** section, throughout every lesson's **Structures** section, and in each end-of-unit **Savoir-faire** section.
- **ESPACES** offers **Coup de main** boxes with on-the-spot linguistic, cultural, and language-learning information, as well as **ressources** boxes with on-page correlations of student supplements, to increase students' comfort level and to save them time.
- **ESPACES** integrates grammar and practice activities in a more supportive way to facilitate learning. It provides students with immediate access to information essential for communication by having each grammar explanation and its activities appear on one self-contained spread of two facing pages.
- **ESPACES** provides a unique four-part practice sequence for every grammar point. It moves from form-focused **Essayez!** activities to directed, yet meaningful, **Mise en pratique** activities to communicative, interactive **Communication** activities, and lastly to cumulative, open-ended **Synthèse** activities.
- **ESPACES** incorporates groundbreaking technology to expand students' learning and instructors' teaching options like the **ESPACES** supersite where you and your students can access all of the textbook's multimedia (audio, video, and TV clips), plus a wealth of practice and Internet activities.

To get the most out of pages IAE-6 – IAE-16 in your Instructor's Annotated Edition, you should familiarize yourself with these pages of the StudentText front matter: page iii (To the Student), pages xii–xxv (**ESPACES**-At-A-Glance), pages xxvi–xxvii (Video Program), and pages xxviii–xxix (Icons and Ancillaries).

Getting to Know Your Instructor's Annotated Edition

ESPACES offers you a comprehensive, thoroughly developed Instructor's Annotated Edition (IAE). With a trim size slightly larger than that of the student text, it features slightly reduced student text pages overprinted with answers to all activities with discrete responses. Surrounding side and bottom panels place a wealth of teaching resources at your fingertips. The annotations were written to complement and support varied teaching styles, to extend the already rich contents of the student textbook, and to save you time in class preparation and course management.

Because the **ESPACES** IAE is different from instructor's editions available with other French programs, this section is designed as a quick orientation to the principal types of instructor annotations it contains. As you familiarize yourself with them, it is important to know that the annotations are suggestions only. Any French questions, sentences, models, or simulated instructor-student exchanges are not meant to be prescriptive or limiting. You are encouraged to view these suggested "scripts" as flexible points of departure that will help you achieve your instructional goals.

On the Unit Opening Page

- **Unit Goals** A list of the lexical, grammatical, and socio-cultural goals of each unit, including language-learning strategies and skill-building techniques
- **Pour commencer** The answers to the **Pour commencer** activity in the student text
- **Instructional Resources** A correlation to all student and instructor supplements available to reinforce the unit

In the Side Panels

- **Section Goals** A list of the lexical, grammatical, and/or socio-cultural goals of the corresponding section
- **Instructional Resources** A correlation to all ancillaries
- **Suggestion** Teaching suggestions for leading into the corresponding section, working with on-page materials, and carrying out specific activities, as well as quick ways for starting classes or activities by recycling language or ideas
- **Expansion** Expansions and variations on activities
- **Script** Printed transcripts of the recordings on the Textbook Audio Program for the first **Mise en pratique** activity in each **Contextes** section and the **Stratégie** and **À vous d'écouter** features in each **À l'écoute** section
- **Video Recap** Questions or a true/false activity to help students recall the events of the previous lesson's **Roman-photo** episode
- **Video Synopsis** Summaries of the **Roman-photo** sections that recap that lesson's video module
- **Expressions utiles** Suggestions for introducing upcoming **Structures** grammar points incorporated into the **Roman-photo** episode

- **Stratégie** Suggestions for working with the reading, listening, and writing strategies presented in the **Lecture, À l'écoute,** and **Écriture** sections, respectively
- **Thème** Ideas for presenting and expanding the writing assignment topic in **Écriture**
- **Map-related Annotations** Suggestions for working with the maps in the **Panorama** sections
- **Le pays, la région, la province, l'archipel en chiffres** Additional information expanding on the data presented for each French-speaking area or country featured in the **Panorama** sections
- **Incroyable mais vrai!** Curious facts about a lesser-known aspect of the area or country featured in the **Panorama** sections
- **Section-specific Annotations** Suggestions for presenting, expanding, varying, and reinforcing individual instructional elements
- **Successful Language Learning** Tips and strategies to enhance students' language-learning experience

In the Options Boxes

- **Content-based Annotations With French Titles** More detailed information about an interesting aspect of the history, geography, culture, or peoples of the French-speaking world
- **Extra Practice, Pairs, and Small Groups** Activities in addition to those already in the student textbook
- **Game** Games that practice the language of the section and/or recycle previously learned language
- **TPR** Total Physical Response activities that engage students physically in learning French
- **Cultural Comparison** Suggestions to help students compare the culture they are learning with their own culture
- **Avant de regarder la vidéo/Regarder la vidéo** Techniques and activities for using the dramatic episodes of the **ESPACES** Video in the **Roman-photo** sections
- **Video** Suggestions for using the dramatic episodes of the **ESPACES** Video in the **Structures** sections
- **Proofreading Activity** Activities exclusive to the **Écriture** sections that guide students in the development of good proofreading skills. Each item contains errors related to a structure taught in the unit's **Structures** sections and/or a spelling rule taught in its **Les sons et les lettres** sections
- **Evaluation** Suggested rubrics in **Écriture** and **Projet** for grading students' writing efforts and oral presentations

Please check the **ESPACES** supersite at **espaces.vhlcentral.com** for additional teaching support.

General Teaching Considerations

Orienting Students to the Student Textbook

Because **ESPACES** treats interior and graphic design as an integral part of students' language-learning experience, you may want to take a few minutes to orient students to the student textbook. Have them flip through one unit, and point out that they are all organized exactly the same way with two short lessons and a concluding **Savoir-faire** section. Also point out how the major sections of each lesson are color-coded for easy navigation: blue for **Espace contextes**, green for **Espace roman-photo**, purple for **Espace culture**, orange for **Espace structures**, red for **Savoir-faire**, and blue for **Vocabulaire**. Let them know that, because of these design elements, they can be confident that they will always know "where they are" in their textbook.

Emphasize that sections are self-contained, occupying either a full page or a spread of two facing pages, thereby eliminating "bad breaks" and the need to flip back and forth to do activities or to work with explanatory material. Finally, call students' attention to the use of color to highlight key information in elements such as charts, diagrams, word lists, activity models, titles, and help boxes such as **Attention!**, **Coup de main**, and **Boîte à outils**.

Flexible Lesson Organization

ESPACES uses a flexible lesson organization designed to meet the needs of diverse teaching styles, institutions, and instructional goals. For example, you can begin with the unit opening page and progress sequentially through a unit. If you do not want to devote class time to grammar, you can assign the **Structures** explanations for outside study, freeing up class time for other purposes like developing oral communication skills; increasing awareness of French music and television broadcasts; building listening, reading, or writing skills; learning more about the French-speaking world; or working with the video program. You might decide to work extensively with the **Savoir-faire** sections in order to focus on students' reading, writing, and listening skills and their knowledge of the French-speaking world. On the other hand, you might prefer to skip these sections entirely, exploiting them periodically in response to your students' interests as the opportunity arises. If you plan on using the **ESPACES** Testing Program, however, be aware that its tests and exams check language presented in **Contextes**, **Structures**, and the **Expressions utiles** boxes of **Roman-photo**.

Identifying Active Vocabulary

All words and expressions taught in the illustrations, **Vocabulaire** lists, and **Attention!** boxes in **Contextes** are considered active, testable vocabulary. The words and expressions in the **Expressions utiles** boxes in **Roman-photo**, as well as words in charts, word lists, and sample sentences in **Structures** are also part of the active vocabulary load. At the end of each unit, **Vocabulaire** provides a convenient one-page summary of the items students should know and that may appear on tests and exams. You will want to point this out to students. You might also tell them that an easy way to study from **Vocabulaire** is to cover up the French half of each section, leaving only the English equivalents exposed. They can then quiz themselves on the French items. To focus on the English equivalents of the French entries, they simply reverse this process.

Taking into Account the Affective Dimension

While many factors contribute to the quality and success rate of learning experiences, two factors are particularly germane to language learning. One is students' beliefs about how language is learned; the other is language-learning anxiety.

As studies show and experienced instructors know, students often come to modern languages courses either with a lack of knowledge about how to approach language learning or with mistaken notions about how to do so. For example, many students believe that making mistakes when speaking the target language must be avoided because doing so will lead to permanent errors. Others are convinced that learning another language is like learning any other academic subject. In other words, they believe that success is guaranteed, provided they attend class regularly, learn the assigned vocabulary words and grammar rules, and study for exams. In fact, in a study of college-level beginning language learners in the United States, over one-third of the participants thought that they could become fluent if they studied the language for only one hour a day for two years or less. Mistaken and unrealistic beliefs such as these can cause frustration and ultimately demotivation, thereby significantly undermining students' ability to achieve a successful language-learning experience.

Another factor that can negatively impact students' language-learning experiences is language-learning anxiety. As Professor Elaine K. Horwitz of The University of Texas at Austin and Senior Consulting Editor of **VISTAS**, First Edition, wrote, "Surveys indicate that up to one-third of American foreign language students feel moderately to highly anxious about studying another language. Physical symptoms of foreign language anxiety can include heart-pounding or palpitations, sweating, trembling, fast breathing, and general feelings of unease." The late Dr. Philip Redwine Donley, **VISTAS** co-author and author of articles on language-learning anxiety, spoke with many students who reported feeling nervous or apprehensive in their classes. They mentioned freezing when called on by their instructors or going inexplicably blank when taking tests. Some so dreaded their classes that they skipped them or dropped the course.

Based on what Vista Higher Learning learned from instructors and students using **VISTAS**, **AVENTURAS**, and its other successful introductory Spanish programs, **ESPACES** contains several features aimed at reducing students' language anxiety and supporting their successful language learning. First of all, the highly structured, visually dramatic interior design of the **ESPACES** student text was conceived as a learning tool to make students feel comfortable with the content and confident about navigating the lessons. The Instructor's Annotated Edition also includes *Successful Language Learning* annotations with suggestions for managing and/or reducing language-learning anxieties and for enhancing students' learning experiences. In addition, the student text provides on-the-spot **Attention!**, **Coup de main**, and **Boîte à outils** boxes that assist students by making immediately relevant connections with new information or reminding them of previously learned concepts.

ESPACES and *the Standards for Foreign Language Learning*

Since 1982, when the *ACTFL Proficiency Guidelines* were first published, that seminal document and its subsequent revisions have influenced the teaching of modern languages in the United States. **ESPACES** was written with the concerns and philosophy of the *ACTFL Proficiency Guidelines* in mind, incorporating a proficiency-oriented approach from its planning stages.

ESPACES' pedagogy was also informed from its inception by the *Standards for Foreign Language Learning in the 21st Century*. First published in 1996 under the auspices of the National Standards in Foreign Language Education Project, the Standards are organized into five goal areas, often called the Five Cs: Communication, Cultures, Connections, Comparisons, and Communities.

Since **ESPACES** takes a communicative approach to the teaching and learning of French, the Communication goal is central to the student text. For example, the diverse formats used in the **Communication** and **Synthèse** activities in each lesson—pair work, small group work, class circulation, information gap, task-based, and so forth—engage students in communicative exchanges, providing and obtaining information, and expressing feelings and emotions. The **Projet** sections guide students in presenting information, concepts, and ideas to their classmates on a variety of topics and in varied ways—oral, written, recorded, and videotaped, whereas the **À l'écoute** and **Écriture** sections focus on developing students' communication skills in listening and writing.

The Cultures goal is most overtly evident on four pages of each lesson in the **Roman-photo** and **Espace culture** sections, as well as in the two-page **Panorama** section at the end of each unit. However, **ESPACES** also weaves culture into virtually every page, exposing students to the multiple facets of practices, products, and perspectives of the French-speaking world. In keeping with the Connections goal, students can connect with other disciplines such as music, communications, business, geography, history, fine arts, and science in the **Projet**, **Interlude**, **Le zapping**, and **Panorama** sections; they can acquire information and recognize distinctive cultural viewpoints in the non-literary and literary texts of the **Lecture** sections. Moreover, **Sur Internet** boxes in **Espace culture**, **Projet**, **Le zapping**, **Interlude**, and **Panorama** support the Connections and Communities goals as students work through those sections and complete the related activities on the **ESPACES** supersite. As for the Comparisons goal, it is reflected in **Les sons et les lettres** pronunciation and spelling sections and the **Structures** sections.

Special Standards icons also appear on the student text pages of your Instructor's Annotated Edition to call out sections that have a particularly strong relationship with the Standards. These are a few examples of how **ESPACES** was written with the Standards firmly in mind, but you will find many more as you work with the student textbook and its ancillaries.

General Suggestions for Using the ESPACES *Roman-photo* Video Episodes

The **Roman-photo** section in each of the student textbook's lessons and the **ESPACES** Video were created as interlocking pieces. All photos in **Roman-photo** are actual video stills from the corresponding video episode, while the printed conversations are abbreviated versions of the dramatic segment. Both the **Roman-photo** conversations and their expanded video versions represent comprehensible input at the discourse level; they were purposely written to use language from the corresponding lesson's **Contextes** and **Structures** sections. Thus, as of **Leçon 2**, they recycle known language, preview grammar points students will study later in the lesson, and, in keeping with the concept of "i + 1," contain a small amount of unknown language.

Because the **Roman-photo** textbook sections and the dramatic episodes of the **ESPACES** Video are so closely connected, you may use them in many different ways. For instance, you can use **Roman-photo** as an advance organizer, presenting it before showing the video episode. You can also show the video episode first and follow up with **Roman-photo**. You can even use **Roman-photo** as a stand-alone, video-independent section.

Depending on your teaching preferences and campus facilities, you might decide to show all video episodes in class or to assign them solely for viewing outside of the classroom. You could begin by showing the first one or two episodes in class to familiarize yourself and students with the characters, storyline, style, and **Reprise** sections. After that, you could work in class only with **Roman-photo** and have students view the remaining video episodes outside of class. No matter which approach you choose, students have ample materials to support viewing the video independently and processing it in a meaningful way. For each video episode, there are activities in the **Roman-photo** section of the corresponding textbook lesson, as well as pre-, while-, and post-viewing activities in the Workbook/Video Manual.

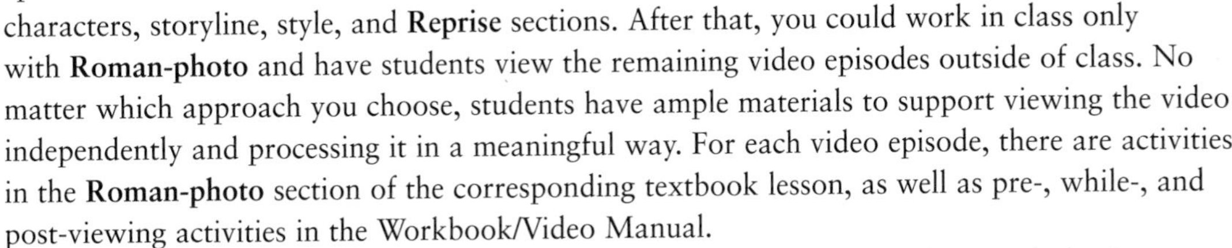

You might also want to use the **ESPACES** Video in class when working with the **Structures** sections. You could play the parts of the dramatic episode that correspond to the video stills in the grammar explanations or show selected scenes and ask students to identify certain grammar points.

You could also focus on the **Reprise** sections that appear at the end of each lesson's dramatic episode to summarize the key language functions and grammar points used. In class, you could play the parts of the **Reprise** section that exemplify individual grammar points as you progress through each **Structures** section. You could also wait until you complete a **Structures** section and review it and the lesson's **Contextes** section by showing the corresponding **Reprise** section in its entirety.

General Suggestions for Using the ESPACES *Flash culture* Video Episodes

The **Flash culture** video segments were specially planned and shot for **ESPACES** to bring France and the French-speaking world "alive" to students within the context of the themes of the textbook's units. The footage was selected for visual appeal and information of interest that both reinforces content presented in the textbook's lessons and goes beyond it. The segments are hosted by the **ESPACES** narrators, Csilla and Benjamin who alternate between odd-numbered and even-numbered segments, respectively. Csilla and Benjamin introduce each segment, provide transitions between topics, and, as appropriate, hold micro-interviews with French speakers whom they encounter as they visit parks, public squares, schools, stores, cafés, markets, and more.

Like the conversations in the **Roman-photo** dramatic episodes, the **Flash culture** narrations represent comprehensible input. Each was written to make the most of the vocabulary and grammar students learned in the corresponding and previous units while still providing a small amount of unknown language and/or cognates. In Units 1–7, the narrators begin the segments in English, but, as much as possible, use French that will be comprehensible to students to explain and describe the images shown. As of Unit 8, the **Flash culture** segments are entirely in French.

Each segment is approximately two-to-three minutes long and is correlated in the **ESPACES** student text in the **Flash culture** box on the **Écriture** page of the each unit's **Savoir-faire** section.

Flash culture Video Segments Table of Contents

Unité 1: greetings and farewells
Unité 2: colleges, universities, and school life
Unité 3: family and friends
Unité 4: cafés, food, and drink
Unité 5: leisure-time activities and sports
Unité 6: holidays and festivals
Unité 7: travel and vacation-related activities
Unité 8: apartments, homes, and other types of housing
Unité 9: an open-air food market
Unité 10: a pharmacy and other health-related locations
Unité 11: cars, transportation, and traffic-related items
Unité 12: the post office, banks, small and large stores
Unité 13: jobs, professions, and careers
Unité 14: parts of France and French-speaking countries
Unité 15: films, documentaries, books, magazines, and newspapers

Activities for the **Flash culture** video are located in the Video Manual section of the **ESPACES** Workbook/Video Manual. They follow a process approach of pre-viewing, while-viewing, and post-viewing and use a variety of formats to prepare students for watching the video segments, to focus them while watching, and to check comprehension after they have watched the footage.

When showing the **Flash culture** video segments in your classes, you might also want to implement a process approach. You could start with an activity that prepares students for the video segment by taking advantage of what they learned in the unit's two lessons. This could be followed by an activity that students do while you play parts of or the entire video segment. The final activity, done in the same class period or in the next one as warm-up, could recap what students saw and heard and move beyond the video segment's topic. The following suggestions for working with the **Flash culture** video segments in class, which are in addition to those on the individual pages of the Instructor's Annotated Edition, can be carried out as described or expanded upon in any number of ways.

Before viewing

- Ask students to guess what the segment might be about based on what they've learned about the unit's theme over the unit's two lessons, especially in the **Contextes**, **Roman-photo**, and **Espace culture** sections.
- Have pairs make a list of the unit vocabulary they expect to hear in the video segment.
- Read the class a list of true-false or multiple-choice questions about the video. Students must use what they learned over the unit to guess the answers. Confirm their guesses after watching the segment.

While viewing

- Show the video segment with the audio turned off and ask students to use unit vocabulary and structures to describe what they see. Have them confirm their guesses by showing the segment again with the audio on.
- Have students refer to the list of words they brainstormed before viewing the video and put a check in front of any words they actually hear or see in the segment.
- First, have students simply watch the video. Then, show it again and ask students to take notes on what they see and hear. Finally, have them compare their notes in pairs or groups for confirmation.
- Photocopy the segment's videoscript from the Instructor's Resource Manual and white out words and expressions related to the unit theme. Distribute the scripts for pairs or groups to complete as cloze paragraphs.
- After having introduced the unit's theme using the unit-opening page in the student text, show the video segment before moving on to **Contextes** to jump-start the unit's vocabulary, grammar, and cultural focus. Have students tell you what vocabulary and grammar they recognize from previous lessons.

After viewing

- Have students say what aspects of the information presented in the corresponding textbook unit are observable in the video segment.
- Ask groups to write a brief summary of the content of the video segment. Have them exchange papers with another group for peer editing.
- Have students pick one new aspect of the corresponding textbook unit's cultural theme that they learned about from watching the video segment. Have them research more about that topic and write a list or paragraph to expand on it.

About Le zapping, Projet, and Interlude

One of three sections appears at the end of each textbook lesson: **Le zapping, Projet,** or **Interlude**, all of which are related to the lesson's theme. **Le zapping** features TV commercials and a weather broadcast so your students can experience the language and culture contained in authentic television pieces. In **Projet**, students are asked to give oral presentations, using tangible products that they create to help them convey meaning and hold their classmates' interest. **Interlude** connects the unit's theme to French music and fine art. For your convenient reference, following are lists of the television clips, projects, singers, artists, and/or fine art pieces by unit and lesson:

Le zapping TV Clips

Unité 1	**Leçon 1**	(23 seconds) *La triplette de Moulinex… un, deux trois!*
Unité 2	**Leçon 4**	(25 seconds) *Clairefontaine: l'écrit du cœur*
Unité 4	**Leçon 7**	(18 seconds) *Bon appétit, bon Baguépi!*
Unité 5	**Leçon 10**	(2 minutes, 20 seconds) *La météo*
Unité 7	**Leçon 13**	(35 seconds) *Air Afrique*
Unité 8	**Leçon 16**	(22 seconds) *Mr. Propre*
Unité 10	**Leçon 19**	(24 seconds) *Diadermine*
Unité 11	**Leçon 22**	(50 seconds) *C'est la Renault 6!*
Unité 13	**Leçon 25**	(1 minute 2 seconds) *DHL*
Unité 14	**Leçon 28**	(33 seconds) *Le Végétarium*

Projet Tasks

Unité 1	**Leçon 2**	*The influence of French-speaking cultures on a city in the United States or Canada based on visuals and graphics*
Unité 3	**Leçon 5**	*A famous family, using an illustrated family tree*
Unité 4	**Leçon 8**	*An imaginary French restaurant, including its menu*
Unité 6	**Leçon 11**	*A report on a holiday in the French-speaking world with visuals*
Unité 7	**Leçon 14**	*A web site for a travel agency about tourist activities in Paris*
Unité 9	**Leçon 17**	*A recipe for a dish from a French-speaking region or country*
Unité 10	**Leçon 20**	*A speech about medical care in Switzerland*
Unité 12	**Leçon 23**	*A brochure for a planned community in Québec province*
Unité 13	**Leçon 26**	*A diagram with text and photos of a career plan for a job in France*
Unité 15	**Leçon 29**	*A report on an artist from the French Caribbean with examples of his or her paintings*

Interlude Sections

		Singer	Painter/Poster
Unité 2	**Leçon 3**	*Amadou & Mariam*	*Cyprien Tokoudagba*
Unité 3	**Leçon 6**	*Tino Rossi*	*Pierre-Auguste Renior*
Unité 5	**Leçon 9**	*Yves Montand*	*Jean Béraud*
Unité 6	**Leçon 12**	*Édith Piaf*	*Henri de Toulouse-Lautrec*
Unité 8	**Leçon 15**	*Lynda Lemay*	*Pascal-Adolphe-Jean Dagnan-Bouveret*
Unité 9	**Leçon 18**	*Thomas Fersen*	*Camille Pissarro*
Unité 11	**Leçon 21**	*Bénabar*	*poster for* **Amilcar**
Unité 12	**Leçon 24**	*Charles Trenet*	*Berthe Morisot*
Unité 14	**Leçon 27**	*Jacques Brel*	*Georges de Feure*
Unité 15	**Leçon 30**	*France Gall*	*Paul Cézanne*

About Lecture, À l'écoute, and Écriture

ESPACES takes a process approach to the development of reading, listening, and writing skills. Here are lists of the strategies taught in each unit so that you may refer to them in one convenient place.

Lecture

- **Unité 1** Recognizing cognates
- **Unité 2** Predicting content through formats
- **Unité 3** Predicting content from visuals
- **Unité 4** Scanning
- **Unité 5** Skimming
- **Unité 6** Recognizing word families
- **Unité 7** Predicting content from the title
- **Unité 8** Guessing meaning from context
- **Unité 9** Reading for the main idea
- **Unité 10** Activating background knowledge
- **Unité 11** Recognizing the purpose of a text
- **Unité 12** Identifying point of view
- **Unité 13** Summarizing a text in your own words
- **Unité 14** Recognizing chronological order
- **Unité 15** Making inferences and recognizing metaphors

À l'écoute

- **Unité 1** Listening for words you know
- **Unité 2** Listening for cognates
- **Unité 3** Asking for repetition / Replaying the recording
- **Unité 4** Listening for the gist
- **Unité 5** Listening for key words
- **Unité 6** Listening for linguistic cues
- **Unité 7** Recognizing the genre of spoken discourse
- **Unité 8** Using visual cues
- **Unité 9** Jotting down notes as you listen
- **Unité 10** Listening for specific information
- **Unité 11** Guessing the meaning of words through context
- **Unité 12** Using background information
- **Unité 13** Using background knowledge / Listening for specific information
- **Unité 14** Listening for the gist / Listening for cognates
- **Unité 15** Listening for key words / Using the context

Écriture

- **Unité 1** Writing in French
- **Unité 2** Brainstorming
- **Unité 3** Using idea maps
- **Unité 4** Adding details
- **Unité 5** Using a dictionary
- **Unité 6** How to report an interview
- **Unité 7** Making an outline
- **Unité 8** Mastering the simple past tenses
- **Unité 9** Expressing and supporting opinions
- **Unité 10** Sequencing events
- **Unité 11** Listing key words
- **Unité 12** Using linking words
- **Unité 13** Using note cards
- **Unité 14** Considering audience and purpose
- **Unité 15** Writing strong introductions and conclusions

COURSE PLANNING

The entire **ESPACES** program was developed with an eye to flexibility and ease of use in a wide variety of course configurations. **ESPACES** can be used in courses taught on semester or quarter systems, and in courses that complete the book in two or three semesters. Here are some sample course plans that illustrate how **ESPACES** can be used in different academic situations. You should, of course, feel free to organize your courses in the way that best suits your students' needs and your instructional objectives.

Two-Semester System

The following chart illustrates how **ESPACES** can be completed in a two-semester course. This division of material allows the present tense, the near future, the **passé composé** with **avoir** and **être**, and the imperative to be presented in the first semester; the second semester focuses on the introduction of some irregular verbs, the imperfect, the **passé composé** vs. the imperfect, the future, the conditional, and the present subjunctive.

Semester 1	**Semester 2**
Units 1–7	Units 8–15

Three-Semester or Quarter System

This chart shows how **ESPACES** can be used in a three-semester or quarter course. The units are equally divided over each semester/quarter, allowing students to absorb the material at a steady pace.

Semester/Quarter 1	**Semester/Quarter 2**	**Semester/Quarter 3**
Units 1–5	Units 6–10	Units 11–15

Lesson Plans

Lesson plans for each unit of **ESPACES** are available on the instructor's part of the **ESPACES** supersite at **espaces.vhlcentral.com**. You will find plans for the two lessons in each unit, as well as each end-of-unit **Savoir-faire** section. The lesson plans are not prescriptive. You should feel free to present lesson materials as you see fit, tailoring them to your own teaching preferences and to your students' learning styles. You may, for example, want to allow extra time for concepts students find challenging. You may want to allot less time to topics they comprehend without difficulty or to group topics together when making assignments. Based on your students' needs and the contact hours of your course, you may want to omit certain topics or activities altogether. It is our hope that you will find the **ESPACES** program very flexible: simply pick and choose from its array of instructional resources and sequence them in the way that makes the most sense for your course.

ESPACES

Rendez-vous avec le monde francophone

Cherie Mitschke
Southwestern University

Cheryl Tano
Emmanuel College and Tufts University

Valérie Thiers-Thiam
Borough of Manhattan Community College

Boston, Massachusetts

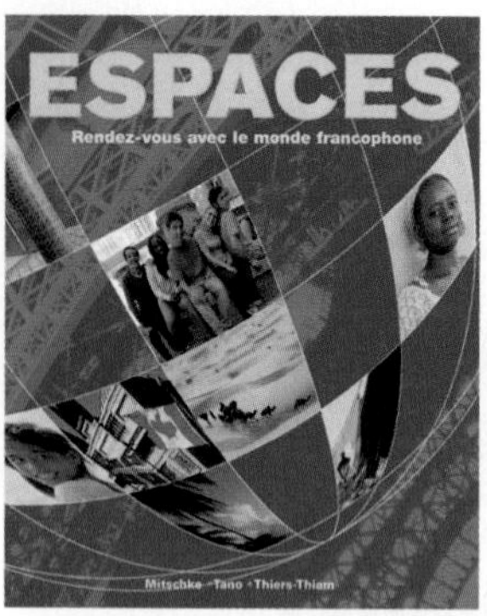

The **ESPACES** cover celebrates the diversity of the French-speaking world that you will find throughout the text and its ancillaries. Cover photos include images of (top left) a doorway in Telouet, Morocco; (middle far left) a Tahitian girl; (middle left) the flags of Quebec and Canada in Hull, Quebec; (middle right) the Sahara Desert, Algeria; (middle far right) a Senegalese woman; (bottom left) flags in Geneva, Switzerland.

Publisher: José Blanco
Senior Vice President, General Manager: Janet Dracksdorf
Vice President & Editorial Director: Denise St. Jean
Director of Art & Design: Linda Jurras
Director of Production & Manufacturing: Lisa Flanagan Perrier
Project Managers: Armando Brito, Sarah Kenney, Jason Velázquez
Editors: Isabelle Alouane, Julie Cormier, Emmanuelle Deschutter, Véronique Drissi, Thomas Keon, Laurent Martein, Julia Noguchi, Sylvie Updegraff
Contributing Writers: Myriam Arcangeli, Dominique Astier, Séverine Champeny, Nora Corral, Virginia Dosher, Carole Figuet, Annick Penant
Design Manager: Polo Barrera
Designers: Andrea Golden, Deborah Rodman
Photo Researcher & Art Buyer: Linde Gee
Production Team: Oscar Diez, María Eugenia Castaño, Mauricio Henao, Kathryn Sala
Manufacturing Coordinator: Gustavo Cinci
Senior Vice President, Operations: Tom Delano
Executive Marketing Manager: Ben Rivera

Student Text ISBN-13: 978-1-59334-836-6
ISBN-10: 1-59334-836-3
Instructor's Annotated Edition ISBN-13: 978-1-59334-833-5
ISBN-10: 1-59334-833-9
Library of Congress Card Number: 2005937387

1 2 3 4 5 6 7 8 9 VH 10 09 08 07 06

TO THE STUDENT

Welcome to **ESPACES**, a brand-new introductory French program from Vista Higher Learning. In French, **espaces** means *spaces* in the sense of spaces reserved for a particular purpose. The spaces in **ESPACES** are its major sections, and they are reserved for helping you to learn French and to explore the cultures of the French-speaking world in the most user-friendly way possible. In light of this goal, here are some of the features you will encounter in **ESPACES**.

- A unique, easy-to-navigate design built around color-coded sections that appear either completely on one page or on spreads of two facing pages
- Abundant illustrations, photos, charts, graphs, diagrams, and other graphic elements, all specially created or chosen to help you learn
- Distinctive integration of a specially shot video, up-front in each lesson of the student text
- Clear, concise grammar explanations in an innovative format that supports you as you work through the practice activities
- Practical, high-frequency vocabulary for use in real-life situations
- Ample guided vocabulary and grammar exercises to give you a solid foundation for communicating in French
- An emphasis on communicative interactions with a classmate, small groups, the whole class, and your instructor
- Systematic development of reading, writing, and listening skills incorporating learning strategies and a process approach
- A rich, contemporary cultural presentation of the everyday life of French speakers and the diverse cultures of the countries and areas of the entire French-speaking world
- Exciting integration of culture and multimedia, including task-based projects, music, fine art and TV clips
- A full set of completely integrated print and technology ancillaries to make learning French easier
- Built-in correlation of all ancillaries, right down to the page numbers

ESPACES has fifteen units with two lessons in each unit followed by an end-of-unit **Savoir-faire** section and a list of active vocabulary. To familiarize yourself with the textbook's organization, features, and ancillary package, turn to page xii and take the **ESPACES**-at-a-glance tour.

TABLE OF CONTENTS

		espace contextes	espace roman-photo

espace culture	espace structures	savoir-faire
Culture à la loupe La poignée de main ou la bise? 8 **Portrait** Aix-en-Provence: ville d'eau, ville d'art 9	1.1 Nouns and articles. . . . . . . 10 1.2 Numbers 0–60 . . . . 12 **Le zapping**. 15	**Panorama:** *Le monde francophone*. . . . . . 30 **Lecture:** *Un carnet d'adresses*. . 32 **À l'écoute** . . . . 34 **Écriture**. 35
Culture à la loupe Qu'est-ce qu'un Français typique? . . . . 22 **Portrait** Superdupont 23	2.1 The verb **être**. . . . . 24 2.2 Adjective agreement. . . . . . 26 **Projet** 29	
Culture à la loupe À l'université. . . . . 44 **Portrait** La Sorbonne 45	3.1 Present tense of regular **–er** verbs . . . . 46 3.2 Forming questions and expressing negation. . . . . 48 **Interlude** 51	**Panorama:** *La France* . . . . 66 **Lecture:** *École de français (pour étrangers) de Lille* . . . . . 68 **À l'écoute** . . . . 70 **Écriture**. 71
Culture à la loupe Les cours universitaires. . . . . 58 **Portrait** Le bac 59	4.1 Present tense of **avoir** . . . . 60 4.2 Telling time . . . . 62 **Le zapping**. 65	
Culture à la loupe La famille française . . . . 80 **Portrait** Jacques Chirac, président et père. 81	5.1 Descriptive adjectives. . . . . 82 5.2 Possessive adjectives . . . . 84 **Projet** 87	**Panorama:** *Paris*. . . . . 102 **Lecture:** *Fido en famille* . . . . . 104 **À l'écoute** . . . . 106 **Écriture**. 107
Culture à la loupe L'amitié . . . . 94 **Portrait** Les Depardieu. 95	6.1 Numbers 61–100 . . . . 96 6.2 Prepositions of location . . . 98 **Interlude** 101	
Culture à la loupe Les passe-temps des jeunes Français. . . . . . . 116 **Portrait** Le parc Astérix 117	7.1 The verb **aller** . . . . 118 7.2 Interrogative words. . . . . . 120 **Le zapping**. 123	**Panorama:** *La Normandie et la Bretagne* . . . . 138 **Lecture:** *Cybercafé Le connecté* . . . . 140 **À l'écoute** . . . . 142 **Écriture** 143
Culture à la loupe Le café français . . . . 130 **Portrait** Les cafés célèbres de Saint-Germain-des-Prés 131	8.1 The verbs **prendre** and **boire** . . . . 132 8.2 Partitives. . . . . 134 **Projet** 137	

TABLE OF CONTENTS

TABLE OF CONTENTS

		espace contextes	espace roman-photo

espace culture	espace structures	savoir-faire

TABLE OF CONTENTS

espace culture	espace structures	savoir-faire

UNIT OPENERS

outline the content and features of each unit.

La famille et les copains
UNITÉ 3
Leçon 5
ESPACE CONTEXTES
pages 74–77
• Family, friends, and pets
• L'accent aigu and l'accent grave
ESPACE ROMAN-PHOTO
pages 78–79
• L'album de photos
ESPACE CULTURE
pages 80–81
• The French family
ESPACE STRUCTURES
pages 82–87
• Descriptive adjectives
• Possessive adjectives
• Synthèse
• Projet
Leçon 6
ESPACE CONTEXTES
pages 88–91
• More descriptive adjectives
• Professions and occupations
• L'accent circonflexe, la cédille, and le tréma
ESPACE ROMAN-PHOTO
pages 92–93
• On travaille chez moi!
ESPACE CULTURE
pages 94–95
• Relationships
ESPACE STRUCTURES
pages 96–101
• Numbers 61–100
• Prepositions of location
• Synthèse
• Interlude
Pour commencer
• Combien de personnes y a-t-il?
• Sont-elles dans un café?
• Mangent-elles? Parlent-elles?
• Ont-elles l'air agréables ou désagréables?
• Aiment-elles les ordinateurs?
Savoir-faire
pages 102–107
Panorama: Paris
Lecture: Read a short article about pets.
À l'écoute: Listen to a conversation between friends.
Écriture: Write a letter to a friend.
Flash culture

Pour commencer activities jump-start the units, allowing you to use the French you know to talk about the photos.

Content thumbnails break down each unit into its two lessons and one **Savoir-faire** section, giving you an at-a-glance summary of the vocabulary, grammar, cultural topics, and language skills on which you will focus.

ESPACE CONTEXTES

presents vocabulary in meaningful contexts.

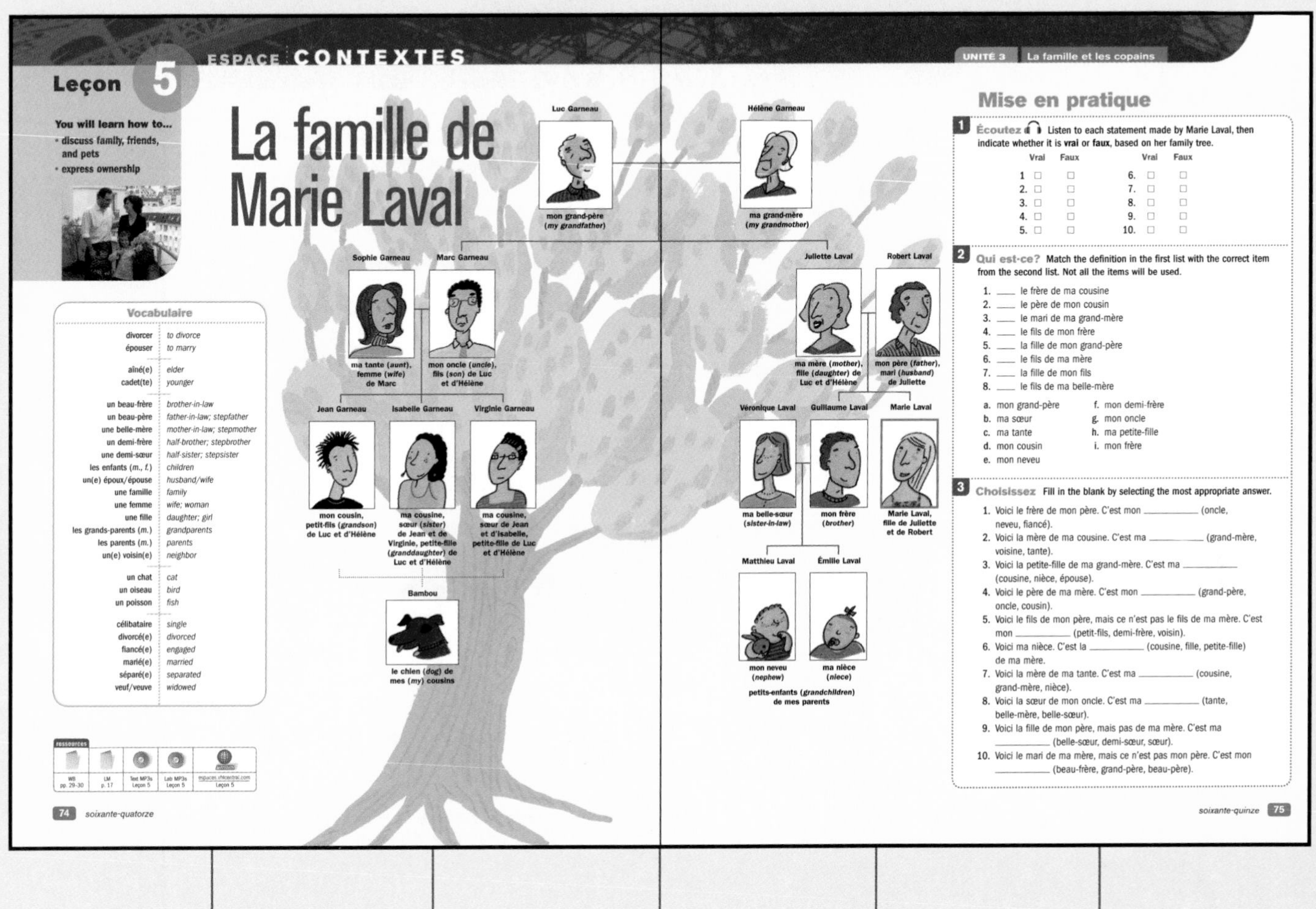

ESPACE CONTEXTES

Leçon 5

You will learn how to...
- discuss family, friends, and pets
- express ownership

La famille de Marie Laval

Luc Garneau — mon grand-père (*my grandfather*)

Hélène Garneau — ma grand-mère (*my grandmother*)

Sophie Garneau — ma tante (*aunt*), femme (*wife*) de Marc

Marc Garneau — mon oncle (*uncle*), fils (*son*) de Luc et d'Hélène

Jean Garneau — mon cousin, petit-fils (*grandson*) de Luc et d'Hélène

Isabelle Garneau — ma cousine, sœur (*sister*) de Jean et de Virginie, petite-fille (*granddaughter*) de Luc et d'Hélène

Virginie Garneau — ma cousine, sœur de Jean et d'Isabelle, petite-fille de Luc et d'Hélène

Bambou — le chien (*dog*) de mes (*my*) cousins

Juliette Laval — ma mère (*mother*), fille (*daughter*) de Luc et d'Hélène

Robert Laval — mon père (*father*), mari (*husband*) de Juliette

Véronique Laval — ma belle-sœur (*sister-in-law*)

Guillaume Laval — mon frère (*brother*)

Marie Laval — Marie Laval, fille de Juliette et de Robert

Matthieu Laval — mon neveu (*nephew*)

Émilie Laval — ma nièce (*niece*)

petits-enfants (*grandchildren*) de mes parents

Vocabulaire

divorcer	*to divorce*
épouser	*to marry*
aîné(e)	*elder*
cadet(te)	*younger*
un beau-frère	*brother-in-law*
un beau-père	*father-in-law; stepfather*
une belle-mère	*mother-in-law; stepmother*
un demi-frère	*half-brother; stepbrother*
une demi-sœur	*half-sister; stepsister*
les enfants (*m., f.*)	*children*
un(e) époux/épouse	*husband/wife*
une famille	*family*
une femme	*wife; woman*
une fille	*daughter; girl*
les grands-parents (*m.*)	*grandparents*
les parents (*m.*)	*parents*
un(e) voisin(e)	*neighbor*
un chat	*cat*
un oiseau	*bird*
un poisson	*fish*
célibataire	*single*
divorcé(e)	*divorced*
fiancé(e)	*engaged*
marié(e)	*married*
séparé(e)	*separated*
veuf/veuve	*widowed*

ressources: WB pp. 29-30 | LM p. 17 | Text MP3s Leçon 5 | Lab MP3s Leçon 5 | espaces.vhlcentral.com Leçon 5

74 soixante-quatorze

UNITÉ 3 La famille et les copains

Mise en pratique

1 Écoutez Listen to each statement made by Marie Laval, then indicate whether it is **vrai** or **faux**, based on her family tree.

	Vrai	Faux		Vrai	Faux
1	☐	☐	6.	☐	☐
2.	☐	☐	7.	☐	☐
3.	☐	☐	8.	☐	☐
4.	☐	☐	9.	☐	☐
5.	☐	☐	10.	☐	☐

2 Qui est-ce? Match the definition in the first list with the correct item from the second list. Not all the items will be used.

1. ____ le frère de ma cousine
2. ____ le père de mon cousin
3. ____ le mari de ma grand-mère
4. ____ le fils de mon frère
5. ____ la fille de mon grand-père
6. ____ le fils de ma mère
7. ____ la fille de mon fils
8. ____ le fils de ma belle-mère

a. mon grand-père
b. ma sœur
c. ma tante
d. mon cousin
e. mon neveu
f. mon demi-frère
g. mon oncle
h. ma petite-fille
i. mon frère

3 Choisissez Fill in the blank by selecting the most appropriate answer.

1. Voici le frère de mon père. C'est mon ________ (oncle, neveu, fiancé).
2. Voici la mère de ma cousine. C'est ma ________ (grand-mère, voisine, tante).
3. Voici la petite-fille de ma grand-mère. C'est ma ________ (cousine, nièce, épouse).
4. Voici le père de ma mère. C'est mon ________ (grand-père, oncle, cousin).
5. Voici le fils de mon père, mais ce n'est pas le fils de ma mère. C'est mon ________ (petit-fils, demi-frère, voisin).
6. Voici ma nièce. C'est la ________ (cousine, fille, petite-fille) de ma mère.
7. Voici la mère de ma tante. C'est ma ________ (cousine, grand-mère, nièce).
8. Voici la sœur de mon oncle. C'est ma ________ (tante, belle-mère, belle-sœur).
9. Voici la fille de mon père, mais pas de ma mère. C'est ma ________ (belle-sœur, demi-sœur, sœur).
10. Voici le mari de ma mère, mais ce n'est pas mon père. C'est mon ________ (beau-frère, grand-père, beau-père).

soixante-quinze 75

Communicative goals highlight the real-life tasks you will be able to carry out in French by the end of each lesson.

Illustrations High-frequency vocabulary is introduced through expansive, full-color illustrations.

Vocabulaire boxes call out other important theme-related vocabulary in easy-to-reference French-English lists.

Mise en pratique always begins with a listening activity and continues with activities that practice the new vocabulary in meaningful contexts.

Ressources boxes let you know exactly what print and technology ancillaries you can use to reinforce and expand on every section of every lesson in your textbook.

ESPACE CONTEXTES

practices vocabulary in a variety of formats.

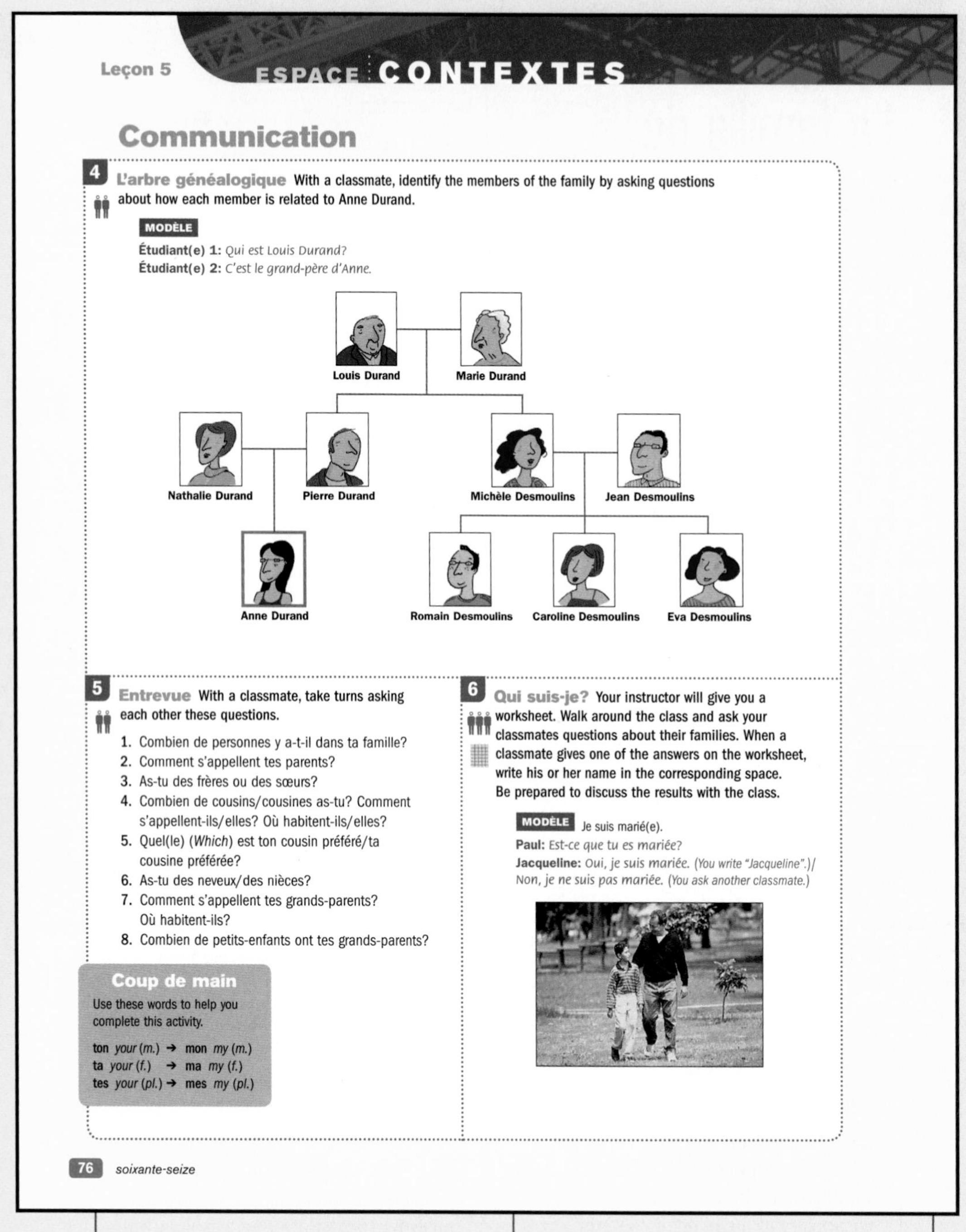

Leçon 5 ESPACE CONTEXTES

Communication

4 L'arbre généalogique With a classmate, identify the members of the family by asking questions about how each member is related to Anne Durand.

MODÈLE

Étudiant(e) 1: *Qui est Louis Durand?*
Étudiant(e) 2: *C'est le grand-père d'Anne.*

5 Entrevue With a classmate, take turns asking each other these questions.

1. Combien de personnes y a-t-il dans ta famille?
2. Comment s'appellent tes parents?
3. As-tu des frères ou des sœurs?
4. Combien de cousins/cousines as-tu? Comment s'appellent-ils/elles? Où habitent-ils/elles?
5. Quel(le) (*Which*) est ton cousin préféré/ta cousine préférée?
6. As-tu des neveux/des nièces?
7. Comment s'appellent tes grands-parents? Où habitent-ils?
8. Combien de petits-enfants ont tes grands-parents?

Coup de main

Use these words to help you complete this activity.

ton *your (m.)* → **mon** *my (m.)*
ta *your (f.)* → **ma** *my (f.)*
tes *your (pl.)* → **mes** *my (pl.)*

6 Qui suis-je? Your instructor will give you a worksheet. Walk around the class and ask your classmates questions about their families. When a classmate gives one of the answers on the worksheet, write his or her name in the corresponding space. Be prepared to discuss the results with the class.

MODÈLE Je suis marié(e).

Paul: *Est-ce que tu es mariée?*
Jacqueline: *Oui, je suis mariée.* (You write "Jacqueline".)/ *Non, je ne suis pas mariée.* (You ask another classmate.)

76 *soixante-seize*

Coup de main provides handy, on-the-spot information that helps you complete the activities.

Communication activities allow you to use the vocabulary creatively in interactions with a partner, a small group, or the entire class.

Icons provide on-the-spot visual cues for various types of activities: pair, small group, listening-based, video-related, handout-based, and information gap. For a legend explaining all icons used in the student text, see page xxviii.

ESPACE CONTEXTES

Les sons et les lettres presents the rules of French pronunciation and spelling.

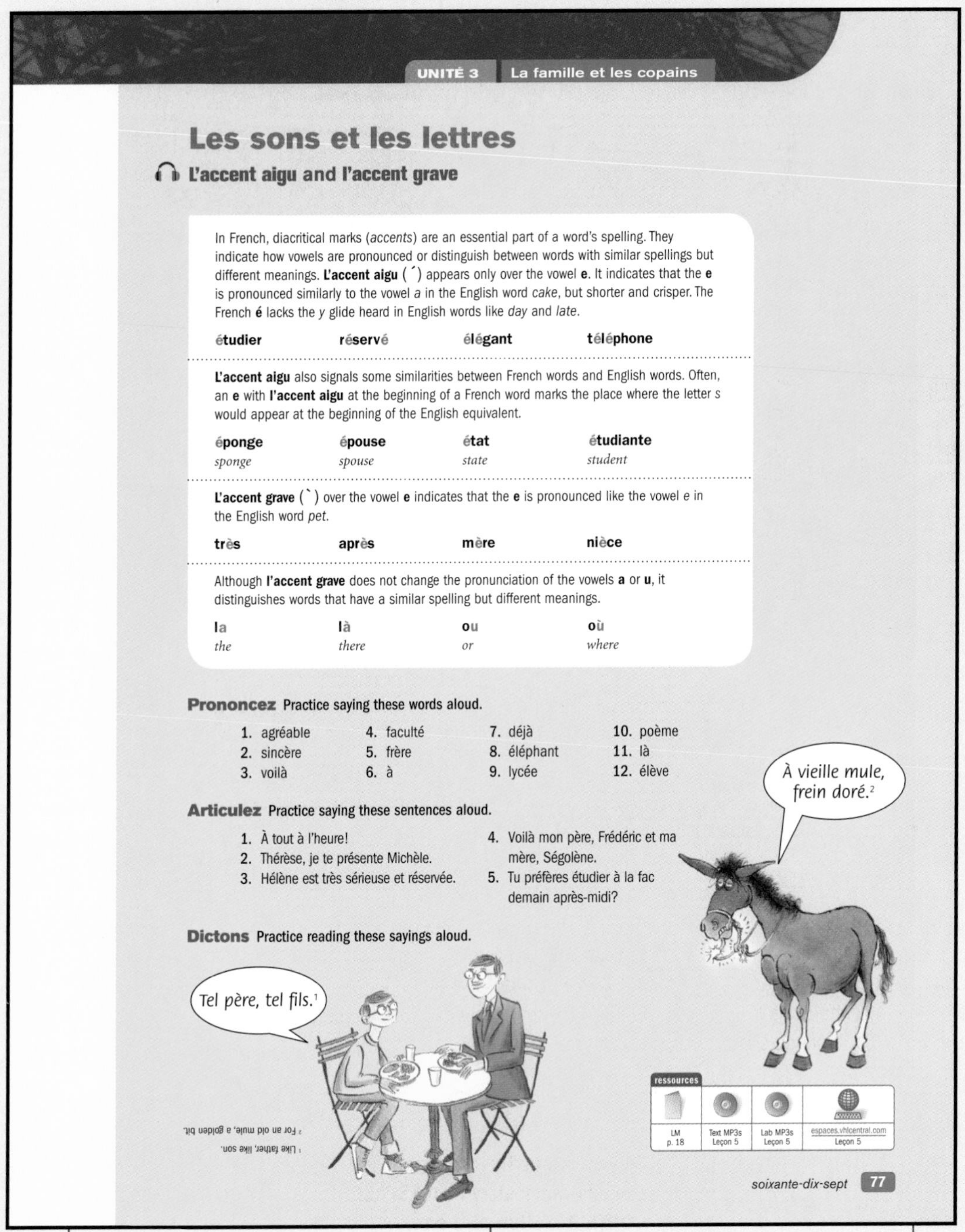

UNITÉ 3 La famille et les copains

Les sons et les lettres

L'accent aigu and l'accent grave

In French, diacritical marks (*accents*) are an essential part of a word's spelling. They indicate how vowels are pronounced or distinguish between words with similar spellings but different meanings. **L'accent aigu** (´) appears only over the vowel **e**. It indicates that the **e** is pronounced similarly to the vowel *a* in the English word *cake*, but shorter and crisper. The French **é** lacks the *y* glide heard in English words like *day* and *late*.

étudier	**réservé**	**élégant**	**téléphone**

L'accent aigu also signals some similarities between French words and English words. Often, an **e** with **l'accent aigu** at the beginning of a French word marks the place where the letter *s* would appear at the beginning of the English equivalent.

éponge	**épouse**	**état**	**étudiante**
sponge	*spouse*	*state*	*student*

L'accent grave (`) over the vowel **e** indicates that the **e** is pronounced like the vowel *e* in the English word *pet*.

très	**après**	**mère**	**nièce**

Although **l'accent grave** does not change the pronunciation of the vowels **a** or **u**, it distinguishes words that have a similar spelling but different meanings.

la	**là**	**ou**	**où**
the	*there*	*or*	*where*

Prononcez Practice saying these words aloud.

1. agréable
2. sincère
3. voilà
4. faculté
5. frère
6. à
7. déjà
8. éléphant
9. lycée
10. poème
11. là
12. élève

Articulez Practice saying these sentences aloud.

1. À tout à l'heure!
2. Thérèse, je te présente Michèle.
3. Hélène est très sérieuse et réservée.
4. Voilà mon père, Frédéric et ma mère, Ségolène.
5. Tu préfères étudier à la fac demain après-midi?

Dictons Practice reading these sayings aloud.

Tel père, tel fils.[1]
À vieille mule, frein doré.[2]

[1] Like father, like son.
[2] For an old mule, a golden bit.

ressources: LM p. 18 | Text MP3s Leçon 5 | Lab MP3s Leçon 5 | espaces.vhlcentral.com Leçon 5

soixante-dix-sept 77

Explanation Rules and tips to help you learn French pronunciation and spelling are presented clearly with abundant model words and phrases.

Practice Pronunciation and spelling practice is provided at the word- and sentence-levels. The final activity features illustrated sayings and proverbs so you can practice the pronunciation or spelling point in an entertaining cultural context.

The headset icon at the top of the page indicates when an explanation and activities are recorded for convenient use in or outside of class.

ESPACE ROMAN-PHOTO

tells the story of a group of students living in Aix-en-Provence, France.

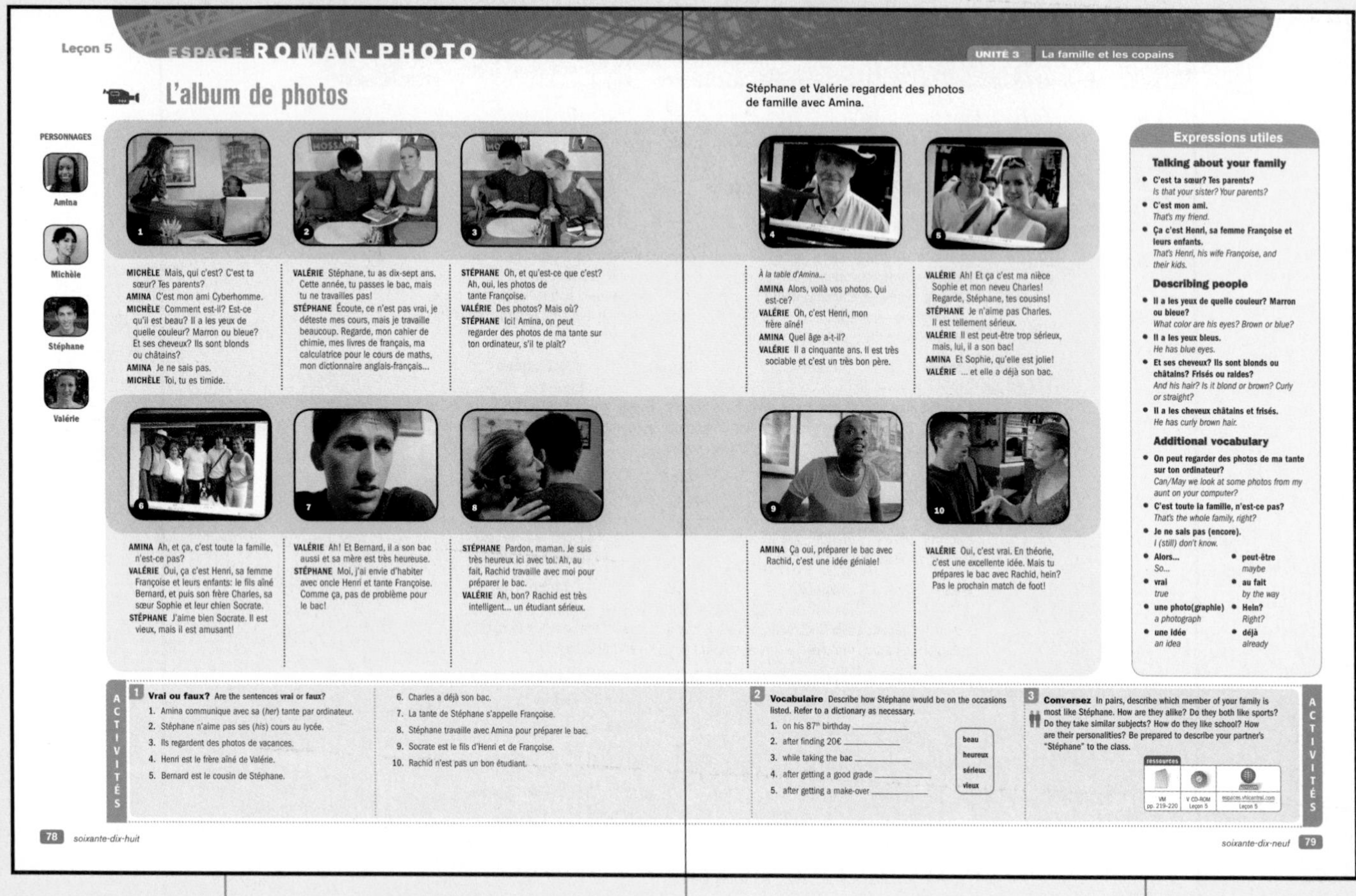

Leçon 5

ESPACE ROMAN-PHOTO

UNITÉ 3 La famille et les copains

L'album de photos

Stéphane et Valérie regardent des photos de famille avec Amina.

PERSONNAGES

Amina

Michèle

Stéphane

Valérie

1 **MICHÈLE** Mais, qui c'est? C'est ta sœur? Tes parents?
AMINA C'est mon ami Cyberhomme.
MICHÈLE Comment est-il? Est-ce qu'il est beau? Il a les yeux de quelle couleur? Marron ou bleue? Et ses cheveux? Ils sont blonds ou châtains?
AMINA Je ne sais pas.
MICHÈLE Toi, tu es timide.

2 **VALÉRIE** Stéphane, tu as dix-sept ans. Cette année, tu passes le bac, mais tu ne travailles pas!
STÉPHANE Écoute, ce n'est pas vrai, je déteste mes cours, mais je travaille beaucoup. Regarde, mon cahier de chimie, mes livres de français, ma calculatrice pour le cours de maths, mon dictionnaire anglais-français...

3 **STÉPHANE** Oh, et qu'est-ce que c'est? Ah, oui, les photos de tante Françoise.
VALÉRIE Des photos? Mais où?
STÉPHANE Ici! Amina, on peut regarder des photos de ma tante sur ton ordinateur, s'il te plaît?

4 *À la table d'Amina...*
AMINA Alors, voilà vos photos. Qui est-ce?
VALÉRIE Oh, c'est Henri, mon frère aîné!
AMINA Quel âge a-t-il?
VALÉRIE Il a cinquante ans. Il est très sociable et c'est un très bon père.

5 **VALÉRIE** Ah! Et ça c'est ma nièce Sophie et mon neveu Charles! Regarde, Stéphane, tes cousins!
STÉPHANE Je n'aime pas Charles. Il est tellement sérieux.
VALÉRIE Il est peut-être trop sérieux, mais, lui, il a son bac!
AMINA Et Sophie, qu'elle est jolie!
VALÉRIE ... et elle a déjà son bac.

6 **AMINA** Ah, et ça, c'est toute la famille, n'est-ce pas?
VALÉRIE Oui, ça c'est Henri, sa femme Françoise et leurs enfants: le fils aîné Bernard, et puis son frère Charles, sa sœur Sophie et leur chien Socrate.
STÉPHANE J'aime bien Socrate. Il est vieux, mais il est amusant!

7 **VALÉRIE** Ah! Et Bernard, il a son bac aussi et sa mère est très heureuse.
STÉPHANE Moi, j'ai envie d'habiter avec oncle Henri et tante Françoise. Comme ça, pas de problème pour le bac!

8 **STÉPHANE** Pardon, maman. Je suis très heureux ici avec toi. Ah, au fait, Rachid travaille avec moi pour préparer le bac.
VALÉRIE Ah, bon? Rachid est très intelligent... un étudiant sérieux.

9 **AMINA** Ça oui, préparer le bac avec Rachid, c'est une idée géniale!

10 **VALÉRIE** Oui, c'est vrai. En théorie, c'est une excellente idée. Mais tu prépares le bac avec Rachid, hein? Pas le prochain match de foot!

Expressions utiles

Talking about your family
- **C'est ta sœur? Tes parents?** *Is that your sister? Your parents?*
- **C'est mon ami.** *That's my friend.*
- **Ça c'est Henri, sa femme Françoise et leurs enfants.** *That's Henri, his wife Françoise, and their kids.*

Describing people
- **Il a les yeux de quelle couleur? Marron ou bleue?** *What color are his eyes? Brown or blue?*
- **Il a les yeux bleus.** *He has blue eyes.*
- **Et ses cheveux? Ils sont blonds ou châtains? Frisés ou raides?** *And his hair? Is it blond or brown? Curly or straight?*
- **Il a les cheveux châtains et frisés.** *He has curly brown hair.*

Additional vocabulary
- **On peut regarder des photos de ma tante sur ton ordinateur?** *Can/May we look at some photos from my aunt on your computer?*
- **C'est toute la famille, n'est-ce pas?** *That's the whole family, right?*
- **Je ne sais pas (encore).** *I (still) don't know.*
- **Alors...** *So...*
- **peut-être** *maybe*
- **vrai** *true*
- **au fait** *by the way*
- **une photo(graphie)** *a photograph*
- **Hein?** *Right?*
- **une idée** *an idea*
- **déjà** *already*

ACTIVITÉS

1 **Vrai ou faux?** Are the sentences **vrai** or **faux**?
1. Amina communique avec sa (*her*) tante par ordinateur.
2. Stéphane n'aime pas ses (*his*) cours au lycée.
3. Ils regardent des photos de vacances.
4. Henri est le frère aîné de Valérie.
5. Bernard est le cousin de Stéphane.
6. Charles a déjà son bac.
7. La tante de Stéphane s'appelle Françoise.
8. Stéphane travaille avec Amina pour préparer le bac.
9. Socrate est le fils d'Henri et de Françoise.
10. Rachid n'est pas un bon étudiant.

2 **Vocabulaire** Describe how Stéphane would be on the occasions listed. Refer to a dictionary as necessary.
1. on his 87th birthday ________
2. after finding 20€ ________
3. while taking the bac ________
4. after getting a good grade ________
5. after getting a make-over ________

beau / heureux / sérieux / vieux

3 **Conversez** In pairs, describe which member of your family is most like Stéphane. How are they alike? Do they both like sports? Do they take similar subjects? How do they like school? How are their personalities? Be prepared to describe your partner's "Stéphane" to the class.

ressources: VM pp. 219-220 | V CD-ROM Leçon 5 | espaces.vhlcentral.com Leçon 5

78 soixante-dix-huit

soixante-dix-neuf 79

Personnages The photo-based conversations take place among a cast of recurring characters—four college students, their landlady (who owns the café downstairs), and her teenage son.

***Roman-photo* video episodes** The **Roman-photo** episode appears in the **Roman-photo** part of the Video Program. To learn more about the video, turn to page xxvi.

Expressions utiles organizes new, active words and expressions by language function so you can focus on using them for real-life, practical purposes.

Conversations The conversations reinforce vocabulary from **ESPACE CONTEXTES**. They also preview structures from the upcoming **ESPACE STRUCTURES** section in context and in a comprehensible way.

ESPACE CULTURE

explores cultural themes introduced in **ESPACE CONTEXTES** and **ESPACE ROMAN-PHOTO.**

Leçon 5 ESPACE CULTURE

UNITÉ 3 La famille et les copains

CULTURE À LA LOUPE

La famille française

Comment est la famille française? Est-elle différente de la famille américaine? La structure familiale traditionnelle existe-t-elle toujours°? La majorité des Français sont-ils mariés, divorcés ou célibataires?

Il n'y a pas de réponse simple à ces questions. Si on regarde la population française d'aujourd'hui, on observe que les familles françaises sont très diverses. Le mariage est toujours très populaire: la majorité des hommes et des femmes sont mariés. Mais attention! Le nombre de personnes divorcées augmente chaque° année, tout comme° le nombre de personnes célibataires.

Selon° l'âge et les circonstances individuelles, les couples vivent° avec ou sans° enfants. La structure familiale traditionnelle existe toujours en France, mais il y a aussi des structures moins traditionnelles, comme les familles monoparentales, où° l'unique parent est divorcé, séparé ou veuf. Il y a aussi des familles qui combinent deux familles, avec un beau-père, une belle-mère, des demi-frères et des demi-sœurs. Certains couples choisissent° le Pacte Civil de Solidarité (PACS), qui offre certains droits° et protections aux couples qui habitent ensemble° mais qui ne sont pas mariés.

Oubliez les stéréotypes des familles françaises. Elles sont grandes et elles sont petites; elles sont traditionnelles et non-conventionnelles; elles changent et elles sont toujours les mêmes°.

Coup de main

Remember to read decimal places in **French** using the French word **virgule** (*comma*) where you would normally say *point* in English. To say *percent*, use **pour cent**.

64,3% soixante-quatre virgule trois pour cent

sixty-four point three percent

La situation familiale des Français
(par tranche° d'âge)

ÂGE	CÉLIBATAIRE	EN COUPLE SANS ENFANTS	EN COUPLE AVEC ENFANTS	PARENT D'UNE FAMILLE MONOPARENTALE
< 25 ans	3,6%	2,8%	1%	0,3%
25–29 ans	16,7%	26,5%	26,2%	2,6%
30–44 ans	10,9%	9,8%	64,3%	6,2%
45–59 ans	11,7%	29,9%	47,2%	5,9%
> 60 ans	20.3%	59.2%	11.7%	2.9%

toujours *still* **chaque** *each* **tout comme** *just like* **Selon** *According to* **vivent** *live* **sans** *without* **où** *where* **choisissent** *choose* **droits** *rights* **ensemble** *together* **mêmes** *same* **tranche** *bracket*

LE FRANÇAIS QUOTIDIEN

La famille

frangin	*brother*
frangine	*sister*
maman	*Mom, Mum*
mamie	*Nana, Grandma*
minou	*kitty*
papa	*Dad*
papi	*Granddad*
tata	*Auntie*
tonton	*Uncle*
toutou	*doggy*

LE MONDE FRANCOPHONE

Les fêtes et la famille

Les États-Unis ont quelques fêtes° en commun avec le monde francophone, mais les dates et les traditions de ces fêtes diffèrent d'un pays° à l'autre°. Voici deux fêtes associées à la famille.

La Fête des mères
En France le dernier° dimanche de mai ou le premier° dimanche de juin
En Belgique le deuxième° dimanche de mai
À l'île Maurice le dernier dimanche de mai
Au Canada le deuxième dimanche de mai

La Fête des pères
En France le troisième° dimanche de juin
En Belgique le deuxième dimanche de juin
Au Canada le troisième dimanche de juin

quelques fêtes *some holidays* **pays** *country* **autre** *other* **dernier** *last* **premier** *first* **deuxième** *second* **troisième** *third*

PORTRAIT

Jacques Chirac, président et père

Jacques Chirac, élu° président de la République française en 1995 (mille neuf cent quatre-vingt-quinze), est père de famille et enfant unique, mais il n'est pas le seul° Chirac dans l'arène politique. Claude Chirac, seconde fille de° Monsieur Chirac et de son° épouse Bernadette, travaille avec son père à Paris. Experte en communication et surnommée° «Madame fille» par la presse française, Claude est aussi mère de famille. Son° fils est né° en 1995, l'année de l'élection présidentielle de son grand-père, Jacques Chirac.

élu *elected* **seul** *only* **de** *of* **son** *his* **surnommée** *nicknamed* **Son** *Her* **est né** *was born*

SUR INTERNET

Le divorce en France est-il épidémique?

Go to espaces.vhlcentral.com to find more cultural information related to this **ESPACE CULTURE.**

ACTIVITÉS

1 Complétez Provide logical answers.

1. Si on regarde la population française d'aujourd'hui, on observe que les familles françaises sont très ________.
2. Le ________ est toujours très populaire en France.
3. La majorité des hommes et des femmes sont ________.
4. Le nombre de Français qui restent ________ augmente.
5. Les Français vivent en couple, avec ou sans ________.
6. Dans les familles ________, l'unique parent est divorcé, séparé ou veuf.
7. Il y a des familles qui combinent ________ familles.
8. Le ________ offre certains droits et protections aux couples qui ne sont pas mariés.
9. Oubliez les ________ des familles françaises.
10. Les familles françaises changent et elles sont toujours ________.

2 Vrai ou faux? Are these statements **vrai** or **faux**?

1. Claude Chirac est enfant unique.
2. Jacques Chirac est grand-père.
3. «Madame fille» est la femme de Jacques Chirac.
4. Claude Chirac a un fils.
5. La famille Chirac célèbre une fête le troisième dimanche de juin.
6. Le deuxième dimanche de mai, c'est la Fête des mères en Belgique et au Canada.

3 À vous... With a partner, write six sentences using the vocabulary in **Le français quotidien**. Be prepared to share them with your classmates.

ressources
espaces.vhlcentral.com
Leçon 5

80 quatre-vingts

quatre-vingt-un 81

Video icon The video icon at the top of the page tells you that topics in the two-page spread are directly related to events, locations, or other cultural phenomena in the lesson's **Roman-photo** video episode.

Culture à la loupe presents a main, in-depth reading about the lesson's cultural theme. Full-color photos bring to life important aspects of the topic, while charts with statistics and/or intriguing facts support and extend the information.

Le français quotidien exposes you to current, contemporary language by presenting familiar words and phrases related to the lesson's theme that are used in everyday spoken French.

Le monde francophone puts the spotlight on the peoples, places, and traditions of the countries and areas of the French-speaking world.

Portrait profiles people, places, and events throughout the French-speaking world, highlighting their importance, accomplishments, and/or contributions to the cultures of the French-speaking peoples and the global community.

Sur Internet boxes, with their provocative questions and photos, direct you to the **ESPACES** supersite where you can continue to learn more about the topics of **ESPACE CULTURE** and the lesson's theme.

ESPACE STRUCTURES

uses innovative design to support the learning of French.

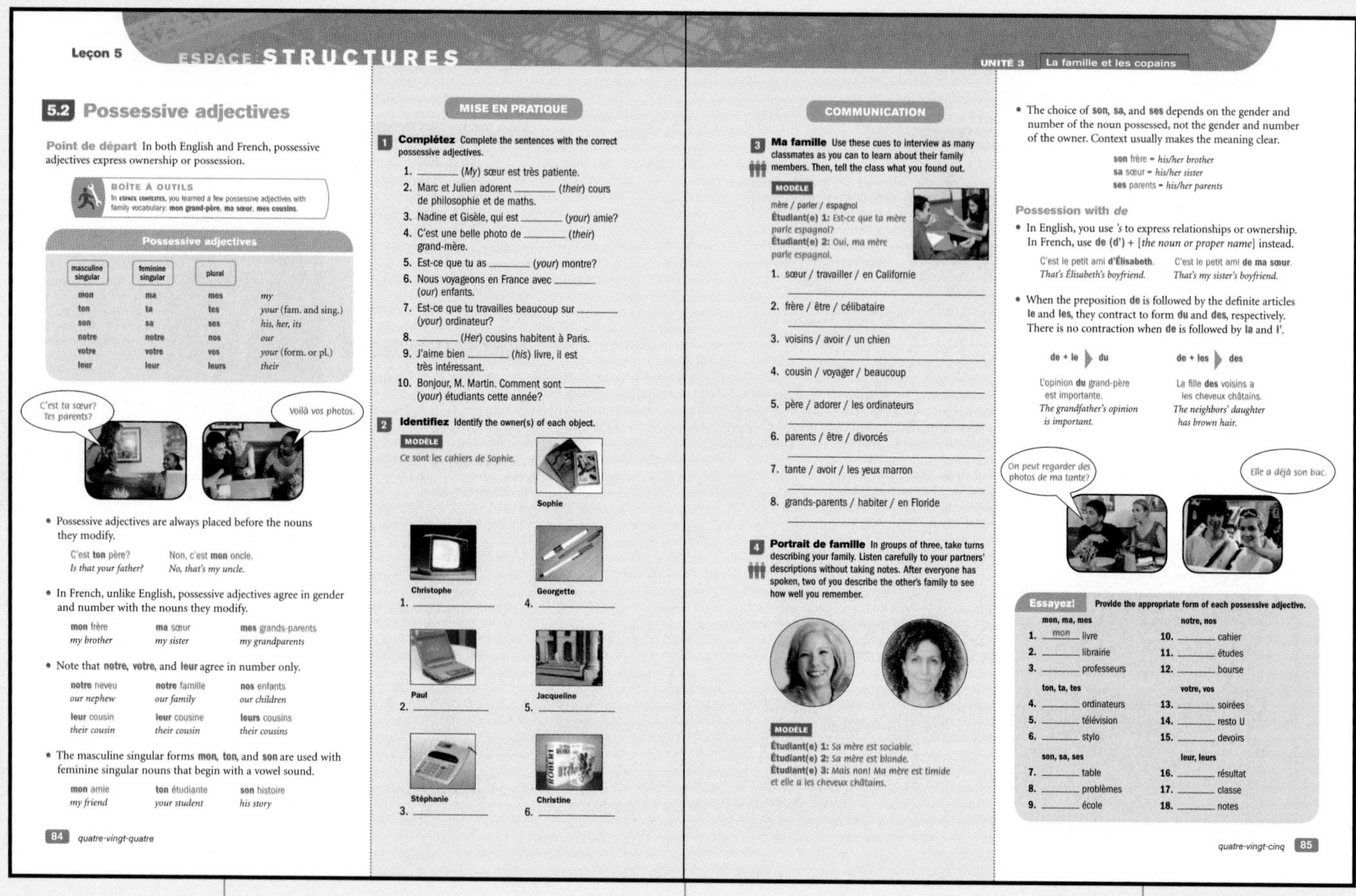
Leçon 5 ESPACE STRUCTURES

5.2 Possessive adjectives

Point de départ In both English and French, possessive adjectives express ownership or possession.

BOÎTE À OUTILS
In ESPACE CONTEXTES, you learned a few possessive adjectives with family vocabulary: **mon grand-père**, **ma sœur**, **mes cousins**.

Possessive adjectives

masculine singular	feminine singular	plural	
mon	ma	mes	*my*
ton	ta	tes	*your* (fam. and sing.)
son	sa	ses	*his, her, its*
notre	notre	nos	*our*
votre	votre	vos	*your* (form. or pl.)
leur	leur	leurs	*their*

- Possessive adjectives are always placed before the nouns they modify.

C'est **ton** père? *Is that your father?* Non, c'est **mon** oncle. *No, that's my uncle.*

- In French, unlike English, possessive adjectives agree in gender and number with the nouns they modify.

mon frère *my brother* / **ma** sœur *my sister* / **mes** grands-parents *my grandparents*

- Note that **notre**, **votre**, and **leur** agree in number only.

notre neveu *our nephew* / **notre** famille *our family* / **nos** enfants *our children*
leur cousin *their cousin* / **leur** cousine *their cousin* / **leurs** cousins *their cousins*

- The masculine singular forms **mon**, **ton**, and **son** are used with feminine singular nouns that begin with a vowel sound.

mon amie *my friend* / **ton** étudiante *your student* / **son** histoire *his story*

84 quatre-vingt-quatre

MISE EN PRATIQUE

1 **Complétez** Complete the sentences with the correct possessive adjectives.

1. _______ (*My*) sœur est très patiente.
2. Marc et Julien adorent _______ (*their*) cours de philosophie et de maths.
3. Nadine et Gisèle, qui est _______ (*your*) amie?
4. C'est une belle photo de _______ (*their*) grand-mère.
5. Est-ce que tu as _______ (*your*) montre?
6. Nous voyageons en France avec _______ (*our*) enfants.
7. Est-ce que tu travailles beaucoup sur _______ (*your*) ordinateur?
8. _______ (*Her*) cousins habitent à Paris.
9. J'aime bien _______ (*his*) livre, il est très intéressant.
10. Bonjour, M. Martin. Comment sont _______ (*your*) étudiants cette année?

2 **Identifiez** Identify the owner(s) of each object.

MODÈLE
Ce sont les cahiers de Sophie.

Sophie

1. Christophe _______
2. Paul _______
3. Stéphanie _______
4. Georgette _______
5. Jacqueline _______
6. Christine _______

UNITÉ 3 La famille et les copains

COMMUNICATION

3 **Ma famille** Use these cues to interview as many classmates as you can to learn about their family members. Then, tell the class what you found out.

MODÈLE
mère / parler / espagnol
Étudiant(e) 1: *Est-ce que ta mère parle espagnol?*
Étudiant(e) 2: *Oui, ma mère parle espagnol.*

1. sœur / travailler / en Californie
2. frère / être / célibataire
3. voisins / avoir / un chien
4. cousin / voyager / beaucoup
5. père / adorer / les ordinateurs
6. parents / être / divorcés
7. tante / avoir / les yeux marron
8. grands-parents / habiter / en Floride

4 **Portrait de famille** In groups of three, take turns describing your family. Listen carefully to your partners' descriptions without taking notes. After everyone has spoken, two of you describe the other's family to see how well you remember.

MODÈLE
Étudiant(e) 1: *Sa mère est sociable.*
Étudiant(e) 2: *Sa mère est blonde.*
Étudiant(e) 3: *Mais non! Ma mère est timide et elle a les cheveux châtains.*

- The choice of **son**, **sa**, and **ses** depends on the gender and number of the noun possessed, not the gender and number of the owner. Context usually makes the meaning clear.

son frère = *his/her brother*
sa sœur = *his/her sister*
ses parents = *his/her parents*

Possession with *de*

- In English, you use *'s* to express relationships or ownership. In French, use **de (d')** + [*the noun or proper name*] instead.

C'est le petit ami **d'Élisabeth**. *That's Élisabeth's boyfriend.* C'est le petit ami **de ma sœur**. *That's my sister's boyfriend.*

- When the preposition **de** is followed by the definite articles **le** and **les**, they contract to form **du** and **des**, respectively. There is no contraction when **de** is followed by **la** and **l'**.

de + le ▶ du / de + les ▶ des

L'opinion **du** grand-père est importante. *The grandfather's opinion is important.*
La fille **des** voisins a les cheveux châtains. *The neighbors' daughter has brown hair.*

Essayez! Provide the appropriate form of each possessive adjective.

mon, ma, mes
1. mon livre
2. _______ librairie
3. _______ professeurs

ton, ta, tes
4. _______ ordinateurs
5. _______ télévision
6. _______ stylo

son, sa, ses
7. _______ table
8. _______ problèmes
9. _______ école

notre, nos
10. _______ cahier
11. _______ études
12. _______ bourse

votre, vos
13. _______ soirées
14. _______ resto U
15. _______ devoirs

leur, leurs
16. _______ résultat
17. _______ classe
18. _______ notes

quatre-vingt-cinq 85

Text format For each grammar point, the explanation and practice activities appear on one self-contained spread of two facing pages. Grammar explanations in the outside panels offer handy on-page support for the activities in the central, inside panels, providing you with immediate access to information essential to communication.

Charts and diagrams Within the clear, easy-to-grasp grammar explanations, colorful, carefully designed charts and diagrams call out key grammatical structures and forms, as well as important related vocabulary.

Graphics-intensive design Photos from the **ESPACES** Video Program consistently integrate the lesson's video episode and **ESPACE ROMAN-PHOTO** section with the grammar explanations. Additional photos, drawings, and graphic devices enliven activities and heighten visual interest.

ESPACE STRUCTURES

provides varied types of directed and communicative practice.

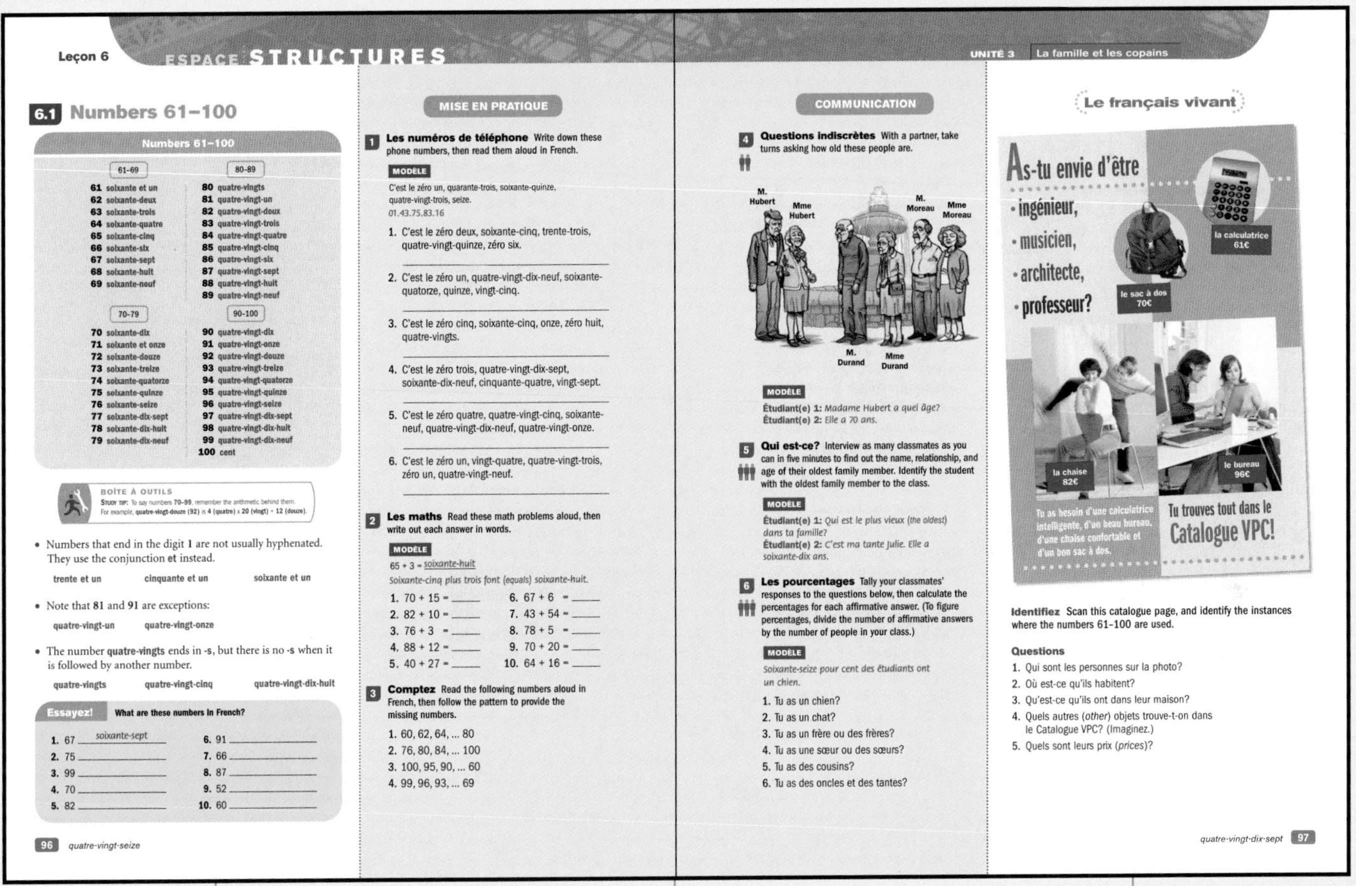

Leçon 6 ESPACE STRUCTURES

6.1 Numbers 61–100

Numbers 61–100

61–69	80–89
61 soixante et un	**80** quatre-vingts
62 soixante-deux	**81** quatre-vingt-un
63 soixante-trois	**82** quatre-vingt-deux
64 soixante-quatre	**83** quatre-vingt-trois
65 soixante-cinq	**84** quatre-vingt-quatre
66 soixante-six	**85** quatre-vingt-cinq
67 soixante-sept	**86** quatre-vingt-six
68 soixante-huit	**87** quatre-vingt-sept
69 soixante-neuf	**88** quatre-vingt-huit
	89 quatre-vingt-neuf
70–79	**90–100**
70 soixante-dix	**90** quatre-vingt-dix
71 soixante et onze	**91** quatre-vingt-onze
72 soixante-douze	**92** quatre-vingt-douze
73 soixante-treize	**93** quatre-vingt-treize
74 soixante-quatorze	**94** quatre-vingt-quatorze
75 soixante-quinze	**95** quatre-vingt-quinze
76 soixante-seize	**96** quatre-vingt-seize
77 soixante-dix-sept	**97** quatre-vingt-dix-sept
78 soixante-dix-huit	**98** quatre-vingt-dix-huit
79 soixante-dix-neuf	**99** quatre-vingt-dix-neuf
	100 cent

BOÎTE À OUTILS
STUDY TIP: To say numbers **70–99**, remember the arithmetic behind them. For example, **quatre-vingt-douze (92)** is **4 (quatre)** x **20 (vingt)** + **12 (douze)**.

- Numbers that end in the digit **1** are not usually hyphenated. They use the conjunction **et** instead.

  trente et un — cinquante et un — soixante et un

- Note that **81** and **91** are exceptions:

  quatre-vingt-un — quatre-vingt-onze

- The number **quatre-vingts** ends in **-s**, but there is no **-s** when it is followed by another number.

  quatre-vingts — quatre-vingt-cinq — quatre-vingt-dix-huit

Essayez! What are these numbers in French?

1. 67 *soixante-sept*
2. 75 ______
3. 99 ______
4. 70 ______
5. 82 ______
6. 91 ______
7. 66 ______
8. 87 ______
9. 52 ______
10. 60 ______

96 *quatre-vingt-seize*

MISE EN PRATIQUE

1 Les numéros de téléphone Write down these phone numbers, then read them aloud in French.

MODÈLE
C'est le zéro un, quarante-trois, soixante-quinze, quatre-vingt-trois, seize.
01.43.75.83.16

1. C'est le zéro deux, soixante-cinq, trente-trois, quatre-vingt-quinze, zéro six.
2. C'est le zéro un, quatre-vingt-dix-neuf, soixante-quatorze, quinze, vingt-cinq.
3. C'est le zéro cinq, soixante-cinq, onze, zéro huit, quatre-vingts.
4. C'est le zéro trois, quatre-vingt-dix-sept, soixante-dix-neuf, cinquante-quatre, vingt-sept.
5. C'est le zéro quatre, quatre-vingt-cinq, soixante-neuf, quatre-vingt-dix-neuf, quatre-vingt-onze.
6. C'est le zéro un, vingt-quatre, quatre-vingt-trois, zéro un, quatre-vingt-neuf.

2 Les maths Read these math problems aloud, then write out each answer in words.

MODÈLE
65 + 3 = *soixante-huit*
Soixante-cinq plus trois font (equals) soixante-huit.

1. 70 + 15 = ____
2. 82 + 10 = ____
3. 76 + 3 = ____
4. 88 + 12 = ____
5. 40 + 27 = ____
6. 67 + 6 = ____
7. 43 + 54 = ____
8. 78 + 5 = ____
9. 70 + 20 = ____
10. 64 + 16 = ____

3 Comptez Read the following numbers aloud in French, then follow the pattern to provide the missing numbers.

1. 60, 62, 64, ... 80
2. 76, 80, 84, ... 100
3. 100, 95, 90, ... 60
4. 99, 96, 93, ... 69

UNITÉ 3 La famille et les copains

COMMUNICATION

4 Questions indiscrètes With a partner, take turns asking how old these people are.

M. Hubert — Mme Hubert — M. Durand — Mme Durand — M. Moreau — Mme Moreau

MODÈLE
Étudiant(e) 1: *Madame Hubert a quel âge?*
Étudiant(e) 2: *Elle a 70 ans.*

5 Qui est-ce? Interview as many classmates as you can in five minutes to find out the name, relationship, and age of their oldest family member. Identify the student with the oldest family member to the class.

MODÈLE
Étudiant(e) 1: *Qui est le plus vieux (the oldest) dans ta famille?*
Étudiant(e) 2: *C'est ma tante Julie. Elle a soixante-dix ans.*

6 Les pourcentages Tally your classmates' responses to the questions below, then calculate the percentages for each affirmative answer. (To figure percentages, divide the number of affirmative answers by the number of people in your class.)

MODÈLE
Soixante-seize pour cent des étudiants ont un chien.

1. Tu as un chien?
2. Tu as un chat?
3. Tu as un frère ou des frères?
4. Tu as une sœur ou des sœurs?
5. Tu as des cousins?
6. Tu as des oncles et des tantes?

Le français vivant

As-tu envie d'être
- ingénieur,
- musicien,
- architecte,
- professeur?

la calculatrice 61€
le sac à dos 70€
la chaise 82€
le bureau 96€

Tu as besoin d'une calculatrice intelligente, d'un beau bureau, d'une chaise confortable et d'un bon sac à dos.

Tu trouves tout dans le Catalogue VPC!

Identifiez Scan this catalogue page, and identify the instances where the numbers 61–100 are used.

Questions
1. Qui sont les personnes sur la photo?
2. Où est-ce qu'ils habitent?
3. Qu'est-ce qu'ils ont dans leur maison?
4. Quels autres (*other*) objets trouve-t-on dans le Catalogue VPC? (Imaginez.)
5. Quels sont leurs prix (*prices*)?

quatre-vingt-dix-sept 97

Essayez! activities are your first step in practicing each new grammar point. They get you working with the grammar point right away in simple, easy-to-understand formats.

Mise en pratique activities provide a wide range of guided exercises in contexts that combine current and previously learned vocabulary with the current grammar point.

Le français vivant activities incorporate authentic documents, like advertisements and posters, into the grammar practice, highlighting the new grammar point in a real-life context.

Communication offers opportunities for creative expression using the lesson's grammar and vocabulary. Activities take place with a partner, in small groups, or with the whole class.

ESPACE STRUCTURES

pulls the lesson together with cumulative practice.

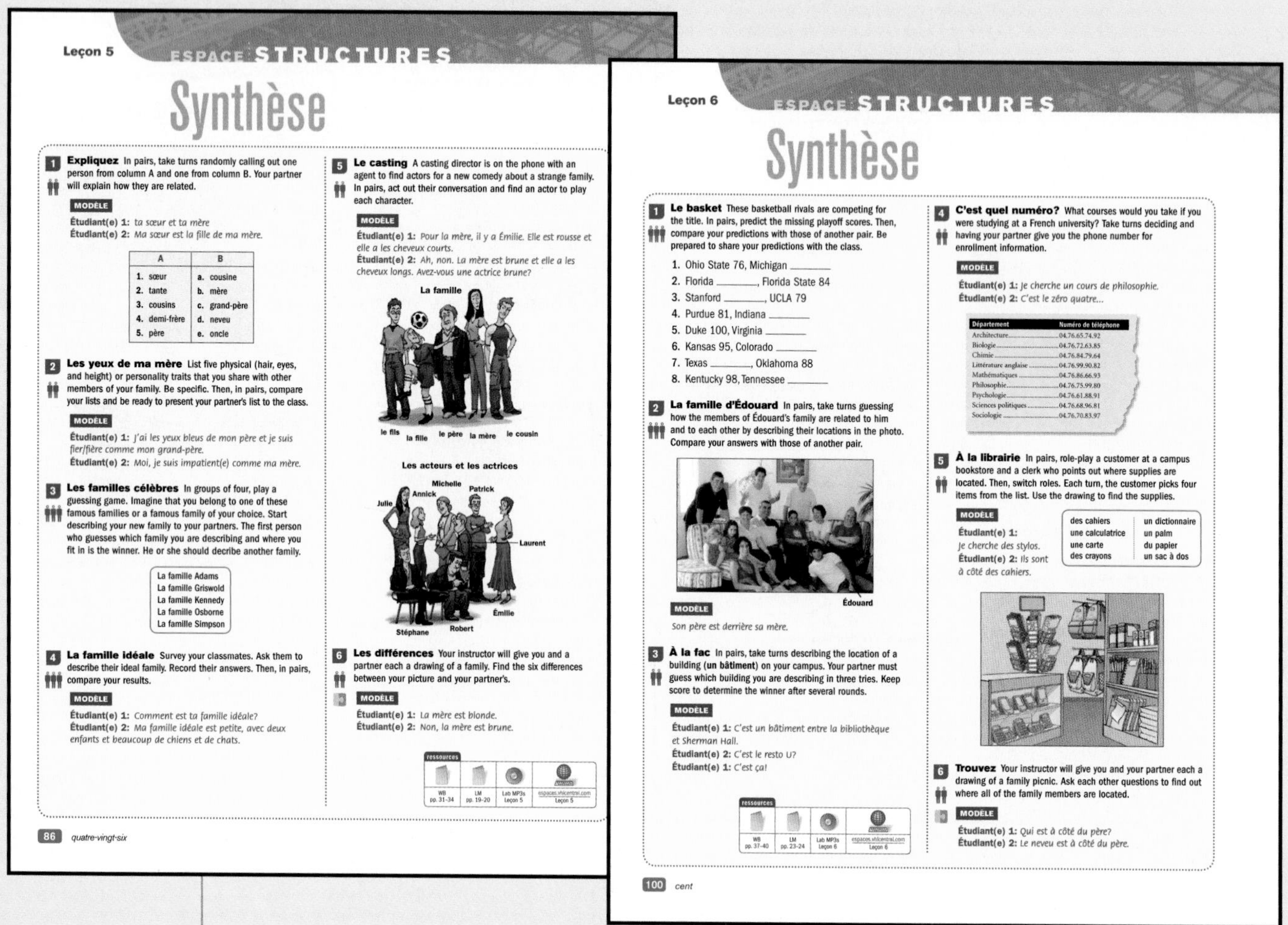

Leçon 5

ESPACE STRUCTURES

Synthèse

1 Expliquez In pairs, take turns randomly calling out one person from column A and one from column B. Your partner will explain how they are related.

MODÈLE

Étudiant(e) 1: *ta sœur et ta mère*
Étudiant(e) 2: *Ma sœur est la fille de ma mère.*

A	B
1. sœur	a. cousine
2. tante	b. mère
3. cousins	c. grand-père
4. demi-frère	d. neveu
5. père	e. oncle

2 Les yeux de ma mère List five physical (hair, eyes, and height) or personality traits that you share with other members of your family. Be specific. Then, in pairs, compare your lists and be ready to present your partner's list to the class.

MODÈLE

Étudiant(e) 1: *J'ai les yeux bleus de mon père et je suis fier/fière comme mon grand-père.*
Étudiant(e) 2: *Moi, je suis impatient(e) comme ma mère.*

3 Les familles célèbres In groups of four, play a guessing game. Imagine that you belong to one of these famous families or a famous family of your choice. Start describing your new family to your partners. The first person who guesses which family you are describing and where you fit in is the winner. He or she should decribe another family.

La famille Adams
La famille Griswold
La famille Kennedy
La famille Osborne
La famille Simpson

4 La famille idéale Survey your classmates. Ask them to describe their ideal family. Record their answers. Then, in pairs, compare your results.

MODÈLE

Étudiant(e) 1: *Comment est ta famille idéale?*
Étudiant(e) 2: *Ma famille idéale est petite, avec deux enfants et beaucoup de chiens et de chats.*

5 Le casting A casting director is on the phone with an agent to find actors for a new comedy about a strange family. In pairs, act out their conversation and find an actor to play each character.

MODÈLE

Étudiant(e) 1: *Pour la mère, il y a Émilie. Elle est rousse et elle a les cheveux courts.*
Étudiant(e) 2: *Ah, non. La mère est brune et elle a les cheveux longs. Avez-vous une actrice brune?*

La famille

le fils la fille le père la mère le cousin

Les acteurs et les actrices

Julie Annick Michelle Patrick Laurent Émilie Robert Stéphane

6 Les différences Your instructor will give you and a partner each a drawing of a family. Find the six differences between your picture and your partner's.

MODÈLE

Étudiant(e) 1: *La mère est blonde.*
Étudiant(e) 2: *Non, la mère est brune.*

ressources

WB pp. 31-34	LM pp. 19-20	Lab MP3s Leçon 5	espaces.vhlcentral.com Leçon 5

86 *quatre-vingt-six*

Leçon 6

ESPACE STRUCTURES

Synthèse

1 Le basket These basketball rivals are competing for the title. In pairs, predict the missing playoff scores. Then, compare your predictions with those of another pair. Be prepared to share your predictions with the class.

1. Ohio State 76, Michigan ______
2. Florida ______, Florida State 84
3. Stanford ______, UCLA 79
4. Purdue 81, Indiana ______
5. Duke 100, Virginia ______
6. Kansas 95, Colorado ______
7. Texas ______, Oklahoma 88
8. Kentucky 98, Tennessee ______

2 La famille d'Édouard In pairs, take turns guessing how the members of Édouard's family are related to him and to each other by describing their locations in the photo. Compare your answers with those of another pair.

Édouard

MODÈLE

Son père est derrière sa mère.

3 À la fac In pairs, take turns describing the location of a building (**un bâtiment**) on your campus. Your partner must guess which building you are describing in three tries. Keep score to determine the winner after several rounds.

MODÈLE

Étudiant(e) 1: *C'est un bâtiment entre la bibliothèque et Sherman Hall.*
Étudiant(e) 2: *C'est le resto U?*
Étudiant(e) 1: *C'est ça!*

ressources

WB pp. 37-40	LM pp. 23-24	Lab MP3s Leçon 6	espaces.vhlcentral.com Leçon 6

4 C'est quel numéro? What courses would you take if you were studying at a French university? Take turns deciding and having your partner give you the phone number for enrollment information.

MODÈLE

Étudiant(e) 1: *Je cherche un cours de philosophie.*
Étudiant(e) 2: *C'est le zéro quatre...*

Département	Numéro de téléphone
Architecture	04.76.65.74.92
Biologie	04.76.72.63.85
Chimie	04.76.84.79.64
Littérature anglaise	04.76.99.90.82
Mathématiques	04.76.86.66.93
Philosophie	04.76.75.99.80
Psychologie	04.76.61.88.91
Sciences politiques	04.76.68.96.81
Sociologie	04.76.70.83.97

5 À la librairie In pairs, role-play a customer at a campus bookstore and a clerk who points out where supplies are located. Then, switch roles. Each turn, the customer picks four items from the list. Use the drawing to find the supplies.

MODÈLE

Étudiant(e) 1: *Je cherche des stylos.*
Étudiant(e) 2: *Ils sont à côté des cahiers.*

des cahiers	un dictionnaire
une calculatrice	un palm
une carte	du papier
des crayons	un sac à dos

6 Trouvez Your instructor will give you and your partner each a drawing of a family picnic. Ask each other questions to find out where all of the family members are located.

MODÈLE

Étudiant(e) 1: *Qui est à côté du père?*
Étudiant(e) 2: *Le neveu est à côté du père.*

100 *cent*

Synthèse activities integrate the lesson's two grammar points with previously learned vocabulary and structures, providing consistent, built-in review and recycling as you progress through the text.

Pair and group icons call out the communicative nature of the activities. Situations, role plays, games, personal questions, interviews, and surveys are just some of the types of activities that you will experience.

Information gap activities engage you and a partner in problem-solving and other situations based on handouts your instructor gives you. You and your partner each have only half of the information you need, so you must work together to accomplish the task at hand.

ESPACE STRUCTURES

wraps up with three types of culturally-based, multimedia-oriented activities.

Projet gets you involved in a task-based project for which you research a topic and create a tangible product like a poster or a brochure.

Interlude connects the unit's theme to French music and fine art.

Le zapping features television clips in French—commercials and a weather report—supported by background information, images from the clips, and activities to help you understand and to check your comprehension of what you see.

Sur Internet lets you know that research tips and support for **Projet**, **Interlude**, and **Le zapping** are accessible on the **ESPACES** supersite. You can even watch the TV clips there.

SAVOIR-FAIRE

Panorama presents the French-speaking world.

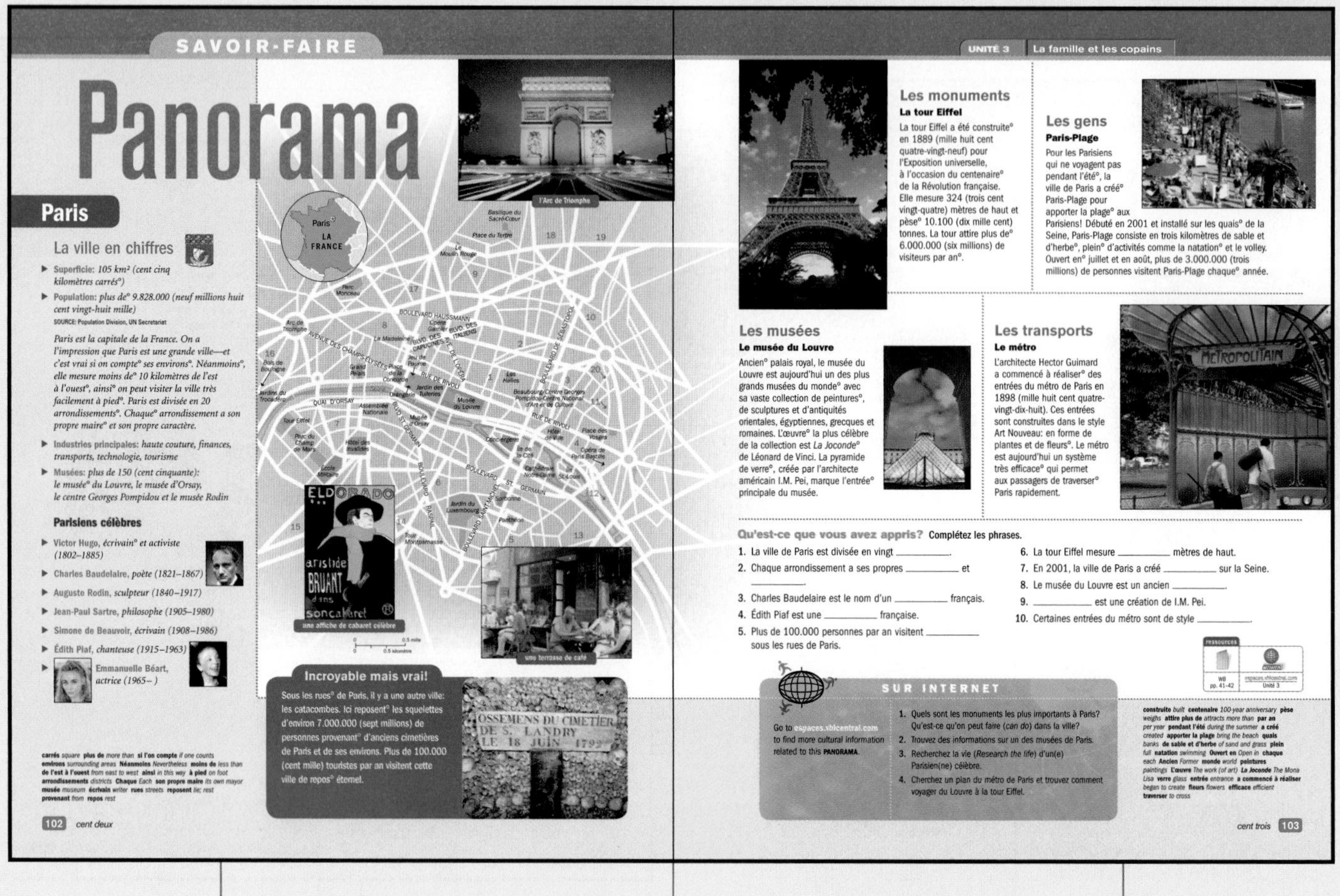

SAVOIR-FAIRE

UNITÉ 3 La famille et les copains

Panorama

Paris

La ville en chiffres

- **Superficie:** *105 km² (cent cinq kilomètres carrés°)*
- **Population:** *plus de° 9.828.000 (neuf millions huit cent vingt-huit mille)*

SOURCE: Population Division, UN Secretariat

Paris est la capitale de la France. On a l'impression que Paris est une grande ville—et c'est vrai si on compte° ses environs°. Néanmoins°, elle mesure moins de° 10 kilomètres de l'est à l'ouest°, ainsi° on peut visiter la ville très facilement à pied°. Paris est divisée en 20 arrondissements°. Chaque° arrondissement a son propre maire° et son propre caractère.

- **Industries principales:** *haute couture, finances, transports, technologie, tourisme*
- **Musées:** *plus de 150 (cent cinquante): le musée° du Louvre, le musée d'Orsay, le centre Georges Pompidou et le musée Rodin*

Parisiens célèbres

- Victor Hugo, *écrivain° et activiste (1802–1885)*
- Charles Baudelaire, *poète (1821–1867)*
- Auguste Rodin, *sculpteur (1840–1917)*
- Jean-Paul Sartre, *philosophe (1905–1980)*
- Simone de Beauvoir, *écrivain (1908–1986)*
- Édith Piaf, *chanteuse (1915–1963)*
- Emmanuelle Béart, *actrice (1965–)*

l'Arc de Triomphe

une affiche de cabaret célèbre

une terrasse de café

Incroyable mais vrai!

Sous les rues° de Paris, il y a une autre ville: les catacombes. Ici reposent° les squelettes d'environ 7.000.000 (sept millions) de personnes provenant° d'anciens cimetières de Paris et de ses environs. Plus de 100.000 (cent mille) touristes par an visitent cette ville de repos° éternel.

Les monuments

La tour Eiffel

La tour Eiffel a été construite° en 1889 (mille huit cent quatre-vingt-neuf) pour l'Exposition universelle, à l'occasion du centenaire° de la Révolution française. Elle mesure 324 (trois cent vingt-quatre) mètres de haut et pèse° 10.100 (dix mille cent) tonnes. La tour attire plus de° 6.000.000 (six millions) de visiteurs par an°.

Les gens

Paris-Plage

Pour les Parisiens qui ne voyagent pas pendant l'été°, la ville de Paris a créé° Paris-Plage pour apporter la plage° aux Parisiens! Débuté en 2001 et installé sur les quais° de la Seine, Paris-Plage consiste en trois kilomètres de sable et d'herbe°, plein° d'activités comme la natation° et le volley. Ouvert en° juillet et en août, plus de 3.000.000 (trois millions) de personnes visitent Paris-Plage chaque° année.

Les musées

Le musée du Louvre

Ancien° palais royal, le musée du Louvre est aujourd'hui un des plus grands musées du monde° avec sa vaste collection de peintures°, de sculptures et d'antiquités orientales, égyptiennes, grecques et romaines. L'œuvre° la plus célèbre de la collection est *La Joconde*° de Léonard de Vinci. La pyramide de verre°, créée par l'architecte américain I.M. Pei, marque l'entrée° principale du musée.

Les transports

Le métro

L'architecte Hector Guimard a commencé à réaliser° des entrées du métro de Paris en 1898 (mille huit cent quatre-vingt-dix-huit). Ces entrées sont construites dans le style Art Nouveau: en forme de plantes et de fleurs°. Le métro est aujourd'hui un système très efficace° qui permet aux passagers de traverser° Paris rapidement.

Qu'est-ce que vous avez appris? Complétez les phrases.

1. La ville de Paris est divisée en vingt ________.
2. Chaque arrondissement a ses propres ________ et ________.
3. Charles Baudelaire est le nom d'un ________ français.
4. Édith Piaf est une ________ française.
5. Plus de 100.000 personnes par an visitent ________ sous les rues de Paris.
6. La tour Eiffel mesure ________ mètres de haut.
7. En 2001, la ville de Paris a créé ________ sur la Seine.
8. Le musée du Louvre est un ancien ________.
9. ________ est une création de I.M. Pei.
10. Certaines entrées du métro sont de style ________.

SUR INTERNET

Go to espaces.vhlcentral.com to find more cultural information related to this **PANORAMA**.

1. Quels sont les monuments les plus importants à Paris? Qu'est-ce qu'on peut faire (*can do*) dans la ville?
2. Trouvez des informations sur un des musées de Paris.
3. Recherchez la vie (*Research the life*) d'un(e) Parisien(ne) célèbre.
4. Cherchez un plan du métro de Paris et trouvez comment voyager du Louvre à la tour Eiffel.

102 cent deux

cent trois 103

La ville/Le pays/La région en chiffres provides interesting key facts about the featured city, country, or region.

Maps point out major cities, rivers, and other geographical features and situate the featured place in the context of its immediate surroundings and the world.

Readings A series of brief paragraphs explores facets of the featured place's culture such as history, landmarks, fine art, literature, and aspects of everyday life.

Incroyable mais vrai! highlights an intriguing fact about the featured place or its people.

Qu'est-ce que vous avez appris? exercises check your understanding of key ideas, and **ressources** boxes reference the two pages of additional activities in the **ESPACES** Workbook.

Sur Internet offers Internet activities on the **ESPACES** supersite for additional avenues of discovery.

SAVOIR-FAIRE

Lecture develops reading skills in the context of the unit's theme.

SAVOIR-FAIRE

UNITÉ 3 La famille et les copains

Lecture

Avant la lecture

STRATÉGIE

Predicting content from visuals

When you are reading in French, be sure to look for visual clues that will orient you as to the content and purpose of what you are reading. Photos and illustrations, for example, will often give you a good idea of the main points that the reading covers. You may also encounter helpful visuals that summarize large amounts of data in a way that is easy to comprehend; these visuals include bar graphs, pie charts, flow charts, lists of percentages, and other diagrams.

Le Top 10 des chiens de race°
% DE FOYERS° POSSESSEURS
les caniches° **9,3%**
les labradors **7,8%**
les yorkshires **5,6%**
les épagneuls bretons° **4,6%**
les bergers allemands° **4,1%**
les autres bergers **3,3%**
les bichons **2,7%**
les cockers/fox-terriers **2,2%**
les boxers **2%**
les colleys **1,6%**

Examinez le texte

Take a quick look at the visual elements of the article in order to generate a list of ideas about its content. Then, compare your list with a classmate's. Are your lists the same or are they different? Discuss your lists and make any changes needed to produce a final list of ideas.

race *breed* **foyers** *households* **caniches** *poodles* **épagneuls bretons** *Brittany Spaniels* **bergers allemands** *German Shepherds*

104 *cent quatre*

Fido en famille

Les Français adorent les animaux. Plus de la moitié° des foyers en France ont un chien, un chat ou un autre animal familier°. Les chiens sont particulièrement appréciés et intégrés dans la famille et la société françaises.

Qui possède un chien en France et pourquoi? Souvent°, la présence d'un chien en famille suit l'arrivée° d'enfants, parce que les parents pensent qu'un chien contribue positivement à leur développement. Il est aussi commun de trouver deux chiens ou plus dans le même° foyer.

Les chiens sont d'excellents compagnons. Leurs maîtres° sont moins seuls° et déclarent avoir moins de stress. Certaines personnes possèdent un chien pour avoir plus d'exercice physique. Et il y a aussi des personnes qui possèdent un chien parce qu'elles en ont toujours eu un° et n'imaginent pas une vie° sans° chien.

Les chiens ont parfois° les mêmes droits° que les autres membres de la famille, et parfois des droits spéciaux. Bien sûr, ils accompagnent leurs maîtres pour les courses en ville° et les promenades dans le parc, et ils entrent même dans certains magasins°. Ne trouvez-vous pas parfois un caniche ou un labrador, les deux races les plus° populaires en France, avec son maître dans un restaurant?

En France, il n'est pas difficile d'observer que les chiens ont une place privilégiée au sein de° la famille.

Pourquoi avoir un animal familier?

RAISON	CHIENS	CHATS	OISEAUX	POISSONS
Pour l'amour des animaux	61,4%	60,5%	61%	33%
Pour avoir de la compagnie	43,5%	38,2%	37%	10%
Pour s'occuper°	40,4%	37,7%	0%	0%
Parce que j'en ai toujours eu un°	31,8%	28,9%	0%	0%
Pour le bien-être° personnel	29,2%	26,2%	0%	0%
Pour les enfants	23,7%	21,3%	30%	48%

Plus de la moitié *More than half* **animal familier** *pet* **Souvent** *Often* **suit l'arrivée** *follows the arrival* **même** *same* **maîtres** *owners* **moins seuls** *less lonely* **en ont toujours eu un** *have always had one* **vie** *life* **sans** *without* **parfois** *sometimes* **droits** *rights* **courses en ville** *errands in town* **magasins** *stores* **les plus** *the most* **au sein de** *in the heart of* **s'occuper** *keep busy* **Parce que j'en ai toujours eu un** *Because I've always had one* **bien-être** *well-being*

Après la lecture

Vrai ou faux? Indicate whether these items are **vrai** or **faux**, based on the reading.

	Vrai	Faux
1. Les chiens accompagnent leurs maîtres pour les promenades dans le parc.	☐	☐
2. Parfois, les chiens accompagnent leurs maîtres dans les restaurants.	☐	☐
3. Le chat n'est pas un animal apprécié en France.	☐	☐
4. Certaines personnes déclarent posséder un chien pour avoir plus d'exercice physique.	☐	☐
5. Certaines personnes déclarent posséder un chien pour avoir plus de stress.	☐	☐
6. En France, les familles avec enfants n'ont pas de chien.	☐	☐

Fido en famille Choose the correct response according to the article.

1. Combien de foyers en France ont au moins (*at least*) un animal familier?
   a. 20%–25%
   b. 40%–45%
   c. 50%–55%
2. Pourquoi est-ce une bonne idée d'avoir un chien?
   a. pour plus de compagnie et plus de stress
   b. pour l'exercice physique et être seul
   c. pour la compagnie et le développement des enfants
3. Que pensent les familles françaises de leurs chiens?
   a. Les chiens sont plus importants que les enfants.
   b. Les chiens font partie (*are part*) de la famille et participent aux activités quotidiennes (*daily*).
   c. Le rôle des chiens est limité aux promenades.
4. Quelles races de chien les Français préfèrent-ils?
   a. les caniches et les oiseaux
   b. les labradors et les bergers allemands
   c. les caniches et les labradors
5. Y a-t-il des familles avec plus d'un chien?
   a. Non
   b. Oui
   c. les caniches et les labradors

cent cinq 105

Avant la lecture presents valuable reading strategies and pre-reading activities that strengthen your reading abilities in French.

Readings are directly tied to the lesson theme and recycle vocabulary and grammar you have learned. The selections in Units 1–11 are cultural texts, while those in Units 12–15 are literary pieces.

Après la lecture includes post-reading activities that check your comprehension of the reading.

SAVOIR-FAIRE

À l'écoute and **Écriture** develop listening and writing skills in the context of the unit's theme.

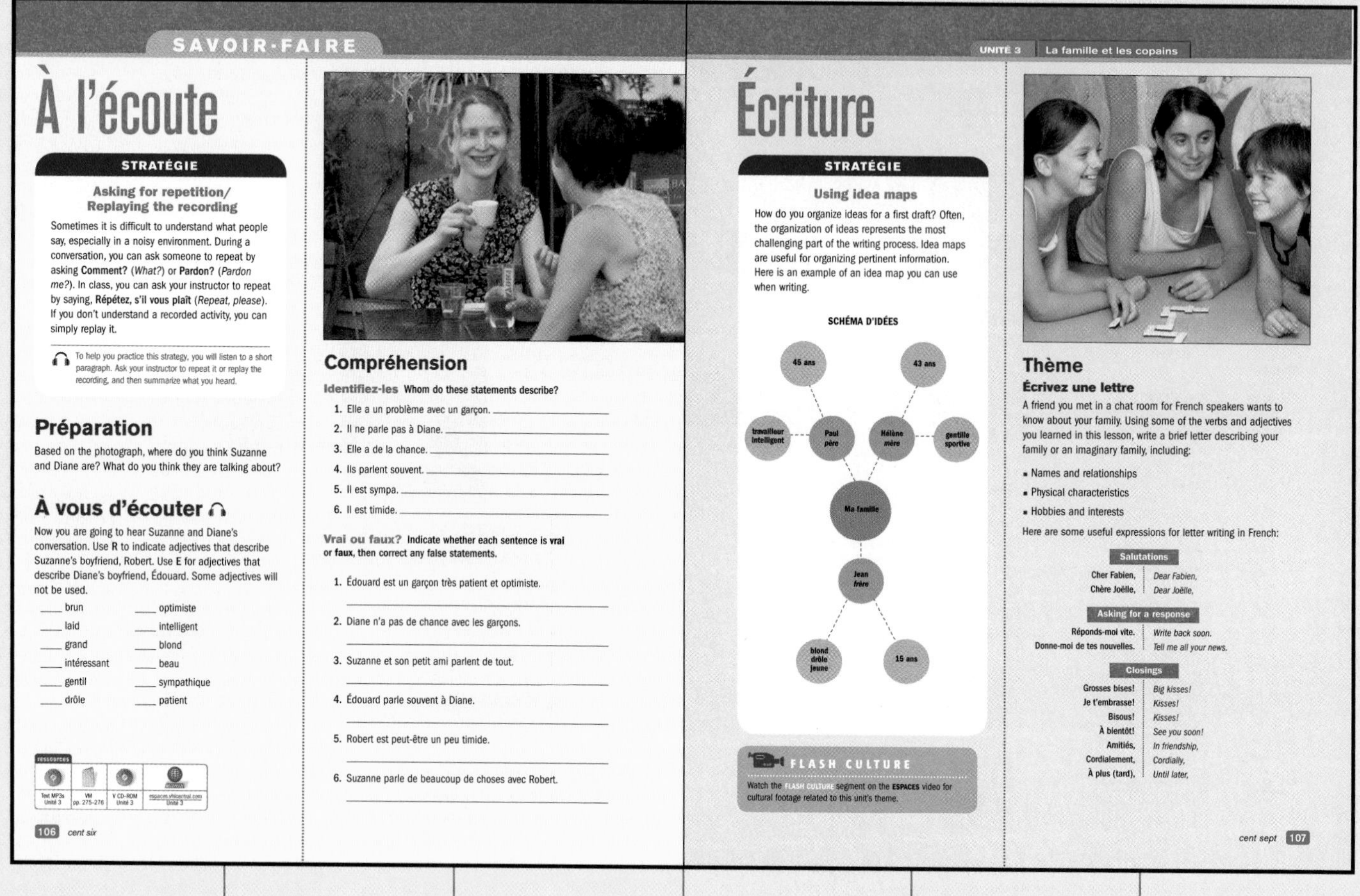
SAVOIR-FAIRE

À l'écoute

STRATÉGIE

Asking for repetition/ Replaying the recording

Sometimes it is difficult to understand what people say, especially in a noisy environment. During a conversation, you can ask someone to repeat by asking **Comment?** (*What?*) or **Pardon?** (*Pardon me?*). In class, you can ask your instructor to repeat by saying, **Répétez, s'il vous plaît** (*Repeat, please*). If you don't understand a recorded activity, you can simply replay it.

To help you practice this strategy, you will listen to a short paragraph. Ask your instructor to repeat it or replay the recording, and then summarize what you heard.

Préparation

Based on the photograph, where do you think Suzanne and Diane are? What do you think they are talking about?

À vous d'écouter

Now you are going to hear Suzanne and Diane's conversation. Use **R** to indicate adjectives that describe Suzanne's boyfriend, Robert. Use **E** for adjectives that describe Diane's boyfriend, Édouard. Some adjectives will not be used.

___ brun	___ optimiste
___ laid	___ intelligent
___ grand	___ blond
___ intéressant	___ beau
___ gentil	___ sympathique
___ drôle	___ patient

106 cent six

Compréhension

Identifiez-les Whom do these statements describe?

1. Elle a un problème avec un garçon. ___
2. Il ne parle pas à Diane. ___
3. Elle a de la chance. ___
4. Ils parlent souvent. ___
5. Il est sympa. ___
6. Il est timide. ___

Vrai ou faux? Indicate whether each sentence is **vrai** or **faux**, then correct any false statements.

1. Édouard est un garçon très patient et optimiste.
2. Diane n'a pas de chance avec les garçons.
3. Suzanne et son petit ami parlent de tout.
4. Édouard parle souvent à Diane.
5. Robert est peut-être un peu timide.
6. Suzanne parle de beaucoup de choses avec Robert.

UNITÉ 3 La famille et les copains

Écriture

STRATÉGIE

Using idea maps

How do you organize ideas for a first draft? Often, the organization of ideas represents the most challenging part of the writing process. Idea maps are useful for organizing pertinent information. Here is an example of an idea map you can use when writing.

SCHÉMA D'IDÉES

45 ans
43 ans
travailleur intelligent
Paul père
Hélène mère
gentille sportive
Ma famille
Jean frère
blond drôle jeune
15 ans

FLASH CULTURE

Watch the FLASH CULTURE segment on the ESPACES video for cultural footage related to this unit's theme.

Thème

Écrivez une lettre

A friend you met in a chat room for French speakers wants to know about your family. Using some of the verbs and adjectives you learned in this lesson, write a brief letter describing your family or an imaginary family, including:

- Names and relationships
- Physical characteristics
- Hobbies and interests

Here are some useful expressions for letter writing in French:

Salutations	
Cher Fabien,	*Dear Fabien,*
Chère Joëlle,	*Dear Joëlle,*
Asking for a response	
Réponds-moi vite.	*Write back soon.*
Donne-moi de tes nouvelles.	*Tell me all your news.*
Closings	
Grosses bises!	*Big kisses!*
Je t'embrasse!	*Kisses!*
Bisous!	*Kisses!*
À bientôt!	*See you soon!*
Amitiés,	*In friendship,*
Cordialement,	*Cordially,*
À plus (tard),	*Until later,*

cent sept 107

À l'écoute presents a recorded conversation or narration to develop your listening skills in French. **Stratégie** and **Préparation** prepare you for listening to the recorded passage.

À vous d'écouter tracks you through the recorded passage, and **Compréhension** checks your understanding of what you heard.

Stratégie in **Écriture** provides useful strategies that prepare you for the writing task presented in **Thème**.

Thème describes the writing topic and includes suggestions for approaching it.

Flash culture lets you know that specially shot cultural footage related to the unit's theme is available for viewing in the **ESPACES** Video Program. To learn more about the video, turn to page xxvii.

Vocabulaire

summarizes all the active vocabulary of the unit.

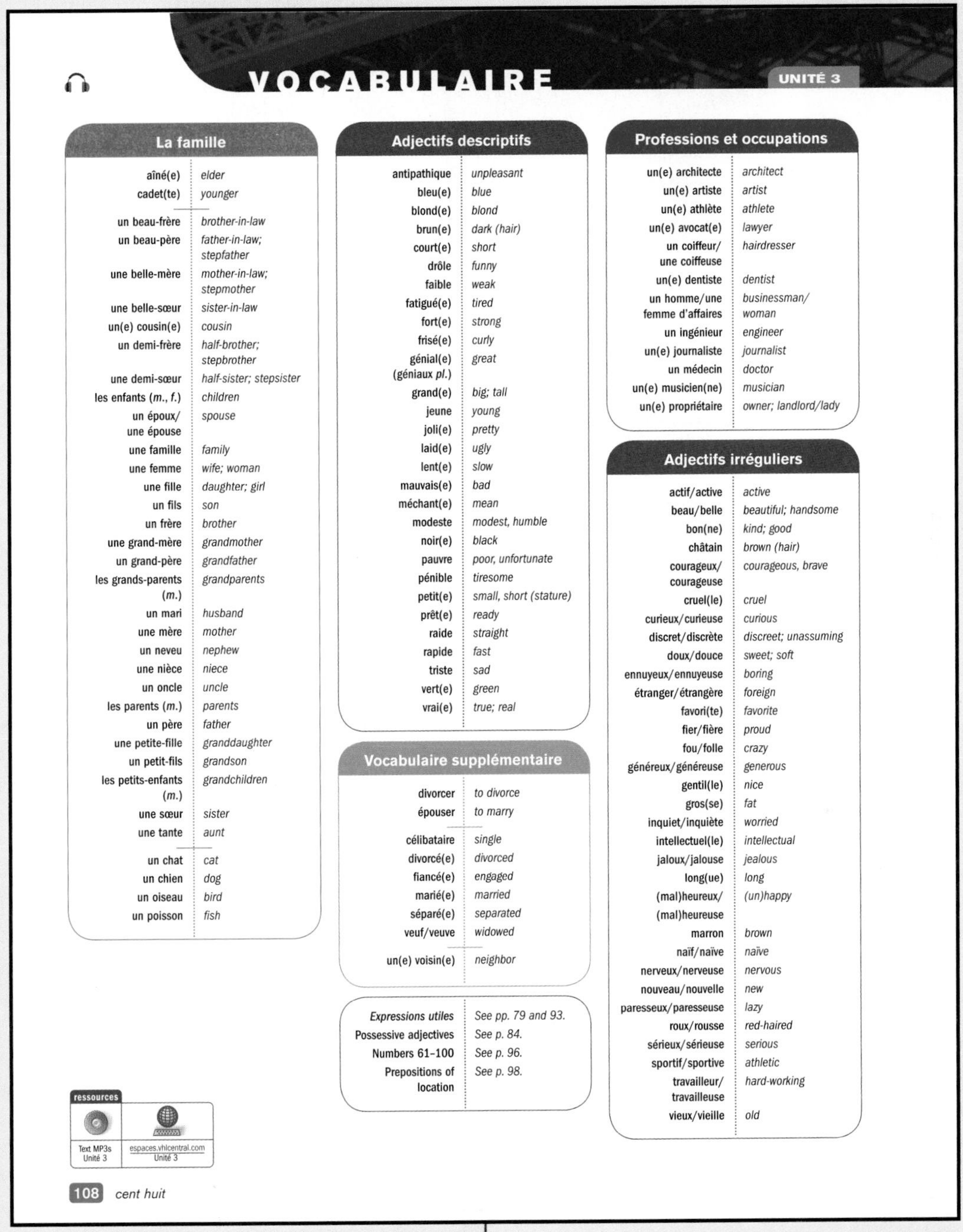

VOCABULAIRE

UNITÉ 3

La famille

aîné(e)	*elder*
cadet(te)	*younger*
un beau-frère	*brother-in-law*
un beau-père	*father-in-law; stepfather*
une belle-mère	*mother-in-law; stepmother*
une belle-sœur	*sister-in-law*
un(e) cousin(e)	*cousin*
un demi-frère	*half-brother; stepbrother*
une demi-sœur	*half-sister; stepsister*
les enfants (*m., f.*)	*children*
un époux/ une épouse	*spouse*
une famille	*family*
une femme	*wife; woman*
une fille	*daughter; girl*
un fils	*son*
un frère	*brother*
une grand-mère	*grandmother*
un grand-père	*grandfather*
les grands-parents (*m.*)	*grandparents*
un mari	*husband*
une mère	*mother*
un neveu	*nephew*
une nièce	*niece*
un oncle	*uncle*
les parents (*m.*)	*parents*
un père	*father*
une petite-fille	*granddaughter*
un petit-fils	*grandson*
les petits-enfants (*m.*)	*grandchildren*
une sœur	*sister*
une tante	*aunt*
un chat	*cat*
un chien	*dog*
un oiseau	*bird*
un poisson	*fish*

Adjectifs descriptifs

antipathique	*unpleasant*
bleu(e)	*blue*
blond(e)	*blond*
brun(e)	*dark (hair)*
court(e)	*short*
drôle	*funny*
faible	*weak*
fatigué(e)	*tired*
fort(e)	*strong*
frisé(e)	*curly*
génial(e) (géniaux *pl.*)	*great*
grand(e)	*big; tall*
jeune	*young*
joli(e)	*pretty*
laid(e)	*ugly*
lent(e)	*slow*
mauvais(e)	*bad*
méchant(e)	*mean*
modeste	*modest, humble*
noir(e)	*black*
pauvre	*poor, unfortunate*
pénible	*tiresome*
petit(e)	*small, short (stature)*
prêt(e)	*ready*
raide	*straight*
rapide	*fast*
triste	*sad*
vert(e)	*green*
vrai(e)	*true; real*

Vocabulaire supplémentaire

divorcer	*to divorce*
épouser	*to marry*
célibataire	*single*
divorcé(e)	*divorced*
fiancé(e)	*engaged*
marié(e)	*married*
séparé(e)	*separated*
veuf/veuve	*widowed*
un(e) voisin(e)	*neighbor*

Expressions utiles	*See pp. 79 and 93.*
Possessive adjectives	*See p. 84.*
Numbers 61–100	*See p. 96.*
Prepositions of location	*See p. 98.*

Professions et occupations

un(e) architecte	*architect*
un(e) artiste	*artist*
un(e) athlète	*athlete*
un(e) avocat(e)	*lawyer*
un coiffeur/ une coiffeuse	*hairdresser*
un(e) dentiste	*dentist*
un homme/une femme d'affaires	*businessman/ woman*
un ingénieur	*engineer*
un(e) journaliste	*journalist*
un médecin	*doctor*
un(e) musicien(ne)	*musician*
un(e) propriétaire	*owner; landlord/lady*

Adjectifs irréguliers

actif/active	*active*
beau/belle	*beautiful; handsome*
bon(ne)	*kind; good*
châtain	*brown (hair)*
courageux/ courageuse	*courageous, brave*
cruel(le)	*cruel*
curieux/curieuse	*curious*
discret/discrète	*discreet; unassuming*
doux/douce	*sweet; soft*
ennuyeux/ennuyeuse	*boring*
étranger/étrangère	*foreign*
favori(te)	*favorite*
fier/fière	*proud*
fou/folle	*crazy*
généreux/généreuse	*generous*
gentil(le)	*nice*
gros(se)	*fat*
inquiet/inquiète	*worried*
intellectuel(le)	*intellectual*
jaloux/jalouse	*jealous*
long(ue)	*long*
(mal)heureux/ (mal)heureuse	*(un)happy*
marron	*brown*
naïf/naïve	*naive*
nerveux/nerveuse	*nervous*
nouveau/nouvelle	*new*
paresseux/paresseuse	*lazy*
roux/rousse	*red-haired*
sérieux/sérieuse	*serious*
sportif/sportive	*athletic*
travailleur/ travailleuse	*hard-working*
vieux/vieille	*old*

ressources

Text MP3s Unité 3

espaces.vhlcentral.com Unité 3

108 *cent huit*

Recorded vocabulary The headset icon at the top of the page and the **ressources** box at the bottom of the page highlight that the active lesson vocabulary is recorded for convenient study and practice on both the Text MP3s CD-ROM and the **ESPACES** supersite.

THE *ROMAN-PHOTO* EPISODES

Fully integrated with your textbook, the **ESPACES** Video contains thirty dramatic episodes, one for each lesson of the text. The episodes present the adventures of four college students who are studying in the south of France at the **Université Aix-Marseille**. They live in apartments above **Le P'tit Bistrot**, a café owned by their landlady, Valérie Forestier. The video tells their story and the story of Madame Forestier and her teenage son, Stéphane.

The **ESPACE ROMAN-PHOTO** section in each textbook lesson is actually an abbreviated version of the dramatic episode featured in the video. Therefore, each **ESPACE ROMAN-PHOTO** section can be done before you see the corresponding video episode, after it, or as a section that stands alone in its own right.

As you watch each video episode, you will first see a live segment in which the characters interact using vocabulary and grammar you are studying. As the video progresses, the live segments carefully combine new vocabulary and grammar with previously taught language. You will then see a **Reprise** segment that summarizes the key language functions and/or grammar points used in the dramatic episode.

THE CAST

Here are the main characters you will meet when you watch the ESPACES Video:

Of Senegalese heritage
Amina Mbaye

From Washington, D.C.
David Duchesne

From Paris
Sandrine Aubry

From Aix-en-Provence
Valérie Forestier

Of Algerian heritage
Rachid Khalil

And, also from Aix-en-Provence
Stéphane Forestier

Salut!

UNITÉ 1

Pour commencer

- What are these young women saying?
  a. Excusez-moi. b. Bonjour! c. Merci.
- How many women are there in the photo?
  a. une b. deux c. trois
- What do you think is an appropriate title for one of these women?
  a. Monsieur b. Madame c. Mademoiselle

Unit Goals

Leçon 1

In this lesson, students will learn:
- terms for greetings, farewells, and introductions
- expressions of courtesy
- the French alphabet and the names of accent marks
- about shaking hands and **bises**
- gender of nouns
- articles (definite and indefinite)
- the numbers 0–60
- the expresion **il y a**
- about the company Moulinex

Leçon 2

In this lesson, students will learn:
- terms to identify people
- terms for objects in the classroom
- rules for silent letters
- about France's multicultural society
- subject pronouns
- the present tense of **être**
- **c'est** and **il/elle est**
- adjective agreement
- some descriptive adjectives and adjectives of nationality
- to give an oral report on the influence of French-speaking cultures on cities in the U.S. and Canada

Savoir-faire

In this section, students will learn:
- cultural, linguistic, and historical information about the francophone world
- to recognize cognates
- to listen for familiar words
- strategies for writing in French
- to write a telephone/address book
- more about greetings and farewells through specially shot video footage

Pour commencer

- **b. Bonjour!**
- **b. deux**
- **c. Mademoiselle**

RESOURCES

Workbook/Video Manual: WB Activities, pp. 1–14
Laboratory Manual: Lab Activities, pp. 1–8
Workbook/Video Manual: Video Activities, pp. 211–214; pp. 271–272
WB/VM/LM Answer Key
Instructor's Resource CD-ROM [IRCD-ROM]:
Instructor's Resource Manual [IRM] (Textbook Audioscript; Lab Audioscript; Videoscript; **Roman-photo** Translations; **Vocabulaire supplémentaire**; **Feuilles d'activités**; Info Gap Activities; **Le zapping** TV clip transcription; **Essayez!** and **Mise en pratique** answers); Transparencies #13, #14, #15, #16; Testing Program, pp. 1–8; Test Files; Testing Program MP3s; Test Generator
Lab MP3s
Textbook MP3s
Video CD-ROM
Video on DVD
espaces.vhlcentral.com

Section Goals

In this section, students will learn and practice vocabulary related to:

- basic greetings and farewells
- introductions
- courtesy expressions

Instructional Resources
*IRCD-ROM: Transparencies #13, #14; IRM (**Vocabulaire supplémentaire; Mise en pratique** answers; Textbook Audioscript; Lab Audioscript)*
Textbook MP3s
WB/VM: Workbook, pp. 1–6
Lab Manual, p. 1
Lab MP3s
WB/VM/LM Answer Key
espaces.vhlcentral.com: activities, downloads, reference tools

Suggestions

- To familiarize students with the meanings of headings used in the lessons and important vocabulary for classroom interactions, pass out **Vocabulaire supplémentaire: vocabulaire pour la classe de français** from the IRM on the IRCD-ROM.
- For complete lesson plans, go to **espaces.vhlcentral.com** to access the instructor's part of the **ESPACES** companion web site.
- With books closed, write a few greetings, farewells, and courtesy expressions on the board, explain their meaning, and model their pronunciation. Circulate around the room, greeting students, making introductions, and encouraging responses. Then, have students open their books to pages 2–3. Ask them to identify which conversations are exchanges between friends and which seem more formal. Then point out the use of **vous** vs. **tu** in each conversation. Give examples of different situations in which each form would be appropriate.

Successful Language Learning Encourage students to make flash cards to help them memorize or review vocabulary.

Leçon 1

You will learn how to...

- greet people in French
- say good-bye

Ça va?

GEORGES Ça va, Henri?
HENRI Oui, ça va très bien, merci. Et vous, comment allez-vous?
GEORGES Je vais bien, merci.
PAUL Merci!
JEAN Il n'y a pas de quoi.
MARIE À plus tard, Guillaume!
GUILLAUME À tout à l'heure, Marie!
JACQUES Bonjour, Monsieur Boniface. Je vous présente Thérèse Lemaire.
M. BONIFACE Bonjour, Mademoiselle.
THÉRÈSE Enchantée.

Vocabulaire

Bonsoir.	*Good evening.; Hello.*
À bientôt.	*See you soon.*
À demain.	*See you tomorrow.*
Bonne journée!	*Have a good day!*
Au revoir.	*Good-bye.*
Comme ci, comme ça.	*So-so.*
Je vais bien/mal.	*I am doing well/badly.*
Moi aussi.	*Me too.*
Comment t'appelles-tu? (*fam.*)	*What is your name?*
Je vous/te présente... (*form./fam.*)	*I would like to introduce (name) to you.*
De rien.	*You're welcome.*
Excusez-moi. (*form.*)	*Excuse me.*
Excuse-moi. (*fam.*)	*Excuse me.*
Merci beaucoup.	*Thanks a lot.*
Pardon.	*Pardon (me).*
S'il vous/te plaît. (*form./fam.*)	*Please.*
Je vous en prie. (*form.*)	*Please.; You're welcome.*
Monsieur (M.)	*Sir (Mr.)*
Madame (Mme)	*Ma'am (Mrs.)*
Mademoiselle (Mlle)	*Miss*
ici	*here*
là	*there*
là-bas	*over there*

ressources

WB pp. 1–2	LM p. 1	Text MP3s Leçon 1	Lab MP3s Leçon 1	espaces.vhlcentral.com Leçon 1

OPTIONS

Language Notes Point out that **Salut** and **À plus**, the shortened form of **À plus tard**, are familiar expressions. Explain that the translation of **Je vais bien/mal** is not literal. **Je vais** means *I go*, but **je vais bien** means *I am doing well.*

Game Divide the class into two teams. Create sentences and questions based on the **Vocabulaire** and the illustrated conversations. Choose one person at a time, alternating between teams. Tell students to respond logically to your statement or question. Award a point for each correct response. The team with the most points at the end of the game wins.

MARC Bonjour, je m'appelle Marc, et vous, comment vous appelez-vous?
ANNIE Je m'appelle Annie.
MARC Enchanté.
SOPHIE Bonjour, Catherine!
CATHERINE Salut, Sophie!
SOPHIE Ça va?
CATHERINE Oui, ça va bien, merci. Et toi, comment vas-tu?
SOPHIE Pas mal.

Attention!

In French, people can be addressed formally or informally. Use the **tu/toi** forms with close friends or someone younger than you. Use the **vous** forms with groups, a boss, someone older than you, or someone you do not know.

Mise en pratique

1 Écoutez Listen to each of these questions or statements and select the most appropriate response.

1.	Enchanté.	☐	Je m'appelle Thérèse.	☑
2.	Merci beaucoup.	☐	Il n'y a pas de quoi.	☑
3.	Comme ci, comme ça.	☑	De rien.	☐
4.	Bonsoir, Monsieur.	☑	Moi aussi.	☐
5.	Enchanté.	☑	Et toi?	☐
6.	Bonjour.	☐	À demain.	☑
7.	Pas mal.	☑	Pardon.	☐
8.	Il n'y a pas de quoi.	☑	Moi aussi.	☐
9.	Enchanté.	☐	Très bien. Et vous?	☑
10.	À bientôt.	☑	Mal.	☐

2 Chassez l'intrus Circle the word or expression that does not belong.

1. a. Bonjour.
   b. Bonsoir.
   c. Salut.
   (d.) Pardon.
2. a. Bien.
   b. Très bien.
   (c.) De rien.
   d. Comme ci, comme ça.
3. a. À bientôt.
   b. À demain.
   c. À tout à l'heure.
   (d.) Enchanté.
4. a. Comment allez-vous?
   (b.) Comment vous appelez-vous?
   c. Ça va?
   d. Comment vas-tu?
5. (a.) Pas mal.
   b. Excuse-moi.
   c. Je vous en prie.
   d. Il n'y a pas de quoi.
6. a. Comment vous appelez-vous?
   b. Je vous présente Dominique.
   c. Enchanté.
   (d.) Comment allez-vous?
7. a. Pas mal.
   b. Très bien.
   c. Mal.
   (d.) Et vous?
8. a. Comment allez-vous?
   b. Comment vous appelez-vous?
   (c.) Et toi?
   d. Je vous en prie.

3 Conversez Madeleine is introducing her classmate Khaled to Libby, an American exchange student. Complete their conversation, using a different expression from **ESPACE CONTEXTES** in each blank. Answers will vary.

MADELEINE (1) ___________!
KHALED Salut, Madeleine. (2) ___________?
MADELEINE Pas mal. (3) ___________?
KHALED (4) ___________, merci.
MADELEINE (5) ___________ Libby. Elle est de (*She is from*) Boston.
KHALED (6) ___________ Libby. (7) ___________ Khaled. (8) ___________?
LIBBY (9) ___________, merci.
KHALED Oh, là, là. Je vais rater (*I am going to miss*) le bus. À bientôt.
MADELEINE (10) ___________.
LIBBY (11) ___________.

1 Tapescript
1. Comment vous appelez-vous?
2. Excusez-moi.
3. Comment allez-vous?
4. Bonsoir, Mademoiselle.
5. Je te présente Thérèse.
6. À bientôt.
7. Comment vas-tu?
8. Merci.
9. Bonjour, comment allez-vous?
10. Au revoir.
(On Textbook MP3s)

1 Suggestion Before students listen, tell them to read the possible responses provided and write down the questions or statements that they think would elicit each response. After completing the listening activity, go over the answers to check whether students' predictions were accurate.

2 Suggestion Go over the answers with the class and have students explain why each expression does not belong.

3 Suggestion Have students work in groups of three on the activity. Tell them to choose a role and complete the conversation. Then ask groups to act out their conversation for the class.

OPTIONS

Pairs Have students work in pairs. Tell them to write an original conversation with six to eight lines. After completing this task, they should rewrite the conversation and scramble the order of the sentences. Have pairs exchange their scrambled conversations and put them in a logical order. Remind students that they should verify the answers.

Small Groups Have small groups role-play a conversation in which other adults, children, and college-age people interact. Remind students to use formal and informal expressions in the appropriate situations. Give them time to prepare, and then have a few groups present their conversations to the class.

4 Suggestions
- Before beginning the activity, encourage students to use as many different words and expressions as they can from the **Vocabulaire** on page 2 rather than repeating the same expressions in each conversation.
- Have a few volunteers write their conversations on the board. Ask the class to identify, correct, and explain any errors.

4 Expansions
- Have students look at the photo, identify the conversation it most likely corresponds to (**Conversation 3**), and explain their reasoning. Point out that nearly all formal greetings are accompanied by a handshake. Tell the class that they will learn more about gestures used in greetings in the **Culture** section of this lesson.
- Have students rewrite **Conversation 1** in the formal register, and **Conversations 2** and **3** in the informal register.

5 Suggestions
- Before beginning this activity, ask students if they would use **tu** or **vous** in each situation.
- If class time is limited, assign a specific situation to each pair.
- Call on volunteers to act out their conversations for the class.

6 Suggestion Have two volunteers read the **modèle** aloud. Remind students to use **vous** when addressing more than one classmate at a time.

Communication

NATIONAL communication STANDARDS

4 Conversez With a partner, complete these conversations. Then act them out. Answers will vary.

Conversation 1 Salut! Je m'appelle François. Et toi, comment t'appelles-tu?

____

Ça va?

____

Conversation 2 _______________

Comme ci, comme ça. Et vous?

____

Bon (*Well*), à demain.

____

Conversation 3 Bonsoir, je vous présente Mademoiselle Barnard.

____

Enchanté(e).

____

Très bien, merci. Et vous?

____

5 C'est à vous! How would you greet these people, ask them for their names, and ask them how they are doing? With a partner, write a short dialogue for each item and act them out. Pay attention to the use of **tu** and **vous**. Answers will vary.

1. Madame Colombier

2. Mademoiselle Estèves

3. Monsieur Marchand

4. Marie, Guillaume et Geneviève

6 Présentations Form groups of three. Introduce yourself, and ask your partners their names and how they are doing. Then, join another group and take turns introducing your partners. Answers will vary.

MODÈLE

Étudiant(e) 1: *Bonjour. Je m'appelle Fatima. Et toi?*
Étudiant(e) 2: *Je m'appelle Fabienne.*
Étudiant(e) 1: *Comment vas-tu?*
Étudiant(e) 2: *Bien, merci. Et toi?*
Étudiant(e) 1: *Comme ci, comme ça.*

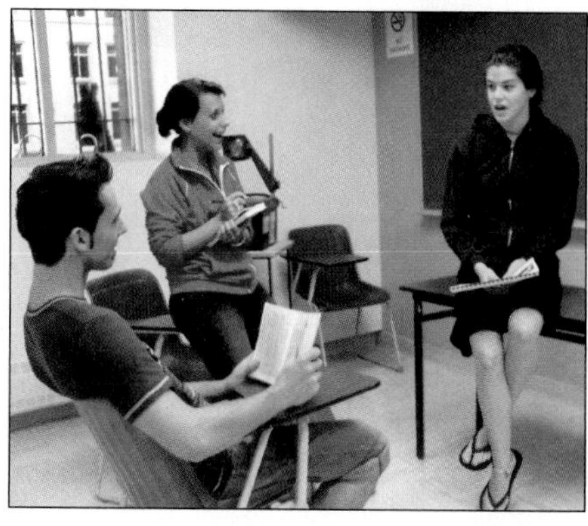

OPTIONS

Extra Practice Read some sentences to the class and ask if they would use them with another student of the same age or an older person. Examples: **1. Je te présente Guillaume.** (student) **2. Merci beaucoup, Monsieur.** (older person) **3. Comment vas-tu?** (student) **4. Bonjour, professeur ____.** (older person) **5. Comment vous appelez-vous?** (older person)

Extra Practice Have students circulate around the classroom and conduct mini-conversations in French with other students, using the words and expressions they learned on pages 2–3. As students are carrying out the activity, move around the room, monitoring their work and offering assistance if requested.

Les sons et les lettres

NATIONAL STANDARDS comparisons

The French alphabet

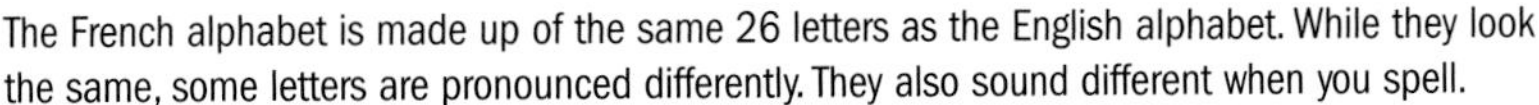

The French alphabet is made up of the same 26 letters as the English alphabet. While they look the same, some letters are pronounced differently. They also sound different when you spell.

lettre	exemple	lettre	exemple	lettre	exemple
a (a)	**a**dresse	**j** (ji)	**j**ustice	**s** (esse)	**s**pécial
b (bé)	**b**anane	**k** (ka)	**k**ilomètre	**t** (té)	**t**able
c (cé)	**c**arotte	**l** (elle)	**l**ion	**u** (u)	**u**nique
d (dé)	**d**essert	**m** (emme)	**m**ariage	**v** (vé)	**v**idéo
e (e)	**e**uro	**n** (enne)	**n**ature	**w** (double vé)	**w**agon
f (effe)	**f**ragile	**o** (o)	**o**live	**x** (iks)	**x**ylophone
g (gé)	**g**enre	**p** (pé)	**p**ersonne	**y** (i grec)	**y**oga
h (hache)	**h**éritage	**q** (ku)	**q**uiche	**z** (zède)	**z**éro
i (i)	**i**nnocent	**r** (erre)	**r**adio		

Notice that some letters in French words have accents. You'll learn how they influence pronunciation in later lessons. Whenever you spell a word in French, include the name of the accent after the letter.

accent	nom	exemple	orthographe
´	*accent aigu*	**identité**	*I-D-E-N-T-I-T-E-accent aigu*
`	*accent grave*	**problème**	*P-R-O-B-L-E-accent grave-M-E*
ˆ	*accent circonflexe*	**hôpital**	*H-O-accent circonflexe-P-I-T-A-L*
¨	*tréma*	**naïve**	*N-A-I-tréma-V-E*
¸	*cédille*	**ça**	*C-cédille-A*

L'alphabet Practice saying the French alphabet and example words aloud.

Ça s'écrit comment? Spell these words aloud in French. For double letters, use **deux: ss=deux s.**

1. judo
2. yacht
3. forêt
4. zèbre
5. existe
6. clown
7. numéro
8. français
9. musique
10. favorite
11. kangourou
12. parachute
13. différence
14. intelligent
15. dictionnaire
16. alphabet

Dictons Practice reading these sayings aloud.

Grande invitation, petites portions.[1]

Tout est bien qui finit bien.[2]
Lundi
Mardi

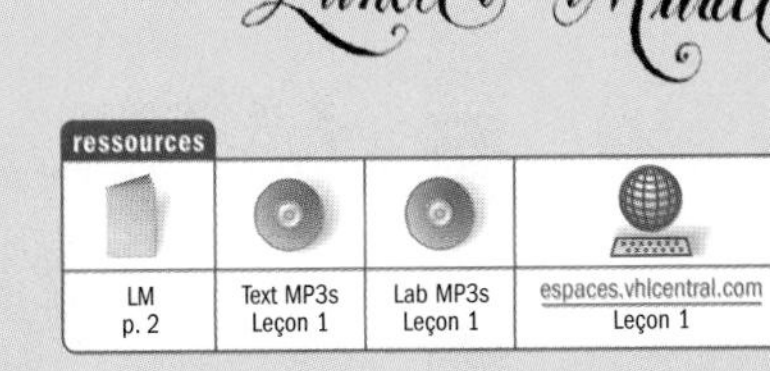

ressources
LM p. 2
Text MP3s Leçon 1
Lab MP3s Leçon 1
espaces.vhlcentral.com Leçon 1

[1] Great boast, small roast.
[2] All's well that ends well.

Section Goals

In this section, students will learn about:

- the French alphabet and how it contrasts with the English alphabet
- the names of the letters
- the names of the accent marks

Instructional Resources
Textbook MP3s
Lab Manual, p. 2
Lab MP3s
WB/VM/LM Answer Key
IRCD-ROM: IRM (Textbook Audioscript; Lab Audioscript)
espaces.vhlcentral.com: activities, downloads, reference tools

Suggestions

- Model the pronunciation of the French alphabet and the example words. Have students repeat.
- Point out that vowel sounds can have many different pronunciations when combined with other vowels or when spelled with accents, particularly the **e**.
- Point out the different diacritical marks and model their pronunciation. For a detailed explanation of **l'accent aigu** and **l'accent grave**, see **Leçon 5**, page 77. For an explanation of **l'accent circonflexe, le tréma**, and **la cédille**, see **Leçon 6**, page 91.
- Draw attention to any posters, signs, or maps in the classroom. Point out individual letters, and ask the class to identify them in French.
- Write on the board the French abbreviations of several famous organizations (Examples: **ONU**, **OPEP**), and have students spell them in French. Explain what each abbreviation represents: **ONU** = **l'Organisation des Nations Unies** (*United Nations, UN*); **OPEP** = **l'Organisation des pays exportateurs de pétrole** (*Organization of Petroleum-Exporting Countries, OPEC*).
- Have students work on the **Ça s'écrit comment?** activity in pairs.
- The explanation and exercises are recorded on the Textbook MP3s CD-ROM and are available on the **ESPACES** web site. You may want to play them in class so students hear French speakers other than yourself.

OPTIONS

Extra Practice Do a dictation activity in which you spell out a list of words in French to the class. Spell each word twice to allow students sufficient time to write. After you have finished, write your list on the board or project it on a transparency and have students check their work.

Extra Practice Tell students to greet two classmates that they haven't met yet, ask each person his or her name, and ask the person to spell the last name as they write it down. Tell them to verify the spelling with the person to make sure it is correct. Before beginning the activity, write this question on the board and model the pronunciation: **Comment s'écrit** *last name* ?

Section Goals

In this section, students will learn functional phrases for making introductions and speaking on the telephone through comprehensible input.

Instructional Resources
WB/VM: Video Manual, pp. 211–212
WB/VM/LM Answer Key
Video CD-ROM
Video on DVD
IRCD-ROM: IRM (Videoscript; ***Roman-photo*** *Translations)*
espaces.vhlcentral.com: activities, downloads, reference tools

Video Synopsis Sandrine buys a magazine at Monsieur Hulot's newsstand. At **Le P'tit Bistrot**, Rachid introduces David, his American friend, to Sandrine and Amina. Madame Forestier, who owns the café, gets a phone call from her son's high school French teacher because he didn't do well on his French exam. Stéphane tells Rachid to introduce David to his mother so he can avoid talking to her.

Suggestions

- Have students cover the French captions and guess the plot based only on the video stills. Write their predictions on the board.
- Have students volunteer to read the characters' parts in the **Roman-photo** aloud. Then have them get together in groups of eight to act out the episode.
- After students have read the **Roman-photo**, quickly review their predictions, and ask them which ones were correct.
- Point out that 100 centimes = 1 euro, the monetary unit of the European Union, which includes France.

Au café

PERSONNAGES

Amina

David

Monsieur Hulot

Michèle

Rachid

Sandrine

Stéphane

Valérie

1

Au kiosque...
SANDRINE Bonjour, Monsieur Hulot!
M. HULOT Bonjour, Mademoiselle Aubry! Comment allez-vous?
SANDRINE Très bien, merci! Et vous?
M. HULOT Euh, ça va. Voici 45 (quarante-cinq) centimes. Bonne journée!
SANDRINE Merci, au revoir!

2

À la terrasse du café...
AMINA Salut!
SANDRINE Bonjour, Amina. Ça va?
AMINA Ben... ça va. Et toi?
SANDRINE Oui, je vais bien, merci.
AMINA Regarde! Voilà Rachid et... un ami?

3

RACHID Bonjour!
AMINA ET SANDRINE Salut!
RACHID Je vous présente un ami, David Duchesne.
SANDRINE Je m'appelle Sandrine.
DAVID Enchanté.

6

STÉPHANE Oh, non! Madame Richard! Le professeur de français!
DAVID Il y a un problème?

7

STÉPHANE Oui! L'examen de français! Présentez-vous, je vous en prie!

8

VALÉRIE Oh... l'examen de français! Oui, merci, merci Madame Richard, merci beaucoup! De rien, au revoir!

ACTIVITÉS

1 Vrai ou faux? Choose whether each statement is **vrai** or **faux**.

1. Sandrine va (*is doing*) bien. Vrai.
2. Sandrine et Amina sont (*are*) amies. Vrai.
3. David est français. Faux.
4. David est de Washington. Vrai.
5. Rachid présente son frère (*his brother*) David à Sandrine et Amina. Faux.
6. Stéphane est étudiant à l'université. Faux.
7. Il y a un problème avec l'examen de sciences politiques. Faux.
8. Amina, Rachid et Sandrine sont (*are*) à Paris. Faux.
9. Michèle est au P'tit Bistrot. Vrai.
10. Madame Richard est le professeur de Stéphane. Vrai.
11. Madame Forestier va mal. Vrai.
12. Rachid a (*has*) cours de français dans 30 minutes. Faux.

OPTIONS

Video Tips General suggestions for using video clips in the classroom can be found on page IAE-11 of this Instructor's Annotated Edition.

Avant de regarder la vidéo Before showing the video episode, have students brainstorm some greetings and some other expressions that they might hear in an episode in which some of the characters meet each other for the first time.

Regarder la vidéo Play the episode once and tell the class to listen for basic greetings. After the video is over, have students recall the greetings they heard and write them on the board. Show the episode again and ask the class to write down all of the courtesy expressions that they hear, including ways to say *pleased to meet you.*

Les étudiants se retrouvent (*meet*) au café.

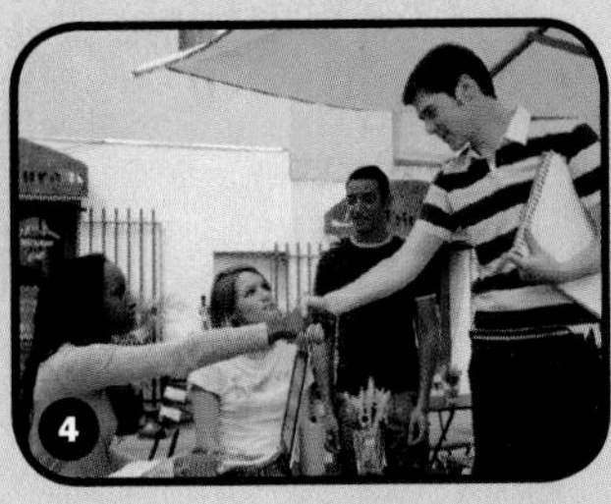
4

DAVID Et toi..., comment t'appelles-tu?
AMINA Je m'appelle Amina.
RACHID David est un étudiant américain. Il est de Washington, la capitale des États-Unis.
AMINA Ah, oui! Bienvenue à Aix-en-Provence.
RACHID Bon..., à tout à l'heure.
SANDRINE À bientôt, David.

5

À l'intérieur (inside) *du café...*
MICHÈLE Allô. Le P'tit Bistrot. Oui, un moment, s'il vous plaît. Madame Forestier! Le lycée de Stéphane
VALÉRIE Allô. Oui. Bonjour, Madame Richard. Oui. Oui. Stéphane? Il y a un problème au lycée?

9

RACHID Bonjour, Madame Forestier. Comment allez-vous?
VALÉRIE Ah, ça va mal.
RACHID Oui? Moi, je vais bien. Je vous présente David Duchesne, étudiant américain de Washington.

10

DAVID Bonjour, Madame. Enchanté!
RACHID Ah, j'ai cours de sciences politiques dans 30 (trente) minutes. Au revoir, Madame Forestier. À tout à l'heure, David.

Expressions utiles

Introductions

- **David est un étudiant américain. Il est de Washington.**
  David is an American student. He's from Washington.
- **Présentez-vous, je vous en prie!**
  Introduce yourselves, please!
- **Il/Elle s'appelle...**
  His/Her name is...
- **Bienvenue à Aix-en-Provence.**
  Welcome to Aix-en-Provence.

Speaking on the telephone

- **Allô.**
  Hello.
- **Un moment, s'il vous plaît.**
  One moment, please.

Additional vocabulary

- **Regarde! Voilà Rachid et... un ami?**
  Look! There's Rachid and... a friend?
- **J'ai cours de sciences politiques dans 30 (trente) minutes.**
  I have political science class in thirty minutes.
- **Il y a un problème au lycée?**
  Is there a problem at the high school?
- **Il y a...**
  There is/are...
- **Il/Elle est**
  He/She is...
- **Voici...**
  Here's...
- **Voilà...**
  There's...
- **euh**
  um
- **bon**
  well; good
- **centimes**
  cents

2 Complétez Fill in the blanks with the words from the list. Refer to the video scenes as necessary.

ai	est
bienvenue	voici
capitale	

1. __Bienvenue__ à Aix-en-Provence.
2. Il est de Washington, la __capitale__ des États-Unis.
3. __Voici__ 45 (quarante-cinq) centimes. Bonne journée!
4. J'__ai__ cours de sciences politiques.
5. David __est__ un étudiant américain.

3 Conversez In groups of three, write a conversation where you introduce an exchange student to a friend. Be prepared to present your conversation to the class.

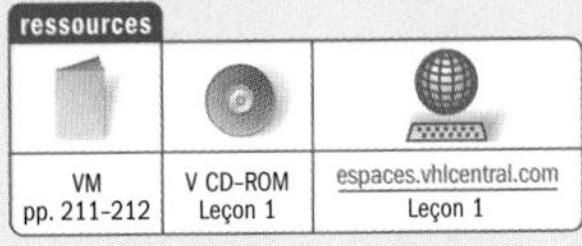

ACTIVITÉS

Successful Language Learning Tell your students that their conversational skills will grow more quickly as they learn each lesson's **Expressions utiles**. This feature is designed to teach phrases that will be useful in conversation, and it will also help students understand key phrases in each **Roman-photo**.

Expressions utiles
- Tell students that all the items in **Expressions utiles** are active vocabulary for which they are responsible. Model the pronunciation of the words and expressions and have the class repeat.
- As you work through the list, point out examples of nouns with indefinite articles (**un étudiant, un moment, un ami, un problème**). Tell students that nouns and articles will be formally presented in the **Structures** section.

1 Suggestion Have students correct the false statements.

2 Expansion Tell students to write three additional fill-in-the-blank statements based on the **Roman-photo**. Then have them exchange papers with a classmate and complete the sentences.

3 Suggestion Have volunteers act out their conversations for the class or another group.

OPTIONS

Extra Practice Choose four or five lines of the **Roman-photo** to use as a dictation. Read each line twice, pausing after each line so that students have time to write. Have students check their own work by comparing it with the **Roman-photo** text.

Cultural Comparison Have students make observations about the places and people that they saw in the video. Ask what was surprising or different about any of the scenes or the characters' mannerisms. Did they notice anything different about the way that the American student, David, introduced himself compared to the others?

Point out that greeting friends, family members, and loved ones with a kiss on both cheeks is not unique to the French-speaking world. This custom is common throughout Europe and in other parts of the world.

connections cultures NATIONAL STANDARDS

Section Goals

In this section, students will:
- learn about gestures used with greetings
- learn some familiar greetings and farewells
- learn some tips about good manners in different francophone countries
- read about Aix-en-Provence

Instructional Resources
espaces.vhlcentral.com: activities, downloads, reference tools

Culture à la loupe

Avant la lecture Ask students how they greet their friends, family members, fellow students, co-workers, and people they meet for the first time. Ask them for some examples of regional variations in greetings in the United States.

Lecture
- Ask students what information the map on this page shows. (It shows the number of kisses traditionally given by region.)
- Explain that **faire la bise** does not actually mean to kiss another's cheek, but rather to kiss parallel to the other person's face, so that physical contact is limited to a grazing of cheeks.

Après la lecture Have students compare French and American greetings or any other method of greeting with which they are familiar.

1 Expansion Have students work in pairs. Tell them to role-play the situations in items 1–6. Example: 1. Students give each other four kisses because they are in northwestern France.

CULTURE À LA LOUPE

La poignée de main ou la bise?

French friends and relatives usually exchange a kiss (la bise) on alternating cheeks whenever they meet and again when they say good-bye. Friends of friends may also kiss when introduced, even though they have just met. This is particularly true among students and young adults. It is not unusual for men of the same family to exchange **la bise**; otherwise, men generally greet one another with a handshake (**la poignée de main**). As the map shows, the number of kisses varies from place to place in France. In some regions, two kisses (one on each cheek) is the standard while in others, people may exchange as many as four kisses. Whatever the number, each kiss is accompanied by a slight kissing sound.

Unless they are also friends, business acquaintances and co-workers usually shake hands each time they meet and do so again upon leaving. A French handshake is brief and firm, with a single downward motion.

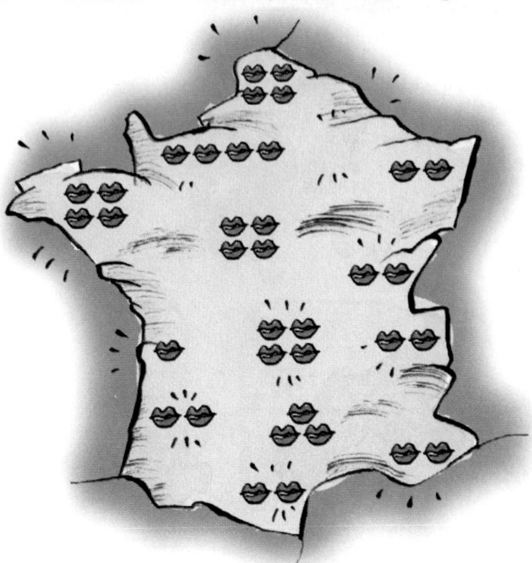

Combien de° bises?

Coup de main

If you are not sure whether you should shake hands or kiss someone, or if you don't know which side to start on, you can always follow the other person's lead. When in doubt, start on your right.

Combien de *How many*

ACTIVITÉS

1 Vrai ou faux? Indicate whether each statement is **vrai** or **faux**. Correct any false statements.

1. In northwestern France, giving four kisses is common. Vrai.
2. Business acquaintances usually kiss one another on the cheek. Faux. They usually shake hands.
3. French people may give someone they've just met **la bise**. Vrai.
4. **Bises** exchanged between French men at a family gathering are common. Vrai.
5. In a business setting, French people often shake hands when they meet each day and again when they leave. Vrai.
6. When shaking hands, French people prefer a long and soft handshake. Faux. A French handshake is brief and firm.
7. The number of kisses given can vary from one region to another. Vrai.
8. It is customary for kisses to be given silently. Faux. Each kiss is accompanied by a slight kissing sound.

OPTIONS

La bise Tell students that, although people in some social circles in the United States commonly kiss each other on the cheek once, this is not common practice in France. It could be considered impolite to give only one **bise** since the other person would be waiting for the second kiss. In some regions of France and Switzerland, people may even give three **bises**, but just one is rare.

Game Divide the class into two teams. Indicate one team member at a time, alternating between teams. Give situations in which people are greeting each other. Students should say if the people should greet each other with **la poignée de main** or **la bise**. Examples: female friends (**la bise**); male and female business associates (**la poignée de main**). Give a point for each correct answer. The team with the most points at the end of the game wins.

LE FRANÇAIS QUOTIDIEN

Les salutations

À la prochaine!	*Until next time!*
À plus!	*See you later!*
Ciao!	*Bye!*
Coucou!	*Hi there!/Hey!*
Pas grand-chose.	*Nothing much.*
Quoi de neuf?	*What's new?*
Rien de nouveau.	*Nothing new.*

LE MONDE FRANCOPHONE

Les bonnes manières

In any country where a foreign language is spoken, an effort to speak the native language is always appreciated. Using titles of respect and learning a few polite expressions, such as **excusez-moi**, **merci**, and **s'il vous plaît**, can take you a long way when conversing with native Francophones.

Dos and don'ts in the francophone world:

France Always greet shopkeepers upon entering a store and say good-bye upon leaving.

Northern Africa Use your right hand when handing items to others.

Quebec Province Make eye contact when shaking hands.

Sub-Saharan Africa Do not show the soles of your feet when sitting.

Switzerland Do not litter or jaywalk.

PORTRAIT

Aix-en-Provence: ville d'eau, ville d'art°

Aix-en-Provence is a vibrant university town that welcomes international students. Its main boulevard, **le cours Mirabeau**, is great for people-watching or just relaxing in a sidewalk café. One can discover interesting boutiques, traditional and ethnic restaurants, and the daily vegetable and flower market among the winding, narrow streets of **la vieille ville** (*old town*).

Aix is also renowned for its dedication to the arts, hosting numerous cultural festivals every year such as **le Festival International d'Art Lyrique**, **Aix en Musique**, and **Danse à Aix**. For centuries, artists have been drawn to Provence for its natural beauty and its unique quality of light. Paul Cézanne, artist and native son of Provence, spent his days painting the surrounding countryside.

ville d'eau, ville d'art *city of water, city of art*

SUR INTERNET

What behaviors are socially unacceptable in French-speaking countries?

Go to **espaces.vhlcentral.com** to find more cultural information related to this **ESPACE CULTURE**.

ACTIVITÉS

2 **Les bonnes manières** In which places might these behaviors be particularly offensive?

1. littering
   Switzerland
2. offering a business card with the left hand
   Northern Africa
3. sitting with the bottom of your foot facing your host
   Sub-Saharan Africa
4. failing to greet a salesperson
   France
5. looking away when shaking hands
   Quebec Province

3 **À vous** With a partner, practice meeting and greeting people in various social situations in French.

1. Your good friend from Provence introduces you to her close friend.
2. You walk into your neighborhood bakery.
3. You arrive for a job interview and meet your prospective employer.

ressources

Le français quotidien

- Model the pronunciation of each expression and have students repeat.
- Tell students to list all the situations they can think of in which they could use these expressions. Then have them compare their lists in pairs or small groups.

Portrait Mention that Aix-en-Provence is often referred to simply as Aix. Ask students why Aix is called **ville d'eau, ville d'art** in the title. Then ask if they would like to visit Aix, and which aspects of the town attract them the most.

Le monde francophone Ask students which dos and don'ts in the francophone world should be followed in the anglophone world, too. Have the class think of logical reasons for following each custom or social convention, especially for North Africa and Sub-Saharan Africa. Example: In North Africa, the left hand is reserved for using the toilets.

Sur Internet Point out to students that they will find supporting activities and information at **espaces.vhlcentral.com.**

2 Suggestion Have students check their answers with a partner.

3 Suggestion Before beginning this activity, ask students if they would use **tu** or **vous** in each situation. Remind them to use appropriate gestures and manners.

OPTIONS

Cultural Activity Have students choose one of these topics to research on the Internet: **Aix-en-Provence, le Festival International d'Art Lyrique, Aix en Musique, Danse à Aix**, or **Paul Cézanne**. Tell them to come to the next class with printouts of two photos illustrating their topic and a sentence or two in French, if possible, about each photo. Divide the class into groups of three or four students so that they can present the material to one another while looking at the images.

Small Groups Have students work in groups of three or four. Tell them to create an informal conversation using the expressions in **Le français quotidien** and appropriate gestures. Have a few groups act out their conversations for the class.

National Standards: comparisons

Section Goals

In this section, students will learn:

- gender and number of nouns
- definite and indefinite articles

Instructional Resources
WB/VM: Workbook, pp. 3–4
Lab Manual, p. 3
Lab MP3s
WB/VM/LM Answer Key
*IRCD-ROM: IRM (**Essayez!** and **Mise en pratique** answers; Lab Audioscript)*
espaces.vhlcentral.com: activities, downloads, reference tools

Suggestions

- Explain what a noun is by giving examples of people (**professeur**), places (**café**), things (**examen**), and ideas (**problème**). Then write these nouns on the board: **ami, amie, cours, télévision**. Point out the gender of each noun. Explain that nouns for male beings are usually masculine, and nouns for female beings are usually feminine. All other nouns can be either masculine or feminine. Tell students that they should memorize the gender of a noun along with the word.
- Write these nouns on the board: **professeur, professeurs, étudiante, étudiantes**. Ask students to point out the singular and plural nouns and to explain why. Then have students pronounce the words. Point out that the **-s** is not pronounced in French.
- Write **bureau** and **bureaux** on the board. Explain that words ending in **-eau** add **-x** to form the plural.
- Write these words on the board: **le café, les cafés, l'ami, les amis, la personne, les personnes**. Explain the use of the definite article. Point out that singular nouns beginning with a vowel or silent **h** use **l'**.
- Follow the same procedure for indefinite articles using these words: **un café, des cafés, un ami, des amis, une personne, des personnes**. Point out that the **-n** of **un** is pronounced before a vowel.
- Model how to pronounce **les** and **des** before words beginning with a consonant and a vowel.

1.1 Nouns and articles

Point de départ A noun designates a person, place, or thing. As in English, nouns in French have number (singular or plural). However, French nouns also have gender (masculine or feminine).

masculine singular	masculine plural	feminine singular	feminine plural
le café *the café*	**les cafés** *the cafés*	**la bibliothèque** *the library*	**les bibliothèques** *the libraries*

- Nouns that designate a male are usually masculine. Nouns that designate a female are usually feminine.

masculine		feminine	
l'acteur	*the actor*	**l'actrice**	*the actress*
l'ami	*the (male) friend*	**l'amie**	*the (female) friend*
le chanteur	*the (male) singer*	**la chanteuse**	*the (female) singer*
l'étudiant	*the (male) student*	**l'étudiante**	*the (female) student*
le petit ami	*the boyfriend*	**la petite amie**	*the girlfriend*

- Some nouns can designate either a male or a female regardless of their grammatical gender.

un professeur *a (male or female) professor* — **une personne** *a (male or female) person*

- Nouns for objects that have no natural gender can be either masculine or feminine.

masculine		feminine	
le bureau	*the office; desk*	**la chose**	*the thing*
le lycée	*the high school*	**la différence**	*the difference*
l'examen	*the test, exam*	**la faculté**	*the university; faculty*
l'objet	*the object*	**la littérature**	*literature*
l'ordinateur	*the computer*	**la sociologie**	*sociology*
le problème	*the problem*	**la télévision**	*the television*

- You can usually form the plural of a noun by adding **-s**, regardless of gender. However, in the case of words that end in **-eau** in the singular, add **-x** to the end to form the plural. For most nouns ending in **-al**, drop the **-al** and add **-aux**.

	singular		plural	
typical masculine noun	**l'objet**	*the object*	**les objets**	*the objects*
typical feminine noun	**la télévision**	*the television*	**les télévisions**	*the televisions*
noun ending in **-eau**	**le bureau**	*the office*	**les bureaux**	*the offices*
noun ending in **-al**	**l'animal**	*the animal*	**les animaux**	*the animals*

MISE EN PRATIQUE

1 Les singuliers et les pluriels Make the singular nouns plural, and vice versa.

1. l'actrice — les actrices
2. les lycées — le lycée
3. les différences — la différence
4. la chose — les choses
5. le bureau — les bureaux
6. le café — les cafés
7. les librairies — la librairie
8. la faculté — les facultés
9. les acteurs — l'acteur
10. l'ami — les amis
11. l'université — les universités
12. les tableaux — le tableau
13. le problème — les problèmes
14. les bibliothèques — la bibliothèque

2 Les mots Find ten words (**mots**) hidden in this word jumble. Then, provide the corresponding indefinite articles. une amie; des bureaux; un café; une chose; une faculté; un lycée; des objets; des ordinateurs; une librairie; un tableau

G	N	I	O	R	Z	Y	M	I	P	X	L	R	W
E	B	U	R	E	A	U	X	U	J	V	C	B	N
C	A	F	B	S	M	V	B	G	H	M	N	I	P
A	N	R	Y	E	I	H	K	B	E	F	K	V	F
J	G	O	S	T	E	J	B	O	B	E	G	D	D
E	K	E	L	H	N	U	Q	R	V	F	D	B	M
G	W	F	G	E	R	E	S	D	C	N	U	H	E
P	S	V	B	C	H	O	S	I	U	K	H	S	C
U	Q	K	S	I	Y	M	F	N	A	D	O	X	R
A	B	V	Z	R	I	V	V	A	J	H	W	I	J
E	I	W	Q	L	P	W	J	T	C	P	Y	E	Y
L	I	B	R	A	I	R	I	E	D	U	E	K	L
B	D	O	I	B	S	S	E	U	C	H	L	D	Y
A	Y	P	E	P	J	C	N	R	L	S	G	T	C
T	D	G	A	E	S	Y	L	S	V	C	A	F	E
S	I	J	E	M	X	K	P	Z	A	A	S	O	E
R	I	A	R	B	I	L	A	D	S	F	H	C	W

3 L'université Complete the sentences with an appropriate word from the list. Don't forget to provide the missing articles. Answers may slightly vary. Suggested answers below.

bibliothèque	faculté	petit ami
bureau	littérature	sociologie
chanteuse	ordinateurs	tableaux

1. À (a) __la faculté__, (b) __les tableaux__ et (c) __les ordinateurs__ sont (*are*) modernes.
2. Marc, c'est (d) __le petit ami__ de (*of*) Marie. Marc étudie (*studies*) (e) __la littérature__.
3. Marie étudie (f) __la sociologie__. Elle (*She*) est dans (g) __la bibliothèque__ de l'université.

OPTIONS

Extra Practice Write ten singular nouns on the board. In a rapid-response drill, call on students to give the appropriate gender. Examples: **bureau** (masculine), **étudiante** (feminine). You may also do this activity without writing the words on the board.

Game Divide the class into groups of three to four students. Bring in photos or magazine pictures, point to various objects or people, and say the French word without saying the article. Call on groups to indicate the person's or object's gender. Give a point for each correct answer. Deduct a point for each wrong answer. The group with the most points at the end wins.

COMMUNICATION

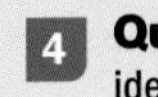

4 Qu'est-ce que c'est? In pairs, take turns identifying each drawing.

MODÈLE

Étudiant(e) 1: *Qu'est-ce que c'est?*
Étudiant(e) 2: *C'est un ordinateur.*

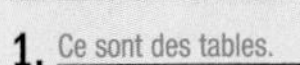

1. Ce sont des tables.

4. Ce sont des télévisions.

2. Ce sont des étudiants.

5. C'est une bibliothèque.

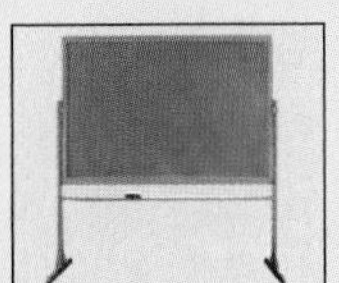

3. C'est un tableau.

6. Ce sont des cafés.

5 Identifiez In pairs, take turns providing a category for each item.

MODÈLE

Michigan, UCLA, Rutgers, Duke
Ce sont des universités.

1. saxophone C'est un instrument.
2. Ross, Rachel, Joey, Monica, Chandler, Phoebe Ce sont des amis.
3. SAT C'est un examen.
4. Library of Congress C'est une bibliothèque.
5. Sharon Stone, Deborah Messing, Catherine Deneuve Ce sont des actrices.
6. Céline Dion, Bruce Springsteen Ce sont des chanteurs.

6 Pictogrammes In groups of four, someone draws a person, object, or concept for the others to guess. Whoever guesses correctly draws next. Continue until everyone has drawn at least once. Answers will vary.

- Refer to a group composed of males and females with a masculine plural noun.

les amis	**les étudiants**
the (male and female) friends	*the (male and female) students*

- The English definite article *the* never varies for number or gender. However, the French definite article takes different forms according to the gender and number of the noun that it accompanies.

	singular noun beginning with a consonant	singular noun beginning with a vowel sound	plural noun
masculine	**le tableau** *the picture/ blackboard*	**l'ami** *the (male) friend*	**les cafés** *the cafés*
feminine	**la librairie** *the bookstore*	**l'université** *the university*	**les télévisions** *the televisions*

- In English, the singular indefinite article is *a/an*, and the plural indefinite article is *some*. Although *some* is often omitted in English, the plural indefinite article cannot be omitted in French.

	singular		plural	
masculine	**un instrument**	*an instrument*	**des instruments**	*(some) instruments*
feminine	**une table**	*a table*	**des tables**	*(some) tables*

Il y a **un ordinateur** ici.
There's a computer here.

Il y a **des ordinateurs** ici.
There are (some) computers here.

Il y a **une bibliothèque** ici.
There's a library here.

Il y a **des bibliothèques** ici.
There are (some) libraries here.

- Use **c'est** followed by a singular article and noun or **ce sont** followed by a plural article and noun to identify people and objects.

Qu'est-ce que c'est?	**C'est une librairie.**	**Ce sont des bureaux.**
What is that?	*It's a bookstore.*	*They're offices.*

Essayez! Select the correct article for each noun.

le, la, l' ou les?	**un, une ou des?**
1. le café	1. un bureau
2. la bibliothèque	2. une différence
3. l' acteur	3. un objet
4. l' amie	4. des amis
5. les problèmes	5. des amies
6. le lycée	6. une université
7. les examens	7. un ordinateur
8. la littérature	8. des tableaux

Essayez! Have students change the singular nouns and articles to the plural and vice versa.

1 Suggestion To check students' answers, have volunteers write them on the board or spell out the nouns orally.

1 Expansion Have students close their books. Tell them to change the plural nouns they hear to the singular and vice versa. Then randomly give them the answers to the items in the activity.

2 Suggestion This activity can also be done in pairs or groups.

3 Expansion Have students create additional sentences with the words in the list. Example: **Britney Spears est chanteuse.**

4 Suggestion Before beginning this activity, have students identify the objects in the photos. Then read the **modèle** aloud with a volunteer. Remind them that **Ce sont** is used with plural nouns.

5 Expansion Have students work in pairs. Tell them to write two more items for the activity. Example: GRE, GMAT, LSAT **(Ce sont des examens.)** Then have volunteers read their items aloud, while the rest of the class guesses the category.

6 Suggestion Before beginning the activity, remind students that they must choose something the class knows how to say in French, and that to guess what the picture is, they should say: **C'est un(e) ____?** or **Ce sont des ____?**

OPTIONS

TPR Assign a different definite article to each of four students. Then line up ten students, each of whom is assigned a noun. Include a mix of masculine, feminine, singular, and plural nouns. Say one of the nouns (without the article), and that student must step forward. The student assigned the corresponding article has five seconds to join the student with the noun.

Video Show the video episode again to offer more input on singular and plural nouns and their articles. With their books closed, have students write down every noun and article that they hear. After viewing the video, ask volunteers to list the nouns and articles they heard.

NATIONAL STANDARDS comparisons

Section Goals

In this section, students will learn:

- numbers 0–60
- the expression **il y a**

Instructional Resources
WB/VM: Workbook, pp. 5–6
Lab Manual, p. 4
Lab MP3s
WB/VM/LM Answer Key
*IRCD-ROM: IRM (**Essayez!** and **Mise en pratique** answers; Lab Audioscript)*
espaces.vhlcentral.com: activities, downloads, reference tools

Suggestions

- Introduce numbers by asking students how many of them can count to ten in French. Hold up varying numbers of fingers and ask students to shout out the corresponding number in French.
- Go through the numbers, modeling the pronunciation of each. Write individual numbers on the board and call on students at random to say each number as you point to it.
- Assign each student a number at random that they must remember. When finished, have the student assigned **un** say his or her number aloud, then **deux**, **trois**, etc. Help anyone who struggles with his or her number.
- Emphasize the variable forms of **un** and **une**, **vingt et un**, and **vingt et une**, giving examples of each. Examples: **vingt et un étudiants, vingt et une personnes.**
- Ask questions like the following: **Il y a combien d'étudiants dans la classe? (Il y a seize étudiants dans la classe.)**

1.2 Numbers 0–60

Point de départ Numbers in French follow patterns, as they do in English. First, learn the numbers **0–30**. The patterns they follow will help you learn the numbers **31–60**.

Numbers 0–30

0-10	11-20	21-30
0 zéro		
1 un	**11** onze	**21** vingt et un
2 deux	**12** douze	**22** vingt-deux
3 trois	**13** treize	**23** vingt-trois
4 quatre	**14** quatorze	**24** vingt-quatre
5 cinq	**15** quinze	**25** vingt-cinq
6 six	**16** seize	**26** vingt-six
7 sept	**17** dix-sept	**27** vingt-sept
8 huit	**18** dix-huit	**28** vingt-huit
9 neuf	**19** dix-neuf	**29** vingt-neuf
10 dix	**20** vingt	**30** trente

- When counting, use **un** for *one*. Use **une** before a feminine noun.

un objet *an/one object* — **une télévision** *a/one television*

- Note that the number **21** (**vingt et un**) follows a different pattern than the numbers **22–30**. When **vingt et un** precedes a feminine noun, add **-e** to the end of it: **vingt et une.**

vingt et un objets *twenty-one objects* — **vingt et une choses** *twenty-one things*

- Notice that the numbers **31–39**, **41–49**, and **51–59** follow the same pattern as the numbers **21–29**.

Numbers 31–60

31-34	35-38	39, 40, 50, 60
31 trente et un	**35** trente-cinq	**39** trente-neuf
32 trente-deux	**36** trente-six	**40** quarante
33 trente-trois	**37** trente-sept	**50** cinquante
34 trente-quatre	**38** trente-huit	**60** soixante

- To indicate a count of **31**, **41**, or **51** for a feminine noun, change the **un** to **une**.

trente et un objets *thirty-one objects* — **trente et une choses** *thirty-one things*

cinquante et un objets *fifty-one objects* — **cinquante et une choses** *fifty-one things*

MISE EN PRATIQUE

1 Logique Provide the number that completes each series. Then, write out the number in French.

MODÈLE
2, 4, 6, 8, 10; six

1. 9, 12, 15, 18, 21; quinze
2. 15, 20, 25, 30, 35; vingt-cinq
3. 2, 9, 16, 23, 30; seize
4. 0, 10, 20, 30, 40; trente
5. 15, 17, 19, 21, 23; dix-sept
6. 29, 26, 23, 20, 17; vingt-trois
7. 2, 5, 9, 14, 20, 27; quatorze
8. 30, 22, 16, 12, 10; dix

2 Il y a combien de...? Provide the number that you associate with these pairs of words.

MODÈLE
lettres: l'alphabet *vingt-six*

1. mois (*months*): année (*year*) douze
2. états (*states*): USA cinquante
3. semaines (*weeks*): année cinquante-deux
4. jours (*days*): octobre trente et un
5. âge: le vote dix-huit
6. Noël: décembre vingt-cinq

3 Numéros de téléphone Your roommate left behind a list of phone numbers to call today. Now he or she calls you and asks you to read them off. (Note that French phone numbers are read as double, not single, digits.)

MODÈLE
Le bureau, c'est le zéro un, vingt-trois, quarante-cinq, vingt-six, dix-neuf.

1. *bureau: 01.23.45.26.19*
2. *bibliothèque: 01.47.15.54.17* La bibliothèque, c'est le zéro un, quarante-sept, quinze, cinquante-quatre, dix-sept.
3. *café: 01.41.38.16.29* Le café, c'est le zéro un, quarante et un, trente-huit, seize, vingt-neuf.
4. *librairie: 01.10.13.60.23* La librairie, c'est le zéro un, dix, treize, soixante, vingt-trois.
5. *faculté: 01.58.36.14.12* La faculté, c'est le zéro un, cinquante-huit, trente-six, quatorze, douze.

OPTIONS

TPR Assign ten students a number from 0–60 and line them up in front of the class. Call out one of the numbers at random and have the student assigned to that number take a step forward. When two students have stepped forward, ask them to repeat their numbers. Then ask individuals to add (say: **plus**) or subtract (say: **moins**) the two numbers.

Game Hand out Bingo cards with B-I-N-G-O across the top of five columns. The 25 squares underneath will contain random numbers. From a hat, draw letters and numbers and call them out in French. The first student that can fill in a number in each one of the lettered columns yells "Bingo!" and wins.

COMMUNICATION

4 **Contradiction** Thierry is describing the new Internet café in the neighborhood, but Paul is in a bad mood and contradicts everything he says. In pairs, act out the roles using words from the list. Answers will vary.

MODÈLE

Étudiant(e) 1: *Dans (In) le café, il y a des tables.*
Étudiant(e) 2: *Non, il n'y a pas de tables.*

actrices	professeurs
bureau	tableau
étudiants	tables
ordinateur	télévision

5 **Sur le campus** Nathalie's inquisitive best friend wants to know everything about her new campus. In pairs, take turns acting out the roles.

MODÈLE

bibliothèques: 3
Étudiant(e) 1: *Il y a combien de bibliothèques?*
Étudiant(e) 2: *Il y a trois bibliothèques.*

1. professeurs de littérature: 22 Il y a vingt-deux professeurs de littérature.
2. étudiants dans (*in*) la classe de français: 15 Il y a quinze étudiants dans la classe de français.
3. télévision dans la classe de sociologie: 0 Il n'y a pas de télévision dans la classe de sociologie.
4. ordinateurs dans le café: 8 Il y a huit ordinateurs dans le café.
5. employés dans la librairie: 51 Il y a cinquante et un employés dans la librairie.
6. tables dans le café: 21 Il y a vingt et une tables dans le café.

6 **Choses et personnes** In groups of three, make a list of ten things or people that you see or don't see in the classroom. Use **il y a** and **il n'y a pas de**, and specify the number of items you can find. Then, compare your list with that of another pair. Answers will vary.

MODÈLE

Étudiant(e) 1: *Il y a un étudiant français.*
Étudiant(e) 2: *Il n'y a pas de télévision.*

- Use **il y a** to say *there is* or *there are* in French. This expression doesn't change, even if the noun that follows it is plural.

Il y a un ordinateur dans le bureau.
There is a computer in the office.

Il y a des tables dans le café.
There are tables in the café.

- In most cases, the indefinite article (**un**, **une**, or **des**) is used with **il y a**, rather than the definite article (**le**, **la**, **l'**, or **les**).

Il y a un professeur de biologie américain.
There's an American biology professor.

Il y a des étudiants français et anglais.
There are French and English students.

- Use the expression **il n'y a pas de/d'** followed by a noun to express *there isn't a...* or *there aren't any....* Note that no article (definite or indefinite) is used in this case. Use **de** before a consonant sound and **d'** before a vowel sound.

before a consonant

Il n'y a pas de tables dans le café.
There aren't any tables in the café.

before a vowel sound

Il n'y a pas d'ordinateur dans le bureau.
There isn't a computer in the office.

- Use **combien de/d'** to ask how many of something there are.

Il y a **combien de tables**?
How many tables are there?

Il y a **combien d'ordinateurs**?
How many computers are there?

Essayez! Write out or say the French word for each number below.

1. 15 quinze	6. 8 huit	11. 44 quarante-quatre
2. 6 six	7. 30 trente	12. 14 quatorze
3. 22 vingt-deux	8. 21 vingt et un	13. 38 trente-huit
4. 5 cinq	9. 1 un	14. 56 cinquante-six
5. 12 douze	10. 17 dix-sept	15. 19 dix-neuf

Essayez! Have students write four more numbers from 0–60. Tell them to exchange papers with a classmate and write the numbers as words.

1 Expansion Ask the class to list the prime numbers (**les nombres premiers**) up to 30. Explain that a prime number is any number that can only be divided by itself and 1. Prime numbers to 30 are: 1, 2, 3, 5, 7, 11, 13, 17, 19, 23, 29.

2 Suggestion Have students form complete sentences using **Il y a** when answering. Example: **Il y a douze mois dans une année.**

2 Expansion For additional practice, give students these items. **7. jours: semaine (sept) 8. jours: novembre (trente) 9. minutes: heure (*hour*) (soixante) 10. saisons (*seasons*): année (quatre)**

3 Expansion Write on the board three more telephone numbers for real places on campus or in town with their area codes, using double digits as in the activity. Call on volunteers to read the numbers aloud. Permit students to say the digits one by one if the numbers exceed 60.

4 Suggestion Have two volunteers read the **modèle** aloud. Remind students that they shouldn't use any article (definite or indefinite) after **Il n'y a pas de/d'**.

5 Suggestion Have two volunteers read the **modèle** aloud. Remind students to use **combien d'** before a noun that begins with a vowel sound.

6 Expansion After groups have compared their answers, convert the statements into questions. Example: **Il y a combien d'étudiants?**

OPTIONS

TPR Give ten students a card with a number from 0–60. (You may want to assign numbers in fives to simplify the activity.) The card must be visible to the other students. Then call out simple math problems (addition or subtraction) involving the assigned numbers. When the first two numbers are called, each student steps forward. The student whose assigned number completes the math problem has five seconds to join them.

Extra Practice Ask questions about the university and the town or city in which it is located. Examples: **Il y a combien de professeurs dans le département de français? Il y a combien de bibliothèques sur le campus? Il y a combien d'universités à ____?** Encourage students to guess the number if they don't know it.

Suggestion Tell students that this section reviews and recycles the lesson vocabulary and grammar points.

Instructional Resources
IRCD-ROM: IRM (Info Gap Activities); Testing Program, pp. 1–4; Test Files; Testing Program MP3s; Test Generator
espaces.vhlcentral.com: activities, downloads, reference tools

1 Suggestion Before beginning this activity, you may wish to review the alphabet and how to say the accent marks.

2 Suggestion Tell students not to accept a guess if the letter is not pronounced correctly in French.

3 Suggestion Before beginning the activity, have two volunteers read the **modèle** aloud.

4 Suggestion Remind students to use appropriate gestures and encourage them to add information to the introduction, such as the person's hometown.

5 Suggestions
- Before beginning this activity, quickly review the numbers 0–60. Hold up cards with various numbers, and have the class or individuals say them in French.
- Read the **modèle** aloud with a volunteer.

6 Suggestion Divide the class into pairs and distribute the Info Gap Handouts in the IRM on the IRCD-ROM for this activity. Give students ten minutes to complete the activity.

Synthèse

1 Des lettres In pairs, take turns choosing nouns. One partner chooses only masculine nouns, while the other chooses only feminine. Slowly spell each noun for your partner, who will guess the word. Find out who can give the quickest answers. Answers will vary.

2 Le pendu In groups of four, play hangman (**le pendu**). Form two teams of two partners each. Take turns choosing a French word or expression you learned in this lesson for the other team to guess. Continue to play until your team guesses at least one word or expression from each category. Answers will vary.

1. un nom féminin
2. un nom masculin
3. un nombre entre (*number between*) 0 et 30
4. un nombre entre 31 et 60
5. une expression

3 C'est... Ce sont... Doug is spending a week in Paris with his French e-mail pal, Marc. As Doug points out what he sees, Marc corrects him sometimes. In pairs, act out the roles. Doug should be right half the time. Answers will vary.

MODÈLE

Étudiant(e) 1: *C'est une bibliothèque?*
Étudiant(e) 2: *Non, c'est une librairie.*

1. C'est une bibliothèque.

2. C'est un café.

3. C'est une actrice.

4. Ce sont des acteurs.

5. C'est une université.

6. Ce sont des amies.

4 Les présentations In pairs, introduce yourselves. Together, meet another pair. One person per pair should introduce him or herself and his or her partner. Use the items from the list in your conversations. Switch roles until you have met all of the other pairs in the class. Answers will vary.

ami	étudiant
c'est	petit(e) ami(e)
ce sont	professeur

5 S'il te plaît You are new on campus and ask another student for help finding these places. He or she gives you the building (**le bâtiment**) and room (**la salle**) number and you thank him or her. Then, switch roles and repeat with another place from the list. Answers will vary.

MODÈLE

Étudiant(e) 1: *Pardon... l'examen de sociologie, s'il te plaît?*
Étudiant(e) 2: *Ah oui... le bâtiment E, la salle dix-sept.*
Étudiant(e) 1: *Merci beaucoup!*
Étudiant(e) 2: *De rien.*

Bibliothèque d'anglais	Bâtiment C Salle 11
Bureau de Mme Girard	Bâtiment A Salle 35
Bureau de M. Brachet	Bâtiment J Salle 42
Café	Bâtiment H Salle 59
Littérature française	Bâtiment B Salle 46
Examen de littérature	Bâtiment E Salle 24
Examen de sociologie	Bâtiment E Salle 17
Salle de télévision	Bâtiment F Salle 33
Salle des ordinateurs	Bâtiment D Salle 40

6 Mots mélangés You and a partner each have half the words of a wordsearch (**des mots mélangés**). Pick a number and a letter and say them to your partner, who must tell you if he or she has a letter in the corresponding space. Do not look at each other's worksheet. Answers will vary.

ressources

WB pp. 3-6	LM pp. 3-4	Lab MP3s Leçon 1	espaces.vhlcentral.com Leçon 1

OPTIONS

Extra Practice Bring in pictures from newspapers, magazines, or the Internet of nouns that students have learned, and ask them to identify the people or objects. Examples: **C'est un(e) ____? Ce sont des ____? Qu'est-ce que c'est?** You might also ask how many people or objects are in the picture if there are more than one. Example: **Il y a combien de(d') ____?**

Small Groups Bring in family photos or magazine pictures showing people greeting or introducing each other in different situations. Assign a photo to each group or allow them to choose one. Tell students to write a brief conversation based on the photo. Remind the class to use formal and informal expressions as appropriate.

La Triplette de Moulinex... un, deux, trois!

The story of Moulinex started with an invention. In 1932, Jean Mantelet invented the electric potato masher to help his wife. Later, he invented an electric coffee grinder called **Moulin° X**, which went on to become the company brand. After World War II, Moulinex came up with the famous slogan, **Moulinex libère la femme** (*Moulinex liberates women*). In the 1980s, Moulinex started facing tough competition and in 2001 was bought out by Seb, another French company specializing in small appliances and kitchen equipment.

Coup de main

Moulin X is a play on words. **Moulin** means *grinder* and you need to pronounce the **x** the English way, not the French way. That's how you obtain Moulinex.

—Un, deux, trois, elle fait° la raclette.

—Un, deux, trois, elle fait des crêpes.

Compréhension Answer these questions. Some answers will vary.

1. What numbers and articles did you recognize? un, deux, trois, la, des
2. What is special about this device?

Discussion In groups of four, discuss the answers to these questions. Use as much French as you can. Answers will vary.

1. Have you ever eaten **raclette** or **crêpes** before? Where?
2. When would one use **la Triplette**?
3. What other appliance can you think of that performs more than one job?
4. If you could invent an appliance with several functions, what would it do? What would you name it?

SUR INTERNET

Go to **espaces.vhlcentral.com** to watch the TV clip featured in this **Le zapping**.

Moulin *grinder* **elle fait** *it makes*

Section Goals

In this section, students will:
- read about Moulinex, a company that makes small household appliances
- watch the commercial for one of its devices, the **Triplette**
- answer questions about the device and Moulinex

Instructional Resources
*IRCD-ROM: IRM (**Le zapping** TV clip transcription)*
espaces.vhlcentral.com: activities, downloads, reference tools, TV clip

Introduction
To check comprehension, ask these questions.
1. What did Jean Mantelet invent? (He invented an electric potato masher and an electric coffee grinder.)
2. What was Moulinex's slogan after World War II? (**«Moulinex libère la femme»**)
3. Who bought Moulinex in 2001? (Seb, another French company specializing in small appliances and kitchen equipment)

Avant de regarder la vidéo
- Have students look at the video stills, read the captions, and describe the device and what it is used for. (It's an electric cooking device that you can use to prepare **raclette** and **crêpes**.)
- Before showing the video, explain to students that they do not need to understand every word they hear. Tell them to listen for numbers, articles, and cognates.

Compréhension Have students work in pairs or groups for this activity. Tell them to write their answers. Then show the video again so that they can check their answers and add any missing information.

Discussion
- Have volunteers report their answers to the class.
- Take a quick class survey to find out who likes or would like to try either **raclette** or **crêpes**.

OPTIONS

Les appareils ménagers There are more than 280 million small appliances in French households. The three most common appliances are irons, vacuum cleaners, and hair dryers. In the kitchen, the three main types of appliances are coffee makers, toasters, and food processors. Seventy-five percent of households buy one or more small household appliances per year. These new products represent an increasing part of the market: steam irons and espresso makers. Twenty-five percent of all appliances are offered as gifts.

Section Goals

In this section, students will learn and practice vocabulary related to:
- objects in the classroom
- identifying people

Instructional Resources

*IRCD-ROM: Transparency #15; IRM (**Vocabulaire supplémentaire; Mise en pratique** answers; Textbook Audioscript; Lab Audioscript; Info Gap Activities)*
Textbook MP3s
WB/VM: Workbook, pp. 7–8
Lab Manual, p. 5
Lab MP3s
WB/VM/LM Answer Key
espaces.vhlcentral.com: activities, downloads, reference tools

Suggestions

- Introduce vocabulary for classroom objects, such as **un cahier, une carte, un dictionnaire, un stylo**. Hold up or point to an object and say: **C'est un stylo.**
- Hold up or point to an object and ask either/or questions. Examples: **C'est un crayon ou un stylo? C'est une porte ou une fenêtre?**
- Using either objects in the classroom or **Transparency #15**, point to items or people and ask questions, such as **Qu'est-ce que c'est? Qui est-ce? C'est un stylo? C'est un professeur?**
- Have students pick up or point out objects you name. You might want to teach them the expression **Montrez-moi un/une ____.**
- Additional vocabulary for this lesson can be found in the **Vocabulaire supplémentaire** in the IRM on the IRCD-ROM.

Leçon 2

You will learn how to...
- identify yourself and others
- ask yes/no questions

En classe

Vocabulaire

Qui est-ce?	*Who is it?*
Quoi?	*What?*
une calculatrice	*calculator*
une montre	*watch*
un palm	*Palm Pilot; PDA*
une porte	*door*
un résultat	*result*
une salle de classe	*classroom*
un(e) camarade de chambre	*roommate*
un(e) camarade de classe	*classmate*
une classe	*class (group of students)*
un copain/ une copine (*fam.*)	*friend*
un(e) élève	*pupil, student*
une femme	*woman*
une fille	*girl*
un garçon	*boy*
un homme	*man*

ressources

WB pp. 7–8	LM p. 6	Text MP3s Leçon 2	Lab MP3s Leçon 2	espaces.vhlcentral.com Leçon 2

OPTIONS

Pairs Have students work in pairs and take an inventory of all the people and items in the classroom. Tell them to write their list in French using the expression **Il y a ____**. After students have finished, tell them to compare their lists with another pair to see if they are the same.

Game Divide the class into teams. Then, in English, say the name of a classroom object and ask one of the teams to provide the French equivalent. If the team provides the correct term, it gets a point. If not, the second team gets a chance to give the correct term. Alternate giving items to the two teams. The team with the most points at the end of the game wins.

une carte

une chaise

Mise en pratique

1 **Écoutez** Listen to Madame Arnaud as she describes her French classroom, then check the items she mentions.

1. une porte ☑
2. un professeur ☐
3. une feuille de papier ☐
4. un dictionnaire ☑
5. une carte ☑
6. vingt-quatre cahiers ☐
7. une calculatrice ☐
8. vingt-sept chaises ☑
9. une corbeille à papier ☑
10. un stylo ☑

2 **Chassez l'intrus** Circle the word that does not belong.

1. étudiants, élèves, (professeur)
2. un stylo, un crayon, (un cahier)
3. un livre, un dictionnaire, (un stylo)
4. un homme, (un crayon), un garçon
5. une copine, (une carte), une femme
6. une porte, une fenêtre, (une chaise)
7. une chaise, (un professeur), une fenêtre
8. (un crayon), une feuille de papier, un cahier
9. un palm, une montre, (une copine)
10. une fille, (un sac à dos), un garçon

3 **C'est...** Work with a partner to identify the items you see in the image.

MODÈLE

Étudiant(e) 1: *Qu'est-ce que c'est?*
Étudiant(e) 2: *C'est un tableau.*

1. un tableau
2. une porte
3. un crayon/stylo
4. un livre
5. une calculatrice
6. un stylo/crayon
7. une feuille
8. un bureau
9. un dictionnaire
10. une corbeille à papier
11. une chaise
12. un professeur

1 Tapescript Bonjour! Dans la salle de classe, il y a beaucoup de choses! Il y a trois fenêtres, une porte, une carte, un tableau, vingt-sept chaises et une corbeille à papier. Il y a aussi vingt-quatre étudiants et vingt-quatre sacs à dos. Dans les sacs à dos, il y a généralement un cahier, un crayon ou un stylo, un livre et un dictionnaire pour le cours de français.
(On Textbook MP3s)

1 Suggestion Have students check their answers by going over **Activité 1** with the whole class. Repeat any sections of the recording that the students missed or did not understand.

2 Suggestion Have students compare their answers in pairs or small groups. Tell them to explain why a word does not belong if they don't have the same answer.

2 Expansion For additional practice, read these items aloud or write them on the board.
11. une calculatrice, un étudiant, un professeur (une calculatrice)
12. une femme, un garçon, une fille (un garçon)
13. un palm, un copain, un camarade de chambre (un palm)

3 Suggestion Remind students to use the appropriate form of the indefinite article when doing this activity.

3 Expansion In pairs, tell students to take turns pointing to the items in the drawing and asking: **C'est un(e) ____?** If it's correct, the other person says: **Oui, c'est un(e) ____.** If it is not correct, the persons says: **Non, c'est un(e) ____.**

OPTIONS

Extra Practice Review numbers and practice vocabulary for classroom objects using printouts of advertisements in French from stores that sell school supplies, such as Monoprix. Make sure the ads include prices. As you show the pictures, ask students about the prices. Examples: **La corbeille à papier est à 15 euros ou à 20 euros? C'est combien, la calculatrice?**

Game Have the class do a chain activity in which the first student says a word in French, for example, **chaise**. The next student has to think of a word that begins with the last letter of the first person's word, such as **étudiant**. If a student can't think of a word, he or she is out of the game, and it's the next person's turn. The last student left in the game is the winner.

4 Expansion For additional practice, point to different students' desks that have objects on them and ask: **Qu'est ce qu'il y a sur le bureau de ____?** You might also ask: **Qu'est-ce qu'il y a sur mon bureau?**

5 Suggestion Before beginning the activity, have a few volunteers demonstrate what students should do using the **modèle**.

Successful Language Learning Remind the class that errors are a natural part of language learning. Point out that it is impossible to speak "perfectly" in any language. Emphasize that their spoken and written French will improve if they make an effort to practice.

6 Suggestions
- Divide the class into pairs and distribute the Info Gap Handouts in the IRM on the IRCD-ROM for this activity. Give students ten minutes to complete the activity.
- Have two volunteers read the **modèle** aloud.

6 Expansion Have students describe the people and objects in the photo using **Il y a.**

7 Suggestion Before beginning the activity, remind students that to guess what the drawing represents they should say: **C'est un(e) ____?** or **Ce sont des ____?**

Communication

NATIONAL STANDARDS communication

4 Qu'est-ce qu'il y a dans mon sac à dos? Make a list of six different items that you have in your backpack, then work with a partner to compare your answers. Answers will vary.

Dans mon (*my*) sac à dos, il y a	Dans le sac à dos de *nom*, il y a
1. ____	1. ____
2. ____	2. ____
3. ____	3. ____
4. ____	4. ____
5. ____	5. ____
6. ____	6. ____

5 Qu'est-ce que c'est? Point at eight different items around the classroom and ask a classmate to identify them. Write your partner's responses on the spaces provided below. Answers will vary.

MODÈLE
Étudiant(e) 1: *Qu'est-ce que c'est?*
Étudiant(e) 2: *C'est un stylo.*

1. ____	5. ____
2. ____	6. ____
3. ____	7. ____
4. ____	8. ____

6 Sept différences Your instructor will give you and a partner two different drawings of a classroom. Do not look at each other's worksheet. Find seven differences between your picture and your partner's by asking each other questions and describing what you see.

MODÈLE
Étudiant(e) 1: *Il y a une fenêtre dans ma (my) salle de classe.*
Étudiant(e) 2: *Oh! Il n'y a pas de fenêtre dans ma salle de classe.*

7 Pictogrammes As a class, play pictionary. Answers will vary.
- Take turns going to the board and drawing words you learned on pp. 16–17.
- The person drawing may not speak and may not write any letters or numbers.
- The person who guesses correctly in French what the **grand artiste** is drawing will go next.
- Your instructor will time each turn and tell you if your time runs out.

OPTIONS

Game Divide the class into two teams. Put labels of classroom vocabulary in a box. Alternating between teams, one person picks a label out of the box without showing it to anyone. This person must place the label on the correct person or object in the classroom and say the word aloud. Each player is allowed only 15 seconds and one guess per turn. Award a point for a correct response. If a player is incorrect, the next player on the opposing team may "steal" the point by placing the label on the correct person or object. The team with the most points at the end of the game wins.

Les sons et les lettres

NATIONAL
comparisons
STANDARDS

Silent letters

Final consonants of French words are usually silent.

françai~~s~~ **spor~~t~~** **vou~~s~~** **salu~~t~~**

An unaccented **-e** (or **-es**) at the end of a word is silent, but the preceding consonant *is* pronounced.

français~~e~~ **américain~~e~~** **orang~~es~~** **japonais~~es~~**

The consonants **-c**, **-r**, **-f**, and **-l** are usually pronounced at the ends of words. To remember these exceptions, think of the consonants in the word **c**a**r**e**f**u**l**.

parc	**bonjour**	**actif**	**animal**
lac	**professeur**	**naïf**	**mal**

Prononcez Practice saying these words aloud.

1. traditionnel
2. étudiante
3. généreuse
4. téléphones
5. chocolat
6. Monsieur
7. journalistes
8. hôtel
9. sac
10. concert
11. timide
12. sénégalais
13. objet
14. normal
15. importante

Articulez Practice saying these sentences aloud.

1. Au revoir, Paul. À plus tard!
2. Je vais très bien. Et vous, Monsieur Dubois?
3. Qu'est-ce que c'est? C'est une calculatrice.
4. Il y a un ordinateur, une table et une chaise.
5. Frédéric et Chantal, je vous présente Michel et Éric.
6. Voici un sac à dos, des crayons et des feuilles de papier.

Dictons Practice reading these sayings aloud.

Mieux vaut tard que jamais.[1]

Aussitôt dit, aussitôt fait.[2]

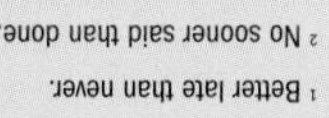
[1] Better late than never.
[2] No sooner said than done.

ressources

LM p. 6	Text MP3s Leçon 2	Lab MP3s Leçon 2	espaces.vhlcentral.com Leçon 2

OPTIONS

Extra Practice Write on the board or an overhead transparency a list of words that have silent letters. Call on volunteers to spell each word in French and then pronounce it. Examples: **art**, **comment**, **sont**, **est**, **intelligent**, **sac à dos**, and **résultat**.

Small Groups Working in groups of three or four, have students practice pronunciation by reading the vocabulary words aloud on pages 16–17. Circulate among the groups and model correct pronunciation as needed. When they have finished, ask them if they discovered any exceptions to the pronunciation rules. (**palm, cahier, papier**)

Section Goals

In this section, students will learn about:

- silent letters
- a strategy for remembering which consonants are pronounced at the end of words

Instructional Resources
Textbook MP3s
Lab Manual, p. 6
Lab MP3s
WB/VM/LM Answer Key
IRCD-ROM: IRM (Textbook Audioscript; Lab Audioscript)
espaces.vhlcentral.com: activities, downloads, reference tools

Suggestions

- Write the sentences below on the board or a transparency. Then say each sentence and ask students which letters are silent. Draw a slash through the silent letters as students say them. **Qui est-ce? C'est Gilbert. Il est français.** **Qu'est-ce que c'est? C'est un éléphant.**
- Work through the example words. Model the pronunciation of each word and have students repeat after you.
- Tell students that the final consonants of a few words that end in **c**, **r**, **f** or **l** are silent. Examples: **porc** (*pork*), **blanc** (*white*), **nerf** (*nerve*), and **gentil** (*nice*).
- Point out that the letters **-er** at the end of a word are pronounced like the vowel sound in the English word *say*. Examples: **cahier** and **papier.**
- Explain that numbers are exceptions to pronunciation rules. When counting, some final consonants are pronounced. Have students compare the pronunciation of the following: **six, sept, huit; six cahiers, sept stylos, huit crayons.**
- Tell students that the final consonants of words borrowed from other languages are often pronounced. Examples: **palm, snob, autobus**, and **club**. This topic will be presented in **Leçon 21.**
- The explanations and exercises are recorded on the Textbook MP3s CD-ROM and are available on the **ESPACES** web site. You may want to play them in class so students hear French speakers other than yourself.

Section Goals

In this section, students will learn functional phrases for describing people's character traits and talking about their nationalities through comprehensible input.

Instructional Resources
WB/VM: Video Manual, pp. 213–214
WB/VM/LM Answer Key
Video CD-ROM
Video on DVD
*IRCD-ROM: IRM (Videoscript; **Roman-photo** Translations)*
espaces.vhlcentral.com: activities, downloads, reference tools

Video Recap: Leçon 1
Before doing this **Roman-photo**, review the previous one. Write the names of the main characters on the board and ask students with whom they associate the following people, places, or objects.

1. un étudiant américain (David)
2. Le P'tit Bistrot (Madame Forestier et Stéphane)
3. un magazine (Sandrine)
4. un examen de français (Stéphane)
5. un cours de sciences politiques (Rachid)
6. le lycée (Stéphane)

Video Synopsis At the café, Valérie waits on some tourists. Valérie argues with Stéphane about his failed math test. While Michèle and Valérie prepare the tourists' orders, Michèle advises Valérie to be patient with her son. At another table, David asks Amina about herself, Rachid, and Sandrine. David repeats his questions about the others to Valérie, who warns him not to get involved with Sandrine because she is seeing Pascal.

Suggestions

- Have students scan the captions and find six adjectives of nationality plus five phrases that describe people's personality or character. Call on volunteers to read the adjectives or phrases they found aloud.
- Have students volunteer to read the characters' parts in the **Roman-photo** aloud.

Les copains

PERSONNAGES

Amina

David

Michèle

Stéphane

Touriste

Valérie

1

À la terrasse du café...
VALÉRIE Alors, un croissant, une crêpe et trois cafés.
TOURISTE Merci, Madame.
VALÉRIE Ah, vous êtes... américain?
TOURISTE Um, non, je suis anglais. Il est canadien et elle est italienne.
VALÉRIE Moi, je suis française.

2

À l'intérieur du café...
VALÉRIE Stéphane!!!
STÉPHANE Quoi?! Qu'est-ce que c'est?
VALÉRIE Qu'est-ce que c'est! Qu'est-ce que c'est! Une feuille de papier! C'est l'examen de maths! Qu'est-ce que c'est?
STÉPHANE Oui, euh, les maths, c'est difficile.

3

VALÉRIE Stéphane, tu es intelligent, mais tu n'es pas brillant! En classe, on fait attention au professeur, au cahier et au livre! Pas aux fenêtres. Et. Pas. Aux. Filles!
STÉPHANE Oh, oh, ça va!!

6

À la table d'Amina et de David...
DAVID Et Rachid, mon colocataire? Comment est-il?
AMINA Il est agréable et très poli... plutôt réservé mais c'est un étudiant brillant. Il est d'origine algérienne.

7

DAVID Et toi, Amina. Tu es de quelle origine?
AMINA D'origine sénégalaise.
DAVID Et Sandrine?

8

AMINA Sandrine? Elle est française.
DAVID Mais non... Comment est-elle?
AMINA Bon, elle est chanteuse, alors elle est un peu égoïste. Mais elle est très sociable. Et charmante. Mais attention! Elle est avec Pascal.
DAVID Pfft, Pascal, Pascal...

ACTIVITÉS

1 Identifiez Indicate which character would make each statement: Amina (**A**), David (**D**), Michèle (**M**), Sandrine (**S**), Stéphane (**St**), or Valérie (**V**).

1. Les maths, c'est difficile. St
2. En classe, on fait attention au professeur! V
3. Michèle, les trois cafés sont pour les trois touristes. V
4. Ah, Madame, du calme! M
5. Ma mère est très impatiente! St
6. J'ai (*I have*) de la famille au Sénégal. A
7. Je suis une grande chanteuse! S
8. Mon colocataire est très poli et intelligent. D
9. Pfft, Pascal, Pascal... D
10. Attention, David! Sandrine est avec Pascal. A/V

OPTIONS

Video Tips General suggestions for using video clips in the classroom can be found on page IAE-11 of the Instructor's Annotated Edition.

Avant de regarder la vidéo Before showing the video episode, have students brainstorm the type of information they might give when describing people.

Regarder la vidéo Show the video episode and have students give you a play-by-play description of the action. Write their descriptions on the board. Then show the episode a second time so students can add details if necessary, or simply consolidate information. Finally, discuss the material on the board and call attention to any incorrect information. Help students prepare a brief plot summary.

Amina, David et Stéphane passent la matinée (*spend the morning*) au café.

Au bar...
VALÉRIE Le croissant, c'est pour l'Anglais, et la crêpe, c'est pour l'Italienne.
MICHÈLE Mais, Madame. Ça va? Qu'est-ce qu'il y a?
VALÉRIE Ben, c'est Stéphane. Des résultats d'examens, des professeurs... des problèmes!

MICHÈLE Ah, Madame, du calme! Je suis optimiste. C'est un garçon intelligent. Et vous, êtes-vous une femme patiente?
VALÉRIE Oui... oui, je suis patiente. Mais le Canadien, l'Anglais et l'Italienne sont impatients. Allez! Vite!

VALÉRIE Alors, ça va bien?
AMINA Ah, oui, merci.
DAVID Amina est une fille élégante et sincère.
VALÉRIE Oui! Elle est charmante.
DAVID Et Rachid, comment est-il?
VALÉRIE Oh! Rachid! C'est un ange! Il est intelligent, poli et modeste. Un excellent camarade de chambre.

DAVID Et Sandrine? Comment est-elle?
VALÉRIE Sandrine?! Oh, là, là. Non, non, non. Elle est avec Pascal.

Expressions utiles

Describing people

- **Vous êtes/Tu es américain?**
  You're American?
- **Je suis anglais. Il est canadien et elle est italienne.**
  I'm English. He's Canadian, and she's Italian.
- **Et Rachid, mon colocataire? Comment est-il?**
  And Rachid, my roommate (in an apartment)? What's he like?
- **Il est agréable et très poli... plutôt réservé mais c'est un étudiant brillant.**
  He's nice and polite... rather reserved, but a brilliant student.
- **Tu es de quelle origine?**
  (Of) What heritage are you?
- **Je suis d'origine algérienne/sénégalaise.**
  I'm of Algerian/Senegalese heritage.
- **Elle est avec Pascal.**
  She's with (dating) Pascal.
- **Rachid! C'est un ange!**
  Rachid! He's an angel!

Asking questions

- **Ça va? Qu'est-ce qu'il y a?**
  Are you OK? What is it?/What's wrong?

Additional vocabulary

- **Ah, Madame, du calme!**
  Oh, ma'am, calm down!
- **On fait attention à...**
  One pays attention to...
- **Mais attention!**
  But watch out!
- **Allez! Vite!**
  Go! Quickly!
- **Mais non...**
  Of course not...
- **alors**
  so
- **mais**
  but
- **un peu**
  a little

2 Complétez Use words from the list to describe these people in French. Refer to the video scenes and a dictionary as necessary.

1. Michèle always looks on the bright side. optimiste
2. Rachid gets great grades. intelligent
3. Amina is very honest. sincère
4. Sandrine thinks about herself a lot. égoïste
5. Sandrine has a lot of friends. sociable

égoïste
intelligent
optimiste
sincère
sociable

3 Conversez In pairs, choose the words from this list you would use to describe yourselves. What personality traits do you have in common? Be prepared to share your answers with the class.

brillant	modeste
charmant	optimiste
égoïste	patient
élégant	sincère
intelligent	sociable

ressources
VM pp. 213-214 | V CD-ROM Leçon 2 | espaces.vhlcentral.com Leçon 2

ACTIVITÉS

Expressions utiles

- Model the pronunciation of the **Expressions utiles** and have students repeat after you.
- Point out forms of the verb **être** and adjective agreement in the captions and in the **Expressions utiles**. Tell students that this material will be formally presented in the **Structures** section.
- Ask a few questions based on the **Expressions utiles**. Examples: **Et ____, vous êtes américain(e) [canadien(ne)/ italien(ne)]? Ça va? Qu'est-ce qu'il y a?**

1 Expansion For additional practice, read these items aloud or write them on the board.
11. Je suis optimiste. (Michèle)
12. Je suis anglais. (le touriste)
13. Rachid! C'est un ange! (Valérie)

2 Expansion Write the following adjectives on the board and ask students which video character they describe.
1. sénégalais(e) (Amina)
2. algérien(ne) (Rachid)
3. français(e) (Sandrine, Stéphane, Valérie, Michèle)
4. charmant(e) (Sandrine)
5. réservé (Rachid)

3 Expansion After the students complete the activity, tell them to write a brief description of themselves using **Je suis ____**. Read some of the descriptions aloud and have the class guess who wrote them.

OPTIONS

Extra Practice Choose four or five lines of the **Roman-photo** to use as a dictation. Read each line twice, pausing after each line so that students have time to write. Have students check their own work by comparing it with the **Roman-photo** text.

Pairs Have students work in pairs. Tell them to look at video stills 2–3 and 6–8, and choose a situation to ad-lib. Assure them that it is not necessary to follow or memorize the **Roman-photo** word for word. Students should be creative while getting the general meaning across with the vocabulary and expressions they know.

Section Goals

In this section, students will:
- learn about France's multicultural society
- learn some familiar terms for identifying people
- read the mottos of some francophone countries
- read about ***Superdupont***, a popular comic-strip character

Instructional Resources
espaces.vhlcentral.com: activities, downloads, reference tools

Culture à la loupe
Avant la lecture Have students discuss what their idea of a typical French person is.

Lecture
- Point out the regions where Provençal **(Provence)**, Breton **(Bretagne)**, and Basque **(Le Pays basque)** are spoken on the map of France in **Appendice A.**
- Explain that there are other regional languages not mentioned in the text: Alsatian, Caribbean Creole, Catalan, Corsican, Dutch, Gascon, Lorraine German dialect, and Occitan.

Après la lecture Ask students what facts in this reading are interesting or surprising to them.

1 Expansion For additional practice, give students these items. 11. There are several official languages in France. (**Faux.** French is the only official language.) 12. South Africans represent a significant immigrant population in France. (**Faux.** North and West Africans represent significant immigrant populations.) 13. There are more immigrants in France from both Italy and Spain than from Tunisia. (**Vrai.**) 14. There aren't many Asians in France (**Faux.** There are significant Indo-Chinese populations.)

CULTURE À LA LOUPE

Qu'est-ce qu'un Français typique?

What is your idea of a typical Frenchman? Do you picture a man wearing a **béret**? How about French women? Are they all fashionable and stylish? Do you picture what is shown in these photos? While real French people fitting one aspect or another of these cultural stereotypes do exist, rarely do you find individuals who fit all aspects.

France is a multicultural society with no single, national ethnicity. While the majority of French people are of Celtic or Latin descent, France has significant North and West African (e.g., Algeria, Morocco, Senegal) and Indo-Chinese (e.g., Vietnam, Laos, Cambodia) populations as well. Long a **terre d'accueil**°, France today has over four million foreigners and immigrants. Even as France has maintained a strong concept of its culture through the preservation of its language, history, and traditions, French culture has been ultimately enriched by the contributions of its immigrant populations. Each region of the country also has its own traditions, folklore, and, often, its own language. Regional languages, such as Provençal, Breton, and Basque, are still spoken in some areas, but the official language is, of course, French.

terre d'accueil *a land welcoming of newcomers*

Immigrants in France, by country of birth

COUNTRY NAME	NUMBER OF PEOPLE
Algeria	574,200
Portugal	571,900
Other European countries	568,800
Morocco	522,500
Italy	378,700
Spain	316,200
Tunisia	201,600
Turkey	174,200
Cambodia, Laos, Vietnam	159,800
Poland	98,600

ACTIVITÉS

1 Vrai ou faux? Indicate whether each statement is **vrai** or **faux.**

1. Cultural stereotypes are generally true for most people in France. Faux. Rarely do you find individuals who fit all aspects of a stereotype.
2. People in France no longer speak regional languages. Faux. Regional languages are still spoken in some areas.
3. Many immigrants from North Africa live in France. Vrai.
4. More immigrants in France come from Portugal than from Morocco. Vrai.
5. Algerians and Moroccans represent the largest immigrant populations in France. Faux. Algerians and Portuguese have the largest immigrant populations.
6. Immigrant cultures have little impact on French culture. Faux. French culture has been enriched by immigrant cultures.
7. Because of immigration, France is losing its cultural identity. Faux. France has maintained its culture.
8. French culture differs from region to region. Vrai.
9. Most French people are of Anglo-saxon heritage. Faux. The majority of French people are of Celtic or Latin descent.
10. For many years, France has received immigrants from many countries. Vrai.

OPTIONS

Cultural Activity Ask students what stereotypical ideas a French person might have of Americans. If students have difficulty answering, then give them a few examples of American stereotypes and ask them if they are true or valid. Examples: Americans are loud and obnoxious. Americans only speak English. Americans are overweight.

Small Groups Divide the class into groups of three or four. Give groups five minutes to brainstorm names of cities, states, lakes, rivers, mountain ranges, and so forth in the United States that have French origins. One member of each group should write down the names. Then have groups share their lists with the class.

LE FRANÇAIS QUOTIDIEN

Les gens

ado (*m./f.*)	*adolescent, teen*
bonhomme (*m.*)	*fellow*
gars (*m.*)	*guy*
mec (*m.*)	*guy*
minette (*f.*)	*young woman, sweetie*
nana (*f.*)	*young woman, girl*
pote (*m.*)	*buddy*
type (*m.*)	*guy*

LE MONDE FRANCOPHONE

Les devises

Here are the **devises** (*national mottos*) of some francophone countries.

Belgium **L'union fait la force** (*Unity is strength*)
Ivory Coast **Union, Discipline, Travail** (*Unity, Discipline, Work*)
France **Liberté, Égalité, Fraternité** (*Liberty, Equality, Fraternity*)
Monaco **Avec l'aide de Dieu** (*With the help of God*)
Morocco **Dieu, la Patrie, le Roi** (*God, Country, King*)
Senegal **Un Peuple, un But, une Foi** (*One People, one Goal, one Faith*)
Switzerland **Un pour tous, tous pour un** (*One for all, all for one*)
Tunisia **Liberté, Ordre, Justice** (*Liberty, Order, Justice*)

PORTRAIT

Superdupont

Superdupont is an ultra-French superhero in a popular comic strip parodying French nationalism. The protector of all things French, he battles the secret enemy organization **Anti-France**, whose agents speak **anti-français**, a mixture of English, Spanish, Italian, Russian, and German. *Superdupont* embodies just about every French stereotype imaginable. For example, the name Dupont, much like Smith in the United States, is extremely common in France. In addition to his **béret** and moustache, he wears a blue, white, and red belt around his waist representing **le drapeau français** (*the French flag*). Physically, he is overweight and has a red nose—signs that he appreciates rich French food and wine. Finally, on his arm is **un coq** (*a rooster*), the national symbol of France. The Latin word for rooster (*gallus*) also means "inhabitant of Gaul," as France used to be called.

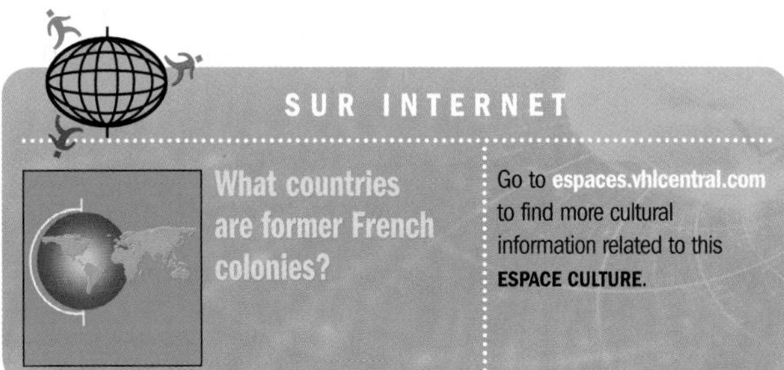

SUR INTERNET

What countries are former French colonies?

Go to espaces.vhlcentral.com to find more cultural information related to this **ESPACE CULTURE**.

ACTIVITÉS

2 Complétez Provide responses to these questions.

1. France is often symbolized by this bird: ___the rooster___.
2. ___Blue, white, and red___ are the colors of the French flag.
3. France was once named ___Gaul___.
4. The French term ___ado___ refers to a person aged 15 or 16.
5. ___Liberty, equality, and fraternity___ are three basic principles of French society.

3 Et les Américains? What might a comic-book character based on a "typical American" be like? With a partner, brainstorm a list of stereotypes to create a profile for such a character. Compare the profile you create with your classmates'. Do they fairly represent Americans? Why or why not?

ressources

Le français quotidien

- Point out that this vocabulary is very familiar. These words are usually used in informal conversations among young people.
- Model the pronunciation of each term and have students repeat.

Portrait

- Explain that this political comic strip is not unique and that **la bande dessinée (B.D.)** represents serious reading for young and old alike in France. An international comic-book festival takes place every year in the small town of Angoulême, France.
- Ask students why they think ***Superdupont*** is so popular in France.

Le monde francophone

- Have students locate the countries listed here on the world map in **Appendice A.**
- To check comprehension, ask these questions. 1. Which countries' mottos include the word *union*? (Belgium and Ivory Coast) 2. How do other mottos express this same idea? (Senegal: **Un peuple, un But, une Foi** and Switzerland: **Un pour tous, tous pour un**) 3. Whose motto mentions freedom? (France and Tunisia) 4. Whose motto mentions God? (Monaco and Morocco) 5. What other country considers religion important? (Senegal: **une Foi**) 6. What does Morocco's motto tell you about the country's political structure? (It's a monarchy.)

Sur Internet Point out to students that they will find supporting activities and information at **espaces.vhlcentral.com**.

2 Expansion Have students write four more fill-in-the-blank statements based on the information on this page. Then tell them to exchange papers with a classmate and complete the activity.

3 Expansion Have students draw a picture of their comic-book character or find a photo in a newspaper or magazine to illustrate the character's profile.

OPTIONS

Cultural Comparison Have students compare ***Superdupont*** to American comic-book superheroes, such as Superman, Batman, and Wonder Woman. Bring in pictures of these comic-book characters, if possible, to facilitate the discussion. Have students discuss the following aspects: their clothing and general appearance, the reason for their existence or purpose, what they represent, and why they are so popular.

Les devises Tell students to take out a coin and find mottos of the United States. ("In God We Trust" and "*E Pluribus Unum*") Point out that "*E Pluribus Unum*" means "*One Out of Many*". Then ask students which countries in the francophone world have mottos that express similar ideas. "In God We Trust" is the official national motto according to a law passed in 1956.

comparisons NATIONAL STANDARDS

Section Goals

In this section, students will learn:

- subject pronouns
- the verb **être**
- **c'est** and **il/elle est**

Instructional Resources
WB/VM: Workbook, pp. 9–10
Lab Manual, p. 7
Lab MP3s
WB/VM/LM Answer Key
*IRCD-ROM: IRM (**Essayez!** and **Mise en pratique** answers; Lab Audioscript)*
espaces.vhlcentral.com: activities, downloads, reference tools

Suggestions

- Point to yourself and say: **Je suis professeur**. Then walk up to a student and say: **Tu es…**The student should say: **étudiant(e)**. Once the pattern has been established, include other subject pronouns and forms of **être** while pointing to other students. Examples: **Il est étudiant. Elle est étudiante. Elles sont étudiantes.**
- Ask students a few simple questions and tell them to respond **Oui** or **Non**. Examples: **Brad Pitt est acteur? Jennifer Aniston est chanteuse?**
- Point out that in French you do not use an article before a profession after **il/elle est** and **ils/elles sont.** You say: **Il est acteur,** not **Il est un acteur.**
- Ask students to give examples of situations in which they would use the **tu** and **vous** forms of **être**.
- Give examples of how **on** can mean *we* in casual conversation: **On est copains.**
- Point out the liaison in **vous êtes**. Also point out that the **-n** in **on est** is pronounced. Have students pronounce these phrases.
- When teaching the difference between **c'est/ce sont** and **il(s)/elle(s) est/sont**, explain that **c'est/ce sont** is most often followed by a noun and **il(s)/elle(s) est/sont** is most often followed by an adjective. Point out the exceptions: **C'est très bien. Elle est chanteuse.**
- Tell students that the term **la photo**, which appears in the example **Ce sont des photos**, comes from the word **la photographie.**

2.1 The verb *être*

Point de départ In French, as in English, the subject of a verb is the person or thing that carries out the action. The verb expresses the action itself.

SUBJECT ⟷	VERB
Le professeur	parle français.
The professor	*speaks French.*

Subject pronouns

- Subject pronouns replace a noun that is the subject of a verb.

SUBJECT PRONOUN ⟷	VERB
Il	parle français.
He	*speaks French.*

French subject pronouns

	singular		plural	
first person	**je**	*I*	**nous**	*we*
second person	**tu**	*you*	**vous**	*you*
third person	**il**	*he/it* (masc.)	**ils**	*they* (masc.)
	elle	*she/it* (fem.)	**elles**	*they* (fem.)
	on	*one*		

- Subject pronouns in French show number (singular vs. plural) and gender (masculine vs. feminine). When a subject consists of both genders, use the masculine form.

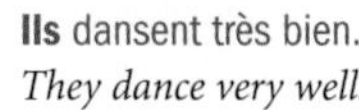

Ils dansent très bien.
They dance very well.

Ils sont de Dakar.
They are from Dakar.

- Use **tu** for informal address and **vous** for formal. **Vous** is also the plural form of *you*, both informal and formal.

Comment vas-**tu**?	Comment allez-**vous**?
How's it going?	*How are you?*

- The subject pronoun **on** refers to people in general, just as the English subject pronouns *one, they,* or *you* sometimes do. **On** can also mean *we* in a casual style. **On** always takes the same verb form as **il** and **elle.**

En France, **on** parle français.	**On** est au café.
In France, they speak French.	*We are at the coffee shop.*

MISE EN PRATIQUE

1 Pascal répète Pascal repeats everything his friend Odile says to be sure he understands. Give the question he asks after each statement, using subject pronouns.

MODÈLE Chantal est étudiante. *Elle est étudiante?*

1. Les professeurs sont en Tunisie. Ils sont en Tunisie?
2. Mon (*My*) petit ami Charles n'est pas ici. Il n'est pas ici?
3. Moi, je suis chanteuse. Tu es chanteuse?
4. Nadège et moi, nous sommes à l'université. Vous êtes à l'université?
5. Tu es un ami. Je suis un ami?
6. L'ordinateur est dans (*in*) la chambre. Il est dans la chambre?
7. Claude et Charles sont là. Ils sont là?
8. Lucien et toi, vous êtes copains. Nous sommes copains?

2 Où sont-ils? Thérèse wants to know where all her friends are. Tell her by completing the sentences with the appropriate subjects and the correct forms of **être.**

MODÈLE Sylvie / au café *Elle est au café.*

1. Georges / à la faculté de médecine Il est à la faculté de médec
2. Marie et moi / dans (*in*) la salle de classe Nous sommes d la salle de class
3. Christine et Anne / à la bibliothèque Elles sont à la bibliothèqu
4. Richard et Vincent / là-bas Ils sont là-bas.
5. Véronique, Marc et Anne / à la librairie Ils sont à la librairie.
6. Jeanne / au bureau Elle est au bureau.

3 Identifiez Describe these photos using **c'est, ce sont, il/elle est,** or **ils/elles sont.**

1. C'est un acteur.

2. Il est ici.

3. Elles sont copines.

4. Elle est chanteuse.

5. Elle est là.

6. Ce sont des montres.

OPTIONS

Extra Practice As a rapid-response drill, call out subject pronouns and have students respond with the correct form of **être**. Examples: **tu (es)** and **vous (êtes)**. Then reverse the drill; say the forms of **être** and have students give the subject pronouns. Accept multiple answers for **est** and **sont**.

Extra Practice Ask students to indicate whether the following people would be addressed as **vous** or **tu**. Examples: a roommate, a friend's grandmother, a doctor, and a neighbor's child.

Extra Practice Bring in pictures of people and objects and ask students to describe them using **c'est**, **ce sont**, **il/elle est**, or **ils/elles sont.**

COMMUNICATION

4 Questions In pairs, ask each other these questions. Be prepared to share what you learn with the class.
Answers will vary.

1. Tu es étudiant?
2. Ton (*Your*) camarade de chambre et toi, vous êtes copains?
3. Tes (*Your*) profs sont-ils intéressants?
4. Tes cours sont-ils difficiles?
5. Nous deux, nous sommes dans combien de classes?
6. Tu es de New York?

5 Qui est-ce? In pairs, identify who or what is in each picture. If possible, use **il/elle est** or **ils/elles sont** to add something else about each person or place.
Answers will vary.

MODÈLE

C'est Céline Dion. Elle est chanteuse.

1.

4.

2.

5.

3.

6.

6 Enchanté You and your roommate are in a campus bookstore. You run into one of his or her classmates, whom you've never met. In a brief conversation, introduce yourselves, ask how you are, and say something about yourselves using a form of **être**.
Answers will vary.

The verb *être*

- **Être** (*to be*) is an irregular verb; its conjugation (set of forms for different subjects) does not follow a pattern. The form **être** is called the infinitive; it does not correspond to any particular subject.

être **(to be)**			
je suis	*I am*	**nous sommes**	*we are*
tu es	*you are*	**vous êtes**	*you are*
il/elle est	*he/she/it is*	**ils/elles sont**	*they are*
on est	*one is*		

- Note that the **-s** of the subject pronoun **vous** is pronounced as an English *z* in the phrase **vous êtes.**

Vous êtes à Paris.
You are in Paris.

Vous êtes M. Leclerc? Enchantée.
Are you Mr. Leclerc? Pleased to meet you.

C'est and *il/elle est*

- Use **c'est** or its plural form **ce sont** plus a noun to identify who or what someone or something is. Except with proper names, an article must always precede the noun.

C'est un téléphone.
That's a phone.

Ce sont des photos.
Those are pictures.

C'est Émilie.
That's Émilie.

- Use the phrases **il/elle est** and **ils/elles sont** to refer to someone or something previously mentioned. Any noun that follows directly must not be accompanied by an article or adjective.

La bibliothèque?
Elle est moderne.
The library?
It's modern.

Voilà M. Richard.
Il est professeur.
There's Mr. Richard.
He's a professor.

BOÎTE À OUTILS

Note that in French, unlike English, you cannot use an article before a profession after **il/elle est** and **ils/elles sont**: **il est chanteur** (*he is a singer*); **elles sont actrices** (*they are actresses*).

Essayez! **Fill in the blanks with the correct forms of the verb être.**

1. Je ___suis___ ici.
2. Ils ___sont___ intelligents.
3. Tu ___es___ étudiante.
4. Nous ___sommes___ à Québec.
5. Vous ___êtes___ Mme Lacroix?
6. Marie ___est___ chanteuse.

Essayez! Have students create additional simple sentences using the verb **être**.

1 Suggestion Have students work on this activity in pairs. Tell them to switch roles for items 5–8.

2 Suggestion To check students' answers, call on volunteers to read the sentences aloud or write them on the board.

3 Suggestion Before beginning the activity, have students quickly identify the items or people in the photos.

4 Suggestion Tell students to add two questions of their own to the list and to jot down notes during their interviews.

5 Suggestion Tell students to write down their descriptions. After they have completed the activity, call on volunteers to read their descriptions.

6 Suggestion Have volunteers act out their conversations for the class.

OPTIONS

Video Replay the video episode, having students focus on subject pronouns and the verb **être**. Ask them to write down as many examples of sentences that use forms of **être** as they can. Stop the video where appropriate to ask comprehension questions about what the characters said.

Small Groups Working in small groups, have students invent a story about the people in the photo of **Activité 6**. Tell them to include who the people are, where they are from, and what they do in their story. Circulate around the room and assist with unfamiliar vocabulary as necessary, but encourage students to use terms they already know.

NATIONAL STANDARDS comparisons

Section Goals

In this section, students will learn:

- forms, agreement, and position of adjectives
- some descriptive adjectives
- adjectives of nationality

Instructional Resources

WB/VM: Workbook, pp. 11–12
Lab Manual, p. 8
Lab MP3s
WB/VM/LM Answer Key
*IRCD-ROM: IRM (**Essayez!** and **Mise en pratique** answers; Lab Audioscript)*
espaces.vhlcentral.com: activities, downloads, reference tools

Suggestions

- Write these adjectives on the board: **impatient, impatiente, impatients, impatientes**. Model each adjective in a sentence and ask volunteers to tell you whether it is masculine or feminine and singular or plural.
- Model the pronunciation of adjectives of nationality and have students repeat them. Point out that the feminine forms ending in **-ienne**.
- Go around the room asking **Quelle est votre nationalité?** Also have a few students ask each other their nationalities.
- Use pictures and the names of celebrities to practice other adjectives of nationality. Examples: **Tony Blair, est-il canadien? (Non, il est anglais.) Julia Roberts, est-elle française? (Non, elle est américaine.)**
- Explain that adjectives of nationality can be used as nouns as well. Examples: **La femme anglaise est réservée. L'Anglaise est réservée.**
- Point out that in English most adjectives are placed before the noun, but in French they are placed after the noun. Write the following example on the board, circle the adjective, and draw an arrow pointing to the noun. Example: **C'est un examen difficile.**
- At this point you may want to present the adjectives in the **Vocabulaire supplémentaire** in the IRM on the IRCD-ROM.

2.2 Adjective agreement

Point de départ Adjectives are words that describe people, places, and things. In French, adjectives are often used with the verb **être** to point out the qualities of nouns or pronouns.

- Many adjectives in French are cognates; that is, they have the same or similar spellings and meanings in French and English.

Cognate descriptive adjectives

agréable	*pleasant*	**intelligent(e)**	*intelligent*
amusant(e)	*fun*	**intéressant(e)**	*interesting*
brillant(e)	*bright*	**occupé(e)**	*busy*
charmant(e)	*charming*	**optimiste**	*optimistic*
désagréable	*unpleasant*	**patient(e)**	*patient*
différent(e)	*different*	**pessimiste**	*pessimistic*
difficile	*difficult*	**poli(e)**	*polite*
égoïste	*selfish*	**réservé(e)**	*reserved*
élégant(e)	*elegant*	**sincère**	*sincere*
impatient(e)	*impatient*	**sociable**	*sociable*
important(e)	*important*	**sympathique (sympa)**	*nice*
indépendant(e)	*independent*	**timide**	*shy*

- In French, most adjectives agree in number and gender with the nouns they describe. Most adjectives form the feminine by adding a silent **-e** (no accent) to the end of the masculine form, unless one is already there. Adding a silent **-s** to the end of masculine and feminine forms gives you the plural forms of both.

MASCULINE SINGULAR — MASCULINE SINGULAR
Henri est **élégant**.
Henri is elegant.

FEMININE SINGULAR — FEMININE SINGULAR
Patricia est **élégante**.
Patricia is elegant.

MASCULINE PLURAL — MASCULINE PLURAL
Henri et Jérôme sont **élégants**.
Henri and Jérôme are elegant.

FEMININE PLURAL — FEMININE PLURAL
Patricia et Marie sont **élégantes**.
Patricia and Marie are elegant.

BOÎTE À OUTILS
Use the masculine plural form of an adjective to describe a group composed of masculine and feminine nouns: **Henri et Patricia sont élégants.**

MISE EN PRATIQUE

1 Nous aussi! Jean-Paul is bragging about himself, but his younger sisters Stéphanie and Gisèle believe they possess the same attributes. Tell what they say.

MODÈLE
Je suis amusant. *Nous aussi, nous sommes amusantes.*

1. Je suis intelligent. Nous aussi, nous sommes intelligentes.
2. Je suis sincère. Nous aussi, nous sommes sincères.
3. Je suis élégant. Nous aussi, nous sommes élégantes.
4. Je suis patient. Nous aussi, nous sommes patientes.
5. Je suis sociable. Nous aussi, nous sommes sociables.
6. Je suis poli. Nous aussi, nous sommes polies.

2 Les nationalités You are with a group of students from all over the world. Indicate their nationalities according to the cities from which they come.

MODÈLE
Monique est de (*from*) Paris. *Elle est française.*

1. Fumiko et Keiko sont de Tokyo. Elles sont japonaises.
2. Hans est de Berlin. Il est allemand.
3. Juan et Pablo sont de Guadalajara. Ils sont mexicains.
4. Wendy est de Londres. Elle est anglaise.
5. Jared est de San Francisco. Il est américain.
6. Francesca est de Rome. Elle est italienne.
7. Aboud et Moustafa sont de Casablanca. Ils sont marocains.
8. Jean-Pierre et Mario sont de Québec. Ils sont québécois.

3 Voilà Mme... Your parents are having a party and you point out different people to your friend. Use a word from this grammar point each time. Answers will vary.

MODÈLE
Voilà M. Duval. Il est sénégalais. C'est un ami.

OPTIONS

Extra Practice As a rapid-response drill, say the name of a country and have students respond with the appropriate adjective of nationality. For variation, have students write the adjective on the board or tell them to spell the adjective after they say it.

Extra Practice Write each descriptive adjective on two cards or slips of paper and put them in two separate piles in random order. Hand out one card to each student. Tell students they have to find the person who has the same adjective as they do. Example: **Étudiant(e) 1: Tu es optimiste? Étudiant(e) 2: Oui, je suis optimiste./Non, je suis sociable.** For variation, this activity can also be used to practice adjectives of nationality.

COMMUNICATION

4 **Interview** You are looking for a roommate and interview someone to see what he or she is like. In pairs, play both roles. Are you compatible roommates? Answers will vary.

MODÈLE

américain
Étudiant(e) 1: *Tu es américain?*
Étudiant(e) 2: *Non, je suis suisse.*

1. impatient
2. modeste
3. timide
4. sincère
5. égoïste
6. sociable
7. indépendant
8. amusant

5 **Ils sont comment?** In pairs, take turns describing each item below. Tell your partner whether you agree (**C'est vrai**) or disagree (**C'est faux**) with the descriptions. Answers will vary.

MODÈLE

Johnny Depp
Étudiant(e) 1: *C'est un acteur désagréable.*
Étudiant(e) 2: *C'est faux. Il est charmant.*

1. Beyoncé et Céline Dion
2. les étudiants de Harvard
3. Bono
4. la classe de français
5. le président des États-Unis (*United States*)
6. Tom Hanks et Gérard Depardieu
7. le prof de français
8. Steven Spielberg
9. notre (*our*) université
10. Melanie Griffith et Julia Roberts

6 **Au café** You and two classmates are talking about your new bosses (**patrons**), each of whom is very different from the other two. In groups of three, create a dialogue in which you greet one another and describe your bosses. Answers will vary.

- French adjectives are usually placed after the noun they modify when they don't directly follow a form of **être**.

Ce sont des **étudiantes brillantes**.	Bernard est un homme **agréable et poli**.
They're brilliant students.	*Bernard is a pleasant and polite man.*

- Here are some adjectives of nationality. Note that the **-n** of adjectives that end in **-ien** doubles before the final **-e** of the feminine form: **algérienne, canadienne, italienne, vietnamienne.**

Adjectives of nationality

algérien(ne)	*Algerian*	**japonais(e)**	*Japanese*
allemand(e)	*German*	**marocain(e)**	*Moroccan*
anglais(e)	*English*	**martiniquais(e)**	*from Martinique*
américain(e)	*American*	**mexicain(e)**	*Mexican*
canadien(ne)	*Canadian*	**québécois(e)**	*from Quebec*
espagnol(e)	*Spanish*	**sénégalais(e)**	*Senegalese*
français(e)	*French*	**suisse**	*Swiss*
italien(ne)	*Italian*	**vietnamien(ne)**	*Vietnamese*

- The first letter of adjectives of nationality is not capitalized.

Il est américain.

Elle est française.

- An adjective whose masculine singular form already ends in **-s** keeps the identical form in the masculine plural.

Pierre est **un ami sénégalais**.	Pierre et Yves sont **des amis sénégalais**.
Pierre is a Senegalese friend.	*Pierre and Yves are Senegalese friends.*

- To ask someone's nationality or heritage, use **Quelle est ta/votre nationalité?** or **Tu es/Vous êtes de quelle origine?**

Quelle est votre nationalité?	**Je suis de nationalité canadienne.**
What is your nationality?	*I'm of Canadian nationality.*
Tu es de quelle origine?	**Je suis d'origine italienne.**
What is your heritage?	*I'm of Italian heritage.*

Essayez! **Write in the correct forms of the adjectives.**

1. Marc est _timide_ (timide).
2. Ils sont _anglais_ (anglais).
3. Elle adore la littérature _française_ (français).
4. Ce sont des actrices _suisses_ (suisse).
5. Elles sont _réservées_ (réservé).
6. Il y a des universités _importantes_ (important).
7. Christelle est _amusante_ (amusant).
8. Les étudiants sont _polis_ (poli) en cours.

1 Suggestion Before beginning the activity, make sure students understand that they should use feminine plural forms of the adjectives. For each item, call on one student to read the sentence in the book and another student to respond.

2 Expansion For additional practice, change the subject of the sentence and have students restate or write the sentences. Examples: **1. Kazumi est de Tokyo. (Il est japonais.) 2. Gerta et Katarina sont de Berlin. (Elles sont allemandes.) 3. Carmen est de Guadalajara. (Elle est mexicaine.) 4. Tom et Susan sont de Londres. (Ils sont anglais.) 5. Linda est de San Francisco. (Elle est américaine.) 6. Luciano et Gino sont de Rome. (Ils sont italiens.) 7. Fatima est de Casablanca. (Elle est marocaine.) 8. Denise et Monique sont de Québec. (Elles sont canadiennes/québécoises.)**

3 Expansion Have students say what each person in the drawing is not. Example: **Madame Malbon n'est pas sociable.**

4 Suggestions
- Have students add two more qualities to the list that are important to them.
- After students have completed the activity, ask them if they are compatible roommates and to explain why or why not.

5 Suggestion Have two volunteers read the **modèle** aloud.

5 Expansion Have small groups brainstorm names of famous people, places, and things not found in the activity and write them in a list. Tell them to include some plural items. Then ask the groups to exchange lists and describe the people, places, and things on that list.

6 Suggestion Tell students to give their bosses a name so that it is obvious if they are male or female. Also encourage students to ask each other questions about their bosses during the conversation.

OPTIONS

Extra Practice Do a quick class survey to find out how many nationalities are represented in your class. As students respond, write the nationality and number of students on the board. Ask: **Combien d'étudiants sont d'origine américaine? Mexicaine? Vietnamienne?** If students ask, clarify that the gender of the adjective of nationality agrees with the word **origine**, which is feminine.

Extra Practice Have students collect several interesting pictures of people from magazines or newspapers. Have them prepare a description of one of the pictures ahead of time. Invite them to show the pictures to the class and then give their descriptions orally without indicating which picture they are talking about. The class will guess which of the pictures is being described.

Instructional Resources
*IRCD-ROM: IRM (**Feuilles d'activités**; Info Gap Activities); Testing Program, pp. 5–8; Test Files; Testing Program MP3s; Test Generator espaces.vhlcentral.com: activities, downloads, reference tools*

1 Suggestion Have pairs act out their conversations for the rest of the class.

2 Suggestion Before students begin to make corrections on their classmates' papers, tell them to check the following: correct use of articles and subject pronouns, subject-verb agreement, and adjective agreement.

3 Expansion Have students repeat the activity and describe their differences this time.

4 Suggestion Because this is the first activity in which the **Feuilles d'activités** (found in the IRM on the IRCD-ROM) are used, tell students that they use the **feuilles** to complete the corresponding activity. Explain that they must approach their classmates with their paper in hand and ask questions following the **modèle**. When they find someone who answers affirmatively, that student signs his or her name.

5 Expansion Have a few volunteers read their descriptions to the class. Then ask the class to point out the differences between the various descriptions.

6 Suggestions
- Divide the class into pairs and distribute the Info Gap Handouts in the IRM on the IRCD-ROM for this activity. Give students ten minutes to complete the activity.
- Have two volunteers read the **modèle** aloud.

Synthèse

1 **Festival francophone** With a partner, choose two characters from the list and act out a conversation between them. The people are meeting for the first time at a francophone festival. Then, change characters and repeat. Answers will vary.

Angélique, Sénégal

Abdel, Algérie

Laurent, Martinique

Sylvain, Suisse

Hélène, Canada

Daniel, France

Mai, Viêt-Nam

Nora, Maroc

2 **Tu ou vous?** How would the conversations between the characters in **Activité 1** differ if they were all 19-year-old students at a university orientation? Write out what you would have said differently. Then, exchange papers with a new partner and make corrections. Return the paper to your partner and act out the conversation using a different character from last time. Answers will vary.

3 **En commun** In pairs, tell your partner the name of a friend. Use adjectives to say what you both (**tous les deux**) have in common. Then, share with the class what you learned about your partner and his or her friend. Answers will vary.

MODÈLE

Charles est un ami. Nous sommes tous les deux amusants. Nous sommes patients aussi.

4 **Comment es-tu?** Your instructor will give you a worksheet. Survey as many classmates as possible to ask if they would use the adjectives listed to describe themselves. Then, decide which two students in the class are most similar. Answers will vary.

MODÈLE

Étudiant(e) 1: *Tu es timide?*
Étudiant(e) 2: *Non. Je suis sociable.*

Adjectifs	*Nom*
1. timide	*Éric*
2. impatient (e)	
3. optimiste	
4. réservé (e)	
5. charmant (e)	
6. poli (e)	
7. agréable	
8. amusant (e)	

5 **Mes camarades de classe** Write a brief description of the students in your French class. What are their names? What are their personalities like? What is their heritage? Use all the French you have learned so far. Your paragraph should be at least eight sentences long. Remember, be complimentary! Answers will vary.

6 **Les descriptions** Your instructor will give you one set of drawings of eight people and a different set to your partner. Each person in your drawings has something in common with a person in your partner's drawings. Find out what it is without looking at your partner's sheet. Answers will vary.

MODÈLE

Étudiant(e) 1: *Jean est à la bibliothèque.*
Étudiant(e) 2: *Gina est à la bibliothèque.*
Étudiant(e) 1: *Jean et Gina sont à la bibliothèque.*

ressources

WB	LM	Lab MP3s	espaces.vhlcentral.com
pp. 9–12	pp. 7–8	Leçon 2	Leçon 2

OPTIONS

Small Groups Have students work in groups of three or four. Tell them to prepare a skit on any situation they wish, provided that they use material presented in this lesson. Possible situations can include meeting at a café (as in **Roman-photo**), meeting in between classes, and introducing friends to professors. Remind them to use as many adjectives as possible. Encourage students to have fun with the skit and be creative.

Extra Practice To practice **vous**, have students ask you yes/no questions. First, have them guess your nationality. Example: **Vous êtes français(e)?** Then have them ask you about your personality. Example: **Vous êtes impatient(e)?**

Projet

Décrivez° une ville

Imagine that you are a journalist reporting on the influence of French-speaking cultures on cities in the United States and Canada. You have been asked to present a report focusing on one American or Canadian city to a French class.

1 Préparez un exposé°

Prepare a brief presentation about how French-speaking cultures have influenced a city in the United States or Canada. Using the research tools in **Sur Internet**, choose a city and take notes about how it has been affected by French-speaking cultures. Your presentation might include these elements:

- A description of the city, its location, its history, and its population
- Explanations of how the city has been influenced by French-speaking cultures, for example, its cuisine, arts, politics, and architecture
- Descriptions and photos of famous people, places, and things in the city that are related to French-speaking cultures

2 Présentez votre travail°

Using an outline and images, tell the class about the city you chose and how it reflects the influence of French-speaking cultures. Make your presentation vivid so that your classmates will want to learn more about the influence of French-speaking cultures in the United States and Canada. Use as much French as possible in your presentation, especially to greet the class, to introduce yourself, to say where you are from, and to state that you are a journalist (**Je suis journaliste**).

Décrivez *Describe* **un exposé** *an oral presentation* **votre travail** *your work*

SUR INTERNET

Go to **espaces.vhlcentral.com** for more information related to this **Projet**.

Section Goals

In this section, students will:
- learn about how French-speaking cultures have influenced a city in the United States and Canada
- use French as they research and interact with the wider world
- give an oral presentation

Instructional Resources
espaces.vhlcentral.com: activities, downloads, reference tools

Suggestion Students might need a week to complete the project, so at the beginning of that time period, have them open their books to this page and read through **Projet**. Explain that they are going to use their research skills to prepare an oral report in which they describe how French-speaking cultures have influenced a city in the United States or Canada (**une ville américaine/canadienne**).

Préparez un exposé
- If students choose a city they live in or visit, they may seek information from French-speaking members of the community, the Chamber of Commerce, or other French-speaking organizations. There may be a French Consulate, a French library, or a chapter of the **Alliance française** in certain cities.
- Students' presentations will be more interesting if they incorporate visual aids such as posters and brochures, or integrate music or audio recordings. Some students may want to use PowerPoint to display their visuals.

Présentez votre travail
- Have students practice before a small group of classmates who can make suggestions before the students present in front of the whole class.
- Extend the presentations over more than one class period so that each student has sufficient time to present.

EVALUATION

Criteria	Scale
Content	1 2 3 4
Comprehensibility	1 2 3 4
Organization	1 2 3 4
Accuracy	1 2 3 4
Use of visuals	1 2 3 4

Scoring	
Excellent	18–20 points
Good	14–17 points
Satisfactory	10–13 points
Unsatisfactory	< 10 points

Section Goals

In this section, students will:

- read statistics and cultural information about the French language and the francophone world
- learn historical and cultural information about Québec, Louisiana, and Algeria

Instructional Resources
IRCD-ROM: Transparency #16,
WB/VM: Workbook, pp. 13–14
WB/VM/LM Answer Key
espaces.vhlcentral.com: activities; downloads; reference tools

Carte du monde francophone Have students look at the map or use **Transparency #16**. Ask them to identify the continents where French is spoken. Then ask them to make inferences about why French is spoken in these regions.

Les pays en chiffres

- Call on volunteers to read the sections. Point out cognates and clarify unfamiliar words.
- Have students locate the capitals of the countries listed in **Villes capitales** on the maps in **Appendice A.**
- After reading **Francophones célèbres**, ask students if they know any additional information about these people.

Incroyable mais vrai! UNESCO is the United Nations Educational Scientific and Cultural Organization. UNESCO not only builds classrooms in impoverished countries, but it also brings nations together on social issues.

Panorama

Le monde francophone

Les pays en chiffres°

Organisation internationale de la Francophonie

- **Nombre de pays° où le français est langue° officielle:** *28*
- **Nombre de pays où le français est parlé°:** *plus de° 60*
- **Nombre de francophones dans le monde°:** *175.000.000 (cent soixante-quinze millions)*

SOURCE: Organisation internationale de la Francophonie

Villes capitales

- **Algérie:** *Alger*
- **Cameroun:** *Yaoundé*
- **France:** *Paris*
- **Guinée:** *Conakry*
- **Haïti:** *Port-au-Prince*
- **Laos:** *Vientiane*
- **Mali:** *Bamako*
- **Rwanda:** *Kigali*
- **Seychelles:** *Victoria*
- **Suisse:** *Berne*

Francophones célèbres

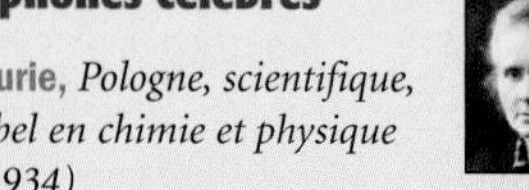
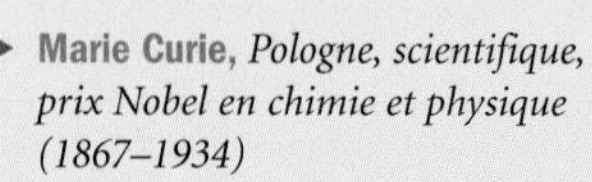

- **Marie Curie,** *Pologne, scientifique, prix Nobel en chimie et physique (1867–1934)*
- **René Magritte,** *Belgique, peintre° (1898–1967)*
- **Ousmane Sembène,** *Sénégal, cinéaste° et écrivain° (1923–)*

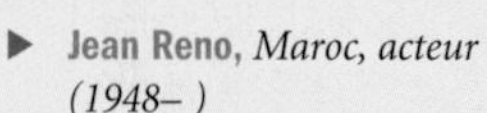

- **Jean Reno,** *Maroc, acteur (1948–)*

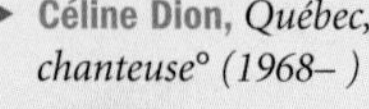

- **Céline Dion,** *Québec, chanteuse° (1968–)*

- **Marie-José Pérec,** *Guadeloupe, coureuse° olympique (1968–)*

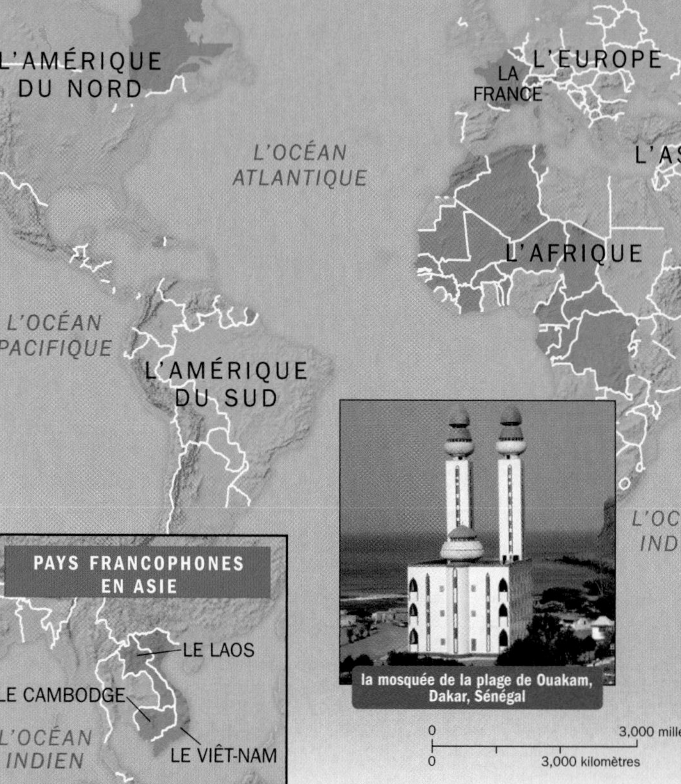

Heiva°, Papeete, Tahiti

la mosquée de la plage de Ouakam, Dakar, Sénégal

Incroyable mais vrai!

La langue française est une des rares langues à être parlées sur° cinq continents. C'est aussi la langue officielle de beaucoup d'organisations internationales comme° l'OTAN°, les Nations unies, l'Union européenne, et aussi des Jeux° Olympiques! Le français est la deuxième° langue enseignée° dans le monde, après l'anglais.

chiffres *numbers* **pays** *countries* **langue** *language* **parlé** *spoken* **plus de** *more than* **monde** *world* **peintre** *painter* **cinéaste** *filmmaker* **écrivain** *writer* **chanteuse** *singer* **coureuse** *runner* **sur** *on* **comme** *such as* **l'OTAN** *NATO* **Jeux** *Games* **deuxième** *second* **enseignée** *taught* **Heiva** *an annual Tahitian festival*

OPTIONS

Francophones célèbres **Marie Curie** received Nobel Prizes for the discovery of radioactivity and the isolation of radium. **René Magritte** was one of the most prominent surrealist painters. For more information on **Magritte**, see **Unité 11, Panorama**, page 391. **Ousmane Sembène** is considered one of the founders of the African realist tradition and the first African to produce a film.

Jean Reno has played a variety of roles in French and American films. **Céline Dion** has received Grammy awards in the U.S., Juno and Felix awards in Canada, and World Music Awards in Europe for her vocal talents. **Marie-José Pérec** is the first sprinter to win consecutive gold medals in the 400-meter dash.

La société

Le français au Québec

Au Québec, province du Canada, le français est la langue officielle, parlée par° 82% (quatre-vingt-deux pour cent) de la population. Les Québécois, pour° préserver l'usage de la langue, ont° une loi° qui oblige l'affichage° en français dans les lieux° publics. Le français est aussi la langue co-officielle du Canada: les employés du gouvernement doivent° être bilingues.

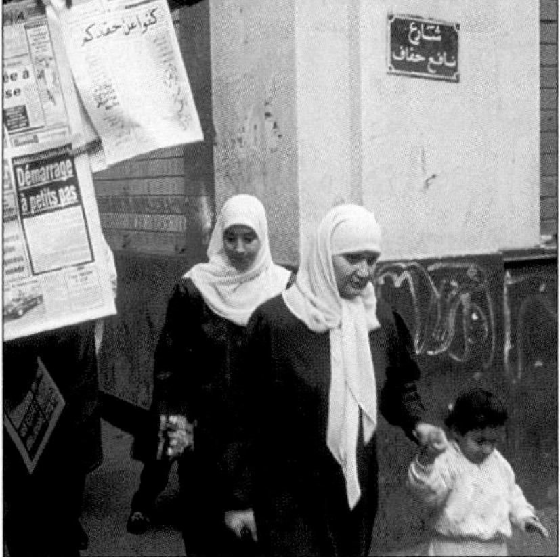

Les gens

Les francophones d'Algérie

Depuis° 1830 (mille huit cent trente), date de l'acquisition de l'Algérie par la France, l'influence culturelle française y° est très importante. À présent ancienne° colonie, l'Algérie est un des plus grands° pays francophones au monde. L'arabe est la langue officielle, mais le français est la deuxième langue parlée et est compris° par la majorité de la population algérienne.

Les destinations

La Louisiane

Ce territoire au sud° des États-Unis a été nommé° «Louisiane» en l'honneur du Roi° de France Louis XIV. En 1803 (mille huit cent trois), Napoléon Bonaparte vend° la colonie aux États-Unis pour 15 millions de dollars, pour empêcher° son acquisition par les Britanniques. Aujourd'hui° en Louisiane, 200.000 (deux cent mille) personnes parlent° le français cajun. La Louisiane est connue° pour sa° cuisine cajun, comme° le jambalaya, ici sur° la photo avec le chef Paul Prudhomme.

Les traditions

La Journée internationale de la Francophonie

Chaque année°, l'Organisation internationale de la Francophonie (O.I.F.) coordonne la Journée internationale de la Francophonie: dans plus de° 100 (cent) pays et sur cinq continents, on célèbre la langue française et la diversité culturelle francophone avec des festivals de musique, de gastronomie, de théâtre, de danse et de cinéma. Le rôle principal de l'O.I.F. est la promotion de la langue française et la défense de la diversité culturelle et linguistique du monde francophone.

Qu'est-ce que vous avez appris? Complete the sentences.

1. Ousmane Sembène est un cinéaste africain.
2. 175 millions de personnes parlent français dans le monde.
3. L'Organisation internationale de la Francophonie est responsable de la promotion de la diversité culturelle francophone.
4. Les employés du gouvernement du Canada parlent anglais et français.
5. En Algérie, la langue officielle est l'arabe.
6. Une majorité d'Algériens comprend (*understands*) le français.
7. Le nom «Louisiane» vient du (*comes from the*) nom de Louis XIV.
8. Plus de 100 pays célèbrent la Journée internationale de la Francophonie.
9. Le français est parlé sur cinq continents.
10. En 1803, Napoléon Bonaparte vend la Louisiane aux États-Unis.

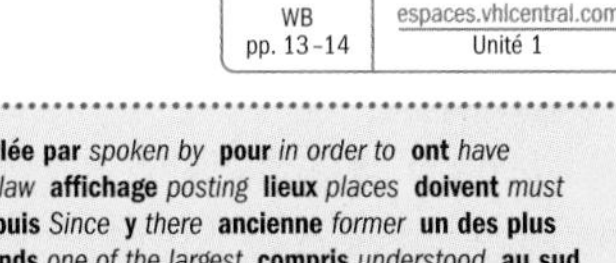

ressources
WB
pp. 13-14
espaces.vhlcentral.com
Unité 1

SUR INTERNET

Go to **espaces.vhlcentral.com** to find more cultural information related to this **PANORAMA**.

1. Les États-Unis célèbrent la Journée internationale de la Francophonie: faites (*make*) une liste de trois événements (*events*) et où ils ont lieu (*take place*).
2. Trouvez des informations sur un(e) chanteur/chanteuse francophone célèbre aux États-Unis. Citez (*Cite*) trois titres de chanson (*song titles*).

parlée par *spoken by* **pour** *in order to* **ont** *have* **loi** *law* **affichage** *posting* **lieux** *places* **doivent** *must* **Depuis** *Since* **y** *there* **ancienne** *former* **un des plus grands** *one of the largest* **compris** *understood* **au sud** *in the South* **a été nommé** *was named* **Roi** *King* **vend** *sells* **empêcher** *to prevent* **Aujourd'hui** *Today* **parlent** *speak* **connue** *known* **sa** *its* **comme** *such as* **sur** *in* **Chaque année** *Each year* **dans plus de** *in more than*

Le français au Québec Since Jacques Cartier first arrived in the Gaspé and claimed the land for the French king in 1534, the people of Québec have maintained their language and culture, despite being outnumbered and surrounded by English speakers. French became an official language of Canada in 1867. Ask students if they know of any places in the United States where people speak two languages or they can see bilingual signs.

Les francophones d'Algérie Algeria gained its independence from France in 1962, but French is still taught from primary school through high school. French is principally used in business relations, some social situations, and in the information industries. Some newspapers, as well as several television and radio broadcasts, are produced in French.

La Louisiane The early settlers of Louisiana came from France and Acadia (now Nova Scotia and adjacent areas) during the seventeenth and eighteenth centuries. The Acadian settlers were descendents of French Canadians who were exiled from Acadia by the English and eventually settled in the bayou region. Cajun French evolved over time borrowing terms from American Indian, German, English, African, and Spanish speakers.

La Journée internationale de la Francophonie

- The members of **l'Organisation internationale de la Francophonie** comprise 63 states and governments. The celebrations in the various Francophone regions take place throughout the month of March. The name **20 mars** was chosen to commemorate the signature of a treaty which created **l'Agence intergouvernementale de la Francophonie.**
- Point out the symbol of **l'Organisation internationale de la Francophonie** on page 30 next to the heading **Les pays en chiffres.**

OPTIONS

Pairs Have students work in pairs. Tell them to look at the maps in **Appendice A** and make a list of the francophone countries and capitals that do not appear in the section **Villes capitales**. Point out that they need to find eighteen countries.

Cultural Comparison In groups of three, have students compare **la Journée internationale de la Francophonie** to a cultural celebration held in their town or city. Tell them to discuss the purpose of each celebration, the reasons why people attend them, and the types of events or activities that are part of the celebration.

Section Goals
In this section, students will:
- learn to recognize cognates
- use context to guess the meaning of new words
- read some pages from an address book in French

Stratégie Tell students that cognates are words in one language that have identical or similar counterparts in another language. True cognates are close in meaning, so recognizing French words that are cognates of English words can help them read French. To help students recognize cognates, write these common correspondences between French and English on the board: **-ie** = *-y* (**sociologie**); **-ique** = *-ic* (**fantastique**); **-if(-ive)** = *-ive* (**active**).

Successful Language Learning Tell students that reading in French will be less anxiety provoking if they follow the advice in the **Stratégie** sections, which are designed to reinforce and improve reading comprehension skills.

Examinez le texte Ask students to tell you what type of text this is and how they can tell. (It's an excerpt from an address book. You can tell because it contains names and telephone numbers.)

Mots apparentés
- Check to see if students found all of the cognates from the **Stratégie** box in the reading: **pharmacie, dentiste, télévision, médecin, banque,** and **restaurant**.
- If students are having trouble finding other cognates in the reading, point out a few to get them started: **route** (*route*), **avenue** (*avenue*), **boulevard** (*boulevard*), **théâtre** (*theater*), **comédie** (*comedy*), **dîner** (*dinner*), and **municipale** (*municipal*).

Devinez Ask volunteers to share their responses with the class. Find out how many were able to guess the meanings correctly: **horaires** (*schedule [hours open]*), **lundi** (*Monday*), **ouvert** (*open*), **soirs** (*evenings; nights*), and **tous** (*all; every*).

Lecture

Avant la lecture

STRATÉGIE

Recognizing cognates

Cognates are words that share similar meanings and spellings in two or more languages. When reading in French, it's helpful to look for cognates and use them to guess the meaning of what you're reading. However, watch out for false cognates. For example, **librairie** means *bookstore*, not *library*, and **coin** means *corner*, not *coin*. Look at this list of French words. Can you guess the meaning of each word?

important	**banque**
pharmacie	**culture**
intelligent	**actif**
dentiste	**sociologie**
décision	**fantastique**
télévision	**restaurant**
médecine	**police**

Examinez le texte

Briefly look at the document. What kind of information is listed? In what order is it listed? Where do you usually find such information? Can you guess what this document is?

Mots apparentés

Read the list of cognates in the **Stratégie** box again. How many cognates can you find in the reading selection? Are there additional cognates in the reading? Which ones? Can you guess their English equivalents?

Devinez

In addition to using cognates and words you already know, you can also use context to guess the meaning of words you do not know. Find the following words in the reading selection and try to guess what they mean. Compare your answers with those of a classmate.

horaires   lundi   ouvert   soirs   tous

Un carnet d'adresses

DAMERY Jean-Claude, dentiste
18, rue des Lilas 02 38 23 45 46
45000 Orléans

Café de la Poste
Ouvert tous les jours°, de 7h00° à 22h00
25, place de la Poste 02 38 27 18 00
45000 Orléans

Librairie Balzac
Horaires: 9h00–12h00 et 14h00–18h00
18, route de Lorient 02 38 18 60 36
45000 Orléans

DANTEC Pierre-Henri, médecin généraliste
23, rue du lac 02 38 47 34 20
45000 Orléans

Banque du Centre
Ouvert de 9h00 à 17h00 du lundi° au vendredi°
17, boulevard Giroud 02 38 58 35 00
45000 Orléans

Dîner vendredi
8h00

Restaurant du
Chat qui dort

OPTIONS

Extra Practice Write these words on the board and have students guess the English meaning: **un agent** (*agent*), **un concert** (*concert*), **la géographie** (*geography*), **une guitare** (*guitar*), **la musique** (*music*), **un réfrigérateur** (*refrigerator*), **confortable** (*comfortable*), **courageux** (*courageous*), **riche** (*rich*), and **typique** (*typical*). Then have them look at the **Vocabulaire** on page 36 and identify all the cognates they have learned.

Small Groups Have students work in groups of three or four. Assign four letters of the alphabet to each group. (Adjust the number of letters according to your class size so that the entire alphabet is covered.) Tell students to use a French-English dictionary and make a list of all the cognates they find beginning with their assigned letters. Have groups read their list of cognates to the rest of the class.

Messier et fils°
Réparations ordinateurs et télévisions
56, boulevard Henri IV 02 38 44 42 59
45000 Orléans

Théâtre de la Comédie
11, place de la Comédie 02 38 45 32 11
45000 Orléans

Pharmacie Vidal
45, rue des Acacias 02 38 13 57 53
45000 Orléans

Restaurant du Chat qui dort°
Ouvert tous les soirs pour le dîner
Horaires: 19h00 à 23h00
29, avenue des Rosiers 02 38 45 35 08
45000 Orléans

Bibliothèque municipale
Place de la gare 02 38 56 43 22
45000 Orléans

Lycée Molière
15, rue Molière 02 38 29 23 04
45000 Orléans

tous les jours *everyday* **7h00 (sept heures)** *7:00* **lundi** *Monday* **vendredi** *Friday* **fils** *son(s)*
Chat qui dort *Sleeping cat*

Après la lecture

Où aller? Tell where each of these people should go based on what they need or want to do.

MODÈLE

Camille's daughter is starting high school.
Lycée Molière

1. Mrs. Leroy needs to deposit her paycheck.
   Banque du Centre
2. Laurent would like to take his girlfriend out for a special dinner.
   Restaurant du Chat qui dort
3. Marc has a toothache.
   DAMERY Jean-Claude, dentiste
4. Céleste would like to go see a play tonight.
   Théâtre de la Comédie
5. Pauline's computer is broken.
   Messier et fils, Réparations ordinateurs et télévisions
6. Mr. Duchemin needs to buy some aspirin for his son.
   Pharmacie Vidal
7. Jean-Marie needs a book on French history but he doesn't want to buy one.
   Bibliothèque municipale
8. Noémie thinks she has the flu.
   DANTEC Pierre-Henri, médecin généraliste
9. Mr. and Mrs. Prudhomme want to go out for breakfast this morning.
   Café de la Poste
10. Jonathan wants to buy a new book for his sister's birthday.
    Librairie Balzac

Notre annuaire With a classmate, select three of the listings from the reading and use them as models to create similar listings in French advertising places or services in your area.

MODÈLE

Restaurant du Chat qui dort
Ouvert tous les soirs pour le dîner
Horaires: 19h00 à 23h00
29, avenue des Rosiers 02 38 45 35 08
45000 Orléans

Always Good Eats Restaurant
Ouvert tous les jours
Horaires: 6h00 à 19h00
1250 9th Avenue San Diego, CA 92108 224-0932

Où aller? Go over the activity with the class. If students have trouble inferring the answer to any question, help them identify the cognate or provide additional context clues.

Notre annuaire

- Before beginning the activity, have students brainstorm places and services in the area, and write a list on the board. You might also want to bring in a few local telephone books for students to use as references for addresses and phone numbers.
- You may wish to have students include e-mail addresses (**les adresses e-mail**) in their lists.

OPTIONS

Pairs To review numbers 0–60, have students work in pairs and take turns asking each other the phone numbers and addresses of the people and places listed in the reading. Example: **Étudiant(e) 1: Le numéro de téléphone du dentiste Jean-Claude DAMERY? Étudiant(e) 2: C'est le zéro deux, trente-huit, vingt-trois, quarante-cinq, quarante-six. Étudiant(e) 1: Et l'adresse? Étudiant(e) 2: Dix-huit, rue des Lilas, Orléans.**

Extra Practice Have several students select one of the three listings they created for the **Notre annuaire** activity to read aloud. Instruct the rest of the class to write down the information they hear. To check students' work, have the students who read the listings write the information on the board.

Section Goals

In this section, students will:
- learn to listen for known vocabulary
- listen to sentences containing familiar and unfamiliar vocabulary
- listen to a conversation and complete several activities

Instructional Resources
Textbook MP3s
IRCD-ROM: IRM (Textbook Audioscript)
espaces.vhlcentral.com: downloads, reference tools

Stratégie
Script Je vous présente une amie, Juliette Lenormand. Elle étudie la sociologie à la faculté.

Successful Language Learning Tell your students that many people feel nervous about their ability to comprehend what they learn in a foreign language. Tell them that they will probably feel less anxious if they follow the advice for increasing listening comprehension in the **Stratégie** sections.

Préparation Have students look at the photo and describe what they see. Ask them to justify their responses based on the visual clues.

À vous d'écouter
Script
HERVÉ: Salut, Laure! Ça va?
LAURE: Bonjour, Hervé. Ça va bien. Et toi?
HERVÉ: Pas mal, merci.
LAURE: Je te présente un copain de l'université. Lucas, Hervé. Hervé, Lucas.
LUCAS: Enchanté.
H: Bonjour, Lucas. Comment vas-tu?
LU: Très bien, merci.
LA: Qu'est-ce que tu fais, Hervé?
H: Je vais à la librairie pour acheter un livre sur la littérature.
LA: Pour un examen?
H: Oui, pour un examen. Et vous?
LA: Nous, on va au café.
H: Alors, à plus tard.
LA: Oui, salut.
LU: Au revoir, Hervé.
H: À bientôt.

À l'écoute

STRATÉGIE

Listening for words you know

You can get the gist of a conversation by listening for words and phrases you already know.

 To help you practice this strategy, listen to this sentence and make a list of the words you have already learned.

__________ __________
__________ __________

Préparation

Look at the photograph. Where are these people? What are they doing? In your opinion, do they know one another? Why or why not? What do you think they're talking about?

À vous d'écouter

As you listen, circle the items you associate with Hervé and those you associate with Laure and Lucas.

HERVÉ	LAURE ET LUCAS
(la littérature)	(le café)
(l'examen)	la littérature
le bureau	la sociologie
le café	la librairie
la bibliothèque	le lycée
(la librairie)	l'examen
le tableau	(l'université)

ressources

Text MP3s Unité 1	VM pp. 271-272	V CD-ROM Unité 1	espaces.vhlcentral.com Unité 1

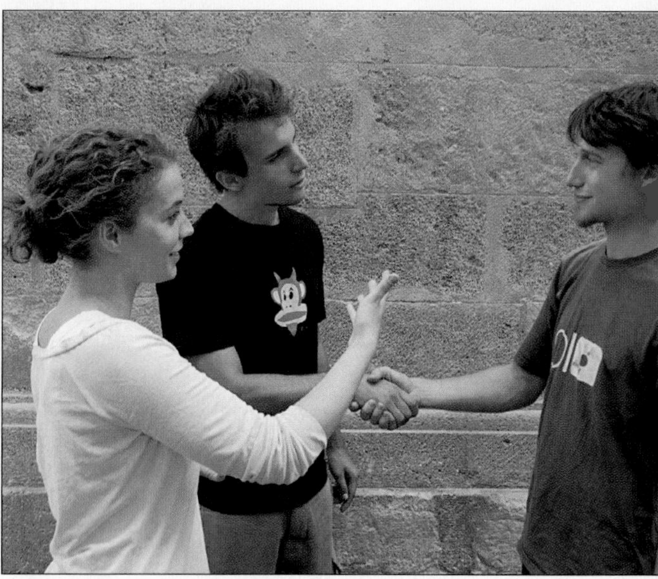

Compréhension

Vrai ou faux? Based on the conversation you heard, indicate whether each of the following statements is **vrai** or **faux**.

	Vrai	Faux
1. Lucas and Hervé are good friends.	☐	☑
2. Hervé is preparing for an exam.	☑	☐
3. Laure and Lucas know each other from school.	☑	☐
4. Hervé is on his way to the library.	☐	☑
5. Lucas and Laure are going to a café.	☑	☐
6. Lucas studies literature.	☐	☑
7. Laure is in high school.	☐	☑
8. Laure is not feeling well today.	☐	☑

Présentations It's your turn to get to know your classmates. Using the conversation you heard as a model, select a partner you do not know and introduce yourself to him or her in French. Follow the steps below.

- Greet your partner.
- Find out his or her name.
- Ask how he or she is doing.
- Introduce your partner to another student.
- Say good-bye.

Écriture

STRATÉGIE

Writing in French

Why do we write? All writing has a purpose. For example, we may write a poem to reveal our innermost feelings, a letter to share information, or an essay to persuade others to accept a point of view. People are not born proficient writers, however. Writing requires time, thought, effort, and a lot of practice. Here are some tips to help you write more effectively in French.

DO

- **Try to write your ideas in French**
- **Try to make an outline of your ideas**
- **Decide what the purpose of your writing will be**
- **Use the grammar and vocabulary that you know**
- **Use your textbook for examples of style, format, and expressions in French**
- **Use your imagination and creativity to make your writing more interesting**
- **Put yourself in your reader's place to determine if your writing is interesting**

AVOID

- **Translating your ideas from English to French**
- **Simply repeating what is in the textbook or on a web page**
- **Using a bilingual dictionary until you have learned how to use one effectively**

Watch the FLASH CULTURE segment on the **ESPACES** video for cultural footage related to this unit's theme.

Thème

Faites une liste!

Imagine that several French-speaking students will be spending a year at your school. You've been asked to put together a list of people and places that might be useful and of interest to them. Your list should include:

- Your name, address, phone number(s) (home and/or mobile), and e-mail address
- The names of two or three other students in your French class, their addresses, phone numbers, and e-mail addresses
- Your French teacher's name, office and/or mobile phone number(s), e-mail address, as well as his or her office hours
- Your school library's phone number and hours
- The names, addresses, and phone numbers of three places near your school where students like to go (a bookstore, a coffee shop or restaurant, a theater, a skate park, etc.)

NOM: *Madame Smith (professeur de français)*
ADRESSE: *McNeil University*
NUMÉRO DE TÉLÉPHONE: *645-3458 (bureau)*
NUMÉRO DE PORTABLE: *919-0040*
ADRESSE E-MAIL: *absmith@yahoo.com*
NOTES: *Heures de bureau: 8h00–9h00*

NOM: *Skate World*
ADRESSE: *8970 McNeil Road*
NUMÉRO DE TÉLÉPHONE: *658-0349*
NUMÉRO DE PORTABLE: –
ADRESSE E-MAIL: *skate@skateworld.com*
NOTES: —

Section Goals

In this section, students will:

- learn strategies for writing in French
- learn to write a telephone/address book in French
- integrate vocabulary and structures taught in **Leçons 1–2**
- view authentic cultural footage of greetings and farewells in formal and informal situations

Instructional Resources
WB/VM: Video Manual pp. 271–272
WB/VM/LM Answer Key
IRCD-ROM: IRM (Videoscript)
Video CD-ROM
Video on DVD
espaces.vhlcentral.com: activities, downloads, reference tools

Stratégie Have students focus on the final point under the "Do" section. Ask them to think about the types of writing that most interests them as readers. Why? Is it that the writer supplies vivid detail? Interesting anecdotes? An easy-to-read style? Is it simply that the subject is important to them? This shows the value of putting themselves in their reader's place.

Thème Introduce students to standard headings used in a telephone/address list: **Nom**, **Adresse**, **Numéro de téléphone**, **Numéro de portable**, and **Adresse e-mail**. Students may wish to add notes pertaining to home (**Numéro du domicile**) or office (**Numéro de bureau**) telephone numbers, fax numbers (**Numéro de fax**), or office hours (**Horaires de bureau**).

Flash culture Tell students that they will learn more about greetings and farewells in French by watching a variety of real-life images narrated by Csilla. Show the video segment, then have students jot down in French at least three examples of situations or things they saw. You can also use the activities in the video manual in class to reinforce this **Flash culture** or assign them as homework.

EVALUATION

Criteria	Scale
Content	1 2 3 4 5
Organization	1 2 3 4 5
Accuracy	1 2 3 4 5
Creativity	1 2 3 4 5

Scoring	
Excellent	18–20 points
Good	14–17 points
Satisfactory	10–13 points
Unsatisfactory	< 10 points

Instructional Resources
Textbook MP3s
IRCD-ROM: IRM (Textbook Audioscript)
espaces.vhlcentral.com: downloads, reference tools

Suggestion Tell students that this is active vocabulary for which they are responsible and that it will appear on tests and exams.

Le campus

une bibliothèque	*library*
un café	*café*
une faculté	*university; faculty*
une librairie	*bookstore*
un lycée	*high school*
une salle de classe	*classroom*
une université	*university*
un dictionnaire	*dictionary*
une différence	*difference*
un examen	*exam, test*
la littérature	*literature*
un livre	*book*
un problème	*problem*
un résultat	*result*
la sociologie	*sociology*
un bureau	*desk; office*
une carte	*map*
une chaise	*chair*
une fenêtre	*window*
une horloge	*clock*
un ordinateur	*computer*
une porte	*door*
une table	*table*
un tableau	*blackboard; picture*
la télévision	*television*
un cahier	*notebook*
une calculatrice	*calculator*
une chose	*thing*
une corbeille (à papier)	*wastebasket*
un crayon	*pencil*
une feuille de papier	*sheet of paper*
un instrument	*instrument*
une montre	*watch*
un objet	*object*
un palm	*Palm Pilot; PDA*
un sac à dos	*backpack*
un stylo	*pen*

Les personnes

un(e) ami(e)	*friend*
un(e) camarade de chambre	*roommate*
un(e) camarade de classe	*classmate*
une classe	*class (group of students)*
un copain/une copine (*fam.*)	*friend*
un(e) élève	*pupil, student*
un(e) étudiant(e)	*student*
un(e) petit(e) ami(e)	*boyfriend/girlfriend*
une femme	*woman*
une fille	*girl*
un garçon	*boy*
un homme	*man*
une personne	*person*
un acteur/une actrice	*actor*
un chanteur/une chanteuse	*singer*
un professeur	*teacher, professor*

Les présentations

Comment vous appelez-vous? (*form.*)	*What is your name?*
Comment t'appelles-tu? (*fam.*)	*What is your name?*
Enchanté(e).	*Delighted.*
Et vous/toi? (*form./fam.*)	*And you?*
Je m'appelle...	*My name is...*
Je vous/te présente... (*form./fam.*)	*I would like to introduce (name) to you.*

Identifier

c'est/ce sont	*it's/they are*
Combien...?	*How much/many...?*
ici	*here*
Il y a...	*There is/are...*
là	*there*
là-bas	*over there*
Qu'est-ce que c'est?	*What is it?*
Qui est-ce?	*Who is it?*
Quoi?	*What?*
voici	*here is/are*
voilà	*there is/are*

Bonjour et au revoir

À bientôt.	*See you soon.*
À demain.	*See you tomorrow.*
À plus tard.	*See you later.*
À tout à l'heure.	*See you later.*
Au revoir.	*Good-bye.*
Bonne journée!	*Have a good day!*
Bonjour.	*Good morning.; Hello.*
Bonsoir.	*Good evening.; Hello.*
Salut!	*Hi!; Bye!*

Comment ça va?

Ça va?	*What's up?; How are things?*
Comment allez-vous? (*form.*)	*How are you?*
Comment vas-tu? (*fam.*)	*How are you?*
Comme ci, comme ça.	*So-so.*
Je vais bien/mal.	*I am doing well/badly.*
Moi aussi.	*Me too.*
Pas mal.	*Not badly.*
Très bien.	*Very well.*

Expressions de politesse

De rien.	*You're welcome.*
Excusez-moi. (*form.*)	*Excuse me.*
Excuse-moi. (*fam.*)	*Excuse me.*
Il n'y a pas de quoi.	*It's nothing.; You're welcome.*
Je vous en prie. (*form.*)	*Please.; You're welcome.*
Merci beaucoup.	*Thank you very much.*
Monsieur (M.) Madame (Mme) Mademoiselle (Mlle)	*Sir (Mr.) Ma'am (Mrs.) Miss*
Pardon.	*Pardon (me).*
S'il vous/te plaît. (*form./fam.*)	*Please.*

Expressions utiles	*See pp. 7 and 21.*
Numbers 0-60	*See p. 12.*
Subject pronouns	*See p. 24.*
être	*See p. 25.*
Descriptive adjectives	*See p. 26.*
Adjectives of nationality	*See p. 27.*

ressources
Text MP3s Unité 1
espaces.vhlcentral.com Unité 1

À la fac

UNITÉ 2

Leçon 3

ESPACE CONTEXTES
pages 38–41
- Academic life
- Liaisons

ESPACE ROMAN-PHOTO
pages 42–43
- **Trop de devoirs!**

ESPACE CULTURE
pages 44–45
- The French university system

ESPACE STRUCTURES
pages 46–51
- Present tense of regular **-er** verbs
- Forming questions and expressing negation
- **Synthèse**
- **Interlude**

Leçon 4

ESPACE CONTEXTES
pages 52–55
- Everyday activities
- The letter **r**

ESPACE ROMAN-PHOTO
pages 56–57
- **On trouve une solution.**

ESPACE CULTURE
pages 58–59
- University life

ESPACE STRUCTURES
pages 60–65
- Present tense of **avoir**
- Telling time
- **Synthèse**
- **Le zapping**

Pour commencer
- What object is on the table?
  a. une montre b. un stylo c. un tableau
- What is Rachid looking at?
  a. un cahier b. un ordinateur c. un livre
- How does Rachid look in this photo?
  a. intelligent b. sociable c. égoïste
- Which word describes what he is doing?
  a. arriver b. voyager c. étudier

Savoir-faire

pages 66–71
Panorama: **La France**
Lecture: Read an academic brochure.
À l'écoute: Listen to some students talk about their schedules.
Écriture: Write a description of yourself.
Flash culture

Unit Goals

Leçon 3

In this lesson, students will learn:
- terms for courses and places at the university
- to express likes and dislikes
- about liaisons
- about the French university system and **la Sorbonne**
- the present tense of regular **-er** verbs
- about spelling changes in **-cer** and **-ger** verbs
- to ask questions and express negation
- about the singers Amadou Bagayoko and Mariam Doumbia and the painter Cyprien Tokoudagba

Leçon 4

In this lesson, students will learn:
- terms for talking about schedules and when things happen
- to pronounce the French **r**
- about university courses and **le bac** in France
- the present tense of **avoir**
- some expressions with **avoir**
- to tell time
- about the French company Clairefontaine

Savoir-faire

In this section, students will learn:
- cultural, economic, geographical, and historical information about France
- to use text formats to predict content
- to listen for cognates
- to brainstorm before writing
- to write a personal description
- more about university life through specially shot video footage

Pour commencer

- **b. un stylo**
- **b. un ordinateur**
- **a. intelligent**
- **c. étudier**

RESOURCES

Workbook/Video Manual: WB Activities, pp. 15–28
Laboratory Manual: Lab Activities, pp. 9–16
Workbook/Video Manual: Video Activities, pp. 215–218; pp. 273–274
WB/VM/LM Answer Key
Instructor's Resource CD-ROM [IRCD-ROM]: Instructor's Resource Manual [IRM] (Textbook Audioscript; Lab Audioscript; Videoscript; **Roman-photo** Translations; **Vocabulaire supplémentaire**; **Feuilles d'activités**; Info Gap Activities; **Le zapping** TV clip transcription; **Essayez!** and **Mise en pratique** answers); Transparencies #17, #18, #19, #20; Testing Program, pp. 9–16; Test Files; Testing Program MP3s;
Test Generator
Lab MP3s
Textbook MP3s
Video CD-ROM
Video on DVD
espaces.vhlcentral.com

Section Goals

In this section, students will learn and practice vocabulary related to:

- courses and fields of study
- places at the university
- expressing likes and dislikes

Instructional Resources

*IRCD-ROM: Transparency #17; IRM (**Vocabulaire supplémentaire; Mise en pratique** answers, Textbook Audioscript; Lab Audioscript; **Feuilles d'activités**)*
Textbook MP3s
WB/VM: Workbook, pp. 15–16
Lab Manual, p. 9
Lab MP3s
WB/VM/LM Answer Key
espaces.vhlcentral.com: activities, downloads, reference tools

Suggestions

- Have students look at the new vocabulary and identify cognates. Say the words and have students guess the meaning. Point out that the words **lettres** and **note** are **faux amis** in this context.
- Call students' attention to the pronunciation of **ps** in **psychologie**.
- Point out that abbreviations, such as **sciences po** and **resto U**, are common. For more examples, see **Le français quotidien** on page 45.
- To review classroom objects and practice new vocabulary, show items and ask what courses they might be used for. Example: **Un dictionnaire, c'est pour quel cours?**
- Explain that many of the adjectives they learned for nationalities in **Leçon 2** are also used for languages and language classes. Examples: **le cours de français (d'anglais, d'italien, d'espagnol)**
- Introduce vocabulary for expressing likes and dislikes by talking about your own. Use facial and hand gestures to convey meaning. Examples: **J'adore la littérature française. J'aime bien l'histoire. Je n'aime pas tellement la biologie. Je déteste l'informatique.**
- Additional vocabulary for this lesson can be found in the **Vocabulaire supplémentaire** in the IRM on the IRCD-ROM.

Leçon 3

You will learn how to...

- talk about your classes
- ask questions and express negation

Les cours

Vocabulaire

J'aime bien...	*I like...*
Je n'aime pas tellement...	*I don't like... very much*
être reçu(e) à un examen	*to pass an exam*
l'art (*m.*)	*art*
la chimie	*chemistry*
le droit	*law*
l'éducation physique (*f.*)	*physical education*
la géographie	*geography*
la gestion	*business administration*
les lettres (*f.*)	*humanities*
la philosophie	*philosophy*
les sciences (politiques / po) (*f.*)	*(political) science*
une bourse	*scholarship, grant*
un cours	*class, course*
un devoir	*homework*
un diplôme	*diploma, degree*
l'école (*f.*)	*school*
les études (supérieures) (*f.*)	*(higher) education; studies*
le gymnase	*gymnasium*
une note	*grade*
un restaurant universitaire (un resto U)	*university cafeteria*
difficile	*difficult*
facile	*easy*
inutile	*useless*
utile	*useful*
surtout	*especially; above all*

ressources

WB pp. 15-16	LM p. 9	Text MP3s Leçon 3	Lab MP3s Leçon 3	espaces.vhlcentral.com Leçon 3

OPTIONS

Extra Practice Ask students questions using the new vocabulary words. Examples: **La physique, c'est facile ou difficile? Une bourse, c'est utile ou inutile?**

Extra Practice Have them brainstorm adjectives that can describe their courses and write them: **facile, difficile, utile, inutile, intéressant, amusant, agréable, différent,** and **important**. Ask students to describe various courses. Example: **Le cours de philosophie est difficile.**

Game Divide the class into teams. Say the name of a course in English and ask one team to say it in French. If the team is correct, it gets a point. If not, the other team gets a chance to say it and "steal" the point. Alternate giving words to the two teams.

Attention!

The French system of grading is based on a scale of 0–20. A score below 10 is not a passing grade. It is rare to earn a grade between 18–20. Most students are happy to earn a grade between 12–14.

les langues étrangères (f.)

l'économie (f.)

l'histoire (f.)

la psychologie

Mise en pratique

1 Écoutez On their first day back to school, Aurélie and Hassim are discussing their classes, likes, and dislikes. Indicate the name of the person most likely to use the books listed below: Aurélie (**A**), Hassim (**H**), both (**A & H**), or neither (**X**). Not all items will be used.

1. Informatique et statistiques __A & H__
2. L'économie de la France __A__
3. L'architecture japonaise __X__
4. Histoire de France __H__
5. Études Freudiennes __H__
6. La géographie de l'Europe __H__
7. L'italien, c'est facile! __A & H__
8. Le droit international __A__

2 Associez Which classes, activities, or places do you associate with these words? Not all items in the second column will be used.

1. __d__	manger	a.	les mathématiques
2. __e__	un ordinateur	b.	la physique
3. __i__	le français	c.	l'histoire
4. __a__	une calculatrice	d.	un restaurant universitaire
5. __f__	le sport	e.	l'informatique
6. __h__	Socrate	f.	l'éducation physique
7. __b__	$E=MC^2$	g.	la biologie
8. __c__	Napoléon	h.	la philosophie
		i.	les langues étrangères
		j.	l'art

3 Qu'est-ce que j'aime? Read each statement and indicate whether you think it is **vrai** or **faux**. Compare your answers with a classmate's. Do you agree? Why? Answers will vary.

	Vrai	Faux
1. C'est facile d'être reçu à l'examen de mathématiques.	☐	☐
2. Je déteste manger au restaurant universitaire.	☐	☐
3. Je vais recevoir (*receive*) une bourse; c'est très utile.	☐	☐
4. La mode, c'est inutile.	☐	☐
5. Avoir un diplôme de l'université, c'est facile.	☐	☐
6. La chimie, c'est un cours difficile.	☐	☐
7. Je déteste les lettres.	☐	☐
8. 18 est une très bonne note.	☐	☐
9. Je n'aime pas tellement les études.	☐	☐
10. J'adore les langues étrangères.	☐	☐

OPTIONS

Small Groups Write the names of different fields of study across the board (for example, **les langues**, **les sciences naturelles**, **les sciences humaines**, **les cours techniques**). Working in groups of three or four, have students list the courses under the appropriate category.

Extra Practice Using **Transparency #17**, point to various people in the drawing and ask general questions about them. Examples: **Les étudiants sont au resto U? Il aime la physique?**

1 Tapescript AURÉLIE: Bonjour, Hassim. Comment ça va?
HASSIM: Bien. Et toi?
A: Pas mal, merci.
H: Tu aimes le cours d'informatique?
A: Oui, j'adore et j'aime bien l'économie et le droit aussi.
H: Moi, je n'aime pas tellement l'informatique, c'est difficile. J'aime l'histoire, la géographie et la psychologie. C'est très intéressant.
A: Tu aimes la gestion?
H: Ah non, je déteste!
A: Mais c'est très utile!
H: Mais non! Les langues, oui, sont utiles. J'aime bien l'italien.
A: Oui, j'adore l'italien, moi aussi!
H: Bon, à tout à l'heure, Aurélie!
A: Oui, à bientôt!
(On Textbook MP3s)

1 Expansion Play the recording again and ask students these true/false statements or write them on the board. **1. Aurélie n'aime pas le cours d'économie. (Faux.) 2. Hassim déteste le cours de gestion. (Vrai.) 3. Pour Hassim, le cours d'informatique est facile. (Faux.) 4. Hassim aime la psychologie et la géographie. (Vrai.) 5. Aurélie et Hassim aiment bien l'italien. (Vrai.)**

2 Expansions

- Items g. and j. were not used. Ask the class what words they associate with **la biologie** and **l'art**.
- Have students brainstorm a list of famous people that they associate with the following fields: **le stylisme de mode** (Ralph Lauren, Vera Wang); **l'informatique** (Bill Gates, Michael Dell); and **la gestion** (Donald Trump, Lee Iacocca). Then have the class guess the field associated with each of the following people: Louis Pasteur **(la biologie)**, Alan Greenspan **(l'économie)**, and Maya Angelou **(les lettres)**.

3 Expansion Take a class survey of students' responses to each question and tally the results on the board. Ask students which questions are most controversial. Then ask them on which questions they agree. You might want to introduce the expression **être d'accord**, which will be presented later in **Leçon 3**.

4 Suggestion Before doing this activity, complete a similar exchange; scramble the order of the sentences and write them on the board or on a transparency. Tell students to put the sentences in order to make a logical conversation.

5 Suggestion Have several volunteers write their captions on the board.

6 Suggestions
- To save time in class, photocopy and distribute a page from a French **agenda** the day before. Introduce the days of the week and have students fill in their class schedule for homework. The days of the week will be formally presented in **Leçon 4.**
- Before beginning the activity, give students a model. Example: **Mon** (*My*) **cours d'histoire est le mardi et le jeudi. Et toi?**

7 Suggestions
- Read the **modèle** aloud with a volunteer. Then distribute the **Feuilles d'activités** from the IRM on the IRCD-ROM
- Have volunteers share their findings with the class.

NATIONAL STANDARDS communication

Communication

4 Conversez Get together with a partner and fill in the blanks according to your own situations. Then, act out the conversation for the class. Answers will vary.

Étudiant(e) A: ______, comment ça va?
Étudiant(e) B: ______. Et toi?
Étudiant(e) A: ______ merci.
Étudiant(e) B: Est-ce que tu aimes le cours de ______?
Étudiant(e) A: J'adore le cours de ______.
Étudiant(e) B: Moi aussi. Tu aimes ______?
Étudiant(e) A: Non, j'aime mieux (*better*) ______.
Étudiant(e) B: Bon, à bientôt.
Étudiant(e) A: À ______.

5 Qu'est-ce que c'est? Write a caption for each image, stating where the students are and how they feel about the classes they are attending. Then, get together with a partner and take turns reading one of your captions and have him or her guess about whom you are talking. Answers will vary. Suggested answers.

MODÈLE

C'est le cours de français. Le français, c'est facile.

1. C'est le cours d'informatique. L'informatique, je déteste.

2. Être reçu à l'examen / Avoir le diplôme de l'université, c'est difficile.

3. C'est la philosophie. La philosophie, j'adore.

4. C'est le cours de chimie. La chimie, c'est facile.

5. C'est le cours d'éducation physique / le restaurant universitaire, je n'aime pas tellement...

6. C'est un devoir d'architecture / de stylisme de mode, j'aime bien...

6 L'emploi du temps In pairs, take turns describing your class schedules (**l'emploi du temps**). Then, get together with another pair and take turns describing your respective partner's schedule. How many classes do you have in common? Answers will vary.

Emploi du temps		
	lundi	*mardi*
8h30-9h30	*français*	*philosophie*
9h30-10h30	*histoire*	*géographie*
10h45-11h45	*maths*	*français*

7 Sondage Your instructor will give you a worksheet to conduct a survey (**un sondage**). Go around the room to find people that study the subjects listed. Ask what your classmates think about their subjects. Keep a record of their answers to discuss with the class. Answers will vary.

MODÈLE

Étudiant(e) 1: *Jean, est-ce que tu étudies (do you study) le droit?*
Étudiant(e) 2: *Oui. J'aime bien le droit. C'est un cours utile.*

OPTIONS

Game Divide the class into two teams. Write names of courses or people on index cards and tape them face down on the board. Play a game of Concentration in which students match courses with an expert in the field. Examples: **le stylisme de mode/**Jean-Paul Gautier, **l'art/**Claude Monet, and **la philosophie/**Jean-Paul Sartre. As students turn over a card, they must read it aloud. If a player has a match, that player's team collects those cards. When all the cards have been matched, the team with the most cards wins.

Extra Practice To practice expressing likes and dislikes, ask students yes/no and either/or questions. Examples: **Vous aimez bien la psychologie? Vous détestez la géographie? Vous adorez les lettres ou les sciences?**

Les sons et les lettres

Liaisons

In French, the final sound of a word sometimes links with the first letter of the following word. Consonants at the end of French words are generally silent, but are usually pronounced when the word that follows begins with a vowel sound. This linking of sounds is called a liaison.

À tout à l'heure! **Comment allez-vous?**

An **s** or an **x** in a liaison sounds like the letter **z**.

les étudiants **trois élèves** **six élèves** **deux hommes**

Always make a liaison between a subject pronoun and a verb that begins with a vowel sound; always make a liaison between an article and a noun that begins with a vowel sound.

nous aimons **ils ont** **un étudiant** **les ordinateurs**

Always make a liaison between **est** (a form of **être**) and a word that begins with a vowel or a vowel sound. Never make a liaison with the final consonant of a proper name.

Robert est anglais. **Paris est exceptionnelle.**

Never make a liaison with the conjunction **et** (*and*).

Carole et Hélène **Jacques et Antoinette**

Never make a liaison between a singular noun and an adjective that follows it.

un cours horrible **un instrument élégant**

Prononcez Practice saying these words and expressions aloud.

1. un examen
2. des étudiants
3. les hôtels
4. dix acteurs
5. Paul et Yvette
6. cours important
7. des informations
8. les études
9. deux hommes
10. Bernard aime
11. chocolat italien
12. Louis est

Articulez Practice saying these sentences aloud.

1. Nous aimons les arts.
2. Albert habite à Paris.
3. C'est un objet intéressant.
4. Sylvie est avec Anne.
5. Ils adorent les deux universités.

Dictons Practice reading these sayings aloud.

Un hôte non invité doit apporter son siège.[2]

Les amis de nos amis sont nos amis.[1]

ressources
LM p. 10
Text MP3s Leçon 3
Lab MP3s Leçon 3
espaces.vhlcentral.com Leçon 3

[1] Friends of our friends are our friends.
[2] An uninvited guest must bring his own chair.

Section Goals

In this section, students will learn about liaisons.

Instructional Resources
Textbook MP3s
Lab Manual, p. 10
Lab MP3s
WB/VM/LM Answer Key
IRCD-ROM: IRM (Textbook Audioscript; Lab Audioscript)
espaces.vhlcentral.com: activities, downloads, reference tools

Suggestions

- Model the pronunciation of each phrase and have students repeat. Explain the liaison for each case.
- Point out expressions with liaison in **Contextes** or ask students to find them. Have them repeat after you. Example: **les études.**
- Ask students to provide expressions from **Leçons 1–2** that contain a liaison. Examples: **les États-Unis** and **Comment allez-vous?**
- Write the sentences in the **Articulez** on the board or a transparency. Have students listen to the recording and tell you where they hear liaisons. Alternately, have students write the sentences on a sheet of paper, draw lines linking letters that form liaisons, and cross out silent final consonants.
- **Liaisons obligatoires** and **liaisons interdites** will be formally presented in **Leçon 29.**
- The explanation and exercises are recorded on the Textbook MP3s CD-ROM and are available on the **ESPACES** web site. You may want to play them in class so students practice listening to French speakers other than yourself.

Dictons Tell students to pronounce the liaison between **n** and **in** in **non invité**. Have students compare the saying **«Un hôte non invité doit apporter son siège»** with its literal translation. Ask what they think it means figuratively. (Possible answer: People who show up unexpectedly have no right to complain about the service.) Ask: What do the two sayings in this section reveal about French culture?

OPTIONS

Extra Practice Dictate the following phrases with liaisons, saying each one at least two times. Then write them on the board or on a transparency and have students check what they wrote. **1. dix-huit étudiants 2. les mathématiques 3. un cours utile 4. la chimie et l'architecture 5. les langues étrangères**

Extra Practice Here are additional sentences with liaisons to use for oral practice or dictation. **1. Robert et Alex sont anglais. 2. C'est un film très intéressant. 3. Il y a trois enfants. 4. C'est un restaurant italien.**

Section Goals

In this section, students will learn functional phrases for talking about their courses.

Instructional Resources
WB/VM: Video Manual, pp. 215–216
WB/VM/LM Answer Key
Video CD-ROM
Video on DVD
*IRCD-ROM: IRM (Videoscript; **Roman-photo** Translations)*
espaces.vhlcentral.com: activities, downloads, reference tools

Video Recap: Leçon 2
Before doing this **Roman-photo**, review the previous one.
1. Le cours d'histoire est difficile pour Stéphane, n'est-ce pas? (Non, les maths et le français sont difficiles pour Stéphane.)
2. Comment est Sandrine? (égoïste, sociable et charmante)
3. De quelle origine est Amina? (sénégalaise) Et Rachid? (algérienne)
4. Comment est Amina? (charmante, sincère et élégante)
5. Comment est Rachid? (intelligent, poli, modeste, réservé et brillant)

Video Synopsis Rachid and Antoine discuss their political science class. As they are walking, David joins them, and Rachid introduces him. Then Antoine leaves. When the two roommates get to Rachid's car, Sandrine and Amina are waiting for them. The girls ask David about school and his classes. Later, at **Le P'tit Bistrot**, Stéphane joins the four friends and they continue their discussion about classes. Stéphane hates all of his courses.

Suggestions
- Have students predict what they think the episode will be about. Record predictions on the board.
- Have students work in groups of six. Tell them to choose a role and read the **Roman-photo** conversation aloud. Ask one or two groups to act out the conversation for the class.
- After students read the **Roman-photo**, review their predictions and ask which ones were correct. Then ask a few questions to guide them in summarizing this episode.

NATIONAL STANDARDS communication cultures

Trop de devoirs!

PERSONNAGES

Amina

Antoine

David

Rachid

Sandrine

Stéphane

ANTOINE Je déteste le cours de sciences po.
RACHID Oh? Mais pourquoi? Je n'aime pas tellement le prof, Monsieur Dupré, mais c'est un cours intéressant et utile!
ANTOINE Tu crois? Moi, je pense que c'est très difficile, et il y a beaucoup de devoirs. Avec Dupré, je travaille, mais je n'ai pas de bons résultats.

RACHID Si on est optimiste et si on travaille, on est reçu à l'examen.
ANTOINE Toi, oui, mais pas moi! Toi, tu es un étudiant brillant! Mais moi, les études, oh, là, là.
DAVID Eh! Rachid! Oh! Est-ce que tu oublies ton coloc'?

RACHID Pas du tout, pas du tout. Antoine, voilà, je te présente David, mon colocataire américain.
DAVID Nous partageons un des appartements du P'tit Bistrot.
ANTOINE Le P'tit Bistrot? Sympa!

SANDRINE Salut! Alors, ça va l'université française?
DAVID Bien, oui. C'est différent de l'université américaine, mais c'est intéressant.
AMINA Tu aimes les cours?
DAVID J'aime bien les cours de littérature et d'histoire françaises. Demain on étudie *les Trois Mousquetaires* d'Alexandre Dumas.

SANDRINE J'adore Dumas. Mon livre préféré, c'est *le Comte de Monte-Cristo*.
RACHID Sandrine! S'il te plaît! *Le Comte de Monte-Cristo*?
SANDRINE Pourquoi pas? Je suis chanteuse, mais j'adore les classiques de la littérature.
DAVID Donne-moi le sac à dos, Sandrine.

Au P'tit Bistrot...
RACHID Moi, j'aime le cours de sciences po, mais Antoine n'aime pas Dupré. Il pense qu'il donne trop de devoirs.

ACTIVITÉS

1 Vrai ou faux? Choose whether each statement is **vrai** or **faux**.

1. Rachid et Antoine n'aiment pas le professeur Dupré. Vrai.
2. Antoine aime bien le cours de sciences po. Faux.
3. Rachid et Antoine partagent (*share*) un appartement. Faux.
4. David et Rachid cherchent (*look for*) Amina et Sandrine après (*after*) les cours. Vrai.
5. Le livre préféré de Sandrine est *le Comte de Monte-Cristo*. Vrai.
6. L'université française est très différente de l'université américaine. Vrai.
7. Stéphane aime la chimie. Faux.
8. Monsieur Dupré est professeur de maths. Faux.
9. Antoine a (*has*) beaucoup de devoirs. Vrai.
10. Stéphane adore l'anglais. Faux.

OPTIONS

Avant de regarder la vidéo Before showing the video episode, have students brainstorm some expressions people might use when talking about their classes and professors.

Regarder la vidéo Photocopy the videoscript and opaque out ten words or expressions with white correction fluid in order to create a master for a cloze activity. Hand out the photocopies and tell students to fill in the missing words as they watch the video episode. You may want to show the episode twice if students have difficulty with the activity. Then have students compare their answers in small groups.

Antoine, David, Rachid et Stéphane parlent (*talk*) de leurs (*their*) cours.

RACHID Ah... on a rendez-vous avec Amina et Sandrine. On y va?
DAVID Ah, oui, bon, ben, salut, Antoine!
ANTOINE Salut, David. À demain, Rachid!

SANDRINE Bon, Pascal, au revoir, chéri.
RACHID Bonjour, chérie. Comme j'adore parler avec toi au téléphone! Comme j'adore penser à toi!

STÉPHANE Dupré? Ha! C'est Madame Richard, mon prof de français. Elle, elle donne trop de devoirs.
AMINA Bonjour, comment ça va?
STÉPHANE Plutôt mal. Je n'aime pas Madame Richard. Je déteste les maths. La chimie n'est pas intéressante. L'histoire-géo, c'est l'horreur. Les études, c'est le désastre!

DAVID Le français, les maths, la chimie, l'histoire-géo... mais on n'étudie pas les langues étrangères au lycée en France?
STÉPHANE Si, malheureusement! Moi, j'étudie l'anglais. C'est une langue très désagréable! Oh, non, non, ha, ha, c'est une blague, ha, ha. L'anglais, j'adore l'anglais. C'est une langue charmante....

Expressions utiles

Talking about classes

- **Tu aimes les cours?**
  Do you like the classes?
- **Antoine n'aime pas Dupré.**
  Antoine doesn't like Dupré.
- **Il pense qu'il donne trop de devoirs.**
  He thinks he gives too much homework.
- **Tu crois? Mais pourquoi?**
  You think? But why?
- **Avec Dupré, je travaille, mais je n'ai pas de bon résultats.**
  With Dupré, I work, but I don't get good results (grades).
- **Demain on étudie *les Trois Mousquetaires*.**
  Tomorrow we're studying The Three Musketeers.
- **C'est mon livre préféré.**
  It's my favorite book.

Additional vocabulary

- **On a rendez-vous.**
  We have a meeting.
- **Comme j'adore...**
  How I love...
- **parler au téléphone**
  to talk on the phone
- **C'est une blague.**
  It's a joke.
- **Si, malheureusement!**
  Yes, unfortunately!
- **On y va?**
  Let's go?
- **Eh!**
  Hey!
- **pas du tout**
  not at all
- **Chéri(e)**
  Darling

2 Complétez Match the people in the second column with the verbs in the first. Refer to a dictionary, the dialogue, and the video stills as necessary. Use each option once.

1. b/e travailler
2. c partager
3. a oublier
4. b/e étudier
5. d donner

a. Sandrine is very forgetful.
b. Rachid is very studious.
c. David can't afford his own apartment.
d. Amina is very generous.
e. Stéphane needs to get good grades.

3 Conversez In this episode, Rachid, Antoine, David, and Stéphane talk about the subjects they are studying. Get together with a partner. Do any of the characters' complaints or preferences remind you of your own? Whose opinions do you agree with? Whom do you disagree with?

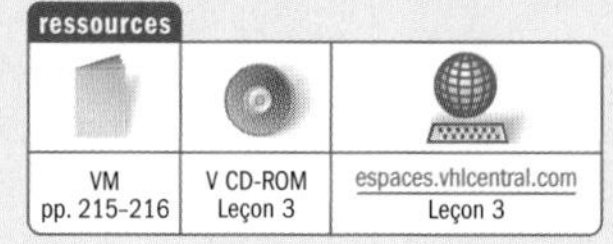

ressources
VM pp. 215-216
V CD-ROM Leçon 3
espaces.vhlcentral.com Leçon 3

ACTIVITÉS

Expressions utiles
- Model the pronunciation of the **Expressions utiles** and have students repeat after you.
- As you work through the list, point out forms of **-er** verbs. Also identify examples of negation. Tell students that **-er** verbs and negation will be formally presented in the **Structures** section.
- Ask students a few questions about their classes and professors. Examples: **Vous aimez le cours de sciences po? Comment s'appelle le prof de sciences po? Est-ce que ____ donne trop de devoirs?**
- Point out that **si** is used instead of **oui** to contradict a negative statement or question. Example: **Si, malheureusement!**

1 Suggestion Have students correct the false statements.

1 Expansion For additional practice, give students these items. **11. Rachid pense que le cours de sciences po est inutile. (Faux.) 12. Madame Richard est prof de français. (Vrai.) 13. Pour Stéphane, les études, c'est le désastre. (Vrai.)**

2 Expansion Write these verbs on the board: **aimer, détester, adorer**, and **penser**. Have students create additional statements about the video characters that relate to each verb.

3 Suggestion Encourage students to express their opinions in simple French. Write a few sentence starters on the board. Examples: **Comme Stéphane, moi, je n'aime pas...** and **Je suis d'accord avec Rachid...**

OPTIONS

Alexandre Dumas Alexandre Dumas (**père**) (1802–1870) was a prolific French novelist and dramatist. With the assistance of a group of collaborators, he wrote almost 300 works. *The Three Musketeers (**Les Trois Mousquetaires**), The Count of Monte Cristo (**le Comte de Monte-Cristo**),* and *The Black Tulip (**La Tulipe noire**)* are among his most famous and popular novels. These historical romances feature swashbuckling characters. Ask students if they have read any of these books or seen any movies based on them.

Small Groups Working in groups of four, have students create a short skit similar to the scenes in video stills 6–10 in which some students are talking about their classes and professors. Give students about ten minutes to prepare, and then call on groups to perform their skits for the class.

NATIONAL STANDARDS connections cultures

Section Goals

In this section, students will:

- learn about French universities and **les grandes écoles**
- learn some familiar terms for talking about academic courses
- learn the names of some well-known universities in the francophone world
- read about **la Sorbonne**

Instructional Resources
espaces.vhlcentral.com: activities, downloads, reference tools

Culture à la loupe

Avant la lecture Have the class brainstorm and make a list of the different types of educational institutions that exist in the United States.

Lecture

- Point out the chart **Les étudiants en France**. Ask students what information the chart shows. (The percentages of students enrolled at different types of educational institutions in France.) Then ask them to name the types of institutions that exist.
- Tell students that an urban university system may have many individual campuses that operate autonomously. The **Université de Paris**, for example, comprises 13 campuses that are located within the city and in its suburbs.

Après la lecture Working in small groups, have students compare French and American universities. Tell them to make a list of the similarities and differences. Then ask several groups to read their lists to the class.

1 Expansion For additional practice, give students these items. 11. Students need to pass an exam in order to advance to a university. (**Vrai.**) 12. France changed its university system in 1998. (**Faux.** France changed its university system in 2005.) 13. A **Master** is the highest degree awarded at a French university. (**Faux.** A **Doctorat** is the highest degree awarded.)

CULTURE À LA LOUPE

À l'université

French students who pass le bac° may continue on to study in a university. By American standards, university tuition is low. In 1999, 29 European countries, including France, decided to reform their university systems in order to create a more uniform European system. France began implementing these reforms in 2005. As a result, French students' degrees (**diplômes**) are now accepted in most European countries. It is also easier for French students to study in other European countries for a semester, and for other European students to study in France, because studies are now organized by semesters. Students are awarded a **Licence°** after six semesters (usually three years). If they continue their studies, they can earn a **Master°** after the fifth year and then proceed to a **Doctorat°**. If students choose technical studies, they receive a **BTS** (**Brevet de Technicien Supérieur**) after two years.

In addition to universities, France has an extremely competitive, elite branch of higher education called **les grandes écoles°**. These schools train most of the high-level administrators, scientists, businesspeople, and engineers in the country. There are about 300 of them, including **ENA** (**École Nationale d'Administration**), **HEC** (**Hautes° Études Commerciales**), and **IEP** (**Institut d'Études Politiques, «Sciences Po»**).

Some French universities are city-based, lacking campuses and offering few extra-curricular activities like organized sports or fraternities and sororities. Others boast both a more defined campus and a great number of student **associations**. Many students live with their families, in a **résidence universitaire,** or in an apartment.

Les étudiants en France	
Universités	64,5%
Sections de Techniciens Supérieurs	11,1%
Autres Écoles ou Formations	6,6%
Instituts Universitaires de Technologie	5,2%
Écoles Paramédicales et Sociales	5,1%
Formation d'Ingénieurs	4,6%
Instituts Universitaires de Formation de Maîtres°	4,0%
Classes Préparatoires aux grandes écoles	3,4%
Écoles de Commerce°	2,2%

bac *exit exam taken after high school* **Licence** *the equivalent of a Bachelor's degree* **Master** *Master's degree* **Doctorat** *Ph.D.* **grandes écoles** *competitive, prestigious university-level schools* **Hautes** *High* **Formation de Maîtres** *teacher training* **Écoles de Commerce** *business schools*

ACTIVITÉS

1 Vrai ou faux? Indicate whether each statement is **vrai** or **faux**.

1. French university students can earn a **Licence** after only three years of study.
   Vrai.
2. It takes five years to earn a **BTS**.
   Faux. It takes two years to earn a BTS.
3. Entry into the **grandes écoles** is not competitive.
   Faux. Entry into the grandes écoles is extremely competitive.
4. The **grandes écoles** train high-level engineers.
   Vrai.
5. Some French universities lack campuses.
   Vrai.
6. Extra-curricular activities are uncommon in some French universities.
   Vrai.
7. All French students live at home with their families.
   Faux. Some students also live in résidences universitaires or in an apartment.
8. About 5% of French students are in business school.
   Faux. Only 2.2% of French students are in business school.
9. More French students study business than engineering.
   Faux. More French students study engineering.
10. About 4% of French students are studying for a teaching degree.
   Vrai.

OPTIONS

Pairs Explain how to read percentages so students can quiz each other in pairs about the information in the chart **Les étudiants en France**. Model how to say percentages. Example: 64,5% (**soixante-quatre virgule cinq pour cent**). To help students, write some sample questions on the board. Examples: **Il y a plus** (*more*) **d'étudiants dans les universités ou dans les écoles de Commerce? Il y a moins** (*less*) **d'étudiants dans les instituts de technologie ou dans les écoles vétérinaires?**

À l'université Despite France's longstanding low fees for a university education, tuition has increased rapidly. France has only recently needed seriously to consider a federal program of low-interest student loans to offset rising tuition costs since it is unusual for students to work while studying.

LE FRANÇAIS QUOTIDIEN

Les études

être fort(e) en...	*to be good at...*
être nul(le) en...	*to be bad at...*
bio	*biology*
éco	*economics*
géo	*geography*
maths	*math*
philo	*philosophy*
psycho	*psychology*

LE MONDE FRANCOPHONE

Des universités francophones

Voici quelques-unes° des universités du monde francophone où vous pouvez étudier°.

En Belgique Université Libre de Bruxelles

En Côte d'Ivoire Université d'Abobo-Adjamé

En France Université de Paris

Au Maroc Université Mohammed V Souissi à Rabat

En Polynésie française Université de la Polynésie française, à Faa'a, à Tahiti

Au Québec Université de Montréal

Au Sénégal Université Cheikh Anta Diop de Dakar

En Suisse Université de Genève

En Tunisie Université Libre de Tunis

quelques-unes *some* **où vous pouvez étudier** *where you can study*

PORTRAIT

La Sorbonne

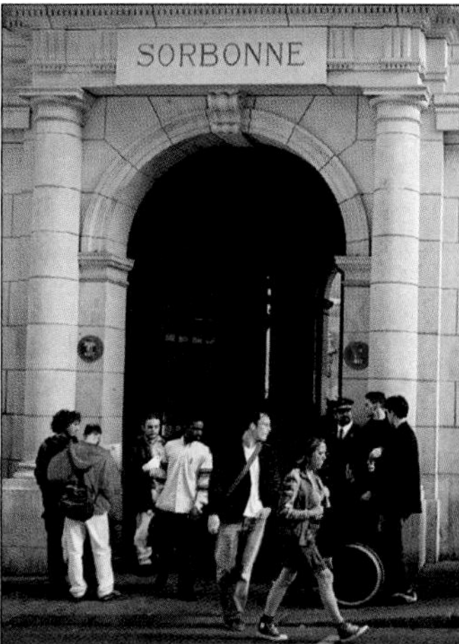

Fondée° à Paris au XIIIe (treizième) siècle°, la prestigieuse Sorbonne est une des plus vieilles° universités du monde et un des symboles de l'intellect français. Aujourd'hui, la Sorbonne comprend° quatre universités: Université de Paris I, III, IV et V. Les études proposées sont diverses et d'excellente qualité: les arts et sciences humaines, la littérature, les langues, les sciences, les technologies, les sciences juridiques° et politiques. La Sorbonne prépare aussi des étudiants pour les **grandes écoles**. À l'Université Paris Sorbonne-Paris IV, les étudiants étrangers peuvent suivre° des cours de langue et de civilisation françaises.

Fondée *Founded* **XIIIe siècle** *13th century* **des plus vieilles** *of the oldest* **comprend** *includes* **juridiques** *legal* **peuvent suivre** *can take*

Coup de main

In French, a superscript -e following a numeral tells you that it is an ordinal number. It is the equivalent of a -th after a numeral in English: $4^e = 4^{th}$.

SUR INTERNET

Quelles (*What*) sont les caractéristiques d'un campus universitaire en France?

Go to **espaces.vhlcentral.com** to find more cultural information related to this **ESPACE CULTURE.**

ACTIVITÉS

2 La Sorbonne Provide completions for these statements.

1. La Sorbonne est une des plus vieilles universités du monde.
2. La Sorbonne comprend quatre universités.
3. Les étudiants de la Sorbonne peuvent (*can*) étudier Answers will vary.
4. La Sorbonne est un symbole de la vie intellectuelle française.
5. La Sorbonne prépare des étudiants pour les grandes écoles.
6. Les étudiants étrangers peuvent étudier la langue et la civilisation françaises.

3 Les cours Research two of the universities mentioned in **Le monde francophone** and, in French, make a list of at least five courses taught at each. You may search in your library or online.

ressources

espaces.vhlcentral.com Leçon 3

Le français quotidien Have students work in pairs. Tell them to take turns describing the courses they are good and bad at using the vocabulary in this section. Examples: **Je suis nul(le) en maths. Je suis fort(e) en géo.**

Portrait

- Show the class a photo of **la Sorbonne**. Ask: **Qu'est-ce que c'est? (une université) Comment s'appelle-t-elle?** Then ask students if they know why it is famous.
- Point out the **Coup de main** box. Say the ordinal numbers in French and have volunteers write them on the board using a superscript.

Le monde francophone Have students read the list. Ask: What do you notice about the names of these schools? (All include the name of the city in which they are located, except for two. **L'Université Mohammed V Souissi** in Rabat is named after the king of Morocco from 1957–1961, and **l'Université d'Adobo-Adjamé** is named after two of the ten municipalities in the city of Abidjan.)

2 Suggestion Have students compare their answers with a classmate.

3 Expansion Have students find out the following information as part of their research: when the universities were founded, how many languages are taught, and whether or not they have programs for foreign students and study abroad programs.

OPTIONS

Cultural Comparison Have students compare their university to **la Sorbonne**. Begin by having students look at the photo and discuss the architecture and campus. Then have them compare other aspects mentioned in the reading, such as fields of study, number of campuses or universities, and courses for foreign students.

Des universités francophones Tell students to imagine that they have the opportunity to go on a study abroad program at one of the universities listed in **Le monde francophone**. Have them choose a location and explain why they would like to attend that particular school.

Section Goals

NATIONAL STANDARDS comparisons

In this section, students will learn:
- the present tense of regular **-er** verbs
- spelling changes in **-cer** and **-ger** verbs

Instructional Resources
WB/VM: Workbook, pp. 17–18
Lab Manual, p. 11
Lab MP3s
WB/VM/LM Answer Key
*IRCD-ROM: IRM (**Mise en pratique** answers; Lab Audioscript)*
espaces.vhlcentral.com: activities, downloads, reference tools

Suggestions
- Point out that students have been using verbs from the start: **Comment t'appelles-tu?, il y a,** forms of **être**, etc. Ask the class: **Quels cours aimez-vous?** Model the response **J'aime....** Ask a student: ____ **aime quels cours?** Model **Il/Elle aime....** Give other subjects.
- Introduce the idea of a "boot verb." Write the conjugation of a common **-er** verb on the board with the singular forms in the first column and the plural forms in the second column. Draw a line around **je**, **tu**, **il/elle**, and **ils/elles**, forming the shape of a boot. The four verb forms inside the "boot" are pronounced alike.
- Model the pronunciation of each infinitive, having students repeat. Create sentences with **j'aime...** and **j'adore...** followed by infinitives. Stress that **je** changes to **j'** before verbs starting with a vowel and most verbs starting with **h**. Ask if students like some of the activities. Example: **Vous aimez voyager?**
- Explain that the French present tense equals four English present tenses. Ask volunteers to translate examples like these: **À l'université, je mange bien.** (*At college, I eat well.*) **Excusez-moi, je mange.** (*Excuse me, I'm eating.*)
- Point out that verbs ending in **-cer** and **-ger** have a spelling change in the **nous** form. Write **commençons** and **mangeons** on the board, and circle the change.
- Model the pronunciation of adverbs in **Boîte à outils.** Have students repeat. Ask volunteers for sentences using each word.

3.1 Present tense of regular *-er* verbs

- The infinitives of most French verbs end in **-er**. To form the present tense of regular **-er** verbs, drop the **-er** from the infinitive and add the corresponding endings for the different subject pronouns. This chart demonstrates how to conjugate regular **-er** verbs.

parler **(to speak)**

je parle	*I speak*	**nous parlons**	*we speak*
tu parles	*you speak*	**vous parlez**	*you speak*
il/elle parle	*he/she/it speaks*	**ils/elles parlent**	*they speak*

- Here are some other verbs that are conjugated the same way as **parler**.

Common *-er* verbs

adorer	*to love*	**habiter (à)**	*to live (in)*
aimer	*to like; to love*	**manger**	*to eat*
aimer mieux	*to prefer (to like better)*	**oublier**	*to forget*
		partager	*to share*
arriver	*to arrive*	**penser (que/qu'...)**	*to think (that...)*
chercher	*to look for*	**regarder**	*to look (at)*
commencer	*to begin, to start*	**rencontrer**	*to meet*
dessiner	*to draw; to design*	**retrouver**	*to meet up with; to find (again)*
détester	*to hate*		
donner	*to give*	**travailler**	*to work*
étudier	*to study*	**voyager**	*to travel*

- Note that **je** becomes **j'** when it appears before a verb that begins with a vowel sound.

J'habite à Bruxelles.
I live in Brussels.

J'étudie la psychologie.
I study psychology.

- With the verbs **adorer, aimer,** and **détester**, use the definite article before a noun to tell what someone loves, what someone likes, or what someone hates.

J'aime mieux **l'**art.
I prefer art.

Marine déteste **les** devoirs.
Marine hates homework.

- Use infinitive forms after the verbs **adorer, aimer,** and **détester** to say that you like (or hate, etc.) to do something. Only the first verb should be conjugated.

Ils **adorent travailler** ici.
They love to work here.

Ils **détestent étudier** ensemble.
They hate to study together.

MISE EN PRATIQUE

1 Complétez Complete the conversation with the correct forms of the verbs.

ARTHUR Tu (1) parles (parler) bien français!

OLIVIER Mon colocataire Marc et moi, nous (2) retrouvons (retrouver) un professeur de français et nous (3) étudions (étudier) ensemble. Et toi, tu (4) travailles (travailler)?

ARTHUR Non, j' (5) étudie (étudier) l'art et l'économie. Je (6) dessine (dessiner) bien et j' (7) aime (aimer) beaucoup l'art moderne. Marc et toi, vous (8) habitez (habiter) à Paris?

2 Phrases Form sentences using the words provided. Conjugate the verbs and add any necessary words.

1. je / oublier / devoir de littérature
J'oublie le devoir de littérature.
2. nous / commencer / études supérieures
Nous commençons des études supérieures.
3. vous / rencontrer / amis / à / fac
Vous rencontrez des amis à la fac.
4. Hélène / détester / travailler
Hélène déteste travailler.
5. tu / chercher / cours / facile
Tu cherches un cours facile.
6. élèves / arriver / avec / dictionnaires
Les élèves arrivent avec des dictionnaires.

3 Après l'école Say what Stéphanie and her friends are doing after (**après**) school.

MODÈLE
Nathalie cherche un livre.

1. André travaille à la bibliothèque.

4. Julien et Audrey parlent avec Simon.

2. Édouard retrouve Caroline au café.

5. Robin et toi, vous voyagez avec la classe.

3. Jérôme et moi, nous dessinons.

6. Je mange.

OPTIONS

Extra Practice Do a rapid-response drill. Write an infinitive from the list of **-er** verbs on the board. Call out subject pronouns and/or names, and have students respond with the correct verb form. Then reverse the drill; write a verb form on the board and have students say the subject pronouns.

Game Divide the class into two teams. Choose one team member at a time to go to the board, alternating between teams. Say an infinitive and a subject pronoun. The person at the board must write and say the correct present tense form. Example: **parler: vous (vous parlez).** Give a point for each correct answer. The team with the most points at the end of the game wins.

COMMUNICATION

4 Activités In pairs, say which of these activities you and your roommate both do. Be prepared to share your partner's answers with the class. Then, get together with another partner and report to the class again. Answers will vary.

MODÈLE

Étudiant(e) 1: *Nous parlons au téléphone, nous...*
Étudiant(e) 2: *Ils/Elles parlent au téléphone, ils/elles...*

manger au resto U	étudier une langue étrangère
partager un appartement	commencer les devoirs
retrouver des amis au café	arriver en classe
travailler	voyager

5 Les études In pairs, take turns asking your partner if he or she likes one academic subject or another. If you don't like a subject, mention one you do like. Then, use **tous les deux** (*both of us*) to tell the class what subjects both of you like or hate. Answers will vary.

MODÈLE

Étudiant(e) 1: *Tu aimes la chimie?*
Étudiant(e) 2: *Non, je déteste la chimie. J'aime mieux les langues.*
Étudiant(e) 1: *Moi aussi... Nous adorons tous les deux les langues.*

6 Adorer, aimer, détester In groups of four, ask each other if you like to do these activities. Then, use an adjective to tell why you like them or not and say whether you do them often (**souvent**), sometimes (**parfois**), or rarely (**rarement**). Answers will vary.

MODÈLE

Étudiant(e) 1: *Tu aimes voyager?*
Étudiant(e) 2: *Oui, j'adore voyager. C'est amusant! Je voyage souvent.*
Étudiant(e) 3: *Moi, je n'aime pas tellement voyager. C'est désagréable! Je voyage rarement.*

dessiner	partager un appartement
étudier le week-end	retrouver des amis
manger au restaurant	travailler à la bibliothèque
oublier les devoirs	voyager
parler avec les professeurs	

- The present tense in French can be translated in different ways in English. The English equivalent for a sentence depends on its context.

Éric et Nadine **étudient** le droit.	Nous **travaillons** à Paris demain.
Éric and Nadine study law.	*We work in Paris tomorrow.*
Éric and Nadine are studying law.	*We are working in Paris tomorrow.*
Éric and Nadine do study law.	*We will work in Paris tomorrow.*

- Verbs ending in **-ger** (**manger**, **partager**, **voyager**) and **-cer** (**commencer**) have a spelling change in the **nous** form.

manger ▸ **nous mangeons** **commencer** ▸ **nous commençons**

Nous **voyageons** avec une amie.	Nous **commençons** les devoirs.
We are traveling with a friend.	*We are starting the homework.*

- Unlike the English *to look for*, the French **chercher** requires no preposition before the noun that follows it.

Nous **cherchons les stylos**.	Vous **cherchez la montre**?
We are looking for the pens.	*Are you looking for the watch?*

Est-ce que tu oublies ton coloc'?

Nous partageons un des appartements du P'tit Bistrot.

BOÎTE À OUTILS

To express yourself with greater accuracy, use these adverbs: **assez** (*enough*), **d'habitude** (*usually*), **de temps en temps** (*from time to time*), **parfois** (*sometimes*), **rarement** (*rarely*), **souvent** (*often*), **toujours** (*always*).

Essayez! Complete the sentences with the correct present tense forms of the verbs.

1. Je __parle__ (parler) français en classe.
2. Nous __habitons__ (habiter) près de (*near*) l'université.
3. Ils __aiment__ (aimer) le cours de sciences politiques.
4. Vous __mangez__ (manger) en classe?!
5. Le cours __commence__ (commencer) à huit heures (*at eight o'clock*).
6. Marie-Claire __cherche__ (chercher) un stylo.
7. Nous __partageons__ (partager) un crayon en cours de maths.
8. Tu __étudies__ (étudier) l'économie.

Essayez! Have students create new sentences orally or in writing by changing the subject of the sentence.

1 Suggestion Go over the answers quickly in class, then ask several pairs of students to act out the conversation and add at least two lines of their own at the end.

2 Suggestion To check students' answers, have volunteers write the sentences on the board and read them aloud.

2 Expansion For additional practice, change the subjects of the sentences and have students restate or write the sentences. Examples: **1. Tu (Tu oublies le devoir de littérature.) 2. Chantal (Chantal commence des études supérieures.) 3. Je (Je rencontre des amis à la fac.) 4. Les étudiants (Les étudiants détestent travailler.) 5. Nous (Nous cherchons un cours facile.) 6. Pascale (Pascale arrive avec des dictionnaires.)**

3 Expansion Have students add additional sentences to the captions below the drawings. Example: **1. Il étudie l'histoire. Il y a un examen.**

4 Suggestion Encourage students to personalize the information and to add additional information. Examples: **étudier** __a different subject__, **travailler dans** __a place__, and **regarder la télé.**

5 Suggestion Before beginning the activity, tell students to jot down a list of academic subjects that they can ask their partner about and to note their partner's responses. Examples: **Il/Elle aime** or **Il/Elle déteste**.

6 Suggestion Before beginning the activity, have students brainstorm adjectives they can use and write them on the board.

OPTIONS

Video Show the video episode again to give students additional input on verbs. Pause the video where appropriate to discuss how certain verbs were used and to ask comprehension questions.

Game Have students play a game of charades (**charades**) in groups of four or five. Tell students to pick a verb from the list on page 46 and act out the word. The other members of the group have to guess what the person is doing. Example: **Tu travailles?** The first person to guess correctly acts out the next charade.

National Standards: comparisons

Section Goals

In this section, students will learn:
- to form questions
- to express negation
- expressions for agreeing and disagreeing

Instructional Resources
WB/VM: Workbook, pp. 19–20
Lab Manual, p. 12
Lab MP3s
WB/VM/LM Answer Key
*IRCD-ROM: IRM (**Mise en pratique** answers; Lab Audioscript)*
espaces.vhlcentral.com: activities, downloads, reference tools

Suggestions
- Model the pronunciation and intonation of the different types of example questions. Point out that the questions on page 48 signal yes-no responses.
- Explain how to form inverted questions. Point out that inversion is usually used in written and formal language. Inversion with **je** is rare in spoken French, but seen in literary language, especially questions. Examples: **Ai-je le droit? Qui suis-je?**
- Point out that any question word can go before **est-ce que.** Example: **Que** as in **Qu'est-ce que c'est?**
- Explain the positions of **ne (n')** and **pas** in negative phrases and in inverted questions. If an infinitive follows a conjugated verb, **ne (n')** and **pas** surround the conjugated verb. Example: **Tu n'aimes pas regarder la vidéo?**
- Tell students that **ne (n')** in negative sentences is sometimes dropped in informal speech.
- Model the expressions indicating agreement and disagreement. Show how **mais** can precede **oui** as well as **non** if you want to say yes or no more emphatically.
- Make sure students grasp when to say **si** instead of **oui** by asking questions like these: **Tu n'étudies pas le français? (Si, j'étudie le français.) Je ne suis pas le professeur? (Si, vous êtes le professeur.)** Choose two students that are friends and ask: ____ **et** ____ **ne sont pas copains/copines? (Si, nous sommes copains/copines.)** Tell students to say, **Mais si!** if they want to contradict a negative question more forcefully.

3.2 Forming questions and expressing negation

Point de départ You have learned how to make affirmative and declarative statements in French. Now you will learn how to form questions and make negative statements.

Forming questions

- There are several ways to ask a question in French. The simplest way is to use the same wording as for a statement but with rising intonation (when speaking) or setting a question mark at the end (when writing). This method is considered informal.

Vous habitez à Bordeaux?	**Tu aimes le cours de français?**
You live in Bordeaux?	*You like French class?*

- A second way is to place the phrase **Est-ce que...** directly before a statement. If the next word begins with a vowel sound, use **Est-ce qu'**. Questions with **est-ce que** are somewhat formal.

Est-ce que vous parlez français?	**Est-ce qu'**il aime dessiner?
Do you speak French?	*Does he like to draw?*

- A third way is to place a tag question at the end of a statement. This method can be formal or informal.

On commence à deux heures, **d'accord**?	Nous mangeons à midi, **n'est-ce pas**?
We're starting at two o'clock, OK?	*We eat at noon, don't we?*

- A fourth way is to invert the order of the subject pronoun and the verb and hyphenate them. If the verb ends in a vowel and the subject pronoun is **il** or **elle**, **-t-** is inserted between the verb and the pronoun. Inversion is considered more formal.

Parlez-vous français?	**Mange-t-il** à midi?	**Est-elle** étudiante?
Do you speak French?	*Does he eat at noon?*	*Is she a student?*

- If the subject is a noun rather than a pronoun, invert the pronoun and the verb, and place the noun before them.

Le professeur parle-t-il français?	**Nina arrive-t-elle** demain?
Does the professor speak French?	*Does Nina arrive tomorrow?*

- The inverted form of **il y a** is **y a-t-il. C'est** becomes **est-ce.**

Y a-t-il une horloge dans la classe?	**Est-ce** le professeur de lettres?
Is there a clock in the class?	*Is he the humanities professor?*

- Use **pourquoi** to ask *why?* Use **parce que** (**parce qu'** before a vowel sound) in the answer to express *because.*

Pourquoi retrouves-tu Sophie ici?	**Parce qu'**elle habite près d'ici.
Why are you meeting Sophie here?	*Because she lives near here.*

MISE EN PRATIQUE

1 L'inversion Restate the questions using inversion.

1. Est-ce que vous parlez espagnol? Parlez-vous espagnol?
2. Est-ce qu'il étudie à Paris? Étudie-t-il à Paris?
3. Est-ce qu'ils voyagent avec des amis? Voyagent-ils avec des amis?
4. Est-ce que tu aimes les cours de langues? Aimes-tu les cours de langues?
5. Est-ce que le professeur parle anglais? Le professeur parle-t-il anglais?
6. Est-ce que les étudiants aiment dessiner? Les étudiants aiment-ils dessiner?

2 Les questions Ask the questions that correspond to the answers. Use **est-ce que/qu'** and inversion for each item.

MODÈLE

Nous habitons sur le campus.
Est-ce que vous habitez sur le campus? / Habitez-vous sur le campus?

1. Il mange au resto U. Est-ce qu'il mange au resto U? / Mange-t-il au resto U?
2. J'oublie les examens. Est-ce que tu oublies les examens? / Oublies-tu les examens?
3. François déteste les maths. Est-ce que François déteste les maths? / François déteste-t-il les maths?
4. Nous adorons voyager. Est-ce que vous adorez voyager? / Adorez-vous voyager?
5. Les cours ne commencent pas demain. Est-ce que les cours ne commencent pas demain? / Les cours ne commencent-ils pas demain?
6. Les étudiantes arrivent en classe. Est-ce que les étudiantes arrivent en classe? / Les étudiantes arrivent-elles en classe?

3 Complétez Complete the conversation with the correct forms of the verbs. Act it out with a partner. Suggested answers

MYLÈNE Salut, Arnaud. Ça va?
ARNAUD Oui, ça va. Alors (*So*)... (1) Tu aimes les cours?
MYLÈNE J'adore le cours de sciences po, mais je déteste l'informatique.
ARNAUD (2) Pourquoi est-ce que tu détestes l'informatique?
MYLÈNE Parce que le prof est très strict.
ARNAUD (3) Il y a des étudiants sympathiques, n'est-ce pas?
MYLÈNE Oui, il y a des étudiants sympathiques... Et demain? (4) Tu retrouves Béatrice?
ARNAUD Peut-être, mais demain je retrouve aussi Dominique.
MYLÈNE (5) Tu cherches une petite amie?
ARNAUD Pas du tout!

OPTIONS

Pairs Write ten statements on the board or a transparency. Have students work in pairs. Tell them to convert the statements into questions by inverting the subject and verb. When they have finished writing the questions, call on volunteers to read their questions aloud. This activity can also be done orally with the class.

Extra Practice Using the same ten statements from the previous activity, ask students to form tag questions. Encourage them to use both **d'accord?** and **n'est-ce pas?** Have students answer some of the questions. Then add a few negative statements so that students will have to respond with **si**.

COMMUNICATION

4 **Au café** In pairs, take turns asking each other questions about the drawing. Use verbs from the list as well as your own. Answers will vary.

MODÈLE

Étudiant(e) 1: *Monsieur Laurent parle à Madame Martin, n'est-ce pas?*
Étudiant(e) 2: *Mais non. Il déteste parler!*

arriver	dessiner	manger	partager
chercher	étudier	oublier	rencontrer

5 **Questions** You and your partner want to know each other better. Take turns asking each other questions. Modify or add elements as needed. Some answers will vary.

MODÈLE aimer / l'art

Étudiant(e) 1: *Est-ce que tu aimes l'art?*
Étudiant(e) 2: *Oui, j'adore l'art.*

1. habiter / à l'université
   Est-ce que tu habites à l'université?
2. étudier / avec / amis
   Est-ce que tu étudies avec des amis?
3. penser qu'il y a / cours / intéressant / à la fac
   Est-ce que tu penses qu'il y a des cours intéressants à la fac?
4. cours de sciences / être / facile
   Est-ce que les cours de sciences sont faciles?
5. aimer mieux / biologie / ou / physique
   Est-ce que tu aimes mieux la biologie ou la physique?
6. retrouver / copains / au resto U
   Est-ce que tu retrouves des copains au resto U?

6 **Confirmez** In groups of three, confirm whether the statements are true of your school. Correct any untrue statements by making them negative. Answers will vary.

MODÈLE

Les profs sont désagréables.
Pas du tout, les profs ne sont pas désagréables.

1. Les cours d'informatique sont inutiles.
2. Il y a des étudiants de nationalité allemande.
3. Nous mangeons une cuisine excellente au resto U.
4. Tous (*All*) les étudiants habitent sur le campus.
5. Les cours de chimie sont faciles.
6. Nous travaillons pour obtenir un diplôme.

Expressing negation

- To make a sentence negative in French, place **ne** (**n'** before a vowel sound) before the conjugated verb and **pas** after it.

Je **ne dessine pas** bien.
I don't draw well.

Elles **n'étudient pas** la chimie.
They don't study chemistry.

- In the construction [*conjugated verb* + *infinitive*], **ne** (**n'**) comes before the conjugated verb and **pas** after it.

Abdel **n'aime pas étudier**.
Abdel doesn't like to study.

Vous **ne détestez pas travailler**?
You don't hate to work?

- In questions with inversion, place **ne** before the inversion and **pas** after it.

Abdel **n'aime-t-il pas** étudier?
Doesn't Abdel like to study?

Ne détestez-vous pas travailler?
Don't you hate to work?

- Use these expressions to respond to a statement or a question that requires a *yes* or *no* answer.

Expressions of agreement and disagreement

oui	*yes*	**(mais) non**	*no (but of course not)*
bien sûr	*of course*	**pas du tout**	*not at all*
moi/toi non plus	*me/you neither*	**peut-être**	*maybe, perhaps*

Vous mangez souvent au resto U?
Do you eat often in the cafeteria?

Non, pas du tout.
No, not at all.

- Use **si** instead of **oui** to contradict a negative question.

Il **ne cherche pas** le sac à dos?
Isn't he looking for the backpack?

Si. Il cherche aussi les crayons.
Yes. He's looking for the pencils too.

Essayez! Make questions out of these statements. Use **est-ce que/qu'** in items 1–6 and inversion in 7–12.

	Statement	Question
1.	Vous mangez au resto U.	*Est-ce que vous mangez au resto U?*
2.	Ils adorent les devoirs.	Est-ce qu'ils adorent les devoirs?
3.	La biologie est difficile.	Est-ce que la biologie est difficile?
4.	Tu travailles.	Est-ce que tu travailles?
5.	Elles cherchent le prof.	Est-ce qu'elles cherchent le prof?
6.	Aude voyage beaucoup.	Est-ce qu'Aude voyage beaucoup?
7.	Vous arrivez demain.	*Arrivez-vous demain?*
8.	L'étudiante oublie.	L'étudiante oublie-t-elle?
9.	La physique est utile.	La physique est-elle utile?
10.	Il y a deux salles de classe.	Y a-t-il deux salles de classe?
11.	Ils n'habitent pas à Québec.	N'habitent-ils pas à Québec?
12.	C'est le professeur de gestion.	Est-ce le professeur de gestion?

Essayez! Have students repeat using inversion for items 1–6 and **est-ce que/qu'** in 7–12.

1 Expansion Have students work in pairs, and take turns asking and answering the questions in the negative.

2 Expansion Have students write two additional statements. Tell them to exchange papers with a partner who will ask the questions that would elicit those statements.

3 Expansion Have pairs of students create a similar conversation, replacing the answers and some of the questions with information that is true for them. Then have volunteers act out their conversations for the class.

4 Suggestion Tell students to vary the method of asking questions instead of always using a tag question as in the **modèle**.

5 Suggestions
- Have two volunteers read the **modèle** aloud.
- After students have completed the activity, ask volunteers to report what they learned about their partner.

6 Suggestion Encourage students to use as many expressions indicating agreement or disagreement as they can.

6 Expansion Have groups write three additional true/false statements about their school. Ask several groups to read their statements and have the class respond to them. Encourage students to respond with **Mais oui!** or **Mais non!** where appropriate.

OPTIONS

Video Replay the video episode, having students focus on the different forms of questions used. Tell them to write down each question they hear. Stop the video where suitable to give students time to write and to discuss what was heard.

Extra Practice Prepare eight questions. Write their answers on the board in random order. Then read your questions aloud, having students match the question to the appropriate answer. Make sure that only one of the possible answers corresponds logically to the questions you ask. Example: **Pourquoi ____ déteste-t-il les maths? (Il n'aime pas le prof.)**

Synthèse

Instructional Resources
IRCD-ROM: IRM (Info Gap Activities); Testing Program, pp. 9–12; Test Files; Testing Program MP3s; Test Generator espaces.vhlcentral.com: activities, downloads, reference tools

1 Expansion Have students compare two of their own classes that are very different, such as a large lecture and a small class, and explain which one they prefer. This activity can be done orally or in writing.

2 Suggestion Have two volunteers read the **modèle** aloud. Tell students to add at least two more items to the list, one that applies to both of them and one that does not.

3 Suggestion As students share their responses with the class, make a list of their likes and dislikes on the board under the headings **Nous aimons** and **Nous n'aimons pas.**

4 Suggestion Tell students they may use adjectives that are not in the list.

5 Suggestion Before beginning the activity, have the class decide on names for the people in the drawings. Also have them brainstorm possible relationships between the people, for example, strangers meeting for the first time or classmates.

6 Suggestion Divide the class into pairs and distribute the Info Gap Handouts in the IRM on the IRCD-ROM for this activity. Give students ten minutes to complete the activity.

6 Expansion Have pairs compare their answers with another pair to confirm the people's likes and dislikes. Then ask a few groups to share some of their sentences with the class.

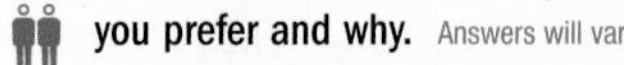

1 Des styles différents In pairs, compare these two very different classes. Then, tell your partner which class you prefer and why. Answers will vary.

2 Les activités In pairs, discuss whether these expressions apply to both of you. React to every answer you hear. Answers will vary.

MODÈLE

Étudiant(e) 1: *Est-ce que tu étudies le week-end?*
Étudiant(e) 2: *Non! Je n'aime pas travailler le week-end.*
Étudiant(e) 1: *Moi non plus. J'aime mieux travailler le soir.*

1. adorer le resto U
2. être reçu à un examen difficile
3. étudier au café
4. manger souvent (*often*) des sushis
5. oublier les devoirs
6. parler espagnol
7. travailler le soir à la bibliothèque
8. voyager souvent

3 Le campus In pairs, prepare ten questions inspired by the list and what you know about your campus. Together, survey as many classmates as possible to find out what they like and dislike on campus. Answers will vary.

MODÈLE

Étudiant(e) 1: *Est-ce que tu aimes travailler à la bibliothèque?*
Étudiant(e) 2: *Non, pas trop. Je travaille plutôt au café.*

bibliothèque	étudiant	resto U
bureau	gymnase	salle de classe
cours	librairie	salle d'ordinateurs

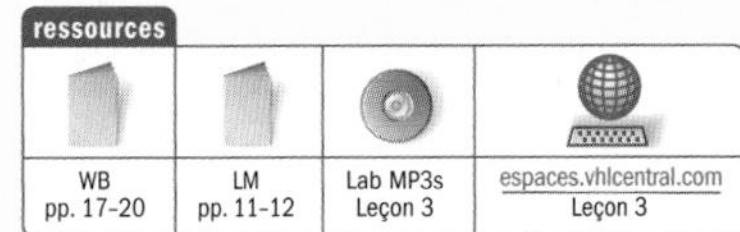

ressources
WB pp. 17-20
LM pp. 11-12
Lab MP3s Leçon 3
espaces.vhlcentral.com Leçon 3

4 Pourquoi? Survey as many classmates as possible to find out what adjectives they would pick to describe these academic subjects. Ask if they like them and why. Tally the most popular answers for each subject. Answers will vary.

MODÈLE

Étudiant(e) 1: *Est-ce que tu aimes la philosophie?*
Étudiant(e) 2: *Pas tellement.*
Étudiant(e) 1: *Pourquoi?*
Étudiant(e) 2: *Parce que c'est trop difficile.*

1. la biologie	a. agréable
2. la chimie	b. amusant
3. l'histoire de l'art	c. désagréable
4. l'économie	d. difficile
5. la gestion	e. facile
6. les langues	f. important
7. les mathématiques	g. inutile
8. la psychologie	h. utile

5 Les conversations In pairs, act out a short conversation between the people shown in each drawing. They should greet each other, describe what they are doing, and discuss their likes or dislikes. Choose your favorite skit and role-play it for another pair. Answers will vary.

MODÈLE

Étudiant(e) 1: *Bonjour, Aurélie.*
Étudiant(e) 2: *Salut! Tu travailles, n'est-ce pas?*

6 Les portraits Your instructor will give you and a partner a set of drawings showing the likes and dislikes of eight people. Discuss each person's tastes. Do not look at each other's worksheet. Answers will vary.

MODÈLE

Étudiant(e) 1: *Sarah n'aime pas travailler.*
Étudiant(e) 2: *Mais elle adore manger.*

OPTIONS

Extra Practice Have students write a brief paragraph describing the activities they like or don't like to do. Collect the descriptions and read a few of them to the class. Have the class guess who wrote each description by asking: **Est-ce que c'est...?**

Small Groups Tell students to turn to the **Roman-photo** on pages 47–48 and write five comprehension questions based on the dialogue. Then have them get together in groups of three or four, and take turns asking and answering each other's questions.

Interlude

Sénégal fast-food

*The song **Sénégal fast-food** deals with the immigration of Africans to other countries like France, Italy, and Japan. The song's narrator is getting married one day and leaving Mali the next. When it's midnight in Tokyo, it is 5:00 p.m. in Mali. He is wondering what time it is in Heaven. Those who leave the country hope that the children who stay behind will not forget them.*

*AMADOU BAGAYOKO (1954–) and MARIAM DOUMBIA (1958–) were born in Bamako, the capital of Mali. He lost his eyesight as a teenager, and she lost hers at age five. They met at the **Institut des jeunes aveugles** (Institute for Blind Youth), which opened in 1973 in Bamako. They got married in 1980 and had three children. They became famous all over Africa but it was only in the late 1990s that they became known in Europe. They write their songs in Bambara, their native language, and then translate them into French.*

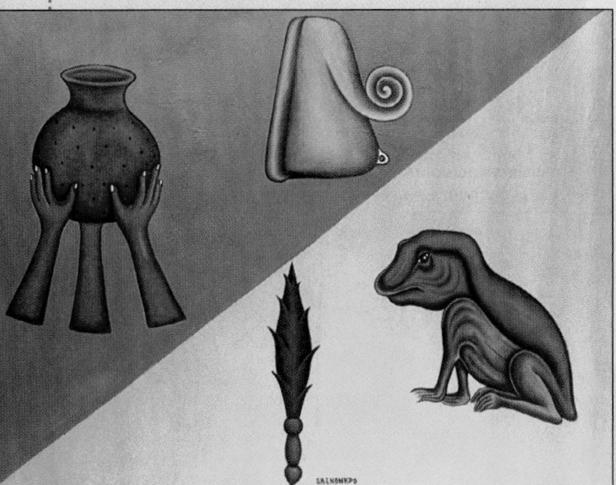

Gbenonkpo

*CYPRIEN TOKOUDAGBA (1939–) is a renowned artist from Benin, West Africa. Master of voodoo, he became famous by painting murals on temples. Gbenonkpo is the name of the movement fighting for the development of the Wémê valley in Benin, which has always been marginalized. The painting represented here depicts the will to leave the sand behind and make water accessible to everyone as a means of curbing emigration, a topic also central to the song **Sénégal fast-food**.*

Activité

Choose the best option. Some answers may vary. Suggested answers below.

1. Which of these statements might the singers of ***Sénégal fast-food*** say?
   - **a.** Nous sommes japonais.
   - **(b.)** Nous sommes maliens.
   - **c.** Nous sommes italiens.
2. Which of these excerpts from ***Sénégal fast-food*** refers to the process of applying for an immigrant visa?
   - **a.** Il n'y a pas de problèmes, j'aime!
   - **b.** Moi ici, toi là-bas...
   - **(c.)** Au consulat numéro 39...
3. Which adjectives would you pick to describe the painting?
   - **a.** sincère et pessimiste
   - **(b.)** intéressante et différente
   - **c.** désagréable et charmante

SUR INTERNET

Go to espaces.vhlcentral.com for more information related to this **Interlude**.

Section Goals

In this section, students will learn about:

- Amadou Bagayoko and Mariam Doumbia
- Cyprien Tokoudagba

Instructional Resources
espaces.vhlcentral.com: activities, downloads, reference tools

Sénégal fast-food

- To check comprehension, ask these questions.

1. What social issue does the song ***Sénégal fast-food*** highlight? (the immigration of Africans to other countries like France, Italy, and Spain)
2. Where were Amadou Bagayoko and Mariam Doumbia born? (Bamako, Mali)
3. In what language do they write their songs? (Bambara)
4. Why is their success remarkable? (They are both blind.)

- Have students locate the following places on the map of Africa in **Appendice A**, page 546: Benin, Senegal, and Bamako, Mali.

Gbenonkpo

- Point out that Tokoudagba's art is characterized by simple shapes, vivid colors, and strong contours. The imagery often recalls ceremonies and talismans.
- Have students describe the images in the painting. Then ask: Which part of the painting represents the water? (the blue area) Which part represents the sand? (the yellow area)
- Tokoudagba lives in Abomey, Benin. Since 1987, he has worked as a restorer at the **Musée historique d'Abomey**. He began sketching figures and sculpting in clay when he was in primary school. In addition to his paintings, he has created bas-reliefs, sculptures, and wall paintings for temples in Abomey, Ghana, Togo, and Nigeria.

OPTIONS

Amadou et Mariam The Afro-Pop music of Amadou (vocalist and guitarist) and Mariam (vocalist) is a combination of blues, rock, and Malian. As children, both demonstrated their musical talents at an early age. Amadou was learning to play the harmonica and flute by the time he was ten. At the age of six, Mariam was performing at weddings and baptisms. The couple began making music together in 1977. ***Mon amour, ma chérie*** (1998) was their first hit single. Their album ***Dimanche à Bamako*** (2004) went platinum and was considered one of the best world music records of the year.

Extra Practice Bring in pictures from books or the Internet of additional artworks by Tokoudagba or other modern African artists. Have students discuss and compare them.

Section Goals

In this section, students will learn and practice vocabulary related to:
- talking about schedules
- the days of the week
- sequencing events

Instructional Resources

*IRCD-ROM: Transparency #18; IRM (**Vocabulaire supplémentaire; Mise en pratique** answers; Textbook Audioscript; Lab Audioscript; **Feuilles d'activités**)*
Textbook MP3s
WB/VM: Workbook, pp. 21–22
Lab Manual, p. 13
Lab MP3s
WB/VM/LM Answer Key
espaces.vhlcentral.com: activities, downloads, reference tools

Suggestions

- Write days of the week across the board and present them like this: **Aujourd'hui, c'est ____. Demain, c'est ____. Après, c'est ____.**
- Write the following questions and answers on the board, explaining their meaning:
  —Quel jour sommes-nous?
  —Nous sommes ____.
  —C'est quel jour demain?
  —Demain, c'est ____.
  —C'est quand l'examen?
  —L'examen est ____.
  Ask students the questions.
- Tell students Monday is the first day of the week in France.
- Point out that days of the week are masculine and lowercase.
- Explain the differences between **le matin/la matinée, le soir/la soirée,** and **le jour/la journée.**
- Introduce new vocabulary using **Transparency #18**. Give the student a name, for example, Henri. Ask students picture-based questions. Examples: **Quel jour Henri assiste-t-il au cours d'économie? Il assiste au cours d'économie le matin ou le soir? Quels jours visite-t-il Paris avec Annette?**
- Point out that **visiter** is used with places, not people.
- Additional vocabulary for this lesson can be found in the **Vocabulaire supplémentaire** in the IRM on the IRCD-ROM.

Leçon 4

You will learn how to...
- say when things happen
- discuss your schedule

Une semaine à la fac

Vocabulaire

demander	*to ask*
échouer	*to fail*
écouter	*to listen (to)*
enseigner	*to teach*
expliquer	*to explain*
trouver	*to find; to think*
Quel jour sommes-nous?	*What day is it?*
un an	*year*
une/cette année	*one/this year*
après	*after*
après-demain	*day after tomorrow*
un/cet après-midi	*a/this afternoon*
aujourd'hui	*today*
demain (matin/après-midi/soir)	*tomorrow (morning/afternoon/evening)*
un jour	*day*
une journée	*day*
un/ce matin	*a/this morning*
la matinée	*morning*
un mois/ce mois-ci	*month/this month*
une/cette nuit	*a/this night*
une/cette semaine	*a/this week*
un/ce soir	*an/this evening*
une soirée	*evening*
un/le/ce week-end	*a/the/this weekend*
dernier/dernière	*last*
premier/première	*first*
prochain(e)	*next*

ressources

WB pp. 21-22	LM p. 13	Text MP3s Leçon 4	Lab MP3s Leçon 4	espaces.vhlcentral.com Leçon 4

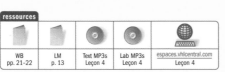

OPTIONS

Extra Practice Write **le matin, l'après-midi,** and **le soir** on the board or a transparency. Have your students tell when they do various activites, such as **préparer les cours, assister aux cours, téléphoner à des amis, écouter de la musique, regarder la télévision, rentrer à la maison,** and **dîner.**

Pairs Have the class brainstorm a list of nouns associated with verbs from the **Contextes**. For example, for the verb **regarder**, students might think of **télévision** or **vidéo**. Write the verbs and nouns on the board as students say them. Then have students work in pairs. Give them five minutes to write original sentences using these words. Ask volunteers to write their sentences on the board.

Attention!

Use the masculine definite article **le** + [*day of the week*] when an activity is done on a weekly basis. Omit **le** when it is done on a specific day.

Le prof enseigne le lundi.
The professor teaches on Mondays.

Je passe un examen lundi.
I take a test on Monday.

samedi | dimanche

visiter Paris avec Annette

rentrer à la maison

Mise en pratique

1 Écoutez You will hear Lorraine describing her schedule. Listen carefully and indicate whether the statements are **vrai** or **faux**.

	Vrai	Faux
1. Lorraine étudie à l'université le soir.	☐	☑
2. Elle trouve le cours de mathématiques facile.	☐	☑
3. Elle étudie le week-end.	☐	☑
4. Lorraine étudie la chimie le mardi et le jeudi matin.	☐	☑
5. Le professeur de mathématiques explique bien.	☐	☑
6. Lorraine regarde la télévision, écoute de la musique ou téléphone à Claire et Anne le soir.	☑	☐
7. Lorraine travaille dans (*in*) une librairie.	☐	☑
8. Elle étudie l'histoire le mardi et le jeudi matin.	☑	☐
9. Lorraine adore dîner avec sa famille le week-end.	☑	☐
10. Lorraine rentre à la maison le soir.	☐	☑

2 Quel jour sommes-nous? Complete each statement with the correct day of the week.

1. Aujourd'hui, c'est ___Answers will vary.___.
2. Demain, c'est ___Answers will vary.___.
3. Après-demain, c'est ___Answers will vary.___.
4. Le week-end, c'est le ___samedi et le dimanche___.
5. Le premier jour de la semaine en France, c'est le ___lundi___.
6. Les jours du cours de français sont ___Answers will vary.___.
7. Mon (*My*) jour préféré de la semaine, c'est le ___Answers will vary.___.
8. Je travaille à la bibliothèque le ___Answers will vary.___.

3 La classe de Mme Arnaud Complete this paragraph by selecting the correct verb from the list below. Make sure to change the verb form. Some verbs will not be used.

demander	expliquer	rentrer
écouter	passer un examen	travailler
enseigner	préparer	trouver
étudier	regarder	visiter

Madame Arnaud (1) ___travaille___ à l'université. Elle (2) ___enseigne___ un cours de français. Elle (3) ___explique___ les verbes et la grammaire aux étudiants. Le vendredi, en classe, les étudiants (4) ___regardent___ une vidéo en français ou (*or*) (5) ___écoutent___ de la musique française. Ce week-end, ils (6) ___étudient___ pour (*for*) (7) ___préparer___ un examen très difficile lundi matin. Je (8) ___travaille___ beaucoup pour ce cours, mais mes (*my*) amis et moi, nous (9) ___trouvons___ la classe sympa.

1 Tapescript Cette année à l'université j'étudie: la chimie, le lundi et le mercredi matin; l'histoire, le mardi et le jeudi matin; l'art, le vendredi matin et les mathématiques, le lundi et le mercredi après-midi. Je déteste les mathématiques; le professeur n'explique pas bien et je trouve le cours difficile. J'étudie l'après-midi quand je rentre à la maison. Le soir, je ne travaille pas, alors je regarde la télévision, j'écoute de la musique ou je téléphone à mes amies, Claire et Anne. Le week-end, j'adore rendre visite à ma famille pour dîner! *(On Textbook MP3s)*

1 Suggestions

- Before playing the recording, have students read the statements and identify the expressions that describe when things occur. Examples: **le soir, le week-end**, and **le jeudi matin.**
- Go over the answers with the class. If students have difficulty, replay the recording.

2 Expansions

- Give these items for more practice. **9. Le jour après lundi, c'est ____. 10. Il n'y a pas de cours de français le ____.**
- Have students repeat items 1–5 from the perspective of a different day of the week.

3 Expansion Have pairs write original sentences about Madame Arnaud and her class using the verbs that weren't in this paragraph. Ask volunteers to read their sentences aloud.

OPTIONS

TPR Create a schedule for an imaginary student using the whole class. Assign each day of the week to a different student and assign each of the remaining students a different activity. As you describe the schedule, students arrange themselves as a page in a weekly day-planner, starting with the day of the week and then each activity you mention. Example: **Le lundi matin, j'assiste au cours. L'après-midi, je passe un examen de français. Le soir, je dîne au resto U.**

Extra Practice Have students write a paragraph similar to the one in **Activité 3** describing your French class or a different class. They should use as many verbs from the list as possible. Ask volunteers to read their paragraph aloud.

4 Suggestion Before doing this activity, you may want to write a short list of musical genres on the board for item 5. Also tell students that **quand** means *when.*

4 Expansions
- Have volunteers report what they learned about their classmate.
- To practice the **nous** forms, ask students what they have in common with their partner.

5 Suggestion Tell students to switch roles after completing the conversation so that both students have the opportunity to ask and answer questions.

6 Suggestion To save time in class, assign the written part of this activity the day before as homework.

7 Suggestions
- Have two volunteers read the **modèle** aloud. Make sure students understand the directions. Then distribute the **Feuilles d'activités** from the IRM on the IRCD-ROM.
- Have students repeat the activity with a different partner.

Communication

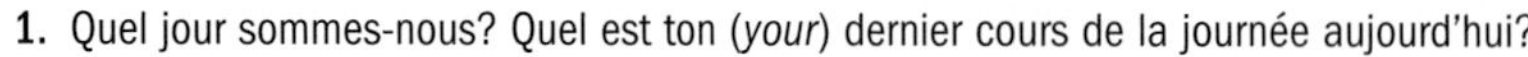

4 Conversez Interview a classmate. Answers will vary.

1. Quel jour sommes-nous? Quel est ton (*your*) dernier cours de la journée aujourd'hui?
2. Quand est le prochain cours de français?
3. Quand rentres-tu à la maison? Demain soir? Après-demain?
4. Est-ce que tu prépares un examen cette année?
5. Est-ce que tu écoutes la radio? Quel genre de musique?
6. Quand téléphones-tu à tes (*your*) amis?
7. Est-ce que tu regardes la télévision le matin, l'après-midi ou (*or*) le soir?
8. Est-ce que tu dînes dans un restaurant ce mois-ci?

5 Le premier jour à la fac You make a new friend in your French class and want to know what his or her class schedule is like this semester. With a partner, prepare a conversation to perform for the class where you: Answers will vary.

- ask his or her name
- ask what classes he or she is taking
- ask on which days of the week he or she has class
- ask at which times of day (morning or afternoon) he or she has class

6 Le week-end Write your schedule for a typical weekend where you show the activities you do. Use the verbs you know. Compare your schedule with a classmate's, and talk about the different activities that you do and when. Be prepared to discuss your results with the class. Answers will vary.

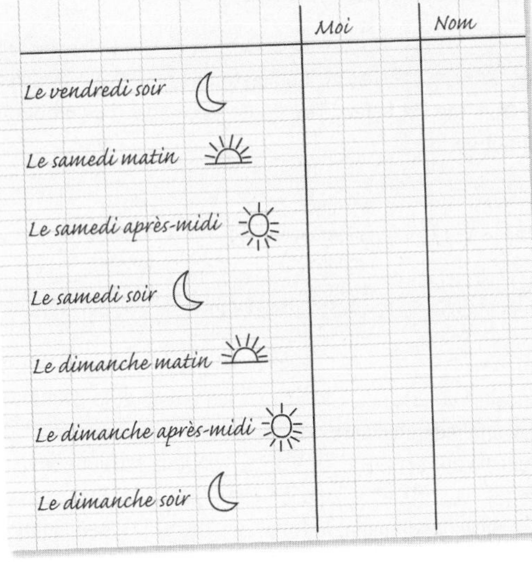

7 Bataille navale Your instructor will give you a worksheet. Choose four spaces on your chart and mark them with a battleship. Work with a partner and formulate questions by using the subjects in the first column and the verbs in the first row to find out where he or she has placed his or her submarines. Whoever "sinks" the most battleships wins. Answers will vary.

MODÈLE

Étudiant(e) 1: *Est-ce que Luc et Sabine travaillent le week-end?*
Étudiant(e) 2: *Oui, ils travaillent le week-end.*
(if you marked that square.)
Non, ils ne travaillent pas le week-end.
(if you didn't mark that square.)

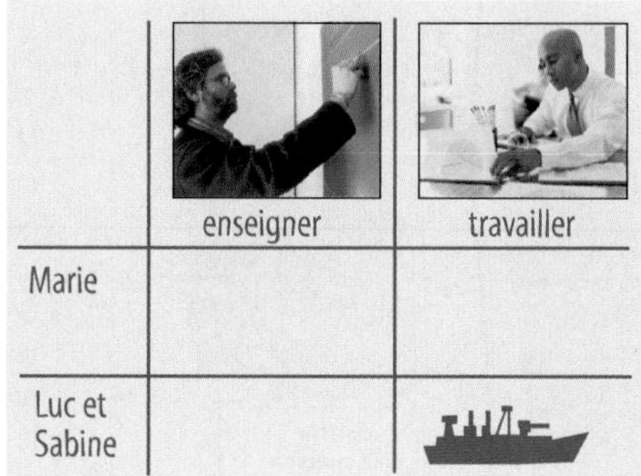

OPTIONS

Game Play a memory game in which the first player says one activity he or she does on a particular day of the week. The next player repeats what the first person said, then adds what he or she does on the following day. The third player must remember what the first two people said before saying what he or she does on the next day. Continue until the end of a week. If someone makes a mistake, then choose another student to continue.

Small Groups Have students work in groups of three. Tell them to take turns asking what days of the week TV shows are on and answering. Example: **Quel(s) jour(s) est l'émission *CSI*?**

Les sons et les lettres

The letter r

The French **r** is very different from the English *r*. In English, an *r* is pronounced in the middle and toward the front of the mouth. The French **r** is pronounced in the throat.

You have seen that an **-er** at the end of a word is usually pronounced **-ay**, as in the English word *way*, but without the glide sound.

chanter **manger** **expliquer** **aimer**

In most other circumstances, the French **r** has a very different sound. Pronunciation of the French **r** varies according to its position in a word. Note the different ways the **r** is pronounced in these words.

rivière **littérature** **ordinateur** **devoir**

If an **r** falls between two vowels or before a vowel, it is pronounced with slightly more friction.

rare **garage** **Europe** **rose**

An **r** sound before a consonant or at the end of a word is pronounced with slightly less friction.

porte **bourse** **adore** **jour**

Prononcez Practice saying the following words aloud.

1. crayon
2. professeur
3. plaisir
4. différent
5. terrible
6. architecture
7. trouver
8. restaurant
9. rentrer
10. regarder
11. lettres
12. réservé
13. être
14. dernière
15. arriver
16. après

Articulez Practice saying the following sentences aloud.

1. Au revoir, Professeur Colbert!
2. Rose arrive en retard mardi.
3. Mercredi, c'est le dernier jour des cours.
4. Robert et Roger adorent écouter la radio.
5. La corbeille à papier, c'est quarante-quatre euros!
6. Les parents de Richard sont brillants et très agréables.

Dictons Practice reading these sayings aloud.

Quand le renard prêche, gare aux oies.[2]

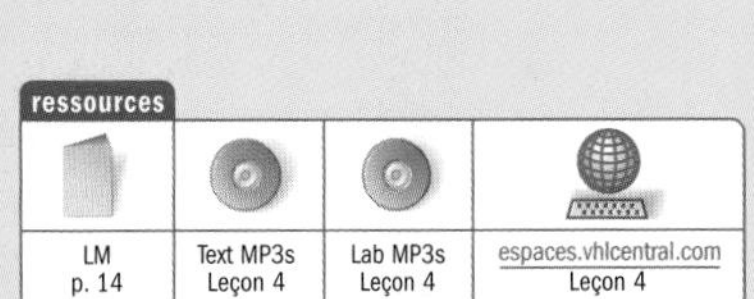

[1] Nothing ventured, nothing gained.
[2] When the fox preaches, watch your geese.

Section Goals

In this section, students will learn about the letter **r**.

Instructional Resources
Textbook MP3s
Lab Manual, p. 14
Lab MP3s
WB/VM/LM Answer Key
IRCD-ROM: IRM (Textbook Audioscript; Lab Audioscript)
espaces.vhlcentral.com: activities, downloads, reference tools

Suggestions

- Model the pronunciation of words and expressions with **r** from **Contextes**. Then have students repeat. Examples: **regarder, préparer un examen**, etc.
- Explain that the French **r** is more like the **k** sound than the English **r**. The **k** is produced by totally blocking, then releasing the air passage in the back of the mouth. Pronouncing a French **r** is similar, but instead of totally blocking the air passage, the passage is only partially blocked with the back of the tongue.
- Model the pronunciation of each example word and have students repeat.
- Ask students to provide words or expressions from previous lessons that contain the letter **r**. Examples: **au revoir, très bien, professeur**, and **merci**.
- The explanation and exercises are recorded on the Textbook MP3s CD-ROM and are available on the **ESPACES** web site. You may want to play them in class so students hear French speakers other than yourself.

Dictons Ask students if they can think of an English saying that is similar to **«Quand le renard prêche, gare aux oies.»** (*Don't let a fox guard the hen house.*)

OPTIONS

Extra Practice Dictate five familiar words with the **r** in different places, saying each one at least two times. Examples: **librairie, résultat, jour, chercher**, and **montre**. Then write them on the board or a transparency and have students check their spelling.

Extra Practice Use these sentences with the letter **r** for additional oral practice or dictation. **1. Renée regarde un garçon américain. 2. Le colocataire de Grégoire est réservé. 3. Je travaille le mercredi après-midi et le vendredi soir. 4. Nous trouvons le cours d'histoire très intéressant.**

Section Goals

In this section, students will learn functional phrases for talking about their schedules and classes and telling time.

Instructional Resources
WB/VM: Video Manual, pp. 217–218
WB/VM/LM Answer Key
Video CD-ROM
Video on DVD
*IRCD-ROM: IRM (Videoscript; **Roman-photo** Translations)*
espaces.vhlcentral.com: activities, downloads, reference tools

Video Recap: Leçon 3 Before doing this **Roman-photo**, review the previous one with this activity.

1. Comment est-ce que Rachid trouve le cours de sciences po? (intéressant et utile)
2. Comment s'appelle le colocataire de Rachid? (David)
3. Comment est-ce que David trouve l'université française? (C'est différent de l'université américaine, mais c'est intéressant.)
4. Quels cours est-ce que David aime? (littérature et histoire françaises)
5. Stéphane a des problèmes dans quels cours? (français, maths, chimie et histoire-géo)

Video Synopsis At **Le P'tit Bistrot**, Rachid, Sandrine, Amina and David discuss their schedules. Astrid arrives; she is supposed to study with Stéphane. While she waits, Astrid talks about **le bac** and how Stéphane never does his homework. Rachid and Astrid decide to go to the park because they think Stéphane is there. At the park, Astrid and Stéphane argue. When Stéphane complains about his problems at school, Rachid offers to help him study.

Suggestions

- Have volunteers play the roles of Rachid, Sandrine, Amina, David, and Astrid in the scenes that match video stills 1–5.
- Have the class predict what will happen in scenes 6–10. Write predictions on the board.
- Read remaining scenes correcting the predictions. Ask questions to help students summarize this episode.

NATIONAL STANDARDS communication cultures

On trouve une solution.

PERSONNAGES

Amina

Astrid

David

Rachid

Sandrine

Stéphane

1

À la terrasse du café...
RACHID Alors, on a rendez-vous avec David demain à cinq heures moins le quart, pour rentrer chez nous.
SANDRINE Aujourd'hui, c'est mercredi. Demain... jeudi. Le mardi et le jeudi j'ai cours de chant de trois heures vingt à quatre heures et demie. C'est parfait!
AMINA Pas de problème. J'ai cours de stylisme...

2

AMINA Salut, Astrid!
ASTRID Bonjour.
RACHID Astrid, je te présente David, mon (*my*) coloc' américain.
DAVID Alors, cette année, tu as des cours très difficiles, n'est-ce pas?

3

ASTRID Oui? Pourquoi?
DAVID Ben, Stéphane pense que les cours sont très difficiles.
ASTRID Ouais, Stéphane, il assiste au cours mais... il ne fait pas ses (*his*) devoirs et il n'écoute pas les profs. Cette année est très importante, parce que nous avons le bac...
DAVID Ah, le bac...

6

Au parc...
ASTRID Stéphane! Quelle heure est-il? Tu n'as pas de montre?
STÉPHANE Oh, Astrid, excuse-moi! Le mercredi, je travaille avec Astrid au café sur le cours de maths...
ASTRID Et le mercredi après-midi, il oublie! Tu n'as pas peur du bac, toi!

7

STÉPHANE Tu as tort, j'ai très peur du bac! Mais je n'ai pas envie de passer mes (*my*) journées, mes soirées et mes week-ends avec des livres!
ASTRID Je suis d'accord avec toi, Stéphane! J'ai envie de passer les week-ends avec mes copains... des copains qui n'oublient pas les rendez-vous!

8

RACHID Écoute, Stéphane, tu as des problèmes avec ta (*your*) mère, avec Astrid aussi.
STÉPHANE Oui, et j'ai d'énormes problèmes au lycée. Je déteste le bac.
RACHID Il n'est pas tard pour commencer à travailler pour être reçu au bac.
STÉPHANE Tu crois, Rachid?

ACTIVITÉS

1 Vrai ou faux? Choose whether each statement is **vrai** or **faux.**

1. Le mardi et le mercredi, Sandrine a (*has*) cours de chant. Faux.
2. Le jeudi, Amina a cours de stylisme. Vrai.
3. Astrid pense que le bac est impossible. Faux.
4. La famille de David est allemande. Faux.
5. Le mercredi, Stéphane travaille avec Astrid au café sur le cours de maths. Vrai.
6. Stéphane a beaucoup de problèmes. Vrai.
7. Rachid est optimiste. Vrai.
8. Stéphane dîne chez Rachid le samedi. Faux.
9. Le sport est très important pour Stéphane. Vrai.
10. Astrid est fâchée (*angry*) contre Stéphane. Vrai.

OPTIONS

Avant de regarder la vidéo Write the title **On trouve une solution** on the board. Ask the class: Who has a problem in the video? What is it? Then ask the class to predict how the problem will be solved.

Regarder la vidéo Show the video episode and have students give you a play-by-play description of the action. Write their descriptions on the board. Then show the episode again so students can add more details to the description.

Les amis organisent des rendez-vous.

4

5

RACHID C'est un examen très important que les élèves français passent la dernière année de lycée pour continuer en études supérieures.
DAVID Euh, n'oublie pas, je suis de famille française.
ASTRID Oui, et c'est difficile, mais ce n'est pas impossible. Stéphane trouve que les études ne sont pas intéressantes. Le sport, oui, mais pas les études.

RACHID Le sport? Tu cherches Stéphane, n'est-ce pas? On trouve Stéphane au parc! Allons-y, Astrid.
ASTRID D'accord. À demain!

9

10

RACHID Oui. Mais le sport, c'est la dernière des priorités. Écoute, dimanche prochain, tu dînes chez moi et on trouve une solution.
STÉPHANE Rachid, tu n'as pas envie de donner des cours à un lycéen nul comme moi!
RACHID Mais si, j'ai très envie d'enseigner les maths...

STÉPHANE Bon, j'accepte. Merci, Rachid. C'est sympa.
RACHID De rien. À plus tard!

Expressions utiles

Talking about your schedule

- **Alors, on a rendez-vous demain à cinq heures moins le quart, pour rentrer chez nous.**
  So, we're meeting tomorrow at quarter to five to go home (our home).
- **J'ai cours de chant de trois heures vingt à quatre heures et demie.**
  I have voice (singing) class from three-twenty to four-thirty.
- **J'ai cours de stylisme de deux heures à quatre heures vingt.**
  I have fashion design class from two o'clock to four-twenty.
- **Quelle heure est-il?**
  What time is it?
- **Tu n'as pas de montre?**
  You don't have a watch?

Talking about school

- **Nous avons le bac.**
  We have the **bac**.
- **Il ne fait pas ses devoirs.**
  He doesn't do his homework.
- **Tu n'as pas peur du bac!**
  You're not afraid of the **bac**!
- **Tu as tort, j'ai très peur du bac!**
  You're wrong, I'm very afraid of the **bac**!
- **Je suis d'accord avec toi.**
  I agree with you.
- **J'ai d'énormes problèmes.**
  I have big/enormous problems.
- **Tu n'as pas envie de donner des cours à un(e) lycéen(ne) nul(le) comme moi.**
  You don't want to teach a high school student as bad as myself.

Useful expressions

- **C'est parfait!**
  That's perfect!
- **Allons-y!**
  Let's go!
- **D'accord.**
  OK, all right.
- **Ouais.**
  Yeah.
- **C'est sympa.**
  That's nice/fun.

ACTIVITÉS

2 Répondez Answer these questions. Refer to the video scenes and a dictionary as necessary. You do not have to answer in complete sentences. Answers will vary.

1. Où est-ce que tu as envie de voyager?
2. Est-ce que tu as peur de quelque chose? De quoi?
3. Qu'est-ce que tu dis (*say*) quand tu as tort?

3 À vous! With a partner, describe someone you know whose personality, likes, or dislikes resemble those of Rachid or Stéphane.

MODÈLE

Paul est comme (like) Rachid... il est sérieux.

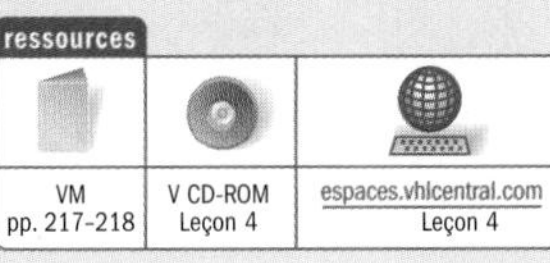

Expressions utiles
- Model the pronunciation of the **Expressions utiles** and have students repeat after you.
- As you work through the list, point out forms of **avoir**, idiomatic expressions with **avoir**, and expressions for telling time. Tell students that these concepts will be formally presented in **Structures**.
- Respond briefly to questions about **avoir** and reinforce correct forms, but do not expect students to produce them consistently at this time.
- Ask students a few questions based on the **Expressions utiles**. Examples: **Tu as cours de chant aujourd'hui? Tu as cours de stylisme de mode?**
- Have students scan the video-still captions for phrases or sentences that show a sequence of time or events. Examples: **Aujourd'hui c'est mercredi. Demain jeudi....**

1 Suggestion Have students correct the false statements.

2 Expansion For additional practice, ask these questions. **4. Où est-ce que tu as envie de dîner? 5. À qui est-ce que tu as envie de téléphoner? 6. Est-ce que tu as peur de regarder les films d'horreur?**

3 Suggestion Before beginning the activity, tell pairs to brainstorm and write a list of adjectives or phrases that describe Rachid and Stéphane.

OPTIONS

Small Groups Working in groups of three, have students create a short skit similar to the scenes in video stills 6–10 in which one of the students forgets to show up for a study session or a meeting. Give students ten minutes to prepare, then call on groups to perform their skits for the class.

Pairs Have students work in pairs. Tell them to create two-line conversations using as many of the **Expressions utiles** as they can. Example:
—Alors on a rendez-vous à cinq heures?
—Ouais! C'est parfait!

Section Goals

In this section, students will:

- learn about university courses in France
- learn familiar terms for talking about classes and exams
- learn the names of some universities with French programs for foreigners
- read about **le bac**

Instructional Resources
espaces.vhlcentral.com: activities, downloads, reference tools

Culture à la loupe

Avant la lecture Ask students: What would you want to know about the classes at **la Sorbonne** if you were going there to study for a year?

Lecture

- Tell students that the word **amphi** is often used instead of **amphithéâtre**. Similarly, the word **fac** (for **faculté**) is used more often than **université**. The start of the school year is also known as the **rentrée scolaire**.
- Point out the **Coup de main**. Explain that commas are used instead of periods in percentages.
- Explain that French students rarely get praise from teachers. While American teachers are trained to encourage students for effort, the French typically reserve approbation for only truly excellent work.

Après la lecture Ask students if they prefer the French or American university system and to explain why.

1 Expansion For extra practice, give students these items. 11. Lecture courses are rare in France. (**Faux**. They are common.) 12. The French discourage open debate. (**Faux.**) 13. The French university system relies heavily on exams for assessment. (**Vrai.**) 14. After studying abroad in France, a student needs to make sure that the overseas university provides information about grade conversion to the home institution. (**Vrai.**)

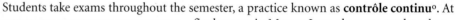

CULTURE À LA LOUPE

Les cours universitaires

French university courses often consist of lectures in large halls called amphithéâtres. Some also include discussion-based sessions with fewer students. Other than in the **grandes écoles** and specialized schools, class attendance is not mandatory in most universities. Students are motivated to attend by their desire to pass. Course grades may be based upon only one or two exams or term papers, so students generally take their studies seriously. They often form study groups to discuss the lectures and share class notes. This practice encourages open exchange of ideas and debate, a tradition that continues well past university life in France.

The start of classes each year is known as the **rentrée universitaire** and takes place at the beginning of October. The academic year is divided into two semesters. Four to six classes each semester is typical.

Students take exams throughout the semester, a practice known as **contrôle continu°**. At

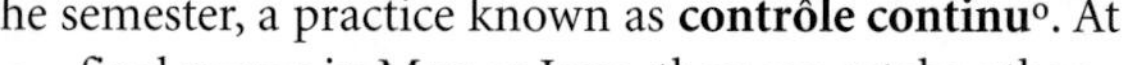

final exams in May or June, they can retake other exams they might have failed during that year or the preceding year. French grades range from 0–20, rather than from 0–100. Scores over 17 or 18 are rare and even the best students do not expect to score consistently in the near-perfect range. A grade of 10 is a passing grade, and is therefore not the equivalent of a 50 in the American system. If you plan to study abroad for credit, ask the foreign institution to provide your school with grade equivalents.

contrôle continu *continuous assessment*

Système français de notation

NOTE FRANÇAISE	NOTE AMÉRICAINE	%	NOTE FRANÇAISE	NOTE AMÉRICAINE	%
0	F	0	11	A-	85
2	F	3	12	A	90
3	F	8	13	A	93
4	F	18	14	A+	96
5	F	28	15	A+	99
6	F	38	16	A+	99.5
7	D-	50	17	A+	99.7
8	C-	60	18	A+	99.9
9	B-	70	19	A+	99.99
10	B	78	20	A+	over 99.99

Coup de main

To read decimal places in French, use the French word **virgule** (*comma*) where you would normally say *point* in English. To say *percent*, use **pour cent**.

60,4% soixante virgule quatre pour cent
sixty point four percent

ACTIVITÉS

1 Vrai ou faux? Indicate whether each statement is **vrai** or **faux**. Correct any false statements.

1. Class attendance is optional in some French universities.
   Vrai.
2. Final course grades are usually based on several exam grades and class participation.
   Faux. Grades may be based upon only one or two exams or papers.
3. The French university system discourages note sharing.
   Faux. Note sharing is completely normal.
4. The French grading system is similar to the American system.
   Faux. The French and American grading systems are very different.
5. The **rentrée universitaire** happens each year in June.
   Faux. The rentrée happens in October.
6. A grade of 11 is not a passing grade.
   Faux. A grade of 11 is equal to an A- in the United States.
7. The academic year in France is typically divided into trimesters.
   Faux. The academic year is divided into two semesters.
8. Scores of 18 or 19 are very rare.
   Vrai.
9. French students typically take three classes each semester.
   Faux. They typically take four to six classes.
10. The final exams in May or June are called the **contrôle continu**.
    Faux. The exams given throughout the semester are called the contrôle continu.

OPTIONS

Pairs To review numbers and the alphabet, have students take turns making true/false statements about the French and American grading systems based on the information in the chart. Write on the board: a plus sign = **plus**; a minus sign = **moins**. Example: **Un vingt en France est un A plus plus plus plus plus plus aux États-Unis. (Vrai.)**

Small Groups Working in groups of three, have students describe the photos on this page. Tell them to create as many sentences in French as they can about the people, what they are doing, and why they are there. Then have volunteers read their descriptions to the class.

LE FRANÇAIS QUOTIDIEN

Les cours et les examens

cours (*m.*) magistral	*lecture*
cours (*m.*) de rattrapage	*remedial class*
bosser	*to work hard*
cartonner à un examen	*to ace an exam*
potasser	*to cram*
rater (un examen)	*to fail (an exam)*
sécher un cours	*to skip a class*

LE MONDE FRANCOPHONE

Le français langue étrangère

Voici quelques° écoles du monde francophone où vous pouvez aller° pour étudier le français.

En Belgique Université de Liège

En France Université de Franche-Comté–Centre de linguistique appliquée, Université de Grenoble, Université de Paris IV-Sorbonne

À la Martinique Institut Supérieur d'Études Francophones, à Schoelcher

En Nouvelle-Calédonie Centre de Rencontres et d'Échanges Internationaux du Pacifique, à Nouméa

Au Québec Université Laval, Université de Montréal

Aux îles Saint-Pierre et Miquelon Le FrancoForum, à Saint-Pierre

En Suisse Université Populaire de Lausanne, Université de Neuchâtel

quelques *some* **pouvez aller** *can go*

PORTRAIT

Le bac

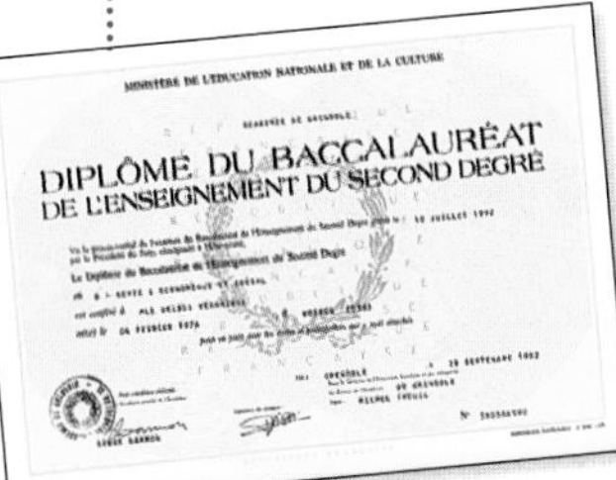

Au lycée, les élèves ont des cours communs, comme le français, l'histoire et les maths, et aussi un choix° de spécialisation. À la fin° du lycée, à l'âge de dix-sept ou dix-huit ans, les jeunes Français passent un examen très important: le baccalauréat. Le bac est nécessaire pour continuer des études supérieures. Les lycéens° passent des bacs différents: le bac L (littéraire), le bac ES (économique et social) et le bac S (scientifique) sont des bacs généraux. Il y a aussi des bacs techniques et des bacs technologiques, comme° le bac STI (sciences et technologies industrielles) ou le bac SMS (sciences et techniques médico-sociales). Il y a même° un bac technique de la musique et de la danse et un bac hôtellerie°! Entre 70 (soixante-dix) et 80 (quatre-vingts) pour cent des élèves passent le bac avec succès.

choix *choice* **À la fin** *At the end* **lycéens** *high school students* **comme** *such as* **même** *even* **hôtellerie** *hotel trade*

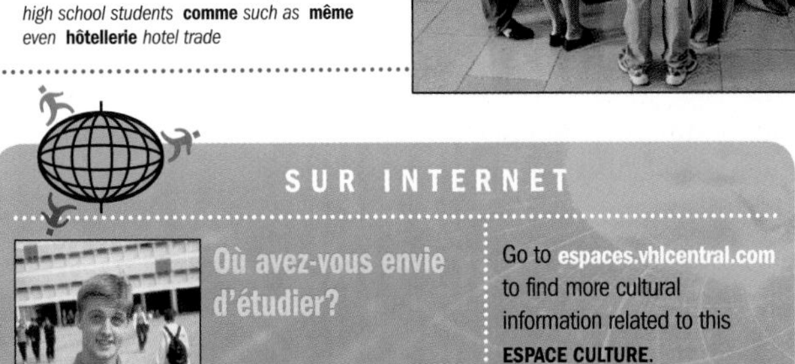

SUR INTERNET

Où avez-vous envie d'étudier?

Go to **espaces.vhlcentral.com** to find more cultural information related to this **ESPACE CULTURE.**

ACTIVITÉS

2 Quel bac? Which bac best fits the following interests?

1. le ballet *le bac technique de la musique et de la danse*
2. la littérature *le bac littéraire*
3. la médecine *le bac sciences et techniques médico-sociales*
4. le tourisme *le bac hôtellerie*
5. la technologie *le bac sciences et technologies industrielles*
6. le piano et la flûte *le bac technique de la musique et de la danse*

3 Et les cours? In French, name two courses you might take in preparation for each of these **baccalauréat** exams. *Answers will vary. Possible answers shown.*

1. un bac L *le français et la philosophie*
2. un bac SMS *la biologie et la psychologie*
3. un bac ES *l'économie et la sociologie*
4. un bac STI *la physique et les maths*

ressources

espaces.vhlcentral.com Leçon 4

Le français quotidien Model the pronunciation of each term and have students repeat it. You might also add these words to this list: **une dissert(ation)** (*writing assignment*), **réussir à un examen** (*to pass an exam*), **recaler** (*to fail*), and **les travaux pratiques (TP)** (*labs*).

Portrait Explain that, if a student fails the **bac**, he or she must complete a **cours de rattrapage** successfully or repeat **terminale** and retake the exam the next year in order to pursue further study.

Le monde francophone Have students read the list. Use this as an opportunity to explain the importance of language immersion in a French-speaking country and to encourage students to start thinking about study abroad. If possible, bring in brochures or refer students to web sites for study abroad programs.

2 Expansion For additional practice, give students these items. **7. l'histoire (le bac littéraire) 8. la biologie (le bac scientifique) 9. l'informatique (le bac sciences et technologies industrielles) 10. les sciences po (le bac économique et social)**

3 Expansion Tell students to imagine that they are in high school. Given their interests or major, ask them which **bac** they are preparing for. Example: **Quel bac est-ce que vous préparez? (Je prépare le bac S parce que j'étudie la chimie et la physique.)**

OPTIONS

Cultural Comparison Have students compare the French **lycée** to an American high school. Have them discuss the differences between the two educational systems. Then ask them what determines a student's ability to enroll in a university in France versus in the United States.

Pairs Have students work in pairs. Tell them to take turns asking and answering questions using the expressions in **Le français quotidien**. Examples: **Tu bosses pour le cours de français? Tu aimes les cours magistraux?**

NATIONAL comparisons STANDARDS

Section Goals

In this section, students will learn:

- the verb **avoir**
- some common expressions with **avoir**

Instructional Resources

WB/VM: Workbook, pp. 23–24
Lab Manual, p. 15
Lab MP3s
WB/VM/LM Answer Key
*IRCD-ROM: IRM (**Mise en pratique** answers*
Lab Audioscript;
***Feuilles d'activités**)*
espaces.vhlcentral.com: activities, downloads, reference tools

Suggestions

- Model **avoir** by asking questions such as: **Avez-vous un examen cette semaine? Avez-vous un palm? ____ a-t-il/elle un palm?** Point out that forms of **avoir** were in the **Roman-photo.**
- Explain that **avoir** is irregular and must be memorized. Begin a paradigm for **avoir** by writing **j'ai** on the board and asking volunteers questions that elicit **j'ai**. Examples: **J'ai un stylo. Qui a un crayon?**
- Add **tu as** and **il/elle a** to the paradigm on the board. Point out that **as** and **a** are pronounced alike. Tell students that **avoir** has no real stem apart from the letter **a**.
- Write **nous avons** and **vous avez**. Point out that **-ons** and **-ez** are the same endings as in **-er** verbs. Add **ils/elles ont.**
- Remind students of liaisons in the plural forms of **avoir** and have them pronounce these forms again.
- Tell the class that many French expressions use **avoir** + *noun* instead of **être** to say *to be* + *adjective* in English. Also point out that, to ask people if they feel like doing something, use **avoir envie de** + *infinitive*.
- Model the use of the expressions by talking about yourself while gesturing and asking students questions about themselves. Examples: **J'ai froid ce matin/cet après-midi. Vous avez froid aussi ou vous avez chaud? J'ai besoin d'un dictionnaire. Avez-vous un dictionnaire?**

4.1 Present tense of *avoir*

Point de départ The verb **avoir** (*to have*) is frequently used. You will have to memorize each of its present tense forms because they are irregular.

Present tense of *avoir*

j'ai	*I have*	**nous avons**	*we have*
tu as	*you have*	**vous avez**	*you have*
il/elle a	*he/she/it has*	**ils/elles ont**	*they have*

On a rendez-vous avec David demain.
Cette année, nous avons le bac.

- Liaison is required between the final consonants of **on, nous, vous, ils,** and **elles** and the forms of **avoir** that follow them. When the final consonant is an **-s**, pronounce it as a *z* before the verb forms.

On a un prof sympa.
We have a nice professor.

Nous avons un cours d'art.
We have an art class.

- Keep in mind that an indefinite article, whether singular or plural, usually becomes **de/d'** after a negation.

J'ai **un** cours difficile.
I have a difficult class.

Je n'ai pas **de** cours difficile.
I do not have a difficult class.

Il a **des** examens.
He has exams.

Il n'a pas **d'**examens.
He does not have exams.

MISE EN PRATIQUE

1 On a... Use the correct forms of **avoir** to form questions from these elements. Use inversion and provide an affirmative or negative answer as cued.

MODÈLE

tu / bourse (oui)
As-tu une bourse? Oui, j'ai une bourse.

1. nous / dictionnaire (oui)
   Avons-nous un dictionnaire? Oui, nous avons un dictionnaire.
2. Luc / diplôme (non)
   Luc a-t-il un diplôme? Non, il n'a pas de diplôme.
3. elles / montres (non)
   Ont-elles des montres? Non, elles n'ont pas de montres.
4. vous / copains (oui)
   Avez-vous des copains? Oui, j'ai/nous avons des copains.
5. Thérèse / palm (oui)
   Thérèse a-t-elle un palm? Oui, elle a un palm.
6. Charles et Jacques / calculatrice (non)
   Charles et Jacques ont-ils une calculatrice? Non, ils n'ont pas de calculatrice.

2 C'est évident Describe these people using expressions with **avoir.**

1. J' ai de la chance.

3. Vous avez froid.

2. Tu as honte.

4. Elles ont sommeil.

3 Assemblez Use the verb **avoir** and combine elements from the two columns to create sentences about yourself, your class, and your school. Make any necessary changes or additions. Answers will vary.

A	B
Je	cours utiles
L'université	bourses importantes
Les profs	professeurs brillants
Mon (*My*) petit ami	ami(e) mexicain(e) / anglais(e) / canadien(ne) / vietnamien(ne)
Ma (*My*) petite amie	étudiants intéressants
Nous	resto U agréable
	école de droit

OPTIONS

Extra Practice Do a quick substitution drill with **avoir**. Write a sentence on the board and have students read it aloud. Then say a new subject and have students repeat the sentence, substituting the new subject. Examples: **1. J'ai des problèmes. (Éric et moi, tu, Stéphane, vous, les hommes) 2. Pierre a cours de chimie le mardi et le jeudi. (Pierre et Julie, nous, je, vous, tu)**

Game Divide the class into two teams. Choose one team member at a time to go to the board, alternating between teams. Say a subject pronoun. The person at the board must write and say the correct form of **avoir**. Example: **elle (elle a)**. Give a point for each correct answer. The team with the most points at the end of the game wins.

COMMUNICATION

4 **C'est vrai?** Interview a classmate by transforming each of these statements into a question. Be prepared to report the results of your interview to the class. Answers will vary.

MODÈLE J'ai deux ordinateurs.

Étudiant(e) 1: *Tu as deux ordinateurs?*
Étudiant(e) 2: *Non, je n'ai pas deux ordinateurs.*

1. J'ai peur des examens.
2. J'ai vingt et un ans.
3. J'ai envie de visiter Montréal.
4. J'ai un cours de biologie.
5. J'ai sommeil le lundi matin.
6. J'ai un(e) petit(e) ami(e) égoïste.

5 **Besoins** Your instructor will give you a worksheet. Ask different classmates if they need to do these activities. Find at least one person to answer **Oui** and at least one to answer **Non** for each item. Answers will vary.

MODÈLE regarder la télé

Étudiant(e) 1: *Tu as besoin de regarder la télé?*
Étudiant(e) 2: *Oui, j'ai besoin de regarder la télé.*
Étudiant(e) 3: *Non, je n'ai pas besoin de regarder la télé.*

Activités	*Oui*	*Non*
1. regarder la télé	*Anne*	*Louis*
2. étudier ce soir		
3. passer un examen cette semaine		
4. trouver un cours d'informatique		
5. travailler à la bibliothèque		
6. commencer un devoir important		
7. téléphoner à un(e) copain/copine ce week-end		
8. parler avec le professeur		

6 **Interview** You are talking to the campus housing advisor. Answer his or her questions. In pairs, practice the scene and role-play it for the class. Answers will vary.

1. Qu'est-ce que (*What*) vous étudiez?
2. Est-ce que vous avez d'excellentes notes?
3. Est-ce que vous avez envie de partager la chambre?
4. Est-ce que vous mangez au resto U?
5. Est-ce que vous avez un ordinateur?
6. Est-ce que vous retrouvez des amis à la fac?
7. Est-ce que vous écoutez de la musique?
8. Est-ce que vous avez des cours le matin?

- The verb **avoir** is used in certain idiomatic or set expressions where English generally uses *to be* or *to feel*.

Expressions with *avoir*

avoir... ans	*to be... years old*	**avoir froid**	*to be cold*
avoir besoin (de)	*to need*	**avoir honte (de)**	*to be ashamed (of)*
avoir de la chance	*to be lucky*	**avoir l'air**	*to look like*
avoir chaud	*to be hot*	**avoir peur (de)**	*to be afraid (of)*
avoir envie (de)	*to feel like*	**avoir raison**	*to be right*
		avoir sommeil	*to be sleepy*
		avoir tort	*to be wrong*

Il a chaud.

Ils ont froid.

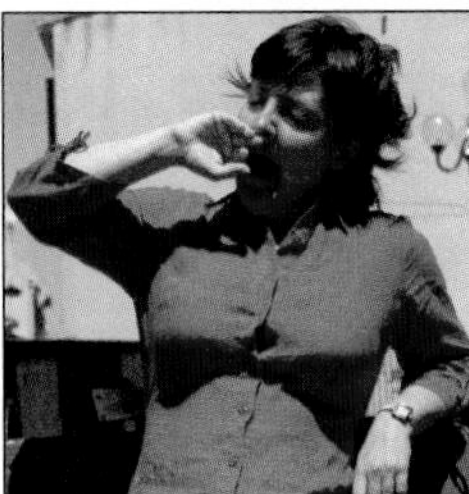
Elle a sommeil.

Il a de la chance.

Essayez! **Complete the sentences with the correct forms of avoir.**

1. La température est de 35 degrés Celsius. Nous ___avons___ chaud.
2. En Alaska, en décembre, vous ___avez___ froid.
3. Martine écoute la radio et elle ___a___ envie de danser.
4. Ils ___ont___ besoin d'une calculatrice pour le devoir.
5. Est-ce que tu ___as___ peur des insectes?
6. Sébastien pense que je travaille aujourd'hui. Il ___a___ raison.
7. J'___ai___ cours d'économie le lundi et le mercredi.
8. Mes amis voyagent beaucoup. Ils ___ont___ de la chance.
9. Mohammed ___a___ deux cousins à Marseille.
10. Vous ___avez___ un grand appartement.

Essayez! Ask students to identify the idiomatic expressions in the sentences. (All are idiomatic expressions, except items 7, 9, and 10.)

1 Suggestion This activity can be done in pairs. Tell students to alternate asking and answering the questions.

2 Expansion For each drawing, ask students how many people there are, their names, and their ages. Example: **Combien de personnes y a-t-il sur le dessin numéro 1? Comment s'appellent-elles? Quel âge a ____?**

3 Suggestion This activity can be done orally or in writing in pairs or groups.

4 Suggestion Have two volunteers read the **modèle** aloud. Remind students that an indefinite article becomes **de (d')** if it follows **avoir** in the negative.

5 Suggestions
- Have three volunteers read the **modèle** aloud. Then distribute the **Feuilles d'activités** from the IRM on the IRCD-ROM.
- Have students add at least two activities of their own.

6 Suggestions
- Remind students to do the interview twice so each person asks and answers the questions.
- Ask volunteers to summarize their partners' responses. Record the responses on the board as a survey (**un sondage**) about the class' characteristics. Then ask questions like this: **Combien d'étudiants dans la classe étudient l'économie?**

OPTIONS

TPR Assign gestures to expressions with **avoir**. Examples: **avoir chaud**: *wipe brow*, **avoir froid**: *wrap arms around oneself and shiver*, **avoir peur**: *hold one's hand over mouth in fear*, **avoir faim**: *rub stomach*, **avoir sommeil**: *yawn and stretch*. Have students stand. Say an expression at random as you point to a student who performs the appropriate gesture. Vary by indicating more than one student at a time.

Small Groups Have students work in groups of three. Tell them to write nine sentences, each of which uses a different expression with **avoir**. Call on volunteers to write some of their group's best sentences on the board. Have the class read the sentences aloud and correct any errors.

Section Goals

In this section, students will learn:
- to tell time
- some time expressions
- the 24-hour system of telling time

Instructional Resources
WB/VM: Workbook, pp. 25–26
Lab Manual, p. 16
Lab MP3s
WB/VM/LM Answer Key
*IRCD-ROM: Transparency #19; IRM (**Essayez!** and **Mise en pratique** answers; Lab Audioscript)*
espaces.vhlcentral.com: activities, downloads, reference tools

Suggestions
- To prepare for telling time, review the meanings of **il est** and numbers 0–60.
- Introduce: **Il est sept heures (huit heures, neuf heures…).**
- Explain to students that **heures** refers to *hours* when telling time, but can also mean *o'clock*.
- Introduce: **Il est ____ heure(s) cinq, dix, et quart,** and **et demie.**
- Using a paper plate clock, display various times on the hour. Ask: **Quelle heure est-il?**
- Introduce and explain: **Il est ____ heure(s) moins cinq, moins dix, moins le quart,** and **moins vingt.** Repeat the procedure above using your movable-hands clock.
- Explain that the French view times of day differently from Americans. In France, they say **«bonjour»** until about 4:00 or 5:00 p.m. After that, they use the greeting **«bonsoir»**. They say **«bonne nuit»** only when going to sleep.
- Explain the use of the 24-hour clock. Have students practice saying times this way by adding 12.
- Model the pronunciation of the time expressions in the box and have students repeat. Point out that a.m. and p.m. are not used in France or most francophone regions. Instead, they use **du matin, de l'après midi,** and **du soir.**

4.2 Telling time

Point de départ Use the verb **être** with numbers to tell time.

- There are two ways to ask what time it is.

Quelle heure est-il?	**Quelle heure avez-vous?**
What time is it?	*What time do you have?*

- Use **heures** by itself to express time on the hour. Use **heure** for one o'clock.

Il est **six heures**.

Il est **une heure**.

- Express time from the hour to the half-hour by adding minutes.

Il est quatre heures **cinq**.

Il est onze heures **vingt**.

- Use **et quart** to say that it is fifteen minutes past the hour. Use **et demie** to say that it is thirty minutes past the hour.

Il est une heure **et quart**.

Il est sept heures **et demie**.

- To express time from the half hour to the hour, subtract minutes or a portion of an hour from the next hour.

Il est trois heures **moins dix**.

Il est une heure **moins le quart**.

- To express at what time something happens, use the preposition **à**.

Céline travaille **à sept heures moins vingt**.	On passe un examen **à une heure**.
Céline works at 6:40.	*We take a test at one o'clock.*

MISE EN PRATIQUE

1 Quelle heure est-il? Give the time shown on each clock or watch.

MODÈLE
Il est quatre heures et quart de l'après-midi.

1. Il est midi/minuit et demie.
2. Il est une heure du matin.
3. Il est huit heures dix.
4. Il est onze heures moins le quart.

5. Il est deux heures douze.
6. Il est sept heures cinq.
7. Il est quatre heures moins cinq.
8. Il est minuit moins vingt-cinq.

2 À quelle heure? Find out when you and your friends are going to do certain things.

MODÈLE
À quelle heure est-ce qu'on étudie? (about 8 p.m.)
On étudie vers huit heures du soir.

À quelle heure...
1. ... est-ce qu'on arrive au café? (at 10:30 a.m.) On arrive au café à dix heures et demie du matin.
2. ... est-ce que vous parlez avec le professeur? (at noon) Nous parlons avec le professeur à midi.
3. ... est-ce que tu rentres? (late, at 11:15 p.m.) Je rentre tard, à onze heures et quart du soir.
4. ... est-ce qu'on regarde la télé? (at 9:00 p.m.) On regarde la télé à neuf heures du soir.
5. ... est-ce que Marlène et Nadine mangent? (around 1:45 p.m.) Elles mangent vers deux heures moins le quart de l'après-midi.
6. ... est-ce que le cours commence? (very early, at 8:20 a.m.) Il commence très tôt, à huit heures vingt du matin.

3 Départ à... Tell what each of these times would be on a 24-hour clock.

MODÈLE
Il est trois heures vingt de l'après-midi.
Il est quinze heures vingt.

1. Il est dix heures et demie du soir. Il est vingt-deux heures trente.
2. Il est deux heures de l'après-midi. Il est quatorze heures.
3. Il est huit heures et quart du soir. Il est vingt heures quinze.
4. Il est minuit moins le quart. Il est vingt-trois heures quarante-cinq.
5. Il est six heures vingt-cinq du soir. Il est dix-huit heures vingt-cinq.
6. Il est trois heures moins cinq du matin. Il est deux heures cinquante-cinq.

OPTIONS

Extra Practice Draw a large clock face on the board with its numbers but without the hands. Say a time and ask a volunteer to come up and draw the hands to indicate that time. The rest of the class verifies whether or not the person has written the correct time, saying: **Il/Elle a raison/tort**. Repeat this procedure a number of times.

Pairs Have pairs take turns telling each other what time their classes are this semester/trimester/term. Example: **J'ai un cours à ____ heures….** For each time given, the other student draws a clock face with the corresponding time. The first student verifies if the clock is correct.

COMMUNICATION

4 **Télémonde** Look at this French TV guide. In pairs, ask questions about program start times. Answers will vary.

MODÈLE

Étudiant(e) 1: *À quelle heure commence Télé-ciné?*
Étudiant(e) 2: *Télé-ciné commence à dix heures dix du soir.*

dessins animés	*cartoons*
feuilleton télévisé	*soap opera*
film policier	*detective film*
informations	*news*
jeu télévisé	*game show*

VENDREDI

Antenne 2	Antenne 4	Antenne 5
15h30 Pomme d'Api (dessins animés) **17h35** Reportage spécial: le sport dans les lycées **20h15** La famille Menet (feuilleton télévisé) **21h35** Télé-ciné: L'inspecteur Duval (film policier)	**14h00** Football: match France-Italie **19h45** Les informations **20h30** Concert: Orchestre de Nice **22h10** Télé-ciné: Une chose difficile (comédie dramatique)	**18h25** Montréal: une ville à visiter **19h30** Des chiffres et des lettres (jeu télévisé) **21h05** Reportage spécial: les Sénégalais **22h05** Les informations

5 **Où es-tu?** In pairs, take turns asking where (**où**) your partner usually is on these days at these times. Choose from the places listed. Answers will vary.

au lit (*bed*)	chez mes (*at my*) parents
au resto U	chez mes copains
à la bibliothèque	chez mon (*my*) petit ami
en ville (*town*)	chez ma (*my*) petite amie
au parc	
en cours	

1. Le samedi: à 8h00 du matin; à midi; à minuit
2. En semaine: à 9h00 du matin; à 3h00 de l'après-midi; à 7h00 du soir
3. Le dimanche: à 4h00 de l'après-midi; à 6h30 du soir; à 10h00 du soir
4. Le vendredi: à 11h00 du matin; à 5h00 de l'après-midi; à 11h00 du soir

6 **Le suspect** A student on campus is a suspect in a crime. You and a partner are detectives. Keeping a log of the student's activities, use the 24-hour clock to say what he or she is doing when. Answers will vary.

MODÈLE

À vingt-deux heures trente-trois, il parle au téléphone.

- **Liaison** occurs between numbers and the word **heure(s)**. Final **-s** and **-x** in **deux, trois, six,** and **dix** are pronounced like a *z*. The final **-f** of **neuf** is pronounced like a *v*.

Il est **deux heures**. *It's two o'clock.*	Il est **neuf heures** et quart. *It's 9:15.*

- You do not usually make a **liaison** between the verb form **est** and a following number that starts with a vowel sound.

Il est **onze** heures. *It's eleven o'clock.*	Il est **une** heure vingt. *It's 1:20.*	Il est **huit** heures et demie. *It's 8:30.*

Expressions for telling time

À quelle heure?	*(At) what time/ when?*	**midi**	*noon*
de l'après-midi	*in the afternoon*	**minuit**	*midnight*
du matin	*in the morning*	**presque**	*almost*
du soir	*in the evening*	**tard**	*late*
en avance	*early*	**tôt**	*early*
en retard	*late*	**vers**	*about*

Il est **minuit** à Paris. *It's midnight in Paris.*	Il est six heures **du soir** à New York. *It's six o'clock in the evening in New York.*

- The 24-hour clock is often used to express official time. Departure times, movie times, and store hours are expressed in this fashion. Only numbers are used to tell time this way. Expressions like **et demie, moins le quart**, etc. are not used.

Le train arrive à **dix-sept heures six**. *The train arrives at 5:06 p.m.*	Le film est à **vingt-deux heures trente sept**. *The film is at 10:37 p.m.*

J'ai cours de trois heures vingt à quatre heures et demie.

Stéphane! Quelle heure est-il?

Essayez! **Complete the sentences by writing out the correct times according to the cues.**

1. (1:00 a.m.) Il est *une heure* du matin.
2. (2:50 a.m.) Il est trois heures moins dix du matin.
3. (8:30 p.m.) Il est huit heures et demie du soir.
4. (12:00 p.m.) Il est midi.
5. (4:05 p.m.) Il est quatre heures cinq de l'après-midi.
6. (4:45 a.m.) Il est cinq heures moins le quart du matin.

Essayez! For additional practice, give students these items. 7. 6:20 p.m. 8. 9:10 a.m. 9. 2:15 p.m. 10. 10:35 a.m. 11. 12:00 a.m. 12. 9:55 p.m.

1 Expansion At random, say the times shown and have students say the number of the clock or watch described. Example: **Il est sept heures cinq. (C'est le numéro six.)**

2 Suggestion Read the **modèle** aloud with a volunteer. Working in pairs, have students take turns asking and answering the questions.

3 Expansion Create a train schedule and write it on the board or use photocopies of a real one. Ask students questions based on the schedule. Example: **À quelle heure est le train Paris-Bordeaux le vendredi soir?**

4 Suggestion Before starting this activity, have students read the TV guide, point out cognates, and predict their meaning. Provide examples for non-cognate categories so students can guess their meaning. Examples: **dessins animés, feuilleton télévisé**, and **jeu télévisé**.

4 Expansion Have pairs ask each other additional questions based on the TV guide. Examples: **Est-ce qu'il y a un reportage à vingt heures dix? (Non, les reportages sont à dix-sept heures trente-cinq et à vingt et une heures cinq.) J'ai envie de regarder le film policier. À quelle heure est-il? (Le film policier est à vingt et une heures trente-cinq.)**

5 Suggestion Before beginning the activity, provide students with a model. Example: **Étudiant(e) 1: Où es-tu le samedi à midi? Étudiant(e) 2: Le samedi à midi, je suis au resto U.**

6 Expansion After completing the activity, ask students if the suspect has an alibi at certain times. Tell them to respond using the information on their logs. Example: **Le suspect a-t-il un alibi à vingt-trois heures? (Oui, à vingt-trois heures il étudie avec un ami.)**

OPTIONS

Video Play the video episode again to give students additional input on telling time and the verb **avoir**. Pause the video where appropriate to discuss how time or **avoir** were used and to ask comprehension questions. Example: **Est-ce que Stéphane a peur de parler à Astrid? (Mais non, il a peur du bac.)**

Small Groups Have students work in groups of three. Tell them to take turns asking what time various TV shows start and answering. Example: **À quelle heure est *60 Minutes*? (C'est à dix-neuf heures.)** Remind students to use the 24-hour system when talking about TV shows.

Synthèse

Instructional Resources
IRCD-ROM: IRM (Info Gap Activities); Testing Program, pp. 13–16; Test Files; Testing Program MP3s; Test Generator
espaces.vhlcentral.com: activities, downloads, reference tools

1 Suggestion Have two volunteers read the **modèle** aloud. Encourage students to add other items to the list.

2 Suggestion Before beginning the activity, tell students to choose two language classes, a science class, and an elective in the list. Then read the **modèle** aloud with a volunteer.

3 Expansion Have volunteers report their findings to the class. Then do a quick class survey to find out how many students are taking the same courses. Example: **Combien d'étudiants ont sciences politiques ce semestre?**

4 Suggestion Before doing the activity, point out the use of the construction **avoir envie de** + *infinitive*. Encourage students to add activities to the list. Examples: **regarder un film, manger/partager une pizza, parler au téléphone,** and **voyager en France/Europe.**

5 Suggestion Ask what expressions express likes and dislikes, and write them on the board before assigning this activity.

6 Suggestions
- Divide the class into pairs and distribute the Info Gap Handouts in the IRM on the IRCD-ROM for this activity. Have two volunteers read the **modèle**. Give students ten minutes to complete the activity.
- After completing the activity, ask students what activities Patrick would like to do this weekend.

1 J'ai besoin de... In pairs, take turns saying which items you need. Your partner will guess why you need them. How many times did each of you guess correctly? Answers will vary.

MODÈLE

Étudiant(e) 1: *J'ai besoin d'un cahier et d'un dictionnaire pour demain.*
Étudiant(e) 2: *Est-ce que tu as un cours de français?*
Étudiant(e) 1: *Non. J'ai un examen d'anglais.*

un cahier	le livre *La physique quantique*
une calculatrice	une montre
une carte	un ordinateur
un dictionnaire	des stylos
une feuille de papier	un téléphone

2 À l'université française To complete your degree, you need two language classes, a science class, and an elective of your choice. Take turns deciding what classes you need or want to take. Your partner will tell you the days and times so you can set up your schedule. Answers will vary.

MODÈLE

Étudiant(e) 1: *J'ai besoin d'un cours de maths, peut-être «Initiation aux maths».*
Étudiant(e) 2: *C'est le mardi et le jeudi après-midi, de deux heures à trois heures et demie.*
Étudiant(e) 1: *J'ai aussi besoin d'un cours de langue...*

Les cours	Jours et heures
Allemand	mardi, jeudi; 14h00-15h30
Biologie II	mardi, jeudi; 9h00-10h30
Chimie générale	lundi, mercredi; 11h00-12h30
Espagnol	lundi, mercredi; 11h00-12h30
Gestion	mercredi; 13h00-14h30
Histoire des États-Unis	jeudi; 12h15-14h15
Initiation à la physique	lundi, mercredi; 12h00-13h30
Initiation aux maths	mardi, jeudi; 14h00-15h30
Italien	lundi, mercredi; 12h00-13h30
Japonais	mardi, jeudi; 9h00-10h30
Les philosophes grecs	lundi; 15h15-16h45
Littérature moderne	mardi; 10h15-11h15

3 Les cours Your partner will tell you what classes he or she is currently taking. Make a list, including the times and days of week. Then, talk to as many classmates as you can, and find at least two students who take at least two of the same classes as your partner. Answers will vary.

4 On y va? Walk around the room and find at least one classmate who feels like doing each of these activities with you. For every affirmative answer, record the name of your classmate and agree on a time and date. Do not speak to the same classmate twice. Answers will vary.

MODÈLE

Étudiant(e) 1: *Tu as envie de retrouver des amis avec moi?*
Étudiant(e) 2: *Oui, pourquoi pas? Samedi, à huit heures du soir, peut-être?*
Étudiant(e) 1: *D'accord!*

chercher un café sympa	regarder la télé française
dîner au resto U	retrouver des amis
écouter des CD	travailler à la bibliothèque
étudier du français cette semaine	visiter un musée

5 Au téléphone Two high school friends are attending different universities. In pairs, imagine a conversation where they discuss the time, their classes, and likes or dislikes about campus life. Then, role-play the conversation for the class and vote for the best skit. Answers will vary.

MODÈLE

Étudiant(e) 1: *J'ai cours de chimie à dix heures et demie.*
Étudiant(e) 2: *Je n'ai pas de cours de chimie cette année.*
Étudiant(e) 1: *N'aimes-tu pas les sciences?*
Étudiant(e) 2: *Si, mais...*

6 La semaine de Patrick Your instructor will give you and a partner different incomplete pages from Patrick's day planner. Do not look at each other's worksheet. Answers will vary.

MODÈLE

Étudiant(e) 1: *Lundi matin Patrick a cours de géographie à dix heures et demie.*
Étudiant(e) 2: *Lundi il a cours de sciences po à deux heures de l'après-midi.*

ressources

WB	LM	Lab MP3s	espaces.vhlcentral.com
pp. 23-26	pp. 15-16	Leçon 4	Leçon 4

OPTIONS

Small Groups Working in groups of three or four, have students create a short skit similar to the scene in video still 1 of the **Roman-photo**. Tell them that they have to decide on a day, time, and place to meet for a study session in order to prepare for the next French test. Have groups perform their skits for the class.

Extra Practice Have students make a list of six items that students normally carry in their backpacks to class. Then tell them to circulate around the room asking their classmates if they have those items in their backpacks. Also tell them to ask how many they have. Example: **As-tu un cahier dans le sac à dos? Combien de cahiers as-tu?**

Clairefontaine: l'écrit du cœur

In 1858, Jean-Baptiste Bichelberger founded a paper factory in eastern France. Soon the company became Clairefontaine and started making envelopes and notebooks. In 1950, Charles Nusse took over the company, offering schoolchildren notebooks made of high-quality paper. He was the creator of the Clairefontaine logo, which became famous. Today, the company has branches all over Europe and even in the United States. It manufactures school supplies, accounting ledgers, and stationery.

—C'est pas vrai...!

—Je suis votre nouveau prof d'histoire.

Compréhension Answer these questions. Answers will vary.

1. What school-related vocabulary did you understand?
2. Why did one of the girls throw the notebook on the ground?

Discussion In pairs, discuss the answers to these questions. Answers will vary.

1. If the commercial were to continue, what would the characters say next?
2. Do you know of any TV commercials advertising stationery?

SUR INTERNET

Go to espaces.vhlcentral.com to watch the TV clip featured in this **Le zapping**.

Section Goals

In this section, students will:

- read about the company Clairefontaine
- watch a commercial for Clairefontaine notebooks
- answer questions about the commercial and Clairefontaine

Instructional Resources
*IRCD-ROM: IRM (**Le zapping** TV clip transcription)*
espaces.vhlcentral.com: activities, downloads, reference tools, TV clip

Introduction
To check students' comprehension, ask these questions.
1. What was the origin of the Clairefontaine company? (It was a paper factory founded in 1858 in eastern France.)
2. What product did Clairefontaine start making after Charles Nusse took over? (It started to make notebooks with high-quality paper.)
3. Is Clairefontaine a successful brand? (Yes. It has a famous logo, and the company has branches in Europe and the United States.)

Avant de regarder la vidéo

- Have students look at the video stills, read the captions, and predict what is happening in the commercial for each visual. (1. Two teenage girls are chatting at school. 2. They meet their new teacher.)
- Before showing the video, explain to students that they do not need to understand every word they hear. Tell them to listen for cognates, school-related vocabulary, and the slogan.

Compréhension Have students work in pairs or groups for this activity. Tell them to write their answers. Then show the video again so that they can check their work and add any missing information.

Discussion After discussing the questions, ask volunteers to report their comments and ideas to the class.

OPTIONS

Le papier Clairefontaine People love Clairefontaine notebooks for the quality of their paper. The company uses ultra-smooth, brushed vellum paper that it manufactures itself. This paper weighs 90 grams per square meter. It is also very white and anti-glare. Clairefontaine is currently the only manufacturer making its own paper for its stationery products. This helps the company maintain consistent paper quality and also controls the environmental impact of the paper manufacturing process. The company uses pulp exclusively from trees grown in certified sustainable forests.

Section Goals

In this section, students will learn historical, cultural, and geographical information about France.

Instructional Resources
IRCD-ROM: Transparency #20
WB/VM: Workbook, pp. 27–28
WB/VM/LM Answer Key
espaces.vhlcentral.com: activities; downloads; reference tools

Carte de la France

- Have students look at the map of France or use **Transparency #20**. Ask volunteers to read the cities' names aloud.
- Have students identify the location of the place or object in each photo.

Le pays en chiffres

- Have students read the section headings. Point out the type of information contained in each section and clarify unfamiliar words.
- Have volunteers read the sections aloud. After each section, ask questions about the content.
- Ask students to share any additional information they might know about the people in **Français célèbres.**

Incroyable mais vrai!
L'Académie française was founded by Cardinal Richelieu during the reign of Louis XIII. In the beginning, the Academy's primary role was to standardize the language for French-speaking people by establishing rules to make it pure, eloquent, and capable of dealing with the arts and sciences.

Panorama

La France

Le pays en chiffres

- **Superficie:** *549.000 km² (cinq cent quarante-neuf mille kilomètres carrés°)*
- **Population:** *61.203.000 (soixante et un millions deux cent trois mille)*
  SOURCE: Population Division, UN Secrétariat
- **Industries principales:** *agro-alimentaires°, assurance°, banques, énergie, produits pharmaceutiques, produits de luxe, télécommunications, tourisme, transports*
  La France est le pays° le plus° visité du monde° avec plus de° 60 millions de touristes chaque° année. Son histoire, sa culture et ses monuments–plus de 12.000 (douze mille)–et musées–plus de 1.200 (mille deux cents)–attirent° des touristes d'Europe et de partout° dans le monde.
- **Villes principales:** *Paris, Lille, Lyon, Marseille, Toulouse*
- **Monnaie°:** *l'euro*
  La France est un pays membre de l'Union Européenne et, en 2002, l'euro a remplacé° le franc français comme° monnaie nationale.

Français célèbres

- **Jeanne d'Arc,** *héroïne française (1412–1431)*
- **Émile Zola,** *écrivain° (1840–1902)*
- **Auguste Renoir,** *peintre° (1841–1919)*
- **Claude Debussy,** *compositeur et musicien (1862–1918)*
- **Camille Claudel,** *femme sculpteur (1864–1943)*
- **Claudie André-Deshays,** *médecin, première astronaute française (1957–)*

un bateau-mouche sur la Seine

le château de Chenonceau

le pont° du Gard

Incroyable mais vrai!

Être «immortel», c'est réguler et défendre le bon usage du français! Les Académiciens de l'Académie française sont élus à vie° et s'appellent les «Immortels». Depuis° 1635 (mille six cent trente-cinq), ils décident de l'orthographe correcte des mots° et publient un dictionnaire. Attention, c'est «courrier° électronique», pas «e-mail»!

carrés *square* **agro-alimentaires** *food processing* **assurance** *insurance* **pays** *country* **le plus** *the most* **monde** *world* **plus de** *more than* **chaque** *each* **attirent** *attract* **partout** *everywhere* **Monnaie** *Currency* **a remplacé** *replaced* **comme** *as* **écrivain** *writer* **peintre** *painter* **élus à vie** *elected for life* **Depuis** *Since* **mots** *words* **courrier** *mail* **pont** *bridge*

OPTIONS

Le pays en chiffres France is the third largest country in Europe. It is divided into 22 **régions** (*regions*), which include **la Corse** (*Corsica*). The **régions** are divided into 95 **départements** (*departments*). France also has four overseas **Départements et régions d'outre-mer (DROM): Guadeloupe, Guyane française, la Réunion,** and **Martinique.** Using the map of France in **Appendice A** that shows the **régions** and **départements,** have students locate various cities as you say the names. Example: **Marseille (C'est dans le département 13.)**

Oral Presentation If a student has visited France (preferably outside Paris), ask him or her to prepare a short presentation about his or her experiences there. Encourage the student to bring in photos and souvenirs of France.

La géographie

L'Hexagone

Surnommé l'Hexagone à cause de° sa forme géométrique, le territoire français a trois fronts maritimes: l'océan Atlantique, la mer° Méditerranée et la Manche°; et trois frontières° naturelles: les Pyrénées, les Ardennes et les Alpes et le Jura. À l'intérieur du pays°, le Massif central et les Vosges ponctuent° un relief composé de vastes plaines et de forêts. La Loire, la Seine, la Garonne, le Rhin et le Rhône sont les fleuves° principaux de l'Hexagone.

La technologie

Le Train à Grande Vitesse

Le chemin de fer° existe en France depuis° 1827 (mille huit cent vingt-sept). Aujourd'hui, la SNCF (Société Nationale des Chemins de Fer) offre la possibilité aux voyageurs de se déplacer° dans tout° le pays et propose des tarifs° avantageux aux étudiants et aux moins de 25 ans°. Le TGV (Train à Grande Vitesse°) roule° à plus de 300 (trois cent) km/h (kilomètres/heure) et emmène° même° les voyageurs jusqu'à° Londres et Bruxelles.

Audrey Tautou

Les arts

Le cinéma, le 7e art!

L'invention du cinématographe par les frères° Lumière en 1895 (mille huit cent quatre-vingt-quinze) marque le début° du «7e (septième) art». Le cinéma français donne naissance° aux prestigieux Césars° en 1976 (mille neuf cent soixante-seize), à des cinéastes talentueux comme° Jean Renoir, François Truffaut et Luc Besson, et à des acteurs mémorables comme Brigitte Bardot, Catherine Deneuve, Olivier Martinez et Audrey Tautou.

L'économie

L'industrie

Avec la richesse de la culture française, il est facile d'oublier que l'économie en France n'est pas limitée à l'artisanat°, à la gastronomie ou à la haute couture°. En fait°, la France est une véritable puissance° industrielle et se classe° parmi° les économies les plus° importantes du monde. Ses° activités dans des secteurs comme la construction automobile (e.g. Peugeot, Citroën, Renault), l'industrie aérospatiale (e.g. Airbus) et l'énergie nucléaire (e.g. Électricité de France) sont considérables.

Qu'est-ce que vous avez appris? Complete these sentences.

1. Camille Claudel est une femme sculpteur française.
2. Les Académiciens sont élus à vie.
3. Le mot correct en français pour «e-mail», c'est courrier électronique.
4. À cause de sa forme, la France s'appelle aussi «l'Hexagone».
5. La SNCF offre la possibilité de voyager dans tout le pays.
6. Avec le TGV, on voyage de Paris à Londres.
7. Les frères Lumières sont les inventeurs du cinéma.
8. Answers will vary. Possible answer: Jean Renoir est un grand cinéaste français.
9. La France est une grande puissance industrielle.
10. Électricité de France produit (*produces*) l'énergie nucléaire.

ressources

WB pp. 27-28	espaces.vhlcentral.com Unité 2

SUR INTERNET

Go to espaces.vhlcentral.com to find more cultural information related to this **PANORAMA**.

1. Cherchez des informations sur l'Académie française. Faites (*Make*) une liste de mots ajoutés à la dernière édition du dictionnaire de l'Académie française.
2. Cherchez des informations sur l'actrice Catherine Deneuve. Quand a-t-elle commencé (*did she begin*) sa (*her*) carrière? Trouvez ses (*her*) trois derniers films.

à cause de *because of* **mer** *sea* **Manche** *English Channel* **frontières** *borders* **pays** *country* **ponctuent** *punctuate* **fleuves** *rivers* **chemin de fer** *railroad* **depuis** *since* **se déplacer** *travel* **dans tout** *throughout* **tarifs** *fares* **moins de 25 ans** *people under 25* **Train à Grande Vitesse** *high speed train* **roule** *rolls, travels* **emmène** *takes* **même** *even* **jusqu'à** *to* **frères** *brothers* **début** *beginning* **donne naissance** *gives birth* **Césars** *equivalent of the Oscars in France* **comme** *such as* **artisanat** *craft/ cottage industry* **haute couture** *high fashion* **En fait** *In fact* **puissance** *power* **se classe** *ranks* **parmi** *among* **les plus** *the most* **Ses** *Its*

L'Hexagone Have students locate the geographical features mentioned on the map or use **Transparency #20**.

Le Train à Grande Vitesse

- The first **TGV** service was from Paris to Lyon in 1981. Since then, its service has expanded. Presently, the high-speed network has over 30,000 kilometers of track that connect over 150 cities and towns in France.
- Have students look at the photo and compare the **TGV** to the trains they have traveled on or seen in the Unites States. Then have them figure out the speed of the **TGV** in miles per hour (1 km = 0.62 mile). (300 km/h = 186 mph)

Le cinéma, le 7e art! Each year the members of **l'Académie des Arts et Techniques du Cinéma** choose the actors, actresses, directors, and others involved in film-making to receive the **César** awards for their outstanding achievements. The **Césars** were named after the artist who designed the award trophies.

L'industrie

- The arts and crafts industry, **l'Artisanat**, can be found throughout France. Using traditional methods that are centuries old, French artisans craft hand-made products, such as pottery, figurines, jewelry, textiles, fabrics, and wood carvings. Each region's products reflect the history and culture of that particular area.
- Bring in some French craft items or magazine photos of items to show the class.

OPTIONS

Game Create categories for the newly learned information on France: **Géographie, Français célèbres, Technologie,** etc. Make index cards with a question on one side and category on the other. Tape cards to the board under the appropriate categories with questions face down. Teams take turns picking a card and answering the question. Give a point for each right answer. The team with the most points at the end wins.

Cultural Comparison Distribute a list in French of the award categories for the **Césars** from the web site of **l'Académie des Arts et Techniques du Cinéma** (**www.lescesarducinema.com**). Ask if the same categories exist for the Oscars. Show them pictures of a **César** and an Oscar. Have students compare the trophies. Ask what other film festivals occur in France. (Cannes Film Festival and the American Film Festival)

Section Goals

In this section, students will:
- learn to use text formats to predict content
- read a brochure for a French language school

Stratégie
Tell students that many documents have easily identifiable formats that can help them predict the content. Have them look at the document in the **Stratégie** box and ask them to identify the recognizable elements:
- days of the week
- times
- classes

Ask what kind of document it is. (a student's weekly schedule)

Examinez le texte Have students look at the headings and ask them what type of information is contained in **École de français (pour étrangers) de Lille**. (lists of courses by level and specialization, a list of supplementary activities, and a list of types of housing available) Then ask students what types of documents contain these elements. (brochures)

Mots apparentés
- In pairs, have students scan the brochure, identify cognates, and guess their meanings.
- Ask students what this document is and its purpose. (It's a brochure. It's advertising a French language and culture immersion program. Its purpose is to attract students.)

Lecture

Avant la lecture

STRATÉGIE

Predicting content through formats

Recognizing the format of a document can help you to predict its content. For instance, invitations, greeting cards, and classified ads follow an easily identifiable format, which usually gives you a general idea of the information they contain. Look at the text and identify it based on its format.

	lundi	mardi	mercredi	jeudi	vendredi
8h30	biologie		biologie		biologie
9h00		histoire		histoire	
9h30	anglais		anglais		anglais
10h00					
10h30					
11h00					
11h30					
12h00					
12h30					
1h00	art		art		art

If you guessed that this is a page from a student's schedule, you are correct. You can now infer that the document contains information about a student's weekly schedule, including days, times, and activities.

Examinez le texte

Briefly look at the document. What is its format? What kind of information is given? How is it organized? Are there any visuals? What kind? What type(s) of documents usually contain these elements?

Mots apparentés

As you have already learned, in addition to format, you can use cognates to help you predict the content of a document. With a classmate, make a list of all the cognates you find in the reading selection. Based on these cognates and the format of the document, can you guess what this document is and what it's for?

ÉCOLE DE FRANÇAIS

(pour étrangers°) DE LILLE

COURS DE FRANÇAIS POUR TOUS°	COURS DE SPÉCIALISATION
Niveau° débutant°	Français pour enfants°
Niveau élémentaire	Français des affaires°
Niveau intermédiaire	Droit° français
Niveau avancé	Français pour le tourisme
Conversation	Culture et civilisation
Grammaire française	Histoire de France
	Art et littérature
	Arts culinaires

26, place d'Arsonval • 59000 Lille
Tél. 03.20.52.48.17 • Fax. 03.20.52.48.18 • www.efpelille.fr

OPTIONS

Extra Practice Have students write a friend's or family member's weekly schedule as homework. Tell them to label the days of the week in French and add notes for that person's appointments and activities. In class, ask students questions about the schedules they wrote. Examples: **Quel cours est-ce que ____ a aujourd'hui? Combien de jours est-ce que ____ travaille cette semaine?**

Cultural Activity Ask students what aspects of this school they find appealing or interesting: **Qu'est-ce que vous trouvez intéressant à l'école?** Jot down their responses on the board. Then do a quick class survey to find out which aspect is the most appealing.

Programmes de 2 à 8 semaines,
4 à 8 heures par jour
Immersion totale
Professeurs diplômés

le Musée des Beaux-Arts, Lille

GRAND CHOIX° D'ACTIVITÉS SUPPLÉMENTAIRES

- Excursions à la journée dans la région
- Visites de monuments et autres sites touristiques
- Sorties° culturelles (théâtre, concert, opéra et autres spectacles°)
- Sports et autres activités de loisir°

HÉBERGEMENT°

- En cité universitaire°
- Dans° une famille française
- À l'hôtel

pour étrangers *for foreigners* **tous** *all* **Niveau** *Level* **débutant** *beginner* **enfants** *children* **affaires** *business* **Droit** *Law* **choix** *choice* **Sorties** *Outings* **spectacles** *shows* **loisir** *leisure* **hébergement** *lodging* **cité universitaire** *university dormitories (on campus)* **Dans** *In*

Après la lecture

Répondez **Select the correct response or completion to each question or statement, based on the reading selection.**

1. C'est une brochure pour...
   (a.) des cours de français pour étrangers.
   b. une université française.
   c. des études supérieures en Belgique.
2. «Histoire de France» est...
   a. un cours pour les professeurs diplômés.
   (b.) un cours de spécialisation.
   c. un cours pour les enfants.
3. Le cours de «Français pour le tourisme» est utile pour...
   a. une étudiante qui (*who*) étudie les sciences po.
   (b.) une femme qui travaille dans un hôtel de luxe.
   c. un professeur d'administration des affaires.
4. Un étudiant étranger qui commence le français assiste probablement à quel (*which*) cours?
   a. Cours de français pour tous, Niveau avancé
   b. Cours de spécialisation, Arts et littérature
   (c.) Cours de français pour tous, Niveau débutant
5. Quel cours est utile pour un homme qui parle assez bien français et qui travaille dans l'économie?
   (a.) Cours de spécialisation, Français des affaires
   b. Cours de spécialisation, Arts culinaires
   c. Cours de spécialisation, Culture et civilisation
6. Le week-end, les étudiants...
   a. passent des examens.
   b. travaillent dans des hôtels.
   (c.) visitent la ville et la région.
7. Les étudiants qui habitent dans une famille...
   (a.) ont envie de rencontrer des Français.
   b. ont des bourses.
   c. ne sont pas reçus aux examens.
8. Un étudiant en architecture va aimer...
   a. le cours de droit français.
   (b.) les visites de monuments et de sites touristiques.
   c. les activités sportives.

Complétez **Complete these sentences.**

1. Le numéro de téléphone est le __03.20.52.48.17__.
2. Le numéro de fax est le __03.20.52.48.18__.
3. L'adresse de l'école est __26, place d'Arsonval, 59000 Lille__.
4. L'école offre des programmes de Français de __2 à 8__ semaines et de __4 à 8 heures__ par jour.

Répondez Go over the answers with the whole class or have students check their answers in pairs.

Complétez For additional practice, give students these items. **5. L'école est à____. (Lille) 6. L'adresse Internet de l'école est ____. (www.efpelille.fr) 7. Grammaire française est un cours de ____. (français pour tous) 8. Les professeurs de l'école sont ____. (diplômés) 9. On habite en cité universitaire, ____ ou à l'hôtel. (dans une famille française)**

Suggestion Encourage students to record unfamiliar words and phrases that they learn in **Lecture** in their notebooks.

OPTIONS

Small Groups Provide students with magazines and newspapers in French. Have groups of three or four students work together to look for documents in French with easily recognizable formats, such as classified ads or other advertisements. Ask them to use cognates and other context clues to predict the content. Then have groups present their examples and findings to the class.

Oral Presentation Invite a student who has studied abroad to come and speak to the class about the school he or she attended, the classes, and any interesting experiences he or she had there. Encourage the class to ask questions.

Section Goals

In this section, students will:

- learn to listen for cognates
- listen to sentences containing familiar and unfamiliar vocabulary
- listen to a conversation, complete a schedule, and answer true/false questions

Instructional Resources
Textbook MP3s
IRCD-ROM: IRM (Textbook Audioscript)
espaces.vhlcentral.com: downloads, reference tools

Stratégie
Script 1. Dans certaines institutions d'études supérieures, les étudiants reçoivent un salaire. 2. Ma cousine étudie la médecine vétérinaire. C'est sa passion!

Préparation Have students describe the photo. Ask them to justify their descriptions based on the visual clues.

Suggestion To check answers for the **À vous d'écouter** activity, have students work in pairs and take turns asking questions about Marie-France's schedule. Example: **Est-ce que Marie-France a cours de biologie à 14h00? (Non, elle a cours de biologie à 9h30.)**

À vous d'écouter
Script DOMINIQUE: Tiens, bonjour, Marie-France. Comment ça va?
MARIE-FRANCE: Salut, Dominique. Ça va bien. Et toi?
D: Très bien, merci. Tu vas en cours?
M: Oui, j'ai cours toute la journée, le lundi. Ce matin, j'ai biologie à neuf heures et demie.
D: Tu aimes la biologie?
M: Oui, j'aime bien. C'est facile. Après, à onze heures, j'ai chimie. Ça, je déteste! C'est difficile! À midi, je mange au resto U avec des copains.
D: Et cet après-midi?
M: Alors, à deux heures, j'ai psychologie et à trois heures et demie, j'ai physique.
D: Est-ce que tu aimes ça, la physique?
M: Oui, mais cette année, le prof n'est pas très intéressant.
D: Ah bon? Qui est-ce?
M: Monsieur Meyer.
D: Ah oui! Tu as raison. Il n'est pas très intéressant. Et il donne des devoirs et des examens très difficiles.
M: C'est vrai. Et toi, tu aimes tes cours cette année?
D: Oui, beaucoup. J'adore l'informatique. Le prof est amusant et il explique bien.
M: Tu as de la chance! Dis, est-ce que tu as envie de dîner au restaurant avec Sophie et moi ce soir? On va au restaurant vietnamien près de l'université.
D: Oui, avec plaisir. À quelle heure?
M: À sept heures et demie.
D: Bon, d'accord. À ce soir.
M: Salut.

À l'écoute

STRATÉGIE

Listening for cognates

You already know that cognates are words that have similar spellings and meanings in two or more languages: for example *group* and **groupe** or *activity* and **activité**. Listen for cognates to increase your comprehension of spoken French.

 To help you practice this strategy, you will listen to two sentences. Make a list of all the cognates you hear.

Préparation

Based on the photograph, who and where do you think Marie-France and Dominique are? Do you think they know each other well? Where are they probably going this morning? What do you think they are talking about?

À vous d'écouter

Listen to the conversation and list any cognates you hear. Listen again and complete the highlighted portions of Marie-France's schedule.

28 OCTOBRE	lundi		
8H00	*jogging*	14H00	psychologie
8H30		14H30	
9H00		15H00	
9H30	biologie	15H30	physique
10H00		16H00	
10H30		16H30	
11H00	chimie	17H00	
11H30		17H30	*étudier*
12H00	resto U	18H00	
12H30		18H30	
13H00	*bibliothèque*	19H00	*téléphoner à papa*
13H30		19H30	*Sophie:* restaurant vietnamien

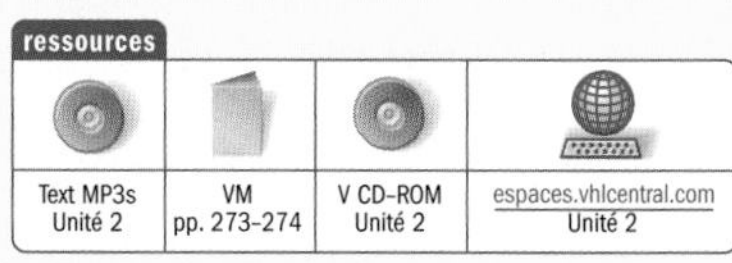

Compréhension

Vrai ou faux? Indicate whether each statement is **vrai** or **faux**. Then correct the false statements.

1. D'après Marie-France, la biologie est facile.
   Vrai.
2. Marie-France adore la chimie.
   Faux. Marie-France déteste la chimie.
3. Marie-France et Dominique mangent au restaurant vietnamien à midi.
   Faux. Marie-France et Dominique mangent au restaurant vietnamien à sept heures et demie du soir.
4. Dominique aime son cours de sciences politiques.
   Faux. Dominique aime son cours d'informatique.
5. Monsieur Meyer est professeur de physique.
   Vrai.
6. Monsieur Meyer donne des devoirs faciles.
   Faux. Monsieur Meyer donne des devoirs très difficiles.
7. Le lundi après-midi, Marie-France a psychologie et physique.
   Vrai.
8. Aujourd'hui, Dominique mange au resto U.
   Faux. Aujourd'hui, Marie-France mange au resto U.

Votre emploi du temps With a partner, discuss the classes you're taking this semester. Be sure to say when you have each one, and give your opinion of at least three courses.

Écriture

STRATÉGIE

Brainstorming

In the early stages of writing, brainstorming can help you generate ideas on a specific topic. You should spend ten to fifteen minutes brainstorming and jotting down any ideas about the topic that occur to you. Whenever possible, try to write down your ideas in French. Express your ideas in single words or phrases, and jot them down in any order. While brainstorming, do not worry about whether your ideas are good or bad. Selecting and organizing ideas should be the second stage of your writing. Remember that the more ideas you write down while you are brainstorming, the more options you will have to choose from later when you start to organize your ideas.

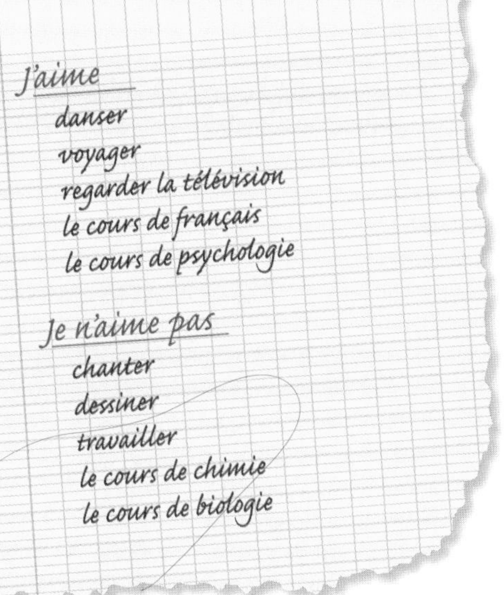

j'aime
danser
voyager
regarder la télévision
le cours de français
le cours de psychologie
Je n'aime pas
chanter
dessiner
travailler
le cours de chimie
le cours de biologie

FLASH CULTURE

Watch the **FLASH CULTURE** segment on the **ESPACES** video for cultural footage related to this unit's theme.

Thème

Une description personnelle

Write a description of yourself to post on a web site in order to find a francophone e-pal. Your description should include:

- your name and where you are from
- the name of your university and where it is located
- the courses you are currently taking and your opinion of each one
- some of your likes and dislikes
- where you work if you have a job
- any other information you would like to include

Bonjour!

Je m'appelle Xavier Dupré.
Je suis québécois, mais j'étudie le droit à l'université de Lyon, en France. J'aime...

Section Goals

In this section, students will:

- learn to brainstorm and organize their ideas for writing
- learn to write a description of themselves
- integrate vocabulary and structures taught in **Leçon 4** and previous lessons
- view authentic cultural footage of university life

Instructional Resources
WB/VM: Video Manual, pp. 273–274
WB/VM/LM Answer Key
IRCD-ROM: IRM (Videoscript)
Video CD-ROM
Video on DVD
espaces.vhlcentral.com: activities, downloads, reference tools

Stratégie Discuss information students might want to include in a self-description, recording their suggestions on the board in French. Quickly review structures students will include in their writing, such as **j'aime** and **je n'aime pas** as well as the first person singular of several verbs. Examples: **je m'appelle, je suis, j'étudie, j'ai cours de...,** and **je travaille**.

Thème Copy on the board the brief chat room description for Xavier Dupré, leaving blanks where his name, nationality, course of study, and university name appear. At the end, add the sentences **J'aime** ____. and **Je n'aime pas** ____. Model completing the description orally with your own information and then ask volunteers to complete it with their own information.

Flash culture Tell students that they will learn more about classes and university life by watching a variety of real-life images narrated by Benjamin. Show the video segment, then have students jot down in French at least three examples of people or things they saw. You can also use the activities in the video manual in class to reinforce this **Flash culture** or assign them as homework.

EVALUATION

Criteria	Scale
Content	1 2 3 4 5
Organization	1 2 3 4 5
Use of vocabulary	1 2 3 4 5
Grammatical accuracy	1 2 3 4 5

Scoring	
Excellent	18–20 points
Good	14–17 points
Satisfactory	10–13 points
Unsatisfactory	< 10 points

VOCABULAIRE

Instructional Resources
Textbook MP3s
IRCD-ROM: IRM (Textbook Audioscript)
espaces.vhlcentral.com: downloads, reference tools

Verbes

adorer	*to love*
aimer	*to like; to love*
aimer mieux	*to prefer*
arriver	*to arrive*
chercher	*to look for*
commencer	*to begin, to start*
dessiner	*to draw; to design*
détester	*to hate*
donner	*to give*
étudier	*to study*
habiter (à)	*to live (in)*
manger	*to eat*
oublier	*to forget*
parler (au téléphone)	*to speak (on the phone)*
partager	*to share*
penser (que/qu')	*to think (that)*
regarder	*to look (at), to watch*
rencontrer	*to meet*
retrouver	*to meet up with; to find (again)*
travailler	*to work*
voyager	*to travel*

Vocabulaire supplémentaire

J'adore...	*I love...*
J'aime bien...	*I like...*
Je n'aime pas tellement...	*I don't like... very much.*
Je déteste...	*I hate...*
être reçu(e) à un examen	*to pass an exam*

Des questions et des opinions

bien sûr	*of course*
d'accord	*OK, all right*
Est-ce que/qu'...?	*question phrase*
(mais) non	*no (but of course not)*
moi/toi non plus	*me/you neither*
ne... pas	*no, not*
n'est-ce pas?	*isn't that right?*
oui/si	*yes*
parce que	*because*
pas du tout	*not at all*
peut-être	*maybe, perhaps*
pourquoi?	*why?*

ressources
Text MP3s Unité 2
espaces.vhlcentral.com Unité 2

L'université

assister	*to attend*
demander	*to ask*
dîner	*to have dinner*
échouer	*to fail*
écouter	*to listen (to)*
enseigner	*to teach*
expliquer	*to explain*
passer un examen	*to take an exam*
préparer	*to prepare (for)*
rentrer (à la maison)	*to return (home)*
téléphoner à	*to telephone*
trouver	*to find; to think*
visiter	*to visit (a place)*
l'architecture (f.)	*architecture*
l'art (m.)	*art*
la biologie	*biology*
la chimie	*chemistry*
le droit	*law*
l'économie (f.)	*economics*
l'éducation physique (f.)	*physical education*
la géographie	*geography*
la gestion	*business administration*
l'histoire (f.)	*history*
l'informatique (f.)	*computer science*
les langues (étrangères) (f.)	*(foreign) languages*
les lettres (f.)	*humanities*
les mathématiques (maths) (f.)	*mathematics*
la philosophie	*philosophy*
la physique	*physics*
la psychologie	*psychology*
les sciences (politiques/po) (f.)	*(political) science*
le stylisme de mode (m.)	*fashion design*
une bourse	*scholarship, grant*
un cours	*class, course*
un devoir	*homework*
un diplôme	*diploma, degree*
l'école (f.)	*school*
les études (supérieures) (f.)	*(higher) education; studies*
le gymnase	*gymnasium*
une note	*grade*
un restaurant universitaire (un resto U)	*university cafeteria*

Expressions utiles	See pp. 43 and 57.
Telling time	See pp. 62–63.

Expressions de temps

Quel jour sommes-nous?	*What day is it?*
un an	*year*
une/cette année	*one/this year*
après	*after*
après-demain	*day after tomorrow*
un/cet après-midi	*an/this afternoon*
aujourd'hui	*today*
demain (matin/après-midi/soir)	*tomorrow (morning/afternoon/evening)*
un jour	*day*
une journée	*day*
(le) lundi, mardi, mercredi, jeudi, vendredi, samedi, dimanche	*(on) Monday(s), Tuesday(s), Wednesday(s), Thursday(s), Friday(s), Saturday(s), Sunday(s)*
un/ce matin	*a/this morning*
la matinée	*morning*
un mois/ce mois-ci	*a month/this month*
une/cette nuit	*a/this night*
une/cette semaine	*a/this week*
un/ce soir	*an/this evening*
une soirée	*evening*
un/le/ce week-end	*a/the/this weekend*
dernier/dernière	*last*
premier/première	*first*
prochain(e)	*next*

Adjectifs et adverbes

difficile	*difficult*
facile	*easy*
inutile	*useless*
utile	*useful*
surtout	*especially; above all*

Expressions avec avoir

avoir	*to have*
avoir... ans	*to be... years old*
avoir besoin (de)	*to need*
avoir chaud	*to be hot*
avoir de la chance	*to be lucky*
avoir envie (de)	*to feel like*
avoir froid	*to be cold*
avoir honte (de)	*to be ashamed (of)*
avoir l'air	*to look like*
avoir peur (de)	*to be afraid (of)*
avoir raison	*to be right*
avoir sommeil	*to be sleepy*
avoir tort	*to be wrong*

La famille et les copains

UNITÉ **3**

Pour commencer

- Combien de personnes y a-t-il?
- Sont-elles dans un café?
- Mangent-elles? Parlent-elles?
- Ont-elles l'air agréables ou désagréables?
- Aiment-elles les ordinateurs?

Unit Goals

Leçon 5
In this lesson, students will learn:
- terms for family members and marital status
- some terms for pets
- usage of **l'accent aigu** and **l'accent grave**
- about the French family
- descriptive adjectives
- possessive adjectives
- to give an oral presentation on a famous family

Leçon 6
In this lesson, students will learn:
- terms for some professions and occupations
- more descriptive adjectives
- usage of **l'accent circonflexe, la cédille**, and **le tréma**
- about different types of friendships and relationships between people
- the numbers 61–100
- some prepositions of location
- disjunctive pronouns
- about singer Tino Rossi and painter Pierre-Auguste Renoir

Savoir-faire
In this section, students will learn:
- historical and cultural information about the city of Paris
- to use visuals and graphic elements to predict content
- to ask for repetition in oral communication
- to use idea maps to organize information
- to write an informal letter
- more about families and friends through specially shot video footage

Pour commencer
- **Il y a trois personnes.**
- **Oui, elles sont dans un café.**
- **Non, elles ne mangent pas. Oui, elles parlent.**
- **Elles ont l'air agréable.**
- **Oui, elles aiment les ordinateurs.**

RESOURCES

Workbook/Video Manual: WB Activities, pp. 29–42
Laboratory Manual: Lab Activities, pp. 17–24
Workbook/Video Manual: Video Activities, pp. 219–222; pp. 275–276
WB/VM/LM Answer Key
Instructor's Resource CD-ROM [IRCD-ROM]: Instructor's Resource Manual [IRM] (Textbook Audioscript; Lab Audioscript; Videoscript; **Roman-photo** Translations; **Vocabulaire supplémentaire**; **Feuilles d'activités**; Info Gap Activities; **Essayez!** and **Mise en pratique** answers; Transparencies #21, #22, #23, #24; Testing Program, pp. 17–24, pp. 121–128; Test Files; Testing Program MP3s; Test Generator
Lab MP3s
Textbook MP3s
Video CD-ROM
Video on DVD
espaces.vhlcentral.com

Section Goals

In this section, students will learn and practice vocabulary related to:
- family members
- some pets
- marital status

Instructional Resources
*IRCD-ROM: Transparencies #21, #22; IRM (**Vocabulaire supplémentaire; Mise en pratique** answers; Textbook Audioscript; Lab Audioscript; **Feuilles d'activités**)*
Textbook MP3s
WB/VM: Workbook, pp. 29–30
Lab Manual, p. 17
Lab MP3s
WB/VM/LM Answer Key
espaces.vhlcentral.com: activities, downloads, reference tools

Suggestions
- Introduce active lesson vocabulary with questions and gestures. Ask: **Comment s'appelle ton frère?** Ask a different student: **Comment s'appelle le frère de ____?** Work your way through various family relationships.
- Point out the meanings of plural family terms so that students understand that the masculine plural forms can refer to mixed groups of males and females:
  les enfants *male children; female children; male and female children*
  les cousins *male cousins; male and female cousins*
  les petits-enfants *male grandchildren; male and female grandchildren*
- Point out the difference in meaning between the noun **mari** (*husband*) and the adjective **marié(e)** (*married*).
- Use **Transparency #21**. Point out that the family tree is drawn from the point of view of Marie Laval. Have students refer to the family tree to answer your questions about it. Example: **Comment s'appelle la mère de Marie?**
- Additional vocabulary for this lesson can be found in the **Vocabulaire supplémentaire** in the IRM on the IRCD-ROM.

Leçon 5

You will learn how to...
- **discuss family, friends, and pets**
- **express ownership**

La famille de Marie Laval

Vocabulaire

divorcer	*to divorce*
épouser	*to marry*
aîné(e)	*elder*
cadet(te)	*younger*
un beau-frère	*brother-in-law*
un beau-père	*father-in-law; stepfather*
une belle-mère	*mother-in-law; stepmother*
un demi-frère	*half-brother; stepbrother*
une demi-sœur	*half-sister; stepsister*
les enfants (*m., f.*)	*children*
un(e) époux/épouse	*husband/wife*
une famille	*family*
une femme	*wife; woman*
une fille	*daughter; girl*
les grands-parents (*m.*)	*grandparents*
les parents (*m.*)	*parents*
un(e) voisin(e)	*neighbor*
un chat	*cat*
un oiseau	*bird*
un poisson	*fish*
célibataire	*single*
divorcé(e)	*divorced*
fiancé(e)	*engaged*
marié(e)	*married*
séparé(e)	*separated*
veuf/veuve	*widowed*

Luc Garneau

mon grand-père (*my grandfather*)

Sophie Garneau

ma tante (*aunt*), femme (*wife*) de Marc

Marc Garneau

mon oncle (*uncle*), fils (*son*) de Luc et d'Hélène

Jean Garneau

mon cousin, petit-fils (*grandson*) de Luc et d'Hélène

Isabelle Garneau

ma cousine, sœur (*sister*) de Jean et de Virginie, petite-fille (*granddaughter*) de Luc et d'Hélène

Virginie Garneau

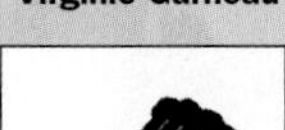

ma cousine, sœur de Jean et d'Isabelle, petite-fille de Luc et d'Hélène

Bambou

le chien (*dog*) de mes (*my*) cousins

ressources

WB pp. 29–30	LM p. 17	Text MP3s Leçon 5	Lab MP3s Leçon 5	espaces.vhlcentral.com Leçon 5

OPTIONS

Extra Practice Draw your own family tree on a transparency or the board and label it with names. Ask students questions about it. Examples: **Est-ce que ____ est ma sœur ou ma tante? Comment s'appelle ma grand-mère? ____ est le neveu ou le frère de ____? Qui est le grand-père de ____?** Help them identify the relationships between members. Then invite them to ask you questions.

Les noms de famille français Ask for a show of hands to see if any students' last names are French in origin. Examples: names that begin with **Fitz____** such as **Fitzgerald** or **Fitzpatrick** (**Fitz-** = **fils de**) and names that begin with **Le____** or **La____** such as **Leblanc** or **Larose**. Ask these students what they know about their French heritage or family history.

Hélène Garneau

ma grand-mère (*my grandmother*)

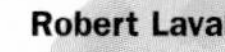

Juliette Laval

ma mère (*mother*), fille (*daughter*) de Luc et d'Hélène

Robert Laval

mon père (*father*), mari (*husband*) de Juliette

Véronique Laval

ma belle-sœur (*sister-in-law*)

Guillaume Laval

mon frère (*brother*)

Marie Laval

Marie Laval, fille de Juliette et de Robert

Matthieu Laval

mon neveu (*nephew*)

Émilie Laval

ma nièce (*niece*)

petits-enfants (*grandchildren*) de mes parents

Mise en pratique

1 Écoutez Listen to each statement made by Marie Laval, then indicate whether it is **vrai** or **faux**, based on her family tree.

	Vrai	Faux		Vrai	Faux
1	☑	☐	6.	☐	☑
2.	☐	☑	7.	☐	☑
3.	☑	☐	8.	☑	☐
4.	☐	☑	9.	☑	☐
5.	☐	☑	10.	☑	☐

2 Qui est-ce? Match the definition in the first list with the correct item from the second list. Not all the items will be used.

1. __d__ le frère de ma cousine
2. __g__ le père de mon cousin
3. __a__ le mari de ma grand-mère
4. __e__ le fils de mon frère
5. __c__ la fille de mon grand-père
6. __i__ le fils de ma mère
7. __h__ la fille de mon fils
8. __f__ le fils de ma belle-mère

a. mon grand-père
b. ma sœur
c. ma tante
d. mon cousin
e. mon neveu
f. mon demi-frère
g. mon oncle
h. ma petite-fille
i. mon frère

3 Choisissez Fill in the blank by selecting the most appropriate answer.

1. Voici le frère de mon père. C'est mon __oncle__ (oncle, neveu, fiancé).
2. Voici la mère de ma cousine. C'est ma __tante__ (grand-mère, voisine, tante).
3. Voici la petite-fille de ma grand-mère. C'est ma __cousine__ (cousine, nièce, épouse).
4. Voici le père de ma mère. C'est mon __grand-père__ (grand-père, oncle, cousin).
5. Voici le fils de mon père, mais ce n'est pas le fils de ma mère. C'est mon __demi-frère__ (petit-fils, demi-frère, voisin).
6. Voici ma nièce. C'est la __petite-fille__ (cousine, fille, petite-fille) de ma mère.
7. Voici la mère de ma tante. C'est ma __grand-mère__ (cousine, grand-mère, nièce).
8. Voici la sœur de mon oncle. C'est ma __tante__ (tante, belle-mère, belle-sœur).
9. Voici la fille de mon père, mais pas de ma mère. C'est ma __demi-sœur__ (belle-sœur, demi-sœur, sœur).
10. Voici le mari de ma mère, mais ce n'est pas mon père. C'est mon __beau-père__ (beau-frère, grand-père, beau-père).

Successful Language Learning Tell students that it isn't necessary to understand every word they hear. They may feel less anxious if they listen for general meaning.

1 Tapescript
1. Marc est mon oncle.
2. Émilie est la nièce de Véronique.
3. Jean est le petit-fils d'Hélène.
4. Robert est mon grand-père.
5. Luc est le père de Sophie.
6. Isabelle est ma tante.
7. Matthieu est le fils de Jean.
8. Émilie est la fille de Guillaume.
9. Juliette est ma mère.
10. Virginie est ma cousine.

(On Textbook MP3s)

1 Expansion Play Marie's statements again, stopping at the end of each. Where the statements are true, have students repeat. Where the statements are false, have students correct them by referring to Marie Laval's family tree.

2 Suggestion Mention that family terms with hyphenated adjectives such as **beau, grand,** and **petit** must agree in gender. Exceptions: **la grand-mère, la demi-sœur.**

3 Expansion Have students provide additional examples for the class to identify.

OPTIONS

Game As a class or group activity, have students state the relationship between people on Marie Laval's family tree. Their classmates will guess which person on the family tree they are describing. Example: **C'est la sœur de Jean et la fille de Sophie. (Isabelle ou Véronique)** Take turns until each member of the class or group has had a chance to state a relationship.

Extra Practice Have students draw their own family tree as homework. Tell them to label each position on the tree with the appropriate French term and the person's name. Also tell them to write five fill-in-the-blank statements based on their family tree. Examples: **Je suis la fille de ____. Mon frère s'appelle ____.** In the next class, have students exchange papers with a classmate and complete the activity.

4 Suggestion You can use **Transparency #22** to do this activity.

5 Suggestion Tell students to jot down their partner's responses.

5 Expansion After they have finished the interview, ask students questions about their partner's answers. Examples: **Combien de personnes y a-t-il dans la famille de ____? Comment s'appellent les parents de ____?**

6 Suggestion Have two volunteers read the **modèle**. Then distribute the **Feuilles d'activités** from the IRM on the IRCD-ROM.

6 Expansion After students have finished, ask true/false questions. Example: **Est-ce que ____ est marié(e)?**

Communication

4 L'arbre généalogique With a classmate, identify the members of the family by asking questions about how each member is related to Anne Durand. Answers will vary.

MODÈLE

Étudiant(e) 1: *Qui est Louis Durand?*
Étudiant(e) 2: *C'est le grand-père d'Anne.*

5 Entrevue With a classmate, take turns asking each other these questions. Answers will vary.

1. Combien de personnes y a-t-il dans ta famille?
2. Comment s'appellent tes parents?
3. As-tu des frères ou des sœurs?
4. Combien de cousins/cousines as-tu? Comment s'appellent-ils/elles? Où habitent-ils/elles?
5. Quel(le) (*Which*) est ton cousin préféré/ta cousine préférée?
6. As-tu des neveux/des nièces?
7. Comment s'appellent tes grands-parents? Où habitent-ils?
8. Combien de petits-enfants ont tes grands-parents?

Coup de main

Use these words to help you complete this activity.

ton *your (m.)* → **mon** *my (m.)*
ta *your (f.)* → **ma** *my (f.)*
tes *your (pl.)* → **mes** *my (pl.)*

6 Qui suis-je? Your instructor will give you a worksheet. Walk around the class and ask your classmates questions about their families. When a classmate gives one of the answers on the worksheet, write his or her name in the corresponding space. Be prepared to discuss the results with the class. Answers will vary.

MODÈLE Je suis marié(e).

Paul: *Est-ce que tu es mariée?*
Jacqueline: *Oui, je suis mariée.* (You write "Jacqueline".)/ *Non, je ne suis pas mariée.* (You ask another classmate.)

OPTIONS

Extra Practice Have students bring in some family photos. In pairs, tell them to take turns pointing to people in their partner's photo and asking who it is. Example: **Qui est-ce? (C'est mon/ma ____.)** Model a few examples. If necessary, write the question and a sample response on the board.

TPR Make a family tree using the whole class. Have each student write down the family designation you assign him or her on a note card or sheet of paper, then arrange students as in a family tree with each one displaying the note card. Then, ask questions about relationships. Examples: **Qui est la mère de ____? Comment s'appelle l'oncle de ____?** Give students the opportunity to ask questions by switching roles with them.

Les sons et les lettres

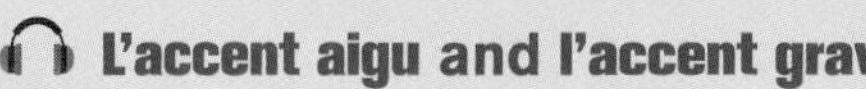

L'accent aigu and l'accent grave

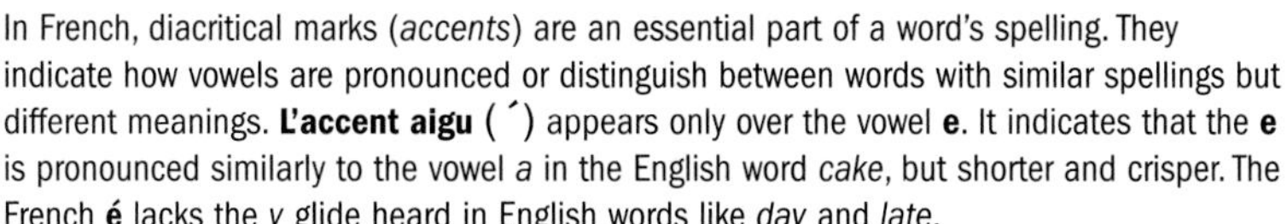

In French, diacritical marks (*accents*) are an essential part of a word's spelling. They indicate how vowels are pronounced or distinguish between words with similar spellings but different meanings. **L'accent aigu** (´) appears only over the vowel **e**. It indicates that the **e** is pronounced similarly to the vowel *a* in the English word *cake*, but shorter and crisper. The French **é** lacks the *y* glide heard in English words like *day* and *late*.

étudier **réservé** **élégant** **téléphone**

L'accent aigu also signals some similarities between French words and English words. Often, an **e** with **l'accent aigu** at the beginning of a French word marks the place where the letter *s* would appear at the beginning of the English equivalent.

éponge	**épouse**	**état**	**étudiante**
sponge	*spouse*	*state*	*student*

L'accent grave (`) over the vowel **e** indicates that the **e** is pronounced like the vowel *e* in the English word *pet*.

très **après** **mère** **nièce**

Although **l'accent grave** does not change the pronunciation of the vowels **a** or **u**, it distinguishes words that have a similar spelling but different meanings.

la	**là**	**ou**	**où**
the	*there*	*or*	*where*

Prononcez Practice saying these words aloud.

1. agréable
2. sincère
3. voilà
4. faculté
5. frère
6. à
7. déjà
8. éléphant
9. lycée
10. poème
11. là
12. élève

Articulez Practice saying these sentences aloud.

1. À tout à l'heure!
2. Thérèse, je te présente Michèle.
3. Hélène est très sérieuse et réservée.
4. Voilà mon père, Frédéric et ma mère, Ségolène.
5. Tu préfères étudier à la fac demain après-midi?

Dictons Practice reading these sayings aloud.

Tel père, tel fils.¹

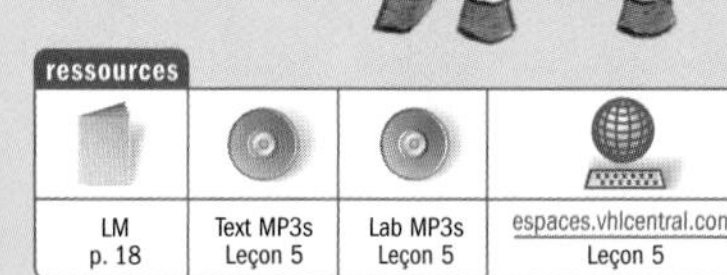

À vieille mule, frein doré.²

ressources: LM p. 18 | Text MP3s Leçon 5 | Lab MP3s Leçon 5 | espaces.vhlcentral.com Leçon 5

¹ Like father, like son.
² For an old mule, a golden bit.

Section Goals

In this section, students will learn about:

- **l'accent aigu**
- **l'accent grave**
- a strategy for recognizing cognates

Instructional Resources

Textbook MP3s
Lab Manual, p. 18
Lab MP3s
WB/VM/LM Answer Key
IRCD-ROM: IRM (Textbook Audioscript; Lab Audioscript)
espaces.vhlcentral.com: activities, downloads, reference tools

Suggestions

- Write **é** on the board. Tell students to watch your mouth as you pronounce the sound. Explain that when **é** appears at the beginning of a word, the corners of your mouth are slightly turned up and your tongue is low behind bottom teeth when you pronounce the sound. Have students repeat **é** after you several times.
- Write words and/or French names from the Laval family with **l'accent aigu** on the board. Pronounce each word as you point to it and have students repeat it after you. Examples: **époux, célibataire, fiancé, séparé, Émilie,** and **Véronique**.
- Give students some sample sentences with **la, là, ou,** or **où** and ask them what the words mean to demonstrate how context clarifies meaning. Examples: **1. Où est la fille? 2. La fille est là. 3. Est-ce que Sophie est la tante ou la grand-mère de Marie Laval?**
- Ask students to provide more examples of words they know with these accents.
- The explanation and exercises are recorded on the Textbook MP3s CD-ROM and are available on the **ESPACES** web site. You may want to play them in class so students hear French speakers besides yourself.

Dictons Explain to students that the saying **«À vieille mule, frein doré»** applies to a situation in which someone tries to sell something old by dressing it up or decorating it. For example, to have a better chance at selling an old car, give it a new paint job.

OPTIONS

Extra Practice Here are additional sentences to use for extra practice with **l'accent aigu** and **l'accent grave. 1. Étienne est mon frère préféré. 2. Ma sœur aînée est très occupée avec les études. 3. André et Geneviève sont séparés. 4. Vous êtes marié ou célibataire? 5. Éric est mon petit ami; nous sommes fiancés.**

Game Have a spelling bee using words with **l'accent aigu** and/or **l'accent grave** from **Leçon 5** or previous lessons. Divide the class into two teams. Call on one team member at a time, alternating between teams. Give a point for each correct answer. The team with the most points at the end of the game wins. Before beginning, remind students that they must indicate the accent marks in the words. Give them an example: **très T-R-E accent grave-S**.

Section Goals

In this section, students will learn functional phrases for talking about their families and describing people through comprehensible input.

Instructional Resources
WB/VM: Video Manual, pp. 219–220
WB/VM/LM Answer Key
Video CD-ROM
Video on DVD
IRCD-ROM: IRM (Videoscript; ***Roman-photo*** *Translations)*
espaces.vhlcentral.com: activities, downloads, reference tools

Video Recap: Leçon 4

Before doing this **Roman-photo**, review the previous one with this activity.

1. Comment s'appelle la copine de Stéphane? (Astrid)
2. Qu'est-ce qu'elle pense de Stéphane? (Answers will vary. **Il n'est pas sérieux. Il ne fait pas ses devoirs. Il n'écoute pas en classe.)**
3. Qui téléphone à Sandrine? (Pascal)
4. On trouve quelle solution pour Stéphane et le bac? (Rachid étudie les maths avec Stéphane.)

Video Synopsis

Michèle wants to know what Amina's friend, Cyberhomme, looks like. Valérie describes her brother's family as she, Stéphane, and Amina look at their photos. Valérie keeps pointing out all the people who have their **bac** because she thinks Stéphane is not studying enough to pass his **bac**. To ease his mother's mind, Stéphane finally tells her that Rachid is helping him study.

Suggestions

- Ask students to read the title, glance at the video stills, and predict what they think the episode will be about. Record their predictions.
- Have students work in groups of four. Tell them to choose a role and read the **Roman-photo** conversation aloud.
- After students have read the **Roman-photo**, quickly review their predictions and ask them which ones were correct. Then ask a few questions to help guide students in summarizing this episode.

NATIONAL STANDARDS communication cultures

L'album de photos

PERSONNAGES

Amina

Michèle

Stéphane

Valérie

1

MICHÈLE Mais, qui c'est? C'est ta sœur? Tes parents?
AMINA C'est mon ami Cyberhomme.
MICHÈLE Comment est-il? Est-ce qu'il est beau? Il a les yeux de quelle couleur? Marron ou bleue? Et ses cheveux? Ils sont blonds ou châtains?
AMINA Je ne sais pas.
MICHÈLE Toi, tu es timide.

2

VALÉRIE Stéphane, tu as dix-sept ans. Cette année, tu passes le bac, mais tu ne travailles pas!
STÉPHANE Écoute, ce n'est pas vrai, je déteste mes cours, mais je travaille beaucoup. Regarde, mon cahier de chimie, mes livres de français, ma calculatrice pour le cours de maths, mon dictionnaire anglais-français...

3

STÉPHANE Oh, et qu'est-ce que c'est? Ah, oui, les photos de tante Françoise.
VALÉRIE Des photos? Mais où?
STÉPHANE Ici! Amina, on peut regarder des photos de ma tante sur ton ordinateur, s'il te plaît?

6

AMINA Ah, et ça, c'est toute la famille, n'est-ce pas?
VALÉRIE Oui, ça c'est Henri, sa femme Françoise et leurs enfants: le fils aîné Bernard, et puis son frère Charles, sa sœur Sophie et leur chien Socrate.
STÉPHANE J'aime bien Socrate. Il est vieux, mais il est amusant!

7

VALÉRIE Ah! Et Bernard, il a son bac aussi et sa mère est très heureuse.
STÉPHANE Moi, j'ai envie d'habiter avec oncle Henri et tante Françoise. Comme ça, pas de problème pour le bac!

8

STÉPHANE Pardon, maman. Je suis très heureux ici avec toi. Ah, au fait, Rachid travaille avec moi pour préparer le bac.
VALÉRIE Ah, bon? Rachid est très intelligent... un étudiant sérieux.

ACTIVITÉS

1 Vrai ou faux? Are the sentences **vrai** or **faux**?

1. Amina communique avec sa (*her*) tante par ordinateur. Faux.
2. Stéphane n'aime pas ses (*his*) cours au lycée. Vrai.
3. Ils regardent des photos de vacances. Faux.
4. Henri est le frère aîné de Valérie. Vrai.
5. Bernard est le cousin de Stéphane. Vrai.
6. Charles a déjà son bac. Vrai.
7. La tante de Stéphane s'appelle Françoise. Vrai.
8. Stéphane travaille avec Amina pour préparer le bac. Faux.
9. Socrate est le fils d'Henri et de Françoise. Faux.
10. Rachid n'est pas un bon étudiant. Faux.

OPTIONS

Avant de regarder la vidéo Before viewing the video episode **L'album de photos**, ask students to brainstorm a list of things someone might say when describing his or her family photos.

Regarder la vidéo Play the first half of the video episode and have students describe what happened. Write their observations on the board. Then ask them to guess what will happen in the second half of the episode. Write their ideas on the board. Play the entire video episode, then help the class summarize the plot.

Stéphane et Valérie regardent des photos de famille avec Amina.

À la table d'Amina...

AMINA Alors, voilà vos photos. Qui est-ce?

VALÉRIE Oh, c'est Henri, mon frère aîné!

AMINA Quel âge a-t-il?

VALÉRIE Il a cinquante ans. Il est très sociable et c'est un très bon père.

5

VALÉRIE Ah! Et ça c'est ma nièce Sophie et mon neveu Charles! Regarde, Stéphane, tes cousins!

STÉPHANE Je n'aime pas Charles. Il est tellement sérieux.

VALÉRIE Il est peut-être trop sérieux, mais, lui, il a son bac!

AMINA Et Sophie, qu'elle est jolie!

VALÉRIE ... et elle a déjà son bac.

AMINA Ça oui, préparer le bac avec Rachid, c'est une idée géniale!

VALÉRIE Oui, c'est vrai. En théorie, c'est une excellente idée. Mais tu prépares le bac avec Rachid, hein? Pas le prochain match de foot!

Expressions utiles

Talking about your family

- **C'est ta sœur? Tes parents?**
  Is that your sister? Your parents?
- **C'est mon ami.**
  That's my friend.
- **Ça c'est Henri, sa femme Françoise et leurs enfants.**
  That's Henri, his wife Françoise, and their kids.

Describing people

- **Il a les yeux de quelle couleur? Marron ou bleue?**
  What color are his eyes? Brown or blue?
- **Il a les yeux bleus.**
  He has blue eyes.
- **Et ses cheveux? Ils sont blonds ou châtains? Frisés ou raides?**
  And his hair? Is it blond or brown? Curly or straight?
- **Il a les cheveux châtains et frisés.**
  He has curly brown hair.

Additional vocabulary

- **On peut regarder des photos de ma tante sur ton ordinateur?**
  Can/May we look at some photos from my aunt on your computer?
- **C'est toute la famille, n'est-ce pas?**
  That's the whole family, right?
- **Je ne sais pas (encore).**
  I (still) don't know.
- **Alors...** *So...*
- **vrai** *true*
- **une photo(graphie)** *a photograph*
- **une idée** *an idea*
- **peut-être** *maybe*
- **au fait** *by the way*
- **Hein?** *Right?*
- **déjà** *already*

ACTIVITÉS

2 Vocabulaire Describe how Stéphane would be on the occasions listed. Refer to a dictionary as necessary.

1. on his 87th birthday _vieux_
2. after finding 20€ _heureux_
3. while taking the **bac** _sérieux_
4. after getting a good grade _heureux_
5. after getting a make-over _beau_

beau
heureux
sérieux
vieux

3 Conversez In pairs, describe which member of your family is most like Stéphane. How are they alike? Do they both like sports? Do they take similar subjects? How do they like school? How are their personalities? Be prepared to describe your partner's "Stéphane" to the class.

ressources: VM pp. 219–220 | V CD-ROM Leçon 5 | espaces.vhlcentral.com Leçon 5

OPTIONS

Pairs Working in pairs, have students draw a family tree based on Valérie's description of her brother's family. Tell them to use the family tree on page 74 as a model. Remind them to include Valérie and Stéphane. Then have them get together with another pair of students and compare their drawings.

Small Groups Have students write four questions about Henri's family based on the conversation and video still #6. Then have them get together in groups of three and take turns asking and answering each other's questions. Examples: **Combien de personnes y a-t-il dans la famille d'Henri? Comment s'appelle le fils aîné? Combien de frères a Sophie?**

Expressions utiles

- Point out the various forms of possessive adjectives and descriptive adjectives in the captions and the **Expressions utiles.** Tell students that this material will be formally presented in the **Structures** section. Do not expect students to produce the forms correctly at this time.
- Model the pronunciation of the **Expressions utiles** and have students repeat them.
- To practice new vocabulary, ask students to describe their classmates' eyes and hair. Examples: ____ **a les yeux de quelle couleur? Marron ou bleue? Avez-vous les yeux bleus?** ____ **a-t-il/elle les cheveux blonds ou châtains? Qui a les cheveux blonds/châtains dans la classe? Est-ce que les cheveux de** ____ **sont frisés ou raides?**

1 Suggestion Have students correct the false statements.

1 Expansion For additional practice, give students these items. **11. Valérie n'aime pas son frère, Henri. (Faux.) 12. Stéphane aime les gens très sérieux. (Faux.) 13. Socrate est un chien. (Vrai.) 14. Stéphane et Rachid préparent le prochain match de foot. (Faux.)**

2 Suggestion Before beginning the activity, you might want to introduce the adjectives in the word list using pictures or people in the video stills rather that having students look them up in the dictionary.

2 Expansion Have students describe Rachid, Charles, and Henri using the adjectives in the word list. At this point, avoid asking students to describe people that would require a feminine or plural form of these adjectives.

3 Suggestion If time is limited, this activity may be assigned as a written composition for homework.

Section Goals

In this section, students will:

- learn about the different types of French families
- learn some informal terms for family members
- find out when Mother's Day and Father's Day are celebrated in various French-speaking regions
- read about Jacques Chirac and his family

Instructional Resources
espaces.vhlcentral.com: activities, downloads, reference tools

Culture à la loupe

Avant la lecture

- Have students look at the photo and describe the family there. Ask: **La famille est-elle traditionnelle ou non-conventionnelle? (Elle est traditionnelle.)**
- Tell students to scan the reading, identify the cognates, and guess their meanings.

Lecture Point out the statistics chart. Tell students that this data refers to Metropolitan France (Source: INSEE). Ask them what information this chart shows. (The percentages of different types of French families by age group.) Ask students to name the types of families. (**Célibataires, couples sans enfants, couples avec enfants,** and **familles monoparentales**)

Après la lecture

- Ask students what facts about French families are new or surprising to them.
- Have students compare French and American families. Ask: **Est-ce qu'il y a des similitudes (*similarities*) entre la famille française et la famille américaine? Et des différences?**

1 Suggestion If students have difficulty filling in the blanks, provide them with a word bank.

1 Expansion Have pairs write four more fill-in-the-blank statements. Tell them to exchange papers with another pair and complete the sentences.

CULTURE À LA LOUPE

La famille française

Comment est la famille française? Est-elle différente de la famille américaine? La structure familiale traditionnelle existe-t-elle toujours°? La majorité des Français sont-ils mariés, divorcés ou célibataires?

Il n'y a pas de réponse simple à ces questions. Si on regarde la population française d'aujourd'hui, on observe que les familles françaises sont très diverses. Le mariage est toujours très populaire: la majorité des hommes et des femmes sont mariés. Mais attention! Le nombre de personnes divorcées augmente chaque° année, tout comme° le nombre de personnes célibataires.

Selon° l'âge et les circonstances individuelles, les couples vivent° avec ou sans° enfants. La structure familiale traditionnelle existe toujours en France, mais il y a aussi des structures moins traditionnelles, comme les familles monoparentales, où° l'unique parent est divorcé, séparé ou veuf. Il y a aussi des familles qui combinent deux familles, avec un beau-père, une belle-mère, des demi-frères et des demi-sœurs. Certains couples choisissent° le Pacte Civil de Solidarité (PACS), qui offre certains droits° et protections aux couples qui habitent ensemble° mais qui ne sont pas mariés.

Oubliez les stéréotypes des familles françaises. Elles sont grandes et elles sont petites; elles sont traditionnelles et non-conventionnelles; elles changent et elles sont toujours les mêmes°.

toujours *still* **chaque** *each* **tout comme** *just like* **Selon** *According to* **vivent** *live* **sans** *without* **où** *where* **choisissent** *choose* **droits** *rights* **ensemble** *together* **mêmes** *same* **tranche** *bracket*

Coup de main

Remember to read decimal places in **French** using the French word **virgule** (*comma*) where you would normally say *point* in English. To say *percent*, use **pour cent.**

64,3% soixante-quatre virgule trois pour cent
sixty-four point three percent

La situation familiale des Français
(par tranche° d'âge)

ÂGE	CÉLIBATAIRE	EN COUPLE SANS ENFANTS	EN COUPLE AVEC ENFANTS	PARENT D'UNE FAMILLE MONOPARENTALE
< 25 ans	3,6%	2,8%	1%	0,3%
25–29 ans	16,7%	26,5%	26,2%	2,6%
30–44 ans	10,9%	9,8%	64,3%	6,2%
45–59 ans	11,7%	29,9%	47,2%	5,9%
> 60 ans	20,3%	59,2%	11,7%	2,9%

ACTIVITÉS

1 Complétez Provide logical answers.

1. Si on regarde la population française d'aujourd'hui, on observe que les familles françaises sont très __diverses__.
2. Le __mariage__ est toujours très populaire en France.
3. La majorité des hommes et des femmes sont __mariés__.
4. Le nombre de Français qui restent __célibataires__ augmente.
5. Les Français vivent en couple, avec ou sans __enfants__.
6. Dans les familles __monoparentales__, l'unique parent est divorcé, séparé ou veuf.
7. Il y a des familles qui combinent __deux__ familles.
8. Le __PACS__ offre certains droits et protections aux couples qui ne sont pas mariés.
9. Oubliez les __stéréotypes__ des familles françaises.
10. Les familles françaises changent et elles sont toujours __les mêmes__.

OPTIONS

La famille française Explain to students that the concept of family is changing in France. In the past, extended families (grandparents, parents, and children) often lived in the same dwelling. Today fewer grandparents live with their children, and the number of traditional nuclear families (mother, father and children) as well as non-traditional families is increasing.

In spite of these changes, family life is still an important social institution in French culture. When people say **la famille**, the majority of them are referring to their extended family. Most holidays are spent with family, and students often choose a university near their home so that they can spend the weekends with their family.

LE FRANÇAIS QUOTIDIEN

La famille

frangin	*brother*
frangine	*sister*
maman	*Mom, Mum*
mamie	*Nana, Grandma*
minou	*kitty*
papa	*Dad*
papi	*Granddad*
tata	*Auntie*
tonton	*Uncle*
toutou	*doggy*

LE MONDE FRANCOPHONE

Les fêtes et la famille

Les États-Unis ont quelques fêtes° en commun avec le monde francophone, mais les dates et les traditions de ces fêtes diffèrent d'un pays° à l'autre°. Voici deux fêtes associées à la famille.

La Fête des mères

En France le dernier° dimanche de mai ou le premier° dimanche de juin
En Belgique le deuxième° dimanche de mai
À l'île Maurice le dernier dimanche de mai
Au Canada le deuxième dimanche de mai

La Fête des pères

En France le troisième° dimanche de juin
En Belgique le deuxième dimanche de juin
Au Canada le troisième dimanche de juin

quelques fêtes *some holidays* **pays** *country* **autre** *other*
dernier *last* **premier** *first* **deuxième** *second* **troisième** *third*

PORTRAIT

Jacques Chirac, président et père

Jacques Chirac, élu° président de la République française en 1995 (mille neuf cent quatre-vingt-quinze), est père de famille et enfant unique, mais il n'est pas le seul° Chirac dans l'arène politique. Claude Chirac, seconde fille de° Monsieur Chirac et de son° épouse Bernadette, travaille avec son père à Paris. Experte en communication et surnommée° «Madame fille» par la presse française, Claude est aussi mère de famille. Son° fils est né° en 1995, l'année de l'élection présidentielle de son grand-père, Jacques Chirac.

élu *elected* **seul** *only* **de** *of* **son** *his*
surnommée *nicknamed* **Son** *Her* **est né** *was born*

SUR INTERNET

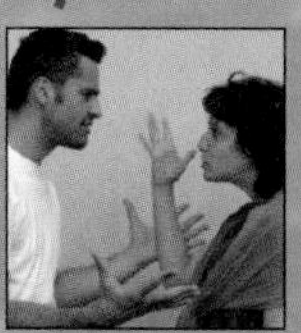

Le divorce en France est-il épidémique?

Go to **espaces.vhlcentral.com** to find more cultural information related to this **ESPACE CULTURE.**

ACTIVITÉS

2 Vrai ou faux? Are these statements **vrai** or **faux**?

1. Claude Chirac est enfant unique. Faux. Jacques Chirac est enfant unique.
2. Jacques Chirac est grand-père. Vrai.
3. «Madame fille» est la femme de Jacques Chirac. Faux. «Madame fille» est la fille de Jacques Chirac.
4. Claude Chirac a un fils. Vrai.
5. La famille Chirac célèbre une fête le troisième dimanche de juin. Vrai.
6. Le deuxième dimanche de mai, c'est la Fête des mères en Belgique et au Canada. Vrai.

3 À vous... With a partner, write six sentences using the vocabulary in **Le français quotidien**. Be prepared to share them with your classmates.

Le français quotidien Point out that this vocabulary, while quite common in day-to-day language, is very familiar. These words are usually used in informal conversations with family members, children, and close friends.

Portrait Show the class a photo of Jacques Chirac. Ask: **Qui est-ce? Comment s'appelle-t-il?** Ask students what they know about President Chirac. Explain that the President of the French Republic, even after he has left office, is still known and referred to as **Monsieur le Président**. For example, after Chirac leaves office, people will still refer to him as the president.

Le monde francophone Explain that Mother's Day and Father's Day did not originate in France. The first **Journée des mères** took place in France in 1926; it became an official holiday **La Fête des mères** in 1950.

2 Suggestion Have students correct the false statements.

2 Expansion Have students write three more true/false statements based on **Portrait** and **Le monde francophone**. Then have them work in groups of three and take turns reading their statements while the other group members respond **vrai** or **faux**.

3 Expansion Have students work in pairs. Tell them to create a brief conversation in which they talk about their families and pets, using vocabulary in **Le français quotidien**. Example: **Est-ce que tu as un minou? Non, mais ma tata, elle a des minous.** Remind students that this level of language is only appropriate when talking to small children.

OPTIONS

Les fêtes de la famille Explain to students that many countries around the world have a special day to honor mothers. **La Fête des mères** and **La Fête des pères** are celebrated somewhat similarly in France, Belgium, and Canada to the way Mother's Day and Father's Day are celebrated in the United States. Children create cards, write poems, and make handicrafts in school to give to their parents on these holidays. Older sons and daughters often give a small gift. On **l'île Maurice**, they do not officially celebrate Father's Day. In other francophone regions, such as North and West Africa, there is no official holiday for either Mother's or Father's Day.

National Standards: comparisons

Section Goals

In this section, students will learn:
- forms, agreement, and position of adjectives
- high-frequency descriptive adjectives and some irregular adjectives

Instructional Resources
WB/VM: Workbook, pp. 31–32
Lab Manual, p. 19
Lab MP3s
WB/VM/LM Answer Key
*IRCD-ROM: IRM (**Essayez!** and **Mise en pratique** answers; Lab Audioscript)*
espaces.vhlcentral.com: activities, downloads, reference tools

Suggestions
- Write these adjectives on the board: **américain, amusant, intelligent, timide, aînée**. Say each word and ask students if it is masculine or feminine. Model one of the adjectives in a sentence and ask volunteers to use the others in sentences.
- Work through the discussion of adjective forms point by point, writing examples on the board. Remind students that grammatical gender doesn't necessarily reflect the actual gender. Example: **Charles est une personne nerveuse.**
- Use magazine pictures and the names of celebrities to teach or practice descriptive adjectives in semantic pairs. Use either/or questions, yes/no questions, or a combination. Examples: **Est-ce que Tiger Woods est grand ou petit? (Il est grand.) Jessica Simpson est-elle brune? (Non, elle est blonde.)**
- Point out the adjectives that have the same masculine and feminine form.
- Teach students the pneumonic device **BAGS** to help them remember the adjectives placed before a noun: **B** as in beauty for **joli, beau**; **A** as in age for **jeune, vieux, nouveau**; **G** as in goodness for **bon, mauvais, pauvre**; and **S** as in size for **grand, petit, long,** and **gros**.

5.1 Descriptive adjectives

Point de départ As you learned in **Leçon 2**, adjectives describe people, places, and things. In French, most adjectives agree in gender and number with the nouns or pronouns they modify.

SINGULAR MASCULINE NOUN ⟷ SINGULAR MASCULINE ADJECTIVE

Le **père** est **américain**.
The father is American.

PLURAL MASCULINE NOUN ⟷ PLURAL MASCULINE ADJECTIVE

As-tu des **cours faciles**?
Do you have easy classes?

- You've already learned several adjectives of nationality and some adjectives to describe your classes. Here are some adjectives used to describe physical characteristics.

Adjectives of physical description

bleu(e)	*blue*	**joli(e)**	*pretty*
blond(e)	*blond*	**laid(e)**	*ugly*
brun(e)	*dark (hair)*	**marron**	*brown*
châtain	*brown (hair)*	**noir(e)**	*black*
court(e)	*short*	**petit(e)**	*small, short (stature)*
grand(e)	*tall, big*	**raide**	*straight*
jeune	*young*	**vert(e)**	*green*

- Notice that, in the examples below, the adjectives agree in gender and number with the subjects.

Elles sont **blondes** et **petites**.
They are blond and short.

L'examen est **long**.
The exam is long.

- Use the expression **de taille moyenne** to describe someone or something of medium size.

Victor est un homme **de taille moyenne**.
Victor is a man of medium height.

C'est une université **de taille moyenne**.
It's a medium-sized university.

- The adjective **marron** is invariable; that is, it does not agree in gender and number with the noun it modifies. The adjective **châtain** is almost exclusively used to describe hair color.

Mon neveu a les **yeux marron**.
My nephew has brown eyes.

Ma nièce a les **cheveux châtains**.
My niece has brown hair.

MISE EN PRATIQUE

1 Ressemblances Family members often look and behave alike. Describe them.

MODÈLE
Caroline est intelligente. Elle a un frère.
Il est intelligent aussi.

1. Jean est curieux. Il a une sœur. Elle est curieuse aussi.
2. Carole est blonde. Elle a un cousin. Il est blond aussi.
3. Albert est gros. Il a trois tantes. Elles sont grosses aussi.
4. Sylvie est fière et heureuse. Elle a un fils. Il est fier et heu[reux] aussi.
5. Christophe est vieux. Il a une demi-sœur. Elle est vieille a[ussi].
6. Martin est laid. Il a une petite-fille. Elle est laide aussi.
7. Sophie est intellectuelle. Elle a deux grands-pères. Ils sont intellectuels aussi.
8. Céline est naïve. Elle a deux frères. Ils sont naïfs aussi.
9. Anne est belle. Elle a cinq neveux. Ils sont beaux aussi.
10. Anissa est rousse. Elle a un mari. Il est roux aussi.

2 Une femme heureuse Christine has a happy life. To know why, complete these sentences.

MODÈLE
Christine / avoir / trois enfants (beau)
Christine a trois beaux enfants.

1. Elle / avoir / des amis (sympathique)
Elle a des amis sympathiques.
2. Elle / habiter / dans un appartement (nouveau)
Elle habite dans un nouvel appartement.
3. Son (*Her*) mari / avoir / un travail (bon)
Son mari a un bon travail.
4. Ses (*Her*) filles / être / des étudiantes (sérieux)
Ses filles sont des étudiantes sérieuses.
5. Christine / être / une femme (heureux)
Christine est une femme heureuse.
6. Son mari / être / un homme (beau)
Son mari est un bel homme.
7. Elle / avoir / des collègues (amusant)
Elle a des collègues amusants.
8. Sa (*Her*) secrétaire / être / une fille (jeune/intellectuel)
Sa secrétaire est une jeune fille intellectuelle.
9. Elle / avoir / des chiens (bon)
Elle a de bons chiens.
10. Ses voisins / être (poli)
Ses voisins sont polis.

OPTIONS

Extra Practice Have pairs of students write sentences using adjectives such as **jeune, grand, joli,** and **court**. When they have finished, ask volunteers to dictate their sentences to you to write on the board. After you have written a sentence and corrected any errors, ask volunteers to suggest a sentence that uses the antonym of the adjective.

Game Divide the class into two teams. Call on one team member at a time, alternating between teams. Give a certain form of an adjective and name another form that the person must say and write on the board. Example: **beau**; feminine plural (**belles**). Give a point for each correct answer. The team with the most points at the end of the game wins.

NATIONAL communication STANDARDS

COMMUNICATION

3 **Comparaisons** In pairs, take turns comparing these brothers and their sister. Make as many comparisons as possible, then share them with the class to see which pair is most perceptive. Answers will vary.

Jean-Paul Tristan Géraldine

MODÈLE

Géraldine et Jean-Paul sont grands mais Tristan est petit.

4 **Qui est-ce?** Choose the name of a classmate. Your partner must guess the person by asking up to 10 **oui** or **non** questions. Then, switch roles. Answers will vary.

MODÈLE

Étudiant(e) 1: *C'est un homme?*
Étudiant(e) 2: *Oui.*
Étudiant(e) 1: *Il est de taille moyenne?*
Étudiant(e) 2: *Non.*

5 **Les bons copains** Interview two classmates to learn about one of their friends, using these questions and descriptive adjectives. Be prepared to report to the class what you learned. Answers will vary.

- Est-ce que tu as un(e) bon(ne) copain/copine?
- Comment est-ce qu'il/elle s'appelle?
- Quel âge est-ce qu'il/elle a?
- Comment est-ce qu'il/elle est?
- Il/Elle est de quelle origine?
- Quels cours est-ce qu'il/elle aime?
- Quels cours est-ce qu'il/elle déteste?

Some irregular adjectives

masculine singular	feminine singular	masculine plural	feminine plural	
beau	**belle**	**beaux**	**belles**	*beautiful; handsome*
bon	**bonne**	**bons**	**bonnes**	*good; kind*
fier	**fière**	**fiers**	**fières**	*proud*
gros	**grosse**	**gros**	**grosses**	*fat*
heureux	**heureuse**	**heureux**	**heureuses**	*happy*
intellectuel	**intellectuelle**	**intellectuels**	**intellectuelles**	*intellectual*
long	**longue**	**longs**	**longues**	*long*
naïf	**naïve**	**naïfs**	**naïves**	*naïve*
roux	**rousse**	**roux**	**rousses**	*red-haired*
vieux	**vieille**	**vieux**	**vieilles**	*old*

- The forms of the adjective **nouveau** (*new*) follow the same pattern as those of **beau**.
- Other adjectives that follow the pattern of **heureux** are **curieux** (*curious*), **malheureux** (*unhappy*), **nerveux** (*nervous*), and **sérieux** (*serious*).

Position of adjectives

- These adjectives are usually placed before the noun they modify: **beau**, **bon**, **grand**, **gros**, **jeune**, **joli**, **long**, **nouveau**, **petit**, and **vieux**.

J'aime bien les **grandes familles**.
I like large families.

Joël est un **vieux copain**.
Joël is an old friend.

- These adjectives are also generally placed before a noun: **mauvais(e)** (*bad*), **pauvre** (*poor, unfortunate*), **vrai(e)** (*true, real*).
- These forms are used before masculine singular nouns that begin with a vowel sound.

beau	**bel**	un **bel** appartement
vieux	**vieil**	un **vieil** homme
nouveau	**nouvel**	un **nouvel** ami

- The plural indefinite article **des** changes to **de** before an adjective followed by a noun.

J'habite avec **des amis sympathiques**.
I live with nice friends.

J'habite avec **de bons amis**.
I live with good friends.

Essayez! Provide all four forms of the adjectives.

1. grand *grand, grande, grands, grandes*
2. nerveux nerveux, nerveuse, nerveux, nerveuses
3. roux roux, rousse, roux, rousses
4. bleu bleu, bleue, bleus, bleues
5. naïf naïf, naïve, naïfs, naïves
6. gros gros, grosse, gros, grosses
7. long long, longue, longs, longues
8. fier fier, fière, fiers, fières

Language Note Point out that the adjective **châtain** comes from the noun **une châtaigne**, which is a type of sweet chestnut. The adjective **marron** is also a noun; **un marron** means horse chestnut.

Essayez! Have students create sentences using these adjectives. Examples: **La tour Eiffel est grande. Les étudiants ne sont pas naïfs.**

1 Expansion Have students restate the answers, except #3, #7, #8 and #9, using the phrase **les deux** to practice plural forms. Example: **1. Les deux sont curieux.**

2 Suggestion To check students' work, have volunteers write their sentences on the board and read them aloud.

2 Expansion For additional practice, change the adjective(s) and have students restate or write the sentences. Examples: **1. bon (Elle a de bons amis.) 2. vieux (Elle habite dans un vieil appartement.) 3. désagréable (Son mari a un travail désagréable.) 4. bon (Ses filles sont de bonnes étudiantes.) 5. indépendant/élégant (Christine est une femme indépendante et élégante.) 6. fier (Son mari est un homme fier.) 7. réservé (Elle a des collègues réservés.) 8. joli/petit (Sa secrétaire est une jolie, petite femme.)**

3 Expansion To practice negation, have students say what the people in the drawings are not. Example: **Géraldine et Jean-Paul ne sont pas petits.**

4 Suggestion This activity can also be done in small groups or with the whole class.

5 Suggestions
- To model this activity, have students look at the photo and respond as you ask the interview questions. Tell them to invent answers, where necessary.
- Tell students to add two questions of their own to the list and to jot down notes during their interviews.
- If time is limited, have students write a description of one of their classmates' friends as written homework.

OPTIONS

Extra Practice Have students brainstorm and make a list of adjectives in French that describe their ideal spouse **(Mon époux idéal/Mon épouse idéale)**. Tell them to rank each adjective in terms of its importance to them. Then take a quick class survey to find out what the most important and least important qualities are in the ideal spouse. Tally the results on the board.

Extra Practice Prepare short descriptions of five easily recognizable people. Write their names on the board in random order. Tell students to write your descriptions as you dictate them. Then have them match the description to the appropriate name. Example: **Elle est jeune, brune, athlétique et intellectuelle. (Serena Williams)**

Section Goals

In this section, students will learn:
- possessive adjectives
- to express possession and relationships with **de**

Instructional Resources
WB/VM: Workbook, pp. 33–34
Lab Manual, p. 20
Lab MP3s
WB/VM/LM Answer Key
*IRCD-ROM: IRM (**Essayez!** and **Mise en pratique** answers; Lab Audioscript)*
espaces.vhlcentral.com: activities, downloads, reference tools

Suggestions
- Introduce the concept of possessive adjectives. Ask volunteers questions, such as: **Est-ce que votre mère est heureuse? Comment est-il, votre oncle préféré?** Point out the possessive adjectives in questions and responses.
- List the possessive adjectives on the board. Use each with a noun to illustrate agreement. Point out that all possessive adjectives agree in number with the noun they modify, but that all singular possessives must agree in gender and number. Examples: **son cousin, sa cousine, ses cousin(e)s; leur cousin, leur cousine, leurs cousin(e)s.** Also point out that **mon**, **ton**, and **son** are used before feminine singular nouns beginning with a vowel sound or silent **h**. Examples: **mon épouse, ton idée, son université.**
- Have students give the plural or singular of possessive adjectives with nouns. Say: **Donne le pluriel: mon étudiant, ton examen, notre cours.** Say: **Donne le singulier: mes sœurs, nos frères, leurs chiens, ses enfants.**
- To introduce possession with **de**, write the following phrases in a list on the board: **l'ordinateur de Monique, l'ordinateur d'Alain, l'ordinateur du professeur, les ordinateurs des professeurs.** Explain the use of the contractions **d'**, **du (de + le)**, and **des (de + les)**.
- Ask students these questions. **C'est mon stylo? C'est votre amie? Ce sont leurs devoirs? C'est sa feuille de papier? Ce sont nos livres de français? C'est l'ordinateur de ____? C'est le C'est le sac à dos de ____?**

5.2 Possessive adjectives

Point de départ In both English and French, possessive adjectives express ownership or possession.

BOÎTE À OUTILS
In ESPACE CONTEXTES, you learned a few possessive adjectives with family vocabulary: **mon grand-père**, **ma sœur**, **mes cousins**.

Possessive adjectives

masculine singular	feminine singular	plural	
mon	**ma**	**mes**	*my*
ton	**ta**	**tes**	*your* (fam. and sing.)
son	**sa**	**ses**	*his, her, its*
notre	**notre**	**nos**	*our*
votre	**votre**	**vos**	*your* (form. or pl.)
leur	**leur**	**leurs**	*their*

- Possessive adjectives are always placed before the nouns they modify.

C'est **ton** père?	Non, c'est **mon** oncle.
Is that your father?	*No, that's my uncle.*

- In French, unlike English, possessive adjectives agree in gender and number with the nouns they modify.

mon frère	**ma** sœur	**mes** grands-parents
my brother	*my sister*	*my grandparents*

- Note that **notre**, **votre**, and **leur** agree in number only.

notre neveu	**notre** famille	**nos** enfants
our nephew	*our family*	*our children*
leur cousin	**leur** cousine	**leurs** cousins
their cousin	*their cousin*	*their cousins*

- The masculine singular forms **mon**, **ton**, and **son** are used with feminine singular nouns that begin with a vowel sound.

mon amie	**ton** étudiante	**son** histoire
my friend	*your student*	*his story*

MISE EN PRATIQUE

1 Complétez Complete the sentences with the correct possessive adjectives.

1. __Ma__ (*My*) sœur est très patiente.
2. Marc et Julien adorent __leurs__ (*their*) cours de philosophie et de maths.
3. Nadine et Gisèle, qui est __votre__ (*your*) amie?
4. C'est une belle photo de __leur__ (*their*) grand-mère.
5. Est-ce que tu as __ta__ (*your*) montre?
6. Nous voyageons en France avec __nos__ (*our*) enfants.
7. Est-ce que tu travailles beaucoup sur __ton__ (*your*) ordinateur?
8. __Ses__ (*Her*) cousins habitent à Paris.
9. J'aime bien __son__ (*his*) livre, il est très intéressant.
10. Bonjour, M. Martin. Comment sont __vos__ (*your*) étudiants cette année?

2 Identifiez Identify the owner(s) of each object.

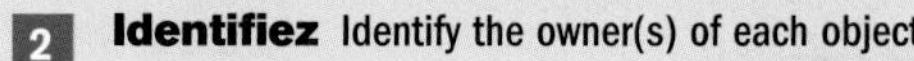

MODÈLE
Ce sont les cahiers de Sophie.

Sophie

Christophe
1. C'est la télévision de Christophe.

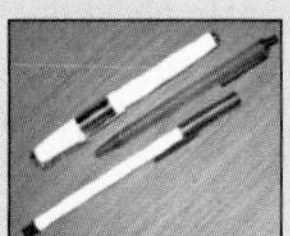
Georgette
4. Ce sont les stylos de Georgette.

Paul
2. C'est l'ordinateur de Paul.

Jacqueline
5. C'est l'université de Jacqueline.

Stéphanie
3. C'est la calculatrice de Stéphanie.

Christine
6. Ce sont les dictionnaires de Christine.

OPTIONS

Video Replay the video episode, having students focus on possessive adjectives. Tell them to write down each one they hear with the noun it modifies. Afterward, ask the class to describe Valérie and Stéphane's family. Remind them to use definite articles and **de** if necessary.

Small Groups Give small groups three minutes to brainstorm how many words they can associate with the phrases **notre université** and **notre cours de français**. Have them model their responses on **Dans notre cours nous avons ____** and **Notre université est ____**. Have the groups share their associations with the rest of the class.

Sandrine perd (*loses*) son téléphone.
Rachid et Stéphane préparent le bac.

STÉPHANE Qui est-ce? C'est moi!
SANDRINE Stéphane! Tu n'es pas drôle!
AMINA Oui, Stéphane. C'est cruel.
STÉPHANE C'est génial...
RACHID Bon, tu es prêt? On travaille chez moi!

À l'appartement de Rachid et de David...
STÉPHANE Sandrine, elle est tellement pénible. Elle parle de Pascal, elle téléphone à Pascal... Pascal, Pascal, Pascal! Que c'est ennuyeux!
RACHID Moi aussi, j'en ai marre.

STÉPHANE Avocate? Moi, j'ai envie d'être architecte.
RACHID Architecte? Alors, c'est pour ça qu'on prépare le bac.

Rachid et Stéphane au travail...
RACHID Allez, si *x* égale 83 et *y* égale 90, la réponse c'est...
STÉPHANE Euh... 100?
RACHID Oui! Bravo!

Expressions utiles

Making complaints

- **Sandrine, elle est tellement pénible.**
  Sandrine, she is so tiresome.
- **J'en ai marre.**
  I'm fed up.
- **Tu sais, David, lui aussi, est pénible.**
  You know, David, he too, he's tiresome.
- **C'est barbant!/C'est la barbe!**
  What a drag!

Reading numbers

- **Numéro de téléphone 06.62.70.94.87 (zéro six, soixante-deux, soixante-dix, quatre-vingt-quatorze, quatre-vingt-sept).**
  Phone number 06.62.70.94.87.
- **Si *x* égale 83 (quatre-vingt-trois) et *y* égale 90 (quatre-vingt-dix)...**
  If x equals 83 and y equals 90...
- **La réponse, c'est 100 (cent).**
  The answer is 100.

Expressing location

- **Où est le téléphone de Sandrine?**
  Where is Sandrine's telephone?
- **Il n'est pas dans son sac à dos.**
  It's not in her backpack.
- **Il est sous ses cahiers.**
  It's under her notebooks.
- **Il est derrière son livre, pas devant.**
  It's behind her book, not in front.
- **Il est à droite ou à gauche?**
  Is it to the right or to the left?
- **Il est sur la table à côté de la porte.**
  It's on the table next to the door.

ACTIVITÉS

2 Vocabulaire Refer to the video stills and dialogues to match these people and objects with their locations.

a/c/e	1. sur la table	a. le téléphone de Sandrine
a	2. pas sous les cahiers	b. Sandrine
b/c/e	3. devant Rachid	c. l'ordinateur de Rachid
b	4. au café	d. la famille de Rachid
f	5. à côté de la porte	e. le café de Rachid
d	6. en Algérie	f. la table

3 Écrivez In pairs, write a brief description in French of one of the video characters. Do not mention the character's name. Describe his or her personality traits, physical characteristics, and career path. Be prepared to read your description aloud to your classmates, who will guess the identity of the character.

ressources
VM pp. 221-222 | V CD-ROM Leçon 6 | espaces.vhlcentral.com Leçon 6

Expressions utiles
- Point out any numbers between 61–100 and prepositions of location in the captions in the **Expressions utiles**. Tell students that this material will be formally presented in the **Structures** section.
- Model the pronunciation of the **Expressions utiles** and have students repeat after you. If available, use a cell phone to model the phrases that express location.
- To practice expressing location, point to different objects in the room and ask students where they are located. Examples: **Est-ce que le livre de ____ est sur le bureau ou sous le bureau? Où est le sac à dos de ____?**

1 Expansion Give students these additional items: **11. Ce n'est pas Pascal! (Sandrine) 12. Elle est avocate. (Rachid) 13. Si x égale 83 et y égale 90, la réponse c'est... (Rachid)**

2 Suggestion To check students' answers, have them form complete sentences using **être**. Examples: **Le téléphone de Sandrine est sur la table. L'ordinateur de Rachid est sur la table.**

3 Suggestions
- Tell pairs to choose a video character and brainstorm a list of adjectives that describe the person before they begin to write their descriptions. Remind them that they can include information from previous episodes.
- Have volunteers read their descriptions and ask the class to guess who it is. Alternatively, you can have students read their descriptions in small groups.

OPTIONS

Extra Practice To practice the terms **à droite** and **à gauche**, ask students to describe the people's positions in reference to each other in the video stills of the **Roman-photo**. Example: **1. Amina est à droite de Sandrine.**

Small Groups Have groups create a short skit similar to the scenes in video stills 1–4 in which someone is searching for a lost object. Provide suggestions for objects. Examples: a notebook (**un cahier**), their homework (**leurs devoirs**), a calculator (**une calculatrice**), a dictionary (**un dictionnaire**), a pen (**un stylo**), and a pencil (**un crayon**). Give students ten minutes to prepare, then call on groups to act out their skits for the class.

Section Goals

In this section, students will:

- learn to distinguish between different types of friendships
- learn some commonly used adjectives to describe people
- learn about some marriage traditions in the francophone world
- read about the Depardieu family

Instructional Resources
espaces.vhlcentral.com: activities, downloads, reference tools

Culture à la loupe

Avant la lecture

- Introduce the reading topic by asking: **Avez-vous beaucoup de copains? Combien d'amis avez-vous? De quoi parlez-vous avec vos copains? Et avec vos amis? Avez-vous un(e) petit(e) ami(e)?**
- Have students look at the photos and describe the people.
- Tell students to scan the reading, identify the cognates, and guess their meanings.

Lecture

- Point out that **un(e) petit(e) ami(e)** is the main term for boyfriend and girlfriend, but **mon ami(e)** or **mon copain/ma copine** without **petit(e)** takes on a similar meaning implying a more romantic relationship.
- Tell students that it is not uncommon to hear people describe their significant others as **fiancé(e)** even if they are not officially engaged.

Après la lecture

- Have students classify the following people as **copains, amis, petits amis**, or **fiancés**. 1. two classmates (**copains**) 2. an engaged couple (**fiancés**) 3. two coworkers (**copains**) 4. you and your best friend (**ami[e]s**) 5. a boyfriend and girlfriend in junior high (**petits amis**)
- Have students identify some differences in French and American dating customs. Ask: **Quelles sont les différences entre les coutumes françaises et américaines des jeunes couples?**

1 Expansion Have students write two more true/false statements. Then tell them to exchange their papers with a classmate and complete the activity.

CULTURE À LA LOUPE

L'amitié

Quelle est la différence entre un copain et un ami? Un petit ami, qu'est-ce que c'est? Avoir plus de copains que° d'amis, c'est normal. Des copains sont des personnes qu'on voit assez souvent°, comme° des gens de l'université ou du travail°, et avec qui on parle de sujets ordinaires. L'amitié° entre copains est souvent éphémère et n'est pas très profonde. D'habitude°, ils ne parlent pas de problèmes très personnels.

Par contre°, des amis parlent de choses plus importantes et plus intimes. L'amitié est plus profonde, solide et stable, même si° on ne voit pas ses amis très souvent. Un ami, c'est une personne très proche° qui vous écoute quand vous avez un problème.

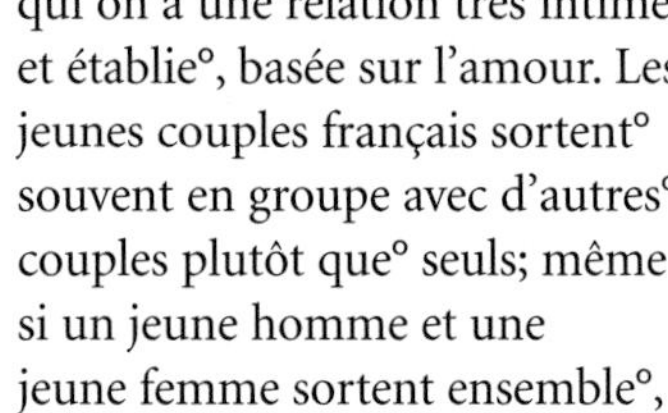

Un(e) petit(e) ami(e) est une personne avec qui on a une relation très intime et établie°, basée sur l'amour. Les jeunes couples français sortent° souvent en groupe avec d'autres° couples plutôt que° seuls; même si un jeune homme et une jeune femme sortent ensemble°, normalement chaque personne paie sa part.

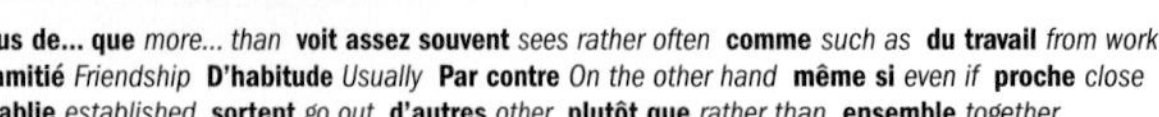

plus de... que *more... than* **voit assez souvent** *sees rather often* **comme** *such as* **du travail** *from work* **L'amitié** *Friendship* **D'habitude** *Usually* **Par contre** *On the other hand* **même si** *even if* **proche** *close* **établie** *established* **sortent** *go out* **d'autres** *other* **plutôt que** *rather than* **ensemble** *together*

Coup de main

To ask *what is* or *what are*, you can use **quel** and a form of the verb **être**. The different forms of **quel** agree in gender and number with the nouns to which they refer:

Quel / Quelle est...?
What is...?

Quels / Quelles sont...?
What are...?

ACTIVITÉS

1 Vrai ou faux? Are these statements **vrai** or **faux**?

1. Un copain est un très bon ami. Faux.
2. D'habitude, on a plus d'amis que de copains. Faux.
3. Un copain est une personne qu'on ne voit pas souvent. Faux.
4. Un ami est une personne avec qui on a une relation très solide. Vrai.
5. Normalement, on ne parle pas de ses problèmes personnels avec ses copains. Vrai.
6. Un ami vous écoute quand vous avez un problème. Vrai.
7. L'amitié entre amis est plus profonde que l'amitié entre copains. Vrai.
8. En général, les jeunes couples français vont au café ou au cinéma en groupe. Vrai.
9. Un petit ami est comme un copain. Faux.
10. En France, les femmes ne paient pas quand elles sortent. Faux.

OPTIONS

Extra Practice In small groups, have students draw a chart with three columns. Tell them to label the columns with the three main types of relationships between people: fellow students or coworkers (**les copains, les collègues**); intimate, platonic friends (**les amis**); and people that are boyfriend and girlfriend (**un[e] petit[e] ami[e]**). Then have students list at least five adjectives in each column in French that apply to the people in that type of relationship. Tell them that they can use adjectives from the reading or others that they know. Examples: **normal, ordinaire, intime, personnel, établi, profond, stable, solide**, and **éphémère**. When students have finished, ask different groups to read their lists of adjectives and compile the results on the board.

LE FRANÇAIS QUOTIDIEN

Pour décrire les gens

bête	*stupid*
borné(e)	*narrow-minded*
canon	*good-looking*
coincé(e)	*inhibited*
cool	*relaxed*
dingue	*crazy*
malin/maligne	*clever*
marrant(e)	*funny*
mignon(ne)	*cute*
zarbi	*weird*

PORTRAIT

Les Depardieu

Gérard

Les Depardieu sont une famille d'acteurs français. Gérard, le père, est l'acteur le plus célèbre° de France. Lauréat° de deux Césars°, un pour *Le Dernier Métro*° et l'autre° pour *Cyrano de Bergerac*, et d'un Golden Globe pour le film américain *Green Card*, il joue depuis trente ans° et a tourné° dans plus de 120 (cent vingt) films. Ses enfants ont aussi du succès dans la profession: Guillaume, son fils, a joué° dans beaucoup de films, y compris° *Tous les matins du monde*° avec son père; Julie, sa fille, a déjà° deux Césars et a joué avec son père dans *Le Comte de Monte-Cristo*.

Guillaume

Julie

le plus célèbre *most famous* **Lauréat** *Winner* **Césars** *César awards (the equivalent of the Oscars in France)* ***Le Dernier Métro*** *The Last Metro* **l'autre** *the other* **il joue depuis trente ans** *he has been acting for thirty years* **a tourné dans** *has been in* **a joué** *has acted* **y compris** *including* ***Tous les matins du monde*** *All the Mornings of the World* **déjà** *already*

LE MONDE FRANCOPHONE

Le mariage et les traditions

Voici des objets et traditions associés au mariage dans le monde francophone.

En France Les jeunes mariés boivent° dans une coupe de mariage°, un objet de famille°.

En Belgique Une femme, à l'occasion de son mariage, porte° le mouchoir° familial où son nom et le nom de toutes les femmes mariées de sa famille sont brodés°.

Au Maroc Les amies de la mariée appliquent° du henné sur les mains° de la mariée.

Au Québec Les jeunes mariés et leurs invités boivent le caribou°.

boivent *drink* **dans une coupe de mariage** *from an engraved, double-handled wedding goblet* **objet de famille** *family heirloom* **porte** *carries* **mouchoir** *handkerchief* **brodés** *embroidered* **appliquent** *apply* **henné sur les mains** *henna to the hands* **caribou** *red wine with whisky*

SUR INTERNET

Quand ils sortent (*go out*), où vont (*go*) les jeunes couples français?

Go to **espaces.vhlcentral.com** to find more cultural information related to this **ESPACE CULTURE.**

ACTIVITÉS

2 Les Depardieu Complete these statements with the correct information.

1. Gérard Depardieu a joué dans plus de ___120___ films.
2. Guillaume est ___le fils___ de Gérard Depardieu.
3. Julie est ___la fille___ de Gérard Depardieu.
4. Julie joue avec Gérard dans ___Le Comte de Monte-Cristo___.
5. Guillaume joue avec Gérard dans ___Tous les matins du monde___.
6. Julie a déjà ___deux___ Césars.

3 Comment sont-ils? Look at the photos of the Depardieu family. With a partner, take turns describing each person in detail in French. How old do you think they are? What do you think their personalities are like? Do you see any family resemblances?

Le français quotidien Have students work in pairs. Tell them to take turns describing their friends or classmates using these words.

Portrait Show the class a photo of Gérard Depardieu. Ask: **Qui est-ce? Comment s'appelle-t-il? Quelle est sa profession?** Repeat the questions with a photo of his son and/or daughter. Then ask students to name any movies starring one or more of the Depardieus that they have seen, for example, *Last Holiday* (2006) or *The Man in the Iron Mask* (1998).

Le monde francophone Ask students which tradition they find most interesting. Then explain that not everyone in these countries follows these customs. The wedding traditions a couple chooses to follow often depend upon their religion. For example, a Jewish couple in France or even the United States might observe Jewish traditions at their wedding, and an Algerian or Moroccan couple might follow Islamic traditions.

2 Expansion To check students' answers, have them work in pairs. Tell students to take turns asking the questions that would elicit each statement and responding with the completed sentence.

3 Expansions
- Give students the following dates of birth and have them calculate the exact age of each person: Gérard (1948), Julie (1973), and Guillaume (1971).
- You might want to tell students that Gérard was born in Châteauroux, France, and that Depardieu is a typical name from the center of France.

OPTIONS

Le mariage et les traditions Here are some other wedding customs or traditions.
- In France, most couples have two wedding ceremonies on the same day. By law, there must be a civil ceremony, and it has to take place before the religious ceremony.
- A traditional Moroccan wedding ceremony lasts from four to seven days. After the couple exchanges vows, the bride walks around the exterior of her new home three times.
- In Belgium, wedding invitations are traditionally printed on two sheets of paper—one sheet is from the bride's family and the other sheet is from the groom's family. The two sheets of paper symbolize the union of two families.

Section Goals

In this section, students will learn numbers 61–100.

Instructional Resources
WB/VM: Workbook, pp. 37–38
Lab Manual, p. 23
Lab MP3s
WB/VM/LM Answer Key
*IRCD-ROM: IRM (**Essayez!** and **Mise en pratique** answers; Lab Audioscript)*
espaces.vhlcentral.com: activities, downloads, reference tools

Suggestions
- Review numbers 0–20 by having the class count with you. Then have them count by tens to 60.
- Model the pronunciation of numbers 61–100 and have students repeat them.
- Explain that the numbers 70–99 follow a slightly different pattern than the numbers 21–69. Point out that 61 and 71 use the conjunction **et**, while 81 and 91 need hyphens.
- Write a few numbers on the board, such as 68, 72, 85, and 99. Have students say each number in French as you point to it. Then have students count by fives from 60–100.
- Numbers 101 and greater are presented in **Leçon 10**.

Essayez! Have students write five more numbers between 61–100. Then tell them to get together with a classmate and take turns dictating their numbers to each other and writing them down. Remind students to check each other's answers.

6.1 Numbers 61–100

Numbers 61–100

61–69	80–89
61 soixante et un	**80** quatre-vingts
62 soixante-deux	**81** quatre-vingt-un
63 soixante-trois	**82** quatre-vingt-deux
64 soixante-quatre	**83** quatre-vingt-trois
65 soixante-cinq	**84** quatre-vingt-quatre
66 soixante-six	**85** quatre-vingt-cinq
67 soixante-sept	**86** quatre-vingt-six
68 soixante-huit	**87** quatre-vingt-sept
69 soixante-neuf	**88** quatre-vingt-huit
	89 quatre-vingt-neuf

70–79	90–100
70 soixante-dix	**90** quatre-vingt-dix
71 soixante et onze	**91** quatre-vingt-onze
72 soixante-douze	**92** quatre-vingt-douze
73 soixante-treize	**93** quatre-vingt-treize
74 soixante-quatorze	**94** quatre-vingt-quatorze
75 soixante-quinze	**95** quatre-vingt-quinze
76 soixante-seize	**96** quatre-vingt-seize
77 soixante-dix-sept	**97** quatre-vingt-dix-sept
78 soixante-dix-huit	**98** quatre-vingt-dix-huit
79 soixante-dix-neuf	**99** quatre-vingt-dix-neuf
	100 cent

BOÎTE À OUTILS
Study tip: To say numbers **70–99**, remember the arithmetic behind them. For example, **quatre-vingt-douze (92)** is **4 (quatre)** x **20 (vingt)** + **12 (douze)**.

- Numbers that end in the digit **1** are not usually hyphenated. They use the conjunction **et** instead.

  trente et un **cinquante et un** **soixante et un**

- Note that **81** and **91** are exceptions:

  quatre-vingt-un **quatre-vingt-onze**

- The number **quatre-vingts** ends in **-s**, but there is no **-s** when it is followed by another number.

  quatre-vingts **quatre-vingt-cinq** **quatre-vingt-dix-huit**

Essayez! What are these numbers in French?

1. 67 soixante-sept
2. 75 soixante-quinze
3. 99 quatre-vingt-dix-neuf
4. 70 soixante-dix
5. 82 quatre-vingt-deux
6. 91 quatre-vingt-onze
7. 66 soixante-six
8. 87 quatre-vingt-sept
9. 52 cinquante-deux
10. 60 soixante

MISE EN PRATIQUE

1 Les numéros de téléphone Write down these phone numbers, then read them aloud in French.

MODÈLE
C'est le zéro un, quarante-trois, soixante-quinze, quatre-vingt-trois, seize.
01.43.75.83.16

1. C'est le zéro deux, soixante-cinq, trente-trois, quatre-vingt-quinze, zéro six. 02.65.33.95.06
2. C'est le zéro un, quatre-vingt-dix-neuf, soixante-quatorze, quinze, vingt-cinq. 01.99.74.15.25
3. C'est le zéro cinq, soixante-cinq, onze, zéro huit, quatre-vingts. 05.65.11.08.80
4. C'est le zéro trois, quatre-vingt-dix-sept, soixante-dix-neuf, cinquante-quatre, vingt-sept. 03.97.79.54.27
5. C'est le zéro quatre, quatre-vingt-cinq, soixante-neuf, quatre-vingt-dix-neuf, quatre-vingt-onze. 04.85.69.99.91
6. C'est le zéro un, vingt-quatre, quatre-vingt-trois, zéro un, quatre-vingt-neuf. 01.24.83.01.89

2 Les maths Read these math problems aloud, then write out each answer in words.

MODÈLE
65 + 3 = soixante-huit
Soixante-cinq plus trois font (equals) soixante-huit.

1. 70 + 15 = quatre-vingt-cinq
2. 82 + 10 = quatre-vingt-douze
3. 76 + 3 = soixante-dix-neuf
4. 88 + 12 = cent
5. 40 + 27 = soixante-sept
6. 67 + 6 = soixante-treize
7. 43 + 54 = quatre-vingt-dix-sept
8. 78 + 5 = quatre-vingt-trois
9. 70 + 20 = quatre-vingt-dix
10. 64 + 16 = quatre-vingts

3 Comptez Read the following numbers aloud in French, then follow the pattern to provide the missing numbers.

1. 60, 62, 64, ... 80 66, 68, 70, 72, 74, 76, 78
2. 76, 80, 84, ... 100 88, 92, 96
3. 100, 95, 90, ... 60 85, 80, 75, 70, 65
4. 99, 96, 93, ... 69 90, 87, 84, 81, 78, 75, 72

OPTIONS

Game Play a game of Bingo. Have students draw a square on a sheet of paper with three horizontal and three vertical rows. Tell them to write nine different numbers between 61–100 in the boxes. Explain that they should cross out the numbers as they hear them and that they should say "Bingo!" if they have three numbers in a horizontal, vertical, or diagonal row. Then call out numbers at random and write them down to verify.

TPR Assign ten students a number from 0–100 and line them up in front of the class. As you call out a number at random, that student should take a step forward. When two students have stepped forward, ask them to repeat their numbers. Then ask volunteers to add or subtract the two numbers given. Make sure the resulting sum is not greater than 100.

COMMUNICATION

4 Questions indiscrètes With a partner, take turns asking how old these people are. Answers will vary.

MODÈLE

Étudiant(e) 1: *Madame Hubert a quel âge?*
Étudiant(e) 2: *Elle a 70 ans.*

5 Qui est-ce? Interview as many classmates as you can in five minutes to find out the name, relationship, and age of their oldest family member. Identify the student with the oldest family member to the class. Answers will vary.

MODÈLE

Étudiant(e) 1: *Qui est le plus vieux* (the oldest) *dans ta famille?*
Étudiant(e) 2: *C'est ma tante Julie. Elle a soixante-dix ans.*

6 Les pourcentages Tally your classmates' responses to the questions below, then calculate the percentages for each affirmative answer. (To figure percentages, divide the number of affirmative answers by the number of people in your class.) Answers will vary.

MODÈLE

Soixante-seize pour cent des étudiants ont un chien.

1. Tu as un chien?
2. Tu as un chat?
3. Tu as un frère ou des frères?
4. Tu as une sœur ou des sœurs?
5. Tu as des cousins?
6. Tu as des oncles et des tantes?

Le français vivant

As-tu envie d'être
• ingénieur,
• musicien,
• architecte,
• professeur?
la calculatrice 61€
le sac à dos 70€
la chaise 82€
le bureau 96€
Tu as besoin d'une calculatrice intelligente, d'un beau bureau, d'une chaise confortable et d'un bon sac à dos.
Tu trouves tout dans le Catalogue VPC!

Identifiez Scan this catalogue page, and identify the instances where the numbers 61–100 are used. Answers will vary.

Questions Answers will vary.

1. Qui sont les personnes sur la photo?
2. Où est-ce qu'ils habitent?
3. Qu'est-ce qu'ils ont dans leur maison?
4. Quels autres (*other*) objets trouve-t-on dans le Catalogue VPC? (Imaginez.)
5. Quels sont leurs prix (*prices*)?

1 Expansions
- Model the question: **Quel est ton numéro de téléphone?** Then have students circulate around the room asking each other their phone numbers. Tell them to write the person's number next to his or her name and have the person verify it.
- Dictate actual phone numbers to the class and tell them to write the numerals. Examples: your office number, the department's number, etc.

2 Expansion Have each student write five more addition or subtraction problems. Then have students work in pairs and take turns reading their problems aloud while the other person says the answer.

3 Expansion Tell students to write three additional series of numbers. Then have them exchange papers with a classmate and take turns reading the series and filling in the numbers.

4 Expansion To review descriptive adjectives, have students describe the people in the drawing.

5 Suggestions
- Have two volunteers read the **modèle**.
- You may wish to provide a few supplementary terms for family members, such as **l'arrière-grand-mère** and **l'arrière-grand-père**.
- Ask various students to identify the person who has the oldest family member from their interviews. Continue this until students identify the oldest person among all the families.

6 Expansion Have students make a pie chart or bar graph that shows the percentages of affirmative answers to each question. Call on volunteers to present their graphs to the class and to explain them in French.

Le français vivant
- Call on a volunteer to read the catalogue page aloud. Point out the prices in euros.
- Ask students: **Combien d'objets y a-t-il sur la photo?**

OPTIONS

Game Ask for two volunteers and station them at opposite ends of the board so neither one can see what the other is writing. Say a number from 0–100 and tell them to write it on the board. If both students are correct, continue to give numbers until one writes an incorrect number. The winner continues on to play against another student.

Extra Practice Ask students to write down their university mailbox numbers on a slip of paper. Collect the papers. Tell students to say **«C'est ma boite à lettres!»** when they hear their mailbox number. Then proceed to read the numbers aloud at random.

comparisons

Section Goals

In this section, students will learn:
- prepositions of location
- disjunctive pronouns

Instructional Resources
WB/VM: Workbook, pp. 39–40
Lab Manual, p. 24
Lab MP3s
WB/VM/LM Answer Key
*IRCD-ROM: IRM (**Essayez!** and **Mise en pratique** answers; Lab Audioscript)*
espaces.vhlcentral.com: activities, downloads, reference tools

Suggestions
- Explain that prepositions typically indicate where one thing or person is in relation to another: *near, far, on, between, under.* Model the pronunciation of the prepositions and have students repeat.
- Remind students that they may need to use the contractions **du** and **des**.
- Take a book or other object and place it in various locations in relation to your desk or a student's desk as you ask individual students about its location. Examples: **Où est le livre? Est-ce qu'il est derrière le bureau? Quel objet est à côté du livre?** Work through various locations, eliciting all prepositions of location.
- Ask where different students are in relation to one another. Example: ____, **où est** ____? **(Il/Elle est à côté de [à droite de, à gauche de, derrière]** ____**.)**
- Model the pronunciation of the disjunctive pronouns and have students repeat them. Explain that these pronouns are used in prepositional phrases. Examples: **1. Ma famille vient** (*comes*) **souvent chez moi. 2. Je suis en face de toi.** Then ask volunteers for examples.
- Write the following in a column on the board and explain each usage of **chez**: **chez** + *person's name or person* (**chez Rachid, chez des amis**); **chez** + *professional's office or business* (**chez le docteur**); and **chez** + *disjunctive pronoun* (**chez toi**).

6.2 Prepositions of location

Point de départ You have already learned expressions in French containing prepositions like **à**, **de**, and **en**. Prepositions of location describe the location of something or someone in relation to something or someone else.

- Use the preposition **à** before the name of any city to express *in, to*. The preposition that accompanies the name of a country varies, but you can use **en** in many cases. In **Leçon 13**, you will learn more names of countries and their corresponding prepositions.

Il étudie **à Nice**. *He studies in Nice.*	Je voyage **en France** et **en Belgique**. *I'm traveling in France and Belgium.*

Prepositions of location

à côté de	*next to*	**en face de**	*facing, across from*
à droite de	*to the right of*	**entre**	*between*
à gauche de	*to the left of*	**loin de**	*far from*
dans	*in*	**par**	*by*
derrière	*behind*	**près de**	*close to, near*
devant	*in front of*	**sous**	*under*
en	*in*	**sur**	*on*

- Use the contractions **du** and **des** in prepositional expressions when they are appropriate.

Le resto U est **à côté du** gymnase. *The cafeteria is next to the gym.*	Notre chien aime manger **près des** enfants. *Our dog likes to eat close to the children.*

- You can further modify prepositions of location by using intensifiers such as **tout** (*very, really*) and **juste** (*just, right*).

Ma sœur habite **juste à côté de** l'université. *My sister lives right next to the university.*	Jules et Alain travaillent **tout près de** la fac. *Jules and Alain work really close to campus.*

- You may use prepositions without the word **de** when they are not followed by a noun.

Ma sœur habite **juste à côté**. *My sister lives right next door.*	Elle travaille **tout près**. *She works really close by.*

Il n'est pas sous les cahiers.

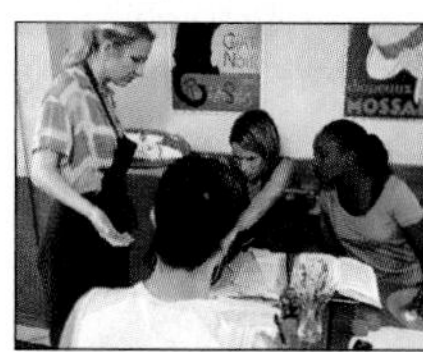

Pas derrière! Pas à droite!

MISE EN PRATIQUE

1 Où est ma montre? Claude has lost her watch. Choose the appropriate prepositions to complete her friend Pauline's questions.

1. Elle est (sur / entre) le bureau? sur
2. Elle est (par / derrière) la télévision? derrière
3. Elle est (entre / dans) le lit et la table? entre
4. Elle est (en / sous) la chaise? sous
5. Elle est (sur / à côté de) la fenêtre? à côté de
6. Elle est (près du / entre le) sac à dos? près du
7. Elle est (devant / sur) la porte? devant
8. Elle est (dans / sous) la corbeille? dans

2 Complétez Complete these sentences with the appropriate prepositions. Suggested answers

MODÈLE
Nous sommes chez nos cousins.

1. Nous sommes devant la maison de notre tante.
2. Michel est loin de Béatrice.
3. Entre Jasmine et Laure, il y a le petit cousin, Adrien.
4. Béatrice est à côté de Jasmine.
5. Jasmine est tout près de Béatrice.
6. Michel est derrière Laure.
7. Un oiseau est sur la maison.
8. Laure est à droite d' Adrien.

OPTIONS

Video Show the video episode again to give students more input containing prepositions and disjunctive pronouns. Stop the video where appropriate to discuss how the prepositions of location and disjunctive pronouns were used. Ask comprehension questions.

TPR Have one student start with a small beanbag or rubber ball. You call out another student identified only by his or her location with reference to other students. Example: **C'est la personne derrière** ____. The student with the beanbag or ball has to throw it to the student identified. The latter student must then throw the object to the next person you identify.

COMMUNICATION

3 **Où est l'objet?** In pairs, take turns asking where these items are in the classroom. Use prepositions of location. Answers will vary.

MODÈLE la carte
Étudiant(e) 1: *Où est la carte?*
Étudiant(e) 2: *Elle est devant la classe.*

1. l'horloge
2. l'ordinateur
3. le tableau
4. la fenêtre
5. le bureau du professeur
6. ton livre de français
7. la corbeille
8. la porte

4 **Qui est-ce?** Choose someone in the room. The rest of the class will guess whom you chose by asking yes/no questions that use prepositions of location. Answers will vary.

MODÈLE
Est-ce qu'il/elle est derrière Dominique?
Est-ce qu'il/elle est entre Jean-Pierre et Suzanne?

5 **S'il vous plaît...?** A tourist stops someone on the street to ask where certain places are located. In pairs, play these roles using the map to locate the places. Answers will vary.

MODÈLE la Banque Nationale de Paris (BNP)
Étudiant(e) 1: *La BNP, s'il vous plaît?*
Étudiant(e) 2: *Elle est en face de l'hôpital.*

1. le cinéma Ambassadeur
2. le restaurant Chez Marlène
3. la librairie Antoine
4. le lycée Camus
5. l'hôtel Royal
6. le café de la Place

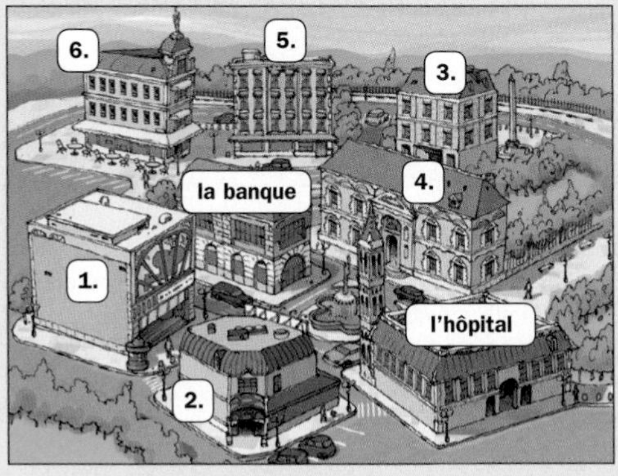

- The preposition **chez** has no exact English equivalent. It expresses the idea of *at* or *to someone's house* or *place*.

  Louise n'aime pas étudier **chez** Arnaud parce qu'il parle beaucoup.
  Louise doesn't like studying at Arnaud's because he talks a lot.

  Ce matin, elle n'étudie pas parce qu'elle est **chez** sa cousine.
  This morning she's not studying because she's at her cousin's.

- The preposition **chez** is also used to express the idea of *at* or *to a professional's office* or *business*.

  chez le docteur — *at the doctor's*
  chez la coiffeuse — *to the hairdresser's*

On travaille chez moi!

Stéphane est chez Rachid.

- Use disjunctive pronouns after prepositions instead of subject pronouns:

singular		plural	
je	moi	nous	nous
tu	toi	vous	vous
il	lui	ils	eux
elle	elle	elles	elles

Maryse travaille **à côté de moi**.
Maryse is working next to me.

J'aime mieux dîner **chez eux**.
I prefer to dine at their house.

Nous pensons **à lui**.
We're thinking about him.

Essayez! **Provide the preposition indicated in parentheses.**

1. La librairie est _derrière_ (*behind*) le resto U.
2. J'habite _près de_ (*close to*) leur lycée.
3. Le laboratoire est _à côté de_ (*next to*) ma résidence.
4. Tu retournes _chez_ (*to the house of*) tes parents ce week-end?
5. La fenêtre est _en face de_ (*across from*) la porte.
6. Mon sac à dos est _sous_ (*under*) la chaise.
7. Ses crayons sont _sur_ (*on*) la table.
8. Votre ordinateur est _dans_ (*in*) la corbeille!
9. Il n'y a pas de secrets _entre_ (*between*) amis.
10. Le professeur est _devant_ (*in front of*) les étudiants.

Essayez! Have students write three more fill-in-the-blank sentences describing where certain objects are located in their dorm room or apartment. Then tell them to exchange papers with a classmate and complete the sentences.

1 Suggestion To check students' answers, have them work in pairs and take turns asking the completed questions and answering them in the affirmative or negative.

2 Suggestion Before beginning the activity, have students identify the people, places, and other objects in the drawing. Example: **Il y a un oiseau.**

2 Expansion Have students create additional sentences about the location of the people or objects in the drawing. To practice negation, have students describe where the people and other objects are not located. Example: **La famille n'est pas devant la bibliothèque.**

3 Suggestion Have two volunteers read the **modèle** aloud. Remind students to pay attention to the gender of the nouns when responding.

3 Expansion For additional practice, give students these items if they are present in the classroom. **9. le dictionnaire de français 10. la calculatrice 11. les examens**

4 Suggestion To continue this activity, allow the student who guessed the correct person to choose another person and have the class ask the student yes/no questions.

5 Suggestion Before beginning this activity, make sure that students understand that the numbers on the illustration correspond to the places on the list. Have two volunteers read the **modèle** aloud.

OPTIONS

Extra Practice Have students look at the world map in **Appendice A** or use **Transparencies #1** and **#2**. Make true/false statements about the locations of various countries. Examples: **1. La Chine est près des États-Unis. (Faux.) 2. Le Luxembourg est entre la France et l'Allemagne. (Vrai.)** For variation, you can make statements or ask true/false questions about the location of various cities in France.

Small Groups In groups of three or four, have students think of a city or town within a 100-mile radius of your university city or town. They need to figure out how many miles away it is and what other cities or towns are nearby (**La ville est près de**...). Then have them get together with another group and read their descriptions. The other group has to guess which city or town is being described.

Instructional Resources
IRCD-ROM: IRM (Info Gap Activities); Testing Program, pp. 21–24; Test Files; Testing Program MP3s; Test Generator
espaces.vhlcentral.com: activities, downloads, reference tools

1 Suggestion Point out that in France and most francophone countries (except Canada) the general public doesn't usually follow college sports. Also, it is not common for universities to have sports teams, but if they do, their fans are usually limited to university students.

2 Expansion To review descriptive adjectives, ask students to give physical descriptions of the people.

3 Suggestion You might want to make photocopies of your university's campus map and distribute them to the class for this activity since some students might not know the campus well.

4 Suggestion To practice listening skills, tell students to cover the phone numbers with one hand and write the phone numbers down as their partner says them.

5 Suggestion Encourage students to ask questions when they are playing the role of the customer. For example, they can ask if the store has certain brands of an item, backpacks and notebooks in certain colors, or a specific type of dictionary.

6 Suggestion Divide the class into pairs and distribute the Info Gap Handouts in the IRM on the IRCD-ROM for this activity. Give students ten minutes to complete the activity.

6 Expansion Ask students questions based on the artwork. Example: **Est-ce que le neveu est à côté de la mère?**

Synthèse

1 Le basket These basketball rivals are competing for the title. In pairs, predict the missing playoff scores. Then, compare your predictions with those of another pair. Be prepared to share your predictions with the class. Answers will vary.

1. Ohio State 76, Michigan ________
2. Florida ________, Florida State 84
3. Stanford ________, UCLA 79
4. Purdue 81, Indiana ________
5. Duke 100, Virginia ________
6. Kansas 95, Colorado ________
7. Texas ________, Oklahoma 88
8. Kentucky 98, Tennessee ________

2 La famille d'Édouard In pairs, take turns guessing how the members of Édouard's family are related to him and to each other by describing their locations in the photo. Compare your answers with those of another pair. Answers will vary.

Édouard

MODÈLE

Son père est derrière sa mère.

3 À la fac In pairs, take turns describing the location of a building (**un bâtiment**) on your campus. Your partner must guess which building you are describing in three tries. Keep score to determine the winner after several rounds. Answers will vary.

MODÈLE

Étudiant(e) 1: *C'est un bâtiment entre la bibliothèque et Sherman Hall.*
Étudiant(e) 2: *C'est le resto U?*
Étudiant(e) 1: *C'est ça!*

ressources

WB	LM	Lab MP3s	espaces.vhlcentral.com
pp. 37–40	pp. 23–24	Leçon 6	Leçon 6

4 C'est quel numéro? What courses would you take if you were studying at a French university? Take turns deciding and having your partner give you the phone number for enrollment information. Answers will vary.

MODÈLE

Étudiant(e) 1: *Je cherche un cours de philosophie.*
Étudiant(e) 2: *C'est le zéro quatre...*

Département	Numéro de téléphone
Architecture	04.76.65.74.92
Biologie	04.76.72.63.85
Chimie	04.76.84.79.64
Littérature anglaise	04.76.99.90.82
Mathématiques	04.76.86.66.93
Philosophie	04.76.75.99.80
Psychologie	04.76.61.88.91
Sciences politiques	04.76.68.96.81
Sociologie	04.76.70.83.97

5 À la librairie In pairs, role-play a customer at a campus bookstore and a clerk who points out where supplies are located. Then, switch roles. Each turn, the customer picks four items from the list. Use the drawing to find the supplies. Answers will vary.

MODÈLE

Étudiant(e) 1: *Je cherche des stylos.*
Étudiant(e) 2: *Ils sont à côté des cahiers.*

des cahiers	un dictionnaire
une calculatrice	un palm
une carte	du papier
des crayons	un sac à dos

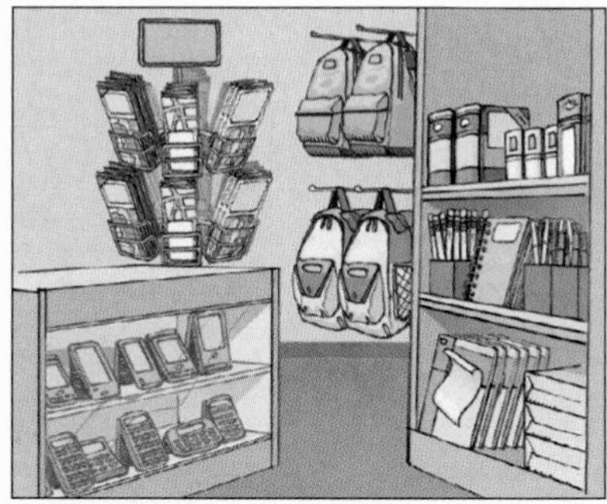

6 Trouvez Your instructor will give you and your partner each a drawing of a family picnic. Ask each other questions to find out where all of the family members are located. Answers will vary.

MODÈLE

Étudiant(e) 1: *Qui est à côté du père?*
Étudiant(e) 2: *Le neveu est à côté du père.*

OPTIONS

Game Divide the class into two teams. Select a student from the first team to choose an item in the classroom and to write it down. Call on five students from the other team one at a time to ask questions in French about where this item is. The first student can respond only with **oui**, **non**, **chaud** (*hot*), or **froid** (*cold*). If a team guesses the item within five tries, give them a point. The team with the most points wins.

Extra Practice Have students work in pairs. Tell them to take turns reading phone numbers at random from the list in **Activité 4** without mentioning the department. The person who responds should say the name of the department. Example: **Étudiant(e) 1: 04.76.65.74.92 Étudiant(e) 2: C'est le département d'architecture.**

NATIONAL STANDARDS communication cultures

NATIONAL STANDARDS connections communities

Interlude

Maman la plus belle du monde

The universal theme of family and friends finds a unique expression in the song ***Maman la plus belle du monde****, which is about the love of a son for his mother. He's seen much beauty in his life, but none of it compares to his mother's. In her eyes, he is still a small child, and when everything collapses in his life, she is always there for him.*

TINO ROSSI (1907–1983) made ***Maman la plus belle du monde*** *a hit in 1958. Born in Corsica, Rossi became a superstar in France, on stage and on screen. He starred in a number of movies and operettas. During his 50-year career, he sold 300 million records. His biggest hit is* ***Petit Papa Noël*** *(1946). Most French children know this song, with recordings still sold every year at Christmas time. The Sunlights, a 1960s group that performed old songs, later rerecorded* ***Maman la plus belle du monde****.*

La mère et l'enfant

PIERRE-AUGUSTE RENOIR (1841–1919) was a French impressionist painter. Impressionists broke with conventional themes and techniques which were often dictated by civil and religious institutions. Instead, they painted for themselves, portraying subjects like the family and life outdoors. Renoir portrayed personal feelings and moments. He captures the theme of family masterfully in the painting ***La mère et l'enfant****.*

Activité

Both Rossi's song and Renoir's painting show a positive representation of family members and relationships. Using the French you know, create your own tribute to a member of your family or to someone who is important in your life. Write a brief description in French that addresses these points. Answers will vary.

- What is the name of the person you have chosen?
- How is this person related to you?
- What is this person like physically?
- What personality traits distinguish this person as someone special?
- Why is this person so important to you?

SUR INTERNET

Go to **espaces.vhlcentral.com** for more information related to this **Interlude**.

Section Goals

In this section, students will learn about:
- Tino Rossi
- Pierre-Auguste Renoir

Instructional Resources
espaces.vhlcentral.com: activities, downloads, reference tools

Maman la plus belle du monde
To check comprehension, ask these questions.
1. Why is Tino Rossi considered a superstar? (He starred in a number of movies and operettas. He sold 300 million records.)
2. What is this song about? (the love of a son for his mother)
3. What was this singer's biggest hit? (***Petit Papa Noël***)

La mère et l'enfant
- Point out that Renoir is one of the most famous and important French painters of the nineteenth century. Claude Monet was also an important impressionist painter.
- Have students describe the mother and child in the painting. Ask them what elements of impressionism are exhibited in the painting.
- Have students brainstorm a list of words they associate with the term mother and write them on the board.

OPTIONS

Tino Rossi Born Constantino Rossi, Tino began his career singing in a church choir, and in his late teens he performed at amateur singing contests. He made his first record in 1932. During his career, he was often compared to Rudolph Valentino because of his dark, good looks. He recorded approximately 1,000 songs, mostly romantic ballads and love songs.

Cultural Activity Have students work in pairs. Tell them to compare the paintings ***Gbenonkpo*** (page 51) and ***La mère et l'enfant***. They should discuss the general style (realistic, idealistic, objective, subjective, abstract, etc.); the subject matter; the types of colors used; and the background or setting of the paintings. Then have pairs share their ideas with the class.

Section Goals

In this section, students will learn historical and cultural information about the city of Paris.

NATIONAL STANDARDS connections cultures

Instructional Resources
IRCD-ROM: Transparency #24,
WB/VM: Workbook
WB/VM/LM Answer Key
espaces.vhlcentral.com: activities; downloads; reference tools

Plan de Paris

- Have students look at the map of Paris or use **Transparency #24**. Point out that **Paris** and its surrounding areas **(la banlieue)** are called **l'Île-de-France**. This area is also known as **la Région parisienne.** Ask students to locate places mentioned in the **Panorama** on the map. Examples: **le musée du Louvre, le musée d'Orsay, le centre Georges Pompidou, l'Arc de Triomphe,** and **la tour Eiffel.**
- Point out that the Seine River (**La Seine**) divides Paris into two parts: the Left Bank (**la Rive Gauche**) and the Right Bank (**la Rive Droite**).

La ville en chiffres

- Point out the city's coat of arms.
- Call on volunteers to read the sections. After each section, ask questions about content.
- Point out that the population figure for Paris includes the city and the surrounding areas.
- Tell students that there is a Rodin Museum in Paris and one in Philadelphia. If possible, show students pictures of two of Rodin's most famous sculptures: *The Kiss (**le Baiser**)* and *The Thinker (**le Penseur**)*.

Incroyable mais vrai! The miles of tunnels and catacombs under Paris used to be quarries; the city was built with much of the stone dug from them. Some of these quarries date back to Roman times. The skeletons in the catacombs are Parisians who were moved from overcrowded cemeteries in the late 1700s.

Panorama

Paris

La ville en chiffres

- **Superficie:** *105 km² (cent cinq kilomètres carrés°)*
- **Population:** *plus de° 9.828.000 (neuf millions huit cent vingt-huit mille)*
  SOURCE: Population Division, UN Secretariat

Paris est la capitale de la France. On a l'impression que Paris est une grande ville—et c'est vrai si on compte° ses environs°. Néanmoins°, elle mesure moins de° 10 kilomètres de l'est à l'ouest°, ainsi° on peut visiter la ville très facilement à pied°. Paris est divisée en 20 arrondissements°. Chaque° arrondissement a son propre maire° et son propre caractère.

- **Industries principales:** *haute couture, finances, transports, technologie, tourisme*
- **Musées:** *plus de 150 (cent cinquante): le musée° du Louvre, le musée d'Orsay, le centre Georges Pompidou et le musée Rodin*

Parisiens célèbres

- **Victor Hugo,** *écrivain° et activiste (1802–1885)*
- **Charles Baudelaire,** *poète (1821–1867)*
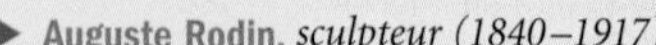
- **Auguste Rodin,** *sculpteur (1840–1917)*
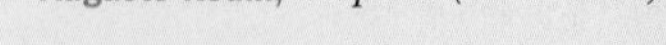
- **Jean-Paul Sartre,** *philosophe (1905–1980)*
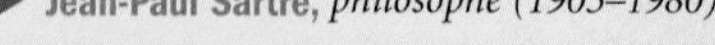
- **Simone de Beauvoir,** *écrivain (1908–1986)*
- **Édith Piaf,** *chanteuse (1915–1963)*

- **Emmanuelle Béart,** *actrice (1965–)*

une affiche de cabaret célèbre

une terrasse de café

Incroyable mais vrai!

Sous les rues° de Paris, il y a une autre ville: les catacombes. Ici reposent° les squelettes d'environ 7.000.000 (sept millions) de personnes provenant° d'anciens cimetières de Paris et de ses environs. Plus de 100.000 (cent mille) touristes par an visitent cette ville de repos° éternel.

carrés *square* **plus de** *more than* **si l'on compte** *if one counts* **environs** *surrounding areas* **Néanmoins** *Nevertheless* **moins de** *less than* **de l'est à l'ouest** *from east to west* **ainsi** *in this way* **à pied** *on foot* **arrondissements** *districts* **Chaque** *Each* **son propre maire** *its own mayor* **musée** *museum* **écrivain** *writer* **rues** *streets* **reposent** *lie; rest* **provenant** *from* **repos** *rest*

OPTIONS

Oral Presentation If a student has visited Paris, ask the person to prepare a short presentation about his or her experiences there. Encourage the student to bring in photos and souvenirs. If no students have been to Paris, then invite a French graduate student who has been there to speak to the class. Tell the presenter to include what his or her favorite place or activity is in Paris and to explain why.

Parisiens célèbres Jean-Paul Sartre and **Simone de Beauvoir** had a personal and professional relationship. Sartre became famous as the leader of a group of intellectuals who used to gather regularly at the **Café de Flore**. This group included Simone de Beauvoir and **Albert Camus**. Ask students to name some works they may have read or heard of by Sartre, de Beauvoir, or Camus.

Les monuments

La tour Eiffel

La tour Eiffel a été construite° en 1889 (mille huit cent quatre-vingt-neuf) pour l'Exposition universelle, à l'occasion du centenaire° de la Révolution française. Elle mesure 324 (trois cent vingt-quatre) mètres de haut et pèse° 10.100 (dix mille cent) tonnes. La tour attire plus de° 6.000.000 (six millions) de visiteurs par an°.

Les gens

Paris-Plage

Pour les Parisiens qui ne voyagent pas pendant l'été°, la ville de Paris a créé° Paris-Plage pour apporter la plage° aux Parisiens! Débuté en 2001 et installé sur les quais° de la Seine, Paris-Plage consiste en trois kilomètres de sable et d'herbe°, plein° d'activités comme la natation° et le volley. Ouvert en° juillet et en août, plus de 3.000.000 (trois millions) de personnes visitent Paris-Plage chaque° année.

Les musées

Le musée du Louvre

Ancien° palais royal, le musée du Louvre est aujourd'hui un des plus grands musées du monde° avec sa vaste collection de peintures°, de sculptures et d'antiquités orientales, égyptiennes, grecques et romaines. L'œuvre° la plus célèbre de la collection est *La Joconde*° de Léonard de Vinci. La pyramide de verre°, créée par l'architecte américain I.M. Pei, marque l'entrée° principale du musée.

Les transports

Le métro

L'architecte Hector Guimard a commencé à réaliser° des entrées du métro de Paris en 1898 (mille huit cent quatre-vingt-dix-huit). Ces entrées sont construites dans le style Art Nouveau: en forme de plantes et de fleurs°. Le métro est aujourd'hui un système très efficace° qui permet aux passagers de traverser° Paris rapidement.

Qu'est-ce que vous avez appris? Complétez les phrases.

1. La ville de Paris est divisée en vingt arrondissements.
2. Chaque arrondissement a ses propres maire et caractère.
3. Charles Baudelaire est le nom d'un poète français.
4. Édith Piaf est une chanteuse française.
5. Plus de 100.000 personnes par an visitent les catacombes sous les rues de Paris.
6. La tour Eiffel mesure 324 mètres de haut.
7. En 2001, la ville de Paris a créé Paris-Plage sur la Seine.
8. Le musée du Louvre est un ancien palais.
9. La pyramide de verre est une création de I.M. Pei.
10. Certaines entrées du métro sont de style Art Nouveau.

ressources: WB pp. 41-42 | espaces.vhlcentral.com Unité 3

SUR INTERNET

Go to **espaces.vhlcentral.com** to find more cultural information related to this **PANORAMA**.

1. Quels sont les monuments les plus importants à Paris? Qu'est-ce qu'on peut faire (*can do*) dans la ville?
2. Trouvez des informations sur un des musées de Paris.
3. Recherchez la vie (*Research the life*) d'un(e) Parisien(ne) célèbre.
4. Cherchez un plan du métro de Paris et trouvez comment voyager du Louvre à la tour Eiffel.

construite *built* **centenaire** *100-year anniversary* **pèse** *weighs* **attire plus de** *attracts more than* **par an** *per year* **pendant l'été** *during the summer* **a créé** *created* **apporter la plage** *bring the beach* **quais** *banks* **de sable et d'herbe** *of sand and grass* **plein** *full* **natation** *swimming* **Ouvert en** *Open in* **chaque** *each* **Ancien** *Former* **monde** *world* **peintures** *paintings* **L'œuvre** *The work (of art)* **La Joconde** *The Mona Lisa* **verre** *glass* **entrée** *entrance* **a commencé à réaliser** *began to create* **fleurs** *flowers* **efficace** *efficient* **traverser** *to cross*

La tour Eiffel Constructed of wrought iron, the architectural design of the Eiffel Tower was an engineering masterpiece for its time. Critics of Gustave Eiffel's design said it couldn't be built, but he proved them wrong. Later, some of the engineering techniques employed would be used to build the first steel skyscrapers. The Eiffel Tower remained the world's tallest building until 1930.

Paris-Plage To create this manmade beach, each year about 2,000 tons of sand are spread over what is a busy highway the rest of the year. In 2004, it cost two million euros to create the beach. A swimming pool was added in 2004 because the Seine is too dirty to swim in. When it is open, **Paris-Plage** is a popular center for relaxation and fun with numerous organized sports activities and concerts. Ask students if they think that **Paris-Plage** is worth the money.

Le musée du Louvre Bring in photos or slides of the **Louvre** and some of the most famous artworks in its collection, such as the *Mona Lisa*, the *Venus de Milo*, the *Winged Victory of Samothrace*, *Vermeer's Lacemaker*, and *Delacroix's Liberty Leading the People* (***La liberté guidant le peuple***). Ask students to describe the woman in the *Mona Lisa*. Point out that only a fraction of the 300,000 works owned by the museum are on display.

Le métro The Paris public transportation system, **le métro** (short for **le Métropolitain**), has 14 lines. It is the most convenient and popular means of transportation in the city since every building in Paris is within 500 meters of a **métro** station. Ask students what cities in the United States have metro or subway systems.

OPTIONS

Cultural Activity Assign each student a famous sight in Paris. Examples: **l'Île de la Cité, la Sainte-Chapelle, le Quartier latin**, etc. Tell students to research the sight and write a brief description. Encourage them to include photos from the Internet or magazines. Ask a few volunteers to share their descriptions with the class.

Pairs Have students work in pairs. Tell them that they have three days in Paris, and they have to make a list of places they want to see or visit each day so that they can make the most of their time there. Remind students that many famous sights, other than those mentioned in the text, appear on the map. Example: **Jour 1: visiter le musée du Louvre.** Ask volunteers to share their lists with the class.

Section Goals
In this section, students will:
- learn to use visuals and graphic elements to predict content
- read an article about pets in France

Stratégie Tell students that they can infer a great deal of information about the content of an article or text by examining the visual and graphic elements. Some items they should look at are:
- titles and headings
- photos
- photo captions
- graphs, tables, and diagrams

To practice this strategy, have students read the headings in the chart **Le Top 10 des chiens de race.** Ask: What information does this chart contain? (It lists the top ten dog breeds and the percentage of households that owns each breed.)

Examinez le texte After students have finished the activity, tell them to look at the visual elements in the article again. Then ask them the following questions and have them explain their answers.
1. What is the article about? (It is about dogs as family pets. The title of the article and the photos of dogs indicate the main topic.)
2. What information does the table on page 105 contain? (It lists the reasons why people have pets and shows the percentages of people who own dogs, cats, birds, and fish for each reason.)
3. What can you learn from the photo on page 105? (Answers will vary.)

Lecture

Avant la lecture

STRATÉGIE

Predicting content from visuals

When you are reading in French, be sure to look for visual clues that will orient you as to the content and purpose of what you are reading. Photos and illustrations, for example, will often give you a good idea of the main points that the reading covers. You may also encounter helpful visuals that summarize large amounts of data in a way that is easy to comprehend; these visuals include bar graphs, pie charts, flow charts, lists of percentages, and other diagrams.

Le Top 10 des chiens de race°
% DE FOYERS° POSSESSEURS
les caniches° **9,3%**
les labradors **7,8%**
les yorkshires **5,6%**
les épagneuls bretons° **4,6%**
les bergers allemands° **4,1%**
les autres bergers **3,3%**
les bichons **2,7%**
les cockers/fox-terriers **2,2%**
les boxers **2%**
les colleys **1,6%**

Examinez le texte

Take a quick look at the visual elements of the article in order to generate a list of ideas about its content. Then, compare your list with a classmate's. Are your lists the same or are they different? Discuss your lists and make any changes needed to produce a final list of ideas.

race *breed* **foyers** *households* **caniches** *poodles* **épagneuls bretons** *Brittany Spaniels* **bergers allemands** *German Shepherds*

Fido

Les Français adorent les animaux. Plus de la moitié° des foyers en France ont un chien, un chat ou un autre animal familier°. Les chiens sont particulièrement appréciés et intégrés dans la famille et la société françaises.

Qui possède un chien en France et pourquoi? Souvent°, la présence d'un chien en famille suit l'arrivée° d'enfants, parce que les parents pensent qu'un chien contribue positivement à leur développement. Il est aussi commun de trouver deux chiens ou plus dans le même° foyer.

Les chiens sont d'excellents compagnons. Leurs maîtres° sont moins seuls° et déclarent avoir moins de stress. Certaines personnes possèdent un chien pour avoir plus d'exercice physique. Et il y a aussi des personnes qui possèdent

OPTIONS

Pairs Working in pairs, have students read the article aloud and write four questions about it. After they have finished, tell them to exchange their papers with another pair and answer the questions.

Extra Practice Tell students to read the chart **Le Top 10 des chiens de race**. Then pronounce the name of each dog breed and have students repeat it after you. To check comprehension, give students these true/false statements. **1. Le caniche est la race de chien la plus populaire. (Vrai.) 2. Les boxers n'existent pas en France. (Faux.) 3. Les labradors sont moins populaires que les épagneuls. (Faux.) 4. Les Français aiment mieux les yorkshires que les bergers. (Faux.) 5. Les colleys sont le numéro dix sur la liste. (Vrai.)**

en famille

un chien parce qu'elles en ont toujours eu un° et n'imaginent pas une vie° sans° chien.

Les chiens ont parfois° les mêmes droits° que les autres membres de la famille, et parfois des droits spéciaux. Bien sûr, ils accompagnent leurs maîtres pour les courses en ville° et les promenades dans le parc, et ils entrent même dans certains magasins°. Ne trouvez-vous pas parfois un caniche ou un labrador, les deux races les plus° populaires en France, avec son maître dans un restaurant?

En France, il n'est pas difficile d'observer que les chiens ont une place privilégiée au sein de° la famille.

Pourquoi avoir un animal familier?

RAISON	CHIENS	CHATS	OISEAUX	POISSONS
Pour l'amour des animaux	61,4%	60,5%	61%	33%
Pour avoir de la compagnie	43,5%	38,2%	37%	10%
Pour s'occuper°	40,4%	37,7%	0%	0%
Parce que j'en ai toujours eu un°	31,8%	28,9%	0%	0%
Pour le bien-être° personnel	29,2%	26,2%	0%	0%
Pour les enfants	23,7%	21,3%	30%	48%

Plus de la moitié *More than half* **animal familier** *pet* **Souvent** *Often* **suit l'arrivée** *follows the arrival* **même** *same* **maîtres** *owners* **moins seuls** *less lonely* **en ont toujours eu un** *have always had one* **vie** *life* **sans** *without* **parfois** *sometimes* **droits** *rights* **courses en ville** *errands in town* **magasins** *stores* **les plus** *the most* **au sein de** *in the heart of* **s'occuper** *keep busy* **Parce que j'en ai toujours eu un** *Because I've always had one* **bien-être** *well-being*

Après la lecture

Vrai ou faux? Indicate whether these items are **vrai** or **faux**, based on the reading.

	Vrai	Faux
1. Les chiens accompagnent leurs maîtres pour les promenades dans le parc.	☑	☐
2. Parfois, les chiens accompagnent leurs maîtres dans les restaurants.	☑	☐
3. Le chat n'est pas un animal apprécié en France.	☐	☑
4. Certaines personnes déclarent posséder un chien pour avoir plus d'exercice physique.	☑	☐
5. Certaines personnes déclarent posséder un chien pour avoir plus de stress.	☐	☑
6. En France, les familles avec enfants n'ont pas de chien.	☐	☑

Fido en famille Choose the correct response according to the article.

1. Combien de foyers en France ont au moins (*at least*) un animal familier?
   a. 20%-25%
   b. 40%-45%
   (c.) 50%-55%
2. Pourquoi est-ce une bonne idée d'avoir un chien?
   a. pour plus de compagnie et plus de stress
   b. pour l'exercice physique et être seul
   (c.) pour la compagnie et le développement des enfants
3. Que pensent les familles françaises de leurs chiens?
   a. Les chiens sont plus importants que les enfants.
   (b.) Les chiens font partie (*are part*) de la famille et participent aux activités quotidiennes (*daily*).
   c. Le rôle des chiens est limité aux promenades.
4. Quelles races de chien les Français préfèrent-ils?
   a. les caniches et les oiseaux
   b. les labradors et les bergers allemands
   (c.) les caniches et les labradors
5. Y a-t-il des familles avec plus d'un chien?
   a. Non
   (b.) Oui
   c. les caniches et les labradors

Vrai ou faux? Have students correct the false statements and check their answers with a partner.

Fido en famille Go over the answers with the class. Ask students to read the corresponding line(s) of the text that contain the answer to each question.

Suggestion Encourage students to record unfamiliar words and phrases that they learn in **Lecture** in their notebooks.

Expansions

- Ask students to describe their pets. If they don't own a pet, then tell them to describe someone else's pet. Example: **Mon chat s'appelle Tyler. Il est très gentil avec tout le monde. Il est noir et c'est un bon copain.**
- Write these headings on the board: **animaux familiers, chiens, chats, oiseaux, poissons,** and **autres animaux**. Do a quick class survey to find out how many have pets in general and how many have dogs, cats, birds, fish, and other animals. Record the results on the board. Then ask them why they have a pet. If students need help expressing their reasons, tell them to look at the reasons in the chart on this page.

OPTIONS

Cultural Comparison Have students work in pairs or groups of three. Tell them to draw a two-column chart and write the headings **Similitudes** (*Similarities*) and **Différences** (*Differences*). Then, tell them to list the similarities and differences between the French and American attitudes toward dogs based on the facts in the reading and what they know about Americans and their pets. Allow students to use their books for this activity. After pairs have completed their charts, call on volunteers to read their lists. Ask the class if they agree or disagree with the similarities.

Section Goals
In this section, students will:
- learn to ask for repetition in oral communication
- listen to and summarize a short paragraph
- listen to a conversation and complete several activities

Instructional Resources
Textbook MP3s
IRCD-ROM: IRM (Textbook Audioscript)
espaces.vhlcentral.com: downloads, reference tools

Stratégie
Script Bonjour, je m'appelle Christine Dupont. Je suis médecin et mère de famille. Mon mari, Richard, est ingénieur. Il est intelligent et très drôle aussi. Nous avons trois enfants charmants: deux fils et une fille. Les garçons sont roux et notre fille est blonde. Notre fils aîné, Marc, a 17 ans. Le cadet, Pascal, a 15 ans. Leur petite sœur, Véronique, a 12 ans.

Préparation Before doing the activity, tell students to look at the photo and describe what they see. Ask students to justify their responses based on visual clues in the photo.

Suggestion To check students' answers for the **À vous d'écouter** activity, have them work in pairs and take turns asking and answering questions using the adjectives listed. Example: **Est-ce que Robert est brun? Non, Édouard est brun.**

À vous d'écouter
Script
SUZANNE: Salut, Diane. Est-ce que ça va?
DIANE: Oh, comme ci, comme ça. J'ai un petit problème. Ce n'est pas grand-chose, mais...
S: Quel genre de problème?
D: Tu sais que j'aime bien Édouard.
S: Oui.
D: Le problème, c'est qu'il ne me parle pas!
S: Il t'aime bien aussi. Il est peut-être un peu timide?
D: Tu crois? ...Il est si beau! Grand, brun... Et puis il est gentil, très intelligent et aussi très intéressant. Et Robert et toi, comment ça va?
S: Euh... plutôt bien. Robert est sympa. Je l'aime beaucoup. Il est patient, optimiste et très drôle.
D: Vous parlez souvent?
S: Oui. Nous parlons deux à trois heures par jour. Nous parlons de beaucoup de choses! De nos cours, de nos amis, de nos familles... de tout.
D: C'est super! Tu as de la chance.

À l'écoute

STRATÉGIE

Asking for repetition/ Replaying the recording

Sometimes it is difficult to understand what people say, especially in a noisy environment. During a conversation, you can ask someone to repeat by asking **Comment?** (*What?*) or **Pardon?** (*Pardon me?*). In class, you can ask your instructor to repeat by saying, **Répétez, s'il vous plaît** (*Repeat, please*). If you don't understand a recorded activity, you can simply replay it.

 To help you practice this strategy, you will listen to a short paragraph. Ask your instructor to repeat it or replay the recording, and then summarize what you heard.

Préparation

Based on the photograph, where do you think Suzanne and Diane are? What do you think they are talking about?

À vous d'écouter

Now you are going to hear Suzanne and Diane's conversation. Use **R** to indicate adjectives that describe Suzanne's boyfriend, Robert. Use **E** for adjectives that describe Diane's boyfriend, Édouard. Some adjectives will not be used.

E brun	R optimiste
___ laid	E intelligent
E grand	___ blond
E intéressant	E beau
E gentil	R sympathique
R drôle	R patient

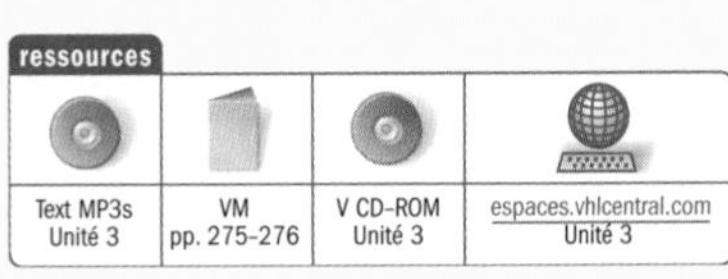

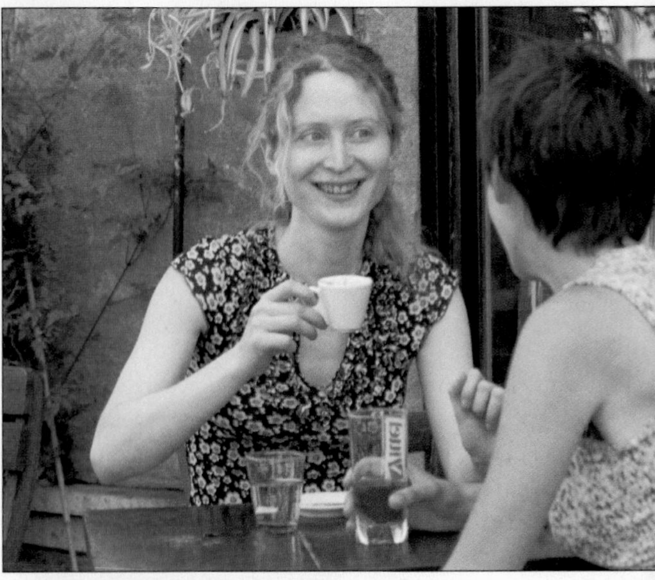

Compréhension

Identifiez-les Whom do these statements describe?

1. Elle a un problème avec un garçon. Diane
2. Il ne parle pas à Diane. Édouard
3. Elle a de la chance. Suzanne
4. Ils parlent souvent. Suzanne et Robert
5. Il est sympa. Robert
6. Il est timide. Édouard

Vrai ou faux? Indicate whether each sentence is **vrai** or **faux**, then correct any false statements.

1. Édouard est un garçon très patient et optimiste.
   Faux. Robert est très patient et optimiste.
2. Diane n'a pas de chance avec les garçons.
   Vrai.
3. Suzanne et son petit ami parlent de tout.
   Vrai.
4. Édouard parle souvent à Diane.
   Faux. Édouard ne parle pas à Diane.
5. Robert est peut-être un peu timide.
   Faux. Édouard est peut-être un peu timide.
6. Suzanne parle de beaucoup de choses avec Robert.
   Vrai.

Écriture

STRATÉGIE

Using idea maps

How do you organize ideas for a first draft? Often, the organization of ideas represents the most challenging part of the writing process. Idea maps are useful for organizing pertinent information. Here is an example of an idea map you can use when writing.

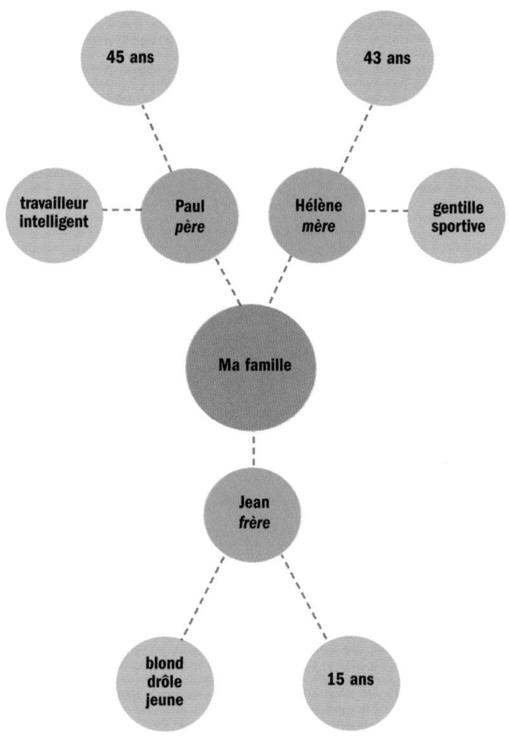

Watch the FLASH CULTURE segment on the **ESPACES** video for cultural footage related to this unit's theme.

Thème

Écrivez une lettre

A friend you met in a chat room for French speakers wants to know about your family. Using some of the verbs and adjectives you learned in this lesson, write a brief letter describing your family or an imaginary family, including:

- Names and relationships
- Physical characteristics
- Hobbies and interests

Here are some useful expressions for letter writing in French:

Salutations

Cher Fabien,	*Dear Fabien,*
Chère Joëlle,	*Dear Joëlle,*

Asking for a response

Réponds-moi vite.	*Write back soon.*
Donne-moi de tes nouvelles.	*Tell me all your news.*

Closings

Grosses bises!	*Big kisses!*
Je t'embrasse!	*Kisses!*
Bisous!	*Kisses!*
À bientôt!	*See you soon!*
Amitiés,	*In friendship,*
Cordialement,	*Cordially,*
À plus (tard),	*Until later,*

Section Goals

In this section, students will:
- learn to use idea maps to organize information
- learn to write an informal letter in French
- view authentic cultural footage of families and friends

Instructional Resources
WB/VM: Video Manual, pp. 275–276
WB/VM/LM Answer Key
IRCD-ROM: IRM (Videoscript)
Video CD-ROM
Video on DVD
espaces.vhlcentral.com: activities, downloads, reference tools

Stratégie Tell students that they might find it helpful to use note cards to create idea maps. Writing each detail on a separate card will allow them to rearrange ideas and experiment with organization. Remind students to write their ideas in French, since they may not have the vocabulary or structures for some English terms they generate.

Thème Introduce the common salutations and closings used in informal letters in French. Point out the difference between **cher** (masculine) and **chère** (feminine). Model the pronunciation to show students that the two words sound virtually the same. Explain that the closings **Grosses bises!** and **Bisous!** are often used with close friends. If the relationship is informal but the person is not a close friend, then **À plus** is an appropriate choice. **Amitiés** and **Cordialement** are less familiar than the other options.

Flash culture Tell students that they will learn more about family and friends by watching a variety of real-life images narrated by Csilla. Show the video segment, then have students jot down in French at least three examples of people or things they saw. You can also use the activities in the video manual in class to reinforce this **Flash culture** or assign them as homework.

EVALUATION

Criteria	Scale
Appropriate salutation/closings	1 2 3 4 5
Appropriate details	1 2 3 4 5
Organization	1 2 3 4 5
Accuracy	1 2 3 4 5

Scoring	
Excellent	18–20 points
Good	14–17 points
Satisfactory	10–13 points
Unsatisfactory	< 10 points

Instructional Resources
Textbook MP3s
IRCD-ROM: IRM (Textbook Audioscript)
espaces.vhlcentral.com: downloads, reference tools

La famille

aîné(e)	*elder*
cadet(te)	*younger*
un beau-frère	*brother-in-law*
un beau-père	*father-in-law; stepfather*
une belle-mère	*mother-in-law; stepmother*
une belle-sœur	*sister-in-law*
un(e) cousin(e)	*cousin*
un demi-frère	*half-brother; stepbrother*
une demi-sœur	*half-sister; stepsister*
les enfants (*m., f.*)	*children*
un époux/une épouse	*spouse*
une famille	*family*
une femme	*wife; woman*
une fille	*daughter; girl*
un fils	*son*
un frère	*brother*
une grand-mère	*grandmother*
un grand-père	*grandfather*
les grands-parents (*m.*)	*grandparents*
un mari	*husband*
une mère	*mother*
un neveu	*nephew*
une nièce	*niece*
un oncle	*uncle*
les parents (*m.*)	*parents*
un père	*father*
une petite-fille	*granddaughter*
un petit-fils	*grandson*
les petits-enfants (*m.*)	*grandchildren*
une sœur	*sister*
une tante	*aunt*
un chat	*cat*
un chien	*dog*
un oiseau	*bird*
un poisson	*fish*

Adjectifs descriptifs

antipathique	*unpleasant*
bleu(e)	*blue*
blond(e)	*blond*
brun(e)	*dark (hair)*
court(e)	*short*
drôle	*funny*
faible	*weak*
fatigué(e)	*tired*
fort(e)	*strong*
frisé(e)	*curly*
génial(e) (géniaux *pl.*)	*great*
grand(e)	*big; tall*
jeune	*young*
joli(e)	*pretty*
laid(e)	*ugly*
lent(e)	*slow*
mauvais(e)	*bad*
méchant(e)	*mean*
modeste	*modest, humble*
noir(e)	*black*
pauvre	*poor, unfortunate*
pénible	*tiresome*
petit(e)	*small, short (stature)*
prêt(e)	*ready*
raide	*straight*
rapide	*fast*
triste	*sad*
vert(e)	*green*
vrai(e)	*true; real*

Vocabulaire supplémentaire

divorcer	*to divorce*
épouser	*to marry*
célibataire	*single*
divorcé(e)	*divorced*
fiancé(e)	*engaged*
marié(e)	*married*
séparé(e)	*separated*
veuf/veuve	*widowed*
un(e) voisin(e)	*neighbor*

Expressions utiles	See pp. 79 and 93.
Possessive adjectives	See p. 84.
Numbers 61–100	See p. 96.
Prepositions of location	See p. 98.

Professions et occupations

un(e) architecte	*architect*
un(e) artiste	*artist*
un(e) athlète	*athlete*
un(e) avocat(e)	*lawyer*
un coiffeur/une coiffeuse	*hairdresser*
un(e) dentiste	*dentist*
un homme/une femme d'affaires	*businessman/woman*
un ingénieur	*engineer*
un(e) journaliste	*journalist*
un médecin	*doctor*
un(e) musicien(ne)	*musician*
un(e) propriétaire	*owner; landlord/lady*

Adjectifs irréguliers

actif/active	*active*
beau/belle	*beautiful; handsome*
bon(ne)	*kind; good*
châtain	*brown (hair)*
courageux/courageuse	*courageous, brave*
cruel(le)	*cruel*
curieux/curieuse	*curious*
discret/discrète	*discreet; unassuming*
doux/douce	*sweet; soft*
ennuyeux/ennuyeuse	*boring*
étranger/étrangère	*foreign*
favori(te)	*favorite*
fier/fière	*proud*
fou/folle	*crazy*
généreux/généreuse	*generous*
gentil(le)	*nice*
gros(se)	*fat*
inquiet/inquiète	*worried*
intellectuel(le)	*intellectual*
jaloux/jalouse	*jealous*
long(ue)	*long*
(mal)heureux/(mal)heureuse	*(un)happy*
marron	*brown*
naïf/naïve	*naïve*
nerveux/nerveuse	*nervous*
nouveau/nouvelle	*new*
paresseux/paresseuse	*lazy*
roux/rousse	*red-haired*
sérieux/sérieuse	*serious*
sportif/sportive	*athletic*
travailleur/travailleuse	*hard-working*
vieux/vieille	*old*

ressources

Text MP3s Unité 3	espaces.vhlcentral.com Unité 3

Au café

UNITÉ

4

Leçon 7

Leçon 8

Pour commencer

- Quelle heure est-il?
  a. 7h00 du matin b. midi c. minuit
- Qu'est-ce qu'il y a sur la table?
  a. une soupe b. une limonade
  c. des sandwichs
- Qu'est-ce que Sandrine et David ont envie de faire (*do*)?
  a. manger b. partager c. échouer

Savoir-faire

Unit Goals

Leçon 7

In this lesson, students will learn:
- names for places around town
- terms for activities around town
- to pronounce oral vowels
- about pastimes of young French people and **le verlan**
- the verb **aller** and to express future actions with it
- the preposition **à** and contractions with it
- interrogative words
- about Baguépi, a French bread brand

Leçon 8

In this lesson, students will learn:
- terms for food items at a café
- expressions of quantity
- to pronounce nasal vowels in French
- about the role of the café in France and famous cafés of Paris
- the present tense of **prendre** and **boire**
- the formation and use of partitive articles
- to create a menu for a new café

Savoir-faire

In this section, students will learn:
- cultural and historical information about the French regions of **Normandie** and **Bretagne**
- to scan a text to improve comprehension
- to listen for the gist in oral communication
- to add details in French to make writing more interesting
- more about cafés and food items through specially shot video footage

Pour commencer

- **b. midi**
- **c. des sandwichs**
- **a. manger**

RESOURCES

Workbook/Video Manual: WB Activities, pp. 43–56
Laboratory Manual: Lab Activities, pp. 25–32
Workbook/Video Manual: Video Activities, pp. 223–226; pp. 277–278
WB/VM/LM Answer Key
Instructor's Resource CD-ROM [IRCD-ROM]: Instructor's Resource Manual [IRM] (Textbook Audioscript; Lab Audioscript; Videoscript; **Roman-photo** Translations; **Vocabulaire supplémentaire**; **Feuilles d'activités**; Info Gap Activities; **Le zapping** TV clip transcription; **Essayez!** and **Mise en pratique** answers); Transparencies #25, #26, #27; Testing Program, pp. 25–32; Test Files; Testing Program MP3s; Test Generator
Lab MP3s
Textbook MP3s
Video CD-ROM
Video on DVD
espaces.vhlcentral.com

Section Goals

In this section, students will learn and practice vocabulary related to:

- places in a city
- pastimes

Instructional Resources
*IRCD-ROM: Transparency #25; IRM (**Vocabulaire supplémentaire**; **Mise en pratique** answers; Textbook Audioscript; Lab Audioscript; Info Gap Activities)*
Textbook MP3s
WB/VM: Workbook, pp. 43–44
Lab Manual, p. 25
Lab MP3s
WB/VM/LM Answer Key
espaces.vhlcentral.com: activities, downloads, reference tools

Suggestions

- Have students look at the new vocabulary and identify the cognates.
- Use **Transparency #25**. As you point to different people, describe where they are and what they are doing. Examples: **Ils sont à la terrasse d'un café. Elles bavardent.** Follow up with simple questions based on your narrative.
- Ask students yes/no and either/or questions about their preferences using the new vocabulary. Examples: **Aimez-vous nager? Préférez-vous regarder un film au cinéma ou à la maison?**
- Tell students that proper names of places, like adjectives, usually follow generic nouns. Examples: **le cinéma Rex** and **le parc Monceau.**
- Point out that the term **une boîte de nuit** is familiar and usually used among young people. **Une discothèque** is the more formal word for *nightclub.*
- Point out that **un gymnase** in France generally has a track, exercise equipment, basketball or tennis courts, showers, but no pool.
- Additional vocabulary for this lesson can be found in the **Vocabulaire supplémentaire** in the IRM on the IRCD-ROM.

Leçon 7

You will learn how to...

- say where you are going
- say what you are going to do

Où allons-nous?

Vocabulaire

danser	*to dance*
explorer	*to explore*
fréquenter	*to frequent; to visit*
inviter	*to invite*
nager	*to swim*
patiner	*to skate*
une banlieue	*suburbs*
une boîte (de nuit)	*nightclub*
un bureau	*office; desk*
un centre commercial	*shopping center, mall*
un centre-ville	*city/town center, downtown*
un cinéma (ciné)	*movie theater, movies*
un endroit	*place*
un grand magasin	*department store*
un gymnase	*gym*
un hôpital	*hospital*
un lieu	*place*
un magasin	*store*
un marché	*market*
un musée	*museum*
un parc	*park*
une piscine	*pool*
un restaurant	*restaurant*
une ville	*city, town*

une montagne
une maison
Il passe chez quelqu'un. (passer)
Elle quitte la maison. (quitter)
Ils déjeunent. (déjeuner)
une place
une terrasse de café
Elles bavardent. (bavarder)
poissonnerie
café

ressources

WB pp. 43–44	LM p. 25	Text MP3s Leçon 7	Lab MP3s Leçon 7	espaces.vhlcentral.com Leçon 7

OPTIONS

Game Divide the class into two teams. Put objects related to different places in a box (for example, movie ticket stubs, sunglasses, and a coffee cup). Without looking, have a student reach into the box and pick out an object. The next player on that person's team has five seconds to name a place associated with the object. If the person cannot do so within the time limit, the other team may "steal" the point by giving a correct response. When the box is empty, the team with the most points wins.

Extra Practice Use magazine photos or clip art from the Internet to make flash cards representing places in and around town. As you show each image, students should say the name of the place and as many activities associated with it as they can think of.

Attention!

Remember that nouns that end in **-al** have an irregular plural. Replace **-al** with **-aux**.
un hôpital → deux hôpitaux

À (*to, at*) before **le** or **les** makes these contractions:
à + le = au **à + les = aux**
À does NOT contract with **l'** or **la**.

Mise en pratique

1 Écoutez Jamila parle de sa journée à son amie Samira. Écoutez la conversation et mettez (*put*) les lieux listés dans l'ordre chronologique. Il y a deux lieux en trop (*extra*).

- 3 a. à l'hôpital
- 8 b. à la maison
- 1 c. à la piscine
- 5 d. au centre commercial
- 6 e. au cinéma
- NA f. à l'église
- 2 g. au musée
- 7 h. au bureau
- NA i. au parc
- 4 j. au restaurant

Coup de main

Note that the French **Je vais...** is the equivalent of the English *I am going to...*

2 Associez Quels lieux associez-vous aux activités listées?

1. nager ___une piscine___
2. danser ___une boîte (de nuit)___
3. dîner ___un restaurant___
4. travailler ___un bureau___
5. habiter ___une maison___
6. épouser ___une église___
7. voir (*to see*) un film ___un cinéma___
8. acheter (*to buy*) des fruits ___un marché, une épicerie___

3 Logique ou illogique Lisez chaque phrase et déterminez si l'action est logique ou illogique. Corrigez si nécessaire. Suggested answers

	logique	illogique
1. Maurice invite Delphine à une épicerie. *Maurice invite Delphine au musée.*	☐	☑
2. Caroline et Aurélie bavardent au marché.	☑	☐
3. Nous déjeunons à l'épicerie. *Nous déjeunons au restaurant.*	☐	☑
4. Ils dépensent beaucoup d'argent au centre commercial.	☑	☐
5. Vous explorez une ville.	☑	☐
6. Vous escaladez (*climb*) une montagne.	☑	☐
7. J'habite en banlieue.	☑	☐
8. Tu danses dans un marché. *Tu danses dans une boîte (de nuit).*	☐	☑

1 Tapescript JAMILA: Allô, Samira. Comment ça va?
SAMIRA: Très bien, et toi?
J: Aujourd'hui très bien, mais alors demain, quelle journée!
S: Comment ça?
J: Et bien… demain matin, je vais à la piscine avec mon frère, Hassan, à 8h00. À 10h00, je vais au musée Rodin avec ma classe. À 11h00, je passe un moment avec grand-mère à l'hôpital. À midi, je vais au restaurant Chez Benoît, près de la place Carnot. L'après-midi, je vais au centre commercial et au cinéma voir le dernier film de Jean Reno. Pour terminer, à 17h00 je vais au bureau de maman pour travailler un peu et nous rentrons à la maison ensemble.
S: Quel programme! Bon, courage Jamila et à bientôt.
J: Merci, bonne soirée.
(On Textbook MP3s)

1 Suggestion Before beginning the activity, have students read the list of places and the **Coup de main**.

2 Expansions
- For additional practice, give students these items. **9. chanter (une église) 10. manger (un restaurant/un café) 11. dessiner (un musée)**
- Do this activity in reverse. Name places and have students say what activities can be done there.

3 Suggestion Tell students to write their corrections. Then have volunteers write their sentences on the board.

3 Expansion For additional practice, give students these items. **9. Vous dansez au magasin. (illogique) 10. Je nage au musée. (illogique) 11. Madame Ducharme habite dans une maison. (logique)**

OPTIONS

TPR Have students represent various stores and places in town by giving them signs to hold. Ask them where one does various activities. Examples: **Où est-ce qu'on regarde un film/mange/nage?** The student with the appropriate sign should step forward and answer. Examples: **On regarde un film au cinéma. On mange au restaurant. On nage à la piscine.**

Extra Practice Ask students about their favorite places. Tell them to use generic place names in front of proper nouns, such as **le parc Zilker** and **le musée du Louvre**. Ask: **Quel(le) est votre restaurant/musée/épicerie préféré(e)?**

4 Suggestion Have two volunteers read the **modèle** aloud.

4 Expansion After completing the activity, have students share their partner's opinions with the rest of the class.

5 Suggestion Divide the class into pairs and distribute the Info Gap Handouts in the IRM on the IRCD-ROM for this activity. Give students ten minutes to complete the activity.

6 Suggestion Tell students that they should use the salutation **chère** if they are writing to a female. Remind them to include expressions of time, such as **le lundi après-midi** and **le samedi soir** in their letters.

Successful Language Learning Remind students that it's important to proofread their work. Have them brainstorm a checklist of potential errors, for example, accents, adjective agreement, and subject-verb agreement. Tell students to add grammar points to their checklists as they learn new structures and make mistakes.

NATIONAL communication STANDARDS

Communication

4  **Conversez** Avec un(e) partenaire, échangez vos opinions sur ces activités. Utilisez un élément de chaque colonne dans vos réponses. Answers will vary.

MODÈLE

Étudiant(e) 1: *Moi, j'adore bavarder au restaurant, mais je déteste nager au gymnase.*
Étudiant(e) 2: *Moi aussi, j'adore bavarder au restaurant. Je ne déteste pas nager au gymnase, mais j'aime mieux patiner au gymnase.*

Opinion	Activité	Lieu
adorer	bavarder	au bureau
aimer (mieux)	danser	au centre commercial
ne pas tellement aimer	déjeuner	au centre-ville
détester	dépenser de l'argent	au cinéma
	étudier	au gymnase
	inviter	au musée
	nager	au parc
	parler	à la piscine
	patiner	au restaurant

5 **La journée d'Anne** Votre professeur va vous donner, à vous et à votre partenaire, une feuille d'activités partiellement illustrée. À tour de rôle, posez-vous des questions pour compléter vos feuilles respectives. Utilisez le vocabulaire de la leçon. Attention! Ne regardez pas la feuille de votre partenaire. Answers will vary.

MODÈLE

Étudiant(e) 1: *À 7h30, Anne quitte la maison. Qu'est-ce qu'elle fait ensuite (do next)?*
Étudiant(e) 2: *À 8h00, elle...*

Anne

6 **Une lettre** Écrivez une lettre à un(e) ami(e) dans laquelle (*in which*) vous décrivez vos activités de la semaine. Utilisez les expressions listées. Answers will vary.

bavarder	passer chez quelqu'un
déjeuner	travailler
dépenser de l'argent	quitter la maison
étudier	un centre commercial
manger au restaurant	une boîte de nuit

Cher Paul,

Comment vas-tu? Moi, tout va bien. Je suis très actif/active à l'université. Je travaille beaucoup et j'ai beaucoup d'amis. En général, le samedi à midi, je déjeune au restaurant Le Lion d'Or avec mes copains. L'après-midi, je bavarde avec mes amis...

OPTIONS

Extra Practice On a sheet of paper, have students write down six places they like to go and what they like to do there. Tell them to circulate around the room trying to find other students who also like to go those places or do those things. Remind them to jot down the names of people who share something in common with them. Then have them report what they have in common with their classmates.

Small Groups Have small groups plan and design an ideal town or neighborhood. Have them draw the plan, label each place, and list fun activities to do at each one. One person from each group should present the plan to the class. Hold a secret vote and give prizes for the best plan in various categories, such as **le plus amusant**, **le plus créateur**, and **le plus réaliste**.

Les sons et les lettres

Oral vowels

French has two basic kinds of vowel sounds. Oral vowels, the subject of this discussion, are produced by releasing air through the mouth; for nasal vowels, presented in **Leçon 8**, the air is also released through the nose. The pronunciation of French vowels is consistent and predictable.

In short words (usually two-letter words), **e** is pronounced like the vowel sound in *bug*.

le **que** **ce** **de**

The letter **a** alone is pronounced like the *a* in *father*.

la **ça** **ma** **ta**

The letter **i** by itself and the letter **y** are pronounced like the vowel sound in the word *bee*.

ici **livre** **stylo** **lycée**

The letter combination **ou** sounds like the vowel sound in the English word *who*.

vous **nous** **oublier** **écouter**

The French **u** sound does not exist in English. To produce this sound, say *ee* with your lips rounded.

tu **du** **une** **étudier**

Prononcez Répétez les mots suivants à voix haute.

1. je
2. chat
3. fou
4. ville
5. utile
6. place
7. jour
8. triste
9. mari
10. active
11. Sylvie
12. rapide
13. gymnase
14. antipathique
15. calculatrice
16. piscine

Articulez Répétez les phrases suivantes à voix haute.

1. Salut, Luc. Ça va?
2. La philosophie est difficile.
3. Brigitte est une actrice fantastique.
4. Suzanne va à son cours de physique.
5. Tu trouves le cours de maths facile?
6. Viviane a une bourse universitaire.

Dictons Répétez les dictons à voix haute.

Plus on est de fous, plus on rit.[2]

[1] He who steps out of line loses his place.
[2] The more the merrier.

ressources

LM p. 26	Text MP3s Leçon 7	Lab MP3s Leçon 7	espaces.vhlcentral.com Leçon 7

Section Goals

In this section, students will learn about oral vowels.

Instructional Resources
Textbook MP3s
Lab Manual, p.26
Lab MP3s
WB/VM/LM Answer Key
IRCD-ROM: IRM (Textbook Audioscript; Lab Audioscript)
espaces.vhlcentral.com: activities, downloads, reference tools

Suggestions

- Model the pronunciation of each vowel sound. Have students watch the shape of your mouth, then repeat the sound after you. Pronounce each of the example words and have students repeat them.
- Tell students that an unaccented **e** at the end of a word is silent, but will cause a consonant that precedes it to be pronounced. Example: **petit/petite**.
- Contrast the pronunciation of words containing **u** and **ou**. Examples: **vous/vu** and **tous/tu**.
- Point out that this lesson primarily addresses the pronunciation of single oral vowels. Tell them that like **ou**, various vowel pairs create different sounds when combined. They will learn about these letter combinations in other lessons.
- Dictate five familiar words containing oral vowels to the class, repeating each one at least two times. Then write them on the board or on a transparency and have students check their spelling.

Dictons Ask students if they can think of a saying in English that is similar to **«Qui va à la chasse perd sa place.»** (*You snooze, you lose.*)

OPTIONS

Game Have a spelling bee using vocabulary words from **Leçons 1–7** that contain oral vowel sounds. Pronounce each word, use it in a sentence, and then say the individual word again. Tell students that they must spell the words in French and include the diacritical marks.

Extra Practice Use these sentences with oral vowels for additional practice or dictation. **1. Madame Duclos et son mari sont séparés. 2. Marianne prépare le bac. 3. Tu aimes mieux le parc ou le gymnase? 4. Coralie nage à la piscine.**

Section Goals

In this section, students will learn functional phrases for talking about their plans through comprehensible input.

Instructional Resources
WB/VM: Video Manual, pp. 223–224
WB/VM/LM Answer Key
Video CD-ROM
Video on DVD
IRCD-ROM: IRM (Videoscript; ***Roman-photo*** *Translations)*
espaces.vhlcentral.com: activities, downloads, reference tools

Video Recap: Leçon 6
Before doing this **Roman-photo**, review the previous one with this activity.
1. De qui Sandrine parle-t-elle souvent? (de Pascal)
2. Où Rachid et Stéphane travaillent-ils? (chez Rachid)
3. Quelle est la profession du père de Rachid? (médecin)
4. Quelle est la profession de la mère de Rachid? (avocate)
5. Qui a envie d'être architecte? (Stéphane)

Video Synopsis David thinks he sees the actress Juliette Binoche in a grocery store. He runs to tell Sandrine. At the café, Sandrine is on the phone with Pascal; he wants to know her weekend plans. David arrives with his news. He, Sandrine, and Amina rush off to try to catch a glimpse of the actress, but have difficulty locating the correct store. At the store, they discover that David saw a store clerk, not Juliette Binoche.

Suggestions
- Ask students to read the title, glance at the video stills, and predict what they think the episode will be about. Record their predictions.
- Have students work in groups and read the **Roman-photo** conversation aloud.
- After students have read the **Roman-photo**, review their predictions and ask them which ones were correct. Then ask a few questions to help them summarize this episode.

Star du cinéma

PERSONNAGES

Amina

David

Pascal

Sandrine

1

À l'épicerie...
DAVID Juliette Binoche? Pas possible! Je vais chercher Sandrine!

2

Au café...
PASCAL Alors chérie, tu vas faire quoi de ton week-end?
SANDRINE Euh, demain je vais déjeuner au centre-ville.
PASCAL Bon... et quand est-ce que tu vas rentrer?
SANDRINE Euh, je ne sais pas. Pourquoi?

3

PASCAL Pour rien. Et demain soir, tu vas danser?
SANDRINE Ça dépend. Je vais passer chez Amina pour bavarder avec elle.
PASCAL Combien d'amis as-tu à Aix-en-Provence?
SANDRINE Oh, Pascal...
PASCAL Bon, moi, je vais continuer à penser à toi jour et nuit.

6

DAVID Mais l'actrice! Juliette Binoche!
SANDRINE Allons-y! Vite! C'est une de mes actrices préférées! J'adore le film *Chocolat*!
AMINA Et comme elle est chic! C'est une vraie star!
DAVID Elle est à l'épicerie! Ce n'est pas loin d'ici!

7

Dans la rue...
AMINA Mais elle est où, cette épicerie? Nous allons explorer toute la ville pour rencontrer Juliette Binoche?
SANDRINE C'est là, l'épicerie Pierre Dubois à côté du cinéma?
DAVID Mais non, elle n'est pas à l'épicerie Pierre Dubois, elle est à l'épicerie près de l'église, en face du parc.

8

AMINA Et combien d'églises est-ce qu'il y a à Aix?
SANDRINE Il n'y a pas d'église en face du parc!
DAVID Bon, hum, l'église sur la place.
AMINA D'accord, et ton église sur la place, elle est ici au centre-ville ou en banlieue?

ACTIVITÉS

1 Vrai ou faux? **Indiquez pour chaque phrase si l'affirmation est vraie ou fausse et corrigez si nécessaire.**

1. David va chercher Pascal. Faux. David va chercher Sandrine.
2. Sandrine va déjeuner au centre-ville. Vrai.
3. Pascal va passer chez Amina. Faux. Sandrine va passer chez Amina.
4. Pascal va continuer à penser à Sandrine jour et nuit. Vrai.
5. Pascal va bien. Vrai.
6. Juliette Binoche est l'actrice préférée de Sandrine. Vrai.
7. L'épicerie est loin du café. Faux. L'épicerie n'est pas loin.
8. L'épicerie Pierre Dubois est à côté de l'église. Faux. L'épicerie Pierre Dubois est à côté du cinéma.
9. Il n'y a pas d'église en face du parc. Vrai.
10. Juliette Binoche fréquente le P'tit Bistrot. Faux. Juliette Binoche ne fréquente pas le P'tit Bistrot.

OPTIONS

Avant de regarder la vidéo Before viewing the video, have students brainstorm possible activities that Sandrine might include in her weekend plans. Write their predictions on the board.

Regarder la vidéo Photocopy the videoscript and opaque out ten key words or phrases with white correction fluid in order to create a master for a cloze activity. Hand out photocopies and tell students to fill in the missing words as they watch the video episode. You may want to show the episode twice if students have difficulty with the activity. Then have students compare their answers in small groups.

David et les filles à la recherche de (*in search of*) leur actrice préférée.

4

SANDRINE Oui. Génial. Au revoir, Pascal.
AMINA Salut Sandrine. Comment va Pascal?
SANDRINE Il va bien mais il adore bavarder.

5

DAVID Elle est là, elle est là!
SANDRINE Mais, qui est là?
AMINA Et c'est où, «là»?
DAVID Juliette Binoche! Mais non, pas ici!
SANDRINE ET AMINA Quoi? Qui? Où?

9

Devant l'épicerie...
DAVID C'est elle, là! Hé, JULIETTE!
AMINA Oh, elle est belle!
SANDRINE Elle est jolie, élégante!
AMINA Elle est... petite?
DAVID Elle, elle... est... vieille?!?

10

AMINA Ce n'est pas du tout Juliette Binoche!
SANDRINE David, tu es complètement fou! Juliette Binoche, au centre-ville d'Aix?
AMINA Pourquoi est-ce qu'elle ne fréquente pas le P'tit Bistrot?

Expressions utiles

Talking about your plans

- **Tu vas faire quoi de ton week-end?**
  What are you doing this weekend?
- **Je vais déjeuner au centre-ville.**
  I'm going to have lunch downtown.
- **Quand est-ce que tu vas rentrer?**
  When are you coming back?
- **Je ne sais pas.**
  I don't know.
- **Je vais passer chez Amina.**
  I am going to Amina's (house).
- **Nous allons explorer toute la ville.**
  We're going to explore the whole city.

Additional vocabulary

- **C'est une de mes actrices préférées.**
  She's one of my favorite actresses.
- **Comme elle est chic!**
  She is so chic!
- **Ce n'est pas loin d'ici!**
  It's not far from here!
- **Ce n'est pas du tout...**
  It's not... at all.
- **Ça dépend.**
  It depends.
- **Pour rien.**
  No reason.
- **Vite!**
  Quick!, Hurry!

ACTIVITÉS

2 Questions À l'aide (*the help*) d'un dictionnaire, choisissez le bon mot pour chaque question.

1. (Avec qui, Quoi) Sandrine parle-t-elle au téléphone?
2. (Où, Parce que) Sandrine va-t-elle déjeuner?
3. (Qui, Pourquoi) Pascal demande-t-il à Sandrine quand elle va rentrer?
4. (Combien, Comment) d'amis Sandrine a-t-elle?
5. (Combien, À qui) Amina demande-t-elle comment va Pascal?
6. (Quand, Où) est Juliette Binoche?

3 Écrivez Pensez à votre acteur ou actrice préféré(e) et préparez un paragraphe où vous décrivez son apparence, sa personnalité et sa carrière. Comment est-il/elle? Dans quel(s) (*which*) film(s) joue-t-il/elle? Si un jour vous rencontrez cet acteur/cette actrice, qu'est-ce que vous allez lui dire (*say to him or her*)?

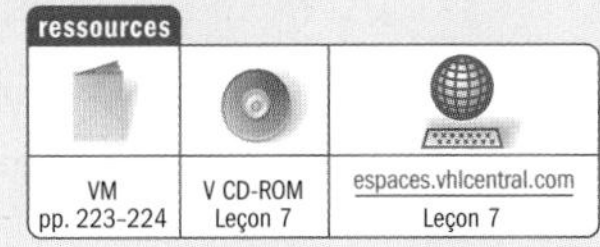

Expressions utiles

- Model the pronunciation of the **Expressions utiles** and have students repeat after you.
- As you work through the list, point out forms of **aller** and the interrogative words. Tell students that these concepts will be formally presented in the **Structures** section.
- Point out that, like the English verb *to go*, the verb **aller** is used to express future actions.
- Write **je vais** and **tu vas** on the board. Ask students the questions in the **Expressions utiles** and have them respond. Examples: **Tu vas faire quoi de ton week-end? Quand est-ce que tu vas rentrer?**
- Have students scan the video-still captions for interrogative words that are not in the list and read the sentences. Examples: **combien de, comment, qui, où,** and **pourquoi**.

1 Suggestion Have students write the correct answers to the false statements on the board.

1 Expansion For additional practice, give students these items. **11. Juliette Binoche est vieille. (Faux. Elle n'est pas vieille.) 12. Amina pense que Juliette Binoche est chic. (Vrai.)**

2 Expansion For additional practice, give students these items. **7. (Qui, Comment) est-ce que David voit (*see*) à l'épicerie? (Qui) 8. (Pourquoi, Comment) est Juliette Binoche? (Comment) 9. (Quand, Où) est-ce que Pascal va penser à Sandrine? (Quand)**

3 Suggestion Have students exchange papers for peer editing. Remind them to pay particular attention to adjective agreement and subject-verb agreement.

OPTIONS

Juliette Binoche Juliette Binoche (1964–), often referred to by the French press simply as "La Binoche", was born in Paris. In addition to being an actress, she is a poster designer and avid painter. Her first film was *Liberty Bell* (1983). She has now acted in more that 30 films. She won an Oscar for "Best Supporting Actress" in *The English Patient* (1996). *Chocolat* (2000) is the film version of the novel *Chocolat* by Joanne Harris, in which a single mother (Binoche) opens a chocolaterie in a small French village.

Small Groups Working in groups of three, have students create a short skit similar to the scenes in video stills 5–10 in which someone thinks they have seen a famous person. Give students ten minutes to prepare, then call on groups to perform their skits for the class.

Section Goals

In this section, students will:
- learn about popular French pastimes
- learn about **le verlan**
- learn about **le maquis** and **le tangana** in Africa
- read about **le parc Astérix**

Instructional Resources
espaces.vhlcentral.com: activities, downloads, reference tools

Culture à la loupe
Avant la lecture Have students read the title and look at the photos. Ask: **À votre avis** (*In your opinion*)**, quelles sont les activités préférées des jeunes Français?** Write a list on the board.

Lecture
- Point out the chart **Les activités culturelles des Français**. Ask students what information the chart shows. (The percentages of French people 15 years and older who participate in various cultural activities.)
- Have students verify their predictions and add any missing activities to the list.

Après la lecture Working in small groups, have students compare French and American pastimes. Tell them to make a list of the similarities and differences in French. Then ask several groups to read their lists to the class.

1 Expansion For additional practice, give students these items. **11. Les jeunes Français ne regardent pas souvent la télévision. (Faux.) 12. Les jeux vidéo ne sont pas très populaires en France. (Faux.) 13. Les Français aiment passer du temps avec leurs amis. (Vrai.) 14. L'écriture est plus (*more*) populaire que la danse en France. (Vrai.)**

CULTURE À LA LOUPE

Les passe-temps des jeunes Français

Comment est-ce que les jeunes occupent leur temps libre° en France? Les jeunes de 15 à 25 ans passent beaucoup de temps à regarder la télévision: environ° 14 heures par° semaine. Ils écoutent aussi beaucoup de musique: environ 16 heures par semaine, et surfent souvent° sur Internet (11 heures). Les jeux° vidéo sont aussi très populaires: les jeunes jouent° en moyenne° 12 heures par semaine.

En France, les jeunes aiment également° les activités culturelles, en particulier le cinéma: en moyenne, ils y° vont une fois° par semaine. Ils aiment aussi la littérature et l'art: presque° 50% (pour cent) visitent des musées ou des monuments historiques chaque année et plus de° 40% vont au théâtre ou à des concerts. Un jeune sur cinq° joue d'un instrument de musique ou chante°, et environ 20% d'entre eux° pratiquent une activité artistique, comme la danse, le théâtre, la sculpture, le dessin° ou la peinture°. La photographie et la vidéo sont aussi très appréciées.

Il ne faut pas° oublier de mentionner que les jeunes Français sont aussi très sportifs. Bien sûr, comme tous les jeunes, ils préfèrent parfois° simplement se détendre° et bavarder avec des amis.

Finalement, les passe-temps des jeunes Français sont similaires aux activités des jeunes Américains!

temps libre *free time* **environ** *around* **par** *per* **souvent** *often* **jeux** *games* **jouent** *play* **en moyenne** *on average* **également** *also* **y** *there* **fois** *time* **presque** *almost* **plus de** *more than* **un... sur cinq** *one... in five* **chante** *sings* **d'entre eux** *of them* **dessin** *drawing* **peinture** *painting* **Il ne faut pas** *One must not* **parfois** *sometimes* **se détendre** *relax* **les** *them* **écriture** *writing*

Les activités culturelles des Français

(% des Français qui les° pratiquent)

le dessin	7%
l'écriture°	4%
la peinture	4%
le piano	3%
autre instrument de musique	3%
la danse	2%
la guitare	2%
la sculpture	1%
le théâtre	1%

ACTIVITÉS

1 Vrai ou faux? Indiquez si les phrases sont **vraies** ou **fausses**.

1. Les jeunes Français n'écoutent pas de musique. Faux.
2. Les jeunes Français n'utilisent pas Internet. Faux.
3. Les jeunes Français aiment aller au musée. Vrai.
4. Les jeunes Français n'aiment pas beaucoup les livres. Faux.
5. Les jeunes Français n'aiment pas pratiquer d'activités artistiques. Faux.
6. Les Français entre 15 et 25 ans ne font pas de sport. Faux.
7. Les passe-temps des jeunes Américains sont similaires aux passe-temps des jeunes Français. Vrai.
8. L'instrument de musique le plus (*the most*) populaire en France est le piano. Vrai.
9. Plus de (*More*) gens pratiquent la peinture que la sculpture. Vrai.
10. Environ 10% des Français pratiquent la sculpture. Faux.

OPTIONS

Pairs Have students work in pairs and ask each other about the information in the chart **Les activités culturelles des Français**. To help them, write a model on the board. Example: **Étudiant(e) 1: Est-ce que le dessin est un passe-temps populaire en France? Étudiant(e) 2: Oui, sept pour cent des jeunes Français dessinent.**

Cultural Activity Distribute photocopies of the cinematic and cultural activities in the weekly ***Pariscope*** or ***Officiel des spectacles***. Tell students to make a list of the ones they would like to attend. Then have them compare their lists in small groups.

LE FRANÇAIS QUOTIDIEN

Le verlan

En France, on entend parfois° des jeunes parler en **verlan**. En verlan, les syllabes des mots sont inversées°:

l'envers° → vers-l'en → verlan.

Voici quelques exemples:

français	verlan	anglais
louche	chelou	*shady*
café	féca	*café*
mec	keum	*guy*
femme	meuf	*woman*

parfois *sometimes* **inversées** *inverted* **l'envers** *the reverse*

LE MONDE FRANCOPHONE

Où passer le temps

Voici quelques endroits typiques où les jeunes francophones aiment se restaurer° et passer du temps.

En Afrique de l'ouest

Le maquis Commun dans beaucoup de pays° d'Afrique de l'ouest°, le maquis est un restaurant où on peut manger à bas prix°. Situé en ville ou en bord de route°, le maquis est typiquement en plein air°.

Au Sénégal

Le tangana Le terme «tang» signifie «chaud» en wolof, une des langues nationales du Sénégal. Le tangana est un lieu populaire pour se restaurer. On trouve souvent les tanganas au coin de la rue°, en plein air, avec des tables et des bancs°.

se restaurer *have something to eat* **pays** *countries* **ouest** *west* **à bas prix** *inexpensively* **en bord de route** *on the side of the road* **en plein air** *outdoors* **coin de la rue** *street corner* **bancs** *benches*

PORTRAIT

Le parc Astérix

Situé° à 30 kilomètres de Paris, en Picardie, le parc Astérix est le premier parc à thème français. Le parc d'attractions°, ouvert° en 1989, est basé sur la bande dessinée° française, *Astérix le Gaulois*. Création de René Goscinny et d'Albert Uderzo, Astérix est un guerrier gaulois° qui lutte° contre l'invasion des Romains. Au parc Astérix, il y a des montagnes russes°, des petits trains et des spectacles, tous° basés sur les aventures d'Astérix et de son meilleur ami, Obélix. Une des attractions, *le Tonnerre° de Zeus*, est la plus grande° montagne russe en bois° d'Europe.

Situé *Located* **parc d'attractions** *amusement park* **ouvert** *opened* **bande dessinée** *comic strip* **guerrier gaulois** *Gallic warrior* **lutte** *fights* **montagnes russes** *roller coasters* **tous** *all* **Tonnerre** *Thunder* **la plus grande** *the largest* **en bois** *wooden*

SUR INTERNET

Comment sont les parcs d'attractions dans les autres pays francophones?

Go to **espaces.vhlcentral.com** to find more cultural information related to this **ESPACE CULTURE.**

ACTIVITÉS

2 Compréhension Complétez les phrases.

1. Le parc Astérix est basé sur *Astérix le Gaulois*, une bande dessinée.
2. Astérix le Gaulois est une création de René Goscinny et d'Albert Uderzo.
3. Le parc Astérix est près de la ville de Paris.
4. Astérix est un guerrier gaulois.
5. En verlan, on peut passer du temps avec ses copains au féca.
6. Si ce n'est pas une «meuf», c'est un «keum».

3 Vos activités préférées Posez des questions à trois ou quatre de vos camarades de classe à propos de leurs activités favorites. Comparez vos résultats avec ceux (*those*) d'un autre groupe.

Le français quotidien Model the pronunciation of each term and have students repeat it. Ask students what language or jargon in English is similar to **verlan**. (pig latin)

Portrait Point out Astérix and Obélix in the photo. If possible, bring in an Astérix comic strip to show the students.

Le monde francophone Have students read the text. Then ask a few comprehension questions. Examples: **1. Pourquoi les jeunes fréquentent-ils les maquis et les tanganas? (pour manger et passer le temps) 2. On trouve les maquis en ville ou en bord de route? (les deux) Et les tanganas? (Ils sont souvent au coin d'une rue.) 3. On mange à l'intérieur ou en plein air dans le maquis et le tangana? (en plein air)**

2 Expansion For additional practice, give students these items. **7. Le parc Astérix est le premier ____ à thème français. (parc) 8. Astérix lutte (*fights*) contre les ____. (Romains) 9. Au parc Astérix, il y a des montagnes ____. (russes) 10. L'ami d'Astérix s'appelle ____. (Obélix)**

3 Expansion Do a quick class survey to find out how many students like each activity and which one is the most popular. Tally the results on the board. Example: **Combien d'étudiants surfent sur Internet?**

OPTIONS

Le verlan Write on the board: **1. une piscine 2. une bande 3. la musique 4. le métro 5. le prof 6. manger 7. bonjour 8. fou** Have students work in pairs. Tell them to copy the words and write the equivalents in **verlan**. Call on volunteers to write their answers on the board. Then have students pronounce the words. Answers: **1. une cinepi 2. une deban 3. la siquemu/sicmu 4. le tromé 5. le fepro 6. géman 7. jourbon 8. ouf**

Le parc Astérix Some other popular attractions at the park are **La Galère** (a giant swinging ship), **Les Chaises Volantes** (flying chairs), **Le Cheval de Troie** (the Trojan horse), and **Transdemonium** (a ghost train through a castle dungeon). Have students take a virtual tour of the park by going to **www.parcasterix.com**.

Section Goals

In this section, students will learn:
- the verb **aller**
- the **futur proche** with **aller**
- the preposition **à**

Instructional Resources
WB/VM: Workbook, pp. 45–46
Lab Manual, p. 27
Lab MP3s
WB/VM/LM Answer Key
*IRCD-ROM: IRM (**Essayez!** and **Mise en pratique** answers; Lab Audioscript; Info Gap Activities)*
espaces.vhlcentral.com: activities, downloads, reference tools

Suggestions
- Write the paradigm of **aller** on the board and model the pronunciation. Ask students what forms of **aller** are irregular.
- Write your next day's schedule on the board using infinitives and nouns. Examples: **8h00: bibliothèque; 10h00: cours de français; 12h00: déjeuner** Explain what you are going to do using the verb **aller**. Examples: **Je vais (aller) à la bibliothèque à huit heures. Je vais déjeuner à midi**. Ask students questions about their schedules using forms of **aller**.
- Ask individuals questions about their future plans using **aller**. Examples: **Allez-vous chez vos parents ce week-end? Allez-vous manger avec des copains vendredi soir?**
- Bring in pictures of people dressed for different activities. Describe them to the class using the verb **aller**. Example: Showing a picture of a swimmer, say: **Il/Elle va à la piscine.** Then explain the contractions **à** + **le** = **au** and **à** + **les** = **aux**.
- Model the pronunciation of the list of prepositions with places. Tell students that they should memorize these phrases.

7.1 The verb *aller*

Point de départ In **Leçon 1**, you saw a form of the verb **aller** (*to go*) in the expression **ça va**. Now you will use this verb to talk about going places and to express actions that take place in the immediate future.

aller			
je vais	*I go*	**nous allons**	*we go*
tu vas	*you go*	**vous allez**	*you go*
il/elle va	*he/she/it goes*	**ils/elles vont**	*they go*

- Note that **aller** is irregular. Only the **nous** and **vous** forms resemble the infinitive.

Tu **vas** souvent au cinéma?
Do you go often to the movies?

Je **vais** à la piscine.
I'm going to the pool.

Nous **allons** au marché le samedi.
We go to the market on Saturdays.

Vous **allez** au parc aussi?
Are you going to the park too?

- **Aller** can also be used with another verb to tell what is going to happen. This construction is called **le futur proche** (*immediate future*). Conjugate **aller** in the present tense and place the other verb's infinitive form directly after it.

Nous **allons déjeuner** sur la terrasse.
We're going to eat lunch on the terrace.

Marc et Julie **vont explorer** le centre-ville.
Marc and Julie are going to explore downtown.

Demain, je vais déjeuner au centre-ville.

Et quand est-ce que tu vas rentrer?

- To negate an expression in **le futur proche**, place **ne/n'** before the conjugated form of **aller** and **pas** after it.

Je **ne vais pas** faire mes devoirs.
I'm not going to do my homework.

Nous **n'allons pas** quitter la maison.
We're not going to leave the house.

- Note that this construction can be used with the infinitive of **aller** to mean *going to go (somewhere)*.

Elle **va aller** à la piscine.
She's going to go to the pool.

Vous **allez aller** au gymnase ce soir?
You're going to go to the gym tonight?

MISE EN PRATIQUE

1 Questions parentales Votre père est très curieux. Trouvez les questions qu'il pose.

MODÈLE
tes frères / piscine *Tes frères vont à la piscine?*

1. tu / cinéma / ce soir
   Tu vas au cinéma ce soir?
2. tes amis et toi, vous / boîte
   Tes amis et toi, vous allez en boîte?
3. ta mère et moi, nous / ville / vendredi
   Ta mère et moi, nous allons en ville vendredi?
4. ta petite amie / souvent / marché
   Ta petite amie va souvent au marché?
5. je / musée / avec toi / demain
   Je vais au musée avec toi demain?
6. tes amis / parc
   Tes amis vont au parc?

2 Samedi prochain Voici ce que (*what*) vous et vos amis faites (*are doing*) aujourd'hui. Indiquez que vous allez faire les mêmes (*same*) choses samedi prochain.

MODÈLE
Je nage. *Samedi prochain aussi, je vais nager.*

1. Paul bavarde avec ses copains.
   Samedi prochain aussi, Paul va bavarder avec ses copains.
2. Nous dansons.
   ... nous allons danser.
3. Je dépense de l'argent dans un magasin.
   ... je vais dépenser de l'argent dans un magasin.
4. Luc et Sylvie déjeunent au restaurant.
   ... Luc et Sylvie vont déjeuner au restaurant.
5. Vous explorez le centre-ville.
   ... vous allez explorer le centre-ville.
6. Tu patines.
   ... tu vas patiner.

3 Où vont-ils? Avec un(e) partenaire, regardez les images et indiquez où vont les personnages. Answers will vary.

MODÈLE
Henri va au cinéma.

Henri

1. je

3. Paul et Luc

2. nous

4. vous

OPTIONS

TPR Invent gestures to pantomime some activities taught in **Leçon 4**. Examples: **nager:** *move arms as if swimming;* **bavarder:** *make talking gestures with hands;* **dépenser de l'argent:** *turn pockets inside out.* Signal individuals to gesture appropriately as you cue activities by saying: **Nous allons…** or **On va…**.

Extra Practice Do a quick substitution drill to practice **aller**. Write a sentence on the board and have students read it aloud. Then say a new subject and have students repeat the sentence, substituting the new subject. Examples: **1. Tu vas à l'hôpital. (nous, mon frère, vous, mes parents, je) 2. Il va aller au kiosque. (je, Claudine, nous, tu, les enfants, vous)**

COMMUNICATION

4 Activités du week-end Avec un(e) partenaire, assemblez les éléments des colonnes pour poser des questions. Rajoutez (*Add*) d'autres éléments utiles. Answers will vary.

MODÈLE

Étudiant(e) 1: *Est-ce que tu vas déjeuner avec tes copains?*
Étudiant(e) 2: *Oui, je vais déjeuner avec mes copains.*

A	B	C	D
ta sœur	aller	voyager	professeur
vous		aller	cinéma
tes copains		déjeuner	boîte de nuit
nous		bavarder	piscine
tu		nager	centre commercial
ton petit ami		danser	café
ta petite amie		parler	parents
tes grands-parents			copains
			petit(e) ami(e)

5 Le grand voyage Vous avez gagné (*have won*) un voyage dans un lieu de votre choix. Par groupes de trois, expliquez à vos camarades ce que vous allez faire pendant (*during*) le voyage. Vos camarades vont deviner (*to guess*) où vous allez. Answers will vary.

MODÈLE

Étudiant(e) 1: *Je vais visiter le musée du Louvre.*
Étudiant(e) 2: *Est-ce que tu vas aller à Paris?*

6 À Deauville Votre professeur va vous donner, à vous et à votre partenaire, un plan (*map*) de Deauville. Attention! Ne regardez pas la feuille de votre partenaire. Answers will vary.

MODÈLE

Étudiant(e) 1: *Où va Simon?*
Étudiant(e) 2: *Il va au kiosque.*

The preposition à

- The preposition **à** contracts with the definite articles **le** and **les**. It does not contract with **la** and **l'**.

à + le ▸ au | à + les ▸ aux

Nous allons **au** magasin.
We're going to the store.

Ils parlent **aux** profs.
They speak to the professors.

Je rentre **à la** maison.
I'm going back home.

Il va **à l'**épicerie.
He's going to the grocery store.

- The preposition **à** can be translated in various ways in English: *to, in, at*. It often indicates a physical location, as with **aller à** and **habiter à**. However, it can have other meanings depending on the verb used.

Verbs with the preposition à

commencer à [+ *infinitive*]	*to start (doing something)*	**penser à**	*to think about*
parler à	*to talk to*	**téléphoner à**	*to phone (someone)*

Elle va **parler au** professeur.
She's going to talk to the professor.

Il **commence à travailler** demain.
He starts working tomorrow.

- In general, **à** is used to mean *at* or *in*, whereas **dans** is used to mean *inside*. When learning a place name in French, learn the preposition that accompanies it.

Prepositions with place names

à la maison	*at home*	**dans la maison**	*inside the house*
à Paris	*in Paris*	**dans Paris**	*inside Paris*
en ville	*in town*	**dans la ville**	*inside the town*
sur la place	*in the square*	**à/sur la terrasse**	*on the terrace*

Tu travailles **à la maison**?
Are you working at home?

On mange **dans la maison**.
We'll eat inside the house.

Essayez! **Utilisez la forme correcte du verbe aller.**

1. Comment ça ___va___?
2. Tu ___vas___ à la piscine pour nager.
3. Ils ___vont___ au centre-ville.
4. Nous ___allons___ bavarder au café.
5. Vous ___allez___ aller au restaurant ce soir?
6. Elle ___va___ aller à l'église dimanche matin.
7. Ce soir, je ___vais___ danser en boîte.
8. On ne ___va___ pas passer par l'épicerie cet après-midi.

Essayez! Have students create a few additional sentences using the verb **aller**.

1 Suggestion To check students' answers, have a volunteer say the question, then call on another student to answer it.

2 Expansion For additional practice, give students these items. **7. Nous passons chez Martine. (Samedi prochain aussi, nous allons passer chez Martine.) 8. André travaille le matin. (... André va travailler le matin.) 9. Je dîne avec un ami. (... je vais dîner avec un ami.)**

3 Suggestion Have students take turns asking where the people in the drawings are going and answering the questions. Example: **Où va Henri? (Henri va au cinéma.)**

4 Suggestion Have two volunteers read the **modèle**. Remind students that they can answer in the negative. Encourage them to expand on their answers. Examples: **Oui, je vais déjeuner avec mes copains au Petit Croissant./Non, je ne vais pas déjeuner avec mes copains, mais je vais aller au centre commercial avec ma mère.**

5 Suggestion Have two volunteers read the **modèle**. Encourage students to choose famous places in the francophone world.

6 Suggestions
- Tell students that Deauville is a fashionable seaside resort in Normandy frequented by the rich and famous.
- Divide the class into pairs and distribute the Info Gap Handouts in the IRM on the IRCD-ROM for this activity. Give students ten minutes to complete the activity.

OPTIONS

Game Divide the class into four-member teams. Using the immediate future, each team will write a description of tomorrow's events for a well-known fictional character. Teams take turns reading and/or writing the description on the board without giving the character's name. The other teams will guess the identity. Each correct guess earns a point. If a team fools the others, it earns two points. The team with the most points wins.

Video Show the video episode again to give students additional input on the verb **aller**. Pause the video where appropriate to discuss how **aller** was used and to ask comprehension questions.

National Standards: comparisons

Section Goals

In this section, students will learn interrogative words.

Instructional Resources
WB/VM: Workbook, pp. 47–48
Lab Manual, p. 28
Lab MP3s
WB/VM/LM Answer Key
*IRCD-ROM: IRM (**Essayez!** and **Mise en pratique** answers; Lab Audioscript)*
espaces.vhlcentral.com: activities, downloads, reference tools

Suggestions

- Write the interrogative words on the board. Have students identify the words they know. Examples: **comment?, combien?, pourquoi?, qui?**, and **quel(s)/quelle(s)?** Model the pronunciation of the new words and have students repeat.
- Point out that in informal conversation interrogative words can be placed after the verb. Examples: **Tu vas où? Il s'appelle comment?**
- Explain that **que/qu'...?, quel(le)(s)?**, and **quoi?** cannot be used interchangeably. **Que?** is often used in more formal questions or with **est-ce que**. Examples: **Que cherchez-vous? Qu'est-ce que vous cherchez?**
- Point out that **que?** and **quoi?** are used to ask about things. A preposition usually precedes **quoi?** or the word appears at the end of an informal question. Examples: **De quoi parlez-vous? Tu manges quoi?**
- Point out that **qui?** is used to ask about people. **Qui?** takes the third person singular verb form. You may also wish to introduce the expression **Qui est-ce qui...?**

7.2 Interrogative words

Point de départ In **Leçon 3**, you learned four ways to formulate yes or no questions in French. However, many questions seek information that can't be provided by a simple yes or no answer.

- Use these words with **est-ce que** or inversion.

Interrogative words			
à quelle heure?	*at what time?*	**quand?**	*when?*
combien (de)?	*how many?; how much?*	**que/qu'...?**	*what?*
		quel(le)(s)?	*which?; what?*
comment?	*how?; what?*	**(à/avec/pour) qui?**	*(to/with/for) who(m)?*
où?	*where?*		
pourquoi?	*why?*	**quoi?**	*what?*

À qui le professeur parle-t-il ce matin?
Whom is the professor talking to this morning?

Combien de villes **y a-t-il** en Suisse?
How many cities are there in Switzerland?

Pourquoi est-ce que tu danses?
Why are you dancing?

Que vas-tu manger?
What are you going to eat?

- Although **quand?** and **à quelle heure?** can be translated as *when?* in English, they are not interchangeable. Use **quand** to talk about a day or date, and **à quelle heure** to talk about a particular time of day.

Quand est-ce que le cours commence?
When does the class start?

À quelle heure est-ce qu'il commence?
At what time does it begin?

Il commence **le lundi 28 août**.
It starts Monday, August 28.

Il commence **à dix heures et demie**.
It starts at 10:30.

- Another way to formulate questions with most interrogative words is by placing them after a verb. This kind of formulation is very informal but very common.

Tu t'appelles **comment**?
What's your name?

Tu habites **où**?
Where do you live?

- Note that **quoi?** (*what?*) must immediately follow a preposition in order to be used with **est-ce que** or inversion. If no preposition is necessary, place **quoi** after the verb.

À quoi pensez-vous?
What are you thinking about?

Elle étudie **quoi**?
What does she study?

De quoi est-ce qu'il parle?
What is he talking about?

Tu regardes **quoi**?
What are you looking at?

MISE EN PRATIQUE

1 La paire Trouvez la paire et formez des phrases complètes. Utilisez chaque (*each*) phrase une fois (*once*).

1. À quelle heure d
2. Comment f
3. Combien de g
4. Avec qui h
5. Où b
6. Pourquoi c
7. Qu' a
8. Quelle e

a. est-ce que tu regardes?
b. habitent-ils?
c. est-ce que tu habites dans le centre-ville?
d. est-ce que le cours commence?
e. heure est-il?
f. vous appelez-vous?
g. villes est-ce qu'il y a aux États-Unis?
h. parlez-vous?

2 Le français familier Utilisez l'inversion pour refaire les questions.

MODÈLE
Tu t'appelles comment?
Comment t'appelles-tu?

1. Tu habites où? Où habites-tu?
2. Le film commence à quelle heure? À quelle heure le film commence-t-il?
3. Il est quelle heure? Quelle heure est-il?
4. Tu as combien de frères? Combien de frères as-tu?
5. Le prof parle quand? Quand le prof parle-t-il?
6. Vous aimez quoi? Qu'aimez-vous?
7. Elle téléphone à qui? À qui téléphone-t-elle?
8. Il étudie comment? Comment étudie-t-il?

3 La question Vous avez les réponses. Quelles sont les questions? Some answers will vary.

MODÈLE
Il est midi.
Quelle heure est-il?

1. Les cours commencent à huit heures. À quelle heure est-ce que les cours commencent?
2. Stéphanie habite à Paris. Où est-ce que Stéphanie habite?
3. Julien danse avec Caroline. Avec qui est-ce que Julien danse?
4. Elle s'appelle Julie. Comment s'appelle-t-elle?
5. Laetitia a deux chiens. Combien de chiens Laetitia a-t-elle?
6. Elle déjeune dans ce restaurant parce qu'il est à côté de son bureau. Pourquoi déjeune-t-elle dans ce restaurant?
7. Nous allons bien, merci. Comment allez-vous?
8. Je vais au marché mardi. Quand est-ce que tu vas au marché?

OPTIONS

Extra Practice Divide the class in two. Give a strip of paper with a question on it to each member of one group. Example: **Où va-t-on pour dépenser de l'argent?** Give an answer to each member of the other group. Example: **On va au centre commercial.** Have students circulate around the room asking their questions until they find the person with the appropriate response. Write only one possible answer for each question.

Extra Practice Have students turn to the **Roman-photo** on pages 114–115. Tell them to write as many questions as they can based on the photos. Example: **Où est David? (Il est à l'épicerie.)** Ask volunteers to read their questions aloud and then call other students to answer them. You may also have students ask their questions in pairs.

COMMUNICATION

4 **Questions et réponses** À tour de rôle, posez une question à un(e) partenaire au sujet de chaque (*each*) thème de la liste. Posez une deuxième (*second*) question basée sur sa réponse. Answers will vary.

MODÈLE

Étudiant(e) 1: *Où est-ce que tu habites?*
Étudiant(e) 2: *J'habite chez mes parents.*
Étudiant(e) 1: *Pourquoi est-ce que tu habites chez tes parents?*

Thèmes

- où vous habitez
- ce que vous faites (*do*) le week-end
- à qui vous téléphonez
- combien de frères et sœurs vous avez
- les endroits que vous fréquentez avec vos copains

5 **La montagne** Par groupes de quatre, lisez (*read*) avec attention la lettre de Céline. Fermez votre livre. Une personne du groupe va poser une question basée sur l'information donnée. La personne qui répond pose une autre question au groupe, etc. Answers will vary.

Bonjour. Je m'appelle Céline. J'ai 20 ans. Je suis grande, mince et sportive. J'habite à Grenoble dans une maison agréable. Je suis étudiante à l'université. J'adore la montagne.

Tous les week-ends, je vais skier à Chamrousse avec mes trois amis Alain, Catherine et Pascal. Nous skions de midi à cinq heures. À six heures, nous prenons un chocolat chaud à la terrasse d'un café ou nous allons manger des crêpes dans un restaurant. Nous rencontrons souvent d'autres étudiants et nous allons en boîte tous ensemble.

- To answer a question formulated with **pourquoi**, use **parce que/qu'** (*because*).

Pourquoi habites-tu la banlieue?	**Parce que** je n'aime pas le centre-ville.
Why do you live in the suburbs?	*Because I don't like downtown.*

- It's impolite to use **Quoi?** to indicate that you don't understand what's being said. Use **Comment?** or **Pardon?** instead.

Vous allez voyager cette année?	**Comment?**
Are you going to travel this year?	*I beg your pardon?*

- Note that when **qui?** is used as a subject, the verb that follows is always singular.

Qui fréquente le café?	Nora et Angélique fréquentent le café.
Who goes to the café?	*Nora and Angélique go to the café.*

- **Quel(le)(s)** agrees in gender and number with the noun it modifies.

The interrogative adjective *quel(le)(s)*

	singular		plural	
masculine	**quel hôpital?**	*which hospital?*	**quels restaurants?**	*which restaurants?*
feminine	**quelle place?**	*which public square?*	**quelles montagnes?**	*which mountains?*

- **Quel(le)(s)?** can be placed before a form of the verb **être**.

Quels problèmes as-tu?	*but*	**Quels sont** tes problèmes?
What problems do you have?		*What are your problems?*

Tu es de quelle origine?
Quel jour sommes-nous?

Essayez! **Donnez les mots (*words*) interrogatifs.**

1. Comment allez-vous?
2. Qu' est-ce que vous allez faire (*do*) après le cours?
3. Le cours de français commence à quelle heure?
4. Pourquoi est-ce que tu ne travailles pas?
5. Avec qui est-ce qu'on va au cinéma ce soir?
6. Combien d'étudiants y a-t-il dans la salle de classe?

Essayez! Have one student read the question aloud, then call on another student to respond.

1 Suggestion Have students compare their answers with a classmate.

2 Suggestion Have one student say the question and call on another student to answer it.

3 Suggestion Before beginning the activity, point out that there is more than one way to form some of the questions. Have students work in pairs. Tell them to take turns asking and answering the questions.

4 Suggestion Have two volunteers read the **modèle** aloud. Tell students to jot down their partner's responses.

5 Suggestion Circulate among the groups, lending help where necessary. You might want to have one person in each group keep the book open to verify answers.

OPTIONS

Extra Practice Bring in pictures or magazine photos of people doing various activities. Have students, as a class, create as many questions as they can about the pictures. Also, call on individuals to answer each question.

Extra Practice Tell students to write a simple statement about something they like, love, or hate. Have the first student say the statement. The next student asks **Pourquoi?** and the first student answers. Then the second student says his or her statement, and a third student asks why. Examples: **Étudiant(e) 1: Je déteste étudier le samedi soir. Étudiant(e) 2: Pourquoi? Étudiant(e) 1: Parce que c'est la barbe/barbant!**

Synthèse

Instructional Resources
IRCD-ROM: IRM (Info Gap Activities); Testing Program, pp. 25–28; Test Files; Testing Program MP3s; Test Generator espaces.vhlcentral.com: activities, downloads, reference tools

1 Suggestion Model the activity with a volunteer by asking questions about **le café**. Tell students to jot down notes during the interviews. Encourage them to add other places to the list.

2 Suggestion Photocopy and distribute a page from a French day planner so that students can make a note of the activities in the appropriate place. To review telling time, tell students to say the time at which they do the activities as well as the day.

3 Suggestion Before beginning the activity, have students make a list of possible activities for the weekend.

4 Suggestion Before beginning the activity, give students a few minutes to make a list of possible activities in their hometown to discuss.

5 Suggestion Have two volunteers to read the **modèle** aloud. Then have students brainstorm places they could go and things they could do in each city. Write their suggestions on the board.

6 Suggestion Divide the class into pairs and distribute the Info Gap Handouts in the IRM on the IRCD-ROM for this activity. Give students ten minutes to complete the activity.

6 Expansion Call on volunteers to read their descriptions aloud and have the class compare them.

1 En ville Par groupes de trois, interviewez vos camarades. Où allez-vous en ville? Quand ils mentionnent un endroit de la liste, demandez des détails (quand? avec qui? pourquoi? etc.). Présentez les réponses à la classe. Answers will vary.

le café	le musée
le centre commercial	le parc
le cinéma	la piscine
le marché	le restaurant

2 La semaine prochaine Voici votre agenda (*day planner*). Parlez de votre semaine avec un(e) partenaire. Mentionnez trois activités associées au travail et trois activités d'un autre type. Deux des activités devraient (*should*) être des activités de groupe. Answers will vary.

MODÈLE

Lundi je vais préparer un examen, mais samedi je vais danser en boîte.

	L	M	M	J	V	S	D
8h30							
9h00							
9h30							
10h00							
10h30							
11h00							
11h30							
12h00							
12h30							

3 Le week-end Par groupes de trois, posez-vous des questions sur vos projets (*plans*) pour le week-end prochain. Donnez des détails. Mentionnez aussi des activités faites (*made*) pour deux personnes. Answers will vary.

MODÈLE

Étudiant(e) 1: *Quels projets avez-vous pour ce week-end?*
Étudiant(e) 2: *Nous allons au marché samedi.*
Étudiant(e) 3: *Et nous allons au café dimanche.*

4 Ma ville À tour de rôle, vous invitez votre partenaire dans votre ville d'origine pour une visite d'une semaine. Proposez des activités variées et préparez une liste. Ensuite (*Then*), comparez vos villes et vos projets (*plans*) avec ceux (*those*) d'un autre groupe. Answers will vary.

MODÈLE

Étudiant(e) 1: *Samedi, on va au centre-ville.*
Étudiant(e) 2: *Nous allons dépenser de l'argent!*

5 Où passer un long week-end? Vous et votre partenaire avez la possibilité de passer un long week-end à Montréal ou à La Nouvelle-Orléans, mais vous préférez chacun(e) (*each one*) une ville différente. Jouez la conversation pour la classe. Answers will vary.

MODÈLE

Étudiant(e) 1: *À Montréal, on va visiter les librairies!*
Étudiant(e) 2: *Oui, mais à La Nouvelle-Orléans, je vais danser dans les boîtes cajuns!*

Montréal

La Nouvelle-Orléans

6 La semaine de Martine Votre professeur va vous donner, à vous et à votre partenaire, des informations sur la semaine de Martine. Attention! Ne regardez pas la feuille de votre partenaire. Answers will vary.

MODÈLE

Lundi matin, Martine va dessiner au parc.

ressources

WB	LM	Lab MP3s	espaces.vhlcentral.com
pp. 45–48	pp. 27–28	Leçon 7	Leçon 7

OPTIONS

Cultural Activity Invite a native French speaker to class. Before the person arrives, have students prepare a list of questions that they would like to ask this person. For example, they could ask about the person's job, family, leisure-time activities, weekend plans, and the places he or she frequents. Have students use their questions to interview the person.

Pairs Give pairs three minutes to write as many questions as they can using interrogative words. Then have them get together with another pair and take turns asking and answering the questions.

Amina et Sandrine déjeunent au café.

4

SANDRINE Oh, Madame Forestier, j'adore! Un jour, je vais apprendre à préparer des éclairs. Et une bonne soupe maison. Et beaucoup d'autres choses.
AMINA Mais pas aujourd'hui. J'ai trop faim!
SANDRINE Alors, je prends la soupe et un sandwich au fromage.

5

VALÉRIE Et comme boisson?
SANDRINE Une bouteille d'eau minérale, s'il vous plaît. Tu bois de l'eau aussi? Avec deux verres, alors.

9

VALÉRIE Ah, ça y est! Je comprends! La boisson gazeuse coûte un euro vingt-cinq, pas un euro soixante-quinze. C'est noté, Michèle?
MICHÈLE Merci, Madame Forestier. Excusez-moi. Je vais expliquer ça au monsieur. Et voilà, tout est prêt pour la table d'Amina et Sandrine.
VALÉRIE Merci, Michèle.

10

À la table des filles...
VALÉRIE Voilà, une limonade, un café, un jus d'orange et trois croissants.
AMINA Oh? Mais Madame Forestier, je ne bois pas de limonade!
VALÉRIE Et vous prenez du jus d'orange uniquement le matin, n'est-ce pas? Ah! Excusez-moi, les filles!

Expressions utiles

Talking about food

- **Moi aussi, j'ai faim, et puis j'ai soif.** *Me too, I am hungry, and I am thirsty as well.*
- **J'ai envie d'une bonne boisson.** *I feel like having a nice drink.*
- **Qu'est-ce qu'il y a de bon à manger aujourd'hui?** *What looks good on the menu today?*
- **Une soupe de poisson maison délicieuse.** *A delicious homemade fish soup.*
- **Je vais apprendre à préparer des éclairs.** *I am going to learn (how) to prepare éclairs.*
- **Je prends la soupe.** *I'll have the soup.*
- **Tu bois de l'eau aussi?** *Are you drinking water too?*
- **Vous prenez du jus d'orange uniquement le matin.** *You only have orange juice in the morning.*

Additional vocabulary

- **On va au café?** *Shall we go to the café?*
- **Bof, ça va.** *So-so.*
- **comme d'habitude** *as usual*
- **Le monsieur ne comprend pas pourquoi ça coûte onze euros cinquante.** *The gentleman doesn't understand why this costs 11,50€.*
- **Je ne comprends pas non plus.** *I don't understand either.*
- **Je prépare ça tout de suite.** *I am going to prepare this right away.*
- **Ça y est! Je comprends!** *That's it! I get it!*
- **C'est noté?** *Understood?/Got it?*
- **Tout est prêt.** *Everything is ready.*

ACTIVITÉS

2 Mettez dans l'ordre Numérotez les phrases suivantes dans l'ordre correspondant à l'histoire.

a. 5 Michèle a un problème avec l'addition.
b. 3 Amina prend (*gets*) un sandwich jambon-fromage.
c. 1 Sandrine dit qu'elle (*says that she*) a soif.
d. 2 Rachid rentre à l'appartement.
e. 4 Valérie va chercher du pain.
f. 6 Tout est prêt pour la table d'Amina et Sandrine.

3 Conversez Au moment où Valérie apporte le plateau (*tray*) de la table sept à Sandrine et Amina, Michèle apporte le plateau de Sandrine et Amina à la table sept. Avec trois partenaires, écrivez la conversation entre Michèle et les client(e)s et jouez-la devant la classe.

ressources

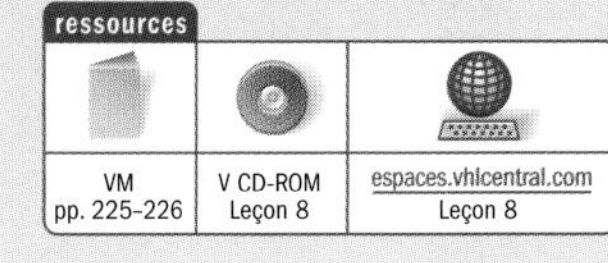

Expressions utiles
- Model the pronunciation of the **Expressions utiles** and have students repeat after you.
- As you work through the list, point out the forms of the verbs **prendre** and **boire** and the partitive articles. Tell students that these verbs and the partitive articles will be formally presented in the **Structures** section.
- Ask students questions about foods and beverages using the vocabulary in the **Expressions utiles**. Examples: **Vous prenez du jus d'orange uniquement le matin? Quand est-ce que vous avez envie de boire de l'eau?**

1 Expansions
- For additional practice, give students these items. **11. Le monsieur ne comprend pas pourquoi ça coûte 11,50€. (M) 12. J'ai faim et puis j'ai soif. (S) 13. Mais pas aujourd'hui. J'ai trop faim! (A) 14. Non, je rentre avec toi. (D)**
- Write these adverbial expressions on the board: **non plus**, **aussi**, and **toute de suite**. Have students create sentences with them.

2 Suggestion Have students work in groups of six. Write each sentence on a strip of paper. Make a set of sentences for each group, then distribute them to students. Tell them to read their sentences aloud and arrange them in the proper order.

2 Expansion Have students create sentences to fill in the missing parts of the story.

3 Suggestion Before doing this activity, have the class brainstorm vocabulary and expressions they might use in this activity and write their ideas on the board.

OPTIONS

Pairs Have students work in pairs. Tell them to combine sentences in **Expressions utiles** with other words and expressions they know to create mini-dialogues. Example:
—Qu'est-ce qu'il y a de bon aujourd'hui?
—Il y a une soupe de poisson maison délicieuse.

Extra Practice Ask volunteers to ad-lib the **Roman-photo** episode for the class. Tell them that it is not necessary to memorize the episode or to stick strictly to its content. They should try to get the general meaning across with the vocabulary and expressions they know, and they should also feel free to be creative. Give them time to prepare.

Section Goals

In this section, students will:

- learn about the role of the café in French life
- learn some terms for describing how people eat and drink
- learn about some common snacks in different francophone countries
- read about the famous cafés in **Saint-Germain-des-Prés**

Instructional Resources
espaces.vhlcentral.com: activities, downloads, reference tools

Culture à la loupe

Avant la lecture Have students look at the photos and describe what they see. Then ask: **Allez-vous au café? Où? Quand?**

Lecture Point out that you can order a drink or food at the bar (**le bar**) and pay less than sitting at a table. Sitting on the **terrasse** is even more expensive. The menu posted outside a café usually indicates the different **tarifs**.

Après la lecture Ask students what aspects of French cafés they find interesting or appealing.

1 Expansion For additional practice, give students these items. **11. Aller au café est une tradition récente en France. (Faux.) 12. Les enfants et les adultes fréquentent les cafés en France. (Vrai.)**

CULTURE À LA LOUPE

Le café français

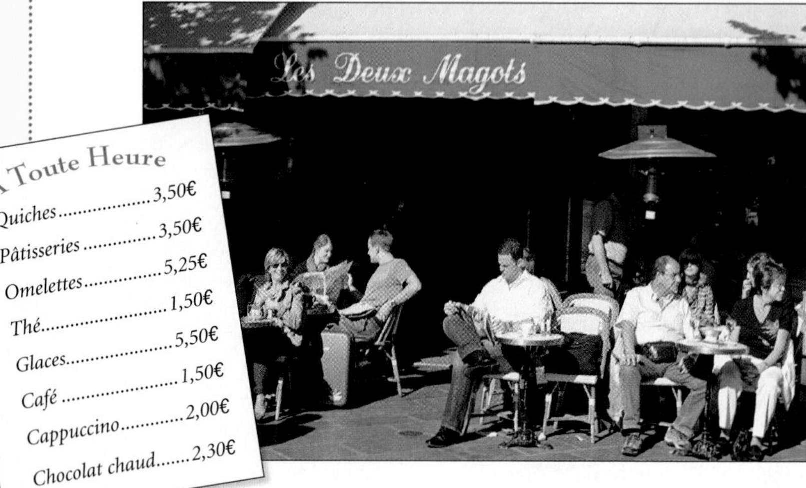

Les Deux Magots
À Toute Heure
Quiches.......3,50€
Pâtisseries.......3,50€
Omelettes.......5,25€
Thé.......1,50€
Glaces.......5,50€
Café.......1,50€
Cappuccino.......2,00€
Chocolat chaud.......2,30€

Le premier café français a ouvert° ses portes à Paris au 17e (dix-septième) siècle°. Depuis°, passer du temps° au café est une tradition. C'est un lieu° de rendez-vous pour beaucoup: le matin, les gens° y° vont pour un café et un croissant; à midi, on y déjeune pour le plaisir ou pour des rendez-vous d'affaires, parce que c'est moins cher° et plus rapide qu'°au restaurant. Après le travail, les gens y vont pour prendre l'apéritif°. Les étudiants ont souvent «leur» café de quartier° où ils vont déjeuner, étudier ou se détendre° avec des amis. Il est aussi très commun pour des amis de se retrouver° au café plutôt qu'°à la maison.

Les cafés servent une grande variété de boissons: café, thé, chocolat chaud, eau minérale, sodas, jus de fruit, etc. En général, les cafés proposent aussi un menu léger°: sandwichs, omelettes, quiches, soupes, salades, hot-dogs et, pour le dessert, des pâtisseries° et des glaces°. La terrasse d'un café est l'endroit° idéal pour se détendre, lire° ou pour observer la vie° de tous les jours et regarder passer les gens.

a ouvert *opened* **siècle** *century* **Depuis** *Since* **passer du temps** *spending time* **lieu** *place* **gens** *people* **y** *there* **moins cher** *less expensive* **plus rapide qu'** *faster than* **apéritif** *before-dinner drink* **quartier** *neighborhood* **se détendre** *relax* **se retrouver** *get together* **plutôt qu'** *rather than* **menu léger** *light menu* **pâtisseries** *pastries* **glaces** *ice cream* **endroit** *place* **lire** *read* **vie** *life*

ACTIVITÉS

1 Vrai ou faux? Indiquez si les phrases sont **vraies** ou **fausses**.

1. Le premier café parisien date des années 1600. Vrai.
2. Les Français vont au café uniquement aux grandes occasions. Faux.
3. Le matin, les Français prennent du jambon et du fromage. Faux.
4. En général, les cafés en France coûtent plus chers que les restaurants. Faux.
5. Les étudiants ont souvent un café où ils vont tous les jours. Vrai.
6. En France, les gens se retrouvent parfois (*sometimes*) au café au lieu de se retrouver à la maison. Vrai.
7. Au café, on trouve des sandwichs et des salades, mais pas de dessert. Faux.
8. En France, on mange rarement (*rarely*) dans les cafés. Faux.
9. Les cafés ont une grande variété de boissons. Vrai.
10. On peut se détendre au café et observer la vie de tous les jours. Vrai.

OPTIONS

Cultural Comparison Have students work in groups of three and compare French cafés to the cafés they frequent. Tell them to list the similarities and differences in a two-column chart under the headings **Similitudes** and **Différences**. After completing their charts, have two groups get together and compare their lists.

Extra Practice Have students look at the **À Toute Heure** menu. Ask them what they are having and how much it costs. Examples: **Qu'est-ce que vous prenez? Combien coûte le chocolat chaud?** Alternatively, this activity can be done in pairs.

LE FRANÇAIS QUOTIDIEN

J'ai faim!

avoir les crocs	*to be hungry*
avoir un petit creux	*to be slightly hungry*
boire à petites gorgées	*to sip*
bouffer	*to eat*
dévorer	*to devour*
grignoter	*to snack on*
mourir de faim	*to be starving*
siroter	*to sip (with pleasure)*

PORTRAIT

Les cafés célèbres de Saint-Germain-des-Prés

Le quartier° de Saint-Germain-des-Prés, à Paris, a plusieurs cafés célèbres°. Le Procope est le plus vieux° café de France: il date de 1686 (mille six cent quatre-vingt-six). Benjamin Franklin et Napoléon Bonaparte sont deux des clients les plus légendaires de son histoire. Pas très loin du Procope se trouvent° le café Les Deux Magots et le Café de Flore. Situés° l'un en face de l'autre°, ils sont fréquentés pendant° les années 1920 (mille neuf cent vingt) et 1930 (mille neuf cent trente) par des intellectuels, des peintres°, des éditeurs, des écrivains et des cinéastes°. Pablo Picasso, Ernest Hemingway, Jean-Paul Sartre et Simone de Beauvoir sont tous des clients réguliers de ces cafés.

quartier *neighborhood* **célèbres** *famous* **le plus vieux** *the oldest* **se trouvent** *are found* **Situés** *Located* **autre** *other* **pendant** *during* **peintres** *painters* **cinéastes** *filmmakers*

LE MONDE FRANCOPHONE

Des spécialités à grignoter

Voici quelques spécialités à grignoter dans les pays et régions francophones.

En Afrique du Nord la merguez (saucisse épicée°) et le makroud (pâtisserie° au miel° et aux dattes)

En Côte d'Ivoire l'aloco (bananes plantains frites°)

En France le pan-bagnat (sandwich avec de la salade, des tomates, des œufs durs° et du thon°) et les crêpes (pâte° cuite° composée de farine° et de lait, de forme ronde)

À la Martinique les accras de morue° (beignets° à la morue)

Au Québec la poutine (frites avec du fromage fondu° et de la sauce)

Au Sénégal le chawarma (de la viande°, des oignons et des tomates dans du pain pita)

saucisse épicée *spicy sausage* **pâtisserie** *pastry* **miel** *honey* **frites** *fried* **œufs durs** *hard-boiled eggs* **thon** *tuna* **pâte** *batter* **cuite** *cooked* **farine** *flour* **morue** *cod* **beignets** *fritters* **fondu** *melted* **viande** *meat*

SUR INTERNET

Quels sont les noms de cafés célèbres dans les autres pays francophones?

Go to **espaces.vhlcentral.com** to find more cultural information related to this **ESPACE CULTURE.**

ACTIVITÉS

2 Compréhension Complétez les phrases.

1. Quand on a un peu soif, on a tendance à (*tends to*) boire __à petite gorgée__.
2. Le plus vieux café français s'appelle __Le Procope__.
3. Pendant les années 1920, on trouve souvent l'artiste __Pablo Picasso__ dans les cafés de Saint-Germain-des-Prés.
4. Si (*If*) vous aimez les frites, vous allez manger de la __poutine__ au Québec.

3 Un café francophone Un(e) ami(e) a envie de créer un café francophone. Par groupes de quatre, préparez une liste de suggestions pour aider votre ami(e): noms pour le café, idées (*ideas*) pour le menu, prix, heures, etc. Indiquez où le café va être situé et qui va fréquenter ce café.

ressources

espaces.vhlcentral.com Leçon 8

Le français quotidien Model the pronunciation of each term and have students repeat it. Then ask questions based on the vocabulary. Examples: **Avez-vous les crocs? Vous mangez quoi quand vous avez les crocs? Vous dévorez votre déjeuner?**

Portrait Point out that Hemingway wrote much of his novel *The Sun Also Rises* at the nearby café **La Closerie de Lilas**. F. Scott Fitzgerald, Gertrude Stein, Ezra Pound, and e. e. cummings were also in Paris during the 1920s and 1930s.

Le monde francophone Have students read the text. Tell them to choose a specialty they would like to eat from the list. Then ask: **Quelle spécialité préférez-vous manger? Pourquoi?**

2 Expansion For additional practice, give students these items. **5. Le Procope date de ____. (1686) 6. ____ est un client américain célèbre du Procope. (Benjamin Franklin) 7. ____ est un écrivain qui fréquente les cafés de Saint-Germain-des-Prés pendant les années 1920. (Ernest Hemmingway/ Jean-Paul Sartre)**

3 Expansion Have groups present their suggestions to the class. Then have the class discuss the role that the country's culture played in forming their ideas. For example, did it affect the name, the hours of operation, the menu, or the prices?

OPTIONS

Pairs Have students work in pairs. Tell them to take turns stating that they like one of the specialties in the list **Des spécialités à grignoter** at their house. The other person should guess where they live based on the snack named. Example: **Étudiant(e) 1: Chez moi, on aime les accras de morue. Étudiant(e) 2: Alors tu habites à la Martinique, n'est-ce pas?**

Extra Practice Have students write five true/false statements based on the information in the **J'ai faim!** and **Des spécialités à grignoter** sections. Then tell them to exchange papers with a classmate and complete the activity. Remind them to verify their answers.

NATIONAL comparisons STANDARDS

Section Goals

In this section, students will learn:

- the verbs **prendre**, **apprendre**, and **comprendre**
- the verb **boire**

Instructional Resources
WB/VM: Workbook, pp. 51–52
Lab Manual, p. 31
Lab MP3s
WB/VM/LM Answer Key
*IRCD-ROM: IRM (**Essayez!** and **Mise en pratique** answers; Lab Audioscript)*
espaces.vhlcentral.com: activities, downloads, reference tools

Suggestions

- Model **prendre** by taking objects from around the room and describing your actions. Example: **Je prends un crayon**. Then have students take objects from their neighbors and describe their own or someone else's actions. Examples: **Je prends un stylo. Il prend mon stylo. Nous prenons des feuilles de papier. Ils prennent un livre.**
- Point out that **prendre** means *to have* when saying what one is having to eat or drink, but it cannot be used to express possession. For possession, **avoir** must be used.
- Ask students if they can think of any English words related to **apprendre** (*apprentice*) and **comprendre** (*comprehend*).
- Work through the forms of **boire**, asking students what they drink most often or rarely. Model a response by first saying what you drink: **Je bois souvent ____. Je bois rarement ____. Qu'est-ce que vous buvez?**
- Write the conjugation of **boire** on the board with the singular forms in one column and the plural forms in another column. Draw a line around the forms that have **oi**. Tell students that **boire** is a "boot verb." Also mention that the singular **je**, **tu**, and **il/elle** forms are pronounced the same.

Essayez! Have students create new sentences orally or in writing by changing the subjects of the sentences.

8.1 The verbs *prendre* and *boire*

Point de départ The verbs **prendre** (*to take, to have*) and **boire** (*to drink*), like **être**, **avoir**, and **aller**, are irregular.

Je prends la soupe et un sandwich au fromage.

Je ne bois pas de limonade.

prendre

je prends	*I take*	**nous prenons**	*we take*
tu prends	*you take*	**vous prenez**	*you take*
il/elle prend	*he/she/it takes*	**ils/elles prennent**	*they take*

Brigitte **prend** le métro le soir.
Brigitte takes the subway in the evening.

Nous **prenons** un café chez moi.
We are having a coffee at my house.

- The forms of the verbs **apprendre** (*to learn*) and **comprendre** (*to understand*) follow the same pattern as that of **prendre**.

Tu ne **comprends** pas l'espagnol?
Don't you understand Spanish?

Elles **apprennent** beaucoup.
They're learning a lot.

boire

je bois	*I drink*	**nous buvons**	*we drink*
tu bois	*you drink*	**vous buvez**	*you drink*
il/elle boit	*he/she/it drinks*	**ils/elles boivent**	*they drink*

Ton père **boit** un jus d'orange.
Your father is drinking an orange juice.

Vous **buvez** un chocolat, M. Dion?
Are you drinking hot chocolate, Mr. Dion?

Essayez! **Utilisez la forme correcte du verbe entre parenthèses.**

1. Ma sœur ___prend___ (prendre) une salade au déjeuner.
2. Tes parents ___prennent___ (prendre) un taxi ce soir?
3. Tu ___bois___ (boire) une eau minérale?
4. Si vous êtes fatigués, vous ___buvez___ (boire) un café.
5. Je vais ___apprendre___ (apprendre) à parler japonais.
6. Vous ___apprenez___ (apprendre) très vite (*fast*) les leçons.

MISE EN PRATIQUE

1 À la bibliothèque Un groupe d'amis parle des livres qu'ils cherchent à la bibliothèque. Complétez leurs phrases.

MODÈLE
je / livre de sciences po
Je prends un livre de sciences po.

1. nous / livre de psychologie
   Nous prenons un livre de psychologie.
2. moi, je / livres d'histoire
   Moi, je prends des livres d'histoire.
3. Micheline / deux livres d'art
   Micheline prend deux livres d'art.
4. vous / romans (*novels*) de Stendhal
   Vous prenez des romans de Stendhal.
5. tu / ne / pas / livre
   Tu ne prends pas de livre.
6. Marc et Abdel / livres sur le sport
   Marc et Abdel prennent des livres sur le sport.

2 Au restaurant Alain est au restaurant avec toute sa famille. Il note les préférences de tout le monde. Complétez ses phrases.

MODÈLE
Oncle Lucien aime bien le café. (prendre) *Il prend un café.*

1. Marie-Hélène et papa adorent le thé. (prendre)
   Ils prennent un thé.
2. Tu adores le chocolat chaud. (boire)
   Tu bois un chocolat chaud.
3. Vous aimez bien le jus de pomme. (prendre)
   Vous prenez un jus de pomme.
4. Mes nièces aiment la limonade. (boire)
   Elles boivent une limonade.
5. Tu aimes les boissons gazeuses. (prendre)
   Tu prends une boisson gazeuse.
6. Vous adorez le café. (boire)
   Vous buvez un café.

3 Les langues étrangères Avec un(e) partenaire, regardez les images et indiquez les langues étrangères parlées par (*spoken by*) les étudiants. Answers will vary.

MODÈLE
Étudiant(e) 1: *Julie apprend l'espagnol?*
Étudiant(e) 2: *Non, mais elle comprend l'anglais.*

Julie / espagnol

1. vous / français

3. Nicole / italien

2. tes cousins / anglais

4. nous / japonais

OPTIONS

Game Divide the class into two teams. Choose one team member at a time to go to the board, alternating between teams. Say an infinitive and a subject pronoun. The person at the board must write and say the correct present tense form. Example: **prendre: ils (ils prennent).** Give a point for each correct answer. The team with the most points at the end of the game wins.

Extra Practice Bring in pictures or magazine photos of people consuming food, drink, or taking various things. Have students describe what the people in the pictures are doing using **boire** and **prendre**.

COMMUNICATION

4 Questions Avec un(e) partenaire, posez-vous des questions en utilisant un élément de chaque (*each*) colonne. Si vous donnez une réponse négative, elle doit (*must*) correspondre à la réalité. Answers will vary.

MODÈLE

Étudiant(e) 1: *Est-ce que tu apprends l'italien cette année?*
Étudiant(e) 2: *Non, mais j'apprends le français.*

A	B	C
apprendre	dessiner	aujourd'hui
boire	parler japonais	cette année
comprendre	un café	cette semaine
prendre	un cahier	en classe
	les devoirs	à la fac
	l'italien	à la librairie
	un Orangina	au resto U
	les femmes	
	les hommes	
	le professeur	

5 Échanges Posez les questions à un(e) partenaire. Answers will vary.

1. Qu'est-ce que tu bois quand tu as très soif?
2. Qu'est-ce que tu apprends à la fac?
3. Quelles langues est-ce que tes parents comprennent?
4. Est-ce que tu bois beaucoup de café? Pourquoi?
5. Qu'est-ce que tu prends pour aller en cours?
6. Quelle langue est-ce que ton/ta camarade de chambre apprend?
7. Où est-ce que tu prends tes repas (*meals*)?
8. Qu'est-ce que tu bois le matin? À midi? Le soir?

6 Un ami et sa famille Un ami va passer le week-end chez vous, et vous êtes au supermarché. Il va arriver avec sa femme, ses deux fils (âgés de deux et cinq ans) et sa belle-mère. Avec un(e) partenaire, imaginez ce qu'ils vont boire et prendre. Answers will vary.

Au supermarché, j'ai besoin de...
—deux bouteilles d'eau minérale

Le français vivant

Buvez de l'eau.
Pure, claire, fraîche,
elle arrive de la montagne.
Vous avez soif, vous prenez un verre,
vous buvez de l'eau et vous allez boire
toute la bouteille!
0€,92
Vittel
Vittel
Perrier
Volvic
Volvic
0€,93

Questions Avec un(e) partenaire, regardez la publicité (*ad*) et répondez aux questions. Some answers will vary.

1. Quelles formes des verbes **prendre** et **boire** trouvez-vous dans la pub? Buvez, prenez, boire
2. Selon (*According to*) la pub, pourquoi l'eau minérale est-elle bonne?
3. Buvez-vous de l'eau minérale? Pourquoi? Achetez-vous (*Do you buy*) une des eaux mentionnées dans la pub?
4. Avez-vous soif quand vous regardez la pub? Que buvez-vous quand vous avez soif?
5. Trouve-t-on toutes ces marques (*these brands*) d'eau minérale dans les supermarchés américains? Quelles autres marques trouve-t-on?

1 Suggestion Have volunteers write the sentences on the board.

2 Suggestion This activity can also be done in pairs. One person should say the sentence and the other person responds. Remind students to switch roles after items 1–3.

3 Suggestion Have two volunteers read the **modèle** aloud.

3 Expansion Ask students what languages they understand. Examples: **Comprenez-vous l'espagnol? ____ comprend-il l'anglais? Quelles langues comprenez-vous?**

4 Suggestion Tell students that they may add other items to column B and other places to column C.

5 Suggestion Have students create two additional questions with **boire**, **apprendre**, **prendre**, or **comprendre** to ask their partner.

6 Suggestion When comparing lists, have pairs take turns stating items they need and asking the other pair if they need the same item. Example: **Nous avons besoin de trois bouteilles de lait. Vous aussi, avez-vous besoin de trois bouteilles de lait?**

Le français vivant

- Call on a volunteer to read the ad aloud. Point out that there are two types of **eau minérale: gazeuse** (Perrier) and **non-gazeuse** (Vittel and Evian).
- Ask students how much each item costs. Example: **Combien coûte la bouteille d'eau Vittel? (Elle coûte quatre-vingt-douze centimes.)**

OPTIONS

Extra Practice Arrange students in rows of six. The first person in each row has a piece of paper. Call out the infinitive of **boire**, **prendre**, **apprendre**, or **comprendre**. Silently, the first student writes the **je** form and passes the paper to the student behind him or her. That student writes the **tu** form and passes the paper on. The last person holds up the completed paper. Have students rotate places before the next verb.

Extra Practice Take a quick class survey of students' eating and drinking habits. Tally the results on the board. Examples: **Qui boit du thé? Du café? De la limonade? Qui prend de la soupe pour le déjeuner? Et des frites? Et un sandwich?**

NATIONAL comparisons STANDARDS

Section Goals

In this section, students will learn partitive articles.

Instructional Resources
WB/VM: Workbook, pp. 53–54
Lab Manual, p. 32
Lab MP3s
WB/VM/LM Answer Key
*IRCD-ROM: IRM (**Essayez!** and **Mise en pratique** answers; Lab Audioscript; **Feuilles d'activités**)*
espaces.vhlcentral.com: activities, downloads, reference tools

Suggestions
- Write a summary chart of the articles on the board with these headings: Definite Articles, Indefinite Articles, and Partitive Articles. Briefly review definite and indefinite articles.
- Explain that **de la**, **du**, and **de l'** are not always partitives. Example: **La table est à côté de la porte**. Point out the partitive is required in French even though it is optional in English.
- Model the pronunciation of the example sentences and have students repeat them.
- Make sure students understand the idea of count nouns and non-count nouns. Have students classify vocabulary from **Contextes** as count nouns (**une boisson, un café, un chocolat**) and non-count nouns (**le beurre, le lait, le sucre**).
- Point out that some nouns can be both count and non-count, depending on context. Examples: **Il y a trois fromages sur la table: le camembert, le roquefort et le reblochon.** (**Fromages** is a count noun, no partitive.) **Prenez-vous du fromage avec votre pain?** (**Fromage** is a non-count noun, with partitive.)

Essayez! For additional practice, give students these items. **7. Pour leur déjeuner, les enfants prennent ____ sandwichs et ____ jus de pomme. (des, du) 8. J'ai toujours envie de boire ____ café le matin. (du)**

8.2 Partitives

- Use partitive articles in French to express *some* or *any*. To form the partitive, use the preposition **de** followed by a definite article. Although the words *some* and *any* are often omitted in English, the partitive must always be used in French.

Je bois **du** thé chaud.	Tu bois **de la** limonade?	Elle prend **de l'**eau?
I drink (some) hot tea.	*Are you drinking (any) lemon soda?*	*Is she having (some) water?*

- Note that partitive articles are only used with non-count nouns (nouns whose quantity cannot be expressed by a number).

PARTITIVE ARTICLE / NON-COUNT NOUN	INDEFINITE ARTICLE / COUNT NOUN
Tu prends **de la soupe** tous les jours.	Tu prends **une banane**, aussi.
You have (some) soup every day.	*You have a banana, too.*

- The article **des** also means *some*, but it is the plural form of the indefinite article, not the partitive.

PARTITIVE ARTICLE	INDEFINITE ARTICLE
Vous prenez **de la limonade**.	Nous prenons **des croissants**.
You're having (some) lemon soda.	*We're having (some) croissants.*

- To give a negative response to a question asked using the partitive structure, as with indefinite articles, always use **pas de**.

Est-ce qu'il y a **du** lait?	Non, il n'y a **pas de** lait.
Is there (any) milk?	*No, there isn't (any) milk.*
Prends-tu **de la** soupe?	Non, je ne prends **pas de** soupe.
Will you have (some) soup?	*No, I'm not having (any) soup.*

Essayez! **Complétez les phrases. Choisissez le partitif, l'article indéfini ou pas de/d'.**

1. Samira boit _de l'_ eau minérale tous les soirs.
2. Son frère mange _des_ éclairs.
3. Est-ce qu'il y a _du_ sucre pour le café?
4. Il y a _un_ kilo de sucre sur la table.
5. Non, merci, je ne prends _pas de_ frites.
6. Nous buvons _de la_ limonade.

MISE EN PRATIQUE

1 Au café Indiquez l'article correct.

MODÈLE
Prenez-vous _du_ thé glacé?

1. Avez-vous _du_ lait froid?
2. Je voudrais _une_ baguette, s'il vous plaît.
3. Elle prend _un_ croissant.
4. Nous ne prenons pas _de_ sucre dans le café.
5. Thérèse ne laisse pas _de_ pourboire.
6. Vous mangez _des_ frites.
7. Zeina commande _une_ boisson gazeuse.
8. Voici _de l'_ eau minérale.
9. Nous mangeons _du_ pain.
10. Je ne prends pas _de_ fromage.

2 Des suggestions Laurent est au café avec des amis et il fait (*makes*) des suggestions. Que suggère-t-il?

MODÈLE
On prend du jus d'orange?

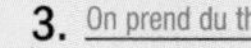

1. _On prend de la limonade?_
3. _On prend du thé?_

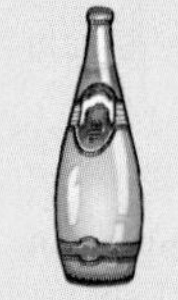

2. _On prend de l'eau minérale?_
4. _On prend des sandwichs?_

3 Mauvais appétit Gérard est difficile. Sa petite amie prépare le dîner, mais il refuse toutes ses suggestions. Avec un(e) partenaire, jouez (*play*) les deux rôles. Answers will vary.

MODÈLE
Étudiant(e) 1: *Je vais préparer du jambon.*
Étudiant(e) 2: *Mais, je ne mange pas de jambon!*

dessert	fromage	pain	sandwich
frites	hamburgers	pizza	soupe

OPTIONS

Extra Practice Distribute empty food and drink containers with labels or pictures of items to groups of three students. Call out the items saying: **du lait**, **des frites**, etc. The group with the item should hold up the package or photo and say: **Voici/Nous avons du lait!** To practice negative partitives, have them say: **Il n'y a pas de ____.**

Extra Practice Show **Transparency #26**. Point to different items and have students identify them. Example: **Il y a des croissants.** Then ask questions about what the people are having to eat and drink. Example: **Qu'est-ce que les garçons prennent avec leurs éclairs? (Ils prennent/boivent du café.)**

COMMUNICATION

4 **Au menu** Vous allez dans un petit café où il y a peu de choix. Vous demandez au serveur/à la serveuse s'il/si elle a d'autres options. Avec un(e) partenaire, jouez (*play*) les deux rôles. Answers will vary.

CAFÉ "LE BON PRIX"

Soupe à l'oignon	3,50€
Sandwich fromage	4€
Frites maison	2,75€
Eau minérale	2€
Jus de pomme	2,50€

MODÈLE

Étudiant(e) 1: *Vous avez du chocolat chaud?*
Étudiant(e) 2: *Non, je n'ai pas de chocolat chaud, mais j'ai...*

5 **Je bois, je prends** Votre professeur va vous donner une feuille d'activités. Circulez dans la classe pour demander à vos camarades s'ils prennent rarement, une fois (*once*) par semaine ou tous les jours la boisson ou le plat (*dish*) indiqués. Écrivez (*Write*) les noms sur la feuille, puis présentez vos réponses à la classe. Answers will vary.

MODÈLE

Étudiant(e) 1: *Est-ce que tu bois du café?*
Étudiant(e) 2: *Oui, je bois du café une fois par semaine. Et toi?*

Boisson ou plat	rarement	une fois par semaine	tous les jours
1. café		Didier	
2. fromage			
3. thé			
4. soupe			
5. chocolat chaud			
6. jambon			

6 **Après les cours** Vous retrouvez des amis au café. Par groupes de quatre, jouez (*play*) les rôles d'un(e) serveur/serveuse et de trois clients. Utilisez les mots de la liste et présentez la scène à la classe. Answers will vary.

addition	chocolat chaud	frites
avoir faim	coûter	prix
avoir soif	croissant	sandwich
boisson	eau minérale	soupe

Le français vivant

Mangez du pain.
Prenez une baguette et du beurre. Le matin, du pain avec du café ou du chocolat chaud. À midi, un morceau de pain pour un sandwich, avec du jambon et du fromage. Le soir, du pain avec de la soupe. Vive le pain!
Savourez le pain. C'est si bon!
1€
1,50€
0,68€
2,50€
francine
PAIN
1,77€

Identifiez Regardez la publicité (*ad*) et trouvez les articles partitifs et les articles indéfinis. du, de la, un, une

Questions Avec un(e) partenaire, répondez aux questions. Answers will vary.

1. Selon (*According to*) la pub, de quelles façons (*ways*) mange-t-on du pain?
2. Mangez-vous souvent (*often*) du pain? À quelle heure? À quelles occasions?
3. Quand vous regardez la pub, avez-vous envie de manger du pain? Pourquoi?

1 Expansion Have students write two more fill-in-the-blank sentences. Tell them to exchange papers with a partner and complete the sentences.

2 Suggestion Have students say the questions, then call on other individuals to answer them. Examples: **Oui, on prend ____.** **Non, on ne prend pas de/d' ____.**

3 Suggestion Have two volunteers read the **modèle** aloud. Remind students to switch roles after they complete four items.

4 Suggestion Tell students that the customer should also ask about the price of the items. Example: **Combien coûte la soupe à l'oignon?**

5 Suggestion Have two volunteers read the **modèle** aloud. Then distribute the **Feuilles d'activités** from the IRM on the IRCD-ROM.

6 Suggestions
- Bring in a few props, such as cups, bottles and plates, for students to use in their role plays.
- Have volunteers perform their role plays for the class, then vote on the best one.

Le français vivant
- Call on a volunteer to read the ad aloud.
- Have volunteers read the phrases with partitives first, and then those with indefinite articles. Write them on the board.

OPTIONS

Extra Practice Write this activity on the board. Tell students to add the missing words and form complete sentences.
1. Marc / boire / eau / et / prendre / sandwich / jambon
2. Solange / prendre / soupe / et / boire / boisson gazeuse
3. Nous / boire / café / lait / et / prendre / éclairs
4. Henri et Paul / prendre / hot-dogs / et / frites
5. Anne / prendre / soupe / poisson / et / verre / thé glacé

Video Show the video episode again to give additional input on partitive articles. Tell students to write down the partitive articles they hear with the nouns. After viewing the video, call on various volunteers to read an example from their list.

Instructional Resources
IRCD-ROM: IRM (Info Gap Activities); Testing Program, pp. 29–32; Test Files; Testing Program MP3s; Test Generator espaces.vhlcentral.com: activities, downloads, reference tools

1 Suggestion Have two volunteers read the **modèle** aloud.

1 Expansion Have students write three things they are learning to do. Then have them exchange papers with a partner and ask each other why they are learning to do those things.

2 Suggestion Tell students to jot down notes during their interviews.

3 Suggestion Tell students that a few **centimes** are almost always added to the price of each item if the people sit on the **terrasse**.

4 Suggestion After completing the activity, call on volunteers to state one difference until all options are exhausted.

5 Suggestion Give students two minutes to jot down a drink and/or dish for each family member.

6 Suggestion Divide the class into pairs and distribute the Info Gap Handouts in the IRM on the IRCD-ROM for this activity. Give students ten minutes to complete the activity.

Synthèse

1 Ils aiment apprendre Vous demandez à Sylvie et à Jérôme pourquoi ils aiment apprendre. Un(e) partenaire va poser des questions et l'autre partenaire va jouer les rôles de Jérôme et de Sylvie. Answers will vary.

MODÈLE

Étudiant(e) 1: *Pourquoi est-ce que tu apprends à travailler sur l'ordinateur?*
Étudiant(e) 2: *J'apprends parce que j'aime les ordinateurs.*

1.

4.

2.

5.

3.

6.

2 Quelle boisson? Interviewez un(e) partenaire. Que boit-on dans ces circonstances? Ensuite (*Then*), posez les questions à un(e) partenaire différent(e). Présentez la comparaison à la classe. Answers will vary.

1. au café
2. au cinéma
3. en classe
4. le dimanche matin
5. le matin très tôt
6. quand il/elle passe des examens
7. quand il/elle a très soif
8. quand il/elle étudie toute la nuit

3 Notre café Vous et votre partenaire allez créer un café français. Sélectionnez le nom du café et huit boissons. Pour chaque (*each*) boisson, inventez deux prix, un pour le comptoir (*bar*) et un pour la terrasse. Comparez votre café au café d'un autre groupe. Answers will vary.

4 La terrasse du café Avec un(e) partenaire, observez les deux dessins et trouvez au minimum quatre différences. Comparez votre liste à la liste d'un autre groupe. Answers will vary.

MODÈLE

Étudiant(e) 1: *Mylène prend une limonade.*
Étudiant(e) 2: *Mylène prend de la soupe.*

5 Elle prend... Vous êtes dans un café avec cinq membres de votre famille. Quelles boissons et quels plats (*dishes*) de la liste prennent-ils? Parlez avec un(e) partenaire. Les membres de sa famille prennent-ils les mêmes (*same*) choses? Answers will vary.

boisson gazeuse	frites	limonade
café	fromage	pain
chocolat chaud	jambon	sandwich au...
croissant	jus de...	soupe
eau minérale	lait	thé

6 La famille Arnal au café Votre professeur va vous donner, à vous et à votre partenaire, des photos de la famille Arnal. Attention! Ne regardez pas la feuille de votre partenaire. Answers will vary.

MODÈLE

Étudiant(e) 1: *Qui prend un sandwich?*
Étudiant(e) 2: *La grand-mère prend un sandwich.*

ressources

WB	LM	Lab MP3s	espaces.vhlcentral.com
pp. 51-54	pp. 31-32	Leçon 8	Leçon 8

OPTIONS

Extra Practice Have students write a brief story about inviting some friends or a date to go to a café and what happens when they are at the café. Tell students that the story can be real or imaginary. Encourage them to be creative.

Extra Practice Have students write five questions that they would like to ask you using the verbs **apprendre**, **comprendre**, **boire**, and **prendre**. Then allow each student the opportunity to ask you one question.

Projet

Créez un nouveau café français

Vous allez ouvrir° un café à Paris. Décidez quels plats° vous allez servir et à quels prix, et cherchez une adresse dans Paris pour votre café.

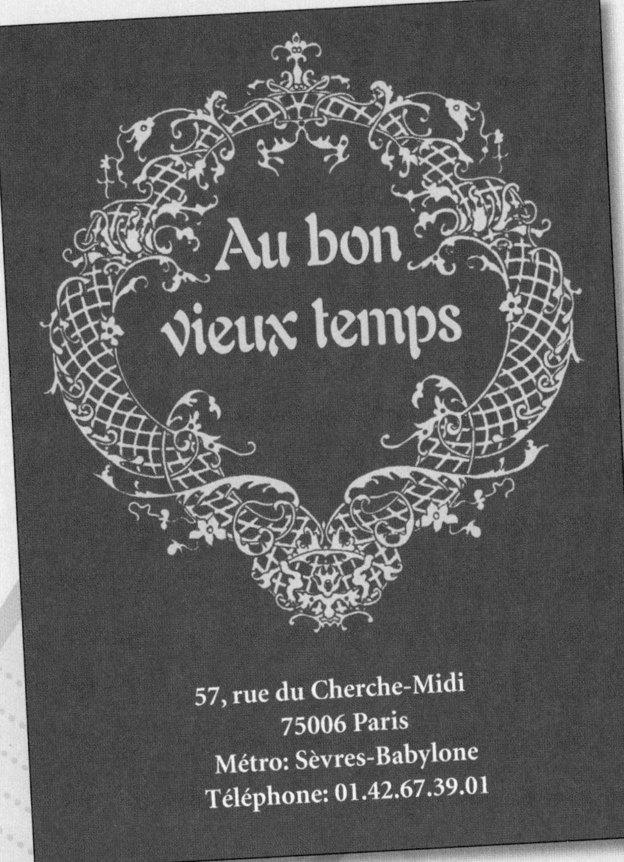

Au bon
vieux temps
57, rue du Cherche-Midi
75006 Paris
Métro: Sèvres-Babylone
Téléphone: 01.42.67.39.01

1 Planifiez° le menu

La carte° est un aspect très important de votre futur café. Pour découvrir° des plats français typiques et des prix de plats en euros, explorez le lien° dans la boîte° **Sur Internet.** N'oubliez pas d'inclure ces° éléments:

- le nom du café
- l'adresse du café
- les plats et les boissons que vous allez servir
- les prix en euros des plats et des boissons

2 Présentez l'information

Parlez de votre projet de café avec trois camarades. Parlez des plats que vous allez servir. Demandez à vos camarades quels sont les plats les plus savoureux°.

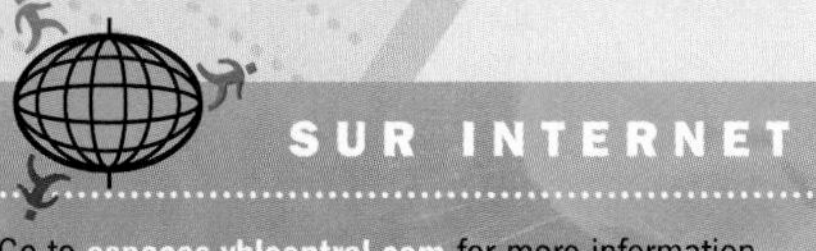

SUR INTERNET

Go to **espaces.vhlcentral.com** for more information related to this **Projet**.

ouvrir *to open* **plats** *dishes* **Planifiez** *Plan* **carte** *menu* **découvrir** *to discover* **lien** *link* **boîte** *box* **ces** *these* **les plus savoureux** *the tastiest*

Section Goals

In this section, students will:

- plan a menu for a new café
- design a menu
- integrate vocabulary and structures from this unit

Instructional Resources
espaces.vhlcentral.com: activities, downloads, reference tools

Suggestion Students might need a week to complete the project, so at the beginning of that time period, have them read through **Projet**. Explain that they are going to open a French café and design its menu.

Planifiez le menu

- Provide students with several menus written in French and English. Ask them to discuss the good and bad points of the design features of each, integrating what works well into their menus.
- Students can search for recipes or information on French dishes on the Internet by using the key words **cuisine française**.

Présentez l'information

- Have students present their menus and plans in small groups.
- Encourage students to bring in dishes they have prepared.

EVALUATION

Criteria	Scale
Content	1 2 3 4
Organization	1 2 3 4
Accuracy	1 2 3 4
Oral presentation	1 2 3 4
Creativity	1 2 3 4

Scoring	
Excellent	18–20 points
Good	14–17 points
Satisfactory	10–13 points
Unsatisfactory	< 10 points

NATIONAL STANDARDS connections cultures

Section Goals

In this section, students will learn historical and cultural information about Normandy and Brittany.

Instructional Resources
IRCD-ROM: Transparency #27,
WB/VM: Workbook, pp. 55–56
WB/VM/LM Answer Key
espaces.vhlcentral.com: activities; downloads; reference tools

Carte de la Normandie et de la Bretagne
- Have students look at the map of Normandy and Brittany or use **Transparency #27**. Ask volunteers to read the cities' names aloud.
- Have students read the photo captions and locate the places on the map.

La région en chiffres
- Have volunteers read the sections aloud. After each section, ask questions about the content.
- Have students compare the industries of these two regions.
- Ask students to share any information they might know about the **Personnages célèbres**.

Incroyable mais vrai! The Abbey of Mont-Saint-Michel was a small chapel in the eighth century. In 966 it became a Benedictine monastery. After the French Revolution, the abbey was a political prison. In 1874, it was declared a national monument, and it presently houses a small monastic community.

Panorama

La Normandie

La région en chiffres

- **Superficie:** *29.906 km² (vingt-neuf mille neuf cent six kilomètres carrés°)*
- **Population:** *3.248.000 (trois millions deux cent quarante-huit mille)*
SOURCE: Institut National de la Statistique et des Études Économiques (INSEE)
- **Industries principales:** *élevage bovin°, énergie nucléaire, raffinage° du pétrole*
- **Villes principales:** *Alençon, Caen, Évreux, Le Havre, Rouen*

Personnages célèbres

- **la comtesse de Ségur,** *écrivain (1799–1874)*
- **Guy de Maupassant,** *écrivain (1850–1893)*
- **Christian Dior,** *couturier° (1905–1957)*

La Bretagne

La région en chiffres

- **Superficie:** *27.208 km² (vingt-sept mille deux cent huit kilomètres carrés)*
- **Population:** *3.011.000 (trois millions onze mille)*
- **Industries principales:** *agriculture, élevage°, pêche°, tourisme*
- **Villes principales:** *Brest, Quimper, Rennes, Saint-Brieuc, Vannes*

Personnages célèbres

- **Anne de Bretagne,** *reine° de France (1477–1514)*
- **Jacques Cartier,** *explorateur (1491–1557)*
- **Bernard Hinault,** *cycliste (1954–)*

carrés *squared* **élevage bovin** *cattle raising* **raffinage** *refining* **couturier** *fashion designer* **élevage** *livestock raising* **pêche** *fishing* **reine** *queen* **les plus grandes marées** *the highest tides* **presqu'île** *peninsula* **entourée de sables mouvants** *surrounded by quicksand* **basse** *low* **île** *island* **haute** *high* **chaque** *each* **onzième siècle** *11th century* **pèlerinage** *pilgrimage* **falaises** *cliffs* **moulin** *mill*

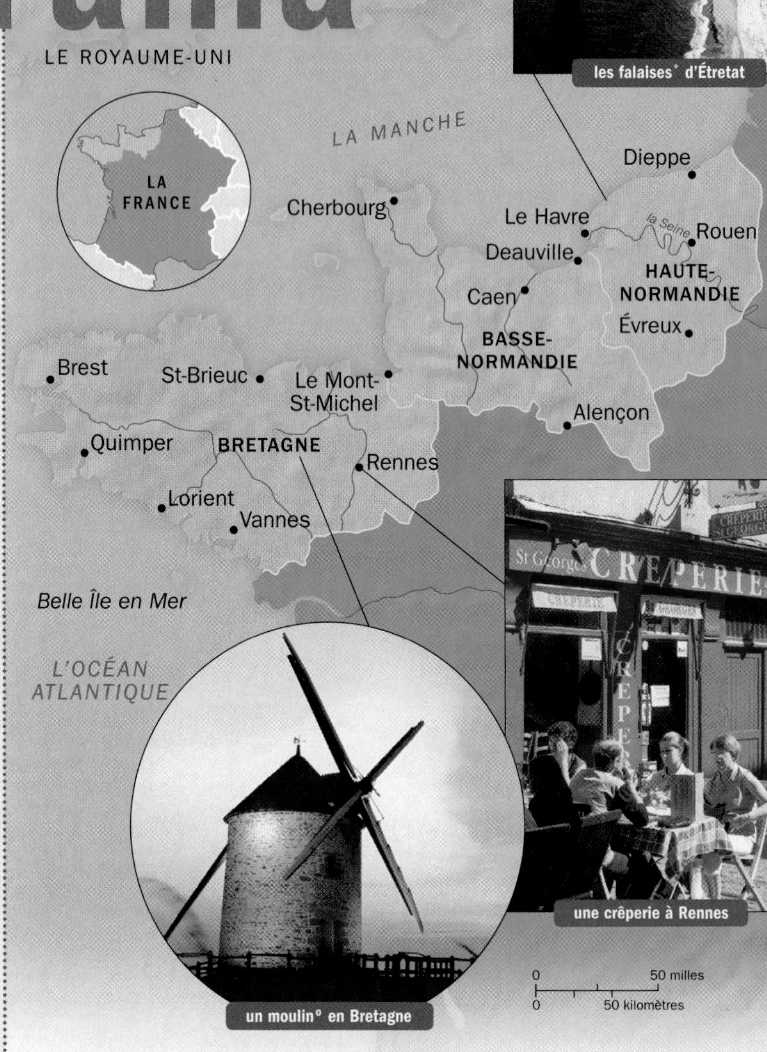

les falaises° d'Étretat

une crêperie à Rennes

un moulin° en Bretagne

Incroyable mais vrai!

C'est au Mont-Saint-Michel qu'il y a les plus grandes marées° d'Europe. Une presqu'île° entourée de sables mouvants° à marée basse°, le Mont-Saint-Michel est transformé en île° à marée haute°. Trois millions de touristes visitent chaque° année l'église du onzième siècle°, centre de pèlerinage° depuis 1000 (mille) ans.

OPTIONS

Personnages célèbres La comtesse de Ségur wrote 25 novels, notably ***les Malheurs de Sophie***. **Guy de Maupassant** published some 300 short stories and 6 novels. His stories present a picture of French life from 1870–1890. **Christian Dior** dominated post-World War II fashion. Today Christian Dior S.A. runs 160 boutiques worldwide. The company also markets lingerie, cosmetics, perfumes, handbags, watches, and accessories under the Dior name. **Anne de Bretagne** was Queen of France twice by marriage. She married Charles VIII in 1491 and Louis XII in 1499. **Jacques Cartier** explored the St. Lawrence River region during his three voyages to North America (1534, 1535, and 1541–1542). France based its claims to that area on Cartier's discoveries. **Bernard Hinault** won the **Tour de France** five times and dominated international cycling from 1977–1987.

La gastronomie

Les crêpes bretonnes et le camembert normand

Les crêpes sont une des spécialités culinaires de Bretagne; en Normandie, c'est le camembert. Les crêpes sont appréciées sucrées, salées°, flambées... Dans les crêperies°, le menu est complètement composé de crêpes! Le camembert normand est un des grands symboles gastronomiques de la France. Il est vendu° dans la fameuse boîte en bois ronde° pour une bonne conservation.

Les arts

Giverny et les impressionnistes

La maison° de Claude Monet, maître du mouvement impressionniste, est à Giverny, en Normandie. Après des rénovations, la résidence et les deux jardins° ont aujourd'hui leur ancienne° splendeur. Le légendaire jardin d'eau est la source d'inspiration pour les peintures° célèbres, «Les Nymphéas°» et «Le pont japonais°». Depuis la fin° du dix-neuvième siècle°, beaucoup d'artistes américains, influencés par les techniques impressionnistes, font de la peinture à Giverny.

Les monuments

Les menhirs et les dolmens

À Carnac, en Bretagne, il y a 3.000 (trois milles) menhirs et dolmens. Les menhirs sont d'énormes pierres° verticales. Alignés ou en cercle, ils ont une fonction rituelle associée au culte de la fécondité ou à des cérémonies en l'honneur du soleil°. Les plus anciens° datent de 4.500 (quatre mille cinq cents) ans avant J.-C.° Les dolmens servent de° sépultures° collectives et ont une fonction culturelle comme° le rite funéraire du passage de la vie° à la mort°.

Les destinations

Deauville: station balnéaire de réputation internationale

Deauville, en Normandie, est une station balnéaire° de luxe et un centre de thalassothérapie°. La ville est célèbre pour sa marina, ses courses hippiques°, son casino, ses grands hôtels et son festival du film américain. La clientèle internationale apprécie beaucoup la plage°, le polo et le golf. L'hôtel le Royal Barrière est un palace° du début° du vingtième° siècle.

Compréhension Complétez ces phrases.

1. Jacques Cartier est un explorateur breton.
2. Le Mont-Saint-Michel est une île à marée haute.
3. Les crêpes sont une spécialité bretonne.
4. Dans les crêperies, on mange uniquement des crêpes.
5. Le camembert est vendu dans une boîte en bois ronde.
6. Le jardin d'eau de Monet est la source d'inspiration de beaucoup de peintures.
7. Beaucoup d'artistes américains font de la peinture à Giverny.
8. Les menhirs ont une fonction rituelle.
9. Les dolmens servent de sépultures.
10. Deauville est une station balnéaire de luxe.

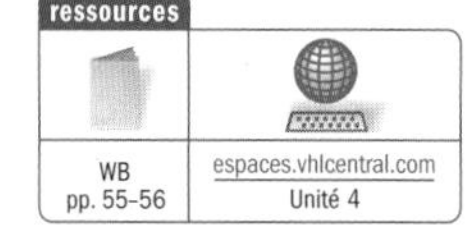

ressources
WB pp. 55-56
espaces.vhlcentral.com Unité 4

SUR INTERNET

Go to **espaces.vhlcentral.com** to find more cultural information related to this **PANORAMA**.

1. Cherchez des informations sur les marées du Mont-Saint-Michel. À quelle heure est la marée haute aujourd'hui?
2. Cherchez des informations sur deux autres impressionnistes. Trouvez deux peintures que vous aimez et dites (*say*) pourquoi.

salées *salty* **crêperies** *crêpes restaurants* **vendu** *sold* **boîte en bois ronde** *round, wooden box* **maison** *house* **jardins** *gardens* **ancienne** *former* **peintures** *paintings* **Nymphéas** *Waterlilies* **pont japonais** *Japanese Bridge* **Depuis la fin** *Since the end* **dix-neuvième siècle** *19th century* **pierres** *stones* **soleil** *sun* **Les plus anciens** *The oldest* **avant J.-C.** *B.C.* **servent de** *serve as* **sépultures** *graves* **comme** *such as* **vie** *life* **mort** *death* **station balnéaire** *seaside resort* **thalassothérapie** *seawater therapy* **courses hippiques** *horse races* **plage** *beach* **palace** *luxury hotel* **début** *beginning* **vingtième** *twentieth*

Les crêpes bretonnes et le camembert normand

- There are various types of crêpes. In Brittany, the **galettes de blé noir** (buckwheat crêpes) are often filled with foods such as egg, ham and cheese, or mushrooms. The **crêpes de froment** (wheat flour crêpes) frequently have sweet fillings such as honey, sugar, jam, or chocolate. Normandy has been known for its cheeses since the sixteenth century. Created in 1890, the wooden container permitted Camembert to be exported worldwide.
- Ask students if they have eaten crêpes or Camembert and if they like them. Or bring in some Camembert and a baguette for students to sample.

Giverny et les impressionnistes Considered one of the greatest landscape painters, Claude Monet lived in the village of Giverny from 1883 until his death in 1926. Bring in photos of ***les Nymphéas*** or ***Le pont japonais*** and briefly comment on the style and colors.

Les menhirs et les dolmens The megaliths, which are ancient granite blocks, can be found all over Brittany. The **menhir** is the most common form of megalith. The **dolmen** has two upright stones with a flat stone on top, like a table. The words **menhir** and **dolmen** come from Breton; **men** means *stone*, **hir** means *long*, and **dol** means *table*.

Deauville: station balnéaire de réputation internationale Founded by the Duke of Normandy in the 1860s, Deauville is famous for its **Promenade des Planches**, the wooden boardwalk alongside the beach, which was created so women wouldn't have to walk in the sand. Ask students: **Avez-vous envie de visiter Deauville? Pourquoi?**

OPTIONS

Cultural Comparison Working in small groups, have students compare Deauville to a famous American seaside resort. Tell them to list the similarities and differences in a two-column chart under the headings **Similitudes** and **Différences**. After completing their charts, call on volunteers to read their lists.

La Chandeleur On February 2, friends and family gather to celebrate the holiday **la Chandeleur** by cooking and eating crêpes and hoping for a prosperous year. Originally a religious celebration, **la Chandeleur** attracted pilgrims to Rome, and according to legend, the pope gave the pilgrims crêpes. Since then, crêpes have been associated with the holiday.

Section Goals

In this section, students will:

- learn to scan a text for specific information
- read an advertisement for a cybercafé

Stratégie Tell students that a good way to get an idea of what an article or other text is about is to scan it before reading. Scanning means running one's eyes over a text in search of specific information that can be used to infer the text's content. Explain that scanning a text before reading it is a good way to improve reading comprehension.

Examinez le texte Call on volunteers to identify the cognates. Then ask the class what the text is about. (a cybercafé)

Trouvez Have students give details about the information they found in the document. Examples: **une adresse (24 place Joliet 69006 LYON), les noms des propriétaires (Bernard et Marie-Claude Fouchier), les heures d'ouverture (7h à 20h),** and **le numéro de téléphone (04.72.45.87.90).**

Décrivez Tell students to proofread each other's descriptions for spelling, verb agreement, and accuracy of information.

Lecture

Avant la lecture

STRATÉGIE

Scanning

Scanning involves glancing over a document in search of specific information. For example, you can scan a document to identify its format, to find cognates, to locate visual clues about the document's content, or to find specific facts. Scanning allows you to learn a great deal about a text without having to read it word-for-word.

Examinez le texte

Regardez le texte et indiquez huit mots apparentés (*cognates*) que vous trouvez. Answers may vary.

1. Chocolat
2. Cybercafé
3. Accès Internet
4. Omelette
5. Salade
6. Tarte
7. Soupe
8. Snack

Trouvez

Regardez le document. Indiquez si les informations suivantes sont présentes dans le texte.

1. ✓ une adresse
2. ___ le nombre d'ordinateurs
3. ___ un plat du jour (*daily special*)
4. ✓ une terrasse
5. ✓ les noms des propriétaires
6. ___ des prix réduits pour étudiants
7. ___ de la musique live
8. ✓ les heures d'ouverture (*business hours*)
9. ✓ un numéro de téléphone
10. ___ une librairie à l'intérieur

Décrivez

Regardez les photos. Écrivez un paragraphe succinct pour décrire (*describe*) le cybercafé. Comparez votre paragraphe avec le paragraphe d'un(e) camarade.

Cybercafé Le

- Ouvert° du lundi au samedi, de 7h00 à 20h00
- Snack et restauration rapide
- Accès Internet et jeux° vidéo

Cybercafé Le connecté

MENU

PETIT-DÉJEUNER° FRANÇAIS 12,00€
Café, thé, chocolat chaud ou lait
Pain, beurre et confiture°
Orange pressée

VIENNOISERIES° 3,00€
Croissant, pain au chocolat, brioche°, pain aux raisins

SANDWICHS ET SALADES 7,50€
Sandwich (jambon ou fromage; baguette ou pain de campagne) 7,80€
Croque-monsieur° 6,20€
Salade verte°

BOISSONS CHAUDES 3,80€
Café/Déca 5,50€
Grand crème 5,80€
Chocolat chaud 5,50€
Thé 4,80€
Lait chaud

Propriétaires: Bernard et Marie-Claude Fouchier

PETIT-DÉJEUNER ANGLAIS 15,00€
Café, thé, chocolat chaud ou lait
Œufs° (au plat° ou brouillés°), bacon, toasts
Orange pressée

DESSERTS 7,50€
Tarte aux fruits 6,40€
Banana split

AUTRES SÉLECTIONS CHAUDES 4,30€
Frites 6,40€
Soupe à l'oignon 8,50€
Omelette au fromage 8,50€
Omelette au jambon

BOISSONS FROIDES 5,50€
Eau minérale non gazeuse 6,00€
Eau minérale gazeuse 5,80€
Jus de fruits (orange...) 5,50€
Soda/limonade 5,20€
Café/thé glacé°

OPTIONS

Game Have students work in pairs and play a game of **Dix questions**. The first person thinks of a food or beverage listed in the **Cybercafé Le connecté** menu. The second person must guess the item by asking yes/no questions. Remind students that they may only ask ten questions.

Small Groups Have students work in groups of three or four. Tell them that they are going to open up a new cybercafé and they need to create a "must-have" list of services and foods for their establishment. After groups have completed their lists, have them describe their café to the class. Then have the class vote on the cybercafé with the best features.

connecté

- Le connecté, le cybercafé préféré des étudiants
- Ordinateurs disponibles° de 10h00 à 18h00, 1,50€ les 10 minutes

24, place des Terreaux
69001 LYON
Tél. 04.72.45.87.90
www.leconnecte.fr

Situé en face du musée des Beaux-Arts

Ouvert *Open* **jeux** *games* **Petit-déjeuner** *Breakfast* **confiture** *jam* **Viennoiseries** *Breakfast pastries* **brioche** *a light, slightly-sweet bread* **Croque-monsieur** *Grilled sandwich with cheese and ham* **verte** *green* **Œufs** *Eggs* **au plat** *fried* **brouillés** *scrambled* **glacé** *iced* **disponibles** *available*

Après la lecture

Répondez **Répondez aux questions suivantes par des phrases complètes.**

1. Combien coûte un sandwich au café?
   Un sandwich coûte 7,50€.
2. Quand est-ce qu'on peut (*can*) surfer sur Internet?
   On peut surfer sur Internet de 10h00 à 18h00.
3. Qui adore ce cybercafé?
   Les étudiants adorent ce cybercafé.
4. Quelles sont deux des boissons gazeuses? Combien coûtent-elles?
   L'eau minérale gazeuse coûte 5,80€. Un soda coûte 5,20€.
5. Combien de desserts sont proposés?
   Deux desserts sont proposés.
6. Vous aimez le sucre. Qu'est-ce que vous allez manger? (2 sélections) Answers may vary. Je vais manger… Any two of the following: un croissant, un pain au chocolat, une brioche, un pain aux raisins, une tarte aux fruits, un banana split.

Choisissez **Indiquez qui va prendre quoi. Écrivez des phrases complètes.** Answers may vary. Possible answers provided.

MODÈLE

Julie a soif. Elle n'aime pas les boissons gazeuses. Elle a 6 euros.
Julie va prendre un jus d'orange.

1. Lise a froid. Elle a besoin d'une boisson chaude. Elle a 4 euros et 90 centimes.
   Lise va prendre un café.
2. Nathan a faim et soif. Il a 14 euros.
   Nathan va prendre un croque-monsieur et un soda.
3. Julien va prendre un plat chaud. Il a 8 euros et 80 centimes.
   Julien va prendre une omelette au jambon.
4. Annie a chaud et elle a très soif. Elle a 5 euros et 75 centimes.
   Annie va prendre un thé glacé.
5. Martine va prendre une boisson gazeuse. Elle a 6 euros et 20 centimes.
   Martine va prendre une eau minérale gazeuse.
6. Ève va prendre un dessert. Elle n'aime pas les bananes. Elle a 8 euros.
   Ève va prendre une tarte aux fruits.

L'invitation **Avec un(e) camarade, jouez (*play*) cette scène: vous invitez un ami à déjeuner au cybercafé Le connecté. Parlez de ce que vous allez manger et boire. Puis (*Then*), bavardez de vos activités de l'après-midi et du soir.**

Répondez Go over the answers with the class. Take a quick class poll to find out what is the most popular food chosen for question 6.

Choisissez Have students write two more situations similar to those in the activity. Then tell them to exchange papers with a partner, write the answers, and verify the answers.

L'invitation Before beginning the activity, tell students that they only have 20€ to spend at the **Cybercafé Le connecté**.

OPTIONS

Cultural Comparison Working in groups of three, have students compare the **Cybercafé Le connecté** menu to a typical menu found at an American Internet café. Tell them to list the similarities and differences in a two-column chart under the headings **Similitudes** and **Différences**. After completing their charts, call on volunteers to read their lists.

Extra Practice To practice scanning written material, bring in short, simple French-language magazine or newspaper articles you have read. Have pairs or small groups scan the articles to determine what they are about. Have them write down all the clues that help them. When each group has come to a decision, ask it to present its findings to the class. Confirm the accuracy of their inferences.

Section Goals

In this section, students will:
- learn to listen for the gist
- listen to and summarize a short paragraph
- listen to a conversation and complete several activities

Instructional Resources
Textbook MP3s
IRCD-ROM: IRM (Textbook Audioscript)
espaces.vhlcentral.com: downloads, reference tools

Stratégie
Script Aujourd'hui, c'est dimanche. Ce matin, Marie va aller au café avec une copine. Cet après-midi, elle va aller au centre commercial et ce soir, elle va aller danser.

Préparation Have students look at the photo and describe what they see. Ask them to justify their responses based on visual clues. Then have them guess what they might order at the café and what they might do this afternoon.

À vous d'écouter
Script CHARLES: Alors, Gina, où est-ce que tu vas cet après-midi? Au centre-ville pour du shopping?
GINA: Eh bien, oui. Je cherche un livre pour mon frère. Je vais aller à la librairie Monet, près de l'hôpital. Il y a beaucoup de livres intéres-sants là-bas.
C: Et après, où vas-tu?
G: Euh... Je vais peut-être aller au cinéma...
SERVEUR: Bonjour. Vous désirez?
C: Pour moi, un sandwich au jambon et une eau minérale, s'il vous plaît.
S: Pour le sandwich, de la baguette ou du pain de campagne?
C: De la baguette, s'il vous plaît.
S: Très bien. Et pour vous, Mademoiselle?
G: Euh... Je ne sais pas...euh...un café, s'il vous plaît. Et un croissant. Je n'ai pas très faim ce midi.
S: D'accord. Merci.
G: Et toi, tu vas où cet après-midi?
C: Je vais aller au gymnase avec Pierre. Et ce soir, je vais manger au restaurant avec des copains et après, on va aller danser.
G: Ah oui? Où ça? En banlieue, près du centre commercial?
C: Non, à la nouvelle boîte de nuit, au centre-ville, près du parc. Tu as envie d'y aller?
G: Au restaurant, non. Je vais manger chez mes grands-parents ce soir, mais en boîte de nuit, oui, pourquoi pas. À quelle heure?
C: Ben, je passe chez toi après le restaurant, vers onze heures, d'accord?
G: D'accord.
C: Excusez-moi Monsieur, l'addition, s'il vous plaît.
S: Voilà.
G: C'est combien, pour mon croissant et mon café?
C: Alors, c'est 2,50 pour le croissant et pour le café, c'est... Oh, allez, je t'invite.
G: Merci. C'est gentil.

À l'écoute

STRATÉGIE

Listening for the gist

Listening for the general idea, or gist, can help you follow what someone is saying even if you can't hear or understand some of the words. When you listen for the gist, you try to capture the essence of what you hear without focusing on individual words.

 To help you practice this strategy, you will listen to three sentences. Jot down a brief summary of what you hear.

Préparation

Regardez la photo. Combien de personnes y a-t-il? Où sont Charles et Gina? Qu'est-ce qu'ils vont manger? Boire? Quelle heure est-il? Qu'est-ce qu'ils vont faire (*to do*) cet après-midi?

À vous d'écouter

Écoutez la conversation entre Charles, Gina et leur serveur. Écoutez une deuxième fois (*a second time*) et indiquez quelles activités ils vont faire.

1. ✓ acheter un livre
2. ✓ aller à la librairie
3. ____ aller à l'église
4. ✓ aller chez des grands-parents
5. ____ boire un coca
6. ✓ danser
7. ✓ dépenser de l'argent
8. ____ étudier
9. ✓ manger au restaurant
10. ✓ manger un sandwich

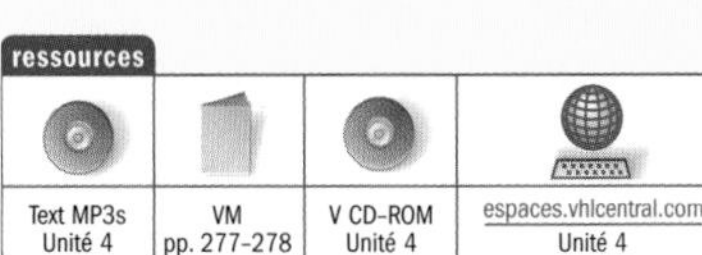

ressources
Text MP3s Unité 4
VM pp. 277-278
V CD-ROM Unité 4
espaces.vhlcentral.com Unité 4

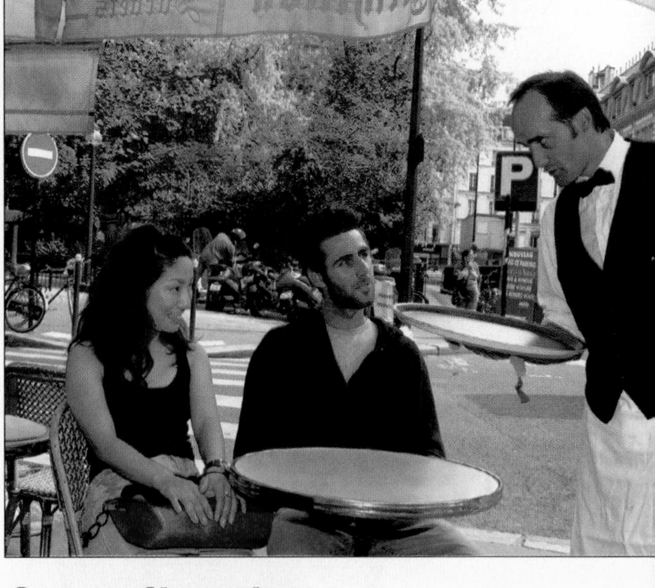

Compréhension

Un résumé Complétez ce résumé (*summary*) de la conversation entre Charles et Gina avec des mots et expressions de la liste.

aller au cinéma	une eau minérale
aller au gymnase	en boîte de nuit
avec son frère	faim
café	un jus d'orange
chez ses grands-parents	manger au restaurant
des copains	du pain
un croissant	soif

Charles et Gina sont au (1) café. Charles va boire (2) une eau minérale. Gina n'a pas très (3) faim. Elle va manger (4) un croissant. Cet après-midi, Charles va (5) aller au gymnase. Ce soir, il va (6) manger au restaurant avec (7) des copains. Cet après-midi, Gina va peut-être (8) aller au cinéma. Ce soir, elle va manger (9) chez ses grands-parents. À onze heures, elle va aller (10) en boîte de nuit avec Charles.

Et vous? Avec un(e) camarade, discutez de vos projets (*plans*) pour ce week-end. Où est-ce que vous allez aller? Qu'est-ce que vous allez faire (*to do*)?

Écriture

STRATÉGIE

Adding details

How can you make your writing more informative or more interesting? You can add details by answering the "W" questions: Who? What? When? Where? Why? The answers to these questions will provide useful and interesting details that can be incorporated into your writing. You can use the same strategy when writing in French. Here are some useful question words that you have already learned:

(À/Avec) Qui?	À quelle heure?
Quoi?	Où?
Quand?	Pourquoi?

Compare these two sentences.

Je vais aller nager.

Aujourd'hui, à quatre heures, je vais aller nager à la piscine du parc avec mon ami Paul, parce que nous avons chaud.

While both sentences give the same basic information (the writer is going to go swimming), the second, with its detail, is much more informative.

Watch the FLASH CULTURE segment on the ESPACES video for cultural footage related to this unit's theme.

Thème

Un petit mot

Vous passez un an en France et vous vivez (*are living*) dans une famille d'accueil (*host family*). C'est samedi, et vous allez passer la journée en ville avec des amis. Écrivez un petit mot (*note*) pour informer votre famille de vos projets (*plans*) pour la journée. Listez cinq activités et répondez aux pronoms interrogatifs (**qui? quoi? quand? où? pourquoi?**) pour détailler votre description.

Chère famille,
Aujourd'hui, je vais visiter la ville avec Xavier et Laurent, deux étudiants belges de l'université.

Section Goals

In this section, students will:
- learn to add informative details
- learn to write an informative note
- view authentic cultural footage of various French cafés

Instructional Resources
WB/VM: Video Manual, pp. 277–278
WB/VM/LM Answer Key
IRCD-ROM: IRM (Videoscript
Video CD-ROM
Video on DVD
espaces.vhlcentral.com: activities, downloads, reference tools

Stratégie Discuss the importance of being informative when writing a note and answering the "W" questions. For example, someone calls while you are out, and your roommate answers the phone. If your note has enough information, your roommate can answer the person's questions about where you are or when you will return.

Thème Have students read the model note and identify the details. (**aujourd'hui; avec Xavier et Laurent, deux étudiants belges de l'université**)

Proofreading Activity Have the class correct these sentences. **1. Ou est-ce que tu va après le cours? 2. Il vont à le magasin cet après-midi. 3. Est-ce que tu prend de le sucre dans le café? 4. Dominique bois de la thé avec le petit-déjeuner.**

Flash culture Tell students that they will learn more about French cafés by watching a variety of real-life images narrated by Benjamin. Show the video segment, then have students jot down at least three examples of things they see. You can also use the activities in the video manual in class to reinforce this **Flash culture** or assign them as homework.

EVALUATION

Criteria	Scale
Content	1 2 3 4 5
Use of vocabulary	1 2 3 4 5
Appropriate details	1 2 3 4 5
Accuracy	1 2 3 4 5

Scoring	
Excellent	18–20 points
Good	14–17 points
Satisfactory	10–13 points
Unsatisfactory	< 10 points

Instructional Resources
Textbook MP3s
IRCD-ROM: IRM (Textbook Audioscript)
espaces.vhlcentral.com: downloads, reference tools

Dans la ville

une boîte (de nuit)	*nightclub*
un bureau	*office; desk*
un centre commercial	*shopping center, mall*
un cinéma (ciné)	*movie theater, movies*
une église	*church*
une épicerie	*grocery store*
un grand magasin	*department store*
un gymnase	*gym*
un hôpital	*hospital*
un kiosque	*kiosk*
un magasin	*store*
une maison	*house*
un marché	*market*
un musée	*museum*
un parc	*park*
une piscine	*pool*
une place	*square; place*
un restaurant	*restaurant*
une terrasse de café	*café terrace*
une banlieue	*suburbs*
un centre-ville	*city/town center, downtown*
un endroit	*place*
un lieu	*place*
une montagne	*mountain*
une ville	*city, town*

Les questions

à quelle heure?	*at what time?*
à qui?	*to whom?*
avec qui?	*with whom?*
combien (de)?	*how many?; how much?*
comment?	*how?; what?*
où?	*where?*
parce que	*because*
pour qui?	*for whom?*
pourquoi?	*why?*
quand?	*when?*
quel(le)(s)?	*which?; what?*
que/qu'...?	*what?*
qui?	*who?; whom?*
quoi?	*what?*

À table

avoir faim	*to be hungry*
avoir soif	*to be thirsty*
manger quelque chose	*to eat something*
une baguette	*baguette (long, thin loaf of bread)*
le beurre	*butter*
un croissant	*croissant (flaky, crescent-shaped roll)*
un éclair	*éclair (pastry filled with cream)*
des frites (*f.*)	*French fries*
un fromage	*cheese*
le jambon	*ham*
un pain (de campagne)	*(country-style) bread*
un sandwich	*sandwich*
une soupe	*soup*
le sucre	*sugar*
une boisson (gazeuse)	*(soft) (carbonated) drink/beverage*
un café	*coffee*
un chocolat (chaud)	*(hot) chocolate*
une eau (minérale)	*(mineral) water*
un jus (d'orange, de pomme, etc.)	*(orange, apple, etc.) juice*
le lait	*milk*
une limonade	*lemon soda*
un thé (glacé)	*(iced) tea*

Activités

bavarder	*to chat*
danser	*to dance*
déjeuner	*to eat lunch*
dépenser de l'argent (*m.*)	*to spend money*
explorer	*to explore*
fréquenter	*to frequent; to visit*
inviter	*to invite*
nager	*to swim*
passer chez quelqu'un	*to stop by someone's house*
patiner	*to skate*
quitter la maison	*to leave the house*

Expressions de quantité

(pas) assez (de)	*(not) enough (of)*
beaucoup (de)	*a lot (of)*
d'autres	*others*
une bouteille (de)	*bottle (of)*
un morceau (de)	*piece, bit (of)*
un peu (plus/moins) (de)	*little (more/less) (of)*
plusieurs	*several*
quelque chose	*something; anything*
quelques	*some*
une tasse (de)	*cup (of)*
tous (*m. pl.*)	*all*
tout (*m. sing.*)	*all*
tout (tous) le/les (*m.*)	*all the*
toute(s) la/les (*f.*)	*all the*
trop (de)	*too many/much (of)*
un verre (de)	*glass (of)*

Au café

apporter l'addition (*f.*)	*to bring the check/bill*
coûter	*to cost*
laisser un pourboire	*to leave a tip*
Combien coûte(nt)...?	*How much is/are...?*
un prix	*price*
un serveur/une serveuse	*server*

Verbes

aller	*to go*
apprendre	*to learn*
boire	*to drink*
comprendre	*to understand*
prendre	*to take; to have*

Expressions utiles	*See pp. 115 and 129.*
Prepositions	*See p. 119.*
Partitives	*See p. 134.*

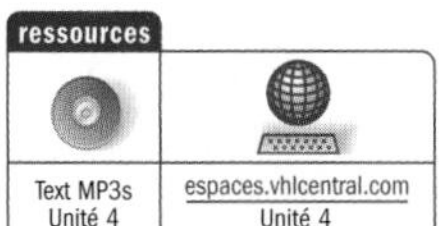

Les loisirs

UNITÉ

Pour commencer

- Où est Stéphane?
- A-t-il froid?
- Pensez-vous qu'il aime le sport?
- Quel sport pratique-t-il, le football ou le basket-ball?
- Quel mois sommes-nous? En septembre ou en décembre?

Unit Goals

Leçon 9

In this lesson, students will learn:
- terms for sports and leisure activities
- adverbs of frequency
- about intonation
- about **le football** in France
- the verb **faire**
- expressions with **faire**
- the expression **il faut**
- irregular **-ir** verbs
- about the singer and actor Yves Montand and painter Jean Béraud

Leçon 10

In this lesson, students will learn:
- terms for seasons and months
- weather expressions
- to tell the date
- differences between open and closed vowels
- about public gardens and parks in the francophone world
- the numbers 101 and higher
- **-er** verbs with spelling changes
- about meteorology and weather forecasts in France

Savoir-faire

In this section, students will learn:
- cultural and historical information about the French regions of **Pays de la Loire** and **Centre**
- to skim a text
- to listen for key words in oral communication
- to use a French-English dictionary
- more about sports and leisure activities through specially shot video footage

Pour commencer

- **Il est dans le parc.**
- **Non, il n'a pas froid.**
- **Oui, je pense qu'il aime le sport.**
- **Il pratique le football.**
- **Nous sommes en septembre.**

RESOURCES

Workbook/Video Manual: WB Activities, pp. 57–70
Laboratory Manual: Lab Activities, pp. 33–40
Workbook/Video Manual: Video Activities, pp. 227–230; pp. 279–280
WB/VM/LM Answer Key
Instructor's Resource CD-ROM [IRCD-ROM]: Instructor's Resource Manual [IRM] (Textbook Audioscript; Lab Audioscript; Videoscript; **Roman-photo** Translations; **Vocabulaire supplémentaire**; **Feuilles d'activités**; Info Gap Activities; **Interlude** song lyrics; **Le zapping** TV clip transcription; **Essayez!** and **Mise en pratique** answers); Transparencies #28, #29, #30; Testing Program, pp. 33–40, pp. 185–196; Test Files; Testing Program MP3s; Test Generator
Lab MP3s
Textbook MP3s
Video CD-ROM
Video on DVD
espaces.vhlcentral.com

Section Goals

In this section, students will learn and practice vocabulary related to:

- sports and leisure activities
- adverbs of frequency

Instructional Resources

*IRCD-ROM: Transparency #28; IRM (**Vocabulaire supplémentaire; Mise en pratique** answers; Textbook Audioscript; Lab Audioscript; **Feuilles d'activités**)*
Textbook MP3s
WB/VM: Workbook, pp. 57–58
Lab Manual, p. 33
Lab MP3s
WB/VM/LM Answer Key
espaces.vhlcentral.com: activities, downloads, reference tools

Suggestions

- Have students look over the new vocabulary, covering the translations. Guide them to notice the numerous cognates for sports terms. See how many words students know without looking at the English.
- Use **Transparency #28** to describe what people are doing. Examples: **Ils jouent au football. Elles jouent au tennis.** Encourage students to add their remarks.
- Teach students the expression **aider quelqu'un à... (étudier, bricoler, travailler)**. Pointing to the person toward the right helping his injured friend, say: **Il aide son copain à marcher.**
- Point out the differences between the words **un jeu**, **jouer**, **un joueur**, and **une joueuse**.
- Ask students closed-ended questions about their favorite activities: **Tu préfère jouer au tennis ou aller à la pêche? Aller à un spectacle ou jouer au golf?**
- Tell students that **pratiquer** can also mean *to play (on a regular basis)*.
- Call out sports and activities from this section and have students classify them as either **un sport** or **un loisir**. List them on the board in two columns.
- Additional vocabulary for this lesson can be found in the **Vocabulaire supplémentaire** in the IRM on the IRCD-ROM.

Leçon 9

You will learn how to...

- talk about activities
- tell how often and how well you do things

Le temps libre

Vocabulaire

aller à la pêche	*to go fishing*
bricoler	*to tinker; to do odd jobs*
désirer	*to want*
jouer (à/de)	*to play*
pratiquer	*to practice*
skier	*to ski*
le baseball	*baseball*
le cinéma	*movies*
le foot(ball)	*soccer*
le football américain	*football*
le golf	*golf*
un jeu	*game*
un loisir	*leisure activity*
un passe-temps	*pastime, hobby*
un spectacle	*show*
un stade	*stadium*
le temps libre	*free time*
le volley(-ball)	*volleyball*
une/deux fois	*one/two time(s)*
par jour, semaine, mois, an, etc.	*per day, week, month, year, etc.*
déjà	*already*
encore	*again; still*
jamais	*never*
longtemps	*long time*
maintenant	*now*
parfois	*sometimes*
rarement	*rarely*
souvent	*often*

les joueuses (*f.*)
un match de tennis (*m.*)
Elle marche. (marcher)
le sport
une équipe
les joueurs (*m.*)
Il joue au foot. (jouer)
Il gagne. (gagner)
les cartes (*f.*)
une bande dessinée (B.D.)

ressources

WB pp. 57–58	LM p. 33	Text MP3s Leçon 9	Lab MP3s Leçon 9	espaces.vhlcentral.com Leçon 9

OPTIONS

Extra Practice Have students give their opinions about activities in **Contextes**. Brainstorm pairs of adjectives that apply to activities and write them on the board or on a transparency. Examples: **agréable/désagréable, intéressant/ennuyeux, utile/inutile, génial/nul, facile/difficile**. Then ask questions like these: **Le football, c'est intéressant ou c'est ennuyeux? Les échecs, c'est facile ou difficile?**

Game Play a game of **Jacques a dit** (*Simon says*) using the activities in this section. Tell students to mime each activity only if they hear the words **Jacques a dit**. If a student mimes an activity not preceded by **Jacques a dit**, he or she is eliminated from the game. The last person standing wins. You might want students to take turns calling out activities.

Attention!

Use **jouer à** with games and sports.
Elle joue aux cartes/ au baseball.
She plays cards/baseball.
Use **jouer de** with musical instruments.
Vous jouez de la guitare/ du piano.
You play the guitar/piano.

le basket(-ball)
Il aide le joueur. (aider)
Il chante. (chanter)
Il indique. (indiquer)
les échecs (m.)

Mise en pratique

1 Écoutez Écoutez Sabine et Marc parler de leurs passe-temps préférés. Dans le tableau suivant, écrivez un **S** pour Sabine et un **M** pour Marc pour indiquer s'ils pratiquent ces activités **souvent**, **parfois**, **rarement** ou **jamais**. Attention, toutes les activités ne sont pas utilisées.

Activité	Souvent	Parfois	Rarement	Jamais
1. chanter	S			
2. le basket	S	M		
3. les cartes				
4. le tennis	M	S		
5. aller à la pêche			M	S
6. le golf				M
7. le cinéma	M, S			
8. le spectacle	M		S	

2 Remplissez Choisissez dans la liste le mot qui convient (*the word that fits*) et remplissez (*fill*) les espaces. N'oubliez pas de conjuguer les verbes.

aider	jeu	pratiquer
bande dessinée	jouer	skier
bricoler	marcher	sport
équipe		

1. Notre ___équipe___ joue un match cet après-midi.
2. Le ___jeu___ de cette équipe n'est pas très bon.
3. Mon livre préféré, c'est une ___bande dessinée___ de Tintin, *Le sceptre d'Ottokar.*
4. J'aime ___jouer___ aux cartes avec ma grand-mère.
5. Pour devenir (*To become*) champion de volley, je ___pratique___ tous les jours.
6. Le dimanche, nous ___marchons___ beaucoup, environ (*about*) cinq kilomètres.
7. Mon ___sport___ préféré, c'est le foot.
8. Mon père ___aide___ mon frère à préparer son match de tennis.
9. J'aime mieux ___skier___ dans les Alpes que dans le Colorado.
10. Il faut réparer la table, mais je n'aime pas ___bricoler___.

3 Les loisirs Utilisez un élément de chaque colonne pour former huit phrases au sujet des loisirs de ces personnes. N'oubliez pas les accords (*agreements*). Answers will vary.

Personnes	Activités	Fréquence
Je	jouer aux échecs	maintenant
Ma sœur	chanter	parfois
Mes parents	jouer au tennis	rarement
Christian	gagner le match	souvent
Sandrine et Cédric	skier	déjà
Les étudiants	regarder un spectacle	une fois par semaine
Élise	jouer au basket	une fois par mois
Mon ami(e)	aller à la pêche	encore

1 Tapescript SABINE: Bonjour, Marc, comment ça va?
MARC: Pas mal. Et toi?
S: Très bien, merci. Est-ce que tu joues au golf?
M: Non, jamais. Je n'aime pas ce sport. Je préfère jouer au tennis. En général je joue au tennis trois fois par semaine. Et toi?
S: Moi? Jouer au tennis? Oui, parfois, mais j'aime mieux le basket. C'est un sport que je pratique souvent.
M: Ah le basket, je n'aime pas tellement, je joue parfois avec des amis, mais ce n'est pas mon sport préféré. Le soir, j'aime bien aller au spectacle ou au cinéma. Et toi, qu'est-ce que tu aimes faire le soir?
S: Oh je vais rarement au spectacle mais j'adore aller au cinéma, j'y vais très souvent.
M: C'est quoi ton passe-temps préféré?
S: Mon passe-temps préféré, c'est le chant. J'aime chanter tous les jours.
M: Moi j'adore aller à la pêche quand j'ai du temps libre, mais ce n'est que très rarement.
S: La pêche? Oh moi jamais, je trouve ça ennuyeux.
M: Et est-ce que tu aimes le baseball?
S: Je ne sais pas; je n'ai jamais regardé un match de baseball.
M: Il y a un match toutes les semaines. C'est très intéressant.
(On Textbook MP3s)

1 Expansion Have students tell a partner how often they, themselves, do these activities.

2 Suggestions
- To review **-er** verb forms, conjugate on the board one of the verbs from the list.
- Tell students to use each item in the word box only once.

3 Suggestion Ask volunteers to write one of their sentences on the board, making sure to have one example sentence for each of the verbs listed in this activity.

3 Expansion Ask students how frequently they do each of the activities listed. Encourage them to use as many different adverbial expressions as possible.

OPTIONS

Extra Practice Call out names of famous athletes and have students say: **Ils jouent au** ___*sport*___. Examples: Tiger Woods, Arnold Palmer (**golf**), David Beckham, Zinedine Zidane (**football**), Serena Williams, André Agassi (**tennis**), Donovan McNabb, Troy Aikman (**football américain**), Shaquille O'Neal, Larry Bird (**basket-ball**), and Babe Ruth, Mark McGwire (**baseball**).

Game Write each of the words or expressions in **Activité 3** on an index card. Label three boxes **Personnes**, **Activités**, and **Fréquence**. Then place the cards in their respective boxes. Divide the class into two teams. Students take turns drawing one card from each box. Each player has five seconds to form a sentence using all of the words on the three cards. If they do not make a mistake, they score a point for their team.

4 Suggestion Follow up this activity by asking students about their partners' favorite sports and activities. Examples: **Est-ce que ____ est sportif/sportive? Quel sport pratique-t-il/elle? Combien de fois par mois est-ce que ____ va au cinéma?**

4 Expansion Have students conduct an informal survey by circulating around the room and asking these questions to five other students. Tell them to write down all of the responses for each question. As a class, share and compare students' findings.

5 Suggestion Call on two students to read the **modèle** before assigning this activity.

6 Suggestions
- Have two volunteers read the **modèle** aloud to make sure students understand the directions. Then distribute the **Feuilles d'activités** from the IRM on the IRCD-ROM.
- Combine pairs of students to form groups of four. Have students share with the other pair what they learned about their partner.

6 Expansion Tally the results of the survey to determine the most and least popular activities among your students.

7 Suggestion Have students exchange letters with a classmate. Remind them to begin the letter with **chère** if they are writing to a woman.

Successful Language Learning Suggest that students use mnemonics devices to memorize vocabulary. Examples: Use alliteration for interrogative words like **qui**, **quand**, and **quoi**. Group words in categories, such as team sports (**football, basketball, volley-ball**) versus those that are usually played one-on-one (**échecs, cartes, tennis**). Learn word "families," such as **un jeu**, **jouer**, **un joueur**, and **une joueuse**.

Communication

4 Répondez Avec un(e) partenaire, posez-vous (*ask each other*) les questions suivantes et répondez (*answer*) à tour de rôle. Answers will vary.

1. Quel est votre loisir préféré?
2. Quel est votre sport préféré à la télévision?
3. Êtes-vous sportif/sportive? Si oui, quel sport pratiquez-vous?
4. Qu'est-ce que vous désirez faire (*to do*) ce week-end?
5. Combien de fois par mois allez-vous au cinéma?
6. Que faites-vous (*do you do*) quand vous avez du temps libre?
7. Est-ce que vous aidez quelqu'un? Qui? À faire quoi? Comment?
8. Quel est votre jeu de société (*board game*) préféré? Pourquoi?

5 Conversez Avec un(e) partenaire, utilisez les expressions de la liste et les mots de la section **ESPACE CONTEXTES** et écrivez une conversation au sujet de vos loisirs. Présentez votre travail au reste de la classe. Answers will vary.

Avec qui?	Pourquoi?
Combien de fois par...?	Quand?
Comment?	Quel(le)(s)?
Où?	Quoi?

MODÈLE

Jacques: *Que fais-tu (do you do) comme sport?*
Clothilde: *Je joue au volley.*
Jacques: *Tu joues souvent?*
Clothilde: *Oui, trois fois par semaine, avec mon amie Julie. C'est un sport que j'adore. Et toi, quel est ton passe-temps préféré?*

6 Sondage Avec la feuille d'activités que votre professeur va vous donner, circulez dans la classe et demandez à vos camarades s'ils pratiquent ces activités et si oui (*if so*), à quelle fréquence. Quelle est l'activité la plus pratiquée (*the most practiced*) de la classe? Answers will vary.

MODÈLE

aller à la pêche
Simone: *Est-ce que tu vas à la pêche?*
François: *Oui, je vais parfois à la pêche.*

Activité	*Nom*	*Fréquence*
1. aller à la pêche	*François*	*parfois*
2. jouer au tennis	______	______
3. jouer au foot	______	______
4. skier	______	______

7 La lettre Écrivez une lettre à un(e) ami(e). Dites ce que vous faites (*do*) pendant vos loisirs, quand, avec qui et avec quelle fréquence.

Cher Marc,

Pendant (during) mon temps libre, j'aime bien jouer au basket et au tennis. J'aime gagner, mais ce n'est pas souvent! Je joue au tennis avec mes amis deux fois par semaine, le mardi et le vendredi, et au basket le samedi. J'adore les films et je vais souvent au cinéma avec ma sœur ou mes amis. Le soir...

OPTIONS

Extra Practice Give students five minutes to jot down a description of their typical weekend, including what they do, where they go, and with whom they spend time. Circulate among the class to help with unfamiliar vocabulary. Then have volunteers share their information with the rest of the class. The class decides whether or not each volunteer represents a "typical" student.

Game Play a game of **Dix questions**. Ask a volunteer to think of a sport, activity, person, or place from the vocabulary drawing or list. Other students get one chance to ask a yes/no question and make a guess until someone guesses the word. Limit attempts to 10 questions per word. You may want to write some phrases on the board to cue students' questions.

NATIONAL STANDARDS comparisons

Les sons et les lettres

Intonation

In short, declarative sentences, the pitch of your voice, or intonation, falls on the final word or syllable.

Nathalie est française. **Hector joue au football.**

In longer, declarative sentences, intonation rises, then falls.

À trois heures et demie, j'ai sciences politiques.

In sentences containing lists, intonation rises for each item in the list and falls on the last syllable of the last one.

Martine est jeune, blonde et jolie.

In long, declarative sentences, such as those containing clauses, intonation may rise several times, falling on the final syllable.

Le samedi, à dix heures du matin, je vais au centre commercial.

Questions that require a yes or no answer have rising intonation. Information questions have falling intonation.

C'est ta mère? **Est-ce qu'elle joue au tennis?**

Quelle heure est-il? **Quand est-ce que tu arrives?**

Prononcez Répétez les phrases suivantes à voix haute.

1. J'ai dix-neuf ans.
2. Tu fais du sport?
3. Quel jour sommes-nous?
4. Sandrine n'habite pas à Paris.
5. Quand est-ce que Marc arrive?
6. Charlotte est sérieuse et intellectuelle.

Articulez Répétez les dialogues à voix haute.

1. –Qu'est-ce que c'est?
   –C'est un ordinateur.
2. –Tu es américaine?
   –Non, je suis canadienne.
3. –Qu'est-ce que Christine étudie?
   –Elle étudie l'anglais et l'espagnol.
4. –Où est le musée?
   –Il est en face de l'église.

Dictons Répétez les dictons à voix haute.

Petit à petit, l'oiseau fait son nid.[2]

Si le renard court, le poulet a des ailes.[1]

1 Though the fox runs, the chicken has wings.
2 Little by little, a bird builds its nest.

ressources

LM p. 34	Text MP3s Leçon 9	Lab MP3s Leçon 9	espaces.vhlcentral.com Leçon 9

Section Goals

In this section, students will learn about using intonation.

Instructional Resources
Textbook MP3s
Lab Manual, p. 34
Lab MP3s
WB/VM/LM Answer Key
IRCD-ROM: IRM (Textbook Audioscript; Lab Audioscript)
espaces.vhlcentral.com: activities, downloads, reference tools

Suggestions

- Model the intonation of each of the example sentences and have students repeat them after you.
- Make sure students can recognize an information question. Tell them that information questions contain question words: **qui**, **qu'est-ce que**, **quand**, **comment**, **pourquoi**, etc. Remind students that the question word is not always the first word of the sentence. Examples: **À qui parles-tu? Ils arrivent quand?**
- Contrast the intonation of various types of declarative sentences (short, long, and those containing lists).
- Point out that the sentences without question words in the **Prononcez** activity (all except items 3 and 5) can be changed from a question to a statement and vice-versa simply by changing the intonation.

Dictons

- Ask students if they can think of sayings in English that are similar to **«Petit à petit, l'oiseau fait son nid.»** (*Rome wasn't built in a day. Slow and steady wins the race.*)
- Have students discuss the meaning of **«Si le renard court, le poulet a des ailes.»** (Students may mention *To each his own.*)

OPTIONS

Extra Practice Here are some sentences to use for additional practice with intonation: **1. Il a deux frères? 2. Il a deux frères. 3. Combien de frères est-ce qu'il a? 4. Vous jouez au tennis? 5. Vous jouez au tennis. 6. Avec qui est-ce que vous jouez au tennis?** Make sure students hear the difference between declarative and interrogative statements.

Game Divide the class into small groups. Pronounce ten phrases based on those in the examples and in **Prononcez**. Have students silently pass one piece of paper, numbered 1–10, around their group. Members of each group take turns recording whether the statements are declarative or interrogative. Collect the papers, one per group, when you finish saying the phrases. The group with the most correct answers wins.

Section Goals

In this section, students will learn functional phrases for talking about leisure activities through comprehensible input.

Instructional Resources
WB/VM: Video Manual, pp. 227–228
WB/VM/LM Answer Key
Video CD-ROM
Video on DVD
IRCD-ROM: IRM (Videoscript; ***Roman-photo*** *Translations)*
espaces.vhlcentral.com: activities, downloads, reference tools

Video Recap: Leçon 8
Before doing this **Roman-photo**, review the previous episode.
1. Amina et Sandrine vont au café, mais David et Rachid… (rentrent à leur appartement)
2. Rachid va étudier et David a envie de… (dessiner un peu)
3. Sandrine a envie d'apprendre à… (préparer des éclairs)
4. Amina commande… (un sandwich jambon-fromage et des frites)

Video Synopsis In a park, Rachid, David, and Sandrine talk about their favorite pastimes. David likes to draw; Rachid plays soccer. They run into Stéphane. He and Rachid talk about Stéphane's studies. Stéphane doesn't like his classes; he prefers sports. Sandrine tells David she doesn't like sports, but prefers movies and concerts. She also wants to be singer.

Suggestions
- Ask students to predict what the episode will be about.
- Have pairs of students list words they expect to hear in a video about sports and activities. As they watch, have them mark the words and expressions they hear.
- Have students scan the captions to find phrases used to talk about sports and activities. Examples: **Rachid, lui, c'est un grand sportif. Je fais du ski, de la planche à voile, du vélo… et j'adore nager.**
- Ask students to read the **Roman-photo** in groups of four. Ask groups to present their dramatic readings to the class.
- Review the predictions and confirm the correct ones. Have students summarize this episode.

NATIONAL STANDARDS communication cultures

Au parc

PERSONNAGES

David

Rachid

Sandrine

Stéphane

1

DAVID Oh, là, là… On fait du sport aujourd'hui!
RACHID C'est normal! On est dimanche. Tous les week-ends à Aix, on fait du vélo, on joue au foot…
SANDRINE Oh, quelle belle journée! Faisons une promenade!
DAVID D'accord.

2

DAVID Moi, le week-end, je sors souvent. Mon passe-temps favori, c'est de dessiner la nature et les belles femmes. Mais Rachid, lui, c'est un grand sportif.
RACHID Oui, je joue au foot très souvent et j'adore.

3

RACHID Tiens, Stéphane! Déjà? Il est en avance.
SANDRINE Salut.
STÉPHANE Salut. Ça va?
DAVID Ça va.
STÉPHANE Salut.
RACHID Salut.

6

STÉPHANE Pfft! Je n'aime pas l'histoire-géo.
RACHID Mais, qu'est-ce que tu aimes alors, à part le foot?
STÉPHANE Moi? J'aime presque tous les sports. Je fais du ski, de la planche à voile, du vélo… et j'adore nager.
RACHID Oui, mais tu sais, le sport ne joue pas un grand rôle au bac.

7

RACHID Et puis les études, c'est comme le sport. Pour être bon, il faut travailler!
STÉPHANE Ouais, ouais.
RACHID Allez, commençons. En quelle année Napoléon a-t-il…

8

SANDRINE Dis-moi David, c'est comment chez toi, aux États-Unis? Quels sont les sports favoris des Américains?
DAVID Euh… chez moi? Beaucoup pratiquent le baseball ou le basket et surtout, on adore regarder le football américain. Mais toi, Sandrine, qu'est-ce que tu fais de tes loisirs? Tu aimes le sport? Tu sors?

ACTIVITÉS

1 Les événements Mettez les événements suivants dans l'ordre chronologique.

a. 10 David dessine un portrait de Sandrine.
b. 6 Stéphane se plaint (*complains*) de ses cours.
c. 4 Rachid parle du match de foot.
d. 9 David complimente Sandrine.
e. 2 David mentionne une activité que Rachid aime faire.
f. 7 Sandrine est curieuse de savoir (*to know*) quels sont les sports favoris des Américains.
g. 5 Stéphane dit (*says*) qu'il ne sait (*knows*) pas s'il va gagner son prochain match.
h. 3 Stéphane arrive.
i. 1 David parle de son passe-temps favori.
j. 8 Sandrine parle de sa passion.

OPTIONS

Avant de regarder la vidéo Before viewing the **Au parc** episode, ask students to consider both the title and video still 1. Then brainstorm what David, Sandrine, and Rachid might talk about in an episode set in a park. Examples: sports and activities: **On fait du sport aujourd'hui!** or the weather: **Quelle belle journée!**

Regarder la vidéo Play the video episode once without sound and have the class create a plot summary based on the visual cues. Afterward, show the video with sound and have the class correct any mistaken guesses and fill in any gaps in the plot summary they created.

Les amis parlent de leurs loisirs.

4

5

RACHID Alors, Stéphane, tu crois que tu vas gagner ton prochain match?
STÉPHANE Hmm, ce n'est pas garanti! L'équipe de Marseille est très forte.
RACHID C'est vrai, mais tu es très motivé, n'est-ce pas?
STÉPHANE Bien sûr.

RACHID Et, pour les études, tu es motivé? Qu'est-ce que vous faites en histoire-géo en ce moment?
STÉPHANE Oh, on étudie Napoléon.
RACHID C'est intéressant! Les cent jours, la bataille de Waterloo...

9

10

SANDRINE Bof, je n'aime pas tellement le sport, mais j'aime bien sortir le week-end. Je vais au cinéma ou à des concerts avec mes amis. Ma vraie passion, c'est la musique. Je désire être chanteuse professionnelle.

DAVID Mais tu es déjà une chanteuse extraordinaire! Eh! J'ai une idée. Je peux faire un portrait de toi?
SANDRINE De moi? Vraiment? Oui, si tu insistes!

Expressions utiles

Talking about your activities

- **Qu'est-ce que tu fais de tes loisirs? Tu sors?**
  What do you do in your free time? Do you go out?
- **Le week-end, je sors souvent.**
  On weekends I often go out.
- **J'aime bien sortir.**
  I like to go out.
- **Tous les week-ends, on/tout le monde fait du sport.**
  Every weekend, people play/everyone plays sports.
- **Qu'est-ce que tu aimes alors, à part le foot?**
  What else do you like then, besides soccer?
- **J'aime presque tous les sports.**
  I like almost all sports.
- **Je peux faire un portrait de toi?**
  Can/May I do a portrait of you?
- **Qu'est-ce que vous faites en histoire-géo en ce moment?**
  What are you doing in history-geography at this moment?
- **Les études, c'est comme le sport. Pour être bon, il faut travailler!**
  Studies are like sports. To be good, you have to work!
- **Faisons une promenade!**
  Let's take a walk!

Additional vocabulary

- **Dis-moi.** *Tell me.*
- **Bien sûr.** *Of course.*
- **Tu sais.** *You know.*
- **Tiens.** *Hold on./Here you are.*
- **Ce n'est pas garanti!** *It's not guaranteed!*
- **Vraiment?** *Really?*

ACTIVITÉS

2 Questions Choisissez la traduction (*translation*) qui convient pour chaque activité. Essayez de ne pas utiliser de dictionnaire. Combien de traductions y a-t-il pour le verbe **faire**?

1. _c_ faire du ski
2. _d_ faire une promenade
3. _b_ faire du vélo
4. _a_ faire du sport

a. to play sports
b. to go biking
c. to ski
d. to take a walk

3 À vous! David et Rachid parlent de faire des projets (*plans*) pour le week-end, mais les loisirs qu'ils aiment sont très différents. Ils discutent de leurs préférences et finalement choisissent (*choose*) une activité qu'ils vont pratiquer ensemble (*together*). Avec un(e) partenaire, écrivez la conversation et jouez la scène devant la classe.

Expressions utiles
- Draw attention to the forms of the verb **faire** and irregular **-ir** verbs in the captions, in the **Expressions utiles** box, and as they occur in your conversation with students. Tell students that this material will be presented in **Structures**.
- Respond briefly to questions about **faire** and irregular **-ir** verbs. Reinforce correct forms, but do not expect students to produce them consistently at this time.
- Work through the **Expressions utiles** by asking students about their activities. As you do, respond to the content of their responses and ask other students questions about their classmates' answers. Example: **Qu'est-ce que tu fais de tes loisirs? Tu sors?**
- Remind students that the **nous** form of a verb can be used to say *Let's...* Example: **Faisons une promenade!** = *Let's take a walk!*

1 Suggestion Form several groups of eight students. Write each of these sentences on individual strips of paper and distribute them among the students in each group. Make a set of sentences for each group. Have students read their sentences aloud in the correct order.

1 Expansion Have students make sentences to fill in parts of the story not mentioned in this activity.

2 Suggestion Remind students that **faire** has several English translations.

3 Suggestion Remind students of expressions like **On...?** for suggesting activities and **D'accord** and **Non, je préfère...** for accepting or rejecting suggestions. As students write their scenes, circulate around the room to help with unfamiliar vocabulary and expressions.

OPTIONS

Pairs Have pairs of students create two-line mini-conversations using as many **Expressions utiles** as they can. Example:
—**Qu'est-ce que tu aimes alors, à part le foot?**
—**J'aime presque tous les sports.**
Then have them use the vocabulary in this section to talk about their own activities and those of their friends and family.

Extra Practice Ask volunteers to ad-lib the **Roman-photo** episode for the class. Assure them that it is not necessary to memorize the episode or to stick strictly to its content. They should try to get the general meaning across with the vocabulary and expressions they know. Encourage creativity. Give them time to prepare. You may want to assign this as homework and do it the next class period as a review activity.

Section Goals

In this section, students will:
- learn about a popular French sport
- learn sports terms
- learn names of champions from French-speaking regions
- read about two celebrated French athletes

Instructional Resources
espaces.vhlcentral.com: activities, downloads, reference tools

Culture à la loupe

Avant la lecture Before opening their books, ask students to call out as many sports-related words as they can remember in French. Ask them to name the most popular sports in the United States and those that they associate with the French.

Lecture
- Point out the chart **Nombre de membres des fédérations sportives en France**. Ask students what information the chart shows. (The number of members of athletic federations in France for each sport listed.)
- Point out that the term **le foot** is a common abbreviation for **le football**. Make sure your class understands that **le football américain** is *football* and **le foot** is *soccer.*

Après la lecture Have students prepare a list of questions with **jouer** and frequency expressions to ask a classmate. Have them present the other person's preferences to the class. Example: **Étudiant(e) 1: Est-ce que tu joues parfois au volley-ball? Étudiant(e) 2: Non, je joue rarement au volley-ball.**

1 Expansion Continue the activity with these true/false statements.
11. En France, le basket-ball est plus populaire que la natation. (Vrai.) 12. On fait moins de rugby que de vélo en France. (Faux.) 13. L'équipe de foot de Marseille est très populaire. (Vrai.) 14. Les femmes jouent rarement au foot en France. (Faux.)

CULTURE À LA LOUPE

Les Français et le football

Le vélo°, le tennis, la natation° et le ski sont tous des sports très appréciés des Français, mais le sport le plus° populaire en France, c'est le football. Tous les quatre ans, des centaines de milliers de° fans, ou «supporters», regardent la Coupe du Monde°: le championnat de foot(ball) le plus important du monde. En 1998 (mille neuf cent quatre-vingt-dix-huit), l'équipe de France gagne la Coupe du Monde et en 2000 (deux mille), elle gagne la Coupe d'Europe, autre championnat important.

En France, il y a deux ligues professionnelles de vingt équipes chacune°. Ça fait° quarante équipes professionnelles de football pour un pays plus petit que l'État° du Texas! Certaines équipes, comme l'équipe de Paris Saint-Germain («le P.S.G.») ou l'Olympique de Marseille («l'O.M.»), ont beaucoup de supporters. Chaque semaine, plus de° 200.000 (deux cent mille) personnes vont dans les stades pour assister à des matchs de foot.

à l'intérieur du stade de France

Les Français adorent regarder le football, mais ils sont aussi des joueurs très sérieux: aujourd'hui, il y a plus de 19.000 (dix-neuf mille) clubs amateurs de football et plus de deux millions de joueurs, hommes et femmes.

Nombre de membres des fédérations sportives en France

Football	2.066.000
Tennis	1.068.000
Judo-jujitsu	577.000
Basket-ball	427.000
Golf	325.000
Rugby	253.000
Natation	214.000
Ski	152.000
Escrime°	116.000
Vélo	99.000

vélo *cycling* **natation** *swimming* **le plus** *the most* **centaines de milliers de** *hundreds of thousands of* **Coupe du Monde** *World Cup* **chacune** *each* **Ça fait** *That makes* **un pays plus petit que l'État** *a country smaller than the state* **plus de** *more than* **Escrime** *Fencing*

ACTIVITÉS

1 Vrai ou faux? Indiquez si ces phrases sont **vraies** ou **fausses.**

1. Le football est le sport le plus populaire en France. Vrai.
2. La Coupe du Monde a lieu (*takes place*) tous les deux ans. Faux.
3. La Coupe d'Europe est le championnat de foot le plus important du monde. Faux.
4. En 2000, l'équipe de France gagne la Coupe du Monde. Faux.
5. En France, il y a vingt équipes professionnelles de football. Faux.
6. La France est plus petite que le Texas. Vrai.
7. L'Olympique de Marseille est un stade de football célèbre. Faux.
8. Les Français aiment aller au stade pour regarder les matchs de football. Vrai.
9. Les Français aiment jouer au football. Vrai.
10. Les femmes françaises ne jouent pas au foot. Faux.

OPTIONS

Extra Practice Provide groups of three students with a list of words that are relevant to **Les Français et le football** like **gagner, longtemps, courir** from the **Leçon 9** vocabulary list. Ask them to work together to create sentences about the reading by incorporating the lexical items you have prompted. Example: **gagner (En 1998, la France gagne la Coupe du Monde.)** Answers will vary in an open-ended activity like this, but remind the class to stick to learned material. Follow up by creating a column on the board for each word that you prompted so students can share sentences they consider successful. After at least one student has written a response for each word, correct the sentences as a class.

LE FRANÇAIS QUOTIDIEN

Le sport

arbitre (*m./f.*)	*referee*
ballon (*m.*)	*ball*
coup de sifflet (*m.*)	*whistle*
entraîneur/ entraîneuse	*coach*
maillot (*m.*)	*jersey*
terrain (*m.*)	*playing field*
hors-jeu	*off-side*
marquer	*to score*

PORTRAIT

Zinédine Zidane et Laura Flessel

Zinédine Zidane, ou «Zizou», est un footballeur français. Né° à Marseille, il joue dans différentes équipes françaises. Nommé trois fois «Joueur de l'année» par la FIFA (la Fédération Internationale de Football Association), il gagne la Coupe du Monde avec l'équipe de France en 1998 (mille neuf cent quatre-vingt-dix-huit). Pendant° sa carrière, il joue aussi pour l'équipe d'Italie et pour le Real Madrid, en Espagne°.

Née à la Guadeloupe, **Laura Flessel** commence l'escrime à l'âge de sept ans. Après plusieurs titres° de championne de Guadeloupe, elle va en France pour continuer sa carrière. En 1991 (mille neuf cent quatre-vingt-onze), à 20 ans, elle est championne de France et cinq ans plus tard, elle est double championne olympique à Atlanta en 1996.

Né *Born* **Pendant** *During* **Espagne** *Spain* **plusieurs titres** *several titles*

LE MONDE FRANCOPHONE

Des champions

Voici quelques champions olympiques récents.

Algérie Nouria Merah-Benida, athlétisme°, or°, Sydney, 2000
Burundi Venuste Niyongabo, athlétisme, or, Atlanta, 1996
Cameroun Patrick Mboma Dem, football, or, Sydney, 2000
Canada Jamie Salé et David Pelletier, patinage artistique°, or, Salt Lake City, 2002
France Laure Manaudou, natation, or, Athènes, 2004
Maroc Hicham El Guerrouj, athlétisme, or, Athènes, 2004
Suisse Simon Ammann, saut à skis°, or, Salt Lake City, 2002
Tunisie Fathi Missaoui, boxe°, bronze, Atlanta, 1996

athlétisme *track and field* **or** *gold* **patinage artistique** *figure skating* **saut à skis** *ski jumping* **boxe** *boxing*

SUR INTERNET

Qu'est-ce que le «free-running»?

Go to **espaces.vhlcentral.com** to find more cultural information related to this **ESPACE CULTURE.**

ACTIVITÉS

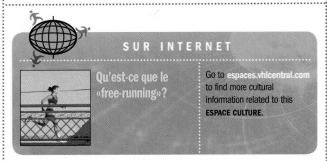

2 Zinédine ou Laura? Indiquez de qui on parle.

1. ___Zinédine___ est de France.
2. ___Laura___ est née à la Guadeloupe.
3. ___Zinédine___ gagne la Coupe du Monde pour la France en 1998.
4. ___Laura___ est championne de Guadeloupe en 1991.
5. ___Laura___ est double championne olympique en 1996.
6. ___Zinédine___ a été trois fois joueur de l'année.

3 Une interview Avec un(e) partenaire, préparez une interview entre un(e) journaliste et un(e) athlète que vous aimez. Jouez la scène devant la classe. Est-ce que vos camarades peuvent deviner (*can guess*) le nom de l'athlète?

ressources: espaces.vhlcentral.com Leçon 9

Le français quotidien You might extend this list to include **le poteau de but** (*goalpost*), **le coup d'envoi** (*kickoff*), **un penalty** (*penalty kick*), and **une faute** (*foul*).

Portrait Zinédine Zidane became the most expensive player in the history of soccer when Real Madrid acquired him for the equivalent of about $66 million American dollars. «Zizou» also made history as Christian Dior's first male model. Laura Flessel is a left-handed fencer called «la Guêpe» because of her competitive and dangerous attack. She works at **l'Office du tourisme** in Paris when not competing.

Le monde francophone Model the pronunciation of names and places in this box. Then ask students if they know of any other athletes from the francophone world.

2 Expansion Continue the activity with additional fill-in-the-blank statements such as these.
7. ____ joue aussi pour l'équipe d'Espagne. (Zinédine)
8. ____ est championne aux jeux olympiques de 1996. (Laura)

3 Expansion Have students prepare five sentences in the first person for homework, describing themselves as a well-known athlete. Ask students to introduce themselves to the class. The class tries to guess the presenter's identity.

OPTIONS

Des champions Look at the map of the world in **Appendice A** to remind students where francophone countries featured in **Le monde francophone** are located. Ask students to pick one of the athletes from this list to research for homework. They should come to the next class with five French sentences about that athlete's life and career. You may want to have students bring an image from the Internet of the athlete they chose to research. Collect the photos and gather different images of the same athlete. Have students who researched the same champion work together as a group to present that athlete while the rest of the class looks at the images they found.

comparisons NATIONAL STANDARDS

Section Goals

In this section, students will learn:
- the verb **faire**
- expressions with **faire**
- the expression **il faut**

Instructional Resources
WB/VM: Workbook, pp. 59–60
Lab Manual, p. 35
Lab MP3s
WB/VM/LM Answer Key
*IRCD-ROM: Transparency #28; IRM (**Essayez!** and **Mise en pratique** answers; Lab Audioscript, **Feuilles d'activités**)*
espaces.vhlcentral.com: activities, downloads, reference tools

Suggestions
- Point out that students have seen **faire** in previous lessons. Example: **faire ses devoirs** in **Leçon 4 Roman-photo.**
- Model **faire** with the whole class by asking: **Qu'est-ce que vous faites? Je fais...** Then, using **Transparency #28**, ask what people in the image are doing.
- Write the forms of **faire** on the board as students hear them in your questions. If **tu** and **nous** forms are missing, complete the conjugation by asking a student: **Tu fais attention?** Then ask: **Qu'est-ce que nous faisons? (Nous apprenons/ faisons attention.)**
- Point out that **fai-** in **nous faisons** is pronounced differently than **fai-** in all other forms. Underline the first syllable of the **nous** form and have students repeat.
- Ask students where they have seen the **-s, -s, -t** pattern. (**boire: je bois, tu bois, il/elle boit**)
- To facilitate memorization, have students compare **faire** with **aller**, **avoir**, and **être**, noting similarities in the forms. Examples: **tu fais, vas, as, es**; **nous faisons, avons, allons**; **vous êtes, faites**; etc.
- Explain that **il faut** is a very common expression in French even though its English translations are not as widely used in everyday language.

9.1 The verb *faire*

Point de départ Like other commonly used verbs, the verb **faire** (*to do, to make*) is irregular in the present tense.

faire (to do, to make)	
je fais	nous faisons
tu fais	vous faites
il/elle fait	ils/elles font

Il ne **fait** pas ses devoirs.
He's not doing his homework.

Qu'est-ce que vous **faites** ce soir?
What are you doing this evening?

On fait du sport aujourd'hui!

Qu'est-ce que vous faites en histoire-géo?

- Use the verb **faire** in these idiomatic expressions. Note that it is not always translated into English as *to do* or *to make*.

Expressions with *faire*			
faire de l'aérobic	*to do aerobics*	faire de la planche à voile	*to go wind-surfing*
faire attention (à)	*to pay attention (to)*	faire une promenade	*to go for a walk*
faire du camping	*to go camping*	faire une randonnée	*to go for a hike*
faire du cheval	*to go horseback riding*	faire du ski	*to go skiing*
faire la connaissance de...	*to meet (someone)*	faire du sport	*to do sports*
faire la cuisine	*to cook*	faire un tour (en voiture)	*to go for a walk (drive)*
faire de la gym	*to work out*	faire du vélo	*to go bike riding*
faire du jogging	*to go jogging*		

Tu **fais** souvent **du sport**?
Do you do sports often?

Nous **faisons attention** en classe.
We pay attention in class.

Elles **font du camping**.
They go camping.

Yves **fait la cuisine**.
Yves is cooking.

Je **fais de la gym**.
I'm working out.

Faites-vous **une promenade**?
Are you going for a walk?

MISE EN PRATIQUE

1 Que font-ils? Regardez les dessins. Que font les personnages?

MODÈLE
Julien fait du jogging.

Julien

1. je Je fais du cheval.

3. Anne Anne fait de l'aérobic.

2. tu Tu fais de la planche à voile.

4. Louis et Paul Louis et Paul font du camping.

2 Chassez l'intrus Quelle activité ne fait pas partie du groupe?

1. a. faire du jogging b. faire une randonnée (c.) faire de la planche à voile
2. a. faire du vélo (b.) faire du camping c. faire du jogging
3. a. faire une promenade (b.) faire la cuisine c. faire un tour
4. a. faire du sport b. faire du vélo (c.) faire la connaissance
5. (a.) faire ses devoirs b. faire du ski c. faire du camping
6. (a.) faire la cuisine b. faire du sport c. faire de la planche à voile

3 La paire Appareillez (*Match*) les éléments des deux colonnes et rajoutez (*add*) la forme correcte du verbe **faire**.

1. Elle aime courir (*to run*), alors elle... e. fait du jogging.
2. Ils adorent les animaux. Ils... d. font du cheval.
3. Quand j'ai faim, je... b. fais la cuisine.
4. L'hiver, vous... g. faites du ski.
5. Pour marcher, nous... f. faisons une promenade.
6. Tiger Woods... a. fait du golf.

a. du golf.
b. la cuisine.
c. les devoirs.
d. du cheval.
e. du jogging.
f. une promenade.
g. du ski.
h. de l'aérobic.

OPTIONS

TPR Assign gestures to pantomime some of the expressions with **faire**. Examples: **faire de l'aérobic, la connaissance de..., du jogging, du ski**. Signal to individuals or pairs to gesture appropriately as you cue activities by saying: **Vous faites...** ____ **fait...** Then ask for a few volunteers to take your place calling out the activities.

Extra Practice Write on the board two headings: **Il faut...** and **Il ne faut pas...** Have students think of as many general pieces of advice (**les conseils**) as possible. Tell them to use **être**, any **-er** verbs, **avoir** and expressions with **avoir, aller, prendre, boire,** and **faire** to formulate the sentences. Examples: **Il faut souvent boire de l'eau. Il ne faut pas manger trop de sucre.** See how many sentences the class can write.

COMMUNICATION

4 Ce week-end Que faites-vous ce week-end? Avec un(e) partenaire, posez les questions à tour de rôle. Some answers will vary.

MODÈLE

tu / jogging
Étudiant(e) 1: *Est-ce que tu fais du jogging ce week-end?*
Étudiant(e) 2: *Non, je ne fais pas de jogging. Je fais un tour en voiture.*

1. tu / le vélo
   Est-ce que tu fais du vélo ce week-end?
2. tes amis / la cuisine
   Est-ce que tes amis font la cuisine ce week-end?
3. ton/ta petit(e) ami(e) et toi, vous / le jogging
   Est-ce que ton/ta petit(e) ami(e) et toi, vous faites du jogging ce week-end?
4. toi et moi, nous / une randonnée
   Est-ce que toi et moi, nous faisons une randonnée ce week-end?
5. tu / la gym
   Est-ce que tu fais de la gym ce week-end?
6. ton/ta camarade de chambre / le sport
   Est-ce que ton/ta camarade de chambre fait du sport ce week-end?

5 De bons conseils Avec un(e) partenaire, donnez de bons conseils (*advice*). À tour de rôle, posez des questions et utilisez les éléments de la liste. Présentez vos idées à la classe. Answers will vary.

MODÈLE

Étudiant(e) 1: *Qu'est-ce qu'il faut faire pour avoir de bonnes notes?*
Étudiant(e) 2: *Il faut étudier jour et nuit.*

être en pleine forme (*great shape*)	avoir de bonnes notes
avoir de l'argent	gagner une course (*race*)
avoir beaucoup d'amis	bien manger
être champion de ski	réussir (*succeed*) aux examens

6 Les sportifs Votre professeur va vous donner une feuille d'activités. Faites une enquête sur le nombre d'étudiants qui pratiquent certains sports dans votre classe. Présentez les résultats à la classe. Answers will vary.

MODÈLE

Étudiant(e) 1: *Est-ce que tu fais du jogging?*
Étudiant(e) 2: *Oui, je fais du jogging.*

Sport	Nom
1. jogging	Carole
2. vélo	
3. planche à voile	
4. cuisine	
5. camping	
6. cheval	

- Make sure to learn the correct article with each **faire** expression that calls for one. For **faire** expressions requiring a partitive or indefinite article, the article is replaced with **de** when the expression is negated.

Elles font **de la** gym trois fois par semaine.	Elles ne font pas **de** gym le dimanche.
They work out three times a week.	*They don't work out on Sundays.*

- Use **faire la connaissance de** before someone's name or another noun that identifies a person.

Je vais **faire la connaissance de Martin**.	Je vais **faire la connaissance des joueurs**.
I'm going to meet Martin.	*I'm going to meet the players.*

The expression *il faut*

Pour être bon, il faut travailler!
Il ne faut pas regarder la télé.

- When followed by a verb in the infinitive, the expression **il faut...** means *it is necessary to...* or *one must...*

Il faut faire attention en cours de maths.	**Il ne faut pas manger** après dix heures.
It is necessary to pay attention in math class.	*One must not eat after 10 o'clock.*
Faut-il laisser un pourboire?	**Il faut gagner** le match!
Is it necessary to leave a tip?	*We must win the game!*

Essayez! Complétez chaque phrase avec la forme correcte du verbe **faire** au présent.

1. Tu ___fais___ tes devoirs le samedi?
2. Vous ne ___faites___ pas attention au professeur.
3. Nous ___faisons___ du camping.
4. Ils ___font___ du jogging.
5. On ___fait___ une promenade au parc.
6. Il ___fait___ du ski en montagne.
7. Je ___fais___ de l'aérobic.
8. Elles ___font___ un tour en voiture.
9. Est-ce que vous ___faites___ la cuisine?
10. Nous ne ___faisons___ pas de sport.

Essayez! Have students check each other's answers.

1 Suggestion Bring in images of people doing other activities with **faire** expressions. Ask: **Que fait-il/elle?**

2 Suggestion Have pairs of students drill each other on the meanings of expressions with **faire** (that are not cognates). Then tell them to cover that half of the page with paper or a book before doing this activity.

3 Suggestion Have students check their answers with a partner. If partners disagree, have them say: **Mais non, il ne fait pas...** Remind students that any expression with the partitive must use **pas de** when negative.

4 Expansion Have students come up with four more activities using expressions with **faire** that they would like to ask their partner about. Encourage students to include adverbs or other logical additions in their answers.

5 Expansion Write **Qu'est-ce qu'il faut faire pour...** on the board followed by a few of the most talked about expressions from the box. Have volunteers write their ideas under each expression, forming columns of categories. Accept several answers for each. Ask: **Êtes-vous d'accord? Pourquoi?**

6 Suggestions
- Read the **modèle** aloud with a volunteer. Then distribute the **Feuilles d'activités** from the IRM on the IRCD-ROM.
- Have students say how popular these activities are among classmates. Tell them to be prepared to justify their statements by citing how many students participate in each. Example: **Faire du jogging, c'est très populaire. Quinze étudiants de notre classe font du jogging.**

OPTIONS

Game Divide the class into two teams. Pick one team member at a time to go to the board, alternating between teams. Give a subject pronoun that the team member must write and say aloud with the correct form of **faire**. Example: **vous (vous faites)**. Give a point for each correct answer. The game ends when all students have had a chance to go to the board. The team with the most points at the end of the game wins.

Extra Practice Have students study the captions from **Roman-photo**. In small groups, tell them to think of additional phrases containing **faire** expressions and **il faut** that the characters would likely say. Write the main characters' names on the board in a row and have volunteers put their ideas underneath. Ask what can be concluded about each character. Example: **Rachid donne beaucoup de conseils.**

comparisons
NATIONAL STANDARDS

Section Goals

In this section, students will learn:
- the verbs **sortir** and **partir**
- other irregular **-ir** verbs

Instructional Resources
WB/VM: Workbook, pp. 61–62
Lab Manual, p. 36
Lab MP3s
WB/VM/LM Answer Key
*IRCD-ROM: IRM (**Essayez!** and **Mise en pratique** answers; Lab Audioscript)*
espaces.vhlcentral.com: activities, downloads, reference tools

Suggestions
- Ask students where they have heard irregular **-ir** verbs before. (They heard **sortir** in this lesson's **Roman-photo**. If students have been to French-speaking places, they may have noticed the noun derived from **sortir**, **la sortie**, on **SORTIE** signs.)
- Model the pronunciation of forms for **sortir** and **partir**. Ask students simple questions. Example: **Je sors d'habitude le vendredi soir. Quand sortez-vous? (Je sors le samedi soir.)** As you elicit responses, write the present-tense forms of **sortir** on the board until the conjugation is complete. Underline the endings.
- Point out the recurrence of the **-s, -s, -t** pattern in singular forms.
- Reiterate that **sortir** is used as *to go out* or *to exit* while **partir** means *to leave*. Ask students to think of more examples comparing the two verbs. Then remind them of the note about **quitter** in the **Boîte à outils**. Using ideas from students, write on the board a short paragraph (two to three sentences) that contains at least one form of each of the three verbs mentioned above. Make sure the context defines the meanings well.
- Go over other irregular **-ir** verbs, pointing out that they are all in the same grammatical "verb family" as **sortir** and **partir**. Note that all verbs of this type have two stems: **sortir:** singular stem **sor-** and plural stem **sort-**.

9.2 Irregular *-ir* verbs

Point de départ You are familiar with the class of French verbs whose infinitives end in **-er**. The infinitives of a second class of French verbs end in **-ir**. Some of the most commonly used verbs in this class are irregular.

- **Sortir** is used to express leaving a room or a building. It also expresses the idea of going out, as with friends or on a date. The preposition **de** is used after **sortir** when the place someone is leaving is expressed.

sortir

je sors	nous sortons
tu sors	vous sortez
il/elle sort	ils/elles sortent

Tu **sors** souvent avec tes copains?
Do you go out often with your friends?

Pierre et moi **sortons de** la salle de classe.
Pierre and I leave the classroom.

Le week-end, je sors souvent.

Ils partent pour la fac.

- **Partir** is generally used to say someone is leaving a large place such as a city, country, or region. Often, a form of **partir** is accompanied by the preposition **pour** and a destination name to say *to leave for (a place)*.

partir

je pars	nous partons
tu pars	vous partez
il/elle part	ils/elles partent

Je **pars pour** l'Algérie.
I'm leaving for Algeria.

Ils **partent pour** Genève demain.
They're leaving for Geneva tomorrow.

BOÎTE À OUTILS
As you learned in **Leçon 7**, **quitter** is used to say that someone leaves a place or another person: **Tu quittes la maison?** (*Are you leaving the house?*)

MISE EN PRATIQUE

1 Choisissez Monique et ses amis aiment bien sortir. Choisissez la forme correcte des verbes **partir** et **sortir** pour compléter la description de leurs activités.

1. Samedi soir, je __sors__ avec mes copains.
2. Mes copines Magali et Anissa __partent__ pour New York.
3. Nous __sortons__ du cinéma.
4. Nicolas __part__ pour Dakar vers 10 heures du soir.
5. À minuit, vous __partez__ pour la boîte.
6. Je __pars__ pour le Maroc dans une semaine.
7. Tu __sors__ avec ton petit ami ce week-end.
8. Olivier et Bernard __sortent__ tard du bureau.

2 Vos habitudes Utilisez les éléments des colonnes pour décrire (*describe*) les habitudes de votre famille et de vos amis. Answers will vary.

A	B	C
je mon frère ma sœur mes parents mes cousins mon petit ami ma petite amie mes copains ?	(ne pas) courir (ne pas) dormir (ne pas) partir (ne pas) sortir	jusqu'à (*until*) midi tous les week-ends tous les jours souvent rarement jamais une (deux, etc.) fois par jour/semaine ?

3 La question Vincent parle au téléphone avec sa mère. Vous entendez (*hear*) ses réponses, mais pas les questions. Avec un(e) partenaire, reconstruisez la conversation. Answers will vary.

MODÈLE
Comment vas-tu? Ça va bien, merci.

1. ______ Oui, je sors avec mes amis ce soir.
2. ______ Nous partons à six heures.
3. ______ Oui, nous allons jouer au tennis.
4. ______ Après, nous allons au restaurant.
5. ______ Nous sortons du restaurant à neuf heures.
6. ______ Marc et Audrey partent pour Nice le week-end prochain.

OPTIONS

TPR Tell students that they will act out the appropriate gestures when you say what certain people in the class are doing. Examples: ____ **dort.** (The student gestures sleeping.) ____ **et** ____ **courent**. (The two students indicated run in place briefly.) Repeat verbs and vary forms as much as possible.

Extra Practice Dictate sentences like these to the class, saying each one twice and pausing between. **1. Je pars pour la France la semaine prochaine. 2. Mon copain et moi, nous sortons ce soir. 3. Les étudiants ne dorment jamais en classe. 4. Le café sent bon. 5. Tu cours vite. 6. Que servez-vous au restaurant?** Advise students to pay attention to the verbs.

COMMUNICATION

4 Descriptions Avec un(e) partenaire, complétez les phrases avec la forme correcte d'un verbe de la liste.

courir dormir partir sentir servir sortir

1. Véronique /  / tard
   Véronique dort tard.
2. je /  / sandwichs
   Je sers des sandwichs.
3. les enfants /  / le chocolat chaud
   Les enfants sentent le chocolat chaud.
4. nous / / souvent
   Nous courons souvent.
5. tu / / de l'hôpital
   Tu sors de l'hôpital.
6. vous /  / pour la France demain
   Vous partez pour la France demain.

5 Indiscrétions Votre partenaire est curieux/curieuse et désire savoir (*to know*) ce que vous faites chez vous. Répondez à ses questions. Answers will vary.

1. Jusqu'à (*Until*) quelle heure dors-tu le week-end?
2. Dors-tu pendant (*during*) les cours à la fac? Pendant quels cours? Pourquoi?
3. À quelle heure sors-tu le samedi soir?
4. Avec qui sors-tu le samedi soir?
5. Que sers-tu quand tu as des invités à la maison?
6. Pars-tu bientôt en vacances (*vacation*)? Où?

6 Dispute Laëtitia est très active. Son petit ami Bertrand ne sort pas beaucoup, alors ils ont souvent des disputes. Avec un(e) partenaire, jouez les deux rôles. Utilisez les mots et les expressions de la liste.
Answers will vary.

dormir	partir
faire des promenades	un passe-temps
faire un tour (en voiture)	sentir
par semaine	sortir
	rarement
	souvent

Other irregular *-ir* verbs

	dormir (*to sleep*)	servir (*to serve*)	sentir (*to feel*)	courir (*to run*)
je	dors	sers	sens	cours
tu	dors	sers	sens	cours
il/elle	dort	sert	sent	court
nous	dormons	servons	sentons	courons
vous	dormez	servez	sentez	courez
ils/elles	dorment	servent	sentent	courent

Rachid dort.

Nous courons.

Elles **dorment** jusqu'à midi.
They sleep until noon.

Vous **courez** vite!
You run fast!

Je **sers** du fromage à la fête.
I'm serving cheese at the party.

Nous **servons** du thé glacé.
We are serving iced tea.

- **Sentir** can mean *to feel, to smell,* or *to sense.*

Je **sens** qu'il arrive.
I sense that he's arriving.

Ça **sent** bon!
That smells good!

Vous **sentez** le café?
Do you smell the coffee?

Ils **sentent** sa présence.
They feel his presence.

Essayez! Complétez les phrases avec la forme correcte du verbe.

1. Nous ___sortons___ (sortir) vers neuf heures.
2. Je ___sers___ (servir) des boissons gazeuses aux invités.
3. Tu ___pars___ (partir) quand pour le Canada?
4. Nous ne ___dormons___ (dormir) pas en cours.
5. Ils ___courent___ (courir) pour attraper (*to catch*) le bus.
6. Tu manges des oignons? Ça ___sent___ (sentir) mauvais.
7. Vous ___sortez___ (sortir) avec des copains ce soir.
8. Elle ___part___ (partir) pour Dijon ce week-end.

Essayez! Give these items for additional practice, having students choose which **-ir** verb(s) to use. **1. J'adore ____. Je ____ vingt à trente kilomètres par semaine. (courir, cours) 2. Les enfants ne ____ pas parce qu'ils ne sont pas fatigués. (dorment) 3. Qu'est-ce qu'on ____ au café en face de chez toi? (sert) 4. Merci pour les fleurs. Elles ____ très bon. (sentent)**

1 Suggestion Give a tip on how to choose between **sortir** and **partir**. Remind students that **partir** is often followed by the preposition **pour**.

2 Suggestions
- Have students write as least five sentences describing their family's and friends' habits.
- In pairs, have students compare the information. Example:
  Étudiant(e) 1: Est-ce que tu dors jusqu'à midi?
  Étudiant(e) 2: Oui, mais rarement.
  Étudiant(e) 1: Moi, jamais!
- Ask for volunteers to share some of their sentences with the class.

3 Expansion Ask students to imagine they are on the telephone and a classmate can overhear them. Have students write three answers to say in front of a partner who will guess the questions. Example: **Non, maman, on ne sort pas trop souvent. Je fais mes devoirs tous les soirs. (Tu ne sors pas trop souvent avec tes copains?)**

4 Suggestion Find a photo to use for a **modèle**. Example: Put on the board **Les chiens** / image of dogs sleeping / **beaucoup**. Have students ask **Que fait Véronique? Qu'est-ce que je fais?** etc. before partners answer.

5 Suggestion Remind students to answer in complete sentences.

6 Suggestion Have a couple of volunteer pairs act out their conversations for the class.

OPTIONS

Game Divide the class into two teams. Announce an infinitive and a subject pronoun. Example: **dormir**; **elle**. At the board, have the first member of Team A say and write down the given subject and the conjugated form of the verb. If the team member answers correctly, Team A gets one point. If not, give the first member of Team B the same example. The team with the most points at the end of the game wins.

Small Groups Have small groups of students create a short story in the present tense or a conversation in which they logically mention as many verb forms as possible of **sortir**, **partir**, **dormir**, **servir**, **sentir**, and **courir**. If the class is advanced, add **mentir**. Call on groups to tell their story to the class or act out their conversation. Have students vote on the best story or conversation.

Instructional Resources
IRCD-ROM: IRM (Info Gap Activities); Testing Program pp. 33–36; Test Files; Testing Program MP3s; Test Generator espaces.vhlcentral.com: activities, downloads, reference tools

1 Suggestion After collaborating on their efforts, ask groups how many activities they described. Have the group with most sentences share them with the class.

2 Suggestion Remind students that adverbs like **rarement**, **souvent**, and **toujours** should be placed immediately after the verb, not at the end of a sentence or anywhere else as one can say in English. Example: **Je fais rarement du cheval.** They should never say: **je fais du cheval rarement** or **je rarement fais du cheval**.

3 Suggestion Have students say what their partners are going to do on vacation, when, where, and with whom.

4 Suggestion Call on two volunteers to do the **modèle**.

4 Expansion Have students continue the activity with additional places, such as **à la faculté**, **au resto U**, **au centre-ville**, etc.

5 Suggestion Tell students to use as many irregular **-ir** verbs and **faire** expressions as possible.

6 Suggestion Divide the class into pairs and distribute the Info Gap Handouts in the IRM on the IRCD-ROM for this activity. Give students ten minutes to complete the activity.

Synthèse

1 Au parc C'est dimanche au parc. Avec un(e) partenaire, décrivez les activités de tous les personnages. Comparez vos observations avec les observations d'un autre groupe pour compléter votre description. Answers will vary.

2 Mes habitudes Avec un(e) partenaire, parlez de vos habitudes de la semaine. Que faites-vous régulièrement? Utilisez tous les mots de la liste. Answers will vary.

MODÈLE

Étudiant(e) 1: *Je fais de la gym parfois le lundi. Et toi?*
Étudiant(e) 2: *Moi, je fais la cuisine parfois le lundi.*

parfois le lundi	souvent à midi
le mercredi à midi	toujours le vendredi
le jeudi soir	tous les jours
le vendredi matin	trois fois par semaine
rarement le matin	une fois par semaine

3 Mes vacances Parlez de vos prochaines vacances (*vacation*) avec un(e) partenaire. Mentionnez cinq de vos passe-temps habituels en vacances et cinq nouvelles activités que vous allez essayer (*to try*). Comparez votre liste avec la liste de votre partenaire puis présentez les réponses à la classe. Answers will vary.

4 Que faire ici? Avec un(e) partenaire, trouvez au minimum quatre choses à faire dans chaque (*each*) endroit. Quel endroit préférez-vous et pourquoi? Comparez votre liste avec un autre groupe et parlez de vos préférences avec la classe. Answers will vary.

MODÈLE

Étudiant(e) 1: *À la montagne, on fait des randonnées à cheval.*
Étudiant(e) 2: *Oui, et il faut marcher.*

1.

3.

2.

4.

5 Le conseiller Un(e) conseiller/conseillère à la fac suggère des stratégies à un(e) étudiant(e) pour l'aider (*help him or her*) à préparer les examens. Avec un(e) partenaire, jouez les deux rôles. Vos camarades vont sélectionner les meilleurs conseils (*best advice*). Answers will vary.

MODÈLE

Il faut faire tous ses devoirs.

6 Quelles activités? Votre professeur va vous donner, à vous et à votre partenaire, deux feuilles d'activités différentes pour le week-end. Attention! Ne regardez pas la feuille de votre partenaire. Answers will vary.

MODÈLE

Étudiant(e) 1: *Est-ce que tu fais une randonnée dimanche après-midi?*
Étudiant(e) 2: *Oui, je fais une randonnée dimanche après-midi.*

ressources

WB	LM	Lab MP3s	espaces.vhlcentral.com
pp. 59-62	pp. 35-36	Leçon 9	Leçon 9

OPTIONS

Extra Practice Ask students to write five sentences individually, at least two with **faire**, at least one with **il faut**, and at least three with different irregular **-ir** verbs. Tell them to try to include more than one requirement in each sentence. Have students dictate their sentences to their partner. After both students in each pair have finished dictating their sentences, have them exchange papers for correction.

Pairs Have students take turns telling their partners about a memorable vacation experience, who they were with, what they did, etc. Encourage students to express themselves using as much variety as possible in terms of vocabulary and grammar structures. Have students take notes as their partner narrates to reveal to the class later what was said.

Interlude

Les grands boulevards

The song ***Les grands boulevards*** *(1945) illustrates the theme of pastimes through the story of a blue-collar worker who, on his day off, loves to stroll the main thoroughfares of Paris. There is much to see on the boulevards, like markets, shops, and street vendors. Much has taken place there across the years as well, like political demonstrations.*

The singer of ***Les grands boulevards****, YVES MONTAND (1921–1991), whose real name was Ivo Livi, was born in Italy. In 1923, his family fled the fascist regime and settled in Marseilles, in the south of France. Montand acquired French citizenship in 1929 and later became both a famous singer and a beloved star of the stage and screen. Montand was also very vocal about politics and injustice and took a stand on various issues throughout his life.*

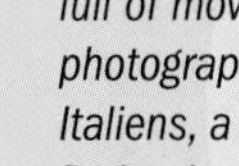

Boulevard des Italiens à Paris

The impressionist painter JEAN BÉRAUD (1849–1935) was known as "the most Parisian of the painters of the ***Belle Époque****." He loved representing his city full of movement and life, with the spontaneity of a photograph. Pictured is a view of the Boulevard des Italiens, a wide and lively thoroughfare in the heart of Paris where, as in the song, people go for shopping and entertainment.*

Activité

Choisissez une de ces options et écrivez un paragraphe sur les loisirs. Écrivez au moins six phrases complètes. Answers will vary.

1. Où aimez-vous faire une promenade: en ville, comme dans la chanson (*song*), ou à la campagne? Pourquoi? Y a-t-il d'autres endroits où vous aimez faire une promenade? Où? Quelles autres activités aimez-vous pratiquer en ville? Et à la campagne?
2. Vous vous trouvez (*You find yourself*) à l'endroit que vous voyez (*see*) sur la peinture (*painting*). Comment allez-vous passer la journée? Mentionnez au moins trois activités. Est-ce que vous pratiquez souvent ces activités?

SUR INTERNET

Go to **espaces.vhlcentral.com** for more information related to this **Interlude**.

Section Goals

In this section, students will learn about:
- Yves Montand
- Jean Béraud

Instructional Resources
espaces.vhlcentral.com: activities, downloads, reference tools

Les grands boulevards
To check comprehension, ask these questions.
1. When did Yves Montand's family move to France? (1923) Why? (They were fleeing the fascist regime in Italy.)
2. In addition to being a singer, how did Yves Montand gain celebrity status? (He was an actor on the stage and in the movies.)
3. Why is the song entitled ***Les grands boulevards***? (Answers may vary. Because the worker in the song loves to spend his day off strolling the boulevards of Paris looking at the street vendors and places.)

Boulevard des Italiens à Paris
- Have students describe the painting. Then ask: What elements indicate that this is not a painting of Paris today?
- Explain that the **boulevard des Italiens** was constructed during the reign of King Louis XIV. It has always been an avenue where people like to stroll. It changed names several times, and finally in the nineteenth century took the name of **Italiens**, because it is near **La comédie des Italiens**, which later became **L'Opéra comique**. The **boulevard des Italiens** has been the subject of a number of paintings, including one by Camille Pissarro. Today this avenue is famous for its restaurants, cafés, cinemas, theaters, and strollers.
- Point out that the **Belle Époque** was a period during which art and innovation flourished in France. It began in the late nineteenth century and lasted until World War I.

OPTIONS

Yves Montand et le cinéma Yves Montand was Marilyn Monroe's co-star in ***Le milliardaire***, a comedy directed by George Cukor in 1960. If students are interested in watching one of Yves Montand's movies, you may wish to suggest ***Le salaire de la peur*** by Henri-Georges Clouzot (1953), ***César et Rosalie*** by Claude Sautet (1972) or ***Jean de Florette*** and ***Manon des Sources*** by Claude Berri (1986), both adapted from books by the famous author Marcel Pagnol. You may want to preview these movies for appropriateness before recommending them to your class.

Section Goals

In this section, students will learn and practice vocabulary related to:
- the weather
- seasons and dates

Instructional Resources
IRCD-ROM: Transparency #29;
*IRM (**Vocabulaire supplémentaire; Mise en pratique** answers;*
Textbook Audioscript;
Lab Audioscript; Info Gap Activities)
Textbook MP3s
WB/VM: Workbook, pp. 63–64
Lab Manual, p. 37
Lab MP3s
WB/VM/LM Answer Key
espaces.vhlcentral.com: activities, downloads, reference tools

Suggestions
- Introduce weather-related vocabulary by describing the weather in your area today. Example: **Aujourd'hui, il pleut et il fait du vent.**
- Before going over the **Vocabulaire**, ask students to brainstorm the kinds of expressions they use to talk about the weather.
- Use **Transparency #29** to present new vocabulary. See how many of the words and expressions your students can understand without looking at their translations.
- Tell students that most weather expressions use the verb **faire**, but **neiger** and **pleuvoir** stand alone. Point out that they are only used in the third person singular.
- Point out that the expressions **avoir froid** and **avoir chaud** refer to people, but **faire froid** and **faire chaud** describe weather. Bring in photos that include people to illustrate this distinction.
- Mention to students that **temps** in this context means *weather*, not *time*.
- Using magazine photos of weather conditions and seasons, describe each image. Show photos again one at a time. Then ask: **En quelle saison sommes-nous? Quel temps fait-il?**
- Additional terms for this lesson can be found in the **Vocabulaire supplémentaire** in the IRM.

Leçon 10

You will learn how to...
- talk about seasons and the date
- discuss the weather

Quel temps fait-il?

Vocabulaire

Il fait 18 degrés.	*It is 18 degrees.*
Il fait beau.	*The weather is nice.*
Il fait bon.	*The weather is good/warm.*
Il fait mauvais.	*The weather is bad.*
Il fait un temps épouvantable.	*The weather is dreadful.*
Le temps est orageux.	*It is stormy.*
Quel temps fait-il?	*What is the weather like?*
Quelle température fait-il?	*What is the temperature?*
une saison	*season*
à l'automne	*in the fall*
en été	*in the summer*
en hiver	*in the winter*
au printemps	*in the spring*
Quelle est la date?	*What's the date?*
C'est le 1er (premier) octobre.	*It's the first of October.*
C'est quand votre/ton anniversaire?	*When is your birthday?*
C'est le 2 mai.	*It's the second of May.*
C'est quand l'anniversaire de Paul?	*When is Paul's birthday?*
C'est le 15 mars.	*It's March 15th.*
un anniversaire	*birthday*

L'hiver: décembre, janvier, février

L'été: juin, juillet, août

ressources

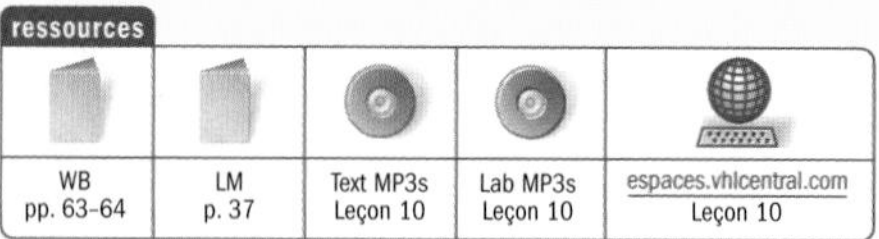

OPTIONS

Pairs Distribute a set of illustrations of various weather conditions to pairs of students. Choose images with variety and have students write detailed descriptions of each one. They should describe the weather, the season, and any activities represented.

Extra Practice Distribute a calendar that shows **les fêtes**. First, call out dates and have students give the corresponding name on the calendar. Then call out names on the calendar and have students provide the date. Example: **la Saint-Valentin (le 14 février).**

Mise en pratique

Attention!

In France and in most of the francophone world, temperature is given in Celsius. Convert from Celsius to Fahrenheit with this formula: F = (C x 1.8) + 32. Convert from Fahrenheit to Celsius with this formula: C = (F - 32) x 0.56.

11°C = 52°F   78°F = 26°C

Le printemps: mars, avril, mai

L'automne: septembre, octobre, novembre

1 Écoutez Écoutez le bulletin météorologique et répondez aux questions suivantes.

		Vrai	Faux
1.	C'est l'été.	☐	☑
2.	Le printemps commence le 21 mars.	☑	☐
3.	Il fait 11 degrés vendredi.	☑	☐
4.	Il fait du vent vendredi.	☐	☑
5.	Il va faire soleil samedi.	☐	☑
6.	Il faut utiliser le parapluie et l'imperméable vendredi.	☐	☑
7.	Il va faire un temps épouvantable dimanche.	☑	☐
8.	Il ne va pas faire chaud samedi.	☑	☐

2 Les fêtes et les jours fériés Indiquez la date et la saison de chaque jour férié.

		Date	Saison
1.	la fête nationale française	le 14 juillet	l'été
2.	l'indépendance des États-Unis	le 4 juillet	l'été
3.	la Saint-Patrick	le 17 mars	l'hiver/le printemps
4.	Noël	le 25 décembre	l'hiver
5.	la Saint-Valentin	le 14 février	l'hiver
6.	le Nouvel An	le 1er janvier	l'hiver
7.	Halloween	le 31 octobre	l'automne
8.	l'anniversaire de Washington	le 22 février	l'hiver

3 Quel temps fait-il? Répondez aux questions suivantes par des phrases complètes. Answers will vary.

1. Quel temps fait-il en été?
2. Quel temps fait-il à l'automne?
3. Quel temps fait-il au printemps?
4. Quel temps fait-il en hiver?
5. Où est-ce qu'il neige?
6. Quel est votre mois préféré de l'année? Pourquoi?
7. Quand est-ce qu'il pleut où vous habitez?
8. Quand est-ce que le temps est orageux où vous habitez?

1 Tapescript Aujourd'hui vendredi 21 mars, nous commençons le printemps avec une température de 11 degrés; il n'y a pas de vent, mais il y a quelques nuages.
Votre météo du week-end: samedi, il ne va pas faire soleil; il va faire frais avec une température de 13 degrés; dimanche, encore 13 degrés, mais il va faire un temps épouvantable; il va pleuvoir toute la journée, alors, n'oubliez pas votre parapluie et votre imperméable!
(On Textbook MP3s)

1 Suggestion Have students correct the false items.

2 Suggestion Remind students to give the date in the correct order (day before month) and to include **le** before the day.

2 Expansion Using this year's calendar, have students find the dates of these holidays. **9. la fête du travail aux États-Unis 10.** *Thanksgiving* **(le jour d'Action de Grâces) 11.** *Easter* **(Pâques) 12.** *Memorial Day* You may ask students to look up dates of other secular celebrations or religious holidays from various faiths. Answers will vary from year to year.

3 Suggestions

- Have students work in pairs or small groups to answer these questions.
- Tell students that how to say *in the fall* is optional: **en automne** or **à l'automne**. For other seasons, make sure they know to use **en** before those starting with vowels and **au** with **printemps**, as it starts with a consonant.

OPTIONS

Le calendrier républicain During the French Revolution, the official calendar was changed. The New Year began on September 22 (the autumnal equinox), and the year was divided into 30-day months named as follows: **Vendémiaire** (*Vintage*), **Brumaire** (*Mist*), **Frimaire** (*Frost*), **Nivôse** (*Snow*), **Pluviôse** (*Rain*), **Ventôse** (*Wind*), **Germinal** (*Seed time*), **Floréal** (*Flower*), **Prairial** (*Meadow*), **Messidor** (*Harvest*), **Thermidor** (*Heat*), and **Fructidor** (*Fruits*).

Game Have students take turns guessing another student's birthday. He or she responds by saying **avant** or **après** until someone guesses correctly. The class then tries to guess the winning student's birthday. Play several rounds of this game to give all students as many opportunities as possible to guess.

Communication

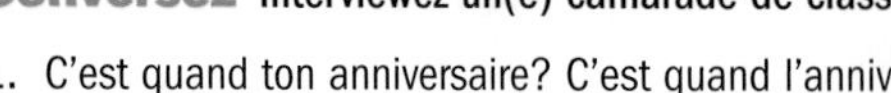

4 Conversez Interviewez un(e) camarade de classe. Answers will vary.

1. C'est quand ton anniversaire? C'est quand l'anniversaire de ton père? Et de ta mère?
2. En quelle saison est ton anniversaire? Quel temps fait-il?
3. Quelle est ta saison préférée? Pourquoi? Quelles activités aimes-tu pratiquer?
4. En quelles saisons utilises-tu un parapluie et un imperméable? Pourquoi?
5. À quel moment de l'année es-tu en vacances? Précise les mois. Pendant (*During*) quels mois de l'année préfères-tu voyager? Pourquoi?
6. À quelle période de l'année étudies-tu? Précise les mois.
7. Quelle saison détestes-tu le plus (*the most*)? Pourquoi?
8. Quand tu vas au café en janvier, qu'est-ce que tu bois? En juillet? En septembre?

5 Une lettre Vous avez un correspondant (*pen pal*) en France qui veut (*wants*) vous rendre visite (*to visit you*). Écrivez une lettre à votre ami(e) où vous décrivez le temps qu'il fait à chaque saison et les activités que vous pouvez (*can*) pratiquer ensemble (*together*). Comparez votre lettre avec la lettre d'un(e) camarade de classe. Answers will vary.

Cher Thomas,

Ici à Boston, il fait très froid en hiver et il neige souvent. Est-ce que tu aimes la neige? Moi, j'adore parce que je fais du ski tous les week-ends. Et toi, tu fais du ski? ...

6 Quel temps fait-il en France? Votre professeur va vous donner, à vous et à votre partenaire, deux feuilles d'activités différentes. Attention! Ne regardez pas la feuille de votre partenaire.

MODÈLE

Étudiant(e) 1: *Quel temps fait-il à Paris?*
Étudiant(e) 2: *À Paris, il fait beau; il fait du soleil et la température est de dix degrés.*

7 La météo Préparez avec un(e) camarade de classe une présentation où vous: Answers will vary.

- mentionnez le jour, la date et la saison.
- présentez la météo d'une ville francophone.
- présentez les prévisions météo (*weather forecasts*) pour le reste de la semaine.
- préparez une affiche pour illustrer votre présentation.

La météo d'Haïti en juillet – Port-au-Prince

samedi 23	dimanche 24	lundi 25
27°C	35°C	37°C
soleil	très nuageux	orageux

Aujourd'hui samedi, c'est le 23 juillet. C'est l'été et il fait soleil...

4 Suggestion Have students share what they've learned about their partners with another pair of students or with the rest of the class.

5 Suggestion Encourage students to use a wide variety of expressions for seasons and activities. Have them exchange papers for peer editing.

6 Suggestions
- Divide the class into pairs and distribute the Info Gap Handouts in the IRM on the IRCD-ROM for this activity. Give students ten minutes to complete the activity.
- Have two volunteers read the **modèle**.

7 Expansion Assign a different francophone location to each pair of students and have them research its weather forecast on the Internet. Hold a vote without revealing names of students, and give prizes for the best presentation in various categories (**le plus amusant, créateur, utile,** and so on).

Successful Language Learning Tell students that when looking at materials intended for native speakers like weather forecasts, they should pay attention to visual cues and use their background knowledge about the subject to help them understand. They should try to anticipate vocabulary they might hear, listen for familiar sounding words, and make intelligent guesses.

OPTIONS

TPR Write **C'est quand ton anniversaire?** on the board or on a transparency. Make a "human calendar" using students to represent various days. Have them form 12 rows (one for each month) and put themselves in order according to their birthdays by asking and answering the question. Give the person with the first birthday in each month a sign for that month. Call out each month and have students give their birthdays in order.

Small Groups Have students form groups of two to four. Hand out cards with the name of a holiday or other annual event. Instruct each group to hide their card from other groups. Groups come up with three sentences to describe the holiday or occasion without mentioning its name. They can mention the season. The other groups must first guess the month and day on which the event takes place, then name the event itself.

Les sons et les lettres

Open vs. closed vowels: Part 1

You have already learned that **é** is pronounced like the vowel *a* in the English word *cake*. This is a closed **e** sound.

étudiant **agréable** **nationalité** **enchanté**

The letter combinations **-er** and **-ez** at the end of a word are pronounced the same way, as is the vowel sound in single-syllable words ending in **-es**.

travailler **avez** **mes** **les**

The vowels spelled **è** and **ê** are pronounced like the vowel in the English word *pet*, as is an **e** followed by a double consonant. These are open **e** sounds.

répète **première** **pêche** **italienne**

The vowel sound in *pet* may also be spelled **et**, **ai**, or **ei**.

secret **français** **fait** **seize**

Compare these pairs of words. To make the vowel sound in *cake*, your mouth should be slightly more closed than when you make the vowel sound in *pet*.

mes mais **ces cette** **théâtre thème**

Prononcez Répétez les mots suivants à voix haute.

1. thé
2. lait
3. belle
4. été
5. neige
6. aider
7. degrés
8. anglais
9. cassette
10. discret
11. treize
12. mauvais

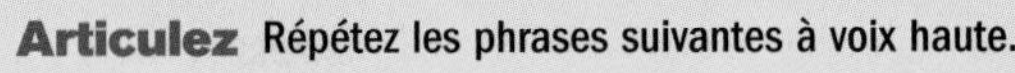

Articulez Répétez les phrases suivantes à voix haute.

1. Hélène est très discrète.
2. Céleste achète un vélo laid.
3. Il neige souvent en février et en décembre.
4. Désirée est canadienne; elle n'est pas française.

Dictons Répétez les dictons à voix haute.

Qui sème le vent récolte la tempête.[2]

ressources: LM p. 38 | Text MP3s Leçon 10 | Lab MP3s Leçon 10 | espaces.vhlcentral.com Leçon 10

1 An offense admitted is half pardoned.
2 You reap what you sow. (lit. He who sows the wind reaps a storm.)

Section Goals

In this section, students will learn about open and closed vowels.

Instructional Resources
Textbook MP3s
Lab Manual, p. 38
Lab MP3s
WB/VM/LM Answer Key
IRCD-ROM: IRM (Textbook Audioscript; Lab Audioscript)
espaces.vhlcentral.com: activities, downloads, reference tools

Suggestions

- Model the pronunciation of these open and closed vowel sounds and have students watch the shape of your mouth, then repeat each sound after you. Then pronounce each of the example words and have students repeat them.
- Mention words and expressions from the **Vocabulaire** on page 160 that contain the open and closed vowels presented on this page. Alternately, ask students to recall such vocabulary. Then have them repeat after you. Examples: **février**, **Il fait frais**, etc. See if a volunteer is able to recall any expression from previous lessons. Examples: **seize**, **vélo**, **aérobic**.
- Dictate five familiar words containing the open and closed vowels presented on this page, repeating each one at least two times. Then write them on the board or on a transparency and have students check and correct their spelling.
- Remind students that **ai** and **ei** are nasalized when followed by **m** or **n**. Compare the following words: **français** / **faim**, **seize** / **hein**.
- Point out that, unlike English, there is no diphthong or glide in these vowel sounds. To illustrate this, contrast the pronunciation of the English word *may* with that of the French word **mai**.

OPTIONS

Extra Practice Here are some sentences to use for additional practice with these open and closed vowel sounds. **1. Il fait du soleil. 2. En janvier, il neige et il fait mauvais. 3. Toute la journée j'aide ma mère. 4. Didier est français, mais Hélène est belge.**

Game Have a spelling bee using vocabulary words from **Leçons 1–10** that contain the two open and closed vowel sounds featured on this page. Pronounce each word, use it in a sentence, and then say the individual word again. Tell students that they must spell the words in French and include all diacritical marks.

Section Goals

In this section, students will learn functional phrases for talking about seasons, the weather, and birthdays through comprehensible input.

Instructional Resources
WB/VM: Video Manual, pp. 229–230
WB/VM/LM Answer Key
Video CD-ROM
Video on DVD
*IRCD-ROM: IRM (Videoscript; **Roman-photo** Translations)*
espaces.vhlcentral.com: activities, downloads, reference tools

Video Recap: Leçon 9
Before doing this **Roman-photo**, review the previous one with this activity.
1. Où sont les jeunes dans cet épisode? (Ils sont au parc.)
2. Que font Rachid et Stéphane? (Ils jouent au football.)
3. Qu'est-ce que Stéphane étudie? (Napoléon)
4. Qu'est-ce que Sandrine aime faire de ses loisirs? (aller au cinéma ou à des concerts)

Video Synopsis Rachid and Stéphane are in the park playing soccer. They talk about the weather. Meanwhile, David is sketching Sandrine at his apartment. They talk about the weather in Washington and things they like to do. Sandrine tells David that Stéphane's 18th birthday is next Saturday and invites him to the surprise party. Rachid arrives home and admires the portrait. Sandrine offers to make them all dinner.

Suggestions
- Ask students to predict what the episode will be about.
- Have students make a list of vocabulary they expect to see in an episode about weather and seasons.
- Ask students to read the **Roman-photo** conversation in groups of four. Ask one or two groups to present their dramatic readings to the class.
- Quickly review the predictions and confirm the correct ones.

Quel temps!

PERSONNAGES

David

Rachid

Sandrine

Stéphane

Au parc...
RACHID Napoléon établit le Premier Empire en quelle année?
STÉPHANE Euh... mille huit cent quatre?
RACHID Exact! On est au mois de novembre et il fait toujours chaud.
STÉPHANE Oui, il fait bon!... dix-neuf, dix-huit degrés!

RACHID Et on a chaud aussi parce qu'on court.
STÉPHANE Bon, allez, je rentre faire mes devoirs d'histoire-géo.
RACHID Et moi, je rentre boire une grande bouteille d'eau.

RACHID À demain, Stéph! Et n'oublie pas: le cours du jeudi avec ton professeur, Monsieur Rachid Kahlid, commence à dix-huit heures, pas à dix-huit heures vingt!
STÉPHANE Pas de problème! Merci et à demain!

SANDRINE Et puis, en juillet, le Tour de France commence. J'aime bien regarder à la télévision. Et après, c'est mon anniversaire, le 20. Cette année, je fête mes vingt et un ans. Tous les ans, pour célébrer mon anniversaire, j'invite mes amis et je prépare une super soirée. J'adore faire la cuisine, c'est une vraie passion!
DAVID Ah, oui?

SANDRINE En parlant d'anniversaire, Stéphane célèbre ses dix-huit ans samedi prochain. C'est un anniversaire important. ...On organise une surprise. Tu es invité!
DAVID Hmm, c'est très gentil, mais... Tu essaies de ne pas parler deux minutes, s'il te plaît? Parfait!

SANDRINE Pascal! Qu'est-ce que tu fais aujourd'hui? Il fait beau à Paris?
DAVID Encore un peu de patience! Allez, encore dix secondes... Voilà!

ACTIVITÉS

1 Qui? Identifiez les personnages pour chaque phrase. Écrivez S pour Sandrine, St pour Stéphane, R pour Rachid et D pour David.

1. Cette personne aime faire la cuisine. S
2. Cette personne sort quand il fait froid. D
3. Cette personne aime le Tour de France. S
4. Cette personne n'aime pas la pluie. S
5. Cette personne va boire de l'eau. R
6. Ces personnes ont rendez-vous tous les jeudis. R, St
7. Cette personne fête son anniversaire en janvier. D
8. Ces personnes célèbrent un joli portrait. D, R, S
9. Cette personne fête ses dix-huit ans samedi prochain. St
10. Cette personne prépare des crêpes pour le dîner. S

OPTIONS

Avant de regarder la vidéo Before showing the video, show students individual photos and have them write their own captions. Ask volunteers to write their captions on the board.

Regarder la vidéo Photocopy the videoscript from the IRM, and white out months, seasons, weather-related expressions, and other new vocabulary items. Distribute the scripts for pairs or groups to complete as cloze paragraphs as they watch the video.

Les anniversaires à travers (*through*) les saisons.

4

5

À l'appartement de David et de Rachid...

SANDRINE C'est quand, ton anniversaire?

DAVID Qui, moi? Oh, c'est le quinze janvier.

SANDRINE Il neige en janvier, à Washington?

DAVID Parfois... et il pleut souvent à l'automne et en hiver.

SANDRINE Je déteste la pluie. C'est pénible. Qu'est-ce que tu aimes faire quand il pleut, toi?

DAVID Oh, beaucoup de choses! Dessiner, écouter de la musique. J'aime tellement la nature, je sors même quand il fait très froid.

SANDRINE Moi, je préfère l'été. Il fait chaud. On fait des promenades.

9

10

RACHID Oh là, là, j'ai soif! Mais... qu'est-ce que vous faites, tous les deux?

DAVID Oh, rien! Je fais juste un portrait de Sandrine.

RACHID Bravo, c'est pas mal du tout! Hmm, mais quelque chose ne va pas, David. Sandrine n'a pas de téléphone dans la main!

SANDRINE Oh, Rachid, ça suffit! C'est vrai, tu as vraiment du talent, David. Pourquoi ne pas célébrer mon joli portrait? Vous avez faim, les garçons?

RACHID ET DAVID Oui!

SANDRINE Je prépare le dîner. Vous aimez les crêpes ou vous préférez une omelette?

RACHID ET DAVID Des crêpes... Miam!

Expressions utiles

Talking about birthdays

- **Cette année, je fête mes vingt et un ans.**
  This year, I celebrate my twenty-first birthday.
- **Pour célébrer mon anniversaire, je prépare une super soirée.**
  To celebrate my birthday, I plan a great party.
- **Stéphane célèbre ses dix-huit ans samedi prochain.**
  Stéphane celebrates his eighteenth birthday next Saturday.
- **On organise une surprise.**
  We are planning a surprise.

Talking about hopes and preferences

- **Tu essaies de ne pas parler deux minutes, s'il te plaît?**
  Could you try not to talk for two minutes, please?
- **J'aime tellement la nature, je sors même quand il fait très froid.**
  I like nature so much, I go out even when it's very cold.
- **Moi, je préfère l'été.**
  Me, I prefer summer.
- **Vous aimez les crêpes ou vous préférez une omelette?**
  Do you like crêpes or do you prefer an omelette?

Additional vocabulary

- **encore un peu**
  a little more
- **Quelque chose ne va pas.**
  Something's not right/working.
- **main**
  hand
- **Ça suffit!**
  That's enough!
- **Miam!**
  Yum!

2 Faux! Toutes ces phrases contiennent une information qui est fausse. Corrigez chaque phrase. Answers will vary. Suggested answers below.

1. Stéphane a dix-huit ans. Stéphane a dix-sept ans.
2. David et Rachid préfèrent une omelette. Ils préfèrent les crêpes.
3. Il fait froid et il pleut. Il fait beau/bon.
4. On n'organise rien (*anything*) pour l'anniversaire de Stéphane. On organise une surprise pour l'anniversaire de Stéphane.
5. L'anniversaire de Stéphane est au printemps. L'anniversaire de Stéphane est à l'automne.
6. Rachid et Stéphane ont froid. Ils ont chaud.

3 Conversez Parlez avec vos camarades de classe pour découvrir (*find out*) qui a l'anniversaire le plus proche du vôtre (*closest to yours*). Qui est-ce? Quand est son anniversaire? En quelle saison? Quel mois? En général, quel temps fait-il le jour de son anniversaire?

ressources

VM pp. 229–230	V CD-ROM Leçon 10	espaces.vhlcentral.com Leçon 10

ACTIVITÉS

Expressions utiles

- Draw attention to numbers 101 and higher and spelling-change **-er** verbs in the video-still captions, in the **Expressions utiles** box, and as they occur in your conversation with students.
- Have students scan the video-still captions and the **Expressions utiles** box for expressions related to hopes and preferences.
- Ask students about their own preferences. You might ask questions like: **Vous préférez l'été ou l'hiver? l'automne ou le printemps? janvier ou décembre? regarder la télé ou aller au cinéma?** For a more challenging activity, follow up by asking **Pourquoi?**

1 Expansions

- Continue the activity with more statements like these. **11. Cette personne fête son anniversaire samedi prochain. (St) 12. Cette personne parle souvent au téléphone. (S) 13. Ces personnes aiment écouter de la musique. (D, S)**
- Assign one of the four main characters in this episode to a small group. Each group should write a brief description of their character's likes, dislikes, and preferences.

2 Suggestion Have students correct false statements on the board.

2 Expansion Give these true/false items for extra practice. **1. Sandrine n'aime pas parler au téléphone (Faux.) 2. Stéphane et Rachid étudient la psychologie aujourd'hui. (Faux.) 3. Sandrine aime bien regarder la télé. (Vrai.) 4. Sur son portrait, Sandrine a un téléphone dans la main. (Faux.)**

3 Suggestion Brainstorm questions students might ask to find the person whose birthday is closest to their own. Once they have found that person, have them do this activity in pairs. Ask volunteers to tell the class what they learned about their partner.

OPTIONS

Extra Practice Ask volunteers to ad-lib the episode for the class. Assure them that it is not necessary to memorize the episode or to stick strictly to its content. They should try to get the general meaning across with the vocabulary and expressions they know, and they should feel free to be creative. Give them time to prepare. You may want to assign this as homework and do it the next class period as a review activity.

Game Play a memory game. The first player tells his or her birthday. The next player repeats what the first said, then adds his or her birthday. The third player must state the first two birthdays, then his or her own. Continue until someone makes an error. Replay the game until everyone has had a turn. Or, form teams and alternate sides. If a player makes a mistake, that team gets a strike. After three strikes, the game is over.

connections cultures
NATIONAL STANDARDS

Section Goals

In this section, students will:

- learn about French public gardens
- learn terms for natural disasters
- learn names of public gardens and parks in various French-speaking regions
- read about cycling in France

Instructional Resources
espaces.vhlcentral.com: activities, downloads, reference tools

Culture à la loupe

Avant la lecture

- Take a poll of students to find out how many of them come from towns with or without public parks.
- Ask if students know of any French parks or if anyone visited a park in Paris. If so, ask what they remember about them.

Lecture

- Point out the chart comparing **Le bois de Vincennes et le bois de Boulogne**. Ask students what information is shown. Have them compare details about the two parks.
- Look at a detailed map of Paris with the class, so students visualize where **le bois de Vincennes** and **le bois de Boulogne** are located. Introduce **le jardin des Plantes, le parc Monceau, le parc Montsouris**, and **le parc des Buttes Chaumont**.

Après la lecture Have students think of parks in the United States. Have them compare the roles and levels of popularity between French and American parks.

1 Expansion Continue the activity with additional questions like these.
11. Quelles activités y a-t-il pour les adultes au bois de Boulogne? 12. Quels sont les quatre parcs parisiens dans ce texte? 13. À quel parc trouve-t-on une cascade?

CULTURE À LA LOUPE

Les jardins publics français

le jardin du Luxembourg

Dans toutes les villes françaises, la plupart° du temps au centre-ville, on trouve des jardins° publics. Ils sont en général entourés° d'une grille° et ouverts° au public pendant° la journée. Certains sont très petits et très simples; d'autres sont très grands avec d'immenses pelouses°, des plantes, des arbres° et de jolis parterres de fleurs°. Il y a aussi des sentiers° pour faire des promenades, des bancs°, des aires de jeux° pour les enfants, des statues, des fontaines ou des bassins°. On y° trouve des parents avec leurs enfants, des personnes qui font un pique-nique, qui jouent à la pétanque° ou au football, etc.

À Paris, le jardin des Tuileries et le jardin du Luxembourg sont deux jardins publics de style classique, très appréciés des Parisiens. Il y a aussi deux grands parcs à côté de Paris: le bois° de Vincennes, à l'est°, qui a un zoo, un jardin tropical et la foire° du Trône, la plus grande fête foraine° de France; et le bois de Boulogne, à l'ouest°, qui a un parc d'attractions° pour les enfants. Tous les deux ont aussi des cafés et des restaurants. Quand il fait beau, on peut faire du canotage° sur leurs lacs° ou pratiquer des activités sportives diverses.

la plupart *most* **jardins** *gardens/parks* **entourés** *surrounded* **grille** *fence* **ouverts** *open* **pendant** *during* **pelouses** *lawns* **arbres** *trees* **parterres de fleurs** *flower beds* **sentiers** *paths* **bancs** *benches* **aires de jeux** *playgrounds* **bassins** *ponds* **y** *there* **pétanque** *a popular game similar to the Italian game of bocce* **bois** *forest/wooded park* **est** *east* **foire** *fair* **fête foraine** *carnival* **ouest** *west* **parc d'attractions** *amusement park* **canotage** *boating* **lacs** *lakes* **superficie** *area* **Ferme** *Farm* **entrées** *entrances* **cascade** *waterfall* **de large** *wide* **de haut** *high* **hippodromes** *horse racetracks*

Le bois de Vincennes et le bois de Boulogne

VINCENNES	BOULOGNE
• une superficie° totale de 995 hectares	• une superficie totale de 863 hectares
• un zoo de 15 hectares	• cinq entrées°
• 19 km de sentiers pour les promenades à cheval et à vélo	• 95 km d'allées
• 32 km d'allées pour le jogging	• une cascade° de 10 mètres de large° et 14 mètres de haut°
• la Ferme° de Paris, une ferme de 5 hectares	• deux hippodromes°

Coup de main

In France and elsewhere, units of measurement are different than those used in the United States.

1 hectare = *2.47 acres*

1 kilomètre = *0.62 mile*

1 mètre = *approximately 1 yard (3 feet)*

ACTIVITÉS

1 Répondez Répondez aux questions par des phrases complètes.

1. Où trouve-t-on, en général, des jardins publics? En général, on trouve des jardins publics dans toutes les villes françaises, la plupart du temps au centre-ville.
2. Quel type de végétation y a-t-il dans les jardins publics français? Il y a des pelouses, des arbres, des plantes et des parterres de fleurs.
3. Qu'y a-t-il pour les enfants dans les jardins et les parcs français? Il y a des aires de jeux, des parcs d'attractions et des zoos.
4. Où va-t-on, à Paris, si on a envie de voir des animaux? On va au zoo du bois de Vincennes.
5. Quel type de plantes, en particulier, peut-on trouver au bois de Vincennes? On peut trouver des plantes tropicales au bois de Vincennes.
6. Comment s'appelle la plus grande fête foraine de France? Elle s'appelle la foire du Trône.
7. Où les enfants peuvent-ils visiter un parc d'attractions? Les enfants peuvent visiter un parc d'attractions au bois de Boulogne.
8. Que peut-on faire au bois de Vincennes? Answers may vary. Possible answers: On peut faire du jogging, ou des promenades à cheval ou à vélo.
9. Citez deux activités que les Français aiment faire dans les jardins publics. Answers may vary. Possible answers: Ils font des promenades et des pique-niques.
10. Est-il possible de manger dans les jardins et les parcs? Expliquez votre réponse. Answers may vary. Possible answer: Oui. Il y a parfois des restaurants et des cafés, et des personnes font aussi des pique-niques.

OPTIONS

Les jardins publics français Explain the longstanding reputations of **le bois de Vincennes** and **le bois de Boulogne**. **Le bois de Vincennes** was a working-class destination where marginal characters did their business. **Le bois de Boulogne** was a place where the well-heeled hoped to be seen. Eighteenth-century associations say it all: the Marquis de Sade was imprisoned at **le bois de Vincennes**, and Marie Antoinette lived in **le château de Bagatelle**, which she commissioned at the western end of **le bois de Boulogne**. There is no longer a socio-economic status attached to each of these green spaces, but many Parisians are familiar with their reputations.

LE FRANÇAIS QUOTIDIEN

Les catastrophes naturelles

blizzard (*m.*)	*blizzard*
canicule (*f.*)	*heat wave*
inondation (*f.*)	*flood*
ouragan (*m.*)	*hurricane*
raz-de-marée (*m.*)	*tidal wave, tsunami*
sécheresse (*f.*)	*drought*
tornade (*f.*)	*tornado*
tremblement (*m.*) de terre	*earthquake*

LE MONDE FRANCOPHONE

Des parcs publics

Voici quelques parcs publics du monde francophone.

Bruxelles, Belgique

le bois de la Cambre 123 hectares, un lac° avec une île° au centre

Casablanca, Maroc

le parc de la Ligue Arabe des palmiers°, un parc d'attractions pour enfants, des cafés et restaurants

Québec, Canada

le parc des Champs de Batailles («Plaines d'Abraham») 107 hectares, 6.000 arbres°

Tunis, Tunisie

le parc du Belvédère 110 hectares, un zoo de 13 hectares, 230.000 arbres (80 espèces° différentes), situé° sur une colline°

lac *lake* **île** *island* **palmiers** *palm trees* **arbres** *trees* **espèces** *species* **situé** *located* **colline** *hill*

PORTRAIT

Les Français et le vélo

Tous les étés, la course° cycliste du Tour de France attire° un grand nombre de spectateurs, Français et étrangers, surtout lors de° son arrivée sur les Champs-Élysées, à Paris. C'est le grand événement° sportif de l'année pour les amoureux du cyclisme. Les Français adorent aussi faire du vélo pendant° leur temps libre. Beaucoup de clubs organisent des randonnées en vélo de course° le week-end. Pour les personnes qui préfèrent le vélo tout terrain (VTT)°, il y a des sentiers° adaptés dans les parcs régionaux et nationaux. Certaines agences de voyage proposent aussi des vacances «vélo» en France ou à l'étranger°.

course *race* **attire** *attracts* **lors de** *at the time of* **événement** *event* **pendant** *during* **vélo de course** *road bike* **vélo tout terrain (VTT)** *mountain biking* **sentiers** *paths* **à l'étranger** *abroad*

le Tour de France sur les Champs-Élysées

SUR INTERNET

Qu'est-ce que Jacques Anquetil, Eddy Merckx et Bernard Hinault ont en commun?

Go to espaces.vhlcentral.com to find more cultural information related to this ESPACE CULTURE.

ACTIVITÉS

2 Vrai ou faux? Indiquez si les phrases sont **vraies** ou **fausses**. Corrigez les phrases fausses.

1. Les Français ne font pas de vélo. Faux. Les Français adorent faire du vélo pendant leur temps libre.
2. Les membres de clubs de vélo font des promenades le week-end. Vrai.
3. Les agences de voyage offrent des vacances «vélo». Vrai.
4. On utilise un VTT quand on fait du vélo sur la route. Faux. On utilise un vélo de course.
5. Le Tour de France arrive sur les Champs-Élysées à Paris. Vrai.

3 Les catastrophes naturelles Avec un(e) partenaire, parlez de trois catastrophes naturelles. Quel temps fait-il, en général, pendant (*during*) chaque catastrophe? Choisissez une catastrophe et décrivez-la à vos camarades. Peuvent-ils deviner (*Can they guess*) de quelle catastrophe vous parlez?

ressources

espaces.vhlcentral.com Leçon 10

Le français quotidien After studying the vocabulary, ask students to close their books and to number from one to five on a piece of paper. Describe five of these **catastrophes naturelles** with new lexical items from **Leçon 10.** Have the class write down the event you are describing. Go over the answers as a class.

Portrait
- Ask students what they know about the **Tour de France**. They may mention Lance Armstrong, **le maillot jaune** (*yellow jersey*), etc.
- Find out if the class has heard of stereotypes about the French and cycling. Have them list ideas in small groups.

Le monde francophone
- Look at the francophone world map in **Appendice A** to remind students where these countries are located.
- Practice pronunciation with the descriptions of these parks.

2 Expansion Continue the activity with more true/false statements like these.
6. Le Tour de France est une grande course cycliste. (Vrai.)
7. Le Tour de France est au printemps. (Faux, en été)
8. Les Français et les étrangers sont spectateurs du Tour de France. (Vrai.)

3 Expansion Students can use this as an opportunity to practice contradicting while quizzing each other about weather in the context of these new expressions. Example: **Étudiant(e) 1: Quand il y a un ouragan, fait-il du soleil? Étudiant(e) 2: Pas du tout! Il pleut beaucoup.**

OPTIONS

Des parcs publics Assign a francophone country to several students in class. Have everyone do individual research on gardens or a park in the country he or she has been assigned. Students should be prepared to present their findings about the park in at least three clear sentences in French and an image from the Internet, if possible.

Les Français et le vélo Bring in an example of francophone music or film about cycling. For example, play the song ***Mon vélo est blanc*** by Anne Sylvestre. Screen part of the Belgian film ***Le vélo de Ghislain Lambert***. There are also scenes with Charlotte Gainsbourg riding a bicycle in ***La petite voleuse***.

NATIONAL STANDARDS comparisons

Section Goals

In this section, students will learn numbers 101 and higher.

Instructional Resources
WB/VM: Workbook, pp. 65–66
Lab Manual, p. 39
Lab MP3s
WB/VM/LM Answer Key
*IRCD-ROM: IRM (**Essayez!** and **Mise en pratique** answers; Lab Audioscript)*
espaces.vhlcentral.com: activities, downloads, reference tools

Suggestions

- Review numbers 0–100 by asking students questions that call for a number in the answer. Examples: **Combien d'étudiants y a-t-il dans la classe? Quel âge avez-vous? Quel âge a votre grand-mère? Anne a trois crayons. J'ai quatre boîtes de vingt crayons. Combien de crayons avons-nous? (quatre-vingt-trois)**
- Write on the board: **quatre cents étudiants, neuf cents personnes, deux mille livres, onze millions de voyageurs**. Help students deduce the meanings of the numbers.
- Model pronunciation of example numbers. Write other three- to seven-digit numbers on the board and have students read them.
- Go over the example sentences containing **cent**, **mille**, and **million**. Explain that the rules for when to pluralize are different from English.
- Inform students that years before 2000 can be said in two ways: 1939 **mille neuf cent trente-neuf / dix-neuf cent trente-neuf.**

Successful Language Learning Explain that to count from 101–199, say **cent** followed by 1–99. So, 101: **cent un**, 102: **cent deux**, 103: **cent trois**, and so forth up to 199: **cent quatre-vingt-dix-neuf**. Use the same strategy after **deux cent**, **trois cent**, etc.

Essayez! Have students think of four more numbers for their partner to write out in French.

10.1 Numbers 101 and higher

Numbers 101 and higher

101 cent un	**800** huit cents
125 cent vingt-cinq	**900** neuf cents
198 cent quatre-vingt-dix-huit	**1.000** mille
200 deux cents	**1.100** mille cent
245 deux cent quarante-cinq	**2.000** deux mille
300 trois cents	**5.000** cinq mille
400 quatre cents	**100.000** cent mille
500 cinq cents	**550.000** cinq cent cinquante mille
600 six cents	**1.000.000** un million
700 sept cents	**8.000.000** huit millions

- Note that French uses a period, rather than a comma, to indicate thousands and millions.
- The word **cent** does not take a final **-s** when it is followed by the numbers **1-99**.

Il y a **deux cent cinquante** jours de soleil.
There are 250 sunny days.

but

J'ai **quatre cents** bandes dessinées.
I have 400 comic books.

- The number **un** is not used before the word **mille** to mean *a/one thousand*. It is used, however, before **million** to say *a/one million*.

Mille personnes habitent le village.
One thousand people live in the village.

but

Un million de personnes habitent la région.
One million people live in the region.

- **Mille**, unlike **cent** and **million**, is invariable. It never takes an **-s**.

Aimez-vous *les Mille et Une Nuits*?
Do you like "The Thousand and One Nights"?

Onze mille étudiants sont inscrits.
Eleven thousand students are registered.

- Before a noun, **million** and **millions** are followed by **de/d'**.

Deux millions de personnes sont en vacances.
Two million people are on vacation.

Il y a **onze millions d'habitants** dans la capitale.
There are 11,000,000 inhabitants in the capital.

Essayez! Donnez les équivalents en français.

1. 10.000 ___dix mille___
2. 620 ___six cent vingt___
3. 365 ___trois cent soixante-cinq___
4. 42.000 ___quarante deux mille___
5. 200.000.000 ___deux cents millions___
6. 480 ___quatre cent quatre-vingts___
7. 1.789 ___mille sept cent quatre-vingt-neuf___
8. 400 ___quatre cents___

MISE EN PRATIQUE

1 Quelle adresse? Vous allez distribuer des journaux (*newspapers*) et vous téléphonez aux clients pour avoir leur adresse. Écrivez les adresses.

MODÈLE
cent deux, rue Lafayette
102, rue Lafayette

1. deux cent cinquante-deux, rue de Bretagne 252, rue de Bretagne
2. quatre cents, avenue Malbon 400, avenue Malbon
3. cent soixante-dix-sept, rue Jeanne d'Arc 177, rue Jeanne d'Arc
4. cinq cent quarante-six, boulevard St. Marc 546, boulevard St. Marc
5. six cent quatre-vingt-huit, avenue des Gaulois 688, avenue des Gaulois
6. trois cent quatre-vingt-douze, boulevard Micheline 392, boulevard Micheline
7. cent vingt-cinq, rue des Pierres 125, rue des Pierres
8. trois cent quatre, avenue St. Germain 304, avenue St. Germain

2 Faisons des calculs Faites les additions et écrivez les réponses.

MODÈLE
200 + 300 =
Deux cents plus trois cents font cinq cents.

1. 5.000 + 3.000 = Cinq mille plus trois mille font huit mille.
2. 650 + 750 = Six cent cinquante plus sept cent cinquante font mille quatre cents.
3. 2.000.000 + 3.000.000 = Deux millions plus trois millions font cinq millions.
4. 4.400 + 3.600 = Quatre mille quatre cents plus trois mille six cents font huit mille.
5. 155 + 310 = Cent cinquante-cinq plus trois cent dix font quatre cent soixante-cinq.
6. 7.000 + 3.000 = Sept mille plus trois mille font dix mille.
7. 9.000.000 + 2.000.000 = Neuf millions plus deux millions font onze millions.
8. 1.250 + 2.250 = Mille deux cent cinquante plus deux mille deux cent cinquante font trois mille cinq cents.

3 Combien d'habitants? À tour de rôle, demandez à votre partenaire combien d'habitants il y a dans chaque ville d'après (*according to*) les statistiques.

MODÈLE
Dijon: 153.813
Étudiant(e) 1: *Combien d'habitants y a-t-il à Dijon?*
Étudiant(e) 2: *Il y a cent cinquante-trois mille huit cent treize habitants.*

1. Toulouse: 398.423 Il y a trois cent quatre-vingt-dix-huit mille quatre cent vingt-trois habitants.
2. Abidjan: 2.877.948 Il y a deux millions huit cent soixante-dix-sept mille neuf cent quarante-huit habitants.
3. Lyon: 453.187 Il y a quatre cent cinquante-trois mille cent quatre-vingt-sept habitants.
4. Québec: 510.559 Il y a cinq cent dix mille cinq cent cinquante-neuf habitants.
5. Marseille: 807.071 Il y a huit cent sept mille soixante et onze habitants.
6. Papeete: 26.181 Il y a vingt-six mille cent quatre-vingt-un habitants.

OPTIONS

Game Ask students to stand up to create a number chain. The first student states the number 25. The next student says 50. Students continue the chain, using multiples of 25. If a student misses the next number in sequence, he or she must sit down. Continue play until only one student is left standing. If a challenge is required to break a tie, play the game with multiples of 30.

Extra Practice Ask students to make a list of nine items containing the following: a variety of plural and singular nouns, three numerals in the hundreds, three in the thousands, and three in the millions. Once lists are completed, have students exchange them and read the items off their partners' lists aloud. Partners should listen for the correct number and any agreement errors.

COMMUNICATION

4 Quand? Avec un(e) partenaire, regardez les dates et dites quand ces événements ont lieu (*take place*).

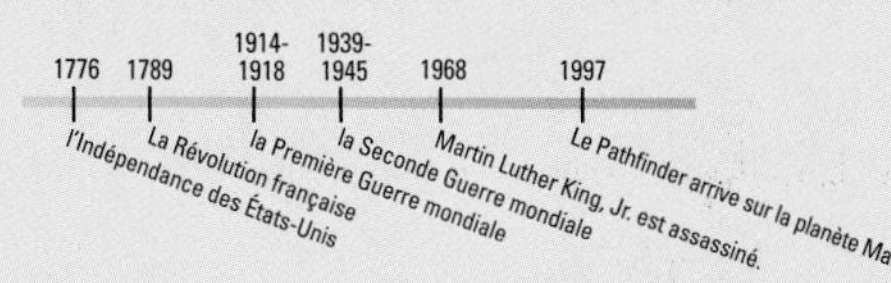

1. Le Pathfinder arrive sur la planète Mars. Il arrive en mille neuf cent quatre-vingt-dix-sept.
2. La Première Guerre mondiale commence. Elle commence en mille neuf cent quatorze.
3. La Seconde Guerre mondiale prend fin (*ends*). Elle prend fin en mille neuf cent quarante-cinq.
4. L'Amérique déclare son indépendance. Elle déclare son indépendance en mille sept cent soixante-seize.
5. Martin Luther King, Jr. est assassiné. Il est assassiné en mille neuf cent soixante-huit.
6. La Première Guerre Mondiale prend fin. Elle prend fin en mille neuf cent dix-huit.

5 Combien ça coûte? Vous regardez un catalogue avec un(e) ami(e). À tour de rôle, demandez à votre partenaire le prix des choses. Answers will vary.

MODÈLE

Étudiant(e) 1: *Combien coûte l'ordinateur?*
Étudiant(e) 2: *Il coûte mille huit cents euros.*

1. É1: ... la montre? É2: Elle ... quatre cent trente-deux ...

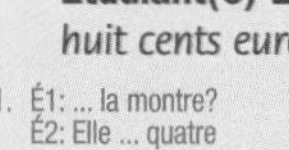

2. É1: ... le palm? É2: Il ... cent trente-sept ...

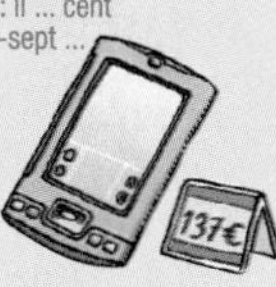

3. É1: ... le sac à dos? É2: Il ... cent dix-huit ...

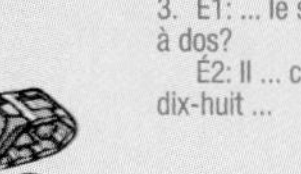

4. É1: ... le vélo? É2: Il ... six cent soixante-quinze ...

6 Dépensez de l'argent Vous et votre partenaire avez 100.000€. Décidez quels articles de la liste vous allez prendre. Justifiez vos choix à la classe. Answers will vary.

MODÈLE

Étudiant(e) 1: *On prend un rendez-vous avec Brad Pitt.*
Étudiant(e) 2: *Alors, nous n'avons pas assez d'argent pour la voiture!*

un ordinateur... 2.000€	des vacances à Tahiti... 7.000€
un rendez-vous avec Brad Pitt... 50.000€	un vélo... 1.000€
un rendez-vous avec Madonna... 50.000€	une voiture de luxe... 60.000€

Le français vivant

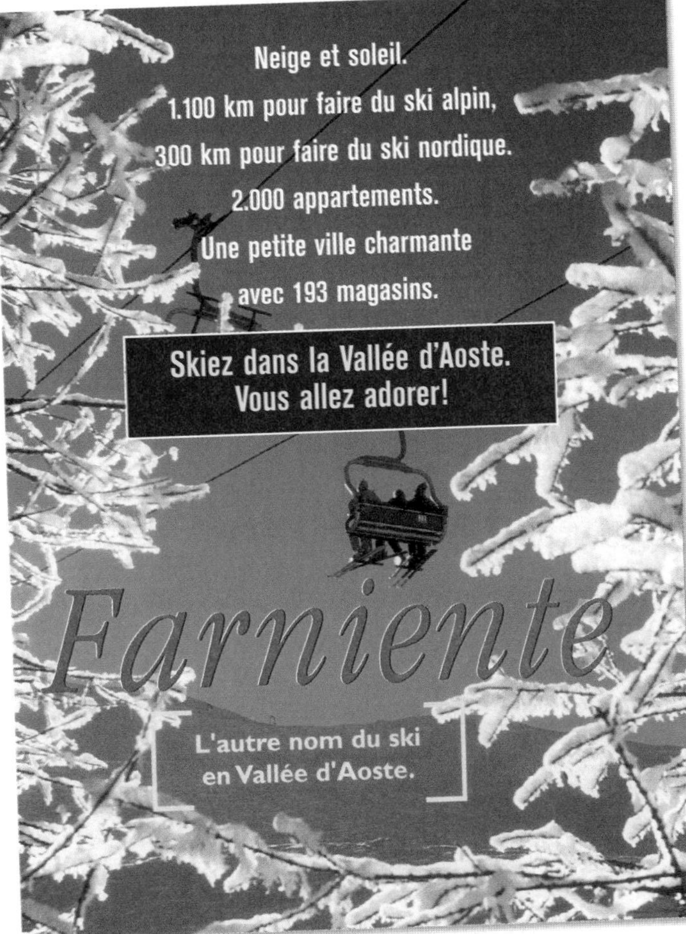

Neige et soleil.
1.100 km pour faire du ski alpin,
300 km pour faire du ski nordique.
2.000 appartements.
Une petite ville charmante
avec 193 magasins.
Skiez dans la Vallée d'Aoste.
Vous allez adorer!
Farniente
L'autre nom du ski
en Vallée d'Aoste.

Questions Avec un(e) partenaire, regardez la publicité (*ad*) et répondez aux questions. Écrivez les nombres en toutes lettres. (*Write out the numbers.*) Some answers will vary.

1. Combien de kilomètres y a-t-il pour faire du ski alpin? Pour faire du ski nordique? mille cent kilomètres; trois cents kilomètres
2. Combien d'appartements y a-t-il dans la ville? Combien de magasins? deux mille appartements; cent quatre-vingt-treize magasins
3. Quelles autres activités sportives sont possibles, à votre avis (*in your opinion*), dans la Vallée d'Aoste?
4. Faites-vous du ski? Avez-vous envie de faire du ski en Vallée d'Aoste? Pourquoi?
5. Quel temps fait-il en Vallée d'Aoste?

1 Suggestion For listening comprehension, have students read numbers from the activity to a partner.

1 Expansion Give students these real addresses in regions **Centre** and **Pays de la Loire**. Model how to pronounce the postal codes. Example: 45000: **quarante-cinq mille**. **(1) Préfecture de la Région Centre et du Loiret: 181, rue de Bourgogne - 45042 ORLÉANS (2) Espace Région Centre de Tours: 1, rue des Ursulines - 37000 TOURS (3) Auberge de Jeunesse: 23, Avenue Neigre - CHARTRES 28000 (4) Médiathèque Louis Aragon: 54, rue du Port - 72015 LE MANS**

2 Suggestions
- Call on pairs of students to say some of the calculations aloud.
- Give additional math problems if more practice is needed.

2 Expansion Have pairs convert a **calcul** into a word problem. Example: **J'ai deux cents dollars. Ma sœur a trois cents dollars. Combien de dollars avons-nous?**

3 Expansion Write on the board some well-known American cities and your university's city or town. Ask students: **Combien d'habitants...?** Have them guess if they don't know. Then write the accurate number next to each city. Have students come to the board to write out the populations in French.

4 Expansion Ask students to brainstorm other famous years throughout history.

5 & 6 Suggestions
- Before beginning each activity, make sure students know the vocabulary.
- Do the **modèles** with a volunteer to make sure students understand the activities.

Le français vivant Have students look at the picture and guess what the ad is for. Call on a volunteer to read the text aloud. Have other students help if the volunteer has trouble with the numbers.

OPTIONS

Extra Practice Have small groups of students work together to create a worksheet consisting of five math word problems for their classmates to complete. Have students take turns reading problems to the class or one of the other small groups, who, in turn, will solve the problems. Have groups include an answer key with their worksheets.

Groups Divide the class into groups of ten. Give a flashcard with a number from 0–9 to each person in each group. If one group is smaller, distribute extra numbers to group members, as needed, so some students have more than one card. Call out a three- to nine-digit number in which none of the digits is repeated. Students arrange themselves, showing their flashcard(s) to reflect the number. Repeat with other numbers.

comparisons NATIONAL STANDARDS

Section Goals

In this section, students will learn **-er** verbs with spelling changes.

Instructional Resources
WB/VM: Workbook, pp. 67–68
Lab Manual, p. 40
Lab MP3s
WB/VM/LM Answer Key
*IRCD-ROM: IRM (**Essayez!** and **Mise en pratique** answers; Lab Audioscript, **Feuilles d'activités**)*
espaces.vhlcentral.com: activities, downloads, reference tools

Suggestions

- Model pronunciations of forms of **acheter**, **espérer**, and **envoyer**. Go over the example statements as a class.
- Guide students to notice that, like regular **-er** verbs, spelling-change **-er** verbs are "boot verbs."
- Point out that infinitives often follow forms of **espérer**.
- Ask questions using verbs from this section, encouraging student responses. Examples: **Où est-ce que vous achetez du pain? Quelle saison préférez-vous: l'été ou l'hiver?**
- Explain that when the letter **e** is followed by one pronounced consonant and a silent **e**, add an **accent grave** over the first **e**. If the first **e** already has an **accent aigu**, it becomes an **accent grave**. This causes spelling changes in some verbs, adjectives, and nouns. Remind students to apply this rule whenever this pattern of letters occurs. Exception: **e** with an **accent circonflexe**.
- Go through the meanings of verbs. Note the number of cognates. Make sure students understand that **amener** and **emmener** are only used for people. Ask: What verbs would you use to say *to take* and *to bring* objects? (**prendre**; **apporter**)

10.2 Spelling-change *-er* verbs

Point de départ Some **-er** verbs, though regular with respect to their verb endings, have spelling changes that occur in the verb stem (what remains after the **-er** is dropped).

- Most infinitives whose next-to-last syllable contains an **e** (no accent) change this letter to **è** in all forms except **nous** and **vous**.

acheter (to buy)	
j'achète	nous achetons
tu achètes	vous achetez
il/elle achète	ils/elles achètent

Où est-ce que tu **achètes** des skis?
Where do you buy skis?

Ils **achètent** beaucoup sur Internet.
They buy a lot on the Internet.

- Infinitives whose next-to-last syllable contains an **é** change this letter to **è** in all forms except **nous** and **vous**.

espérer (to hope)	
j'espère	nous espérons
tu espères	vous espérez
il/elle espère	ils/elles espèrent

Elle **espère** arriver tôt aujourd'hui.
She hopes to arrive early today.

Nos profs **espèrent** commencer les cours.
Our professors hope to start classes.

Elle achète quelque chose.

Ils répètent.

- Infinitives ending in **-yer** change **y** to **i** in all forms except **nous** and **vous**.

envoyer (to send)	
j'envoie	nous envoyons
tu envoies	vous envoyez
il/elle envoie	ils/elles envoient

J'**envoie** une lettre.
I'm sending a letter.

Tes amis **envoient** un e-mail.
Your friends send an e-mail.

MISE EN PRATIQUE

1 Passe-temps Chaque membre de la famille Desrosiers a son passe-temps préféré. Utilisez les éléments pour dire comment ils préparent leur week-end.

MODÈLE
Tante Manon fait une randonnée. (acheter / sandwichs)
Elle achète des sandwichs.

1. Nous faisons du vélo. (essayer / vélo) Nous essayons le vélo.
2. Christiane aime chanter. (répéter) Elle répète.
3. Les filles jouent au foot. (espérer / gagner) Elles espèrent gagner.
4. Vous allez à la pêche. (emmener / enfants) Vous emmenez les enfants.
5. Papa fait un tour en voiture. (nettoyer / voiture) Il nettoie la voiture.
6. Mes frères font du camping. (préférer / partir tôt) Ils préfèrent partir tôt.

2 Que font-ils? Avec un(e) partenaire, dites ce que font les personnages. Answers will vary.

MODÈLE
Il achète une baguette.

acheter

1. envoyer

3. répéter

2. payer

4. nettoyer

3 Invitation au cinéma Avec un(e) partenaire, jouez les rôles de Halouk et de Thomas. Ensuite, présentez la scène à la classe.

THOMAS J'ai envie d'aller au cinéma.
HALOUK Bonne idée. Nous (1) emmenons (emmener, protéger) Véronique avec nous?
THOMAS J' (2) espère (acheter, espérer) qu'elle a du temps libre.
HALOUK Peut-être, mais j' (3) envoie (envoyer, payer) des e-mails tous les jours et elle ne répond pas.
THOMAS Parce que son ordinateur ne fonctionne pas. Elle (4) préfère (essayer, préférer) parler au téléphone.
HALOUK D'accord. Alors toi, tu (5) achètes (acheter, répéter) les tickets au cinéma et moi, je vais chercher Véronique.

OPTIONS

Game Divide the class into two teams. Announce one of the infinitives and a subject pronoun. Example: **emmener**; **ils**. At the board, have the first member of Team A say and write the given subject and the conjugated form of the verb. If the team member answers correctly, Team A gets one point. If not, give the first member of Team B the same example. The team with the most points at the end of the game wins.

Video Replay the video episode, having students focus on **-er** verbs with spelling changes. Have them note each one they hear, with subjects if conjugated. Find out how many occurrences students heard before pointing out these examples: **je préfère, célébrer, célèbre, tu essaies,** and **préférer.** Ask for remarks with spelling-change **-er** verbs that describe the characters. Example: **Rachid possède un palm.**

COMMUNICATION

4 **Questions** À tour de rôle, posez les questions à un(e) partenaire. Answers will vary.

1. Qu'est-ce que tu achètes tous les jours?
2. Qu'est-ce que tu achètes tous les mois?
3. Quand tu sors avec ton/ta petit(e) ami(e), qui paie?
4. Est-ce que toi et ton/ta camarade de chambre partagez les frais (*expenses*)? Qui paie quoi?
5. Est-ce que tu possèdes une voiture?
6. Qui nettoie ta chambre?
7. À qui est-ce que tu envoies des e-mails?
8. Qu'est-ce que tu espères faire cet été?

5 **Réponses affirmatives** Votre professeur va vous donner une feuille d'activités. Trouvez au moins deux camarades de classe pour répondre à chaque question par l'affirmative. Et si vous, vous répondez aux questions par l'affirmative, écrivez votre nom. Answers will vary.

MODÈLE

Étudiant(e) 1: *Est-ce que tu achètes exclusivement sur Internet?*
Étudiant(e) 2: *Oui, j'achète exclusivement sur Internet.*

Questions	Noms
1. acheter exclusivement sur Internet	Virginie, Éric
2. posséder un palm	
3. envoyer des lettres à ses grands-parents	
4. célébrer une occasion spéciale demain	

6 **E-mail à l'oncle Marcel** Xavier va écrire un e-mail à son oncle pour raconter (*to tell*) ses activités de la semaine prochaine. Il prépare une liste des choses qu'il veut dire (*wants to say*). Avec un(e) partenaire, écrivez son e-mail. Answers will vary.

- lundi: emmener maman chez le médecin
- mercredi: fac envoyer notes
- jeudi: répéter rôle Roméo et Juliette
- vendredi: célébrer anniversaire papa
- vendredi: essayer faire gym
- samedi: parents acheter voiture

- The change of **y** to **i** is optional in verbs whose infinitives end in **-ayer**.

Je **paie** avec une carte de crédit.
I pay with a credit card.

Comment est-ce que tu **payes**?
How do you pay?

Other spelling-change -er verbs

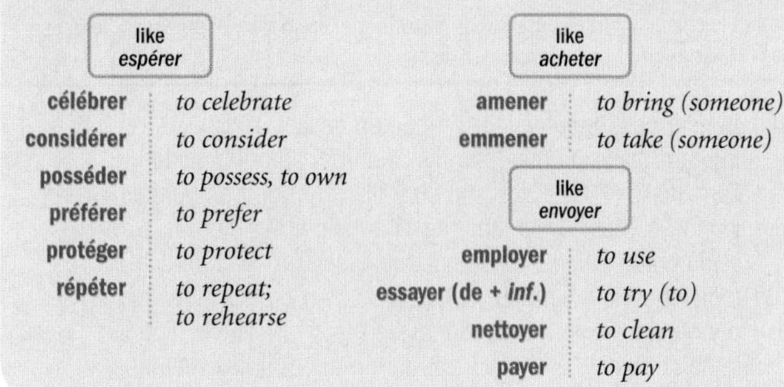

like espérer		like acheter	
célébrer	*to celebrate*	**amener**	*to bring (someone)*
considérer	*to consider*	**emmener**	*to take (someone)*
posséder	*to possess, to own*	**like envoyer**	
préférer	*to prefer*	**employer**	*to use*
protéger	*to protect*	**essayer (de + inf.)**	*to try (to)*
répéter	*to repeat; to rehearse*	**nettoyer**	*to clean*
		payer	*to pay*

Je préfère l'été. Il fait chaud.

- Note that the **nous** and **vous** forms of the verbs presented in this section have no spelling changes.

Vous **achetez** des sandwichs aussi.
You're buying sandwiches, too.

Nous **espérons** partir à huit heures.
We hope to leave at 8 o'clock.

Nous **envoyons** les enfants à l'école.
We're sending the children to school.

Vous **payez** avec une carte de crédit.
You pay with a credit card.

Essayez! **Complétez les phrases avec la forme correcte du verbe.**

1. Les bibliothèques emploient (employer) beaucoup d'étudiants.
2. Vous répétez (répéter) les phrases en français.
3. Nous payons (payer) assez pour les livres.
4. Mon camarade de chambre ne nettoie (nettoyer) pas son bureau.
5. Est-ce que tu espères (espérer) gagner?
6. Vous essayez (essayer) parfois d'arriver à l'heure.
7. Tu préfères (préférer) prendre du thé ou du café?
8. Elle emmène (emmener) sa mère au cinéma.
9. On célèbre (célébrer) une occasion spéciale.
10. Les parents protègent (protéger) leurs enfants?

Essayez! For additional drills with spelling-change **-er** verbs for the whole class or those who need extra practice, do this activity orally and on the board with different subjects.

1 Suggestion Ask for a volunteer to demonstrate the **modèle**.

1 Expansion Have students write four additional statements modeled on the activity about their own family members.

2 Expansion Show additional pictures of people cleaning, using something, trying, sending, etc. Ask a yes/no question about each picture. Example: Showing an image of someone sending a letter, ask: **Est-ce qu'il nettoie?** Students answer: **Mais non, il envoie une lettre.**

3 Suggestion Explain that students must first choose the logical verb, then write the correct form.

4 Expansion Have students write two more questions containing spelling-change **-er** verbs that they would like to ask their partner.

5 Suggestion Call on two volunteers to read the **modèle** aloud. Then distribute the **Feuilles d'activités** from the IRM on the IRCD-ROM.

6 Expansion Have students think of a family member or friend to whom they would likely write an e-mail. Tell them to first list at least five ideas using as many spelling-change **-er** verbs as possible. Then have them write an e-mail of at least five sentences.

OPTIONS

Extra Practice Arrange students in rows of six. The first person in each row has a piece of paper. Call out an infinitive. Silently, the first student writes the **je** form and passes the paper to the student behind him or her. That student writes the **tu** form and passes the paper on. The last person in the row holds up the paper to show completion. Have students rotate places before calling out another verb.

Small Groups Have small groups write dehydrated sentences with only subjects and infinitives. Examples: **1. Tu / amener / ??? 2. Sylvie et Véronique / espérer / ???** Tell groups to switch with another group, who will form a complete sentence by conjugating the verb and inventing an appropriate ending. Ask for volunteers to write one of their group's sentences on the board.

Instructional Resources
IRCD-ROM: IRM (Info Gap Activities); Testing Program, pp. 37–40; Test Files; Testing Program MP3s; Test Generator
espaces.vhlcentral.com: activities, downloads, reference tools

1 Expansion Have students write a story about their preferred sport modeled on the paragraph in this activity.

2 Suggestion Have pairs get together to form groups of four to review each others' sentences. Have students explain any corrections or suggested changes.

3 Suggestion Encourage students to choose places from the French-speaking world that they have learned about in **Espace culture** and **Panorama** sections.

3 Expansion Have students create more questions based on those in the activity to ask their partner. Guide the class to ask about where the partner hopes or prefers to go for various vacations throughout the year. Students may combine reusing weather conditions described in the box and using additional weather descriptions.

4 Expansion For additional numbers practice, have students ask each other: **Combien coûte ___________ (type de voyage) avec la commission?**

5 Suggestion Ask for volunteers to do the **modèle** and auction off a few more items to set further examples.

6 Suggestions
- Divide the class into pairs and distribute the Info Gap Handouts in the IRM on the IRCD-ROM for this activity. Give students ten minutes to complete the activity.
- Act out the **modèle** with a student volunteer playing the role of **Étudiant(e) 2**.

NATIONAL communication STANDARDS

Synthèse

1 Le basket Avec un(e) partenaire, utilisez les verbes de la liste pour compléter le paragraphe.

acheter	considérer	envoyer	essayer	préférer
amener	employer	espérer	payer	répéter

Je m'appelle Stéphanie et je joue au basket. J' (1) _amène_ toujours (*always*) mes parents avec moi aux matchs le samedi. Ils (2) _considèrent_ que les filles sont de très bonnes joueuses. Mes parents font aussi du sport. Ma mère fait du vélo et mon père (3) _espère_ gagner son prochain match de foot! Le vendredi matin, j' (4) _envoie_ un e-mail à ma mère pour lui rappeler (*remind her of*) le match. Mais elle n'oublie jamais! Ils n' (5) _achètent_ pas de tickets pour les matchs, parce que les parents des joueurs ne (6) _paient_ pas. Nous (7) _essayons_ toujours d'arriver une demi-heure avant le match, parce que maman et papa (8) _préfèrent, espèrent_ s'asseoir (*to sit*) tout près du terrain (*court*). Ils sont tellement fiers!

2 Que font-ils? Avec un(e) partenaire, parlez des activités des personnages et écrivez une phrase par illustration. Answers will vary.

1. ___________ 2. ___________ 3. ___________

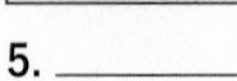

4. ___________ 5. ___________ 6. ___________

3 Où partir? Avec un(e) partenaire, choisissez cinq endroits intéressants à visiter où il fait le temps indiqué sur la liste. Ensuite, répondez aux questions. Answers will vary.

Il fait chaud.	Il fait soleil.	Il fait du vent.	Il neige.	Il pleut.

1. Où essayez-vous d'aller cet été? Pourquoi?
2. Où préférez-vous partir cet hiver? Pourquoi?
3. Quelle est la première destination que vous espérez visiter? La dernière? Pourquoi?
4. Qui emmenez-vous avec vous? Pourquoi?

4 J'achète Vous allez payer un voyage aux membres de votre famille et à vos amis. À tour de rôle, choisissez un voyage et donnez à votre partenaire la liste des personnes qui partent. Votre partenaire va vous donner le prix à payer. Answers will vary.

MODÈLE

Étudiant(e) 1: *J'achète un voyage de dix jours dans les Pays de la Loire à ma cousine Pauline et à mon frère Alexandre.*
Étudiant(e) 2: *D'accord. Tu paies deux mille cinq cent soixante-deux euros.*

Voyages	Prix par personne	Commission
Dix jours dans les Pays de la Loire	1.250	62
Deux semaines de camping	660	35
Sept jours au soleil en hiver	2.100	78
Trois jours à Paris en avril	500	55
Trois mois en Europe en été	10.400	47
Un week-end à Nice en septembre	350	80
Une semaine à la montagne en juin	990	66
Une semaine à la neige	1.800	73

5 La vente aux enchères Par groupes de quatre, organisez une vente aux enchères (*auction*) pour vendre les affaires (*things*) du professeur. À tour de rôle, un(e) étudiant(e) joue le rôle du/de la vendeur/vendeuse et les autres étudiants jouent le rôle des enchérisseurs (*bidders*). Vous avez 5.000 euros et toutes les enchères (*bids*) commencent à cent euros. Answers will vary.

MODÈLE

Étudiant(e) 1: *J'ai le cahier du professeur. Qui paie cent euros?*
Étudiant(e) 2: *Moi, je paie cent euros.*
Étudiant(e) 1: *Qui paie cent cinquante euros?*

6 À la bibliothèque Votre professeur va vous donner, à vous et à votre partenaire, deux feuilles d'activités différentes. Attention! Ne regardez pas la feuille de votre partenaire. Answers will vary.

MODÈLE

Étudiant(e) 1: *Est-ce que tu as le livre «Candide»?*
Étudiant(e) 2: *Oui, son numéro de référence est P, Q, deux cent soixante-six, cent quarante-sept, cent dix.*

ressources
WB pp. 65–68 | LM pp. 39–40 | Lab MP3s Leçon 10 | espaces.vhlcentral.com Leçon 10

OPTIONS

Small Groups Have students write a conversation between two friends. One friend tries to convince the other to go out. The other makes excuses to not go. Students should include as many spelling-change **-er** verbs and weather expressions as possible. Example: **Étudiant(e) 1: Faisons une randonnée! Étudiant(e) 2: Mais je nettoie ma chambre. Étudiant(e) 1: Mais il fait beau. Étudiant(e) 2: Il va pleuvoir plus tard.**

Pairs Ask students to imagine they are going on an extended trip. Have them make a list of at least five things they are to do (buy things, take someone somewhere, send mail, etc.) before leaving. Examples: **Je vais acheter un nouveau parapluie. J'espère envoyer une carte d'anniversaire.**

La météo

In 1854, a French fleet was destroyed in a violent storm on the Black Sea. The astronomer Le Verrier realized that this disaster could have been avoided; if weather observations had been made, the ships could have been warned. Le Verrier laid the foundation of the French national weather service with a network of thirteen stations, and he started a system that allows European countries to share weather observations. In 1946, the first French weather forecast was broadcast on TV.

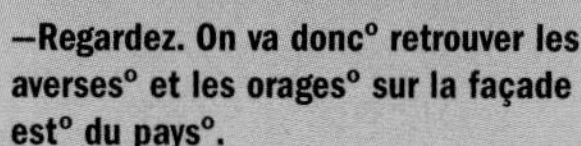

—Regardez. On va donc° retrouver les averses° et les orages° sur la façade est° du pays°.

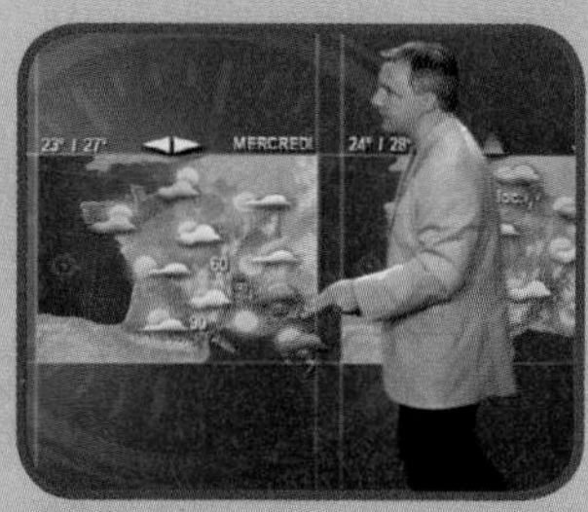

—Quelques gouttes° de pluie sur les Alpes et sur la Corse, et globalement c'est plutôt du beau temps.

Compréhension Answer the questions in French. Some answers may vary. Suggested answers.

1. What is the date of the forecast? Is the weather nice today? Explain. C'est le 1er août. Non, le temps est moyen. Il y a des averses et des orages.
2. What is the weather going to be like tomorrow? C'est le même temps avec des averses et des orages.
3. On Wednesday and Thursday, is the weather going to be nicer? Explain. Oui, c'est plutôt du beau temps.
4. How are the temperatures in general? Mild, hot, cold? Answers will vary.

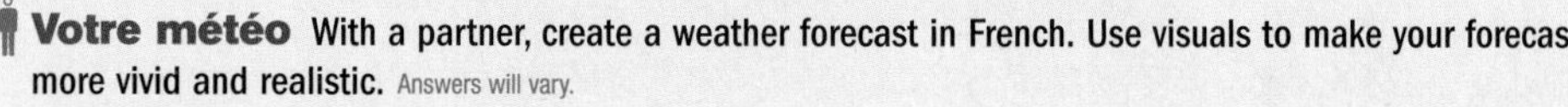

Votre météo With a partner, create a weather forecast in French. Use visuals to make your forecast more vivid and realistic. Answers will vary.

SUR INTERNET

Go to **espaces.vhlcentral.com** to watch the TV clip featured in this **Le zapping**.

donc *so* **averses** *showers* **orages** *thunderstorms* **est** *east* **pays** *country* **gouttes** *drops*

Section Goals

In this section, students will:

- read about the history of the French national weather service
- watch a video clip of the weather forecast
- answer questions about the weather forecast

Instructional Resources
*IRCD-ROM: IRM (**Le zapping** TV clip transcription)*
espaces.vhlcentral.com: activities, downloads, reference tools, TV clip

Introduction To check comprehension, ask these questions.
1. Why is it important to know what the weather will be like? (It helps predict storms, for example, and can save lives.)
2. Do you find it helpful to know the weather ahead of time? Why?

Avant de regarder la vidéo

- Have students look at the video stills, read the captions, and predict what is happening in the forecast for each visual. **(1. L'homme parle du temps qu'il va faire demain matin. Il va pleuvoir et il va faire [du] soleil. 2. L'homme parle du temps qu'il va faire mercredi. Il va faire beau, mais avec des nuages.)**
- Before showing the video, explain to students that they do not need to understand every word they hear. Tell them to listen for greetings, cognates, and vocabulary related to the weather.

Compréhension Have students work in pairs or groups for this activity. Tell them to write down their answers. Then show the video again so that they can check their work and add any missing information.

Votre météo Suggest that they choose a specific region in the United States for their weather forecast. Have pairs present their work to the class.

OPTIONS

Language Notes At one point in the forecast, the anchor says the temperatures are going down **«un peu comme le Livret A»**. He is referring to a savings account from **La Poste** (which acts also as a bank) and to its interest rate.

At the end of the forecast, the anchor says **«On se retrouve dans un instant. Embrassez les Julien.»** because the day following this broadcast was to be **«la saint Julien»**. To celebrate, usually people would say to the person **«Bonne fête!»** and do **la bise** with them. People may offer flowers to women or send a card to men and women. In France, **«Bonne fête»** cards are as common as birthday cards.

Section Goals

In this section, students will learn historical and cultural information about **Pays de la Loire** and **Centre**.

Instructional Resources

IRCD-ROM: Transparency #30,
WB/VM: Workbook, pp. 69–70
WB/VM/LM Answer Key
espaces.vhlcentral.com: activities; downloads; reference tools

Carte des Pays de la Loire et du Centre

- Have students look at the map of the regions **Pays de la Loire** and **Centre** or use **Transparency #30**. Have volunteers read aloud the cities and geographic features. Model French pronunciation of city names, as necessary.
- Ask students to name a geographical feature that was likely an asset to these regions during their development. (the many major rivers)
- Ask students if they recognize any of the town names and to share any prior knowledge they have about the locations.

La région en chiffres

- Ask volunteers to read the sections. After each section, ask other students questions about the content.
- Have students list the many cognates that appear in this section and state the likely English equivalent or what the word might relate to.

Incroyable mais vrai!

Chambord's construction began in 1519 under François Ier, continued under Henri II, and was finally completed in 1685 under Louis XIV.

Panorama

Les Pays de la Loire

La région en chiffres

- **Superficie:** *32.082 km^2°*
- **Population:** *3.344.000*
  SOURCE: INSEE
- **Industries principales:** *aéronautique, agriculture, informatique, tourisme, viticulture°*
- **Villes principales:** *Angers, Laval, Le Mans, Nantes, Saint Nazaire*

Personnages célèbres

- **Claire Bretécher,** *dessinatrice de bandes dessinées (1940–)*
- **Léon Bollée,** *inventeur d'automobiles (1870–1913)*
- **Jules Verne,** *écrivain° (1828–1905)*

Le Centre

La région en chiffres

- **Superficie:** *39.152 km^2*
- **Population:** *2.480.000*
- **Industrie principale:** *tourisme*
- **Villes principales:** *Bourges, Chartres, Orléans, Tours, Vierzon*

Personnages célèbres

- **Honoré de Balzac,** *écrivain (1799–1850)*
- **George Sand,** *écrivain (1804–1876)*
- **Gérard Depardieu,** *acteur (1948–)*

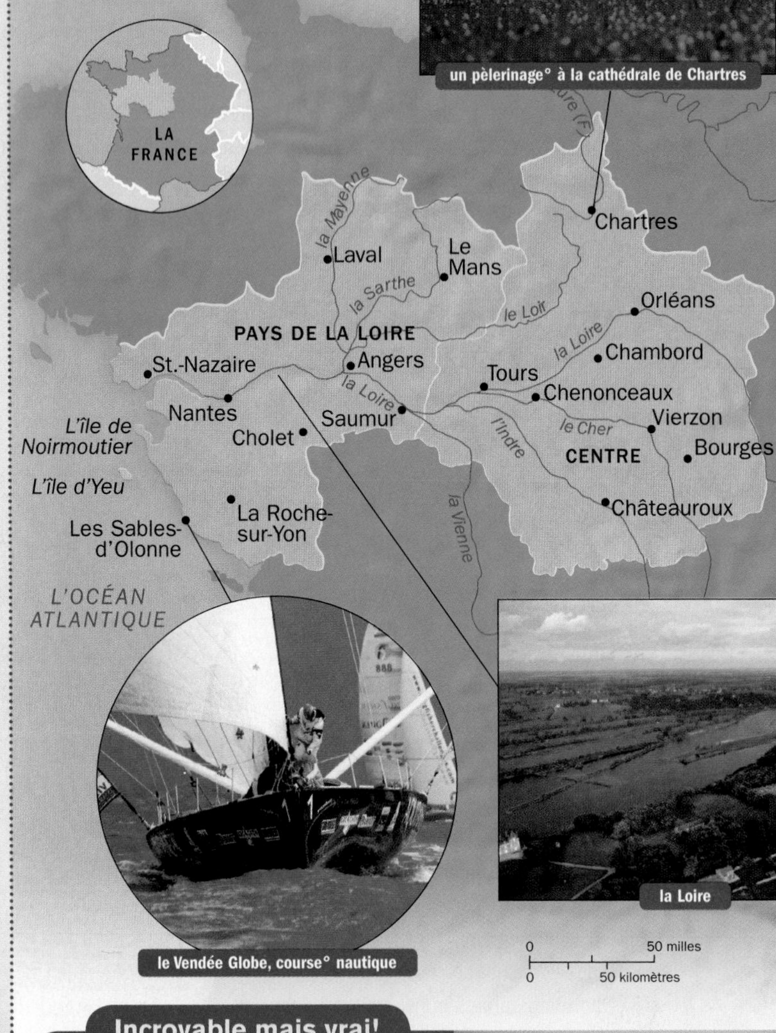

un pèlerinage° à la cathédrale de Chartres

le Vendée Globe, course° nautique

la Loire

Incroyable mais vrai!

Construit° au XVIe (seizième) siècle°, l'architecture du château de Chambord est influencée par Léonard de Vinci. Le château a 440 pièces°, 84 escaliers° et 365 cheminées (une pour chaque° jour de l'année). Le logis° central a deux escaliers en forme de double hélice°. Les escaliers vont dans la même° direction, mais ne se croisent jamais°.

km² (kilomètres carrés) *square kilometers* **viticulture** *wine-growing* **écrivain** *writer* **Construit** *Constructed* **siècle** *century* **pièces** *rooms* **escaliers** *staircases* **chaque** *each* **logis** *living area* **hélice** *helix* **même** *same* **ne se croisent jamais** *never cross* **pèlerinage** *pilgrimage* **course** *race*

OPTIONS

Tours et Chartres Tours and Chartres are lively cities that have thriving industries and are considered historical, academic, and cultural centers. Tours was at one time the capital of France and the residence of kings. Built on the site of a Roman town, it has remnants of medieval architecture such as the timber-framed houses present in **place Plumereau**, which is the pedestrian-zoned, medieval heart of the city.

Chartres was named after the Celtic tribe, the Carnutes. The city was attacked and many of its structures destroyed. However, many efforts were put into its restoration. One of the most magnificent architectural masterpieces is **la cathédrale Notre-Dame de Chartres**. The cathedral marks the high point of gothic and medieval art, featuring fine sculptures, over 170 stained-glass windows, and flying buttresses.

Les monuments

La vallée des rois

La vallée de la Loire, avec ses châteaux, est appelée la vallée des rois°. C'est au XVIe (seizième) siècle° que les Valois° quittent Paris pour habiter dans la région, où ils construisent° de nombreux° châteaux de style Renaissance. François Ier inaugure le siècle des «rois voyageurs»: ceux° qui vont d'un château à l'autre avec leur cour° et toutes leurs possessions. Chenonceau, Chambord et Amboise sont aujourd'hui les châteaux les plus° visités.

Les festivals

Le Printemps de Bourges

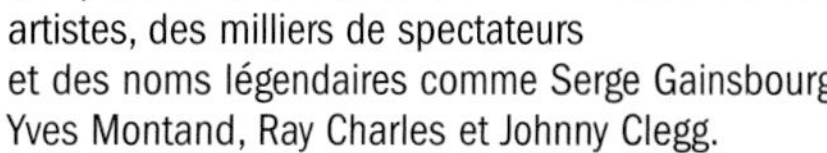

Le Printemps de Bourges est un festival de musique qui a lieu° chaque année, en avril. Pendant° une semaine, tous les styles de musique sont représentés: variété française, musiques du monde°, rock, musique électronique, reggae, hip-hop, etc... Il y a des dizaines° de spectacles, de nombreux artistes, des milliers de spectateurs et des noms légendaires comme Serge Gainsbourg, Yves Montand, Ray Charles et Johnny Clegg.

Les sports

Les 24 heures du Mans

Les 24 heures du Mans, c'est la course° d'endurance automobile la plus célèbre° du monde. Depuis° 1923, de prestigieuses marques° y° participent. C'est sur ce circuit de 13,6 km que Ferrari gagne neuf victoires et que Porsche détient° le record de 16 victoires avec une vitesse moyenne° de 222 km/h sur 5.335 km. Il existe aussi les 24 heures du Mans moto°.

Les destinations

La route des vins

La vallée de la Loire est réputée pour ses vignobles°, en particulier pour ses vins blancs°. Le Sauvignon et le Chardonnay, par exemple, constituent environ° 75% (pour cent) de la production. La vigne est cultivée dans la vallée depuis l'an 380. Aujourd'hui, les vignerons° de la région produisent 400 millions de bouteilles par an. Pour apprécier le vin, il est nécessaire de l'observer°, de le sentir, de le goûter° et de le déguster°. C'est tout un art!

Qu'est-ce que vous avez appris? Répondez aux questions par des phrases complètes.

1. Quel événement peut-on voir aux Sables d'Olonne? *On peut voir le Vendée Globe, une course nautique, aux Sables d'Olonne.*
2. Au seizième siècle, qui influence le style de construction de Chambord? *Léonard de Vinci influence le style de construction de Chambord.*
3. Combien de cheminées y a-t-il à Chambord? *Il y a 365 cheminées à Chambord.*
4. De quel style sont les châteaux de la Loire? *Les châteaux de la Loire sont de style Renaissance.*
5. Pourquoi les Valois sont-ils «les rois voyageurs»? *Ils sont «les rois voyageurs» parce qu'ils vont d'un château à l'autre avec toutes leurs possessions.*
6. Combien de spectateurs vont au Printemps de Bourges chaque année? *Des milliers de spectateurs vont au Printemps de Bourges chaque année.*
7. Qu'est-ce que les 24 heures du Mans? *C'est une course d'endurance automobile.*
8. Quel autre type de course existe-t-il au Mans? *Il existe aussi une course de moto.*
9. Quels vins sont produits dans la vallée de la Loire? *Les vins blancs sont principalement produits dans la vallée de la Loire.*
10. Combien de bouteilles y sont produites chaque année? *400 millions de bouteilles de vin sont produites chaque année dans la vallée de la Loire.*

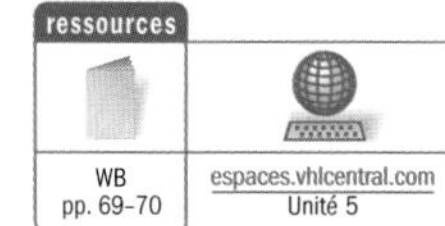

ressources
WB pp. 69–70
espaces.vhlcentral.com Unité 5

SUR INTERNET

Go to **espaces.vhlcentral.com** to find more cultural information related to this **PANORAMA**.

1. Trouvez des informations sur le Vendée Globe. Quel est l'itinéraire de la course? Combien de bateaux (*boats*) y participent chaque année?
2. Qui étaient (*were*) les artistes invités au dernier Printemps de Bourges? En connaissez-vous quelques-uns? (*Do you know some of them?*)

rois *kings* **siècle** *century* **les Valois** *name of a royal dynasty* **construisent** *build* **de nombreux** *numerous* **ceux** *those* **cour** *court* **les plus** *the most* **a lieu** *takes place* **Pendant** *For* **monde** *world* **dizaines** *dozens* **course** *race* **célèbre** *famous* **Depuis** *Since* **marques** *brands* **y** *there* **détient** *holds* **vitesse moyenne** *average speed* **moto** *motorcycle* **vignobles** *vineyards* **vins blancs** *white wines* **environ** *around* **vignerons** *wine-growers* **l'observer** *observe it* **le goûter** *taste it* **le déguster** *savor it*

La vallée des rois François Ier (1515–1547) and his court resided and traveled between his châteaux in Amboise, Blois, and Chambord. The castles were first built as defense structures but later evolved into decorative palaces. With less of a need for defense, elements like moats and towers remained as symbols of rank and ancestry. Other magnificent châteaux of the area are Azay-le-Rideau, Chenonceau, Villandry, Saumur, Ussé, Chaumont, Beauregard, and Cour-Cheverny.

Le Printemps de Bourges This music festival has been taking place every spring since its creation in 1977. Festival goers can listen to the music of the latest up-and-coming talent as well as world-renowned artists. Music shows can be found close to downtown. Musicians also play in restaurants, bars, and at outdoor and indoor stages. Some shows are free to the public.

Les 24 heures du Mans The biggest names in sports car racing come to test their speed, endurance, and reliability on the 13.6 km (8.5 mile) track. The driver of the car to travel the greatest distance within the 24-hour period is the champion. Close to 200,000 fans and 2,000 journalists come to Le Mans in June for one of the best-known automobile races in the world.

La route des vins The Loire River flows through the heart of the Loire Valley, connecting many of the major wine producing towns. Nantes, home of the Muscadet grape, produces dry white wines. There is a concentration of vineyards closer to the center of the Loire Valley in Saumur, Vouvray, Azay-le-Rideau, Chinon, Bourgueil, among others. Classic white wines are found further east in Pouilly-sur-Loire. The Loire Valley is known for all sorts of white wines, but also produces some red and rosé wines.

OPTIONS

Cultural Activity Considering the historical, architectural, and cultural richness of the regions **Pays de la Loire** and **Centre**, it's no wonder they are part of the World Heritage List of UNESCO (United Nations Education, Scientific, and Cultural Organization). Have students explore UNESCO's web site to find out more. Ask students to search the World Heritage List for other places from these regions.

Small Groups During the reign of François Ier, the Renaissance period was at its height. There was an increasing interest in arts and humanism, which was evident in the court life at the châteaux. Have small groups research various aspects of court life, such as the food they ate, activities they participated in, and what kinds of music, literature, and art were preferred. Have each group make a short presentation on their findings.

Section Goals

In this section, students will:
- learn to skim a text
- read a weekly city guide about Montréal

Stratégie Tell students that they can often predict the content of an unfamiliar document in French by skimming it and looking for recognizable format elements.

Examinez le texte Have students skim the text at the top of this calendar of events in and around Montréal. Point out the cognates **arts**, **culture**, **festival**, **musique classique**, and **manifestations culturelles**. Ask them to predict what type of document it is (city guide/calendar of events in a newspaper/weekly). Then ask students to scan the rest of the calendar of events.

Catégories Before students do this activity, ask them to think of three words or expressions that fit each of the three given categories (**les loisirs culturels, les activités sportives, les activités de plein air**) in English.

Trouvez Go over answers with the whole class by pointing out where in the text each piece of information is found. Expand the activity by having students write additional entries for the calendar of events that include information for the unchecked items (**où manger cette semaine, le temps qu'il va faire cette semaine, des prix d'entrée, des adresses**).

Language Note Point out that French-speaking Canadians say **la fin de semaine** instead of **le week-end**.

Lecture

Avant la lecture

STRATÉGIE

Skimming

Skimming involves quickly reading through a document to absorb its general meaning. This allows you to understand the main ideas without having to read word-for-word. When you skim a text, you might want to look at its title and subtitles. You might also want to read the first sentence of each paragraph.

Examinez le texte

Regardez rapidement le texte. Quel est le titre (*title*) du texte? En combien de parties le texte est-il divisé? Quels sont les titres des parties? Maintenant, regardez les photos. Quel est le sujet de l'article?

Catégories

Dans le texte, trouvez trois mots ou expressions qui représentent chaque catégorie. Answers will vary. Suggested answers below.

les loisirs culturels
musique classique | cinéma africain | musée des Beaux-Arts

les activités sportives
golf | ski | tennis

les activités de plein air (*outdoor*)
camping | randonnées | équitation

Trouvez

Regardez le document. Indiquez si vous trouvez les informations suivantes.

1. ____ où manger cette semaine
2. ____ le temps qu'il va faire cette semaine
3. _✓_ où aller à la pêche
4. ____ des prix d'entrée (*entrance*)
5. _✓_ des numéros de téléphone
6. _✓_ des sports
7. _✓_ des spectacles
8. ____ des adresses

CETTE SEMAINE À MONTRÉAL ET DANS LA RÉGION

ARTS ET CULTURE

Festivals et autres manifestations culturelles à explorer:

- Festival de musique classique, samedi de 16h00 à 22h00, à la Salle de concerts Richelieu, à Montréal
- Festival du cinéma africain, dans tous les cinémas de Montréal
- Journée de la bande dessinée, samedi toute la journée, à la Librairie Rochefort, à Montréal
- Festival de reggae, dimanche tout l'après-midi, à l'Espace Lemay, à Montréal

Spectacle à voir°:

- *La Cantatrice chauve*, pièce° d'Eugène Ionesco, samedi et dimanche à 20h00, au Théâtre du Chat Bleu, à Montréal

À ne pas oublier°:

- Le musée des Beaux-Arts de Montréal, avec sa collection de plus de° 30.000 objets d'art du monde entier°

OPTIONS

TPR Write activities from the calendar of events (**aller à la pêche, jouer au baseball, faire de l'équitation,** etc.) on slips of paper. Divide the class into two teams. Have a member of one team draw a paper. That team member mimes the chosen activity. The other team guesses what it is. Give points for correct answers. The team with the most points wins.

Small Groups Have groups of three students work together to read aloud each section of the calendar of events (**Arts et culture, Sports et jeux, Exploration**). Each student will then write two questions about the section that he or she read. After they have finished, ask groups to exchange their questions with another group. Have groups read the questions to the class and ask volunteers to answer them.

SPORTS ET JEUX

- L'Académie de golf de Montréal organise un grand tournoi° le mois prochain. Pour plus d'informations, contactez le (514) 846-1225.
- Tous les dimanches, le Club d'échecs de Montréal organise des tournois d'échecs en plein air° dans le parc Champellier. Pour plus d'informations, appelez le (514) 846-1085.
- Skiez! Passez la fin de semaine dans les Laurentides° ou dans les Cantons-de-l'Est!
- Et pour la famille sportive: essayez le parc Lafontaine, un centre d'amusement pour tous qui offre: volley-ball, tennis, football et baseball.

PASSIONNÉ° DE PÊCHE? N'OUBLIEZ PAS LES NOMBREUX LACS° OÙ LA PÊCHE EST AUTORISÉE.

EXPLORATION

Redécouvrez la nature grâce à° ces activités à ne pas manquer°:

Visite du parc national de la Jacques-Cartier°
- Camping
- Promenades et randonnées
- Observation de la faune et de la flore

Région des Laurentides et Gaspésie°
- Équitation°
- Randonnées à cheval de 2 à 5 jours en camping

voir *see* **pièce (de théâtre)** *play* **À ne pas oublier** *Not to be forgotten* **plus de** *more than* **du monde entier** *from around the world* **tournoi** *tournament* **en plein air** *outdoor* **Laurentides** *region of eastern Quebec* **Passionné** *Enthusiast* **lacs** *lakes* **grâce à** *thanks to* **à ne pas manquer** *not to be missed* **la Jacques-Cartier** *the Jacques-Cartier river in Quebec* **Gaspésie** *peninsula of Quebec* **Équitation** *Horseback riding*

Après la lecture

Répondez Répondez aux questions avec des phrases complètes.

1. Citez deux activités sportives qu'on peut pratiquer à l'extérieur.
   Answers will vary.
2. À quel jeu est-ce qu'on joue dans le parc Champellier?
   On joue aux échecs dans le parc Champellier.
3. Où va peut-être aller un passionné de lecture et de dessin?
   Un passionné de lecture et de dessin va peut-être aller à la Journée de la bande dessinée.
4. Où pratique-t-on des sports d'équipe?
   On pratique des sports d'équipe au parc Lafontaine.
5. Où y a-t-il de la neige au Québec en cette saison?
   Il y a de la neige dans les Laurentides et dans les Cantons-de-l'Est.
6. Si on aime beaucoup la musique, où peut-on aller?
   On peut aller au Festival de musique classique ou au Festival de reggae.

Suggestions **Lucille est étudiante au Québec. Ce week-end, elle invite sa famille à explorer la région. Listez une activité à faire ou un lieu à visiter que chaque membre de sa famille va aimer.**

MODÈLE

La sœur cadette de Lucille adore le ski.
Elle va aimer les Laurentides et les Cantons-de-l'Est.

1. La mère de Lucille est artiste.
   Elle va aimer le musée des Beaux-Arts de Montréal.
2. Le frère de Lucille joue au volley-ball à l'université.
   Il va aimer le parc Lafontaine.
3. La sœur aînée de Lucille a envie de voir un film sénégalais.
   Elle va aimer le Festival du cinéma africain.
4. Le grand-père de Lucille joue souvent aux échecs.
   Il va aimer les tournois d'échecs en plein air dans le parc Champellier.
5. La grand-mère de Lucille est fan de théâtre.
   Elle va aimer *La Cantatrice chauve* au Théâtre du Chat Bleu.
6. Le père de Lucille adore la nature et les animaux, mais il n'est pas très sportif.
   Answers will vary. Possible answer: Il va aimer les promenades dans le parc national de la Jacques-Cartier.

Une invitation **Vous allez passer le week-end au Québec. Qu'est-ce que vous allez faire? Par groupes de quatre, discutez des activités qui vous intéressent (*that interest you*) et essayez de trouver trois ou quatre activités que vous avez en commun. Attention! Il va peut-être pleuvoir ce week-end, alors ne choisissez pas (*don't choose*) uniquement des activités de plein air!**

Répondez Present these as items 7–10. **7. Où peut-on voir des films africains? (On peut voir des films africains dans tous les cinémas de Montréal.) 8. Combien d'objets d'art y a-t-il au musée des Beaux-Arts de Montréal? (Il y a plus de 30.000 objets d'art.) 9. Quels sports pratique-t-on au parc Lafontaine? (On propose le volley-ball, le tennis, le football et le baseball.) 10. Si on aime beaucoup les animaux et les fleurs, où peut-on aller? (On peut aller au parc national de la Jacques-Cartier.)**

Suggestion Ask students to write about three more members of Lucille's family. They should model their sentences after the ones in the activity, saying what each person enjoys doing. Then have students read their sentences to a partner. The partner will come up with a suggested activity or place to visit that will suit each person.

Une invitation Give students a couple of minutes to review the **Vocabulaire** on page 146, **Expressions utiles** on page 151, and Expressions with **faire** on page 154. Add activities, such as **faire du surf des neiges, prendre des photos, faire des arts martiaux**, and **faire du skateboard**.

Expansion Have one or two groups act out their conversation from **Une invitation** for the rest of the class. Before the groups begin, have the listeners in the class write a list of ten activities that they think will be mentioned in each of the presentations. As students listen, have them check off on their list the activities they hear.

OPTIONS

Extra Practice Give students true or false statements about the **Lecture.** Example: **On peut faire des randonnées à cheval au parc national de la Jacques-Cartier. (Faux. On peut faire des randonnées à cheval en Région des Laurentides et Gaspésie.)**

Extra Practice Ask students to go through the selection and locate all of the activities that require usage of **faire.** (Encourage them to use their dictionaries, if necessary.) Then have them write sentences saying whether or not they like doing those activities. Example: **Activités avec faire: faire du vélo, faire de l'équitation,** etc. **J'aime faire du vélo. Je n'aime pas faire de l'équitation.**

Section Goals

In this section, students will:

- learn to listen for key words
- listen to a short paragraph and note the key words
- answer questions based on the content of a recorded weather forecast

Instructional Resources
Textbook MP3s
IRCD-ROM: IRM (Textbook Audioscript)
espaces.vhlcentral.com: downloads, reference tools

Stratégie
Script Qu'est-ce que je fais quand j'ai du temps libre? Eh bien, l'hiver, j'aime faire du ski. Au printemps et à l'automne, quand il fait bon, je fais du vélo et du cheval. Et l'été, je fais de la planche à voile.

Préparation Have students look at the map and describe what they see. Guide them to think about expressions that are commonly mentioned during a weather forecast. Ask them to brainstorm and write a list of as much weather-related vocabulary as they can in five minutes.

À vous d'écouter
Script Mesdames, Mesdemoiselles, Messieurs, bonjour et bienvenue sur Radio Satellite. Il est 10h00 et voici la météo.
Aujourd'hui, sur la capitale, des nuages toute la journée. Eh oui, il fait frais à Paris ce matin, avec une température maximale de huit degrés. À Lille, on va avoir un temps épouvantable. Il fait froid avec six degrés seulement et il va pleuvoir tout l'après-midi et toute la soirée. À Strasbourg, il fait cinq degrés et il neige encore. Il fait assez frais à Brest, avec dix degrés et beaucoup de nuages. À Lyon, il fait neuf degrés aussi avec un temps très orageux, alors ne sortez pas sans votre parapluie! À Bordeaux, il fait bon, onze degrés et quelques nuages. Toulouse va avoir du soleil toute la journée et il va faire douze degrés. À Marseille, la température est de douze degrés maintenant, mais il va pleuvoir dans l'après-midi. Sur la Côte d'Azur, il fait treize degrés à Nice, et il y a beaucoup de vent. Bonne journée!

À l'écoute

STRATÉGIE

Listening for key words

By listening for key words (**mots-clés**) or phrases, you can identify the subject and main ideas of what you hear, as well as some of the details.

To practice this strategy, you will listen to a short paragraph. Jot down the key words that help you identify the subject of the paragraph and its main ideas.

Préparation

Regardez l'image. Où trouve-t-on ce type d'image? Manque-t-il des éléments (*Is anything missing*) sur cette carte? Faites une liste de mots-clés qui vont vous aider à trouver ces informations quand vous allez écouter la météo (*the weather*).

À vous d'écouter

Écoutez la météo. Puis, écoutez une deuxième fois et complétez le tableau. Notez la température et écrivez un **X** pour indiquer le temps qu'il fait dans chaque ville.

Ville	(soleil)	(soleil et nuages)	(nuages)	(pluie)	(vent)	(neige)	Température
Paris			X				8°C
Lille				X			6°C
Strasbourg						X	5°C
Brest			X				10°C
Lyon				X			9°C
Bordeaux		X					11°C
Toulouse	X						12°C
Marseille				X			12°C
Nice					X		13°C

ressources

Text MP3s Unité 5	VM pp. 279–280	V CD-ROM Unité 5	espaces.vhlcentral.com Unité 5

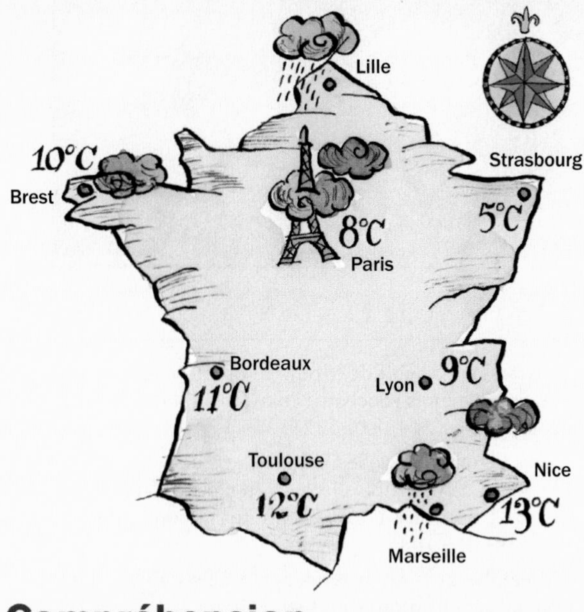

Compréhension

Probable ou improbable? Indiquez si les phrases suivantes sont probables ou improbables, d'après la météo d'aujourd'hui.

MODÈLE

	Probable	Improbable
Ève va nager à Strasbourg.		✓
1. Lucie fait du vélo à Lille.		✓
2. Il fait un temps épouvantable à Toulouse.		✓
3. Émilien joue aux cartes à la maison à Lyon.	✓	
4. Il va neiger à Marseille.		✓
5. Jérome et Yves jouent au golf à Bordeaux.	✓	
6. À Lyon, on a besoin d'un imperméable.	✓	
7. Il fait froid à Strasbourg.	✓	
8. Nous allons nager à Nice cet après-midi.		✓

Quelle ville choisir? Imaginez qu'aujourd'hui vous êtes en France. Décidez dans quelle ville vous avez envie de passer la journée. Pourquoi? Décrivez le temps qu'il fait et citez des activités que vous allez peut-être faire.

MODÈLE

J'ai envie d'aller à Strasbourg parce que j'aime l'hiver et la neige. Aujourd'hui, il fait froid et il neige. Je vais faire une promenade en ville et après, je vais boire un chocolat chaud au café.

Écriture

STRATÉGIE

Using a dictionary

A common mistake made by beginning language learners is to embrace the dictionary as the ultimate resource for reading, writing, and speaking. While it is true that the dictionary is a useful tool that can provide valuable information about vocabulary, using the dictionary correctly requires that you understand the elements of each entry.

If you glance at a French-English dictionary, you will notice that its format is similar to that of an English dictionary. The word is listed first, usually followed by its pronunciation. Then come the definitions, organized by parts of speech. Sometimes, the most frequently used meanings are listed first.

To find the best word for your needs, you should refer to the abbreviations and the explanatory notes that appear next to the entries. For example, imagine that you are writing about your pastimes. You want to write *I want to buy a new racket for my match tomorrow*, but you don't know the French word for *racket*.

In the dictionary, you might find an entry like this one:

racket n 1. boucan; 2. raquette (sport)

The abbreviation key at the front of the dictionary says that *n* corresponds to **nom** (*noun*). Then, the first word you see is **boucan**. The definition of **boucan** is *noise* or *racket*, so **boucan** is probably not the word you want. The second word is **raquette**, followed by the word *sport*, which indicates that it is related to **sports**. This detail indicates that the word **raquette** is the best choice for your needs.

Watch the FLASH CULTURE segment on the ESPACES video for cultural footage related to this unit's theme.

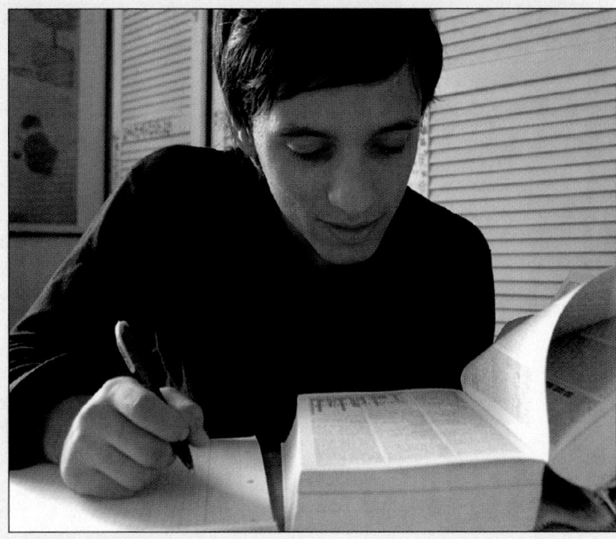

Thème

Écrire une brochure

Choisissez un sujet:

1. Vous travaillez à la Chambre de Commerce de votre région pour l'été. Des hommes et des femmes d'affaires québécois vont visiter votre région cette année, mais ils n'ont pas encore décidé (*have not yet decided*) quand. La Chambre de Commerce vous demande de créer (*asks you to create*) une petite brochure sur le temps qu'il fait dans votre région aux différentes saisons de l'année. Dites quelle saison, à votre avis (*in your opinion*), est idéale pour visiter votre région et expliquez pourquoi.
2. Vous avez une réunion familiale pour décider où aller en vacances cette année, mais chaque membre de la famille suggère un endroit différent. Choisissez un lieu de vacances où vous avez envie d'aller et créez une brochure pour montrer à votre famille pourquoi vous devriez (*should*) tous y aller (*go there*). Décrivez la météo de l'endroit et indiquez les différentes activités culturelles et sportives qu'on peut y faire.
3. Vous passez un semestre/trimestre dans le pays francophone de votre choix (*of your choice*). Deux étudiants de votre cours de français ont aussi envie de visiter ce pays. Créez une petite brochure pour partager vos impressions du pays. Présentez le pays, donnez des informations météorologiques et décrivez vos activités préférées.

Section Goals

In this section, students will:

- learn to use a French-English dictionary
- write a brochure including weather-related information and seasonal activities
- view authentic cultural footage of people engaged in sports and leisure activities

Instructional Resources
WB/VM: Video Manual, pp. 279–280
WB/VM/LM Answer Key
IRCD-ROM: IRM (Videoscript)
Video CD-ROM
Video on DVD
espaces.vhlcentral.com: activities, downloads, reference tools

Stratégie Explain to students that when they look up a translation of an English word in a French-English dictionary, they will frequently find more than one translation. They must decide which one best fits the context. Discuss the meanings of *racket* that might be found in an entry in a French-English dictionary and the usefulness of the explanatory notes and abbreviations found in dictionary entries. Tell them that a good way of checking the meaning of a French translation of an English word is to look up the French word and see how it is translated in English.

Thème Discuss the three topics students may wish to write about. You may wish to introduce terms like **comité, guide d'orientation,** and **chambre de commerce**. Remind students of some of the common graphic features used in brochures: headings, times and places, brief descriptions of events, and prices.

Flash culture Tell students that they will learn more about sports and leisure activities by watching a variety of real-life images narrated by Csilla. Show the video, and then have students close their eyes and describe from memory what they saw. Write their descriptions on the board. You can also use the activities in the video manual in class to reinforce this **Flash culture** or assign them as homework.

EVALUATION

Criteria	Scale
Appropriate details	1 2 3 4 5
Organization	1 2 3 4 5
Use of vocabulary	1 2 3 4 5
Accuracy	1 2 3 4 5

Scoring	
Excellent	18–20 points
Good	14–17 points
Satisfactory	10–13 points
Unsatisfactory	< 10 points

Instructional Resources
Textbook MP3s
IRCD-ROM: IRM (Textbook Audioscript)
espaces.vhlcentral.com: downloads, reference tools

Activités sportives et loisirs

aider	*to help*
aller à la pêche	*to go fishing*
bricoler	*to tinker; to do odd jobs*
chanter	*to sing*
désirer	*to want*
gagner	*to win*
indiquer	*to indicate*
jouer (à/de)	*to play*
marcher	*to walk (person); to work (thing)*
pratiquer	*to practice*
skier	*to ski*
une bande dessinée (B.D.)	*comic strip*
le baseball	*baseball*
le basket(-ball)	*basketball*
les cartes (*f.*)	*cards*
le cinéma	*movies*
les échecs (*m.*)	*chess*
une équipe	*team*
le foot(ball)	*soccer*
le football américain	*football*
le golf	*golf*
un jeu	*game*
un joueur/une joueuse	*player*
un loisir	*leisure activity*
un match	*game*
un passe-temps	*pastime, hobby*
un spectacle	*show*
le sport	*sport*
un stade	*stadium*
le temps libre	*free time*
le tennis	*tennis*
le volley(-ball)	*volleyball*

Verbes irréguliers en -ir

courir	*to run*
dormir	*to sleep*
partir	*to leave*
sentir	*to feel; to smell; to sense*
servir	*to serve*
sortir	*to go out, to leave*

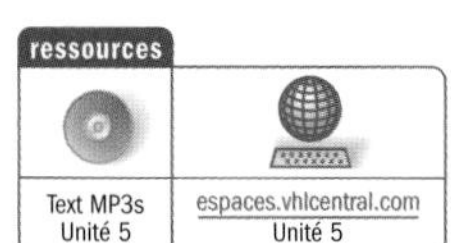

Le temps qu'il fait

Il fait 18 degrés.	*It is 18 degrees.*
Il fait beau.	*The weather is nice.*
Il fait bon.	*The weather is good/warm.*
Il fait chaud.	*It is hot (out).*
Il fait (du) soleil.	*It is sunny.*
Il fait du vent.	*It is windy.*
Il fait frais.	*It is cool.*
Il fait froid.	*It is cold.*
Il fait mauvais.	*The weather is bad.*
Il fait un temps épouvantable.	*The weather is dreadful.*
Il neige. (neiger)	*It is snowing. (to snow)*
Il pleut. (pleuvoir)	*It is raining. (to rain)*
Le temps est nuageux.	*It is cloudy.*
Le temps est orageux.	*It is stormy.*
Quel temps fait-il?	*What is the weather like?*
Quelle température fait-il?	*What is the temperature?*
un imperméable	*rain jacket*
un parapluie	*umbrella*

Verbes

acheter	*to buy*
amener	*to bring (someone)*
célébrer	*to celebrate*
considérer	*to consider*
emmener	*to take (someone)*
employer	*to use*
envoyer	*to send*
espérer	*to hope*
essayer (de + *inf.*)	*to try (to)*
nettoyer	*to clean*
payer	*to pay*
posséder	*to possess, to own*
préférer	*to prefer*
protéger	*to protect*
répéter	*to repeat; to rehearse*

La fréquence

une/deux fois	*one/two time(s)*
par jour, semaine, mois, an, etc.	*per day, week, month, year, etc.*
déjà	*already*
encore	*again; still*
jamais	*never*
longtemps	*long time*
maintenant	*now*
parfois	*sometimes*
rarement	*rarely*
souvent	*often*

Les saisons, les mois, les dates

une saison	*season*
l'automne (*m.*)/ à l'automne	*fall/in the fall*
l'été (*m.*)/en été	*summer/in the summer*
l'hiver (*m.*)/en hiver	*winter/in the winter*
le printemps (*m.*)/ au printemps	*spring/in the spring*
Quelle est la date?	*What's the date?*
C'est le 1er (premier) octobre.	*It's the first of October.*
C'est quand votre/ton anniversaire?	*When is your birthday?*
C'est le 2 mai.	*It's the second of May.*
C'est quand l'anniversaire de Paul?	*When is Paul's birthday?*
C'est le 15 mars.	*It's March 15th.*
un anniversaire	*birthday*
janvier	*January*
février	*February*
mars	*March*
avril	*April*
mai	*May*
juin	*June*
juillet	*July*
août	*August*
septembre	*September*
octobre	*October*
novembre	*November*
décembre	*December*

Expressions utiles	See pp. 151 and 165.
Expressions with *faire*	See p. 154.
faire	See p. 154.
Il faut...	See p. 155.
Numbers 101 and higher	See p. 168.

Les fêtes

UNITÉ

6

Leçon 11

Leçon 12

Pour commencer

- Qui est la propriétaire sur la photo?
- Qu'est-ce qu'Amina et Valérie vont faire?
- Qu'est-ce qu'elles vont manger, du jambon ou un dessert?
- De quelle couleur est le tee-shirt d'Amina, orange ou violet?

Savoir-faire

Unit Goals

Leçon 11

In this lesson, students will learn:
- terms for parties and celebrations
- terms for the stages of life
- more differences between open and closed vowels
- about **carnaval** and France's Bastille Day
- demonstrative adjectives
- the **passé composé** with **avoir**
- some irregular past participles
- to write an article on a French holiday

Leçon 12

In this lesson, students will learn:
- terms for clothing, shopping, and colors
- more about open and closed vowels
- about the fashion industry in France
- indirect object pronouns
- more uses of disjunctive pronouns
- regular and irregular **-re** verbs
- about singer Édith Piaf and painter Henri de Toulouse-Lautrec

Savoir-faire

In this section, students will learn:
- cultural and historical information about the French regions of **Aquitaine**, **Midi-Pyrénées**, and **Languedoc-Roussillon**
- to recognize word families
- to listen for linguistic cues in oral communication
- how to report an interview
- more about festivals and holiday celebrations through specially shot video footage

Pour commencer

- **Valérie est la propriétaire.**
- **Elles vont faire la fête.**
- **Elles vont manger un dessert.**
- **Son tee-shirt est orange.**

RESOURCES

Workbook/Video Manual: WB Activities, pp. 71–84
Laboratory Manual: Lab Activities, pp. 41–48
Workbook/Video Manual: Video Activities, pp. 231–234; pp. 281–282
WB/VM/LM Answer Key
Instructor's Resource CD-ROM [IRCD-ROM]: Instructor's Resource Manual [IRM] (Textbook Audioscript; Lab Audioscript; Videoscript; **Roman-photo** Translations; **Vocabulaire supplémentaire**; **Feuilles d'activités**; Info Gap Activities; **Essayez!** and **Mise en pratique** answers); Transparencies #31, #32, #33; Testing Program, pp. 41–48; pp. 129–136; Test Files; Testing Program MP3s; Test Generator
Lab MP3s
Textbook MP3s
Video CD-ROM
Video on DVD
espaces.vhlcentral.com

Section Goals

In this section, students will learn and practice vocabulary related to:

- parties and celebrations
- stages of life and interpersonal relationships

Instructional Resources
*IRCD-ROM: Transparency #31; IRM (**Vocabulaire supplémentaire; Mise en pratique** answers; Textbook Audioscript; Lab Audioscript; Info Gap Activities)*
Textbook MP3s
WB/VM: Workbook, pp. 71–72
Lab Manual, p. 41
Lab MP3s
WB/VM/LM Answer Key
espaces.vhlcentral.com: activities, downloads, reference tools

Suggestions

- Have students look over the new vocabulary and identify the cognates. Examples: **organiser, fiancé(e), mariage,** and **divorce.**
- Describe what people are doing in the drawing using **Transparency #31.** Examples: **Ils font la fête. Ils boivent du vin.** Follow up with simple questions based on your narrative.
- Point out the banner and the cake in the illustration. Ask students what **Bon anniversaire** and **Joyeux anniversaire** mean. (*Happy birthday*)
- Point out the similarities and differences between these related words: **aimer, ami(e), l'amitié, un amour, amoureux,** and **amoureuse.**
- Additional vocabulary for this lesson can be found in the **Vocabulaire supplémentaire** in the IRM on the IRCD-ROM.

Leçon 11

You will learn how to...

- talk about celebrations
- talk about the stages of life

Surprise!

Vocabulaire

faire la fête	*to party*
faire une surprise (à quelqu'un)	*to surprise (someone)*
fêter	*to celebrate*
organiser une fête	*to organize a party*
une fête	*party; celebration*
un jour férié	*holiday*
une bière	*beer*
le vin	*wine*
une amitié	*friendship*
un amour	*love*
le bonheur	*happiness*
un(e) fiancé(e)	*fiancé*
des jeunes mariés (*m.*)	*newlyweds*
un rendez-vous	*date; appointment*
l'adolescence (*f.*)	*adolescence*
l'âge adulte (*m.*)	*adulthood*
un divorce	*divorce*
l'enfance (*f.*)	*childhood*
une étape	*stage*
l'état civil (*m.*)	*marital status*
la jeunesse	*youth*
un mariage	*marriage; wedding*
la mort	*death*
la naissance	*birth*
la vie	*life*
la vieillesse	*old age*
prendre sa retraite	*to retire*
tomber amoureux/amoureuse	*to fall in love*
ensemble	*together*

ressources

WB pp. 71–72	LM p. 41	Text MP3s Leçon 11	Lab MP3s Leçon 11	espaces.vhlcentral.com Leçon 11

OPTIONS

Les fêtes Point out that, in addition to celebrating birthdays, many people in French-speaking cultures celebrate **la fête**, or saint's day, which is based upon their given name. Bring in a French calendar that has the names of **fêtes** and have students find their own saint's day. You may need to help students find the name that most closely resembles their own.

Extra Practice Have students write three fill-in-the-blank sentences based on the drawing above, using the new vocabulary. Then have students exchange papers with a classmate and complete the sentences. Remind them to verify their answers.

BON ANNIVERSAIRE, MARC!

la surprise

le couple

le cadeau

Mise en pratique

1 **Écoutez** Écoutez la conversation entre Anne et Nathalie. Indiquez si les affirmations sont **vraies** ou **fausses.**

	Vrai	Faux
1. Jean-Marc va prendre sa retraite dans six mois.	☐	☑
2. Nathalie a l'idée d'organiser une fête pour Jean-Marc.	☐	☑
3. Anne et Nathalie essaient de trouver un cadeau original.	☑	☐
4. Anne va acheter un gâteau.	☑	☐
5. Nathalie va apporter de la glace.	☐	☑
6. La fête est une surprise.	☑	☐
7. Nathalie va envoyer les invitations par e-mail.	☑	☐
8. La fête va avoir lieu (*take place*) dans le bureau d'Anne.	☐	☑
9. Elles ont besoin de beaucoup de décorations.	☐	☑
10. Tout le monde va donner des idées pour le cadeau.	☑	☐

2 **Chassez l'intrus** Indiquez le mot ou l'expression qui n'appartient pas (*doesn't belong*) à la liste.

1. l'amour, tomber amoureux, un fiancé, (un divorce)
2. un mariage, un couple, (un jour férié), un fiancé
3. un biscuit, (une bière), un dessert, un gâteau
4. (une glace), une bière, le champagne, le vin
5. (la vieillesse), la naissance, l'enfance, la jeunesse
6. faire la fête, un hôte, des invités, (une étape)
7. fêter, un cadeau, (la vie), une surprise
8. (l'état civil), la naissance, la mort, l'adolescence

3 **Associez** Faites correspondre les mots et expressions de la colonne de gauche avec les définitions de la colonne de droite. Notez que tous les éléments ne sont pas utilisés. Ensuite (*Then*), avec un(e) partenaire, donnez votre propre définition de quatre expressions de la première colonne. Votre partenaire doit deviner (*must guess*) de quoi vous parlez.

1. __b__ la naissance
2. ____ l'enfance
3. __c__ l'adolescence
4. ____ l'âge adulte
5. __e__ tomber amoureux
6. __a__ un jour férié
7. __g__ le mariage
8. __f__ le divorce
9. __h__ prendre sa retraite
10. __d__ la mort

a. C'est une date importante, comme le 4 juillet aux États-Unis.
b. C'est la première étape de la vie.
c. C'est l'étape de la vie pendant laquelle (*during which*) on va au lycée.
d. C'est un événement très triste.
e. C'est faire une rencontre romantique comme dans un conte de fées (*fairy tale*).
f. C'est le futur probable d'un couple qui se dispute (*fights*) tout le temps.
g. C'est un jour de bonheur et de célébration de l'amour.
h. C'est quand une personne décide de ne plus travailler.

1 Tapescript ANNE: Nathalie, je vais organiser une fête pour Jean-Marc. Il va prendre sa retraite dans un mois. Ça va être une surprise. Je vais acheter un gâteau.
NATHALIE: Oh, et moi, qu'est-ce que je fais pour aider, Anne? J'apporte des biscuits?
A: Oui, c'est une bonne idée. Il faut aussi trouver un cadeau original.
N: D'accord, mais je vais avoir besoin d'un peu de temps pour y penser.
A: Qu'est-ce qu'on fait pour les invités?
N: Pour faire une vraie surprise à Jean-Marc, il faut être discrètes. Je propose d'envoyer un e-mail à tout le monde. En plus, comme ça, c'est rapide.
A: Et qu'est-ce qu'on fait pour la décoration?
N: Pourquoi ne pas fêter la retraite chez moi? Ma maison est très belle, on n'a pas besoin de beaucoup de décoration.
A: Oui, pourquoi pas! Maintenant il ne reste plus qu'à trouver un cadeau. Pourquoi est-ce qu'on ne demande pas aux autres de donner des idées par e-mail?
N: Oui et quel beau cadeau pour Jean-Marc si tout le monde participe et donne un peu d'argent!
(On Textbook MP3s)

1 Suggestion Play the conversation again, stopping at the end of each sentence that contains the answer to one of these items. Have students verify true statements and correct the false ones.

2 Expansions
- For additional practice, give students these items. **9. la vieillesse, la jeunesse, la fête, l'âge adulte (la fête) 10. le bonheur, une fête, un rendez-vous, une surprise (le bonheur) 11. l'amour, le bonheur, l'amitié, la retraite (la retraite)**
- Have students create one or two additional items using at least three of the new vocabulary words in each one. Collect their papers and write some of their items on the board.

3 Suggestion Have volunteers share their definitions with the class.

OPTIONS

Game Write vocabulary words related to celebrations on index cards. On another set of cards, draw or paste pictures to match each term. Tape them face down on the board in random order. Divide the class into two teams. Then play a game of Concentration, matching words with pictures. When a player has a match, that team collects those cards. When all the cards have been matched, the team with the most cards wins.

Extra Practice Say vocabulary words aloud and have students write or say opposite terms. Examples: **la jeunesse (la vieillesse), le divorce (le mariage), la naissance (la mort), travailler (prendre sa retraite), séparé (ensemble),** and **enfant (adulte).**

4 Suggestions
- Go over the answers to the activity with the class before students write their own sentences.
- Ask volunteers to write their sentences on the board and have the class make corrections as needed.

5 Suggestion Tell students that they should plan the party first by answering the questions. Then they should use those answers to write the conversation discussing the details of the party.

6 Suggestion Have two volunteers read the **modèle** aloud. Then divide the class into pairs and distribute the Info Gap Handouts in the IRM on the IRCD-ROM for this activity. Give students ten minutes to complete the activity.

Communication

communication NATIONAL STANDARDS

4 Le mot juste Remplissez les espaces avec le mot illustré. Faites les accords nécessaires. Ensuite (*Then*), avec un(e) partenaire, créez (*create*) une phrase pour laquelle (*for which*) vous illustrez trois mots d'**ESPACE CONTEXTES**. Échangez votre phrase avec celle d'un autre groupe et résolvez le rébus.

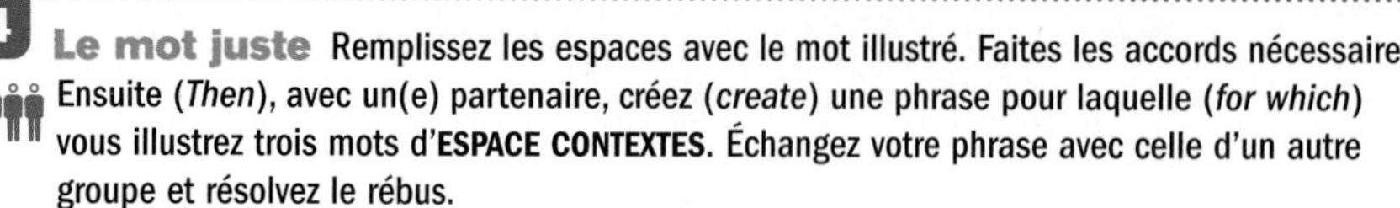

1. Caroline est une amie d' _enfance_ . Je vais lui faire _une surprise_  samedi. C'est son anniversaire.
2. Marc et Sophie sont inséparables. Ils sont toujours _ensemble_ . C'est le bonheur et le grand _amour_.
3. Le _vin_  rouge va bien avec les viandes rouges alors que le _champagne_  va mieux avec les _desserts_.
4. Les _(jeunes) mariés_  ont beaucoup de _cadeaux_ .
5. La _naissance_ de ma sœur est un grand _bonheur_  pour mes parents.

5 C'est la fête! Vous avez terminé (*have finished*) les examens de fin d'année et vouz allez faire la fête! Avec un(e) partenaire, écrivez une conversation au sujet de la préparation de cette fête. N'oubliez pas de répondre aux questions suivantes. Ensuite (*Then*), jouez (*act out*) votre dialogue devant la classe. Answers will vary.

1. Quand et où allez-vous organiser la fête?
2. Qui vont être les invités?
3. Qui est l'hôte?
4. Qu'allez-vous manger? Qu'allez-vous boire?
5. Qui va apporter quoi?
6. Qui se charge (*is in charge*) de la musique? De la décoration?
7. Qu'allez-vous faire pendant (*during*) la fête?
8. Qui va nettoyer après la fête?

6 Sept différences Votre professeur va vous donner, à vous et à votre partenaire, deux feuilles d'activités différentes. À tour de rôle, posez-vous des questions pour trouver les sept différences entre les illustrations de l'anniversaire des jumeaux (*twins*) Boniface. Attention! Ne regardez pas la feuille de votre partenaire.

MODÈLE

Étudiant(e) 1: *Sur mon image, il y a trois cadeaux. Combien de cadeaux y a-t-il sur ton image?*
Étudiant(e) 2: *Sur mon image, il y a quatre cadeaux.*

OPTIONS

Small Groups In groups of three or four, have students plan and perform a skit in which they depict a particular stage of life (youth, old age, etc.) or marital status (engaged, single, divorced). The rest of the class tries to guess which stage of life or marital status the skit represents.

Pairs Have students write four or five true/false statements based on the illustration on pages 182–183. Then have them get together with a partner and take turns saying their statements and responding **C'est vrai** or **C'est faux.** Call on volunteers to correct the false statements, pointing out the changes on **Transparency #31**.

Les sons et les lettres

NATIONAL
comparisons
STANDARDS

Open vs. closed vowels: Part 2

The letter combinations **au** and **eau** are pronounced like the vowel sound in the English word *coat*, but without the glide heard in English. These are closed **o** sounds.

chaud **aussi** **beaucoup** **tableau**

When the letter **o** is followed by a consonant sound, it is usually pronounced like the vowel in the English word *raw*. This is an open **o** sound.

homme **téléphone** **ordinateur** **orange**

When the letter **o** occurs as the last sound of a word or is followed by a *z* sound, such as a single **s** between two vowels, it is usually pronounced with the closed **o** sound.

trop **héros** **rose** **chose**

When the letter **o** has an **accent circonflexe**, it is usually pronounced with the closed **o** sound.

drôle **bientôt** **pôle** **côté**

Prononcez Répétez les mots suivants à voix haute.

1. rôle
2. porte
3. dos
4. chaud
5. prose
6. gros
7. oiseau
8. encore
9. mauvais
10. nouveau
11. restaurant
12. bibliothèque

Articulez Répétez les phrases suivantes à voix haute.

1. À l'automne, on n'a pas trop chaud.
2. Aurélie a une bonne note en biologie.
3. Votre colocataire est d'origine japonaise?
4. Sophie aime beaucoup l'informatique et la psychologie.
5. Nos copains mangent au restaurant marocain aujourd'hui.
6. Comme cadeau, Robert et Corinne vont préparer un gâteau.

Dictons Répétez les dictons à voix haute.

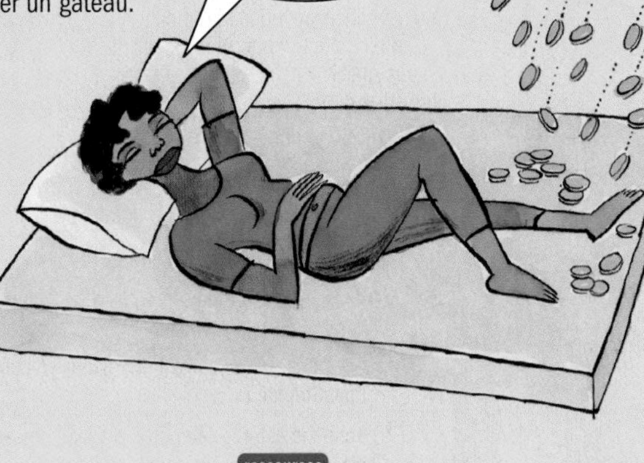
La fortune vient en dormant.[2]

Tout nouveau, tout beau.[1]

[1] Shiny and new.
[2] Fortune comes while you sleep.

ressources			
LM p. 42	Text MP3s Leçon 11	Lab MP3s Leçon 11	espaces.vhlcentral.com Leçon 11

Section Goals

In this section, students will learn more about open and closed vowels.

Instructional Resources
Textbook MP3s
Lab Manual, p. 42
Lab MP3s
WB/VM/LM Answer Key
IRCD-ROM: IRM (Textbook Audioscript; Lab Audioscript)
espaces.vhlcentral.com: activities, downloads, reference tools

Suggestions

- Model the pronunciation of each open and closed vowel sound. Have students watch the shape of your mouth, then repeat the sound after you. Pronounce each of the example words and have students repeat them.
- Remind students that **o** is sometimes nasalized when followed by **m** or **n**. Compare the following words: **bon, nom,** and **bonne, homme.**
- Ask students to provide more examples of words from this lesson or previous lessons with these vowel sounds. Examples: **cadeau, gâteau, hôte, octobre,** and **beau.**
- Dictate five familiar words containing the open and closed vowels presented here, repeating each one at least two times. Then write them on the board or on a transparency and have students check their spelling.

Dictons Ask students if they can think of sayings in English that are similar to **«La fortune vient en dormant.»** (*Good things come to those who wait. Patience is a virtue.*)

OPTIONS

Extra Practice Use these sentences with open and closed vowel sounds for additional practice or dictation. **1. Octobre est en automne. 2. Est-ce qu'il fait mauvais aujourd'hui? 3. En août, il fait beau, mais il fait chaud. 4. Aurélie est aussi drôle que Paul.**

Extra Practice Teach students this French tongue-twister that contains a variety of vowel sounds. **Paul se pèle au pôle dans sa pile de pulls et polos pâles. Pas plus d'appel de la poule à l'Opel que d'opale dans la pelle à Paul.**

Section Goals

In this section, students will learn functional phrases for talking about the past and celebrations through comprehensible input.

Instructional Resources
WB/VM: Video Manual, pp. 231–232
WB/VM/LM Answer Key
Video CD-ROM
Video on DVD
IRCD-ROM: IRM (Videoscript; ***Roman-photo*** *Translations)*
espaces.vhlcentral.com: activities, downloads, reference tools

Video Recap: Leçon 10
Before doing this **Roman-photo**, review the previous one with this true/false activity.

1. Rachid aime boire de l'eau. (Vrai.)
2. L'anniversaire de Stéphane est le 15 janvier. (Faux.)
3. Sandrine déteste la pluie. (Vrai.)
4. Stéphane va avoir 18 ans. (Vrai.)
5. Rachid n'aime pas le portrait de Sandrine. (Faux.)

Video Synopsis Sandrine tells Pascal about her preparations for Stéphane's party. Valérie arrives and offers to help Sandrine carry the desserts to **Le P'tit Bistrot**. Meanwhile, Astrid and Rachid are shopping for birthday gifts. They buy gag gifts and a watch. At the café, Astrid helps Valérie with decorations while Rachid goes to get Stéphane. Amina is in a good mood because her parents are coming to visit.

Suggestions
- Ask students to read the title, glance at the video stills, and predict what they think the episode will be about. Record their predictions.
- Have students scan the video-still captions and find sentences with words or expressions related to party preparations. Have volunteers read their phrases.
- After reading the **Roman-photo**, review their predictions and ask which ones were correct.

Les cadeaux

PERSONNAGES

Amina

Astrid

Rachid

Sandrine

Valérie

Vendeuse

1 *À l'appartement de Sandrine...*
SANDRINE Allô, Pascal? Tu m'as téléphoné? Écoute, je suis très occupée là. Je prépare un gâteau d'anniversaire pour Stéphane... Il a dix-huit ans aujourd'hui... On organise une fête surprise au P'tit Bistrot.

2 **SANDRINE** J'ai fait une mousse au chocolat, comme pour ton anniversaire. Stéphane adore ça! J'ai aussi préparé des biscuits que David aime bien.

3 **SANDRINE** Quoi? David!... Mais non, il n'est pas marié. C'est un bon copain, c'est tout!... Désolée, je n'ai pas le temps de discuter. À bientôt.

6 **RACHID** Écoute, Astrid. Il faut trouver un cadeau... un *vrai* cadeau d'anniversaire.
ASTRID Excusez-moi, Madame. Combien coûte cette montre, s'il vous plaît?
VENDEUSE Quarante euros.
ASTRID Que penses-tu de cette montre, Rachid?
RACHID Bonne idée.

7 **VENDEUSE** Je fais un paquet cadeau?
ASTRID Oui, merci.
RACHID Eh, Astrid, il faut y aller!
VENDEUSE Et voilà dix euros. Merci, Mademoiselle, bonne fin de journée.

8 *Au café...*
VALÉRIE Ah, vous voilà! Astrid, aide-nous avec les décorations, s'il te plaît. La fête commence à six heures. Sandrine a tout préparé.
ASTRID Quelle heure est-il? Zut, déjà? En tout cas, on a trouvé des cadeaux.
RACHID Je vais chercher Stéphane.

ACTIVITÉS

1 Vrai ou faux? Indiquez si les affirmations suivantes sont **vraies** ou **fausses**.

1. Sandrine prépare un gâteau d'anniversaire pour Stéphane. Vrai.
2. Sandrine est désolée parce qu'elle n'a pas le temps de discuter avec Rachid. Faux.
3. Rachid ne comprend pas la blague. Vrai.
4. Pour aider Sandrine, Valérie va apporter les desserts. Vrai.
5. Rachid et Astrid trouvent un cadeau pour Valérie. Faux.
6. Rachid n'aime pas l'idée de la montre pour Stéphane. Faux.
7. La fête d'anniversaire surprise pour Stéphane commence à huit heures. Faux.
8. Sandrine va chercher Stéphane. Faux.
9. Amina a aussi apporté de la glace au chocolat. Vrai.
10. Les parents d'Amina vont passer l'été à Aix-en-Provence. Vrai.

OPTIONS

Avant de regarder la vidéo Before viewing the video, have students brainstorm a list of words or expressions that someone might say when preparing for a party and discussing gifts. Write their ideas on the board.

Regarder la vidéo Show the video in three parts, pausing the video before each location change. Have students describe what happens in each place. Write their observations on the board. Then show the entire episode again without pausing and have the class fill in any missing details to summarize the plot.

Tout le monde prépare la surprise pour Stéphane.

VALÉRIE Oh là là! Tu as fait tout ça pour Stéphane?!
SANDRINE Oh, ce n'est pas grand-chose.
VALÉRIE Tu es un ange! Stéphane va bientôt arriver. Je t'aide à apporter ces desserts?
SANDRINE Oh, merci, c'est gentil.

Dans un magasin...
ASTRID Eh Rachid, j'ai eu une idée géniale... Des cadeaux parfaits pour Stéphane. Regarde! Ce matin, j'ai acheté cette calculatrice et ces livres.
RACHID Mais enfin, Astrid, Stéphane n'aime pas les livres.
ASTRID Oh Rachid, tu ne comprends rien, c'est une blague.

AMINA Bonjour! Désolée, je suis en retard!
VALÉRIE Ce n'est pas grave. Tu es toute belle ce soir!

AMINA Vous trouvez? J'ai acheté ce cadeau pour Stéphane. Et j'ai apporté de la glace au chocolat aussi.
VALÉRIE Oh, merci! Il faut aider Astrid avec les décorations.
ASTRID Salut, Amina. Ça va?
AMINA Oui, super. Mes parents ont téléphoné du Sénégal ce matin! Ils vont passer l'été ici. C'est le bonheur!

Expressions utiles

Talking about celebrations

- **J'ai fait une mousse au chocolat, comme pour ton anniversaire.**
  I made a chocolate mousse, (just) like for your birthday.
- **J'ai aussi préparé des biscuits que David aime bien.**
  I have also prepared cookies that David likes.
- **Je fais un paquet cadeau?**
  Shall I wrap the present?
- **En tout cas, on a trouvé des cadeaux.**
  In any case, we have found some presents.
- **Et j'ai apporté de la glace au chocolat.**
  And I brought some chocolate ice cream.

Talking about the past

- **Tu m'as téléphoné?**
  Did you call me?
- **Tu as fait tout ça pour Stéphane?!**
  You did all that for Stéphane?!
- **J'ai eu une idée géniale.**
  I had a great idea.
- **Sandrine a tout préparé.**
  Sandrine prepared everything.

Pointing out things

- **Je t'aide à apporter ces desserts?**
  Can I help you to bring these desserts?
- **J'ai acheté cette calculatrice et ces livres.**
  I bought this calculator and these books.
- **J'ai acheté ce cadeau pour Stéphane.**
  I bought this present for Stéphane.

Additional vocabulary

- **Ce n'est pas grave.**
  It's okay./No problem.
- **Tu ne comprends rien.**
  You don't understand a thing.
- **désolé(e)**
  sorry
- **discuter**
  to talk
- **zut**
  darn

ACTIVITÉS

2 **Le bon mot** Choisissez le bon mot entre **ce** (*m.*), **cette** (*f.*) et **ces** (*pl.*) pour compléter les phrases. Utilisez un dictionnaire. Attention, les phrases ne sont pas identiques aux dialogues!

1. Je t'aide à apporter __ce__ gâteau?
2. Ce matin, j'ai acheté __ces__ calculatrices et __ce__ livre.
3. Rachid ne comprend pas __cette__ blague.
4. Combien coûtent __ces__ montres?
5. À quelle heure commence __cette__ classe?

3 **Imaginez** Avec un(e) partenaire, imaginez qu'Amina est dans un grand magasin et qu'elle téléphone à Madame Forestier pour l'aider à choisir le cadeau idéal pour Stéphane. Amina propose et décrit plusieurs possibilités de cadeaux et Madame Forestier donne son avis (*opinion*) sur chacune d'entre elles (*each of them*).

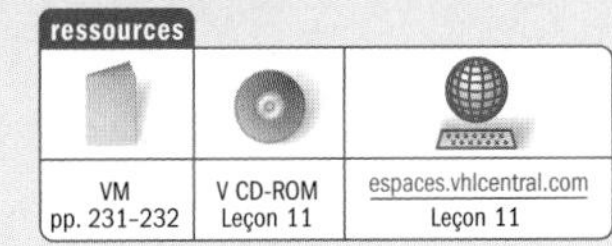

ressources
VM pp. 231-232
V CD-ROM Leçon 11
espaces.vhlcentral.com Leçon 11

Expressions utiles

- Model the pronunciation of the **Expressions utiles** and have students repeat them.
- As you work through the list, point out forms of the **passé composé** and demonstrative adjectives. Tell students that these grammar structures will be formally presented in the **Structures** section.
- Respond briefly to questions about the **passé composé** and demonstrative adjectives. Reinforce correct forms, but do not expect students to produce them consistently at this time.
- Say some of the **Expressions utiles** and have students react to them. Examples:
  1. J'ai eu une idée géniale! (Ah oui? Quelle est ton idée?)
  2. Sandrine a tout préparé. (Oh, c'est gentil!)

1 Suggestion Have students correct the false statements.

1 Expansion For additional practice, give students these items. **11. Sandrine prépare une mousse au chocolat. (Vrai.) 12. David n'aime pas les biscuits. (Faux.) 13. Astrid achète une calculatrice pour Stéphane. (Vrai.)**

2 Suggestion Before beginning the activity, point out the gender of each demonstrative adjective given. Tell students that demonstrative adjectives must agree with the noun they modify just like articles and descriptive adjectives.

2 Expansion For additional practice, give students these items. **6. Je t'aide à apporter ____ desserts? (ces) 7. Tu es très belle ____ soir. (ce) 8. Mes parents ont téléphoné du Sénégal ____ matin. (ce)**

3 Suggestion If time is limited, assign students the roles of Madame Forestier or Amina and tell them to prepare for homework a list of possible questions or responses according to their role. Then allow partners a few minutes to work together before presenting their conversations.

OPTIONS

Les cadeaux Point out the question **Je fais un paquet cadeau?** Explain that many stores gift wrap items free of charge, especially small items. The wrapping is often a simple sack sealed with a small ribbon and a sticker, which usually bears the name of the store.

L'étiquette Point out some basic etiquette regarding gifts in France. For example, if invited to eat at someone's house, one should not bring wine because the host or hostess most certainly will have chosen an appropriate wine to accompany the meal. Instead, choose candy or flowers.

connections cultures NATIONAL STANDARDS

Section Goals

In this section, students will:

- learn about **carnaval**
- learn to express congratulations and best wishes
- learn about some festivals and holidays in various francophone regions
- read about Bastille Day

Instructional Resources
espaces.vhlcentral.com: activities, downloads, reference tools

Culture à la loupe

Avant la lecture Ask if anyone has attended **carnaval** or **Mardi gras** or seen TV news clips of these celebrations. Then ask students to share what they know about these celebrations.

Lecture

- The word **carnaval** is from the Italian *carnevale*, an alteration of the medieval Latin *carnelevare*, meaning *removal of meat*.
- Point out that the plural of **carnaval** is **carnavals**.

Après la lecture Ask students: **Où désirez-vous assister à une célébration: à Nice, à la Nouvelle-Orléans, à Québec ou à la Martinique? Pourquoi?**

1 Expansion For additional practice, give students these items. **11. Quel événement** (*event*) **est-ce qu'on fête au carnaval? (la fin de l'hiver et l'arrivée du printemps) 12. Où est-ce qu'il fait très froid lors du carnaval? (à Québec) 13. Combien de défilés y a-t-il typiquement pendant le carnaval de la Nouvelle-Orléans? (plus de 70)**

CULTURE À LA LOUPE

Le carnaval

le roi du carnaval de Nice

Tous les ans, beaucoup de pays° et de régions francophones célèbrent le carnaval. Cette tradition est l'occasion de fêter la fin° de l'hiver et l'arrivée° du printemps. En général, la période de fête commence la semaine avant le Carême° et se termine° le jour du Mardi gras. Le carnaval demande très souvent des mois de préparation. La ville organise des défilés° de musique, de masques, de costumes et de chars fleuris°. La fête finit souvent par la crémation du roi° Carnaval, personnage de papier qui représente le carnaval et l'hiver.

Certaines villes et certaines régions sont réputées° pour leur carnaval: Nice, en France, la ville de Québec, au Canada, la Nouvelle-Orléans, aux États-Unis et la Martinique. Chaque ville a ses traditions particulières. La ville de Nice, lieu du plus grand carnaval français, organise une grande bataille de fleurs° où des jeunes, sur des chars, envoient des milliers° de fleurs aux spectateurs. À Québec, le climat intense transforme le carnaval en une célébration de l'hiver. Le symbole officiel de la fête est le «Bonhomme» (de neige°) et les gens font du ski, de la pêche sous la glace ou des courses de traîneaux à chiens°. À la Martinique, le carnaval continue jusqu'au° mercredi des Cendres°, à minuit: les gens, tout en noir° et blanc°, regardent la crémation de Vaval, le roi Carnaval. Le carnaval de la Nouvelle-Orléans est célébré avec de nombreux bals° et défilés costumés. Ses couleurs officielles sont l'or°, le vert et le violet.

le carnaval de Québec

pays *countries* **fin** *end* **arrivée** *arrival* **Carême** *Lent* **se termine** *ends* **défilés** *parades* **chars fleuris** *floats decorated with flowers* **roi** *king* **réputées** *famous* **bataille de fleurs** *flower battle* **milliers** *thousands* **«Bonhomme» (de neige)** *snowman* **courses de traîneaux à chiens** *dogsled races* **jusqu'au** *until* **mercredi des Cendres** *Ash Wednesday* **noir** *black* **blanc** *white* **bals** *balls (dances)* **or** *gold* **choisit** *chooses* **reine** *queen* **a eu lieu** *took place* **pendant** *during*

Le carnaval en chiffres

Martinique	Chaque ville choisit° une reine°.
Nice	La première bataille de fleurs a eu lieu° en 1876. On envoie entre 80.000 et 100.000 fleurs aux spectateurs.
la Nouvelle-Orléans	Il y a plus de 70 défilés pendant° le carnaval.
la ville de Québec	Le premier carnaval a eu lieu en 1894.

ACTIVITÉS

1 Compréhension Répondez par des phrases complètes.

1. En général, quel est le dernier jour du carnaval?
   En général, le dernier jour du carnaval est le jour du Mardi gras.
2. Dans quelle ville des États-Unis est-ce qu'on célèbre le carnaval?
   On célèbre le carnaval à la Nouvelle-Orléans.
3. Où a lieu le plus grand carnaval français?
   Le plus grand carnaval français a lieu à Nice.
4. Qu'est-ce que les jeunes envoient aux spectateurs du carnaval de Nice?
   Les jeunes envoient des fleurs aux spectateurs.
5. Quel est le symbole officiel du carnaval de Québec?
   Le «Bonhomme» est le symbole officiel du carnaval de Québec.
6. Que fait-on pendant (*during*) le carnaval de Québec?
   On pratique des activités d'hiver pendant le carnaval de Québec.
7. Qu'est-ce qui est différent au carnaval de la Martinique?
   Il continue jusqu'au mercredi des Cendres.
8. Qui est Vaval?
   Vaval est le roi du carnaval à la Martinique.
9. Comment est-ce qu'on célèbre le carnaval à la Nouvelle-Orléans?
   On célèbre le carnaval à la Nouvelle-Orléans avec des bals et des défilés.
10. Quelles sont les couleurs officielles du carnaval de la Nouvelle-Orléans?
    Les couleurs officielles du carnaval de la Nouvelle-Orléans sont l'or, le vert et le violet.

OPTIONS

Small Groups Have students work in groups of three. They should choose a country, research its **carnaval**, and create an Internet home page for next year's **carnaval** in that country. Tell them that the home page should include the dates, a list of events with short descriptions, and any other important or interesting information. Have students present their home pages to the class.

Pairs Working in pairs, have students write a conversation between two people who are trying to decide if they should go to the **carnaval** in Nice or in Québec City. After they have finished, have volunteers act out their conversations for the class.

COMMUNICATION

4 **La semaine** À tour de rôle, assemblez les éléments des colonnes pour raconter (*to tell*) à votre partenaire ce que (*what*) tout le monde (*everyone*) a fait cette semaine. Answers will vary.

A	B	C
je	acheter	bonbons
Luc	apprendre	café
mon prof	boire	cartes
Sylvie	enseigner	l'espagnol
mes parents	étudier	famille
mes copains et moi	faire	foot
tu	jouer	glace
vous	manger	jogging
?	parler	les maths
	prendre	promenade
	regarder	vélo
	?	?

5 **L'été dernier** Vous avez passé l'été dernier avec deux amis, mais vos souvenirs (*memories*) diffèrent. Par groupes de trois, utilisez les expressions de la liste et imaginez le dialogue. Answers will vary.

MODÈLE

Étudiant(e) 1: *Nous avons fait du cheval tous les matins.*
Étudiant(e) 2: *Mais non! Moi, j'ai fait du cheval. Vous deux, vous avez fait du jogging.*
Étudiant(e) 3: *Je n'ai pas fait de jogging. J'ai dormi!*

acheter	essayer	faire une promenade
courir	faire du cheval	jouer aux cartes
dormir	faire du jogging	jouer au foot
emmener	faire la fête	manger

6 **Qu'est-ce que tu as fait?** Avec un(e) partenaire, posez-vous les questions à tour de rôle. Ensuite, présentez vos réponses à la classe. Answers will vary.

1. As-tu fait la fête samedi dernier? Où? Avec qui?
2. Est-ce que tu as célébré une occasion importante cette année? Quelle occasion?
3. As-tu organisé une fête? Pour qui?
4. Qui est-ce que tu as invité à ta dernière fête?
5. Qu'est-ce que tu as fait pour fêter ton dernier anniversaire?
6. Est-ce que tu as préparé quelque chose à manger pour une fête ou un dîner? Quoi?

- The adverbs **hier** (*yesterday*) and **avant-hier** (*the day before yesterday*) are used often with the **passé composé**.
- Place the adverbs **déjà**, **encore**, **bien**, **mal**, and **beaucoup** between the auxiliary verb or **pas** and the past participle.

Tu as **déjà** mangé ta part de gâteau.
You already ate your piece of cake.

Elle n'a pas **encore** visité notre ville.
She hasn't visited our town yet.

- The past participles of spelling-change **-er** verbs have no spelling changes.

Laurent a-t-il **acheté** le champagne?
Did Laurent buy the champagne?

Vous avez **envoyé** des bonbons.
You sent candy.

- The past participle of most **-ir** verbs is formed by replacing the **-ir** ending with **-i**.

Sylvie a **dormi** jusqu'à dix heures.
Sylvie slept until 10 o'clock.

On a **senti** leurs regards.
We felt their stares.

Some irregular past participles

apprendre	appris	être	été
avoir	eu	faire	fait
boire	bu	pleuvoir	plu
comprendre	compris	prendre	pris
courir	couru	surprendre	surpris

Nous avons **bu** du vin.
We drank wine.

Ils ont **été** très en retard.
They have been very late.

- The **passé composé** of **il faut** is **il a fallu**; that of **il y a** is **il y a eu**.

Il a fallu passer par le supermarché.
It was necessary to stop by the supermarket.

Il y a eu deux fêtes hier soir.
There were two parties last night.

BOÎTE À OUTILS
Some verbs, like **aller**, use **être** instead of **avoir** to form the **passé composé**. You will learn more about these verbs in **Leçon 13**.

Essayez! **Indiquez les formes du passé composé des verbes.**

1. j' ai commencé, ai payé, ai bavardé (commencer, payer, bavarder)
2. tu as servi, as compris, as donné (servir, comprendre, donner)
3. on a parlé, a eu, a dormi (parler, avoir, dormir)
4. nous avons adoré, avons fait, avons amené (adorer, faire, amener)
5. vous avez pris, avez employé, avez couru (prendre, employer, courir)
6. elles ont espéré, ont bu, ont appris (espérer, boire, apprendre)

Essayez! For additional practice, have students create complete sentences orally or in writing using the subjects and verbs given.

1 Expansion Ask follow-up questions about Laurent's weekend. Examples: **1. Qu'est-ce qu'ils ont mangé? 2. Qui a acheté une montre? 3. Qui a pris une glace à la terrasse d'un café? 4. Qu'est-ce que leurs parents ont célébré? 5. Quand est-ce que Laurent et sa famille ont eu sommeil?**

2 Suggestion To check answers, have one student ask the question and call on another student to answer it. This activity can also be done in pairs.

2 Expansion For additional practice, give students these items. **9. parler à ses parents (Stéphane) 10. boire du café (toi et ton copain)**

3 Suggestion Before beginning the activity, have students describe what the people are doing in the present tense.

4 Suggestion Before beginning this activity, call on volunteers to give the past participles of verbs listed.

5 Suggestion Have three volunteers read the **modèle** aloud. Encourage students to be creative.

6 Suggestion Tell students to jot down notes on their partner's responses and to add two of their own questions to the list.

OPTIONS

TPR Working in groups of three, have students write three sentences in the **passé composé**, each with a different verb. After they have finished, have each group mime its sentences for the class. When someone guesses the mimed action, the group writes the sentence on the board.

Extra Practice Have students write a paragraph about what they did yesterday or last weekend for homework. Then in class have them exchange papers with a classmate and peer edit each other's work.

Synthèse

Instructional Resources
*IRCD-ROM: IRM (**Feuilles d'activités**; Info Gap Activities); Testing Program, pp. 41–44; Test Files; Testing Program MP3s; Test Generator*
espaces.vhlcentral.com: activities, downloads, reference tools

1 Suggestion Before beginning this activity, give students a few minutes to jot down some notes about the previous Thanksgiving.

2 Expansion Have a few volunteers report the common activities they and their partner did.

3 Suggestion Before beginning the activity, have students identify the items on the table.

4 Suggestion Distribute the **Feuilles d'activités** from the IRM on the IRCD-ROM.

5 Suggestion Tell students that they can talk about a real or imaginary dinner. Encourage students to be creative.

6 Suggestion Divide the class into pairs and distribute the Info Gap Handouts in the IRM on the IRCD-ROM for this activity. Give students ten minutes to complete the activity.

1 L'année dernière et cette année Décrivez vos dernières fêtes du jour d'Action de Grâces (*Thanksgiving*) à votre partenaire. Utilisez les verbes de la liste. Parlez aussi de vos projets (*plans*) pour le prochain jour d'Action de Grâces.
Answers will vary.

MODÈLE

Étudiant(e) 1: *L'année dernière, nous avons fêté le jour d'Action de Grâces chez mes grands-parents. Cette année, je vais manger au restaurant avec mes parents.*

Étudiant(e) 2: *Moi, j'ai fait la fête avec mes amis l'année dernière. Cette année, je vais visiter New York avec ma sœur.*

acheter	dormir	manger	regarder
boire	faire	prendre	téléphoner
donner	fêter	préparer	visiter

2 Ce musée, cette ville Faites par écrit (*Write*) une liste de cinq lieux (villes, musées, restaurants, etc.) que vous avez visités. Avec un(e) partenaire, comparez vos listes. Utilisez des adjectifs démonstratifs dans vos phrases. Answers will vary.

MODÈLE

Étudiant(e) 1: *Ah, tu as visité Bruxelles. Moi aussi, j'ai visité cette ville. Elle est charmante.*

Étudiant(e) 2: *Tu as mangé au restaurant La Douce France. Je n'aime pas du tout ce restaurant!*

3 La fête Vous et votre partenaire avez préparé une fête avec vos amis. Vous avez acheté des cadeaux, des boissons et des snacks. À tour de rôle, parlez de ce qu'il y a sur l'illustration.
Answers will vary.

MODÈLE

Étudiant(e) 1: *J'aime bien ces biscuits-là.*

Étudiant(e) 2: *Moi, j'ai apporté cette glace-ci.*

4 Enquête Qu'est-ce que vos camarades ont fait de différent dans leur vie? Votre professeur va vous donner une feuille d'activités. Parlez à vos camarades pour trouver une personne différente pour chaque expérience, puis écrivez son nom.
Answers will vary.

MODÈLE

Étudiant(e) 1: *As-tu parlé à un acteur?*

Étudiant(e) 2: *Oui! Une fois, j'ai parlé à Bruce Willis!*

Expérience	Nom
1. parler à un(e) acteur/actrice	Julien
2. passer une nuit entière sans dormir	
3. dépenser plus de $100 pour des CD en une fois	
4. faire la fête un lundi soir	
5. courir cinq kilomètres ou plus	
6. surprendre un(e) ami(e) pour son anniversaire	

5 Conversez Avec un(e) partenaire, préparez une conversation où un(e) copain/copine demande à un(e) autre copain/copine les détails d'un dîner romantique du week-end dernier. N'oubliez pas de mentionner dans la conversation:
Answers will vary.

- où ils/elles ont mangé
- les thèmes de la conversation
- qui a payé
- qui a parlé de quoi
- la date du prochain rendez-vous

6 Magali fait la fête Votre professeur va vous donner, à vous et à votre partenaire, deux feuilles d'activités différentes. Attention! Ne regardez pas la feuille de votre partenaire.
Answers will vary.

MODÈLE

Étudiant(e) 1: *Magali a parlé avec un homme. Cet homme n'a pas l'air intéressant du tout!*

Étudiant(e) 2: *Après,...*

ressources

WB	LM	Lab MP3s	espaces.vhlcentral.com
pp. 73-76	pp. 43-44	Leçon 11	Leçon 11

OPTIONS

Extra Practice Have students create a continuous narration about a person who had a very bad day. Begin the story by saying: **Hier, Robert a passé une très mauvaise journée.** Call on a student at one corner of the class to continue the story by telling how Robert began his day. The second person tells what happened next. Students continue adding sentences until only one student remains. He or she must conclude the story.

Extra Practice Have students make a "to do" list (**à faire...**) at the beginning of their day. Then, tell students to review their list at the end of the day and write down which activities they completed and which ones they didn't complete. Example: **acheter de la nourriture: Non, je n'ai pas acheté de nourriture.**

Projet

Préparez un article

C'est un jour de fête en France. Vous êtes journaliste. Vous allez écrire° un article sur cette fête et ses origines et vous allez expliquer comment on célèbre cet événement.

1 Écrivez un article

Écrivez un article sur un jour de fête en France. Pour découvrir quels sont les jours fériés en France, explorez le lien° dans la boîte° **Sur Internet**. Donnez le plus de détails possibles°:

- le nom de la fête
- la date de la fête chaque° année
- une brève° histoire de la fête
- une description des festivités
- des images des activités typiques de la fête

2 Présentez votre travail°

Faites un exposé° devant la classe sur la fête que vous avez choisie°. Vous pouvez° distribuer des photocopies de votre article à vos camarades. N'oubliez pas de montrer° les images que vous avez trouvées.

SUR INTERNET

Go to **espaces.vhlcentral.com** for more information related to this **Projet**.

écrire *to write* **lien** *link* **boîte** *box* **le plus de détails possibles** *as many details as possible* **chaque** *each* **brève** *brief, short* **travail** *work* **exposé** *presentation* **choisie** *chosen* **pouvez** *can* **montrer** *to show*

Section Goals

In this section, students will:

- use French to carry out research and to interact with the wider world
- write an article about a holiday in France

Instructional Resources
espaces.vhlcentral.com: activities, downloads, reference tools

Suggestion Students might need a week to complete the project, so at the beginning of that time period, have them read through **Projet**. Explain that they are going to carry out research and write an article on a holiday in France. Examples: **la Toussaint** (November 1), **la fête des Rois** (January 6), **la Chandeleur** (February 2), or **la fête nationale** (July 14).

Écrivez un article

- Provide students with examples of articles written in French about holidays in France.
- Remind them to include the information in the list.

Présentez votre travail

- Have students present the articles as though they were at a live broadcast of the event.
- Do a few presentations at a time over several days.

EVALUATION

Criteria	Scale
Content	1 2 3 4
Organization	1 2 3 4
Comprehensibility	1 2 3 4
Accuracy	1 2 3 4
Use of visuals	1 2 3 4

Scoring	
Excellent	18–20 points
Good	14–17 points
Satisfactory	10–13 points
Unsatisfactory	< 10 points

Section Goals

In this section, students will learn and practice vocabulary related to:

- clothing and accessories
- shopping
- colors

Instructional Resources

*IRCD-ROM: Transparency #32; IRM (**Vocabulaire supplémentaire; Mise en pratique** answers; Textbook Audioscript; Lab Audioscript)*
Textbook MP3s
WB/VM: Workbook, pp. 77–78
Lab Manual, p. 45
Lab MP3s
WB/VM/LM Answer Key
espaces.vhlcentral.com: activities, downloads, reference tools

Suggestions

- Use **Transparency #32.** Point out clothing items in the store and describe what the people in the illustration are wearing. Examples: **Cette femme porte une robe. Ce sont des sous-vêtements.**
- After presenting the new vocabulary, briefly describe what you are wearing.
- Have students name one item of clothing they are wearing today. Then ask: **Qu'est-ce que ____ porte? De quelle couleur est ____?**
- Point out the difference between **une écharpe** (a heavier scarf or wrap worn in fall or winter) and **un foulard** (a lighter scarf usually worn in spring or summer).
- Tell students that the word **taille** is used to talk about *clothing sizes.* **Pointure** refers to *shoe sizes.*
- Point out the title of this lesson. Tell students that **chic** is an invariable adjective.
- Tell students that the verb **porter** means *to wear* or *to carry.* The verb **mettre** (*to wear; to put on*) is presented on page 207.
- Additional vocabulary for this lesson can be found in the **Vocabulaire supplémentaire** in the IRM on the IRCD-ROM.

Leçon 12

You will learn how to...

- describe clothing
- offer and accept gifts

Très chic!

Vocabulaire

aller avec	*to go with*
un anorak	*ski jacket, parka*
une chaussette	*sock*
une chemise (à manches courtes/longues)	*shirt (short-/long-sleeved)*
un chemisier	*blouse*
un gant	*glove*
un jean	*jeans*
une jupe	*skirt*
un manteau	*coat*
un pantalon	*pants*
un pull	*sweater*
un sous-vêtement	*underwear*
une taille	*clothing size*
un tailleur	*(woman's) suit; tailor*
un tee-shirt	*tee shirt*
un vendeur/une vendeuse	*salesman/saleswoman*
des vêtements (*m.*)	*clothing*
De quelle couleur...?	*In what color...?*
des soldes (*m.*)	*sales*
chaque	*each*
large	*loose; big*
serré(e)	*tight*

ressources

WB	LM	Text MP3s	Lab MP3s	espaces.vhlcentral.com
pp. 77–78	p. 45	Leçon 12	Leçon 12	Leçon 12

OPTIONS

Game Have students stand. Toss a beanbag to a student at random and say the name of a sport, place, or activity. The person has four seconds to name a clothing item or accessory that goes with it. That person then tosses the beanbag to another student and says a sport, place, or activity. Students who cannot think of an item in time or repeat an item that has already been mentioned are eliminated. The last person standing wins.

Extra Practice Review the weather and seasons by asking students what they wear in various circumstances. Examples: **Que portez-vous quand il fait chaud/quand il fait frais/quand il neige/au printemps/en hiver?**

Attention!

Note that the adjective **orange** is invariable; it does not vary its gender or number to match the noun it modifies.
J'aime l'anorak orange.
Il porte des chaussures orange.

des lunettes (de soleil) (f.)
une casquette
une écharpe
bon marché
un blouson

Mise en pratique

1 Écoutez Guillaume prépare ses vacances d'hiver (*winter vacation*). Indiquez quels vêtements il va acheter pour son voyage.

	Oui	Non
1. des baskets	☑	☐
2. un maillot de bain	☐	☑
3. des chemises	☐	☑
4. un pantalon noir	☑	☐
5. un manteau	☑	☐
6. un anorak	☐	☑
7. un jean	☑	☐
8. un short	☐	☑
9. un pull	☐	☑
10. une robe	☐	☑

Guillaume

2 Les vêtements Chassez l'intrus et choisissez le mot qui ne va pas avec les autres.

1. des baskets, (une cravate), une chaussure
2. un jean, un pantalon, (une jupe)
3. un tailleur, un costume, (un short)
4. (des lunettes), un chemisier, une chemise
5. (un tee-shirt), un pull, un anorak
6. une casquette, (une ceinture), un chapeau
7. un sous-vêtement, une chaussette, (un sac à main)
8. une jupe, une robe, (une écharpe)

3 De quelle couleur? Indiquez de quelle(s) couleur(s) sont les choses suivantes.

MODÈLE

l'océan
Il est bleu.
la statue de la Liberté
Elle est grise.

1. le drapeau français Il est bleu, blanc et rouge.
2. les dollars américains Ils sont verts.
3. les pommes Answers will vary. Elles sont rouges, vertes ou jaunes.
4. le soleil Il est jaune.
5. la nuit Elle est noire.
6. le zèbre Il est blanc et noir.
7. la neige Elle est blanche.
8. les oranges Elles sont orange.
9. le vin Answers will vary. Il est blanc, rouge ou rose.
10. les bananes Elles sont jaunes.

1 Tapescript Bonjour! Je m'appelle Guillaume. Je vais aller en Suisse pour mes vacances d'hiver. J'ai besoin d'acheter un manteau parce qu'il va faire froid. J'ai déjà acheté un pull gris. J'ai aussi un bel anorak bleu qui est un peu vieux, mais chaud. Pour faire des randonnées, j'ai besoin d'un jean et de nouvelles baskets. Pour aller en boîte, je vais acheter un pantalon noir qui va aller avec toutes mes chemises: j'ai des chemises de toutes les couleurs, des chemises à manches longues, à manches courtes. Bien sûr, je ne vais pas avoir besoin d'un short parce qu'il ne va pas faire chaud. *(On Textbook MP3s)*

1 Expansion Play the recording again. Ask students why Guillaume is not going to buy the items marked **Non**. Example: **Pourquoi Guillaume ne va-t-il pas acheter un maillot de bain? (parce qu'il va faire froid en Suisse)**

2 Expansions
- For additional practice, give students these items. **9. un sac à main, une ceinture, une robe (une robe) 10. un tailleur, un maillot de bain, un costume (un maillot de bain) 11. un pantalon, un blouson, un anorak (un pantalon) 12. des chaussettes, des baskets, un chapeau (un chapeau)**
- Have students create one or two additional items using at least three new vocabulary words in each one. Collect their papers and write some of the items on the board.

3 Expansions
- Point out items in the classroom and have students tell what color they are. Examples: **le tableau, ce sac à dos,** and **mon stylo**.
- Have students name items of various colors. Example: **Nommez** (*Name*) **quelque chose de rouge. (le chemisier de ____)**

OPTIONS

TPR Play a game of **Jacques a dit** (*Simon says*). Write **asseyez-vous** and **levez-vous** on the board and model them by sitting and standing as you say them. Start by saying: **Jacques a dit: Si vous portez un jean noir, levez-vous.** Students wearing black jeans stand up and remain standing until further instruction. Work through various items of clothing. Give instructions without saying **Jacques a dit...** once in a while.

Small Groups Divide the class into small groups. Assign each group a season and a vacation destination. Have groups brainstorm a list of items to pack and write a brief explanation for each item. You might want to have groups write two lists, one for a female traveler and one for a male.

4 Suggestion Tell students to write their descriptions. Then have volunteers write a description for each picture on the board.

4 Expansion Have students describe what they are wearing in detail, including accessories and colors of each item.

5 Suggestion Remind students to include greetings and other polite expressions in their role plays. Have volunteers perform their role plays for the rest of the class.

6 Expansion Take a quick class survey to find out students' clothing preferences. Tally the results on the board.

7 Suggestion Have a volunteer read the **modèle** aloud.

NATIONAL communication STANDARDS

Communication

4 Qu'est-ce qu'ils portent? Avec un(e) camarade de classe, regardez les images et à tour de rôle, décrivez ce que les personnages portent. Answers will vary.

MODÈLE

Elle porte un maillot de bain rouge.

1.

2.

3.

4.

5 On fait du shopping Choisissez deux partenaires et préparez une conversation. Deux client(e)s et un vendeur/une vendeuse sont dans un grand magasin; les client(e)s sont invité(e)s à un événement très chic, mais ils ou elles ne veulent pas (*don't want*) dépenser beaucoup d'argent. Answers will vary.

Client(e)s

- Décrivez l'événement auquel (*to which*) vous êtes invité(e)s.
- Parlez des vêtements que vous cherchez, de vos couleurs préférées, de votre taille. Trouvez-vous le vêtement trop large, trop serré, etc.?
- Demandez les prix et dites si vous trouvez que c'est cher, bon marché, etc.

Vendeur/Vendeuse

- Demandez les tailles, préférences, etc. des client(e)s.
- Répondez à toutes les questions de vos client(e)s.
- Suggérez des vêtements appropriés.

Coup de main

To compare French and American sizes, see the chart on p. 202.

6 Conversez Interviewez un(e) camarade de classe. Answers will vary.

1. Qu'est-ce que tu portes l'hiver? Et l'été?
2. Qu'est-ce que tu portes pour aller à l'université?
3. Qu'est-ce que tu portes pour aller à la plage?
4. Qu'est-ce que tu portes pour faire une randonnée?
5. Qu'est-ce que tu portes pour aller en boîte de nuit?
6. Qu'est-ce que tu portes pour un entretien d'embauche (*job interview*)?
7. Quelle est ta couleur préférée? Pourquoi?
8. Qu'est-ce que tu portes pour aller dans un restaurant très élégant?
9. Où est-ce que tu achètes tes vêtements? Pourquoi?
10. Est-ce que tu prêtes (*lend*) tes vêtements à tes ami(e)s?

7 Défilé de mode Votre classe a organisé un défilé de mode (*fashion show*). Votre partenaire est mannequin (*model*) et vous représentez la marque (*brand*) de vêtements. Pendant que votre partenaire défile, vous décrivez à la classe les vêtements qu'il ou elle porte. Après, échangez les rôles. Answers will vary.

MODÈLE

Et voici la charmante Julie, qui porte les modèles de la dernière collection H&M: une chemise à manches courtes et un pantalon noir, ensemble idéal pour aller en boîte de nuit. Ses chaussures blanches vont parfaitement avec l'ensemble. Cette collection H&M est très à la mode et très bon marché.

OPTIONS

Extra Practice Have students write a paragraph about a real or imaginary vacation they plan to take and the clothing they will take with them. Tell them to include what kind of weather they expect at their destination and any weather-specific clothing they will need. Ask volunteers to share their paragraphs with the class.

Extra Practice Have students write descriptions of an article of clothing or a complete outfit that best describes them without indicating who they are. Collect the papers and read the descriptions aloud. The rest of the class has to guess who wrote each one.

Les sons et les lettres

Open vs. closed vowels: Part 3

The letter combination **eu** can be pronounced two different ways, open and closed. Compare the pronunciation of the vowel sounds in these words.

heure **meilleur** **cheveux** **neveu**

When **eu** is the last sound of a syllable, it has a closed vowel sound, sort of like the vowel sound in the English word *full*. While this exact sound does not exist in English, you can make the closed **eu** sound by saying **é** with your lips rounded.

deux **bleu** **peu** **mieux**

When **eu** is followed by a *z* sound, such as a single **s** between two vowels, it is usually pronounced with the closed **eu** sound.

chanteuse **généreuse** **sérieuse** **curieuse**

When **eu** is followed by a pronounced consonant, it has a more open sound. The open **eu** sound does not exist in English. To pronounce it, say **è** with your lips only slightly rounded.

peur **jeune** **chanteur** **beurre**

The letter combination **œu** is usually pronounced with an open **eu** sound.

sœur **bœuf** **œuf** **chœur**

Prononcez Répétez les mots suivants à voix haute.

1. leur	4. vieux	7. monsieur	10. tailleur
2. veuve	5. curieux	8. coiffeuse	11. vendeuse
3. neuf	6. acteur	9. ordinateur	12. couleur

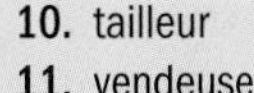

Articulez Répétez les phrases suivantes à voix haute.

1. Le professeur Heudier a soixante-deux ans.
2. Est-ce que Matthieu est jeune ou vieux?
3. Monsieur Eustache est un chanteur fabuleux.
4. Eugène a les yeux bleus et les cheveux bruns.

Dictons Répétez les dictons à voix haute.

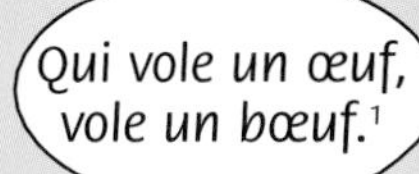

ressources

LM p. 46	Text MP3s Leçon 12	Lab MP3s Leçon 12	espaces.vhlcentral.com Leçon 12

[1] He who steals an egg would steal an ox.
[2] Those who give advice are not the ones who pay the price.

Section Goals

In this section, students will learn about additional open and closed vowel sounds.

Instructional Resources
Textbook MP3s
Lab Manual, p. 46
Lab MP3s
WB/VM/LM Answer Key
IRCD-ROM: IRM (Textbook Audioscript; Lab Audioscript)
espaces.vhlcentral.com: activities, downloads, reference tools

Suggestions

- Model the pronunciation of each open and closed vowel sound. Have students watch the shape of your mouth, then repeat each sound after you. Pronounce each of the example words and have students repeat them.
- Point out that the letters **o** and **e** together are usually written as the single character **œ**.
- Ask students to provide more examples of words from this lesson or previous lessons with these vowel sounds. Examples: **tailleur, vendeuse, peur, sœur,** and **chanteuse.**
- Dictate five familiar words containing the open and closed vowels presented in this section to the class, repeating each one at least two times. Then write them on the board or on a transparency and have students check their spelling.

Dictons Ask students to explain the two sayings in their own words.

OPTIONS

Extra Practice Use these sentences with open and closed vowel sounds for additional practice or dictation. **1. Elle a deux ordinateurs neufs. 2. Ma sœur est jeune et sérieuse. 3. J'aime mieux être coiffeur ou ingénieur. 4. Tu veux ce vieux tailleur?**

Extra Practice Teach students this French tongue-twister that contains the open and closed vowel sounds on this page. **Un généreux déjeuner régénérerait des généraux dégénérés.**

Section Goals

In this section, students will learn functional phrases for talking about clothing and gifts through comprehensible input.

Instructional Resources
WB/VM: Video Manual, pp. 233–234
WB/VM/LM Answer Key
Video CD-ROM
Video on DVD
*IRCD-ROM: IRM (Videoscript; **Roman-photo** Translations)*
espaces.vhlcentral.com: activities, downloads, reference tools

Video Recap: Leçon 11 Before doing this **Roman-photo**, review the previous one with this activity.

1. Qu'est-ce que Sandrine a préparé pour l'anniversaire de Stéphane? (les desserts: une mousse au chocolat, des biscuits et un gâteau)
2. Qu'est-ce que Rachid et Astrid ont acheté comme cadeaux? (une calculatrice, des livres et une montre)
3. Qui a fait la décoration au café? (Astrid, Valérie et Amina)
4. Qu'est-ce qu'Amina a apporté à la fête? (un cadeau et de la glace au chocolat)

Video Synopsis Stéphane arrives at his surprise party. Sandrine explains that David is in Paris with his parents. Sandrine admires Amina's outfit, and Stéphane opens his presents. Valérie gives him a leather jacket and gloves. When he opens the books and calculator from Rachid and Astrid, he tries to act pleased. Then he realizes they were gag gifts when he sees the watch.

Suggestions

- Have students read the title, glance at the video stills, and predict what the episode will be about. Record their predictions.
- Have students read the **Roman-photo** conversation in groups of six.
- Have students scan the captions for vocabulary related to clothing and colors.
- Review students' predictions and ask them which ones were correct.

communication cultures NATIONAL STANDARDS

L'anniversaire

PERSONNAGES

Amina

Astrid

Rachid

Sandrine

Stéphane

Valérie

1

Au café...

VALÉRIE, SANDRINE, AMINA, ASTRID ET RACHID Surprise! Joyeux anniversaire, STÉPHANE!
STÉPHANE Alors là, je suis agréablement surpris!
VALÉRIE Bon anniversaire, mon chéri!
SANDRINE On a organisé cette surprise ensemble...

2

VALÉRIE Pas du tout! C'est Sandrine qui a presque tout préparé.
SANDRINE Oh, je n'ai fait que les desserts et ton gâteau d'anniversaire.
STÉPHANE Tu es un ange.
RACHID Bon anniversaire, Stéphane. Tu sais, à ton âge, il ne faut pas perdre son temps, alors cette année, tu travailles sérieusement, c'est promis?
STÉPHANE Oui, oui.

3

AMINA Rachid a raison. Dix-huit ans, c'est une étape importante dans la vie! Il faut fêter ça.
ASTRID Joyeux anniversaire, Stéphane.
STÉPHANE Oh, et en plus, vous m'avez apporté des cadeaux!

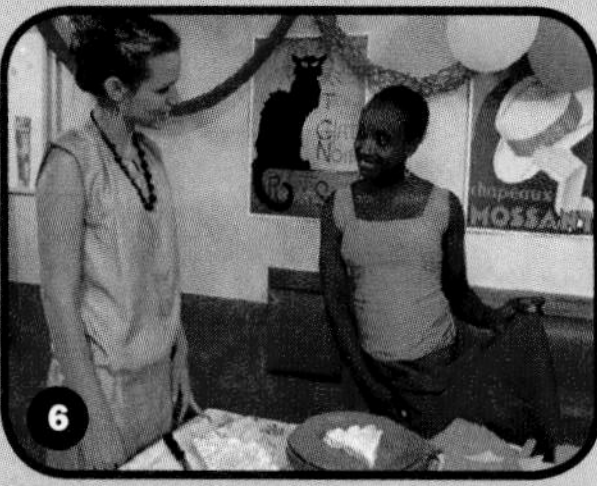

6

AMINA Oui. J'ai tout fait moi-même: ce t-shirt, cette jupe et j'ai acheté ces chaussures.
SANDRINE Tu es une véritable artiste, Amina! Ta jupe est très originale! J'adore!
AMINA J'ai une idée. Tu me prêtes ta robe grise samedi et je te prête ma jupe. D'accord?
SANDRINE Bonne idée!

7

STÉPHANE Eh! C'est super cool, ce blouson en cuir noir. Avec des gants en plus! Merci, maman!
AMINA Ces gants vont très bien avec le blouson! Très à la mode!
STÉPHANE Tu trouves?

8

RACHID Tiens, Stéphane.
STÉPHANE Mais qu'est-ce que c'est? Des livres?
RACHID Oui, la littérature, c'est important pour la culture générale!
VALÉRIE Tu as raison, Rachid.
STÉPHANE Euh oui... euh... c'est gentil... euh... merci, Rachid.

ACTIVITÉS

1 Vrai ou faux? Indiquez si les affirmations suivantes sont **vraies** ou **fausses**. Corrigez les phrases fausses.

1. David ne veut pas (*doesn't want*) aller à la fête.
   Faux. David est désolé de ne pas être là.
2. Sandrine porte une jupe bleue.
   Faux. Sandrine porte une robe grise.
3. Amina a fait sa jupe elle-même (*herself*).
   Vrai.
4. La jupe d'Amina, c'est de la soie.
   Vrai.
5. Valérie donne un blouson en cuir et une ceinture à Stéphane.
   Faux. Valérie donne un blouson en cuir et des gants à Stéphane.
6. Sandrine n'aime pas partager ses vêtements.
   Faux. Sandrine va prêter sa robe à Amina.
7. Pour Amina, 18 ans, c'est une étape importante.
   Vrai.
8. Sandrine n'a rien fait (*didn't do anything*) pour la fête.
   Faux. Sandrine a fait le gâteau et les desserts.
9. Rachid donne des livres de littérature à Stéphane.
   Vrai.
10. Stéphane pense que ses amis sont drôles.
    Faux. Stéphane pense que ses amis ne sont pas drôles.

OPTIONS

Avant de regarder la vidéo Before viewing the video, have students work in pairs and make a list of words and expressions they might hear at a surprise birthday party.

Regarder la vidéo Show the video episode and tell students to check off the words or expressions they hear on their lists. Then show the episode again and have students give you a play-by-play description of the action. Write their descriptions on the board.

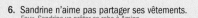

Les amis fêtent l'anniversaire de Stéphane.

4

5

SANDRINE Ah au fait, David est désolé de ne pas être là. Ce week-end, il visite Paris avec ses parents. Mais il pense à toi.
STÉPHANE Je comprends tout à fait. Les parents de David sont de Washington, n'est-ce pas?
SANDRINE Oui, c'est ça.

AMINA Merci, Sandrine. Je trouve que tu es très élégante dans cette robe grise! La couleur te va très bien.
SANDRINE Vraiment? Et toi, tu es très chic. C'est du coton?
AMINA Non, de la soie.
SANDRINE Cet ensemble, c'est une de tes créations, n'est-ce pas?

9

10

STÉPHANE Une calculatrice rose... pour moi?
ASTRID Oui, c'est pour t'aider à répondre à toutes les questions en maths et avec le sourire.
STÉPHANE Euh, merci beaucoup! C'est très... utile.
ASTRID Attends! Il y a encore un cadeau pour toi...

STÉPHANE Ouah, cette montre est géniale, merci!
ASTRID Tu as aimé notre petite blague? Nous, on a bien ri.
RACHID Eh Stéphane! Tu as vraiment aimé tes livres et ta calculatrice?
STÉPHANE Ouais, vous deux, ce que vous êtes drôles.

Expressions utiles

Talking about your clothes

- **Et toi, tu es très chic. C'est du coton/de la soie?**
  And you, you are very chic. Is it cotton/silk?
- **J'ai tout fait moi-même.**
  I did/made everything myself.
- **La couleur te va très bien.**
  The color suits you well.
- **Tu es une véritable artiste! Ta jupe est très originale!**
  You are a true artist! Your skirt is very original!
- **Tu me prêtes ta robe grise samedi et je te prête ma jupe.**
  You lend me your gray dress Saturday and I'll lend you my skirt.
- **C'est super cool, ce blouson en cuir/laine/velours noir(e). Avec des gants en plus!**
  It's really cool, this black leather/wool/velvet jacket. With gloves as well!

Additional vocabulary

- **Vous m'avez apporté des cadeaux!**
  You brought me gifts!
- **Tu sais, à ton âge, il ne faut pas perdre son temps.**
  You know, at your age, one should not waste time.
- **C'est pour t'aider à répondre à toutes les questions en maths et avec le sourire.**
  It's to help you answer all math questions with a smile.

- **agréablement surpris(e)** *pleasantly surprised*
- **C'est promis?** *Promise?*
- **Il pense à toi.** *He's thinking of you.*
- **tout à fait** *absolutely*
- **Vraiment?** *Really?*
- **véritable** *true, genuine*
- **Pour moi?** *For me?*
- **Attends!** *Wait!*
- **On a bien ri.** *We had a good laugh.*

ACTIVITÉS

2 Identifiez Indiquez qui a dit (*said*) les phrases suivantes: Valérie **(V)**, Sandrine **(S)**, Amina **(A)**, Astrid **(As)**, Rachid **(R)** ou Stéphane **(St)**.

S 1. Tu es une véritable artiste.
As 2. On a bien ri.
A 3. Très à la mode.
St 4. Je comprends tout à fait.
V 5. C'est Sandrine qui a presque tout préparé.
R 6. C'est promis?

3 À vous! Ce sont les soldes. Sandrine, David et Amina vont dans un magasin pour acheter des vêtements. Ils essaient différentes choses, donnent leurs avis (*opinions*) et parlent de leurs préférences, des prix et des matières (*fabrics*). Avec un(e) partenaire, écrivez la conversation et jouez la scène devant la classe.

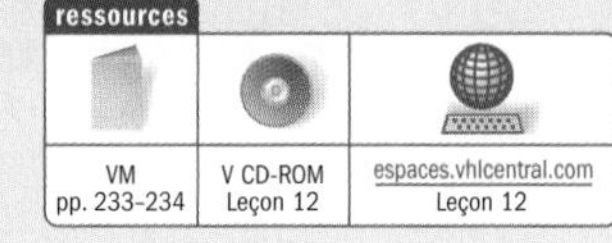

ressources
VM pp. 233-234
V CD-ROM Leçon 12
espaces.vhlcentral.com Leçon 12

Expressions utiles
- Model the pronunciation of the **Expressions utiles** and have students repeat them.
- As you work through the list, point out expressions with indirect object pronouns, disjunctive pronouns, and **-re** verbs. Tell students that these grammar structures will be formally presented in the **Structures** section.
- Respond briefly to questions about indirect object pronouns and **-re** verbs. Reinforce correct forms, but do not expect students to produce them consistently at this time.
- Point out that the pronouns **tu**, **te**, and **toi** all mean *you*, but they cannot be used interchangeably because they are different parts of speech.
- To practice different fabrics and other materials, ask students yes/no and either/or questions about their clothing. Examples: ____, **votre chemisier, c'est du coton ou de la soie?** ____, **votre blouson, c'est du cuir ou de la laine? Avez-vous des gants en cuir noir?**

1 Suggestion Have students write their corrections for false statements on the board.

1 Expansion For additional practice, give students these items. **11. Stéphane n'est pas content de la fête. (Faux.) 12. David est à Paris avec ses parents (Vrai.) 13. Sandrine aime bien la jupe d'Amina. (Vrai.) 14. Stéphane n'aime pas la montre. (Faux.)**

2 Expansion In addition to identifying the speaker, have students give the name of the person to whom each one is speaking. **1. Amina 2. Stéphane 3. Stéphane 4. Sandrine 5. Stéphane 6. Stéphane**

3 Suggestion Tell students to use an idea map or outline to plan their conversation before they begin to write it.

OPTIONS

Game Divide the class into two teams. Give one team member a card with the name of an item of clothing or an accessory. This person has 30 seconds to draw the item and one player on his or her team has to guess what it is. Give a point for each correct answer. If a player cannot guess the item within the time limit, the next player on the opposing team may "steal" the point.

Extra Practice Bring in photos from French fashion magazines or catalogues, such as ***3 Suisses*** or ***La Redoute***, and have students give their opinions about the clothing and accessories.

Section Goals

NATIONAL STANDARDS: connections, cultures

In this section, students will:
- learn about the fashion industry in France and where to buy clothes
- learn terms related to fashion
- read about traditional clothing and fabrics in some francophone regions
- read about Coco Chanel

Instructional Resources
espaces.vhlcentral.com: activities, downloads, reference tools

Culture à la loupe

Avant la lecture Have students read the title, look at the photos, and predict what this reading is about. Then ask them to share any information they know about French fashion or the fashion industry in France.

Lecture
- Point out the **Coup de main** and have students compare the clothing sizes. Example: **Si une femme porte la taille 8 aux États-Unis, quelle taille porte-t-elle en France? (38)**
- Explain that a **hypermarché** is similar to a Wal-Mart in the United States.

Après la lecture Ask students: **Où les Français achètent-ils leurs vêtements? (dans les boutiques indépendantes, dans les chaînes de magasins spécialisés, dans les hypermarchés, dans les centres commerciaux, au marché aux puces, sur catalogue et sur Internet)**

1 Expansion For additional practice, give students these items. **11. Les couturiers ne dessinent pas de modèles pour le prêt-à-porter. (Faux.) 12. On peut (*can*) acheter des vêtements aux marchés aux puces en France. (Vrai.)**

CULTURE À LA LOUPE

La mode en France

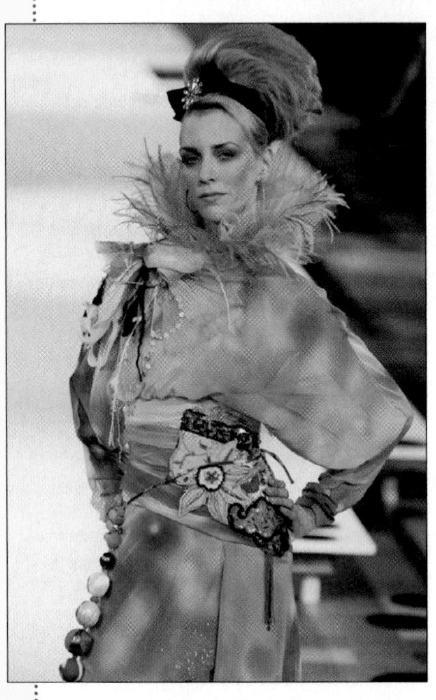

Paris est la capitale de la mode et les maisons de haute couture° françaises, comme Chanel, Yves Saint Laurent, Dior ou Christian Lacroix, sont connues° dans le monde entier°. Pendant° une semaine, en été et en hiver, elles présentent leurs collections à la presse et à un public privilégié, au cours de° défilés de mode°. Les modèles° sont uniques et très chers. Certains couturiers° dessinent° aussi des modèles pour le prêt-à-porter°. Ils vendent° ces collections plus abordables° dans leurs boutiques et parfois dans les grands magasins, comme les Galeries Lafayette ou le Printemps à Paris.

Pour la majorité des Français, la mode est un moyen° d'expression. Beaucoup de jeunes, par exemple, personnalisent leurs vêtements «basiques», ce qu'on appelle «customiser». Les magasins préférés des Français sont les boutiques indépendantes et, pour les jeunes, les chaînes de magasins spécialisés, comme Naf Naf ou Kookaï. Les Français achètent également° des vêtements dans les hypermarchés° et les centres commerciaux, comme Auchan ou Carrefour. Des vêtements sont aussi vendus° sur les marchés aux puces°, et par correspondance, dans des catalogues et sur Internet.

Coup de main

Comparaison des tailles°

FEMMES						
France	36	38	40	42	44	46
USA	6	8	10	12	14	16
HOMMES (PANTALONS)						
France	36	38	40	42	44	46
USA	26	28	30	32	34	36

Évolution des dépenses des Français pour la mode (en % du budget)

maisons de haute couture *high fashion houses* **connues** *known* **monde entier** *entire world* **Pendant** *For* **au cours de** *during* **défilés de mode** *fashion shows* **modèles** *creations (clothing)* **couturiers** *fashion designers* **dessinent** *design* **prêt-à-porter** *ready-to-wear* **vendent** *sell* **plus abordables** *more affordable* **moyen** *means* **également** *also* **hypermarchés** *large supermarkets* **vendus** *sold* **marchés aux puces** *flea markets* **tailles** *sizes (clothing)*

ACTIVITÉS

1 Vrai ou faux? Indiquez si les phrases sont **vraies** ou **fausses**. Corrigez les phrases fausses.

1. Les grands couturiers français dessinent des modèles de haute couture. Vrai.
2. Les défilés de haute couture ont lieu (*take place*) en mai. Faux. Ils ont lieu en été et en hiver.
3. Le prêt-à-porter est plus cher que (*more expensive than*) la haute couture. Faux. La haute couture est plus chère.
4. Les vêtements de prêt-à-porter sont parfois vendus dans les grands magasins. Vrai.
5. Les jeunes Français aiment personnaliser leurs vêtements. Vrai.
6. En France, on vend des vêtements par correspondance. Vrai.
7. Aujourd'hui, les Français dépensent plus (*more*) d'argent pour leurs vêtements qu'en (*than in*) 1980. Faux. Ils dépensent moins d'argent aujourd'hui.
8. Naf Naf est une maison de haute couture française. Faux. Naf Naf est une chaîne de magasins.
9. On vend des vêtements dans les hypermarchés en France. Vrai.
10. Les Français n'achètent pas de vêtements sur Internet. Faux. Ils achètent des vêtements sur Internet.

OPTIONS

Cultural Comparison Have students work in groups of three and compare where the French people and Americans shop for clothing. Tell them to list the similarities and differences in a two-column chart under the headings **Similitudes** and **Différences**. After completing their charts, have two groups get together and compare their lists.

Extra Practice First, ask students what information the graph **Évolution des dépenses des Français pour la mode** shows. (The percentage of total budget that the French spent on fashion from 1960–2000.) Then ask: **Quel pourcentage de leur budget les Français ont-ils dépensé pour la mode en 1960? (10,0%) Et en 1970? (8,2%) En 1980? (6,3%) En 1990? (5,5%) En 2000? (3,7%)** (Accept approximate answers.)

LE FRANÇAIS QUOTIDIEN

Les vêtements et la mode

fringues (*f.*)	*clothes*
look (*m.*)	*style*
vintage (*m.*)	*vintage clothing*
BCBG (bon chic bon genre)	*chic and conservative*
ringard(e)	*out-of-style*
être bien/ mal sapé(e)	*to be well/ badly dressed*
être sur son 31	*to be well-dressed*

PORTRAIT

Coco Chanel, styliste parisienne

«La mode se démode°, le style jamais.»
—*Coco Chanel*

Coco Chanel (1883–1971) est considérée comme étant° l'icône du parfum et de la mode du vingtième siècle°. Dans les années 1910, elle a l'idée audacieuse° d'intégrer la mode «à la garçonne» dans ses créations: les lignes féminines empruntent aux° éléments de la mode masculine. C'est la naissance du fameux tailleur Chanel. Pour «Mademoiselle Chanel», l'important dans la mode, c'est que les vêtements permettent de bouger°; ils doivent° être simples et confortables. Son invention de «la petite robe noire» illustre l'esprit° classique et élégant de ses collections. De nombreuses célébrités ont immortalisé le nom de Chanel: Jacqueline Kennedy avec le tailleur et Marilyn Monroe avec le parfum No. 5 par exemple.

se démode *goes out of fashion* **étant** *being* **vingtième siècle** *twentieth century* **idée audacieuse** *daring idea* **empruntent aux** *borrow* **bouger** *move* **doivent** *have to* **esprit** *spirit*

LE MONDE FRANCOPHONE

Vêtements et tissus

Voici quelques vêtements et tissus traditionnels du monde francophone.

En Afrique centrale et de l'ouest

Le boubou tunique plus ou moins° longue et souvent très colorée portée par les hommes et les femmes
Les batiks tissus° traditionnels très colorés

En Afrique du Nord

La djellaba longue tunique à capuche° portée par les hommes et les femmes
Le kaftan sorte de djellaba portée à la maison

À la Martinique

Le madras tissu typique aux couleurs vives

À Tahiti

Le paréo morceau° de tissu attaché au-dessus de la poitrine° ou à la taille°

plus ou moins *more or less* **tissus** *fabrics* **à capuche** *hooded* **morceau** *piece* **poitrine** *chest* **taille** *waist*

SUR INTERNET

Combien de couturiers présentent leurs collections dans les défilés de mode, à Paris, chaque hiver?

Go to **espaces.vhlcentral.com** to find more cultural information related to this **ESPACE CULTURE**.

ACTIVITÉS

2 Coco Chanel Complétez les phrases.

1. Coco Chanel était (*was*) __styliste de mode__.
2. Le style Chanel est inspiré de __la mode masculine__.
3. Les vêtements Chanel sont __simples et confortables__.
4. Jacqueline Kennedy portait souvent des __tailleurs__ Chanel.
5. D'après «Mademoiselle Chanel», il est très important de pouvoir (*to be able to*) __bouger__ dans ses vêtements.
6. C'est Coco Chanel qui a inventé __la petite robe noire__.

3 Le «relookage» Vous êtes conseillers/conseillères en image (*image counselors*), spécialisé(es) dans le «relookage». Votre nouveau (nouvelle) client(e), une célébrité, vous demande de l'aider à sélectionner un nouveau style. Discutez de ce nouveau look avec un(e) partenaire.

Le français quotidien
- Model the pronunciation of each term and have students repeat it.
- Ask students to give some examples of vintage clothing.
- Have volunteers create sentences using these words.

Portrait Have students look at the photos of Coco Chanel and describe her appearance and clothing. Encourage them to use some of the expressions from **Le français quotidien**.

Le monde francophone
- Bring in photos from magazines or the Internet of people wearing these types of clothing and fabrics to show the class.
- Ask a few content questions based on the reading. Examples: **1. Comment s'appelle la tunique que les gens portent en Afrique centrale? (le boubou) 2. Qu'est-ce qu'une djellaba? (C'est une longue tunique à capuche.) 3. À la Martinique, on porte des vêtements faits de batik ou de madras? (des vêtements faits de madras) 4. Où porte-t-on le kaftan? (en Afrique du Nord)**

2 Expansion For additional practice, give students these items. **7. Les collections de Chanel sont classiques et ____. (élégantes) 8. Marilyn Monroe a immortalisé ____ de Chanel. (le parfum No. 5)**

3 Suggestions
- Tell students that they can change the person's hairstyle as well as the clothing. Encourage them to include what is wrong with the person's present style in their discussion.
- Have students write their descriptions and read them aloud for the class.

OPTIONS

Vêtements et tissus Have students create five true/false statements based on the content in **Le monde francophone**. Then have students get together with a classmate and take turns reading their statements and responding **vrai** or **faux**.

Les couturiers Have students research one of the couturiers from the **Sur Internet** activity and write a short paragraph about the person. Tell them to include information about the person's accomplishments, type(s) of clothing he or she designs, where it is sold, and any other important details.

comparisons NATIONAL STANDARDS

Section Goals

In this section, students will learn:
- indirect object pronouns
- some additional uses of disjunctive pronouns

Instructional Resources
WB/VM: Workbook, pp. 79–80
Lab Manual, p. 47
Lab MP3s
WB/VM/LM Answer Key
*IRCD-ROM: IRM (**Essayez!** and **Mise en pratique** answers; Lab Audioscript)*
espaces.vhlcentral.com: activities, downloads, reference tools

Suggestions
- Say and write on the board: **Valérie achète un blouson à Stéphane.** Tell students that an indirect object is a noun or pronoun that answers the question *to whom* or *for whom* an action is done. Ask them what the indirect object of the verb is in the sentence. (Stéphane) Explain that indirect object nouns are introduced by the preposition **à**. Point out that **un blouson** is the direct object of the verb.
- Write the indirect object pronouns on the board. Show students some photos and say: **Je vous montre mes photos.** Give a student an object, such as a book, and say: **Je vous prête mon livre.** Continue the same procedure with the remaining indirect object pronouns.
- Explain that, in French, indirect object pronouns do not follow verbs as they do in English. The word order in French is *subject* + (**ne**) *indirect object pronoun* + *verb* or *subject* + *conjugated verb* + *indirect object pronoun* + *infinitive*.
- Point out that they should use **m'** and **t'** before a verb beginning with a vowel sound. Example: **Ma mère m'achète des baskets.**
- Ask students to call out the disjunctive pronouns. Explain the use of **-même(s)** and provide a few examples. Then have students create some sentences with the disjunctive pronouns.

12.1 Indirect object pronouns

- An indirect object expresses *to whom* or *for whom* an action is done. In the example below, the indirect object answers this question: **À qui parle Gisèle?** (*To whom does Gisèle speak?*)

SUBJECT VERB INDIRECT OBJECT NOUN

Gisèle parle à sa mère.
Gisèle speaks to her mother.

Indirect object pronouns

singular			plural		
me	te	lui	nous	vous	leur

- Indirect object pronouns replace indirect object nouns.

Gisèle parle à **sa mère**. *Gisèle speaks to her mother.*	Gisèle **lui** parle. *Gisèle speaks to her.*
J'envoie des cadeaux à **mes nièces**. *I send gifts to my nieces.*	Je **leur** envoie des cadeaux. *I send them gifts.*

Vous m'avez apporté des cadeaux!

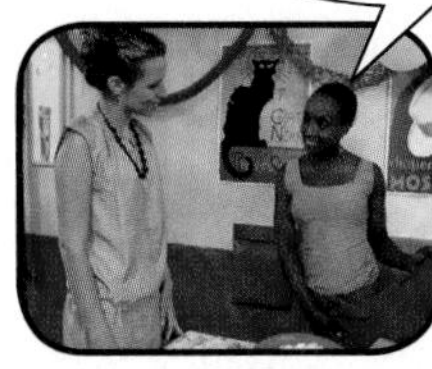

Je te prête ma jupe. D'accord?

- The indirect object pronoun usually precedes the conjugated verb.

Antoine, je **te** parle.
Antoine, I'm speaking to you.

Notre père **nous** a envoyé un poème.
Our father sent us a poem.

- In a negative statement, place the indirect object pronoun between **ne** and the conjugated verb.

Antoine, je **ne te parle** pas de ça.
Antoine, I'm not speaking to you about that.

Notre père **ne nous a** pas envoyé de poème.
Our father didn't send us a poem.

- When an infinitive follows a conjugated verb, the indirect object pronoun precedes the infinitive.

Nous allons **lui donner** la cravate.
We're going to give him the tie.

Ils espèrent **vous prêter** le costume.
They hope to lend you the suit.

MISE EN PRATIQUE

1 Complétez Corinne fait du shopping avec sa copine Célia. Trouvez le bon pronom d'objet indirect pour compléter ses phrases.

1. Je ___leur___ achète des baskets. (à mes cousins)
2. Je ___te___ prends une ceinture. (à toi, Célia)
3. Nous ___lui___ achetons une jupe. (à notre copine Christelle)
4. Célia ___nous___ prend des lunettes de soleil. (à ma mère et à moi)
5. Je ___vous___ achète des gants. (à ta mère et à toi, Célia)
6. Célia ___m'___ achète un pantalon. (à moi)

2 Dialogues Complétez les dialogues.

1. M. SAUNIER Tu m'as posé une question, chérie?
   MME SAUNIER Oui. Je ___t'___ ai demandé l'heure.
2. CLIENT Je cherche un beau pull.
   VENDEUSE Je vais ___vous___ montrer ce pull noir.
3. PROF 1 Mes étudiants ont passé l'examen.
   PROF 2 Tu ___leur___ envoies les résultats?
4. MÈRE Qu'est-ce que vous allez faire?
   ENFANTS On va aller au cinéma. Tu ___nous___ donnes de l'argent?
5. PIERRE Tu ___me___ téléphones ce soir?
   CHARLOTTE D'accord. Je te téléphone.
6. GÉRARD Christophe a oublié son pull. Il a froid!
   VALENTIN Je ___lui___ prête mon blouson.

3 Assemblez Avec un(e) partenaire, assemblez les éléments pour comparer vos familles et vos amis.
Answers will vary.

MODÈLE
Étudiant(e) 1: *Mon père me prête souvent sa voiture.*
Étudiant(e) 2: *Mon père, lui, il nous prête de l'argent.*

A	B	C
je	acheter	argent
tu	apporter	biscuits
mon père	envoyer	cadeaux
ma mère	expliquer	devoirs
mon frère	faire	e-mails
ma sœur	montrer	problèmes
mon/ma petit(e) ami(e)	parler	vêtements
mes copains	payer	voiture
?	prêter	?
	?	

OPTIONS

Extra Practice Write sentences with indirect objects on the board. Examples: **Anne-Laure ne te donne pas de biscuits. Pierre ne me parle pas. Loïc prête de l'argent à Louise. Marie nous pose une question. Je téléphone à mes amis.** Have students come to the board and circle the indirect objects.

Small Groups Working in groups of three, the first student lends an object to the second and says: **Je te prête mon/ma….** The second student responds: **Tu me prêtes ton/ta….** The third student says: **Marc lui prête son/sa….** Groups repeat the procedure until everyone has begun the chain twice. To practice plural pronouns, have two groups get together. Then two students lend something to two other students.

COMMUNICATION

4 Qu'allez-vous faire? Avec un(e) partenaire, dites ce que vous allez faire pour aider ces personnes. Employez les verbes de la liste et présentez vos réponses à la classe. Answers will vary.

MODÈLE

Un ami a soif.
On va lui donner de l'eau.

apporter	parler
demander	poser des questions
donner	préparer
envoyer	prêter
faire	téléphoner

1. Une personne âgée a froid.
2. Des touristes sont perdus (*lost*).
3. Un homme est sans abri (*homeless*).
4. Votre professeur est à l'hôpital.
5. Des amis vous invitent à manger chez eux.
6. Vos nièces ont faim.
7. Votre petit(e) ami(e) fête son anniversaire.
8. Votre meilleur(e) (*best*) ami(e) a des problèmes.

5 Les cadeaux de l'année dernière Par groupes de trois, parlez des cadeaux que vous avez achetés à votre famille et à vos amis l'année dernière. Que vous ont-ils acheté? Présentez vos réponses à la classe. Answers will vary.

MODÈLE

Étudiant(e) 1: *Qu'est-ce que tu as acheté à ta mère?*
Étudiant(e) 2: *Je lui ai acheté un ordinateur.*
Étudiant(e) 3: *Ma copine Dominique m'a donné une montre.*

6 Au grand magasin Par groupes de trois, jouez les rôles de deux client(e)s et d'un(e) vendeur/vendeuse. Les client(e)s cherchent des vêtements pour faire des cadeaux. Ils parlent de ce qu'ils (*what they*) cherchent et le/la vendeur/vendeuse leur fait des suggestions. Answers will vary.

Verbs used with indirect object pronouns

demander à	*to ask, to request*	**parler à**	*to speak to*
donner à	*to give to*	**poser une question à**	*to pose/ ask a question (to)*
envoyer à	*to send to*	**prêter à**	*to lend to*
montrer à	*to show to*	**téléphoner à**	*to phone, to call*

- The indirect object pronouns **me** and **te** become **m'** and **t'** before a verb beginning with a vowel sound.

Ton petit ami **t'envoie** des e-mails.
Your boyfriend sends you e-mails.

Isabelle **m'a** prêté son sac à main.
Isabelle lent me her handbag.

Disjunctive pronouns

BOÎTE À OUTILS
In **Leçon 6**, you learned to use disjunctive pronouns (**moi**, **toi**, **lui**, **elle**, **nous**, **vous**, **eux**, **elles**) after prepositions: **J'ai une écharpe pour ton frère/pour lui.** (*I have a scarf for your brother/for him.*)

- Disjunctive pronouns can also be used alone or in phrases without a verb.

Qui prend du café?	**Moi**!	**Eux** aussi?
Who's having coffee?	*Me!*	*Them, too?*

- Disjunctive pronouns emphasize the person to whom they refer.

Moi, je porte souvent une casquette.
Me, I often wear a cap.

Mon frère, **lui**, il déteste les casquettes.
My brother, him, he hates caps.

- To say *myself*, *ourselves*, etc., add **-même(s)** after the disjunctive pronoun.

Tu fais ça **toi-même**?
Are you doing that yourself?

Ils organisent la fête **eux-mêmes**.
They're organizing the party themselves.

Essayez! **Complétez les phrases avec le pronom d'objet indirect approprié.**

1. Tu __nous__ montres tes photos? (*us*)
2. Luc, je __te__ donne ma nouvelle adresse. (*you, fam.*)
3. Vous __me__ posez de bonnes questions. (*me*)
4. Nous __leur__ avons demandé. (*them*)
5. On __vous__ achète une nouvelle robe. (*you, form.*)
6. Ses parents __lui__ ont acheté un tailleur. (*her*)
7. Je vais __lui__ téléphoner à dix heures. (*him*)
8. Elle va __me__ prêter sa jupe. (*me*)

Essayez! Have students restate items 1, 2, 4, 5, and 6 using the **futur proche**. Example: **1. Tu vas nous montrer tes photos?**

1 Expansion Have students write four more sentences with indirect objects (not pronouns). Tell them to exchange papers with a classmate and rewrite the sentences, replacing the indirect object with the corresponding indirect object pronoun.

2 Suggestion To check students' answers, have volunteers read different roles aloud.

3 Expansion Have students convert three of their statements into questions for their partner, using **Qui...?** or **À qui...?** Example: **Qui te prête sa voiture?**

4 Suggestion Have pairs write their suggestions. Encourage them to come up with multiple responses for each item.

5 Suggestion Before beginning the activity, give students a few minutes to jot down a list of gifts they bought for their family last year. Then have three volunteers read the **modèle** aloud.

6 Suggestions
- Before beginning the activity, have students describe what is happening in the photo.
- Videotape the scenes in class or have students videotape themselves outside of class. Show the videos so students can critique their role plays.

OPTIONS

Video Have students read along as you show the video episode again. Tell them to note each time an indirect object pronoun or a disjunctive pronoun is used. After the video, ask them to read the sentences they identified and to say to whom each pronoun refers.

Pairs Have students work in pairs. Tell them to write five questions they would like to ask their partner that require an indirect object pronoun in the answer. Then they should take turns asking and answering each other's questions.

comparisons — NATIONAL STANDARDS

Section Goals

In this section, students will learn:
- regular **-re** verbs
- irregular **-re** verbs

Instructional Resources
WB/VM: Workbook, pp. 81–82
Lab Manual, p. 48
Lab MP3s
WB/VM/LM Answer Key
*IRCD-ROM: IRM (**Essayez!** and **Mise en pratique** answers; Lab Audioscript; Info Gap Activities)*
espaces.vhlcentral.com: activities, downloads, reference tools

Suggestions
- Model the pronunciation of the **-re** verbs and have students repeat them.
- Introduce the verbs by talking about yourself and asking students follow-up questions. Examples: **Je conduis à la fac en voiture tous les jours. Conduisez-vous à la fac? Où conduisez-vous? D'habitude, je mets un pantalon. Aujourd'hui, j'ai mis une jupe/un costume. Et vous, que mettez-vous en général? Je rends visite à ma famille le week-end. Rendez-vous visite à votre famille le week-end?**
- Ask a volunteer to go to the board and write the conjugation of **donner** as you write the conjugation of **attendre**. Have students compare the endings of the two verb conjugations, noting the similarities and differences.
- Follow the same procedure with the conjugations of **conduire** and **mettre**. Point out that many irregular **-re** verbs have two stems. Examples: **conduire (condui-, conduis-)** and **mettre (met-, mett-)**.
- Explain that the past participles of regular **-re** verbs add **-u** to the stem. Example: **attendre: attendu**. Then say the verbs listed and have students respond with the past participles.
- Point out the irregular past participles.

12.2 Regular and irregular *-re* verbs

Point de départ You've already seen infinitives that end in **-er** and **-ir**. The infinitive forms of some French verbs end in **-re**.

- Many **-re** verbs, such as **attendre** (*to wait*), follow a regular pattern of conjugation, as shown below.

attendre	
j'attends	nous attendons
tu attends	vous attendez
il/elle attend	ils/elles attendent

Tu **attends** des soldes? *Are you waiting for a sale?*	Nous **attendons** dans le magasin. *We're waiting in the store.*

Other regular *-re* verbs			
descendre	*to go down; to take down*	rendre (à)	*to give back, to return (to)*
entendre	*to hear*	rendre visite (à)	*to visit someone*
perdre (son temps)	*to lose (one's time)*	répondre (à)	*to respond, to answer (to)*
		vendre	*to sell*

- The verb **attendre** means *to wait* or *to wait for*. Unlike English, it does not require a preposition.

Marc **attend le bus**. *Marc is waiting for the bus.*	Ils **attendent Robert**. *They're waiting for Robert.*

- To form the past participle of regular **-re** verbs, drop the **-re** from the infinitive and add **-u**.

Les étudiants ont **vendu** leurs livres. *The students sold their books.*	Il a **entendu** arriver la voiture de sa femme. *He heard his wife's car arrive.*
J'ai **répondu** à ton e-mail. *I answered your e-mail.*	Nous avons **perdu** patience. *We lost patience.*

- **Rendre visite à** means *to visit a person*, while **visiter** means *to visit a place*.

Tu **rends visite à ta grand-mère** le lundi. *You visit your grandmother on Mondays.*	Cécile va **visiter le musée** aujourd'hui. *Cécile is going to visit the museum today.*

MISE EN PRATIQUE

1 Qui fait quoi? Quelles phrases vont avec les illustrations?

1.

3.

2.

4.

3 a. Martin attend ses copains.
4 b. Nous rendons visite à notre grand-mère.
1 c. Tu vends de jolis vêtements.
2 d. Je ris en regardant un film.

2 Les clients difficiles Henri et Gilbert travaillent pour un grand magasin. Complétez leur conversation.

GILBERT Tu n'as pas encore mangé?
HENRI Non, j' (1) attends (attendre) Jean-Michel.
GILBERT Il ne (2) descend (descendre) pas tout de suite. Il (3) perd (perdre) son temps avec un client difficile. Il (4) met (mettre) des cravates, des costumes, des chaussures...
HENRI Nous ne (5) vendons (vendre) pas souvent à des clients comme ça.
GILBERT C'est vrai. Ils (6) promettent (promettre) d'acheter quelque chose, puis ils partent les mains vides (*empty*).

3 La journée de Béatrice Hier, Béatrice a fait une liste des choses à faire. Avec un(e) partenaire, utilisez les verbes de la liste au passé composé pour dire (*to say*) tout ce qu'elle a fait. Answers will vary.

attendre	rendre visite
conduire	traduire
mettre	vendre

1. devoir d'espagnol	*4. tante Albertine*
2. centre commercial	*5. gants dans mon sac*
3. e-mail de Sébastien	*6. vieille voiture*

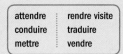

OPTIONS

Extra Practice Do a rapid-response drill. Write an infinitive from the list of **-re** verbs on the board. Call out subject pronouns and/or names, and have students respond with the correct verb form. Then repeat the drill, having students respond with the correct forms of the **passé composé**.

Pairs Have students make a list of five things their parents allow them to do and five things their parents don't allow them to do. Then have them get together in pairs and compare their lists. Have volunteers report to the class the items they have in common. Example: **Mes parents ne me permettent pas de mettre des vêtements trop serrés. Ils me permettent parfois de conduire leur voiture.**

COMMUNICATION

4 Fréquence Employez les verbes de la liste et d'autres verbes pour dire (*to tell*) à un(e) partenaire ce que (*what*) vous faites tous les jours, une fois par mois et une fois par an. Alternez les rôles. Answers will vary.

MODÈLE

Étudiant(e) 1: *J'attends mes copains au resto U tous les jours.*
Étudiant(e) 2: *Moi, je rends visite à mes grands-parents une fois par mois.*

attendre	perdre
conduire	rendre
entendre	répondre
mettre	sourire
?	?

5 Les charades Par groupes de quatre, jouez aux charades. Chaque étudiant(e) pense à une phrase différente avec un des verbes en **-re**. La première personne qui devine (*guesses*) propose la prochaine charade. Answers will vary.

6 La journée des vendeuses Votre professeur va vous donner, à vous et à votre partenaire, une série d'illustrations qui montrent la journée d'Aude et d'Aurélie. Attention! Ne regardez pas la feuille de votre partenaire. Answers will vary.

MODÈLE

Étudiant(e) 1: *Le matin, elles ont conduit pour aller au magasin.*
Étudiant(e) 2: *Après,...*

- Some verbs whose infinitives end in **-re** are irregular.

Irregular *-re* verbs

	conduire *(to drive)*	**mettre** *(to put (on))*	**rire** *(to laugh)*
je	conduis	mets	ris
tu	conduis	mets	ris
il/elle	conduit	met	rit
nous	conduisons	mettons	rions
vous	conduisez	mettez	riez
ils/elles	conduisent	mettent	rient

Je **conduis** la voiture.
I'm driving the car.

Thérèse **met** ses gants.
Thérèse puts on her gloves.

Elles **rient** pendant le spectacle.
They laugh during the show.

Other irregular *-re* verbs

like *conduire*

construire	*to build, to construct*
détruire	*to destroy*
produire	*to produce*
réduire	*to reduce*
traduire	*to translate*

like *mettre*

permettre	*to allow*
promettre	*to promise*

like *rire*

sourire	*to smile*

- The past participle of the verb **mettre** is **mis**. Verbs derived from **mettre** (**permettre**, **promettre**) follow the same pattern: **permis, promis.**
- The past participle of **conduire** is **conduit**. Verbs like it follow the same pattern: **construire → construit**; **détruire → détruit**; **produire → produit**; **réduire → réduit**; **traduire → traduit.**
- The past participle of **rire** is **ri**. The past participle of **sourire** is **souri.**

Essayez! **Complétez les phrases avec la forme correcte du présent du verbe.**

1. Ils ___attendent___ (attendre) l'arrivée du train.
2. Nous ___répondons___ (répondre) aux questions du professeur.
3. Je ___souris___ (sourire) quand je suis heureuse.
4. Si on ___construit___ (construire) trop, on ___détruit___ (détruire) la nature.
5. Quand il fait froid, vous ___mettez___ (mettre) un pull.
6. Est-ce que les étudiants ___entendent___ (entendre) le professeur?
7. Keiko ___conduit___ (conduire) sa voiture ce week-end.
8. Si le café n'est pas bon, je ___mets___ (mettre) du sucre (*sugar*).

Essayez! For additional practice, change the subjects of the sentences and have students restate them.

1 Expansion Have students create short descriptions of the people, places, and objects in the drawings by putting in additional information.

2 Expansion Ask students comprehension questions about the dialogue. Examples: **1. Pourquoi Henri n'a-t-il pas encore mangé? (Il attend Jean-Michel.) 2. Où est Jean-Michel? (Il est avec un client difficile.) 3. Pourquoi ce client est-il difficile? (parce qu'il met tout, mais il part les mains vides)**

3 Expansion Have students also say what Béatrice did not do.

4 Suggestion Have two volunteers read the **modèle** aloud.

4 Expansion To practice the **passé composé**, have students specify when they did these things. Example: **J'ai rendu visite à mes grands-parents en avril.**

5 Suggestion This activity can also be used as a game by dividing the class into two teams with players from each team acting out the charades.

6 Suggestion Divide the class into pairs and distribute the Info Gap Handouts in the IRM on the IRCD-ROM for this activity.

OPTIONS

Extra Practice Ask students personalized questions using **-re** verbs. Examples: **1. Comment les étudiants perdent-ils leur temps? 2. Est-ce que l'argent rend les gens heureux? 3. Que vend-on dans une boutique? 4. Vos parents vous permettent-ils d'avoir une voiture à la fac? 5. Conduisez-vous rapidement? 6. Où mettez-vous vos livres en classe?**

Pairs Have students work in pairs. Tell them to write a conversation between a clerk in a clothing store and a customer who has lost some item like sunglasses, a scarf, or gloves. The customer should explain the situation, and the clerk should ask for details, such as when the item was lost and a description. Alternatively, pairs can role-play this situation.

Instructional Resources
IRCD-ROM: IRM (Info Gap Activities); Testing Program, pp. 45–48; Test Files; Testing Program MP3s; Test Generator espaces.vhlcentral.com: activities, downloads, reference tools

1 Suggestion Have two volunteers read the **modèle** aloud. Remind students that they need to use the preposition **à** before the indirect object in the questions.

2 Expansion Take a quick class survey of students' reactions to each type of e-mail. Tally the results on the board.

3 Suggestion Before beginning the activity, have students jot down a list of objects.

4 Suggestion Before beginning, have the class identify the items in each **ensemble**.

4 Expansion Have students think of two new destinations. Tell them to switch roles and repeat the activity.

5 Suggestion Encourage students to use some of the comments in the **Expressions utiles** on page 201 in their role plays.

6 Suggestion Divide the class into pairs and distribute the Info Gap Handouts in the IRM on the IRCD-ROM for this activity.

communication NATIONAL STANDARDS

Synthèse

1 Je leur téléphone Par groupes de quatre, interviewez vos camarades. Comment entrent-ils en contact avec eux? Préparez dix questions avec un verbe et une personne de la liste. Écrivez les réponses. Answers will vary.

MODÈLE

Étudiant(e) 1: *Est-ce que tu parles souvent à ton frère?*
Étudiant(e) 2: *Oui, je lui parle le lundi.*

verbes	personnes
donner un cadeau	copain ou copine d'enfance
envoyer une carte/un e-mail	cousin ou cousine
parler	grands-parents
rendre visite	petit(e) ami(e)
téléphoner	sœur ou frère

2 Mes e-mails Ces personnes vous envoient des e-mails. Que faites-vous? Vous ne répondez pas, vous attendez quelques jours, vous leur téléphonez? Par groupes de trois, comparez vos réactions. Answers will vary.

MODÈLE

Étudiant(e) 1: *Ma mère m'envoie un e-mail tous les jours.*
Étudiant(e) 2: *Tu lui réponds tout de suite?*
Étudiant(e) 3: *Tu préfères lui téléphoner?*

1. un e-mail anonyme
2. un e-mail d'un(e) camarade de classe
3. un e-mail d'un professeur
4. un e-mail d'un(e) ami(e) d'enfance
5. un e-mail d'un(e) ex-petit(e) ami(e)
6. un e-mail de vos parents

3 Une liste Des membres de votre famille ou des amis vous ont donné, prêté ou acheté des objets que vous n'aimez pas du tout. Faites une liste de quatre ou cinq de ces objets. Comparez votre liste à la liste d'un(e) camarade. Answers will vary.

MODÈLE

Étudiant(e) 1: *Ma sœur m'a prêté une écharpe verte et laide et mon père m'a acheté des chaussettes marron trop petites!*
Étudiant(e) 2: *L'année dernière, mon petit ami m'a donné...*

4 Quoi mettre? Vous et votre partenaire allez faire des choses différentes. Un(e) partenaire va fêter la retraite de ses grands-parents à Tahiti. L'autre va skier dans les Alpes. Qu'allez-vous porter? Demandez des vêtements à votre partenaire si vous n'aimez pas tous les vêtements de votre ensemble. Answers will vary.

MODÈLE

Étudiant(e) 1: *Est-ce que tu me prêtes ton blouson jaune?*
Étudiant(e) 2: *Ah non, j'ai besoin de ce blouson. Tu me prêtes ton pantalon?*

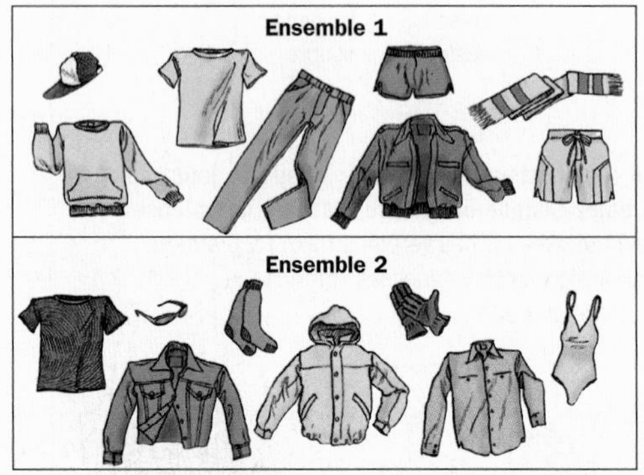

5 S'il te plaît Votre ami(e) a acheté un nouveau vêtement que vous aimez beaucoup. Vous essayez de convaincre (*to convince*) cet(te) ami(e) de vous prêter ce vêtement. Préparez un dialogue avec un(e) partenaire où vous employez tous les verbes. Jouez la scène pour la classe. Answers will vary.

aller avec	montrer
aller bien	prêter
donner	promettre
mettre	rendre

6 Bon anniversaire, Nicolas! Votre professeur va vous donner, à vous et à votre partenaire, deux feuilles d'activités différentes. Attention! Ne regardez pas la feuille de votre partenaire. Answers will vary.

MODÈLE

Étudiant(e) 1: *Les amis de Nicolas lui téléphonent.*
Étudiant(e) 2: *Ensuite,...*

ressources

WB	LM	Lab MP3s	espaces.vhlcentral.com
pp. 79–82	pp. 47–48	Leçon 12	Leçon 12

OPTIONS

Small Groups Have students work in groups of three. Tell them to imagine that it is the holiday season. They have to create a radio commercial for a clothing store. The commercials should include gift ideas for prospective customers, such as what they can buy, for whom, and at what price.

Extra Practice Have students write a conversation between two people sitting at a busy sidewalk café in the city. They are watching the people who walk by, asking each other questions about what the passersby are doing, and making comments about their clothing. Tell students to use as many **-re** verbs and verbs that take indirect object pronouns as possible.

Interlude

NATIONAL
connections
communities
STANDARDS

Bal dans ma rue

*Pour illustrer le thème des fêtes, la chanson, **Bal dans ma rue** (1949), décrit° un bal dans une rue° de Paris. Les musiciens sont dans un café, où il y a beaucoup de monde°. La chanteuse a présenté son petit ami à sa meilleure° amie. Ils se sont mariés° ce matin et voilà pourquoi il y a un bal ce soir.*

*ÉDITH PIAF (1915–1963), l'interprète° de **Bal dans ma rue**, est née° à Paris, sous le nom d'Édith Gassion. À 15 ans, pour manger, elle commence à chanter dans les rues de Paris. En 1932, le directeur d'un cabaret l'entend chanter et l'engage°. Il l'appelle «la Môme Piaf», qui signifie en argot° «le petit moineau°». Elle devient° très vite une grande vedette° et adopte le nom d'Édith Piaf. Elle est encore maintenant le symbole de la chanson française.*

Marcelle Lender dansant le boléro dans «Chilpéric»

HENRI DE TOULOUSE-LAUTREC (1864–1901), né aristocrate et infirme, est un peintre français considéré comme une des sources de l'Expressionnisme. Il se différencie des artistes impressionnistes par des œuvres plus crues°. Il fréquente les cabarets de Paris où il aime représenter l'ambiance chaude des soirées. Le thème de la fête est très présent dans son travail, comme ici avec une actrice dansant dans une pièce° de théâtre.

Activité

Répondez aux questions. Answers will vary.

1. Y a-t-il des fêtes en plein air (*outdoors*) dans votre ville? À quelle occasion? Qu'est-ce que vous portez pour ces fêtes? Quelles sortes de personnes y a-t-il?
2. Qu'est-ce qu'Édith Piaf porte sur la photo? Et les gens dans le tableau (*painting*)?
3. Qu'est-ce que fait la femme dans le tableau? D'après vous (*In your opinion*), que font les gens autour d'elle?
4. Quelle fête préférez-vous, le bal en plein air ou le spectacle au cabaret? Pourquoi?

SUR INTERNET

Go to **espaces.vhlcentral.com** for more information related to this **Interlude**.

décrit *describes* **rue** *street* **beaucoup de monde** *a lot of people* **meilleure** *best* **se sont mariés** *got married* **interprète** *performer* **est née** *was born* **l'engage** *hires her* **en argot** *in slang* **moineau** *sparrow* **devient** *becomes* **vedette** *star* **œuvres plus crues** *more crude works (i.e., depicting lower classes of society)* **pièce** *play*

Section Goals

In this section, students will learn about:
- Édith Piaf
- Henri de Toulouse-Lautrec

Instructional Resources
espaces.vhlcentral.com: activities, downloads, reference tools

Bal dans ma rue
To check comprehension, ask these questions.

1. À quel âge est-ce qu'Édith Piaf commence à chanter? (à 15 ans) Pourquoi? (pour manger)
2. De quoi est-elle le symbole? (la chanson française)
3. Quel événement décrit la chanson? (un bal dans une rue de Paris)
4. Pourquoi y a-t-il un bal? (Sa meilleure amie et son petit ami se sont mariés.)

Marcelle Lender dansant le boléro dans «Chilpéric»
Marcelle Lender (1862–1926) was a French singer, dancer, and entertainer who gained fame performing at the **Théâtre des Variétés** in Montmartre. She appears in several of Toulouse-Lautrec's works. This painting depicts her performance in Florimond Hervé's operetta ***Chilpéric*** in 1895.

OPTIONS

Édith Piaf At one point in her life, Édith Piaf was romantically involved with Yves Montand, whose song ***Les grands boulevards*** was featured in the **Leçon 9 Interlude**, page 159. Ask students if they are familiar with the song ***La vie en rose***, which is Édith Piaf's most famous song. Louis Armstrong, Grace Jones, and Donna Summer are among the many artists who have sung their own versions of this timeless ballad.

Les bals populaires Like the one described in the song, **bals populaires** are still popular throughout France. These street dances often feature music, dancing, food, and sometimes fireworks. They are usually held on special occasions, such as for Bastille Day (**le 14 juillet**).

Section Goals

In this section, students will read historical and cultural information about **Aquitaine**, **Midi-Pyrénées**, and **Languedoc-Roussillon**.

Instructional Resources
IRCD-ROM: Transparency #33,
WB/VM: Workbook, pp. 83–84
WB/VM/LM Answer Key
espaces.vhlcentral.com: activities; downloads; reference tools

Carte des régions Aquitaine, Midi-Pyrénées et Languedoc-Roussillon

- Have students look at the map or use **Transparency #33**. Ask volunteers to read aloud the names of cities and geographical features. Model French pronunciation as necessary. Point out the locations of Spain and Andorra.
- Have students identify the locations of the places in the photos.

La région en chiffres

- Point out the three different coats of arms for the regions.
- Have volunteers read the sections aloud. After each section, ask questions about the content.
- Point out that the Bordeaux region is one of the largest producers of fine wines in the world.
- Ask students to share any information they might know about the **Personnages célèbres**.

Incroyable mais vrai! The original cave at Lascaux was closed in 1963 in order to save the paintings from deterioration. A replica of the cave, known as Lascaux II, was built nearby and contains reproductions of the Great Hall of Bulls and the Painted Gallery.

SAVOIR-FAIRE

Panorama

Aquitaine

La région en chiffres

- **Superficie:** *41.308 km²*
- **Population:** *3.049.000*
- **Industrie principale:** *agriculture*
- **Villes principales:** *Bordeaux, Pau, Périgueux*

Midi-Pyrénées

La région en chiffres

- **Superficie:** *45.348 km²*
- **Population:** *2.687.000*
- **Industries principales:** *aéronautique, agriculture*
- **Villes principales:** *Auch, Toulouse, Rodez*

Languedoc-Roussillon

La région en chiffres

- **Superficie:** *27.376 km²*
- **Population:** *2.458.000*
- **Industrie principale:** *agriculture*
- **Villes principales:** *Montpellier, Nîmes, Perpignan*

Personnages célèbres

- **Aliénor d'Aquitaine,** *Aquitaine, reine° de France (1122–1204)*
- **Jean Jaurès,** *Midi-Pyrénées, homme politique (1859–1914)* 

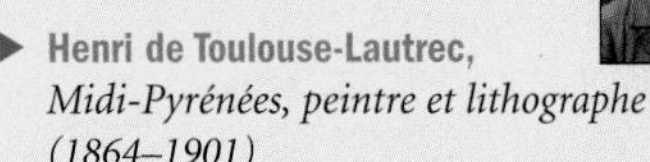

- **Henri de Toulouse-Lautrec,** *Midi-Pyrénées, peintre et lithographe (1864–1901)*
- **Georges Brassens,** *Languedoc-Roussillon, chanteur (1921–1981)*
- **Francis Cabrel,** *Aquitaine, chanteur (1953–)*

reine *queen* **grotte** *cave* **gravures** *carvings* **peintures** *paintings* **découvrent** *discover*

la dune du Pilat

le canal du Midi

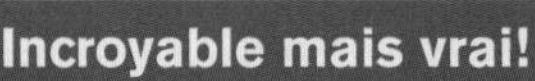

la cité de Carcassonne

Incroyable mais vrai!

Appelée parfois «la chapelle Sixtine préhistorique», la grotte° de Lascaux, en Aquitaine, est décorée de 1.500 gravures° et de 600 peintures°, vieilles de plus de 17.000 ans. En 1940, quatre garçons découvrent° ce sanctuaire. Les fresques, composées de plusieurs animaux, ont jusqu'à ce jour une signification mystérieuse.

OPTIONS

Personnages célèbres **Eleanor of Aquitaine** was one of the most powerful women in Europe during her time. Her first husband was King Louis VIII of France. She later became Queen of England when she married Henry II. **Francis Cabrel** is a guitarist, composer, and singer of blues-rock, pop, and contemporary folk music. **Jean Jaurès** was a leader of the French socialist movement. **Toulouse-Lautrec** established lithography as a major art form with his vivid posters depicting Parisian nightlife in Montmartre. **Georges Brassens** was a poetic songwriter and performer who used his lyrics to address social issues.

La gastronomie

Le foie gras et le cassoulet

Le foie gras° et le cassoulet sont des spécialités du Sud-Ouest° de la France. Le foie gras est un produit° de luxe, en général réservé aux grandes occasions. On le mange sur du pain grillé ou comme ingrédient d'un plat° élaboré. Le cassoulet est un plat populaire, préparé à l'origine dans une «cassole°». Les ingrédients varient, mais en général cette spécialité est composée d'haricots° blancs, de viande° de porc et de canard, de saucisses°, de tomates, d'ail° et d'herbes.

Les monuments

Les arènes de Nîmes

Inspirées du Colisée de Rome, les arènes° de Nîmes, en Languedoc-Roussillon, datent de la fin du premier siècle. C'est l'amphithéâtre le plus grand° de France et le mieux° conservé de l'ère° romaine. Les spectacles de gladiateurs d'autrefois°, appréciés par plus de° 20.000 spectateurs, sont aujourd'hui remplacés° par des corridas° et des spectacles musicaux pour le plaisir de 15.000 spectateurs en été et 7.000 spectateurs en hiver.

Le sport

La pelote basque

L'origine de la pelote est ancienne°: on retrouve des versions du jeu chez les Mayas, les Grecs et les Romains. C'est au Pays Basque, à la frontière° entre la France et l'Espagne, en Aquitaine, que le jeu se transforme en véritable sport. La pelote basque existe sous sept formes différentes; le principe de base est de lancer° une balle en cuir°, la «pelote», contre un mur° avec la «paleta», une raquette en bois°, et le «chistera», un grand gant en osier°.

Les traditions

La langue d'Oc

La langue d'Oc (l'occitan) est une langue romane° développée dans le sud de la France. Cette langue a donné son nom à la région: Languedoc-Roussillon. La poésie lyrique occitane et l'idéologie des troubadours° du Moyen Âge° influencent les valeurs° culturelles et intellectuelles européennes. Il existe plusieurs dialectes de l'occitan. «Los cats fan pas de chins» (les chats ne font pas des chiens) et «la bornicarié porta pas pa a casa» (la beauté n'apporte pas de pain à la maison) sont deux proverbes occitans connus°.

Qu'est-ce que vous avez appris? Répondez aux questions par des phrases complètes.

1. Qui était (*was*) peintre, lithographe et d'origine midi-pyrénéenne?
   Henri de Toulouse-Lautrec était peintre, lithographe et d'origine midi-pyrénéenne.
2. Quel est le surnom (*nickname*) de la grotte de Lascaux?
   Le surnom de la grotte de Lascaux est «la chapelle Sixtine».
3. Que trouve-t-on dans la grotte de Lascaux?
   On trouve des peintures et des gravures dans la grotte de Lascaux.
4. Quand mange-t-on du foie gras en général?
   En général, le foie gras est réservé aux grandes occasions.
5. Quels ingrédients utilise-t-on pour le cassoulet?
   On utilise des haricots blancs, de la viande, des saucisses, des tomates, de l'ail et des herbes.
6. Quand les arènes de Nîmes ont-elles été construites?
   Les arènes de Nîmes datent de la fin du premier siècle.
7. Combien de spectateurs y a-t-il dans les arènes de Nîmes en hiver?
   Il y a 7.000 personnes dans les arènes de Nîmes en hiver.
8. Quelles civilisations ont une version de la pelote?
   Les civilisations des Mayas, des Romains et des Grecs ont une version de la pelote.
9. Combien de formes différentes de pelote basque y a-t-il?
   Il y a sept formes différentes de pelote basque.
10. Qu'est-ce qui influence les valeurs culturelles et intellectuelles européennes? Ce sont la poésie occitane et l'idéologie des troubadours du Moyen Âge.

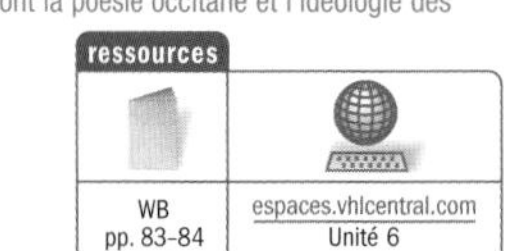

ressources

WB pp. 83–84	espaces.vhlcentral.com Unité 6

SUR INTERNET

Go to **espaces.vhlcentral.com** to find more cultural information related to this **PANORAMA**.

1. Il existe une forme de la pelote basque aux États-Unis. Comment s'appelle ce sport?
2. Cherchez des peintures de la grotte de Lascaux. Quelles sont vos préférées? Pourquoi?
3. Cherchez plus d'informations sur Henri de Toulouse-Lautrec. Avez-vous déjà vu quelques-unes de ses peintures? Où?

foie gras *fatted liver of an animal served in the form of a pâté* **Sud-Ouest** *Southwest* **produit** *product* **plat** *dish* **cassole** *pottery dish* **haricots** *beans* **viande** *meat* **saucisses** *sausages* **ail** *garlic* **arènes** *amphitheaters* **le plus grand** *the largest* **le mieux** *the most* **ère** *era* **autrefois** *long ago* **plus de** *more than* **remplacés** *replaced* **corridas** *bullfights* **ancienne** *ancient* **frontière** *border* **lancer** *throw* **cuir** *leather* **mur** *wall* **bois** *wood* **osier** *wicker* **langue romane** *romance language* **troubadours** *minstrels* **Moyen Âge** *Middle Ages* **valeurs** *values* **connus** *well-known*

Le foie gras et le cassoulet
- The raising of geese and ducks for **foie gras** dates back to ancient Egypt, Greece, Rome, and Gaul. There is a rivalry amongst the southwestern regions for the best variety of **cassoulet**. The differences occur mostly in the type of meat used.
- Ask students to name some regional dishes in the United States. Also ask if they know of a dish similar to **cassoulet**.

Les arènes de Nîmes
- Throughout the centuries the amphitheater always remained in use. At one time, residences were built within the arena and during another period it was used as a fortress and refuge. In 1909, it was restored to its original design as an arena for entertainment.
- Have students compare today's amphitheaters or arenas to the amphitheaters of the Romans.

La pelote basque
- The courts, gear, and rules used to play **pelote basque** can vary from village to village. But no matter which variety of the game is played, it is always lively and fast. The speed of the **pelote** can get up to 250–300 km/hr or about 155–186 mph.
- Ask students what sports are similar to **pelote basque**.

La langue d'Oc **La langue d'Oc** is spoken by approximately 1.5 million people in the south of France. Although the Occitan dialects have been influenced by modern French, they still strongly resemble dialects of the Middle Ages in which the phonology and grammar are more closely related to Spanish.

OPTIONS

La langue d'Oc The troubadours of southern France were traveling poet-musicians. They wrote and performed courtly love poems or songs for the ladies of the courts in the Occitan dialect Provençal. Eleanor of Aquitaine, a patron of troubadours, used her influence to introduce Provençal poetry at the courts in northern France. This type of poetry thrived in the twelfth and thirteenth centuries, and had a great influence on later lyric poetry.

Cultural Activity Point out that France and Spain share a border. Ask students to give some examples of cross-cultural influences. (**les corridas à Nîmes, la pelote basque,** or jai-alai, and **la poésie lyrique des troubadours**)

Section Goals

In this section, students will:

- learn to recognize word families
- read an invitation to an engagement celebration

Stratégie Write **inviter** on the board and ask students what it means in English. Next to it, write **invitation** and **invité(e)**, then ask them the meaning of these words. Point out that all three words have the same root and belong to a word family. Explain that recognizing the relationship between a known word and unfamiliar words can help them infer the meaning of words they don't know.

Examinez le texte Tell students to scan the text for the new words and try to guess their meaning based on the root and context before they look them up in the dictionary.

Familles de mots Point out the three categories of words. You might want to tell students to look for the words in the **Vocabulaire** on page 216.

Lecture

Avant la lecture

STRATÉGIE

Recognizing word families

Recognizing related words can help you guess the meaning of words in context, ensuring better comprehension of a reading selection. Using this strategy will enrich your French vocabulary.

Examinez le texte

Voici quelques mots que vous avez déjà appris. Pour chaque mot, trouvez un terme de la même famille dans le texte et utilisez un dictionnaire pour donner son équivalent anglais.

MODÈLE

amour *amoureux* *lovers*

1	marié	(se) marier	*to get married*
2.	fiancé	les fiançailles	*engagement*
3.	sortir	la sortie	*exit*
4.	timide	la timidité	*shyness*
5.	difficile	les difficultés	*difficulties*
6.	attendre	inattendue	*unexpected*

Familles de mots 

Avec un(e) partenaire, trouvez le bon mot pour compléter chaque famille de mots. (Note: vous avez appris tous les mots qui manquent (*all the missing words*) dans cette unité et il y a un mot de chaque famille dans le texte.)

MODÈLE

(se) fiancer *fiancé(e)* fiancé(e)

	VERBE	NOM	ADJECTIF
1.	blanchir	la blancheur	blanc/blanche
2.	construire	la construction	construit(e)
3.	aimer	l'amour	amoureux/amoureuse
4.	rajeunir	la jeunesse	jeune
5.	surprendre	la surprise	surpris(e)
6.	répondre	la réponse	répondu(e)

Ça y est,° c'est officiel!

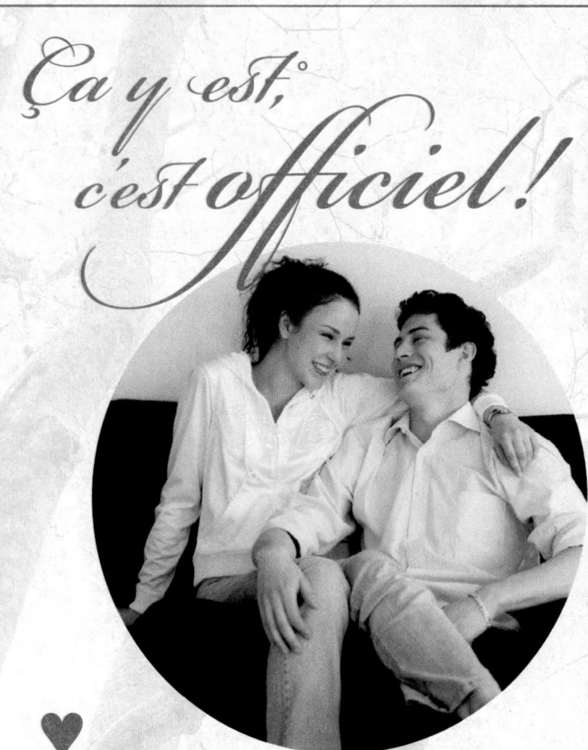

♥

Mathilde et Thierry ont décidé de construire une vie à deux! Ils vont se marier° cet été!

En attendant° le mariage, vous êtes tous invités à un week-end de camping pour fêter les fiançailles° des jeunes amoureux, Mathilde Lopez et Thierry Monet!

À laisser chez vous:
L'élégance, la timidité, les soucis° et les difficultés de la semaine

Quoi d'autre?
Une surprise très inattendue° pour le jeune couple samedi soir!

OPTIONS

Extra Practice Write these words on the board. At least one form will be familiar to students. Have them discuss the relationship between the words and their meanings. **1. idée, idéal(e), idéaliste, idéalement, idéaliser 2. organiser, organisateur/organisatrice, organisation, organisationnel(le), 3. chanter, chanteur/chanteuse, chansonnette, chanson, chantable**

Pairs Working in pairs, have students discuss whether or not they would attend a weekend celebration like the one in the selection. Tell them to talk about the aspects of the camping trip that they do and do not like. Afterwards, ask them if they have ever attended a similar event and what types of activities were planned for the guests.

À apporter:
Matériel de camping
Vêtements: Rien d'élégant! Shorts, tee-shirts, baskets pour la journée; blousons, jeans, chemises à manches longues et pulls pour le soir (Il va faire frais!)

Quand:
Le week-end du 15 et 16 mai (de 10h00 du matin samedi à 18h00 dimanche)

Où:
Chez les grands-parents de Thierry, 14 route des Mines, Allouagne, Nord-Pas-de-Calais

Comment y aller°:
À la sortie d'Allouagne, prenez la route de Lozinghem. Tournez à gauche sur la route des Mines. Le numéro 14 est la grande ferme° sur la droite. (Nous allons mettre des ballons blancs sur la route pour indiquer l'endroit.)

Où loger°:
Amenez vos tentes pour faire du camping près de la ferme ou logez à l'hôtel des Lilas, à Allouagne.

Au programme:
Faire la fête, bien sûr! Boire, manger (samedi soir: grillades°, salades, fruits et gâteaux; vin, bière et champagne), rire, danser, s'amuser° et célébrer l'amour!

Autres activités:
Promenades à cheval et à vélo et randonnées dans la nature

Pour répondre à cette invitation:
Téléphonez à Laurence Monet (avant le 5 mai, svp) au 06.14.55.85.80 ou par e-mail: **laurence.monet@courriel.fr**

Ça y est! *That's it!* **se marier** *get married* **En attendant** *While waiting for* **fiançailles** *engagement* **soucis** *worries* **inattendue** *unexpected* **y aller** *get there* **ferme** *farm* **Où loger** *Where to stay* **grillades** *grilled meats* **s'amuser** *to have fun*

Après la lecture

Vrai ou faux? **Indiquez si les phrases sont vraies ou fausses. Corrigez les phrases fausses.**

1. C'est une invitation à une fête d'anniversaire.
   Faux. C'est une invitation pour fêter les fiançailles.
2. Mathilde et Thierry sont des jeunes mariés.
   Faux. Ils sont fiancés.
3. On va boire du vin et manger des gâteaux samedi soir.
   Vrai.
4. On va porter des vêtements élégants.
   Faux. On va porter des jeans, des pulls, des shorts, etc.
5. Les fiancés vont avoir une surprise.
   Vrai.
6. Le jeune couple va se marier cet été.
   Vrai.

Conseillez **Vous êtes Laurence Monet, l'organisatrice de la fête. Les amis de Mathilde et Thierry veulent (*want*) assister à la fête, mais ils vous contactent pour parler de leurs soucis respectifs. Donnez-leur des conseils (*advice*) pour les mettre à l'aise (*at ease*).** Answers may vary. Suggested answers below.

MODÈLE

Isabelle: J'ai beaucoup de soucis cette semaine.
Vous: *Tu vas laisser tes soucis à la maison et venir (come) à la fête.*

1. Thomas: Je n'ai pas de tente.
   Vous: Tu vas loger à l'hôtel des Lilas.
2. Sarah: Je me perds (*get lost*) facilement quand je conduis.
   Vous: Tu vas chercher les ballons blancs sur la route.
3. Sylvie: J'ai souvent froid.
   Vous: Tu vas apporter des jeans et des pulls.
4. M. Briteaux: Je veux (*want*) répondre à l'invitation, mais je n'ai pas d'ordinateur.
   Vous: Tu vas me téléphoner.
5. Denise: Je n'aime pas le gâteau comme dessert.
   Vous: Tu vas manger des fruits.
6. Véronique: J'aime les promenades, mais je n'aime pas les animaux ou la nature.
   Vous: Tu vas faire une promenade à vélo.

On va à la fête? **Vous êtes invité(e) aux fiançailles de Mathilde et Thierry et vous allez amener un(e) ami(e). Téléphonez à cet(te) ami(e) (votre partenaire) pour l'inviter à la fête. Donnez des détails et répondez aux questions de votre ami(e) sur le jeune couple, les activités du week-end, les vêtements à apporter, etc.**

Vrai ou faux? Go over the answers with the class. For the false items, have students point out where they found the correct answer in the text.

Conseillez
- This activity can be done in pairs. Remind students to switch roles after items 1–3.
- Have pairs write two more situations for the activity. Then have them exchange papers with another pair and complete the situations.

On va à la fête? After students have completed the activity, take a quick class poll. Ask: **Qui va assister à la fête? Qui ne va pas assister à la fête? Pourquoi?**

OPTIONS

Small Groups Have students write an invitation to a birthday party, an anniversary party, or a holiday celebration. Tell them to include the name(s) of the host(s); date, time, and place of the event; what is being celebrated; and any other important details. If possible, provide students with examples of other invitations in French to use as models.

Pairs Working in pairs, have students write three content questions based on the reading. When they have finished, have them get together with another pair and take turns asking and answering each other's questions.

Section Goals

In this section, students will:
- learn to listen for specific linguistic cues
- listen for temporal cues in sentences
- listen to a conversation and complete several activities

Instructional Resources
Textbook MP3s
IRCD-ROM: IRM (Textbook Audioscript)
espaces.vhlcentral.com: downloads, reference tools

Stratégie
Script 1. Est-ce que tu vas aller au mariage de tes cousins? (*future*) 2. Elles ont acheté dix nouveaux maillots de bain pour cet été! (*past*) 3. Noémie a envie de parler à Martha de son rendez-vous avec Julien. (*present*) 4. Vous avez vendu tous les tee-shirts? (*past*)

Préparation Have students look at the photo of Pauline and Sarah, describe what they see, and predict what they are talking about.

À vous d'écouter
Script PAULINE: Tiens, bonjour, Sarah. Ça va?
SARAH: Ah, bonjour Pauline! Oui, très bien et toi?
P: Bien, merci. Dis, je t'ai cherchée hier soir à la fête de ma cousine...
S: Excuse-moi. J'ai passé une mauvaise journée hier et j'ai complètement oublié. Mais... Et toi? Tu as aimé la fête?
P: Oui, j'ai beaucoup dansé et j'ai rencontré un garçon intéressant. Il s'appelle Boris et il est musicien. Je vais déjeuner avec lui demain midi, alors je cherche de nouveaux vêtements pour notre rendez-vous. Qu'est-ce que tu penses de ce pantalon noir avec cette chemise rose?
S: Oui, c'est bien. Et qu'est-ce que tu vas mettre comme chaussures?
P: Ben, ces baskets roses, non?
S: Ah non. Des chaussures en cuir noir, c'est plus élégant.
P: Oui, tu as raison. Et toi, qu'est-ce que tu cherches?
S: Une jolie robe pas trop chère.
P: Tu as un rendez-vous, toi aussi?
S: Non, c'est pour la fête de retraite de mon père. C'est samedi prochain.
P: Regarde cette robe rouge en coton. Elle est jolie, non?
S: Oui, mais elle a l'air un peu serrée. Je préfère les robes larges.
P: Et cette belle robe en soie à manches courtes?
S: Je déteste le vert. Ils l'ont en bleu?
P: Oui, et en blanc aussi.
S: Super. Je vais prendre la bleue.

À l'écoute

STRATÉGIE

Listening for linguistic cues

You can enhance your listening comprehension by listening for specific linguistic cues. For example, if you listen for the endings of conjugated verbs, or for familiar constructions, such as the **passé composé** with **avoir**, **avoir envie de** + [*infinitive*] or **aller** + [*infinitive*], you can find out whether a person did something in the past, wants to do something, or will do something in the future.

To practice listening for linguistic cues, you will listen to four sentences. As you listen, note whether each sentence refers to a past, present, or future action.

Préparation

Regardez la photo. Où sont Pauline et Sarah? Que font-elles? Décrivez les vêtements qu'elles regardent. À votre avis, pour quelle occasion cherchent-elles des vêtements?

À vous d'écouter

Écoutez la conversation entre Pauline et Sarah. Après une deuxième écoute, indiquez si les actions suivantes sont du **passé (p)**, du **présent (pr)** ou du **futur (f)**.

1. aller à la fête de la cousine de Pauline p
2. beaucoup danser p
3. rencontrer un musicien p
4. déjeuner avec un garçon intéressant f
5. chercher de nouveaux vêtements pr
6. mettre des chaussures en cuir noir f
7. aimer une robe bleue pr
8. acheter la robe bleue f

ressources

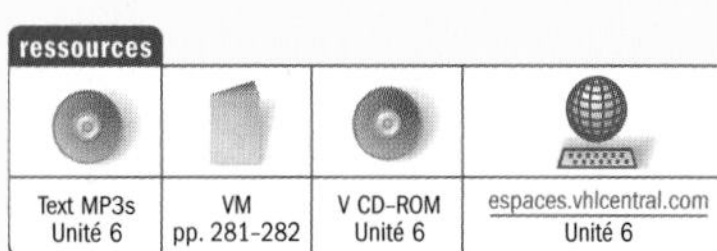

Text MP3s Unité 6
VM pp. 281–282
V CD-ROM Unité 6
espaces.vhlcentral.com Unité 6

Compréhension

Complétez Complétez les phrases.

1. Pauline cherche des vêtements pour __c__.
   a. un dîner **b.** une fête **c.** un rendez-vous
2. Pauline va acheter un pantalon noir et __b__.
   a. un tee-shirt **b.** une chemise rose **c.** un maillot de bain
3. Sarah pense que __b__ ne vont pas avec les nouveaux vêtements.
   a. l'écharpe verte **b.** les baskets roses **c.** les lunettes de soleil
4. D'après Sarah, les chaussures __a__ sont élégantes.
   a. en cuir noir **b.** roses **c.** en soie
5. La couleur préférée de Sarah n'est pas le __c__.
   a. rose **b.** jaune **c.** vert
6. Sarah cherche un vêtement pour __b__.
   a. un déjeuner **b.** la fête de retraite de son père **c.** un mariage
7. Sarah va acheter une robe en soie __a__.
   a. à manches courtes **b.** à manches longues **c.** rouge
8. La robe existe en vert, en bleu et en __c__.
   a. noir **b.** marron **c.** blanc

Une occasion spéciale **Décrivez la dernière fois que vous avez fêté une occasion spéciale. Qu'est-ce que vous avez fêté? Où? Comment? Avec qui? Qu'est-ce que vous avez mis comme vêtements? Et les autres?**

MODÈLE

Samedi, nous avons fêté l'anniversaire de mon fiancé. Nous avons invité nos amis Paul, Marc, Julia et Naomi dans un restaurant élégant. Moi, j'ai mis une belle robe verte en coton. Mon fiancé a mis un costume gris. Paul a mis...

Écriture

STRATÉGIE

How to report an interview

There are several ways to prepare a written report about an interview. For example, you can transcribe the interview verbatim, or you can summarize it. In any event, the report should begin with an interesting title and a brief introduction including the five *W*'s (*who, what, when, where, why*) and the H (*how*) of the interview. The report should end with an interesting conclusion. Note that when you transcribe a conversation in French, you should pay careful attention to format and punctuation.

Écrire une conversation en français

- Pour indiquer qui parle dans une conversation, on peut mettre le nom de la personne qui parle devant sa phrase.

  MONIQUE Lucie, qu'est-ce que tu vas mettre pour l'anniversaire de Jean-Louis?

  LUCIE Je vais mettre ma robe en soie bleue à manches courtes. Et toi, tu vas mettre quoi?

  MONIQUE Eh bien, une jupe en coton et un chemisier, je pense. Ou peut-être mon pantalon en cuir avec... Tiens, tu me prêtes ta chemise jaune et blanche?

  LUCIE Oui, si tu me la rends (*return it to me*) dimanche. Elle va avec le pantalon que je vais porter la semaine prochaine.

- On peut aussi commencer les phrases avec des tirets (*dashes*) pour indiquer quand une nouvelle personne parle.

  – Qu'est-ce que tu as acheté comme cadeau pour Jean-Louis?

  – Une cravate noire et violette. Elle est très jolie. Et toi?

  – Je n'ai pas encore acheté son cadeau. Des lunettes de soleil peut-être?

  – Oui, c'est une bonne idée! Et il y a des soldes à Saint-Louis Lunettes.

Thème

Écrire une interview

Clarisse Deschamps est une styliste de mode suisse. Elle dessine des vêtements pour les jeunes et va présenter sa nouvelle collection sur votre campus. Vous allez interviewer Clarisse pour le journal de votre université.

- Commencez par une courte introduction.

  MODÈLE *Voici une interview de Clarisse Deschamps, une styliste de mode suisse.*

- Préparez une liste de questions à poser à Clarisse Deschamps sur sa nouvelle collection. Vous pouvez (*can*) poser des questions sur:
  - les types de vêtements
  - les couleurs
  - le style
  - les prix
- Inventez une conversation de 10 à 12 lignes entre vous et Clarisse. Indiquez qui parle, avec des tirets ou avec les noms des personnes.
- Terminez par une brève (*brief*) conclusion.

  MODÈLE *On vend la collection de Clarisse Deschamps à Fun Clothes à côté de l'université. Cette semaine, il y a des soldes!*

FLASH CULTURE

Watch the FLASH CULTURE segment on the **ESPACES** video for cultural footage related to this unit's theme.

Section Goals

In this section, students will:
- learn to report an interview
- learn to conduct an interview
- view authentic cultural footage of French festivals and holiday celebrations

Instructional Resources
WB/VM: Video Manual, pp. 281–282
WB/VM/LM Answer Key
IRCD-ROM: IRM (Videoscript)
Video CD-ROM
Video on DVD
espaces.vhlcentral.com: activities, downloads, reference tools

Stratégie Play the role of an interviewee. Tell students to interview you about your clothing preferences. Allow recording so students can transcribe the interview. Then choose volunteers to report on the interview, transcribing it verbatim, summarizing it, or summarizing and quoting you occasionally.

Proofreading Activity Have the class correct these sentences. **1. Quand est-ce vous avez achete ces vetements? 2. Cette blouson-la est tres cher, mais c'est parfait. 3. Est-ce que vous déjà avez travaille comme styliste? 4. Vous allez parler moi de votre travail?**

Flash culture Tell students that they will learn more about French festivals and holiday celebrations by watching a variety of real-life images narrated by Benjamin. Show the video segment, and then have students jot down at least three examples of things they saw. You can also use the activities in the video manual in class to reinforce this **Flash culture** or assign them as homework.

EVALUATION

Criteria	Scale
Content	1 2 3 4 5
Organization	1 2 3 4 5
Accuracy	1 2 3 4 5
Creativity	1 2 3 4 5

Scoring	
Excellent	18–20 points
Good	14–17 points
Satisfactory	10–13 points
Unsatisfactory	< 10 points

Instructional Resources
Textbook MP3s
IRCD-ROM: IRM (Textbook Audioscript)
espaces.vhlcentral.com: downloads, reference tools

Les vêtements

aller avec	*to go with*
porter	*to wear*
un anorak	*ski jacket, parka*
des baskets (*f.*)	*tennis shoes*
un blouson	*jacket*
une casquette	*(baseball) cap*
une ceinture	*belt*
un chapeau	*hat*
une chaussette	*sock*
une chaussure	*shoe*
une chemise (à manches courtes/longues)	*shirt (short-/long-sleeved)*
un chemisier	*blouse*
un costume	*(man's) suit*
une cravate	*tie*
une écharpe	*scarf*
un gant	*glove*
un jean	*jeans*
une jupe	*skirt*
des lunettes (de soleil) (*f.*)	*(sun)glasses*
un maillot de bain	*swimsuit, bathing suit*
un manteau	*coat*
un pantalon	*pants*
un pull	*sweater*
une robe	*dress*
un sac à main	*purse, handbag*
un short	*shorts*
un sous-vêtement	*underwear*
une taille	*clothing size*
un tailleur	*(woman's) suit; tailor*
un tee-shirt	*tee shirt*
des vêtements (*m.*)	*clothing*
des soldes (*m.*)	*sales*
un vendeur/une vendeuse	*salesman/saleswoman*
bon marché	*inexpensive*
chaque	*each*
cher/chère	*expensive*
large	*loose; big*
serré(e)	*tight*

Les fêtes

faire la fête	*to party*
faire une surprise (à quelqu'un)	*to surprise (someone)*
fêter	*to celebrate*
organiser une fête	*to organize a party*
une bière	*beer*
un biscuit	*cookie*
un bonbon	*candy*
le champagne	*champagne*
un dessert	*dessert*
un gâteau	*cake*
la glace	*ice cream*
un glaçon	*ice cube*
le vin	*wine*
un cadeau	*gift*
une fête	*party; celebration*
un hôte/une hôtesse	*host(ess)*
un(e) invité(e)	*guest*
un jour férié	*holiday*
une surprise	*surprise*

Périodes de la vie

l'adolescence (*f.*)	*adolescence*
l'âge adulte (*m.*)	*adulthood*
un divorce	*divorce*
l'enfance (*f.*)	*childhood*
une étape	*stage*
l'état civil (*m.*)	*marital status*
la jeunesse	*youth*
un mariage	*marriage; wedding*
la mort	*death*
la naissance	*birth*
la vie	*life*
la vieillesse	*old age*
prendre sa retraite	*to retire*
tomber amoureux/amoureuse	*to fall in love*
avant-hier	*the day before yesterday*
hier	*yesterday*

Expressions utiles	*See pp. 187 and 201.*
Demonstrative adjectives	*See p. 190.*
Indirect object pronouns	*See p. 204.*
Disjunctive pronouns	*See p. 205.*

Les relations

une amitié	*friendship*
un amour	*love*
le bonheur	*happiness*
un couple	*couple*
un(e) fiancé(e)	*fiancé*
des jeunes mariés (*m.*)	*newlyweds*
un rendez-vous	*date; appointment*
ensemble	*together*

Les couleurs

De quelle couleur...?	*In what color...?*
blanc(he)	*white*
bleu(e)	*blue*
gris(e)	*gray*
jaune	*yellow*
marron	*brown*
noir(e)	*black*
orange	*orange*
rose	*pink*
rouge	*red*
vert(e)	*green*
violet(te)	*purple; violet*

Verbes en -re

attendre	*to wait*
conduire	*to drive*
construire	*to build; to construct*
descendre	*to go down; to take down*
détruire	*to destroy*
entendre	*to hear*
mettre	*to put (on); to place*
perdre (son temps)	*to lose (one's time)*
permettre	*to allow*
produire	*to produce*
promettre	*to promise*
réduire	*to reduce*
rendre (à)	*to give back; to return (to)*
rendre visite (à)	*to visit someone*
répondre (à)	*to respond, to answer (to)*
rire	*to laugh*
sourire	*to smile*
traduire	*to translate*
vendre	*to sell*

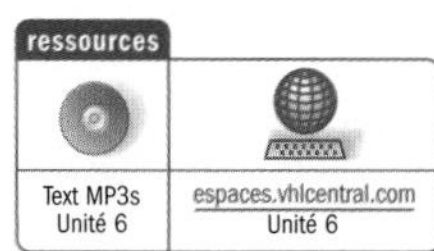

LE FRANÇAIS QUOTIDIEN

À la gare

contrôleur	*ticket inspector*
couchette	*berth*
guichet	*ticket window*
horaire	*schedule*
quai	*train/metro platform*
voie	*track*
wagon-lit	*sleeper car*
composter	*to punch one's (train) ticket*

LE MONDE FRANCOPHONE

Les transports

Voici quelques faits insolites° dans les transports.

Au Canada Inauguré en 1966, le métro de Montréal est le premier du monde à rouler° sur des pneus° plutôt que° sur des roues° en métal. Chaque station a été conçue° par un architecte différent.

En France L'Eurotunnel (le tunnel sous la Manche°) permet aux trains Eurostar de transporter des voyageurs et des marchandises entre la France et l'Angleterre.

En Mauritanie Le train du désert, en Mauritanie, en Afrique, est peut-être le train de marchandises le plus long° du monde. Long de 3 km en général, le train fait deux ou trois voyages chaque jour du Sahara à la côte ouest°. C'est un voyage de plus de 600 km qui dure° 12 heures. Un des seuls moyens° de transport dans la région, ce train est aussi un train de voyageurs.

faits insolites *unusual facts* **rouler** *ride* **pneus** *tires* **plutôt que** *rather than* **roues** *wheels* **conçue** *designed* **Manche** *English Channel* **le plus long** *the longest* **côte ouest** *west coast* **dure** *lasts* **seuls moyens** *only means*

PORTRAIT

Le musée d'Orsay

Le musée d'Orsay est un des musées parisiens les plus° visités. Le lieu n'a pourtant° pas toujours été un musée. À l'origine, ce bâtiment° est une gare, construite par l'architecte Victor Laloux et inaugurée en 1900 à l'occasion de l'Exposition universelle. Les voies° de la gare d'Orsay deviennent° trop courtes et en 1939, on décide de limiter le service aux trains de banlieue. Plus tard, la gare sert de décor à des films, comme *Le Procès* de Kafka adapté par Orson Welles, puis° elle devient théâtre, puis salle de ventes aux enchères°. En 1986, le bâtiment est transformé en musée. Il est principalement dédié° à l'art du dix-neuvième siècle°, avec une collection magnifique d'art impressionniste.

Danseuses en bleu, Edgar Degas

les plus *the most* **pourtant** *however* **bâtiment** *building* **voies** *tracks* **deviennent** *become* **puis** *then* **ventes aux enchères** *auction* **principalement dédié** *mainly dedicated* **siècle** *century*

SUR INTERNET

Qu'est-ce que le funiculaire de Montmartre?

Go to **espaces.vhlcentral.com** to find more cultural information related to this **ESPACE CULTURE**.

ACTIVITÉS

2 **Vrai ou faux?** Indiquez si les phrases sont vraies ou fausses. Corrigez les phrases fausses.

1. Le musée d'Orsay a été un théâtre. Vrai.
2. Le musée d'Orsay a été une station de métro. Faux. Il a été une gare.
3. Le musée d'Orsay est dédié à la sculpture moderne. Faux. Le musée d'Orsay est dédié à l'art du dix-neuvième siècle.
4. Il y a un tunnel entre la France et la Guyane française. Faux. Il y a un tunnel entre la France et l'Angleterre.
5. Le métro de Montréal roule sur des roues en métal. Faux. Le métro de Montréal roule sur des pneus.
6. Le train du désert transporte aussi des voyageurs. Vrai.

3 **Comment voyager?** Vous allez passer deux semaines en France. Vous avez envie de visiter Paris et deux autres régions. Par petits groupes, parlez des moyens (*means*) de transport que vous allez utiliser pendant votre voyage. Expliquez vos choix (*choices*).

ressources

espaces.vhlcentral.com Leçon 13

Le français quotidien Explain that French people visit **la SNCF (Société Nationale des Chemins de Fer)** to get information about rates and to buy train tickets (just as Americans go to an Amtrak station). Bring in a map showing train routes, so students understand the viability of train travel to and from big cities and small towns alike. Remind students of what they learned about **le TGV** in **Unité 2, Panorama**, page 67.

Portrait Show photos of Claude Monet's train paintings ***La Gare Saint-Lazare***, ***Le train dans la neige***, and ***Un train dans la campagne***, the last of which is in **le musée d'Orsay**.

Le monde francophone Have students work in pairs to ask each other content questions. Examples: **1. Quel est le nom du tunnel entre la France et l'Angleterre? (L'Eurotunnel/ le tunnel sous la Manche) 2. Quelle est une des différences entre le métro de Montréal et le métro de Paris? (Le métro de Montréal roule sur des pneus.) 3. Comment peut-on voyager en Afrique, du Sahara à la côte ouest? (On prend le train du désert.)**

2 Expansion Continue the activity with these true/false statements. **7. La gare d'Orsay a servi de décor à des films. (Vrai.) 8. Quand les voies deviennent trop courtes, la gare d'Orsay est limitée au métro. (Faux, aux trains de banlieue) 9. Au musée d'Orsay on peut admirer de l'art surréaliste. (Faux, de l'art impressionniste)**

3 Expansion Once students have agreed on the areas they would like to visit, they should consult road and train maps to see which **moyen de transport** would work best.

OPTIONS

Cultural Comparison Bring in maps of the Paris **métro** and **RER** along with maps of a well-known American public transportation system, such as the New York City subway. Ask students: **Quel moyen de transport préférez-vous à Paris? à New York?** Then have them discuss their answers and plan mock commutes to various destinations in the two cities. Tell them to list similarities (**Similitudes**) and differences (**Différences**) between the American and French subway systems. Have groups compare lists.

Les transports You may want to supplement this section by telling students about travel between **Tanger (Maroc)** and **Algeciras (Espagne)** via hydrofoil; between **la Corse**, **l'Italie**, and **la Tunisie** by ferry; **le funiculaire de Montmartre**; **les canaux** in France; and **le bus amphibie** in **Montréal**.

NATIONAL STANDARDS comparisons

Section Goals

In this section, students will learn the **passé composé** with **être**.

Instructional Resources
WB/VM: Workbook, pp. 87–88
Lab Manual, p. 51
Lab MP3s
WB/VM/LM Answer Key
*IRCD-ROM: Transparency #34; IRM (**Essayez!** and **Mise en pratique** answers; Lab Audioscript; **Feuilles d'activités**)*
espaces.vhlcentral.com: activities, downloads, reference tools

Suggestions

- Quickly review the **passé composé** with **avoir**.
- Introduce the **passé composé** with **être** by describing where you went yesterday. Example: **Hier, je suis allé(e) à la bibliothèque de la faculté. Ensuite, je suis allé(e) chez moi.** Then ask students: **Et vous, où êtes-vous allé(e) hier?**
- Write the **passé composé** of **donner** and **aller** on the board. Have students compare the forms of the **passé composé** with **avoir** and **être**.
- Explain the agreement of past participles in the **passé composé** with **être**.
- Point out the verbs that form the **passé composé** with **être** as well as the irregular past participles **mort** and **né**.
- Tell students that the present tense forms of **naître** and **mourir** are rarely used.
- Have students turn to the illustration on pages 218–219 or use **Transparency #34** and have them describe the scene in the past.

13.1 The *passé composé* with *être*

Point de départ In **Leçon 11**, you learned to form the **passé composé** with **avoir**. Some verbs, however, form the **passé composé** with **être**.

- To form the **passé composé** of these verbs, use a present-tense form of **être** and the past participle of the verb that expresses the action.

	PRESENT TENSE	PAST PARTICIPLE		PRESENT TENSE	PAST PARTICIPLE
Je	**suis**	**allé.**	Il	**est**	**sorti.**

- Many of the verbs that take **être** in the **passé composé** involve motion. You have already learned a few of them: **aller**, **arriver**, **descendre**, **partir**, **passer**, **rentrer**, **sortir**, and **tomber**.

Jean-Luc **est parti** en vacances.
Jean-Luc left on vacation.

Je **suis tombé** de la chaise.
I fell from the chair.

Tu es parti pour Paris.
Mes parents sont arrivés des États-Unis.

- The past participles of verbs conjugated with **être** agree with their subjects in number and gender.

Charles, tu **es allé** à Montréal?
Charles, did you go to Montreal?

Florence **est partie** en vacances.
Florence left on vacation.

Mes frères **sont rentrés**.
My brothers came back.

Elles **sont arrivées** hier soir.
They arrived last night.

- To make a verb negative in the **passé composé**, place **ne/n'** and **pas** around the auxiliary verb, in this case, **être**.

Marie-Thérèse **n'est pas sortie**?
Marie-Thérèse didn't go out?

Nous **ne sommes pas allées** à la plage.
We didn't go to the beach.

Je **ne suis pas passé** chez mon amie.
I didn't drop by my friend's house.

Tu **n'es pas rentré** à la maison hier.
You didn't come home yesterday.

MISE EN PRATIQUE

1 Un week-end sympa Carole raconte son week-end à Paris. Complétez l'histoire avec les formes correctes des verbes au passé composé.

Thomas et moi, nous (1) sommes partis (partir) de Lyon samedi et nous (2) sommes arrivés (arriver) à Paris à onze heures. Nous (3) sommes passés (passer) à l'hôtel et puis je (4) suis allée (aller) au Louvre. En route, je (5) suis tombée (tomber) sur un vieil ami, et nous (6) sommes allés (aller) prendre un café. Ensuite, je (7) suis entrée (entrer) dans le musée. Samedi soir, Thomas et moi (8) sommes montés (monter) au sommet de la tour Eiffel et après nous (9) sommes sortis (sortir) en boîte. Dimanche, nous (10) sommes retournés (retourner) au Louvre. Ouf... je suis fatiguée.

2 Dimanche dernier Dites ce que (*what*) ces personnes ont fait dimanche dernier. Utilisez les verbes de la liste. Suggested answers

MODÈLE
Laure est allée à la piscine.

aller	rentrer
arriver	rester
monter	sortir

Laure

1. je Je suis rentré tard.

3. nous Nous sommes allés à l'église.

2. tu Tu es restée à l'hôtel.

4. Pamela et Caroline Pamela et Caroline sont sorties.

3 L'accident Le mois dernier, Djénaba et Safiatou sont allées au Sénégal. Racontez (*Tell*) leur histoire. Avec un(e) partenaire, complétez les phrases au passé composé. Ensuite, mettez-les dans l'ordre chronologique.

1 a. les filles / partir pour Dakar en avion
Les filles sont parties pour Dakar en avion.
5 b. Djénaba / tomber de vélo
Djénaba est tombée de vélo.
4 c. elles / aller faire du vélo dimanche matin
Elles sont allées faire du vélo dimanche matin.
2 d. elles / arriver à Dakar tard le soir
Elles sont arrivées à Dakar tard le soir.
3 e. elles / rester à l'hôtel Sofitel
Elles sont restées à l'hôtel Sofitel.
6 f. elle / aller à l'hôpital
Elle est allée à l'hôpital.

OPTIONS

Extra Practice To practice discriminating between the **passé composé** with **être** and the **passé composé** with **avoir**, call out infinitives and have students respond with **avoir** or **être** and the past participle. Examples: **1. voyager (avoir voyagé) 2. entrer (être entré) 3. aller (être allé) 4. parler (avoir parlé) 5. retourner (être retourné)**

Game Divide the class into two teams. Choose one team member at a time to go to the board, alternating between teams. Say a subject pronoun and an infinitive. The person at the board must write and say the correct **passé composé** form. Example: **je: aller (je suis allé[e])**. Give a point for each correct answer. The team with the most points at the end of the game wins.

COMMUNICATION

4 **Les vacances de printemps** Avec un(e) partenaire, parlez de vos dernières vacances de printemps. Répondez à toutes ses questions.

Answers will vary.

MODÈLE

quand / partir
Étudiant(e) 1: *Quand es-tu parti(e)?*
Étudiant(e) 2: *Je suis parti(e) vendredi soir.*

1. où / aller
2. avec qui / partir
3. comment / voyager
4. à quelle heure / arriver
5. où / rester
6. combien de temps / rester
7. que / visiter
8. sortir / souvent le soir
9. que / acheter
10. quand / rentrer

5 **Enquête** Votre professeur va vous donner une feuille d'activités. Circulez dans la classe et demandez à des camarades différents s'ils ont fait ces choses récemment (*recently*). Présentez les résultats de votre enquête à la classe. Answers will vary.

MODÈLE

Étudiant(e) 1: *Es-tu allé(e) au musée récemment?*
Étudiant(e) 2: *Oui, je suis allé(e) au musée jeudi dernier.*

Questions	*Nom*
1. aller au musée	*François*
2. passer chez ses amis	
3. sortir en boîte	
4. rester à la maison pour écouter de la musique	
5. partir en week-end avec un copain	
6. monter en avion	

6 **À l'aéroport** Par groupes de quatre, parlez d'une mauvaise expérience dans un aéroport. À tour de rôle, racontez (*tell*) vos aventures et posez le plus (*most*) de questions possible. Utilisez les expressions de la liste et d'autres aussi. Answers will vary.

MODÈLE

Étudiant(e) 1: *Quand je suis rentré(e) de la Martinique, j'ai attendu trois heures à la douane.*
Étudiant(e) 2: *Quelle horreur! Pourquoi?*

arriver	partir
attendre	perdre
avion	prendre un avion
billet (aller-retour)	sortir
douane	vol

- Here are a few more verbs that take **être** instead of **avoir** in the **passé composé.**

Some verbs used with *être*

entrer	*to enter*	**naître**	*to be born*
monter	*to go up; to get in/on*	**rester**	*to stay*
mourir	*to die*	**retourner**	*to return*

Mes parents **sont nés** en 1958 à Paris.
My parents were born in 1958 in Paris.

Ma grand-mère maternelle **est morte** l'année dernière.
My maternal grandmother died last year.

- Note that the verb **passer** takes **être** when it means *to pass by*, but it takes **avoir** when it means *to spend time.*

Maryse **est passée** par la douane.
Maryse passed through customs.

Maryse **a passé** trois jours à la campagne.
Maryse spent three days in the country.

- To form a question using inversion in the **passé composé**, invert the subject pronoun and the conjugated form of **être**. Note that this does not apply to other types of question formation.

Est-elle restée à l'hôtel Aquabella?
Did she stay at the Hotel Aquabella?

Vous êtes arrivée ce matin, Madame Roch?
Did you arrive this morning, Mrs. Roch?

- Place short adverbs such as **déjà**, **encore**, **bien**, **mal**, and **beaucoup** between the auxiliary verb **être** or **pas** and the past participle.

Elle **est déjà rentrée** de vacances?
She already came back from vacation?

Nous **ne sommes pas encore arrivés** à Aix-en-Provence.
We haven't arrived in Aix-en-Provence yet.

Essayez! Choisissez le participe passé approprié.

1. Vous êtes (nés/né) en 1959, Monsieur?
2. Les élèves sont (partis/parti) le 2 juin.
3. Les filles sont (rentrées/rentrés) de vacances.
4. Simone de Beauvoir est-elle (mort/morte) en 1986?
5. Mes frères sont (sortis/sortie).
6. Paul n'est pas (resté/restée) chez sa grand-mère.
7. Tu es (arrivés/arrivée) avant dix heures, Sophie.
8. Jacqueline a (passée/passé) une semaine en Suisse.

Essayez! For additional practice, change the subjects of the sentences (except items 1 and 7), and have students restate or rewrite them.

1 Suggestion Before beginning the activity, have students identify the past participles of the verbs in parentheses.

2 Expansion Ask students what they did last Sunday.

3 Expansion Have two volunteers play the roles of Djénaba and Safiatou. Tell the rest of the class to ask them questions about their trip. Example: **Quand êtes-vous arrivées à Dakar?**

4 Suggestion Have two volunteers read the **modèle** aloud.

5 Suggestion Distribute the **Feuilles d'activités** from the IRM on the IRCD-ROM.

6 Suggestion Before beginning the activity, ask the students about their travel experiences. Example: **Avez-vous déjà voyagé dans un autre pays?**

OPTIONS

Video Show the video episode again to give students more input regarding the **passé composé** with **être** and **avoir**. Pause the video where appropriate to discuss how certain verbs were used and to ask comprehension questions.

Extra Practice Using the information in the **Roman-photo**, have students write a summary of David's trip to Paris. Then have students get together with a partner and exchange papers. Tell them to peer edit each other's work. Remind them to check for the correct usage of **avoir** and **être** in the **passé composé,** subject-verb agreement, and the correct forms of past participles.

Section Goals

In this section, students will learn direct object pronouns.

Instructional Resources
WB/VM: Workbook, pp. 89–90
Lab Manual, p. 52
Lab MP3s
WB/VM/LM Answer Key
*IRCD-ROM: IRM (**Essayez!** and **Mise en pratique** answers; Lab Audioscript)*
espaces.vhlcentral.com: activities, downloads, reference tools

Suggestions

- Write these sentences on the board: **Qui a les tickets? Roger les a**. Underline **les tickets** and explain that it is the direct object. The direct object receives the action of the verb. It answers the questions *what?* or *whom?* Then underline **les** and explain that it is the plural direct object pronoun. Translate both sentences, pointing out the word order. Follow the same procedure with these sentences.
  —Qui prend le bus?
  —Les étudiants le prennent.
  —Qui écrit la lettre?
  —Mon père l'écrit.
- Take various objects from students' desks and ask: **Qui a ____?** Have students respond using the direct object pronoun: **Vous ____ avez.**
- Point out that direct objects are never preceded by a preposition.
- Continue asking questions to elicit other direct object pronouns. Examples: **M'entendez-vous? (Oui, nous vous entendons.) Qui achète vos vêtements? (Je les achète.)**
- Explain the agreement of past participles with direct object pronouns in the **passé composé**.

13.2 Direct object pronouns

Point de départ In **Leçon 12**, you learned about indirect objects. You are now going to learn about direct objects.

DIRECT OBJECT / INDIRECT OBJECT

J'ai donné **un cadeau à ma sœur**.
I gave a gift to my sister.

- Note that a direct object receives the action of a verb directly and an indirect object receives the action of a verb indirectly. While indirect objects are frequently preceded by the preposition **à**, no preposition is needed before the direct object.

J'emmène **mes parents**. *I'm taking my parents.* *but* Je parle **à mes parents**. *I'm speaking to my parents.*

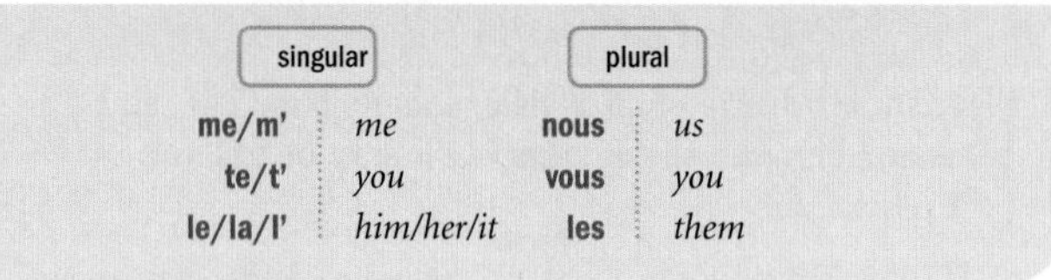

Tes parents sont allés te chercher?
Tu m'excuses une minute?

Direct object pronouns

singular		plural	
me/m'	*me*	nous	*us*
te/t'	*you*	vous	*you*
le/la/l'	*him/her/it*	les	*them*

- You can use a direct object pronoun in the place of a direct object noun.

Tu fais **les valises**? *Are you packing the suitcases?* → Tu **les** fais? *Are you packing them?*

Ils retrouvent **Luc** à la gare. *They're meeting Luc at the station.* → Ils **le** retrouvent à la gare. *They're meeting him at the station.*

- Place a direct object pronoun before the conjugated verb.

Les langues? Laurent et Xavier **les** étudient. *Languages? Laurent and Xavier study them.*

Les étudiants **vous** ont entendu. *The students heard you.*

MISE EN PRATIQUE

1 On fait beaucoup Dites ce que (*what*) ces gens font le week-end. Employez les pronoms d'objet direct.

MODÈLE
Il l'écoute.

Dominique écoute ce CD.

1. Benoît regarde ses films.
Il les regarde.

3. Il mange son gâteau.
Il le mange.

2. Ma mère admire cette robe.
Elle l'admire.

4. Ils achètent ces lunettes.
Ils les achètent.

2 À la plage La famille de Dalila a passé une semaine à la mer. Dalila parle de ce que (*what*) chaque membre de sa famille a fait. Employez des pronoms d'objet direct.

MODÈLE
J'ai conduit Yassim à la plage. *Je l'ai conduit à la plage.*

1. Mon père a acheté le journal tous les matins. Il l'a acheté tous les matins.
2. Ma sœur a retrouvé son petit ami au café. Elle l'a retrouvé au café.
3. Mes parents ont emmené les enfants au cinéma. Ils les ont emmenés au cinéma.
4. Mon frère a invité sa fiancée au restaurant. Il l'a invitée au restaurant.
5. Anissa a porté ses lunettes de soleil. Elle les a portées.
6. À midi, Chekib a pris des baguettes. À midi, il les a prises.

3 Des doutes Julien et sa petite amie Caroline sont au café. Il est inquiet et lui pose des questions sur leurs vacances avec ses parents. Avec un(e) partenaire, jouez les deux rôles. Ensuite, présentez la scène à la classe.

Suggested answers

1. Tes parents m'invitent au bord de la mer? Oui, ils t'invitent au bord de la mer.
2. Tes parents vont m'écouter? Oui, ils vont t'écouter.
3. Quelqu'un va m'attendre à l'aéroport? Oui, je vais t'attendre à l'aéroport.
4. Ton frère va nous emmener sur son bateau? Oui, il va nous emmener sur son bateau.
5. Tu penses que ta famille va m'aimer? Oui, je pense qu'elle va t'aimer.
6. Tu m'adores? Oui, je t'adore.

OPTIONS

Game Send a student out of the room. Give his or her belongings to other students to hide. Then have the person return. To get the belongings back, the person must ask students yes/no questions. They should respond using direct object pronouns. Example: **Tu as mon livre? (Oui, je l'ai./Non, je ne l'ai pas.)**

Pairs Have students work in pairs. Write the following list on the board. Tell them to take turns asking each other who does these activities: **écouter de la musique, parler l'espagnol, prendre le bus, aimer les sports, porter des baskets, jouer au foot, étudier les mathématiques,** and **boire de l'eau minérale.** Example: **Qui parle l'espagnol? (Mon ami Diego le parle.)**

COMMUNICATION

4 **Le départ** Clémentine va partir au Cameroun chez sa correspondante (*pen pal*) Léa. Sa mère est avec elle et veut (*wants*) être sûre qu'elle n'a pas oublié un objet important, mais sa fille n'a presque rien (*nothing*) fait. Avec un(e) partenaire, jouez leur conversation en utilisant les phrases de la liste. Answers will vary.

MODÈLE

Étudiant(e) 1: *Tu as acheté le cadeau pour ton amie?*
Étudiant(e) 2: *Non, je ne l'ai pas encore acheté.*
Étudiant(e) 1: *Quand vas-tu l'acheter?*
Étudiant(e) 2: *Je vais l'acheter cet après-midi.*

acheter ton billet d'avion	faire tes valises
avoir l'adresse de Léa	prendre tes lunettes
chercher un maillot de bain	préparer tes vêtements
confirmer l'heure de l'arrivée	trouver ton passeport

5 **À Tahiti** Imaginez que vous allez partir à Tahiti. Avec un(e) partenaire, posez-vous ces questions. Il/Elle vous répond en utilisant le pronom d'objet direct approprié. Ensuite, alternez les rôles. Answers will vary.

MODÈLE

Est-ce que tu prends le bus pour aller à la plage?
Non, je ne le prends pas.

1. Est-ce que tu prends l'avion?
2. Qui va t'attendre à l'aéroport?
3. Quand as-tu fait tes valises?
4. Est-ce que tu as acheté ton maillot de bain?
5. Est-ce que tu prends ton appareil photo?
6. Où as-tu acheté tes vêtements?
7. Tu vas regarder la télévision tahitienne?
8. Vas-tu essayer les plats typiques de Tahiti?

- In a negative statement, place the direct object pronoun between **ne/n'** and the conjugated verb.

Le chinois? Je **ne le parle pas**.	Elle **ne l'a pas** pris à 14 heures?
Chinese? I don't speak it.	*She didn't take it at 2 o'clock?*

- When an infinitive follows a conjugated verb, the direct object pronoun precedes the infinitive.

Marcel va **nous écouter**.	Tu ne préfères pas **la porter** demain?
Marcel is going to listen to us.	*Don't you prefer to wear it tomorrow?*

Et le gâteau, je l'ai adoré!
Les musées, je les ai adorés!

- When a direct object pronoun is used with the **passé composé**, the past participle must agree with it in both gender and number.

J'ai mis **la valise** dans la voiture ce matin. *I put the suitcase in the car this morning.*	Je **l'**ai **mise** dans la voiture ce matin. *I put it in the car. this morning.*
J'ai attendu **les filles** à la gare. *I waited for the girls at the station.*	Je **les** ai **attendues** à la gare. *I waited for them at the station.*

Essayez! **Répondez aux questions en remplaçant l'objet direct par un pronom d'objet direct.**

1. Thierry prend le train? Oui, il __le__ prend.
2. Tu attends ta mère? Oui, je __l'__ attends.
3. Vous entendez Olivier et Vincent? Oui, on __les__ entend.
4. Le professeur te cherche? Oui, il __me__ cherche.
5. Barbara et Caroline retrouvent Linda? Oui, elles __la__ retrouvent.
6. Vous m'invitez? Oui, nous __t'__ invitons.
7. Tu nous comprends? Oui, je __vous__ comprends.
8. Elles regardent la mer? Oui, elles __la__ regardent.
9. Chloé aime écouter la musique classique? Oui, elle aime __l'__ écouter.
10. Vous avez regardé le film *Chacun cherche son chat*? Oui, nous __l'__ avons regardé.

Essayez! For additional practice, have students restate or rewrite the answers in the negative.

1 Suggestion Have students ask questions with a direct obect pronoun for each item. Example: **Qui l'écoute?**

2 Suggestion Before beginning the activity, have students identify the direct objects.

3 Suggestion Tell students to add two of their own questions to the list.

4 Suggestions
- Before beginning the activity, have students underline the direct objects in the phrases.
- Have two volunteers read the **modèle** aloud.

5 Suggestions
- Before beginning the activity, have students describe the photo.
- Tell students to add three of their own questions with direct objects to the list.

OPTIONS

Extra Practice Make a list of twenty questions requiring direct object pronouns in the answer. Arrange students in two concentric circles. Students in the inner circle ask questions from the list to those in the outer circle until you say stop (**Arrêtez-vous**). The outer circle then moves one person to the right and the questions begin again. Continue for five minutes, and then have the students in the outer circle ask the questions.

Pairs Have students work in pairs. Tell them to invent a romantic dialogue between Simone and Jean-Claude, two protagonists of a soap opera. They should include direct object pronouns in their dialogues and at least three of these verbs: **adorer, aimer, détester, avoir besoin de, penser,** and **attendre.** Example: **Jean-Claude: Simone, je t'adore.**

Synthèse

Instructional Resources
*IRCD-ROM: IRM (**Feuilles d'activités**; Info Gap Activities); Testing Program, pp. 49–52; Test Files; Testing Program MP3s; Test Generator)*
espaces.vhlcentral.com: activities, downloads, reference tools

1 Suggestion Tell students to write their sentences. Remind them that verbs that indicate motion often require the **passé composé** with **être**.

2 Suggestions
- Distribute the **Feuilles d'activités** from the IRM on the IRCD-ROM.
- Have two volunteers read the **modèle** aloud. Remind students to use direct object pronouns in their responses.

3 Suggestion Tell students to jot down notes during their interviews.

4 Suggestion Before beginning the activity, have the class identify the items.

4 Expansion To practice **vous** forms, bring in a small suitcase with various items and tell the class you just returned from a trip. Students must ask you questions about your vacation based on the items and figure out where you went. Example: a suitcase with gloves, a hat, a parka, and ski goggles.

5 Expansion Have groups decide who had the best or most interesting weekend, then ask them to tell the class about it.

6 Suggestion Divide the class into pairs and distribute the Info Gap Handouts in the IRM on the IRCD-ROM for this activity. Give students ten minutes to complete the activity.

1 Il y a dix minutes Avec un(e) partenaire, décrivez dans cette scène les actions qui se sont passées (*happened*) il y a dix minutes. Utilisez les verbes de la liste pour faire des phrases. Ensuite, comparez vos phrases avec les phrases d'un autre groupe. Answers will vary.

MODÈLE

Étudiant(e) 1: *Il y a dix minutes, M. Hamid est parti.*
Étudiant(e) 2: *Il y a dix minutes,...*

aller	partir
arriver	rentrer
descendre	sortir
monter	tomber

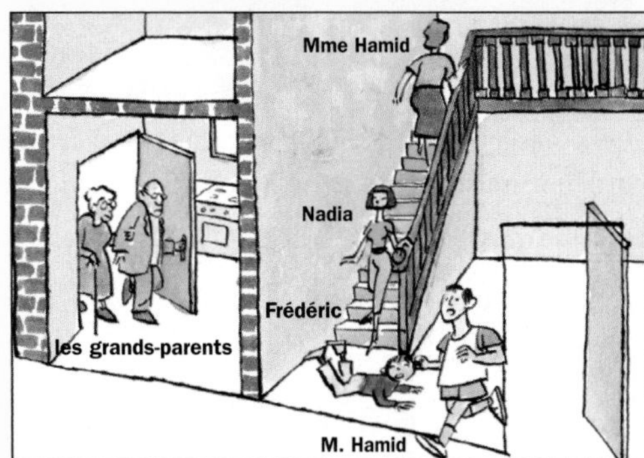

2 Qui aime quoi? Votre professeur va vous donner une feuille d'activités. Circulez dans la classe pour trouver un(e) camarade différent(e) qui aime ou qui n'aime pas chaque lieu de la liste. Answers will vary.

MODÈLE

Étudiant(e) 1: *Est-ce que tu aimes les aéroports?*
Étudiant(e) 2: *Je ne les aime pas du tout, je les déteste.*

3 Les pays étrangers Par groupes de quatre, interviewez vos camarades. Dans quels pays étrangers sont-ils déjà allés? Dans quelles villes? Comparez vos destinations puis présentez toutes les réponses à la classe. N'oubliez pas de demander: Answers will vary.

- quand vos camarades sont parti(e)s
- où ils/elles sont allé(e)s
- où ils/elles sont resté(e)s
- combien de temps ils/elles ont passé là-bas

4 La valise Sandra et Jean sont partis en vacances. Voici leur valise. Avec un(e) partenaire, faites une description écrite (*written*) de leurs vacances. Où sont-ils allés? Comment sont-ils partis? Answers will vary.

5 Un long week-end Avec un(e) partenaire, préparez huit questions sur le dernier long week-end. Utilisez les verbes de la liste. Ensuite, par groupes de quatre, répondez à toutes les questions. Answers will vary.

MODÈLE

Étudiant(e) 1: *Où es-tu allé(e) vendredi soir?*
Étudiant(e) 2: *Vendredi soir je suis resté(e) chez moi. Mais samedi je suis sorti(e)!*

aller	sortir
arriver	rentrer
partir	rester
passer	retourner

6 Mireille et les Girard Votre professeur va vous donner, à vous et à votre partenaire, une feuille sur le week-end de Mireille et de la famille Girard. Attention! Ne regardez pas la feuille de votre partenaire. Answers will vary.

MODÈLE

Étudiant(e) 1: *Qu'est-ce que Mireille a fait vendredi soir?*
Étudiant(e) 2: *Elle est allée au cinéma.*

ressources

WB	LM	Lab MP3s	espaces.vhlcentral.com
pp. 87-90	pp. 51-52	Leçon 13	Leçon 13

OPTIONS

Extra Practice Write these phrases on the board. Tell students to write complete sentences, using the **passé composé**. **1. Janine et moi / faire du shopping 2. Nous / partir / une heure 3. Nous / prendre / métro / Galeries Lafayette / et / nous / passer / après-midi / là 4. Nous / arriver / chez Janine / fatigué 5. Elle / ne pas / avoir besoin / sortir / pour manger / et / nous / rester / la maison**

Extra Practice Have students write a composition about a memorable vacation they took with friends or family. Remind them to use the **passé composé** and object pronouns to avoid unnecessary repetition.

Air Afrique

En 1961, 11 pays d'Afrique francophone fondent une compagnie aérienne° nationale africaine, appelée Air Afrique. En collaboration avec UTA (ancienne compagnie aérienne française) et Air France, elle connaît un grand succès° jusqu'en 1974. Puis elle commence à perdre de l'argent et finalement fait faillite° en 2001. Aujourd'hui, on parle de la fondation d'une nouvelle compagnie aérienne nationale africaine.

AIR AFRIQUE

LIGNE DE VIE POUR LE NOUVEAU MILLENAIRE

—Où que vous soyez°, où que vous alliez°...

—Air Afrique, ligne de vie pour le nouveau millénaire.

Compréhension Répondez aux questions. Answers will vary.

1. À votre avis (*In your opinion*), pourquoi le petit garçon voyage-t-il?
2. La pub (*commercial*) montre des enfants. Pourquoi est-ce un message important?

Discussion Par groupes de quatre, répondez aux questions. Answers will vary.

1. Êtes-vous déjà allé(e) en Afrique francophone? Si oui, dans quel pays? Si non, quel pays d'Afrique francophone avez-vous envie de visiter? Pourquoi?
2. Vous allez fonder votre propre compagnie aérienne. Dans quels pays ou quelles régions va-t-elle aller?

SUR INTERNET

Go to **espaces.vhlcentral.com** to watch the TV clip featured in this **Le zapping.**

compagnie aérienne *airline* **connaît un grand succès** *is a big success* **fait faillite** *goes bankrupt* **soyez** *are, may be* **alliez** *go, may go*

OPTIONS

Air Afrique The disappearance of the transnational airline company Air Afrique left many West African countries without good air transportation. Particularly affected were the countries of Chad, Nigeria, the Central African Republic, Mali, Benin, Togo and the Republic of Congo. On the other hand, it made space for new successful ventures. For example, the company Air Sénégal International (ASI) was created in 2001 by merging airline companies from Morocco and Senegal. Today ASI transports more than 350,000 passengers a year and has a growing market in African international transportation.

Section Goals

In this section, students will:

- read about the airline company Air Afrique
- watch a commercial for the company
- answer questions about the commercial and Air Afrique

Instructional Resources
*IRCD-ROM: IRM (**Le zapping** TV clip transcription)*
espaces.vhlcentral.com: activities, downloads, reference tools, TV clip

Introduction
To check comprehension, ask these questions.
1. Qu'est-ce qu'Air Afrique? (C'est une compagnie aérienne nationale africaine fondée par 11 pays d'Afrique francophones en 1961.)
2. Quand est-ce qu'Air Afrique a commencé à avoir des problèmes d'argent? (La compagnie a commencé à perdre de l'argent après 1974.)
3. Quand est-ce qu'Air Afrique a fait faillite? (Elle a fait faillite en 2001.)

Avant de regarder la vidéo

- Have students look at the video stills, read the captions, and predict what is happening in the commercial for each visual. (**1. Le garçon africain prend un avion. 2. Le garçon africain fait la connaissance d'un autre garçon.**)
- Before showing the video, tell students to listen for the slogan and for cognates.

Compréhension Have students work in pairs or groups for this activity. Tell them to write their answers.

Discussion

- Take a quick class survey to find out which students have gone to Africa and where they went or where students would like to go.
- Have volunteers name the countries their airline would go to and explain why.

Section Goals

In this section, students will learn and practice vocabulary related to:
- hotels
- ordinal numbers
- sequencing events

Instructional Resources
*IRCD-ROM: Transparency #35; IRM (**Vocabulaire supplémentaire; Mise en pratique** answers; Textbook Audioscript; Lab Audioscript)*
Textbook MP3s
WB/VM: Workbook, pp. 91–92
Lab Manual, p. 53
Lab MP3s
WB/VM/LM Answer Key
espaces.vhlcentral.com: activities, downloads, reference tools

Suggestions
- Use **Transparency #35.** Point out people and things in the illustration and describe what the people are doing. Example: **Ils sont à la réception d'un hôtel. Ils ont une réservation. Voici la clé de leur chambre.**
- Have students look over the new vocabulary. They should notice that many terms related to hotels and travel are cognates (**réservation, réception, passeport,** and **passager**).
- Point out that **passeport** has an **e** and **passager/passagère** have no **n**.
- Model the difference in pronunciation between **deuxième** and **douzième**, and have students repeat.
- Point out that the word **libre** means *free*, as in *available*, not *free of charge.*
- Emphasize that, in this context, **complet/complète** means *full*, not *complete.*
- Tell students that the word **second(e)** is used instead of **deuxième** when there are only two items to list. Example: **La Seconde Guerre mondiale**.
- Additional vocabulary for this lesson can be found in the **Vocabulaire supplémentaire** in the IRM on the IRCD-ROM.

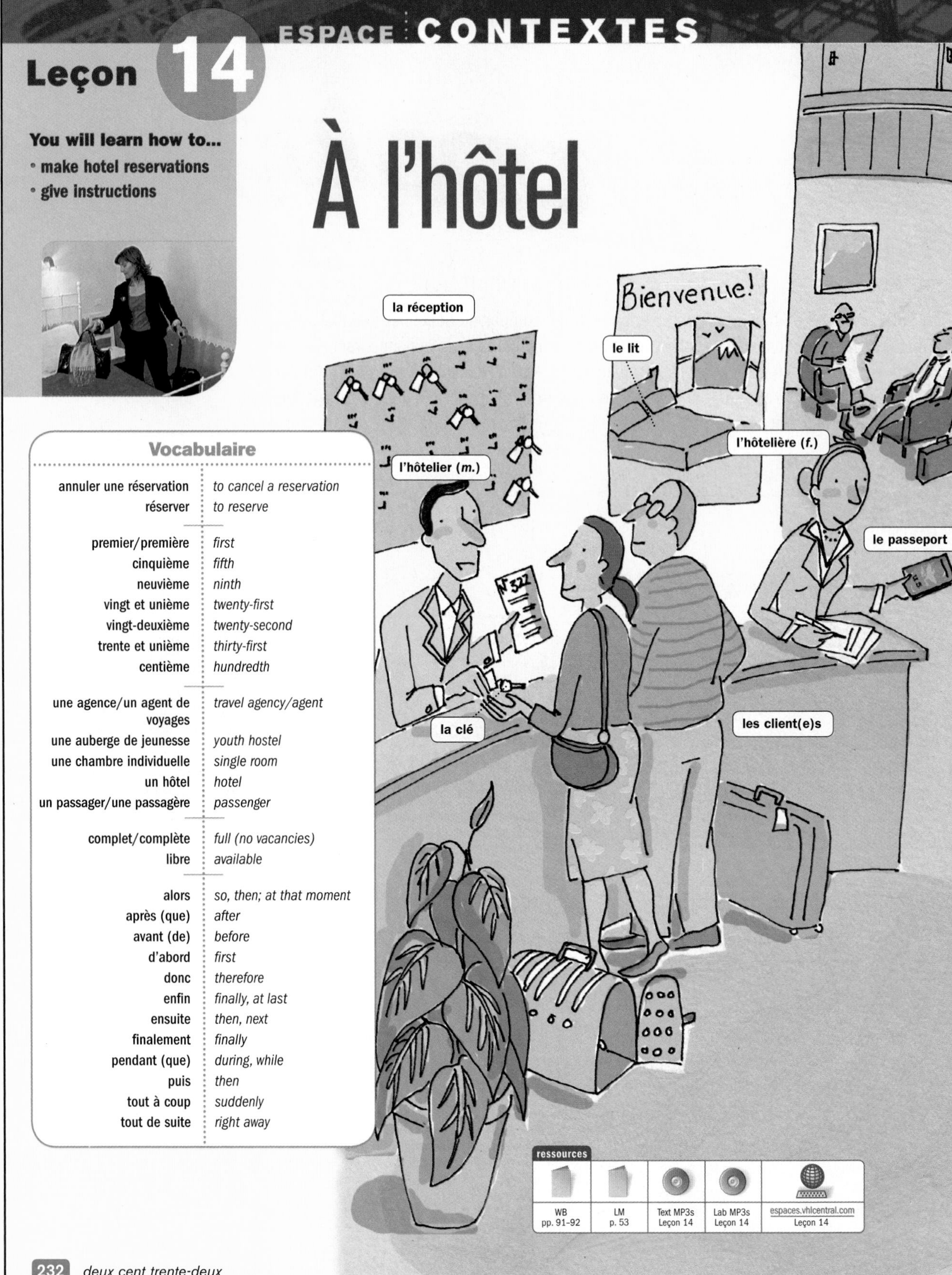

Leçon 14

You will learn how to...
- make hotel reservations
- give instructions

À l'hôtel

Vocabulaire

annuler une réservation	*to cancel a reservation*
réserver	*to reserve*
premier/première	*first*
cinquième	*fifth*
neuvième	*ninth*
vingt et unième	*twenty-first*
vingt-deuxième	*twenty-second*
trente et unième	*thirty-first*
centième	*hundredth*
une agence/un agent de voyages	*travel agency/agent*
une auberge de jeunesse	*youth hostel*
une chambre individuelle	*single room*
un hôtel	*hotel*
un passager/une passagère	*passenger*
complet/complète	*full (no vacancies)*
libre	*available*
alors	*so, then; at that moment*
après (que)	*after*
avant (de)	*before*
d'abord	*first*
donc	*therefore*
enfin	*finally, at last*
ensuite	*then, next*
finalement	*finally*
pendant (que)	*during, while*
puis	*then*
tout à coup	*suddenly*
tout de suite	*right away*

ressources
WB pp. 91-92 | LM p. 53 | Text MP3s Leçon 14 | Lab MP3s Leçon 14 | espaces.vhlcentral.com Leçon 14

OPTIONS

TPR Ask ten volunteers to line up facing the class. Make sure students know what number they are in line. Call out ordinal numbers at random. The student whose cardinal number corresponds to the called ordinal number has three seconds to step forward. If that student is too slow, he or she sits down. The order changes for the rest of the students standing further down the line. The last students standing win.

Les étages d'un hôtel Point out to students that a second floor in the U.S. would be called the **premier étage** in France. Tell them that an **étage** is a floor above another floor. Elevators usually indicate the ground floor by the letter **R** (or other abbreviation of **rez-de-chaussée**) or the number **0**. Add that, in buildings with only two floors, people say **à l'étage** for *on the second floor.*

Attention!

In French, form ordinal numbers by placing **-ième** at the end of the cardinal number. If the cardinal number ends in an **-e**, drop it before adding **-ième**. Note the spelling changes in **cinquième** and **neuvième**. Also note that the French word for *first*, **premier/première** (1er/1ère), is an exception.

onze → **onzième** (11e)
vingt → **vingtième** (20e)

Mise en pratique

1 Écoutez Écoutez la conversation entre Mme Renoir et un hôtelier et décidez si les phrases sont **vraies** ou **fausses**.

	Vrai	Faux
1. Mme Renoir est à l'agence de voyages.	☐	☑
2. Mme Renoir a fait une réservation.	☑	☐
3. Mme Renoir prend la chambre au cinquième étage.	☐	☑
4. Il y a un ascenseur dans l'hôtel.	☐	☑
5. Mme Renoir a réservé une chambre à deux lits.	☐	☑
6. La cliente s'appelle Margot Renoir.	☑	☐
7. L' hôtel a des chambres libres.	☐	☑
8. L' hôtelier donne à Mme Renoir la clé de la chambre 27.	☑	☐

2 Hôtel Paradis Virginie téléphone à l'hôtel Paradis pour faire une réservation. Mettez les phrases dans l'ordre chronologique.

a. __6__ Finalement, il me demande le numéro de ma carte de crédit (*credit card*) pour finaliser la réservation.
b. __2__ Pendant la conversation, je demande une chambre individuelle au troisième étage.
c. __1__ D'abord, j'appelle l'hôtel Paradis pour faire une réservation.
d. __4__ Je ne veux (*want*) pas dormir au rez-de-chaussée, donc je demande une chambre au deuxième étage.
e. __3__ Ensuite, l'hôtel me rappelle (*calls me back*) pour annoncer qu'il n'y a plus de chambre libre au troisième étage, donc ma première réservation est annulée.
f. __5__ C'est alors que l'hôtelier me donne une chambre au deuxième étage à côté de l'ascenseur.

3 Complétez Remplissez les espaces avec le nombre ordinal qui convient (*fits*).

MODÈLE

B est la *deuxième* lettre de l'alphabet.

1. Décembre est le __douzième__ mois de l'année.
2. Mercredi est le __troisième__ jour de la semaine.
3. Aux États-Unis, le rez-de-chaussée est le __premier__ étage.
4. Ma classe de français est au __Answers will vary.__ étage.
5. Octobre est le __dixième__ mois de l'année.
6. Z est la __vingt-sixième__ lettre de l'alphabet.
7. Samedi est le __sixième__ jour de la semaine.
8. Je suis le/la __Answers will vary.__ enfant dans ma famille.
9. Mon prénom (*first name*) commence avec la __Answers will vary.__ lettre de l'alphabet.
10. La fête nationale américaine est le __quatrième__ jour du mois de juillet.

1 Tapescript L'HÔTELIER: Bonjour, Madame. Bienvenue à l'hôtel Casablanca! Avez-vous une réservation?
LA CLIENTE: Bonjour, Monsieur. Oui, mon mari et moi avons fait une réservation.
H: Et c'est à quel nom?
C: Je l'ai faite à mon nom, Renoir.
H: Excellent! Vous avez réservé une chambre avec un grand lit. Votre chambre est la numéro 57 au cinquième étage.
C: Ah non, il y a une erreur. J'ai réservé la chambre numéro 27 au deuxième étage. Je refuse de prendre cette chambre, il n'y a pas d'ascenseur dans votre hôtel. Est-ce que vous avez une autre solution?
H: Madame Renoir, je suis désolé mais l'hôtel est complet.
C: Oh là là. Ce n'est pas possible! Qu'est-ce que je vais faire?
H: Un instant, êtes-vous Marguerite Renoir?
C: Non, je suis Margot Renoir.
H: Madame Renoir, pardonnez-moi. Voici votre clé, chambre 27 au deuxième étage.
(On Textbook MP3s)

2 Suggestion Call students' attention to the sequencing words in these sentences. Examples: **Finalement**, **Pendant**, **D'abord**, etc.

2 Expansion Have pairs of students rewrite the story using the sequencing words, but changing the details. Example: reserve a different kind of room, encounter a different problem, and find a different solution.

3 Expansions
- Give students these items. **11. Aujourd'hui est le ____ jour de la semaine. 12. Ce cours est mon ____ cours aujourd'hui. 13. Ma chambre est au ____ étage. 14. Mon anniversaire est dans le ____ mois de l'année.** (Answers will vary.)
- Have students invent riddles using ordinal numbers. Example: **Je suis le seizième président des États-Unis. Qui suis-je?** (Abraham Lincoln)

OPTIONS

Extra Practice Review seasons, months, and days while practicing ordinal numbers by asking questions like the following: **Quel est le septième mois de l'année? Quelle est la troisième saison de l'année? Quel est le dernier jour de la semaine?**

Extra Practice Ask questions about the **À l'hôtel** illustration. Examples: **Cet hôtel a combien d'étages? Ce monsieur a un passeport de quel pays? Qu'est-ce que la femme à la réception donne aux clients?** Then ask students personalized questions. Examples: **Préférez-vous aller à une agence de voyages ou faire les réservations sur Internet? Aimez-vous voyager seul(e) ou en groupe? Avez-vous un hôtel préféré?**

4 Expansions
- After students have answered the questions, have them make up a conversation between a customer and a travel agent to arrange the trip.
- Ask volunteers to describe their **vacances idéales** to the class.

5 Suggestion Have students consider other details that might come up while making a hotel reservation and include them in their conversation. Examples: **Est-ce qu'il y a un ascenseur? Il y a une télévision dans la chambre?** Have them refer to the **Vocabulaire supplémentaire** from the IRM on the IRCD-ROM.

6 Expansion Assign each group a different francophone location. Tell students to include any nearby attractions (**la plage, la campagne, le centre-ville**) and hotel amenities (**la piscine, le restaurant**) in their poster. For inspiration, show some French language brochures from actual hotels.

7 Suggestion Before starting this activity, have students brainstorm a list of steps involved in making a hotel reservation. If students have never reserved a room before, have them make up a scenario that includes at least one complication, for instance, their first choice of hotel is full.

Successful Language Learning Remind students to accept some corrections without explanation, especially when they are attempting to use language and structures above their current level. Tell them not to overanalyze and to trust that it will make more sense as their language skills develop.

National Standards communication

Communication

4 Conversez Imaginez que vous prenez des vacances idéales dans un hôtel. Interviewez un(e) camarade de classe. Answers will vary.

1. Quelles sont les dates de ton séjour?
2. Où vas-tu? Dans quel pays, région ou ville? Vas-tu à la plage, à la campagne, etc.?
3. À quel hôtel descends-tu (*do you stay*)?
4. Qui fait la réservation?
5. Comment est l'hôtel? Est-ce que l'hôtel a un ascenseur, une piscine, etc.?
6. À quel étage est ta chambre?
7. Combien de lits a ta chambre?
8. Laisses-tu ton passeport à la réception?

5 Notre réservation Travaillez avec deux partenaires pour préparer une présentation où deux touristes font une réservation dans un hôtel francophone ou une auberge de jeunesse. N'oubliez pas d'ajouter (*add*) les informations de la liste. Answers will vary.

- le nom de l'hôtel
- le type de chambre(s)
- l'étage
- le nombre de lits
- les dates
- le prix

6 Mon hôtel Vous allez ouvrir (*open*) votre propre hôtel. Avec trois partenaires, créez un poster pour le promouvoir (*promote*) avec l'information de la liste et présentez votre hôtel au reste de la classe. Votre professeur va ensuite donner à chaque groupe un budget. Avec ce budget, vous allez faire la réservation à l'hôtel qui convient le mieux (*best suits*) à votre groupe. Answers will vary.

- le nom de votre hôtel
- le nombre d'étoiles (*stars*)
- les services offerts
- le prix pour une nuit

★ une étoile	★★ deux étoiles	★★★ trois étoiles	★★★★ quatre étoiles	★★★★★ cinq étoiles

7 Votre dernière réservation Écrivez un paragraphe où vous décrivez (*describe*) ce que vous avez fait la dernière fois que vous avez réservé une chambre. Utilisez au moins cinq des mots de la liste. Échangez et comparez votre paragraphe avec un camarade de classe. Answers will vary.

alors	d'abord	puis
après (que)	donc	tout à coup
avant (de)	enfin	tout de suite

OPTIONS

Extra Practice Give each student a card with either (1) a noun from the **Vocabulaire**, such as **chambre, clé,** or **passeport** or (2) a related verb, such as **réserver, prendre, oublier,** or **perdre**. Tell students to find someone whose word can be combined logically with their own. Then have them write an original sentence in the **passé composé**. Compile the sentences on the board. Then use sequencing expressions to combine them into a story.

Combien d'étoiles préférez-vous? Tell students that the French government regulates hotel ratings and requires that they be posted. Hotels must meet standards to qualify for a certain number of stars. A two-star hotel is a comfortable budget hotel. A five-star hotel is luxurious. While the level of comfort is standardized, prices are not.

Les sons et les lettres

ti, sti, and ssi

The letters **ti** followed by a consonant are pronounced like the English word *tea*, but without the puff released in the English pronunciation.

actif **petit** **tigre** **utiles**

When the letter combination **ti** is followed by a vowel sound, it is often pronounced like the sound linking the English words *miss you*.

dictionnaire **patient** **initial** **addition**

Regardless of whether it is followed by a consonant or a vowel, the letter combination **sti** is pronounced *stee*, as in the English word *steep*.

gestion **question** **Sébastien** **artistique**

The letter combination **ssi** followed by another vowel or a consonant is usually pronounced like the sound linking the English words *miss you*.

passion **expression** **mission** **profession**

Words that end in **-sion** or **-tion** are often cognates with English words, but they are pronounced quite differently. In French, these words are never pronounced with a *sh* sound.

compression **nation** **attention** **addition**

Prononcez Répétez les mots suivants à voix haute.

1. artiste
2. mission
3. réservation
4. impatient
5. position
6. initiative
7. possession
8. nationalité
9. compassion
10. possible

Articulez Répétez les phrases suivantes à voix haute.

1. L'addition, s'il vous plaît.
2. Christine est optimiste et active.
3. Elle a fait une bonne première impression.
4. Laëtitia est impatiente parce qu'elle est fatiguée.
5. Tu cherches des expressions idiomatiques dans le dictionnaire.

Dictons Répétez les dictons à voix haute.

De la discussion jaillit la lumière.[1]

Il n'est de règle sans exception.[2]

ressources			
LM p. 54	Text MP3s Leçon 14	Lab MP3s Leçon 14	espaces.vhlcentral.com Leçon 14

1 Discussion brings light.
2 The exception proves the rule.

Section Goals

In this section, students will learn about the letter combinations **ti**, **sti**, and **ssi**.

Instructional Resources
Textbook MP3s
Lab Manual, p. 54
Lab MP3s
WB/VM/LM Answer Key
IRCD-ROM: IRM (Textbook Audioscript; Lab Audioscript
espaces.vhlcentral.com: activities, downloads, reference tools

Suggestions

- Pronounce each of the example words and have students repeat them after you.
- To practice **ti**, have students put the palm of their hand in front of their lips and say the English word *tea*. Ask them if they felt the puff of air when they pronounced the letter **t**. Then have them pronounce the French word **petit** holding their hand in front of their mouth. Explain that they should not feel a puff of air when they pronounce the letters **ti** in French.
- Point out that **-sion** as in the word **télévision** has a [**z**] sound. Additionally, **-cia** as in the name **Patricia** has an unvoiced [**s**] sound
- Many words that end in **-sion**, **-ssion**, **-stion**, and **-tion** are cognates. Contrast the French and English pronunciation of words such as **attention** and **mission**.
- Mention words from the **Vocabulaire** that contain **ti**, **sti**, or **ssi**. Then have students repeat after you. Alternatively, ask students to recall such vocabulary. Examples: **réception, réservation, vingtième**. See if a volunteer is able to recall any words from previous lessons. Examples: **pessimiste, dessiner, l'addition**, and **attention**.

Dictons Tell students that the word **lumière** is used figuratively in the proverb **«De la discussion jaillit la lumière.»** Ask students what they think it means in this context (*clarity, ideas*).

OPTIONS

Extra Practice Here are some sentences to use for additional practice with these letter combinations. **1. C'est utile d'étudier la gestion et l'informatique. 2. La profession de Sébastien? Il est dentiste. 3. Patricia utilise un plan de la station de ski. 4. Martine est-elle pessimiste ou optimiste?**

Extra Practice Teach your students the following French tongue-twisters that contain **ti** and **ssi**: **1. Pauvre petit pêcheur, prend patience pour pouvoir prendre plusieurs petits poissons. 2. Un pâtissier qui pâtissait chez un tapissier qui tapissait, dit un jour au tapissier qui tapissait: vaut-il mieux pâtisser chez un tapissier qui tapisse ou tapisser chez un pâtissier qui pâtisse?**

Section Goals

In this section, students will learn functional phrases for getting help and making reservations.

Instructional Resources
WB/VM: Video Manual, pp. 237–238
WB/VM/LM Answer Key
Video CD-ROM
Video on DVD
IRCD-ROM: IRM (Videoscript; ***Roman-photo*** *Translations)*
espaces.vhlcentral.com: activities, downloads, reference tools

Video Recap: Leçon 13
Before doing this **Roman-photo**, review the previous one with this activity.
1. Où est allé David? (à Paris)
2. Avec qui a-t-il visité Paris? (avec ses parents)
3. Qu'a-t-il fait à Paris? (Il a visité les musées et les monuments. Il a pris un bateau-mouche.)
4. Qu'est-ce qu'il a apporté à Stéphane? (des lunettes de soleil)
5. Où Sandrine va-t-elle passer ses vacances d'hiver? (à Albertville)

Video Synopsis Sandrine goes to a travel agency to find a hotel in Albertville. They are all too expensive, so she leaves without making a reservation. She asks Amina to help find a cheaper hotel. Then Pascal says he can't go to Albertville after all. Disappointed, Sandrine tells Amina to cancel the reservation because she and Pascal are finished. Amina then tells Sandrine about Cyberhomme, her electronic pen pal.

Suggestions
- Ask students to read the title, glance at the video stills, and predict what the episode will be about.
- Have students read the **Roman-photo** aloud in groups of four.
- Have students scan the captions to find at least three sentences that contain words and expressions related to travel and accommodations. Examples: **Ou alors à l'hôtel Le Mont Blanc, deux chambres individuelles pour 171 euros par personne. Les hôtels les moins chers sont déjà complets.**
- Review students' predictions and ask which ones were correct.

NATIONAL STANDARDS communication cultures

La réservation d'hôtel

PERSONNAGES

Agent de voyages

Amina

Pascal

Sandrine

1

À l'agence de voyages...

SANDRINE J'ai besoin d'une réservation d'hôtel, s'il vous plaît. C'est pour les vacances de Noël.
AGENT Où allez-vous? En Italie?
SANDRINE Nous allons à Albertville.
AGENT Et c'est pour combien de personnes?
SANDRINE Nous sommes deux, mais il nous faut deux chambres individuelles.

2

AGENT Très bien. Quelles sont les dates du séjour, Mademoiselle?
SANDRINE Alors, le 25, c'est Noël donc je fête en famille. Disons du 26 décembre au 2 janvier.
AGENT Ce n'est pas possible à Albertville, mais à Megève j'ai deux chambres à l'hôtel Le Vieux Moulin pour 143 euros par personne. Ou alors à l'hôtel Le Mont Blanc pour 171 euros par personne.

3

SANDRINE Oh non, mais Megève, ce n'est pas Albertville... et ces prix! C'est vraiment trop cher.
AGENT C'est la saison, Mademoiselle. Les hôtels les moins chers sont déjà complets.
SANDRINE Oh là là. Je ne sais pas quoi faire... J'ai besoin de réfléchir. Merci, Monsieur. Au revoir!
AGENT Au revoir, Mademoiselle.

6

Chez Sandrine...

SANDRINE Oui, Pascal. Amina nous a trouvé une auberge à Albertville. C'est génial, non? En plus, c'est pas cher!
PASCAL Euh, en fait... Albertville, maintenant c'est impossible.
SANDRINE Qu'est-ce que tu dis?

7

PASCAL C'est que... j'ai du travail.
SANDRINE Du travail! Mais c'est Noël! On ne travaille pas à Noël! Et Amina a déjà tout réservé... Oh! C'est pas vrai!
PASCAL (*à lui-même*) Elle n'est pas très heureuse maintenant, mais quelle surprise en perspective!

8

Un peu plus tard...

AMINA On a réussi, Sandrine! La réservation est faite. Tu as de la chance! Mais, qu'est-ce qu'il y a?
SANDRINE Tu es super gentille, Amina, mais Pascal a annulé pour Noël. Il dit qu'il a du travail... Lui et moi, c'est fini. Tu as fait beaucoup d'efforts pour faire la réservation, je suis désolée.

ACTIVITÉS

1 Vrai ou faux? Indiquez si les affirmations suivantes sont vraies ou fausses.

1. Sandrine fait une réservation à l'agence de voyages. Faux.
2. Pascal dit un mensonge (*lie*). Vrai.
3. Amina fait une réservation à l'hôtel Le Mont Blanc. Faux.
4. Il faut annuler la réservation à l'auberge de la Costaroche. Vrai.
5. Amina est fâchée (*angry*) contre Sandrine. Faux.
6. Pascal est fâché contre Sandrine. Faux.
7. Sandrine est fâchée contre Pascal. Vrai.
8. Sandrine a envie de voyager le 25 décembre. Faux.
9. Cent soixante et onze euros, c'est beaucoup d'argent pour Sandrine. Vrai.
10. Il y a beaucoup de touristes à Albertville en décembre. Vrai.

OPTIONS

Avant de regarder la vidéo Before viewing the video episode **La réservation d'hôtel**, have students brainstorm a list of things people might say when arranging a hotel reservation. For example, what questions might a travel agent ask? How might the traveler respond?

Regarder la vidéo Play the video episode once without sound and have the class create a plot summary based on the visual cues. Afterward, show the video with sound and have the class correct any mistaken guesses and fill in any gaps in the plot summary they created.

Sandrine essaie d'organiser son voyage.

4

5

Au P'tit Bistrot...

SANDRINE Amina, je n'ai pas réussi à faire une réservation pour Albertville. Tu peux m'aider?

AMINA C'est que... je suis connectée avec Cyberhomme.

SANDRINE Avec qui?

AMINA J'écris un e-mail à... Bon, je t'explique plus tard. Dis-moi, comment est-ce que je peux t'aider?

Un peu plus tard...

AMINA Bon, alors... Sandrine m'a demandé de trouver un hôtel pas cher à Albertville. Pas facile à Noël... Je vais essayer... Voilà! L'auberge de la Costaroche... 39 euros la nuit pour une chambre individuelle. L'hôtel n'est pas complet et il y a deux chambres libres. Quelle chance cette Sandrine! Bon, nom... Sandrine Aubry...

9

10

AMINA Bon, la réservation, ce n'est pas un problème. Mais toi, Sandrine, c'est évident, ça ne va pas.

SANDRINE C'est vrai. Mais, alors, c'est qui, ce «Cyberhomme»?

AMINA Oh, c'est juste un ami virtuel. On correspond sur Internet, c'est tout. Ce soir, c'est son dixième message!

SANDRINE Lis-le-moi!

AMINA Euh non, c'est personnel...

SANDRINE Alors, dis-moi comment il est!

AMINA D'accord... Il est étudiant, sportif mais sérieux. Très intellectuel.

SANDRINE S'il te plaît, écris-lui: «Sandrine cherche aussi un cyberhomme»!

Expressions utiles

Getting help

- **Je ne sais pas quoi faire... J'ai besoin de réfléchir.**
  I don't know what to do... I have to think.
- **Je n'ai pas réussi à faire une réservation pour Albertville.**
  I didn't manage to make a reservation for Albertville.
- **Tu peux m'aider?**
  Can you help me?
- **Dis-moi, comment est-ce que je peux t'aider?**
  Tell me, how can I help you?
- **Qu'est-ce que tu dis?**
  What are you saying/did you say?
- **On a réussi.**
  We succeeded./We got it.
- **S'il te plaît, écris-lui.**
  Please, write to him.

Additional vocabulary

- **C'est trop tard?**
  Is it too late?
- **Disons...**
  Let's say...
- **La réservation est faite.**
  The reservation has been made.
- **C'est fini.**
  It's over.
- **Je suis connectée avec...**
  I am online with...
- **Lis-le-moi.**
  Read it to me.
- **Il dit que...**
  He says that...
- **les moins chers**
  the least expensive
- **en fait**
  in fact

2 Questions Répondez aux questions suivantes.

1. Pourquoi est-il difficile de faire une réservation pour Albertville? C'est difficile parce que c'est Noël.
2. Pourquoi est-ce que Sandrine ne veut pas (*doesn't want*) rester à l'hôtel Le Vieux Moulin? L'hôtel Le Vieux Moulin est très cher.
3. Pourquoi est-ce que Pascal ne peut pas (*can't*) aller à Albertville? Il a du travail.
4. Qui est Cyberhomme? C'est l'ami virtuel d'Amina.
5. À ton avis (*In your opinion*), Sandrine va-t-elle rester (*stay*) avec Pascal? Answers will vary.

3 Devinez Inventez-vous une identité virtuelle. Écrivez un paragraphe dans lequel (*in which*) vous vous décrivez, vous et vos occupations préférées. Donnez votre nom d'internaute (*cybername*). Votre professeur va afficher (*post*) vos messages. Devinez (*Guess*) quelle description correspond à quel(le) camarade de classe.

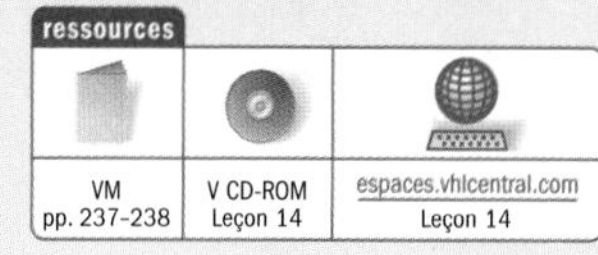

ACTIVITÉS

Expressions utiles
- Draw attention to **-ir** verbs and expressions used to ask for help in the captions, in the **Expressions utiles** box, and as they occur in your conversation with students. Point out that this material will be formally presented in the **Structures** section.
- Respond briefly to questions about regular and irregular **-ir** verbs. Reinforce correct forms, but do not expect students to produce them consistently at this time.
- Contrast the pronunciation of the following expressions: **en fait, on fait**.
- Point out the differences between direct and indirect discourse by writing these two sentences on the board: **Il dit qu'il ne va pas. Il dit: «Je ne vais pas.»**

1 Suggestion Have students correct the items that are false.

1 Expansion Give these statements to the class.
11. Sandrine a besoin de deux chambres individuelles. (Vrai.) 12. Amina ne fait pas de réservation. (Faux.) 13. Cyberhomme est l'ami virtuel de Sandrine. (Faux.)

2 Suggestion Have students discuss these questions in small groups.

2 Expansion Discuss question #5 as a class. Have students make other predictions about what will happen. Ask what kind of surprise they think Pascal has in mind.

3 Suggestion Without revealing students' identities, match students with common interests and have them write back to one another.

OPTIONS

Extra Practice Ask volunteers to ad-lib the **Roman-photo** episode for the class. Assure them that it is not necessary to memorize the episode or to stick strictly to its content. Give them time to prepare. You may want to assign this as homework and do it the next class period as a review activity.

Pairs Have students write a brief paragraph recapping the major events in this episode and using sequencing expressions, such as **d'abord, donc, ensuite, avant de, alors,** etc. Ask volunteers to read their synopses aloud.

Section Goals

In this section, students will:
- learn about how and where the French vacation
- learn some terms used in youth hostels
- find out about vacation spots in the francophone world
- read about the Alps, a popular destination for skiers

Instructional Resources
espaces.vhlcentral.com: activities, downloads, reference tools

Culture à la loupe

Avant la lecture Ask students how much vacation their parents can take annually, how much is typical in this country, and how much they think working people need to be happy in their work. You might also ask what vacation activities Americans enjoy and what the students imagine is popular in France.

Lecture
- Mention to students that when experts anticipate the **grands départs** on the **autoroutes**, these days are labeled **rouge** throughout France.
- Explain the **Coup de main** box on superlatives to help students understand the text.

Après la lecture Ask students to compare American and French vacation habits. Example: **Les étudiants à l'université ici commencent leurs vacances en mai, mais les étudiants en France terminent leurs études en juin.**

1 Expansion Continue the activity with these fill-in-the-blank statements. **11. Les Français d'aujourd'hui prennent des vacances qui durent ____ en moyenne. (sept jours) 12. Les vacances les moins populaires à l'étranger sont ____. (en Asie) 13. Les étudiants commencent leurs vacances d'été en ____. (juin)**

CULTURE À LA LOUPE

Les vacances des Français

une plage à Biarritz, en France

En 1936, les Français obtiennent° leurs premiers congés payés: deux semaines par an. En 1956, les congés payés passent à trois semaines, puis à quatre en 1969, et enfin à cinq semaines en 1982. Aujourd'hui, ce sont les Français qui ont le plus de vacances en Europe. Pendant longtemps, les Français prennent un mois de congés l'été, en août, et beaucoup d'entreprises°, de bureaux et de magasins ferment° tout le mois (la fermeture annuelle). Aujourd'hui, les Français ont tendance à prendre des vacances plus courtes (sept jours en moyenne°) mais plus souvent. Quant aux° destinations de vacances, 90% (pour cent) des Français restent en France. S'ils partent à l'étranger, leurs destinations préférées sont l'Espagne, l'Afrique et l'Italie. Environ° 35% des Français vont à la campagne, 30% vont en ville, 25% vont à la mer et 10% vont à la montagne.

Ce sont les personnes âgées et les agriculteurs° qui partent le moins souvent en vacances et les étudiants qui voyagent le plus, parce qu'ils ont beaucoup de congés. Pour eux, les cours commencent en septembre ou octobre avec la rentrée des classes. Puis, il y a deux semaines de vacances plusieurs fois dans l'année: les vacances de la Toussaint en octobre-novembre, les vacances de Noël en décembre-janvier, les vacances d'hiver en février-mars et les vacances de printemps en avril-mai. L'été, les étudiants ont les grandes vacances de juin jusqu'à° la rentrée.

Les destinations de vacances des Français aujourd'hui

PAYS / CONTINENT	SÉJOURS (EN %)
France	90,1
Espagne	1,9
Afrique	1,8
Italie	1,6
Amérique	1,3
Belgique / Luxembourg	0,9
Grande-Bretagne / Irlande	0,9
Allemagne	0,8
Asie / Océanie	0,7

Coup de main

To form the superlative of nouns, use **le plus (de)** + (*noun*) to say *the most* and **le moins (de)** + (*noun*) to say *the least.*

Les étudiants ont le plus de congés.

Les personnes âgées prennent le moins de congés.

obtiennent *obtain* **entreprises** *companies* **ferment** *close* **en moyenne** *on average* **Quant aux** *As for* **Environ** *Around* **agriculteurs** *farmers* **jusqu'à** *until*

ACTIVITÉS

1 Complétez Complétez les phrases.

1. C'est en 1936 que les Français obtiennent leurs premiers congés payés.
2. Depuis (*Since*) 1982, les Français ont cinq semaines de congés payés.
3. Pendant longtemps, les Français prennent leurs vacances au mois d'août.
4. Pendant la fermeture annuelle, beaucoup de magasins sont fermés.
5. La France est la destination de vacances préférée de 90% des Français.
6. Les destinations étrangères préférées des Français sont l'Espagne, l'Afrique et l'Italie.
7. Le lieu de séjour favori des Français est la campagne.
8. Les personnes âgées et les agriculteurs ne partent pas souvent en vacances.
9. Ce sont les étudiants qui ont le plus de vacances.
10. Les étudiants ont deux semaines de vacances plusieurs fois par an.

OPTIONS

Extra Practice Ask students what they can learn in the chart **Les destinations de vacances des Français aujourd'hui**. (percentages of where the French spend their vacations today) Have students quiz each other on the chart, so they can practice geography and percentages.

Pairs Ask students to work with a partner to tell in their own words three main points described in **Les vacances des Français**. You might brainstorm a list on the board: the history of employee vacations, the change in how the French take their vacations, and the time periods of student vacations.

LE FRANÇAIS QUOTIDIEN

À l'auberge de jeunesse

bagagerie (*f.*)	*baggage check room*
cadenas (*m.*)	*padlock*
casier (*m.*)	*locker*
couvre-feu (*m.*)	*curfew*
dortoir (*m.*)	*dormitory*
sac (*m.*) de couchage	*sleeping bag*
mixte	*coed*

LE MONDE FRANCOPHONE

Des vacances francophones

Voici quelques idées de vacances francophones:

Au soleil

- un séjour ou une croisière (un voyage en bateau) dans les îles° des Antilles, dans la mer des Caraïbes: la Martinique, la Guadeloupe
- un séjour ou une croisière dans les îles de la Polynésie française, dans l'océan Pacifique: les îles de la Société (avec Tahiti), les Marquises, les Tuamotu, les îles Gambier et les îles Australes

Pour de l'aventure

- un trekking (une randonnée à pied) ou une randonnée à dos de chameau° dans le désert du Sahara: Maroc, Tunisie, Algérie
- un circuit-aventure dans les forêts de Madagascar, dans l'océan Indien, ou dans la forêt équatoriale de la Guyane française, en Amérique du sud°

îles *islands* **à dos de chameau** *camelback* **sud** *South*

PORTRAIT

Les Alpes et le ski

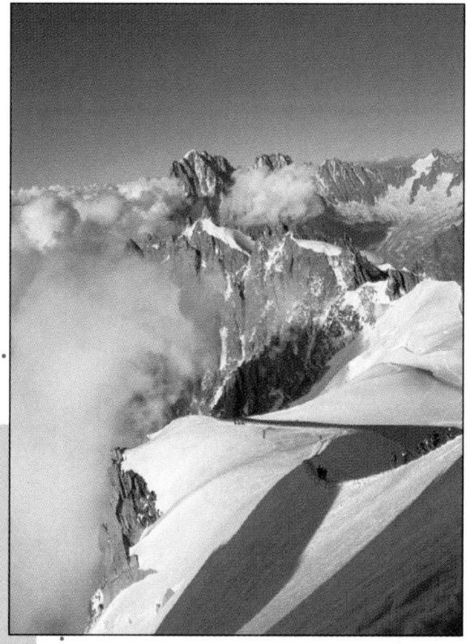

Près de 40% des Français partent à la montagne pour deux semaines en moyenne° pendant les vacances d'hiver. Soixante-dix pour cent d'entre eux° choisissent° une station de ski des Alpes françaises. La chaîne° des Alpes est la plus grande chaîne de montagnes d'Europe. Elle fait plus de 1.000 km de long et va de la Méditerranée à l'Autriche°. Plusieurs pays la partagent: entre autres° la France, la Suisse, l'Allemagne et l'Italie. Le Mont-Blanc, le sommet° le plus haut° d'Europe occidentale°, est à 4.808 mètres d'altitude. On trouve d'excellentes pistes° de ski dans les Alpes, comme à Chamonix, Tignes, Val d'Isère et aux Trois Vallées.

en moyenne *on average* **d'entre eux** *of them* **choisissent** *choose* **chaîne** *range* **l'Autriche** *Austria* **entre autres** *among others* **sommet** *peak* **le plus haut** *the highest* **occidentale** *Western* **pistes** *trails*

SUR INTERNET

Chaque année, depuis (*since*) 1982, plus de 4 millions de Français utilisent des Chèques-Vacances pour payer leurs vacances. Qu'est-ce que c'est, un Chèque-Vacances?

Go to **espaces.vhlcentral.com** to find more cultural information related to this **ESPACE CULTURE.**

ACTIVITÉS

2 Répondez Répondez aux questions par des phrases complètes.

1. Que peut-on utiliser à la place de draps (*instead of sheets*)?
   On peut utiliser un sac de couchage.
2. Quand on passe la nuit dans le dortoir d'une auberge de jeunesse, où met-on ses affaires (*belongings*)?
   On les met dans un casier.
3. Qu'est-ce que c'est, les Alpes?
   C'est une grande chaîne de montagnes partagée entre plusieurs pays d'Europe.
4. Quel est le sommet le plus haut d'Europe occidentale?
   Le Mont-Blanc est le sommet le plus haut d'Europe occidentale.
5. Quel séjour est-ce que vous suggérez à un jeune américain qui aime l'aventure et qui a envie de pratiquer son français?
   Answers will vary.

3 À l'agence de voyages Vous travaillez dans une agence de voyages en France. Votre partenaire, un(e) client(e), va vous parler des activités et du climat qu'il/elle aime. Faites quelques suggestions de destinations. Votre client(e) va vous poser des questions sur les différents voyages que vous suggérez.

ressources

espaces.vhlcentral.com Leçon 14

Le français quotidien Encourage students to try an **auberge de jeunesse** if they travel overseas. They have no frills, sometimes have curfews, can be noisy, and meals (if offered) are during limited hours. **L'auberge de jeunesse** is the best deal, though; many travelers find lifelong international friends and traveling companions there.

Portrait Explain that the Pyrenees are another important ski destination in France. Show their geographical relationship to the Alps on a map and point out that the Pyrenees create a natural border between France and Spain.

Le monde francophone Call on volunteers to read each bulleted item. Then ask for other volunteers to point out each francophone place mentioned on **Transparencies #2** or **#4**.

2 Expansion Continue the activity with these questions. **6. Quel pourcentage des Français part pour la montagne pendant les vacances d'hiver? (près de 40 pour cent) 7. Quels pays partagent les Alpes? (la France, l'Allemagne, la Suisse et l'Italie) 8. Où trouve-t-on de bonnes pistes de ski? (à Chamonix, Tignes, Val d'Isère et aux Trois Vallées)**

3 Expansion After the trip, the **client(e)** returns to the **agent(e)** to discuss what he or she did on the trip. The **agent(e)** asks: **Qu'est-ce que vous avez fait? Et puis, qu'est-ce que vous avez vu? Ensuite, où êtes-vous allé(e)?** The **client(e)** then volunteers as much information as possible about the trip.

OPTIONS

Pairs Have students imagine that, while studying in France, they are planning a trip for an upcoming vacation. They can speak **au présent** and **au futur proche**. Examples: **Où est-ce qu'on va aller? Qui va réserver l'hôtel/l'auberge de jeunesse? Qu'est-ce que tu as envie de faire?** Encourage them to consult **Les vacances des Français** to plan a trip when French universities are actually on break. Then have them refer to **Le monde francophone** to discuss which type of vacation they would like best, **au soleil** or **pour de l'aventure**. You might want to come up with some questions as a class before students continue in pairs. Examples: **Que préférez-vous, la plage ou le désert? Entre le Maroc et la Martinique, qu'aimez-vous mieux? Moi, j'ai envie de faire une croisière, et vous?**

National Standards: comparisons

Section Goals

In this section, students will learn:

- regular **-ir** verbs
- past participles of regular **-ir** verbs

Instructional Resources
WB/VM: Workbook, pp. 93–94
Lab Manual, p. 55
Lab MP3s
WB/VM/LM Answer Key
*IRCD-ROM: IRM (**Essayez!** and **Mise en pratique** answers; Lab Audioscript)*
espaces.vhlcentral.com: activities, downloads, reference tools

Suggestions

- Model the pronunciation of **-ir** verbs and have students repeat them.
- Introduce the verbs by saying when you finish teaching today and asking students when they finish classes. Examples: **Aujourd'hui, je finis d'enseigner à cinq heures. Et vous, ____, à quelle heure finissez-vous les cours?** Then ask students to ask a classmate: **Et toi, ____, à quelle heure finis-tu aujourd'hui?**
- Ask a volunteer to go to the board and write the conjugation of **partir** as you write the conjugation of **finir**. Have students compare the endings of the two verb conjugations noting the similarities and differences.
- Explain that, to form the past participles of regular **-ir** verbs, you drop only the **-r** from the infinitive. Example: **finir: fini**. Then say the verbs listed and have students respond with the past participles.
- Ask students a few questions using **-ir** verbs. Examples: **Quelle profession avez-vous choisie? Quand allez-vous finir vos études? Avez-vous choisi vos cours pour le semestre prochain?**

Essayez! Have students create new sentences orally or in writing by changing the subject of the sentences. Remind them that other elements may have to be changed according to the new subjects.

14.1 Regular *-ir* verbs

Point de départ In **Leçon 9**, you learned several irregular **-ir** verbs. Some **-ir** verbs, like **finir** (*to finish*), are regular in their conjugation.

finir	
je finis	nous finissons
tu finis	vous finissez
il/elle finit	ils/elles finissent

Je **finis** mes devoirs.
I finish my homework.

Alain et Chloé **finissent** de manger.
Alain and Chloé finish eating.

- Here are some other verbs that follow the same pattern as **finir**.

Other regular *-ir* verbs			
choisir	*to choose*	réfléchir (à)	*to think (about), to reflect (on)*
grossir	*to gain weight*	réussir (à)	*to succeed in doing something*
maigrir	*to lose weight*		

Marc **grossit** pendant les vacances.
Marc gains weight during vacation.

Elles **réussissent** à trouver un hôtel au centre-ville.
They succeed in finding a hotel downtown.

- To form the past participle of regular **-ir** verbs, drop the **-r** from the infinitive.

M. Leroy **a** beaucoup **maigri**.
Mr. Leroy lost a lot of weight.

Vous **avez choisi** une chambre?
Did you choose a room?

Une minute... je réfléchis.

On a réussi!

Essayez! Complétez les phrases.

1. Si tu manges de la salade, tu *maigris* (maigrir).
2. Il réussit (réussir) tous ses projets.
3. Vous finissez (finir) vos devoirs?
4. Lundi prochain nous finissons (finir) le livre.
5. Les enfants grossissent (grossir).
6. Vous choisissez (choisir) quel magazine?
7. Son jean est trop grand parce qu'il maigrit (maigrir).
8. Je réfléchis (réfléchir) beaucoup à ce problème.

MISE EN PRATIQUE

1 Notre voyage Complétez le dialogue avec le présent des verbes.

FRÉDÉRIQUE L'agence de voyages (1) finit (finir) d'organiser notre séjour aujourd'hui, n'est-ce pas?
MARC Oui, et elle (2) choisit (choisir) aussi notre hôtel.
LINDA Avez-vous assez d'argent? Est-ce que vous (3) réfléchissez (réfléchir) un peu à ça?
MARC Bien sûr, nous (4) réfléchissons (réfléchir) à ça!
FRÉDÉRIQUE Moi, je (5) réussis (réussir) toujours à dépenser tout mon argent.
LINDA Eh bien moi, je ne dépense pas d'argent pour manger. Je (6) maigris (maigrir) quand je vais à l'étranger.
MARC Moi, je (7) grossis (grossir) quand je voyage parce que je mange trop.
LINDA Est-ce que vous (8) finissez (finir) tous vos devoirs avant de voyager?
FRÉDÉRIQUE Moi, je les (9) finis (finir) rarement!
MARC Et moi, je (10) choisis (choisir) de les finir.

2 Saïda part en voyage Saïda a préparé une liste de choses qu'elle et ses copines, Leyla et Patricia, doivent (*must*) faire avant leur voyage. Elles ont déjà fait plusieurs choses, mais pas toutes. Dites qui a fait quoi.
Answers may vary.

	moi	Leyla	Patricia
1. faire une réservation à l'auberge		✓	
2. réfléchir aux vêtements qu'on va apporter		✓	✓
3. maigrir	✓		
4. choisir une chambre au rez-de-chaussée	✓		✓
5. réussir à trouver un maillot de bain	✓	✓	✓
6. choisir une camarade de chambre			✓

1. Leyla a déjà fait une réservation à l'auberge.
2. Leyla et Patricia ont déjà réfléchi aux vêtements qu'elles vont apporter.
3. J'ai déjà maigri.
4. Patricia et moi, nous avons déjà choisi une chambre au rez-de-chaussée.
5. Nous avons déjà toutes réussi à trouver un maillot.
6. Patricia a déjà choisi une camarade de chambre.

OPTIONS

Game Divide the class into two teams. Choose one team member at a time to go to the board, alternating between teams. Say a subject pronoun and an infinitive. The person at the board must write and say the correct verb form. Example: **tu: choisir (tu choisis)**. Give a point for each correct answer. The team with the most points at the end of the game wins.

Extra Practice Have students write six fill-in-the-blank or dehydrated sentences, one for each verb listed in this section. Then tell them to exchange papers with a partner and complete the activity. Remind students to verify their answers.

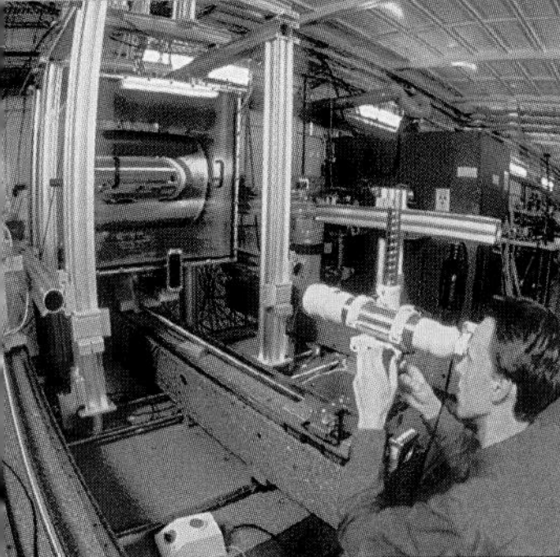

Les destinations

Grenoble

La ville de Grenoble, dans la région Rhône-Alpes, est surnommée «Capitale des Alpes» et «Ville Technologique». Située° à la porte des Alpes, elle donne accès aux grandes stations de ski alpines et elle est le premier centre de recherche° en France après Paris, avec plus de° 15.000 chercheurs°. Le synchrotron de Grenoble, un des plus grands° accélérateurs de particules du monde, permet à 5.000 chercheurs d'étudier la matière°. Grenoble est également° une ville universitaire avec quatre universités et 60.000 étudiants.

Les arts

Le festival de Cannes

Chaque année depuis° 1946, au mois de mai, de nombreux acteurs, réalisateurs° et journalistes viennent à Cannes, sur la Côte d'Azur, pour le Festival International du Film. Avec près de 1.000 films, 4.000 journalistes et plus de 70 pays représentés, c'est la manifestation cinématographique annuelle la plus médiatisée°. Après deux semaines de projections, de fêtes, d'expositions et de concerts, le jury international du festival choisit le meilleur° des vingt films présentés en compétition officielle.

La gastronomie

La raclette et la fondue

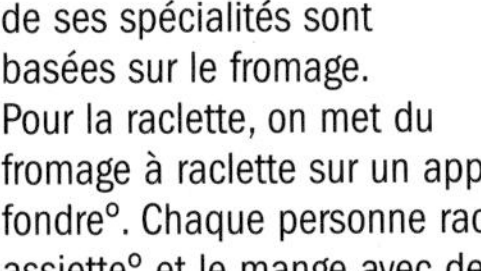

La Savoie, dans la région Rhône-Alpes, est très riche en fromages et deux de ses spécialités sont basées sur le fromage. Pour la raclette, on met du fromage à raclette sur un appareil° à raclette pour le faire fondre°. Chaque personne racle° du fromage dans son assiette° et le mange avec des pommes de terre° et de la charcuterie°. La fondue est un mélange° de fromages fondus°. Avec un bâton°, on trempe° un morceau° de pain dans la fondue. Ne le faites pas tomber!

Les traditions

Grasse, France

La ville de Grasse, sur la Côte d'Azur, est le centre de la parfumerie° française. Capitale mondiale du parfum depuis le dix-huitième siècle, Grasse cultive les fleurs depuis le Moyen Âge°: violette, lavande, rose, plantes aromatiques, etc. Au dix-neuvième siècle, ses parfumeurs, comme Molinard, ont conquis° les marchés du monde grâce à° la fabrication industrielle.

Qu'est-ce que vous avez appris? Répondez aux questions par des phrases complètes.

1. Comment s'appelle la région où les gardians perpétuent les traditions des cow-boys français?
   La région s'appelle la Camargue.
2. Qui a écrit le livre *Le Petit Prince*?
   Antoine de Saint-Exupéry a écrit *Le Petit Prince*.
3. Quel est le rôle des gardians?
   Ils gardent les taureaux.
4. Où est situé Grenoble?
   Grenoble est situé à la porte des Alpes.
5. À Grenoble, qui vient étudier la matière?
   À Grenoble, les chercheurs viennent étudier la matière.
6. Depuis quand existe le festival de Cannes?
   Le festival de Cannes existe depuis 1946.
7. Qui choisit le meilleur film au festival de Cannes?
   Le jury international choisit le meilleur film.
8. Avec quoi mange-t-on la raclette?
   On mange la raclette avec des pommes de terre et de la charcuterie.
9. Quelle ville est le centre de la parfumerie française?
   La ville de Grasse est le centre de la parfumerie française.
10. Pourquoi Grasse est-elle le centre de la parfumerie française?
    Grasse est le centre de la parfumerie française parce que la ville cultive les fleurs / grâce à la fabrication industrielle.

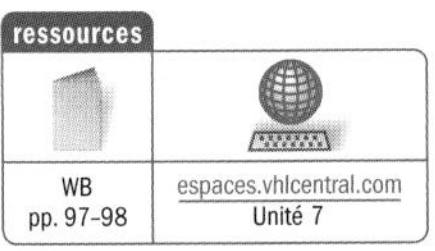

SUR INTERNET

Go to **espaces.vhlcentral.com** to find more cultural information related to this **PANORAMA**.

1. Quels films étaient (*were*) en compétition au dernier festival de Cannes? Qui composait (*made up*) le jury?
2. Trouvez des informations sur la parfumerie à Grasse. Quelles sont deux autres parfumeries qu'on trouve à Grasse?

Située *Located* **recherche** *research* **plus de** *more than* **chercheurs** *researchers* **des plus grands** *of the largest* **matière** *matter* **également** *also* **depuis** *since* **réalisateurs** *filmmakers* **la plus médiatisée** *the most publicized* **meilleur** *best* **appareil** *machine* **fondre** *melt* **racle** *scrapes* **assiette** *plate* **pommes de terre** *potatoes* **charcuterie** *cooked pork meats* **mélange** *mix* **fondus** *melted* **bâton** *stick* **trempe** *dips* **morceau** *piece* **parfumerie** *perfume industry* **Moyen Âge** *Middle Ages* **ont conquis** *conquered* **grâce à** *thanks to*

Grenoble There are a vast number of educational institutions in the city of Grenoble. The city is considered a center for chemical, electronic, and nuclear research. Have students search Grenoble's city web site for information about how many universities are located in Grenoble and in what areas of study they specialize.

Le festival de Cannes Only accredited film industry professionals can attend **le festival de Cannes**. Those not involved in the film industry can obtain invitations to the **Cinéma de la Plage**. Each evening at the **Cinéma de la Plage**, films that are not in the running for the **Palme d'Or** may be viewed on a large open-air screen.

La raclette et la fondue Originally invented by the Swiss, fondue has become an international dish, and each region has adapted the dish to its own taste. In Savoie, instead of the traditional Gruyère cheese, people use Comté and Beaufort as well as Emmental cheeses. Kirsch and dry white wine, preferably from Savoie, are added to the cheese.

Grasse, France Each summer, people in Grasse celebrate the **Fête du Jasmin**. Over 150,000 flowers are used to decorate the floats and in the battle of flowers. Women throw flowers from the floats and spray the audience with jasmine water. Folk dancers, bands, and artists come from all over Europe to celebrate this festival.

OPTIONS

Cultural Activity Have students look at the web sites for **le festival de Cannes, les César du Cinéma**, and a major award show or film festival from their region. Ask students to compare and contrast the award categories, the selection process, the event, and the winners. Have each student share his or her findings with the class.

Pairs Have students imagine that they have gone on vacation in **Provence-Alpes-Côte d'Azur, Rhône-Alpes**, or both. Students will work with a partner telling about his or her experience. Ask students to tell where they went, talk about at least two activities they did there, and what the weather was like. The partner should then ask a question about the trip and tell about his or her vacation.

Section Goals

In this section, students will:
- learn to predict content from the title
- read a travel brochure in French

Stratégie Tell students that they can often predict the content of a newspaper article from its headline. Display or make up several cognate-rich headlines from French newspapers. Examples: **L'ONU critique le changement de règle du vote pour le référendum en Irak; Huit clubs de football français rattrapés par la justice; À la télé américaine, le président est une femme.** Ask students to predict the content of each article.

Examinez le texte Ask volunteers to share their ideas about what type of document it is, and what information they think each section will have. Then go over the correct answers with the entire class.

Des titres Working in pairs to compare their answers, have students discuss how they are able to tell where these titles were found.

Lecture

Avant la lecture

STRATÉGIE

Predicting content from the title

Prediction is an invaluable strategy in reading for comprehension. We can usually predict the content of a newspaper article from its headline, for example. More often than not, we decide whether or not to read the article based on its headline. Predicting content from the title will help you increase your reading comprehension in French.

Examinez le texte

Regardez le titre (*title*) et les sous-titres (*subtitles*) du texte. À votre avis, quel type de document est-ce? Avec un(e) camarade, faites une liste des informations que vous allez probablement trouver dans chaque section du document.

Des titres

Regardez ces titres et indiquez en quelques mots le sujet possible du texte qui suit (*follows*) chaque titre. Où pensez-vous qu'on a trouvé ces titres (dans un journal, un magazine, une brochure, un guide, etc.)?

Cette semaine à Paris:
un journal

Encore un nouveau restaurant pour chiens
un journal, un magazine

L'Égypte des pyramides en 8 jours
une brochure, un guide

L'AÉROPORT CHARLES-DE-GAULLE A PERDU LES VALISES D'UN VOL DE TOURISTES ALLEMANDS
un journal

Plan du centre-ville
un guide

Résultats du septième match de football entre la France et l'Angleterre
un journal

Hôtel confortable près de la gare routière
une brochure

TOUR DE CORSE

Voyage organisé de 12 jours

3.000 euros tout compris°
Promotion spéciale de Vacances-Voyages, agence de voyage certifiée

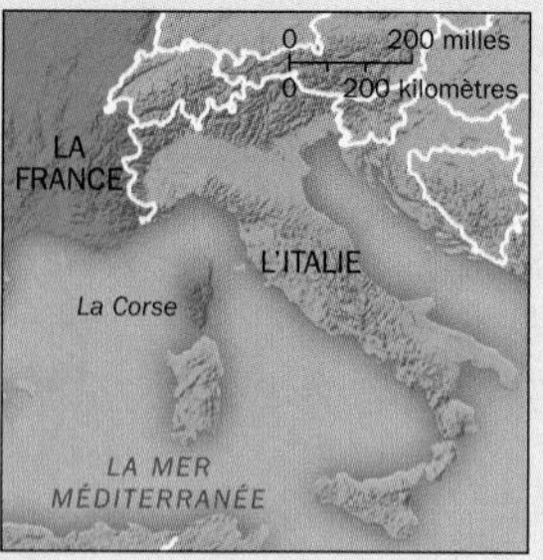

ITINÉRAIRE

JOUR 1 Paris–Ajaccio

Vous partez de Paris en avion pour Ajaccio, en Corse. Vous prenez tout de suite le bus pour aller à votre hôtel. Vous commencez par visiter la ville d'Ajaccio à pied°, puis vous dînez à l'hôtel.

JOUR 2 Ajaccio–Bonifacio

Le matin, vous partez en autobus pour Bonifacio, la belle ville côtière° où vous déjeunez dans un petit restaurant italien avant de visiter la ville. L'après-midi, vous montez à bord° d'un bateau pour une promenade en mer, occasion idéale pour observer les falaises rocailleuses° et les plages blanches de l'île°. Ensuite, vous rentrez à l'hôtel pour dîner et passer la nuit.

JOUR 3 Bonifacio–Corte

La forêt de l'Ospédale est l'endroit idéal pour une randonnée à pied. Vous pique-niquez à Zonza, petite ville montagneuse, avant de continuer vers Corte, l'ancienne° capitale de la Corse. Vous passez la soirée et la nuit à Corte.

JOUR 4 Corte–Bastia

Vous avez la journée pour visiter la ville de Bastia. Vous assistez à un spectacle de danse, puis vous passez la soirée à l'hôtel.

JOUR 5 Bastia–Calvi

Vous visitez d'abord le Cap Corse, la péninsule au nord° de la Corse. Puis, vous continuez vers le désert des Agriates, zone de montagnes désertiques où la chaleur est très forte. Ensuite, c'est l'Île-Rousse et une promenade à vélo dans la ville de Calvi. Vous dînez à votre hôtel.

OPTIONS

Small Groups Have five students work together to brainstorm a list of what would constitute an ideal vacation for them. Each student should contribute at least one idea. Opinions will vary. Ask the group to designate one student to take notes and another to present the information to the class. When each group has its list, ask the presenters to share the group's ideas. How are the group member's ideas similar or different?

Extra Practice Ask students if they have ever been on an organized tour. If students have not been on a tour similar to the one to Corsica described in **Lecture**, have them interview someone they know who has. Have students answer questions like these: **Où êtes-vous allé(e)? Avec quel groupe? Avez-vous aimé toutes les activités organisées? Pourquoi ou pourquoi pas?**

JOUR 6 Calvi–Porto
Vous partez en bus le matin pour la vallée du Fango et le golfe de Galéria à l'ouest° de l'île. Puis, vous visitez le parc naturel régional et le golfe de Porto. Ensuite, vous faites une promenade en bateau avant de passer la soirée dans la ville de Porto.

JOUR 7 Porto–Ajaccio
En bateau, vous visitez des calanques°, particularité géographique de la région méditerranéenne, avant de retourner à Ajaccio.

JOURS 8 à 11 Ajaccio
À Ajaccio, vous avez trois jours pour explorer la ville. Vous avez la possibilité de visiter la cathédrale, la maison natale° de Napoléon ou des musées, et aussi de faire du shopping ou d'aller à la plage.

JOUR 12 Ajaccio–Paris
Vous retournez à Paris en avion.

tout compris *all-inclusive* **à pied** *on foot* **côtière** *coastal* **à bord** *aboard* **falaises rocailleuses** *rocky cliffs* **île** *island* **ancienne** *former* **nord** *north* **ouest** *west* **calanques** *rocky coves or creeks* **natale** *birth*

Après la lecture

Les questions du professeur **Vous avez envie de faire ce voyage en Corse et vous parlez du voyage organisé avec votre professeur de français. Répondez à ses questions par des phrases complètes, d'après la brochure.**

1. Comment allez-vous aller en Corse?
   Je vais prendre l'avion à Paris.
2. Où le vol arrive-t-il en Corse?
   Le vol arrive à Ajaccio.
3. Combien de temps est-ce que vous allez passer en Corse?
   Je vais passer douze jours en Corse.
4. Est-ce que vous allez dormir dans des auberges de jeunesse?
   Non. Je vais dormir à l'hôtel.
5. Qu'est-ce que vous allez faire à Bastia?
   Je vais visiter la ville, aller à un spectacle de danse, puis passer la soirée à l'hôtel.
6. Est-ce que vous retournez à Ajaccio le neuvième jour?
   Non. Je retourne à Ajaccio le septième jour.
7. Qu'est-ce que vous allez prendre comme transports en Corse?
   Je vais prendre l'autobus et des bateaux.
8. Avez-vous besoin de faire toutes les réservations?
   Non. Le voyage est organisé par une agence de voyages.

C'est sûr, je pars en Corse! **Vous allez passer trois semaines en France et vous avez décidé, avec un(e) ami(e), de faire le voyage organisé en Corse au départ de Paris. Vous et votre ami(e) téléphonez à l'agence de voyages pour avoir plus de détails. Posez des questions sur le voyage et demandez des précisions sur les villes visitées, les visites et les activités au programme, les hôtels, les transports, etc.**

- Vous aimez faire des randonnées, mais votre ami(e) préfère voir (*to see*) des spectacles et faire du shopping.
- L'agent va expliquer pourquoi vous aller aimer ce voyage en Corse.
- Demandez à l'agent de vous trouver un billet d'avion aller-retour pour aller de votre ville à Paris.
- Demandez aussi un hôtel à Paris pour la troisième semaine de votre séjour en France.
- L'agent va aussi suggérer des visites et des activités intéressantes à faire à Paris.
- Vous expliquez à l'agent que vous voulez (*want*) avoir du temps libre pendant le voyage.

Les questions du professeur Have students quickly review the brochure before answering the questions. Suggest that pairs take turns answering them. The student who does not answer a question should find the line of text that contains the answer.

C'est sûr, je pars en Corse! Have groups act out their conversations for the rest of the class.

Expansion Tell students that the travel agency is planning to create additional brochures to help them promote their **Tour de Corse** excursion. Their goal is to have several slightly different brochures about the same trip that may appeal to different types of people. Ask students to come up with 3 or 4 short, interesting titles for these new brochures.

OPTIONS

Pairs Have students work together in pairs. Tell them to divide the twelve-day **Tour de Corse** itinerary between them. Each student will then write at least five questions asking about their chosen parts of the trip. They will then answer each other's questions.

Pairs Bring in additional short, simple French-language magazine or newspaper articles you have read. Have pairs scan the headlines/titles of the articles to determine their content. Have them write down all the clues that help them come to these conclusions. Then pairs ask to present their findings to the class. Confirm the correct predictions.

Section Goals

In this section, students will:
- learn to recognize the genre of spoken discourse
- listen to a radio ad for a travel agency

Instructional Resources
Textbook MP3s
IRCD-ROM: IRM (Textbook Audioscript)
espaces.vhlcentral.com: downloads, reference tools

Stratégie
Scripts 1. Bonjour et bienvenue à l'hôtel Belle Plage de Monaco. Nous sommes à quelques minutes de la plage, au 14 avenue des Anges, et nous avons des bus directs pour l'aéroport et la gare routière. Ce week-end, notre hôtel a encore six chambres libres. Si vous désirez des informations sur nos chambres, nos prix et notre hôtel en général, faites le 1. Pour faire ou confirmer une réservation, faites le 2. Pour contacter des clients de l'hôtel, faites le 3. Merci de nous avoir appelés et bonne journée. (message enregistré)
2. Mesdames, Messieurs, nous allons bientôt arriver à notre destination. À l'arrivée à l'aéroport de Montréal, sortez vos passeports pour passer la douane. Ensuite, allez au troisième étage pour prendre vos valises. Nous espérons que vous allez passer un agréable séjour au Canada. Merci d'avoir voyagé avec Air Vacances et à bientôt. (annonce d'avion)

Préparation Have students discuss the questions in pairs or groups. Then have them describe the photo.

À vous d'écouter
Script Envie de partir en vacances? Pour un petit week-end en amoureux ou pour des vacances au soleil, l'agence Vacances Pour Tous a la formule idéale!
Nos promotions de la semaine: Week-end à Venise, en Italie. Avion au départ de Paris vendredi matin, retour dimanche soir. Logement à l'hôtel; 395 euros par personne.
Envie de mer et de plage? Séjour d'une semaine au Brésil; 1.500 euros par personne.
Découvrez la capitale irlandaise avec un séjour de 5 jours à Dublin; 575 euros par personne. En train et bateau.
Autre super promotion pour étudiants: un voyage de deux semaines en Amérique. Une semaine aux États-Unis, quatre jours au Canada et trois jours au Mexique; 2.000 euros par personne. En avion et autobus. Logement en auberge de jeunesse.
Vous n'avez pas envie de partir à l'étranger mais vous avez une semaine de congé? Nous avons une promotion incroyable sur la France. Sept jours à la campagne. Voyage en train. Logement dans un petit hôtel près d'Avignon; 487 euros par personne.
Appelez tout de suite le 01.42.46.46.46 pour faire vos réservations!

À l'écoute

STRATÉGIE

Recognizing the genre of spoken discourse

You will encounter many different types of spoken discourse in French. For example, you may hear a political speech, a radio interview, a commercial, a message on an answering machine, or a news broadcast. Try to identify the context of what you hear so that you can activate your background knowledge about that type of discourse and identify the speakers' motives and intentions.

 To practice this strategy, you will listen to two short selections. Identify the genre of each one.

Préparation

Quand vous partez en vacances, qui décide où aller? Qui fait les réservations? Est-ce que vous utilisez les services d'une agence de voyages? Internet?

À vous d'écouter

Écoutez la publicité. Puis écoutez une deuxième fois et notez les informations qui manquent (*that are missing*). Notez aussi un détail supplémentaire pour chaque voyage.

Pays (ville/région)	Nombre de jours/semaines	Prix par personne	Détail supplémentaire
1. Italie (Venise)	3 jours	395 euros	Answers will vary.
2. Brésil	1 semaine	1.500 euros	Answers will vary.
3. Irlande (Dublin)	5 jours	575 euros	Answers will vary.
4. Amérique du Nord (États-Unis, Canada, Mexique)	14 jours	2.000 euros	Answers will vary.
5. France (Avignon)	7 jours	487 euros	Answers will vary.

ressources
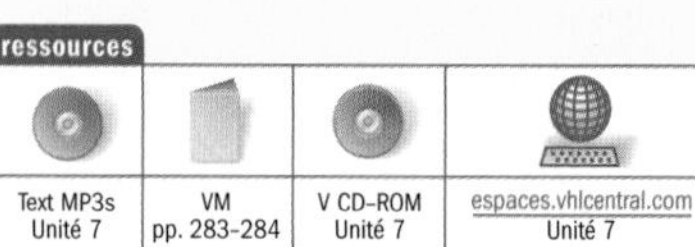

Text MP3s Unité 7
VM pp. 283-284
V CD-ROM Unité 7
espaces.vhlcentral.com Unité 7

Compréhension

Où vont-ils? **Vous travaillez pour l'agence Vacances Pour Tous cet été. Indiquez où chaque personne va aller.**

1. Madame Dupuis n'a pas envie d'aller à l'étranger.
   Madame Dupuis va aller à Avignon.
2. Le fils de Monsieur Girard a besoin de pratiquer son espagnol et son anglais.
   Il va aller en Amérique du Nord.
3. Madame Leroy a envie de visiter une capitale européenne.
   Elle va aller en Irlande.
4. Yves Marignaud a seulement trois jours de congés.
   Il va aller en Italie (Venise).
5. Justine adore la plage et le soleil.
   Elle va aller au Brésil.
6. La famille Abou a envie de passer ses vacances à la campagne.
   Ils vont aller à Avignon.

Votre voyage **Vous avez fait un des voyages proposés par l'agence Voyages Pour Tous. C'est le dernier jour et vous écrivez une carte postale (*postcard*) à un(e) ami(e) francophone. Parlez-lui de votre séjour. Quel voyage avez-vous fait? Pourquoi? Comment avez-vous voyagé? Qu'est-ce que vous avez fait pendant votre séjour? Est-ce que vous avez aimé vos vacances? Pourquoi ou pourquoi pas?**

Écriture

STRATÉGIE

Making an outline

When we write to share information, an outline can serve to separate topics and subtopics, providing a framework for presenting the data. Consider the following excerpt from an outline of the tourist brochure on pages 248–249.

I. Itinéraire et description du voyage
  A. Jour 1
    1. ville: Ajaccio
    2. visites: visite de la ville à pied
    3. activités: dîner
  B. Jour 2
    1. ville: Bonifacio
    2. visites: la ville de Bonifacio
    3. activités: promenade en bateau, dîner
II. Description des hôtels et des transports
  A. Hôtels
  B. Transports

Schéma d'idées

Idea maps can be used to create outlines. The major sections of an idea map correspond to the Roman numerals in an outline. The minor sections correspond to the outline's capital letters, and so on. Consider the idea map that led to the outline above.

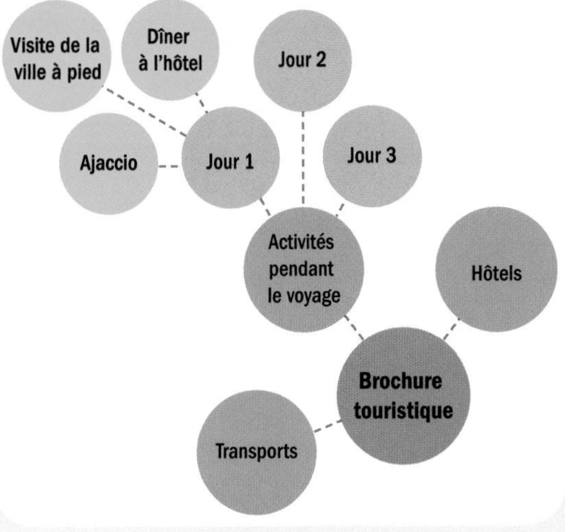

Thème

Écrivez une brochure

Vous allez préparer une brochure pour un voyage organisé que vous avez fait ou que vous avez envie de faire dans un pays francophone. Utilisez un schéma d'idées pour vous aider. Voici des exemples d'informations que votre brochure peut (*can*) donner.

- le pays et la ville
- le nombre de jours
- la date et l'heure du départ et du retour
- les transports utilisés (train, avion,...) et le lieu de départ (aéroport JFK, gare de Lyon,...)
- le temps qu'il va probablement faire et quelques suggestions de vêtements à porter
- où on va dormir (hôtel, auberge de jeunesse, camping,...)
- où on va manger (restaurant, café, pique-nique dans un parc,...)
- les visites culturelles (monuments, musées,...)
- les autres activités au programme (explorer la ville, aller au marché, faire du sport,...)
- le prix du voyage par personne

Watch the FLASH CULTURE segment on the **ESPACES** video for cultural footage related to this unit's theme.

Section Goals

In this section, students will:
- learn to make an outline
- write a travel brochure
- view authentic cultural footage of different kinds of transportation and lodging

Instructional Resources
WB/VM: Video Manual, pp. 283–284
WB/VM/LM Answer Key
IRCD-ROM: IRM (Videoscript)
Video CD-ROM
Video on DVD
espaces.vhlcentral.com: activities, downloads, reference tools

Stratégie Explain that outlines are a great way for a writer to think about what a piece of writing will be like before actually expending much time and effort on writing. An outline is also a great way of keeping a writer on track, and helps him or her keep the whole writing project in mind while focusing on a specific part.

Thème Discuss the travel brochure that students are going to write. Go over the list of information that they might include. You might indicate a specific number of points that should be in the brochure. Tell students that the **Tour de Corse** brochure in **Lecture**, pages 248–249, can serve as a model for their writing. Remind them that they are writing with the purpose of attracting people to take a trip. Suggest that students brainstorm in French as many details as possible about the trip they will describe.

Flash culture Tell students that they will learn more about transportation and lodging by watching a variety of real-life images narrated by Csilla. Show the video segment without sound and tell students to call out what they see. Then show the video segment again with sound. You can also use the activities in the video manual in class to reinforce this **Flash culture** or assign them as homework.

EVALUATION

Criteria	Scale
Appropriate Details	1 2 3 4 5
Organization	1 2 3 4 5
Use of vocabulary	1 2 3 4 5
Grammatical accuracy	1 2 3 4 5

Scoring	
Excellent	18–20 points
Good	14–17 points
Satisfactory	10–13 points
Unsatisfactory	< 10 points

Instructional Resources
Textbook MP3s
IRCD-ROM: IRM (Textbook Audioscript)
espaces.vhlcentral.com: downloads, reference tools

Partir en voyage

un aéroport	*airport*
un arrêt d'autobus (de bus)	*bus stop*
une arrivée	*arrival*
un avion	*plane*
un billet aller-retour	*round-trip ticket*
un billet (d'avion, de train)	*(plane, train) ticket*
un départ	*departure*
une douane	*customs*
une gare (routière)	*train station (bus station)*
une sortie	*exit*
une station (de métro, de train)	*(subway, train) station*
une station de ski	*ski resort*
un ticket de bus, de métro	*bus, subway ticket*
un vol	*flight*
un voyage	*trip*
à l'étranger	*abroad, overseas*
la campagne	*country(side)*
une capitale	*capital*
des gens (*m.*)	*people*
le monde	*world*
un pays	*country*

Les pays

(en/l') Allemagne (*f.*)	*(to, in) Germany*
(en/l') Angleterre (*f.*)	*(to, in) England*
(en/la) Belgique (belge)	*(to, in) Belgium (Belgian)*
(au/le) Brésil (brésilien(ne))	*(to, in) Brazil (Brazilian)*
(au/le) Canada	*(to, in) Canada*
(en/la) Chine (chinois(e))	*(to, in) China (Chinese)*
(en/l') Espagne (*f.*)	*(to, in) Spain*
(aux/les) États-Unis (*m.*)	*(to, in) United States*
(en/la) France	*(to, in) France*
(en/l') Irlande (*f.*) (irlandais(e))	*(to, in) Ireland (Irish)*
(en/l') Italie (*f.*)	*(to, in) Italy*
(au/le) Japon	*(to, in) Japan*
(au/le) Mexique	*(to, in) Mexico*
(en/la) Suisse	*(to, in) Switzerland*

ressources
Text MP3s Unité 7
espaces.vhlcentral.com Unité 7

Les vacances

bronzer	*to tan*
faire du shopping	*to go shopping*
faire les valises	*to pack one's bags*
faire un séjour	*to spend time (somewhere)*
partir en vacances	*to go on vacation*
prendre un train (un avion, un taxi, un (auto)bus, un bateau)	*to take a train (plane, taxi, bus, boat)*
rouler en voiture	*to ride in a car*
utiliser un plan	*to use/read a map*
un (jour de) congé	*day off*
le journal	*newspaper*
la mer	*sea*
une plage	*beach*
des vacances (*f.*)	*vacation*

Adverbes et locutions de temps

alors	*so, then; at that moment*
après (que)	*after*
avant (de)	*before*
d'abord	*first*
donc	*therefore*
enfin	*finally, at last*
ensuite	*then, next*
finalement	*finally*
pendant (que)	*during, while*
puis	*then*
tout à coup	*suddenly*
tout de suite	*right away*

Verbes

aller	*to go*
arriver	*to arrive*
descendre	*to go/take down*
entrer	*to enter*
monter	*to go/come up; to get in/on*
mourir	*to die*
naître	*to be born*
partir	*to leave*
passer	*to pass by; to spend time*
rentrer	*to return*
rester	*to stay*
retourner	*to return*
sortir	*to go out*
tomber (sur quelqu'un)	*to fall (to run into somebody)*

Faire une réservation

annuler une réservation	*to cancel a reservation*
réserver	*to reserve*
une agence/un agent de voyages	*travel agency/agent*
un ascenseur	*elevator*
une auberge de jeunesse	*youth hostel*
une chambre individuelle	*single room*
une clé	*key*
un(e) client(e)	*client; guest*
un étage	*floor*
un hôtel	*hotel*
un hôtelier/une hôtelière	*hotel keeper*
un lit	*bed*
un passager/une passagère	*passenger*
un passeport	*passport*
la réception	*reception desk*
le rez-de-chaussée	*ground floor*
complet/complète	*full (no vacancies)*
libre	*available*

Verbes réguliers en -ir

choisir	*to choose*
finir	*to finish*
grossir	*to gain weight*
maigrir	*to lose weight*
réfléchir (à)	*to think (about), to reflect (on)*
réussir (à)	*to succeed in doing something*

Verbes irréguliers

décrire	*to describe*
dire	*to say*
écrire	*to write*
lire	*to read*

Expressions utiles	*See pp. 223 and 237.*
Direct object pronouns	*See pp. 228–229.*
Ordinal numbers	*See pp. 232–233.*

Chez nous

UNITÉ **8**

Pour commencer
- Qui est passée chez qui?
- Qu'est-ce qu'il y a dans la cafetière? Du lait? De l'eau? Du café?
- Qu'est-ce que fait Sandrine?
- Quelles couleurs porte Sandrine? Et Amina?

Unit Goals

Leçon 15
In this lesson, students will learn:
- terms for parts of the house
- terms for furniture
- the pronunciation of **s** and **ss**
- about housing in France and **le château Frontenac**
- the formation and usage of adverbs
- the **imparfait**
- about the singer Lynda Lemay and painter Pascal-Adolphe-Jean Dagnan-Bouveret

Leçon 16
In this lesson, students will learn:
- terms for household chores
- terms for appliances
- the pronunciation of semi-vowels
- about the interiors of French homes and the French Quarter in New Orleans
- the uses of the **passé composé** and the **imparfait**
- the uses of **savoir** and **connaître**
- about Mr. Propre cleaning products

Savoir-faire
In this section, students will learn:
- cultural and historical information about **Alsace** and **Lorraine**
- to guess the meaning of unknown words from context
- to use visual clues to understand spoken French
- to write a narrative using the **passé composé** and the **imparfait**
- more about housing in France through specially shot video footage

Pour commencer
- **Amina est passée chez Sandrine.**
- **Il y a du café.**
- **Sandrine fait la cuisine.**
- **Sandrine porte de l'orange et du bleu. Amina porte du vert.**

RESOURCES

Workbook/Video Manual: WB Activities, pp. 99–112
Laboratory Manual: Lab Activities, pp. 57–64
Workbook/Video Manual: Video Activities, pp. 239–242; pp. 285–286
WB/VM/LM Answer Key
Instructor's Resource CD-ROM [IRCD-ROM]: Instructor's Resource Manual [IRM] (Textbook Audioscript; Lab Audioscript; Videoscript; **Roman-photo** Translations; **Vocabulaire supplémentaire**; **Feuilles d'activités**; Info Gap Activities; **Le zapping** TV clip transcription; **Essayez!** and **Mise en pratique** answers); Transparencies #37, #38, #39; Testing Program, pp. 57–64; Test Files; Testing Program MP3s; Test Generator
Lab MP3s
Textbook MP3s
Video CD-ROM
Video on DVD
espaces.vhlcentral.com

Section Goals

In this section, students will learn and practice vocabulary related to:

- housing
- rooms and home furnishings

Instructional Resources

*IRCD-ROM: Transparency #37; IRM (**Vocabulaire supplémentaire; Mise en pratique** answers; Textbook Audioscript; Lab Audioscript; Info Gap Activities)*
Textbook MP3s
WB/VM: Workbook, pp. 99–100
Lab Manual, p. 57
Lab MP3s
WB/VM/LM Answer Key
espaces.vhlcentral.com: activities, downloads, reference tools

Suggestions

- Use **Transparency #37**. Point out rooms and furnishings in the illustration. Examples: **Ça, c'est la salle de bains. Voici un canapé.**
- Ask students questions about their homes using the new vocabulary. Examples: **Habitez-vous dans une maison, dans un appartement ou dans une résidence? Avez-vous un balcon? Un garage? Combien de salles de bains y a-t-il chez vous?**
- Point out the difference between **le loyer** (*the rent*) and **louer** (*to rent*).
- Explain that **une chambre** is *a bedroom*, but **une pièce** is the generic term for *a room*.
- Explain that **un salon** is a more formal room used primarily for entertaining guests. Generally, it is not used for watching television or other leisure activities. **Une salle de séjour** is a more functional room, similar to an American family room or den.
- Point out that **un studio** is *an efficiency apartment*, usually equipped with a couch that converts into a bed and a kitchenette. *A studio*, such as that of an artist or craftsperson, is **un atelier**.
- Additional vocabulary for this lesson can be found in the **Vocabulaire supplémentaire** in the IRM on the IRCD-ROM.

Leçon 15

You will learn how to...

- describe your home
- talk about habitual past actions

La maison

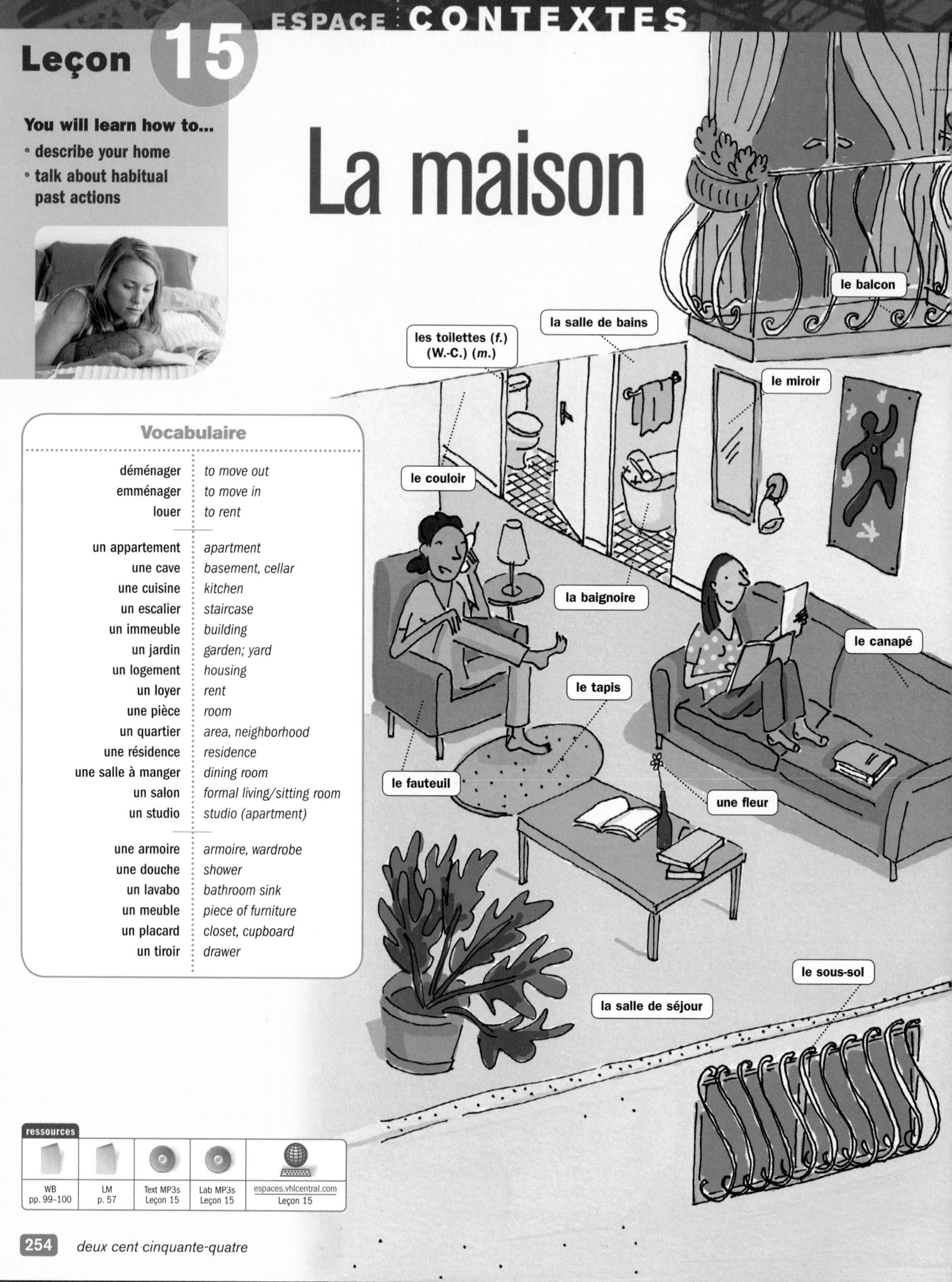

Vocabulaire

déménager	*to move out*
emménager	*to move in*
louer	*to rent*
un appartement	*apartment*
une cave	*basement, cellar*
une cuisine	*kitchen*
un escalier	*staircase*
un immeuble	*building*
un jardin	*garden; yard*
un logement	*housing*
un loyer	*rent*
une pièce	*room*
un quartier	*area, neighborhood*
une résidence	*residence*
une salle à manger	*dining room*
un salon	*formal living/sitting room*
un studio	*studio (apartment)*
une armoire	*armoire, wardrobe*
une douche	*shower*
un lavabo	*bathroom sink*
un meuble	*piece of furniture*
un placard	*closet, cupboard*
un tiroir	*drawer*

ressources

WB pp. 99–100	LM p. 57	Text MP3s Leçon 15	Lab MP3s Leçon 15	espaces.vhlcentral.com Leçon 15

OPTIONS

Extra Practice Ask students what activities they do in various rooms. Examples: **Dans quelle pièce… mangez-vous? étudiez-vous? dormez-vous? faites-vous la cuisine? travaillez-vous sur l'ordinateur? parlez-vous au téléphone?**

TPR Make signs for various rooms in a house and for other parts of a home, such as **le garage** or **le balcon**. Also make several signs for bedrooms and bathrooms. Distribute the signs to students. As other students describe their homes (one floor at a time), those holding signs arrange themselves according to the descriptions. Tell students to use prepositions of location in their descriptions.

Mise en pratique

1 Écoutez Patrice cherche un appartement. Écoutez sa conversation téléphonique et dites si les affirmations sont **vraies** ou **fausses**.

	Vrai	Faux
1. Madame Dautry est la propriétaire de l'appartement.	☑	☐
2. L'appartement est au 24 rue Pasteur.	☑	☐
3. L'appartement est au cinquième étage.	☐	☑
4. L'appartement est dans un vieil immeuble.	☐	☑
5. L'appartement n'a pas de balcon, mais il a un garage.	☐	☑
6. Il y a une baignoire dans la salle de bains.	☐	☑
7. Les toilettes ne sont pas dans la salle de bains.	☑	☐
8. L'appartement est un studio.	☐	☑
9. Le loyer est de 490€.	☑	☐
10. Patrice va emménager tout de suite.	☐	☑

2 Chassez l'intrus Indiquez le mot ou l'expression qui ne convient pas (*that doesn't belong*).

1. un appartement, (un quartier), un logement, un studio
2. une baignoire, une douche, (un sous-sol), un lavabo
3. un salon, une salle à manger, une salle de séjour, (un jardin)
4. un meuble, un canapé, une armoire, (une affiche)
5. (un placard), un balcon, un jardin, un garage
6. une chambre, une cuisine, (un rideau), une pièce
7. un meuble, une commode, (un couloir), un tiroir
8. un mur, (un tapis), une fenêtre, une affiche

3 Définitions Lisez les définitions et trouvez les mots ou expressions d'**ESPACE CONTEXTES** qui correspondent. Ensuite, avec un(e) partenaire, donnez votre propre définition de cinq mots ou expressions. Rejoignez un autre groupe et lisez vos définitions. L'autre groupe doit deviner (*must guess*) de quoi vous parlez.

1. C'est ce que (*what*) vous payez chaque mois quand vous n'êtes pas propriétaire de votre appartement. ___un loyer___
2. Vous passez par ici pour aller d'une pièce à une autre. ___un couloir___
3. C'est le fait de (*act of*) partir de votre appartement. ___déménager___
4. C'est là que vous mettez vos livres. ___une étagère___
5. En général, il y en a quatre dans une pièce et ils sont entre les pièces de votre appartement. ___les murs___
6. C'est ce que vous utilisez pour lire le soir. ___une lampe___
7. C'est là que vous mettez votre voiture. ___un garage___
8. C'est ce que vous utilisez pour aller du premier étage au deuxième étage d'un immeuble. ___un escalier/un ascenseur___
9. Quand vous avez des invités, c'est la pièce dans laquelle (*in which*) vous dînez. ___la salle à manger___
10. En général, il est sur le sol (*floor*) d'une pièce. ___un tapis___

1 Tapescript PATRICE: Allô, Madame Dautry, s'il vous plaît.
MADAME: Oui, c'est moi. J'écoute.
P: Mon nom est Patrice Leconte. Je vous appelle au sujet de votre appartement du 24, rue Pasteur. Est-ce qu'il est toujours libre?
M: Oui, jeune homme. Il est toujours libre.
P: Parfait. Comment est-il?
M: Il est au quatrième étage d'un immeuble moderne. Il y a un balcon mais pas de garage. La chambre est plutôt petite mais il y a beaucoup de placards.
P: Et la salle de bains?
M: Elle est petite aussi avec une douche, un lavabo et un grand miroir. Les toilettes sont séparées.
P: Et le salon?
M: C'est la pièce principale. Elle est plutôt grande. La cuisine est juste à côté.
P: C'est combien le loyer?
M: Le loyer est de 490€.
P: Oh, c'est cher!
M: Mais vous êtes à côté de l'université et l'appartement est libre le premier septembre.
P: Bon, je vais y penser. Merci beaucoup, au revoir, Madame.
M: Au revoir, Monsieur.
(On Textbook MP3s)

1 Expansion Play the recording again, stopping at the end of each sentence that contains an answer. Have students verify true statements and correct the false ones.

2 Expansion Have students create one or two additional sets using at least three of the new vocabulary words in each one. Collect their papers and write some of the items on the board.

3 Suggestion Before beginning this activity, you might want to teach your students expressions for circumlocution. Examples: **C'est un objet qu'on utilise pour.... C'est une pièce où....**

OPTIONS

Game Write vocabulary words related to home furnishings on index cards. On another set of cards, draw or paste pictures to match each term. Tape them face down on the board in random order. Divide the class into two teams. Play a game of Concentration in which students match words with pictures. When a player has a match, that team collects those cards. When all cards are matched, the team with the most cards wins.

Extra Practice Write **Logements** and **Meubles** at the top of two columns on the board or on a transparency. Say vocabulary words and have students classify them in the correct category. Examples: **un appartement (logement), une résidence (logement), un studio (logement), un canapé (meuble), un lit (meuble),** and **une armoire (meuble)**.

4 Suggestion Have students jot down notes during their interviews. Then have them report what they learned to another pair of students.

5 Suggestion Before beginning this activity, have students brainstorm vocabulary for furnishings and other items found in a bedroom. Write the words on the board.

6 Suggestion Divide the class into pairs and distribute the Info Gap Handouts in the IRM on the IRCD-ROM for this activity. Have two volunteers read the **modèle** aloud.

7 Suggestion Tell students to include colors in their descriptions.

Successful Language Learning Suggest to students that they study vocabulary words in varying order to avoid reliance upon the order itself to help them remember. Also, words at the beginning and the end of lists tend to be easier to recall than those in the middle.

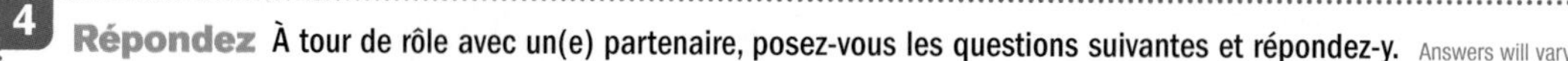

Communication

4 Répondez À tour de rôle avec un(e) partenaire, posez-vous les questions suivantes et répondez-y. Answers will vary.

1. Où est-ce que tu habites?
2. Quelle est la taille de ton appartement ou de ta maison? Combien de pièces y a-t-il?
3. Quand as-tu emménagé?
4. Est-ce que tu as un jardin? Un garage?
5. Combien de placards as-tu? Où sont-ils?
6. Quels meubles as-tu? Comment sont-ils?
7. Quel meuble est-ce que tu voudrais (*would like*) avoir dans ton appartement? (Répondez: Je voudrais...)
8. Qu'est-ce que tu détestes au sujet de ton appartement?

5 Votre chambre Écrivez une description de votre chambre. À tour de rôle, lisez votre description à votre partenaire. Il/Elle va vous demander d'autres détails et dessiner un plan. Ensuite, regardez le dessin (*drawing*) de votre partenaire et dites s'il correspond à votre chambre ou non. Answers will vary.

6 Sept différences Votre professeur va vous donner, à vous et à votre partenaire, deux feuilles d'activités différentes. Il y a sept différences entre les deux images. Comparez vos dessins et faites une liste de ces différences. Quel est le groupe le plus rapide (*the quickest*) de la classe? Attention! Ne regardez pas la feuille de votre partenaire. Answers will vary.

MODÈLE

Étudiant(e) 1: *Dans mon appartement, il y a seulement un lit. Il y a une lampe à côté du lit.*
Étudiant(e) 2: *Dans mon appartement aussi, il y a seulement un lit, mais il n'y a pas de lampe.*

7 La décoration Formez un groupe de trois. L'un de vous est un décorateur d'intérieur qui a rendez-vous avec deux clients qui veulent (*want*) redécorer leur maison. Les clients sont très difficiles. Imaginez votre conversation et jouez la scène devant la classe. Utilisez les mots de la liste. Answers will vary.

un canapé	un fauteuil
une chambre	un meuble
une cuisine	un mur
un escalier	un placard
une étagère	un tapis

OPTIONS

Extra Practice Call out words for furnishings and other objects, and have students write or say the room(s) where they might be found. Examples: **la télévision (la salle de séjour), le lit (la chambre),** and **la table (la salle à manger).**

TPR Have the class label various parts of the classroom with the names of rooms one would typically find in a house. Then have groups of three perform a skit in which the owner of the house is showing it to two exchange students who are going to be spending the semester there.

Les sons et les lettres

 **s and ss**

You've already learned that an **s** at the end of a word is usually silent.

lavabos	**copains**	**vas**	**placards**

An **s** at the beginning of a word, before a consonant, or after a pronounced consonant is pronounced like the *s* in the English word *set*.

soir	**salon**	**studio**	**absolument**

A double **s** is pronounced like the *ss* in the English word *kiss*.

grosse	**assez**	**intéressant**	**rousse**

An **s** at the end of a word is often pronounced when the following word begins with a vowel sound. An **s** in a liaison sounds like a *z*, like the *s* in the English word *rose*.

très élégant **trois hommes**

The other instance where the French **s** has a *z* sound is when there is a single **s** between two vowels within the same word. The **s** is pronounced like the *s* in the English word *music*.

musée	**amusant**	**oiseau**	**besoin**

These words look alike, but have different meanings. Compare the pronunciations of each word pair.

poison	**poisson**	**désert**	**dessert**

Prononcez **Répétez les mots suivants à voix haute.**

1. sac	4. chose	7. surprise	10. expressions
2. triste	5. bourse	8. assister	11. sénégalaise
3. suisse	6. passer	9. magasin	12. sérieusement

Articulez **Répétez les phrases suivantes à voix haute.**

1. Le spectacle est très amusant et la chanteuse est superbe.
2. Est-ce que vous habitez dans une résidence universitaire?
3. De temps en temps, Suzanne assiste à l'inauguration d'expositions au musée.
4. Heureusement, mes professeurs sont sympathiques, sociables et très sincères.

Dictons **Répétez les dictons à voix haute.**

Les oiseaux de même plumage s'assemblent sur le même rivage.[2]

Si jeunesse savait, si vieillesse pouvait.[1]

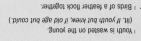

1 Youth is wasted on the young.
(lit. If youth but knew, if old age but could.)
2 Birds of a feather flock together.

ressources

LM p. 58	Text MP3s Leçon 15	Lab MP3s Leçon 15	espaces.vhlcentral.com Leçon 15

Section Goals

In this section, students will learn about the sounds of **s** and **ss**.

Instructional Resources
Textbook MP3s
Lab Manual, p. 58
Lab MP3s
WB/VM/LM Answer Key
IRCD-ROM: IRM (Textbook Audioscript; Lab Audioscript)
espaces.vhlcentral.com: activities, downloads, reference tools

Suggestions

- Model the pronunciation of the example words and have students repeat them after you.
- Ask students to provide more examples of words from this lesson or previous lessons with these sounds. Examples: **cuisine, salon**, and **résidence**.
- Dictate five familiar words containing **s** and **ss**, repeating each one at least two times. Then write them on the board or on a transparency and have students check their spelling.

OPTIONS

Extra Practice Use these sentences for additional practice or dictation. **1. Serge est professeur de sociologie. 2. Solange est paresseuse et pessimiste. 3. Ces étudiants sénégalais sont très intelligents. 4. Sylvain essaie les chaussures sans chaussettes.**

Extra Practice Teach students these French tongue-twisters that contain the **s** and **ss** sounds. **1. Ces six saucissons-ci sont si secs qu'on ne sait si c'en sont. 2. Zazie causait avec sa cousine en cousant.**

Section Goals

In this section, students will learn functional phrases for talking about their home.

Instructional Resources
WB/VM: Video Manual, pp. 239–240
WB/VM/LM Answer Key
Video CD-ROM
Video on DVD
IRCD-ROM: IRM (Videoscript; ***Roman-photo*** *Translations)*
espaces.vhlcentral.com: activities, downloads, reference tools

Video Recap: Leçon 14
Before doing this **Roman-photo**, review the previous one with this activity.

1. Pourquoi Sandrine est-elle allée à l'agence de voyages? (pour faire une réservation d'hôtel à Albertville)
2. Pourquoi n'a-t-elle pas fait la réservation? (Les hôtels moins chers sont complets.)
3. Comment Amina a-t-elle réussi à trouver un hôtel? (Elle utilise son ordinateur.)
4. Pourquoi Sandrine n'est-elle pas contente? (parce que Pascal ne va pas aller à Albertville)

Video Synopsis Pascal arrives in Aix-en-Provence. He runs into Rachid, who helps him pick up his suitcase. He has never met Rachid before. Rachid and David then take a tour of Sandrine's apartment, which is very nice and big. Pascal shows up unexpectedly. She is not pleased by his surprise visit and breaks up with him.

Suggestions
- Have students read the title, glance at the video stills, and predict what the episode will be about. Record their predictions.
- Have students scan the **Roman-photo** and find words related to the home.
- Have students read the **Roman-photo** conversation in groups of four.
- Review students' predictions and ask them which ones were correct.

NATIONAL STANDARDS communication cultures

La visite surprise

PERSONNAGES

David

Pascal

Rachid

Sandrine

1

En ville, Pascal fait tomber (drops) *ses fleurs.*
PASCAL Aïe!
RACHID Tenez. (*Il aide Pascal.*)
PASCAL Oh, merci.
RACHID Aïe!
PASCAL Oh pardon, je suis vraiment désolé!
RACHID Ce n'est rien.
PASCAL Bonne journée!

2

Chez Sandrine...
RACHID Eh, salut, David! Dis donc, ce n'est pas un logement d'étudiants ici! C'est grand chez toi! Tu ne déménages pas, finalement?
DAVID Heureusement, Sandrine a décidé de rester.
SANDRINE Oui, je suis bien dans cet appartement. Seulement les loyers sont très chers au centre-ville.

3

RACHID Oui, malheureusement! Tu as combien de pièces?
SANDRINE Il y a trois pièces: le salon, la salle à manger, ma chambre. Bien sûr il y a une cuisine et j'ai aussi une grande salle de bains. Je te fais visiter?

6

SANDRINE Et voici ma chambre.
RACHID Elle est belle!
SANDRINE Oui... j'aime le vert.

7

RACHID Dis, c'est vrai, Sandrine, ta salle de bains est vraiment grande.
DAVID Oui! Et elle a un beau miroir au-dessus du lavabo et une baignoire!
RACHID Chez nous, on a seulement une douche.
SANDRINE Moi, je préfère les douches en fait.

8

Le téléphone sonne (rings).
RACHID Comparé à cet appartement, le nôtre c'est une cave! Pas de décorations, juste des affiches, un canapé, des étagères et mon bureau.
DAVID C'est vrai. On n'a même pas de rideaux.

ACTIVITÉS

1 Vrai ou faux? Indiquez si les affirmations suivantes sont **vraies** ou **fausses**.

1. C'est la première fois que Rachid visite l'appartement. Vrai.
2. Sandrine ne déménage pas. Vrai.
3. Les loyers au centre-ville ne sont pas chers. Faux.
4. Sandrine invite parfois ses amis à dîner chez elle. Vrai.
5. Rachid préfère son appartement à l'appartement de Sandrine. Faux.
6. Chez les garçons, il y a une baignoire et des rideaux. Faux.
7. Quand Pascal arrive, Sandrine est contente (*pleased*). Faux.
8. Pascal doit (*must*) travailler ce week-end. Faux.

OPTIONS

Avant de regarder la vidéo Before viewing the video, have students read the title and predict what might happen in this episode. Write their predictions on the board.

Regarder la vidéo Show the video episode without sound and have the class create a plot summary based on the visual cues. Then show the video again with sound and have the class correct any mistakes and fill in any gaps in the plot summary they created.

Pascal arrive à Aix-en-Provence.

4

SANDRINE Voici la salle à manger.
RACHID Ça, c'est une pièce très importante pour nous, les invités.

5

SANDRINE Et puis, la cuisine.
RACHID Une pièce très importante pour Sandrine...
DAVID Évidemment!

9

SANDRINE Mais Pascal... je pensais que tu avais du travail... Quoi? Tu es ici, maintenant? C'est une blague!
PASCAL Mais ma chérie, ne sois pas fâchée, c'était une surprise...

10

SANDRINE Une surprise! Nous deux, c'est fini! D'abord, tu me dis que les vacances avec moi, c'est impossible et ensuite tu arrives à Aix sans me téléphoner!
PASCAL Bon, si c'est comme ça, reste où tu es. Ne descends pas. Moi, je m'en vais. Voilà tes fleurs. Tu parles d'une surprise!

Expressions utiles

Talking about your home

- **Tu ne déménages pas, finalement?**
  You are not moving, after all?
- **Heureusement, Sandrine a décidé de rester.**
  Thankfully/Happily, Sandrine decided to stay.
- **Seulement, les loyers sont très chers au centre-ville.**
  However, rents are very expensive downtown.
- **Je te fais visiter?**
  Shall I give you a tour?
- **Ta salle de bains est vraiment grande.**
  Your bathroom is really big.
- **Elle a un beau miroir au-dessus du lavabo.**
  She has a nice mirror above the sink.
- **Chez nous, on a seulement une douche.**
  At our place, we only have a shower.

Additional vocabulary

- **Aïe!**
  Ouch!
- **Tenez.**
  Here.
- **Évidemment!**
  Evidently!
- **Oui, malheureusement!**
  Yes, unfortunately!
- **Je pensais que tu avais du travail.**
  I thought you had to work.
- **Mais ma chérie, ne sois pas fâchée, c'était une surprise.**
  But sweetie, don't be mad, it was a surprise.
- **sans**
  without
- **Moi, je m'en vais.**
  I am leaving/getting out of here.

ACTIVITÉS

2 Quel appartement? Indiquez si les objets suivants sont dans l'appartement de Sandrine **(S)** ou dans l'appartement de David et Rachid **(D & R)**.

1. baignoire S
2. balcon S
3. rideaux S
4. canapé D & R, S
5. trois pièces S
6. étagères D & R
7. miroir S
8. affiches D & R

3 Conversez Sandrine décide que son loyer est vraiment trop cher. Elle cherche un appartement à partager avec Amina. Avec deux partenaires, écrivez leur conversation avec un agent immobilier (*real estate agent*). Elles décrivent l'endroit idéal, le prix et les meubles qu'elles préfèrent. L'agent décrit plusieurs possibilités.

ressources

VM pp. 239-240	V CD-ROM Leçon 15	espaces.vhlcentral.com Leçon 15

Expressions utiles
- Model the pronunciation of the **Expressions utiles** and have students repeat them.
- As you work through the list, point out adverbs ending in **-ment** and verbs in the **imparfait.** You might want to tell students that the ending **-ment** usually corresponds to the English ending *-ly*. Then tell them that these grammar structures will be formally presented in the **Structures** section.
- Respond briefly to questions about the **imparfait.** Reinforce correct forms, but do not expect students to produce them consistently at this time.
- Point out that **être fâché(e) contre quelqu'un** means *to be angry with someone*, but **être fâché(e) avec quelqu'un,** means *to be no longer on speaking terms with someone.*

1 Suggestion Have students write their corrections for false statements on the board.

1 Expansion For additional practice, give students these items. **9. Rachid et Pascal sont de bons amis. (Faux.) 10. La chambre de Sandrine est rose. (Faux.) 11. L'appartement de Sandrine est une cave. (Faux.)**

2 Expansion For additional practice, give students these items. **9. bureau (D & R) 10. grande salle de bains (S) 11. douche (D & R)**

3 Suggestions
- Before writing the conversation, tell students that the person playing the real estate agent should make a list of questions to ask prospective clients, and the two people playing Sandrine and Amina should decide on the features they are looking for in an apartment.
- You might want to bring in some real estate ads in French from newspapers or the Internet for the agents to use as prospective rentals.

OPTIONS

Small Groups Have groups of three interview each other about their dream house, with one student conducting the interview, one answering, and one taking notes. At three-minute intervals, have students switch roles until each has been interviewer, interviewee, and note-taker. Then have two groups get together and take turns describing their dream house to one another using their notes.

Pairs Have students work in pairs. Tell them to write an alternate ending to this episode in which Sandrine is pleased to see Pascal and invites him upstairs to meet Rachid and David. Encourage students to use some of the **Expressions utiles**. Then have volunteers perform their role plays for the class.

Section Goals

In this section, students will:
- learn about different types of housing in France
- learn terms related to renting an apartment
- read about traditional houses in various francophone regions
- read about **le château Frontenac**

Instructional Resources
espaces.vhlcentral.com: activities, downloads, reference tools

Culture à la loupe
Avant la lecture Have students look at the photos and describe what they see.

Lecture
- Point out the **Coup de main**.
- Point out the statistics chart. Ask students what information the chart shows. (the change in percentage between 1962 and 1999 of the size of housing in relation to how many rooms they have) Explain that the kitchen and bathrooms are not included when counting rooms in a French residence.

Après la lecture Ask students: **Dans quelle type de logement désirez-vous habiter en France? Pourquoi?**

1 Expansion For additional practice, give students these items. **11. Plus de la moitié des Français habitent un appartement. (Faux.) 12. Dans le nord, les maisons sont souvent en bois. (Faux. Elles sont en briques.) 13. Cinquante pour cent des Français sont propriétaires. (Vrai.)**

CULTURE À LA LOUPE

Le logement en France

Les trois quarts des gens habitent en ville et un Français sur cinq habite la région parisienne. Quinze pour cent de la population habitent en banlieue dans des HLM (habitations à loyer modéré°), des appartements réservés aux familles qui n'ont pas beaucoup d'argent. Plus de la moitié des Français habitent une maison individuelle et l'autre partie habite un appartement. Cinquante pour cent des Français sont propriétaires, dont° dix pour cent ont une résidence secondaire.

Le type et la taille° des logements varient. Dans les grandes villes, beaucoup d'anciens hôtels particuliers° ont été transformés en appartements. En banlieue, on trouve les grands ensembles°, groupes d'immeubles assez° modernes qui bénéficient de certains équipements collectifs°. En général, dans les petites villes et les villages, les gens habitent de petites maisons qui sont souvent assez vieilles.

Le style et l'architecture varient d'une région à l'autre. La région parisienne a de nombreux pavillons (maisons avec de petits jardins). Dans le nord°, on habite souvent des maisons en briques° avec des toits en ardoise°. En Alsace-Lorraine, il y a de vieilles maisons à colombages avec des parties de mur en bois°. Les maisons traditionnelles de l'ouest° ont des toits de chaume°. Dans le sud°, il y a des villas de style méditerranéen avec des toits en tuiles° rouges et des mas° provençaux (vieilles maisons en pierre°).

habitations à loyer modéré *low-cost government housing* **dont** *of which* **taille** *size* **anciens hôtels particuliers** *former private mansions* **grands ensembles** *high-rise buildings* **assez** *rather* **bénéficient de certains équipements collectifs** *benefit from certain shared facilities* **nord** *north* **briques** *bricks* **toits en ardoise** *slate roofs* **bois** *wood* **ouest** *west* **chaume** *thatch* **sud** *south* **tuiles** *tiles* **mas** *farmhouses* **pierre** *stone*

Coup de main

Here are some terms commonly used in statistics.

un quart = *one quarter*
un tiers = *one third*
la moitié = *half*
la plupart de = *most of*
un sur cinq = *one in five*

Évolution de la taille des logements en France

TAILLE	1962	1999
1 pièce	14,7%	6,4%
2 pièces	24,1%	12,7%
3 pièces	26,8%	22,3%
4 pièces	19,0%	27,0%
5 pièces et plus	15,4%	31,6%

ACTIVITÉS

1 Vrai ou faux? Indiquez si les phrases sont **vraies** ou **fausses**. Corrigez les phrases fausses.

1. Il n'y a pas beaucoup de Français qui habitent la région parisienne. Faux. Un Français sur cinq habite la région parisienne.
2. Les familles sans beaucoup d'argent habitent souvent dans des HLM. Vrai.
3. La moitié des Français ont une résidence secondaire. Faux. Dix pour cent des Français ont une résidence secondaire.
4. On a transformé beaucoup d'anciens hôtels particuliers en appartements. Vrai.
5. Les grands ensembles sont des maisons en pierres. Faux. Les grands ensembles sont des groupes d'immeubles assez modernes.
6. Les maisons françaises ont des styles d'architecture différents d'une région à l'autre. Vrai.
7. En général, les maisons dans les villages sont assez vieilles. Vrai.
8. Dans le sud de la France, il y a beaucoup de pavillons. Faux. Dans le sud de la France, il y a des villas de style méditerranéen et des mas provençaux.
9. Dans le nord de la France, il y a beaucoup de vieilles maisons à colombages. Faux. C'est dans l'est de la France qu'il y a des maisons à colombages.
10. En France, en 1962, plus d'un quart des maisons et des appartements avaient (*had*) seulement trois pièces. Vrai.

OPTIONS

Extra Practice Write the following headings on the board and have students identify the different types of housing in each area: **Les grandes villes, La banlieue, Le nord, L'Alsace-Lorraine, L'ouest,** and **Le sud**.

Cultural Comparison Have students work in groups of three and compare the types of housing in France and the United States. Tell them to list the similarities and differences in a two-column chart under the headings **Similitudes** and **Différences**. After completing their charts, have two groups get together and compare their lists.

NATIONAL
communication
STANDARDS

COMMUNICATION

4 **Quand tu avais seize ans** À tour de rôle, posez ces questions à votre partenaire pour savoir (*to know*) les détails de sa vie quand il/elle avait seize ans. Answers will vary.

1. Où habitais-tu?
2. Est-ce que tu conduisais déjà une voiture?
3. Où est-ce que ta famille et toi alliez en vacances?
4. Pendant combien de temps partiez-vous en vacances?
5. Est-ce que tes amis et toi, vous sortiez tard le soir?
6. Que faisaient tes parents le week-end?
7. Quels sports pratiquais-tu?
8. Quel genre de musique écoutais-tu?
9. Comment était ton école?
10. Aimais-tu l'école? Pourquoi?

5 **La chambre de Rafik** Voici la chambre de Rafik quand il était adolescent. Avec un(e) partenaire, employez des verbes à l'imparfait pour comparer la chambre de Rafik avec votre chambre quand vous aviez son âge. Answers will vary.

MODÈLE

Étudiant(e) 1: *Je n'avais pas de salle de bains à côté de ma chambre. Et toi?*
Étudiant(e) 2: *Moi, je partageais la salle de bains avec ma sœur.*

6 **Une énigme** La nuit dernière, quelqu'un est entré dans le bureau de votre professeur et a emporté (*took away*) l'examen de français. Vous devez (*must*) trouver qui. Qu'est-ce que vos camarades de classe faisaient hier soir? Relisez vos notes et dites qui est le voleur (*thief*). Ensuite, présentez vos conclusions à la classe. Answers will vary.

Je pensais que tu avais du travail.

Mais ma chérie, c'était une surprise.

- Note that the **nous** and **vous** forms of infinitives ending in **-ier** contain a double **i** in the **imparfait**.

Vous **skiiez** dans les Alpes en janvier. *You used to ski in the Alps in January.*	Nous **étudiions** parfois jusqu'à minuit. *We studied until midnight sometimes.*

- The verb **être** is irregular in the **imparfait**.

The *imparfait* of *être*

j'étais	nous étions
tu étais	vous étiez
il/elle était	ils/elles étaient

La cuisine **était** à côté du salon. *The kitchen was next to the living room.*	Les toilettes **étaient** au rez-de-chaussée. *The restrooms were on the ground floor.*

- Note the imperfect forms of these expressions.

Il pleuvait chaque matin. *It rained each morning.*	**Il neigeait** parfois au printemps. *It snowed sometimes in the spring.*
Il y avait deux lits et une lampe dans la chambre. *There were two beds and a lamp in the room.*	**Il fallait** payer un loyer de 1.000 euros. *It was necessary to pay a rent of 1,000 euros.*

Essayez! Choisissez la réponse correcte pour compléter les phrases.

1. Muriel (louait/louais) un appartement en ville.
2. Rodrigue (partageait/partagiez) une chambre avec un autre étudiant.
3. Nous (payait/payions) notre loyer une fois par mois.
4. Il y (avait/était) des balcons au premier étage.
5. Il (neigeait/fallait) mettre le chauffage (*heat*) quand il (faisaient/faisait) froid.
6. Qu'est-ce que tu (faisait/faisais) dans le couloir?
7. Vous (aimiez/aimaient) beaucoup le quartier?
8. Nous (étaient/étions) trois dans le petit studio.

Essayez! Have students identify the infinitive of each verb in the activity. Examples: **1. louer 2. partager**

1 Expansion After completing the activity, have students complete the sentences using the **passé composé**. Compare the meanings of each sentence.

2 Suggestion Before assigning the activity, review the forms of the imperfect by calling out an infinitive and a series of subject pronouns. Ask volunteers to give the corresponding forms. Example: **détester, nous** (**nous détestions**).

3 Suggestion Divide the class into two groups, **l'imparfait** and **le présent**. Have the first group give one phrase about what Emmanuel and his family used to do. The second group should describe what he and his family do differently now, using an opposite verb in the present tense.

4 Expansion Have students share their partner's answers with the class using the third person pronouns **il/elle**.

5 Expansion Have students work in groups of four to list statements about their last childhood bedroom. Example: **Je partageais ma chambre avec mon frère.** Groups then switch surveys and compare answers.

6 Suggestion Before doing this activity, remind students that the imperfect form of **être** is irregular.

OPTIONS

Game Label the four corners of the room different periods throughout history. Examples: **la Préhistoire, le Moyen Âge, la Renaissance,** and **le Dix-Neuvième siècle**. Tell students to go to the corner that best represents the historical period they would visit if they could. Each group then discusses their reasons for picking that period using the **imparfait**. A spokesperson will summarize his or her group's responses to the class.

Extra Practice Bring in or choose a few students to bring in video clips from popular movies. Show clips to the class. Brainstorm important vocabulary. After viewing each clip, have students use the **imparfait** to describe what was happening and what people in the clip were doing.

Synthèse

Instructional Resources
*IRCD-ROM: IRM (**Feuilles d'activités**; Info Gap Activities); Testing Program, pp. 57–60; Test Files; Testing Program MP3s; Test Generator*
espaces.vhlcentral.com: activities, downloads, reference tools

1 Suggestion Have students write out the questions and answers. Check use of subject pronouns and the **imparfait** forms of **être**.

2 Suggestion Have two volunteers model a question and answer for the class.

2 Expansion After group members finish questioning each other, have a student from each group read the answers from another student. The class will then guess which student's childhood birthday celebration was described.

3 Suggestions
- Ask two students to read the **modèle** aloud. Then distribute the **Feuilles d'activités** from the IRM on the IRCD-ROM.
- Encourage students to add activities involving sports and leisure not already found in their survey.

4 Expansion Expand this activity by showing the class an **avant** and **après** picture of a person or place in a magazine. Divide the students into two groups. Have one group describe the person or place in the before picture. Have the other group describe the after picture using the present tense.

5 Expansion Tell students to imagine they are the **ancien(ne) patron(ne)** and have decided to give the employee a second chance. It is time for the three-month review. Have them draft a brief letter to the employee discussing his or her past versus present performance on the job.

6 Suggestion Divide the class into pairs and distribute this activity's Info Gap Handouts in the IRM on the IRCD-ROM. Give students ten minutes to complete the activity.

1 Mes affaires Vous cherchez vos affaires (*belongings*). À tour de rôle, demandez de l'aide à votre partenaire. Où étaient-elles la dernière fois? Utilisez l'illustration pour les trouver. Answers will vary.

MODÈLE

Étudiant(e) 1: *Je cherche mes baskets. Où sont-elles?*
Étudiant(e) 2: *Tu n'as pas cherché sur l'étagère? Elles étaient sur l'étagère.*

baskets	ordinateur
casquette	parapluie
journal	pull
livre	sac à dos

2 Les anniversaires Avec un(e) partenaire, préparez huit questions pour apprendre comment vos camarades de classe célébraient leur anniversaire quand ils étaient enfants. Employez l'imparfait et des adverbes dans vos questions, puis posez-les à un autre groupe. Answers will vary.

MODÈLE

Étudiant(e) 1: *Que faisais-tu souvent pour ton anniversaire?*
Étudiant(e) 2: *Quand j'étais petit, mes parents organisaient souvent une fête.*

3 Sports et loisirs Votre professeur va vous donner une feuille d'activités. Circulez dans la classe et demandez à vos camarades s'ils pratiquaient ces activités avant d'entrer à la fac. Trouvez une personne différente pour chaque réponse affirmative. Présentez les réponses à la classe. Answers will vary.

MODÈLE

Étudiant(e) 1: *Est-ce que tu faisais souvent du jogging avant d'entrer à la fac?*
Étudiant(e) 2: *Oui, je courais souvent le matin.*

4 Avant et après Voici la chambre d'Annette avant et après une visite de sa mère. Comment était sa chambre à l'origine? Avec un(e) partenaire, décrivez la pièce à tour de rôle et cherchez les différences entre les deux illustrations. Answers will vary.

MODÈLE

Avant, la lampe était à côté de l'ordinateur. Maintenant, elle est à côté du canapé.

5 Mes mauvaises habitudes Vous aviez de mauvaises habitudes, mais vous les avez changées. Maintenant, vous parlez avec votre ancien(ne) patron(ne) (*former boss*) pour essayer de récupérer l'emploi que vous avez perdu. Avec un(e) partenaire, préparez la conversation. Answers will vary.

MODÈLE

Étudiant(e) 1: *Impossible de vous employer! Vous dormiez tout le temps.*
Étudiant(e) 2: *Je dormais souvent, mais je travaillais aussi. Cette fois, je vais travailler sérieusement.*

6 Nous cherchons une maison Votre professeur va vous donner, à vous et à votre partenaire, une feuille d'information sur quatre maisons à louer. Attention! Ne regardez pas la feuille de votre partenaire. Answers will vary.

MODÈLE

Étudiant(e) 1: *Malheureusement, la première maison avait un très petit balcon.*
Étudiant(e) 2: *Mais heureusement, elle avait deux salles de bains.*

ressources

WB	LM	Lab MP3s	espaces.vhlcentral.com
pp. 101–104	pp. 59–60	Leçon 15	Leçon 15

OPTIONS

Extra Practice Use these sentences containing regular and irregular verbs in the **imparfait** and adverbs as a dictation. Read each sentence twice, pausing after the second time for students to write. **1. Heureusement, il y avait beaucoup d'étudiants dans la classe. 2. Conduisait-il vite ta voiture? 3. J'étais vraiment très heureuse de te voir. 4. Il fallait travailler constamment le samedi.**

Extra Practice Have small groups organize a skit about a birthday or other party that took place recently. Guide them to first make general comments about the party, such as **C'était vraiment amusant!** Then describe a few specific things that were going on, what people were talking about, what they were wearing, and any other appropriate details. After the skits are performed, have students vote on their favorite one.

Interlude

La place au sous-sol

Pour le thème de la maison, la chanson°, ***La place au sous-sol*** *(2000), parle du problème des parents âgés, placés dans des foyers° par leurs enfants. Dans cette chanson, le personnage regrette beaucoup de l'avoir fait, car° sa mère est morte dans ce foyer. Maintenant, elle nourrit° la perruche° de sa mère, mais pense que sa mère serait° encore vivante° si elle l'avait accueillie° chez elle.*

LYNDA LEMAY (1966–) est née au Québec, à Portneuf, près du fleuve Saint-Laurent. Elle écrit son premier texte à neuf ans. Adolescente, elle apprend à jouer de la guitare et gagne un concours de chansons. Elle enregistre° son premier album en 1991, mais c'est en 1994 qu'elle trouve vraiment le succès avec son deuxième album. Elle reçoit un Félix, au Canada, en 1998 et une Victoire, en France, en 2003 (équivalents des Grammy Awards*). Elle est appréciée pour ses talents d'interprète° et la qualité de ses chansons.*

Un artiste dans son atelier

PASCAL-ADOLPHE-JEAN DAGNAN-BOUVERET (1852–1929) était un peintre° naturaliste français qui n'a pas été influencé par les mouvements de son temps. Il était spécialiste du détail, ce qu'il° montrait dans son travail de style réaliste. Ici, dans ***Un artiste dans son atelier****, on découvre° l'univers d'un artiste, les meubles présents chez lui. Montrer l'intérieur d'une habitation° était alors un thème artistique apprécié.*

Activité

Choisissez une de ces options et écrivez un paragraphe sur le thème de la maison. Écrivez au moins huit phrases complètes. Answers will vary.

1. Dans la chanson, la chanteuse est affectée par les objets de la maison parce que tout lui rappelle (*reminds her of*) sa mère. Pensez à un meuble et à une pièce. À votre avis (*opinion*), à quoi Lemay pense-t-elle quand elle les voit (*sees them*)? Est-ce qu'ils vont l'affecter? Comment?
2. Décrivez tout ce que (*all that*) vous voyez (*see*) dans le tableau (*painting*). Quelle est la fonction de cette pièce? Pourquoi ces objets sont-ils là?
3. Quels objets et quels meubles chez vous ont une valeur sentimentale? Pourquoi?

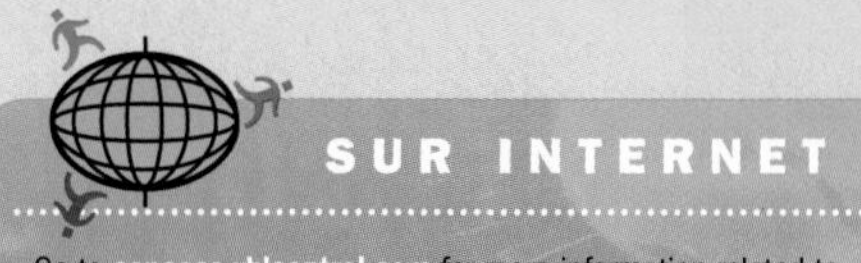

SUR INTERNET

Go to espaces.vhlcentral.com for more information related to this **Interlude**.

chanson *song* **foyers** *nursing homes* **car** *because* **nourrit** *feeds* **perruche** *parakeet* **serait** *would be* **vivante** *alive* **si elle l'avait accueillie** *had she welcomed her* **enregistre** *records* **interprète** *performer* **peintre** *painter* **ce qu'il** *which he* **découvre** *discovers* **habitation** *house*

Section Goals

In this section, students will learn about:
- Lynda Lemay
- Pascal-Adolphe-Jean Dagnan-Bouveret

Instructional Resources
espaces.vhlcentral.com: activities, downloads, reference tools

La place au sous-sol
To check comprehension, ask these questions.
1. De quel problème parle la chanson *La place au sous-sol*? (Elle parle des parents âgés, placés dans des foyers par leurs enfants.)
2. Le ton (*tone*) de cette chanson est-il heureux ou triste? (triste) Pourquoi? (Le personnage dans la chanson regrette son acte.)
3. De quelle nationalité est Lynda Lemay? (québécoise)
4. À quel âge a-t-elle écrit son premier texte? (à neuf ans)
5. Comment savez-vous qu'elle a du succès? (Elle a gagné un Félix, au Canada, en 1998 et une Victoire, en France, en 2003.)

Un artiste dans son atelier
- Dagnan-Bouveret is known for creating photographically accurate compositions. His works often represent scenes of daily life or rural life in Franche-Comté and Brittany. He also painted portraits and, in his later years, religious scenes.
- To check comprehension, give students these true/false items.

1. Dagnan-Bouveret est un peintre impressionniste. (Faux. Il est naturaliste. Son style est réaliste.)
2. Les détails étaient importants pour lui. (Vrai.)
3. Dans le tableau, l'homme travaille. (Faux. Il pense./Il réfléchit.)
4. Il n'y a pas beaucoup de meubles dans l'atelier. (Vrai.)

OPTIONS

Lynda Lemay As a singer-songwriter, Lynda Lemay has a large following of fans in Québec and Europe, with tours in Québec, France, Belgium, and Switzerland. ***Y***, her second album, went double platinum. Lemay uses the dramas of everyday life as the basis for her songs; ***Mon père c'est le plus fort*** is her trademark song. Her album ***Un paradis quelque part*** (2005) includes both ballads and rock numbers, illustrating her versatility. She has also composed a folk opera, ***Un éternel hiver***, which was performed in France in 2005.

Extra Practice Bring in a photo of Dagnan-Bouveret's first popular success, ***Une noce chez le photographe*** (1879), or tell students to print one from the Internet. Have the class compare the style and subject matter of the two paintings.

Section Goals

In this section, students will learn and practice vocabulary related to:

- household chores
- home appliances

Instructional Resources
*IRCD-ROM: Transparency #38; IRM (**Vocabulaire supplémentaire; Mise en pratique** answers; Textbook Audioscript; Lab Audioscript; **Feuilles d'activités**)*
Textbook MP3s
WB/VM: Workbook. pp. 105–106
Lab Manual, p. 61
Lab MP3s
WB/VM/LM Answer Key
espaces.vhlcentral.com: activities, downloads, reference tools

Suggestions

- Use **Transparency #38.** Point out appliances and talk about what people in the illustration are doing. Examples: **Ça, c'est un four à micro-ondes. Cette femme balaie.**
- Ask students questions about chores using the new vocabulary. Examples: **Préférez-vous balayer ou passer l'aspirateur? Faire la cuisine ou faire la lessive? Mettre la table ou sortir la poubelle?**
- Say vocabulary words and tell students to write or say the opposite terms. Examples: **sale (propre), débarrasser la table (mettre la table),** and **salir les vêtements (faire la lessive).**
- Point out the difference between **un évier** (*kitchen sink*) and **un lavabo** (*bathroom sink*).
- Point out the expressions that use **faire**: **faire la lessive, faire la poussière, faire le ménage, faire le lit,** and **faire la vaisselle**.
- Tell students that the names of several appliances are compounds of verbs and nouns. Examples: **grille-pain, lave-vaisselle,** and **sèche-linge**. Other appliances use the preposition **à**: **un fer à repasser, un four à micro-ondes.**
- Additional vocabulary for this lesson can be found in the **Vocabulaire supplémentaire** in the IRM on the IRCD-ROM.

Leçon 16

You will learn how to...

- talk about chores
- talk about appliances

Les tâches ménagères

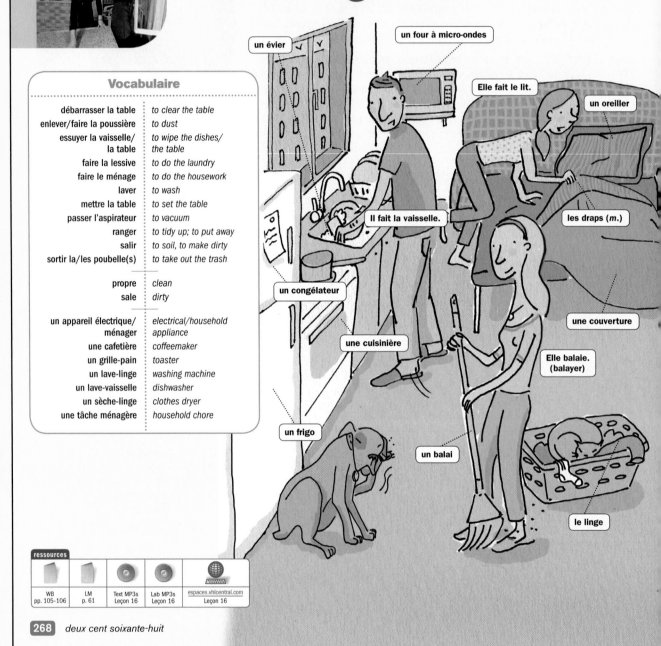

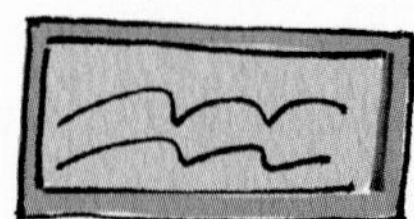

les draps (*m.*)

Elle balaie. (balayer)

Vocabulaire

débarrasser la table	*to clear the table*
enlever/faire la poussière	*to dust*
essuyer la vaisselle/la table	*to wipe the dishes/the table*
faire la lessive	*to do the laundry*
faire le ménage	*to do the housework*
laver	*to wash*
mettre la table	*to set the table*
passer l'aspirateur	*to vacuum*
ranger	*to tidy up; to put away*
salir	*to soil, to make dirty*
sortir la/les poubelle(s)	*to take out the trash*
propre	*clean*
sale	*dirty*
un appareil électrique/ménager	*electrical/household appliance*
une cafetière	*coffeemaker*
un grille-pain	*toaster*
un lave-linge	*washing machine*
un lave-vaisselle	*dishwasher*
un sèche-linge	*clothes dryer*
une tâche ménagère	*household chore*

ressources

WB	LM	Text MP3s	Lab MP3s	espaces.vhlcentral.com
pp. 105-106	p. 61	Leçon 16	Leçon 16	Leçon 16

OPTIONS

Game Write vocabulary words for appliances on index cards. On another set of cards, draw or paste pictures to match each term. Tape them face down on the board in random order. Divide the class into two teams. Then play a game of Concentration in which students match words with pictures. When a player has a match, that player's team collects those cards. When all the cards have been matched, the team with the most cards wins.

Extra Practice Ask students what chores they do in various rooms. Examples: **Dans quelle pièce… faites-vous la vaisselle? faites-vous le lit? mettez-vous la table? passez-vous l'aspirateur? repassez-vous? balayez-vous?**

Il sort la poubelle.
un fer à repasser
Il repasse. (repasser)

Mise en pratique

1 Écoutez Écoutez la conversation téléphonique (*phone call*) entre Édouard, un étudiant, et un psychologue à la radio. Ensuite, indiquez les tâches ménagères que faisaient Édouard et Paul au début du semestre.

	Édouard	Paul
1. Il faisait la cuisine.	☑	☐
2. Il faisait les lits.	☐	☑
3. Il passait l'aspirateur.	☑	☐
4. Il sortait la poubelle.	☐	☑
5. Il balayait.	☐	☑
6. Il faisait la lessive.	☑	☐
7. Il faisait la vaisselle.	☐	☑
8. Il nettoyait le frigo.	☑	☐

2 On fait le ménage Complétez les phrases suivantes avec le bon mot pour faire une phrase logique.

1. On balaie avec un balai.
2. On repasse le linge avec un fer à repasser.
3. On fait la lessive avec un lave-linge.
4. On lave la vaisselle avec un lave-vaisselle.
5. On prépare le café avec une cafetière.
6. On sèche la lessive avec un sèche-linge.
7. On met la glace dans un congélateur.
8. Pour faire le lit, on doit arranger les draps, la couverture et l'oreiller/les oreillers.

3 Les tâches ménagères Avec un(e) partenaire, indiquez quelles tâches ménagères vous faites dans chaque pièce ou partie de votre logement. Il y a plus d'une réponse possible. Answers will vary.

1. La chambre: ____
2. La cuisine: ____
3. La salle de bains: ____
4. La salle à manger: ____
5. La salle de séjour: ____
6. Le garage: ____
7. Le jardin: ____
8. L'escalier: ____

1 Tapescript J'ai un problème avec Paul, mon colocataire, parce qu'il ne m'aide pas à faire le ménage. Quand le semestre a commencé, il faisait la vaisselle, il sortait la poubelle et il balayait. Parfois, il faisait même mon lit. Paul ne faisait jamais la cuisine parce qu'il détestait ça, c'est moi qui la faisais. Je faisais aussi la lessive, je passais l'aspirateur et je nettoyais le frigo. Maintenant, Paul ne fait jamais son lit et il ne m'aide pas. C'est moi qui fais tout. Qu'est-ce que vous me suggérez de faire?
(On Textbook MP3s)

1 Suggestion After listening to the recording, have students identify Paul and Édouard in the photo and describe what they are doing.

1 Expansion Have students describe how they share household chores with their roommate or others in their household.

2 Expansion Reverse this activity and ask students what each appliance is used for. Example: **Que fait-on avec une cuisinière? (On fait la cuisine.)**

3 Suggestion Have students get together with another pair and compare their answers.

OPTIONS

Extra Practice Have students complete these analogies.
1. passer l'aspirateur : tapis :: lave-vaisselle: ____ (verre/tasse)
2. chaud : froid :: cuisinière : ____ (congélateur)
3. ordinateur : bureau :: armoire : ____ (chambre)
4. tasse : cuisine :: voiture : ____ (garage)
5. café : cafetière :: pain : ____ (grille-pain)
6. mauvais : bon :: sale : ____ (propre)
7. chaud : four à micro-ondes :: froid : ____ (frigo)
8. arriver : partir :: nettoyer : ____ (salir)
9. table: verre :: lit: ____ (draps/couverture)

4 Suggestion Have students jot down notes during their interviews. Then ask them to report what they learned about their partner.

4 Expansion Take a quick survey about household chores using items 4 and 6. Tally the results on the board.

5 Suggestion Before beginning this activity, have students brainstorm desirable and undesirable qualities or habits of roommates. Write a list on the board.

6 Suggestion Distribute the **Feuilles d'activités** from the IRM on the IRCD-ROM. Have two volunteers read the **modèle**.

7 Suggestion Have students exchange paragraphs for peer editing. Tell them to underline, rather than correct, grammar and spelling errors.

Communication

NATIONAL STANDARDS communication

4 Conversez Interviewez un(e) camarade de classe. Answers will vary.

1. Qui fait la vaisselle chez toi?
2. Qui fait la lessive chez toi?
3. Fais-tu ton lit tous les jours?
4. Quelles tâches ménagères as-tu faites le week-end dernier?
5. Repasses-tu tous tes vêtements?
6. Quelles tâches ménagères détestes-tu faire?
7. Quels appareils électriques as-tu chez toi?
8. Ranges-tu souvent ta chambre?

5 Camarade de chambre Vous cherchez un(e) camarade de chambre pour habiter dans une résidence universitaire et deux personnes ont répondu à votre petite annonce (*ad*) dans le journal. Travaillez avec deux camarades de classe et préparez un dialogue dans lequel (*in which*) vous: Answers will vary.

- parlez des tâches ménagères que vous détestez/aimez faire.
- parlez des responsabilités de votre nouveau/nouvelle camarade de chambre.
- parlez de vos passions et de vos habitudes.
- décidez quelle est la personne qui vous convient le mieux (*suits you the best*).

6 Qui fait quoi? Votre professeur va vous donner une feuille d'activités. Dites si vous faites les tâches indiquées en écrivant **Oui** ou **Non** dans la première colonne. Ensuite, posez des questions à vos camarades de classe; écrivez leur nom dans la deuxième colonne quand ils répondent **Oui**. Présentez vos réponses à la classe. Answers will vary.

MODÈLE

mettre la table pour prendre le petit-déjeuner
Étudiant(e) 1: *Est-ce que tu mets la table pour prendre le petit-déjeuner?*
Étudiant(e) 2: *Oui, je mets la table chaque matin./ Non, je prends le petit-déjeuner au resto U, donc je ne mets pas la table.*

Activités	Moi	Mes camarades de classe
1. mettre la table pour prendre le petit-déjeuner		
2. passer l'aspirateur tous les jours		
3. salir ses vêtements quand on mange		
4. nettoyer les toilettes		
5. balayer la cuisine		
6. débarrasser la table après le dîner		
7. enlever souvent la poussière sur son ordinateur		
8. laver les vitres (*windows*)		

7 Écrivez L'appartement de Martine est un désastre: la cuisine est sale et comme vous pouvez (*can*) l'imaginer, le reste de l'appartement est encore pire (*worse*). Préparez un paragraphe où vous décrivez les problèmes que vous voyez (*see*) et que vous imaginez. Ensuite, écrivez la liste des tâches que Martine va faire pour tout nettoyer. Answers will vary.

OPTIONS

Small Groups Have groups of three write riddles about furnishings or appliances. For each riddle, the group comes up with at least three hints. Example: **Je suis très doux. On me met sur le lit. Je vous aide à bien dormir. (Je suis un oreiller.)** Ask them to read their riddles to the class, who will guess the answer.

Extra Practice Have students complete this paragraph. **L'appartement de Roger est un désastre. Il a rarement le temps de faire les ____ (ménage). Il ____ (passe) l'aspirateur une fois par semestre et il n'____ (enlève) pas la poussière. Il y a des tasses et des verres dans l'____ (évier) parce qu'il oublie de les mettre dans le ____ (lave-vaisselle). L'appartement sent mauvais parce qu'il ne sort pas la ____ (poubelle).**

Les sons et les lettres

NATIONAL
comparisons
STANDARDS

Semi-vowels

French has three semi-vowels. Semi-vowels are sounds that are produced in much the same way as vowels, but also have many properties in common with consonants. Semi-vowels are also sometimes referred to as *glides* because they glide from or into the vowel they accompany.

hier **chien** **soif** **nuit**

The semi-vowel that occurs in the word **bien** is very much like the *y* in the English word *yes*. It is usually spelled with an **i** or a **y** (pronounced *ee*), then glides into the following sound. This semi-vowel sound may also be spelled **ll** after an **i**.

nation **balayer** **bien** **brillant**

The semi-vowel that occurs in the word **soif** is like the *w* in the English word *was*. It usually begins with **o** or **ou**, then glides into the following vowel.

trois **froid** **oui** **Louis**

The third semi-vowel sound occurs in the word **nuit**. It is spelled with the vowel **u**, as in the French word **tu**, then glides into the following sound.

lui **suis** **cruel** **intellectuel**

Prononcez Répétez les mots suivants à voix haute.

1. oui
2. taille
3. suisse
4. fille
5. mois
6. cruel
7. minuit
8. jouer
9. cuisine
10. juillet
11. échouer
12. croissant

Articulez Répétez les phrases suivantes à voix haute.

1. Voici trois poissons noirs.
2. Louis et sa famille sont suisses.
3. Parfois, Grégoire fait de la cuisine chinoise.
4. Aujourd'hui, Matthieu et Damien vont travailler.
5. Françoise a besoin de faire ses devoirs d'histoire.
6. La fille de Monsieur Poirot va conduire pour la première fois.

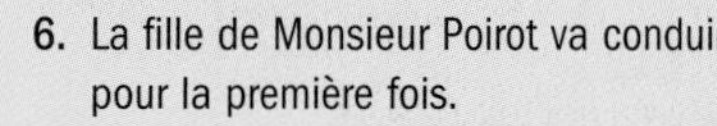

Dictons Répétez les dictons à voix haute.

Vouloir, c'est pouvoir.[2]

La nuit, tous les chats sont gris.[1]

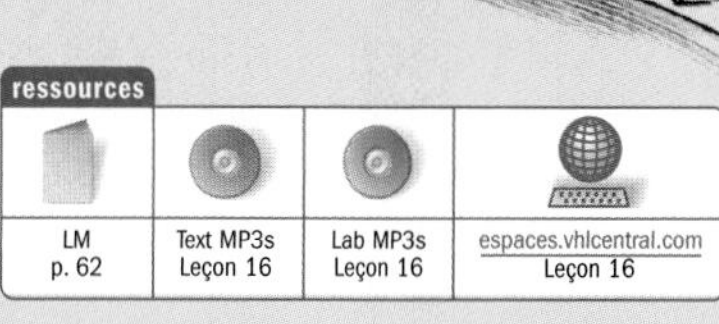

ressources

LM p. 62	Text MP3s Leçon 16	Lab MP3s Leçon 16	espaces.vhlcentral.com Leçon 16

[1] All cats are gray in the dark.
[2] Where there's a will, there's a way.

Section Goals

In this section, students will learn about semi-vowels.

Instructional Resources
Textbook MP3s
Lab Manual, p. 62
Lab MP3s
WB/VM/LM Answer Key
IRCD-ROM: IRM (Textbook Audioscript; Lab Audioscript)
espaces.vhlcentral.com: activities, downloads, reference tools

Suggestions

- Model the pronunciation of the example words and have students repeat them after you.
- Ask students to provide more examples of words from this lesson or previous lessons with these sounds. Examples: **balayer, essuyer,** and **évier**.
- Dictate five familiar words containing semi-vowels, repeating each one at least two times. Then write them on the board or on a transparency and have students check their spelling.
- Remind students that many vowels combine to make a single sound with no glide. Examples: **ai** and **ou**.

OPTIONS

Extra Practice Use these sentences with semi-vowels for additional practice or dictation. **1. Nous balayons bien la cuisine. 2. J'ai soif mais tu as froid. 3. Une fois, ma fille a oublié son parapluie. 4. Parfois, mon chien aime jouer entre minuit et trois heures du matin.**

Extra Practice Teach students these French tongue-twisters that contain semi-vowels. **1. Trois petites truites non cuites, trois petites truites crues. 2. Une bête noire se baigne dans une baignoire noire.**

Section Goals

In this section, students will learn functional phrases for talking about who and what they know.

Instructional Resources
WB/VM: Video Manual, pp. 241–242
WB/VM/LM Answer Key
Video CD-ROM
Video on DVD
IRCD-ROM: IRM (Videoscript; ***Roman-photo*** *Translations)*
espaces.vhlcentral.com: activities, downloads, reference tools

Video Recap: Leçon 15
Before doing this **Roman-photo**, review the previous one with this activity.
1. Qui a fait une visite surprise à Aix-en-Provence? (Pascal)
2. Combien de pièces y a-t-il chez Sandrine? (trois)
3. Comment est l'appartement de Sandrine? (grand et beau)
4. Comment est l'appartement de Rachid et David? (petit, pas de décorations et pas beaucoup de meubles)
5. Que pense Sandrine de la visite surprise de Pascal? (Elle n'est pas contente.)

Video Synopsis
At the café, Amina talks to Sandrine on the phone. Valérie questions Stéphane about his chores and reminds him to do the dishes before he leaves. Amina arrives at Sandrine's. As Sandrine is baking cookies, she breaks a plate. The two girls talk about how annoying Pascal is. Sandrine asks if Amina plans to meet Cyberhomme in person. Amina is not sure that's a good idea.

Suggestions
- Have students predict what the episode will be about based on the title and video stills.
- Have students scan the **Roman-photo** and find sentences related to chores.
- After reading the captions, review students' predictions.

communication cultures — NATIONAL STANDARDS

La vie sans Pascal

PERSONNAGES

Amina

Michèle

Sandrine

Stéphane

Valérie

1

Au P'tit Bistrot...
MICHÈLE Tout va bien, Amina?
AMINA Oui, ça va, merci. (*Au téléphone*) Allô?... Qu'est-ce qu'il y a Sandrine?... Non, je ne le savais pas, mais franchement, ça ne me surprend pas... Écoute, j'arrive chez toi dans quinze minutes, d'accord? ... À tout à l'heure!

2

MICHÈLE Je débarrasse la table?
AMINA Oui, merci et apporte-moi l'addition, s'il te plaît.
MICHÈLE Tout de suite.

3

VALÉRIE Tu as fait ton lit ce matin?
STÉPHANE Oui, maman.
VALÉRIE Est-ce que tu as rangé ta chambre?
STÉPHANE Euh... oui, ce matin pendant que tu faisais la lessive.

6

Chez Sandrine...
SANDRINE Salut, Amina! Merci d'être venue.
AMINA Mmmm. Qu'est-ce qui sent si bon?
SANDRINE Il y a des biscuits au chocolat dans le four.
AMINA Oh, est-ce que tu les préparais quand tu m'as téléphoné?

7

SANDRINE Tu as soif?
AMINA Un peu, oui.
SANDRINE Sers-toi, j'ai des jus de fruits au frigo.

8

Sandrine casse (breaks) une assiette.
SANDRINE Et zut!
AMINA Ça va, Sandrine?
SANDRINE Oui, oui... passe-moi le balai, s'il te plaît.
AMINA N'oublie pas de balayer sous la cuisinière.
SANDRINE Je sais! Excuse-moi, Amina. Comme je t'ai dit au téléphone, Pascal et moi, c'est fini.

ACTIVITÉS

1 Questions Répondez aux questions suivantes par des phrases complètes. Answers may vary slightly.

1. Avec qui Amina parle-t-elle au téléphone? Elle parle avec Sandrine.
2. Comment est Sandrine aujourd'hui? Pourquoi? Elle est de mauvaise humeur parce que c'est fini avec Pascal.
3. Est-ce que Stéphane a fait toutes ses tâches ménagères? Non, il n'a pas fait toutes ses tâches ménagères.
4. Qu'est-ce que Sandrine préparait quand elle a téléphoné à Amina? Elle préparait des biscuits au chocolat.
5. Amina a faim et a soif. À votre avis (*opinion*), qu'est-ce qu'elle va prendre? Elle va prendre un jus de fruits et elle va manger des biscuits.
6. Pourquoi Amina n'est-elle pas fâchée (*angry*) contre Sandrine? Elle comprend pourquoi Sandrine est un peu triste/de mauvaise humeur.
7. Pourquoi Amina pense-t-elle que Sandrine aimerait (*would like*) un cyberhomme américain? Amina pense que Sandrine aime David.
8. Sandrine pense qu'Amina devrait (*should*) rencontrer Cyberhomme, mais Amina pense que ce n'est pas une bonne idée. À votre avis, qui a raison? Answers will vary.

OPTIONS

Avant de regarder la vidéo Before playing the video, show students individual photos from the **Roman-photo**, #5 or #8 for example, and have them write their own captions. Ask volunteers to write their captions on the board.

Regarder la vidéo Photocopy the videoscript from the IRM, then white out words related to household chores and other key vocabulary in order to create a master for a cloze activity. Distribute the photocopies and tell students to fill in the missing information as they watch the video episode.

Amina console Sandrine.

4

VALÉRIE Hmm... et la vaisselle? Tu as fait la vaisselle?
STÉPHANE Non, pas encore, mais...
MICHÈLE Il me faut l'addition pour Amina.
VALÉRIE Stéphane, tu dois faire la vaisselle avant de sortir.
STÉPHANE Bon ça va, j'y vais!

5

VALÉRIE Ah Michèle, il faut sortir les poubelles pour ce soir!
MICHÈLE Oui, comptez sur moi, Madame Forestier.
VALÉRIE Très bien! Moi, je rentre, il est l'heure de préparer le dîner.

9

SANDRINE Il était tellement pénible. Bref je suis de mauvaise humeur aujourd'hui.
AMINA Ne t'en fais pas, je comprends.
SANDRINE Toi, tu as de la chance.
AMINA Pourquoi tu dis ça?
SANDRINE Tu as ton Cyberhomme. Tu vas le rencontrer un de ces jours?
AMINA Oh... Je ne sais pas si c'est une bonne idée.

10

SANDRINE Pourquoi pas?
AMINA Sandrine, il faut être prudent dans la vie, je ne le connais pas vraiment, tu sais.
SANDRINE Comme d'habitude, tu as raison. Mais finalement, un cyberhomme c'est peut-être mieux qu'un petit ami. Ou alors un petit ami artistique, charmant et beau garçon.
AMINA Et américain?

Expressions utiles

Talking about what you know

- **Je ne le savais pas, mais franchement, ça ne me surprend pas.**
  I didn't know that, but frankly, I'm not surprised.
- **Je sais!**
  I know!
- **Je ne sais pas si c'est une bonne idée.**
  I don't know if that's a good idea.
- **Je ne le connais pas vraiment, tu sais.**
  I don't really know him, you know.

Additional vocabulary

- **Comptez sur moi.**
  Count on me.
- **Ne t'en fais pas.**
  Don't worry about it.
- **J'y vais!**
  I'm going there!/I'm on my way!
- **pas encore**
  not yet
- **tu dois**
  you must
- **être de bonne/mauvaise humeur**
  to be in a good/bad mood

ACTIVITÉS

2 Le ménage Indiquez qui a fait ou va faire les tâches ménagères suivantes: Michèle (**M**), Stéphane (**St**), Valérie (**V**), Sandrine (**S**), Amina (**A**) ou personne (*no one*) (**P**).

1. sortir la poubelle M
2. balayer S & A
3. passer l'aspirateur P
4. faire la vaisselle St
5. faire le lit St
6. débarrasser la table M
7. faire la lessive V
8. ranger sa chambre St

3 Écrivez Vous avez gagné un pari (*bet*) avec votre colocataire et il/elle doit faire (*must do*) en conséquence toutes les tâches ménagères que vous lui indiquez pendant un mois. Écrivez une liste de dix tâches minimum. Pour chaque tâche, précisez la pièce du logement et combien de fois par semaine il/elle doit l'exécuter.

ressources

VM pp. 241–242	V CD-ROM Leçon 16	espaces.vhlcentral.com Leçon 16

Expressions utiles
- Model the pronunciation of the **Expressions utiles** and have students repeat them.
- As you work through the list, point out the forms of **savoir** and **connaître**. See if students can discern the difference in meaning between the two verbs from the example sentences. Respond briefly to their questions, but tell them that these verbs will be formally presented in **Structures 16.2**.

1 Suggestion Have volunteers write their answers on the board. Go over them as a class.

2 Expansion Ask students who works the hardest of all these people. Have them support their opinion with details from this episode and previous ones.

3 Suggestion Have students use commands in their lists for review.

OPTIONS

Extra Practice Divide the class into two groups based on their answers to question 8 on page 272 (whether or not Amina should meet Cyberhomme) and have a debate about who is right. Tell groups to brainstorm a list of arguments to support their point of view and anticipate rebuttals for what the other team might say.

Pairs Have students work in pairs. Tell them to reread the last lines of the **Roman-photo** and write a short paragraph predicting what will happen in future episodes. Do they think Amina will meet Cyberhomme in person? What do they think will happen in Sandrine's love life? Have volunteers read their paragraphs to the class aloud.

connections cultures NATIONAL STANDARDS

Section Goals

In this section, students will:
- learn about the interior of French homes
- learn some colloquial terms for describing a home or room
- learn the names of some famous homes in the francophone world
- read about the French Quarter in New Orleans

Instructional Resources
espaces.vhlcentral.com: activities, downloads, reference tools

Culture à la loupe

Avant la lecture
- Have students look at the photos and describe what they see.
- Tell students to read the first sentence of the text. Then ask: **Quel est le sujet du texte?**

Lecture
- Point out the **Coup de main** and have two volunteers read the examples. Demonstrative pronouns will be presented in **Leçon 27**.
- Point out the statistics chart. Ask students what information the chart shows. (the percentage of French residences that have the appliances listed)

Après la lecture Ask students: **Quelles sont les différences entre l'intérieur des logements français et l'intérieur des logements américains?**

1 Suggestion Go over the answers with the class.

CULTURE À LA LOUPE

L'intérieur des logements français

L'intérieur des maisons et des appartements français est assez° différent de celui des Américains. Quand on entre dans un vieil immeuble en France, on est dans un hall° où il y a des boîtes aux lettres°. Ensuite, il y a souvent une deuxième porte. Celle-ci conduit à° l'escalier. Il n'y a pas souvent d'ascenseur, mais s'il y en a un°, en général, il est très petit et il est au milieu de° l'escalier. Le hall de l'immeuble peut aussi avoir une porte qui donne sur une cour° ou un jardin, souvent derrière le bâtiment°.

À l'intérieur des logements, les pièces sont en général plus petites que° les pièces américaines, surtout les cuisines et les salles de bains. Dans la cuisine, on trouve tous les appareils ménagers nécessaires (cuisinière, four, four à micro-ondes, frigo), mais ils sont plus petits qu'aux États-Unis. Les lave-vaisselle sont assez rares dans les appartements et plus communs dans les maisons. On a souvent une seule° salle de bains et les toilettes sont en général dans une autre petite pièce séparée°. Les lave-linge sont aussi assez petits et on les trouve dans la cuisine ou dans la salle de bains. Dans les chambres en France il n'y a pas de grands placards et les vêtements sont rangés la plupart° du temps dans une armoire. Les fenêtres s'ouvrent° sur l'intérieur, un peu comme des portes, et il est très rare d'avoir des moustiquaires°. Par contre°, il y a souvent des volets°.

Combien de logements ont ces appareils ménagers?

Réfrigérateur	97%
Lave-linge	95%
Cuisinière/Four	94%
Four à micro-ondes	70%
Congélateur	58%
Lave-vaisselle	45%
Sèche-linge	28%

Coup de main

Demonstrative pronouns help to avoid repetition.

	S.	P.
M.	**celui**	**ceux**
F.	**celle**	**celles**

Ce lit est grand, mais le lit de Monique est petit.

Ce lit est grand, mais celui de Monique est petit.

assez *rather* **hall** *entryway* **boîtes aux lettres** *mailboxes* **conduit à** *leads to* **s'il y en a un** *if there is one* **au milieu de** *in the middle of* **cour** *courtyard* **bâtiment** *building* **plus petites que** *smaller than* **une seule** *only one* **séparée** *separate* **la plupart** *most* **s'ouvrent** *open* **moustiquaires** *screens* **Par contre** *On the other hand* **volets** *shutters*

ACTIVITÉS

1 Complétez Complétez chaque phrase logiquement.
Answers will vary. Possible answers provided.

1. Dans le hall d'un immeuble français, on trouve... des boîtes aux lettres et des portes.
2. Au milieu de l'escalier, dans les vieux immeubles français,... il y a parfois un ascenseur.
3. Derrière les vieux immeubles, on trouve souvent... une cour ou un jardin.
4. Les cuisines et les salles de bains françaises sont... assez petites.
5. Dans les appartements français, il est assez rare d'avoir... un lave-vaisselle.
6. Les logements français ont souvent une seule... salle de bains.
7. En France, les toilettes sont souvent... dans une pièce séparée.
8. Les Français rangent souvent leurs vêtements dans une armoire parce qu'ils... n'ont pas souvent de placards.
9. On trouve souvent le lave-linge... dans la cuisine ou dans la salle de bains.
10. En général, les fenêtres dans les logements français... ont des volets.

OPTIONS

Cultural Comparison Take a quick class survey to find out how many students have the appliances listed in the chart in their homes. Tally the results on the board and have students calculate the percentages. Example: **Combien de personnes ont un réfrigérateur à la maison?** Then have students compare the results of this survey with those in the chart. Examples: **Plus d'Américains ont un sèche-linge dans leur maison./Moins de Français ont un sèche-linge dans leur maison.**

LE FRANÇAIS QUOTIDIEN

Quelles conditions!

boxon (*m.*)	*shambles*
gourbis (*m.*)	*pigsty*
piaule (*f.*)	*pad, room*
souk (*m.*)	*mess*
dégueulasse	*disgusting*
impeccable	*spic-and-span*
ringard	*cheesy, old-fashioned*
crécher	*to live*
semer la pagaille	*to make a mess*

LE MONDE FRANCOPHONE

Résidences célèbres

Voici quelques résidences célèbres.

En France

l'hôtel Matignon la résidence du Premier ministre°

Au Maroc

le Palais royal de Rabat la résidence du roi° et de sa famille

À la Martinique

la Pagerie la maison natale° de Joséphine de Beauharnais (femme de Napoléon Bonaparte)

À Monaco

le Palais du Prince la résidence de la famille princière° de Monaco (la famille Grimaldi)

Au Sénégal

le Palais présidentiel de Dakar la résidence du président du Sénégal, dans un jardin tropical

Premier ministre *Prime Minister* **roi** *king* **la maison natale** *birthplace* **la famille princière** *the prince and his family*

PORTRAIT

Le Vieux Carré

Le Quartier Français, ou Vieux Carré, est le centre historique de la Nouvelle-Orléans. Il est connu pour sa culture créole, sa vie nocturne°, sa musique et sa fameuse «joie de vivre». Beaucoup de visiteurs viennent° participer à ses fêtes, comme le carnaval du Mardi Gras ou le festival de jazz, en avril. Ils aiment aussi admirer ses nombreux bâtiments classés monuments historiques, comme le palais° du Cabildo ou la cathédrale Saint-Louis, la plus vieille° cathédrale des États-Unis. On ne doit pas quitter le Vieux Carré sans explorer les jardins et les patios cachés° de ses vieilles maisons de planteurs.

vie nocturne *night life* **viennent** *come* **palais** *palace* **la plus vieille** *the oldest* **cachés** *hidden*

SUR INTERNET

Qu'est-ce qu'on peut voir (*see*) au musée des Arts décoratifs de Paris?

Go to **espaces.vhlcentral.com** to find more cultural information related to this **ESPACE CULTURE**.

ACTIVITÉS

2 Complétez Complétez les phrases.

1. Le Vieux Carré est le centre historique de la Nouvelle-Orléans.
2. Il est connu pour sa culture créole, sa vie nocturne, sa musique et sa «joie de vivre».
3. Dans le Vieux Carré, il faut explorer les jardins et les patios cachés des vieilles maisons de planteurs.
4. Les Grimaldi habitent dans le Palais du Prince à Monaco.
5. L'hôtel Matignon est la résidence du Premier ministre français
6. L'impératrice Joséphine est née à la Pagerie, à la Martinique.

3 C'est le souk! Vos parents viennent vous rendre visite ce soir et votre colocataire a semé la pagaille dans tout l'appartement. C'est le souk! Avec un(e) partenaire, inventez une conversation où vous lui donnez des ordres pour nettoyer avant l'arrivée de vos parents. Jouez la scène devant la classe.

ressources

espaces.vhlcentral.com Leçon 16

Le français quotidien
- Model the pronunciation of each term and have students repeat it.
- Have volunteers create sentences using these words.

Portrait Ask students: **Que désirez-vous faire ou visiter dans le Vieux Carré de la Nouvelle-Orléans?**

Le monde francophone
- Bring in photos from magazines, books, or the Internet of these famous homes to show the class.
- Ask a few content questions based on the text. Examples: **1. Où est le Palais du Prince? (Il est à Monaco.) 2. Où habite le Premier ministre de la France? (l'hôtel Matignon) 3. Qui habite le Palais du Prince? (la famille princière de Monaco) 4. Comment s'appelle la maison natale de la femme de Napoléon? (la Pagerie)**

2 Expansion For additional practice, give students these items. **7. ____ sont deux fêtes célèbres à la Nouvelle-Orléans. (Le carnaval du Mardi Gras et le festival de jazz) 8. Le palais du Cabildo est à ____. (la Nouvelle-Orléans) 9. Le roi du Maroc habite ____. (le Palais royal de Rabat)**

3 Suggestion Encourage students to use terms in **Le français quotidien** in their role plays.

OPTIONS

Le Vieux Carré **Le palais du Cabildo** was completed in 1799. The ceremonies finalizing the Louisiana Purchase were held there in 1803. Since 1903, it has been the Louisiana State Museum. The museum contains a number of objects from Napoleonic history. The present-day **cathédrale Saint-Louis** was completed in 1851. Made of wood, the cathedral is dedicated to King Louis IX of France (1214–1279), who was canonized in 1297. His life is depicted in ten of the stained glass windows. This building is actually the third cathedral to occupy this site. The first cathedral was completed in 1727, but it burned down in 1788. The second was completed in 1794, but collapsed in 1849.

Section Goals

In this section, students will learn:
- to compare and contrast the uses and meanings of the **passé composé** and the **imparfait**
- common expressions indicating past tenses

Instructional Resources
WB/VM: Workbook, pp. 107–108
Lab Manual, p. 63
Lab MP3s
WB/VM/LM Answer Key
IRCD-ROM: Transparency #38
*IRM (**Essayez!** and **Mise en pratique** answers; Lab Audioscript)*
espaces.vhlcentral.com: activities, downloads, reference tools

Suggestions
- Have students make two flashcards. On one they write **passé composé** and on the other they write **imparfait**. Read a short text in which both verb tenses are used. As you read each verb, students show the appropriate card. Then call on a volunteer to write the conjugated verb form on the board.
- Give personalized examples as you contrast the **passé composé** and the **imparfait**. Examples: **La semaine dernière quand je faisais le ménage, quelqu'un m'a téléphoné. Je n'ai pas entendu le téléphone parce que je passais l'aspirateur.** Write your examples on the board and call on a volunteer to read the statements. Ask which verbs are in the **imparfait** and which are in the **passé composé**. Repeat with additional examples.
- Using **Transparency #38**, have students find examples of interrupted versus ongoing actions.
- Involve the class in a conversation about what they did in the past. Ask: ____, **faisiez-vous du vélo quand vous étiez petit(e)? Êtes-vous tombé(e) une fois? Et vous,** ____, **quand vous étiez petit(e), alliez-vous souvent en vacances avec votre famille? Où êtes-vous allé(e)?**

16.1 The *passé composé* vs. the *imparfait*

Point de départ Although the **passé composé** and the **imparfait** are both past tenses, they have very distinct uses and are not interchangeable. The choice between these two tenses depends on the context and on the point of view of the speaker.

J'ai rangé ma chambre pendant que tu faisais la lessive.

Tu les préparais quand tu m'as téléphoné?

Uses of the *passé composé*

To express actions that started and ended in the past and are viewed by the speaker as completed	J'**ai balayé** l'escalier deux fois. *I swept the stairs twice.*
To express the beginning or end of a past action	Le film **a commencé** à huit heures. *The movie began at 8 o'clock.* Ils **ont fini** le devoir hier. *They finished the homework yesterday.*
To narrate a series of past actions or events	Nous **avons fait** les lits, nous **avons rangé** les chambres et nous **avons passé** l'aspirateur. *We made the beds, tidied up the rooms, and vacuumed.*

Uses of the *imparfait*

To describe an ongoing past action with no reference to its beginning or end	Vous **faisiez** la lessive très tôt. *You were doing laundry very early.* Tu **attendais** dans le café? *Were you waiting in the café?*
To express habitual past actions and events	On **débarrassait** toujours la table à neuf heures. *We always cleared the table at 9 o'clock.*
To describe mental, physical, and emotional states or conditions	Mon ami **avait** faim et il **avait** envie de manger quelque chose. *My friend was hungry and felt like eating something.*

MISE EN PRATIQUE

1 Le week-end dernier Qu'est-ce que la famille Tran a fait le week-end dernier?

MODÈLE nous / passer le week-end / chez des amis
Nous avons passé le week-end chez des amis.

1. faire / beau / quand / nous / arriver
   Il faisait beau quand nous sommes arrivés.
2. nous / être / fatigué / mais content
   Nous étions fatigués mais contents.
3. Audrey et son amie / aller / à la piscine
   Audrey et son amie sont allées à la piscine.
4. moi, je / décider de / dormir un peu
   Moi, j'ai décidé de dormir un peu.
5. samedi soir / pleuvoir / quand / nous / sortir / cinéma
   Samedi soir, il pleuvait quand nous sommes sortis du cinéma.
6. nous / rire / beaucoup / parce que / film / être / amusant
   Nous avons beaucoup ri parce que le film était amusant.
7. minuit / nous / rentrer / chez nous
   À minuit, nous sommes rentrés chez nous.
8. Lanh / regarder / télé / quand / nous / arriver
   Lanh regardait la télé quand nous sommes arrivés.

2 Une surprise désagréable Récemment, Benoît a fait un séjour à Strasbourg avec un collègue. Complétez ses phrases avec l'imparfait ou le passé composé.

Ce matin, il (1) faisait (faire) chaud. J' (2) étais (être) content de partir pour Strasbourg. Je (3) suis parti (partir) pour la gare, où j' (4) ai retrouvé (retrouver) Émile. Le train (5) est arrivé (arriver) à Strasbourg à midi. Nous (6) avons commencé (commencer) notre promenade en ville. Nous (7) avions (avoir) besoin d'un plan. J' (8) ai cherché (chercher) mon portefeuille (*wallet*), mais il (9) était (être) toujours dans le train! Émile et moi, nous (10) avons couru à la gare!

3 Qu'est-ce qu'ils faisaient quand...? Que faisaient ces personnes au moment de l'interruption?
Suggested answers

MODÈLE
Papa débarrassait la table quand mon frère est arrivé.

débarrasser / arriver

1. sortir / dire
Ils sortaient la poubelle quand le voisin a dit bonjour.

3. faire / partir
Sa mère faisait la lessive quand Ann est partie.

2. passer / tomber
Michel passait l'aspirateur quand l'enfant est tombé.

4. laver / commencer
Ils lavaient la voiture quand il a commencé à pleuvoir.

OPTIONS

Pairs Ask students to narrate an embarrassing moment. Tell them to describe what happened and how they felt, using the **passé composé** and **imparfait.** Then have volunteers retell their partner's embarrassing moment using the third person. You may want to let students make up a fake embarrassing moment.

Small Groups Have students work in groups of four to write a short article about an imaginary road trip they took last summer. Students should use the **imparfait** to set the scene and the **passé composé** to narrate events. Each student should contribute three sentences to the article. When finished, have students read their article to the class.

COMMUNICATION

4 Situations Avec un(e) partenaire, parlez de ces situations en utilisant le passé composé ou l'imparfait. Comparez vos réponses, puis présentez-les à la classe. Answers will vary.

MODÈLE

Le premier jour de cours...
Étudiant(e) 1: *Le premier jour de cours, j'étais tellement nerveux que j'ai oublié mes livres.*
Étudiant(e) 2: *Moi, j'étais nerveux aussi, alors j'ai quitté ma résidence très tôt.*

1. Quand j'étais petit(e),...
2. L'été dernier,...
3. Hier soir, mon/ma petit(e) ami(e)...
4. Hier, le professeur...
5. La semaine dernière, mon/ma camarade de chambre...
6. Ce matin, au resto U,...
7. Quand j'étais au lycée,...
8. La dernière fois que j'étais en vacances,...

5 Votre premier/première petit(e) ami(e) Posez ces questions à un(e) partenaire. Ajoutez (*Add*) d'autres questions si vous voulez (*want*). Answers will vary.

1. Qui a été ton/ta premier/première petit(e) ami(e)?
2. Quel âge avais-tu quand tu as fait sa connaissance?
3. Comment était-il/elle?
4. Est-ce que tu as fait la connaissance de sa famille?
5. Pendant combien de temps êtes-vous sortis ensemble?
6. Où alliez-vous quand vous sortiez?
7. Aviez-vous les mêmes (*same*) centres d'intérêt?
8. Pourquoi avez-vous arrêté (*stopped*) de sortir ensemble?

6 Dialogue Jean-Michel, qui a seize ans, est sorti avec des amis hier soir. Quand il est rentré à trois heures du matin, sa mère était furieuse parce que ce n'était pas la première fois qu'il rentrait tard. Avec un(e) partenaire, préparez le dialogue entre Jean-Michel et sa mère. Answers will vary.

MODÈLE

Étudiant(e) 1: *Que faisais-tu à minuit?*
Étudiant(e) 2: *Mes copains et moi, nous sommes allés manger une pizza...*

- When the **passé composé** and the **imparfait** occur in the same sentence, the action in the **passé composé** often interrupts the ongoing action in the **imparfait**.

Vous **dormiez** et tout d'un coup, il **a téléphoné**.
You were sleeping, and all of a sudden he phoned.

Notre père **repassait** le linge quand vous **êtes arrivées**.
Our father was ironing when you arrived.

- Sometimes the use of the **passé composé** and the **imparfait** in the same sentence expresses a cause and effect.

J'**avais** faim, donc j'**ai mangé** quelque chose.
I was hungry so I ate something.

Elle **a dormi** parce qu'elle **avait** sommeil.
She slept because she was sleepy.

- The **passé composé** and the **imparfait** are often used together to narrate. The **imparfait** provides the background description, such as time, weather, and location. The **passé composé** indicates the specific events.

Il **était** deux heures et il **faisait** chaud. Les étudiants **attendaient** impatiemment les vacances d'été. Le prof **est entré** dans la salle pour leur donner les résultats...
It was 2 o'clock and it was hot. The students were waiting impatiently for their summer vacation. The professor came into the classroom to give them the results...

J'**avais** peur parce que j'**étais** seul dans la maison. Mes parents **allaient** chez des amis et le quartier **était** désert. Soudain, j'**ai entendu** quelque chose...
I was afraid because I was alone in the house. My parents were going to some friends' house and the neighborhood was deserted. Suddenly, I heard something...

- Certain adverbs often indicate a particular past tense.

Expressions that signal a past tense

passé composé		imparfait	
soudain	*suddenly*	**autrefois**	*in the past*
tout d'un coup	*all of a sudden*	**d'habitude**	*usually*
une (deux, etc.) fois	*once (twice, etc.)*	**parfois**	*sometimes*
		souvent	*often*
		toujours	*always*
		tous les jours	*every day*

Essayez! Donnez les formes correctes des verbes.

passé composé	imparfait
1. commencer (il) *il a commencé*	1. jouer (nous) *nous jouions*
2. acheter (tu) tu as acheté	2. être (tu) tu étais
3. boire (nous) nous avons bu	3. prendre (elles) elles prenaient
4. apprendre (ils) ils ont appris	4. avoir (vous) vous aviez
5. répondre (je) j'ai répondu	5. conduire (il) il conduisait

Essayez! Give items like these as additional practice. For the **passé composé: 6. descendre (elle) (elle est descendue) 7. lire (je) (j'ai lu)** For the **imparfait: 6. écrire (je) (j'écrivais) 7. dire (on) (on disait)**

1 Expansion Have volunteers explain why they chose the **passé composé** or **imparfait** in each case. Ask them to point out any words or expressions that triggered one tense or the other.

2 Suggestion Before assigning the activity, remind students that actions viewed as completed by the speaker take the **passé composé**. Have students give personal examples of actions in the past using this verb tense.

3 Suggestion Draw a line on the board and explain that it represents an ongoing past action with no beginning or end reference (**imparfait**). Make X marks along the line and explain that these represent actions with a beginning and an end or actions that interrupt the ongoing actions (**passé composé**). Use this visual aid to help students complete the activity aloud.

4 Expansion Have students choose one of these sentences to begin telling a short story in the past. Encourage students to use both the **passé composé** and the **imparfait.**

5 Expansion After completing the pair work, assign this activity as a short written composition.

6 Suggestions
- Act out the **modèle** with a volunteer before assigning this activity to pairs.
- Encourage students to use key adverbs to indicate the appropriate verb tenses in the dialogue. Examples: **soudain, tout d'un coup, autrefois**, etc.

OPTIONS

Extra Practice Make cards that contain adverbs and expressions that signal a past tense. Mix them up in a hat and have each student take one at random. Go around the room and have each student state the adverb or expression he or she has chosen and use it in a sentence with the **passé composé** or the **imparfait**. You may want to have the student say which tense he or she will use before formulating the sentence.

Small Groups Have students work in small groups to discuss their favorite movie or book. Students should use appropriate past tense forms to describe the main characters and give a brief summary of the plot. Encourage students to ask their classmates questions about the film or text.

Section Goals

In this section, students will learn the uses of **savoir** and **connaître**.

Instructional Resources
WB/VM: Workbook, pp. 109–110
Lab Manual, p. 64
Lab MP3s
WB/VM/LM Answer Key
*IRCD-ROM: IRM (**Essayez!** and **Mise en pratique** answers; Lab Audioscript; **Feuilles d'activités**)*
espaces.vhlcentral.com: activities, downloads, reference tools

Suggestions

- Model **savoir** by asking several questions with it. Examples: **____, savez-vous faire du ski? Et vous, ____, savez-vous où est la bibliothèque?** Next, write **connaître** on the board and ask questions, such as: **____, connaissez-vous mon frère? Connaissez-vous la Nouvelle-Orléans?** Ask students further questions using both verbs and help them infer the difference in use between the two.
- Point out that the context of the phrase will indicate which verb to use. Using examples in English, have students say which verb would be used for the French translation. Examples: I know how to swim. (**savoir**) He doesn't know the president. (**connaître**)
- Review the changes in meaning when **savoir** and **connaître** are used in the **imparfait** and **passé composé.**
- Prepare dehydrated sentences such as these: **Tu / savoir / que tu / ne pas connaître / mon petit ami; Nous / connaître / les nouveaux étudiants.** Write them on the board one at a time and have students complete them.

Essayez! Have students change the sentences to the past tense. Examples: **1. Je connaissais de bons restaurants. 2. Ils ne savaient pas parler allemand.**

16.2 The verbs *savoir* and *connaître*

Point de départ **Savoir** and **connaître** both mean *to know.* Their different uses depend on the context.

savoir* and *connaître

	savoir	connaître
je	sais	connais
tu	sais	connais
il/elle	sait	connaît
nous	savons	connaissons
vous	savez	connaissez
ils/elles	savent	connaissent

- **Savoir** means *to know facts* or *to know how to do something.*

Sait-elle chanter? *Does she know how to sing?*	Ils ne **savent** pas qu'il est parti. *They don't know that he left.*

- **Connaître** means *to know* or *be familiar with a person, place, or thing.*

Vous **connaissez** le prof. *You know the professor.*	Tu **connais** ce quartier? *Do you know that neighborhood?*

- In the **passé composé, savoir** and **connaître** have special connotations. **Savoir** in the **passé composé** means *found out.* **Connaître** in the **passé composé** means *met (for the first time).* Their past participles, respectively, are **su** and **connu.**

J'**ai su** qu'il y avait une fête. *I found out there was a party.*	Nous l'**avons connu** à la fac. *We met him at the university.*

- **Reconnaître** means *to recognize.* It follows the same conjugation patterns as **connaître.**

Mes profs de lycée me **reconnaissent** encore. *My high school teachers still recognize me.*	Nous **avons reconnu** vos enfants à la soirée. *We recognized your children at the party.*

Essayez! **Complétez les phrases avec les formes correctes des verbes savoir et connaître.**

1. Je __connais__ de bons restaurants.
2. Ils ne __savent__ pas parler allemand.
3. Vous __savez__ faire du cheval?
4. Tu __connais__ une bonne coiffeuse?
5. Nous ne __connaissons__ pas Jacques.
6. Claudette __sait__ jouer aux échecs.

MISE EN PRATIQUE

1 Les passe-temps Qu'est-ce que ces personnes savent faire?

MODÈLE
Patrick sait skier.

Patrick

1. Halima
Halima sait patiner.

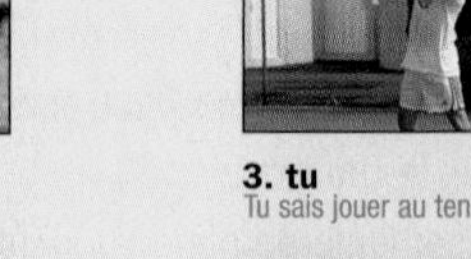
3. tu
Tu sais jouer au tennis.

2. vous
Vous savez nager.

4. nous
Nous savons jouer au foot.

2 Dialogues brefs Complétez les conversations avec le présent du verbe **savoir** ou **connaître.**

1. Marie __sait__ faire la cuisine?
   Oui, mais elle ne __connaît__ pas beaucoup de recettes (*recipes*).
2. Vous __connaissez__ les parents de François?
   Non, je __connais__ seulement sa cousine.
3. Tes enfants __savent__ nager dans la mer.
   Et mon fils aîné __connaît__ toutes les espèces de poissons.
4. Je __sais__ que le train arrive à trois heures.
   Est-ce que tu __sais__ à quelle heure il part?

3 Assemblez Assemblez les éléments des colonnes pour construire des phrases. Answers will vary.

MODÈLE *Je sais parler une langue étrangère.*

A	B	C
Gérard Depardieu Oprah je ton/ta camarade de chambre ?	(ne pas) connaître (ne pas) savoir ?	des célébrités faire la cuisine jouer dans un film Julia Roberts parler une langue étrangère ?

OPTIONS

Video Replay the video episode, having students focus on forms of **savoir** and **connaître**, as well as the use of the **imparfait** and the **passé composé.** Tell them to note when each one is used. Afterward, ask the class to describe the conversations that took place and what tenses were used. Have them identify the reason for this verb choice (a series of past actions, ongoing actions in the past, etc.).

Extra Practice Ask individual students questions using **savoir** and **connaître** that are most likely not true for them. When students give a negative answer, they should indicate someone else who would answer in the affirmative. Example: ____, **connaissez-vous le président des États-Unis? (Non, je ne le connais pas, mais le Premier ministre du Canada le connaît.)**

COMMUNICATION

4 Enquête Votre professeur va vous donner une feuille d'activités. Circulez dans la classe pour trouver au moins une personne différente qui donne une réponse affirmative à chaque question. Answers will vary.

Sujet	*Nom*
1. Sais-tu faire une mousse au chocolat?	*Jacqueline*
2. Connais-tu New York?	
3. Connais-tu le nom des sénateurs de cet état (state)?	
4. Connais-tu quelqu'un qui habite en Californie?	

5 Je sais faire Vous avez l'occasion de travailler chez une célébrité. Par groupes de trois, un(e) étudiant(e) joue le rôle de la personne célèbre et les deux autres jouent le rôle de la personne interviewée. Chacun(e) (*Each one*) essaie de montrer toutes les choses qu'il/elle sait faire. Answers will vary.

MODÈLE

Étudiant(e) 1: *Alors, vous savez faire la vaisselle?*
Étudiant(e) 2: *Je sais faire la vaisselle, et je sais faire la cuisine aussi.*
Étudiant(e) 3: *Moi, je sais faire la cuisine, mais il/elle ne sait pas passer l'aspirateur.*

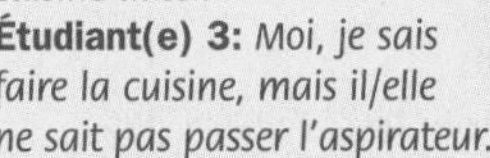

6 Questions À tour de rôle, posez ces questions à un(e) partenaire. Ensuite, présentez vos réponses à la classe. Answers will vary.

1. Quel bon restaurant connais-tu près d'ici? Est-ce que tu manges souvent là?
2. Dans ta famille, qui sait chanter le mieux (*best*)?
3. Connais-tu l'Europe? Quelles villes connais-tu?
4. Reconnais-tu toutes les chansons (*songs*) que tu entends à la radio?
5. Tes parents savent-ils utiliser Internet? Le font-ils bien?
6. Connais-tu un(e) acteur/actrice célèbre? Une autre personne célèbre?
7. Ton/Ta meilleur(e) (*best*) ami(e) sait-il/elle écouter quand tu lui racontes (*tell*) tes problèmes?
8. Connais-tu la date d'anniversaire de tous les membres de ta famille et de tous tes amis? Donne des exemples.

Le français vivant

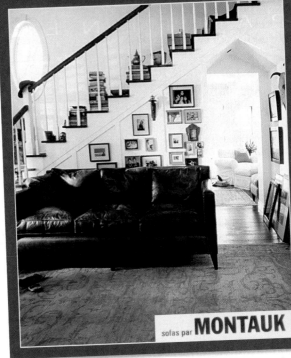

Vous saviez qu'être chez vous, c'est agréable. Avec les sofas par **Montauk**, vous connaissez aussi le confort et la joie d'être chez vous. Les sofas par **Montauk**: savoir qu'on connaît le bonheur.

sofas par **MONTAUK**

Identifiez Regardez la publicité et répondez à ces questions. Some answers will vary.

1. Quelles formes des verbes savoir et connaître avez-vous trouvées dans la pub? saviez, connaissez, savoir, connaît
2. Identifiez les objets sur la photo qui correspondent au vocabulaire de l'Unité 8.

Répondez Par groupes de trois, répondez aux questions. Answers will vary.

1. Aimez-vous être chez vous? Pourquoi?
2. Vos meubles vous donnent-ils envie de rester chez vous? Pourquoi?
3. Un meuble apporte-t-il vraiment du confort et de la joie?
4. Avez-vous envie d'habiter dans une maison comme ça? Pourquoi?
5. Y a-t-il une pièce que vous préférez dans votre maison? Laquelle? (*Which one?*)

1 Expansion Ask individual students questions about what they know how to do. Example: **Savez-vous parler espagnol? (Non, je ne sais pas parler espagnol.)**

2 Expansion Have students work in pairs to write three more sentences similar to those in the activity. Call on volunteers to present their sentences to the class.

3 Expansion Ask students questions about what certain celebrities know how to do or whom they know. Examples: **Est-ce que Brad Pitt connaît Jennifer Aniston? (Oui, il la connaît). Est-ce que Jennifer Lopez sait parler espagnol? (Oui, elle sait le parler).**

4 Suggestions
- Distribute the **Feuilles d'activités** from the IRM on the IRCD-ROM.
- Have students read through the list of questions using **savoir** and **connaître** for comprehension before completing the activity.

5 Suggestions
- Ask for three volunteers to act out the **modèle** for the class.
- Point out that **savoir** + *infinitive* means to know *how* to do something and that the *how* is built into this construction. Avoid the phrase **savoir comment**.

6 Expansion Ask these questions of the whole class. Ask students who answer in the affirmative for additional information. Examples: **Qui sait chanter? Chantez-vous bien? Chantiez-vous avec un groupe quand vous étiez jeune?**

Le français vivant
- Call on a volunteer to read the advertisement aloud.
- After completing **Identifiez**, have students explain and compare the uses of **savoir** and **connaître** in the ad.

OPTIONS

Extra Practice Have students write down three things they know how to do well (using **savoir** + *infinitive* + **bien**). Collect the papers, and then read the sentences. Tell students that they must not identify themselves when they hear their sentence. The rest of the class takes turns trying to guess who wrote each sentence. Repeat this activity with **connaître**.

Pairs Ask students to write brief, but creative, paragraphs in which they use **savoir** and **connaître**. Then have them exchange their papers with a partner. Tell students to help each other, through peer editing, to make the paragraphs as error-free as possible. Collect the papers for grading.

Instructional Resources
*IRCD-ROM: IRM (**Feuilles d'activités**; Info Gap Activities); Testing Program pp. 61–64; Test Files; Testing Program MP3s; Test Generator espaces.vhlcentral.com: activities, downloads, reference tools*

1 Expansion Tell students to imagine they are hosting their own dinner party. Have them make a list of tasks that must be completed before the guests arrive. Have them use the **passé composé**.

2 Suggestions
- Have two students say the **modèle** before distributing the **Feuilles d'activités** from the IRM on the IRCD-ROM.
- Before doing the activity, have students practice creating sentences using **connaître** in the **imparfait** and in the **passé composé**. Example: **J'ai connu la petite amie de Jacques en 2005. Je connais son ancienne petite amie.**

3 Suggestion Review the **imparfait** with the verb phrases listed in this activity. Ask volunteers to supply the correct verb forms for the subjects you suggest. Example: **repasser le ligne: je (je repassais le ligne)**.

4 Suggestion Have students bring photos from magazines or newspapers to supplement this activity. Or, students may prefer to sketch drawings of events.

5 Expansion Ask students to imagine that they are writing an e-mail home to their family expressing what they have learned and whom they have met since arriving at college. Instruct them to use similar sentence constructions as those presented in this activity.

6 Suggestion Divide the class into pairs and distribute the Info Gap Handouts in the IRM on the IRCD-ROM for this activity. Give students ten minutes to complete the activity.

Synthèse

1 Un grand dîner Émilie et son mari Vincent ont invité des amis à dîner ce soir. Qu'ont-ils fait cet après-midi pour préparer la soirée? Que vont-ils faire ce soir après le départ des invités? Conversez avec un(e) partenaire. Answers will vary.

MODÈLE

Étudiant(e) 1: *Cet après-midi, Émilie et Vincent ont mis la table.*

Étudiant(e) 2: *Ce soir, ils vont faire la vaisselle.*

2 Mes connaissances Votre professeur va vous donner une feuille d'activités. Interviewez vos camarades. Pour chaque personne, trouvez un(e) camarade différent(e) qui donne une réponse affirmative. Answers will vary.

Étudiant(e) 1: *Connais-tu une personne qui aime faire le ménage?*

Étudiant(e) 2: *Oui, autrefois mon père aimait bien faire le ménage.*

Activité	Nom
1. ne pas faire souvent la vaisselle	
2. aimer faire le ménage	Farid
3. dormir avec une couverture en été	
4. faire son lit tous les jours	
5. repasser rarement ses vêtements	

3 Qui faisait le ménage? Par groupes de trois, interviewez vos camarades. Qui faisait le ménage à la maison quand ils habitaient encore chez leurs parents? Préparez des questions avec ces expressions et comparez vos réponses. Answers will vary.

balayer	mettre et débarrasser la table
faire la lessive	passer l'aspirateur
faire le lit	ranger
faire la vaisselle	repasser le linge

4 Soudain! Tout était calme quand soudain... Avec un(e) partenaire, choisissez l'une des deux photos et écrivez un texte de dix phrases. Faites cinq phrases pour décrire la photo, et cinq autres pour raconter (*to tell*) un événement qui s'est passé soudainement (*that suddenly happened*). Employez des adverbes et soyez imaginatifs. Answers will vary.

5 J'ai appris... Qu'avez-vous appris ou qui connaissez-vous depuis que (*since*) vous êtes à la fac? Avec un(e) partenaire, faites une liste de cinq choses et de cinq personnes. À chaque fois, utilisez un imparfait et un passé composé dans vos explications. Answers will vary.

MODÈLE

Étudiant(e) 1: *Avant, je ne savais pas comment dire bonjour en français, et puis j'ai commencé ce cours, et maintenant, je sais le dire.*

Étudiant(e) 2: *Avant, je ne connaissais pas tous les pays francophones, et maintenant, je les connais.*

6 Élise fait sa lessive Votre professeur va vous donner, à vous et à votre partenaire, une feuille avec des dessins représentant Élise et sa journée d'hier. Attention! Ne regardez pas la feuille de votre partenaire. Answers will vary.

MODÈLE

Étudiant(e) 1: *Hier matin, Élise avait besoin de faire sa lessive.*

Étudiant(e) 2: *Mais, elle...*

ressources

WB	LM	Lab MP3s	espaces.vhlcentral.com
pp. 107–110	pp. 63–64	Leçon 16	Leçon 16

OPTIONS

Extra Practice Divide the class into three groups. One group is **savoir** (present tense with infinitive, **imparfait**), the second group is **connaître** (present tense, **imparfait**), and the third group is **savoir** and **connaître** (**passé composé**). Have each group brainstorm a list of phrases using their assigned verbs and tenses. A volunteer from each group should present their results to the class.

Example: Group 1 – **Je sais chanter. (présent) Ma mère savait parler français. (imparfait)** Group 2 – **Nous connaissons les nouveaux étudiants. (présent) Il connaissait le président des États-Unis. (imparfait)** Group 3 – **J'ai su que l'examen de français était très difficile. (passé composé) Mon père a connu mon petit ami. (passé composé)**

Mr. Propre

Mr. Clean est né en 1958, à Cincinnati, siège° de la compagnie Procter & Gamble. Il arrive en France en 1966, sous le nom de Mr. Propre. Il est alors fabriqué à Marseille, dans le sud de la France. En 1972, c'est le premier nettoyant° ménager parfumé de l'histoire°, un parfum au citron° qui masque sa forte odeur d'ammoniaque. À la même époque°, on entend ce slogan devenu° célèbre: «Mr. Propre rend° tout si propre que l'on peut se voir dedans°.» Aujourd'hui, Mr. Propre vend un flacon° toutes les secondes, dans plus de cinquante pays.

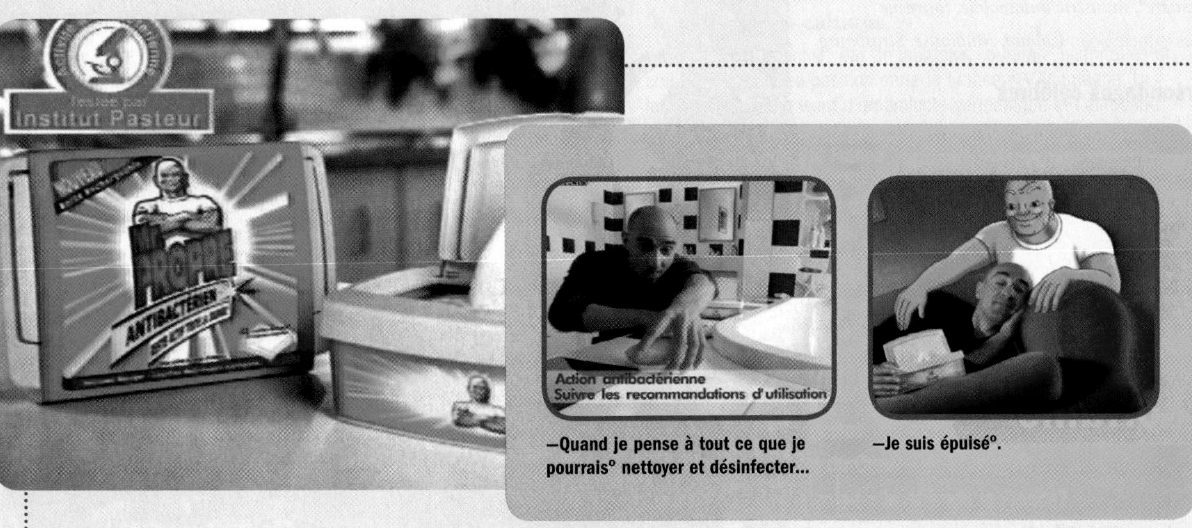

—Quand je pense à tout ce que je pourrais° nettoyer et désinfecter...

—Je suis épuisé°.

Compréhension Répondez aux questions. Answers will vary.

1. Que fait le personnage de la pub (*commercial*)?
2. Pourquoi a-t-il envie de dormir? Que fait Mr. Propre?

Recherche Avec un(e) partenaire, faites une recherche. Puis, comparez vos résultats avec un autre groupe. Answers will vary.

1. Recherchez d'autres produits ménagers dans les régions francophones (Belgique, France, Québec, Suisse).
2. Les produits ont-ils tous le même (*same*) nom qu'aux États-Unis? Comment s'appellent-ils?
3. Que font-ils dans la maison?

SUR INTERNET

Go to **espaces.vhlcentral.com** to watch the TV clip featured in this **Le zapping**.

siège *headquarters* **nettoyant** *cleaner* **de l'histoire** *in history* **citron** *lemon* **À la même époque** *At the same time* **devenu** *that has become* **rend** *makes* **que l'on peut se voir dedans** *that one can see his/her reflection* **flacon** *bottle* **pourrais** *could* **épuisé** *exhausted*

Section Goals

In this section, students will:

- read about Mr. Propre cleaning products
- watch a commercial for Mr. Propre cleaning wipes
- answer questions about the commercial

Instructional Resources
*IRCD-ROM: IRM (**Le zapping** TV clip transcription)*
espaces.vhlcentral.com: activities, downloads, reference tools, TV clip

Introduction
To check comprehension, ask these questions.
1. D'où vient Mr. Propre? (Il vient de Mr. Clean.)
2. Pourquoi Mr. Propre est-il unique en 1972? (parce qu'il est le premier nettoyant ménager parfumé de l'histoire, avec un parfum au citron qui masque sa forte odeur d'ammoniaque)
3. Quel est un slogan célèbre de Mr. Propre? («Mr. Propre rend tout si propre que l'on peut se voir dedans.»)

Avant de regarder la vidéo

- Have students look at the video stills, read the captions, and predict what is happening in the commercial for each visual. **(1. L'homme nettoie la salle de bain. 2. Il dort sur son canapé.)**
- Before showing the video, explain to students that they will hear the two captions for the video stills. Tell them to listen for them to try to complete the whole sentence with the text that comes in between the two.

Compréhension Have students work in pairs or groups for this activity. Tell them to write their answers. Then show the video again so that they can check their answers and add any missing information.

Discussion

- Have volunteers report back to the class the information they found about other cleaning products.
- Take a quick class survey to find out what these products are called and if their names are the same as in the U.S.

OPTIONS

Mr. Propre Mr. Propre was the first cleaning product to use lavender as a perfume in 1994. Lavender is one of the favorite scents of French people. In fact, staying in touch with consumer tastes and desires is one of the strengths of this brand. From 1996 to 1999, Mr. Propre's publicist has alternatively put emphasis on its power, sheen, or genius, to meet the ever-changing demands. Today, Mr. Propre has even managed to become a modern icon for younger people. You can download its ring tone to your cell phones, buy Mr. Propre tee-shirts to wear or get a Mr. Propre plastic bust to decorate your apartment.

Section Goals

In this section, students will learn and practice vocabulary related to:
- foods
- meals

Instructional Resources

*IRCD-ROM: Transparency #40; IRM (**Vocabulaire supplémentaire; Mise en pratique** answers; Textbook Audioscript; Lab Audioscript; **Feuilles d'activités**) Textbook MP3s WB/VM: Workbook, pp. 113–114 Lab Manual, p. 65 Lab MP3s WB/VM/LM Answer Key espaces.vhlcentral.com: activities, downloads, reference tools*

Suggestions

- Use **Transparency #40.** Point out foods as you describe the illustration. Examples: **Voici des fraises. Elle achète une pêche. Le garçon a acheté des œufs, un poivron vert et une laitue.**
- Ask students questions about their food preferences using the new vocabulary. **Préférez-vous les poires ou les fraises? Les oranges ou les bananes? Les tomates ou les champignons? Les escargots ou le thon? Le porc ou le poulet? La viande ou les fruits de mer?**
- Point out that **cuisiner** and **faire la cuisine** both mean *to cook.*
- Name some dishes and have students explain what ingredients are used to make them. Examples: **une salade de fruits, une salade mixte,** and **un sandwich.**
- Say food items and have students classify them in categories under the headings: **les fruits, les légumes, la viande,** and **le poisson.**
- Additional vocabulary for this lesson can be found in the **Vocabulaire supplémentaire** in the IRM on the IRCD-ROM.

Leçon 17

You will learn how to...
- **talk about food**
- **express needs, desires, and abilities**

Quel appétit!

Vocabulaire

cuisiner	*to cook*
faire les courses (*f.*)	*to go (grocery) shopping*
une cantine	*cafeteria*
un supermarché	*supermarket*
un aliment	*food*
un déjeuner	*lunch*
un dîner	*dinner*
un goûter	*afternoon snack*
la nourriture	*food, sustenance*
un petit-déjeuner	*breakfast*
un repas	*meal*
des petits pois (*m.*)	*peas*
une salade	*salad*
le bœuf	*beef*
un escargot	*escargot, snail*
les fruits de mer (*m.*)	*seafood*
un pâté (de campagne)	*pâté, meat spread*
le porc	*pork*
un poulet	*chicken*
une saucisse	*sausage*
un steak	*steak*
le thon	*tuna*
la viande	*meat*
le riz	*rice*
des pâtes (*f.*)	*pasta*
un yaourt	*yogurt*

ressources

WB	LM	Text MP3s	Lab MP3s	espaces.vhlcentral.com
pp. 113–114	p. 65	Leçon 17	Leçon 17	Leçon 17

OPTIONS

Extra Practice To review colors and practice new vocabulary, ask students to name foods that are different colors. Examples: **jaune (les bananes), rouge (les pommes, les tomates et les fraises), vert (les haricots verts et les petits pois), orange (les oranges et les carottes),** and **blanc (les oignons et le riz).**

Game Divide the class into two teams. Give one player a card with the name of a food item. That player is allowed 30 seconds to draw the item for another player on his or her team to guess. Award a point for a correct answer. If a player doesn't guess the correct answer, the next player on the opposing team may "steal" the point.

Projet

Créez une recette de cuisine

Vous êtes auteur de livres de cuisine et vous faites connaître la cuisine de votre région aux francophones du monde entier. Écrivez la recette° d'un plat° typique de votre région. Utilisez le système métrique.

1 Écrivez une recette

Créez une recette pour faire découvrir° aux francophones un plat de votre région. Avant de commencer à écrire, lisez quelques recettes en français pour connaître un peu le vocabulaire de la cuisine. Pour trouver des recettes en français et savoir comment convertir les mesures anglo-saxonnes dans le système métrique, explorez le lien° dans la boîte° **Sur Internet**. N'oubliez pas d'inclure ces éléments dans votre recette:

- le nom du plat
- une petite histoire du plat qui décrit les traditions de la région
- une liste d'ingrédients, avec les quantités indiquées dans le système métrique
- des instructions détaillées sur la préparation avec les verbes à l'infinitif
- une image du plat

2 Présentez la recette

Présentez la recette que vous avez écrite à votre classe avec l'image du plat. Faites goûter° votre plat à vos camarades si possible et répondez à leurs questions.

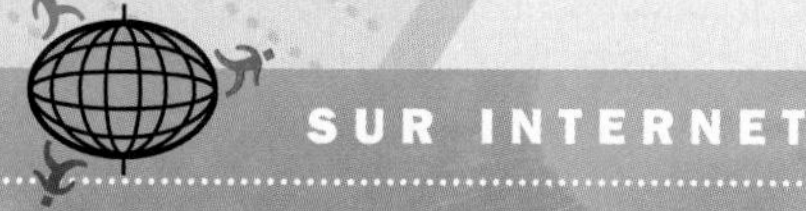

SUR INTERNET

Go to **espaces.vhlcentral.com** for more information related to this **Projet**.

recette *recipe* **plat** *dish* **découvrir** *to discover* **lien** *link* **boîte** *box*
Faites goûter *Have (them) taste*

Section Goals

In this section, students will:

- use French to carry out research and to interact with the wider world
- create a recipe typical of their region
- use the metric system

Instructional Resources
espaces.vhlcentral.com: activities, downloads, reference tools

Suggestion Students might need a week to complete the project, so at the beginning of that time period, have them read through **Projet**. Explain that they are going to write a recipe of a typical dish in their region for a cookbook for French speakers and present the recipe to the class.

Écrivez une recette

- Provide students with several cookbooks or recipes written in French. Ask them to discuss the differences between French recipes and those written in English. (the use of the metric system and weight vs. volume, for example)
- Students can look at several regional American cookbooks to determine some of the best examples of a particular area's cuisine. Have students be prepared to explain why they chose a certain recipe.

Présentez la recette

- Have students present their recipes in small groups. You may want to group students by region (New England, the Southwest, etc.) or by type of dish (breakfast, lunch, dinner, appetizers, main dishes, desserts, etc.)
- Encourage students to bring in dishes they have prepared.

EVALUATION

Criteria	Scale
Content	1 2 3 4
Comprehensibility	1 2 3 4
Organization	1 2 3 4
Accuracy	1 2 3 4
Use of visuals	1 2 3 4

Scoring	
Excellent	18–20 points
Good	14–17 points
Satisfactory	10–13 points
Unsatisfactory	< 10 points

Section Goals

In this section, students will learn and practice vocabulary related to:

- setting the table
- eating in a restaurant
- shopping for food

Instructional Resources
*IRCD-ROM: Transparency #41; IRM (**Vocabulaire supplémentaire; Mise en pratique** answers; Textbook Audioscript; Lab Audioscript; Info Gap Activities)*
Textbook MP3s
WB/VM: Workbook, pp. 119–120
Lab Manual, p. 69
Lab MP3s
WB/VM/LM Answer Key
espaces.vhlcentral.com: activities, downloads, reference tools

Suggestions

- Use **Transparency #41.** Describe what people are doing, then point out eating utensils and other items on the tables. Examples: **Le serveur apporte la carte. La femme commande. C'est une fourchette à côté de la serviette.**
- Ask students simple questions based on your narrative. Example: **Que fait le chef?**
- Bring in items for setting the table. Hold up each one and ask: **Qu'est-ce que c'est?**
- Explain that **le menu (fixe)** is a meal with limited choices from the main menu (**la carte**) for a set price, usually **une entrée**, **un plat**, and **un dessert**. Point out the French expression used in English **à la carte**.
- Point out that **une entrée** is *an appetizer*, not *a main course* as in English.
- Point out that **une assiette** is *a plate*, and **un plat** is *a serving dish* or the *food on the serving dish.*
- Explain the **faux ami: commander** means *to order*, not *to command.*
- Bring in photos from magazines or the Internet to introduce the names of the shops listed. Say: **C'est une boulangerie. On vend du pain à la boulangerie.**
- Additional vocabulary for this lesson can be found in the **Vocabulaire supplémentaire** in the IRM on the IRCD-ROM.

Leçon 18

You will learn how to...

- **describe and discuss food**
- **shop for food**

À table!

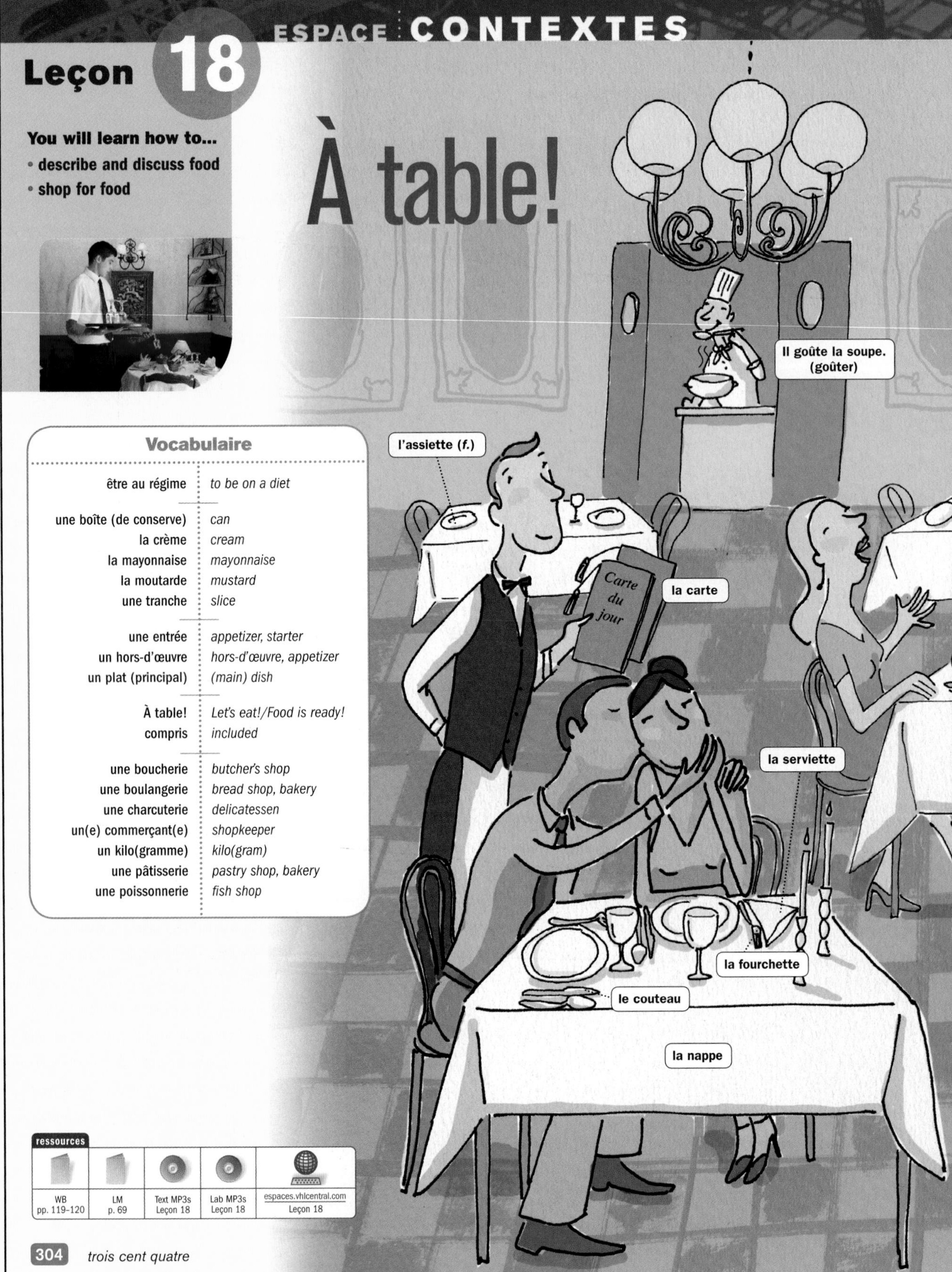

Vocabulaire

être au régime	*to be on a diet*
une boîte (de conserve)	*can*
la crème	*cream*
la mayonnaise	*mayonnaise*
la moutarde	*mustard*
une tranche	*slice*
une entrée	*appetizer, starter*
un hors-d'œuvre	*hors-d'œuvre, appetizer*
un plat (principal)	*(main) dish*
À table!	*Let's eat!/Food is ready!*
compris	*included*
une boucherie	*butcher's shop*
une boulangerie	*bread shop, bakery*
une charcuterie	*delicatessen*
un(e) commerçant(e)	*shopkeeper*
un kilo(gramme)	*kilo(gram)*
une pâtisserie	*pastry shop, bakery*
une poissonnerie	*fish shop*

ressources

WB	LM	Text MP3s	Lab MP3s	espaces.vhlcentral.com
pp. 119–120	p. 69	Leçon 18	Leçon 18	Leçon 18

OPTIONS

Game Write vocabulary words related to setting the table on index cards. On another set of cards, draw or paste pictures for each term. Tape them face down on the board. Divide the class into two teams. Then play a game of Concentration in which students match words with pictures. When a player makes a match, that player's team collects those cards. The team with the most cards at the end of the game wins.

Extra Practice Say the names of foods and have students respond with the type of store that sells each item. Examples: **un steak (une boucherie), des fruits de mer (une poissonnerie), des saucisses (une charcuterie), du pain (une boulangerie), de la moutarde (une épicerie), un gâteau (une pâtisserie), du pâté (une charcuterie),** and **du thon (une poissonnerie).**

Mise en pratique

1 Écoutez Catherine est au régime. Elle parle de ses habitudes alimentaires. Écoutez et indiquez si les affirmations suivantes sont **vraies** ou **fausses**.

	Vrai	Faux
1. Catherine mange beaucoup de desserts.	☐	☑
2. Catherine fait les courses au supermarché.	☐	☑
3. Elle adore la viande.	☐	☑
4. Elle est au régime.	☑	☐
5. Catherine achète des fruits et des légumes au marché.	☑	☐
6. Selon (*According to*) Catherine, le service chez les commerçants est désagréable.	☐	☑
7. Elle va souvent à la boucherie et à la poissonnerie.	☐	☑
8. Elle vient de devenir végétarienne.	☑	☐

2 Le repas Mettez ces différentes étapes dans l'ordre chronologique.

a. __5__ dire «À table!»
b. __7__ servir le plat principal
c. __4__ mettre les assiettes, les fourchettes, les cuillères et les couteaux sur la table
d. __6__ servir l'entrée
e. __2__ faire les courses
f. __1__ organiser un menu
g. __8__ goûter le dessert avec les invités
h. __3__ faire la cuisine

3 Complétez Complétez les phrases suivantes avec le bon mot pour faire une phrase logique.

1. Pour manger de la soupe on utilise...
   a. un couteau.
   (b.) une cuillère.
   c. une fourchette.
2. On sert la soupe dans...
   a. une assiette.
   b. une carafe.
   (c.) un bol.
3. Au restaurant le serveur/ la serveuse doit... la nourriture.
   a. commander
   (b.) apporter
   c. goûter
4. On vend des baguettes à...
   (a.) la boulangerie.
   b. la charcuterie.
   c. la boucherie.
5. On met... dans le café.
   a. du beurre
   b. du poivre
   (c.) de la crème
6. On vend des gâteaux à...
   a. la boucherie.
   (b.) la pâtisserie.
   c. la poissonnerie.
7. Au restaurant, on commande d'abord...
   (a.) une entrée.
   b. un plat principal.
   c. une serviette.
8. On vend du jambon à...
   (a.) la charcuterie.
   b. la boucherie.
   c. la pâtisserie.

1 Tapescript Je suis au régime, alors je ne peux pas manger beaucoup de desserts, ou bien, de pain en général. Parfois, je vais à la boulangerie et j'achète des croissants pour le petit-déjeuner, mais je les prends sans confiture. Quand je mange une salade, je n'utilise jamais d'huile d'olive. Je fais très attention à ce que je mange et je ne mets pas trop de sel dans mes plats. J'utilise très peu de poivre parce que je n'aime pas beaucoup ça. Chaque semaine quand je fais les courses, je vais à la boulangerie pour acheter du pain. Pour les fruits et les légumes, je vais au marché. Je vais rarement au supermarché; je préfère aller chez les commerçants parce que le service est très agréable. Je ne vais jamais ni à la boucherie ni à la poissonnerie parce que je viens de devenir végétarienne. *(On Textbook MP3s)*

1 Suggestion Have students read the true/false sentences before they listen to the recording.

2 Suggestion Have students form groups of eight. Make a set of individual phrases on strips of paper for each group and distribute them. Tell students to arrange the phrases in the proper order and then read them aloud.

3 Expansion For additional practice, give students these items. **9. Pour manger du bœuf on utilise ____. (une fourchette et un couteau) 10. On sert de la salade dans ____. (un bol/une assiette) 11. Au restaurant, après l'entrée on commande ____. (le plat principal) 12. On vend du pâté dans les ____. (charcuteries)**

OPTIONS

Mettre la table A typical French table setting has at least two stemmed glasses per person. If they are not the same size, the larger goblet is for water and the smaller one is for wine. In more formal table settings, there may be several glasses for different types of wine. Champagne is served in tall glasses called **flûtes**; white wine may be served in smaller glasses than red wine. When placing cutlery, knives go on the right with the blade turned toward the plate, and forks go on the left, tines down. Soupspoons are placed next to the forks, on the outside. Teaspoons or dessert forks belong above the plate. A French place setting may also include **un porte-couteau**, which serves to protect the tablecloth.

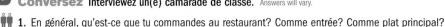

4 Suggestions
- Before beginning the activity, give students a few minutes to think about their responses to these questions.
- Tell students to jot down notes during their interviews. Then have volunteers share their partner's responses with the class.

5 Suggestion Have two volunteers read the **modèle** aloud. Then divide the class into pairs and distribute the Info Gap Handouts in the IRM on the IRCD-ROM for this activity. Give students ten minutes to complete the activity.

6 Suggestion Give each group a menu from a real French restaurant to use in their role plays. Many restaurants include sample menus on their web sites.

7 Suggestions
- Before beginning the activity, have students describe what they see in the drawing.
- Have students exchange paragraphs for peer editing. Students should make sure all required elements are included and underline grammar and spelling errors.

Communication

NATIONAL STANDARDS communication

4 Conversez Interviewez un(e) camarade de classe. Answers will vary.

1. En général, qu'est-ce que tu commandes au restaurant? Comme entrée? Comme plat principal?
2. Qui fait les courses chez toi? Où? Quand?
3. Est-ce que tu préfères faire les courses au supermarché ou chez les commerçants? Pourquoi?
4. Es-tu au régime? Qu'est-ce que tu manges?
5. Quel est ton plat principal préféré?
6. Aimes-tu la moutarde? Avec quel(s) plat(s) l'utilises-tu?
7. Aimes-tu la mayonnaise? Avec quel(s) plat(s) l'utilises-tu?
8. Dans quel(s) plat(s) mets-tu de l'huile d'olive?

5 Sept différences Votre professeur va vous donner, à vous et à votre partenaire, deux feuilles d'activités différentes avec le dessin (*drawing*) d'un restaurant. Il y a sept différences entre les deux images. Sans regarder l'image de votre partenaire, comparez vos dessins et faites une liste de ces différences. Quel est le groupe le plus rapide de la classe?

MODÈLE

Étudiant(e) 1: *Dans mon restaurant, le serveur apporte du beurre à la table.*
Étudiant(e) 2: *Dans mon restaurant aussi, on apporte du beurre à la table, mais c'est une serveuse, pas un serveur.*

6 Au restaurant Travaillez avec deux camarades de classe pour présenter le dialogue suivant. Answers will vary.

- Une personne invite un(e) ami(e) à dîner au restaurant.
- Une personne est le serveur/la serveuse et décrit le menu.
- Vous parlez du menu et de vos préférences.
- Une personne est au régime et ne peut pas manger certains ingrédients.
- Vous commandez les plats.
- Vous parlez des plats que vous mangez.

7 Écriture Écrivez un paragraphe dans lequel vous: Answers will vary.

- parlez de la dernière fois que vous avez préparé un dîner, un déjeuner ou un petit-déjeuner pour quelqu'un.
- décrivez les ingrédients que vous avez utilisés pour préparer le(s) plat(s).
- mentionnez les endroits où vous avez acheté les ingrédients et leurs quantités.
- décrivez comment vous avez mis la table.

OPTIONS

Game Toss a beanbag to a student at random and say the name of a store from this lesson or a previous one. The person has four seconds to name a food that is sold there. That person then tosses the beanbag to another student and names a store. Students who cannot think of a food in time or repeat an item that has already been mentioned are eliminated. The last person standing wins.

Small Groups Have groups of students plan a dinner party for a group of celebrities. Tell them to decide who will attend and what foods will be served. The meal should include several courses and appropriate beverages. You might want to bring in French cookbooks or food magazines for students' reference. Have the class vote on the most delicious-sounding meal and the most interesting guest list.

Les sons et les lettres

Stress and rhythm

In French, all syllables are pronounced with more or less equal stress, but the final syllable in a phrase is elongated slightly.

Je fais souvent du sport, mais aujourd'hui j'ai envie de rester à la maison.

French sentences are divided into three basic kinds of rhythmic groups.

Noun phrase	*Verb phrase*	*Prepositional phrase*
Caroline et Dominique	**sont venues**	**chez moi.**

The final syllable of a rhythmic group may be slightly accentuated either by rising intonation (pitch) or elongation.

Caroline et Dominique sont venues chez moi.

In English, you can add emphasis by placing more stress on certain words. In French, you can repeat the word to be emphasized by adding a pronoun or you can elongate the first consonant sound.

Je ne sais pas, moi. **Quel idiot!** **C'est fantastique!**

Prononcez Répétez les phrases suivantes à voix haute.

1. Ce n'est pas vrai, ça.
2. Bonjour, Mademoiselle.
3. Moi, je m'appelle Florence.
4. La clé de ma chambre, je l'ai perdue.
5. Je voudrais un grand café noir et un croissant, s'il vous plaît.
6. Nous allons tous au marché, mais Marie, elle va au centre commercial.

Articulez Répétez les phrases en mettant l'emphase sur les mots indiqués.

1. C'est *impossible*!
2. Le film était *super*!
3. Cette tarte est *délicieuse*!
4. Quelle idée *extraordinaire*!
5. Ma sœur parle *constamment*.

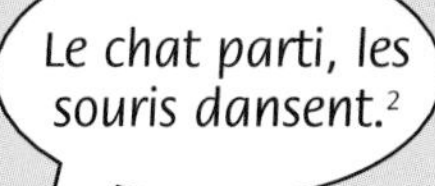

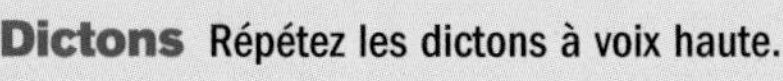

Le chat parti, les souris dansent.[2]

Dictons Répétez les dictons à voix haute.

Les chemins les plus courts ne sont pas toujours les meilleurs.[1]

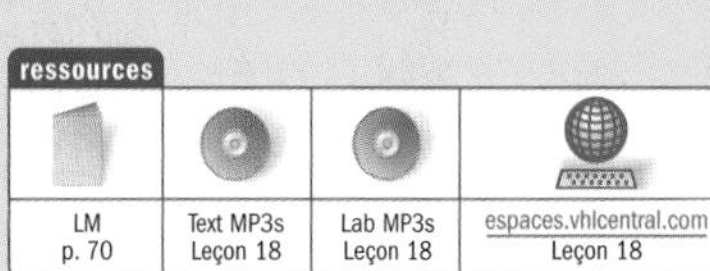

ressources
LM p. 70
Text MP3s Leçon 18
Lab MP3s Leçon 18
espaces.vhlcentral.com Leçon 18

1 The shortest paths aren't always the best.
2 When the cat is away, the mice will play.

Section Goals

In this section, students will learn about:

- stress and rhythm
- a strategy for emphasizing a word

Instructional Resources
Textbook MP3s
Lab Manual, p. 70
Lab MP3s
WB/VM/LM Answer Key
IRCD-ROM: IRM (Textbook Audioscript; Lab Audioscript)
espaces.vhlcentral.com: activities, downloads, reference tools

Suggestions

- Model the pronunciation of the example sentences and have students repeat after you.
- Write these sentences from the **Roman-photo** in **Leçon 17** on the board or a transparency. **1. Mais quelle heure est-il? 2. Bon, une salade, si tu veux. 3. Mais le bœuf bourguignon, c'est long à préparer, non? 4. Il nous faut des champignons, du jambon et du fromage.** Say the sentences and have students repeat after you. Alternately, have students read the entire video episode aloud in small groups, focusing on correct stress and rhythm.
- Have students read the sentences in the **Articulez** activity more than once, using a variety of methods to place emphasis on the appropriate words, for example, pauses before the word or between syllables.
- Prepare a handout that has several sentences with varied rhythm and stress. Tell students to draw arrows to mark rising and falling intonation as you read the sentences aloud.

OPTIONS

Extra Practice Use these sentences for additional practice with stress and rhythm or as a dictation. **1. Ils préfèrent aller au cinéma. 2. Mon anniversaire, c'est le 14 octobre. 3. Charlotte est professeur d'anglais dans un lycée en France. 4. Pour mes vacances, il me faut un maillot de bain, un short et des lunettes de soleil.**

Extra Practice To practice varying stress and rhythm, teach students these French tongue-twisters. **1. Mur pourrit, trou s'y fit, rat s'y mit; chat l'y vit, rat s'enfuit; chat suivit, rat fut pris. 2. Bonjour, Madame Sans Souci. Combien sont ces six saucissons-ci et combien sont ces six saucissons-là? Six sous, Madame, sont ces six saucissons-ci et six sous aussi sont ces six saucissons-là!**

Section Goals

In this section, students will learn functional phrases for making comparisons and discussing a meal.

Instructional Resources
WB/VM: Video Manual, pp. 245–246
WB/VM/LM Answer Key
Video CD-ROM
Video on DVD
IRCD-ROM: IRM (Videoscript; ***Roman-photo*** *Translations)*
espaces.vhlcentral.com: activities, downloads, reference tools

Video Recap: Leçon 17
Before doing this **Roman-photo**, review the previous one with this activity.
1. Pourquoi Sandrine a-t-elle retrouvé Amina et David au supermarché? (pour faire les courses pour son dîner)
2. Pourquoi Stéphane a-t-il voulu parler à Sandrine? (Il a voulu savoir à quelle heure il doit arriver chez elle et s'il doit apporter quelque chose.)
3. Qu'est-ce que Sandrine a décidé de préparer? (un poulet à la crème aux champignons avec un gratin de pommes de terre)
4. Qui a payé les courses au supermarché? (Amina et David)

Video Synopsis
David runs into Rachid in town. Rachid has bought a box of chocolates for Sandrine. David decides to buy her a bouquet of flowers. That evening, the guests arrive at Sandrine's. Sandrine is pleased with her gifts. Amina and Stéphane finish setting the table, and they all sit down to eat. The meal is a great success, and everyone compliments Sandrine on her cooking.

Suggestions
- Have students predict what the episode will be about based on the title and video stills.
- After reading the **Roman-photo**, review students' predictions and have them summarize the episode.

Le dîner

PERSONNAGES

Amina

David

Rachid

Sandrine

Stéphane

Valérie

Au centre-ville...
DAVID Qu'est-ce que tu as fait en ville?
RACHID Des courses à la boulangerie et chez le chocolatier.
DAVID Tu as acheté ces chocolats pour Sandrine?
RACHID Pourquoi? Tu es jaloux? Ne t'en fais pas! Elle nous a invités, il est normal d'apporter quelque chose.

DAVID Je n'ai pas de cadeau pour elle. Qu'est-ce que je peux lui acheter? Je peux lui apporter des fleurs!
Chez le fleuriste...
DAVID Ces roses sont très jolies, non?
RACHID Tu es tombé amoureux?
DAVID Mais non! Pourquoi tu dis ça?
RACHID Des roses, c'est romantique.
DAVID Ah... Ces fleurs-ci sont jolies. C'est mieux?

RACHID Non, c'est pire! Les chrysanthèmes sont réservés aux funérailles.
DAVID Hmmm. Je ne savais pas que c'était aussi difficile de choisir un bouquet de fleurs!
RACHID Regarde! Celles-là sont parfaites!
DAVID Tu es sûr?
RACHID Sûr et certain, achète-les!

AMINA Sandrine, est-ce qu'on peut faire quelque chose pour t'aider?
SANDRINE Oui euh, vous pouvez finir de mettre la table, si vous voulez.
VALÉRIE Je vais t'aider dans la cuisine.
AMINA Tiens, Stéphane. Voilà le sel et le poivre. Tu peux les mettre sur la table, s'il te plaît.
SANDRINE À table!

SANDRINE Je vous sers autre chose? Une deuxième tranche de tarte aux pommes peut-être?
VALÉRIE Merci.
AMINA Merci. Je suis au régime.
SANDRINE Et toi, David?
DAVID Oh! J'ai trop mangé. Je n'en peux plus!
STÉPHANE Moi, je veux bien...
SANDRINE Donne-moi ton assiette.

STÉPHANE Tiens, tu peux la lui passer, s'il te plaît?
VALÉRIE Quel repas fantastique, Sandrine. Tu as beaucoup de talent, tu sais.
RACHID Vous avez raison, Madame Forestier. Ton poulet aux champignons était superbe!

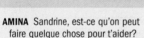

ACTIVITÉS

1 Vrai ou faux? Indiquez si les affirmations suivantes sont **vraies** ou **fausses**.

1. Rachid est allé chez le chocolatier. Vrai.
2. Rachid et David sont arrivés en avance. Faux.
3. David n'a pas apporté de cadeau. Faux.
4. Sandrine aime les fleurs de David. Vrai.
5. Personne (*Nobody*) n'aide Sandrine. Faux.
6. David n'a pas beaucoup mangé. Faux.
7. Stéphane n'est pas au régime. Vrai.
8. Sandrine a fait une tarte aux pêches pour le dîner. Faux.
9. Les plats de Sandrine ne sont pas très bons. Faux.
10. Les invités ont passé une soirée très agréable. Vrai.

OPTIONS

Avant de regarder la vidéo Before viewing the video, have students brainstorm a list of things people might say at a dinner party. What expressions might they use before, during, and after a meal? Write the list on the board.

Regarder la vidéo Photocopy the videoscript from the IRM. Then white out words related to meals, eating, and other key vocabulary in order to create a master for a cloze activity. Distribute the photocopies and tell students to fill in the missing information as they watch the video episode.

Sandrine a préparé un repas fantastique pour ses amis.

Chez Sandrine...

SANDRINE Bonsoir... Entrez! Oh!

DAVID Tiens. C'est pour toi.

SANDRINE Oh, David! Il ne fallait pas, c'est très gentil!

DAVID Je voulais t'apporter quelque chose.

SANDRINE Ce sont les plus belles fleurs que j'aie jamais reçues! Merci!

RACHID Bonsoir, Sandrine.

SANDRINE Oh, du chocolat! Merci beaucoup.

RACHID J'espère qu'on n'est pas trop en retard.

SANDRINE Pas du tout! Venez! On est dans la salle à manger.

STÉPHANE Oui, et tes desserts sont les meilleurs! C'est la tarte la plus délicieuse du monde!

SANDRINE Vous êtes adorables, merci. Moi, je trouve que cette tarte aux pommes est meilleure que la tarte aux pêches que j'ai faite il y a quelques semaines.

AMINA Tout ce que tu prépares est bon, Sandrine.

DAVID À Sandrine, le chef de cuisine le plus génial!

TOUS À Sandrine!

Expressions utiles

Making comparisons and judgments

- **Ces fleurs-ci sont jolies. C'est mieux?**
  These flowers are pretty. Is that better?
- **C'est pire! Les chrysanthèmes sont réservés aux funérailles.**
  It's worse! Chrysanthemums are reserved for funerals.
- **Je ne savais pas que c'était aussi difficile de choisir un bouquet de fleurs!**
  I didn't know it was so hard to choose a bouquet of flowers!
- **Ce sont les plus belles fleurs que j'aie jamais reçues!**
  These are the most beautiful flowers I have ever received!
- **C'est la tarte la plus délicieuse du monde!**
  This is the most delicious tart in the world!
- **Cette tarte aux pommes est meilleure que la tarte aux pêches.**
  This apple tart is better than the peach tart.

Additional vocabulary

- **Ah, tu es jaloux? Ne t'en fais pas!**
  Are you jealous? Don't be!/Don't make anything of it!
- **sûr(e) et certain(e)**
  totally sure/completely certain
- **Il ne fallait pas.**
  You shouldn't have./It wasn't necessary.
- **J'ai trop mangé. Je n'en peux plus!**
  I ate too much. I can't fit anymore!
- **Tu peux la lui passer?**
  Can you pass it to her?

ACTIVITÉS

2 Questions Répondez aux questions suivantes. Answers may vary slightly.

1. Qu'est-ce que Rachid a apporté à Sandrine?
   Il lui a apporté des chocolats.
2. Qu'a fait Amina pour aider?
   Elle a fini de mettre la table.
3. Qui mange une deuxième tranche de tarte aux pommes?
   Stéphane la mange.
4. Quelle type de tarte Sandrine a-t-elle préparée il y a quelques semaines?
   Elle a préparé une tarte aux pêches.
5. Pourquoi David n'a-t-il pas acheté les roses?
   Il ne les a pas achetées parce que (Rachid lui a dit que) les roses sont romantiques.

3 Écrivez David veut raconter le dîner de Sandrine à sa famille. Composez un e-mail. Quels ont été les préparatifs (*preparations*)? Qui a apporté quoi? Qui est venu? Qu'est-ce qu'on a mangé? Relisez l'**ESPACE ROMAN-PHOTO** de la Leçon 17 si nécessaire.

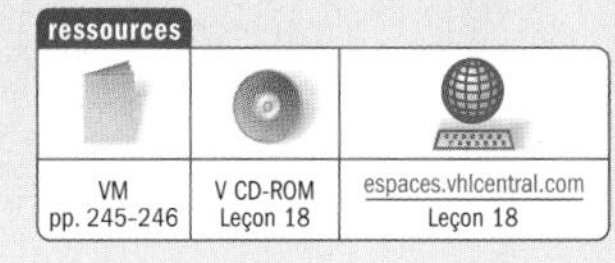

ressources
VM pp. 245-246
V CD-ROM Leçon 18
espaces.vhlcentral.com Leçon 18

Expressions utiles
- Model the pronunciation of the **Expressions utiles** and have students repeat them after you.
- As you work through the list, point out the comparative and superlative expressions and double object pronouns. Explain that **mieux** and **meilleur** both mean *better*, but one is an adverb and one is an adjective. Tell students that these constructions will be formally presented in the **Structures** section.
- Respond briefly to questions about the comparative, the superlative, and double object pronouns. Reinforce correct forms, but do not expect students to produce them consistently at this time.
- Tell students that the expression **je n'en peux plus** is used to say, "*I'm full.*" They should not use the word **plein(e)** in this context.

1 Suggestion Have students correct the false statements and write their corrections on the board.

1 Expansion For additional practice, give students these items. **11. David achète les roses. (Faux.) 12. Valérie aide Sandrine dans la cuisine. (Vrai.) 13. Amina est au régime. (Vrai.) 14. Sandrine n'aime pas sa tarte aux pommes. (Faux.)**

2 Expansion For additional practice, give students these items. **6. Pourquoi est-ce que David et Rachid ont acheté des cadeaux pour Sandrine? (Ils vont dîner chez elle.) 7. Qu'est-ce que Sandrine a préparé pour le dîner? (un poulet aux champignons)**
8. Pourquoi est-ce que David n'a pas acheté les chrysanthèmes? (Les chrysanthèmes sont pour les funérailles.)

3 Suggestion Tell students to jot down the answers to the questions before they begin to compose their e-mail.

OPTIONS

Extra Practice Using the **Roman-photo** as a model, have students write a conversation that takes place at a dinner party. The host or hostess should offer foods, which the guests politely accept or refuse. As each dish is served, guests should comment on the quality of the food. Remind students to use as many of the **Expressions utiles** as they can.

Les fleurs et les sentiments Various flowers are associated with specific sentiments. Much of the symbolism has been forgotten today, but some traditions stemming from the "language" of flowers remain in French culture. For example, red roses are romantic. Chrysanthemums bloom in the fall, so these flowers were placed on graves on All Saints' Day (November 1st). Now they are a traditional flower for funerals.

Section Goals

In this section, students will:
- learn about meals and eating habits in France
- learn some terms for methods of preparing food
- learn some tips about dining manners in France and North Africa
- read about the popularity of North African food in France

Instructional Resources
espaces.vhlcentral.com: activities, downloads, reference tools

Culture à la loupe
Avant la lecture Have students look at the photos, identify the meals, and describe what they see.

Lecture
- Explain that large family meals consisting of many courses typically take place on Sunday afternoons and on holidays.
- Point out the **Coup de main** and model the pronunciation of the terms. Ask: **Comment préférez-vous votre steak? À point? Bien cuit?**
- Point out the chart **Les Français et les repas**. Ask students what type of information is contained in this chart. (statistics about French meals and eating habits)

Après la lecture Ask students to name the courses in a large French meal in chronological order as you write them on the board.

1 Suggestion Have students read the sentences aloud in the text where they found the correct answers.

CULTURE À LA LOUPE

Les repas en France

En France, un grand repas traditionnel peut être composé de beaucoup de plats différents et il peut durer° plusieurs heures. Avant de passer à table, on sert des amuse-gueules° comme des biscuits salés°, des olives ou des cacahuètes°. Ensuite, on commence le repas par un hors-d'œuvre ou directement par une ou deux entrées chaudes ou froides, comme une soupe, de la charcuterie, des escargots, etc. Après l'entrée, on prend parfois un sorbet pour nettoyer le palais°. Puis, on passe au plat principal, qui est en général une viande ou un poisson servi avec des légumes. Après, on apporte la salade, puis le fromage et enfin, on sert le dessert et le café. Le grand repas traditionnel est accompagné de vin, et dans les grandes occasions, de champagne pour le dessert.

Bien sûr, tous les Français ne font pas ce genre de grand repas tous les jours. En général, on mange beaucoup plus simplement. Au petit-déjeuner, on boit du café au lait, du thé ou du chocolat chaud. On mange des tartines° ou du pain grillé° avec du beurre et de la confiture, et des croissants le week-end. Le déjeuner est traditionnellement le repas principal, mais aujourd'hui, les Français n'ont pas souvent le temps de rentrer à la maison. Pour cette raison, on mange de plus en plus° au travail ou au café. Après l'école, les enfants prennent parfois un goûter, par exemple du pain avec du chocolat. Et le soir, on dîne à la maison, en famille.

durer *last* **amuse-gueules** *small appetizers* **salés** *salty* **cacahuètes** *peanuts* **palais** *palate* **tartines** *slices of bread* **pain grillé** *toast* **de plus en plus** *more and more* **moins de** *less than*

Les Français et les repas

- 10% des Français ne prennent pas de petit-déjeuner.
- 60% boivent du café le matin, 20% du thé, 15% du chocolat.
- 99% dînent chez eux en semaine.
- 35% dînent en famille, 30% en couple.
- 75% des dîners consistent en moins de° trois plats successifs.
- Le pain est présent dans plus de 60% des déjeuners et des dîners.

Coup de main

You can use these terms to specify how you would like meat to be cooked.

bleu(e)	*very rare*
saignant(e)	*medium rare*
à point	*medium*
bien cuit(e)	*well-done*

ACTIVITÉS

1 Vrai ou faux? Indiquez si les phrases sont **vraies** ou **fausses**. Corrigez les phrases fausses.

1. On mange les hors-d'œuvres avant les amuse-gueules.
   Faux. On mange les amuse-gueules avant les hors-d'œuvres.
2. On prend parfois un sorbet après l'entrée.
   Vrai.
3. En France, on mange la salade en entrée.
   Faux. On mange la salade après le plat principal.
4. En général, on ne boit pas de vin pendant le repas.
   Faux. En général, on boit du vin pendant le repas.
5. On sert le fromage entre la salade et le dessert.
   Vrai.
6. Les Français mangent souvent des œufs au petit-déjeuner. Faux. Ils mangent des tartines ou du pain grillé avec du beurre et de la confiture ou des croissants le week-end.
7. Tous les Français mangent un grand repas traditionnel chaque soir.
   Faux. En général, on mange plus simplement.
8. Le déjeuner est traditionnellement le repas principal de la journée en France.
   Vrai.
9. À midi, les Français mangent toujours à la maison.
   Faux. Ils mangent de plus en plus souvent au travail ou au café.
10. Les enfants prennent parfois un goûter après l'école.
    Vrai.

OPTIONS

Cultural Comparison Have students work in groups of three and compare a large, traditional French meal with a typical, large American meal. Tell them to list the similarities and differences in a two-column chart under the headings **Similitudes** and **Différences**. After completing the charts, have volunteers read their lists aloud.

Les Français et les repas Have students write five true/false sentences based on the information in the chart. Then tell them to exchange papers with a classmate and complete the activity. Remind them to verify their answers.

LE FRANÇAIS QUOTIDIEN

Au menu

côtelette (*f.*)	*chop*
escalope (*f.*)	*thin slice of meat or fish*
faux-filet (*m.*)	*sirloin steak*
à la vapeur	*steamed*
farci(e)	*stuffed*
frit(e)	*fried*
garni(e)	*garnished*
rôti(e)	*roasted*

PORTRAIT

La couscousmania des Français

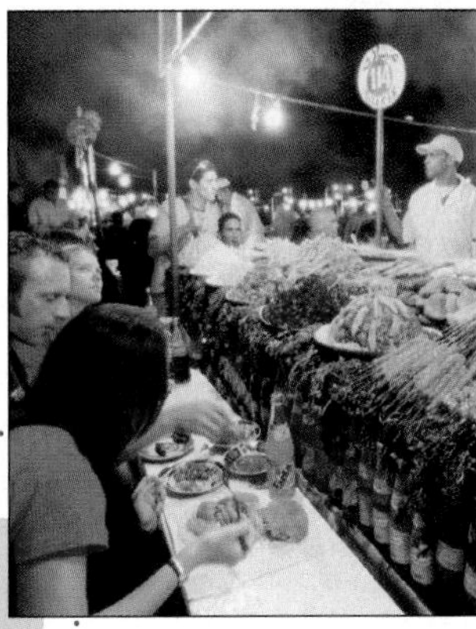

La cuisine du Maghreb est très populaire en France. Les restaurants orientaux sont nombreux et appréciés pour la qualité de leur nourriture et leur ambiance. Les merguez, des petites saucisses rouges pimentées°, sont vendues dans toutes les boucheries. Dans les grandes villes, des pâtisseries au miel° sont dégustées° au goûter. Le plat le plus célèbre reste le couscous, le quatrième plat préféré des Français, devant le steak frites! Aujourd'hui, des restaurants trois étoiles° le proposent en plat du jour et on le sert dans les cantines. Les Français consomment 75.000 tonnes de couscous par an, une vraie couscousmania!

pimentées *spicy* **miel** *honey* **dégustées** *savored* **étoiles** *stars*

LE MONDE FRANCOPHONE

Si on est invité...

Voici quelques bonnes manières à observer quand on dîne chez des amis.

En Afrique du Nord

- Si quelqu'un vous invite à boire un thé à la menthe, ce n'est pas poli de refuser.
- En général, on enlève ses chaussures avant d'entrer dans une maison.
- On mange souvent avec les doigts°.

En France

- Il est poli d'apporter un petit cadeau pour les hôtes, par exemple des bonbons ou des fleurs.
- On dit parfois «Santé!°» ou «À votre santé°!» avant de boire et «Bon appétit!» avant de manger.
- On mange avec la fourchette dans la main gauche et le couteau dans la main droite et on garde toujours les deux mains sur la table.

doigts *fingers* **Santé!** *Cheers!* **santé** *health*

SUR INTERNET

Les Français mangent-ils beaucoup de glace?

Go to **espaces.vhlcentral.com** to find more cultural information related to this **ESPACE CULTURE**.

ACTIVITÉS

2 Répondez Répondez aux questions d'après les textes.

1. Quand on est au régime, il est préférable de manger des plats préparés comment? Il est préférable de manger des plats préparés à la vapeur.
2. Pourquoi les Français apprécient-ils les restaurants orientaux? Ils les apprécient pour leur ambiance et la qualité de leur nourriture.
3. Où sert-on le couscous aujourd'hui? On le sert dans les restaurants trois étoiles et les cantines.
4. Quel cadeau peut-on apporter quand on dîne chez des Français? On peut apporter des bonbons ou des fleurs.
5. Une fourchette et un couteau sont-ils nécessaires en Afrique du Nord? Non, on mange souvent avec les doigts.

3 Que choisir? Avez-vous déjà mangé dans un restaurant nord-africain? Quand? Où? Qu'avez-vous mangé? Du couscous? Si vous n'êtes jamais allé(e) dans un restaurant nord-africain, imaginez que des amis vous invitent à en essayer un. Qu'avez-vous envie de goûter? Pourquoi?

Le français quotidien

- Model the pronunciation of each term and have students repeat it.
- Have volunteers describe different dishes using these terms. Examples: **pommes frites, escalope de poulet, légumes à la vapeur**, and **côtelette de porc**.

Portrait

- Have students look at the map of the French-speaking world in **Appendice A**. Point out the proximity of France to North Africa. Explain that **le Maghreb** refers to the three French-speaking nations in North Africa (**le Maroc, l'Algérie,** and **la Tunisie**).
- Couscous is often considered the national dish of Morocco.

Le monde francophone Bring in a knife and fork. Demonstrate how Americans typically use these eating utensils, then show students how the French use them.

2 Expansion For additional practice, give students these items. **6. Où peut-on acheter des merguez? (dans toutes les boucheries) 7. Quel type de pâtisserie mange-t-on traditionnellement en Afrique du Nord? (les pâtisseries au miel) 8. Combien de tonnes de couscous les Français mangent-ils par an? (75.000 tonnes) 9. Quand peut-on dire «Santé!»? (avant de boire) 10. Que faut-il enlever avant d'entrer dans une maison en Afrique du Nord? (ses chaussures)**

3 Expansion Take a quick class survey to find out how many students have tried couscous and how many like it. Ask: **Combien d'étudiants ont déjà mangé du couscous? Combien de personnes ont aimé ce plat?** Tally the results on the board.

OPTIONS

La couscousmania des Français Traditionally prepared couscous is cooked very slowly with meat and vegetables and served on large platters made of colorful **faïence**. When preparing couscous, it is best to use a special couscous cooker called a **couscoussière**. The couscous found in stores is usually instant and requires only hot water.

Si on est invité... It is customary to drink **thé à la menthe** in small, narrow glasses that are often decorated with faux gold leaf. It is sometimes served with pine nuts floating in the tea. Mint is sold in large bunches at Arab markets in France. For an authentic experience drinking this tea, one should go to the café at **la mosquée** in Paris.

NATIONAL comparisons STANDARDS

Section Goals

In this section, students will learn:

- comparatives and superlatives of adjectives and adverbs
- irregular comparative and superlative forms

Instructional Resources
WB/VM: Workbook, pp. 121–122
Lab Manual, p. 71
Lab MP3s
WB/VM/LM Answer Key
*IRCD-ROM: IRM (**Essayez!** and **Mise en pratique** answers; Lab Audioscript; **Feuilles d'activités**)*
espaces.vhlcentral.com: activities, downloads, reference tools

Suggestions

- Write **plus** + *adjective* + **que** and **moins** + *adjective* + **que** on the board, explaining their meaning. Illustrate with examples like this: **Cette classe est plus grande que la classe de l'année dernière.**
- Practice by asking the class questions whose responses require comparisons. Examples: **Qui est aussi jolie que Gwyneth Paltrow? Qui est aussi riche qu'Oprah Winfrey?**
- Practice superlative questions by asking students their opinions. Example: **Quel cours est le plus difficile? Le plus facile?**
- Use magazine pictures to practice the different irregular comparative and superlative forms, for example: uses of **meilleur(e)** (*adjective*) and **mieux** (*adverb*), **pire / plus mauvais(e)** (*adjective*) and **plus mal** (*adverb*).
- Point out that **que** and what follows it are optional if the items being compared are evident. Example: **Le steak est plus cher (que le poulet).**

18.1 Comparatives and superlatives of adjectives and adverbs

- Comparisons in French are formed by placing the words **plus** (*more*), **moins** (*less*), or **aussi** (*as*) before adjectives and adverbs, and the word **que** (*than, as*) after them.

ADJECTIVE
Simone est **plus âgée que** son mari.
Simone is older than her husband.

ADVERB
Elle parle **plus vite que** son mari.
She speaks more quickly than her husband.

ADJECTIVE
Guillaume est **moins grand que** son père.
Guillaume is less tall than his father.

ADVERB
Il m'écrit **moins souvent que** son père.
He writes me less often than his father.

ADJECTIVE
Nina est **aussi indépendante qu'**Anne.
Nina is as independent as Anne.

ADVERB
Elle joue au golf **aussi bien qu'**Anne.
She plays golf as well as Anne.

- Superlatives are formed by placing the appropriate definite article after the noun, when it is expressed, and before the comparative form. The preposition **de** often follows the superlative to express *in* or *of*.

NOUN — DEFINITE ARTICLE — COMPARATIVE
Les trains? Le TGV est **(le train) le plus rapide du** monde.
Trains? The TGV is the fastest (train) in the world.

- Some adjectives, like **beau**, **bon**, **grand**, and **nouveau**, precede the nouns they modify. Their superlative forms can also precede the nouns they modify or they can follow them.

SUPERLATIVE — NOUN
C'est **la plus grande ville.**
It's the largest city.

NOUN — SUPERLATIVE
C'est **la ville la plus grande.**
It's the largest city.

BOÎTE À OUTILS
You learned many of the adjectives that precede the nouns they modify in **Leçon 5 ESPACE STRUCTURES, page 83.**

MISE EN PRATIQUE

1 Oui, mais... **Deux amis comparent deux restaurants. Complétez les phrases avec bon, bien, meilleur ou mieux.**

1. J'ai mangé au Café du marché dimanche dernier.
   Oui, mais mes amis ont ___mieux___ aimé Chez Charles.
2. Le vin blanc au Café du marché est ___bon___.
   Oui, mais le vin blanc de Chez Charles est meilleur.
3. Mes amis ont bien aimé le Café du marché.
   Oui, mais mes amis ont ___mieux___ aimé Chez Charles.
4. Au Café du marché, le chef prépare ___bien___ le poulet.
   Oui, mais le chef de Chez Charles le prépare mieux.
5. Les salades au Café du marché sont bonnes.
   Oui, mais elles sont ___meilleures___ Chez Charles.
6. Tout est bon au Café du marché!
   Tout est ___meilleur___ Chez Charles!

2 Un nouveau quartier **Vous venez d'emménager. Assemblez les éléments des trois colonnes pour poser des questions à un(e) voisin(e).** Answers will vary.

MODÈLE
Est-ce que le jambon est moins cher au supermarché ou à la charcuterie?

A	B	C
pain	boucherie	aussi
fruits de mer	boulangerie	meilleur(e)
faire les courses	charcuterie	mieux
dîner	pâtisserie	moins
aller	poissonnerie	pire
acheter	voisins	plus
desserts	quartier	
jambon	supermarché	

3 Aujourd'hui et autrefois **Avec un(e) partenaire, comparez la vie domestique d'aujourd'hui et d'autrefois. Utilisez les adjectifs de la liste à tour de rôle. Ensuite, présentez vos opinions à la classe.** Answers will vary.

MODÈLE
Aujourd'hui, les tâches ménagères sont moins difficiles.

compliqué	grand	naturel	rapide
curieux	indépendant	occupé	sophistiqué

1. les congélateurs
2. la nourriture
3. les femmes
4. les voyages
5. les voitures
6. les enfants

OPTIONS

Extra Practice Have students write three original comparative or superlative sentences that describe themselves or compare themselves with a friend, family member, or famous person. Examples: **Je suis la personne la plus intelligente de l'université. Je suis moins égoïste que mon frère.** Then collect the papers and read the sentences aloud. See if the rest of the class can guess who wrote each description.

Game Divide the class into two teams, A and B. Place the names of 20 famous people into a hat. Select a member from each group to draw a name. The student from team A then has ten seconds to compare those two famous people in a complete sentence. If the student has made a logical comparison, team A gets a point. Then it's team B's turn to make a different comparison. The team with the most points at the end wins.

Interlude

NATIONAL communication cultures STANDARDS

NATIONAL connections communities STANDARDS

Pommes, pommes, pommes

*Pour illustrer le thème de la nourriture, la chanson°, **Pommes, pommes, pommes** (1995), parle des enfants qui vont ramasser des marrons°, à l'automne. L'automne est triste. Il pleut. Un balayeur fredonne°: «Pommes, pommes, pommes». La chanson parle aussi des sans-abri° qui dorment sur les bancs° et qui ont froid, l'hiver, sous les ponts°. Ils gèlent jusqu'au trognon°... de pomme.*

THOMAS FERSEN (1963–) est né à Paris. À quinze ans, il apprend à jouer de la guitare jazz. Puis, un peu plus tard, il voyage en Amérique latine et en Scandinavie. C'est là qu'il commence à écrire des chansons. Quand il revient en France, il chante avec son épouse, une pianiste, dans les piano-bars de Paris. Son premier album sort en 1993, et il reçoit une Victoire de la musique° en 1994. Fersen est apprécié pour ses textes poétiques et ses douces mélodies.

La place du marché

*CAMILLE PISSARRO (1830–1903), comme tous les artistes impressionnistes, concentre son travail sur les douceurs° de la vie et le quotidien°. La nourriture prend une place importante dans la vie des Français. Le peintre° montre ici, dans **La place du marché**, des personnes qui achètent de la nourriture. De nos jours°, aller au marché est une activité encore très appréciée en France.*

Activité

Répondez à ces questions par des phrases complètes. Answers will vary.

1. Que peut-on acheter au marché représenté dans le tableau (*painting*), ***La place du marché***?
2. Avez-vous déjà acheté de la nourriture sur un marché? Si oui, qu'est-ce que vous avez acheté? Si non, avez-vous envie d'acheter de la nourriture plus souvent au marché? Pourquoi?
3. Avez-vous déjà ramassé des fruits ou des légumes? Quels fruits ou quels légumes? À quelle saison? Trouvez-vous que c'est bien de manger des fruits ou des légumes qu'on ramasse? Pourquoi?

SUR INTERNET

Go to **espaces.vhlcentral.com** for more information related to this **Interlude**.

chanson *song* **ramasser des marrons** *to gather chestnuts* **Un balayeur fredonne** *A street-cleaner hums* **sans-abri** *homeless* **bancs** *benches* **ponts** *bridges* **Ils gèlent jusqu'au trognon** *They are freezing to the core* **Victoire de la musique** *equivalent of Grammy Award* **douceurs** *simple pleasures* **quotidien** *everyday life* **peintre** *painter* **De nos jours** *Nowadays*

Section Goals

In this section, students will learn about:
- Thomas Fersen
- Camille Pissarro

Instructional Resources
espaces.vhlcentral.com: activities, downloads, reference tools

Pommes, pommes, pommes
To check comprehension, ask these questions.
1. De qui parle la chanson *Pommes, pommes, pommes*? (Elle parle des enfants qui vont ramasser des marrons, d'un balayeur qui fredonne et des sans-abri qui dorment sur les bancs et sous les ponts.)
2. Qu'est-ce que Thomas Fersen a appris à 15 ans? (à jouer de la guitare jazz)
3. Quand a-t-il commencé à écrire des chansons? (pendant un voyage en Scandinavie)
4. Qu'a-t-il fait quand il est revenu à Paris? (Il a chanté avec son épouse, une pianiste, dans les piano-bars de Paris.)

La place du marché
- Camille Pissarro was born in St. Thomas, Danish West Indies (now the Virgin Islands). He moved to Paris in 1855 and spent most of his life in France. A number of impressionists (for example, Renoir, Monet, Degas, and Cézanne) respected his art and regarded him as their teacher. His paintings often feature landscapes or Parisian and provincial scenes.
- Have students brainstorm a list of foods that they expect to find at a French outdoor market. Ask a volunteer to categorize these items on the board. Examples: **les fruits, les légumes**, etc.

OPTIONS

Cultural Comparison Have students work in groups of three and compare the market scene in the painting with an outdoor market today. Tell them to make a list of the similarities and differences in a two-column chart under the headings **Similitudes** and **Différences**. After completing their charts, have two groups get together and compare their lists.

Extra Practice Have students draw a picture to illustrate the song based on the description given. Tell them to label the people in French.

NATIONAL STANDARDS connections cultures

Section Goals

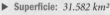

In this section, students will read historical and cultural information about Burgundy and Franche-Comté.

Instructional Resources
IRCD-ROM: Transparency #42
WB/VM: Workbook, pp. 125–126
WB/VM/LM Answer Key
espaces.vhlcentral.com: activities; downloads; reference tools

Carte de la Bourgogne et de la Franche-Comté
- Have students look at the map or use **Transparency #42**. Ask volunteers to read the names of cities and rivers aloud. Model the pronunciation as necessary.
- Ask students to name the country that borders Franche-Comté. (**La Suisse**)

La région en chiffres
- Point out the coats of arms for the regions.
- Have volunteers read the sections. After each section, ask students questions about the content.
- Point out that the vineyards of Burgundy produce some of the world's greatest wines.
- The town of Nevers is famous for its fine, hand-painted, decorative pottery, known as **faïence**.
- In Franche-Comté, many hand-crafted objects are made from wood, such as violins, guitars, pipes, clocks, and toys.

Incroyable mais vrai! Snails have been eaten as food since at least ancient Roman times. They are a rich source of protein and are supposed to help prevent aging.

Panorama

La Bourgogne

La région en chiffres

- **Superficie:** *31.582 km²*
- **Population:** *1.616.000*
  SOURCE: INSEE
- **Industries principales:** *industries automobile et pharmaceutique, tourisme, viticulture°*
- **Villes principales:** *Auxerre, Chalon-sur-Saône, Dijon, Mâcon, Nevers*

Personnages célèbres

- **Gustave Eiffel**, *ingénieur (la tour Eiffel) (1832–1923)*
- **Colette**, *écrivain (1873–1954)*
- **Claude Jade**, *actrice (1948–)*

les vendanges° en Bourgogne

La Franche-Comté

La région en chiffres

- **Superficie:** *16.202 km²*
- **Population:** *1.133.000*
- **Industries principales:** *agriculture, artisanat, industrie automobile, horlogerie°, tourisme*
- **Villes principales:** *Belfort, Besançon, Dole, Pontarlier, Vesoul*

Personnages célèbres

- **Louis (1864–1948) et Auguste (1862–1954) Lumière**, *inventeurs du cinématographe°*
- **Claire Motte**, *danseuse étoile° à l'Opéra de Paris (1937–)*

un marché à Dijon

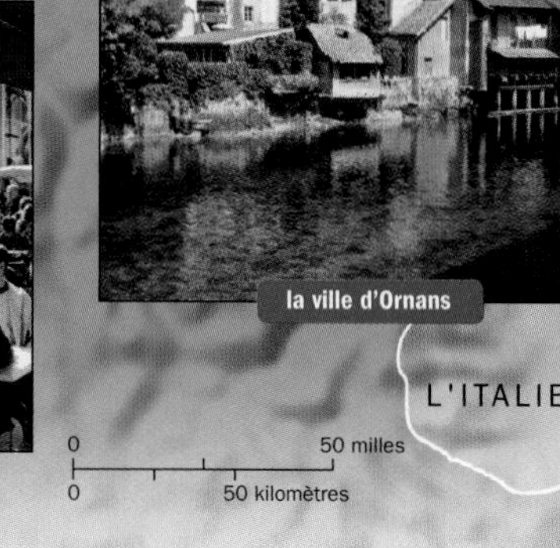

la ville d'Ornans

Incroyable mais vrai!

Au Moyen Âge, les escargots servaient à° la fabrication de sirops contre la toux°. La recette bourguignonne (beurre, ail, persil°) est popularisée au 19e siècle. La France produit 500 à 800 tonnes d'escargots par an, mais en importe 5.000 tonnes. L'escargot aide à lutter contre° le mauvais cholestérol et les maladies cardio-vasculaires.

viticulture *grape growing* **horlogerie** *watch and clock making* **cinématographe** *motion picture camera* **danseuse étoile** *principal dancer* **servaient à** *were used for* **toux** *cough* **persil** *parsley* **lutter contre** *fight against* **vendanges** *grape harvest*

OPTIONS

Personnages célèbres **Claude Jade** is an internationally acclaimed actress and won an award for Best Actress for her performance in ***L'École des femmes***. **Gustave Eiffel** was also a noted bridge designer, and he designed the wrought-iron skeleton for the inside of the Statue of Liberty. **Colette** (the pen name of Sidonie-Gabrielle Colette) wrote novels about women and their lovers; some of her novels were autobiographical. One her best-known works, ***Gigi*** (1945), was made into a musical film in 1958. **Louis** and **Auguste Lumière** created the first motion picture, ***La sortie des ouvriers de l'usine Lumière***, in 1895. They also made the first newsreels.

Les sports

Les sports d'hiver dans le Jura

On peut pratiquer de nombreux sports d'hiver dans les montagnes du Jura, en Franche-Comté: ski alpin, surf°, monoski, planche à voile sur neige. Mais le Jura est surtout le paradis du ski de fond°. Avec des centaines de kilomètres de pistes°, on y skie de décembre à avril, y compris° la nuit, sur des pistes éclairées°. La célèbre Transjurassienne est la 2e course° d'endurance du monde avec un parcours° de 76 km pour les hommes et 50 km pour les femmes. Il y a aussi une minitrans de 10 km pour les enfants.

Les destinations

Besançon: capitale de l'horlogerie

L'artisanat de l'horlogerie commence au 16e siècle avec l'installation de grandes horloges dans les monastères. Au 18e siècle, 400 horlogers suisses viennent s'installer° en Franche-Comté. Au 19e siècle, Montbéliard comptait 5.000 horlogers. En hiver, les paysans°-horlogers s'occupaient°, dans leurs fermes°, de la finition° et de la décoration des horloges. En 1862, une école d'horlogerie est créée° et en 1900, Besançon devient le berceau° de l'horlogerie française avec 8.000 horlogers qui produisent 600.000 montres par an.

L'architecture

Les toits de Bourgogne

Les toits° en tuiles vernissées° multicolores sont typiques de la Bourgogne. Inspirés de l'architecture flamande° et d'Europe centrale, ils forment des dessins géométriques. Le plus célèbre bâtiment° est l'Hôtel-Dieu° de Beaune, construit en 1443 pour accueillir° les pauvres et les victimes de la guerre° de 100 ans. Aujourd'hui, l'Hôtel-Dieu organise la plus célèbre vente aux enchères° de vins du monde.

Les gens

Louis Pasteur (1822–1895)

Louis Pasteur est né à Dole, en Franche-Comté. Il découvre° que les fermentations sont dues à des micro-organismes spécifiques. Dans ses recherches° sur les maladies° contagieuses, il montre la relation entre le microbe et l'apparition d'une maladie. Cette découverte° a des applications dans le monde hospitalier et industriel avec les méthodes de désinfection, de stérilisation et de pasteurisation. Le vaccin contre la rage° est aussi une de ses inventions. L'Institut Pasteur est créé à Paris en 1888. Aujourd'hui, il a des filiales° sur cinq continents.

Qu'est-ce que vous avez appris? Répondez aux questions par des phrases complètes.

1. Comment s'appellent les inventeurs du cinématographe?
   Ils s'appellent Louis et Auguste Lumière.
2. À quoi servaient les escargots au Moyen Âge?
   Ils servaient à fabriquer des sirops contre la toux.
3. Avec quoi sont préparés les escargots de Bourgogne?
   Ils sont préparés avec du beurre, de l'ail et du persil.
4. Quel est le sport le plus pratiqué dans le Jura?
   C'est le ski de fond.
5. Qu'est-ce que la Transjurassienne?
   C'est une course d'endurance.
6. D'où viennent les horlogers au 18e siècle?
   Ils viennent de Suisse.
7. Quel style d'architecture a influencé les toits de Bourgogne?
   L'architecture flamande et d'Europe centrale les a influencés.
8. Quel est le bâtiment avec le toit le plus célèbre en Bourgogne?
   C'est l'Hôtel-Dieu de Beaune, un ancien hôpital.
9. Comment les recherches de Pasteur ont-elles été utilisées par les hôpitaux et l'industrie?
   Elles ont été utilisées dans les méthodes de désinfection, de stérilisation et de pasteurisation.
10. Où trouve-t-on des Instituts Pasteur aujourd'hui?
    On trouve des Instituts Pasteur à Paris et sur cinq continents.

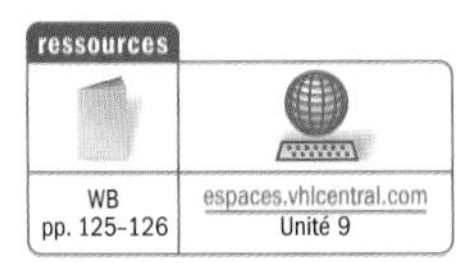

SUR INTERNET

Go to **espaces.vhlcentral.com** to find more cultural information related to this **PANORAMA**.

1. Quand ont lieu les vendanges en Bourgogne?
2. Cherchez trois recettes à base (*using*) d'escargots.
3. Trouvez des informations sur les vacances d'hiver dans le Jura: logement, prix, activités, etc.
4. Cherchez des informations sur Louis Pasteur. Quel effet ont eu ses découvertes sur des produits alimentaires d'usage courant (*everyday use*)?

surf *snowboarding* **ski de fond** *cross-country skiing* **pistes** *trails* **y compris** *including* **éclairées** *lit* **course** *race* **parcours** *course* **s'installer** *settle* **paysans** *peasants* **s'occupaient** *took care* **fermes** *farms* **finition** *finishing* **créée** *created* **berceau** *cradle* **toits** *roofs* **tuiles vernissées** *glazed tiles* **flamande** *Flemish* **bâtiment** *building* **Hôtel-Dieu** *Hospital* **accueillir** *take care of* **guerre** *war* **vente aux enchères** *auction* **découvre** *discovers* **recherches** *research* **maladies** *illnesses* **découverte** *discovery* **rage** *rabies* **filiales** *branches*

Les sports d'hiver dans le Jura
- The Jura Mountains along the Swiss-French border extend from the Rhône River to the Rhine River.
- Ask students: **Que font les gens sur la photo? (Ils font du ski de fond.) Avez-vous envie de visiter les montagnes du Jura? Pourquoi ou pourquoi pas?**

Besançon: capitale de l'horlogerie The **musée du Temps** in the **palais Granvelle** contains all sorts of time pieces from ancient to modern times. It also chronicles the history of the measurement of time.

Les toits de Bourgogne
- The multicolored tiles appear mostly on buildings dating from the late Middle Ages or the Renaissance, but they were sometimes used on houses built or restored during the nineteenth and twentieth centuries.
- Ask students: **De quelles couleurs sont les tuiles vernissées sur la photo? (blanches, rouges, bleues, vertes, marron)**
- **La guerre de 100 ans** began in 1337 and ended in 1453.

Louis Pasteur Louis Pasteur also discovered ways of preventing silkworm diseases, anthrax, and chicken cholera.

OPTIONS

Bourgogne The duchy of Burgundy enjoyed a golden age from the beginning of Duke Philip the Bold's reign in 1342 to the end of Duke Charles the Bold's reign in 1477. During that time Franche-Comté became part of the Burgundian duchy, as did Flanders and parts of the Netherlands. As a result, Burgundy became a powerful economic and cultural force, and it enjoyed prosperous trade in wine, wool, and grain.

Extra Practice After students have read the **Panorama**, ask them to give examples of industries in Burgundy and Franche-Comté that were influenced by the geography or location of these two regions. Examples: **la viticulture, le tourisme ou les sports d'hiver dans les montagnes du Jura, l'horlogerie (qui a commencé avec l'arrivée des horlogers suisses au 18e siècle)**.

Section Goals

In this section, students will:
- learn to identify the main idea in a text
- read a menu and restaurant review

Stratégie Tell students that recognizing the main idea of a text will help them infer the meanings of unfamiliar words they encounter while reading. Tell them to check the title first because the main idea is often expressed there. Also tell them to read the topic sentence of each paragraph before they read the full text so they will get a sense of the main idea.

Examinez le texte First, have students look at the format of the two texts and ask them if the formats are similar or different. Then, tell them to get together with a partner and discuss the reading strategies they can use to identify the texts' genre.

Comparez les deux textes
- Have students look at the first text (the menu) and ask them if it has a title. Then have them identify the subtitles or subheadings and the type of vocabulary used. Finally, ask them to identify the text's genre.
- Have students look at the second text (the review) and identify the different parts of the reading. Then ask them to compare the formats and vocabulary of the two texts. Write a list of the similarities and differences on the board. Finally, have them identify the genre of the second text.

Lecture

Avant la lecture

STRATÉGIE

Reading for the main idea

As you know, you can learn a great deal about a reading selection by looking at its format and by looking for cognates, titles, and subtitles. You can skim to get the gist of the reading selection and scan it for specific information. Reading for the main idea is another useful strategy; it involves locating the topic sentences of each paragraph to determine the author's purpose. Topic sentences can provide clues about the content of each paragraph, as well as the general organization of the reading. Your choice of which reading strategies to use will depend on the style and format of each reading selection.

Examinez le texte

Dans cette lecture, il y a deux textes différents. Regardez ces textes rapidement. Leur format est-il similaire ou différent? Quelles stratégies vont être utiles pour identifier le genre de ces textes, d'après vous? Comparez vos idées avec un(e) camarade.

Comparez les deux textes

Premier texte

Analysez le format du texte. Y a-t-il un titre? Des sous-titres? Plusieurs sections? Comment ce texte est-il organisé? Regardez rapidement le contenu (*content*) du texte. Quel genre de vocabulaire trouvez-vous dans ce texte? D'après vous, qu'est-ce que c'est?

Deuxième texte

Ce texte est-il organisé comme (*like*) le premier texte? Y a-t-il un titre, des sous-titres et plusieurs parties? Y a-t-il des informations similaires aux informations données dans le premier texte? Lesquelles? (*Which ones?*) Le vocabulaire est-il similaire au vocabulaire du premier texte? D'après vous, quel genre de texte est le deuxième texte? Les deux textes parlent-ils du même restaurant?

Chez Michel

12, rue° des Oliviers • 75006 Paris
Tél. 01.42.56.78.90
Ouvert° tous les soirs, de 19h00 à 23h30

Menu à 18 euros • Service compris

Entrée (au choix°)

Assiette de charcuterie
Escargots (1/2 douzaine°)
Salade de tomates au thon
Pâté de campagne
Soupe de légumes

Plat principal (au choix)

Poulet rôti haricots verts
Steak au poivre pommes de terre
Thon à la moutarde (riz ou légumes au choix)
Bœuf aux carottes et aux champignons
Pâtes aux fruits de mer

Salade verte et plateau de fromages°

Dessert (au choix)

Tarte aux pommes
Tarte aux poires
Fruits de saison
Fraises à la crème Chantilly
Sorbet aux pêches
Gâteau au chocolat

OPTIONS

Small Groups Have students work in groups of three. Tell them to create a skit about a waiter or waitress and two customers at **Chez Michel**. The customers should enter the restaurant, ask for a table, order from the menu, and then ask for the check at the end of the meal. The waiter or waitress should respond appropriately and actually write down the customers' orders on a piece of paper.

Cultural Comparison Have students work in pairs. Tell them to compare the menu from **Chez Michel** with the menu of a restaurant that they frequent. Are they similar or different? Have them consider the format of the menu, the number of dishes and types of food served, and the prices.

À essayer: L'Huile d'Olive

Un nouveau restaurant provençal dans le quartier de Montmartre

L'Huile d'Olive
14, rue Molière
75018 Paris
01.44.53.76.35

Ouvert tous les jours sauf° le lundi
Le midi, de 12h00 à 14h30, Menu à 12 euros et Plat du jour
Le soir, de 19h00 à 23h00, Menus à 15 et 20 euros, Carte

De l'extérieur, L'Huile d'Olive est un restaurant aux murs gris, dans une petite rue triste du quartier de Montmartre. Mais à l'intérieur, tout change. C'est la Provence, avec tout son soleil et toute sa beauté. Les propriétaires, Monsieur et Madame Duchesnes, ont transformé ce vieux restaurant qui est maintenant entièrement décoré dans le style provençal, en bleu et jaune. Dans ce nouveau restaurant très sympathique, les propriétaires vous proposent des plats provençaux traditionnels préparés avec soin°. Comme entrée, je vous recommande la salade de tomates à l'ail ou le carpaccio de thon à l'huile d'olive. Comme plat principal, commandez la daube° provençale, si vous aimez le bœuf, ou le poulet au pastis°. Le plateau de fruits de mer est un excellent choix pour les amoureux du poisson. Comme légumes, essayez les pommes de terre au romarin° ou les petits pois aux oignons. Pour les végétariens, Madame Duchesnes propose des pâtes aux légumes avec une sauce à la crème délicieuse ou bien une ratatouille° de légumes fantastique. À la fin° du repas, commandez le fromage de chèvre° ou si vous préférez les desserts, goûtez la tarte poires-chocolat.

*À L'Huile d'Olive, tout est délicieux et le service est impeccable. Alors, n'hésitez pas! Allez à L'Huile d'Olive pour goûter la Provence! ****

rue *street* **Ouvert** *Open* **choix** *choice* **douzaine** *dozen* **plateau de fromages** *cheeseboard* **sauf** *except* **soin** *care* **daube** *beef stew* **pastis** *anise liquor* **romarin** *rosemary* **ratatouille** *vegetable stew* **fin** *end* **chèvre** *goat*

Après la lecture

Vrai ou faux? **Indiquez si les phrases au sujet du premier texte sont vraies ou fausses. Corrigez les phrases fausses.**

1. On peut déjeuner au restaurant Chez Michel.
   Faux. On peut seulement dîner au restaurant Chez Michel.
2. Il n'y a pas de poisson dans les entrées.
   Faux. Il y a du poisson dans la salade de tomates au thon.
3. Comme plat principal, il y a trois viandes.
   Vrai.
4. Le poulet rôti est accompagné de légumes.
   Vrai.
5. Il y a trois plats principaux avec du bœuf.
   Faux. Il y a deux plats principaux avec du bœuf: le steak au poivre pommes de terre et le bœuf aux carottes et aux champignons.
6. On ne peut pas commander de fromage ou de dessert.
   Faux. On peut commander du fromage et des desserts.

Commandez **Suggérez une entrée, un plat et un dessert pour ces personnes qui vont dîner au restaurant Chez Michel.**

Answers will vary. Possible answers provided.

1. Madame Lonier est au régime et elle n'aime pas la viande.
   Elle peut prendre les escargots, le thon et les fruits de saison.
2. Monsieur Sanchez est végétarien. Il n'aime pas le thon. Il adore les légumes, mais il ne mange jamais de fruits.
   Il peut prendre la soupe de légumes, les pâtes aux fruits de mer et le gâteau au chocolat.
3. Madame Petit a envie de manger de la viande, mais elle n'aime pas beaucoup le bœuf. Elle n'aime ni (*neither*) les gâteaux ni (*nor*) les tartes. Elle peut prendre le pâté de campagne, le poulet rôti haricots verts et les fraises à la crème Chantilly.
4. Et vous, qu'est-ce que vous avez envie de goûter au restaurant Chez Michel? Pourquoi?

Répondez **Répondez aux questions par des phrases complètes, d'après le deuxième texte.**

1. Comment s'appelle le restaurant?
   Il s'appelle L'Huile d'Olive.
2. Combien coûtent les menus du soir?
   Ils coûtent 15 et 20 euros.
3. Quel est le style de cuisine du restaurant?
   Le style de cuisine est provençal.
4. Quelles viandes le critique (*critic*) recommande-t-il?
   Il recommande la daube provençale et le poulet au pastis.
5. Comment Madame Duchesnes prépare-t-elle les pâtes?
   Elle les prépare avec des légumes et une sauce à la crème délicieuse.
6. Le critique a-t-il aimé ce restaurant? Justifiez votre réponse. Answers may vary. Sample answer: Oui. Le restaurant est très sympathique. Les plats sont préparés avec soin. Tout est délicieux et le service est impeccable.

À Vous **Vous et votre partenaire allez sortir manger dans un de ces restaurants. Décidez quel restaurant vous préférez. Est-ce que vous allez dîner ou déjeuner? Combien d'argent allez-vous dépenser? Qu'est-ce que vous allez commander?**

Vrai ou faux? Go over the answers with the class.

Commandez
- This activity can be done in pairs.
- For additional practice, give students these situations. **5. David n'aime ni la soupe ni le poisson. Il aime les fruits. 6. Isabelle adore la viande, mais elle n'aime pas les légumes. Elle adore les fruits, surtout les pommes. 7. Claudine adore le thon et les tomates. Elle aime aussi le chocolat.**

Répondez Have students write three more questions about the reading. Then tell them to exchange papers with a partner and answer the questions.

À Vous After completing the activity, take a quick class survey to find out which restaurant was more popular among students. Ask: **Combien de personnes choisissent Chez Michel? Et L'Huile d'Olive?** Tally the results on the board. Then ask pairs to explain why they chose that particular restaurant.

OPTIONS

Montmartre **Le quartier de Montmartre**, located on a hill in Paris (**la butte Montmartre**), is the highest point in the city and a popular tourist site. **La Basilique du Sacré-Cœur,** with its large white dome, sits on the top of the hill. Montmartre is famous for its history of bohemian artists and its nightlife, with the **Moulin Rouge** giving it worldwide acclaim.

Extra Practice For additional practice with the restaurant review, give students these true/false items. **1. Le restaurant se trouve en Provence. (Faux.) 2. Le restaurant est fermé le samedi. (Faux.) 3. L'extérieur du restaurant n'est pas très beau. (Vrai.) 4. Il y a des choix de plats si on est végétarien. (Vrai.)**

Section Goals
In this section, students will:
- learn to take notes as they listen
- listen to a paragraph and jot down the main points
- listen to a cooking program and complete several activities

Instructional Resources
Textbook MP3s
IRCD-ROM: IRM (Textbook Audioscript)
espaces.vhlcentral.com: downloads, reference tools

Stratégie
Script Bon, je vais aller faire les courses. D'abord, je vais passer à la boucherie. J'ai besoin d'un poulet et de quatre steaks. Ensuite, je vais aller à la boulangerie pour acheter du pain et des croissants. Ah oui! Il faut aussi du poisson pour ce soir. Alors, du thon à la poissonnerie. Et au supermarché, des légumes et des fruits.

Préparation Have students look at the photo and describe what they see. Then ask them to guess what dish the chef is preparing.

À vous d'écouter
Script Bonjour à tous et bienvenue à «Cuisiner avec Claude». Aujourd'hui, nous allons préparer une salade bien française: la salade niçoise. C'est une salade très complète qui est parfaite pour l'été. Alors, voici ce que vous devez faire pour préparer cette salade. Tout d'abord, faites cuire les haricots verts et les pommes de terre dans de l'eau très chaude avec un peu de sel. Faites aussi cuire les œufs dans de l'eau. Lavez bien la salade et mettez-la dans une grande assiette. Mettez les pommes de terre et les haricots verts sur la salade. Coupez les œufs, quelques tomates et un poivron et mettez-les dans la salade. Ensuite, mettez du thon et des olives noires. Et maintenant, pour la vinaigrette, mélangez du vinaigre, de l'huile d'olive, de la moutarde et un peu d'ail. Mettez du sel et du poivre dans la vinaigrette et ajoutez-la à la salade. Et voilà! Votre salade est prête! Vous pouvez la servir avec du pain ou bien des croûtons, si vous le désirez. Cette salade délicieuse est rapide à préparer et vous pouvez la servir en entrée ou bien comme plat principal. Allez! À table! Et bon appétit à tous!

À l'écoute

STRATÉGIE

Jotting down notes as you listen

Jotting down notes while you listen to a conversation in French can help you keep track of the important points or details. It will help you to focus actively on comprehension rather than on remembering what you have heard.

 To practice this strategy, you will listen to a paragraph. Jot down the main points you hear.

Préparation

Regardez la photo et décrivez la scène. Où sont ces hommes? Que font-ils? Qui sont-ils, à votre avis? Qu'y a-t-il dans la poêle (*frying pan*)? À votre avis, que préparent ces hommes?

À vous d'écouter 

Écoutez les instructions pour préparer une salade niçoise et notez quelques ingrédients nécessaires.

Pour la salade

des haricots verts	des tomates
des pommes de terre	un poivron
des œufs	du thon
de la salade	des olives noires

Pour la vinaigrette (*dressing*)

de l'huile d'olive	du sel
de la moutarde	du poivre
de l'ail	du vinaigre

ressources

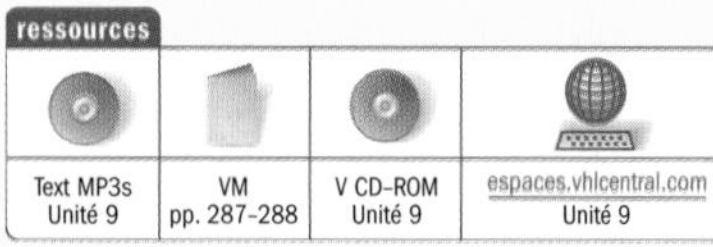

Text MP3s Unité 9
VM pp. 287-288
V CD-ROM Unité 9
espaces.vhlcentral.com Unité 9

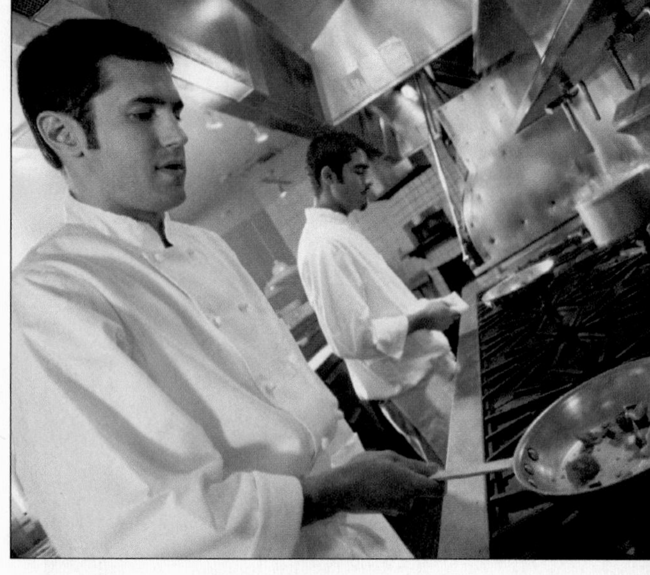

Compréhension

Le bon ordre **Mettez ces instructions simplifiées dans le bon ordre, d'après la recette de la salade niçoise.**

a. _7_ Mélanger (*Mix*) le vinaigre, l'huile d'olive, la moutarde et l'ail pour faire la vinaigrette.

b. _6_ Mettre le thon et les olives sur la salade.

c. _4_ Couper (*Cut*) les œufs et les mettre dans la salade.

d. _1_ Faire cuire (*Cook*) les pommes de terre, les haricots verts et les œufs.

e. _5_ Mettre les morceaux de tomates et de poivron sur la salade.

f. _2_ Laver (*Wash*) la salade et la mettre dans une grande assiette.

g. _3_ Mettre les haricots verts et les pommes de terre sur la salade.

h. _8_ Mettre la vinaigrette sur la salade et servir.

Votre recette préférée **Quel est votre plat ou dessert favori? Donnez la liste des ingrédients qu'il faut pour le préparer, puis expliquez à un groupe de camarades comment le préparer. Ne leur donnez pas le nom du plat. Ils vont prendre des notes et essayer de le deviner (*to guess*). Ensuite, changez de rôles.**

Écriture

STRATÉGIE

Expressing and supporting opinions

Written reviews are just one of the many kinds of writing that require you to state your opinions. In order to convince your reader to take your opinions seriously, it is important to support them as thoroughly as possible. Details, facts, examples, and other forms of evidence are necessary. In a restaurant review, for example, it is not enough just to rate the food, service, and atmosphere. Readers will want details about the dishes you ordered, the kind of service you received, and the type of atmosphere you encountered. If you were writing a concert or album review, what kinds of details might your readers expect to find?

It is easier to include details that support your opinions if you plan ahead. Before going to a place or event that you are planning to review, write a list of questions that your readers might ask. Decide which aspects of the experience you are going to rate, and list the details that will help you decide upon a rating. You can then organize these lists into a questionnaire and a rating sheet. Bring these forms with you to remind you of the kinds of information you need to gather in order to support your opinions. Later, these forms will help you organize your review into logical categories. They can also provide the details and other evidence you need to convince your readers of your opinions.

Watch the FLASH CULTURE segment on the **ESPACES** video for cultural footage related to this unit's theme.

Thème

Écrire une critique

Écrivez la critique d'un restaurant de votre ville pour le journal de l'université. Indiquez d'abord le nom du restaurant et le type de cuisine (cuisine chinoise, indienne, italienne, barbecue, etc.). Ensuite, parlez des catégories de la liste suivante. Enfin, donnez votre opinion personnelle sur le restaurant. Combien d'étoiles (*stars*) mérite-t-il (*deserve*)?

- **Cuisine**

  Quel(s) type(s) de plat(s) y a-t-il au menu? Le restaurant a-t-il une spécialité? Citez quelques plats typiques (entrées et plats principaux) que vous avez goûtés et indiquez les ingrédients utilisés dans ces plats.

- **Service**

  Comment est le service? Les serveurs sont-ils gentils et polis? Sont-ils lents ou rapides à apporter le menu, les boissons et les plats?

- **Ambiance**

  Comment est le restaurant? Est-il beau? Grand? Bien décoré? Est-ce un restaurant simple ou élégant? Y a-t-il une terrasse? Un bar? Des musiciens?

- **Informations pratiques**

  Quel est le prix moyen d'un repas dans ce restaurant (au déjeuner et/ou au dîner)? Où est le restaurant? Donnez son adresse et indiquez comment on y (*there*) va de l'université. Indiquez aussi le numéro de téléphone du restaurant et ses heures d'ouverture (*operating hours*).

Section Goals

In this section, students will:
- learn to express and support opinions
- write a restaurant review
- view authentic cultural footage of a French open-air market

Instructional Resources
WB/VM: Video Manual, pp. 287–288
WB/VM/LM Answer Key
IRCD-ROM: IRM (Videoscript)
Video CD-ROM
Video on DVD
espaces.vhlcentral.com: activities, downloads, reference tools

Stratégie Explain to students that when they write a restaurant review, it is helpful to have some way of organizing the details required to support the rating. Working in groups of three, have students write a list of questions in French that elicit information readers might want to know and use them to create a rating sheet. Tell them to refer to the list of questions in the **Thème** section as a guide. Encourage students to leave space for comments in each category so they can record details that support their opinions. Suggest that they fill out the rating sheet during the various stages of the meal.

Thème Explain that each student will rate a local restaurant and write a review of a meal there, including a recommendation for future patrons.

Flash culture Tell students they will learn more about open-air markets by watching a variety of real-life images narrated by Csilla. Show the video segment without sound and tell students to call out what they see. Then, show the video segment again with sound. You can also use the activities in the video manual in class to reinforce this **Flash culture** or assign them as homework.

EVALUATION

Criteria	Scale
Content	1 2 3 4 5
Organization	1 2 3 4 5
Use of details to support opinions	1 2 3 4 5
Accuracy	1 2 3 4 5

Scoring	
Excellent	18–20 points
Good	14–17 points
Satisfactory	10–13 points
Unsatisfactory	< 10 points

Instructional Resources
Textbook MP3s
IRCD-ROM: IRM (Textbook Audioscript)
espaces.vhlcentral.com: downloads, reference tools

À table!

une assiette	*plate*
un bol	*bowl*
une carafe d'eau	*pitcher of water*
une carte	*menu*
un couteau	*knife*
une cuillère (à soupe/à café)	*spoon (teaspoon/soupspoon)*
une fourchette	*fork*
un menu	*menu*
une nappe	*tablecloth*
une serviette	*napkin*
une boîte (de conserve)	*can*
la crème	*cream*
l'huile (d'olive) (*f.*)	*(olive) oil*
la mayonnaise	*mayonnaise*
la moutarde	*mustard*
le poivre	*pepper*
le sel	*salt*
une tranche	*slice*
une cantine	*cafeteria*
À table!	*Let's eat!/ Food is ready!*
compris	*included*

Les fruits

une banane	*banana*
une fraise	*strawberry*
un fruit	*fruit*
une orange	*orange*
une pêche	*peach*
une poire	*pear*
une pomme	*apple*
une tomate	*tomato*

Autres aliments

un aliment	*food*
la confiture	*jam*
la nourriture	*food, sustenance*
des pâtes (*f.*)	*pasta*
le riz	*rice*
une tarte	*pie, tart*
un yaourt	*yogurt*

Verbes

devenir	*to become*
devoir	*to have to (must); to owe*
maintenir	*to maintain*
pouvoir	*to be able to (can)*
retenir	*to keep, to retain*
revenir	*to come back*
tenir	*to hold*
venir	*to come*
vouloir	*to want; to mean (with dire)*

Autres mots et locutions

depuis [+ *time*]	*since*
il y a [+ *time*]	*ago*
pendant [+ *time*]	*for*

Les repas

commander	*to order*
cuisiner	*to cook*
être au régime	*to be on a diet*
goûter	*to taste*
un déjeuner	*lunch*
un dîner	*dinner*
un goûter	*afternoon snack*
un petit-déjeuner	*breakfast*
un repas	*meal*
une entrée	*appetizer, starter*
un hors-d'œuvre	*hors-d'œuvre, appetizer*
un plat (principal)	*(main) dish*

Les viandes et les poissons

le bœuf	*beef*
un escargot	*escargot, snail*
les fruits de mer (*m.*)	*seafood*
un œuf	*egg*
un pâté (de campagne)	*pâté, meat spread*
le porc	*pork*
un poulet	*chicken*
une saucisse	*sausage*
un steak	*steak*
le thon	*tuna*
la viande	*meat*

Les légumes

l'ail (*m.*)	*garlic*
une carotte	*carrot*
un champignon	*mushroom*
des haricots verts (*m.*)	*green beans*
une laitue	*lettuce*
un légume	*vegetable*
un oignon	*onion*
des petits pois (*m.*)	*peas*
un poivron (vert, rouge)	*(green, red) pepper*
une pomme de terre	*potato*
une salade	*salad*

Les achats

faire les courses (f.)	*to go (grocery) shopping*
une boucherie	*butcher's shop*
une boulangerie	*bread shop, bakery*
une charcuterie	*delicatessen*
une pâtisserie	*pastry shop, bakery*
une poissonnerie	*fish shop*
un supermarché	*supermarket*
un(e) commerçant(e)	*shopkeeper*
un kilo(gramme)	*kilo(gram)*

Expressions utiles	*See pp. 295 and 309.*
Comparatives and superlatives	*See pp. 312–313.*

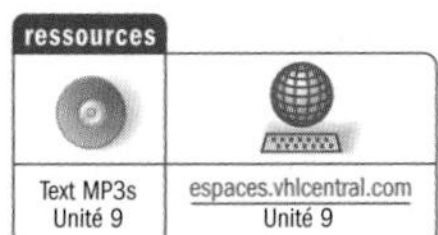

La santé

UNITÉ

10

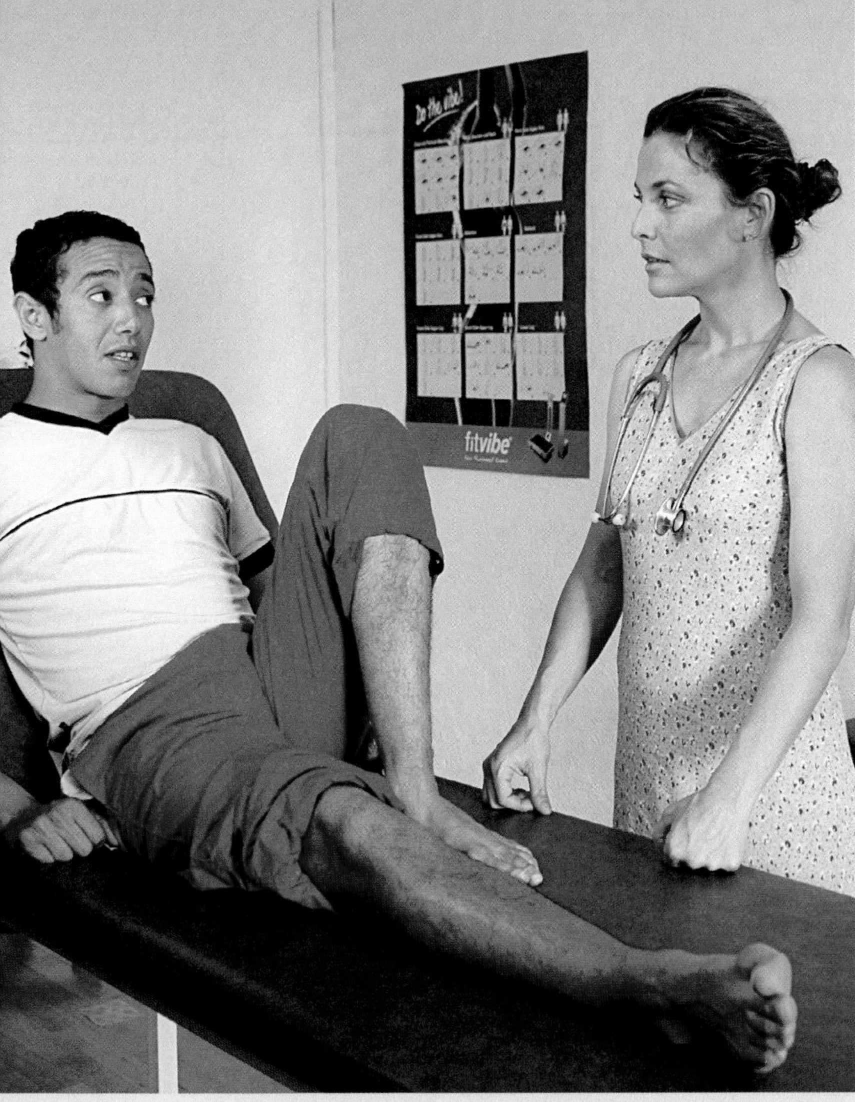

Pour commencer

- Quelle est la profession de la dame, coiffeuse ou médecin?
- Où sont Rachid et cette dame, à l'hôpital ou à l'épicerie?
- Est-ce qu'il veut revenir samedi prochain?
- Qu'est-ce qu'il faisait avant de venir, il jouait au foot ou il faisait les courses?

Unit Goals

Leçon 19
In this lesson, students will learn:
- terms for parts of the body
- terms to discuss one's daily routine
- the role of diacriticals (accents)
- about healthcare in France
- reflexive verbs
- some common idiomatic reflexive verbs
- about the company Diadermine

Leçon 20
In this lesson, students will learn:
- terms to describe one's health
- terms for illnesses and remedies
- terms related to medical visits and treatments
- the pronunciation of **p**, **t**, and **c**
- about the national healthcare system in France
- the **passé composé** of reflexive verbs
- the pronouns **y** and **en**
- about the Swiss healthcare system and give a presentation

Savoir-faire
In this section, students will learn:
- cultural and historical information about Switzerland
- to use background knowledge to increase reading comprehension
- to listen for specific information
- to sequence events in a narration
- more information on pharmacies and health-related businesses through specially shot video footage

Pour commencer
- **Elle est médecin.**
- **Ils sont à l'hôpital.**
- **Non, il ne veut pas revenir.**
- **Il jouait au foot.**

RESOURCES

Workbook/Video Manual: WB Activities, pp. 127–140
Laboratory Manual: Lab Activities, pp. 73–80
Workbook/Video Manual: Video Activities, pp. 247–250; pp. 289–290
WB/VM/LM Answer Key
Instructor's Resource CD-ROM [IRCD-ROM]: Instructor's Resource Manual [IRM] (Textbook Audioscript; Lab Audioscript; Videoscript; **Roman-photo** Translations; **Vocabulaire supplémentaire**; **Feuilles d'activités**; Info Gap Activities; **Le zapping** TV clip transcription; **Essayez!** and **Mise en pratique** answers); Transparencies #43, #44, #45, #46, #47; Testing Program, pp. 73–80, pp. 197–208; Test Files; Testing Program MP3s; Test Generator
Lab MP3s
Textbook MP3s
Video CD-ROM
Video on DVD
espaces.vhlcentral.com

Section Goals

In this section, students will learn and practice vocabulary related to:

- daily routines
- personal hygiene
- some parts of the body

Instructional Resources

*IRCD-ROM: Transparencies #43, #44; IRM (**Vocabulaire supplémentaire; Mise en pratique** answers; Textbook Audioscript; Lab Audioscript; Info Gap Activities)*
Textbook MP3s
WB/VM: Workbook, pp. 127–128
Lab Manual, p. 73
Lab MP3s
WB/VM/LM Answer Key
espaces.vhlcentral.com: activities, downloads, reference tools

Suggestions

- Using **Transparency #43**, describe what the people in the illustration are doing. Then point out objects and parts of the body. Examples: **Il se rase. Elle se maquille. C'est une serviette de bain.**
- Ask students yes/no questions based on the illustration. Examples: **La fille se lève-t-elle? La femme se regarde-t-elle? Est-ce le bras? Est-ce un peigne?**
- Model the pronunciation of **shampooing**. Mention that they may see the alternate spelling **shampoing**.
- Explain the relationships between these terms: **se raser, un rasoir, une crème à raser; se réveiller, un réveil; se coiffer, un coiffeur, une coiffeuse;** and **se brosser les dents, le dentifrice**.
- Remind students that the plural of **l'œil** is **les yeux**.
- Review the use of partitives with non-count nouns using words from **Contextes**. Examples: **du dentifrice** and **du shampooing**.
- Keep in mind that reflexives will only be used in the infinitive and third person singular in the activities until **Structures 19.1**.
- Additional vocabulary for this lesson can be found in the **Vocabulaire supplémentaire** in the IRM on the IRCD-ROM.

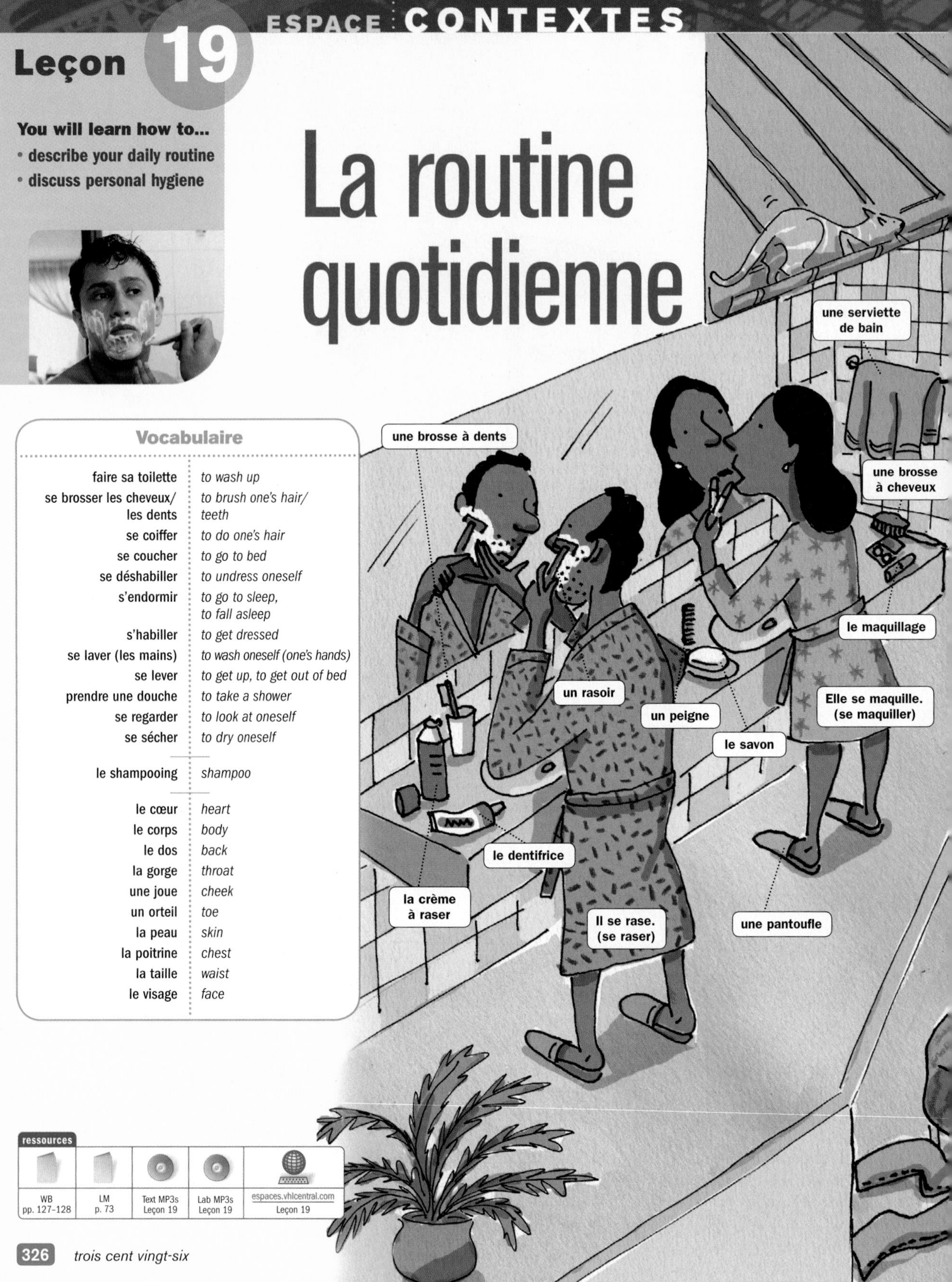

ESPACE CONTEXTES

Leçon 19

You will learn how to...

- **describe your daily routine**
- **discuss personal hygiene**

La routine quotidienne

Vocabulaire

faire sa toilette	*to wash up*
se brosser les cheveux/ les dents	*to brush one's hair/ teeth*
se coiffer	*to do one's hair*
se coucher	*to go to bed*
se déshabiller	*to undress oneself*
s'endormir	*to go to sleep, to fall asleep*
s'habiller	*to get dressed*
se laver (les mains)	*to wash oneself (one's hands)*
se lever	*to get up, to get out of bed*
prendre une douche	*to take a shower*
se regarder	*to look at oneself*
se sécher	*to dry oneself*
le shampooing	*shampoo*
le cœur	*heart*
le corps	*body*
le dos	*back*
la gorge	*throat*
une joue	*cheek*
un orteil	*toe*
la peau	*skin*
la poitrine	*chest*
la taille	*waist*
le visage	*face*

ressources

WB pp. 127–128	LM p. 73	Text MP3s Leçon 19	Lab MP3s Leçon 19	espaces.vhlcentral.com Leçon 19

OPTIONS

Game Write vocabulary words for parts of the body on index cards. On another set of cards, draw or paste pictures to match each term. Tape them face down on the board in random order. Divide the class into two teams. Play a game of Concentration in which students match words with pictures. When a player makes a match, that player's team collects those cards. The team with the most cards at the end of the game wins.

Extra Practice Write two columns on the board: **la routine du matin** and **la routine du soir**. Have students classify the verbs in **Contextes** according to whether people do the actions when they wake up in the morning or in the evening before they go to bed. Then have students order the actions logically. This activity can also be done in pairs.

Attention!

The verbs following the pronoun **se** are called reflexive verbs. You will learn more about them in **ESPACE STRUCTURES**. For now, when talking about another person, place the pronoun **se** between the subject and the verb.

Il se regarde. *He looks at himself.*

Elle se réveille. *She wakes up.*

la tête
un œil (yeux *pl.*)
une oreille
un bras
le nez
la bouche
le cou
le réveil
un doigt
le ventre
un genou (genoux *pl.*)
une jambe
un pied
un doigt de pied
Elle se réveille. (se réveiller)

Mise en pratique

1 Écoutez Sarah, son grand frère Guillaume et leur père parlent de qui va utiliser la salle de bains en premier ce matin. Écoutez la conversation et indiquez si les affirmations suivantes sont **vraies** ou **fausses**.

	Vrai	Faux
1. Guillaume ne va pas se raser.	☐	☑
2. Guillaume doit encore prendre une douche et se brosser les dents.	☑	☐
3. Sarah n'a pas entendu son réveil.	☑	☐
4. Guillaume demande à Sarah de lui apporter de la crème à raser.	☐	☑
5. Guillaume demande à Sarah un savon.	☐	☑
6. Guillaume demande à Sarah une grande serviette de bain.	☑	☐
7. Sarah doit prendre une douche et s'habiller en moins de vingt minutes.	☑	☐
8. Sarah décide de ne pas se maquiller et de ne pas se sécher les cheveux aujourd'hui.	☑	☐

2 Association Associez les activités de la colonne de gauche aux parties du corps correspondantes des colonnes de droite. Notez que certains éléments ne sont pas utilisés et que d'autres sont utilisés plus d'une fois.

1. _e_ écouter	a. la bouche	f. le pied
2. _a/b_ manger	b. la gorge	g. la taille
3. _f_ marcher	c. l'orteil	h. la tête
4. _i_ montrer	d. l'œil	i. le doigt
5. _a/b_ parler	e. l'oreille	j. le nez
6. _h_ penser		
7. _c/i/j/f_ sentir		
8. _d_ regarder		

3 Quel matin! Remplissez les espaces par le mot ou l'expression de la liste qui convient afin de (*in order to*) trouver ce qui est arrivé à Alexandre aujourd'hui. Notez que tous les mots et expressions ne sont pas utilisés. Faites également les accords nécessaires.

le bras	s'habiller	le réveil	la gorge
se brosser les dents	le peigne	se laver	le ventre
se coucher	le pied	le cœur	les yeux

Ce matin, Alexandre n'entend pas son (1) _réveil_. Quand il se lève, il met d'abord le (2) _pied_ gauche par terre. Il entre dans la salle de bains. Là, il ne trouve pas le (3) _peigne_ pour se coiffer ni (*nor*) le dentifrice pour (4) _se brosser les dents_. Il se regarde dans le miroir. Ses (5) _yeux_ sont tout rouges. Comme il a très faim, son (6) _ventre_ commence à faire du bruit (*noise*). Il retourne ensuite dans sa chambre pour (7) _s'habiller_. Il met un pantalon noir et une chemise bleue. Puis, il descend les escaliers et tombe. Après un moment, il retourne dans sa chambre. Après un tel début (*such a beginning*) de journée, Alexandre va (8) _se coucher_.

1 Tapescript SARAH: Allez, Guillaume. J'ai besoin d'utiliser la salle de bains.
GUILLAUME: Une minute! Je viens juste d'y entrer.
S: Mais, je suis en retard pour mes cours. Je n'ai pas entendu mon réveil.
PÈRE: Sarah, laisse ton frère se raser, prendre une douche et se brosser les dents. Il est arrivé le premier.
G: Je fais vite. Tiens! Il n'y a plus de shampooing. Est-ce que tu peux m'apporter une nouvelle bouteille et une grande serviette de bain, s'il te plaît?
S: Et tes pantoufles aussi?
Un peu plus tard…
P: Où est ta sœur?
G: Sarah va prendre sa douche. Elle doit se brosser les dents, s'habiller et se coiffer en moins de vingt minutes. Elle a décidé de ne pas se maquiller et de ne pas se sécher les cheveux pour gagner du temps.
P: Bon, on va te préparer quelque chose à manger dans le bus.
(On Textbook MP3s)

1 Suggestion Have students correct the false statements. If necessary, play the recording again.

2 Expansions
- Have students think of other verbs to add to the list and let the class guess the body part(s) associated with them.
- Do this activity in reverse. Name various parts of the body and have students suggest verbs associated with them.

3 Expansion Ask students comprehension questions based on the paragraph. Examples: **1. Pourquoi Alexandre se lève-t-il tard? (Il n'entend pas son réveil.) 2. Que fait-il d'abord? (Il met le pied par terre.) 3. Où va-t-il? (Il va à la salle de bains.) 4. Ça ne va pas bien. Pourquoi? (Il ne peut pas se coiffer./Il ne trouve pas de dentifrice./Ses yeux sont rouges.) 5. Que met-il quand il s'habille? (un pantalon noir et une chemise bleue) 6. Pourquoi Alexandre veut-t-il se coucher? (parce qu'il tombe quand il descend les escaliers/Il passe une mauvaise matinée.)**

OPTIONS

Pairs Have students write down three daily routine activities. Their partner should ask questions using adverbs of time like **pendant**, **avant**, and **après** in order to guess the activities on their partner's list. Example: **Étudiant(e) 1: C'est avant ou après le petit-déjeuner? Étudiant(e) 2: C'est après le petit-déjeuner. Étudiant(e) 1: C'est se brosser les dents? Étudiant(e) 2: Oui, c'est ça.**

Small Groups Have students work in groups of three. Tell them to draw a picture and write a description of a fantastical alien or monster. Example: **C'est un extraterrestre/un monstre. Il a trois nez, quatre yeux et huit bras.** Then have each group read their description while the class draws a picture of the alien or monster. Have students verify their drawings with the group's picture.

4 Suggestion Have two volunteers read the **modèle** aloud.

4 Expansion For additional practice, give students these items. **13. les doigts de pied 14. la tête 15. le pied**

5 Expansion Use **Transparency #44**. Assign names to the people in the drawings. Then ask questions about the people's actions. Examples: **Qui se lave les mains? Que fait ____?**

6 Expansion Have volunteers read their descriptions to the class without saying the person's name. The class has to guess who it is.

7 Suggestions
- Before beginning this activity, you might want to review telling time and adverbs of time.
- Have two volunteers read the **modèle** aloud. Then divide the class into pairs and distribute the Info Gap Handouts in the IRM on the IRCD-ROM for this activity. Give students ten minutes to complete the activity.

NATIONAL communication STANDARDS

Communication

4 Définition Créez votre propre définition des mots de la liste suivante. Ensuite, à tour de rôle, lisez vos définitions à votre partenaire. Il/Elle doit deviner le mot correspondant. Answers will vary.

MODÈLE

cheveux
Étudiant(e) 1: *On utilise une brosse ou un peigne pour les brosser. Qu'est-ce que c'est?*
Étudiant(e) 2: *Ce sont les cheveux.*

1. le cœur
2. le corps
3. le cou
4. les dents
5. le dos
6. le genou
7. la joue
8. le nez
9. la poitrine
10. le visage
11. l'œil
12. l'orteil

5 Que font-ils? Dites ce que font les personnes suivantes et ce qu'elles utilisent pour le faire. Donnez autant de (*as many*) détails que possible. Ensuite, à tour de rôle avec un(e) partenaire, lisez vos descriptions. Votre partenaire doit deviner quelle image vous décrivez. Answers will vary.

1.

2.

3.

4.

5.

6.

7.

8.

6 Écrivez Pensez à votre acteur/actrice préféré(e). Quelle est sa routine du matin? Décrivez-la et utilisez les adjectifs de la liste suivante et les mots et expressions de la section **ESPACE CONTEXTES**. Answers will vary.

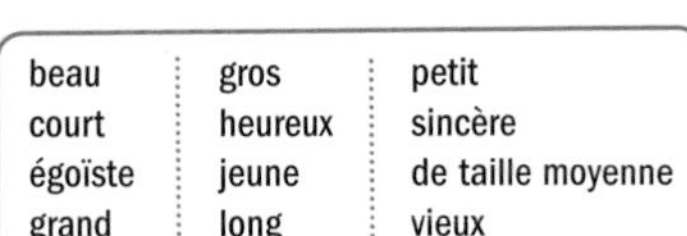

beau	gros	petit
court	heureux	sincère
égoïste	jeune	de taille moyenne
grand	long	vieux

7 Décrivez Votre professeur va vous donner, à vous et à votre partenaire, deux feuilles d'activités différentes. À tour de rôle, posez-vous des questions pour savoir ce que fait Nadia chaque soir et chaque matin. Attention! Ne regardez pas la feuille de votre partenaire. Answers will vary.

MODÈLE

Étudiant(e) 1: *À vingt-trois heures Nadia se déshabille. Que fait-elle ensuite?*
Étudiant(e) 2: *Après, elle...*

OPTIONS

Extra Practice Say the following objects and have students name the body part(s) associated with each one. **1. du shampooing (les cheveux) 2. les lunettes (les yeux) 3. un rasoir (les jambes, le visage) 4. les pantoufles (les pieds) 5. un gant (la main) 6. une écharpe (le cou) 7. un pantalon (les jambes) 8. un peigne (les cheveux) 9. une radio (les oreilles)**

Extra Practice Read these statements to students and have them say whether they are **logique** or **illogique**. **1. Alain prend une douche et puis il se sèche. (logique) 2. Gilles s'habille et puis il se couche. (illogique) 3. Solange se coiffe et puis elle s'endort. (illogique) 4. Isabelle se maquille et puis elle se lave. (illogique) 5. Denis se lève et puis il fait sa toilette. (logique)**

NATIONAL
comparisons
STANDARDS

Les sons et les lettres

Diacriticals for meaning

Some French words with different meanings have nearly identical spellings except for a diacritical mark (*accent*). Sometimes a diacritical does not affect pronunciation at all.

ou	**où**	**a**	**à**
or	*where*	*has*	*to, at*

Sometimes, you can clearly hear the difference between the words.

côte	**côté**	**sale**	**salé**
coast	*side*	*dirty*	*salty*

Very often, two similar-looking words are different parts of speech. Many similar-looking word pairs are those with and without an **-é** at the end.

âge	**âgé**	**entre**	**entré (entrer)**
age (n.)	*elderly* (adj.)	*between* (prep.)	*entered* (p.p.)

In such instances, context should make their meaning clear.

Tu as quel âge?
How old are you? / What is your age?

C'est un homme âgé.
He's an elderly man.

Prononcez Répétez les mots suivants à voix haute.

1. la (*the*) là (*there*)
2. êtes (*are*) étés (*summers*)
3. jeune (*young*) jeûne (*fasting*)
4. pêche (*peach*) pêché (*fished*)

Articulez Répétez les phrases suivantes à voix haute.

1. J'habite dans une ferme (*farm*).
   Le magasin est fermé (*closed*).
2. Les animaux mangent du maïs (*corn*).
   Je suis suisse, mais il est belge.
3. Est-ce que tu es prête?
   J'ai prêté ma voiture à Marcel.
4. La lampe est à côté de la chaise.
   J'adore la côte ouest de la France.

Dictons Répétez les dictons à voix haute.

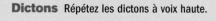

À vos marques, prêts, partez! [1]

C'est un prêté pour un rendu. [2]

[1] On your mark, get set, go!
[2] One good turn deserves another. (lit. It is one loaned for one returned.)

ressources

LM p. 74	Text MP3s Leçon 19	Lab MP3s Leçon 19	espaces.vhlcentral.com Leçon 19

Section Goals

In this section, students will learn about the use of diacriticals to distinguish between words with the same or similar spellings.

Instructional Resources
Textbook MP3s
Lab Manual, p. 74
Lab MP3s
WB/VM/LM Answer Key
IRCD-ROM: IRM (Textbook Audioscript; Lab Audioscript)
espaces.vhlcentral.com: activities, downloads, reference tools

Suggestions

- Model the pronunciation of the example words and have students repeat after you.
- Write examples of other past participles that are used as adjectives on the board. Examples: **réservé** and **préparé**. Ask students to provide more examples.
- Have students give you the English equivalents for the following words in the **Articulez**: **2. mais 3. prête** and **prêté 4. côté** and **côte**.
- Dictate five simple sentences with words that have diacriticals that distinguish meaning, repeating each one at least two times. Then write the sentences on the board or a transparency and have students check their spelling.

Dictons Have students compare the pronunciation and meaning of **prêts** and **prêté**. Then have them identify their parts of speech.

OPTIONS

Extra Practice Use these sentences that contain words with and without diacriticals for additional practice or as a dictation. **1. Quel âge a-t-il? Mon grand-père est âgé. 2. Le bureau est entre le lit et la porte. Marcel est entré dans la salle. 3. La ligne est occupée. Suzanne s'occupe des enfants. 4. J'ai réservé une table au restaurant. Sylvain est réservé.**

Extra Practice Teach students this French tongue-twister that contains diacriticals that affect meaning. **Un pécheur péchait sous un pêcher, le pêcher empêchait le pécheur de pécher, le pécheur coupa le pêcher, le pêcher n'empêcha plus le pécheur de pécher.**

Section Goals

In this section, students will learn functional phrases for talking about daily routines and emotional states.

Instructional Resources
WB/VM: Video Manual, pp. 247–248
WB/VM/LM Answer Key
Video CD-ROM
Video on DVD
*IRCD-ROM: IRM (Videoscript; **Roman-photo** Translations)*
espaces.vhlcentral.com: activities, downloads, reference tools

Video Recap: Leçon 18
Before doing this **Roman-photo**, review the previous one with this activity.
1. Quel cadeau Rachid a-t-il apporté à Sandrine? (des chocolats)
2. Et David, qu'a-t-il apporté à Sandrine? (des fleurs)
3. Qui aide à mettre la table? (Amina et Stéphane)
4. Qui est au régime? (Amina)
5. Qu'est-ce que Sandrine a préparé comme dessert? (une tarte aux pommes)

Video Synopsis
In the bathroom, David notices a rash on his face. Rachid needs to use the bathroom, because he woke up late and doesn't want to be late for class. David is taking a long time to get ready. When David finally opens the door, Rachid tricks him into closing his eyes so that he can slip into the bathroom and lock the door. Rachid also advises David to call a doctor about his rash.

Suggestions
- Have students predict what the episode will be about based on the video stills.
- Tell students to scan the **Roman-photo** and find sentences related to daily routines.
- After reading the **Roman-photo** in pairs, have students summarize the episode.

Drôle de surprise

PERSONNAGES

David

Rachid

1

Chez David et Rachid...
DAVID Oh là là, ça ne va pas du tout, toi!
RACHID David, tu te dépêches? Il est sept heures et quart. Je dois me préparer, moi aussi!

2

DAVID Ne t'inquiète pas. Je finis de me brosser les dents!
RACHID On doit partir dans moins de vingt minutes. Tu ne te rends pas compte!
DAVID Excuse-moi, mais on s'est couché tard hier soir.
RACHID Oui et on ne s'est pas réveillé à l'heure, mais mon prof de sciences po, ça ne l'intéresse pas tout ça.

3

DAVID Attends, je ne trouve pas le peigne... Ah, le voilà. Je me coiffe... Deux secondes!
RACHID C'était vraiment sympa hier soir... On s'entend tous super bien et on ne s'ennuie jamais ensemble... Mais enfin, qu'est-ce que tu fais? Je dois me raser, prendre une douche et m'habiller, en exactement dix-sept minutes!

6

RACHID Bon, tu veux bien me passer ma brosse à dents, le dentifrice et un rasoir, s'il te plaît?
DAVID Attends une minute. Je me dépêche.
RACHID Comment est-ce qu'un mec peut prendre aussi longtemps dans la salle de bains?

7

DAVID Euh, j'ai un petit problème...
RACHID Qu'est-ce que tu as sur le visage?
DAVID Aucune idée.
RACHID Est-ce que tu as mal à la gorge? Fais: Ah!
RACHID Et le ventre, ça va?
DAVID Oui, oui ça va...

8

RACHID Attends, je vais examiner tes yeux... regarde à droite, à gauche... maintenant ferme-les. Bien. Tourne-toi...
DAVID Hé!

ACTIVITÉS

1 Vrai ou faux? Indiquez si les affirmations suivantes sont **vraies** ou **fausses**.

1. David se sent (*feels*) bien ce matin. Faux.
2. Rachid est pressé ce matin. Vrai.
3. David se rase. Faux.
4. David se maquille. Faux.
5. Rachid doit prendre une douche. Vrai.
6. David ne s'est pas réveillé à l'heure. Vrai.
7. David s'est couché tôt hier soir. Faux.
8. Tout le monde s'est bien amusé (*had a good time*) hier soir. Vrai.
9. Les amis se disputent souvent. Faux.
10. Rachid est très inquiet pour David. Faux.

OPTIONS

Avant de regarder la vidéo Tell students to read the title and scene setter. Then have them brainstorm what two roommates might say as they are trying to get ready for class at the same time. Write their ideas on the board.

Regarder la vidéo Show the video episode once without sound and have the class create a plot summary based on the visual cues. Then show the episode with sound and have the class make corrections and fill in any gaps in the plot summary.

LE FRANÇAIS QUOTIDIEN

Les parties du corps

bec (*m.*)	*mouth*
caboche (*f.*)	*head*
carreaux (*m.*)	*eyes*
esgourdes (*f.*)	*ears*
gosier (*m.*)	*throat*
paluche (*f.*)	*hand*
panard (*m.*)	*foot*
pif (*m.*)	*nose*
tifs (*m.*)	*hair*

LE MONDE FRANCOPHONE

Des expressions près du corps

Voici quelques expressions idiomatiques.

En France

avoir le bras long être une personne importante qui peut influencer quelqu'un
avoir un chat dans la gorge ne pas pouvoir parler
casser les pieds à quelqu'un ennuyer une personne
coûter les yeux de la tête coûter très cher
se mettre le doigt dans l'œil faire une erreur

Au Québec

avoir quelqu'un dans le dos détester quelqu'un
coûter un bras coûter très cher
un froid à couper un cheveu un très grand froid
sur le bras gratuit, qu'on n'a pas besoin de payer

En Suisse

avoir des tournements de tête avoir des vertiges°
donner une bonne-main donner un pourboire

vertiges *dizziness, vertigo*

PORTRAIT

L'Occitane

En 1976, un jeune étudiant en littérature de 23 ans, Olivier Baussan, a commencé à fabriquer chez lui de l'huile de romarin° et l'a vendue sur les marchés de Provence. Son huile a été très appréciée par le public et Baussan a fondé° L'Occitane, marque° de produits de beauté. La première boutique a ouvert ses portes dans le sud de la France en 1980 et aujourd'hui, la compagnie a plus de 500 boutiques dans 60 pays, y compris aux États-Unis et au Canada. Les produits de L'Occitane, tous faits d'ingrédients naturels comme la lavande° ou l'olive, s'inspirent de la Provence et sont fabriqués avec des méthodes traditionnelles. L'Occitane offre des produits de beauté, des parfums, du maquillage et des produits pour le bain, pour la douche et pour la maison.

huile de romarin *rosemary oil* **fondé** *founded* **marque** *brand* **lavande** *lavender*

SUR INTERNET

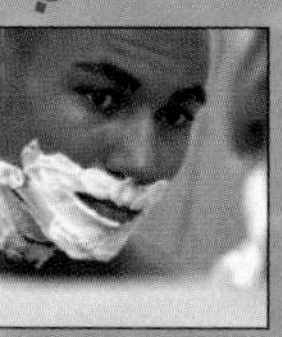

Les hommes en France dépensent-ils beaucoup d'argent pour les produits de beauté ou de soin?

Go to **espaces.vhlcentral.com** to find more cultural information related to this **ESPACE CULTURE**.

ACTIVITÉS

2 Vrai ou faux? Indiquez si les phrases suivantes sont **vraies** ou **fausses**. Corrigez les phrases fausses.

1. La compagnie L'Occitane a été fondée en Provence. Vrai.
2. Le premier magasin L'Occitane a ouvert ses portes en 1976. Faux. La compagnie a été fondée en 1976, mais le premier magasin a ouvert ses portes en 1980.
3. On trouve l'olive dans certains produits de L'Occitane. Vrai.
4. L'Occitane se spécialise dans les produits pour le corps. Faux. L'Occitane offre aussi des parfums, du maquillage et des produits pour la maison.
5. Les produits de L'Occitane utilisent des ingrédients naturels et sont fabriqués avec des méthodes traditionnelles. Vrai.

3 Les expressions idiomatiques Regardez bien la liste des expressions dans **Le monde francophone**. En petits groupes, discutez de ces expressions. Lesquelles (*Which*) aimez-vous? Pourquoi? Essayez de deviner l'équivalent de ces expressions en anglais.

ressources

espaces.vhlcentral.com
Leçon 19

Le français quotidien
- Model the pronunciation of each term and have students repeat it.
- Say the words and have students point to the corresponding body part.

Portrait
- Have students look at the photo and identify the product. Ask students: **Avez-vous déjà utilisé un produit de l'Occitane? Quel produit?**
- These products contain oils used in homeopathic remedies, a form of alternative medicine. Some product lines are based on honey (**le miel**), verbena (**la verveine**), everlasting flower (**l'immortelle**) from Corsica, or shea (**le karité**) from Africa.

Le monde francophone Model the pronunciation of each expression and have students repeat it. You might also give them these expressions: **prendre ses jambes à son cou (partir très vite)** (France), **perdre la tête (devenir fou)** (France), **être beau/belle comme un cœur (être très beau/belle)** (Canada).

2 Expansion For additional practice, give students these items. **6. Les produits de L'Occitane sont vendus seulement en France. (Faux. Il y a plus de 500 boutiques dans 60 pays.) 7. Olivier Baussan étudiait les maths avant de lancer sa compagnie. (Faux. Il étudiait la littérature.) 8. Baussan a d'abord travaillé avec l'huile de lavande. (Faux. Il a d'abord travaillé avec l'huile de romarin.)**

3 Expansion Have students write five sentences using these expressions in a specific context. Example: **Mon billet d'avion m'a coûté les yeux de la tête!**

OPTIONS

Cultural Activity Go to the L'Occitane web site in France at **http://www.loccitane.fr**. Print out a few pages of gift ideas for men and women from their **Boutique cadeaux**, and make photocopies to distribute to pairs. Tell students to take turns asking each other questions about the products and which ones they want to buy.

Les parties du corps Have students write four true/false statements defining the terms from **Le français quotidien**. Examples: **1. Le gosier est le pied. (Faux.) 2. La paluche veut dire la main. (Vrai.)** Then have students get together with a classmate and take turns reading their statements and responding.

Section Goals

In this section, students will learn:
- present-tense reflexive verbs
- the imperative with reflexive verbs

National Standards: comparisons

Instructional Resources
WB/VM: Workbook, pp. 129–130
Lab Manual, p. 75
Lab MP3s
WB/VM/LM Answer Key
*IRCD-ROM: IRM (**Essayez!** and **Mise en pratique** answers; Lab Audioscript; **Feuilles d'activités**)*
espaces.vhlcentral.com: activities, downloads, reference tools

Suggestions
- Model the first person reflexive by talking about yourself. Examples: **Je me réveille très tôt. En général, je me lève à six heures du matin.**
- Model the second person by asking questions using verbs you mentioned in the first person. Examples: **À quelle heure vous réveillez-vous pendant la semaine? Vous levez-vous tôt ou tard en général?** Encourage student responses.
- Introduce the third person by making statements and asking questions about what a student has told you. Examples: ____ **se lève très tard le samedi, n'est-ce pas? (Oui, il/elle se lève entre onze heures et midi.)**
- Write the paradigm of **se laver** on the board and model its pronunciation.
- Use magazine pictures to clarify meanings between third person singular and third person plural forms. Examples: **La femme sur cette photo-ci se maquille. Sur cette photo-là les enfants se couchent.**
- Compare and contrast reflexive and non-reflexive verbs with examples like these: **Il se réveille à six heures et demie. Il réveille les enfants à sept heures.**

19.1 Reflexive verbs

Point de départ A reflexive verb usually describes what a person does to or for himself or herself. In other words, it "reflects" the action of the verb back to the subject. Reflexive verbs always use reflexive pronouns.

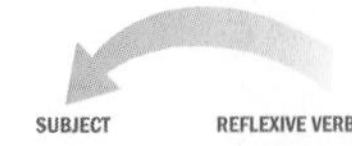

SUBJECT — REFLEXIVE VERB
André **se rase** à huit heures.

Reflexive verbs

	se laver *(to wash oneself)*	
je	**me lave**	*I wash (myself)*
tu	**te laves**	*you wash (yourself)*
il/elle	**se lave**	*he/she/it washes (himself/herself/itself)*
nous	**nous lavons**	*we wash (ourselves)*
vous	**vous lavez**	*you wash (yourself/yourselves)*
ils/elles	**se lavent**	*they wash (themselves)*

- The pronoun **se** before an infinitive identifies the verb as reflexive: **se laver**.

Je me coiffe.
Tu te maquilles, maintenant?

- When a reflexive verb is conjugated, the reflexive pronoun agrees with the subject. Except for **se**, reflexive pronouns have the same forms as direct and indirect object pronouns; **se** is used for both singular and plural subjects.

Tu **te couches**. *You're going to bed.*	Les enfants **se réveillent**. *The children wake up.*
Je **me maquille** aussi. *I put on makeup too.*	Nous **nous levons** très tôt. *We get up very early.*

- Note that the reflexive pronouns **nous** and **vous** are identical to the corresponding subject pronouns.

Nous **nous regardons** dans le miroir. *We look at ourselves in the mirror.*	**Vous habillez**-vous déjà? *Are you getting dressed already?*

MISE EN PRATIQUE

1 Les habitudes Vous descendez chez vos amis Frédéric et Pauline. Tout le monde a ses habitudes. Que fait-on tous les jours?

MODÈLE Frédéric / se raser
Frédéric se rase.

1. vous / se réveiller / à six heures
   Vous vous réveillez à six heures.
2. Frédéric et Pauline / se brosser / dents
   Frédéric et Pauline se brossent les dents.
3. je / se lever / puis / prendre une douche
   Je me lève puis je prends une douche.
4. nous / sécher / cheveux
   Nous nous séchons les cheveux.
5. on / s'habiller / avant le petit-déjeuner
   On s'habille avant le petit-déjeuner.
6. tu / se coiffer / avant / sortir
   Tu te coiffes avant de sortir.
7. Frédéric et Pauline / se déshabiller / et après / se coucher
   Frédéric et Pauline se déshabillent, et après ils se couchent.
8. tout le monde / s'endormir / tout de suite
   Tout le monde s'endort tout de suite.

2 La routine Tous les matins, Juliette suit (*follows*) la même routine. Regardez les illustrations et dites ce que (*what*) fait Juliette.

1. Juliette se réveille.

2. Juliette se lève.

3. Juliette se brosse les dents.

4. Juliette se maquille.

3 L'ordre logique À tour de rôle avec un(e) partenaire, indiquez dans quel ordre vous (ou quelqu'un que vous connaissez) faites ces choses. Suggested answers

MODÈLE se lever / se réveiller
D'abord je me réveille, ensuite je me lève.

1. se laver / se sécher
   D'abord je me lave, ensuite je me sèche.
2. se maquiller / prendre une douche
   D'abord ma sœur prend une douche, ensuite elle se maquille.
3. se lever / s'habiller
   D'abord mon camarade de chambre se lève, ensuite il s'habille.
4. se raser / se réveiller
   D'abord je me réveille, ensuite je me rase.
5. se coucher / se brosser les cheveux
   D'abord nous nous brossons les cheveux, ensuite nous nous couchons.
6. s'endormir / se coucher
   D'abord tu te couches, ensuite tu t'endors.
7. se coucher / se déshabiller
   D'abord je me déshabille, ensuite je me couche.
8. se lever / se réveiller
   D'abord le prof se réveille, ensuite il se lève.

OPTIONS

Extra Practice To provide oral practice with reflexive verbs, create sentences that follow the pattern of the sentences in the examples. Say each sentence, have students repeat it, and then say a different subject. Have students then say the new sentence with the new subject, changing pronouns and verb forms as necessary. Example: **Je me brosse les dents deux fois par jour.: on (On se brosse les dents deux fois par jour.)**

TPR Model gestures for a few of the reflexive verbs. Examples: **se coucher** (*lay head on folded hands*), **se coiffer** (*pretend to fix hair*). Have students stand. Begin by practicing as a class using only the **nous** form, saying an expression at random. Example: **Nous nous lavons les mains.** Then vary the verb forms and point to individuals or groups of students who should perform the appropriate gesture. Keep the pace rapid.

COMMUNICATION

4 Tous les jours Que fait votre partenaire tous les jours? Posez-lui les questions et il/elle vous répond. Some answers will vary.

MODÈLE se lever tôt le matin

Étudiant(e) 1: *Est-ce que tu te lèves tôt le matin?*
Étudiant(e) 2: *Non, je ne me lève pas tôt le matin.*

1. se réveiller tôt ou tard le week-end
   Est-ce que tu te réveilles tôt ou tard le week-end?
2. se lever tout de suite
   Est-ce que tu te lèves tout de suite?
3. se maquiller tous les matins
   Est-ce que tu te maquilles tous les matins?
4. se laver les cheveux tous les jours
   Est-ce que tu te laves les cheveux tous les jours?
5. se raser le soir ou le matin
   Est-ce que tu te rases le soir ou le matin?
6. se coucher avant ou après minuit
   Est-ce que tu te couches avant ou après minuit?

5 Enquête Votre professeur va vous donner une feuille d'activités. Circulez dans la classe et trouvez un(e) camarade différent(e) pour chaque action. Présentez les réponses à la classe. Answers will vary.

MODÈLE

Étudiant(e) 1: *Est-ce que tu te lèves avant six heures du matin?*
Étudiant(e) 2: *Oui, je me lève parfois à cinq heures!*

Activité	Nom
1. se lever avant six heures du matin	Carole
2. se maquiller pour venir en cours	
3. se brosser les dents trois fois par jour	
4. se laver les cheveux le soir	
5. se coiffer à la dernière mode	
6. se reposer le vendredi soir	

6 Jacques a dit Par groupes de quatre, un(e) étudiant(e) donne des ordres au groupe. Attention! Vous devez obéir seulement si l'ordre est précédé de **Jacques a dit...** (*Simon says...*) La personne qui se trompe devient le meneur de jeu (*leader*). Le gagnant (*winner*) est l'étudiant(e) qui n'a pas été le meneur de jeu. Utilisez les expressions de la liste puis trouvez vos propres expressions. Answers will vary.

se brosser les dents	se laver les mains
se coiffer	se lever
s'endormir	se maquiller
s'habiller	se sécher les cheveux

Common reflexive verbs

se brosser les cheveux/ les dents	*to brush one's hair/teeth*	**se laver (les mains)**	*to wash oneself (one's hands)*
se coiffer	*to do one's hair*	**se lever**	*to get up, to get out of bed*
se coucher	*to go to bed*	**se maquiller**	*to put on makeup*
se déshabiller	*to undress*	**se raser**	*to shave oneself*
s'endormir	*to go to sleep, to fall asleep*	**se regarder**	*to look at oneself*
		se réveiller	*to wake up*
s'habiller	*to get dressed*	**se sécher**	*to dry oneself*

- **S'endormir** is conjugated like **dormir. Se lever** and **se sécher** follow the same spelling-change patterns as **acheter** and **espérer**, respectively.

  Il **s'endort** tôt. *He falls asleep early.*
  Tu **te lèves** à quelle heure? *What time do you get up?*
  Elles **se sèchent**. *They dry off.*

- Some verbs can be used reflexively or non-reflexively. If the verb acts upon something other than the subject, the non-reflexive form is used.

  La mère **se réveille** à sept heures. *The mother wakes up at 7 o'clock.*
  Ensuite, elle **réveille** son fils. *Then, she wakes her son up.*

- When a body part is the direct object of a reflexive verb, it is usually preceded by a definite article.

  Je ne **me brosse** pas **les** dents. *I'm not brushing my teeth.*
  Vous **vous lavez les** mains. *You wash your hands.*

- You form the imperative of a reflexive verb as you would a non-reflexive verb. Add the reflexive pronoun to the end of an affirmative command. In negative commands, place the reflexive pronoun between **ne** and the verb. (Remember to change **te** to **toi** in affirmative commands.)

  Réveille-toi, Bruno! *Wake up, Bruno!* *but* **Ne te réveille pas**! *Don't wake up!*

Essayez! Complétez les phrases avec les formes correctes des verbes.

1. Ils *se brossent* (se brosser) les dents.
2. À quelle heure est-ce que vous vous couchez (se coucher)?
3. Tu t'endors (s'endormir) en cours.
4. Nous nous séchons (se sécher) les cheveux.
5. On s'habille (s'habiller) vite! Il faut partir.
6. Les hommes se maquillent (se maquiller) rarement.
7. Tu ne te déshabilles (se déshabiller) pas encore.
8. Je me lève (se lever) vers onze heures.

Essayez! Have students say logical commands for items 2, 3, 4, and 7. (**2. Couchez-vous [de bonne heure]. 3. Ne t'endors pas en cours. 4. Séchons-nous les cheveux. 7. Ne te déshabille pas.)**

1 Suggestion Before assigning this activity, review reflexive verbs by comparing and contrasting weekday versus weekend routines. Example: **Vous couchez-vous plus tôt pendant la semaine?**

2 Expansion Repeat the activity as a pattern drill, supplying different subjects for each drawing. Example: **1. je (Je me réveille.) 2. ils (Ils se lèvent.)**

3 Suggestion Tell students that they may vary the sequencing expressions used, such as **puis** instead of **ensuite**.

3 Expansion Have students say two sentences in which they combine more than two activities. Example: **se lever / se laver / se maquiller (D'abord ma mère se lève, ensuite elle se lave et finalement elle se maquille.)**

4 Expansion Have students come up with four additional items. Pairs then switch papers and form questions.

5 Suggestion Have two students demonstrate the **modèle**. Then distribute the **Feuilles d'activités** from the IRM on the IRCD-ROM.

6 Suggestion To give winners a chance to lead the game, have **le/la gagnant(e)** from each group come to the front of the room to take turns saying **Jacques a dit...**.

OPTIONS

Extra Practice Have students compare their own routines with Juliette's in **Activité 2** on page 334. Have them express each part of the morning routine that they have in common. Example: **Moi aussi, je me réveille et puis je me lève.** Then have them express any differences. Examples: **Je ne me maquille pas (tous les matins). Juliette ne se lave pas le visage. Moi, si, je me lave le visage.**

Small Groups Have groups of three pretend that they share an apartment with only one bathroom. Tell them to have a conversation in which they discuss their morning schedule problems. Example: **Étudiant(e) 1: J'ai cours à huit heures. Je me lève à sept heures et je me lave tout de suite. Étudiant(e) 2: Moi aussi, je dois me laver à sept heures. Étudiant(e) 3: Alors, ____, réveille-toi à sept heures moins le quart.**

comparisons NATIONAL STANDARDS

Section Goals

In this section, students will learn idiomatic reflexive expressions.

Instructional Resources
WB/VM: Workbook, pp. 131–132
Lab Manual, p. 76
Lab MP3s
WB/VM/LM Answer Key
*IRCD-ROM: IRM (**Essayez!** and **Mise en pratique** answers; Lab Audioscript)*
espaces.vhlcentral.com: activities, downloads, reference tools

Suggestions

- Remind students what idiomatic expressions are. Ask which types of these expressions students already know. (idiomatic expressions with **avoir** and **faire**)
- Go through the list of common idiomatic reflexives with the class, pronouncing them and having students repeat. Have them point out which verb(s) they have seen before, such as **s'appeler**.
- Ask students to study the list and note related English words. Examples: **s'amuser** *amuse*, **s'occuper** *occupy*.
- Call attention to the spelling-change verbs and the irregular **s'asseoir**.
- To show how **s'asseoir** can be polite or abrupt in its imperative form, tell students that **Assieds-toi/Asseyez-vous** can mean *Be seated., Have a seat.*, or *Sit down!*
- Point out that when using a verb with **que**, it means *that* as in the example: **Je me souviens que tu m'as téléphoné.** = *I remember (that) you phoned me.* Although the word *that* is optional in English, stress that **que** is required in French.

19.2 Reflexives: *Sens idiomatique*

Point de départ You've learned that reflexive verbs "reflect" the action back to the subject. Some reflexive verbs, however, do not literally express a reflexive meaning.

Common idiomatic reflexives

s'amuser	*to play; to have fun*	**s'intéresser (à)**	*to be interested (in)*
s'appeler	*to be called*	**se mettre à**	*to begin to*
s'arrêter	*to stop*	**se mettre en colère**	*to become angry*
s'asseoir	*to sit down*	**s'occuper (de)**	*to take care of, to keep oneself busy*
se dépêcher	*to hurry*	**se préparer**	*to get ready*
se détendre	*to relax*	**se promener**	*to take a walk*
se disputer (avec)	*to argue (with)*	**se rendre compte**	*to realize*
s'énerver	*to get worked up, to become upset*	**se reposer**	*to rest*
s'ennuyer	*to get bored*	**se souvenir (de)**	*to remember*
s'entendre bien (avec)	*to get along well (with)*	**se tromper**	*to be mistaken*
s'inquiéter	*to worry*	**se trouver**	*to be located*

- **Se souvenir** is conjugated like **venir**.

Souviens-toi de son anniversaire.
Remember her birthday.

Nous nous souvenons de cette date.
We remember that date.

- **S'ennuyer** has the same spelling changes as **envoyer**. **Se promener** and **s'inquiéter** have the same spelling changes as **acheter** and **espérer**, respectively.

Je **m'ennuie** à mourir aujourd'hui.
I'm bored to death today.

On **se promène** dans le parc.
We take a walk in the park.

Ils **s'inquiètent** pour leur fille.
They worry about their daughter.

MISE EN PRATIQUE

1 Ma sœur et moi Complétez ce texte avec les formes correctes des verbes.

Je (1) m'appelle (s'appeler) Anne, et j'ai une sœur, Stéphanie. Nous (2) nous habillons (s'habiller) souvent de la même manière, mais nous sommes très différentes. Stéphanie (3) s'intéresse (s'intéresser) à la politique et elle étudie le droit, et moi, je (4) m'intéresse (s'intéresser) à la peinture et je fais de l'art. Nous habitons ensemble, et nous (5) nous entendons bien (s'entendre bien). On (6) s'assied (s'asseoir) souvent sur un banc (*bench*) pour bavarder. Quelquefois on (7) se met en colère (se mettre en colère). Heureusement, on (8) se rend compte (se rendre compte) que c'est inutile et on (9) s'arrête (s'arrêter). En fait, Stéphanie et moi, nous (10) ne nous ennuyons pas (ne pas s'ennuyer) ensemble.

2 Que faire? Que font Diane et ses copains? Utilisez les verbes de la liste pour compléter les phrases. Suggested answers

s'amuser	se disputer	s'occuper
s'appeler	s'énerver	se préparer
s'asseoir	s'ennuyer	se promener
se dépêcher	s'entendre	se reposer
se détendre	s'inquiéter	se tromper

1. Si j'arrive en retard à mon cours, je me dépêche.
2. Parfois, Toufik se trompe et ne donne pas la bonne réponse.
3. Quand un cours n'est pas intéressant, nous nous ennuyons.
4. Le week-end, Hubert et Édith sont fatigués, alors ils se reposent.
5. Quand je ne comprends pas mon prof, je m'inquiète.
6. Quand il fait beau, vous allez dans le parc et vous vous promenez.

3 La fête Marc a invité ses amis pour célébrer la fin (*end*) du semestre. Avec un(e) partenaire, décrivez la scène à tour de rôle. Utilisez tous les verbes possibles de la liste de l'**Activité 2.** Answers will vary.

OPTIONS

Pairs Have students write a short account of their own daily routine using both types of reflexives. Pairs then compare and contrast their routines using a Venn Diagram. Have the pair write one of their names in the left circle, the other in the right circle, and **les deux** where the circles overlap. They list their activities in the appropriate locations. Remind them to change the subject pronoun to **nous** in the overlapping section.

Game Have two teams write descriptions of five famous people or places (**se trouver**), real or fictional, using idiomatic reflexives. Team members take turns reading their descriptions while the opposing team gets three chances to guess who or what is being described. Each correct guess wins a point, while a team that fools its opponents gets two points. For a tiebreaker, you give clues to both teams. The first to guess correctly wins.

COMMUNICATION

4 Se connaître Vous voulez mieux connaître vos camarades. Par groupes de quatre, posez-vous des questions et puis présentez les réponses à la classe. Answers will vary.

MODÈLE s'intéresser à la politique

Étudiant(e) 1: *Je ne m'intéresse pas à la politique. Et toi, t'intéresses-tu à la politique?*
Étudiant(e) 2: *Je m'intéresse beaucoup à la politique et je lis le journal tous les jours.*

1. s'amuser au cours de français
2. s'inquiéter pour des questions d'argent
3. s'asseoir au premier rang (*row*) dans la classe
4. s'énerver facilement
5. se mettre souvent en colère
6. se reposer le week-end

5 Curieux Utilisez ces verbes et expressions pour interviewer un(e) partenaire. Answers will vary.

MODÈLE s'amuser / avec qui

Étudiant(e) 1: *Avec qui est-ce que tu t'amuses?*
Étudiant(e) 2: *Je m'amuse avec mes amis.*

1. s'entendre bien / avec qui
2. s'intéresser / à quoi
3. s'ennuyer / quand, pourquoi
4. se mettre en colère / pourquoi
5. se détendre / quand, comment
6. se promener / avec qui, où, quand
7. se disputer / avec qui, pourquoi
8. se dépêcher / quand, pourquoi

6 Une mère inquiète La mère de Philippe lui a écrit cet e-mail. Avec un(e) partenaire, préparez par écrit la réponse de Philippe. Employez des verbes réfléchis à sens idiomatique. Answers will vary.

Mon chéri,

Je m'inquiète beaucoup pour toi. Je me rends compte que tu as changé. Tu ne t'amuses pas avec tes amis et tu te mets constamment en colère. Maintenant, tu restes tout le temps dans ta chambre et tu t'intéresses seulement à la télé. Est-ce que tu t'ennuies à l'école? Te souviens-tu que tu as des amis? J'espère que je me trompe.

- Note the spelling changes of **s'appeler** in the present tense.

s'appeler (to be named, to call oneself)	
je m'appelle	nous nous appelons
tu t'appelles	vous vous appelez
il/elle s'appelle	ils/elles s'appellent

Tu **t'appelles** comment?
What is your name?

Vous **vous appelez** Laure?
Is your name Laure?

- Note the irregular conjugation of the verb **s'asseoir**.

s'asseoir (to be seated, to sit down)	
je m'assieds	nous nous asseyons
tu t'assieds	vous vous asseyez
il/elle s'assied	ils/elles s'asseyent

Asseyez-vous, Monsieur.
Have a seat, sir.

Assieds-toi ici sur le canapé.
Sit here on the sofa.

- Many idiomatically reflexive expressions can be used alone, with a preposition, or with the conjunction **que**.

Tu **te trompes**.
You're wrong.

Il **se trompe** toujours **de** date.
He's always mixing up the date.

Marlène **s'énerve** facilement.
Marlène gets mad easily.

Marlène **s'énerve contre** Thierry.
Marlène gets mad at Thierry.

Ils **se souviennent de** ton anniversaire.
They remember your birthday.

Je **me souviens que** tu m'as téléphoné.
I remember you phoned me.

Essayez! Choisissez les formes correctes des verbes.

1. Mes parents *s'inquiètent* (s'inquiéter) beaucoup.
2. Nous ___nous entendons___ (s'entendre) bien, ma sœur et moi.
3. Alexis ne ___se rend___ (se rendre) pas compte que sa petite amie ne l'aime pas.
4. On doit ___se dépêcher___ (se dépêcher) pour arriver à la fac.
5. Papa ___s'occupe___ (s'occuper) toujours de la cuisine.
6. Tu ___t'amuses___ (s'amuser) quand tu vas au cinéma?
7. Vous ___vous intéressez___ (s'intéresser) au cours d'histoire de l'art?
8. Je ne ___me dispute___ (se disputer) pas souvent avec les profs.
9. Tu ___te reposes___ (se reposer) un peu sur le lit.
10. Angélique ___s'assied___ (s'asseoir) toujours près de la porte.
11. Je ___m'appelle___ (s'appeler) Susanne.
12. Elles ___s'ennuient___ (s'ennuyer) chez leurs cousins.

Essayez! Give these sentences for additional practice. Tell students to choose a reflexive verb from the list. **13. La boulangerie ____ à côté de l'épicerie. (se trouve) 14. Cette fête est nulle. On ____. (s'ennuie) 15. Mes copains disent que ce cours est facile, mais je ne suis pas d'accord. Je pense qu'ils ____ (se trompent).**

1 Expansion Give students related sentences like the following. **1. Stéphanie et Anne ____ (se promener) parfois le week-end. (se promènent) 2. Le soir, elles ____ (ne pas s'endormir) tout de suite parce qu'elles parlent beaucoup. (ne s'endorment pas)**

2 Expansion Give additional statements modeled on those in the activity. Examples: **7. Cette étudiante n'est pas très patiente et elle ____ facilement. (s'énerve) 8. Tu t'entends assez bien avec mon frère, mais quelquefois vous ____. (vous disputez)**

3 Suggestion Help pairs get started by asking a question or two to the whole class. Example: **Que fait Fatima? (Elle s'ennuie./ Elle ne parle pas.)**

4 Suggestions
- Have two volunteers act out the **modèle**.
- Give more topics to discuss. Examples: **s'appeler comme son père/sa mère** and **s'entendre bien avec tout le monde**.

5 Expansion Have two pairs form a group of four. Students take turns asking questions in the second person plural. Example: **Vous vous amusez bien avec vos amis? (Oui, nous nous amusons bien avec eux.)** Then have students report back to the class in the third person singular and plural. Examples: ____ **s'entend bien avec sa tante.** ____ **et** ____ **s'intéressent à la médecine.**

6 Suggestion Read the e-mail aloud and ask if students have any questions before assigning this activity.

OPTIONS

Extra Practice Have students think of a friend or family member to whom they are particularly close. Assign a short writing task in which students describe their relationship with this person using at least five different common idiomatic reflexives. Tell them to be creative. They may also refer to **Activité 1** on page 336 for example sentences.

Video Replay the video episode, having students focus on reflexive verbs. Stop the video strategically to discuss how reflexives are used in various structures. Examples: **Je dois me préparer, moi aussi!** (infinitive) **Ne t'inquiète pas.** (command) **Tu ne te rends pas compte!** (present tense) Have students identify the **passé composé** of reflexive verbs, but tell them it will be formally introduced in **Structures 20.1**.

Synthèse

Instructional Resources
IRCD-ROM: IRM (Info Gap Activities); Testing Program, pp. 73–76; Test Files; Testing Program MP3s; Test Generator espaces.vhlcentral.com: activities, downloads, reference tools

1 Suggestion First, have students describe the people physically as a brief review activity. Then have them make up names for the people before describing what they are doing.

2 Suggestion Act out the **modèle** with a volunteer. Then point out the use of double object pronouns. Review the correct order if necessary.

3 Suggestion Before assigning groups, go over some of the things that men and women do differently to get ready to go out. Examples: **Les femmes ne se rasent pas le visage. Les hommes ne se maquillent pas.** Then ask students to give their opinion on the question and divide the class into groups accordingly. Encourage students to use other reflexives during the debate. Compile the most valid reasons on the board for each point of view.

4 Suggestion Ask students what sentence structure they will likely use most in this conversation. (commands)

5 Suggestion When sharing stories with the class, have pairs compare theirs with others. Have students point out any errors or omissions. Vote on the funniest story.

6 Suggestion Divide the class into pairs and distribute the Info Gap Handouts in the IRM on the IRCD-ROM for this activity. Give students ten minutes to complete the activity.

1 Les colocataires Avec un(e) partenaire, décrivez cette maison de colocataires à sept heures du matin. Que font-ils? Answers will vary.

1.

2.

3.

2 Le camping Vous et votre partenaire faites du camping dans un endroit isolé. Malheureusement, vous avez tout oublié. À tour de rôle, parlez de ces problèmes à votre partenaire. Il/Elle va essayer de vous aider. Answers will vary.

MODÈLE

Étudiant(e) 1: *Je veux me laver les cheveux, mais je n'ai pas pris mon shampooing.*
Étudiant(e) 2: *Moi, j'ai apporté mon shampooing. Je te le prête.*

prendre une douche	se laver les cheveux
se brosser les dents	se laver les mains
se coiffer	se sécher les cheveux
se laver le visage	se raser

3 Débat Par groupes de quatre, débattez cette question: Qui prend plus de temps pour se préparer avant de sortir, les hommes ou les femmes? Préparez une liste de raisons pour défendre votre point de vue. Présentez vos arguments à la classe. Answers will vary.

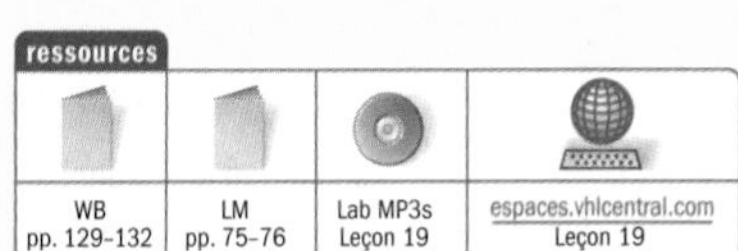

ressources
WB pp. 129-132
LM pp. 75-76
Lab MP3s Leçon 19
espaces.vhlcentral.com Leçon 19

4 Dépêchez-vous! Avec un(e) partenaire, imaginez que vous soyez (*are*) les parents de trois enfants. Ils doivent partir pour l'école dans dix minutes, mais ils viennent juste de se réveiller! Que leur dites-vous? Utilisez des verbes réfléchis. Answers will vary.

MODÈLE

Étudiant(e) 1: *Dépêchez-vous!*
Étudiant(e) 2: *Lève-toi!*

5 Départ de vacances Avec un(e) partenaire, observez les images et décrivez-les. Utilisez tous les verbes de la liste. Ensuite, racontez à la classe l'histoire du départ en vacances de la famille Glassié. Answers will vary.

s'amuser	s'énerver
se dépêcher	se mettre en colère
se détendre	se préparer
se disputer (avec)	se rendre compte

6 La personnalité de Martin Votre professeur va vous donner, à vous et à votre partenaire, une feuille d'information sur Martin. Attention! Ne regardez pas la feuille de votre partenaire. Answers will vary.

MODÈLE

Étudiant(e) 1: *Martin s'habille élégamment.*
Étudiant(e) 2: *Mais...*

OPTIONS

Extra Practice Ask students to translate these sentences into French using the same verb in each item. They choose reflexive or non-reflexive. 1. My dog is called Buddy. When I call him, he doesn't listen to me. (**Mon chien s'appelle Buddy. Quand je l'appelle, il ne m'écoute pas.**) 2. The children are walking the dog while their parents take a walk. (**Les enfants promènent le chien pendant que leurs parents se promènent.**) 3. We have to get ready. Why are you *(pl.)* preparing for the exam now? (**Nous devons nous préparer. Pourquoi préparez-vous l'examen maintenant?**) 4. Wash your *(sing.)* hands. Then wash your little brother. (**Lave-toi les mains. Puis lave ton petit frère.**) 5. The hairdresser does her hair in the morning. She does her clients' hair all day. (**La coiffeuse se coiffe le matin. Elle coiffe ses clients toute la journée.**)

Projet

Participer à une conférence

Vous êtes conférencier/conférencière°. Vous allez faire un discours° pour une conférence sur le système de soins de santé° en Suisse.

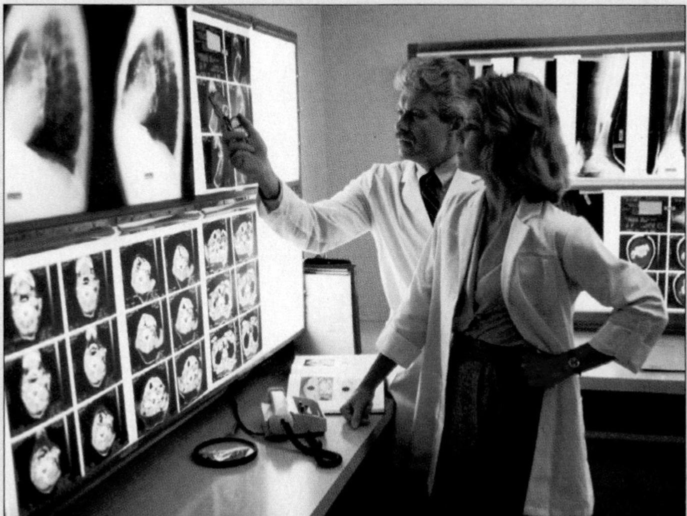

1 Préparez l'exposé°

Préparez une présentation sur le système des soins médicaux en Suisse. Pour mieux connaître le système de soins en Suisse, explorez le lien° dans la boîte° **Sur Internet.** Voici quelques thèmes que vous pouvez explorer:

- Les principes du système
- La qualité des soins proposés par le système
- Le financement du système
- Les cliniques et les comptes d'assurance privés°
- L'avenir° du système

2 Présentez votre travail

Faites votre exposé sur la Sécurité sociale en Suisse et demandez l'avis° de vos camarades sur le système. En quoi le système de soins en Suisse diffère-t-il du système américain? Quels sont les points communs aux deux systèmes?

SUR INTERNET

Go to **espaces.vhlcentral.com** for more information related to this **Projet**.

conférencier/conférencière *lecturer* **discours** *speech* **système de soins de santé** *healthcare system* **exposé** *presentation* **lien** *link* **boîte** *box* **comptes d'assurance privés** *private insurance accounts* **avenir** *future* **avis** *opinion*

Section Goals

In this section, students will:

- use French as they research and interact with the wider world
- write and deliver a speech about the healthcare system in Switzerland

Instructional Resources
espaces.vhlcentral.com: activities, downloads, reference tools

Suggestion Students might need a week to complete the project, so at the beginning of that time period, have them read through **Projet**.

Préparez l'exposé

- Explain to students that Switzerland's healthcare is considered to be of very high quality, but it is very expensive. It is also said to be characterized as consumer-driven.
- Have students work in groups of five to divide up the research (one person could be responsible for each bullet). Then they can designate a group member or group members to give the speech.

Présentez votre travail

- Have the class organize a mock conference in which students give their speech in front of all the conference participants.
- In lieu of the standard presentation to a passive audience, have students conduct an interactive question-and-answer session with their classmates.
- You may wish to set aside sufficient class time to do a few presentations at a time until all students have had a chance to present.

EVALUATION

Criteria	Scale
Content	1 2 3 4
Comprehensibility	1 2 3 4
Organization	1 2 3 4
Accuracy	1 2 3 4
Use of visuals	1 2 3 4

Scoring	
Excellent	18–20 points
Good	14–17 points
Satisfactory	10–13 points
Unsatisfactory	< 10 points

Section Goals

In this section, students will read historical and cultural information about Switzerland.

Instructional Resources
IRCD-ROM: Transparency #47
WB/VM: Workbook, pp. 139–140
WB/VM/LM Answer Key
espaces.vhlcentral.com: activities; downloads; reference tools

Carte de la Suisse

- Have students look at the map or use **Transparency #47**. Ask volunteers to read aloud the names of cities and geographical features. Model the pronunciation as necessary. Explain that about two-thirds of the country is mountainous.
- Point out the francophone region and have students name the cities that are French-speaking.
- Have students name the countries that border Switzerland.

Le pays en chiffres

- Point out the flag of Switzerland. Then ask students to share any information they know about the country.
- Have volunteers read the sections. After each section, ask students questions about the content.
- Tell students the percentage of the population that speaks each language: Swiss German 63.7%, French 20.3%, Italian 6.5%, Romansh 0.5%, and others 9.0%. SOURCE: **Office fédéral de la statistique**.
- Explain that many products in Switzerland have information written in French, German, Italian, and even English.

Incroyable mais vrai! The Swiss play a major role in humanitarian peacekeeping efforts.

Panorama

La Suisse

Le pays en chiffres

- **Superficie:** *41.293 km²*
- **Population:** *7.073.000*
  SOURCE: Population Division, UN Secretariat
- **Industries principales:** *activités financières° (banques, assurances), agroalimentaire°, élevage bovin°, horlogerie°, métallurgie, tourisme*
- **Villes principales:** *Bâle, Berne, Genève, Lausanne, Zurich*
- **Langues:** *allemand, français, italien, romanche*
  L'allemand, le français et l'italien sont les langues officielles, parlées dans les différentes régions du pays. Le romanche, langue d'origine latine, est parlée à l'est° du pays. Langue nationale depuis 1938, elle n'est pas utilisée au niveau° fédéral. Aujourd'hui en Suisse, l'italien et le romanche sont moins parlés que d'autres langues étrangères.
- **Monnaie:** *le franc suisse*

Suisses célèbres

- **Johanna Spyri,** *auteur de «Heidi» (1827–1901)*
- **Louis Chevrolet,** *coureur automobile°, fondateur de la société Chevrolet (1878–1941)*
- **Alberto Giacometti,** *sculpteur (1901–1966)*

- **Charles Édouard Jeanneret Le Corbusier,** *architecte (1887–1965)*
- **Ella Maillart,** *écrivain, journaliste, photographe et sportive (1903–1997)*
- **Jean-Luc Godard,** *cinéaste (1930–)*

financières *financial* **agroalimentaire** *food processing* **élevage bovin** *livestock farming* **horlogerie** *watch and clock making* **est** *east* **niveau** *level* **coureur automobile** *racecar driver* **guerres** *wars* **Battue** *Defeated* **paix** *peace treaty* **statut** *status* **ne... ni** *neither... nor* **OTAN** *NATO*

le château de Chillon sur le lac Léman

des jeunes joueurs de flûte en costume, à Zermatt

Incroyable mais vrai!

La Suisse n'a pas connu de guerres° depuis le 16e siècle! Battue° par la France en 1515, elle signe une paix° perpétuelle avec ce pays et inaugure donc sa période de neutralité. Ce statut° est reconnu par les autres pays européens en 1815 et, depuis, la Suisse ne peut participer à aucune guerre ni° être membre d'alliances militaires comme l'OTAN°.

OPTIONS

Suisses célèbres **Johanna Spyri** began her writing career in order to help refugees of the Franco-Prussian War. **Louis Chevrolet** designed the first Chevrolet automobile sold in 1913. General Motors bought the Chevrolet Motor Company in 1918. **Alberto Giacometti**, a painter as well as a sculptor, was best known for his very thin, metal sculptures. Internationally renowned, **Le Corbusier**'s works and ideas had a profound influence on the development of modern architecture and the field of city planning. **Ella Maillart** traveled to remote regions documenting the lives of people in the former Soviet Union, China, India, and other parts of the Middle and Far East. **Jean-Luc Godard** was born in Paris, but grew up on the Swiss side of Lake Geneva. He is known for his independent vision and his unconventional, often controversial, films.

L'économie

Des montres et des banques

L'économie suisse se caractérise par la présence de grandes entreprises° multinationales et par son secteur financier. Les multinationales sont particulièrement actives dans le domaine des banques, des assurances, de l'agroalimentaire (Nestlé), de l'industrie pharmaceutique et de l'horlogerie (Longines, Rolex, Swatch). Cinquante pour cent de la production mondiale° d'articles° d'horlogerie viennent de la Suisse. Le franc suisse est une des monnaies les plus stables du monde et les banques suisses ont la réputation de bien gérer° les fortunes de leurs clients.

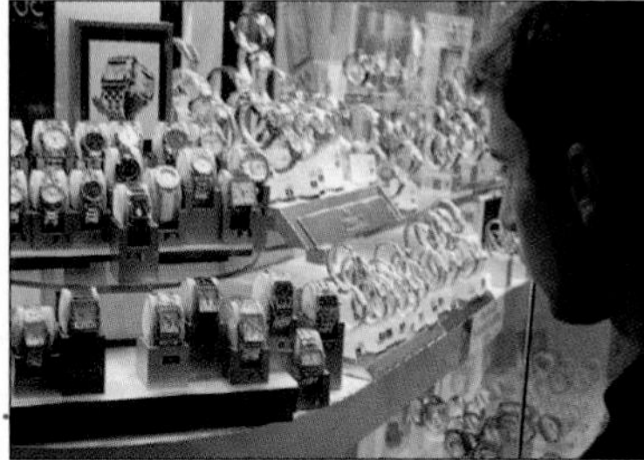

Les gens

Jean-Jacques Rousseau (1712–1778)

Né à Genève, Jean-Jacques Rousseau a passé sa vie entre la France et la Suisse. Vagabond et autodidacte°, Rousseau est devenu écrivain, philosophe, théoricien politique et musicien. Il a comme principe° que l'homme naît bon et que c'est la société qui le corrompt°. Défenseur de la tolérance religieuse et de la liberté de pensée, les principes de Rousseau, exprimés° principalement dans son œuvre° *Du contrat social*, se retrouvent° dans la Révolution française. À la fin de sa vie, il écrit *Les Confessions*, son autobiographie, un genre nouveau pour l'époque°.

Les traditions

Le couteau suisse

En 1884, Carl Elsener, coutelier° suisse, se rend compte que les soldats° suisses portent des couteaux allemands. Il décide donc de fonder sa propre compagnie en Suisse et invente le «couteau du soldat» à quatre outils°. Depuis 1891, chaque soldat de l'armée suisse en a un. En 1897, Elsener développe le «couteau d'officier°» pour l'armée et aujourd'hui, il est vendu au grand public. Le célèbre couteau, orné de la croix° suisse sur fond° rouge, offre un choix de 90 accessoires.

Les destinations

Genève

La ville de Genève, sur la frontière° franco-suisse, est une ville internationale et francophone. C'est une belle ville verte, avec sa rade° sur le lac Léman et son célèbre jet d'eau°. Son horloge fleurie°, ses promenades, ses magasins divers et ses nombreux chocolatiers font de Genève une ville très appréciée des touristes. C'est ici qu'on trouve aussi de nombreuses grandes entreprises internationales et organisations internationales et non gouvernementales, l'O.N.U.°, la Croix-Rouge° et l'O.M.S.° Pour cette raison, 40% de la population de Genève est d'origine étrangère.

Qu'est-ce que vous avez appris? Répondez aux questions par des phrases complètes.

1. Quelles sont les langues officielles de la Suisse?
   L'allemand, le français et l'italien sont les langues officielles de la Suisse.
2. Quand la Suisse a-t-elle commencé sa période de neutralité?
   La Suisse a commencé sa période de neutralité en 1515.
3. Que signifie la neutralité pour la Suisse?
   Elle ne participe pas aux guerres et elle ne peut pas être membre d'alliances militaires.
4. Quels sont deux secteurs importants de l'économie suisse?
   Answers will vary.
5. Quel est le principe fondamental de Rousseau?
   L'homme naît bon, mais c'est la société qui le corrompt.
6. Quel événement a été influencé par les idées de Rousseau?
   La Révolution française a été influencée par les idées de Rousseau.
7. À quoi servait le couteau suisse à l'origine?
   C'était un couteau porté par les soldats de l'armée suisse.
8. Pourquoi Carl Elsener a-t-il inventé le couteau suisse?
   Il a inventé le couteau suisse parce que les soldats suisses portaient des couteaux allemands.
9. Où se trouve la ville de Genève en Suisse?
   Genève se trouve sur la frontière franco-suisse.
10. Quel pourcentage de la population de Genève est d'origine étrangère?
   Quarante pour cent de sa population est d'origine étrangère.

ressources

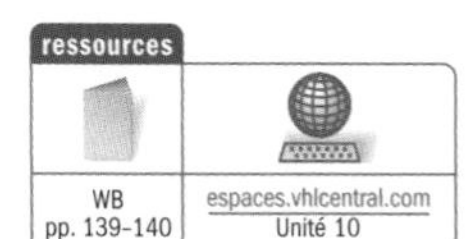

WB pp. 139–140 | espaces.vhlcentral.com Unité 10

SUR INTERNET

Go to **espaces.vhlcentral.com** to find more cultural information related to this **PANORAMA**.

1. Cherchez plus d'informations sur Ella Maillart. Qu'a-t-elle fait de remarquable?
2. Cherchez plus d'informations sur les œuvres de Rousseau. Quelles autres œuvres a-t-il écrites?
3. La Suisse est membre des Nations Unies. Depuis quand en est-elle membre? Quel est son statut (*status*) dans l'Union européenne?

entreprises *companies* **mondiale** *worldwide* **articles** *products* **gérer** *manage* **autodidacte** *self-taught* **comme principe** *as a principle* **corrompt** *corrupts* **exprimés** *expressed* **œuvre** *work* **se retrouvent** *are found* **époque** *time* **coutelier** *knife maker* **soldats** *soldiers* **outils** *tools* **officier** *officer* **orné de la croix** *adorned with the cross* **fond** *background* **frontière** *border* **rade** *harbor* **jet d'eau** *fountain* **horloge fleurie** *flower clock* **O.N.U. (Organisation des Nations Unies)** *U.N.* **Croix-Rouge** *Red Cross* **O.M.S. (Organisation Mondiale de la Santé)** *W.H.O. (World Health Organization)*

Des montres et des banques

- Located in Zurich, Credit Suisse and UBS AG are Switzerland's largest international banks. Swiss banks are known for their discretion, confidentiality, and secrecy. Clients are protected through the use of numbered accounts, and only a few top managers actually know who owns a particular account.
- Have students look at the photo and describe what they see. Then ask: **Combien d'étudiants portent une Swatch? Pourquoi ces montres sont-elles populaires? Connaissez-vous quelqu'un avec une Rolex?**
- Ask students to name some Nestlé products. **Citez quelques produits Nestlé (le chocolat, la nourriture pour bébés, etc.)**

Jean-Jacques Rousseau People's views of society, family values, and political and ethical thinking were directly affected by Rousseau's writings. Through his involvement with the **Philosophes** and Diderot's ***Encyclopédie***, Rousseau influenced society's taste in music, arguing for freedom of expression rather than strict adherence to rules and traditions.

Le couteau suisse

- Victorinox makes 100 models of Swiss Army knives and sells approximately 7 million of them each year. More than 90 percent of the knives are exported.
- Have students look at the photo and identify the implements on the Swiss Army knife. Then ask: **Avez-vous un couteau suisse?**

Genève Known as the "City of Peace", Geneva is considered an ideal neutral site for major diplomatic negotiations. Approximately 190 international organizations are located in Geneva.

OPTIONS

Game Create categories for the information on Switzerland. Examples: **Géographie, Suisses célèbres, Langues,** and **Industries/Produits**. For each category, make cards with a question on one side. Tape the cards to the board under the proper category with the question face down. Divide the class into two teams, and have them take turns picking a card and answering the question. Teams win a point per correct reply.

Les montres suisses Watches, clocks, and alarm clocks manufactured in Switzerland must carry the designation "Swiss made" or "Swiss." A lot of technical expertise goes into fitting very complex mechanisms into small casings. A typical luxury watch usually has over 300 parts. The most complex, luxury watch in the world is probably Calibre 89 by Patek Philippe, which contains 1728 parts.

Section Goals

In this section, students will:

- learn to use background knowledge when reading
- read a magazine article on combating fatigue

Stratégie Explain to students that they will find it easier to understand the content of a text by reviewing previous knowledge about the topic before they begin reading.

Examinez le texte Students should mention that the text is a magazine article written by Dr. Émilie Parmentier and published in France.

Questions personnelles

- Point out to students that by answering these **Questions personnelles** they are activating their background knowledge about health habits and fatigue. This will help them to understand the magazine article.
- Have students discuss their answers to the questions in pairs or small groups.

Lecture

Avant la lecture

STRATÉGIE

Activating background knowledge

Using what you already know about a particular subject will often help you better understand a reading selection. For example, if you read an article about a recent medical discovery, you might think about what you already know about health in order to understand unfamiliar words or concepts.

Examinez le texte

Regardez le document. Analysez le titre de la lecture. Quel est le mot-clé de ce titre? Quel est le sens (*meaning*) du titre? Quel va être le sujet du texte? Faites une liste de vos idées et comparez-les avec les idées d'un(e) camarade. Puis, avec votre partenaire, faites aussi une liste de ce que vous savez déjà sur ce sujet. Essayez de répondre aux questions suivantes.

- Quel type de texte est-ce?
- Où pensez-vous que ce texte a été publié?
- Qui a écrit ce texte?
- Quelle est la profession de l'auteur?

Questions personnelles

Répondez aux questions par des phrases complètes.

1. Vous sentez-vous fatigué(e) parfois pendant la journée? Quand? Pourquoi?
2. Êtes-vous souvent fatigué(e) quand vous avez beaucoup de devoirs ou d'examens? Et quand vous faites beaucoup de sport?
3. Dormez-vous bien en général? Vous couchez-vous tôt ou tard? Et le matin, à quelle heure vous levez-vous en général?
4. Prenez-vous le temps de vous détendre dans la journée? Que faites-vous pour vous détendre?
5. Mangez-vous sainement? Qu'aimez-vous manger?
6. Faites-vous du sport ou d'autres activités physiques? Lesquels (*Which ones*)?

Non à la fatigue!

Par le docteur Émilie Parmentier

Selon un sondage° récent, plus de 50% des Français se sentent souvent fatigués. Que faire pour être moins fatigué? Voici les dix conseils° du docteur Émilie Parmentier.

1 Mangez sainement et évitez les régimes

Vous pouvez garder la ligne et la forme si vous évitez les régimes et choisissez les fruits, les légumes et le poisson au lieu de° la viande et des féculents°. Le matin, prenez le temps de vous préparer un bon petit-déjeuner, mais le soir, mangez léger°.

2 Dormez bien

Chaque personne est différente. Certaines ont besoin de 6 heures de sommeil° par nuit, d'autres de 10 heures. Respectez vos besoins et essayez de dormir assez, mais pas trop.

3 Essayez de respecter des horaires réguliers

Avoir des horaires réguliers°, c'est bon pour la forme. Levez-vous à la même heure chaque jour, si possible, puis le soir, essayez aussi de vous coucher toujours à la même heure.

4 Prenez le temps de vous détendre avant de vous coucher

Le soir avant de vous coucher, prenez quelques minutes pour vous relaxer et oublier vos préoccupations et vos problèmes. Essayez la méditation ou le yoga.

5 Ne vous dépêchez pas tout le temps

Il est très important d'avoir des moments de calme tous les jours et de ne pas toujours se dépêcher. Promenez-vous dans un parc, asseyez-vous et reposez-vous quelques minutes.

OPTIONS

Small Groups Have students work in groups of three or four. Tell them to create a list of possible reasons why more than 50% of French people often feel tired. Example: **Ils travaillent beaucoup**. Then have them get together with another group and compare their lists. Record the most popular reasons on the board.

Pairs Have students work in pairs. Tell them to go through the article and find all the sentences that contain reflexive verbs. Mention that students should watch for reflexive verbs appearing in the infinitive. Example: **... prenez le temps de *vous préparer*...** Then have them point out which verbs are literally reflexive versus those with an idiomatic sense.

Amina découvre l'identité de son ami virtuel.

SANDRINE Il est adorable, ton Cyberhomme! Continue! Est-ce qu'il veux te rencontrer en personne?
VALÉRIE Qui vas-tu rencontrer, Amina? Qui est ce Cyberhomme?
SANDRINE Amina l'a connu sur Internet. Ils s'écrivent depuis longtemps, n'est-ce pas, Amina?

AMINA Oui, mais comme je te l'ai déjà dit, je ne sais pas si c'est une bonne idée de se rencontrer en personne. S'écrire des e-mails, c'est une chose; se donner rendez-vous, ça peut être dangereux.
VALÉRIE Amina a raison, Sandrine. On ne sait jamais.
SANDRINE Mais il est si charmant et tellement romantique...

RACHID Merci, Amina. Tu me sauves la vie aussi. Peut-être que maintenant je vais pouvoir me concentrer.
AMINA Ah? Et tu travailles sur quoi? Ce n'est pas possible!... C'est toi, Cyberhomme?!

RACHID Et toi, tu es Technofemme?!
DAVID Évidemment, tu me l'as dit toi-même: Amina est une pro de l'informatique.

Expressions utiles

Expressing how you communicate with others

- **On arrive enfin à s'entendre parler!**
  Finally we can hear each other speak!
- **On s'entend si bien.**
  We get along so well.
- **On peut tout se dire.**
  We can tell each other everything.
- **Ils s'écrivent depuis longtemps.**
  They've been writing to each other for quite a while.
- **S'écrire des e-mails, c'est une chose; se donner rendez-vous, ça peut être dangereux.**
  Writing each other e-mails, that's one thing; arranging to meet, that can be dangerous.

Additional vocabulary

- **se rencontrer**
  to meet each other
- **On ne sait jamais.**
  You/One never know(s).
- **Au secours!**
  Help!
- **C'est idiot de ma part.**
  It's stupid of me.
- **une dissertation**
  paper
- **pas grand-chose**
  not much

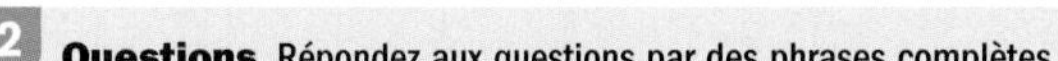

2 Questions Répondez aux questions par des phrases complètes.

1. Pourquoi Rachid se met-il en colère?
   Il se met en colère parce qu'il ne peut pas se concentrer.
2. Pourquoi y a-t-il beaucoup de bruit (*noise*) chez Rachid et David?
   Il y a beaucoup de bruit parce que la chaîne stéréo et la télévision sont allumées.
3. Est-ce qu'Amina s'entend bien avec Cyberhomme?
   Oui, elle s'entend bien avec Cyberhomme.
4. Que pense Valérie de la possibilité d'un rendez-vous avec Cyberhomme? Elle pense que ça peut être dangereux.
5. Qu'est-ce que Rachid fait pendant que David joue au jeu vidéo et écrit sa dissertation? Il écrit des e-mails à Amina/Technofemme.

3 À vous Par rapport aux (*With respect to*) études, David et Rachid sont très différents. David aime les distractions et Rachid a besoin de silence pour travailler. Avec un(e) camarade de classe, décrivez vos habitudes par rapport aux études. Avez-vous les mêmes? Pouvez-vous être de bon(nes) colocataires? Présentez vos conclusions à la classe.

ressources

VM pp. 251-252	V CD-ROM Leçon 21	espaces.vhlcentral.com Leçon 21

ACTIVITÉS

Expressions utiles

- Model the pronunciation of the **Expressions utiles** and have students repeat them after you.
- As you work through the list, point out reciprocal verbs and prepositions used with infinitives. Explain the difference between **entendre** and **s'entendre**. Tell students that these grammar points will be formally presented in the **Structures** section.
- Respond briefly to questions about reciprocal verbs and prepositions with infinitives. Reinforce correct forms, but do not expect students to produce them consistently at this time.
- Ask students what **arriver** means. (*to arrive, to happen*) Then point out that **arriver à** + *infinitive* means *to be able to* or *to manage to do something.* Example: **Je n'arrive pas à travailler.**
- Explain that **une dissertation** is a *paper,* such as an essay, not a *dissertation.* The abbreviated form is **dissert'**.

1 Suggestion Have students correct the false statements.

2 Suggestion Have students compare their answers in pairs or small groups.

2 Expansion For additional practice, give students these items. **6. David éteint la télé et la chaîne stéréo, puis que se met-il à faire? (jouer à un jeu vidéo) 7. Qu'est-ce que Cyberhomme et Technofemme ont en commun? (Ils aiment la technologie.) 8. Selon Sandrine, comment est Cyberhomme? (adorable, charmant et romantique)**

3 Suggestion Before beginning this activity, give students a few minutes to think about their study habits and jot down some ideas.

OPTIONS

Small Groups Working in groups of three, have students role-play this situation. One student is an irate customer in a cybercafé who is annoyed by something the customer seated nearby is doing, for example, playing music too loudly or making noises while playing a game. Another student is the customer who defends his or her own actions. The third student is an employee who tries to resolve the situation.

Pairs Have students work in pairs and discuss these questions. **1. Pourquoi Amina n'a-t-elle pas l'intention d'avoir un rendez-vous avec Cyberhomme? 2. Sandrine pense que Cyberhomme est romantique et elle encourage Amina à fixer un rendez-vous avec lui. Qui a raison, Amina ou Sandrine? Pourquoi?**

NATIONAL STANDARDS: connections, cultures

Section Goals

In this section, students will:

- learn about technology in France
- learn some common Internet terms
- learn about some online francophone radio stations
- read about the Ariane rocket

Instructional Resources
espaces.vhlcentral.com: activities, downloads, reference tools

Culture à la loupe

Avant la lecture Have students look at the photos and describe what the people are doing.

Lecture

- Tell students to make a list of new Internet terms they encounter as they read the article. Examples: **la connexion par câble/ADSL, la connexion haut/bas débit, le graveur**, and **le scanner**.
- In 2004, France was ranked number 9 in the top 15 countries for Internet usage with over 25 million users. Canada is number 12.
- Point out the statistics chart. Ask students what information it shows. (the percentage of French households that have the electronics devices listed)

Après la lecture Ask students: **À votre avis, pourquoi est-ce que les cybercafés sont plus populaires en France qu'aux États-Unis?**

1 Suggestion Have students get together with a classmate to check their answers.

CULTURE À LA LOUPE

La technologie et les Français

le Minitel

Pendant les années 1980, la technologie a connu une grande évolution. En France, cette révolution technologique a commencé par l'invention du Minitel, développé par France Télécom, la compagnie nationale française de téléphone, au début des années 1980. Le Minitel peut être considéré comme le prédécesseur d'Internet. C'est un petit terminal qu'on branche° sur sa ligne de téléphone et qui permet d'accéder à toutes sortes d'informations et de jeux, de faire des réservations de train ou d'hôtel, de commander des articles en ligne ou d'acheter des billets de concert, par exemple. Aujourd'hui, Internet remplace souvent le Minitel et de plus en plus de Français sont équipés chez eux d'un ordinateur et d'une connexion Internet. Environ° 50% d'entre eux ont encore la connexion Internet bas débit°, mais le pourcentage de gens qui ont la connexion haut débit° augmente chaque année et la conversion entre les deux se fait assez rapidement. Les Français ont le choix, pour le haut débit, entre la connexion par câble et la connexion ADSL°. Enfin, pour ceux° qui n'ont pas d'autre manière° de se connecter à Internet, il existe en France—beaucoup plus qu'aux États-Unis—de nombreux cybercafés.

En ce qui concerne les autres appareils électroniques à la mode, on note une augmentation des achats° de consoles de jeux vidéo, de lecteurs de CD/DVD, de caméras vidéo, de palms, d'appareils photos numériques ou de produits périphériques° pour les ordinateurs, comme les imprimantes, les scanners ou les graveurs. Mais l'appareil qui a connu le plus grand succès en France, c'est sans doute le téléphone portable. En 1996, moins de 2,5 millions de Français avaient un téléphone portable. Aujourd'hui, plus de 40 millions de Français en possèdent un.

branche *connects* **Environ** *About* **bas débit** *low-speed* **haut débit** *high-speed* **ADSL** *DSL* **ceux** *those* **manière** *way* **achats** *purchases* **périphériques** *peripheral*

L'équipement technologique des Français (*% de ménages*)

Téléphone	87
Téléphone portable	70
Ordinateur	45
Répondeur	43
Connexion Internet	31
Minitel	13
Palm	6

Coup de main

When saying an e-mail address aloud, follow this example.

claude-monet@yahoo.fr

claude tiret monet arobase yahoo point F R

ACTIVITÉS

1 Répondez Répondez par des phrases complètes.

1. Quelle invention française est le prédécesseur d'Internet? C'est le Minitel.
2. Qu'est-ce que le Minitel? C'est un petit terminal qu'on branche sur sa ligne de téléphone et qui permet d'accéder à toutes sortes d'informations.
3. Quel est le nom de la compagnie nationale française de téléphone? C'est France Télécom.
4. La connexion Internet haut débit existe-t-elle en France? Oui, environ 50% des Français ont la connexion haut débit.
5. Où peut-on aller si on n'a pas d'accès Internet à la maison? On peut aller dans un cybercafé.
6. Quels sont deux appareils électroniques qu'on achète souvent en France en ce moment? Answers will vary. Possible answer: Ce sont les lecteurs de CD/DVD et les consoles de jeux vidéo.
7. Quel appareil électronique a eu le plus de succès depuis 1996? C'est le téléphone portable.
8. Quel est le pourcentage de Français qui possèdent un ordinateur? Quarante-cinq pour cent des Français possèdent un ordinateur.
9. Est-il courant (*common*) d'avoir Internet en France? Oui, 31% des Français ont Internet chez eux et de plus en plus de gens l'ont aussi.
10. La majorité des Français ont-ils encore un Minitel? Non. Seulement 13% des Français ont encore un Minitel.

OPTIONS

Cultural Comparison Take a quick class survey to find out how many students have the electronic devices listed in the chart in their homes. Example: **Combien d'étudiants ont un téléphone à la maison?** Tally the results on the board and have students calculate the percentages.

Then have students compare the results of this survey with the percentages in the chart. Example: **Plus de Français ont un Minitel dans leurs maisons. Plus d'Américains ont un ordinateur chez eux.**

LE FRANÇAIS QUOTIDIEN

Cyberespace

frimousse (*f.*)	*smiley (face)*
grimace (*f.*)	*frown*
message (*m.*) instantané	*instant message*
moteur (*m.*) de recherche	*search engine*
pseudonyme (*m.*)	*screen name*
chatter	*to chat*

PORTRAIT

La fusée Ariane

Après la Seconde Guerre mondiale°, la conquête de l'espace° s'est amplifiée. En Europe, le premier programme spatial, le programme Europa, n'a pas eu beaucoup de succès et il a été abandonné. En 1970, la France a proposé un nouveau programme spatial, le projet Ariane, qui a eu un succès considérable. La fusée° Ariane est un lanceur° civil de satellites européen, à Kourou, en Guyane française, département et région français d'outre-mer°, en Amérique du Sud. Elle transporte des satellites commerciaux dans l'espace. La première fusée Ariane a été lancée en 1979 et il y a eu plusieurs générations de fusées Ariane depuis. Aujourd'hui, Ariane V (cinq), un lanceur beaucoup plus puissant° que ses prédécesseurs, est utilisée.

Guerre mondiale *World War* **espace** *space* **fusée** *rocket* **lanceur** *launcher* **outre-mer** *overseas* **puissant** *powerful*

LE MONDE FRANCOPHONE

Quelques stations de radio francophones

Voici quelques radios francophones en ligne.

En Afrique

Africa 1 radio africaine qui propose des actualités et beaucoup de musique africaine (www.africa1.com)

En Belgique

Classic 21 radio pour les jeunes qui passe° de la musique rock et propose des emplois° pour les étudiants (www.classic21.be)

En France

NRJ radio privée nationale pour les jeunes qui passe tous les grands tubes° (www.nrj.fr)

En Suisse

Fréquence Banane radio universitaire de Lausanne (www.frequencebanane.ch)

passe *plays* **emplois** *jobs* **tubes** *hits*

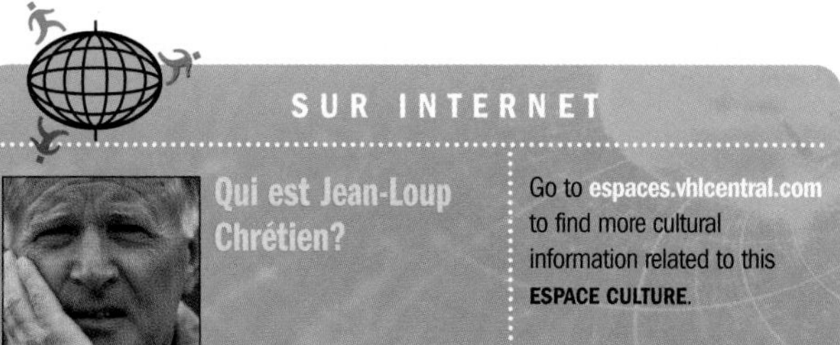

SUR INTERNET

Qui est Jean-Loup Chrétien?

Go to **espaces.vhlcentral.com** to find more cultural information related to this **ESPACE CULTURE**.

ACTIVITÉS

2 Complétez Complétez les phrases d'après les textes.

1. Quand on parle en ligne sur Internet, on ___chatte___.
2. Pour faire une recherche sur Internet, on utilise ___un moteur de recherche___.
3. En Suisse, beaucoup d'étudiants apprécient la radio ___Fréquence Banane___.
4. Le premier programme spatial européen s'appelait ___Europa___.
5. La fusée Ariane est le ___lanceur civil de satellites___ européen.

3 À vous... Avec un(e) partenaire, écrivez six phrases où vous utilisez le vocabulaire du **Français quotidien**. Soyez prêts à les présenter devant la classe.

OPTIONS

Quelques stations de radio francophones Have students write a brief critique of one of the radio stations in **Le monde francophone.** Assign each student a station so that all are covered. Tell them to go to the station's web site and look at the features and type(s) of music offered. They should comment on what they like, dislike, or find interesting about the web site.

Cultural Comparison Have students discuss the similarities and differences between **le projet Ariane** and NASA's Apollo Space Program (**le projet Apollo**), Skylab (**le projet Skylab**), and the space shuttle (**la navette spatiale**).

Le français quotidien

- Model the pronunciation of each term and have students repeat it.
- Ask students questions using these terms. Examples: **1. Écrivez-vous des messages instantanés? Si oui, à qui écrivez-vous? 2. Quel moteur de recherche préférez-vous? 3. Quels sont les pseudonymes de Rachid et d'Amina dans la vidéo? (Cyberhomme et Technofemme) 4. Aimez-vous chatter en ligne? Avec qui chattez-vous?**

Portrait Point out that the space age began in 1957 with the launch of the satellite *Sputnik*. This touched off a "space race" between the United States and Russia, which culminated in the first man landing on the moon in 1969.

Le monde francophone

- You might want to tell students about **RFI (Radio France Internationale)** at **www.rfi.fr**. **RFI** also has a music site at **www.rfimusique.com**.
- After reading the text, ask students what the Internet addresses are for various radio stations. Example: **Quel est l'adresse Internet de Classic 21? (www.classic21.be)**
- Take a quick class survey to find out which radio station(s) they would be interested in listening to and have them explain why. Example: **Combien d'étudiants aimeraient** (*would like*) **écouter la station NRJ? Pourquoi?**

2 Expansion For additional practice, give students these items. **6. Pour une réponse immédiate, on peut envoyer ____. (un message instantané) 7. Pour protéger son identité quand on chatte, on peut employer ____. (un pseudonyme) 8. La première fusée Ariane a été lancée en ____. (1979)**

3 Suggestion Have pairs get together with another pair of students and peer edit each other's sentences.

Section Goals

In this section, students will learn verbs that require a preposition before the infinitive.

Instructional Resources
WB/VM: Workbook, pp. 143–144
Lab Manual, p. 83
Lab MP3s
WB/VM/LM Answer Key
*IRCD-ROM: IRM (**Essayez!** and **Mise en pratique** answers; Lab Audioscript)*
espaces.vhlcentral.com: activities, downloads, reference tools

Suggestions

- Point out that students already know how to use verbs with infinitives by asking questions with **aller**, **pouvoir**, **savoir**, etc. Examples: **Allez-vous faire une promenade après la classe? Pouvons-nous répéter la leçon? Savez-vous danser?**
- Introduce prepositions with the infinitive by using both constructions (*verb + infinitive, verb + preposition + infinitive*) in the same sentence. Ask students what differences they hear. Example: **D'habitude, mon oncle déteste voyager à l'étranger, mais il a décidé d'aller à Paris cet été.**
- After presenting the use of **à** and **de** with the infinitive, write an infinitive on the board and ask volunteers to use it in a sentence with the appropriate preposition. Examples: **hésiter (J'hésite à inviter ton frère à la fête.) rêver (Il rêve d'acheter une nouvelle voiture.)**
- To contrast the use of **à** and **de** with pronouns, review the contractions these prepositions form with definite articles: **au, aux, des.** Point out that prepositions with infinitives and pronouns do not take this form. Example: **Ce film... j'hésite à le voir.**
- Point out that the preposition **pour** + *infinitive* can mean *in order to.* Example: **Nous sommes venus pour t'aider.** *(We came [in order] to help you.)*

21.1 Prepositions with the infinitive

Point de départ Infinitive constructions, where the first verb is conjugated and the second verb is an infinitive, are common in French.

CONJUGATED VERB	INFINITIVE
Vous **pouvez**	**fermer** le document.
You can	*close the document.*

- Some conjugated verbs are followed directly by an infinitive. Others are followed by the preposition **à** or **de** before the infinitive.

verbs followed directly by infinitive	verbs followed by à before infinitive	verbs followed by de before infinitive
adorer	aider à	arrêter de *to stop*
aimer	s'amuser à *to pass time by*	décider de *to decide to*
aller	apprendre à	éviter de
détester	arriver à *to manage to*	finir de
devoir	commencer à	s'occuper de *to take care of, to see to*
espérer	continuer à	oublier de
pouvoir	hésiter à *to hesitate to*	permettre de
préférer	se préparer à	refuser de *to refuse to*
savoir	réussir à	rêver de *to dream about*
vouloir		venir de *to have just*

Nous **allons manger** à midi.
We are going to eat at noon.

Elle **a appris à conduire** ma voiture.
She learned to drive my car.

Il **rêve de visiter** l'Afrique.
He dreams about visiting Africa.

- Place pronouns before infinitives. Unlike definite articles, they do not contract with the prepositions **à** and **de**.

J'**ai décidé de les télécharger**.
I decided to download them.

Il **est arrivé à le nettoyer**.
He managed to clean it.

- The infinitive is also used after the prepositions **pour** and **sans**.

Nous sommes venus **pour t'aider**.
We came to help you.

Elle part **sans manger**.
She's leaving without eating.

Essayez! Décidez s'il faut une préposition ou s'il n'en faut pas. S'il en faut une, choisissez entre **à** et **de**.

1. Tu sais __Ø__ cuisiner.
2. Commencez __à__ travailler.
3. Tu veux __Ø__ goûter la soupe?
4. Elles vont __Ø__ revenir.
5. Je finis __de__ mettre la table.
6. Il hésite __à__ me poser la question.

MISE EN PRATIQUE

1 Les vacances Paul veut voyager cet été. Il vous raconte ses problèmes. Complétez le paragraphe avec les prépositions **à** ou **de**, si nécessaire.

Je n'arrive pas (1) __à__ décider où prendre mes vacances. Je veux (2) __Ø__ visiter un pays chaud et ensoleillé (*sunny*). J'espère (3) __Ø__ trouver des billets d'avion pour la Martinique. Cet après-midi, je me suis amusé (4) __à__ regarder les prix des billets d'avion sur Internet. Je n'ai pas réussi (5) __à__ trouver un tarif (*fare*) intéressant. Je vais continuer (6) __à__ chercher. J'hésite (7) __à__ payer plein tarif mais je refuse (8) __de__ voyager en stand-by.

2 Le week-end dernier Sophie et ses copains ont fait beaucoup de choses le week-end dernier. Regardez les illustrations et dites ce qu'ils (*what they*) ont fait.

Suggested answers

MODÈLE
J'ai décidé de conduire.

je / décider

1. nous / devoir
Nous avons dû nous réveiller tôt.

3. André / refuser
André a refusé de nager.

2. elles / apprendre
Elles ont appris à jouer au tennis.

4. vous / aider
Vous avez aidé à faire la cuisine.

3 Questionnaire Vous cherchez un travail d'été. Complétez les phrases avec les prépositions **à** ou **de**, quand c'est nécessaire. Ensuite, indiquez si vous êtes d'accord avec ces affirmations.

	oui	non	
1.	___	___	Vous savez __Ø__ parler plusieurs langues.
2.	___	___	Vous acceptez __de__ voyager souvent.
3.	___	___	Vous n'hésitez pas __à__ travailler tard.
4.	___	___	Vous oubliez __de__ répondre au téléphone.
5.	___	___	Vous pouvez __Ø__ travailler le week-end.
6.	___	___	Vous commencez __à__ travailler immédiatement.

OPTIONS

Extra Practice Have students write five original sentences using verbs with prepositions and infinitives. Students should use as much active lesson vocabulary as possible. Then have students read their sentences aloud.

Game Divide the class into teams. Call out a verb from the list above. The first member of each team runs to the board and writes a sample sentence, using the verb, its corresponding preposition (if applicable), and an infinitive. If the sentence of the team finishing first is correct, the team gets a point. If not, check the next team, and so on. Practice all verbs from the chart, making sure each team member has had at least two turns. Then tally the points to see which team wins.

COMMUNICATION

4 **Assemblez** Avez-vous eu de bonnes ou de mauvaises expériences avec la technologie? À tour de rôle, avec un(e) partenaire, assemblez les éléments des colonnes.

Answers will vary.

MODÈLE

Étudiant(e) 1: *Je déteste télécharger des logiciels.*
Étudiant(e) 2: *Chez moi, ma mère n'arrive pas à envoyer des e-mails.*

A	B	C	D
ma mère		accepter	composer
mon père		aimer	effacer
mon frère		arriver	envoyer
ma sœur		décider	éteindre
mes copains		détester	être en ligne
mon petit ami	(ne pas)	hésiter	fermer
ma petite amie		oublier	graver
notre prof		refuser	ouvrir
nous		réussir	sauvegarder
?		?	télécharger

5 **Les voyages** Vous et votre partenaire parlez des vacances et des voyages. Utilisez ces éléments pour vous poser des questions. Justifiez vos réponses.

Answers will vary.

MODÈLE aimer / faire des voyage

Étudiant(e) 1: *Aimes-tu faire des voyages?*
Étudiant(e) 2: *Oui, j'aime faire des voyages. J'aime faire la connaissance de personnes différentes.*

1. rêver / aller en Afrique
2. vouloir / visiter des musées
3. préférer / voyager avec un groupe ou seul(e)
4. commencer / lire des guides touristiques
5. réussir / trouver des vols bon marché
6. aimer / rencontrer des amis à l'étranger

6 **Une pub** Par groupes de trois, préparez une publicité pour École-dinateur, une école qui enseigne l'informatique aux technophobes. Utilisez tous les verbes possibles de la liste avec un infinitif. Answers will vary.

MODÈLE *Vous avez toujours rêvé d'écrire des e-mails? Continuez-vous à travailler comme vos grands-parents? Alors...*

aimer	continuer	refuser
s'amuser	détester	réussir
apprendre	hésiter	rêver
arriver	oublier	savoir

Le français vivant

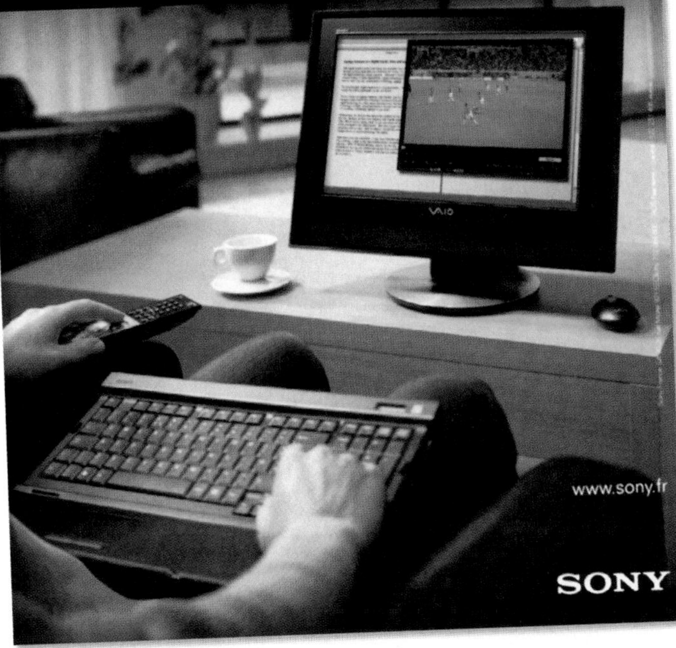

Internet?
Football?
Musique en ligne?
DVD?
Vous avez toujours rêvé de posséder un ordinateur comme ça. Vous vouliez l'acheter, et vous venez de l'allumer. Maintenant, vous commencez à vous rendre compte de ses possibilités. N'hésitez pas à en profiter. En tout confort.
VAIO
www.sony.fr
SONY

Identifiez Quels verbes trouvez-vous devant un infinitif dans le texte de cette publicité (*ad*)? Lesquels (*Which ones*) prennent une préposition? Quelle préposition? rêver de, vouloir, venir de, commencer à, hésiter à

Questions Posez ces questions à un(e) partenaire et répondez à tour de rôle. Answers will vary.

1. As-tu toujours rêvé de posséder quelque chose? De faire quelque chose? Explique.
2. Que veux-tu acheter en ce moment? Pourquoi?
3. D'habitude, qu'hésites-tu à faire?
4. La technologie peut-elle vraiment apporter le confort?
5. Qu'as-tu commencé à faire grâce à (*thanks to*) la technologie? Qu'as-tu arrêté de faire à cause de la technologie?

Essayez! After completing the activity, have students underline the conjugated verb and preposition (if applicable). Ask volunteers to replace the verbs and prepositions with others from the list on page 370.

1 Suggestion Before starting, ask individuals to identify the infinitives of the conjugated verbs.

2 Expansion Ask volunteers to tell two things they did last weekend.

3 Expansion Take a survey of students' responses to the statements. Examples: **Qui sait parler plusieurs langues? Qui accepte de voyager souvent? Qui hésite à travailler tard?** Have students expand on their answers. Example: **Pourquoi hésitez-vous à travailler tard?**

4 Suggestion Before dividing the class into pairs, introduce the activity using your own situation. Example: **Moi, j'aime envoyer des e-mails à mes amis. J'arrive à sauvegarder tous les messages qu'ils m'envoient.**

5 Expansion Have students continue the activity, using these items **7. s'occuper / faire les valises 8. arriver / utiliser un plan 9. éviter / bronzer**

6 Expansion After the groups present their ads, have students from other groups imagine they are potential **École-dinateur** clients and ask questions about their services. Examples: **Nous apprenons à graver des CD? Qui nous aide à télécharger des fichiers?**

Le français vivant

- Ask what the ad is for, and then ask a volunteer to read it aloud.
- Have students describe what the person in the photo is doing and identify all of the objects they see.
- Ask students: **Voulez-vous acheter cet ordinateur? Pourquoi ou pourquoi pas?**

OPTIONS

Extra Practice Have students write three sentences about themselves using three different types of verbs: verbs followed directly by an infinitive, verbs followed by **à** before the infinitive, and verbs followed by **de** before the infinitive. Collect the papers and read them aloud. The rest of the class tries to guess who wrote the sentences.

Video Show the video again to give the students more input with verbs + *infinitives* and verbs + *prepositions* + *infinitives*. Stop the video where appropriate to discuss how these constructions were used and to ask comprehension questions.

comparisons NATIONAL STANDARDS

Section Goals

In this section, students will learn reciprocal reflexives.

Instructional Resources

WB/VM: Workbook, pp. 145–146
Lab Manual, p. 84
Lab MP3s
WB/VM/LM Answer Key
*IRCD-ROM: IRM (**Essayez!** and **Mise en pratique** answers; Lab Audioscript)*
espaces.vhlcentral.com: activities, downloads, reference tools

Suggestions

- Review the reflexive pronouns in the paradigm: **(je) me, (tu) te, (il/elle/on) se, (nous) nous, (vous) vous, (ils/elles) se.**
- Ask volunteers to explain what reflexive verbs are. Ask other students to provide examples. Review reflexive verbs and pronouns by asking students questions about their personal routine. Example: **Je me suis réveillé(e) à sept heures. Et vous, à quelle heure est-ce que vous vous êtes réveillé(e)?**
- Use magazine pictures to introduce the concept of reciprocal reflexive verbs.
- After going over the example sentences, ask students questions using reciprocal constructions. Examples: **Les frères s'entendent-ils bien? Vous écrivez-vous des lettres ou des e-mails? Quand vous êtes-vous rencontrés?**

Essayez! Have volunteers create sentences with the verbs in this activity.

21.2 Reciprocal reflexives

Point de départ In **Leçon 19**, you learned that reflexive verbs indicate that the subject of a sentence does the action to itself. Reciprocal reflexives, on the other hand, express a shared or reciprocal action between two or more people or things. In this context, the pronoun means *(to) each other* or *(to) one another*.

Ils **se regardent** dans le miroir.
They look at themselves in the mirror.

Alain et Diane **se regardent**.
Alain and Diane look at each other.

Common reciprocal verbs

s'adorer	*to adore one another*	**s'entendre bien (avec)**	*to get along well (with one another)*
s'aider	*to help one another*	**se parler**	*to speak to one another*
s'aimer (bien)	*to love (like) one another*	**se quitter**	*to leave one another*
se connaître	*to know one another*	**se regarder**	*to look at one another*
se dire	*to tell one another*	**se rencontrer**	*to meet one another (make an acquaintance)*
se donner	*to give one another*	**se retrouver**	*to meet one another (planned)*
s'écrire	*to write one another*	**se téléphoner**	*to phone one another*
s'embrasser	*to kiss one another*		

Annick et Joël **s'écrivent** tous les jours.
Annick and Joël write one another every day.

Vous **vous donnez** souvent rendez-vous le lundi?
Do you arrange to meet often on Mondays?

- The past participle of a reciprocal verb does not agree with the subject when the subject is also the indirect object of the verb.

Marie et son frère se sont **aidés**.
Marie and her brother helped each other.

but

Les deux sœurs se sont **parlé**.
The two sisters spoke to each other.

Essayez! Donnez les formes correctes des verbes.

1. (s'embrasser) nous *nous embrassons*
2. (se quitter) vous vous quittez
3. (se rencontrer) ils se rencontrent
4. (se dire) nous nous disons
5. (se parler) elles se parlent
6. (se retrouver) ils se retrouvent

MISE EN PRATIQUE

1 L'amour réciproque Employez des verbes réciproques pour raconter l'histoire d'amour de Laure et d'Habib.

MODÈLE Laure retrouve Habib tous les jours. Habib retrouve Laure tous les jours.
Laure et Habib se retrouvent tous les jours.

1. Laure connaît bien Habib. Habib connaît bien Laure. Laure et Habib se connaissent bien.
2. Elle le regarde amoureusement. Il la regarde amoureusement. Ils se regardent amoureusement.
3. Laure écrit des e-mails à Habib. Habib écrit des e-mails à Laure. Laure et Habib s'écrivent des e-mails.
4. Elle lui téléphone tous les soirs. Il lui téléphone tous les soirs. Ils se téléphonent tous les soirs.
5. Elle lui dit tous ses secrets. Il lui dit tous ses secrets. Ils se disent tous leurs secrets.

2 Souvenir Les étudiants de votre classe se retrouvent pour fêter leur réunion. Avec un(e) partenaire, employez l'imparfait pour échanger vos souvenirs.

MODÈLE Marie et moi / s'aider souvent
Marie et moi, nous nous aidions souvent.

1. Marc et toi / se regarder en cours Marc et toi, vous vous regardiez en cours.
2. Anne et Mouna / se téléphoner Anne et Mouna se téléphonaient.
3. François et moi / s'écrire deux fois par semaine François et moi, nous nous écrivions deux fois par semaine.
4. Paul et toi / s'entendre bien Paul et toi, vous vous entendiez bien.
5. Luc et Sylvie / s'adorer Luc et Sylvie s'adoraient.
6. Patrick et moi / se retrouver après les cours Patrick et moi, nous nous retrouvions après les cours.

3 Une rencontre Regardez les illustrations. Qu'est-ce que ces personnages ont fait? Suggested answers

MODÈLE
Ils se sont rencontrés.

ils

1. Arnaud et moi
Arnaud et moi, nous nous sommes embrassés.

3. elles
Elles se sont téléphoné.

2. vous
Vous vous êtes quittés.

4. nous
Nous nous sommes écrit.

OPTIONS

Video Ask students to write two columns on a piece of paper: Reflexive Verbs and Reciprocal Reflexive Verbs. Replay the video episode. Have students write down any examples they hear. Then form groups of three and have students compare their lists.

Extra Practice To provide oral practice with reciprocal reflexive verbs, create sentences that follow the pattern of the sentences in the examples. Say the sentence, have students repeat it, then say a different subject, varying the number. Have students then say the sentence with the new subject, changing pronouns and verbs as necessary.

National Communication Standards

COMMUNICATION

4 **Curieux** Pensez à deux amis qui sont amoureux. Votre partenaire va vous poser beaucoup de questions pour tout savoir sur leur relation. Répondez à ses questions. Answers will vary.

MODÈLE

Étudiant(e) 1: *Est-ce qu'ils se regardent tout le temps?*
Étudiant(e) 2: *Non, ils ne se regardent pas tout le temps, mais ils n'arrêtent pas de se téléphoner!*

s'adorer	bien	se retrouver
s'aimer	mal	se téléphoner
s'écrire	quelquefois	tout le temps
s'embrasser	régulièrement	tous les jours
s'entendre	souvent	?

5 **Un rendez-vous** Avec un(e) partenaire, posez-vous des questions sur la dernière fois que vous êtes sorti(e) avec quelqu'un. Answers will vary.

MODÈLE

à quelle heure / se donner rendez-vous
Étudiant(e) 1: *À quelle heure est-ce que vous vous êtes donné rendez-vous?*
Étudiant(e) 2: *Nous nous sommes donné rendez-vous à sept heures.*

1. où / se retrouver
2. longtemps / se parler
3. s'entendre / bien
4. à quelle heure / se quitter
5. plus tard / se téléphoner

6 **On se quitte** Julie a reçu (*received*) cette lettre de son petit ami Sébastien. Elle ne comprend pas du tout, mais elle doit lui répondre. Avec un(e) partenaire, employez des verbes réciproques pour écrire la réponse. Answers will vary.

Chère Julie,

Nous devons nous quitter, ma chérie. Pourquoi sommes-nous encore ensemble? Nous ne nous sommes pas aimés. Nous nous disputons tout le temps et nous ne nous parlons pas souvent. Soyons réalistes. Je te quitte et j'espère que tu comprends.

Sébastien

Le français vivant

BlackBerry.

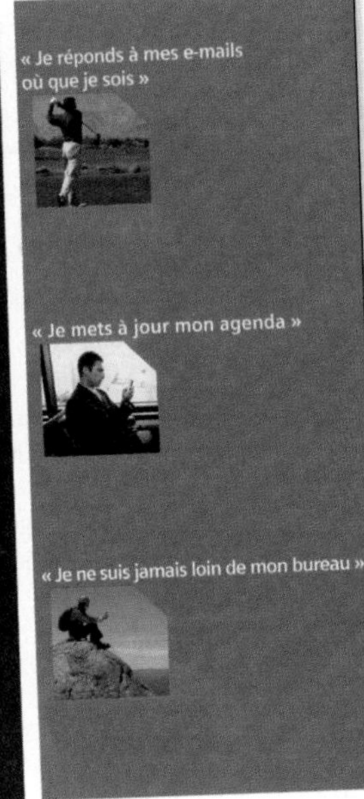

« Je réponds à mes e-mails où que je sois »
« Je mets à jour mon agenda »
« Je ne suis jamais loin de mon bureau »

Avec le palm, je cherche l'heure de mes cours.
Nous nous retrouvons entre amis.
Nous nous écrivons.
Nous nous entendons mieux.
Avec le palm, ce n'est pas difficile de se parler.

Identifiez Quels verbes réciproques avez-vous trouvés dans la publicité (*ad*)? se retrouver, s'écrire, s'entendre mieux, se parler

Questions Posez ces questions à un(e) partenaire et répondez à tour de rôle. Answers will vary.

1. Tes amis et toi, vous écrivez-vous avec un palm? Comment vous écrivez-vous?
2. Penses-tu que les gens s'entendent mieux grâce à (*thanks to*) la technologie? Pourquoi?
3. Quels gadgets technologiques utilises-tu pour communiquer avec tes amis? Pourquoi les utilises-tu?
4. Quels gadgets technologiques utilisaient tes grands-parents pour communiquer avec leurs amis? Pourquoi les utilisaient-ils?

1 Suggestion Do this as a whole-class activity, giving different students the opportunity to form sentences.

2 Expansion Have students imagine that someone from the class contradicts what is said at the reunion. Ask volunteers to change the sentences in the activity to their negative form.

3 Expansion After assigning this activity, have pairs find magazine pictures and create three more sentences using reciprocal reflexives and the **passé composé**.

4 Expansion Have pairs use the reciprocal reflexives from the activity to create a short story about their friends falling in love. Encourage them to use the **passé composé,** the **imparfait**, and the present tense.

5 Expansion After completing the activity, have the students imagine they overheard the conversation about the date. Have pairs retell the facts of the conversation using the **passé composé** and the third person.

6 Suggestion Before assigning the activity, have volunteers identify the infinitive forms of each verb.

Le français vivant

- Have students describe what the people in the photos are doing.
- Call on a volunteer to read the ad aloud.
- Ask: **Possédez-vous un palm?** If any students in the class do own a PDA, have them note which feature(s) in the ad they use or like most or least. Examples: **Je fais tout avec mon palm, mais je l'utilise surtout pour répondre aux e-mails. / Moi, je ne me sers pas de l'agenda.**

OPTIONS

Pairs Have students write and perform a conversation in which one friend discusses a misunderstanding he or she just had with his or her significant other. One student must explain the misunderstanding while the other must ask questions and offer advice. Encourage students to incorporate verbs with infinitives (and prepositions, where needed) and reciprocal reflexive verbs.

TPR Write reciprocal reflexive verbs on index cards and mix them up in a hat. Have volunteers pick a card at random and act out the reciprocal action. The class will guess the action, using the verb in a sentence.

Synthèse

Instructional Resources
*IRCD-ROM: IRM (**Feuilles d'activités**; Info Gap Activities); Testing Program, pp. 81–84; Test Files; Testing Program MP3s; Test Generator espaces.vhlcentral.com: activities, downloads, reference tools*

1 Suggestion Before starting the activity, have students brainstorm a list of reciprocal verbs to use.

2 Suggestion Call on two volunteers to act out the **modèle.** Then distribute the **Feuilles d'activités** from the IRM on the IRCD-ROM.

2 Expansion Have pairs write six original sentences with reciprocal reflexives based on the answers from the survey. Some sentences should be affirmative statements, and some should be negative.

3 Expansion Have pairs invent situations or stories about the people in the drawing.

4 Expansion Ask students questions about how they, their close friends, or family met their significant others. Example: **____, avez-vous un(e) petit(e) ami(e)? Comment vous êtes-vous rencontrés?**

5 Suggestion Before assigning the activity, have a group act out the **modèle** in front of the class. The third group member ad-libs a piece of advice.

6 Suggestion Divide the class into pairs and distribute the Info Gap Handouts in the IRM on the IRCD-ROM for this activity. Give students ten minutes to complete the activity.

1 **À deux** Que peuvent faire deux personnes avec chacun (*each one*) de ces objets? Avec un(e) partenaire, répondez à tour de rôle et employez des verbes réciproques. Answers will vary.

MODÈLE un appareil photo numérique
Avec un appareil photo numérique, deux personnes peuvent s'envoyer des photos tout de suite.

- un portable
- du papier et un stylo
- un ordinateur
- un caméscope
- un fax
- un magnétophone

2 **La communication** Votre professeur va vous donner une feuille d'activités. Circulez dans la classe pour interviewer vos camarades. Comment communiquent-ils avec leurs familles et leurs amis? Pour chaque question, parlez avec des camarades différents qui doivent justifier leurs réponses. Answers will vary.

MODÈLE
Étudiant(e) 1: *Tes amis et toi, vous écrivez-vous plus de cinq e-mails par jour?*
Étudiant(e) 2: *Oui, parfois nous nous écrivons dix e-mails.*
Étudiant(e) 1: *Pourquoi vous écrivez-vous tellement souvent?*

Activité	Oui	Non
1. s'écrire plus de cinq e-mails par jour	Jules	Corinne
2. s'envoyer des lettres par la poste		
3. se téléphoner le week-end		
4. se parler dans les couloirs		
5. se retrouver au resto U		
6. se donner rendez-vous		
7. se rencontrer sur Internet		
8. bien s'entendre		

3 **Dimanche au parc** Ces personnes sont allées au parc dimanche dernier. Avec un(e) partenaire, décrivez à tour de rôle leurs activités. Employez des verbes réciproques. Answers will vary.

4 **Leur rencontre** Comment ces couples se sont-ils rencontrés? Par groupes de trois, inventez une histoire courte pour chaque couple. Utilisez les verbes donnés (*given*) plus des verbes réciproques. Answers will vary.

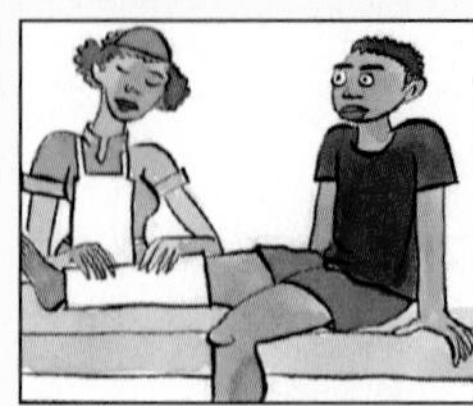

1. venir de

3. continuer à

2. commencer à

4. rêver de

5 **Les bonnes relations** Parlez avec deux camarades. Que faut-il faire pour maintenir de bonnes relations avec ses amis ou sa famille? À tour de rôle, utilisez les verbes de la liste pour donner des conseils (*advice*). Answers will vary.

MODÈLE
Étudiant(e) 1: *Dans une bonne relation, deux personnes peuvent tout se dire.*
Étudiant(e) 2: *Oui, et elles apprennent à se connaître.*

s'adorer	se connaître	hésiter à
s'aider	se dire	oublier de
apprendre à	s'embrasser	pouvoir
arrêter de	espérer	refuser de
commencer à	éviter de	savoir

6 **Rencontre sur Internet** Votre professeur va vous donner, à vous et à votre partenaire, une feuille d'illustrations sur la rencontre sur Internet d'Amandine et de Gilles. Attention! Ne regardez pas la feuille de votre partenaire. Answers will vary.

ressources

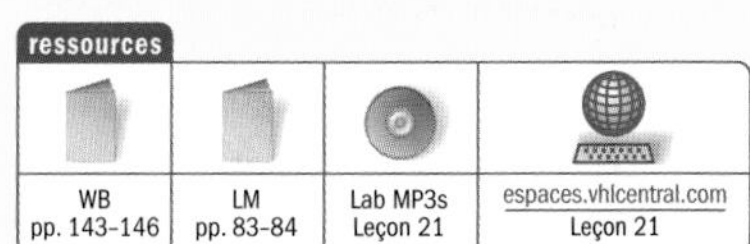

WB pp. 143-146	LM pp. 83-84	Lab MP3s Leçon 21	espaces.vhlcentral.com Leçon 21

OPTIONS

Extra Practice Have students brainstorm a list of chores that must be done every week at their house using vocabulary from previous lessons. Then ask students: **Qui s'occupe de quoi?** After assigning names to each task, have students create sentences telling who forgets to do their chores (**oublier de**), who refuses to do their chores (**refuser de**), and who receives help with their chores (**aider à**).

Game Divide the class into teams of four. Write a reciprocal verb on the board. Groups have 15 seconds to come up with a sentence in the present, the **imparfait**, or the **passé composé.** All groups with correct sentences earn one point.

Interlude

Monospace

Pour le thème de la technologie, la chanson°, ***Monospace*** *(2003), est typique du style de Bénabar: humour un peu caustique et tendresse°. Il est très amoureux d'une fille et pour elle il est prêt à partir en vacances, au mois d'août, dans un monospace°, avec leurs deux enfants, comme la majorité des gens. Il se moque° un peu de ce conformisme°.*

BÉNABAR (1969–) est né dans la banlieue parisienne. À huit ans, il commence à apprendre à jouer de la trompette, parce que c'est l'instrument de musique préféré des clowns. Il adore le cirque. Son pseudonyme est le nom d'un clown, Barnabé, écrit à l'envers°. Il s'intéresse d'abord au cinéma puis écrit des chansons pour un copain. Il finit par écrire des chansons pour lui-même et son premier album sort en 1998. Bénabar est devenu le symbole de la nouvelle chanson française.

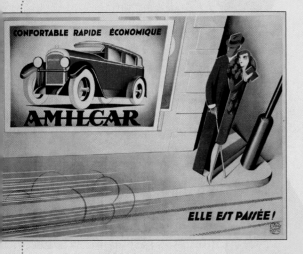

La voiture Amilcar

La marque° française de voitures Amilcar a été créée par Joseph Lamy et Émile Akar en 1920. Cette compagnie a connu un succès important en présentant° des véhicules rapides et bon marché, mais d'une grande qualité, et en améliorant° constamment leur technologie. Aujourd'hui, les grands constructeurs automobiles français produisent des voitures où l'électronique est très présente.

Activité

Cette affiche Amilcar montre un vieux modèle de voiture qui n'a pas tous les gadgets technologiques des voitures contemporaines. Écrivez un paragraphe où vous décrivez l'importance des gadgets technologiques en général, dans le passé et aujourd'hui. Votre paragraphe doit répondre à ces questions: Answers will vary.

- Vos gadgets électroniques sont-ils importants pour vous? Pourquoi?
- Quels gadgets existent aujourd'hui qui n'existaient pas en 1920?
- Est-ce que la technologie rend (*makes*) la vie plus facile ou plus compliquée?
- A-t-on vraiment besoin de tous les gadgets technologiques contemporains?

SUR INTERNET

Go to **espaces.vhlcentral.com** for more information related to this **Interlude**.

chanson *song* **tendresse** *tenderness* **monospace** *minivan* **se moque** *makes fun* **conformisme** *conformity* **à l'envers** *in reverse* **marque** *brand* **en présentant** *by presenting* **en améliorant** *by improving*

Section Goals

In this section, students will learn about:
- Bénabar
- a vintage automobile poster for Amilcar

Instructional Resources
espaces.vhlcentral.com: activities, downloads, reference tools

Monospace
- Point out that Bénabar (whose given name is Bruno Nicolini) is a self-taught musician, as well as a singer and songwriter. He lives part of the time in Brussels and part of the time in France.
- To check comprehension, ask these questions.

1. Quel est le titre (*title*) de la chanson? (*Monospace*) Est-ce un titre approprié? (Oui, c'est approprié.) Pourquoi? (parce que la chanson parle d'un homme qui est prêt à partir en vacances dans un monospace avec une fille et leurs deux enfants)
2. Qu'est-ce que Bénabar a appris à huit ans? (à jouer de la trompette)
3. Pourquoi a-t-il choisi le pseudonyme de Bénabar? (parce qu'il adore le cirque et que Bénabar est le nom d'un clown écrit à l'envers)
4. De quel genre de musique est-il le symbole? (de la nouvelle chanson française)

La voiture Amilcar
- Have students look at the poster. Ask: **Selon l'affiche, pourquoi doit-on acheter une Amilcar? (Elle est confortable, rapide et économique.)** Then have students describe what they see in the poster.
- If possible, bring in a few car ads and have students compare the modern ads to this poster.

OPTIONS

Bénabar Originally trained as a photographer and film technician, Bénabar has three short films to his credit. His film ***José Jeannette*** won three prizes. He also wrote sketches and editorial reviews for the series ***H*** on Canal +. His songwriting often reflects his love for the cinema. His album ***Les risques du métier*** (2003) received a **Victoire de la Musique** in 2004, and the album ***Reprise des négociations*** (2005) was an instant hit. The latter contains some songs in which he talks about his childhood and adolescence.

Extra Practice Take a quick survey of your students to find out how many think taking a vacation in a minivan with their families would be an enjoyable experience. Then have them explain why or why not.

Section Goals

In this section, students will learn and practice vocabulary related to:

- cars and driving
- car maintenance and repair

Instructional Resources

*IRCD-ROM: Transparency #49; IRM (**Vocabulaire supplémentaire; Mise en pratique** answers; Textbook Audioscript; Lab Audioscript; Info Gap Activities)*
Textbook MP3s
WB/VM: Workbook, pp. 147–148
Lab Manual, p. 85
Lab MP3s
WB/VM/LM Answer Key
espaces.vhlcentral.com: activities, downloads, reference tools

Suggestions

- Use **Transparency #49.** Point out objects and describe what the people are doing. Examples: **Ces personnes sont dans une station-service. C'est une voiture. Il a un pneu crevé. Il fait le plein d'essence.**
- Follow up with simple questions based on your narrative. Examples: **C'est un volant? Qu'est-ce que c'est? Le mécanicien vérifie la pression des pneus?**
- Ask students questions about cars and driving using the new vocabulary. Examples: **Avez-vous une voiture? Attachez-vous votre ceinture de sécurité quand vous conduisez? Quand vous allez à la station-service, faites-vous le plein vous-même? Combien coûte l'essence par gallon?**
- Explain that **dépasser** has two meanings: **dépasser la vitesse autorisée/la limitation de vitesse** means *to go over the speed limit* and **dépasser une voiture/un camion** means *to pass a car/truck.*
- Additional vocabulary for this lesson can be found in the **Vocabulaire supplémentaire** in the IRM on the IRCD-ROM.

Leçon 22

You will learn how to...

- **talk about cars**
- **talk about traffic**

En voiture!

Vocabulaire

arrêter (de faire quelque chose)	*to stop (doing something)*
attacher	*to buckle*
avoir un accident	*to have/to be in an accident*
dépasser	*to go over; to pass*
freiner	*to brake*
se garer	*to park*
rentrer (dans)	*to hit*
réparer	*to repair*
tomber en panne	*to break down*
vérifier (l'huile/ la pression des pneus)	*to check (the oil/ the air pressure)*
l'embrayage (*m.*)	*clutch*
les freins (*m.*)	*brakes*
l'huile (*f.*)	*oil*
un pare-chocs (pare-chocs *pl.*)	*bumper*
un réservoir d'essence	*gas tank*
un rétroviseur	*rearview mirror*
une roue (de secours)	*(emergency) tire*
un voyant (d'essence/ d'huile)	*(gas/oil) warning light*
une amende	*fine*
une autoroute	*highway*
un parking	*parking lot*
un permis de conduire	*driver's license*
une rue	*street*

ressources

WB pp. 147-148	LM p. 85	Text MP3s Leçon 22	Lab MP3s Leçon 22	espaces.vhlcentral.com Leçon 22

OPTIONS

Game Play a game of **Dix questions**. Ask a volunteer to think of a car part from the new vocabulary. Other students get to ask one yes/no question, then they can guess what the word is. Limit attempts to ten questions per word. You might want to tell students that they can narrow down the options by asking questions about where the part is on the car and what it does.

Small Groups Distribute pictures of cars to groups of three students. Detailed photos of car interiors and exteriors are available online or from car dealerships. List parts of the car on the board, such as **volant, pneu, coffre,** and **rétroviseur**. Tell students to label the parts on the pictures. Alternatively, ask a student who can draw to sketch a car (inside and out) on the board and have students label its parts.

un pare-brise (pare-brise *pl.*)

la limitation de vitesse

la circulation

un agent de police/un policier (policière *f.*)

les essuie-glaces (*m.*)

les phares (*m.*)

Mise en pratique

1 Écoutez Madeleine a eu une mauvaise journée. Écoutez son histoire, ensuite indiquez si les phrases suivantes sont **vraies** ou **fausses**.

	Vrai	Faux
Madeleine...		
1. a oublié son permis de conduire.	☐	☑
2. a dépassé la limitation de vitesse.	☑	☐
3. a fait le plein avant d'aller à la fac.	☐	☑
4. a attaché sa ceinture de sécurité.	☑	☐
5. s'est garée à l'université.	☑	☐
6. conduisait quand un policier l'a arrêtée.	☑	☐
Sa voiture...		
7. a redémarré.	☐	☑
8. avait un pneu crevé.	☐	☑
9. n'avait pas d'essence.	☑	☐
10. était en panne.	☑	☐

2 Les correspondances Choisissez l'élément de la liste **B** qui convient le mieux à chaque verbe de la liste **A**.

A	B
1. __b__ dépasser	a. les freins
2. __d__ tomber en panne	b. la limitation de vitesse
3. __a__ freiner	c. la ceinture de sécurité
4. __e__ faire le plein	d. une voiture
5. __g__ réparer une voiture	e. l'essence
6. __f__ se garer	f. un parking
7. __c__ attacher	g. un mécanicien
8. __h__ vérifier la pression	h. les pneus

3 Complétez Complétez les phrases suivantes avec le bon mot de vocabulaire pour faire une phrase logique.

1. La personne qui répare une voiture est un __mécanicien__.
2. Il faut ouvrir le __capot__ de la voiture pour vérifier l'huile.
3. On met de l'essence dans le __réservoir d'essence__.
4. Le __permis de conduire__ est un document officiel qui vous autorise à conduire.
5. On utilise les __phares__ pour voir (*see*) quand on conduit la nuit.
6. On utilise les __essuie-glaces__ pour voir à travers (*through*) le pare-brise quand il pleut.
7. Le __volant__ sert à diriger la voiture.
8. Vous utilisez le __rétroviseur__ pour voir la circulation derrière vous.
9. La personne qui peut donner une amende est un __policier/agent de police__.
10. On peut ranger ses valises dans le __coffre__ de la voiture.
11. On utilise les __freins__ quand on veut s'arrêter.
12. Quand il y a beaucoup de voitures sur la route, il y a de la __circulation__.

1 Tapescript Hier, j'ai eu une journée terrible! J'avais un examen de maths à 8h du matin et je me suis levée en retard. J'étais très pressée, donc je conduisais très vite, quand tout à coup j'ai entendu une sirène. Quand j'ai regardé dans le rétroviseur, c'était un policier. Heureusement j'avais mon permis de conduire avec moi et j'avais ma ceinture de sécurité attachée, mais comme je roulais plus vite que la vitesse autorisée, j'ai dû payer une amende. Finalement, je suis arrivée à l'université et j'ai trouvé une place pour me garer sans problème. J'ai passé mon examen de maths et je suis partie. Quand je suis retournée à ma voiture pour partir, elle n'a pas démarré. Un mécanicien est venu, il a vérifié la voiture et il m'a dit qu'elle ne démarrait pas parce qu'elle n'avait pas d'essence.
(On Textbook MP3s)

1 Suggestion Play the recording again, stopping at the end of each sentence that contains an answer so students can check their work.

2 Expansion For additional practice, ask students what parts of a car are associated with these activities. **1. nettoyer le pare-brise (les essuie-glaces) 2. conduire (le volant) 3. arrêter (les freins) 4. changer de vitesse (l'embrayage) 5. regarder ce qui est derrière la voiture (le rétroviseur)**

3 Suggestion Have students work in pairs on this activity. Then go over the answers with the class.

OPTIONS

Les appellations des routes en France The letter preceding the highway number indicates what type of road it is. For example, the **A-8** is an **autoroute** (*freeway*). An **autoroute péage** is a *toll road.* The **N-7** is a **route nationale**, a smaller highway. The **D-15** is a **route départementale**, an even smaller road. **Autoroutes** are much faster than **routes nationales** or **départementales**, but they are usually less scenic.

Extra Practice Propose various driving situations to your students and then ask: **De quoi avez-vous besoin?** Examples: **1. Vous allez en ville en voiture pour faire des courses. (un parking) 2. Vous êtes sur l'autoroute et vous avez un pneu crevé. (une roue de secours) 3. Vous avez 18 ans et vous voulez conduire. (un permis de conduire) 4. Vous conduisez et il commence à pleuvoir. (les essuie-glaces)**

4 Suggestions
- Tell students to jot down notes during their interviews.
- After completing the interviews, ask volunteers to share their partner's responses with the class.

5 Suggestion Have two volunteers read the **modèle** aloud. Then divide the class into pairs and distribute the Info Gap Handouts in the IRM on the IRCD-ROM for this activity. Give students ten minutes to complete the activity.

6 Suggestions
- Before beginning the activity, have students look at the photo and describe what they see.
- Have the class brainstorm a list of potential problems that a car can have and write their suggestions on the board. Example: **Ma voiture consomme beaucoup d'essence.**

7 Suggestion Have students review the use of the **passé composé** and **imparfait** for narrating events in the past before they begin writing. See **Leçon 16**, pages 276–277.

NATIONAL communication STANDARDS

Communication

4 Conversez Interviewez un(e) camarade de classe. Answers will vary.

1. As-tu une voiture? De quelle sorte?
2. À quel âge as-tu obtenu (*obtained*) ton permis de conduire? Comment s'est passé l'examen?
3. Sais-tu comment changer un pneu crevé? En as-tu déjà changé un?
4. Ta voiture est-elle tombée en panne récemment? Qui l'a réparée?
5. Respectes-tu la limitation de vitesse sur l'autoroute? Et tes amis?
6. As-tu déjà été arrêté(e) par un policier? Pour quelle(s) raison(s)?
7. Combien de fois par mois fais-tu le plein (d'essence)? Combien paies-tu à chaque fois?
8. Quelle(s) autoroute(s) utilises-tu pour venir à l'université?
9. Sais-tu comment conduire une voiture à boîte de vitesses manuelle (*manual*)? Et tes amis?
10. As-tu eu des problèmes de pare-chocs récemment? Et des problèmes d'essuie-glaces?

5 Sept différences Votre professeur va vous donner, à vous et à votre partenaire, deux feuilles d'activités différentes. À tour de rôle, posez-vous des questions pour trouver les sept différences entre vos dessins. Attention! Ne regardez pas la feuille de votre partenaire.

MODÈLE

Étudiant(e) 1: *Ma voiture est blanche.*
Étudiant(e) 2: *Oh! Ma voiture est noire.*

6 Chez le mécanicien Travaillez avec un(e) camarade de classe pour présenter un dialogue avec lequel (*with which*) vous jouez les rôles d'un(e) client(e) et d'un(e) mécanicien(ne). Answers will vary.

Le/La client(e)...
- explique le problème qu'il/qu'elle a.
- donne quelques détails sur les problèmes qu'il/qu'elle a eus dans le passé.
- négocie le prix et la date à laquelle il/elle peut venir chercher la voiture.

Le/La mécanicien(ne)...
- demande quand le problème a commencé et s'il y en a d'autres.
- explique le problème et donne le prix des réparations.
- accepte les conditions du/de la client(e).

7 Écriture Écrivez un paragraphe à propos (*about*) d'un accident de la circulation. Suivez les instructions. Answers will vary.
- Parlez d'un accident (voiture, motocyclette, bicyclette) que vous avez eu récemment. Si vous n'avez jamais eu d'accident, inventez-en un.
- Décrivez ce qui s'est passé avant, pendant et après.
- Donnez des détails.
- Comparez votre paragraphe avec celui (*that*) d'un(e) camarade de classe.

OPTIONS

Game Write vocabulary words related to cars on index cards. On another set of cards, draw or paste pictures to match each term. Tape them face down on the board in random order. Divide the class into two teams. Play a game of Concentration in which students match words with pictures. When a player makes a match, that player's team collects those cards. The team with the most cards at the end of the game wins.

Pairs Have students work in pairs. Tell them to take turns explaining to a younger brother or sister how to drive a car. Example: **Tout d'abord, tu attaches ta ceinture de sécurité. Puis...**

Les sons et les lettres

The letter x

The letter **x** in French is sometimes pronounced *-ks*, like the *x* in the English word *axe*.

taxi **expliquer** **mexicain** **texte**

Unlike English, some French words begin with a *ks-* sound.

xylophone **xénon** **xénophile** **Xavière**

The letters **ex-** followed by a vowel are often pronounced like the English word *eggs*.

exemple **examen** **exil** **exact**

Sometimes an **x** is pronounced *s*, as in the following numbers.

soixante **six** **dix**

An **x** is pronounced *z* in a liaison. Otherwise, an **x** at the end of a word is usually silent.

deux enfants **six éléphants** **mieux** **curieux**

Prononcez Répétez les mots suivants à voix haute.

1. fax
2. eux
3. dix
4. prix
5. jeux
6. index
7. excuser
8. exercice
9. orageux
10. expression
11. contexte
12. sérieux

Articulez Répétez les phrases suivantes à voix haute.

1. Les amoureux sont devenus époux.
2. Soixante-dix euros! La note (*bill*) du taxi est exorbitante!
3. Alexandre est nerveux parce qu'il a deux examens.
4. Xavier explore le vieux quartier d'Aix-en-Provence.
5. Le professeur explique l'exercice aux étudiants exceptionnels.

Dictons Répétez les dictons à voix haute.

Les beaux esprits se rencontrent.[1]

[1] Great minds think alike.
[2] Beautiful feathers make beautiful birds.

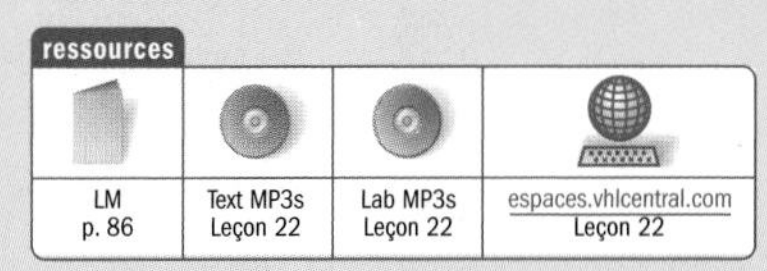

ressources
LM p. 86
Text MP3s Leçon 22
Lab MP3s Leçon 22
espaces.vhlcentral.com Leçon 22

Section Goals

In this section, students will learn about the letter **x**.

Instructional Resources
Textbook MP3s
Lab Manual, p. 86
Lab MP3s
WB/VM/LM Answer Key
IRCD-ROM: IRM (Textbook Audioscript; Lab Audioscript)
espaces.vhlcentral.com: activities, downloads, reference tools

Suggestions

- Model the pronunciation of the example words and have students repeat after you.
- Have students practice saying words that contain the letter **x** in various positions. Examples: Middle: **excellent, expliquer, expérience,** and **extérieur**. End: **yeux, heureux, époux, cheveux, jeux,** and **mieux**.
- Ask students to provide more examples of words with the letter **x**.
- Dictate five simple sentences with words that have the letter **x**, repeating each one at least two times. Then write the sentences on the board or a transparency and have students check their spelling.

Dictons The saying **«Les belles plumes font les beaux oiseaux»** is a quote from the French poet Bonaventure Des Périers (1500–1544).

OPTIONS

Extra Practice For additional practice with the letter **x**, have students write sentences on individual index cards using the words below. Then collect the cards and distribute some of them (at least one for each word) for students to read aloud. **1. excuser 2. deux 3. époux 4. cheveux 5. malheureux 6. roux 7. vieux 8. ennuyeux 9. explorer 10. généreux**

Extra Practice Teach students these French tongue-twisters that contain the letter **x**. **1. Le fisc fixe exprès chaque taxe fixe excessive exclusivement au luxe et à l'acquis. 2. Un taxi attaque six taxis. 3. Je veux et j'exige d'exquises excuses.**

Section Goals
In this section, students will learn functional phrases for talking about dating and cars.

Instructional Resources
WB/VM: Video Manual, pp. 253–254
WB/VM/LM Answer Key
Video CD-ROM
Video on DVD
IRCD-ROM: IRM (Videoscript; ***Roman-photo*** *Translations)*
espaces.vhlcentral.com: activities, downloads, reference tools

Video Recap: Leçon 21
Before doing this **Roman-photo**, review the previous one with this true/false activity.
1. Rachid n'arrive pas à travailler à cause de David. (Vrai.)
2. David ne finit pas sa dissertation. (Faux.)
3. Amina n'a pas l'intention de rencontrer Cyberhomme. (Vrai.)
4. Amina retrouve la dissertation de David. (Vrai.)
5. David, c'est Cyberhomme. (Faux.)

Video Synopsis
Rachid goes to the service station to get some gas. Amina is waiting at **Le P'tit Bistrot** for him to pick her up for a date. Rachid brings her flowers and is very attentive. In the car, Rachid notices that an indicator light is on, so he returns to the service station. The car just needs some oil. After fixing the problem, they take off again, but they don't get very far because they have a flat tire.

Suggestions
- Have students predict what the episode will be about based on the video stills.
- Tell students to scan the captions and find vocabulary related to cars and driving.
- After reading the **Roman-photo**, review students' predictions and have them summarize the episode.

La panne

PERSONNAGES

Amina

Garagiste

Rachid

Sandrine

Valérie

1

À la station-service...
GARAGISTE Elle est belle, votre voiture! Elle est de quelle année?
RACHID Elle est de 2005.
GARAGISTE Je vérifie l'huile ou la pression des pneus?
RACHID Non, merci ça va. Je suis un peu pressé en fait. Au revoir.

2

Au P'tit Bistrot...
SANDRINE Ton Cyberhomme, c'est Rachid! Quelle coïncidence!
AMINA C'est incroyable, non? Je savais qu'il habitait à Aix, mais...
VALÉRIE Une vraie petite histoire d'amour, comme dans les films!
SANDRINE C'est exactement ce que je me disais!

3

AMINA Rachid arrive dans quelques minutes. Est-ce que cette couleur va avec ma jupe?
SANDRINE Vous l'avez entendue? Elle doit être amoureuse.
AMINA Arrête de dire des bêtises.

6

RACHID Oh non!!
AMINA Qu'est-ce qu'il y a? Un problème?
RACHID Je ne sais pas, j'ai un voyant qui s'est allumé.
AMINA Allons à une station-service.
RACHID Oui... c'est une bonne idée.

7

De retour à la station-service...
GARAGISTE Ah! Vous êtes de retour. Mais que se passe-t-il? Je peux vous aider?
RACHID J'espère. Il y a quelque chose qui ne va pas, peut-être avec le moteur, regardez, ce voyant est allumé.
GARAGISTE Ah, ça? C'est l'huile. Je m'en occupe tout de suite.

8

GARAGISTE Vous pouvez redémarrer? Et voilà.
RACHID Parfait. Au revoir. Bonne journée.
GARAGISTE Bonne route!

ACTIVITÉS

1 Vrai ou faux? Indiquez si les affirmations suivantes sont vraies ou fausses.

1. La voiture de Rachid est très vieille. Faux.
2. Quand Rachid va à la station-service la première fois, il a beaucoup de temps. Faux.
3. Amina savait que Cyberhomme habitait à Aix. Vrai.
4. Sandrine trouve l'histoire de Rachid et d'Amina très romantique. Vrai.
5. Amina ouvre la portière de la voiture. Faux.
6. Rachid est galant (*a gentleman*). Vrai.
7. Le premier problème que Rachid rencontre, c'est une panne d'essence. Faux.
8. Le garagiste répare la voiture. Vrai.
9. La voiture a un pneu crevé. Vrai.
10. Rachid n'est pas très fier de lui. Vrai.

OPTIONS

Avant de regarder la vidéo Tell students to read the title and scene setter. Then have them predict what might happen in this episode. Write their predictions on the board. After viewing the episode, have them confirm or correct their predictions.

Regarder la vidéo Photocopy the videoscript from the IRM. Then white out words related to cars and other key vocabulary in order to create a master for a cloze activity. Distribute photocopies and tell students to fill in the missing information as they watch the video episode.

Amina sort avec Rachid pour la première fois.

SANDRINE Oh, regarde, il lui offre des fleurs.
RACHID Bonjour, Amina. Tiens, c'est pour toi.
AMINA Bonjour, Rachid. Oh, merci, c'est très gentil.
RACHID Tu es très belle aujourd'hui.
AMINA Merci.

RACHID Attends, laisse-moi t'ouvrir la portière.
AMINA Merci.
RACHID N'oublie pas d'attacher ta ceinture.
AMINA Oui, bien sûr.

AMINA Heureusement, ce n'était pas bien grave. À quelle heure est notre réservation?
RACHID Oh! C'est pas vrai!

AMINA Qu'est-ce que c'était?
RACHID On a un pneu crevé.
AMINA Oh, non!!

Expressions utiles

Talking about dating

- **Il lui offre des fleurs.**
  He's offering/giving her flowers.
- **Attends, laisse-moi t'ouvrir la portière.**
  Wait, let me open the (car) door for you.

Talking about cars

- **N'oublie pas d'attacher ta ceinture.**
  Don't forget to fasten your seatbelt.
- **J'ai un voyant qui s'est allumé.**
  I have a light that lit up.
- **Il y a quelque chose qui ne va pas.**
  There's something wrong.

Additional vocabulary

- **incroyable**
  incredible

ACTIVITÉS

2 Qui? Indiquez qui dirait (*would say*) les affirmations suivantes: Rachid (**R**), Amina (**A**), Sandrine (**S**), Valérie (**V**) ou le garagiste (**G**).

1. La prochaine fois, je vais suivre les conseils du garagiste. R
2. Je suis un peu anxieuse. A
3. C'est comme un conte de fées (*fairy tale*)! S/V
4. Taisez-vous (*Be quiet*), s'il vous plaît! A
5. Il aurait dû (*should have*) m'écouter. G

3 Écrivez Qu'est-ce qui se passe pour Amina et Rachid après le deuxième incident? Utilisez votre imagination et écrivez un paragraphe qui raconte ce qu'ils ont fait. Est-ce que quelqu'un d'autre les aide? Amina est-elle fâchée? Y aura-t-il (*Will there be*) un deuxième rendez-vous pour Cyberhomme et Technofemme?

ressources

VM pp. 253–254	V CD-ROM Leçon 22	espaces.vhlcentral.com Leçon 22

Expressions utiles

- Model the pronunciation of the **Expressions utiles** and have students repeat them after you.
- As you work through the list, point out forms of **offrir** and **ouvrir**, as well as relative pronouns. Tell students that these verbs and structures will be formally presented in the **Structures** section.
- Respond briefly to questions about verbs like **offrir** and **ouvrir** and relative pronouns. Reinforce correct forms, but do not expect students to produce them consistently at this time.
- Tell students that a **garagiste** is a *garage owner* and a **mécanicien** is a *car mechanic.*
- Explain the different words for *light*: **un voyant** is a *warning light* on a vehicle, **les phares** are *headlights*, and the generic term for *light* is **la lumière**.
- Point out that **une portière** is a *car door*; a door in a room or a house is **une porte**. Similarly, a *car window* is **une vitre**, not **une fenêtre**.

1 Suggestion Have students correct the false statements.

2 Expansion Have students create three more items using lines from the **Roman-photo** conversation. Collect their papers, write some of the items on the board, and ask volunteers to identify the speakers.

3 Expansion Have students exchange papers for peer editing. Then ask volunteers to read their paragraphs aloud.

OPTIONS

Extra Practice Assign students a character (**Rachid, Amina,** or **le garagiste**) and have them prepare a brief summary of the day's events from that character's point of view without saying the person's name. Ask volunteers to read their summaries to the class. Then have the class guess which character would have given each summary.

Le permis de conduire In France, the legal driving age for a regular permit is 18. In order to get a license, students take classes at an **auto-école**. Drivers must know **le code de la route** (*the driving code*) and understand how a car works. Since the lessons are very expensive, it is not unusual for young people to receive them as a gift for their eighteenth birthday.

Section Goals

In this section, students will:

- learn about cars and driving habits in France
- learn some terms for types of vehicles
- learn about the rules of the road in various francophone regions
- read about the car manufacturer Citroën

Instructional Resources
espaces.vhlcentral.com: activities, downloads, reference tools

Culture à la loupe

Avant la lecture Have students look at the photos and describe what they see.

Lecture

- Explain that in Europe gas is sold in liters, not in gallons (1 gallon = 3.79 liters).
- Point out the statistics chart. Ask students what information it shows. (the percentage of French people in rural and urban areas who own a car)

Après la lecture Have students compare French and American cars, driving habits, and car ownership.

1 Suggestion Have students work on this activity in pairs.

CULTURE À LA LOUPE

Les voitures françaises

la Smart

Dans l'ensemble°, les Français utilisent moins leur voiture que les Américains. Il n'est pas rare qu'un couple ou une famille possède une seule voiture. Dans les grandes villes, beaucoup de gens se déplacent° à pied ou utilisent les transports en commun°. Dans les villages ou à la campagne, les gens utilisent un peu plus fréquemment leurs voitures. Pour de longs voyages, pourtant°, ils ont tendance, plus que les Américains, à laisser leurs voitures chez eux et à prendre le train ou l'avion. En général, les voitures en France sont beaucoup plus petites que les voitures qu'on trouve aux États-Unis, mais on y trouve des quatre-quatre°, même dans les grandes villes. La Smart, une voiture minuscule produite par les compagnies Swatch et Mercedes-Benz, a aussi beaucoup de succès en France et en Europe.

Il y a plusieurs raisons qui expliquent ces différences. D'abord, les rues des villes françaises sont beaucoup moins larges. Au centre-ville, beaucoup de rues sont piétonnes° et d'autres sont si petites qu'il est parfois difficile de passer, même pour une petite voiture. Il y a aussi de gros problèmes de parking dans la majorité des villes françaises. Il y a peu de places de parking et elles sont en général assez petites. Il est donc nécessaire de faire un créneau° pour se garer et plus la voiture est petite, plus° on a de chance de le réussir. Les rues en dehors° des villes sont souvent plus larges. En plus, en France, l'essence est plus chère qu'aux États-Unis. Il vaut donc mieux avoir une petite voiture économique qui ne consomme pas beaucoup d'essence, ou prendre les transports en commun quand c'est possible.

Pourcentage de Français qui possèdent une voiture

Dans les villages et à la campagne	92%
Dans les villes de moins de 20.000 habitants	86%
Dans les villes de 20.000 à 100.000 habitants	84%
Dans les villes de plus de 100.000 habitants	75%
En région parisienne	60%
À Paris	45%

Dans l'ensemble *By and large* **se déplacent** *get around* **transports en commun** *public transportation* **pourtant** *however* **quatre-quatre** *sport utility vehicles* **piétonnes** *reserved for pedestrians* **faire un créneau** *parallel park* **plus..., plus...** *the more..., the more...* **en dehors** *outside*

ACTIVITÉS

1 Complétez Donnez un début ou une suite logique à chaque phrase, d'après le texte. Answers may vary. Possible answers provided.

1. ... possèdent parfois une seule voiture. Les familles françaises
2. Les Français qui habitent en ville se déplacent souvent... à pied ou ils utilisent les transports en commun.
3. Beaucoup de Français prennent le train ou l'avion... pour faire de longs voyages.
4. ... sont en général plus petites qu'aux États-Unis. Les voitures en France
5. Comme aux États-Unis, même dans les grandes villes en France, on trouve... des quatre-quatre.
6. ..., on peut facilement faire un créneau pour se garer. Avec la Smart
7. ... sont souvent plus larges. Les rues en dehors des villes
8. Il n'est pas toujours facile de se garer dans les villes françaises... parce qu'il y a peu de places de parking et parce qu'elles sont en général assez petites.
9. ... parce que l'essence coûte cher en France. Il vaut mieux avoir une petite voiture économique
10. ..., la grande majorité des Français ont une voiture. Dans les villages et à la campagne

OPTIONS

Pourcentage de Français qui possèdent une voiture Ask students these questions. **1. Où les gens sont-ils 86% à posséder une voiture? (dans les villes de moins de 20.000 habitants) 2. Qui possède le moins de voitures? (les Parisiens) 3. Quel pourcentage de Français ont une voiture dans les villes de 20.000 à 100.000 habitants? (84%) 4. Les habitants de la région parisienne possèdent-ils plus de voitures que les gens dans les villes de plus de 100.000 habitants? (Non)**

Les parcmètres Parking meters in France are not generally located next to the parking spot. The failure to see a parking meter is not a valid excuse for an expired meter. One should look for a meter down the street to avoid getting a parking ticket and having to pay a fine.

LE FRANÇAIS QUOTIDIEN

Pour parler des voitures

bagnole (*f.*)	*car*
berline (*f.*)	*sedan*
break (*m.*)	*station wagon*
caisse (*f.*)	*car*
char (*m.*)	*car*
coupé (*m.*)	*coupe*
décapotable (*f.*)	*convertible*
monospace (*m.*)	*minivan*
pick-up (*m.*)	*pickup*

PORTRAIT

Le constructeur automobile Citroën

La marque° Citroën est une marque de voitures française créée° en 1919 par André Citroën, ingénieur et industriel français. La marque est réputée pour son utilisation de technologies d'avant-garde et pour ses innovations dans le domaine de l'automobile. Le premier véhicule construit par Citroën, la voiture type A, a été la première voiture européenne construite en série°. En 1924, Citroën a utilisé la première carrosserie° entièrement en acier° d'Europe. Puis, dans les années 1930, Citroën a inventé la traction avant°. Parmi les modèles de voiture les plus vendus de la marque Citroën, on compte la 2CV, ou «deux chevaux», un modèle bon marché et très apprécié des jeunes à l'époque°. En 1976, Citroën a fusionné° avec un autre grand constructeur automobile français, Peugeot, pour former le groupe PSA Peugeot-Citroën.

marque *make* **créée** *created* **en série** *mass-produced* **carrosserie** *body* **acier** *steel* **traction avant** *front-wheel drive* **à l'époque** *at that time* **a fusionné** *merged*

LE MONDE FRANCOPHONE

Conduire une voiture

Voici quelques informations utiles.

En France Il n'existe pas de carrefours° avec quatre panneaux° de stop.

En France, en Belgique et en Suisse Il est interdit d'utiliser un téléphone portable quand on conduit et on n'a pas le droit de tourner à droite quand le feu° est rouge.

À l'île Maurice et aux Seychelles Faites attention! On conduit à gauche.

En Suisse Pour conduire sur l'autoroute, il est nécessaire d'acheter une vignette° et de la mettre sur son pare-brise. On peut l'acheter à la poste ou dans les stations-service, et elle est valable° un an.

Dans l'Union européenne Le permis de conduire d'un pays de l'Union européenne est valable dans tous les autres pays de l'Union.

carrefours *intersections* **panneaux** *signs* **feu** *traffic light* **vignette** *sticker* **valable** *valid*

SUR INTERNET

Qu'est-ce que la Formule 1?

Go to **espaces.vhlcentral.com** to find more cultural information related to this **ESPACE CULTURE**.

ACTIVITÉS

2 Répondez Répondez par des phrases complètes.

1. Quelles sont les caractéristiques de la marque Citroën? Elle est réputée pour son utilisation de technologies d'avant-garde et pour ses innovations.
2. Quelle est une des innovations de la marque Citroën? Answers will vary. Possible answer: La construction en série d'une voiture en Europe a été une innovation.
3. Quel modèle de voiture Citroën a eu beaucoup de succès? La 2CV, ou «deux chevaux», a eu beaucoup de succès.
4. Qu'a fait la compagnie Citroën en 1976? La compagnie a fusionné avec un autre constructeur automobile français, Peugeot.
5. Que faut-il avoir pour conduire sur l'autoroute en Suisse? Il faut avoir une vignette sur le pare-brise.
6. Les résidents d'autres pays de l'U.E. ont-ils le droit de conduire en France? Oui, les permis de conduire des autres pays de l'Union européenne sont valables en France.

3 À vous... Quelle est votre voiture préférée? Pourquoi? Avec un(e) partenaire, discutez de ce sujet et soyez prêts à expliquer vos raisons au reste de la classe.

Le français quotidien
- Model the pronunciation of each term and have students repeat it.
- Point out that **char** is the word for *car* in Quebec.
- Bring in photos of the different types of vehicles from an automotive magazine and have students identify them. Ask: **Qu'est-ce que c'est? C'est un monospace?**

Portrait
- André Citroën (1878–1935) got the idea of mass producing cars when he visited Henry Ford's new Rouge River plant in Detroit. He was also a master at marketing his cars.
- Have students look at the photo of the car. Ask: **Que pensez-vous de la 2CV? Voulez-vous en posséder une? Pourquoi?**

Le monde francophone Have students compare the information given here with driving rules in the United States. Example: **Aux États-Unis, il y a souvent des carrefours avec quatre panneaux de stop. En France, il n'y en a pas.**

2 Expansion For additional practice, give students these items. **7. Qu'est-ce qui-il est interdit de faire au volant dans les pays francophones d'Europe? (utiliser un portable) 8. Dans quels lieux francophones conduit-on à gauche? (à l'île Maurice et aux Seychelles)**

3 Suggestion Have students bring in a photo of their favorite car to use as a visual aid during this activity. Photos can generally be found at a company's or a car dealer's web site.

OPTIONS

Les limitations de vitesse Speed limits are generally higher in France than in the United States. For example, speed limits are 130 km/h (about 80 mph) on **autoroutes**, 110 km/h (about 70 mph) on **routes nationales**, 90 km/h (about 55 mph) on **routes**, and 50 km/h (about 30 mph) in cities and towns.

Cultural Activity Make a color transparency of French road signs (**panneaux de signalisation/signaux routiers**), which can be reproduced from the Internet or other reference sources. Then have the class guess what the signs mean.

Section Goals

In this section, students will learn:

- the verbs **ouvrir** and **offrir**
- other verbs with the same conjugation (**couvrir, souffrir,** etc.)

Instructional Resources

WB/VM: Workbook, pp. 149–150
Lab Manual, p. 87
Lab MP3s
WB/VM/LM Answer Key
*IRCD-ROM: IRM (**Essayez!** and **Mise en pratique** answers; Lab Audioscript)*
espaces.vhlcentral.com: activities, downloads, reference tools

Suggestions

- Review the conjugation of **-er** verbs.
- Write **j'ouvre, tu ouvres, il/elle ouvre** on the board. Point out that the endings are the same as **-er** verbs in the present tense.
- Follow the same procedure with **ouvrir**, but in the imperfect tense. Point out that with this tense, the verb is regular and takes **-ir** verb endings.
- Model verbs like **ouvrir** and **offrir** by asking volunteers questions. Examples: **À quelle heure la bibliothèque ouvre-t-elle? Quels services les grands magasins offrent-ils? Avez-vous souffert quand vous avez eu la varicelle** (*chicken pox*)?

Essayez! Give additional items such as these. **7. Qu'est-ce que je t'____ (offrir) pour ton anniversaire? (offre) 8. Vous ____ (ouvrir) les documents. (ouvrez)**

22.1 The verbs *ouvrir* and *offrir*

Point de départ The verbs **ouvrir** (*to open*) and **offrir** (*to offer*) are irregular. Although they end in **-ir**, they use the endings of regular **-er** verbs in the present tense.

ouvrir* and *offrir

	ouvrir	offrir
j'	ouvre	offre
tu	ouvres	offres
il/elle	ouvre	offre
nous	ouvrons	offrons
vous	ouvrez	offrez
ils/elles	ouvrent	offrent

La boutique **ouvre** à dix heures.
The shop opens at 10 o'clock.

Nous **offrons** soixante-quinze dollars.
We offer seventy-five dollars.

- The verbs **couvrir** (*to cover*), **découvrir** (*to discover*), and **souffrir** (*to suffer*) use the same endings as **ouvrir** and **offrir**.

Elle **souffre** quand elle a des examens.
She suffers when she has exams.

Couvrez la tête d'un enfant quand il fait soleil.
Cover the head of a child when it's sunny.

- The past participles of **ouvrir** and **offrir** are, respectively, **ouvert** and **offert**. Verbs like **ouvrir** and **offrir** follow this pattern.

Nous **avons découvert** un bon logiciel.
We discovered a good software program.

Elles **ont souffert** d'une allergie.
They suffered from an allergy.

- Verbs like **ouvrir** and **offrir** are regular in the **imparfait**.

Nous **souffrions** pendant les moments difficiles.
We suffered during the bad times.

Ils nous **offraient** de beaux cadeaux.
They used to give us nice gifts.

Essayez! **Complétez les phrases avec les formes correctes du présent des verbes.**

1. On _découvre_ (découvrir) beaucoup de choses quand on lit.
2. Vous _ouvrez_ (ouvrir) le livre.
3. Tu _souffres_ (souffrir) beaucoup chez le dentiste?
4. Elle _offre_ (offrir) des fleurs à ses amis.
5. Nous _offrons_ (offrir) dix mille dollars pour la voiture.
6. Les profs _couvrent_ (couvrir) les réponses.

MISE EN PRATIQUE

1 Mais non! **Alexandra et sa copine Djamila parlent en cours de leurs camarades. Que se disent-elles?**

MODÈLE Julianne souffre d'un mal de tête. (je)
Je souffre aussi d'un mal de tête.

1. Jean-Jacques ouvre son livre. (Renée)
Renée ouvre aussi son livre.
2. Antoine souffre d'allergies. (le professeur et moi)
Le professeur et moi, nous souffrons aussi d'allergies.
3. Le professeur découvre la réponse. (nous)
Nous découvrons aussi la réponse.
4. Tu offres ta place à Micheline. (Henri)
Henri offre aussi sa place à Micheline.
5. Je souffre beaucoup avant les examens. (nous)
Nous souffrons aussi beaucoup avant les examens.
6. Vous ouvrez la porte de votre classe. (Luc et Anne)
Luc et Anne ouvrent aussi la porte de leur classe.
7. Odile et Fatou couvrent leurs devoirs. (Lisette)
Lisette couvre aussi ses devoirs.
8. Angèle découvre qu'elle adore les maths. (je)
Je découvre aussi que j'adore les maths.

2 Je l'ai déjà fait **Les parents de Maya et de Sophie partent pour le week-end. Maya parle avec sa sœur des choses qu'elle veut faire pour organiser une fête dans leur nouvelle maison. Sophie lui dit qu'elle les a déjà faites.**

MODÈLE Je veux ouvrir les bouteilles.
Je les ai déjà ouvertes.

1. Je veux couvrir les meubles pour les protéger.
Je les ai déjà couverts.
2. Je veux ouvrir toutes les fenêtres.
Je les ai déjà ouvertes.
3. Je veux découvrir le centre-ville.
Je l'ai déjà découvert.
4. Je veux offrir des cadeaux aux voisins.
Je leur en ai déjà offert.
5. Je veux ouvrir les nouveaux CD.
Je les ai déjà ouverts.
6. Je veux couvrir les murs d'affiches.
Je les ai déjà couverts.
7. Je veux découvrir où papa garde son argent.
Je l'ai déjà découvert.
8. Je veux offrir une fleur aux invités.
Je leur en ai déjà offert une.

3 Que faisaient-ils? **Qu'est-ce que ces personnages faisaient hier à midi? Employez les verbes de la liste.**

couvrir	découvrir	offrir	ouvrir	souffrir

1. Benoît
Benoît ouvrait son livre.

2. tu
Tu souffrais d'une grippe.

3. vous
Vous découvriez de l'argent.

4. ils
Ils offraient un cadeau.

OPTIONS

Video Play the video and have students listen for **-er** and **-ir** verbs. Have them write down those they hear. Afterward, write the verbs on the board. Ask their meanings. Have students write original sentences using each verb.

Extra Practice Here are four sentences containing verbs like **ouvrir** to use as dictation. Read each twice, pausing after the second time for students to write. **1. J'ai découvert que mon frère a eu un accident! 2. Nous couvrons la piscine en hiver. 3. Mon grand-père m'offrait des bonbons après le dîner. 4. Le musée ouvre à dix heures.**

NATIONAL communication STANDARDS

COMMUNICATION

4 **Un cadeau électronique** Vous avez de l'argent et vous voulez acheter un cadeau dans ce magasin. Regardez la photo et dites à un(e) partenaire les choses que vous pouvez acheter. Utilisez les verbes de la liste. Answers will vary.

MODÈLE

Je peux acheter un jeu vidéo pour l'offrir à mon neveu.

couvrir découvrir offrir ouvrir souffrir

5 **Questions** Avec un(e) partenaire, posez-vous ces questions à tour de rôle. Ensuite, présentez les réponses à la classe. Answers will vary.

1. Qu'est-ce que tu as offert à ta mère pour la Fête des mères?
2. En quelle saison souffres-tu le plus? Pourquoi?
3. Est-ce que tu te couvres la tête quand tu bronzes? Avec quoi?
4. Est-ce que tu ouvres la fenêtre de ta chambre quand tu dors? Pourquoi?
5. Qu'est-ce que tes amis t'ont offert pour ton dernier anniversaire?
6. Que fais-tu quand tu souffres d'une grippe?
7. As-tu découvert des sites web intéressants? Quels sites?
8. Quand tu achètes un nouveau CD, est-ce que tu l'ouvres tout de suite? Pourquoi?

6 **Une amende** Un agent de police vous arrête parce que vous n'avez pas respecté la limitation de vitesse. Vous inventez beaucoup d'excuses. Avec un(e) partenaire, créez le dialogue et utilisez ce vocabulaire. Answers will vary.

amende	dépasser	ouvrir
avoir un accident	freiner	permis de conduire
circulation	freins	pneu crevé
coffre	se garer	rentrer dans
couvrir	limitation de vitesse	rue
découvrir	offrir	souffrir

Le français vivant

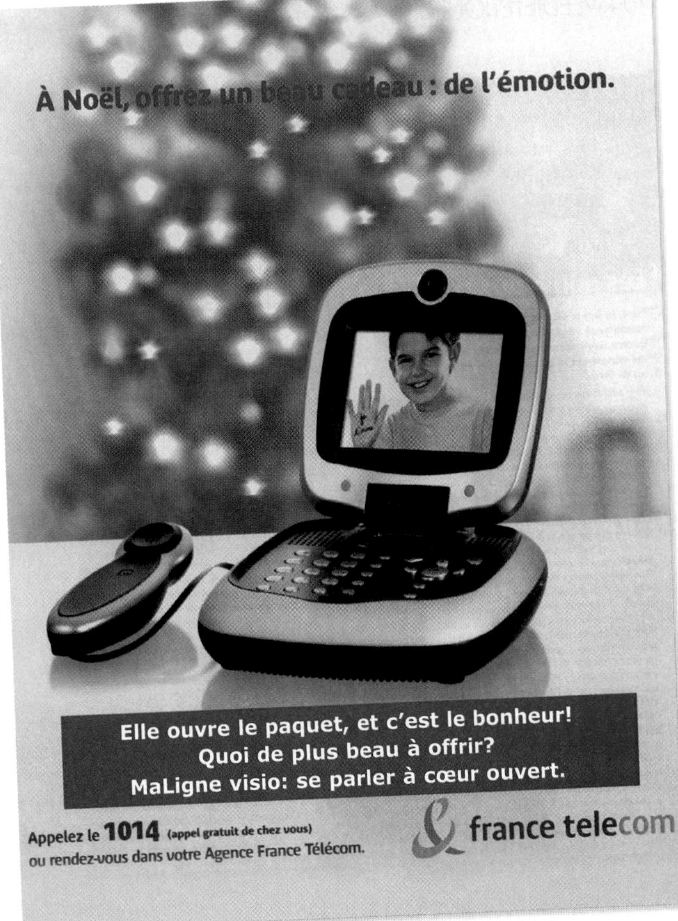

À Noël, offrez un beau cadeau : de l'émotion.
Elle ouvre le paquet, et c'est le bonheur!
Quoi de plus beau à offrir?
MaLigne visio: se parler à cœur ouvert.
Appelez le 1014 (appel gratuit de chez vous)
ou rendez-vous dans votre Agence France Télécom.
france telecom

Identifiez Avez-vous trouvé des formes des verbes **ouvrir** et **offrir** dans cette publicité (*ad*)? Lesquelles (*Which ones*)? offrez, ouvre, offrir, ouvert

Questions Posez ces questions à un(e) partenaire et répondez à tour de rôle. Answers will vary.

1. Qui offre un cadeau dans la pub? Qui reçoit (*receives*) un cadeau?
2. Quel cadeau offre-t-on?
3. Quel est le plus beau cadeau qu'on t'a offert?
4. Quel est le plus beau cadeau que tu as offert à quelqu'un?

1 Suggestion Have students check their answers orally with a partner.

2 Suggestion Before assigning this activity, ask questions using **déjà**. Remind students that **déjà** is placed after the conjugated verb and before the past participle. Example: **Qui a déjà étudié la biologie à l'université?**

3 Expansion Divide the class into groups of four. Have each student pick a photo to present to the group as a verbal portrait. Each one should include an introductory sentence that sets the scene, a body, and a conclusion. The verbal portrait should answer the questions *who, what, where, when,* and *why* based on the photo. After everyone in the group has presented a photo, the group votes on which one to present to the class.

4 Expansion Have pairs use the sentences created in the activity to write a short conversation between two friends shopping for a gift at an electronics store. Then ask for volunteers to present their conversation to the class.

5 Expansion Have pairs create two additional questions using the verbs **couvrir, découvrir, offrir, ouvrir,** and **souffrir**. Then pairs switch their questions with other pairs. Students should answer their classmates' questions in complete sentences.

6 Expansion Ask pairs to perform their conversation for the class or have them videotape it outside of class.

Le français vivant
- Call on a volunteer to read the advertisement aloud.
- Point out the phone number with only four digits. Explain that some toll-free numbers in France are like this. The main format for toll-free numbers is 0800 00 00 00.
- After pairs finish the **Questions** activity, go over the answers as a class.

OPTIONS

Game Divide the class into two teams. Indicate one team member at a time, alternating between teams. Give a certain infinitive from the lesson (**couvrir, découvrir, offrir, ouvrir, souffrir**) and name a subject. The team member uses that subject and verb in a sentence. Give a point per correct sentence. Deduct a point for each erroneous sentence. The team with the most points at the end of play wins.

Small Groups Have small groups prepare a conversation in which two roommates borrow a third roommate's car for the weekend without asking. They returned it in terrible condition. Encourage groups to use vocabulary and verbs from the lesson. Give groups time to prepare and practice their skits before presenting them to the class.

Section Goals

In this section, students will learn the relative pronouns **qui**, **que**, **dont**, and **où**.

Instructional Resources
WB/VM: Workbook, pp. 151–152
Lab Manual, p. 88
Lab MP3s
WB/VM/LM Answer Key
*IRCD-ROM: IRM (**Essayez!** and **Mise en pratique** answers; Lab Audioscript)*
espaces.vhlcentral.com: activities, downloads, reference tools

Suggestions

- Give an example of an optional relative pronoun in English. *The movie (that) we just watched was very sad.* Emphasize to students that relative pronouns are required in French. Example: **Le film que nous venons de regarder était très triste.**
- Explain that **que** can refer to both people and things. Example: **Le chanteur que tu écoutes est très populaire.**
- Point out that the relative pronoun **qui** is always followed by a conjugated verb. **Qui** acts as the subject. **Qui** can also refer to people or things. Example: **Le stylo (qui est) sur la table est vert.**
- Emphasize that, although the interrogative word **où?** means *where?*, the relative pronoun **où** can also be translated as *when* or *in which*.
- Point out that any expression with **de** can use **dont: avoir besoin de, avoir peur de, parler de, rêver de,** etc. Example: **C'est le voyage dont je rêvais.**

22.2 Relative pronouns *qui, que, dont, où*

Point de départ Relative pronouns link two phrases together into a longer, more complex sentence. The second phrase gives additional information about the first phrase. In English, relative pronouns can sometimes be omitted, but the relative pronoun in French cannot be.

Vous téléchargez **le logiciel**? *Are you downloading the software?*
Je préfère **ce logiciel**. *I prefer that software.*

Vous téléchargez le logiciel **que** je préfère? *Are you downloading the software that I prefer?*

J'ai un voyant qui s'est allumé.
C'est l'huile dont je parle.

Relative pronouns

qui	*who, that, which*	**dont**	*of which, of whom*
que	*that, which*	**où**	*where*

- Use **qui** if the final noun of the first phrase is the subject of the second phrase.

FINAL NOUN: Nous écoutons **le prof**. *We listen to the professor.*
SUBJECT: **Le prof** parle vite. *The professor speaks fast.*

Nous écoutons le prof **qui** parle vite. *We listen to the professor who speaks fast.*

FINAL NOUN: Les étudiantes vont au **café**. *The students go to the café.*
SUBJECT: **Le café** se trouve près de la fac. *The café is near the university.*

Les étudiantes vont au café **qui** se trouve près de la fac. *The students go to the café that is near the university.*

MISE EN PRATIQUE

1 Une publicité Complétez les phrases pour une publicité d'un magasin d'appareils électroniques qui vient d'ouvrir. Employez les pronoms relatifs **où**, **dont**, **qui** ou **que**.

MODÈLE
Nous avons des postes de télévision _qui_ ont des écrans géants.

1. Il y a des soldes sur les portables _dont_ vous avez besoin.
2. Il y a des lecteurs de DVD _qui_ ne sont pas chers.
3. Nous avons des claviers _qui_ sont très confortables.
4. Regardez notre site web _où_ nous avons des photos de notre magasin.
5. Nous avons les nouveaux CD _que_ vous désirez.
6. Venez au magasin _où_ vous allez trouver tous les appareils _que_ vous cherchez.

2 À mon avis... La grand-mère d'Édith parle de la technologie avec sa petite-fille. Assemblez les deux phrases avec **où**, **dont**, **qui** ou **que** pour faire une seule phrase.

1. Le fax est une invention récente. Je trouve cette invention formidable. Le fax est une invention récente que je trouve formidable.
2. J'aime bien lire les e-mails. Tu m'envoies des e-mails. J'aime bien lire les e-mails que tu m'envoies.
3. Un jour, ton ordinateur ne va pas fonctionner. Qu'est-ce que tu vas faire ce jour-là? Qu'est-ce que tu vas faire le jour où ton ordinateur ne va pas fonctionner?
4. Tu m'as donné un portable. Je n'utilise pas ce portable parce que je préfère mon téléphone. Je n'utilise pas le portable que tu m'as donné parce que je préfère mon téléphone.
5. Je ne peux pas allumer le poste de télévision. Le poste de télévision est dans ma chambre. Je ne peux pas allumer le poste de télévision qui est dans ma chambre.
6. J'ai visité le site web. On parle de ton université sur ce site. J'ai visité le site web où on parle de ton université.
7. J'ai besoin de ces documents. Explique-moi comment sauvegarder ces documents. Explique-moi comment sauvegarder ces documents dont j'ai besoin.
8. Je voudrais aller au magasin. Tu as acheté ton appareil photo dans ce magasin. Je voudrais aller au magasin où tu as acheté ton appareil photo.

3 Les choses que je préfère Marianne parle des choses qu'elle préfère. À tour de rôle avec un(e) partenaire, utilisez les pronoms relatifs pour écrire ses phrases. Présentez vos phrases à la classe. Answers will vary.

1. Marc est l'ami... (qui, dont)
2. «Chez Henri», c'est le restaurant... (où, que)
3. Ce CD est le cadeau... (que, qui)
4. Ma sœur est la personne... (dont, que)

OPTIONS

Video Replay the video episode, having students focus on relative pronouns. Have students divide their paper into two columns: **qui** and **que**. Ask them to write down each example they hear under its appropriate column. Then form groups of three and have students compare their papers.

Extra Practice Have students make complete sentences with phrases like the following. **1. Le tennis est un sport que... 2. Le tennis est un sport qui... 3. Gwyneth Paltrow est une actrice que... 4. Gwyneth Paltrow est une actrice qui... 5. *Le fabuleux destin d'Amélie Poulain*** (*Amélie*) **est un film que... 6. *Amélie* est un film qui...**

COMMUNICATION

4 **Des opinions** Avec un(e) partenaire, donnez votre opinion sur ces thèmes. Utilisez les pronoms relatifs **qui, que, dont et où.** Answers will vary.

MODÈLE

le printemps / saison
Étudiant(e) 1: *Le printemps est la saison que je préfère parce que j'aime les fleurs.*
Étudiant(e) 2: *L'hiver est la saison que moi, je préfère, parce que j'aime la neige.*

1. le petit-déjeuner / repas
2. surfer sur Internet / passe-temps
3. mon/ma camarade de chambre / personne
4. le samedi / jour
5. la chimie / cours
6. la France / pays
7. Tom Cruise / acteur
8. le prof de français / prof

5 **Des endroits intéressants** Par groupes de trois, organisez un voyage. Parlez des endroits qui vous intéressent et expliquez pourquoi vous voulez y aller. Utilisez des pronoms relatifs dans vos réponses et décidez où vous allez. Answers will vary.

MODÈLE

Allons à Bruxelles où nous pouvons acheter des chocolats délicieux.

6 **Chère Madame** Avec un(e) partenaire, écrivez une lettre à votre professeur où vous lui expliquez pourquoi vous n'avez pas fini votre devoir. Utilisez des pronoms relatifs et le vocabulaire de la Leçon 22. Answers will vary.

Chère Madame,

Je suis désolé(e), mais je n'ai pas fini mon devoir. La bibliothèque où...

- Use **que** if the final noun of the first phrase is the direct object of the second. The past participle following **que** agrees in number and gender with the direct object.

FINAL NOUN	DIRECT OBJECT
J'apporte **les CD**. *I'm bringing the CDs.*	J'ai acheté **les CD** hier. *I bought the CDs yesterday.*

J'apporte les CD **que** j'ai achetés hier.
I'm bringing the CDs (that) I bought yesterday.

FINAL NOUN	DIRECT OBJECT
Samir est à côté de **la porte**. *Samir is by the door.*	Nicole lui a ouvert **la porte**. *Nicole opened the door for him.*

Samir est à côté de la porte **que** Nicole lui a ouverte.
Samir is by the door (that) Nicole opened for him.

- Use **dont**, meaning *that* or *of which*, to replace a noun in the first phrase that is the object of the preposition **de** in the second phrase.

FINAL NOUN	OBJECT OF PREPOSITION DE
Voici **l'huile**. *Here's the oil.*	Tu m'as parlé **de l'huile**. *You talked to me about the oil.*

Voici l'huile **dont** tu m'as parlé.
Here's the oil (that) you talked to me about.

- Use **où**, meaning *where*, *when*, or *in which*, if the final noun of the first phrase is a place or a period of time.

FINAL NOUN	PERIOD OF TIME
Venez me parler à **ce moment-là**. *Come speak with me at that moment.*	Vous arrivez à **ce moment-là**. *You arrive at that moment.*

Venez me parler au moment **où** vous arrivez.
Come speak with me at the moment (that) you arrive.

Essayez! **Complétez les phrases avec qui, que, dont, où.**

1. La France est le pays __que__ j'aime le plus.
2. Tu te souviens du jour __où__ tu as fait ma connaissance?
3. Rocamadour est le village __dont__ mes amis m'ont parlé.
4. C'est la voiture __que__ vous avez louée?
5. Voici l'enveloppe __dont__ tu as besoin.
6. Vous connaissez l'autoroute __qui__ descend à Montpellier?
7. On passe devant la fac __où__ j'ai fait mes études.
8. Je reconnais le mécanicien __qui__ a réparé ma voiture.

Essayez! Ask volunteers to create questions or answers that correspond to the sentences in the activity. Example: **1. Quel est le pays que tu aimes le plus?**

1 Suggestion Ask a volunteer to read the **modèle** aloud. Ask another volunteer to explain the use of the relative pronoun in that example. (The answer is **qui** because it is a subject followed by the verb **ont.**)

2 Expansion Have pairs write two more sentences that contain relative pronouns and refer to Edith's grandmother's views on technology.

3 Expansion Expand the activity by asking students to talk about what they prefer. Have them model their sentences on Marianne's.

4 Expansion In addition to **surfer sur Internet** from #2, brainstorm a list of pastimes with the class. Conduct a conversation with the whole class about which pastimes they prefer and why.

5 Expansion Using magazine or real pictures, have students create a brief travel ad for the destination they chose. The ad should contain at least three uses of relative pronouns. Have students present their ads to the class.

6 Suggestion Do this activity orally, having pairs role-play the professor and the student talking on the telephone.

OPTIONS

Game Ask students to bring in some interesting pictures from magazines or the Internet, but tell them not to show these photos to one another. Divide the class into groups of three. Each group should pick a picture. One student will write an accurate description of it, and the others will write imaginary descriptions. Tell them to use relative pronouns in the descriptions. Each group will read its three descriptions aloud without showing the picture. Give the rest of the class two minutes to ask questions about the descriptions before guessing which is the accurate description. Award one point for a correct guess and two points to a team that fools the class.

Synthèse

Instructional Resources
*IRCD-ROM: IRM (**Feuilles d'activités**; Info Gap Activities); Testing Program, pp. 85–88; Test Files; Testing Program MP3s; Test Generator espaces.vhlcentral.com: activities, downloads, reference tools*

1 Suggestion Have two volunteers act out the **modèle**. Then distribute the **Feuilles d'activités** from the IRM on the IRCD-ROM.

1 Expansion Have pairs write six original sentences with relative pronouns based on the answers from the activity.

2 Suggestion Before assigning the activity, identify the genre of each film.
Le dernier métro: drama / ***Les visiteurs***: comedy, sci-fi / ***Toto le héros***: comedy, drama / ***La chèvre***: comedy / ***L'argent de poche***: documentary-style portrait / ***Le professionnel***: action, thriller

3 Expansion Invite pairs to perform their conversation for the class.

4 Expansion Using magazine and newspaper ads, have pairs invent slogans that advertise an electronic device.

5 Suggestion Before assigning the activity, have volunteers tell about gifts they have received in the past, including the occasion and who gave the gift.

6 Suggestion Divide the class into pairs and distribute the Info Gap Handouts in the IRM on the IRCD-ROM for this activity. Give students ten minutes to complete the activity.

1 Ce type de personne... Votre professeur va vous donner une feuille d'activités. Circulez dans la classe pour interviewer un(e) camarade différent(e) pour chaque question. Utilisez un pronom relatif dans toutes vos questions et mentionnez un détail supplémentaire dans vos réponses. Answers will vary.

MODÈLE

Étudiant(e) 1: *Es-tu quelqu'un qui a peur de conduire?*
Étudiant(e) 2: *Non, je ne suis pas quelqu'un qui a peur de conduire. Mais j'ai peur des agents de police.*

Es-tu quelqu'un qui...	*Nom*
1. a peur de conduire?	*Olivier*
2. aime l'odeur de l'essence?	
3. n'aime pas conduire vite?	
4. n'a jamais eu d'accident?	
5. ne dépasse jamais la limitation de vitesse?	
6. n'a pas son permis de conduire?	
7. ne sait pas ouvrir un capot?	
8. sait vérifier l'huile?	

2 C'est l'histoire de... Avec un(e) partenaire, commentez ces titres de films français et imaginez les histoires. Utilisez des pronoms relatifs. Ensuite, comparez vos histoires avec les histoires d'un autre groupe. Qui a l'histoire la plus proche (*closest*) du vrai film? Answers will vary.

MODÈLE

Étudiant(e) 1: *C'est l'histoire d'un homme qui...*
Étudiant(e) 2: *... et que la police cherche...*

- *Le dernier métro*
- *Les visiteurs*
- *Toto le héros*
- *La chèvre* (goat)
- *L'argent de poche* (pocket)
- *Le professionnel*

3 La leçon de conduite Vous êtes moniteur (*instructor*) et c'est la première leçon de conduite (*driving*) que prend votre partenaire. Inventez une scène où il/elle découvre la voiture et où vous lui expliquez la fonction des différents accessoires. Utilisez plusieurs pronoms relatifs dans votre dialogue. Answers will vary.

MODÈLE

Étudiant(e) 1: *Et ça, c'est le bouton qu'on utilise pour freiner?*
Étudiant(e) 2: *Mais non! C'est le bouton qui sert à allumer les phares que tu dois utiliser la nuit.*

4 Les slogans Avec un(e) partenaire, utilisez ces verbes dans des slogans pour vendre ces voitures. Soyez prêts à voter pour les meilleurs slogans de la classe. Answers will vary.

MODÈLE

Étudiant(e) 1: *Qu'est-ce que tu penses de: «Offrez-vous l'évasion»?*
Étudiant(e) 2: *Ce n'est pas mal, mais j'aime bien aussi: «Le monde vous découvre.»*

couvrir | découvrir | offrir | ouvrir | souffrir

5 Quel cadeau offrir? Vous venez de gagner à la loterie et vous voulez offrir de beaux cadeaux à vos amis et à votre famille. Par groupes de trois, discutez et choisissez quels cadeaux vous allez offrir. Choisissez aussi des cadeaux pour les deux camarades de votre groupe. Answers will vary.

MODÈLE

Étudiant(e) 1: *Je vais offrir une voiture de course à mon père, qui adore la vitesse.*
Étudiant(e) 2: *J'offre une grande limousine blanche à ma sœur, qui veut devenir actrice.*

6 Mots-croisés Votre professeur va vous donner, à vous et à votre partenaire, une grille de mots croisés (*crossword*). Attention! Ne regardez pas la feuille de votre partenaire. Utilisez des pronoms relatifs dans vos définitions.

MODÈLE

Étudiant(e) 1: *Horizontalement, le numéro 1, ce sont des objets dont on se sert pour conduire la nuit.*
Étudiant(e) 2: *Les phares!*

ressources

WB	LM	Lab MP3s	espaces.vhlcentral.com
pp. 149-152	pp. 87-88	Leçon 22	Leçon 22

OPTIONS

Game Place a label with **qui, que, dont,** or **où**, in each corner of the classroom. Divide the class into four groups and have each group gather in one of the sections of the room. Give students three minutes to create as many sentences as they can using their assigned relative pronoun. Every three minutes, have groups rotate to the next relative pronoun. The group with the most correct sentences at the end of the game wins.

Extra Practice Ask students to imagine they have just finished watching a documentary about the effects of technology on a university student's life. Have them think of five possible responses to what they saw and heard, using relative pronouns and active lesson vocabulary.

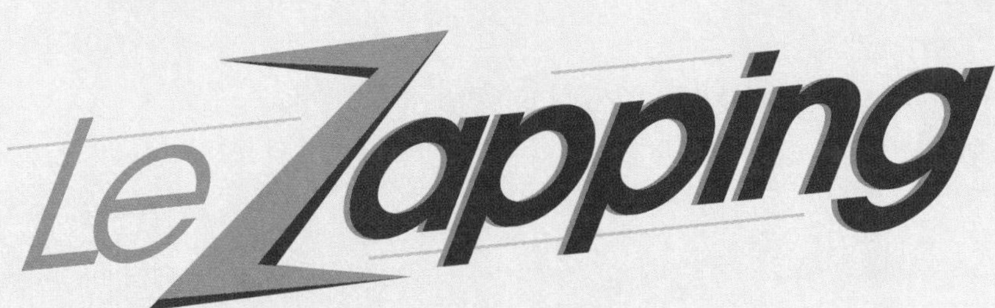

C'est la Renault 6!

Enfant, Louis Renault s'intéresse à toutes les nouvelles technologies et, à vingt ans, en 1897, il convertit son vélo à trois roues en une «Voiturette» à quatre roues. Il l'équipe de son invention: la première boîte de vitesses°.

En 1984, Renault invente le slogan: «Les voitures à vivre°.» Le moteur Renault remporte° de nombreuses courses° automobiles et sera six fois champion du monde. Quelques noms de voitures Renault: Clio, Espace, Laguna, Mégane, Twingo.

elle vous attend
chez votre concessionnaire
ou agent Renault

toutes les Renault sont lubrifiées par elf

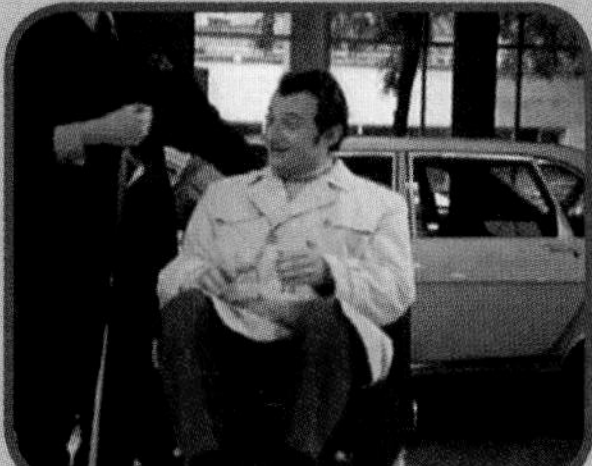

—Essayez le siège°.

—Je la prends! Au fait, comment s'appelle-t-elle?

Compréhension Répondez aux questions. Some answers will vary.

1. Quels mots du vocabulaire de la voiture avez-vous reconnus? un moteur, un coffre
2. Faites un résumé (*summary*) de la conversation. Utilisez des pronoms relatifs (**qui**, **que**, **dont**, **où**).

Discussion Avec un(e) partenaire, posez-vous ces questions et discutez. Answers will vary.

1. Renault est une marque de voiture française. En connais-tu d'autres? Lesquelles (*Which ones*)?
2. Quelle voiture conduis-tu ou quelle voiture as-tu envie de conduire?
3. Renault a gagné des courses automobiles. Que penses-tu des courses automobiles?

boîte de vitesses *transmission* **à vivre** *to live in* **remporte** *wins* **courses** *races* **siège** *seat*

SUR INTERNET

Go to **espaces.vhlcentral.com** to watch the TV clip featured in this **Le zapping**.

Section Goals

In this section, students will:
- read about the car company Renault
- watch a commercial for the Renault 6
- answer questions about the commercial and Renault

Instructional Resources
*IRCD-ROM: IRM (**Le zapping** TV clip transcription)*
espaces.vhlcentral.com: activities, downloads, reference tools, TV clip

Introduction
To check comprehension, ask these questions.
1. Que fait Louis Renault à 20 ans? (Il convertit son vélo à trois roues en une «Voiturette» et invente la boîte de vitesses.)
2. Quel slogan invente Renault? («Les voitures à vivre»)
3. À votre avis, pourquoi Renault remporte-t-il de nombreuses courses? (*Possible answer*: parce que son moteur est de qualité)

Avant de regarder la vidéo
- Have students look at the video stills, read the captions, and predict what is happening in the commercial for each visual. (**1. Le client essaie le siège de la voiture qu'il va peut-être acheter. 2. Le client aime beaucoup la voiture. Il décide de l'acheter, mais il ne sait pas comment l'appeler.**)
- Before showing the video, tell students to listen for car-related vocabulary.

Compréhension Have students work in pairs or groups. Tell them to write their answers. Then show the video again so that they can check their answers and add any missing information.

Discussion
- Find out which other French car companies the students know.
- Have volunteers report to the class what they found about their partner's choice in cars.
- Take a quick class survey to find out if car races are popular among the students.

OPTIONS

Renault In March 1999, Renault bought 36.9% of the Japanese car company Nissan. In 2002, its share rose to 44.4%. Together Renault and Nissan now represent the fourth largest car company in the world. This fits Renault's modern objectives to increase its international presence. In 1999, Renault also bought the Romanian car company Dacia, modernized it, and developed a new "5,000 euros" car for the Eastern European automobile market. As part of this new international strategy, Renault acquired Samsung Motors and created the new Renault Samsung Motors branch. Samsung is particularly strong in the South Korean market.

Section Goals

In this section, students will read historical and cultural information about Belgium.

Instructional Resources
IRCD-ROM: Transparency #50
WB/VM: Workbook, pp. 153–154
WB/VM/LM Answer Key
espaces.vhlcentral.com: activities; downloads; reference tools

Carte de la Belgique

- Have students look at the map or use **Transparency #50**. Ask volunteers to read the names of cities and other geographical features aloud. Model the pronunciation as necessary. Point out the francophone regions.
- Have students identify the countries that border Belgium.

Le pays en chiffres

- Point out the flag of Belgium.
- Have volunteers read the sections aloud. After each section, ask students questions about the content.
- Point out that Belgium is one of the smallest and most densely populated countries of Europe. Have students compare Belgium's size and population to Switzerland's (see page 354).
- About one-tenth of Belgium's population is bilingual, and a majority of the people have some knowledge of both French and Flemish.

Incroyable mais vrai! The beer and cheese made at the monasteries are produced using methods that are centuries old.

Panorama

des péniches° sur l'Escaut

La Belgique

Le pays en chiffres

- **Superficie:** *30.500 km²*
- **Population:** *10.296.000*
  SOURCE: Population Division, UN Secretariat
- **Industries principales:** *agroalimentaire°, chimie, métallurgie, sidérurgie°, textile*
- **Villes principales:** *Anvers, Bruges, Bruxelles, Gand, Liège, Namur*
- **Langues:** *allemand, français, néerlandais°*
  Les Belges néerlandais parlent une variante° de la langue néerlandaise qui s'appelle le flamand°. Environ° 60% de la population belge parlent flamand et habitent dans la partie nord° du pays, la Flandre. Le français est parlé surtout dans la partie sud° du pays, la Wallonie, par environ 40% des Belges. L'allemand est parlé par très peu de gens, environ 1%, dans l'est° du pays.
- **Monnaie:** *l'euro*

Belges célèbres

- **Marguerite Yourcenar,** *écrivain (1903–1987)*
- **Georges Simenon,** *écrivain (1903–1989)*
- **Jacques Brel,** *chanteur (1929–1978)*
- **Eddy Merckx,** *cycliste, cinq fois gagnant° du Tour de France (1945–)*
- **Cécile de France,** *actrice (1975–)*

- **Justine Hénin-Hardenne,** *joueuse de tennis (1982–)*

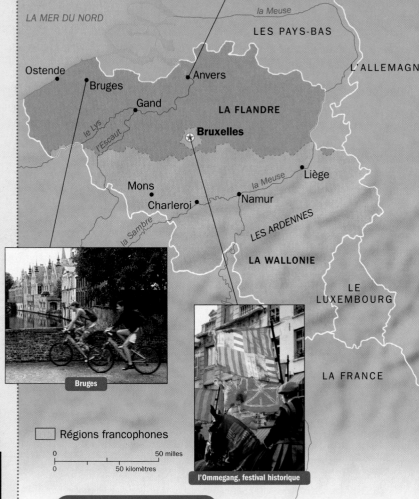

LA MER DU NORD · LES PAYS-BAS · L'ALLEMAGNE · LE LUXEMBOURG · LA FRANCE · LA FLANDRE · LA WALLONIE · LES ARDENNES · Ostende · Bruges · Gand · Anvers · Bruxelles · Mons · Charleroi · Namur · Liège · la Meuse · le Lys · l'Escaut · la Sambre

Régions francophones

0 — 50 milles; 0 — 50 kilomètres

Bruges

l'Ommegang, festival historique

Incroyable mais vrai!

Acheter de la bière ou du fromage au monastère? Pourquoi pas? Les moines° trappistes suivent° des principes monastiques stricts: isolés, ils se consacrent° au travail et à la prière°. Pour subvenir° à leurs besoins, ils font des bières et des fromages de qualité. Seules six bières belges peuvent porter l'appellation «trappiste».

agroalimentaire *food processing* **sidérurgie** *steel industry* **néerlandais** *Dutch* **variante** *variant* **flamand** *Flemish* **Environ** *About* **nord** *north* **sud** *south* **est** *east* **gagnant** *winner* **moines** *monks* **suivent** *follow* **se consacrent** *devote themselves* **prière** *prayer* **subvenir** *provide* **péniches** *barges*

OPTIONS

Belges célèbres Known for her historical novels, **Marguerite Yourcenar** (pen name of Marguerite de Crayencour) was the first woman to be elected to the **Académie française**. A prolific writer, **Georges Simenon** wrote mysteries, psychological novels, and pulp fiction. His *Inspector Maigret* series is sold worldwide. Lyricist, composer, singer, and actor, **Jacques Brel** was known for his passionate style and poetic lyrics. **Eddy Merckx** won numerous international competitions. Besides the **Tour de France**, he won the **Tour d'Italie** five times and the **Tour de Flandres** twice. **Cécile de France** has performed on stage and in films. She won **le César du Meilleur Espoir** for her role in ***L'auberge espagnole***. **Justine Hénin-Hardenne** has won three Grand Slam titles in women's singles and a gold medal at the 2004 Olympics.

Les destinations

Bruxelles, capitale de l'Europe

Fondée au septième siècle, la ville de Bruxelles a été choisie en 1958, en partie pour sa situation géographique centrale, comme siège° de la C.E.E.° Aujourd'hui, elle reste encore le siège de l'Union européenne (l'U.E.), lieu central des institutions et des décisions européennes. On y trouve le Parlement européen, organe législatif de l'U.E., et depuis 1967, le siège de l'OTAN°. Bruxelles est une ville très cosmopolite, avec un grand nombre d'habitants étrangers. Elle est aussi touristique, renommée pour sa Grand-Place, ses nombreux chocolatiers et la grande qualité de sa cuisine.

Les traditions

La bande dessinée

Les dessinateurs° de bandes dessinées (BD) sont très nombreux en Belgique. À Bruxelles, il y a de nombreuses peintures murales° et statues de BD. Le dessinateur Peyo est devenu célèbre avec la création des Schtroumpfs° en 1958, mais le père de la BD belge est Hergé, dessinateur qui a créé Tintin et Milou en 1929. Tintin est un reporter qui a des aventures partout dans° le monde. En 1953, il devient le premier homme, avant Neil Armstrong, à marcher sur la Lune° dans *On a marché sur la Lune*. La BD de Tintin est traduite en 45 langues.

La gastronomie

Les moules frites

Les moules° frites sont une spécialité belge. Les moules, cuites° dans du vin blanc, et les frites sont servies dans des plats séparés mais on les mange ensemble, et c'est délicieux. Beaucoup de gens ne savent pas que les frites ne sont pas françaises mais belges! On peut en acheter dans les nombreuses friteries. Elles sont servies dans un cornet° en papier avec une sauce, souvent de la mayonnaise. Il existe même en Belgique une Semaine nationale de la frite et une Union nationale des frituristes.

Les arts

René Magritte (1898–1967)

René Magritte, peintre surréaliste, s'intéressait à la représentation des images mentales. En montrant° la divergence entre un objet et sa représentation, son désir était de «faire hurler° les objets les plus familiers», mais toujours avec humour. Le musée Magritte à Bruxelles se trouve dans la maison où il a habité pendant 24 ans, et qui était aussi le quartier général° des surréalistes belges. Le portrait de Magritte était sur les billets de 500 francs Belges. Une de ses œuvres° les plus célèbres, à gauche, est *Le fils de l'homme*.

Qu'est-ce que vous avez appris? Répondez aux questions par des phrases complètes.

1. Quelle est la langue la plus parlée en Belgique?
   Le flamand est la langue la plus parlée.
2. Que produisent les moines trappistes?
   Ils produisent de la bière et du fromage.
3. À quelles activités se consacrent-ils?
   Ils se consacrent au travail et à la prière.
4. Pourquoi Bruxelles a-t-elle été choisie comme capitale de l'Europe? Elle a été choisie en partie pour sa situation géographique centrale en Europe.
5. Qui est le père de la bande dessinée belge?
   C'est Hergé.
6. Qui est allé sur la Lune avant Armstrong?
   Tintin est allé sur la Lune avant Armstrong.
7. Quelle bande dessinée a été créée (*created*) par Peyo?
   Les Schtroumpfs ont été créés par Peyo.
8. Où peut-on acheter des frites?
   On peut acheter des frites dans les friteries.
9. Qu'est-ce que Magritte montre dans ses œuvres?
   Il montre la divergence entre un objet et sa représentation.
10. Où se trouvait le quartier général des surréalistes belges?
    Il se trouvait dans la maison de Magritte.

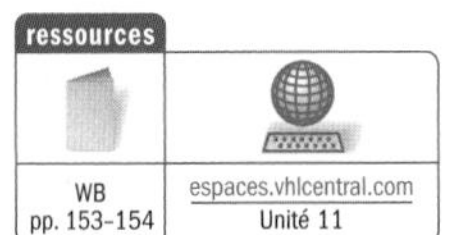

ressources
WB
pp. 153–154
espaces.vhlcentral.com
Unité 11

SUR INTERNET

Go to **espaces.vhlcentral.com** to find more cultural information related to this **PANORAMA**.

1. Quels sont les noms de trois autres personnages de bandes dessinées belges?
2. Dans quelles peintures Magritte a-t-il représenté des parties de la maison (fenêtre, cheminée, escalier)?
3. Cherchez des informations sur la ville de Bruges. Combien de kilomètres de canaux (*canals*) y a-t-il?

siège *headquarters* **C.E.E** *European Economic Community (predecessor of the European Union)* **OTAN** *NATO* **dessinateurs** *artists* **peintures murales** *murals* **Schtroumpfs** *Smurfs* **partout dans** *all over* **Lune** *moon* **moules** *mussels* **cuites** *cooked* **cornet** *cone* **En montrant** *In showing* **faire hurler** *make scream* **quartier général** *headquarters* **œuvres** *works*

Bruxelles, capitale de l'Europe

- The city square, **la Grand-Place**, hosts concerts, festivals, and a flower market during the warmer months. Featuring baroque and gothic guild architecture, **la Grand-Place** was used as a merchant's market during the thirteenth century.
- Point out the abbreviations U.E., C.E.E., and OTAN. Explain that it is not necessary to put periods after the letters in an abbreviation if it can be pronounced as a word, like OTAN. If one says each letter separately, as in U.E. or C.E.E., then periods are required.

La bande dessinée

- In Brussels, one can learn about the creation of comics strips, such as **Tintin** and the **Schtroumpfs,** as well as 670 other cartoonists at the **Centre Belge de la Bande Dessinée**.
- *The Smurfs* was an American TV show from 1981–1990. Ask students: **Combien d'étudiants se souviennent des Schtroumpfs? Qui étaient-ils? Décrivez-les.**

Les moules frites

- Mussels and fries have been served in Belgium since the seventeenth century. The mussels come from the North Sea and are in season from September to February. Although **les moules** are most commonly prepared with white wine, some variations use cream, vegetable stock, or even beer. Today, there are over 4,000 **fritures** in Belgium.
- Ask students: **Voulez-vous goûter des moules frites? Pourquoi?**

René Magritte

- Certain symbols appear repeatedly in Magritte's work, such as a middle-class man wearing a bowler hat, a castle, a window, a rock, and a female torso. Dislocations of space, time, and scale are common elements.
- Have students look at the painting in this section *The Son of Man* (1964) and describe what they see. Then ask: **Que pensez-vous de son style de peinture? Quels objets sont réalistes? Quelle partie est incroyable? Que pensez-vous que la peinture représente?**

OPTIONS

Cultural Comparison Working in small groups, have students compare Brussels to Geneva (page 355), New York City, or Washington, D.C. Tell them to list the similarities and differences in a two-column chart under the headings **Similitudes** and **Différences**. After completing their charts, call on volunteers to read their lists. You might wish to assign a different city to each group.

Le chocolat belge Belgium produces 172,000 tons of chocolate per year and has 2,130 chocolate shops. Godiva, Côte d'Or, Callebaut, and Nirvana are just a few of the many famous Belgian brands. Bring in some Belgian chocolates and conduct a taste test. Ask students how Belgian chocolate compares with well-known American brands of chocolates.

Section Goals
In this section, students will:
- learn to recognize the purpose of a text
- read some cartoons and jokes

Stratégie Tell students that recognizing the writer's purpose will help them understand an unfamiliar text.

Examinez le texte Students should infer that the illustrations are cartoons, the short texts are jokes, the writer's purpose is to make people laugh or to make fun of something or someone, and the language is colloquial.

À propos de l'auteur After reading the text, ask students these comprehension questions.
1. D'où vient Lévy? (Québec)
2. À quel âge a-t-elle commencé à dessiner? (à trois ans)
3. Qui l'a encouragée à être artiste? (son père)
4. Quels sont les sujets de ses dessins humoristiques? (la vie de tous les jours, le travail, les animaux et la politique)

Lecture

Avant la lecture

STRATÉGIE

Recognizing the purpose of a text

When you are faced with an unfamiliar text, it is important to determine the writer's purpose. If you are reading an editorial in a newspaper, for example, you know that the journalist's objective is to persuade you of his or her point of view. Identifying the purpose of a text will help you better comprehend its meaning.

Examinez le texte

Examinez les illustrations. Quel est le genre de ce texte? Décrivez ce qu'il y a dans chaque illustration. Puis, regardez les trois textes courts. Quel est le genre de ces textes? Quel est leur but (*purpose*)? D'après vous, quel genre de vocabulaire allez-vous trouver dans ces textes?

À propos de l'auteur
Renée Lévy

Renée Lévy est une artiste québécoise qui a commencé à dessiner à l'âge de trois ans. Son père, un artiste, lui a expliqué les principes du dessin et l'a encouragée à dessiner. Au lycée, Renée Lévy amusait ses camarades de classe avec ses caricatures de professeurs. Ses dessins humoristiques traitent de° nombreux sujets, comme la vie de tous les jours, le travail, les animaux et la politique. On peut voir ses caricatures et ses dessins humoristiques dans plusieurs publications et sur des sites Internet. Renée Lévy est l'auteur des deux dessins que vous allez voir°.

traitent de *deal with* **voir** *see*

Les Technoblagues

Dessin 1

C'EST UN LECTEUR DE MP3, DE CD ET DE DVD. C'EST AUSSI UN TÉLÉPHONE, UN APPAREIL PHOTO ET UN ORDINATEUR. IL PEUT NUMÉRISER°, TÉLÉCOPIER° ET IMPRIMER.

IL VERROUILLE° MON AUTO, ALLUME MON FOUR ET MESURE MON DIABÈTE. IL ME SERT DE BROSSE À DENTS, D'ASPIRATEUR ET DE RASOIR.

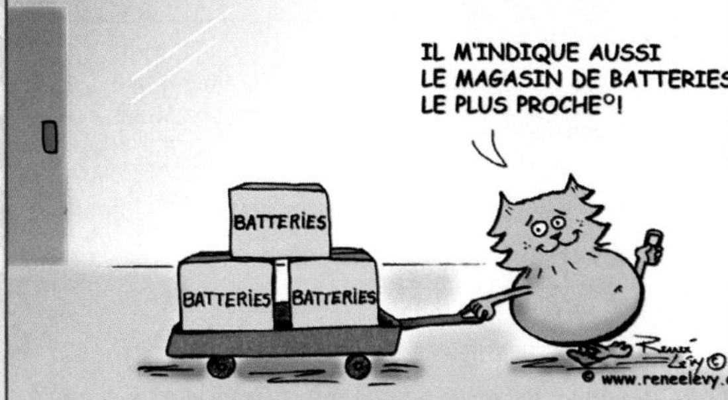

IL M'INDIQUE AUSSI LE MAGASIN DE BATTERIES LE PLUS PROCHE°!
BATTERIES
BATTERIES
BATTERIES
© www.reneelévy.c

Blague 1

Dans un magasin d'ordinateurs, un père se plaint° du manque d'intérêt° de son fils pour le sport. «Il passe son temps devant son écran, avec ses jeux vidéo», explique le père découragé à l'employé. «Tenez, l'autre jour, je lui ai proposé un match de tennis. Savez-vous ce que mon fils m'a répondu? "Quand tu veux, papa, je vais chercher la disquette."»

OPTIONS

Language Notes Point out that several words in the cartoons are specific to **Québécois** French. In the first cartoon, the word **batterie(s)** is used for *battery*, instead of **pile(s)**. In the second cartoon, **V.U.S.** is used for *SUV*, instead of **4x4 (quatre-quatre)**.

Pairs Have students work in pairs. Tell them to go through the cartoons and jokes, and find all of the sentences with relative pronouns. Then have them get together with another pair and verify their answers.

Blague 2

La maîtresse°, absente de sa classe pendant dix minutes, y retourne et entend un véritable vacarme°. «Quand je suis partie, dit-elle, sévèrement, je vous ai interdit° de bavarder entre vous.» «Mais, dit un élève, on ne s'est pas adressé la parole°. Seulement, pour s'occuper, on a tous sorti nos portables et on a passé un coup de fil° à nos parents.»

Blague 3

Un homme vient d'acheter une nouvelle voiture, mais il est obligé de la laisser dans la rue la nuit. Comme il sait que les voleurs° d'autoradios n'hésitent pas à fracturer les portières, il met sur son pare-brise la note suivante: IL N'Y A PAS DE RADIO DANS CETTE VOITURE. Le jour d'après, plus de° voiture. À la place où elle se trouvait, il y a seulement la note sur laquelle° on a écrit: *Ce n'est pas grave, on en fera mettre une*°.

numériser *scan* **télécopier** *fax* **verrouille** *locks* **le plus proche** *the closest* **se plaint** *complains* **manque d'intérêt** *lack of interest* **maîtresse** *school teacher* **vacarme** *racket* **interdit** *forbade* **on ne s'est pas adressé la parole** *we didn't speak to each other* **a passé un coup de fil** *made a call* **V.U.S.** *S.U.V.* **machine à coudre** *sewing machine* **sauf** *except* **il me faudra** *I will need* **fil** *cord* **voleurs** *thieves* **plus de** *no more* **sur laquelle** *on which* **on en fera mettre une** *we'll have one installed*

Après la lecture

Répondez Répondez aux questions par des phrases complètes.

1. Quelles sont trois des fonctions de l'appareil du **dessin 1**?
   Answers will vary. Possible answer: C'est un lecteur de MP3, un téléphone et un aspirateur.
2. De quoi l'appareil du **dessin 1** a-t-il beaucoup besoin?
   L'appareil a besoin de beaucoup de batteries.
3. Pour jouer au tennis, on a besoin d'une raquette. Dans la **blague 1**, quel mot (*word*) le garçon utilise-t-il au lieu de (*instead of*) «raquette»?
   Il utilise le mot «disquette».
4. Dans la **blague 1**, pourquoi le père est-il découragé?
   Il est découragé parce que son fils ne s'intéresse pas au sport et passe son temps devant son écran, avec ses jeux vidéos.
5. Dans la **blague 2**, qu'est-ce que la maîtresse a demandé aux élèves?
   Elle a demandé aux élèves de ne pas bavarder entre eux.
6. Qu'ont fait les élèves de la **blague 2** quand la maîtresse est partie?
   Ils ont téléphoné à leurs parents avec leur portable.
7. Pourquoi faut-il remplacer le moteur du V.U.S. dans le **dessin 2**?
   Il faut le remplacer parce que l'essence coûte très cher.
8. De quoi a-t-il besoin après dans le **dessin 2**?
   Il a besoin d'un plus long fil.
9. Dans la **blague 3**, qu'est-ce que l'homme écrit sur la note qu'il met sur le pare-brise de sa voiture? Pourquoi?
   Il écrit qu'il n'y a pas de radio dans sa voiture. Il pense que les voleurs d'autoradios ne vont pas fracturer les portières s'il n'y a pas de radio dans la voiture.
10. À la fin de la **blague 3**, qu'ont pris les voleurs? Que vont-ils faire?
    Ils ont pris la voiture et vont faire installer un autoradio.

Des inventions L'appareil du **dessin 1** a beaucoup de fonctions. D'après vous, quelle invention dans la liste suivante est la plus utile et pourquoi? Soyez prêt à expliquer votre décision à la classe.

appareil photo	lecteur de CD
aspirateur	lecteur de DVD
fax	lecteur de MP3
imprimante	téléphone

Inventez Électropuissance, une compagnie de technologie, vous demande d'inventer l'appareil idéal pour la vie de tous les jours. Dites comment votre invention va vous aider à la maison, à l'école, dans la voiture, en voyage et pour rester en bonne santé.

Répondez
- Go over the answers with the class.
- Ask various students: **À votre avis, quelle blague est la plus drôle? Quel dessin est le plus drôle? Pourquoi?** Then take a quick poll to find out which cartoon or joke the class considers the funniest or most amusing. Tally the results on the board.

Des inventions
- Give students a few minutes to choose an invention and jot down their reasons before discussing them.
- For each invention listed, ask: **Combien d'étudiants ont choisi ____? Pourquoi?**

Inventez
- If time is limited, you may want to assign this activity as written homework. Then have volunteers present their devices during the next class period. Encourage students to make a drawing of their device so the class can see what it looks like.
- Have the class vote on the most useful invention.

OPTIONS

Pairs Have students work in pairs. Tell them to create a cartoon or write a joke similar to the ones in this reading. They should brainstorm a list of topics first. You might want to suggest that they be related to technology. Then have students present their cartoons or jokes to the class. Have the class vote on the most humorous cartoon and joke.

Cultural Activity Have students go to Renée Lévy's web site to view more of her work. Tell them to find out what other types of artwork she creates, decide which style they prefer, and explain their reasons. Alternatively, you can have them find another cartoon about technology to bring in and share with the class.

À l'écoute

STRATÉGIE

Guessing the meaning of words through context

When you hear an unfamiliar word, you can often guess its meaning by listening to the words and phrases around it.

To practice this strategy, you will listen to a paragraph. Jot down the unfamiliar words that you hear. Then, listen to the paragraph again and jot down the word or words that are the most useful clues to the meaning of each unfamiliar word.

Préparation

Regardez la photo. Que fait la policière? Et l'homme, que fait-il? Où sont-ils? Que se passe-t-il, d'après vous?

À vous d'écouter

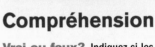

Écoutez la conversation entre la policière et l'homme et utilisez le contexte pour vous aider à comprendre les mots et expressions de la colonne A. Trouvez leur équivalent dans la colonne B.

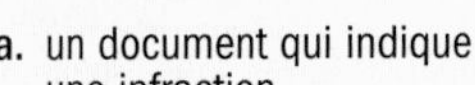

A	B
1. __d__ la moto	a. un document qui indique une infraction
2. __f__ la loi	b. un signal pour indiquer dans quelle direction on va aller
3. __a__ une contravention	c. conduire une voiture
4. __c__ rouler	d. véhicule à deux roues
5. __b__ le clignotant	e. faire attention
6. __e__ être prudent	f. quelque chose qu'il faut respecter

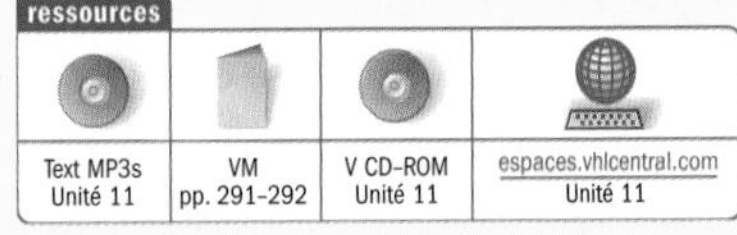

ressources
Text MP3s Unité 11
VM pp. 291–292
V CD-ROM Unité 11
espaces.vhlcentral.com Unité 11

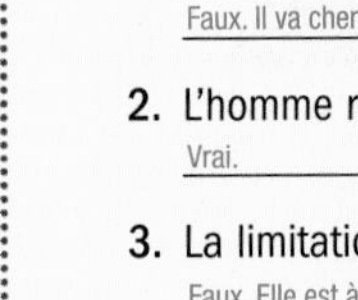

Compréhension

Vrai ou faux? **Indiquez si les phrases sont vraies ou fausses. Corrigez les phrases fausses.**

1. L'homme a oublié son permis de conduire à l'aéroport.

   Faux. Il va chercher son fils à l'aéroport.
2. L'homme roulait trop vite.
   Vrai.
3. La limitation de vitesse est à 150 km/h sur cette route.
   Faux. Elle est à 130.
4. L'homme a dépassé un camion rouge.
   Faux. Il a dépassé la grosse moto.
5. La policière n'accepte pas les excuses de l'homme.
   Vrai.
6. La policière donne une contravention à l'homme.
   Vrai.
7. L'homme préfère payer l'amende tout de suite.
   Faux. Il pense qu'il ne va pas pouvoir payer l'amende.
8. La policière demande à l'homme de faire réparer son rétroviseur avant de redémarrer.
   Faux. Elle lui demande de bien regarder dans son rétroviseur avant de redémarrer.

Racontez **Choisissez un sujet et écrivez un paragraphe.**

1. Avez-vous déjà eu une contravention (*ticket*)? Quand? Où? Que faisiez-vous? Si vous n'avez jamais (*never*) eu de contravention, parlez d'une personne que vous connaissez qui en a déjà eu une.
2. Avez-vous déjà eu de gros problèmes de voiture ou une panne? Quand? Où? Quel était le problème? Êtes-vous allé(e) chez un mécanicien? Qu'a-t-il fait? Est-ce que ça a coûté cher?

Section Goals

In this section, students will:

- learn to guess the meaning of words from context
- listen to a paragraph and jot down unfamiliar words plus clues to their meaning
- listen to a conversation and complete several activities

Instructional Resources
Textbook MP3s
IRCD-ROM: IRM (Textbook Audioscript)
espaces.vhlcentral.com: downloads, reference tools

Stratégie
Script Bonjour Monsieur, j'ai examiné votre voiture. Suite à l'accident, votre voiture a plusieurs problèmes. En particulier, la portière côté passager ne ferme pas et on ne peut plus remonter la vitre. J'ai regardé sous le capot et le moteur est en bon état. Je vais réparer la voiture et vous pouvez venir la chercher demain.

Préparation Have students look at the photo and describe what they see. Then have them guess what the police officer and the man are talking about.

À vous d'écouter
Script LA POLICIÈRE: Bonjour, Monsieur. Votre permis de conduire s'il vous plaît.
L'HOMME: Oui, Madame. Voilà. Euh... Quel est le problème?
P: Vous rouliez à 150 kilomètres/heure quand vous avez dépassé la grosse moto et la limitation de vitesse sur cette autoroute est à 130, Monsieur.
H: Vous êtes sûre que j'allais si vite?
P: Sûre et certaine, Monsieur!
H: Euh... Je suis désolé. C'est que... je suis très, très en retard. Je dois aller chercher mon fils à l'aéroport à vingt heures et...
P: Ce n'est pas une raison, Monsieur. Vous devez respecter la limitation de vitesse comme tout le monde...
H: Oui, je sais. Je suis vraiment désolé. Vous ne pouvez pas...
P: Je dois vous donner une contravention.
H: Oh non! Je vous en prie... Je n'ai vraiment pas beaucoup d'argent en ce moment. Je ne sais pas comment je vais pouvoir payer une amende pareille!
P: Désolée, Monsieur, mais c'est la loi. Tenez. Et roulez moins vite!
H: Oui, Madame.
P: Et n'oubliez pas d'attacher votre ceinture de sécurité, de mettre votre clignotant et de bien regarder dans votre rétroviseur avant de redémarrer.
H: Oui, Madame. Au revoir.
P: Au revoir, Monsieur et soyez prudent.

Écriture

STRATÉGIE

Listing key words

Once you have determined the purpose for a piece of writing and identified your audience, it is helpful to make a list of key words you can use while writing. If you were to write a description of your campus, for example, you would probably need a list of prepositions that describe location, such as **devant**, **à côté de**, and **derrière**. Likewise, a list of descriptive adjectives would be useful if you were writing about the people and places of your childhood.

By preparing a list of potential words ahead of time, you will find it easier to avoid using the dictionary while writing your first draft. You will probably also learn a few new words in French while preparing your list of key words.

Listing useful vocabulary is also a valuable organizational strategy since the act of brainstorming key words will help you form ideas about your topic. In addition, a list of key words can help you avoid redundancy when you write.

If you were going to write a composition about your communication habits with your friends, what words would be the most helpful to you? Jot a few of them down and compare your list with a partner's. Did you choose the same words? Would you choose any different or additional words, based on what your partner wrote?

____

____

____

____

____

____

Thème

Écrire une dissertation

Écrivez une dissertation pour décrire vos préférences et vos habitudes en ce qui concerne (*regarding*) les moyens (*means*) de communication d'hier et d'aujourd'hui.

- Quel est votre moyen de communication préféré (e-mail, téléphone, lettre,...)? Pourquoi?
- En général, comment communiquez-vous avec les gens que vous connaissez? Pourquoi? Avez-vous toujours communiqué avec eux de cette manière (*in this way*)?
- Communiquez-vous avec tout le monde de la même manière ou cela dépend-il des personnes? Par exemple, restez-vous en contact avec vos grands-parents de la même manière qu'avec votre professeur de français? Expliquez.
- Comment restez-vous en contact avec les membres de votre famille? Et avec vos amis et vos camarades de classe?
- Communiquez-vous avec certaines personnes tous les jours? Avec qui? Comment?

Avant de commencer, faites une liste des personnes avec qui vous communiquez régulièrement, et donnez le moyen de communication que vous avez utilisé dans le passé et que vous utilisez aujourd'hui. Utilisez aussi votre liste de mots-clés comme point de départ pour votre dissertation.

Watch the FLASH CULTURE segment on the **ESPACES** video for cultural footage related to this unit's theme.

Section Goals

In this section, students will:
- learn to make a list of key words before writing
- write a composition about their past and present communication habits
- view authentic cultural footage of city streets and people driving

Instructional Resources
WB/VM: Video Manual, pp. 291–292
WB/VM/LM Answer Key
IRCD-ROM: IRM (Videoscript)
Video CD-ROM
Video on DVD
espaces.vhlcentral.com: activities, downloads, reference tools

Stratégie Explain that having a list of key words will allow them to maintain their writing flow rather than stopping every few minutes to try and think of a specific word to use. Encourage students to rely primarily on vocabulary they know when preparing their lists. They should consult a dictionary only if they need a word that is central to their writing.

Thème Tell students to answer the questions first. Then they should make a list of people they communicate with regularly and the means they use to communicate before they begin writing their compositions.

Flash culture Tell students that they will learn more about cars and driving in a city by watching a variety of real-life images narrated by Csilla. Show the video segment. Then ask students to close their eyes and describe from memory what they saw as you write their descriptions on the board. You can also use the activities in the video manual in class to reinforce this **Flash culture** or assign them as homework.

EVALUATION

Criteria	Scale
Content	1 2 3 4 5
Organization	1 2 3 4 5
Use of vocabulary	1 2 3 4 5
Grammatical accuracy	1 2 3 4 5

Scoring	
Excellent	18–20 points
Good	14–17 points
Satisfactory	10–13 points
Unsatisfactory	< 10 points

Instructional Resources
Textbook MP3s
IRCD-ROM: IRM (Textbook Audioscript)
espaces.vhlcentral.com: downloads, reference tools

L'ordinateur

un CD/compact disc/disque compact (CD/compact disc/disques compacts *pl.*)	*CD, compact disc (CDs, compact discs)*
un CD-ROM/cédérom (CD-ROM/cédéroms *pl.*)	*CD-ROM(s)*
un clavier	*keyboard*
un disque dur	*hard drive*
un écran	*screen*
un e-mail	*e-mail*
un fichier	*file*
une imprimante	*printer*
un jeu vidéo (jeux vidéo *pl.*)	*video game(s)*
un logiciel	*software, program*
un moniteur	*monitor*
un mot de passe	*password*
une page d'accueil	*home page*
un site Internet/web	*web site*
une souris	*mouse*
démarrer	*to start up*
être connecté(e) (avec)	*to be connected (with)*
être en ligne (avec)	*to be online/on the phone (with)*
graver	*to record, to burn*
imprimer	*to print*
sauvegarder	*to save*
surfer sur Internet	*to surf the Internet*
télécharger	*to download*

Verbes

couvrir	*to cover*
découvrir	*to discover*
offrir	*to offer*
ouvrir	*to open*
souffrir	*to suffer*

Pronoms relatifs

dont	*of which, of whom*
où	*where*
que	*that, which*
qui	*who, that, which*

Expressions utiles	See pp. 367 and 381.
Prepositions with the infinitive	See p. 370.

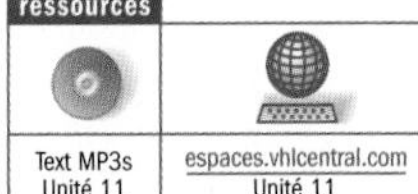

La voiture

arrêter (de faire quelque chose)	*to stop (doing something)*
attacher sa ceinture de sécurité (*f.*)	*to buckle one's seatbelt*
avoir un accident	*to have/to be in an accident*
dépasser	*to go over; to pass*
faire le plein	*to fill the tank*
freiner	*to brake*
se garer	*to park*
rentrer (dans)	*to hit*
réparer	*to repair*
tomber en panne	*to break down*
vérifier (l'huile/la pression des pneus)	*to check (the oil/the air pressure)*
un capot	*hood*
un coffre	*trunk*
l'embrayage (*m.*)	*clutch*
l'essence (*f.*)	*gas*
un essuie-glace (des essuie-glaces)	*windshield wiper(s)*
les freins (*m.*)	*brakes*
l'huile (*f.*)	*oil*
un moteur	*engine*
un pare-brise (pare-brise *pl.*)	*windshield*
un pare-chocs (pare-chocs *pl.*)	*bumper*
les phares (*m.*)	*headlights*
un pneu (crevé)	*(flat) tire*
une portière	*car door*
un réservoir d'essence	*gas tank*
un rétroviseur	*rearview mirror*
une roue (de secours)	*(emergency) tire*
une voiture	*car*
un volant	*steering wheel*
un voyant (d'essence/ d'huile)	*(gas/oil) warning light*
un agent de police/ un(e) policier/policière	*police officer*
une amende	*fine*
une autoroute	*highway*
la circulation	*traffic*
la limitation de vitesse	*speed limit*
un(e) mécanicien(ne)	*mechanic*
un parking	*parking lot*
un permis de conduire	*driver's license*
une rue	*street*
une station-service	*service station*

Verbes pronominaux réciproques

s'adorer	*to adore one another*
s'aider	*to help one another*
s'aimer (bien)	*to love (like) one another*
se connaître	*to know one another*
se dire	*to tell one another*
se donner	*to give one another*
s'écrire	*to write one another*
s'embrasser	*to kiss one another*
s'entendre bien (avec)	*to get along well (with one another)*
se parler	*to speak to one another*
se quitter	*to leave one another*
se regarder	*to look at one another*
se rencontrer	*to meet one another (make an acquaintance)*
se retrouver	*to meet one another (planned)*
se téléphoner	*to phone one another*

L'électronique

un appareil photo (numérique)	*(digital) camera*
un baladeur CD	*personal CD player*
une caméra vidéo/ un caméscope	*camcorder*
une chaîne (de télévision)	*(television) channel*
une chaîne stéréo	*stereo system*
un fax	*fax (machine)*
un lecteur de CD/DVD	*CD/DVD player*
un magnétophone	*tape recorder*
un magnétoscope	*videocassette recorder (VCR)*
un portable	*cell phone*
un poste de télévision	*television set*
un répondeur (téléphonique)	*answering machine*
une télécommande	*remote control*
une vidéocassette	*videotape*
allumer	*to turn on*
composer (un numéro)	*to dial (a number)*
effacer	*to erase*
enregistrer	*to record*
éteindre	*to turn off*
fermer	*to close; to shut off*
fonctionner/marcher	*to work, to function*
sonner	*to ring*

En ville

UNITÉ

12

Pour commencer

- Qu'est-ce que David a dans la main?
- Quel temps fait-il?
- Qu'est-ce que fait Valérie?
- Est-ce que David va conduire jusqu'à sa destination?

Unit Goals

Leçon 23

In this lesson, students will learn:
- terms for banking
- terms for business establishments
- terms for the post office
- the pronunciation of the letter **h**
- about methods of payment in France
- the verbs **recevoir** and **apercevoir**
- negative and affirmative expressions
- to create a brochure for a new, planned community in Québec

Leçon 24

In this lesson, students will learn:
- terms for asking for and giving directions
- rules of French capitalization
- about the centers of French cities and towns
- the formation and usage of **le futur simple**
- irregular future tense forms
- about singer Charles Trenet and painter Berthe Morisot

Savoir-faire

In this section, students will learn:
- cultural and historical, information about the Canadian province of Québec
- to identify the narrator's point of view
- to use background information to understand spoken French
- to use linking words when writing
- more about businesses and small shops through specially shot video footage

Pour commencer

- **Il a un plan dans la main.**
- **Il fait beau./Il fait (du) soleil.**
- **Elle aide David à trouver l'endroit qu'il cherche.**
- **Non, il va y aller à pied.**

RESOURCES

Workbook/Video Manual: WB Activities, pp. 155–168
Laboratory Manual: Lab Activities, pp. 89–96
Workbook/Video Manual: Video Activities, pp. 255–258; pp. 293–294
WB/VM/LM Answer Key
Instructor's Resource CD-ROM [IRCD-ROM]: Instructor's Resource Manual [IRM] (Textbook Audioscript; Lab Audioscript; Videoscript; **Roman-photo** Translations; **Vocabulaire supplémentaire**; **Feuilles d'activités**; Info Gap Activities; **Le zapping** TV clip transcription; **Essayez!** and **Mise en pratique** answers); Transparencies #51, #52, #53; Testing Program, pp. 89–96; pp. 145–152; Test Files; Testing Program MP3s; Test Generator
Lab MP3s
Textbook MP3s
Video CD-ROM
Video on DVD
espaces.vhlcentral.com

Section Goals

In this section, students will learn and practice vocabulary related to:

- banking
- the post office
- business establishments

Instructional Resources
IRCD-ROM: Transparency #51;
*IRM (***Vocabulaire supplémentaire***;* **Mise en pratique** *answers;*
Textbook Audioscript;
Lab Audioscript)
Textbook MP3s
WB/VM: Workbook, pp. 155–156
Lab Manual, p. 89
Lab MP3s
WB/VM/LM Answer Key
espaces.vhlcentral.com: activities, downloads, reference tools

Suggestions

- Use **Transparency #51.** Describe what people are doing. Examples: **Elle poste une lettre. Il retire de l'argent.** Then point out the various stores and other businesses. Have students identify the types of business based on the signs.
- Explain that **un salon de beauté** is a day spa where one gets manicures, pedicures, facials, massages, etc. It is not the same as **un coiffeur/une coiffeuse**.
- Ask students questions using the new vocabulary. Examples: **Que fait le facteur? Que fait l'homme au distributeur automatique? Utilisez-vous les distributeurs automatiques? Que vend-on dans une papeterie? Qu'achète-t-on au marchand de journaux? Où est le cybercafé?**
- To introduce banking terms, mime several transactions. Say: **Quand j'ai besoin de l'argent, je remplis un chèque et je vais à la banque.** Follow the same procedure with the post office vocabulary.
- Let students know that another way to say *a checking account* is **un compte-chèques**.
- Point out the difference in spelling between the French words **adresse** and **enveloppe** and the English words *address* and *envelope*.
- Additional vocabulary for this lesson can be found in the **Vocabulaire supplémentaire** in the IRM on the IRCD-ROM.

Leçon 23

You will learn how to...

- make business transactions
- get around town

Les courses

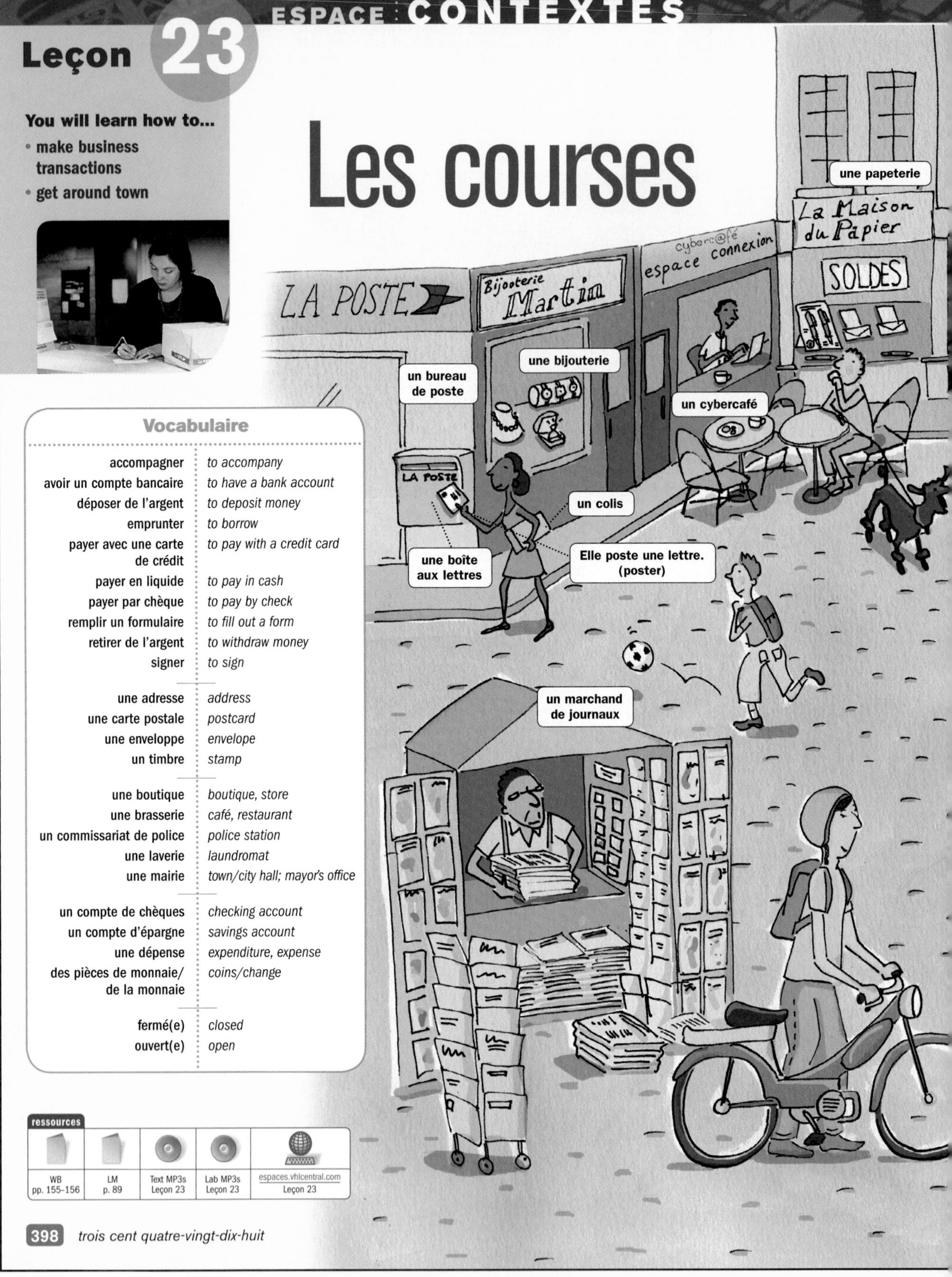

Vocabulaire

accompagner	*to accompany*
avoir un compte bancaire	*to have a bank account*
déposer de l'argent	*to deposit money*
emprunter	*to borrow*
payer avec une carte de crédit	*to pay with a credit card*
payer en liquide	*to pay in cash*
payer par chèque	*to pay by check*
remplir un formulaire	*to fill out a form*
retirer de l'argent	*to withdraw money*
signer	*to sign*
une adresse	*address*
une carte postale	*postcard*
une enveloppe	*envelope*
un timbre	*stamp*
une boutique	*boutique, store*
une brasserie	*café, restaurant*
un commissariat de police	*police station*
une laverie	*laundromat*
une mairie	*town/city hall; mayor's office*
un compte de chèques	*checking account*
un compte d'épargne	*savings account*
une dépense	*expenditure, expense*
des pièces de monnaie/ de la monnaie	*coins/change*
fermé(e)	*closed*
ouvert(e)	*open*

ressources

WB pp. 155–156	LM p. 89	Text MP3s Leçon 23	Lab MP3s Leçon 23	espaces.vhlcentral.com Leçon 23

OPTIONS

Extra Practice For additional practice, ask these questions. **1. Avez-vous un compte de chèques? 2. Avez-vous un compte d'épargne? 3. Où y a-t-il un distributeur automatique? 4. Où y a-t-il un bureau de poste? 5. Où y a-t-il une banque? 6. Quelle est votre papeterie préférée? 7. Quelle est votre boutique préférée?**

Game Play a game of **Dix questions**. Ask a volunteer to think of a place listed in the new vocabulary. Other students get to ask one yes/no question, then they can guess what the word is. Limit attempts to ten questions per word. You might want to tell students that they can narrow down their options by asking questions about what can be done at the location.

un salon de beauté

Salon de Beauté Claude

le facteur

BANQUE

le courrier

une banque

guichet

les billets (*m.*)

un distributeur automatique/de billets

Elle fait la queue.

Mise en pratique

1 Écoutez **Écoutez la conversation entre Jean-Pierre et Carole. Ensuite, complétez les phrases avec le bon mot.**

1. Carole demande à Jean-Pierre d'acheter des timbres et de ___poster___ un colis. (déposer, poster, retirer)
2. Le ___bureau de poste___ se trouve sur la route de Jean-Pierre. (bureau de poste, papeterie, laverie)
3. Jean-Pierre veut ___déposer___ de l'argent à la banque. (retirer, déposer, emprunter)
4. Jean-Pierre doit ___remplir___ et signer des formulaires. (accompagner, remplir, payer)
5. Jean-Pierre a acheté le journal chez le ___marchand de journaux___. (papeterie, marchand de journaux, bureau de poste)
6. Jean-Pierre n'avait pas assez de ___liquide___ sur lui. (compte de chèques, carte de crédit, liquide)

2 Associez **Associez chaque activité de la colonne de gauche avec le lieu qui correspond dans la colonne de droite.**

___d___	1. acheter un chemisier	a. un bureau de poste
___j___	2. acheter du maquillage	b. une banque
___i___	3. acheter un magazine	c. une bijouterie
___c___	4. acheter une montre	d. une boutique
___e___	5. boire un café	e. une brasserie
___a___	6. envoyer une carte	f. un commissariat de police
___g___	7. envoyer un e-mail	g. un cybercafé
___h___	8. faire la lessive	h. une laverie
___b___	9. ouvrir un compte	i. un marchand de journaux
___f___	10. payer une amende	j. un salon de beauté

3 Complétez **Complétez les phrases suivantes avec le mot ou l'expression qui convient le mieux. N'oubliez pas de faire les accords nécessaires.**

1. ___Le facteur___ apporte le courrier tous les jours à la même heure.
2. Quand les magasins sont ___fermés___, on ne peut pas faire de courses.
3. Pour poster une lettre, on peut simplement la mettre dans ___une boîte aux lettres___.
4. Quand on n'a pas beaucoup d'argent, il faut faire attention à ses ___dépenses___.
5. Si la banque n'est pas ouverte, on peut toujours ___retirer de l'argent___ au distributeur automatique.
6. Quand on envoie une lettre, il ne faut pas oublier d'écrire ___l'adresse___ et de mettre ___un timbre___.
7. Pour acheter une voiture, il faut souvent ___emprunter___ de l'argent.
8. Si on n'a pas de lave-linge à la maison, il faut aller à ___la laverie___.

1 Tapescript JEAN-PIERRE: Carole, je vais aller à la banque. Est-ce que tu as besoin de quelque chose en ville?
CAROLE: Oui. Est-ce que tu peux aller faire des courses pour moi? Tu peux prendre le journal chez le marchand de journaux? J'ai aussi un colis à poster et j'ai besoin de timbres.
J: Pas de problème. Le bureau de poste et le marchand de journaux sont sur ma route.
Jean-Pierre est maintenant à la banque.
J: Bonjour, Monsieur. J'ai de l'argent à déposer sur mon compte de chèques et sur mon compte d'épargne, s'il vous plaît.
L'EMPLOYÉ: Oui, bien sûr, Monsieur. Voici les formulaires à remplir et à signer. Si vous avez besoin de liquide pendant le week-end, nous avons un nouveau distributeur de billets à l'extérieur.
J: Très bien, je vous remercie.
Plus tard, à la maison…
C: Alors, tu as fait mes courses?
J: Oui, voici le journal mais je n'ai pas envoyé le colis. La machine ne fonctionnait pas. Je n'ai pas pu payer avec ma carte de crédit et je n'avais pas assez de liquide sur moi. Je suis désolé.
C: Ce n'est pas grave. Je dois aller à la papeterie plus tard, je peux passer à la poste après.
(On Textbook MP3s)

1 Suggestion Have volunteers read the completed sentences aloud.

2 Suggestion Ask students what one does at each place listed. They should respond with the activity. Example: **Que fait-on dans un bureau de poste? (On envoie une lettre/carte.)**

2 Expansion For additional practice, ask students where they might do these activities. **1. poster un colis (au bureau de poste) 2. retirer de l'argent (à la banque/au distributeur automatique) 3. manger quelque chose (dans une brasserie) 4. acheter un cadeau (dans une boutique/dans une bijouterie)**

3 Suggestion Have students check their answers with a classmate.

OPTIONS

Game Toss a beanbag to a student at random and call out the name of a place. You might also recycle places from **Leçon 7**. The person has four seconds to name an activity that goes with it. That person then tosses the beanbag to another student and says another place. Students who cannot think of an activity or repeat one that has already been mentioned are eliminated. The last person standing wins.

Small Groups Have students work in groups of four or five. Give each group a different list of errands. Tell them to create a story in which someone goes to various places to complete the errands. Remind them to use sequencing expressions, such as **d'abord**, **puis**, and **après ça**.

4 Suggestion Encourage students to provide as many details as possible about each photo.

5 Suggestion Tell students to jot down notes during their interviews so that they will remember their partner's responses.

6 Suggestion Encourage students to brainstorm words and expressions they might want to use in their dialogue before they begin writing.

NATIONAL communication STANDARDS

Communication

4 Décrivez Avec un(e) partenaire, regardez les photos et décrivez où et comment Annick et Charles ont passé la journée samedi dernier. Answers will vary.

1.

2.

3.

4.

5.

6.

5 Répondez Avec un(e) partenaire, posez les questions suivantes et répondez-y à tour de rôle. Ensuite, comparez vos réponses avec celles d'un autre groupe. Answers will vary.

1. Vas-tu souvent au bureau de poste? Pour quoi faire?
2. Quel genre de courses fais-tu le week-end?
3. Où est-ce que tu fais souvent la queue? Pourquoi?
4. Y a-t-il une laverie près de chez toi? Combien de fois par mois y vas-tu?
5. Comment préfères-tu payer tes achats (*purchases*)? Pourquoi?
6. Combien de fois par semaine utilises-tu un distributeur de billets?

6 À vous de jouer Par petits groupes, choisissez une des situations suivantes et écrivez un dialogue. Ensuite, jouez la scène. Answers will vary.

1. À la banque, un(e) étudiant(e) veut ouvrir un compte bancaire et connaître les services offerts.
2. À la poste, une vieille dame (*lady*) veut envoyer un colis, acheter des timbres et faire un changement d'adresse. Il y a la queue derrière elle.
3. Dans un salon de beauté, deux femmes discutent de leurs courses à la mairie, à la papeterie et chez le marchand de journaux.
4. Dans un cybercafé, des étudiants font des achats en ligne sur différents sites.

OPTIONS

Extra Practice Have students make signs and set up various businesses around the classroom, such as a bank and a post office. Then give students detailed errands to run and have them role-play the situations at the locations. Example: Go to the bank and withdraw 20 euros, then go to the post office and buy six stamps. Tell students to alternate playing employees and customers.

Game Divide the class into two teams. Have a spelling bee using vocabulary words from the **Contextes**. Pronounce each word, use it in a sentence, and then say the word again. Tell students that they must spell the words in French and include all diacritical marks.

Les sons et les lettres

NATIONAL
comparisons
STANDARDS

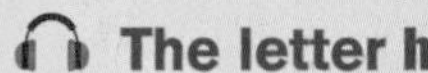

The letter h

You already know that the letter **h** is silent in French, and you are familiar with many French words that begin with an **h muet**. In such words, the letter **h** is treated as if it were a vowel. For example, the articles **le** and **la** become **l'** and there is a liaison between the final consonant of a preceding word and the vowel following the **h**.

l'heure **l'homme** **des hôtels** **des hommes**

Some words begin with an **h aspiré**. In such words, the **h** is still silent, but it is not treated like a vowel. Words beginning with **h aspiré**, like these you've already learned, are not preceded by **l'** and there is no liaison.

la honte **les haricots verts** **le huit mars** **les hors-d'œuvre**

Words that begin with an **h aspiré** are normally indicated in dictionaries by some kind of symbol, usually an asterisk (*).

Prononcez Répétez les mots suivants à voix haute.

1. le hall	5. le héron	9. l'hilarité	13. les hiéroglyphes
2. la hi-fi	6. l'horloge	10. la Hongrie	14. les hors-d'œuvre
3. l'humeur	7. l'horizon	11. l'hélicoptère	15. les hippopotames
4. la honte	8. le hippie	12. les hamburgers	16. l'hiver

Articulez Répétez les phrases suivantes à voix haute.

1. Hélène joue de la harpe.
2. Hier, Honorine est allée à l'hôpital.
3. Le hamster d'Hervé s'appelle Henri.
4. La Havane est la capitale de Cuba.
5. L'anniversaire d'Héloïse est le huit mars.
6. Le hockey et le hand-ball sont mes sports préférés.

Dictons Répétez les dictons à voix haute.

L'heure, c'est l'heure; avant l'heure, c'est pas l'heure; après l'heure, c'est plus l'heure.[2]

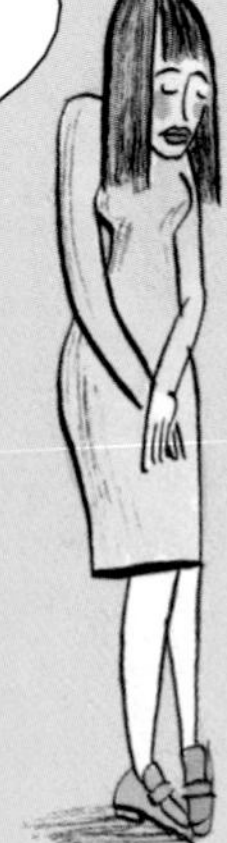
La honte n'est pas d'être inférieur à l'adversaire, c'est d'être inférieur à soi-même.[1]

[1] Shame is not being inferior to an adversary; it's being inferior to oneself.
[2] On time is on time; before the hour is not on time; after the hour is no longer on time.

ressources			
LM p. 90	Text MP3s Leçon 23	Lab MP3s Leçon 23	espaces.vhlcentral.com Leçon 23

Section Goals

In this section, students will learn about the letter **h**.

Instructional Resources
Textbook MP3s
Lab Manual, p. 90
Lab MP3s
WB/VM/LM Answer Key
IRCD-ROM: IRM (Textbook Audioscript; Lab Audioscript)
espaces.vhlcentral.com: activities, downloads, reference tools

Suggestions

- Model the pronunciation of the example words and have students repeat them after you.
- Remind students that **h** often combines with other consonants to make different sounds. Examples: **ch** (**chat, chose**) and **ph** (**téléphone**). The **h** is silent when it combines with the letter **t**. Examples: **thé** and **théâtre**.
- Point out that many words beginning with an **h aspiré** are borrowed from other languages. Examples: **le hall, les hamburgers, le handball,** and **la Hollande**.
- Ask students to provide more examples of words that begin with the letter **h**. Examples: **l'huile, l'hôte, l'hôtesse, des habitants,** and **l'hôtel**.
- Dictate five familiar words containing the letter **h**, repeating each one at least two times. Then write them on the board or a transparency and have students check their spelling.

Dictons The saying **«La honte n'est pas d'être inférieur à l'adversaire, c'est d'être inférieur à soi-même»** is a Manchurian proverb. The saying **«L'heure, c'est l'heure; avant l'heure, c'est pas l'heure; après l'heure, c'est plus l'heure»** is a quote from Jules Jouy.

OPTIONS

Extra Practice Use these sentences with the letter **h** for additional practice or dictation. **1. En hiver, Henri va en Hongrie. 2. Horace a honte d'habiter dans cette habitation. 3. Hélène est heureuse de fêter ses huit ans. 4. Notre hôte Hubert sert des huitres à l'huile d'olive comme hors-d'œuvre.**

Extra Practice Teach students this French tongue-twister that contains the letter **h**. **La pie niche en haut, l'oie niche en bas, le hibou niche ni haut ni bas.**

Section Goals

In this section, students will learn functional phrases for talking about errands and money and expressing negation.

Instructional Resources
WB/VM: Video Manual, pp. 255–256
WB/VM/LM Answer Key
Video CD-ROM
Video on DVD
IRCD-ROM: IRM (Videoscript; ***Roman-photo*** *Translations)*
espaces.vhlcentral.com: activities, downloads, reference tools

Video Recap: Leçon 22
Before doing this **Roman-photo**, review the previous one with this activity.

1. Où est Rachid quand l'épisode commence? (à une station-service)
2. Pourquoi y va-t-il? (pour acheter de l'essence)
3. Qui attend Rachid au P'tit Bistrot? (Amina)
4. Qu'est-ce que Rachid donne à Amina? (des fleurs)
5. Qu'est-ce qui se passe en route? (Un voyant s'allume. Ils ont un pneu crevé.)

Video Synopsis
Rachid and Amina are buying some food at a **charcuterie** for a picnic. Rachid needs some cash, so they head for an ATM. As they are walking, Amina says she has to go to the post office, the jewelry store, and a boutique that afternoon. David invites Sandrine to eat at a **brasserie**. On the way, they run into Rachid and Amina at the ATM. Sandrine and Amina discuss their new relationships.

Suggestions
- Have students predict what the episode will be about based on the video stills.
- Have students scan the captions for sentences related to places in a city.
- After reading the **Roman-photo**, have students summarize the episode.
- Point out that Amina can buy stamps from a machine even when the post office is closed.

On fait des courses

PERSONNAGES

Amina

David

Employée

Rachid

Sandrine

À la charcuterie...
EMPLOYÉE Bonjour, Mademoiselle, Monsieur. Qu'est-ce que je vous sers?
RACHID Bonjour, Madame, quatre tranches de pâté et de la salade de carottes pour deux personnes, s'il vous plaît.
EMPLOYÉE Et avec ça?
RACHID Deux tranches de jambon, s'il vous plaît.

RACHID Vous prenez les cartes de crédit?
EMPLOYÉE Ah désolée, Monsieur, nous n'acceptons que les paiements en liquide ou par chèque.
RACHID Amina, je viens de m'apercevoir que je n'ai pas de liquide sur moi!
AMINA Ce n'est pas grave, j'en ai assez. Tiens.

Dans la rue...
RACHID Merci, chérie. Passons à la banque avant d'aller au parc.
AMINA Mais nous sommes samedi midi, la banque est fermée.
RACHID Peut-être, mais il y a toujours le distributeur automatique.
AMINA Bon d'accord... J'ai quelques courses à faire plus tard cet après-midi. Tu veux m'accompagner?

Dans une autre partie de la ville...
DAVID Tu aimes la cuisine alsacienne?
SANDRINE Oui, j'adore la choucroute!
DAVID Tu veux aller à la brasserie La Petite France? C'est moi qui t'invite.
SANDRINE D'accord, avec plaisir.
DAVID Excellent! Avant d'y aller, il faut trouver un distributeur automatique.
SANDRINE Il y en a un à côté de la banque.

Au distributeur automatique...
SANDRINE Eh regarde qui fait la queue!
RACHID Tiens, salut, qu'est-ce que vous faites de beau, vous deux?
SANDRINE On va à la brasserie. Vous voulez venir avec nous?

AMINA Non non! Euh... je veux dire... Rachid et moi, on va faire un pique-nique dans le parc.
RACHID Oui, et après ça, Amina a des courses importantes à faire.
SANDRINE Je comprends, pas de problème... David et moi, nous avons aussi des choses à faire cet après-midi.

ACTIVITÉS

1 Vrai ou faux? Indiquez si les affirmations suivantes sont **vraies** ou **fausses**.

1. Aujourd'hui, la banque est ouverte. Faux.
2. Amina doit aller à la poste pour envoyer un colis. Faux.
3. Amina doit aller à la poste pour acheter des timbres. Vrai.
4. Amina va mettre ses cartes postales dans une boîte aux lettres à côté de la banque. Faux.
5. Sandrine n'aime pas la cuisine alsacienne. Faux.
6. David et Rachid vont retirer de l'argent. Vrai.
7. Il n'y a pas de queue au distributeur automatique. Faux.
8. David et Sandrine invitent Amina et Rachid à la brasserie. Vrai.
9. Amina et Rachid vont à la brasserie. Faux.
10. Amina va faire ses courses après le pique-nique. Vrai.

OPTIONS

Avant de regarder la vidéo Tell students to read the title and the scene setter. Then have them predict what might happen in this episode. Write their predictions on the board. After viewing the episode, have them confirm or correct their predictions.

Regarder la vidéo Show the video in four parts, pausing the video before each location change. Have students describe what happens in each place. Write their observations on the board. Then show the entire episode again without pausing and have the class fill in any missing details to summarize the plot.

Amina et Rachid préparent un pique-nique.

RACHID Volontiers. Où est-ce que tu vas?
AMINA Je dois aller à la poste pour acheter des timbres et envoyer quelques cartes postales, et puis je voudrais aller à la bijouterie. J'ai reçu un e-mail de la bijouterie qui vend les bijoux que je fais. Regarde.
RACHID Très joli!

AMINA Oui, tu aimes? Et après ça, je dois passer à la boutique Olivia où l'on vend mes vêtements.
RACHID Tu vends aussi des vêtements dans une boutique?
AMINA Oui, mes créations! J'étudie le stylisme de mode, tu ne t'en souviens pas?
RACHID Si, bien sûr, mais... Tu as vraiment du talent.

AMINA Alors! On n'a plus besoin de chercher un Cyberhomme?
SANDRINE Pour le moment, je ne cherche personne. David est super.

DAVID De quoi parlez-vous?
SANDRINE Oh, rien d'important.
RACHID Bon, Amina. On y va?
AMINA Oui. Passez un bon après-midi.
SANDRINE Vous aussi.

Expressions utiles

Dealing with money

- **Nous n'acceptons que les paiements en liquide.**
  We only accept payment in cash.
- **Je viens de m'apercevoir que je n'ai pas de liquide.**
  I just noticed/realized I don't have any cash.
- **Il y a toujours le distributeur automatique.**
  There's always the ATM.

Running errands

- **J'ai quelques courses à faire plus tard cet après-midi.**
  I have a few/some errands to run later this afternoon.
- **Je voudrais aller à la bijouterie qui vend les bijoux que je fais.**
  I would like to go to the jewelry shop that sells the jewelry I make.

Expressing negation

- **Pas de problème.**
  No problem.
- **On n'a plus besoin de chercher un Cyberhomme?**
  We no longer need to look for a Cyberhomme?
- **Pour le moment, je ne cherche personne.**
  For the time being/the moment, I'm not looking for anyone.
- **Rien d'important.**
  Nothing important.

Additional vocabulary

- **J'ai reçu un e-mail.**
  I received an e-mail.
- **Qu'est-ce que vous faites de beau?**
  What are you up to?

2 Complétez Complétez les phrases suivantes.

1. La charcuterie accepte les paiements en liquide et par chèque.
2. Amina veut aller à la poste, à la boutique de vêtements et à la bijouterie.
3. À côté de la banque, il y a un distributeur automatique.
4. Amina paie avec des pièces de monnaie et des billets.
5. Amina a des courses à faire cet après-midi.

3 À vous! Que se passe-t-il au pique-nique ou à la brasserie? Avec un(e) camarade de classe, écrivez une conversation entre Amina et Sandrine ou Rachid et David, dans laquelle elles/ils se racontent ce qu'ils ont fait. Qu'ont-ils mangé? Se sont-ils amusés? Était-ce romantique? Jouez la scène devant la classe.

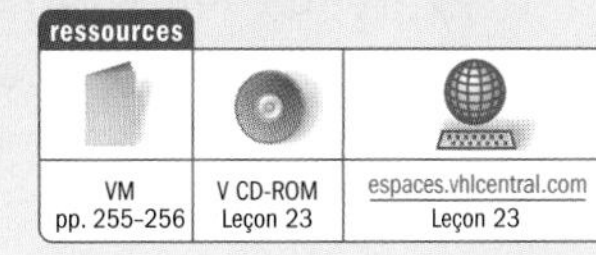

ressources
VM pp. 255–256
V CD-ROM Leçon 23
espaces.vhlcentral.com Leçon 23

ACTIVITÉS

Expressions utiles
- Model the pronunciation of the **Expressions utiles** and have students repeat them.
- As you work through the list, point out the forms of **recevoir** and **apercevoir**, and negative expressions. Tell students that these verbs and constructions will be formally presented in the **Structures** section.
- Respond briefly to questions about **recevoir**, **apercevoir**, and negative expressions. Reinforce correct forms, but do not expect students to produce them consistently at this time.
- Point out that **les brasseries** usually offer quick, hearty meals. They often specialize in Alsatian dishes, such as **la choucroute**.

1 Suggestion Have students correct the false statements.

1 Expansion For additional practice, give students these items. **11. La charcuterie accepte les cartes de crédit. (Faux.) 12. À la charcuterie, Rachid paie par chèque. (Faux.) 13. Rachid va accompagner Amina cet après-midi. (Vrai.) 14. Sandrine cherche toujours un Cyberhomme. (Faux.)**

2 Suggestion Have volunteers read the completed sentences aloud.

3 Suggestion Tell students to choose a situation and brainstorm ideas before writing their conversations. Encourage them to be creative.

OPTIONS

Les heures d'ouverture Many small shops close for an hour or two between 12:00 p.m. and 2:00 p.m. It is common to reopen in the afternoon and stay open until around 7:00 p.m. Most stores are not open late in the evening or on Sundays except around the holidays. Stores near popular tourist attractions are exceptions. For example, many businesses along the Champs-Élysées in Paris are open until midnight.

Extra Practice Ask volunteers to ad-lib the scenes in video stills 5–10 for the class. Tell them it is not necessary to memorize the episode. They should just try to get the general meaning across with the vocabulary they know. Give them time to prepare or have them do their skit as a review activity during the next class period.

Section Goals

connections cultures NATIONAL STANDARDS

In this section, students will:
- learn about methods of payment in France
- learn some terms to talk about the **métro**
- learn about some interesting places to shop in the francophone world
- read about Alain Robert, the French "Spiderman"

Instructional Resources
espaces.vhlcentral.com: activities, downloads, reference tools

Culture à la loupe

Avant la lecture Have students look at the visuals and describe what they see.

Lecture
- Point out that **la Carte Bleue** was widely used in France before the debit card became a common form of payment in the United States.
- Point out the information about opening a bank account in the **Coup de main**.

Après la lecture Ask students: **Comment les Français paient-ils leurs achats et leurs factures? (par prélèvements automatiques sur comptes bancaires, par chèque, par Carte Bleue/carte bancaire/carte de crédit)**

1 Suggestion Have volunteers write the answers on the board. Then go over them with the class.

CULTURE À LA LOUPE

Les moyens de paiement en France

À l'exception des petites courses quotidiennes, les Français paient très rarement leurs achats° et leurs factures° en liquide. Pour les paiements réguliers, comme les factures d'électricité ou de téléphone, les virements° et les prélèvements° automatiques sur comptes bancaires sont souvent utilisés. Pour les autres dépenses, le mode de paiement préféré est la carte bancaire. Les Français sont les plus gros utilisateurs de chèques du monde, mais le système de chèques payants° en France les encourage à se servir de leur carte bancaire. Au départ, les cartes bancaires françaises, émises° uniquement par des banques, servaient seulement à retirer de l'argent dans les distributeurs automatiques. Peu de commerces les acceptaient et il fallait° souvent que les achats dépassent° une certaine somme°. Aujourd'hui, l'usage des cartes bancaires est en hausse°, mais on trouve encore des petits commerces qui ne les acceptent pas.

La plupart des Français possèdent actuellement° une carte de la gamme° Carte Bleue. La carte, qui peut être nationale ou internationale, est une carte bancaire liée° à un compte en banque. Certaines peuvent aussi être utilisées comme des cartes de crédit. Dans ce cas, les sommes sont débitées à la fin de chaque mois ou bien on peut faire des paiements mensuels° à la banque.

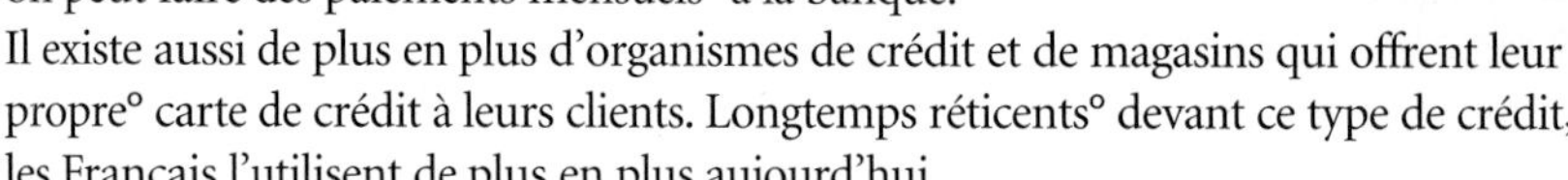

Il existe aussi de plus en plus d'organismes de crédit et de magasins qui offrent leur propre° carte de crédit à leurs clients. Longtemps réticents° devant ce type de crédit, les Français l'utilisent de plus en plus aujourd'hui.

achats *purchases* **factures** *bills* **virements** *transfers* **prélèvements** *withdrawals* **payants** *with a fee* **émises** *issued* **il fallait** *it was necessary* **dépassent** *exceed* **somme** *sum* **en hausse** *increasing* **actuellement** *currently* **gamme** *line* **liée** *linked* **mensuels** *monthly* **propre** *own* **réticents** *hesitant*

Coup de main

If you are in France for more than three months, you may open a bank account as a **résident** by showing three documents.

- your passport
- your **permis de séjour**
- proof of residence (electric, gas or phone bill)

ACTIVITÉS

1 Répondez Répondez aux questions par des phrases complètes.

1. Comment paie-t-on souvent ses factures en France? On les paie souvent par virement ou par prélèvement automatique.
2. Quel mode de paiement est préféré pour faire des achats? C'est la carte bancaire.
3. Pourquoi de plus en plus de Français utilisent-ils leur carte bancaire? Ils utilisent leur carte bancaire parce qu'il y a maintenant en France un système de chèques payants.
4. À quoi servait la carte bancaire quand elle est arrivée en France? Elle servait à retirer de l'argent dans les distributeurs automatiques.
5. À l'origine, pourquoi était-il difficile d'utiliser une carte bancaire? Peu de commerces les acceptaient et il fallait souvent que les achats dépassent une certaine somme.
6. Qu'est-ce qu'une carte bancaire? C'est une carte liée à un compte en banque. Certaines peuvent aussi être utilisées comme des cartes de crédit.
7. Quelle carte peut être utilisée à l'étranger? La carte bancaire internationale peut être utilisée à l'étranger.
8. À quel type de carte américaine ressemble la carte bancaire française? La carte bancaire française ressemble à la *debit card* américaine.
9. Comment en est-elle différente? Quand on utilise une carte bancaire française, les sommes sont débitées du compte à la fin du mois et non pas immédiatement.
10. Quels organismes offrent leur propre carte de crédit à leurs clients? Les organismes de crédit et les magasins les leur offrent.

OPTIONS

Cultural Comparison Have students work in groups of three. Tell them to compare French and American methods for paying for things. Have them list the similarities and differences in a two-column chart under the headings **Similitudes** and **Différences**. Also tell them to discuss which method of payment they prefer.

Les cartes de crédit Many French people do not approve of the American habit of carrying monthly balances on their credit cards and paying interest for daily expenses. Until recently, many French people did not have any credit cards. Now, most of those who do use them often have only one.

LE FRANÇAIS QUOTIDIEN

Le vocabulaire du métro

bouche (*f.*) de métro	*subway station entrance*
correspondance (*f.*)	*connection*
ligne (*f.*) de métro	*subway line*
rame (*f.*) de métro	*subway train*
strapontin (*m.*)	*foldaway seat*
changer	*to change (subway line)*
monter/descendre	*to get on/to get off*
prendre la direction	*to go in the direction*

PORTRAIT

Le «Spiderman» français

Alain Robert, le «Spiderman français», découvre l'escalade° quand il est enfant et devient un des meilleurs grimpeurs° de falaises° du monde. Malgré° deux accidents qui l'ont laissé invalide à 60%°, avec des problèmes de vertiges°, il commence sa carrière de grimpeur «urbain» et escalade son premier gratte-ciel° à Chicago, en 1994. Depuis, il a escaladé plus de 70 gratte-ciel et autres structures du monde, dont la tour Eiffel à Paris et la Sears Tower à Chicago. En 1997, il a été arrêté par la police pendant son ascension du plus grand bâtiment du monde, les tours Petronas en Malaisie. Parfois en costume de Spiderman, mais toujours sans corde° et à mains nues°, Robert fait souvent des escalades pour collecter des dons° et il attire° parfois des milliers de spectateurs.

escalade *climbing* **grimpeurs** *climbers* **falaises** *cliffs* **Malgré** *In spite of* **invalide à 60%** *60% disabled* **vertiges** *vertigo* **gratte-ciel** *skyscraper* **corde** *rope* **nues** *bare* **dons** *charitable donations* **attire** *attracts*

LE MONDE FRANCOPHONE

Où faire des courses?

Voici quelques endroits intéressants où faire des courses.

En Afrique du Nord les souks, quartiers des vieilles villes où il y a une grande concentration de magasins et de stands

En Côte d'Ivoire le marché de Cocody à Abidjan où on trouve des tissus° et des objets locaux

À la Martinique le grand marché de Fort-de-France, un marché couvert°, ouvert tous les jours, qui offre toutes sortes de produits

À Montréal la ville souterraine°, un district du centre-ville où il y a de nombreux centres commerciaux reliés° entre eux par des tunnels

À Paris le marché aux puces° de Saint-Ouen où on trouve des antiquités et des objets divers

À Tahiti le marché couvert de Papeete où on offre des produits pour les touristes et pour les Tahitiens

tissus *fabrics* **couvert** *covered* **souterraine** *underground* **reliés** *connected* **marché aux puces** *flea market*

SUR INTERNET

Que peut-on acheter chez les bouquinistes, à Paris?

Go to **espaces.vhlcentral.com** to find more cultural information related to this **ESPACE CULTURE**.

ACTIVITÉS

2 Vrai ou faux? Indiquez si les phrases sont **vraies** ou **fausses**.

1. Alain Robert escalade seulement des falaises. Faux. Il escalade aussi des gratte-ciel et d'autres structures.
2. Alain Robert a escaladé son premier bâtiment à Chicago. Vrai.
3. Alain Robert n'a jamais eu de problèmes de santé dans sa carrière de grimpeur. Faux. Il a eu deux accidents graves et il a des problèmes de vertiges.
4. À Montréal, il y a un quartier souterrain. Vrai.
5. Il y a des souks dans les marchés d'Abidjan. Faux. Il y a des souks dans les vieilles villes d'Afrique du Nord.

3 Le marchandage En Afrique du Nord, il est très courant de marchander ou de discuter avec un vendeur pour obtenir un meilleur prix. Avez-vous déjà eu l'occasion de marchander? Où? Quand? Qu'avez-vous acheté? Avez-vous obtenu un bon prix? Discutez de ce sujet avec un(e) partenaire.

ressources

espaces.vhlcentral.com Leçon 23

Le français quotidien

- Model the pronunciation of each term and have students repeat it.
- Point out you say **prendre une correspondance.** Remind students that a subway ticket is **un ticket**. In some cities it is possible to purchase **un carnet** or **une carte** for unlimited monthly access.

Portrait

- After two accidents while training in 1982, Robert hasn't suffered any more climbing injuries. He trained in the Alps before starting to climb skyscrapers, which he is now paid to do.
- Ask students: **À votre avis, quel type d'homme est Alain Robert? Avez-vous envie d'escalader un gratte-ciel? Pourquoi?**

Le monde francophone After students have read the text, ask: **Où voulez-vous faire des courses dans le monde francophone? Pourquoi?**

2 Expansion For additional practice, give students these items. **6. Alain Robert escalade les bâtiments en France aussi bien qu'à l'étranger. (Vrai.) 7. Robert réussit à escalader le plus grand bâtiment du monde. (Faux. Il est arrêté par la police.) 8. Le public ne s'intéresse pas aux escalades de Robert. (Faux. Il attire parfois des milliers de spectateurs.)**

3 Expansion Bring in pictures of objects one might find at a market, such as vegetables, pottery, rugs, and shirts. Have students work in pairs and practice bargaining for the objects pictured. They should take turns playing the customer and the vendor.

OPTIONS

Où faire des courses? Bargaining **(le marchandage)** is a common practice in Arab markets in France and throughout the Arab world. If visiting a souk in North Africa, it is best to go with someone who speaks Arabic. If that isn't possible, it's better to speak French than English, since Americans have a reputation for being wealthy.

Pairs Have students work in pairs. Tell them to write a conversation between two tourists who are taking the **métro** in Paris from the Bastille stop to the Franklin D. Roosevelt stop (line 1) to the Trocadéro stop (line 9), using the vocabulary in **Le français quotidien**. Then have pairs role-play their conversations for the class.

Section Goals

In this section, students will learn:
- the verbs **recevoir** and **apercevoir**
- the meaning of **s'apercevoir**

Instructional Resources
WB/VM: Workbook, pp. 157–158
Lab Manual, p. 91
Lab MP3s
WB/VM/LM Answer Key
*IRCD-ROM: IRM (**Essayez!** and **Mise en pratique** answers; **Feuilles d'activités**; Lab Audioscript)*
espaces.vhlcentral.com: activities, downloads, reference tools

Suggestions
- Ask students why they think some forms of **recevoir** and **apercevoir** are spelled with a **cédille**. (It helps the reader know to pronounce the sound as [**s**]. Remind them that the letter **c** is pronounced [**s**] in front of the letters **e** and **i**, and [**k**] in front of the letters **a**, **o**, and **u**.)
- Have students respond **vrai** or **faux** to statements made with forms of **recevoir** that have obvious answers. Examples: **J'ai reçu le prix Nobel de la paix cette année. Vous recevez des cadeaux de temps en temps.**
- You may want to teach the class the verb **décevoir** and the adjective **déçu** along with **recevoir** and **apercevoir**.
- Point out that **s'apercevoir** is followed by **que/qu'** + *another verb* or by **de** + *noun*.
- Since **s'apercevoir** is a difficult verb to conjugate and use, help the class make up a set of sentences with different forms of the verb. Allow them to ask you questions such as **Comment dit-on...?**

Essayez! Have students work in pairs to turn the fragments in the activity into complete sentences. Then have them read their sentences to the class.

23.1 *Recevoir* and *apercevoir*

Point de départ In **Leçon 17**, you learned to conjugate **devoir**. You will now learn two verbs that are conjugated similarly.

recevoir* and *apercevoir

	recevoir (*to receive*)	**apercevoir** (*to see, to catch sight of*)
je/j'	**reçois**	**aperçois**
tu	**reçois**	**aperçois**
il/elle	**reçoit**	**aperçoit**
nous	**recevons**	**apercevons**
vous	**recevez**	**apercevez**
ils/elles	**reçoivent**	**aperçoivent**

Je **reçois** une lettre de mon copain.
I receive a letter from my friend.

Nous **recevons** des colis de notre tante.
We get packages from our aunt.

Les criminels **aperçoivent** le policier.
The criminals catch sight of the police officer.

D'ici, on **aperçoit** le bureau de poste.
From here, you see the post office.

- **Recevoir** and **apercevoir** take **avoir** as the auxiliary verb in the **passé composé**. Their past participles are, respectively, **reçu** and **aperçu**.

Guillaume **a reçu** une carte postale.
Guillaume received a postcard.

J'**ai aperçu** un distributeur automatique.
I saw an ATM.

BOÎTE À OUTILS
Recall that in **Leçon 3**, you learned the expression **être reçu à un examen** (*to pass an exam*).

- The verb **s'apercevoir** means *to notice* or *to realize*.

Elle **s'est aperçue** qu'il fallait faire la queue.
She realized it was necessary to wait in line.

Nous **nous sommes aperçus** du problème hier.
We noticed the problem yesterday.

Essayez! Choisissez la forme appropriée du verbe au présent.

recevoir
1. il *reçoit*
2. nous recevons
3. Paul et Jacques reçoivent
4. je reçois

apercevoir
5. vous *apercevez*
6. tu aperçois
7. elles aperçoivent
8. Houda aperçoit

MISE EN PRATIQUE

1 Recevoir ou apercevoir? Vous parlez avec un(e) ami(e) de votre vie sur le campus. Complétez les phrases avec les verbes appropriés au présent.

1. De sa chambre, mon ami Marc aperçoit le campus.
2. Mon camarade de chambre et moi, nous ne recevons pas de visites pendant la semaine.
3. Tu aperçois parfois des copains au resto U.
4. Ma petite amie et sa sœur reçoivent souvent des colis de leurs parents.
5. Quelquefois, je/j' aperçois mes profs à la bibliothèque.
6. Ton meilleur ami et toi, vous recevez souvent des amis le week-end.

2 À Québec Mélanie a passé une semaine à Québec avec sa famille. Elle en parle avec sa mère et elles se souviennent de leur visite. Utilisez les verbes **recevoir** et **apercevoir** au passé composé.

MODÈLE ton frère / Paul / la Citadelle
Ton frère Paul a aperçu la Citadelle.

1. je / la place d'Armes
   J'ai aperçu la place d'Armes.
2. cousine et toi / Saint-Laurent
   Ta cousine et toi, vous avez aperçu le Saint-Laurent.
3. tu / journal / sept heures / matin
   Tu as reçu le journal à sept heures du matin.
4. ton père et moi / vieille ville
   Ton père et moi, nous avons aperçu la vieille ville.
5. Simon et Théo / mairie
   Simon et Théo ont aperçu la mairie.
6. nous / tante Odile / notre chambre d'hôtel
   Nous avons reçu tante Odile dans notre chambre d'hôtel.

3 Ma vie universitaire Gérard parle de sa vie à la fac. Regardez les illustrations et complétez les phrases avec les verbes **recevoir** et **apercevoir**. Suggested answers

1. Toutes les semaines, je reçois une lettre.

3. La semaine dernière, mon meilleur ami a reçu son diplôme.

2. De leur fenêtre, les étudiants aperçoivent des arbres.

4. Quelquefois, nous apercevons notre prof au resto U.

OPTIONS

Extra Practice Ask students to decide which of the expressions in **Contextes** could serve as a direct object for **recevoir** and **apercevoir**. Examples: **recevoir (une carte postale, une enveloppe); apercevoir (un bureau de poste, un commissariat de police)** Then ask them to make up some sentences with the expressions while you write them on the board.

Game Tell pairs of students to write an obviously illogical sentence with **recevoir** or **apercevoir**. Example: **J'ai reçu une mauvaise note pour mon anniversaire.** Have students read their sentences aloud while their classmates correct the sentences so that they are logical. Then award prizes for the funniest, most ridiculous, and most creative sentences.

COMMUNICATION

4 Enquête Votre professeur va vous donner une feuille d'activités. Circulez dans la classe et demandez à vos camarades s'ils connaissent quelqu'un qui pratique chaque activité de la liste. S'ils répondent par l'affirmative, demandez-leur le nom de la personne et écrivez-le. Ensuite, présentez vos réponses à la classe. Answers will vary.

MODÈLE

Étudiant(e) 1: *Connais-tu quelqu'un qui reçoit rarement des e-mails?*
Étudiant(e) 2: *Oui, mon frère aîné reçoit très peu d'e-mails.*

Activités	*Nom*	*Réponses*
1. recevoir / rarement / e-mails	*Quang*	*son frère aîné*
2. s'inquiéter / quand / ne pas / recevoir / e-mails		
3. apercevoir / e-mail bizarre / le / ouvrir		

5 Assemblez Achetez-vous souvent sur Internet? Avec un(e) partenaire, assemblez les éléments des colonnes pour raconter vos expériences. Utilisez les verbes **recevoir**, **apercevoir** et **s'apercevoir** dans votre conversation. Answers will vary.

MODÈLE

Étudiant(e) 1: *Je commande parfois des livres sur Internet. Une fois, je n'ai pas reçu mes livres!*
Étudiant(e) 2: *Mon père adore acheter sur Internet. Il aperçoit souvent des objets qui l'intéressent.*

A	B	C
je	apercevoir	boîte aux lettres
tu	s'apercevoir	bureau de poste
un(e) ami(e)	commander	colis
nous	envoyer	enveloppe
vous	poster	facteur
tes parents	recevoir	timbre
?	?	?

6 Curieux! Avec un(e) partenaire, posez-vous ces questions à tour de rôle. Answers will vary.

1. Reçois-tu souvent des lettres? De qui? Quand?
2. As-tu reçu une lettre récemment? De qui?
3. Tes parents recevaient-ils souvent des amis quand tu étais petit(e)? Aimais-tu leurs amis?
4. Recevais-tu souvent des amis? Tes parents aimaient-ils tes amis?
5. Qu'aperçois-tu de ta chambre? Des arbres?

Le français vivant

Le plaisir d'offrir,
le bonheur
de recevoir...

Plaisir,
Calme,
Nature.

Les Relais du silence:
Le bonheur de recevoir.

Aux Relais du silence, notre personnel vous reçoit dans le calme. Nous vous recevons avec le plus vrai des plaisirs.

Mais la nature aussi vous reçoit. Le confort et le repos aussi vous reçoivent.

Vous ne vous apercevez pas du temps qui passe.

Identifiez Quelles formes des verbes **recevoir** et **apercevoir** trouvez-vous dans cette publicité (*ad*)? recevoir, reçoit, recevons, reçoivent, apercevez

Questions À tour de rôle, avec un(e) partenaire, posez-vous ces questions et répondez. Some answers will vary.

1. Comment reçoit-on les clients aux Relais du silence? On les reçoit dans le calme et avec le plus vrai des plaisirs.
2. De quoi un(e) client(e) ne s'aperçoit-il/elle pas? Il/Elle ne s'aperçoit pas du temps qui passe.
3. Connais-tu un endroit comme Les Relais du silence? Où est-il? Décris-le.
4. Pourquoi fait-on un séjour dans un endroit comme Les Relais du silence?

1 Suggestion If students find this first activity difficult, provide a list of the conjugated verbs in random order and ask them to pick the correct verb for each sentence.

2 Suggestion You might wish to have students complete this activity in two phases. In the first phase, they decide which verb is appropriate for each sentence. In the second phase, they conjugate the verbs appropriately to complete the sentences.

3 Expansion Have students create sentences with **recevoir** and **apercevoir** that describe their own life at the university. Tell them that they can illustrate the sentences if they wish.

4 Suggestion Call on volunteers to do the **modèle**. Then distribute the **Feuilles d'activités** from the IRM on the IRCD-ROM.

4 Expansion Ask students questions about themselves based on the sentence fragments given for the activity. Examples: **Qui reçoit rarement des e-mails? Vous inquiétez-vous quand vous ne recevez pas d'e-mails?** You may want to let students invent answers.

5 Suggestion Tell students to use each expression in the columns at least once.

6 Expansion Have students retell their partner's answers using third person subjects. Example: **Nathalie a reçu récemment une lettre de son copain au Canada.**

Le français vivant Ask students to assign one to five stars for this hotel, according to how luxurious they think it is. Then have them tell what clues in the ad (language or images) helped determine their decision.

OPTIONS

Extra Practice Tell students to write a paragraph telling what members of their family typically receive as gifts on special occasions. Tell them to make sure to use the pronouns **je**, **il/elle**, **nous**, and **ils/elles**. Examples: **Je reçois souvent de l'argent pour mon anniversaire. Mon père reçoit parfois des cravates.**

Small Groups Ask small groups of students to compose sentences with **s'apercevoir**. Give them a point for each sentence in which the verb is used and conjugated correctly, and a prize to the group with the most points.

Section Goals

In this section, students will learn negative and affirmative expressions.

Instructional Resources
WB/VM: Workbook, pp. 159–160
Lab Manual, p. 92
Lab MP3s
WB/VM/LM Answer Key
*IRCD-ROM: IRM (**Essayez!** and **Mise en pratique** answers; Lab Audioscript)*
espaces.vhlcentral.com: activities, downloads, reference tools

Suggestions

- To help students distinguish between the negative expressions on this page, make a transparency with a set of six fill-in-the-blank sentences with only the second negative particle (**personne, rien,** etc.) missing from each one. Examples: **Je n'ai ____ d'argent! (pas) Il n'y a ____ dans le couloir. (personne)**
- Point out to students that when **personne** and **rien** are used as subjects, the verbs that accompany them are singular. You could also point out that when **de** + *adjective* is used to modify **personne, rien, quelque chose,** and **quelqu'un**, the adjective is a masculine singular form.
- You might give students some more sentences with several negative particles so that they get a feel for those kinds of emphatic constructions. Examples: **Je n'ai jamais rien dit à personne! Il n'y a plus rien dans mon compte à la banque.**
- To practice adverb placement in the **passé composé**, write sentences on sets of index cards, so that a word is on each card. Give out the cards for a sentence to a group of students and have them put the cards in order.

23.2 Negative/affirmative expressions

Point de départ In **Leçon 3**, you learned how to negate verbs with **ne... pas.** You will now learn new ways to make negative as well as affirmative phrases.

- The other ways of negating also require **ne** and a second word that takes the place of **pas**.

Negative expressions

ne... aucun(e)	*none (not any)*	**ne... plus**	*no more (not anymore)*
ne... jamais	*never (not ever)*	**ne... que**	*only*
ne... personne	*nobody, no one*	**ne... rien**	*nothing (not anything)*

Je **n'**ai **aucune** envie de manger.
I have no desire to eat.

Il **n'**a **plus** faim.
He's not hungry anymore.

Le bureau de poste **n'**est **jamais** ouvert.
The post office is never open.

Ils **n'**ont **que** des timbres de la poste aérienne.
They only have airmail stamps.

Elle **ne** parle à **personne**.
She doesn't talk to anyone.

Le facteur **n'**avait **rien** pour nous.
The mailman had nothing for us.

- To negate the expression **il y a**, place **n'** before **y** and the second negative word after the form of **avoir.**

Il **n'**y a **aucune** banque près d'ici?
Aren't there any banks nearby?

Il **n'**y avait **rien** sur mon compte.
There wasn't anything in my account.

- A negative word can be the subject of a verb, in which case it is placed before the verb.

Personne n'était là.
No one was there.

Rien n'est arrivé dans le courrier.
Nothing arrived in the mail.

- Note that **aucun(e)** can be either an adjective or a pronoun. Therefore, it must agree with the noun it modifies. It is always used in the singular.

Tu ne trouves **aucune boîte aux lettres**?
Aren't you finding any mailboxes?

Je n'en trouve **aucune** par ici.
I'm not finding any around here.

- **Jamais**, **personne**, **plus**, and **rien** can be doubled up with **ne**.

Elle **ne** parle **jamais** à **personne**.
She never talks to anyone.

Il **n'**y a **plus personne** ici.
There isn't anyone here anymore.

Elle **ne** dit **jamais rien**.
She never says anything.

Il **n'**y a **plus rien** ici.
There isn't anything here anymore.

MISE EN PRATIQUE

1 Les jumelles Olivia et Anaïs sont des jumelles (*twin sisters*) bien différentes. Expliquez comment.

MODÈLE Olivia est toujours heureuse.
Anaïs n'est jamais heureuse.

1. Olivia rit tout le temps. Anaïs ne rit jamais.
2. Olivia regarde tout. Anaïs ne regarde rien.
3. Olivia voit (*sees*) encore ses amies d'enfance. Anaïs ne voit plus ses amies d'enfance.
4. Olivia aime le chocolat et la glace. Anaïs n'aime ni le chocolat ni la glace.
5. Olivia connaît beaucoup de monde. Anaïs ne connaît personne.
6. Olivia reçoit beaucoup de colis. Anaïs ne reçoit aucun colis.

2 À la banque Vous voulez ouvrir un nouveau compte et le banquier vous explique le processus. Écrivez ses phrases à la forme négative.

MODÈLE La banque ferme-t-elle à midi? (jamais)
Non, la banque ne ferme jamais à midi.

1. La banque est-elle ouverte le samedi? (jamais) Non, la banque n'est jamais ouverte le samedi.
2. Peut-on ouvrir un compte sans papier d'identité? (personne) Non, personne ne peut ouvrir de compte sans papier d'identité.
3. Avez-vous des distributeurs automatiques dans les supermarchés? (aucun) Non, nous n'avons aucun distributeur automatique dans les supermarchés.
4. Pour retirer de l'argent, avons-nous encore besoin de remplir ce document? (plus) Non, vous n'avez plus besoin de remplir ce document.
5. Avez-vous des billets et des pièces dans vos distributeurs automatiques? (que) Non, nous n'avons que des billets dans nos distributeurs automatiques.
6. Est-ce que tout le monde peut retirer de l'argent de notre compte bancaire? (personne) Non, personne ne peut retirer d'argent de votre compte bancaire.

3 Pas exactement Tristan exagère souvent. Il a écrit cet e-mail et vous lui répondez pour dire que les choses ne sont pas arrivées exactement comme ça. Mettez toutes ses phrases à la forme négative dans votre réponse.

MODÈLE
Tu n'es pas arrivé tard à la banque...

Je suis arrivé tard à la banque. Quelqu'un m'a ouvert la porte. J'ai regardé les affiches et les catalogues. J'ai demandé quelque chose. Il y avait encore beaucoup d'argent sur mon compte. Je vais souvent revenir dans cette banque.

Tu n'es pas arrivé tard à la banque. Personne ne t'a ouvert la porte. Tu n'as regardé ni les affiches ni les catalogues. Tu n'as rien demandé. Il n'y avait plus d'argent sur ton compte. Tu ne vas jamais revenir dans cette banque.

OPTIONS

Video Replay the video episode while students listen for negative expressions in the last scene. Tell them to raise their hands when they hear one. Then replay the video, pausing each time a negative expression is used for students to say it aloud or write it down.

Pairs Give pairs of students a set of negative sentences and have them give you an affirmative version of each sentence. Example: **Il n'y a personne à la porte. (Il y a quelqu'un à la porte.)** Go over the sentences with the class, asking students to give all the different positive sentences possible.

COMMUNICATION

4 De mauvaise humeur Aujourd'hui, Anne-Marie contredit son amie chaque fois qu'elle lui pose une question. Avec un(e) partenaire, jouez les rôles d'Anne-Marie et de son amie. Rajoutez (*Add*) deux lignes supplémentaires de dialogue à la fin. Answers will vary.

MODÈLE

tu / sortir avec quelqu'un en ce moment
Étudiant(e) 1: *Est-ce que tu sors avec quelqu'un en ce moment?*
Étudiant(e) 2: *Non, je ne sors avec personne.*

1. tu / faire quelque chose ce soir
2. tes parents / venir chez toi ce week-end
3. ton frère / avoir encore sa vieille voiture
4. tes amis et toi / déjà aller en vacances au Canada
5. quelqu'un / habiter dans ta maison cet été
6. tu / avoir encore faim
7. ?
8. ?

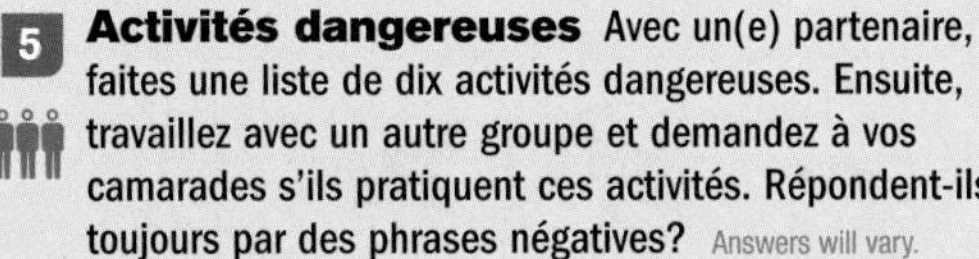

5 Activités dangereuses Avec un(e) partenaire, faites une liste de dix activités dangereuses. Ensuite, travaillez avec un autre groupe et demandez à vos camarades s'ils pratiquent ces activités. Répondent-ils toujours par des phrases négatives? Answers will vary.

MODÈLE

Étudiant(e) 1: *Fais-tu du jogging la nuit?*
Étudiant(e) 2: Non! *Je ne fais jamais de jogging la nuit.*

6 À la banque En vacances, vous vous apercevez que votre valise a disparu (*disappeared*) avec votre argent liquide, vos papiers et vos cartes de crédit. Vous avez besoin de retirer de l'argent à la banque. Préparez un dialogue entre vous et deux employés de banque. Utilisez les expressions de la boîte. Answers will vary.

jamais	ne... que	quelqu'un
ne... aucun(e)	ne... rien	rien
ne... ni... ni...	quelque chose	toujours
ne... plus		

- To say *neither... nor*, you use three negative words: **ne... ni... ni....** Note that partitive and indefinite articles are usually omitted.

Le facteur **n'**est **ni** sympa **ni** sociable. *The mailman is neither nice nor sociable.*	Je **n'**ai **ni** frères **ni** sœurs. *I have neither brothers nor sisters.*

- Note that in the **passé composé**, the words **jamais**, **plus**, and **rien** are placed between the auxiliary verb and the past participle. The placement of **aucun(e)**, **personne**, and **que** varies.

Elle **n'**est **jamais** revenue. *She's never returned.*	Nous **n'**avons **plus** emprunté d'argent. *We haven't borrowed money anymore.*	Je **n'**ai **rien** dit aujourd'hui. *I didn't say anything today.*
Vous **n'**avez signé **aucun** papier. *You didn't sign any paper.*	Il **n'**a entendu **personne**. *He didn't hear anyone.*	Ils **n'**en ont posté **que** deux. *They only mailed two.*

- These expressions can be used in affirmative phrases. Note that when **jamais** is not accompanied by **ne**, it can mean *ever*.

jamais	*ever*	**quelqu'un**	*someone*
quelque chose	*something*	**toujours**	*always; still*

As-tu **jamais** été à cette brasserie? *Have you ever been to that brasserie?*	Il y a **quelqu'un**? *Is someone there?*
Vous cherchez **quelque chose**? *Are you looking for something?*	Il est **toujours** aussi réservé? *Is he still so reserved?*

- Note that **personne**, **quelque chose**, **quelqu'un**, and **rien** can be modified with an adjective after **de**.

Nous cherchons **quelque chose de joli**. *We're looking for something pretty.*	Ce n'est **rien de nouveau**. *It's nothing new.*

BOÎTE À OUTILS
Remember to use **de** instead of the indefinite article in a negative construction: **Il n'y a plus de billets dans le distributeur; personne ne poste de lettre le dimanche.**

Essayez! **Choisissez l'expression correcte.**

1. (Jamais / Personne) ne trouve cet homme agréable.
2. Je ne veux (rien / jamais) faire aujourd'hui.
3. Y a-t-il (quelqu'un / personne) à la banque?
4. Je n'ai reçu (pas de / aucun) colis.
5. Il n'y avait (ne / ni) lettres ni colis dans la boîte aux lettres.
6. Il n'y a (plus / aucun) d'argent à la banque?
7. Jérôme ne va (toujours / jamais) à la poste.
8. Le facteur n'arrive (toujours / qu') à trois heures.

Essayez! Go over the answers to the activity with the class and have students with the correct responses explain them to the class.

1 Expansion Ask students to give additional negative sentences for the activity. Example: **3. Anaïs ne voit jamais ses amies d'enfance.**

2 Suggestion After students have completed item 6, you may wish to teach them the expression **personne d'autre** (*no one else*): **Non, personne d'autre ne peut retirer de l'argent de votre compte bancaire.**

3 Suggestion Have pairs of students complete this activity and act it out in front of the class. One student plays Tristan and one plays his friend.

4 Expansion Once students have written two additional lines of dialogue, alternately call on pairs of students to share the questions they composed and call on other pairs to answer those questions in the negative.

5 Suggestion To get students warmed up for this activity, ask them if they do some unsafe things. Examples: **Vous retirez de l'argent du distributeur automatique à deux heures du matin? Vous ne fermez pas la porte quand vous quittez la maison?**

6 Suggestion Tell students that each member should write the lines for one of the characters (the traveler and the two bank employees). Help them as they collaborate on the dialogue, and encourage them to be as creative as possible.

OPTIONS

Extra Practice Have the class collaborate on a description of a ghost town or a haunted house using expressions from pages 408–409. Write the sentences on the board or on a transparency as they are said and make sure that all seven negative expressions (including **ne... ni... ni...**) are used.

Game Give students index cards with one negative expression from pages 408–409 and another expression that could be used with it on each card. Then tell the students to produce sentences. Example: *(on the card)* **ne... personne + l'école (Personne ne va à l'école le dimanche.)**

Synthèse

Instructional Resources
*IRCD-ROM: IRM (**Feuilles d'activités**; Info Gap Activities); Testing Program, pp. 89–92; Test Files; Testing Program MP3s; Test Generator espaces.vhlcentral.com: activities, downloads, reference tools*

1 Suggestion Have two volunteers read the **modèle** aloud. Then distribute the **Feuilles d'activités** from the IRM on the IRCD-ROM.

2 Expansion Once students have completed this activity, ask them the following questions about other students. **Qu'est-ce que ____ reçoit dans son courrier? Est-ce que ____ envoie des lettres par la poste de temps en temps? Des colis?**

3 Suggestion To get the class started, have students read the instructions and then make up different kinds of questions. Examples: **Y a-t-il un(e) ____ près d'ici? Où se trouve le/la ____ ?**

4 Suggestion Have students formulate **vrai** or **faux** statements about any subject using the negative expressions listed for the activity.

5 Expansion Remind students of the difference in meaning between **apercevoir** and **s'apercevoir**. Then ask them to make up a couple of sentences with the phrases **s'est aperçu(e) de/que** and **sans m'en apercevoir**.

6 Suggestion Divide the class into pairs and distribute the Info Gap Handouts in the IRM on the IRCD-ROM for this activity. Give students ten minutes to complete the activity.

1 Je ne vais jamais... Votre professeur va vous donner une feuille d'activités. Circulez dans la classe pour trouver un(e) camarade différent(e) qui fait ses courses à ces endroits. Où ne vont-ils jamais? Où ne vont-ils plus? Justifiez toutes vos réponses. Answers will vary.

MODÈLE

Étudiant(e) 1: *Vas-tu à la laverie?*
Étudiant(e) 2: *Non, je n'y vais plus parce que j'ai acheté un lave-linge. Mais, je vais toujours à la banque le lundi.*

Endroit	Nom
1. banque	Yvonne
2. bijouterie	
3. boutique de vêtements	
4. cybercafé	
5. laverie	

2 Le courrier Avec un(e) partenaire, préparez six questions pour interviewer vos camarades. Que reçoivent-ils dans leur courrier? Qu'envoient-ils? Utilisez les expressions négatives et les verbes **recevoir** et **envoyer**. Ensuite, par groupes de quatre, posez vos questions et écrivez les réponses. Answers will vary.

MODÈLE

Étudiant(e) 1: *Est-ce que tu ne reçois que des lettres dans ton courrier?*
Étudiant(e) 2: *Non, je reçois des cadeaux parfois, mais je n'en envoie jamais.*

3 Au village Vous visitez un petit village pour la première fois. Malheureusement, tout y est fermé. Vous posez des questions à un(e) habitant(e) sur les endroits de la liste et il/elle vous répond par des expressions négatives. Préparez le dialogue avec un(e) partenaire. Answers will vary.

MODÈLE

Étudiant(e) 1: *À quelle heure le bureau de poste ouvre-t-il aujourd'hui?*
Étudiant(e) 2: *Malheureusement, le bureau de poste n'existe plus, Monsieur!*

banque	laverie
bureau de poste	mairie
commissariat de police	salon de beauté

4 Vrai ou faux? Par groupes de quatre, travaillez avec un(e) partenaire pour préparer huit phrases au sujet des deux autres partenaires de votre groupe. Essayez de deviner ce qu'ils/elles (*what they*) ont fait et n'ont pas fait. Utilisez dans vos phrases le passé composé et les expressions négatives indiquées. Ensuite, lisez les phrases à vos deux camarades, qui vont vous dire si elles sont vraies ou fausses. Answers will vary.

MODÈLE

Étudiant(e) 1: *Tu n'es jamais allée dans le bureau du prof.*
Étudiant(e) 2: *C'est faux. J'ai dû y aller hier pour lui poser une question.*

- ne... aucun(e)
- ne... jamais
- ne... personne
- ne... plus
- ne... que
- ne... rien

5 Au secours! Avec un(e) partenaire, préparez un dialogue pour représenter la scène de cette illustration. Utilisez le verbe **s'apercevoir** et des expressions négatives et affirmatives. Answers will vary.

6 Dix ans plus tard Votre professeur va vous donner, à vous et à votre partenaire, deux plans d'une ville. Attention! Ne regardez pas la feuille de votre partenaire. Answers will vary.

MODÈLE

Étudiant(e) 1: *Il y a dix ans, la laverie avait beaucoup de clients.*
Étudiant(e) 2: *Aujourd'hui, il n'y a personne dans la laverie.*

ressources

WB	LM	Lab MP3s	espaces.vhlcentral.com
pp. 157-160	pp. 91-92	Leçon 23	Leçon 23

OPTIONS

Extra Practice State that someone is wearing a certain article of clothing and then ask students who it is. Example: **Quelqu'un dans la classe porte un tee-shirt rouge. Qui est-ce?** In some cases, name an article not present in the classroom so that students will answer negatively: **Personne ne porte une jupe.**

Extra Practice Read a series of logical and illogical statements that use the verbs **recevoir, apercevoir,** and **s'apercevoir**. Tell students to raise their right hand and say **logique** for logical ones, and to raise their left hand and say **illogique** for illogical ones. Example: **Je reçois toujours de mauvaises notes quand je fais tous mes devoirs. (illogique)**

Projet

Faites de la pub pour une ville nouvelle

Vous faites de la publicité pour une ville nouvelle° au Québec.

1 Préparez une brochure

Préparez une brochure pour un nouveau projet urbain: la construction d'une ville ultra-moderne. La brochure vise à attirer° des résidents aussi bien que des investisseurs potentiels. Pour trouver un site pour votre ville nouvelle, explorez la géographie, le climat et les attraits naturels du Québec grâce au lien° dans la boîte **Sur Internet**. Les éléments suivants peuvent figurer dans votre brochure:

- une carte du Québec qui indique où est située la ville nouvelle
- des photos du site
- un plan de la municipalité, avec les pôles d'intérêt° principaux (magasins, gares routières, centres de loisirs, etc.)
- une description du climat et des attraits naturels de la région
- un plan de développement des transports en commun°

2 Présentez votre brochure

Présentez votre brochure à trois camarades. Essayez de les convaincre° que votre projet de ville nouvelle est un bon investissement. Ensuite, comparez vos plans de développement: Avez-vous choisi le même° site? Quels sont les points forts de chaque projet proposé?

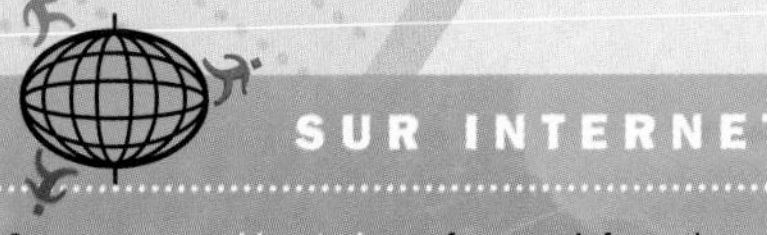

SUR INTERNET

Go to espaces.vhlcentral.com for more information related to this **Projet**.

une ville nouvelle *(literally) a new town, a planned community* **vise à attirer** *is designed to attract* **grâce au lien** *via the link* **pôles d'intérêt** *centers of attraction* **transports en commun** *public transportation* **convaincre** *to convince* **même** *same*

Section Goals

In this section, students will:

- learn about the geography and climate of Québec
- use French as they research and interact with the wider world
- write and present a brochure for a planned community in Québec

Instructional Resources
espaces.vhlcentral.com: activities, downloads, reference tools

Suggestion Students might need a week to complete the project, so at the beginning of that time period have them open their books to this page and read through **Projet**. Explain that they are going to use their research skills to prepare a brochure to promote a planned, modern community in Québec. Ask them to review the list of items to include and have them brainstorm what types of information they want to feature in their brochures.

Préparez une brochure

- Students may wish to interview local community designers or developers to get first-hand information on what goes into developing a community.
- You may wish to have students work in pairs, with one person focusing on the residential areas and the other person on the commercial areas of the community.

Présentez votre brochure
If you assigned partners, give them time to coordinate and practice their individual portions of the presentation.

EVALUATION

Criteria	Scale
Content	1 2 3 4
Organization	1 2 3 4
Grammatical accuracy	1 2 3 4
Creativity	1 2 3 4
Use of visuals	1 2 3 4

Scoring	
Excellent	18–20 points
Good	14–17 points
Satisfactory	10–13 points
Unsatisfactory	< 10 points

Section Goals

In this section, students will learn and practice vocabulary related to:

- asking for and giving directions
- landmarks

Instructional Resources

*IRCD-ROM: Transparency #52; IRM (**Vocabulaire supplémentaire; Mise en pratique** answers; Textbook Audioscript; Lab Audioscript)*
Textbook MP3s
WB/VM: Workbook, pp. 161–162
Lab Manual, p. 93
Lab MP3s
WB/VM/LM Answer Key
espaces.vhlcentral.com: activities, downloads, reference tools

Suggestions

- Tell students to look over the new vocabulary and identify the cognates.
- Use **Transparency #52.** Point out objects and describe what the people are doing. Examples: **Il est perdu. L'homme s'assied sur un banc. C'est une statue. Il y a deux feux de signalisation au carrefour.**
- Define and contrast the words for types of roads: **une rue, une autoroute, un boulevard, une avenue,** and **un chemin**. Also give examples using local roads students know.
- Point out that **coin** and **angle** both mean *corner.*
- Point out the difference between **tout droit** (*straight ahead*) and **à droite** (*to the right*).
- You might want to teach students the expression **point de repère** (*landmark; point of reference*).
- Additional vocabulary for this lesson can be found in the **Vocabulaire supplémentaire** in the IRM on the IRCD-ROM.

Leçon 24

You will learn how to...

- ask for directions
- tell what you will do

Où se trouve...?

Vocabulaire

continuer	*to continue*
se déplacer	*to move (change location)*
suivre	*to follow*
tourner	*to turn*
traverser	*to cross*
un angle	*corner*
une avenue	*avenue*
un bâtiment	*building*
un boulevard	*boulevard*
un chemin	*way; path*
un coin	*corner*
des indications (*f.*)	*directions*
un office du tourisme	*tourist office*
au bout (de)	*at the end (of)*
au coin (de)	*at the corner (of)*
autour (de)	*around*
jusqu'à	*until*
(tout) près (de)	*(very) close (to)*
tout droit	*straight ahead*

ressources

WB pp. 161–162	LM p. 93	Text MP3s Leçon 24	Lab MP3s Leçon 24	espaces.vhlcentral.com Leçon 24

OPTIONS

Extra Practice Ask students which vocabulary words they associate with these verbs. **1. descendre (rue/escalier) 2. suivre (rue/boulevard/chemin) 3. tourner (gauche/droite) 4. demander (indications) 5. monter (escaliers) 6. traverser (un pont/une rue) 7. regarder (une statue) 8. boire (une fontaine) 9. téléphoner (une cabine téléphonique) 10. s'arrêter (un feu de signalisation)**

TPR Label four points in your classroom with the cardinal directions. Play a game of **Jacques a dit** (*Simon says*) in which students respond to commands using the four directions. Example: **Regardez vers le nord.** Tell students to respond only if they hear the words **Jacques a dit**. If a student responds to a command not preceded by **Jacques a dit**, he or she is eliminated. The last person standing wins.

Un touriste se perd à Aix... heureusement, il y a Stéphane!

4

5

SANDRINE Absolument! «Oui, je l'adore, c'est mon amour, mon trésor...»
AMINA Pauline Ester! Tu aimes la musique des années quatre-vingt-dix?
SANDRINE Pas tous les styles de musique, mais Pauline Ester, oui.
AMINA Comme on dit, les goûts et les couleurs, ça ne se discutent pas!
RACHID Tu n'aimes pas Pauline Ester, mon cœur?

TOURISTE Excusez-moi, est-ce que vous savez où se trouve le bureau de poste, s'il vous plaît?
RACHID Oui, ce n'est pas loin d'ici. Vous descendez la rue, juste là, ensuite vous continuez jusqu'au feu rouge et vous tournez à gauche.

9

10

STÉPHANE Le bureau de poste? C'est très simple.
TOURISTE Ah bon! C'est loin d'ici?
STÉPHANE Non, pas du tout. C'est tout près. Vous prenez cette rue, là, à gauche. Vous continuez jusqu'au cours Mirabeau. Vous le connaissez?
TOURISTE Non, je ne suis pas d'ici.
STÉPHANE Bon... Le cours Mirabeau, c'est le boulevard principal de la ville.

STÉPHANE Alors, une fois que vous serez sur le cours Mirabeau, vous tournerez à gauche et suivrez le cours jusqu'à La Rotonde. Vous la verrez... Il y a une grande fontaine. Derrière la fontaine, vous trouverez le bureau de poste, et voilà!
TOURISTE Merci beaucoup.
STÉPHANE De rien. Au revoir!

Expressions utiles

Giving directions

- **Attendez, vous voyez le café qui est juste là?**
  Wait, do you see the café right over there?
- **Il y aura certainement quelqu'un qui saura vous dire comment y aller.**
  There will surely be someone there who will know how to tell you how to get there.
- **Vous tournerez à gauche et suivrez le cours jusqu'à La Rotonde.**
  You will turn left and follow the street until the Rotunda.
- **Vous la verrez.**
  You will see it.
- **Derrière la fontaine, vous trouverez le bureau de poste.**
  Behind the fountain, you will find the post office.

Talking about the weekend

- **Je pense que nous irons faire une randonnée.**
  I think we will go for a hike.
- **J'espère qu'il fera beau!**
  I hope it will be nice/the weather will be good!
- **Nous irons au concert en plein air.**
  We will go to the outdoor concert.

Additional vocabulary

- **voyons**
  let's see
- **le boulevard principal**
  the main drag/principal thoroughfare

ACTIVITÉS

2 Comment y aller? Remettez les indications pour aller du P'tit Bistrot au bureau de poste dans l'ordre. Écrivez un **X** à côté de l'indication que l'on ne doit pas suivre.

a. __3__ Suivez le cours Mirabeau jusqu'à la fontaine.
b. __4__ Le bureau de poste se trouve derrière la fontaine.
c. __2__ Tournez à gauche.
d. __X__ Tournez à droite au feu rouge.
e. __1__ Prenez cette rue à gauche jusqu'au boulevard principal.

3 Écrivez Le touriste est soulagé (*relieved*) d'arriver enfin au bureau de poste. Il était très découragé; presque personne ne savait lui expliquer comment y aller. Il écrit une carte postale à sa femme pour lui raconter son aventure. Composez son message.

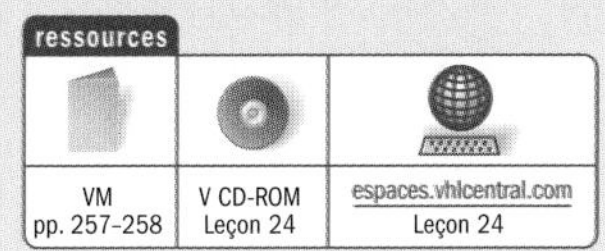

ressources
VM
pp. 257–258
V CD-ROM
Leçon 24
espaces.vhlcentral.com
Leçon 24

Expressions utiles
- Model the pronunciation of the **Expressions utiles** and have students repeat them after you.
- As you work through the list, point out forms of **le futur simple**. Tell students that this tense will be formally presented in the **Structures** section.
- Respond briefly to questions about **le futur**. Reinforce correct forms, but do not expect students to produce them consistently at this time.
- Point out in caption 4 where Amina says: **Les goûts et les couleurs, ça ne se discutent pas**. Ask students to interpret it. Then point out that English expresses the same idea with the saying "*To each his own.*"

1 Suggestions
- Go over the answers with the class.
- For item 4, point out that Pauline Ester recorded the song ***Oui, je l'adore*** in 1989, and it remained popular in the 1990s. In this episode, Amina is surprised that Sandrine likes such an old song.

1 Expansion For additional practice, give students these questions. **9. Où va le touriste pour demander des indications? (chez le marchand de journaux, au café) 10. Que cherche le touriste? (le bureau de poste) 11. Est-ce que le bureau de poste est loin du P'tit Bistrot? (Non, il est tout près.)**

2 Suggestion Have students form groups of five. Make a set of individual sentences on strips of paper for each group and distribute them. Tell students to arrange the sentences in the proper order and then read them aloud. The person who receives the sentence that does not fit should read that sentence last.

3 Suggestions
- Remind students to use appropriate salutations and closings. (See page 107.)
- If time is limited, this activity may be assigned as homework.

OPTIONS

La Rotonde The large fountain located at one end of **le cours Mirabeau** is called **La Rotonde**. Built in 1860, it features bronze lions and stone cherubs riding swans. The source of the water is the city's underground springs. Every evening, this beautiful fountain is illuminated. If possible, bring in photos of **La Rotonde** to show the class.

Extra Practice Have students find the verbs used to give directions in this episode and list them on the board. Examples: **prendre, tourner, descendre, traverser**, and **continuer**. Then have students write directions from campus to various places in town using as many of these verbs as possible. You may wish to assign students different locations.

connections cultures NATIONAL STANDARDS

Section Goals

In this section, students will:
- learn about main squares in French cities and towns
- learn more terms for small shops or businesses
- learn the names of famous areas in the hearts of several francophone cities
- read about the Baron Georges Eugène Haussmann

Instructional Resources
espaces.vhlcentral.com: activities, downloads, reference tools

Culture à la loupe

Avant la lecture Have students read the first sentence of the text. Then ask: **Votre ville natale a-t-elle une place principale ou un centre-ville? Quels bâtiments trouvez-vous souvent dans ces endroits?**

Lecture
- Point out the **Coup de main**. Explain that people in Paris customarily refer to a locale as **le 1er** or **le 13ème**, without using the word **arrondissement**. Paris has 20 **arrondissements**.
- Explain that the term **la mairie** is related to the title of the person who works there, **le maire**.

Après la lecture Have students describe what they see in the photos. Then ask: **Pensez-vous que c'est une photo d'un village, d'une petite ville ou d'une grande ville? Pourquoi?**

1 Suggestion Have students work in pairs on this activity.

CULTURE À LA LOUPE

Villes et villages français

Quand on regarde le plan d'un village, d'une petite ville ou celui d'un quartier d'une grande ville, on remarque qu'il y a souvent une place au centre, autour de laquelle° la ville ou le quartier s'organise. Elle est un peu comme «le cœur» de la ville ou du quartier.

Sur la place principale des villes et villages français, on trouve souvent une église. Il peut s'y trouver aussi l'hôtel de ville (la mairie), ainsi que° d'autres bâtiments administratifs comme la poste, le commissariat de police ou l'office du tourisme, s'il y en a un. La grande place est aussi le quartier commercial d'une petite ville et beaucoup de gens y vont pour faire leurs courses dans les magasins ou pour se détendre dans un café, un restaurant ou au cinéma. On y trouve aussi parfois un musée ou un théâtre. La place peut être piétonne° ou ouverte à la circulation, mais dans les deux cas, elle est souvent très animée°.

En général, la grande place est bien entretenue° et décorée d'une fontaine, d'un parterre de fleurs° ou d'une statue. La majorité des rues principales de la ville ou du quartier partent ensuite de la place. Le nom de la place reflète souvent ce qu'on y trouve, par exemple la place de l'Église, la place de la Mairie ou la place de la Comédie. Beaucoup de rues portent le nom d'un écrivain ou d'un personnage célèbre de l'histoire de France, comme rue Victor Hugo ou avenue du général de Gaulle. Au centre-ville, les rues sont souvent très étroites et beaucoup sont à sens unique°.

laquelle *which* **ainsi que** *as well as* **piétonne** *pedestrian* **animée** *busy* **entretenue** *cared for* **parterre de fleurs** *flower bed* **sens unique** *one-way*

Coup de main

Some major cities in France, such as Paris, Lyon and Marseille, are divided into **arrondissements**, or districts. You can determine in which **arrondissement** something is located by the final numbers of its zip code. For example, 75011 indicates the 11th **arrondissement** in Paris and 13001 is the 1st **arrondissement** in Marseille.

ACTIVITÉS

1 Complétez Donnez un début logique à chaque phrase, d'après le texte. Answers will vary. Possible answers provided.

1. ... au centre de la majorité des petites villes françaises. Il y a une place
2. ... autour de sa grande place. Une petite ville française s'organise
3. ... se situe souvent sur la place principale d'une ville française. Une église
4. ... pour faire leurs courses ou pour se détendre. Beaucoup de gens vont sur la grande place de leur ville
5. ... décorent souvent les places. Une fontaine, une statue ou un parterre de fleurs
6. ... sont réservées exclusivement aux piétons. Les places piétonnes
7. ... détermine souvent le nom d'une place. Un bâtiment
8. ... donnent souvent leur nom aux rues françaises. Des écrivains ou d'autres personnages célèbres
9. ... sont souvent à sens unique. Les rues du centre-ville
10. ... sont parfois divisées en arrondissements. Les grandes villes françaises

OPTIONS

Cultural Comparison Have students work in groups of three. Tell them to compare the center of French towns and cities with the center of the town or city in which their campus is located. Have them list the similarities and differences in a two-column chart under the headings **Similitudes** and **Différences**. Alternatively, you can let students choose another location to compare.

Villes et villages français Having a book of maps (**un plan détaillé**) is essential when visiting a French city because roads are often short, narrow, and organized on uneven grids or no grids at all. Even many lifelong residents of Paris and Lyon keep their maps with them.

LE FRANÇAIS QUOTIDIEN

Des magasins

cordonnerie (*f.*)	*cobbler's*
disquaire (*m.*)	*music store*
fleuriste (*m.*)	*florist*
parfumerie (*f.*)	*perfume/beauty shop*
photographe (*m.*)	*photo shop*
quincaillerie (*f.*)	*hardware store*
tailleur (*m.*)	*tailor's*
teinturerie (*f.*)	*dry cleaner's*
vidéoclub (*m.*)	*video store*

LE MONDE FRANCOPHONE

Le centre des villes

Voici le «cœur» de quelques villes francophones.

En Belgique

la Grand-Place à Bruxelles cœur de la vieille ville avec l'hôtel de ville, la maison du roi et de nombreux restaurants et cafés

Au Maroc

la médina à Fès centre historique avec ses monuments, ses boutiques et surtout ses artisans

En Nouvelle-Calédonie

le marché municipal de Nouméa ouvert tous les jours, on y vend du poisson, des fleurs, des légumes et des fruits

Au Québec

la Place-Royale à Québec rues étroites° et maisons de pierre° restaurées des premiers colons° français

étroites *narrow* **pierre** *stone* **colons** *colonists*

PORTRAIT

Le baron Haussmann

En 1853, Napoléon III demande au baron Georges Eugène Haussmann (1809-1891) de moderniser Paris. Le baron imagine alors un programme de transformation de la ville entière°. Il en est le premier vrai urbaniste. Il multiplie sa surface par deux. Pour améliorer° la circulation, il ouvre de larges avenues et des boulevards, comme le boulevard Haussmann, qu'il borde° d'immeubles bourgeois. Il crée de grands carrefours, comme l'Étoile ou la place de la Concorde, et de nombreux parcs et jardins. Plus de 600 km d'égouts° sont construits. Parce qu'il a aussi détruit beaucoup de bâtiments historiques, les Français ont longtemps détesté le baron Haussmann. Pourtant°, son influence a été remarquable.

entière *entire* **améliorer** *improve* **borde** *lines with* **égouts** *sewers* **Pourtant** *However*

SUR INTERNET

Quelle est la particularité de la ville de Rocamadour, en France?

Go to **espaces.vhlcentral.com** to find more cultural information related to this **ESPACE CULTURE**.

ACTIVITÉS

2 Complétez Donnez une suite logique à chaque phrase.

1. En 1853, Napoléon III demande à Haussmann... de moderniser Paris.
2. Pour améliorer la circulation dans Paris, le baron Haussmann a créé... de larges avenues et des boulevards.
3. Les Français ont longtemps détesté le baron Haussmann... parce qu'il a détruit beaucoup de bâtiments historiques.
4. La médina représente... le centre historique de Fès.
5. Au marché de Nouméa, on peut acheter... du poisson, des fleurs, des légumes ou des fruits.

3 Une école de langues Vous et un(e) partenaire dirigez une école de langues située en plein centre-ville. Préparez une petite présentation de votre école où vous expliquez où elle se situe, les choses à faire au centre-ville, etc. Vos camarades ont-ils envie de s'y inscrire (*enroll*)?

ressources
espaces.vhlcentral.com
Leçon 24

Le français quotidien
- Model the pronunciation of each term and have students repeat it.
- Have volunteers explain what service(s) each store offers or what product(s) each one sells. Example: **Chez le fleuriste, on vend des fleurs.** Alternatively, you can have them write definitions in French. Then tell them to get together with a partner, and take turns reading their definitions and guessing the kind of shop.

Portrait
- Haussmann was born in Paris and began his **carrière préfectorale** in 1831, working in several regions of France before being asked to modernize Paris. The transformation of Paris took place in three stages between 1858 and 1870. The city's sewer system was rebuilt to help prevent disease after a cholera epidemic.
- Have students describe the photos of **le boulevard Haussmann** and **la place de la Concorde**.

Le monde francophone
- After reading the text, ask students in what countries or cities these places are located. Examples: **1. Où est la médina? (Elle est à Fès.) 2. Dans quel pays est la Grand-Place? (en Belgique)**
- Then ask questions about the individual places. Examples: **1. Dans quels endroits pouvez-vous manger? (sur la Grand-Place) 2. Où pouvez-vous trouver des objets artisanaux? (à la médina de Fès) 3. Où pouvez-vous voir des monuments et des bâtiments historiques? (sur la Grand-Place, à la médina et sur la Place-Royale)**

2 Expansion For additional practice, give students these items. **6. Haussmann est le premier vrai... (urbaniste de Paris.) 7. Pour rendre Paris plus beau, Haussmann a créé... (de nombreux parcs et jardins.) 8. Le marché municipal de Nouméa est ouvert... (tous les jours.)**

3 Expansion After the presentations have been completed, have students vote on the school they most wish to attend.

OPTIONS

Le baron Haussmann Have students turn to the map of Paris on page 102. Tell them to find **le boulevard Haussmann, la place de la Concorde,** and **l'Étoile (l'Arc de Triomphe)** and describe each location. Then have them find other boulevards and describe the locations of various parks and gardens.

Small Groups Have students work in groups of three or four. Tell them to discuss these topics: **Les Français ont-ils raison de détester Hausmann? Faut-il détruire des bâtiments historiques au nom du progrès?** Then ask volunteers to report the results of their discussion to the class.

NATIONAL STANDARDS comparisons

Section Goals

In this section, students will learn:

- the **futur simple** of regular verbs
- the **futur simple** with most spelling-change **-er** verbs

Instructional Resources
WB/VM: Workbook, pp. 163–164
Lab Manual, p. 95
Lab MP3s
WB/VM/LM Answer Key
*IRCD-ROM: IRM (**Essayez!** and **Mise en pratique** answers; Lab Audioscript)*
espaces.vhlcentral.com: activities, downloads, reference tools

Suggestions

- Before introducing the **futur simple**, review **futur proche** constructions by asking students questions about their plans for the upcoming weekend. Examples: **Qui va sortir ce week-end? Vous allez faire quoi ce week-end, Samantha?**
- Go over the pronunciation of spelling-change **-er** verbs in the table. Then ask students for other verbs they've learned that end in **-yer** (**employer, essayer, balayer, essuyer,** and **s'ennuyer**).
- You might want to teach the expressions **à l'avenir** and **dans l'avenir** (*in the future*) to the class. In addition, you might give students a list of other adverbial expressions to use with the **futur simple: l'année/la semaine/le mois prochain(e), ...** (*day of the week*) **prochain, dans ... ans/mois/semaines, en ...** (*name of month or year*), etc.

Essayez! Have students create sentences using these phrases.

24.1 *Le futur simple*

Point de départ In **Leçon 7**, you learned to use **aller** + [*infinitive*] to express actions in the immediate future (**le futur proche**). You will now learn the future tense to say what *will happen.*

Future tense of regular verbs

	parler	réussir	attendre
je/j'	parler**ai**	réussir**ai**	attendr**ai**
tu	parler**as**	réussir**as**	attendr**as**
il/elle	parler**a**	réussir**a**	attendr**a**
nous	parler**ons**	réussir**ons**	attendr**ons**
vous	parler**ez**	réussir**ez**	attendr**ez**
ils/elles	parler**ont**	réussir**ont**	attendr**ont**

- Note that you form the future tense of **-er** and **-ir** verbs by adding the future endings to the infinitive. The **-e** of the infinitive is dropped before adding the endings to **-re** verbs.

Nous **voyagerons** cet été. *We will travel this summer.*
Tu ne **sortiras** pas. *You won't go out.*
Ils **attendront** Sophie. *They will wait for Sophie.*

- Note the future tense forms of most spelling-change **-er** verbs:

present form of je	+r	future forms
j'achète	achèter-	j'achèterai
je nettoie	nettoier-	je nettoierai
je paie/paye	paier-/payer-	je paierai/payerai
je m'appelle	m'appeller-	je m'appellerai

- For **-er** verbs with an **é** before the infinitive ending, form the future tense as you would with regular **-er** verbs.

Elle **répétera** ses questions. *She will repeat her questions.*
Elles **considéreront** le pour et le contre. *They'll consider the pros and cons.*

- The words **le futur** and **l'avenir** (*m.*) both mean *future.* Use the first word when referring to the grammatical future; use the second word when referring to events that haven't occurred yet.

On étudie **le futur** en cours. *We're studying the future (tense) in class.*
Je parlerai de **mon avenir** au prof. *I'll speak to the professor about my future.*

Essayez! Remplissez les blancs avec la forme correcte du futur des verbes.

1. je *mangerai* (manger)
2. il prendra (prendre)
3. on boira (boire)
4. ils achèteront (acheter)
5. vous choisirez (choisir)
6. tu connaîtras (connaître)

MISE EN PRATIQUE

1 Projets Cécile et ses amis parlent de leurs projets (*plans*) d'avenir. Employez le futur pour refaire ses phrases.

MODÈLE Je vais chercher une belle maison.
Je chercherai une belle maison.

1. Je vais finir mes études. Je finirai mes études.
2. Philippe va me dire où trouver un travail. Philippe me dira où trouver un travail.
3. Tu vas gagner beaucoup d'argent. Tu gagneras beaucoup d'argent.
4. Mes amis vont habiter près de chez moi. Mes amis habiteront près de chez moi.
5. Mon petit ami et moi, nous allons acheter un chien. Mon petit ami et moi, nous achèterons un chien.
6. Vous allez nous rendre visite de temps en temps. Vous nous rendrez visite de temps en temps.

2 Dans l'avenir Qu'est-ce qu'Habib et sa famille vont faire cet été?

MODÈLE mon cousin / lire / dix / livres
Mon cousin lira dix livres.

1. mon neveu / apprendre / nager Mon neveu apprendra à nager.
2. mes grands-parents / voyager / Montréal Mes grands-parents voyageront à Montréal.
3. en août / je / conduire / ma nouvelle voiture En août, je conduirai ma nouvelle voiture.
4. mon père / écrire / cartes postales Mon père écrira des cartes postales.
5. tante Yamina / maigrir Tante Yamina maigrira.
6. nous / vendre / notre vieille voiture Nous vendrons notre vieille voiture.

3 Je cherche du travail Regardez ces deux annonces (*ads*). Ensuite, avec un(e) partenaire, posez-vous ces questions et parlez du travail que vous préférez. Answers will vary.

NOUVEAU RESTAURANT CHERCHE SERVEUR/ SERVEUSE
Cinq ans d'expérience minimum.
Cuisine française.
Du mardi au samedi de 16h30 à 23h30;
le dimanche de 11h30 à 22h30
Salaire 2.000 euros par mois,
avec une augmentation après six mois
Métro: Goncourt
Téléphonez au: 01.40.96.31.15

TRAVAILLEZ COMME COIFFEUR/ COIFFEUSE
Excellent salaire: 2.500 euros par mois
Deux ans d'expérience
Pour commencer immédiatement
Horaires: mardi, mercredi, jeudi, de 9h00 à 15h00
Téléphonez pour rendez-vous au: 01.38.18.42.90

1. Quel emploi préfères-tu? Pourquoi?
2. À quelle heure arriveras-tu au travail? À quelle heure sortiras-tu?
3. T'amuseras-tu au travail? Pourquoi?
4. Combien gagneras-tu?
5. Prendras-tu le métro? Conduiras-tu? Pourquoi?
6. Chercheras-tu un autre emploi l'année prochaine? Pourquoi?

OPTIONS

Extra Practice Write the following on the board: **L'année prochaine, je/j'....** Then ask students to complete the sentence using a verb in the **futur simple**. If they wish to use a verb with an irregular stem (such as **aller**), give them the form and tell them that they'll learn it in **Structures 24.2**.

Extra Practice Read predictions about the future while students react by saying **Oui, c'est probable** or **Non, c'est peu probable.** Write the two phrases on the board before you get started and be sure to use only verbs with regular stems in the future. Example: **En l'an 3000, personne ne parlera ni français ni anglais.**

COMMUNICATION

4 Chez la voyante Vous voulez savoir ce qui (*what*) vous attend dans l'avenir. Vous allez chez une voyante (*fortune-teller*) et vous lui posez ces questions. Jouez les deux rôles avec un partenaire, puis changez de rôles.
Answers will vary.

1. Où est-ce que je travaillerai après l'université?
2. Où est-ce que j'habiterai dans 20 ans?
3. Avec qui est-ce que je partagerai ma vie?
4. Quelle voiture est-ce que je conduirai?
5. Est-ce que je m'occuperai de ma santé?
6. Qu'est-ce que j'aimerai faire pour m'amuser?
7. Où est-ce que je passerai mes vacances?
8. Où est-ce que je dépenserai mon argent?

5 L'horoscope Avec un(e) partenaire, préparez par écrit l'horoscope d'une célébrité. Ensuite, par groupes de quatre, lisez cet horoscope à vos camarades qui essaieront de découvrir l'identité de la personne.
Answers will vary.

MODÈLE

Vous travaillerez comme acteur de cinéma. Vous jouerez dans beaucoup de films français et américains. Vous jouerez des rôles divers dans des films comiques comme Green Card *et dans des films classiques comme* Jean de Florette. *(réponse: Gérard Depardieu)*

6 Partir très loin Vous et votre partenaire avez décidé de prendre des vacances très loin de chez vous. Regardez les photos et choisissez deux endroits où vous voulez aller, puis comparez-les. Utilisez ces questions pour vous guider. Ensuite, présentez vos réponses à la classe.
Answers will vary.

- Qu'apporterez-vous?
- Quand partirez-vous?
- Que visiterez-vous?
- Comment vous détendrez-vous?
- Quand rentrerez-vous?

Le français vivant

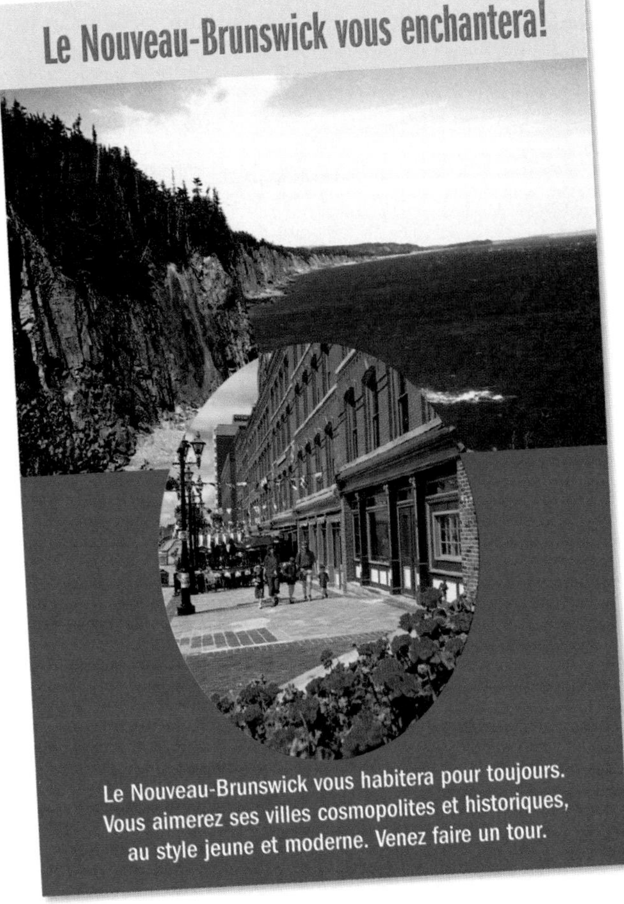

Le Nouveau-Brunswick vous enchantera!
Le Nouveau-Brunswick vous habitera pour toujours. Vous aimerez ses villes cosmopolites et historiques, au style jeune et moderne. Venez faire un tour.

Identifiez Quelles formes de verbes au futur trouvez-vous dans cette publicité (*ad*)? enchantera, habitera, aimerez

Questions À tour de rôle, avec un(e) partenaire, posez-vous ces questions et répondez. Some answers will vary.

1. Que veut dire «Le Nouveau-Brunswick vous habitera pour toujours»?
   a. Vous habiterez toujours au Nouveau-Brunswick.
   (b.) Vous penserez toujours au Nouveau-Brunswick.
   c. Le Nouveau-Brunswick existera toujours.
2. Pourquoi le touriste aimera-t-il le Nouveau-Brunswick?
3. Dans quel pays se trouve le Nouveau-Brunswick? le Canada
4. Dans quelle région du monde veux-tu voyager? Cette région t'enchantera-t-elle?
5. Voyageras-tu un jour au Nouveau-Brunswick? Pourquoi?

1 Suggestion Have students do this activity in pairs. One student should read items 1–3, and the other one should restate the sentence with **futur simple**. Then they should switch roles.

2 Suggestion Students could complete this activity in phases, first writing out the sentences in the present tense and then changing the verbs from the present to the future tense.

3 Expansion When students have finished, have them write an ad for their ideal job and write sentences about it based on the activity's questions. Allow them to create humorous job descriptions, such as for TV watchers.

4 Expansion Have fortune-tellers record predictions. Then ask volunteers to read the most interesting predictions to the class.

5 Suggestion Discreetly assign a picture of a celebrity from magazines or the Internet to each pair.

6 Suggestion You might suggest that students use **on** rather than **nous** in their sentences so that they are typical of informal, everyday speech.

Le français vivant Ask students to find New Brunswick on the map on page 426. Point out that it is an officially bilingual province whose languages are French and English, and that it borders Québec and Maine.

OPTIONS

Extra Practice Read a set of statements about what will happen in the future with some good events and some bad ones. Students should react to the statements by giving a thumbs-up (for good events) or a thumbs-down (for bad events). Example: **On gagnera des millions à la loterie.** (thumbs-up)

Small Groups Have students write a half-page description of a place in the future. It can be a utopia or a dystopia. You might suggest that they use ideas from science fiction. You may need to give them forms for some verbs with irregular stems in the future.

NATIONAL comparisons STANDARDS

Section Goals

In this section, students will learn irregular forms of the **futur simple**.

Instructional Resources
WB/VM: Workbook, pp. 165–166
Lab Manual, p. 96
Lab MP3s
WB/VM/LM Answer Key
*IRCD-ROM: IRM (**Essayez!** and **Mise en pratique** answers; Lab Audioscript)*
espaces.vhlcentral.com: activities, downloads, reference tools

Suggestions

- Ask students if they'll be doing certain things this coming year. Example: **Irez-vous à l'étranger?** As they give you their answers, write the subject pronoun and verb for each statement on the board and have the class repeat the combination after you.
- Ask students: **Que ferez-vous cet été?** As they tell you what they'll be doing, ask the other students if they'll be doing the same thing. Example: **Qui d'autre habitera à New York?**
- Make index cards with future forms of some of the verbs on this page (**j'irai, ils voudront**) and divide them equally between small groups of students. Have the groups formulate a sentence for each verb form with a statement about what will happen in the future. Example: **Rico deviendra médecin.**
- Have the class make a set of resolutions for the new year using the future tense. Write the resolutions on the board. Example: **Je ferai mes devoirs tous les jours.**

Essayez! If students are struggling to remember endings, write a paradigm for a verb in the future tense on the board and underline the endings. Then ask the class what the endings remind them of. (They resemble the present tense of **avoir**.)

24.2 Irregular future forms

Point de départ In the previous grammar point, you learned how to form the future tense. Although the future endings are the same for all verbs, some verbs use irregular stems in the future tense.

Irregular verbs in the future

infinitive	stem	future forms
aller	ir-	j'irai
apercevoir	apercevr-	j'apercevrai
avoir	aur-	j'aurai
devoir	devr-	je devrai
envoyer	enverr-	j'enverrai
être	ser-	je serai
faire	fer-	je ferai
pouvoir	pourr-	je pourrai
recevoir	recevr-	je recevrai
savoir	saur-	je saurai
venir	viendr-	je viendrai
vouloir	voudr-	je voudrai

Vous **aurez** des vacances?
Will you have vacation?

Nous **irons** en Tunisie.
We will go to Tunisia.

Il **enverra** des cartes postales.
He will send postcards.

Tu les **recevras** dans une semaine.
You will receive them in a week.

- The verbs **devenir**, **maintenir**, **retenir**, **revenir**, and **tenir** are patterned after **venir** in the future tense, just as they are in the present tense.

Nous **reviendrons** bientôt.
We will come back soon.

Tu **deviendras** architecte un jour?
Will you become an architect one day?

- The future forms of **il y a**, **il faut**, and **il pleut** are, respectively, **il y aura**, **il faudra**, and **il pleuvra**.

Il **faudra** apporter le parapluie.
We'll need to bring the umbrella.

Tu penses qu'il **pleuvra** ce week-end?
Do you think it will rain this weekend?

Essayez! Conjuguez ces verbes au futur.

1. je/j' (aller, vouloir, savoir) *irai, voudrai, saurai*
2. tu (faire, pouvoir, envoyer) feras, pourras, enverras
3. Marc (venir, être, apercevoir) viendra, sera, apercevra
4. nous (avoir, devoir, faire) aurons, devrons, ferons
5. vous (recevoir, tenir, aller) recevrez, tiendrez, irez
6. elles (vouloir, faire, être) voudront, feront, seront
7. je/j' (devenir, pouvoir, envoyer) deviendrai, pourrai, enverrai
8. elle (aller, avoir, vouloir) ira, aura, voudra

MISE EN PRATIQUE

1 Que ferai-je? Que feront ces personnes la semaine prochaine?

MODÈLE
J'étudierai.

je / étudier

1. nous / faire
Nous ferons du shopping.

3. vous / aller
Vous irez au cinéma.

2. tu / être
Tu seras à la plage.

4. Yves / devoir
Yves devra travailler.

2 Le rêve de Stéphanie Complétez les phrases pour décrire le rêve (*dream*) de Stéphanie. Employez le futur des verbes.

Quand j' (1) aurai (avoir) 26 ans, j' (2) irai (aller) habiter au bord de la mer. Mon beau mari (3) sera (être) avec moi et nous (4) aurons (avoir) une grande maison. Je ne (5) ferai (faire) rien à la maison. Nos amis (6) viendront (venir) nous rendre visite tous les week-ends.

3 Si... Avec un(e) partenaire, finissez ces phrases à tour de rôle. Employez le futur des verbes de la boîte dans toutes vos réponses. Answers will vary.

MODÈLE Si mon ami(e) ne me téléphone pas ce soir, ...
Si mon amie ne me téléphone pas ce soir, je ne ferai pas de gym demain.

aller	devoir	faire	venir
avoir	être	pouvoir	vouloir

1. Si on m'invite à une fête samedi soir, ...
2. Si mes parents me donnent $100, ...
3. Si mon ami(e) me prête sa voiture, ...
4. Si le temps est mauvais, ...
5. Si je suis fatigué(e) vendredi, ...
6. Si ma famille me rend visite, ...

OPTIONS

Video Replay the video episode, having students focus on the conversation at the café. Afterwards, ask them questions about it. Examples: **Pourquoi Amina dit-elle qu'elle espère qu'il fera beau ce week-end? Que feront David et Sandrine ce week-end?**

Game Play a game of Bingo. Distribute Bingo cards with infinitives of verbs written in the squares. Then read aloud sentences, each with a future form of one of the verbs in it. Students should block out the verbs they recognize with tokens or scraps of paper and call Bingo! when they've blocked out a whole row.

NATIONAL communication STANDARDS

COMMUNICATION

4 **Faites des projets** Travaillez avec un(e) camarade de classe pour faire des projets (*plans*) pour ces événements qui auront lieu dans l'avenir. Answers will vary.

MODÈLE

Étudiant(e) 1: *Après l'université, je chercherai un travail à San Diego. J'enseignerai dans un lycée où je pourrai travailler avec les adolescents.*
Étudiant(e) 2: *Moi, après l'université, j'irai en Europe. Je travaillerai comme serveuse dans un café.*

1. Samedi soir: Décidez où vous irez et comment vous y arriverez.
2. Les prochaines vacances: Parlez de ce que (*what*) vous ferez. Que visiterez-vous?
3. Votre prochain anniversaire: Quel âge aurez-vous? Que ferez-vous? Avec qui ferez-vous la fête?
4. Votre vie professionnelle: Que ferez-vous après l'université? Où irez-vous?
5. À 65 ans: Où serez-vous? Que ferez-vous? Avec qui partagerez-vous votre vie?

5 **Prédictions** Par groupes de trois, parlez de comment sera le monde de ces années: 2020, 2050 et 2100. Utilisez votre imagination. Answers will vary.

6 **Demain** Avec un(e) partenaire, parlez de ce que (*what*) vous, votre famille et vos amis ferez demain. Answers will vary.

MODÈLE

Étudiant(e) 1: *Que feras-tu demain à midi?*
Étudiant(e) 2: *Demain à midi, j'irai poster une lettre. Mon camarade de chambre fera ses devoirs.*

vendredi	samedi	dimanche
8h00 ______	8h00 ______	8h00 ______
10h00 ______	10h00 ______	10h00 ______
12h00 ______	12h00 ______	12h00 ______
14h00 ______	14h00 ______	14h00 ______
16h00 ______	16h00 ______	16h00 ______
18h00 ______	18h00 ______	18h00 ______
20h00 ______	20h00 ______	20h00 ______
22h00 ______	22h00 ______	22h00 ______

Le français vivant

Un emplacement unique, près du Parc de Sceaux

Villa Adriana à Antony

À 500 mètres du magnifique parc de Sceaux, il y aura bientôt la Villa Adriana: une belle architecture, de grands appartements, avec terrasses et balcons. Vous viendrez visiter et vous ne voudrez plus repartir. Vous serez charmé.

Bâtir l'excellence

Identifiez Quelles formes de verbes au futur trouvez-vous dans cette publicité (*ad*)? aura, viendrez, voudrez, serez

Questions À tour de rôle, avec un(e) partenaire, posez-vous ces questions et répondez. Some answers will vary.

1. Où se trouvera bientôt la Villa Adriana? Elle se trouvera à 500 mètres du magnifique parc de Sceaux.
2. Quelle sera l'architecture des appartements? L'architecture sera belle avec de grands appartements, avec terrasses et balcons.
3. D'après (*According to*) la pub, quel effet une visite à la Villa Adriana peut-elle avoir? Vous ne voudrez plus repartir. Vous serez charmé.
4. As-tu été dans un appartement que tu n'as pas voulu quitter? Habiteras-tu un jour dans un appartement comme ça?
5. Quelles boutiques et quels bureaux y aura-t-il autour de la Villa Adriana?

1 Expansion Have students create a series of illustrations accompanied by text telling what they'll be doing next week.

2 Suggestion To make sure that students understand the passage they just completed, read each sentence back to them and ask the class if their dream life would be similar. Example: **Et vous? Est-ce que vous rêvez d'avoir une grande maison?**

3 Suggestion Write this paradigm on the board to help students with the activity: **si** + *present tense verb* → *future tense verb.* Make certain that the class remembers and understands the concept of **si** clauses before they complete the activity.

4 Suggestion If students aren't comfortable sharing personal information, tell them that they can answer the questions in the activity for a well-known person (Sarah Michelle Geller, one of the Wayans brothers, etc.) or a fictional character (Rambo, Barbie, etc.).

5 Expansion For the presentation part of this activity, you might write a few reactions on the board for students to repeat. Examples: **Ah, oui, c'est sûr! Mais non! C'est une blague ou quoi?**

6 Suggestion To simplify the presentations, have students present only their partner's plans for tomorrow.

Le français vivant After students have read the ad aloud, point out the phrase **vous ne voudrez plus repartir.** Ask the class what they think it means. Then ask individual students what they think of the building: **Comment trouvez-vous la Villa Adriana?**

OPTIONS

Extra Practice Make up a transparency with a set of **si** clauses, each beginning a sentence. Allow students to complete the sentences by supplying clauses with the verb in the future tense. Example: **S'il pleut cet après-midi... (je resterai à la maison avec mon chat.)**

Pairs Teach the expression **Quand les poules auront des dents** and then add ellipses (...) after it and tell the class to complete the thought by describing an improbable scenario with a partner. Example: **...moi, j'irai à la bibliothèque le samedi soir.** When students have completed their work in pairs, have them share it with the class.

Synthèse

Instructional Resources
IRCD-ROM: IRM (Info Gap Activities); Testing Program, pp. 93–96; Test Files; Testing Program MP3s; Test Generator espaces.vhlcentral.com: activities, downloads, reference tools

1 Suggestion You might wish to hand out campus maps as a visual aid to help students complete this activity. Students with difficulty visualizing space could trace the routes their partner describes to them on their maps. You could mark the classroom with an X and the words **Vous êtes ici.**

2 Suggestion Tell students to include a time reference (**le matin, jeudi soir,** etc.) in each sentence.

3 Suggestion Before students begin this activity, you may wish to review the vocabulary for houses in **Leçon 15.**

4 Suggestion So that students have a point of reference to verify the original instructions, have the student that first gives directions write them. Then he or she can read the directions aloud to the first person and verify them while the second person recalls what he or she heard.

5 Suggestion To get the class warmed up for this activity, read a set of logical and illogical statements about what you will do given certain weather conditions. Tell students to qualify each statement as **logique** or **illogique**. Examples: **Il pleuvra samedi, donc j'irai à la plage. (illogique) S'il fait beau dimanche, on ira au parc. (logique)**

6 Suggestion Divide the class into pairs and distribute the Info Gap Handouts in the IRM on the IRCD-ROM for this activity. Give students ten minutes to complete the activity.

1 Le campus À tour de rôle, donnez des indications à un(e) partenaire pour aller d'où vous vous trouvez en ce moment jusqu'à d'autres endroits sur le campus. Employez le futur. Answers will vary.

MODÈLE

Étudiant(e) 1: *Tu sortiras du bâtiment et tu tourneras à gauche. Ensuite, tu traverseras la rue. Où seras-tu?*
Étudiant(e) 2: *Je serai à la bibliothèque.*

2 La visite de Québec Avec un(e) partenaire, vous visitez la ville de Québec. Préparez un itinéraire de votre visite où vous vous arrêterez souvent pour visiter ou acheter quelque chose, manger, boire, etc. Soyez prêts à présenter votre itinéraire à la classe. Answers will vary.

MODÈLE

Étudiant(e) 1: *Le matin, nous prendrons le petit-déjeuner dans l'hôtel.*
Étudiant(e) 2: *Ensuite, nous irons visiter le musée de la Civilisation.*

Québec vous attend!
Visitez:
· le château Frontenac · la terrasse Dufferin
· le musée de la Civilisation
· la basilique Notre Dame-de-Québec
· le musée de l'Amérique française et beaucoup plus!

3 Ma future maison Avec un(e) partenaire, parlez de votre future maison et de ses pièces, de son jardin, du quartier et de vos voisins. Utilisez le futur et ces prépositions pour les décrire. Ensuite, présentez les projets (*plans*) de votre partenaire à la classe. Answers will vary.

MODÈLE

Étudiant(e) 1: *Il y aura un énorme jardin devant ma future maison.*
Étudiant(e) 2: *Je n'aurai aucun voisin en face de ma future maison.*

à droite (de)	autour (de)	en face (de)
à gauche (de)	derrière	loin (de)
au bout (de)	devant	(tout) près (de)
au milieu de		

4 Ma ville Vous invitez votre partenaire à venir vous rendre visite dans votre ville d'origine. Expliquez-lui le chemin de l'aéroport jusqu'à votre maison. Ensuite, votre partenaire donnera ces indications à un(e) autre camarade, qui vous les répétera. Les indications sont-elles toujours correctes? Utilisez le futur et alternez les rôles. Answers will vary.

MODÈLE

Étudiant(e) 1: *Tu sortiras de l'aéroport et tu passeras la mairie où tu tourneras à droite.*
Étudiant(e) 2: *D'accord, à droite à la mairie. Et après, j'irai où?*

5 Des prévisions météo Avec un(e) partenaire, parlez des prévisions météo pour le week-end prochain. Chacun (*Each one*) doit faire cinq prévisions et dire ce qu'on (*what one*) peut faire par ce temps. Soyez prêts à parler de vos prévisions et des possibilités pour le week-end à la classe. Answers will vary.

MODÈLE

Étudiant(e) 1: *Samedi, il fera beau dans le nord. On pourra faire une promenade.*
Étudiant(e) 2: *Dimanche, il pleuvra dans l'ouest. On devra passer la journée dans l'appartement.*

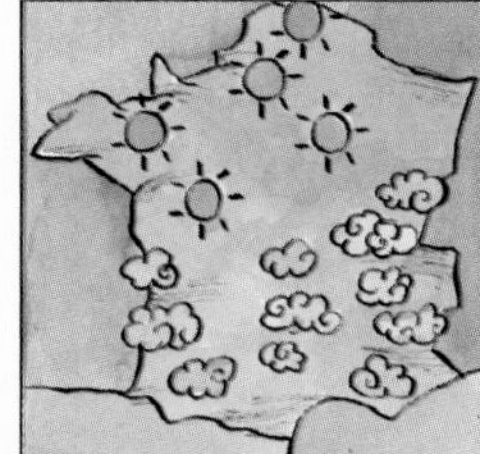
samedi

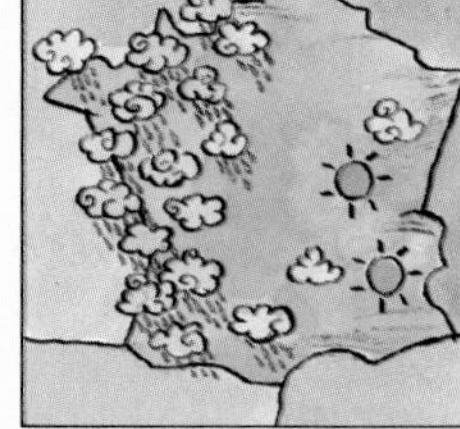
dimanche

6 La vie de Gaëlle et de Jean-Georges Votre professeur va vous donner, à vous et à votre partenaire, deux feuilles d'activités différentes sur l'avenir de Gaëlle et de Jean-Georges. Attention! Ne regardez pas la feuille de votre partenaire. Answers will vary.

MODÈLE

Étudiant(e) 1: *Jean-Georges et Gaëlle finiront leurs études au lycée.*
Étudiant(e) 2: *Ensuite, ...*

ressources

WB	LM	Lab MP3s	espaces.vhlcentral.com
pp. 163–166	pp. 95–96	Leçon 24	Leçon 24

OPTIONS

Extra Practice Read answers and have students produce questions that could have prompted the responses. The answers should contain verbs in the future tense. Challenge the class to come up with as many different questions as possible. Example: **J'habiterai une maison au bord de la mer. (Qu'est-ce que vous ferez après la retraite?)**

Game Make two oversized dice out of paper. Stick labels with subject pronouns on all the facets of one die. Then label the facets of the other die with infinitives of verbs with irregular future stems. Have students take turns rolling the dice so that they know which future-tense verb form to produce for their classmates. Example: **nous + avoir (nous aurons)**

Écriture

STRATÉGIE

Using linking words

You can make your writing more sophisticated by using linking words to connect simple sentences or ideas in order to create more complex sentences. Consider these passages that illustrate this effect:

Without linking words

Aujourd'hui, j'ai fait beaucoup de courses. Je suis allé à la poste. J'ai fait la queue pendant une demi-heure. J'ai acheté des timbres. J'ai aussi posté un colis. Je suis allé à la banque. La banque est rue Girardeau. J'ai perdu ma carte de crédit hier. Je devais aussi retirer de l'argent. Je suis allé à la brasserie pour déjeuner avec un ami. Cet ami s'appelle Marc. Je suis rentré à la maison. Ma mère rentrait du travail.

With linking words

Aujourd'hui, j'ai fait beaucoup de courses. D'abord, je suis allé à la poste où j'ai fait la queue pendant une demi-heure. J'ai acheté des timbres et j'ai aussi posté un colis. Après, je suis allé à la banque qui est rue Girardeau, parce que j'ai perdu ma carte de crédit hier et parce que je devais aussi retirer de l'argent. Ensuite, je suis allé à la brasserie pour déjeuner avec un ami qui s'appelle Marc. Finalement, je suis rentré à la maison alors que ma mère rentrait du travail.

Linking words

alors	*then*	**mais**	*but*
alors que	*as*	**ou**	*or*
après	*then, after that*	**où**	*where*
d'abord	*first*	**parce que**	*because*
donc	*so*	**pendant (que)**	*while*
dont	*of which*	**(et) puis**	*(and) then*
enfin	*finally*	**puisque**	*since*
ensuite	*then, after that*	**quand**	*when*
et	*and*	**que**	*that, which*
finalement	*finally*	**qui**	*who, that*

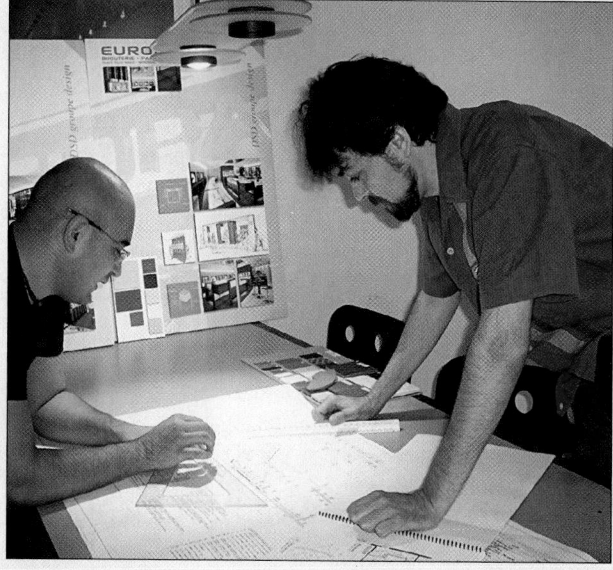

Thème

Faire la description d'un nouveau commerce

Avec des amis, vous allez ouvrir un commerce (*business*) dans le quartier de votre université. Vous voulez créer quelque chose d'original qui n'existe pas encore et qui sera très utile aux étudiants: un endroit où ils pourront faire plusieurs choses en même temps (par exemple, une laverie/salon de coiffure). Préparez une description détaillée de votre idée et de ce que (*what*) votre commerce proposera comme services. Utilisez votre imagination et les questions suivantes comme point de départ de votre description.

- Quel sera le nom du commerce?
- Quel type de commerce voulez-vous ouvrir?
- Quels seront les produits (*products*) que vous vendrez? Quels seront les prix? Donnez quelques détails sur l'activité commerciale.
- Où se trouvera le commerce?
- Comment sera l'intérieur du commerce (style, décoration, etc.)?
- Quels seront ses jours et heures d'ouverture (*business hours*)?
- En quoi consistera l'originalité de votre commerce? Expliquez pourquoi votre commerce sera unique et donnez les raisons pour lesquelles (*which*) des étudiants fréquenteront votre commerce.

Watch the FLASH CULTURE segment on the ESPACES video for cultural footage related to this unit's theme.

Section Goals

In this section, students will:
- learn to use linking words
- write a description of a new business idea
- view authentic cultural footage of various businesses and small shops

Instructional Resources
WB/VM: Video Manual, pp. 293–294
WB/VM/LM Answer Key
IRCD-ROM: IRM (Videoscript)
Video CD-ROM
Video on DVD
espaces.vhlcentral.com: activities, downloads, reference tools

Stratégie Review the list of linking words with the class and have volunteers create sentences with the words. Then have students comment on the writing style in the sample paragraphs.

Thème Tell students to answer the questions first. Remind them to use linking words so that their descriptions won't sound like the first paragraph in the **Stratégie**.

Proofreading Activity Have the class correct these sentences. **1. Je vens de m'apercevoir que je n'ai pas liquide. 2. Il y est toujours le distributeur automatic. 3. Vous tournerez à gauche et suivez le cours jusque à la rotonde. 4. Derriere la fontaine, vous trouverez la bureau poste.**

Flash culture Tell students that they will learn more about businesses and small shops by watching a variety of real-life images narrated by Benjamin. Show the video segment, then have students jot down in French at least three examples of people or things they saw. You can also use the activities in the video manual in class to reinforce this **Flash culture** or assign them as homework.

EVALUATION

Criteria	Scale
Content	1 2 3 4
Organization	1 2 3 4
Use of vocabulary	1 2 3 4
Use of linking words	1 2 3 4
Grammatical accuracy	1 2 3 4

Scoring	
Excellent	18–20 points
Good	14–17 points
Satisfactory	10–13 points
Unsatisfactory	< 10 points

Instructional Resources
Textbook MP3s
IRCD-ROM: IRM (Textbook Audioscript)
espaces.vhlcentral.com: downloads, reference tools

Retrouver son chemin

continuer	*to continue*
se déplacer	*to move (change location)*
descendre	*to go/come down*
être perdu(e)	*to be lost*
monter	*to go up/come up*
s'orienter	*to get one's bearings*
suivre	*to follow*
tourner	*to turn*
traverser	*to cross*
un angle	*corner*
une avenue	*avenue*
un banc	*bench*
un bâtiment	*building*
un boulevard	*boulevard*
une cabine téléphonique	*phone booth*
un carrefour	*intersection*
un chemin	*way; path*
un coin	*corner*
des indications (*f.*)	*directions*
un feu de signalisation (feux *pl.*)	*traffic light(s)*
une fontaine	*fountain*
un office du tourisme	*tourist office*
un pont	*bridge*
une rue	*street*
une statue	*statue*
est	*east*
nord	*north*
ouest	*west*
sud	*south*

Pour donner des indications

au bout (de)	*at the end (of)*
au coin (de)	*at the corner (of)*
autour (de)	*around*
jusqu'à	*until*
(tout) près (de)	*(very) close (to)*
tout droit	*straight ahead*

À la poste

poster une lettre	*to mail a letter*
une adresse	*address*
une boîte aux lettres	*mailbox*
une carte postale	*postcard*
un colis	*package*
le courrier	*mail*
une enveloppe	*envelope*
un facteur	*mailman*
un timbre	*stamp*

À la banque

avoir un compte bancaire	*to have a bank account*
déposer de l'argent	*to deposit money*
emprunter	*to borrow*
payer avec une carte de crédit	*to pay with a credit card*
payer en liquide	*to pay in cash*
payer par chèque	*to pay by check*
retirer de l'argent	*to withdraw money*
les billets (*m.*)	*bills, notes*
un compte de chèques	*checking account*
un compte d'épargne	*savings account*
une dépense	*expenditure, expense*
un distributeur automatique/de billets	*ATM*
les pièces de monnaie (*f.*)/ de la monnaie	*coins/change*

En ville

accompagner	*to accompany*
faire la queue	*to wait in line*
remplir un formulaire	*to fill out a form*
signer	*to sign*
une banque	*bank*
une bijouterie	*jewelry store*
une boutique	*boutique, store*
une brasserie	*café, restaurant*
un bureau de poste	*post office*
un cybercafé	*cybercafé*
une laverie	*laundromat*
un marchand de journaux	*newsstand*
une papeterie	*stationery store*
un salon de beauté	*beauty salon*
un commissariat de police	*police station*
une mairie	*town/city hall; mayor's office*
fermé(e)	*closed*
ouvert(e)	*open*

La négation

jamais	*never; ever*
ne... aucun(e)	*none (not any)*
ne... jamais	*never (not ever)*
ne... ni... ni...	*neither... nor*
ne... personne	*nobody, no one*
ne... plus	*no more (not anymore)*
ne... que	*only*
ne... rien	*nothing (not anything)*
pas (de)	*no, none*
personne	*no one*
quelque chose	*something*
quelqu'un	*someone*
rien	*nothing*
toujours	*always; still*

Verbes

apercevoir	*to see, to catch sight of*
s'apercevoir	*to notice; to realize*
recevoir	*to receive*

Expressions utiles	*See pp. 403 and 417.*
Le futur simple	*See p. 420.*

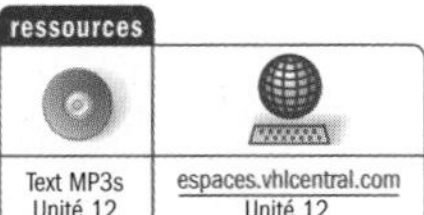

L'avenir et les métiers

UNITÉ **13**

Pour commencer

- Quel genre de travail Amina fera-t-elle?
- Est-ce qu'elle travaillera dans un bureau?
- Est-ce qu'elle aimera son travail?
- Que porte-t-elle aujourd'hui?

Unit Goals

Leçon 25

In this lesson, students will learn:
- terms for the workplace
- terms for job interviews
- terms for making and receiving phone calls
- rules of punctuation in French
- about telephones, text messages, and **les artisans**
- the future tense with **quand** and **dès que**
- interrogative pronouns **lequel**, **laquelle**, **lesquels**, and **lesquelles**
- about the global shipping service DHL

Leçon 26

In this lesson, students will learn:
- terms for professions
- more terms for discussing one's work
- about neologisms and **franglais**
- about labor unions, strikes, and civil servants
- the conditional
- **si** clauses
- to develop a career plan

Savoir-faire

In this section, students will learn:
- cultural, geographical, and historical information about Algeria, Morocco, and Tunisia
- to summarize a text in their own words
- to use background knowledge and listen for specific information
- to use note cards to organize their writing
- more about professions and work through specially shot video footage

Pour commencer

- **Elle fera du stylisme de mode.**
- Answers will vary.
- **Oui, elle l'aimera beaucoup.**
- **Elle porte une robe rose.**

RESOURCES

Workbook/Video Manual: WB Activities, pp. 169–182
Laboratory Manual: Lab Activities, pp. 97–104
Workbook/Video Manual: Video Activities, pp. 259–262; pp. 295–296
WB/VM/LM Answer Key
Instructor's Resource CD-ROM [IRCD-ROM]:
Instructor's Resource Manual [IRM] (Textbook Audioscript; Lab Audioscript; Videoscript; **Roman-photo** Translations; **Vocabulaire supplémentaire**; **Feuilles d'activités**; Info Gap Activities; **Le zapping** TV clip transcription; **Essayez!** and **Mise en pratique** answers); Transparencies #54, #55, #56; Testing Program, pp. 97–104; Test Files;
Testing Program MP3s; Test Generator
Lab MP3s
Textbook MP3s
Video CD-ROM
Video on DVD
espaces.vhlcentral.com

Leçon 25

You will learn how to...
- make and receive phone calls
- talk about your goals

Au bureau

Section Goals

In this section, students will learn and practice vocabulary related to:
- the workplace
- job interviews
- phone calls

Instructional Resources
*IRCD-ROM: Transparency #54; IRM (**Vocabulaire supplémentaire; Mise en pratique** answers; Textbook Audioscript; Lab Audioscript)*
Textbook MP3s
WB/VM: Workbook, pp. 169–170
Lab Manual, p. 97
Lab MP3s
WB/VM/LM Answer Key
espaces.vhlcentral.com: activities, downloads, reference tools

Suggestions

- Tell students to look over the new vocabulary and identify the cognates.
- Use **Transparency #54**. Point out objects and describe what the people are doing. Examples: **Il patiente. C'est une employée. Il passe un entretien.**
- Point out that **un salaire modeste** is a figurative rather than literal equivalent of *low salary*. One might also say **un bas salaire**.
- Point out the difference between **un poste** (*a job*) and **la poste** (*the post office*).
- Explain that **une lettre de motivation** is a letter a job candidate writes in response to a want ad or when introducing him or herself to a prospective employer.
- Point out the **Attention!** Explain that **chercher** is a general term, while **rechercher** refers to more thorough, methodical research.
- Tell students that **les petites annonces** are short, telegraphic-style ads, usually for low-level or temporary jobs rather than career positions.
- Additional vocabulary for this lesson can be found in the **Vocabulaire supplémentaire** in the IRM on the IRCD-ROM.

Vocabulaire

chercher un/du travail	*to look for work*
embaucher	*to hire*
faire des projets	*to make plans*
obtenir	*to get, to obtain*
postuler	*to apply*
prendre (un) rendez-vous	*to make an appointment*
trouver un/du travail	*to find a job*
un(e) candidat(e)	*candidate, applicant*
un conseil	*advice*
un domaine	*field*
une entreprise	*firm, business*
une expérience professionnelle	*professional experience*
une formation	*education; training*
une lettre de recommandation	*letter of reference/ recommendation*
une lettre de motivation	*letter of application*
une mention	*distinction*
un métier	*profession*
un poste	*position*
une référence	*reference*
un salaire (élevé, modeste)	*(high, low) salary*
un(e) spécialiste	*specialist*
un stage	*internship; professional training*
appeler	*to call*
laisser un message	*to leave a message*
l'appareil (m.)	*telephone*
une télécarte	*phone card*
Qui est à l'appareil?	*Who's calling please?*
C'est de la part de qui?	*On behalf of whom?*
C'est M./Mme/Mlle... (à l'appareil.)	*It's Mr./Mrs./Miss... (on the phone.)*
Ne quittez pas.	*Please hold.*

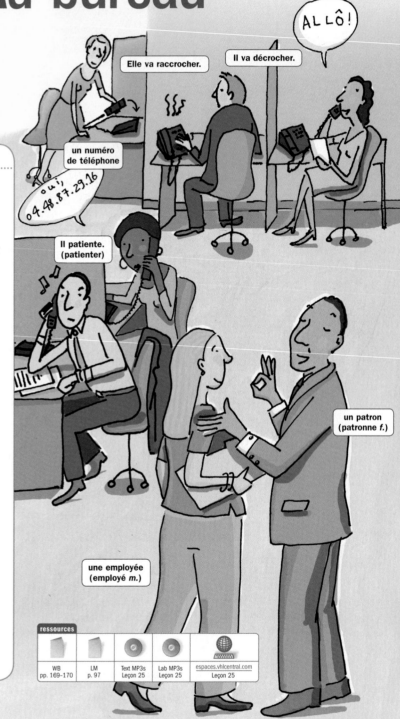

ressources

WB pp. 169–170	LM p. 97	Text MP3s Leçon 25	Lab MP3s Leçon 25	espaces.vhlcentral.com Leçon 25

OPTIONS

Extra Practice For additional practice, ask students these questions. **1. Quel est votre numéro de téléphone? 2. Quels projets avez-vous faits pour votre carrière? 3. Préférez-vous travailler dans une grande entreprise ou dans une petite compagnie? Pourquoi? 4. Est-il plus important d'avoir un salaire élevé ou un métier qu'on aime bien? 5. Avez-vous déjà écrit une lettre de motivation?**

Game Divide the class into two teams. Have a spelling bee using vocabulary words from the **Contextes**. Pronounce each word, use it in a sentence, and then say the word again. Tell students that they must spell the words in French and include all diacritical marks.

Attention!

Note the difference in the usage and meaning of **chercher** and **rechercher**.

Il cherche du travail.
He is looking for work.

Cette compagnie recherche un chef du personnel.
This company is looking for a human resources director.

Mise en pratique

1 Écoutez Armand et Michel cherchent du travail. Écoutez leur conversation et répondez ensuite aux questions.

1. Quel genre de travail Armand recherche-t-il?
   Armand recherche un travail d'assistant.
2. Où est-ce qu'Armand a lu l'annonce?
   Armand a lu l'annonce dans le journal ce matin.
3. Quel(s) document(s) faut-il envoyer pour le stage?
   Il faut envoyer un C.V. accompagné d'une lettre de motivation.
4. Qui est M. Dupont?
   M. Dupont est le chef du personnel.
5. Que doit faire Armand pour obtenir un entretien?
   Armand doit appeler M. Dupont pour prendre (un) rendez-vous.
6. Quel est le domaine professionnel de Michel?
   Son domaine professionnel est l'informatique.
7. Pourquoi Michel a-t-il des difficultés à trouver du travail?
   Michel a des difficultés à trouver du travail parce qu'il ne sait pas où postuler ni comment obtenir un entretien.
8. Comment est-ce qu'Armand aide Michel?
   Armand trouve deux entreprises qui recherchent des spécialistes dans le domaine de Michel.

2 Complétez Complétez les phrases suivantes avec le verbe de la liste qui convient le mieux. N'oubliez pas de faire les accords nécessaires.

appeler	lire les annonces	postuler
décrocher	métier	prendre (un) rendez-vous
conseil	obtenir	raccrocher
embaucher	passer un entretien	salaire
laisser des messages	patienter	trouver un/du travail

1. Quand on cherche du travail, il faut _lire les annonces_ tous les jours.
2. Il est toujours plus facile de trouver un _métier_ intéressant quand on a une bonne formation.
3. Le téléphone sonne. Est-ce que tu peux _décrocher_, s'il te plaît?
4. Il y a peu d'entreprises qui _embauchent_ en ce moment. L'économie ne va pas très bien.
5. —Bonjour, Madame. Je vous _appelle_ pour _prendre (un) rendez-vous_.
   —Vous pouvez venir lundi 15, à 16h00?
6. J'ai envoyé mon C.V. J'espère qu'ils vont m'appeler pour _passer un entretien_.
7. _Patientez_ quelques minutes, s'il vous plaît. Madame Benoît va bientôt arriver.
8. Il _a raccroché_ parce que la ligne n'était pas bonne.
9. Sophie vient juste de _trouver un travail_. Elle va organiser une petite fête vendredi pour célébrer son nouveau poste.
10. Une messagerie permet de _laisser des messages_.

3 Corrigez Lisez les phrases suivantes et dites si elles sont **vraies** ou **fausses**. Corrigez les phrases qui ne sont pas cohérentes.

1. Il faut décrocher le combiné avant de composer un numéro de téléphone.
   Vrai.
2. Quand on appelle d'une cabine téléphonique, on utilise des billets.
   Faux. Quand on appelle d'une cabine téléphonique, on utilise une télécarte.
3. Quand on est embauché, on perd son travail.
   Faux. Quand on est embauché, on trouve un travail.
4. Quand on travaille, on reçoit un salaire à la fin de chaque mois.
   Vrai.
5. À la fin d'un C.V. américain, il ne faut pas oublier de mentionner ses références.
   Vrai.
6. Pour savoir qui vous appelle au téléphone, vous demandez: «Ne quittez pas.»
   Faux. Vous demandez:«Qui est à l'appareil?»
7. Un(e) patron(ne) dirige (*manages*) une entreprise ou des employés.
   Vrai.
8. Avant d'obtenir un poste, il faut souvent passer une entreprise.
   Faux. Il faut souvent passer un entretien.
9. Quand on travaille dans une entreprise, on est un(e) employé(e).
   Vrai.

1 Tapescript MICHEL: Alors Armand, est-ce que tu as trouvé un travail pour l'été?
ARMAND: Chut, je suis au téléphone!
M: Oh, je suis désolé.
A: Allô. Oui, bonjour, Madame. C'est Armand Lemaire à l'appareil. Je vous appelle au sujet de l'annonce que j'ai lue dans le journal ce matin.
LA SECRÉTAIRE: Oui, très bien. Pour le stage, il faut envoyer votre C.V. accompagné d'une lettre de motivation.
A: En fait, je n'appelle pas pour le stage, mais pour le poste d'assistant.
S: Oh, excusez-moi. Dans ce cas, il vous faut appeler Monsieur Dupont, notre chef du personnel, pour prendre un rendez-vous et obtenir un entretien. Ne quittez pas. Je vous le passe. (*Musique*) Je suis désolée, mais ça ne répond pas. Je vous passe sa messagerie. Vous pouvez laisser un message avec votre numéro de téléphone.
A: Je vous remercie, Madame.
Plus tard...
M: Voilà, tu n'as plus besoin de chercher du travail! Je suis sûr qu'ils vont t'embaucher!
A: Je préfère attendre. Et toi, comment ça va, ta recherche de travail?
M: Je ne sais pas vraiment où postuler et je ne sais pas comment obtenir un entretien.
A: Avec ta formation et ton expérience professionnelle, je pense que tu trouveras facilement un travail dans l'informatique. Tiens, regarde le journal, cette compagnie et cette autre entreprise-là recherchent des spécialistes dans ton domaine. En plus, je suis certain qu'elles offrent un bon salaire. Tiens, prends le combiné et appelle-les.
(On Textbook MP3s)

1 Suggestion Go over the answers with the class. If students have difficulty, play the conversation again.

2 Expansion Have students write sentences with the unused words from the list: **conseil, obtenir, postuler,** and **salaire**.

3 Suggestion Have students check their answers with a classmate.

OPTIONS

Pairs Write these expressions for circumlocution on the board: **C'est quand on..., C'est ce qu'on fait quand..., C'est un objet/une machine qu'on utilise pour..., C'est quelqu'un qui....** Then have pairs of students write definitions for the following vocabulary words. **1. chercher du travail 2. postuler 3. un appareil 4. un patron 5. raccrocher 6. un entretien 7. une télécarte 8. un spécialiste**

Have pairs get together with another pair of students and take turns reading their definitions and guessing the words. Ask each group to choose their best definition and write it on the board for the whole class to guess.

4 Suggestions
- Tell students to jot down notes during the interviews.
- After completing the interviews, have pairs get together with another pair and report what they learned about their partner.

5 Suggestion If time is limited, have students role-play the conversations in groups of six. Each pair will act out one of the conversations instead of all three.

6 Suggestions
- Before beginning the activity, ask volunteers to read each ad aloud.
- Have the class brainstorm questions a manager might ask. Write the questions on the board.
- Model the activity by role-playing one of the situations with a student. Remind students to use appropriate greetings.

7 Suggestions
- Before beginning this activity, write a list of professional fields on the board. Examples: **les sciences, les affaires, l'éducation,** and **le commerce**.
- Have the class brainstorm questions an advisor might ask in this situation. Write the questions on the board.

Communication

4 Répondez **Avec un(e) partenaire, posez-vous les questions suivantes à tour de rôle.** Answers will vary.

1. Est-ce que tu as fait des projets d'avenir? Quels sont-ils?
2. Après tes études, dans quel domaine est-ce que tu vas chercher du travail?
3. As-tu déjà fait un stage en entreprise? Comment était-ce?
4. As-tu une expérience professionnelle? Dans quel(s) domaine(s)?
5. As-tu déjà répondu à des annonces pour trouver un travail? Est-ce qu'on t'a embauché(e)?
6. À ton avis, qu'est-ce qui est le plus important pour réussir un entretien d'embauche?
7. Pour qui imagines-tu pouvoir écrire une bonne lettre de recommandation un jour?
8. As-tu déjà préparé ton curriculum vitæ? Quels types d'informations as-tu listées?

5 Les conversations **Avec un(e) partenaire, complétez et remettez dans l'ordre les conversations suivantes. Ensuite, jouez les scènes devant la classe.**

Conversation 1

3 —C'est Mlle Grandjean à l'appareil. Est-ce que vous pouvez me passer le chef du personnel, s'il vous plaît?
1 —__Allô__. Bonjour, Monsieur.
2 —Bonjour. __Qui est à l'appareil?__?
4 —__Ne quittez pas__. Je vous le passe.

Conversation 2

3 —Tu n'as donc pas vu __le poste__ que la compagnie Petit et Fils offre.
1 —Est-ce que tu __as lu les annonces__ ce matin?
4 —Non, mais je connais cette entreprise et elle n'est pas dans __mon domaine__.
2 —Non, je n'ai pas encore acheté le journal.

Conversation 3

2 —Non, appelle plutôt son portable.
4 —C'est le 06-22-28-80-83.
5 —Oh, encore sa __messagerie__! Elle ne décroche jamais.
3 —Tu as raison. Quel est son __numéro de téléphone__?
1 —Stéphanie ne __décroche__ pas. Je vais lui __laisser un message__.

6 Les petites annonces **Lisez les annonces suivantes et choisissez-en une. Avec un(e) partenaire, imaginez votre conversation avec le directeur de l'entreprise que vous avez sélectionnée. Vous devez parler de votre expérience professionnelle, de votre formation et de vos projets. Ensuite, choisissez une autre annonce et changez de rôle.** Answers will vary.

Nous recherchons des professionnels de la gestion. Première expérience ou expert(e) dans votre domaine, notre groupe vous offre d'intéressantes opportunités d'évolution. Retrouvez nos postes sur www.comptaparis.fr/métiers.

France Conseil recherche un analyste financier bilingue anglais. Vous travaillez avec nos bureaux à l'étranger pour développer les projets du département. De formation supérieure, vous avez une expérience de chef de projet de 2 à 4 ans. Nous contacter à: France Conseil, 80, rue du Faubourg Saint-Antoine, 75012 Paris

SARLA recherche un(e) assistant(e) commercial(e) trilingue anglais et espagnol avec expérience en informatique (logiciels et Internet). **Envoyer C.V. et lettre de motivation à SARLA, 155, avenue de Gerland, BP 72, 69007 Lyon**

7 Le poste idéal **Vous souhaitez travailler à l'étranger pendant les vacances d'été, mais vous ne savez pas par où commencer. Vous allez donc dans un Centre d'Information Jeunesse pour rencontrer un conseiller/une conseillère (*advisor*) qui va déterminer le pays et le domaine professionnel les mieux adaptés. Travaillez à deux et échangez les rôles avec votre partenaire.** Answers will vary.

OPTIONS

Extra Practice Brainstorm a list of professions learned in earlier lessons. Have students pick one or randomly assign professions to students. Tell students to write an advertisement in search of someone in that profession, using the ads in **Activité 6** as models.

Pairs Have students role-play a phone call. Tell pairs to sit back-to-back to simulate the phone conversation. Then give them the following situation: The person they want to speak to is not there, so the caller should leave a message. Tell students to use as much phone-related vocabulary as possible in their conversations.

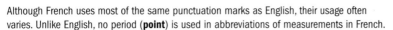

Les sons et les lettres

NATIONAL STANDARDS comparisons

La ponctuation française

Although French uses most of the same punctuation marks as English, their usage often varies. Unlike English, no period (**point**) is used in abbreviations of measurements in French.

200 m (*meters*) **30 min** (*minutes*) **25 cl** (*centiliters*) **500 gr** (*grams*)

In other abbreviations, a period is used only if the last letter of the abbreviation is different from the last letter of the word it represents.

Mme Bonaire = Madame Bonaire **M. Bonaire = Monsieur Bonaire**

French dates are written with the day before the month, so if the month is spelled out, no punctuation is needed. When using digits only, use periods to separate them.

le 25 février 1954 **25.2.1954** **le 15 août 2006** **15.8.2006**

Notice that a comma (**une virgule**) is not used before the last item in a series or list.

Lucie parle français, anglais et allemand. *Lucie speaks French, English, and German.*

Generally, in French, a direct quotation is enclosed in **guillemets**. Notice that a colon (**deux points**), not a comma, is used before the quotation.

Charlotte a dit: «Appelle-moi!» **Marc a demandé: «Qui est à l'appareil?»**

Réécrivez Ajoutez la ponctuation et remplacez les mots en italiques par leurs abréviations.

1. Depuis le *21 mars 1964 Madame* Pagny habite à 500 *mètres* de chez moi
   Depuis le 21.03.1964, Mme Pagny habite à 500 m de chez moi.
2. Ce matin j'ai acheté 2 *kilos* de poires *Monsieur* Florent m'a dit Lucien tu as très bien fait
   Ce matin, j'ai acheté 2 kg de poires. M. Florent m'a dit: «Lucien, tu as très bien fait!»

Corrigez Lisez le paragraphe et ajoutez la bonne ponctuation et les majuscules.

hier michel le frère de ma meilleure amie sylvie m'a téléphoné il a dit carole on va fêter l'anniversaire de sylvie le samedi 13 novembre est-ce que tu peux venir téléphone-moi

Answers may vary. Possible answer: Hier, Michel, le frère de ma meilleure amie, Sylvie, m'a téléphoné. Il a dit: «Carole, on va fêter l'anniversaire de Sylvie, le samedi 13 novembre. Est-ce que tu peux venir? Téléphone-moi!»

Dictons Répétez les dictons à voix haute.

Ne parle jamais des princes: si tu en dis du bien, tu mens; si tu en dis du mal, tu t'exposes.[2]

[1] Time is money.
[2] Never talk about princes. If you talk nicely about them, you lie. If you say bad things about them, you reveal yourself.

ressources

LM p. 98	Lab MP3s Leçon 25	espaces.vhlcentral.com Leçon 25

Section Goals

In this section, students will learn about French punctuation.

Instructional Resources
Lab Manual, p. 98
Lab MP3s
WB/VM/LM Answer Key
IRCD-ROM: IRM (Textbook Audioscript; Lab Audioscript)
espaces.vhlcentral.com: activities, downloads, reference tools

Suggestions

- Tell students that the semi-colon (**le point-virgule**) is used much more often in French than in English. They may also see a space before a colon (**deux-points**), a question mark (**un point d'interrogation**), or an exclamation mark (**un point d'exclamation**).
- Remind students that phone numbers are written in sets of two digits separated by periods or spaces in French. Examples: **01.23.45.67.99** or **01 23 45 67 99**.
- Review the use of a comma (**une virgule**) for decimals and the use a period or a space instead of a comma to separate groups of three digits. Examples: **10,5** = 10.5, **1.000.000** or **1 000 000** = 1,000,000.
- Explain that the lines of different speakers in a dialogue may be preceded by an em dash (**un tiret**):
  —Tu viens avec moi?
  —Non, je reste chez moi.
  —Avez-vous déjà parlé à la patronne?
  —Oui, j'ai un rendez-vous avec elle demain.

Dictons The saying **«Le temps, c'est de l'argent»** is based on an English proverb (*Time is money*).

OPTIONS

Extra Practice Use these sentences for additional practice with French punctuation. Have students replace the italicized words with abbreviations. **1. Mon anniversaire c'est le *17 avril 1988* 2. Est-ce que vous avez bu 75 *centilitres* de lait 3. Caroline a visité le musée du Louvre l'Arc de Triomphe et la tour Eiffel 4. L'homme a crié** (*shouted*) **Au secours**

Extra Practice Teach students this French tongue-twister that models some French punctuation conventions.
—Ta tante t'attend.
—J'ai tant de tantes. Quelle tante m'attend?
—Ta tante Antoinette t'attend.

Section Goals

In this section, students will learn functional phrases for talking about tests, future plans, and successes.

Instructional Resources
WB/VM: Video Manual, pp. 259–260
WB/VM/LM Answer Key
Video CD-ROM
Video on DVD
IRCD-ROM: IRM (Videoscript; ***Roman-photo*** *Translations)*
espaces.vhlcentral.com: activities, downloads, reference tools

Video Recap: Leçon 24
Before doing this **Roman-photo**, review the previous one with this activity.

1. Que cherche le touriste? (le bureau de poste)
2. À qui demande-t-il des indications? (d'abord à M. Hulot, puis à David et à Rachid et finalement à Stéphane)
3. Qui lui donne de bonnes indications? (Stéphane)
4. Où est le bureau de poste? (derrière la fontaine, la Rotonde)

Video Synopsis
Stéphane and Astrid just took their **bac**. Stéphane tells Astrid he wants to study architecture at the **Université de Marseille**. She plans to study medicine at the **Université de Bordeaux**. Stéphane calls his mother to tell her the exam is over. At **Le P'tit Bistrot**, a young woman enquires about a job. Unbeknownst to Valérie, Michèle has an interview for a receptionist's job at Dupont.

Suggestions
- Have students predict what the episode will be about based on the video stills.
- Have students scan the captions to find sentences related to jobs and future plans.
- After reading the **Roman-photo**, have students summarize the episode.

Le bac

PERSONNAGES

Astrid

Jeune femme

Michèle

Stéphane

Valérie

Après le bac...
STÉPHANE Alors, Astrid, tu penses avoir réussi le bac?
ASTRID Franchement, je crois que oui. Et toi?
STÉPHANE Je ne sais pas, c'était plutôt difficile. Mais au moins, c'est fini, et ça, c'est le plus important pour moi!

ASTRID Qu'est-ce que tu vas faire une fois que tu auras le bac?
STÉPHANE Aucune idée, Astrid. J'ai fait une demande à l'université pour étudier l'architecture.
ASTRID Vraiment? Laquelle?
STÉPHANE L'université de Marseille, mais je n'ai pas encore de réponse. Alors, Mademoiselle Je-pense-à-tout, tu sais déjà ce que tu feras?

ASTRID Bien sûr! J'irai à l'université de Bordeaux et dès que je réussirai l'examen de première année, je continuerai en médecine.
STÉPHANE Ah oui? Pour moi, les études, c'est fini pour l'instant. On vient juste de passer le bac, il faut fêter ça! C'est loin, la rentrée.

VALÉRIE Mais bien sûr que je m'inquiète! C'est normal.
STÉPHANE Tu sais, finalement, ce n'était pas si difficile.
VALÉRIE Ah bon? Tu sais quand tu auras les résultats?
STÉPHANE Ils seront affichés dans deux semaines.
VALÉRIE En attendant, il faut prendre des décisions pour préparer l'avenir.

STÉPHANE L'avenir! L'avenir! Vous n'avez que ce mot à la bouche, Astrid et toi. Oh maman, je suis tellement content aujourd'hui. Pour le moment, je voudrais juste faire des projets pour le week-end.
VALÉRIE D'accord, Stéphane. Je comprends. Tu rentres maintenant?
STÉPHANE Oui, maman. J'arrive dans quinze minutes.

Au P'tit Bistrot...
JEUNE FEMME Bonjour, Madame. Je cherche un travail pour cet été. Est-ce que vous embauchez en ce moment?
VALÉRIE Eh bien, c'est possible. L'été en général nous avons beaucoup de clients étrangers. Est-ce que vous parlez anglais?
JEUNE FEMME Oui, c'est ce que j'étudie à l'université.

ACTIVITÉS

1 Complétez Complétez les phrases suivantes.

1. Stéphane et Astrid viennent de passer ___le bac___.
2. Stéphane doit téléphoner à ___sa mère/Valérie___.
3. Astrid prête une ___télécarte___ à Stéphane.
4. Aujourd'hui, Stéphane est très ___content/heureux___.
5. Il aura les résultats du bac dans ___deux semaines___.
6. Stéphane ne veut pas parler de l' ___avenir___.
7. La jeune femme étudie ___l'anglais___ à l'université.
8. Valérie dit que de nombreux clients du P'tit Bistrot sont ___étrangers___.
9. ___Michèle___ est en train (*in the process*) de chercher un nouveau travail.
10. Elle ne veut pas demander ___une lettre de recommandation___ à Valérie.

OPTIONS

Avant de regarder la vidéo Before viewing the video, have students work in pairs and brainstorm a list of things a student might say after taking a difficult exam and what a parent might say to a son or daughter after the exam.

Regarder la vidéo Photocopy the videoscript from the IRM. Then white out words related to tests, jobs, and other key vocabulary in order to create a master for a cloze activity. Distribute the photocopies and tell students to fill in the missing information as they watch the video.

Stéphane et Astrid ont passé l'examen.

4

STÉPHANE Écoute, je dois téléphoner à ma mère. Je peux emprunter ta télécarte, s'il te plaît?
ASTRID Oui, bien sûr. Tiens.
STÉPHANE Merci.
ASTRID Bon... Je dois rentrer chez moi. Ma famille m'attend. Au revoir.
STÉPHANE Salut.

5

Stéphane appelle sa mère...
VALÉRIE Le P'tit Bistrot. Bonjour.
STÉPHANE Allô.
VALÉRIE Allô. Qui est à l'appareil?
STÉPHANE Maman, c'est moi!
VALÉRIE Stéphane! Alors, comment ça a été? Tu penses avoir réussi?
STÉPHANE Oui, bien sûr, maman. Ne t'inquiète pas!

9

VALÉRIE Et vous avez déjà travaillé dans un café?
JEUNE FEMME Eh bien, l'été dernier j'ai travaillé à la brasserie les Deux Escargots. Vous pouvez les appeler pour obtenir une référence si vous le désirez. Voici leur numéro de téléphone.
VALÉRIE Au revoir, et peut-être à bientôt!

10

Près de la terrasse...
MICHÈLE J'ai un rendez-vous pour passer un entretien avec l'entreprise Dupont... C'est la compagnie qui offre ce poste de réceptionniste... Tu es fou, je ne peux pas demander une lettre de recommandation à Madame Forestier... Bien sûr, nous irons dîner pour fêter ça dès que j'aurai un nouveau travail.

Expressions utiles

Talking about tests

- **Tu penses avoir réussi le bac?**
  *Do you think you passed the **bac**?*
- **Je crois que oui.**
  I think so.
- **Qu'est-ce que tu vas faire une fois que tu auras le bac?**
  *What are you going to do once you have the **bac**?*
- **Tu sais quand tu auras les résultats?**
  Do you know when you will have the results?
- **Ils seront affichés dans deux semaines.**
  They will be posted in two weeks.

Enjoying successes

- **L'avenir! Vous n'avez que ce mot à la bouche.**
  The future! That's all you talk about.
- **Je suis tellement content(e) aujourd'hui.**
  I am so happy today.
- **Pour le moment, je voudrais juste faire des projets pour le week-end.**
  For the time being, I would only like to make plans for the weekend.
- **Nous irons dîner pour fêter ça dès que j'aurai un nouveau travail.**
  We will go to dinner to celebrate as soon as I have a new job.

Additional vocabulary

- **laquelle**
  which (f.)

2 **Répondez** Répondez aux questions suivantes par des phrases complètes.

1. Quels sont les projets d'avenir d'Astrid? Elle ira à l'université de Bordeaux et étudiera la médecine.
2. Qu'est-ce que Stéphane veut faire l'année prochaine? Il veut étudier l'architecture à l'université de Marseille.
3. Est-ce que les projets d'Astrid et de Stéphane sont certains? (Supposez que les deux auront le bac.) Les projets d'Astrid sont certains, mais Stéphane n'a pas encore de réponse de l'université de Marseille.
4. Quel est le projet de Michèle pour l'avenir? Michèle veut travailler comme réceptionniste pour une compagnie.
5. Son projet est-il certain? Non, son projet n'est pas certain: elle doit passer l'entretien d'embauche d'abord. Elle ne sait pas encore s'ils vont lui donner le poste.

3 **À vous!** La jeune femme qui veut travailler au P'tit Bistrot rencontre Michèle. Elle veut savoir comment est le travail et comment est Valérie comme patronne. Michèle, qui n'est pas vraiment heureuse au P'tit Bistrot en ce moment, lui raconte tout. Avec un(e) camarade de classe, composez le dialogue et jouez la scène devant la classe.

ressources

VM	V CD-ROM	espaces.vhlcentral.com
pp. 259-260	Leçon 25	Leçon 25

ACTIVITÉS

Expressions utiles
- Model the pronunciation of the **Expressions utiles** and have students repeat them.
- As you work through the list, point out **le futur** with **dès que** and **quand**. Also point out the use of the interrogative pronoun **laquelle** in caption 2. Tell students that these grammar points will be formally presented in the **Structures** section.
- Respond briefly to students' questions about these points.
- Remind students that **le futur** is a grammatical term referring to the future tense. To talk about the future as in time, they should use **l'avenir**.

1 Suggestion Have volunteers read the completed sentences aloud.

1 Expansion Have students write additional sentences to fill in the gaps in the storyline.

2 Suggestion Have volunteers write the answers to the questions on the board. Then go over them with the class.

2 Expansion Ask students personalized questions. Allow students to invent answers if they prefer. Examples: **1. Quels sont vos projets d'avenir? 2. Que voulez-vous faire l'année prochaine? 3. Est-ce que vos projets sont sûrs?**

3 Suggestion If time is limited, this activity may be assigned as homework. Assign each student a role (Michèle or the young woman). Have them prepare their parts at home, then allow partners time to work together before presenting their conversation to the class.

OPTIONS

Extra Practice Ask students yes/no questions based on the **Roman-photo**. Tell them to answer **Je crois que oui** or **Je crois que non**. Examples: **1. Stéphane a-t-il réussi au bac? 2. Stéphane va-t-il étudier l'architecture à l'université? 3. Astrid va-t-elle étudier la médecine? 4. La jeune femme va-t-elle être embauchée au P'tit Bistrot? 5. Michèle va-t-elle trouver un autre travail?**

Small Groups Have students work in groups of three. Tell them to write a résumé for a famous person. Write this format on the board for students to follow: **Objectif(s) professionnel(s), Formation, Expérience professionnelle,** and **Références**. Then have volunteers read the résumé to the class without saying the person's name. The class should try to guess whose résumé it is.

Section Goals

In this section, students will:
- learn about phone usage in France
- learn some common terms used in text messages
- read about well-paying jobs in the francophone world
- read about **les artisans** in France

Instructional Resources
espaces.vhlcentral.com: activities, downloads, reference tools

Culture à la loupe

Avant la lecture
- Have students look at the photos and describe what they see.
- Take a quick class survey to find out how many students use public phones, phone cards, cell phones, and text messaging. Tally the results on the board.

Lecture
- Point out the **Coup de main**. Tell students that the commonly used term **SMS** stands for *short message service*.
- Point out the statistics chart. Ask students what information it shows. (the percentage of French people who had cell phones from 1998–2004)

Après la lecture Have students compare the French usage of telephones and phone cards with their own usage based on the results in the survey in **Avant la lecture**.

1 Suggestion Have students read the completed sentences aloud.

CULTURE À LA LOUPE

Le téléphone en France

Pour téléphoner en France, on peut utiliser une cabine publique avec une télécarte. Les télécartes sont vendues dans les bureaux de tabac°, à la poste et dans tous les endroits qui affichent° «Télécartes en vente ici». Si vous devez téléphoner avec de la monnaie, il vaut mieux° essayer un café ou un hôtel. Les cabines publiques à pièces sont très rares.

Les Français sont surtout accros° à leur téléphone portable. Aujourd'hui, plus de 40 millions de personnes sont abonnées°. Soixante-trois pour cent d'entre elles choisissent le forfait° et payent un tarif mensuel°. Ce type d'abonnement° exige° d'avoir un compte bancaire en France. Sinon, on a la possibilité de choisir des cartes prépayées ou de louer un portable pour une courte période.

Comme les appels sont chers, les gens communiquent beaucoup par SMS°. En moyenne, chaque abonné envoie 24 SMS par mois. Ces messages sont écrits dans un langage particulier, qui permet de taper° plus vite. Le langage SMS est très phonétique et joue avec le son des lettres et des chiffres°. Tous les jeunes l'utilisent. Les jeunes aiment aussi beaucoup télécharger les logos et sonneries° du moment. En France, le marché de la téléphonie mobile a beaucoup d'avenir.

bureaux de tabac *tobacco shops* **affichent** *post* **il vaut mieux** *it is better* **accros** *addicted* **sont abonnées** *have a subscription* **forfait** *package* **tarif mensuel** *monthly fee* **abonnement** *subscription* **exige** *requires* **SMS** *text message* **taper** *type* **chiffres** *numbers* **sonneries** *ringtones*

Coup de main

A cell phone has many names in French: **téléphone, portable, GSM, mobile.**

A text message may be called an **SMS** or a **texto.**

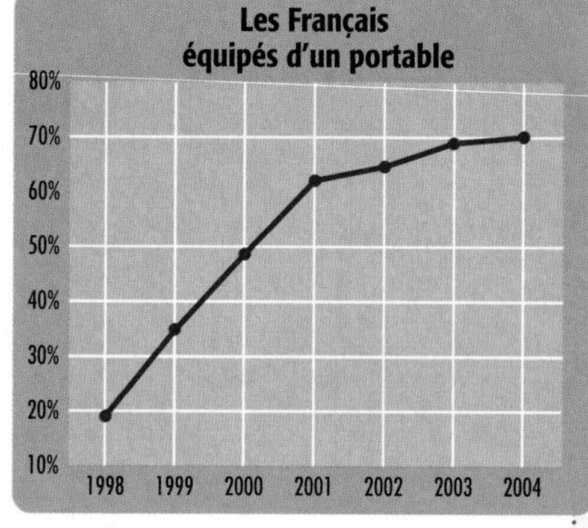

ACTIVITÉS

1 Complétez Donnez le début ou la suite de chaque phrase, d'après le texte et le tableau. Answers may vary. Possible answers provided.

1. Pour téléphoner en France, on peut utiliser... une cabine publique avec une télécarte.
2. ... dans les bureaux de tabac, à la poste et dans tous les endroits qui affichent «Télécartes en vente ici». Les télécartes sont vendues
3. Si vous devez téléphoner avec de la monnaie, il vaut mieux... essayer un café ou un hôtel.
4. ... des abonnés choisissent le forfait. 63%
5. En moyenne, chaque abonné envoie... 24 SMS par mois.
6. ... joue avec le son des lettres et des chiffres. Le langage SMS
7. Les jeunes aiment aussi... télécharger des logos et des sonneries.
8. En 1998, 19% seulement des Français... possédaient un portable.
9. ... sont d'autres noms pour désigner le portable. Téléphone, GSM et mobile
10. Un SMS s'appelle aussi... un texto.

OPTIONS

La télécarte When purchasing **une télécarte**, it is less expensive per unit (**unité**) to buy **une grande** for 120 units than **une petite** for 50 units. The disposable **télécarte** works without a code. The French phone booth has two advantages: the quick, efficient insertion system for **la télécarte** and the caller's ability to view the remaining units on the phone card while talking on the phone.

Pairs Have students work in pairs. Tell them to take turns quizzing each other about the information on cell phones in the chart. Write a sample question on the board for students to use as a model. Example: **En quelle année est-ce que 50 pour cent des Français étaient équipés d'un portable? (2000)**

LE FRANÇAIS QUOTIDIEN

Le SMS, C pratik!

A+	*À plus (tard).*
Bap	*Bon après-midi.*
C pa 5pa	*C'est pas sympa!*
Dak	*D'accord.*
GT o 6né	*J'étais au ciné.*
Je t'M	*Je t'aime.*
Jenémar	*J'en ai marre!*
Kestufé	*Qu'est-ce que tu fais?*
Komencava	*Comment ça va?*
MDR	*Mort de rire!*

LE MONDE FRANCOPHONE

Comment gagner sa vie

Voici des métiers et des secteurs où on peut gagner sa vie dans le monde francophone.

Quelques exemples de métiers bien payés

En France avocat(e)
À Haïti prêtre°
Au Sénégal joueur de football professionnel
En Suisse banquier d'affaires

Quelques exemples de secteurs lucratifs

En Belgique l'industrie chimique, du pétrole
Au Québec l'industrie du papier
En Suisse les banques et les assurances
En Tunisie le tourisme

prêtre *priest*

PORTRAIT

Les artisans

L'artisanat en France emploie 2,3 millions de personnes. On le décrit souvent comme «la plus grande entreprise de France». Bouchers, plombiers, fleuristes, bijoutiers... les artisans travaillent dans plus de 300 secteurs d'activité différents. Leurs entreprises sont de petite taille, avec moins de dix employés. Les artisans sont plus nombreux dans les villes, mais ils jouent un grand rôle en milieu rural. En plus d°'y apporter les services nécessaires, ils aident à créer le «lien social°». Artisans et artisans d'art sont considérés comme les gardiens° de la tradition française et de son savoir-faire°, qu'ils se transmettent depuis des générations, grâce au° système de l'apprentissage°.

En plus de *In addition to* **lien social** *social cohesion* **gardiens** *guardians* **savoir-faire** *expertise* **grâce au** *thanks to* **apprentissage** *apprenticeship*

SUR INTERNET

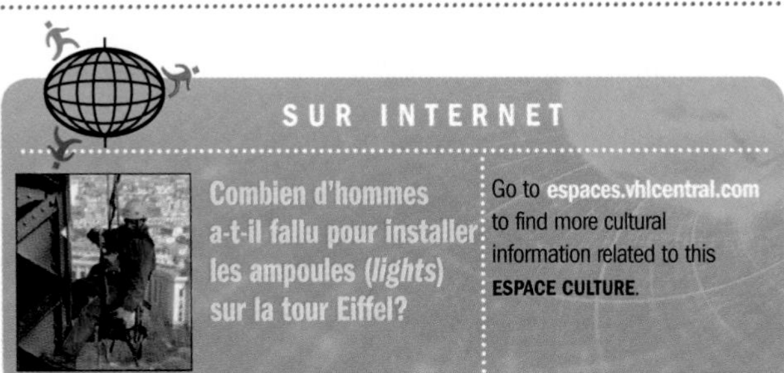

Combien d'hommes a-t-il fallu pour installer les ampoules (*lights*) sur la tour Eiffel?

Go to **espaces.vhlcentral.com** to find more cultural information related to this **ESPACE CULTURE**.

ACTIVITÉS

2 Complétez Complétez les phrases.

1. L'artisanat en France emploie 2,3 millions de personnes.
2. Answer will vary. Possible answer: Bouchers, plombiers, fleuristes, bijoutiers sont des exemples d'artisans.
3. Artisans et artisans d'art sont les gardiens de la tradition française et de son savoir-faire.
4. Le savoir-faire des artisans est transmis grâce au système de l'apprentissage.
5. Au Sénégal, joueur de football professionnel est un métier bien payé.
6. En Tunisie, le tourisme est un secteur lucratif.

3 Échange de textos Vous et un(e) partenaire allez faire connaissance par SMS. Préparez un dialogue en français facile, puis transformez-le en messages SMS. Comparez ensuite votre conversation SMS à la conversation d'un autre groupe. Soyez prêts à les présenter devant la classe.

ressources

espaces.vhlcentral.com Leçon 25

Le français quotidien
- Model the pronunciation of both columns so students can hear the sound-symbol correspondence between the abbreviations and the actual expressions.
- Point out that **après-midi** is one of the few words in French that can be either masculine or feminine. This book refers to it as masculine.

Portrait
- It is a point of pride in France to work as an **artisan** and to sell something one can label **artisanal**.
- Ask students: **Considérez-vous qu'un plombier est un artisan? Pourquoi? Et un fleuriste? Un boucher? Un bijoutier?**

Le monde francophone Ask students: **Quels métiers ou secteurs de la liste sont bien/mal payés aux États-Unis? Pourquoi?**

2 Expansion For additional practice, give students these items. **7. Au Québec ____ est un secteur lucratif. (l'industrie du papier) 8. Si on veut bien gagner sa vie en tant que prêtre, on peut vivre ____. (à Haïti)**

3 Expansion Collect the text messages, choose a few, and write them on the board or a transparency. Tell the class to write the messages in standard French.

OPTIONS

Les artisans The French government supports small family businesses. Also, the general public is accustomed to walking from shop to shop to do errands for services and products that may cost more than in chain stores, but are consistently of higher quality.

Extra Practice Have students write five true/false statements based on the information on this page. Then have them get together with a classmate, and take turns reading their statements aloud and responding.

NATIONAL comparisons STANDARDS

Section Goals

In this section, students will learn the future tense with **quand** and **dès que**.

Instructional Resources
WB/VM: Workbook, pp. 171–172
Lab Manual, p. 99
Lab MP3s
WB/VM/LM Answer Key
*IRCD-ROM: IRM (**Essayez!** and **Mise en pratique** answers; **Feuilles d'activités**; Lab Audioscript)*
espaces.vhlcentral.com: activities, downloads, reference tools

Suggestions

- Quickly review the **futur simple**.
- Explain that the future tense with **quand** and **dès que** is for expressing an act that has not yet taken place. Point out that in English one usually uses the present tense after *when* or *as soon as*. Check for understanding by asking individuals to supply the future tense of phrases using **quand** and **dès que**. Example: **Quand je ____ (voyager) en Europe, je ____ (louer) une voiture. (voyagerai; louerai)** Contrast with the English equivalent *When I travel to Europe, I will rent a car.*
- Explain that expressions with **quand** and **dès que** that express generalities do not use the future tense. Example: **Quand on veut trouver un travail, on doit écrire une lettre de motivation.**
- Write two columns on the board: **quand** and **dès que**. Have students give example sentences using each clause in the present and future tenses.
- Model the use of **quand** and **dès que** by asking questions about what others will do when they begin looking for a job. Examples: **Où habiterez-vous quand vous chercherez un travail? Dès que vous obtiendrez un travail, que ferez-vous?**

Essayez! Before assigning this activity, have students underline the verbs in the sentences and identify their tense. Example: **1. on l'<u>embauchera</u>** (*future*)

25.1 *Le futur simple* with *quand* and *dès que*

Point de départ In **Leçon 24**, you learned how to form **le futur simple**, which is generally equivalent to the English future with *will*. You will now learn how to use **le futur simple** where English uses the present tense.

FUTURE FUTURE
Je me **mettrai** à chercher du travail, quand je n'**aurai** plus d'argent.
*I **will start** looking for work when I **don't have** any more money.*

Dès que je réussirai l'examen de première année, je continuerai en médecine.

Nous irons dîner pour célébrer dès que j'aurai un nouveau travail.

- In a clause that begins with **quand** or **dès que** (*as soon as*), use the future tense if the clause describes an event that will happen in the future.

Il enverra son C.V. **quand il aura** le temps.	Je posterai mon C.V. **dès que je pourrai**.
He will send his résumé when he has time.	*I will post my résumé as soon as I can.*

- If a clause with **quand** or **dès que** does not describe a future action, another tense may be used for the verb.

Quand avez-vous fait le stage?	La patronne nous parle **dès qu'elle arrive**.
When did you do the internship?	*The boss talks to us as soon as she arrives.*

Essayez! **Écrivez la forme correcte des verbes indiqués.**

1. On l'embauchera dès qu'on _aura_ (avoir) de l'argent.
2. Nous commencerons le stage quand nous _connaîtrons_ (connaître) les résultats.
3. Il a téléphoné dès qu'il _a reçu_ (recevoir) la lettre.
4. On a envie de sortir quand il _fait_ (faire) beau.
5. Dès que vous _prendrez_ (prendre) rendez-vous, on vous indiquera le salaire.
6. Ils enverront leurs C.V. dès qu'ils _achèteront_ (acheter) l'ordinateur.
7. Nous passerons un entretien quand il _reviendra_ (revenir) de vacances.
8. Je décroche quand le téléphone _sonne_ (sonner).

MISE EN PRATIQUE

1 **Projets** **Nathalie et Brigitte discutent des problèmes de travail. Nathalie explique ce qu'elle fait quand elle est sans travail. Brigitte approuve.**

MODÈLE Je lis les annonces quand je cherche un travail.
Moi aussi, je lirai les annonces quand je chercherai un travail.

1. J'envoie mon C.V. quand je cherche du travail. Moi aussi, j'enverrai mon C.V. quand je chercherai du travail.
2. Mon mari lit mon C.V. dès qu'il a le temps. Mon mari aussi lira mon C.V. dès qu'il aura le temps.
3. Je suis contente quand tu passes un entretien. Moi aussi, je serai contente quand tu passeras un entretien.
4. Je prends rendez-vous dès que je reçois une lettre d'une compagnie. Moi aussi, je prendrai rendez-vous dès que je recevrai une lettre d'une compagnie.
5. Ta famille et toi, vous êtes heureux quand des chefs du personnel me téléphonent. Ta famille et toi aussi, vous serez heureux quand des chefs du personnel me téléphoneront.
6. Je fais des projets quand j'ai un travail. Moi aussi, je ferai des projets quand j'aurai un travail.

2 **Plus tard** **Aurélien parle de ses projets et des projets de sa famille et de ses amis. Mettez les verbes au futur.**

MODÈLE dès que / je / avoir / le bac / je / aller / à l'université
Dès que j'aurai le bac, j'irai à l'université.

1. quand / je / être / à l'université / ma sœur et moi / habiter ensemble Quand je serai à l'université, ma sœur et moi habiterons ensemble.
2. quand / ma sœur / étudier plus / elle / réussir Quand ma sœur étudiera plus, elle réussira.
3. quand / mes parents / être / à la retraite / je / emprunter pour payer mes études Quand mes parents seront à la retraite, j'emprunterai pour payer mes études.
4. dès que / vous / finir vos études / vous / envoyer vos C.V. / tout / entreprises de la ville Dès que vous finirez vos études, vous enverrez vos C.V. à toutes les entreprises de la ville.
5. quand / tu / travailler / tu / acheter une voiture Quand tu travailleras, tu achèteras une voiture.
6. quand / nous / trouver / nouveau travail / nous / ne plus lire / les annonces Quand nous trouverons un nouveau travail, nous ne lirons plus les annonces.

3 **Conseils** **Quels conseils pouvez-vous donner à un(e) ami(e) qui cherche du travail? Avec un(e) partenaire, assemblez les éléments des colonnes pour formuler vos conseils. Utilisez quand ou dès que.** Answers will vary.

MODÈLE
Quand tu auras ton diplôme, tu chercheras un travail.

A	B
avoir son diplôme	s'amuser
avoir un métier	chercher un travail
passer un entretien	être riche
réussir ses examens	gagner beaucoup d'argent
trouver un emploi	lire les annonces
	se marier
	parler de son expérience professionnelle

OPTIONS

Extra Practice Write these statements on the board, then ask students to finish them using the appropriate verb tense. **1. Quand on a envie de passer un entretien... 2. Dès qu'il a trouvé un travail... 3. Quand je voyagerai à Paris... 4. Quand je recevrai un salaire élevé... 5. Dès que je parlerai avec mon patron...**

Game Have students write three important things they will or will not do when they graduate on a slip of paper and put it in a box. Example: **Quand j'obtiendrai le diplôme, je n'habiterai plus chez mes parents.** Have students draw a paper from the box, then walk around the room, asking others if they will do what is listed, until they find the person who wrote the slip of paper. The first person to find a match wins.

COMMUNICATION

4 **L'avenir** Qu'est-ce que l'avenir nous réserve? Avec un(e) partenaire, complétez ces phrases. Ensuite, présentez vos réponses à la classe. Answers will vary.

1. Dès que je réussirai mes examens, je...
2. Ton ami(e) et toi, vous lirez les annonces quand...
3. Mon/Ma meilleur(e) ami(e) travaillera dès que...
4. Tu enverras ton C.V. quand...
5. Mes amis se marieront dès que...
6. Quand nous aurons beaucoup d'argent, nous...

5 **Les métiers** Vous allez bientôt exercer ces métiers (*have these jobs*). Dites à un(e) partenaire ce qui (*what*) sera possible et ce qui ne sera pas possible quand vous commencerez votre nouveau poste. Alternez les rôles. Answers will vary.

MODÈLE

Étudiant(e) 1: *Dès que je commencerai ce travail, je chercherai un nouvel appartement.*
Étudiant(e) 2: *Je n'aurai plus le temps de sortir quand j'aurai ce poste.*

1.

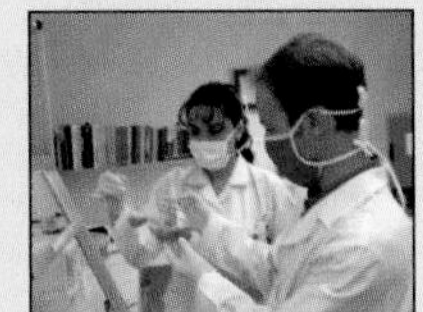
3.

2.

4.

6 **Content(e)** Votre professeur va vous donner une feuille d'activités. Circulez dans la classe pour trouver une réponse affirmative et une réponse négative à chaque question. Justifiez toutes vos réponses. Answers will vary.

MODÈLE

Étudiant(e) 1: *Est-ce que tu seras plus content(e) quand tu auras du temps libre?*
Étudiant(e) 2: *Oui, je serai plus content(e) dès que j'aurai du temps libre, parce que je ferai plus souvent de la gym.*

Le français vivant

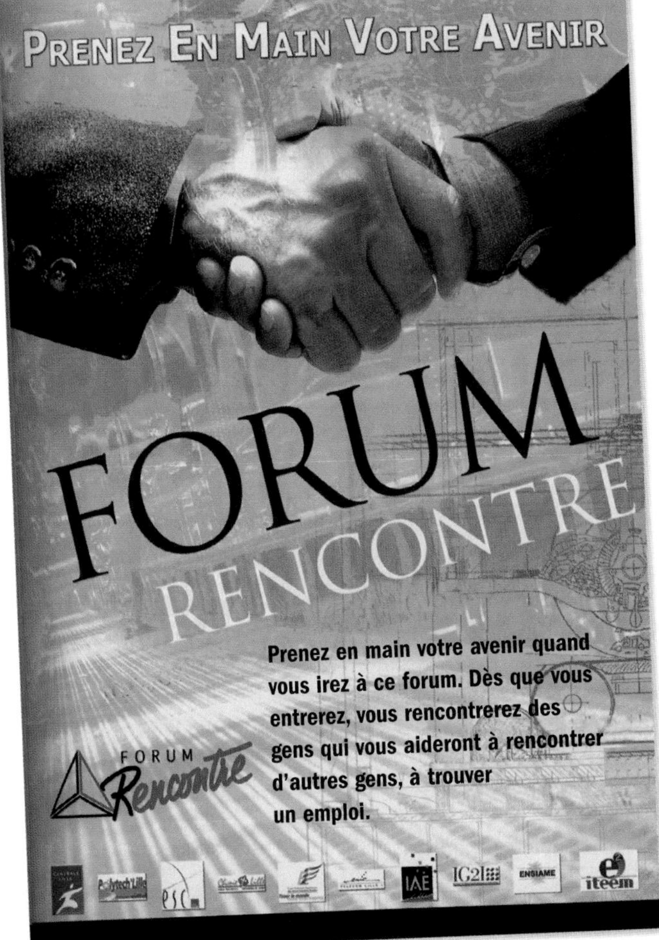

PRENEZ EN MAIN VOTRE AVENIR
FORUM
RENCONTRE
Prenez en main votre avenir quand vous irez à ce forum. Dès que vous entrerez, vous rencontrerez des gens qui vous aideront à rencontrer d'autres gens, à trouver un emploi.
FORUM
Rencontre
IAE
IG2I
iteem

Identifiez Quelles formes de verbes au futur trouvez-vous après **quand** et **dès que** dans cette publicité (*ad*)? Quels autres verbes au futur trouvez-vous? irez, entrerez, rencontrerez, aideront

Questions À tour de rôle, avec un(e) partenaire, posez-vous ces questions. Answers will vary.

1. Qui assistera au Forum rencontre? Pourquoi?
2. Que trouvera-t-on au Forum rencontre? Que fera-t-on?
3. Que feras-tu dès que tu finiras tes études universitaires?
4. Que penses-tu faire pour trouver un emploi quand tu seras prêt(e) à travailler?

1 Expansion Have pairs model the activity and write three more sentences expressing generalities. Then have students switch their sentences with other pairs.

2 Suggestion Have volunteers write each sentence with the future tense on the board. Ask other volunteers to change the sentences into the present or the past tense and discuss how the meanings change.

3 Suggestion Before beginning the activity, have students talk about the last job they had. Encourage them to use **quand** and **dès que** with the past tense.

4 Expansion Have students write three original sentences modeled after the activity. Then ask volunteers to share their sentences with the class.

5 Expansion Ask volunteers to tell you the job of their dreams. Modeling the activity, have them talk about what will and will not be possible once they have begun their job.

6 Suggestion Have two volunteers act out the **modèle**. Then hand out the **Feuilles d'activités** from the IRM on the IRCD-ROM.

Le français vivant Call on a volunteer to read the ad aloud. Ask students: **Quelles sont les questions qu'on doit poser à un forum pour l'emploi?** Encourage students to use the future tense with **quand** and **dès que**.

OPTIONS

Extra Practice Have students imagine they are taking a vacation to Europe. Ask them to write six things they will do when they arrive. Then in pairs have students imagine they are calling home after their first few days of vacation. Have one student ask questions about what they did upon arrival. The second student should answer the questions using **quand** and **dès que.**

Video Show the video episode again to give students more input on the use of the future tense. Ask the students to write down all the examples they hear in the conversation. When the video has finished, review the lists as a class. Discuss the use of **quand**, **dès que**, and **une fois que**.

NATIONAL STANDARDS comparisons

Section Goals

In this section, students will learn:

- interrogative pronouns **lequel, laquelle, lesquels**, and **lesquelles**
- contractions with prepositions and forms of **lequel**

Instructional Resources
WB/VM: Workbook, pp. 173–174
Lab Manual, p. 100
Lab MP3s
WB/VM/LM Answer Key
*IRCD-ROM: IRM (**Essayez!** and **Mise en pratique** answers; **Feuilles d'activités**; Lab Audioscript)*
espaces.vhlcentral.com: activities, downloads, reference tools

Suggestions

- Review the use and forms of **quel: quel(s), quelle(s).** Remind students that **quel** agrees with the noun it modifies.
- Point out that students already use other interrogative pronouns (**qui, que**). **Lequel** differs in that it has a specific antecedent (a person or thing already mentioned).
- Brainstorm a list of movies and write them on the board. Demonstrate the use of **lequel** by pointing to the list and asking students: **Lequel préférez-vous?**
- Practice **de + lequel** and **à + lequel** by asking students questions that elicit its use. Examples: **Je parle des films étrangers avec mes amis. Desquels parlez-vous? Je m'intéresse à l'histoire américaine. À laquelle vous intéressez-vous?**

Essayez! Before assigning this activity, have students underline the noun (and preposition, if applicable) that the appropriate form of **lequel** should replace.

25.2 The interrogative pronoun *lequel*

Point de départ In **Leçon 7**, you learned how to use the interrogative adjective **quel**, as in **Quelle heure est-il?** You will now learn how to use the interrogative pronoun **lequel**.

- If a person or thing has already been mentioned, use a form of **lequel**, translated as *which one(s)*, in place of **quel(le)** [+ *noun*].

Quel métier choisirez-vous? *Which profession will you choose?* ▶ **Lequel** choisirez-vous? *Which one will you choose?*

- **Lequel** agrees with the noun to which it refers.

	singular	plural
masculine	**lequel**	**lesquels**
feminine	**laquelle**	**lesquelles**

Quelle entreprise l'a embauché? *Which company hired him?* ▶ **Laquelle** l'a embauché? *Which one hired him?*

- Place the form of **lequel** wherever you would place **quel(le)(s)** [+ *noun*] in a question.

Dans **quel domaine** travaille-t-il? *Which field does he work in?*
Dans **lequel** travaille-t-il? *Which one does he work in?*

- Remember that past participles agree with preceding direct objects.

Laquelle avez-vous **choisie**? *Which one did you choose?*
Lesquels as-tu **faits**? *Which ones did you do?*

- Forms of **lequel** contract with the prepositions **à** and **de**.

à + form of *lequel*

	singular	plural
masculine	**auquel**	**auxquels**
feminine	**à laquelle**	**auxquelles**

de + form of *lequel*

	singular	plural
masculine	**duquel**	**desquels**
feminine	**de laquelle**	**desquelles**

Auxquels vous intéressez-vous? *Which ones interest you?*
Vous parlez **duquel**? *Which one are you talking about?*

Essayez! **Refaites les phrases avec des formes de lequel.**

1. Pour quelle compagnie travaillez-vous? *Pour laquelle travaillez-vous?*
2. Quel métier préférez-vous? Lequel préférez-vous?
3. À quel métier t'intéresses-tu? Auquel t'intéresses-tu?
4. De quels stages est-ce que vous parlez? Desquels est-ce que vous parlez?

MISE EN PRATIQUE

1 Au bureau Hubert parle à ses collègues. Complétez ses phrases avec une forme du pronom interrogatif **lequel**.

1. J'ai deux stylos. __Lequel__ veux-tu emprunter?
2. Voici la liste des entreprises. À __laquelle__ devons-nous téléphoner?
3. Avez-vous contacté les employés avec __lesquels__ il faut travailler?
4. Sais-tu le nom des stages __auxquels__ tu as assisté?
5. __Lesquelles__ de ces lettres avez-vous lues?
6. Je suis allé dans plusieurs bureaux. __Desquels/Duquel__ parlez-vous?

2 Répétez Vous rencontrez M. Dupont pendant un dîner où il y a beaucoup de bruit (*noise*). Il vous pose des questions, mais il n'entend pas vos réponses. Avec un(e) partenaire, alternez les rôles. Some answers will vary.

MODÈLE examen / avoir réussi

Étudiant(e) 1: *Quel examen avez-vous réussi?*
Étudiant(e) 2: *L'examen de chimie.*
Étudiant(e) 1: *Lequel avez-vous réussi?*

1. métier / s'intéresser à
   À quel métier vous intéressez-vous? Auquel vous intéressez-vous?
2. C.V. / avoir envoyé
   Quel C.V. avez-vous envoyé? Lequel avez-vous envoyé?
3. entreprise / avoir embauché
   Quelle entreprise vous a embauché(e)? Laquelle vous a embauché(e)?
4. candidats / ne pas avoir obtenu de poste
   Quels candidats n'ont pas obtenu de poste? Lesquels n'ont pas obtenu de poste?
5. formations / devoir suivre
   Quelles formations devez-vous suivre? Lesquelles devez-vous suivre?
6. domaine / se spécialiser dans
   Dans quel domaine vous spécialisez-vous? Dans lequel vous spécialisez-vous?

3 La culture francophone Vous voulez savoir si votre partenaire connaît la culture francophone. À tour de rôle, posez-vous ces questions et répondez. Ensuite, posez-vous une question avec une forme de **lequel**. Some answers will vary.

MODÈLE Qui chante en français?
a. Madonna (b.) Céline Dion c. Mariah Carey
Laquelle/Lesquelles de ces chanteuses aimes-tu?

1. Qui est un acteur français?
   (a.) Gérard Depardieu b. Paul Newman c. Johnny Depp
   Lequel/Lesquels de ces acteurs préfères-tu?
2. Où parle-t-on français?
   a. Philadelphie (b.) Montréal c. Athènes
   Laquelle/Lesquelles de ces villes voudras-tu visiter un jour?
3. Quelle voiture est française?
   a. Lotus b. Ferrari (c.) Peugeot
   Laquelle/Lesquelles de ces voitures as-tu déjà conduite(s)?
4. Quelle marque (*brand*) est française?
   a. Mabelle b. Versace (c.) L'Oréal
   Laquelle/Lesquelles de ces marques vas-tu essayer?
5. Qui est un metteur en scène (*director*) français?
   a. Visconti (b.) Besson c. Spielberg
   Lequel/Lesquels de ces metteurs en scène connais-tu?

OPTIONS

Video Replay the video episode, having students focus on the use of **laquelle**. Point out that forms of **lequel** are often used in conversation to clarify a point. Stop the video where appropriate and ask students to which noun each **laquelle** refers.

Game Use a ball to play a game that practices the use of the interrogative pronoun **lequel**. Say a sentence that can be restated using a form of **lequel**. Example: **De quelle université parlez-vous?** Toss the ball to a student who must repeat the sentence using the appropriate form of **lequel**. (**De laquelle parlez-vous?**) When the student has given the appropriate form, he or she tosses the ball back to you. Include both feminine and masculine, singular and plural nouns, and the prepositions **à** and **de** with **lequel**. Keep the pace rapid.

COMMUNICATION

4 Ce semestre Avec un(e) partenaire, parlez des bons et des mauvais aspects de votre vie à la fac ce semestre. Employez des formes du pronom interrogatif **lequel**. Ensuite, présentez vos réponses à la classe. Answers will vary.

MODÈLE

Étudiant(e) 1: *J'ai des cours très difficiles cette année.*
Étudiant(e) 2: *Lesquels?*
Étudiant(e) 1: *Le cours de biologie et le cours de chimie.*

- les cours
- la résidence
- les livres
- les camarades
- les profs
- ?

5 Des choix Cet été, vous irez en vacances avec des amis et vous visiterez plusieurs endroits. Avec un(e) partenaire, parlez de vos projets et posez des questions pour demander des détails. Answers will vary.

MODÈLE visiter des châteaux (*castles*)

Étudiant(e) 1: *Quand je serai en Suisse, je visiterai des châteaux.*
Étudiant(e) 2: *Lesquels visiteras-tu?*

aller dans les musées	marcher dans les rues
bronzer sur la plage	se promener au parc
dîner au restaurant	sortir en boîte
faire du sport	visiter des sites touristiques
?	?

6 Enquête Votre professeur va vous donner une feuille d'activités. Circulez dans la classe et parlez à des camarades différent(e)s pour trouver une réponse affirmative à chaque question. Demandez des détails. Answers will vary.

MODÈLE

Étudiant(e) 1: *Écoutes-tu de la musique?*
Étudiant(e) 2: *Oui.*
Étudiant(e) 1: *Laquelle aimes-tu?*
Étudiant(e) 2: *J'écoute toujours de la musique classique.*

Activités	*Nom*	*Réponse*
1. écouter de la musique	*Delphine*	*musique classique*
2. avoir des passe-temps		
3. bien s'entendre avec des membres de sa famille		
4. s'intéresser aux livres		
5. travailler avec d'autres étudiant(e)s		
6. habiter dans un appartement		

Le français vivant

Identifiez Quelles formes du pronom interrogatif **lequel** trouvez-vous dans cette publicité (*ad*)? Lequel, laquelle, Lesquels

Questions À tour de rôle, avec un(e) partenaire, posez-vous ces questions. Answers will vary.

1. Quel est le but (*goal*) de cette pub?
2. Quelle question posait-on traditionnellement?
3. Quelle question pose-t-on aujourd'hui?
4. Les formations traditionnelles fonctionnent-elles toujours pour trouver un travail? Pourquoi?
5. Pourquoi faut-il aujourd'hui avoir une personnalité inhabituelle?

1 Suggestion Ask six volunteers to write the completed sentences on the board. Have other volunteers correct any spelling or grammar errors.

2 Expansion Have students work in pairs to brainstorm other nouns and verbs similar to those in the activity. Ask volunteers to write their examples on the board. Have other volunteers formulate questions aloud using **lequel.**

3 Suggestion Before assigning the activity, use magazine pictures of popular movies, TV programs, etc., to ask some general questions about students' likes and preferences.

4 Suggestion Brainstorm vocabulary about university life before assigning the activity. Examples: **un emploi sur le campus, les examens**, etc.

5 Expansions
- Have students bring in photos from a past vacation. Working in pairs, students should ask questions similar to those in the activity, but using the past tense.
- Ask volunteers to present their photos to the class. Have classmates ask questions using the appropriate form of **lequel**.

6 Suggestion Have two volunteers act out the **modèle**. Then hand out the **Feuilles d'activités** from the IRM on the IRCD-ROM.

OPTIONS

Pairs Have your students interview each other in pairs about where they want to be and what they want to be doing in five years, in ten years, in thirty years, and so forth. Encourage students to use the future tense and ask clarifying questions using the appropriate forms of **lequel**. Have each student take notes on his or her partner's plans. Then ask for a few volunteers to report on their partner's plans for the future.

Small Groups Divide the class into groups of three. Ask each group to work together to write a prediction of a classmate's future, using the future tense with **quand** and **dès que**. The group should not include the name of their subject. Then circulate the description and ask other groups to identify the name of the classmate whose future is being predicted.

Instructional Resources
IRCD-ROM: IRM (Info Gap Activities); Testing Program, pp. 97–100; Test Files; Testing Program MP3s; Test Generator
espaces.vhlcentral.com: activities, downloads, reference tools

1 Expansion Have pairs repeat the activity referring to their budgets. Example: **Quelles choses achèterez-vous dès que vous aurez le budget nécessaire?** Give students magazine pictures to represent what items they will buy.

2 Suggestion Review the use of the relative pronoun **qui** when giving details about a person.

3 Expansion Have students write a letter to a friend giving career advice. Ask students to include the strategies they developed in the activity as part of their letter.

4 Suggestion Before assigning this activity, do the **modèle** with a volunteer. Ask students to describe any companies for which they have worked. Write two of the company names and characteristics on the board.

5 Suggestion Brainstorm typical interview questions with the class before assigning groups for this activity.

6 Suggestion Divide the class into pairs and distribute the Info Gap Handouts in the IRM on the IRCD-ROM for this activity. Give students ten minutes to complete the activity.

Synthèse

1 Mon premier emploi Avec un(e) partenaire, dites ce que (*what*) vous ferez et utilisez **quand** ou **dès que**. Answers will vary.

MODÈLE

mon premier emploi
Dès que je serai embauché(e), je téléphonerai à ma mère.

1. mon premier entretien
2. mon premier jour dans l'entreprise
3. rencontrer les employés
4. mon premier salaire
5. travailler sur mon premier projet
6. changer de poste
7. me disputer avec le patron
8. quitter l'entreprise

2 Lequel? Avec un(e) partenaire, imaginez un dialogue entre un(e) patron(ne) et son assistant(e). L'assistant(e) demande des précisions. Alternez les rôles. Answers will vary.

MODÈLE

Étudiant(e) 1: *Vous appellerez notre client, s'il vous plaît?*
Étudiant(e) 2: *Oui, mais lequel?*
Étudiant(e) 1: *Le client qui est venu hier après-midi.*

accompagner un visiteur	envoyer un colis
appeler un client	laisser un message à un(e) employé(e)
chercher un numéro de téléphone	prendre un rendez-vous
faire une lettre de recommandation	préparer une réunion (*meeting*)

3 Mes stratégies Avec un(e) partenaire, faites une liste de dix stratégies pour bien mener (*to lead*) votre carrière. Pour chaque stratégie, utilisez **quand** ou **dès que**. Answers will vary.

MODÈLE

Étudiant(e) 1: *Dès que je m'ennuierai, je chercherai un nouveau poste.*
Étudiant(e) 2: *Quand je serai trop fatiguée, je prendrai des vacances.*

4 Laquelle choisir? Deux entreprises différentes vous ont offert un travail. Avec un(e) partenaire, comparez-les. Posez des questions avec le pronom interrogatif **lequel** et donnez des réponses avec **quand** et **dès que**. Choisissez une entreprise et comparez vos réponses avec la classe. Answers will vary.

MODÈLE

Étudiant(e) 1: *Laquelle donne de meilleurs salaires?*
Étudiant(e) 2: *Verrin donne de meilleurs salaires, mais dès que tu commenceras, tu devras travailler jusqu'à neuf heures du soir.*

5 Un entretien Par groupes de trois, jouez cette scène: un chef du personnel visite votre université et vous et un(e) ami(e) passez un entretien informel. Utilisez le pronom interrogatif **lequel** et le futur avec **quand** et **dès que**. Answers will vary.

Le chef du personnel...

- décrit le poste.
- pose des questions.
- répond aux questions des candidat(e)s.
- dit aux candidat(e)s quand il/elle va les contacter.

Les candidat(e)s...

- Un doit donner toutes les bonnes réponses.
- L'autre ne donne que des mauvaises.
- Les deux posent des questions pour en savoir plus sur l'entreprise et sur les postes.

6 Quand nous chercherons du travail... Votre professeur va vous donner, à vous et à votre partenaire, deux feuilles d'activités différentes. Attention! Ne regardez pas la feuille de votre partenaire. Answers will vary.

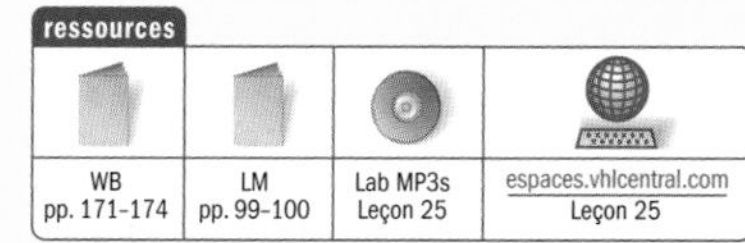

ressources
WB pp. 171-174
LM pp. 99-100
Lab MP3s Leçon 25
espaces.vhlcentral.com Leçon 25

OPTIONS

Extra Practice Tell students to imagine they were fired from a job. Now they must write a letter convincing their **patron(ne)** that they deserve a second chance. Give students fifteen minutes to complete this activity. Encourage the use of the lesson vocabulary and the future tense with **quand** and **dès que**. Then have students switch letters with a classmate for peer editing.

Small Groups Divide the class into groups of three. Have students take turns telling the group three things they hope will be true when they are ten years older. Example: **Quand j'aurai 30 ans, je gagnerai beaucoup d'argent.**

DHL

DHL est créée° en 1969 et ouvre une première ligne, de San Francisco à Honolulu. L'entreprise bâtit° son succès sur une idée nouvelle: envoyer la documentation° avant l'arrivée des marchandises° et accélérer ainsi les procédures d'importation.

En 1983, DHL ouvre des agences en Europe de l'Est. Elle est la première société° de transport express aérien° à le faire. En 1986, des agences sont créées en Chine où cette entreprise est aussi la première à s'implanter°.

ADEATERS

NOUS TENONS VOS PROMESSES.

—Depuis que je travaille avec DHL, je suis beaucoup plus relax.

—Et je sais que cela rassure tout le monde dans l'entreprise.

Compréhension Répondez aux questions. Answers will vary.

1. Résumez (*Summarize*) ce qui se passe dans la pub (*commercial*).
2. Pourquoi est-ce important pour cet employé d'avoir DHL?

Discussion Avec un(e) partenaire, répondez ensemble aux questions et discutez. Answers will vary.

1. À votre avis (*In your opinion*), que signifie le slogan de DHL: «Nous tenons vos promesses»?
2. Est-il possible qu'Internet remplace DHL un jour dans les entreprises? Pourquoi?

SUR INTERNET

Go to espaces.vhlcentral.com to watch the TV clip featured in this **Le zapping**.

créée *created* **bâtit** *builds* **documentation** *paperwork* **marchandises** *goods* **société** *company* **transport express aérien** *express air transportation* **s'implanter** *to establish itself*

Section Goals

In this section, students will:
- read about the company DHL
- watch a commercial for the company
- answer questions about the commercial and DHL

Instructional Resources
*IRCD-ROM: IRM (**Le zapping** TV clip transcription)*
espaces.vhlcentral.com: activities, downloads, reference tools, TV clip

Introduction
To check comprehension, ask these questions.
1. En quelle année DHL est-elle créée? (DHL est créée en 1969.)
2. Où ouvre-t-elle sa première ligne de transport de documents? (Elle ouvre sa première ligne entre San Francisco et Honolulu.)
3. Quelle est l'idée originale de DHL? (Envoyer la documentation avant l'arrivée des marchandises.)

Avant de regarder la vidéo
- Have students look at the video stills, read the captions, and predict what is happening in the commercial for each visual. (**1. Cet homme-ci travaille avec DHL. Il est heureux parce qu'il utilise l'entreprise. 2. Tous les employés sont contents de travailler avec DHL.**)
- Before showing the video, explain to students that they do not need to understand every word they hear. Tell them to listen for the list of people, animals and entities that became more relaxed once the man started using DHL.

Compréhension Have students work in pairs or groups for this activity. Tell them to write their answers. Then show the video again so that they can check their answers and add any missing information.

Discussion Take a quick class survey to find out the opinion of students about the Internet replacing companies like DHL.

OPTIONS

DHL This shipping company provides deliveries to 120,000 destinations in more than 220 countries. DHL has developed a global network of 4,400 offices, 238 gateways and 450 hubs, warehouses and terminals to serve its 4.2 million customers worldwide. It also operates more than 400 aircraft. Its workforce of 170,000 professionals takes care of more than a billion deliveries per year. Since 2002, DHL has been owned by Deutsche Post World Net. You may wish to have students look up additional information on the DHL France Internet address: **www.dhl.fr/publish/fr/fr.high.html.**

Section Goals

In this section, students will learn and practice vocabulary related to:

- professions and occupations
- the workplace

Instructional Resources

*IRCD-ROM: Transparency #55; IRM (**Vocabulaire supplémentaire; Mise en pratique** answers; Textbook Audioscript; Lab Audioscript; Info Gap Activities)*
Textbook MP3s
WB/VM: Workbook, pp. 175–176
Lab Manual, p. 101
Lab MP3s
WB/VM/LM Answer Key
espaces.vhlcentral.com: activities, downloads, reference tools

Suggestions

- Tell students to look over the new vocabulary and identify the cognates.
- Use **Transparency #55.** Identify the professions of people in the illustration. Examples: **C'est un agriculteur. C'est un banquier.**
- Point out that **une profession** is **un métier** that has a certain social or intellectual prestige.
- Explain that whenever there is no feminine form (**un agriculteur/une agricultrice**) nor article change (**un/une psychologue**) nor a term in apposition (**un homme/une femme politique**), the French say **elle est** followed by the masculine form of the profession. Examples: **Elle est plombier. Elle est chef d'entreprise.**
- Ask students questions using the new vocabulary. Examples: **1. Avez-vous un emploi à mi-temps? 2. Êtes-vous au chômage? 3. Avez-vous une assurance maladie? 4. Pourquoi est-il important d'avoir une assurance maladie? 5. Quelles professions sont exigeantes, à votre avis? 6. Connaissez-vous une femme politique célèbre?**
- Additional vocabulary for this lesson can be found in the **Vocabulaire supplémentaire** in the IRM on the IRCD-ROM.

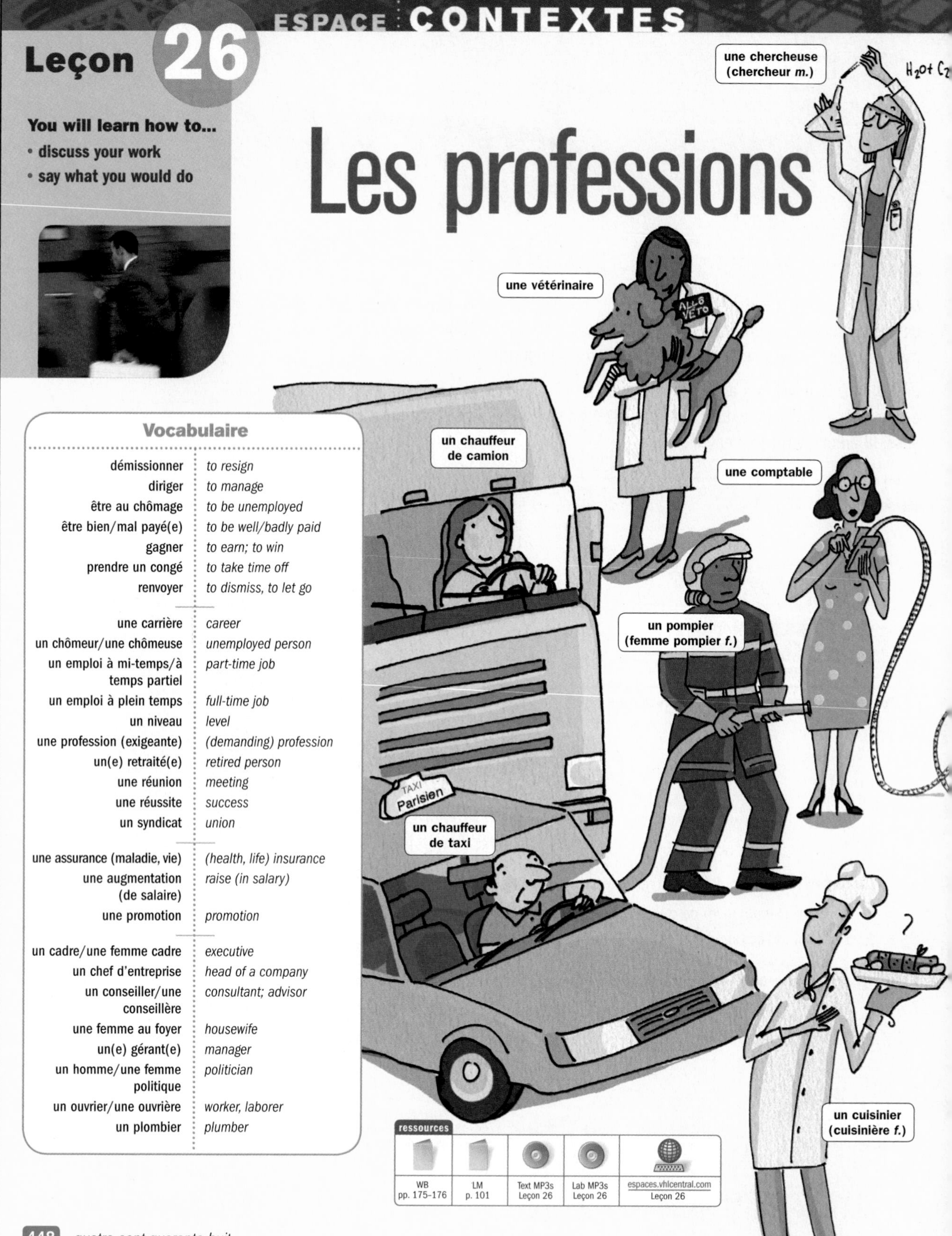

Leçon 26

You will learn how to...

- discuss your work
- say what you would do

Les professions

Vocabulaire

démissionner	*to resign*
diriger	*to manage*
être au chômage	*to be unemployed*
être bien/mal payé(e)	*to be well/badly paid*
gagner	*to earn; to win*
prendre un congé	*to take time off*
renvoyer	*to dismiss, to let go*
une carrière	*career*
un chômeur/une chômeuse	*unemployed person*
un emploi à mi-temps/à temps partiel	*part-time job*
un emploi à plein temps	*full-time job*
un niveau	*level*
une profession (exigeante)	*(demanding) profession*
un(e) retraité(e)	*retired person*
une réunion	*meeting*
une réussite	*success*
un syndicat	*union*
une assurance (maladie, vie)	*(health, life) insurance*
une augmentation (de salaire)	*raise (in salary)*
une promotion	*promotion*
un cadre/une femme cadre	*executive*
un chef d'entreprise	*head of a company*
un conseiller/une conseillère	*consultant; advisor*
une femme au foyer	*housewife*
un(e) gérant(e)	*manager*
un homme/une femme politique	*politician*
un ouvrier/une ouvrière	*worker, laborer*
un plombier	*plumber*

ressources

WB pp. 175–176	LM p. 101	Text MP3s Leçon 26	Lab MP3s Leçon 26	espaces.vhlcentral.com Leçon 26

OPTIONS

TPR Have students mime the work of different professionals. Write the names of professions on slips of paper or whisper them to each person. Examples: **comptable, pompier,** and **chauffeur**. The rest of the class should guess what profession the person is miming. The student who guesses correctly gets to mime the next profession.

Extra Practice Say the French term for a professional, such as **chef de cuisine** or **vétérinaire**. Students should write down as many words as possible that they associate with each profession you mention. Example: **chef de cuisine (la nourriture, un restaurant, cuisiner, une fourchette, un menu, le dîner).**

un banquier (banquière *f.*)

Mise en pratique

1 **Écoutez** Écoutez la conversation entre Henri et Margot, deux jeunes élèves, et indiquez si les phrases suivantes sont **vraies** ou **fausses**.

Henri

Margot

1. Henri veut être comptable. Faux.
2. Il aidera ses employés. Vrai.
3. Ses employés seront bien payés. Vrai.
4. Il offrira à tous une assurance vie. Faux.
5. Margot veut être chef d'entreprise. Faux.
6. Elle aidera les femmes au foyer. Faux.
7. Margot ne parlera pas aux syndicats. Faux.
8. Une de ses priorités sera le chômage. Vrai.

2 **Les professions** Pour chaque profession de la colonne de gauche, trouvez la définition qui correspond dans la colonne de droite.

1. un chef d'entreprise g
2. une femme au foyer j
3. un chauffeur k
4. une banquière i
5. un cuisinier h
6. une comptable a
7. un ouvrier b
8. une vétérinaire f
9. un agent immobilier d
10. un plombier c

a. travaille avec des budgets
b. est employé dans une usine (*factory*)
c. répare les éviers
d. loue, vend et achète des appartements
e. travaille dans un laboratoire
f. s'occupe de la santé des animaux
g. dirige des employés
h. prépare des plats dans un restaurant
i. travaille avec de l'argent
j. s'occupe de la maison et des enfants
k. conduit un taxi ou un camion
l. donne des conseils

3 **Le monde du travail** Complétez le paragraphe en utilisant les mots de vocabulaire de la liste suivante pour faire des phrases cohérentes.

à mi-temps	un conseil
à plein temps	mal payés
l'assurance maladie	un niveau
une augmentation	d'une promotion
leur carrière	un salaire élevé

Quand les étudiants ont un travail, en général c'est un emploi (1) __à mi-temps__ parce qu'ils doivent aussi étudier pour préparer (2) __leur carrière__. Souvent, ils sont (3) __mal payés__. Mais avec leur diplôme, ils auront la possibilité de trouver un poste (4) __à plein temps__, avec (5) __un salaire élevé__ et bien souvent (6) __l'assurance maladie__. Plus tard, ils pourront demander (7) __une augmentation__ de salaire ou bien attendre l'opportunité (8) __d'une promotion__ pour gagner plus d'argent.

1 Tapescript HENRI: Quand je serai grand, je serai chef d'entreprise. J'aiderai mes employés. Ils auront un salaire élevé et bien sûr l'assurance maladie et les congés payés. MARGOT: Moi aussi, quand je serai grande, j'aiderai les gens, spécialement les ouvriers. Je serai femme politique. J'assisterai aux réunions des différents syndicats, j'écouterai les besoins des chômeurs et je travaillerai pour développer les emplois. *(On Textbook MP3s)*

1 Suggestions
- Before playing the recording, have students describe the people in the photos.
- Tell students to correct the false statements.

2 Expansions
- Ask students what professions item e. (**travaille dans un laboratoire**) and item l. (**donne des conseils**) describe. (item e.: **chercheur/chercheuse** and item l.: **conseiller/conseillère**)
- Have students write definitions for other professions not listed. Examples: **un agriculteur, un électricien,** and **un psychologue.**

3 Expansion Have students write three comprehension questions based on the paragraph. Then tell them to get together in groups of three and take turns asking and answering each other's questions.

OPTIONS

Game Brainstorm a list of professions from previous lessons and write them on the board. Distribute or have students make a Bingo card (a 5 X 5 grid of 25 squares) and write the name of a profession from this lesson or a previous one in each square. Write the name of each profession on a separate card and put the cards in a box. Draw cards one by one from the box and read the profession aloud. If students have that profession on their cards, they put a check mark in the corner of the box. To win, a student must have five professions in a row. The first person to have five in a row should say Bingo! To verify a win, have the student read the names of the professions in the winning row.

4 Expansion Have pairs get together with another pair and report what they learned about their partners.

5 Suggestion Before beginning the activity, give students a few minutes to jot down some ideas about their job, boss, and/or employees.

6 Suggestion Have two volunteers read the **modèle** aloud. Then divide the class into pairs and distribute the Info Gap Handouts in the IRM on the IRCD-ROM for this activity. Give students ten minutes to complete the activity.

7 Suggestion Tell students to use the ads on page 436 as models. Encourage them to invent information for the company, such as a telephone number, a street address, or an e-mail address.

Communication

NATIONAL communication STANDARDS

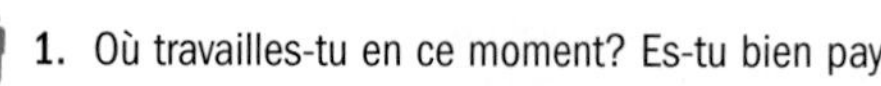

4 Conversez **Interviewez un(e) camarade de classe. Les réponses peuvent être réelles ou imaginaires.** Answers will vary.

1. Où travailles-tu en ce moment? Es-tu bien payé(e)?
2. Préfères-tu travailler à mi-temps ou à plein temps? Pourquoi?
3. Est-ce le métier que tu feras plus tard? Pourquoi?
4. Est-ce que tu as des congés payés? Une assurance maladie? Qu'en penses-tu?
5. As-tu déjà demandé une augmentation de salaire? As-tu réussi à en obtenir une? Comment?
6. As-tu déjà obtenu une promotion? Quand? Pourquoi?
7. As-tu déjà été au chômage? Pendant combien de temps? Qu'est-ce que tu as fait pendant ce temps-là?
8. Quel genre de carrière veux-tu faire? Ta profession sera-t-elle exigeante? Pourquoi?

5 Votre carrière **Voilà cinq ans que vous n'avez pas vu votre ami(e) de la fac. Depuis, vous avez obtenu tous/toutes les deux votre diplôme et trouvé un travail. Travaillez avec un(e) camarade de classe pour présenter le dialogue suivant:** Answers will vary.

- Vous vous retrouvez et vous parlez de votre métier.
- Vous décrivez votre poste.
- Vous parlez de votre patron/patronne et/ou de vos employés.
- Vous parlez des avantages et des inconvénients (*drawbacks*) de votre travail.

6 Décrivez **Votre professeur va vous donner, à vous et à votre partenaire, deux feuilles d'activités différentes. À tour de rôle, posez-vous des questions pour trouver ce que font les personnages de chaque profession pendant la journée.** Answers will vary.

MODÈLE

Étudiant(e) 1: *Sur mon dessin, j'ai un plombier qui répare un évier.*
Étudiant(e) 2: *Moi, j'ai un homme…*

7 L'offre d'emploi **Vous êtes le chef d'entreprise de Cartalis, une agence immobilière. Vous développez votre entreprise et avez besoin d'embaucher une nouvelle personne rapidement. Avec deux partenaires, écrivez une annonce que vous enverrez à votre journal local. Utilisez les mots de la liste suivante.** Answers will vary.

agent immobilier	poste exigeant
carrière	promotion
congés payés	réussite
diriger	salaire élevé
entretien	temps partiel

OPTIONS

Extra Practice Have students categorize professions according to various paradigms. Examples: **les emplois de bureau/les emplois en plein air; les métiers physiques/les métiers intellectuels;** and **les métiers qui exigent une formation longue/les métiers qui n'exigent pas ou peu de formation.**

Pairs Have students work in pairs. Tell them to make a list of reasons people resign from a job (**Raisons pour démissionner d'un poste**) and a list of reasons people are let go from a job (**Raisons pour être renvoyé[e]**). Then call on volunteers to read one item from their list.

NATIONAL
comparisons
STANDARDS

Les sons et les lettres

Les néologismes et le franglais

Many French speakers use **franglais**, words borrowed from English. These words often look identical to the English words, but they are pronounced like French words. Most words in **franglais** are masculine, and many end in **-ing**.

le sweat-shirt **le week-end** **le shopping** **le parking**

Franglais words for foods and sports are very common, as are expressions in popular culture, business, and advertising.

un milk-shake **le base-ball** **le top-modèle** **le marketing**

Many **franglais** words are recently coined terms (**néologismes**). These are common in contemporary fields, such as entertainment and technology. Some of these words do have French equivalents, but the **franglais** terms are used more often.

un e-mail = un courriel **le chat = la causette** **une star = une vedette**

Some **franglais** words do not exist in English at all, or they are used differently.

un brushing = *a blow-dry* **un relooking =** *a makeover* **le zapping =** *channel surfing*

Prononcez Répétez les mots suivants à voix haute.

1. flirter	4. le look	7. un scanneur	10. le shampooing
2. un fax	5. un clown	8. un CD-ROM	11. une speakerine
3. cliquer	6. le planning	9. le volley-ball	12. le chewing-gum

Articulez Répétez les phrases suivantes à voix haute.

1. Le cowboy porte un jean et un tee-shirt.
2. Julien joue au base-ball et il fait du footing.
3. J'ai envie d'un nouveau look, je vais faire du shopping.
4. Au snack-bar, je commande un hamburger, des chips et un milk-shake.
5. Tout ce qu'il veut faire, c'est rester devant la télé dans le living et zapper!

Dictons Répétez les dictons à voix haute.

Ce n'est pas la star qui fait l'audience, mais l'audience qui fait la star.[1]

Un gentleman est un monsieur qui se sert d'une pince à sucre, même lorsqu'il est seul.[2]

ressources

LM p. 102	Text MP3s Leçon 26	Lab MP3s Leçon 26	espaces.vhlcentral.com Leçon 26

[1] It's not the star that makes the fans; it's the fans that make the star.
[2] A gentleman is a man who uses sugar tongs, even when he is alone.

Section Goals

In this section, students will learn about neologisms and **franglais**.

Instructional Resources
Textbook MP3s
Lab Manual, p. 102
Lab MP3s
WB/VM/LM Answer Key
IRCD-ROM: IRM (Textbook Audioscript; Lab Audioscript)
espaces.vhlcentral.com: activities, downloads, reference tools

Suggestions

- Model the pronunciation of the example words and have students repeat after you.
- Ask students to provide more examples of words that are neologisms or **franglais**. Examples: **cool, le basket-ball, un site web, un toaster** and **surfer.**
- Dictate five familiar words that are neologisms or **franglais**, repeating each one at least two times. Then write them on the board or a transparency and have students check their spelling.

Dictons The saying **«Ce n'est pas la star qui fait l'audience, mais l'audience qui fait la star»** is a quote from Noël Mamère, a journalist and politician. The saying **«Un gentleman est un monsieur qui se sert d'une pince à sucre, même lorsqu'il est seul»** is a quote from Alphonse Allais, a writer and humorist.

OPTIONS

Extra Practice Write these Internet words on the board or a transparency. Have the class guess the English equivalents. **1. arrosage** (*spamming*) **2. accès** (*hit*) **3. bombardement** (*bombing*) **4. balise** (*tag*) **5. moteur de recherche** (*search engine*) **6. téléchargement** (*downloading*)

Small Groups Have the class work in groups of three or four. Tell them to write a humorous paragraph using as many neologisms or **franglais** terms as possible. Ask a few volunteers to read their paragraphs to the class.

Section Goals

In this section, students will learn functional phrases for talking about hypothetical situations and making polite requests or suggestions.

Instructional Resources
WB/VM: Video Manual, pp. 261–262
WB/VM/LM Answer Key
Video CD-ROM
Video on DVD
IRCD-ROM: IRM (Videoscript; ***Roman-photo*** *Translations)*
espaces.vhlcentral.com: activities, downloads, reference tools

Video Recap: Leçon 25
Before doing this **Roman-photo**, review the previous one with this activity.

1. Qu'est-ce que Stéphane et Astrid viennent de faire? (passer le bac)
2. Qu'est-ce que Stéphane veut étudier à l'université? (l'architecture)
3. Qu'est-ce qu'Astrid veut étudier à l'université? (la médecine)
4. Qu'est-ce que cherche la jeune femme au P'tit Bistrot? (un emploi)
5. Qu'est-ce que cherche Michèle? (un nouveau travail)

Video Synopsis
Sandrine is anxious about her first public performance as a singer. Amina offers to make her a dress to give her confidence. Stéphane and Astrid get their **bac** results. Astrid passed with honors, but Stéphane has to retake one part of the exam. At **Le P'tit Bistrot**, Michèle asks Valérie for a raise. When Valérie refuses, Michèle quits. Then Stéphane arrives and tells his mother his bad news.

Suggestions
- Have students predict what the episode will be about based on the video stills.
- Tell students to scan the captions to find job-related vocabulary.
- After reading the **Roman-photo**, review students' predictions and have them summarize the episode.

Je démissionne!

PERSONNAGES

Amina

Astrid

Michèle

Sandrine

Stéphane

Valérie

1

En ville...
AMINA Alors, Sandrine, ton concert, ce sera la première fois que tu chantes en public?
SANDRINE Oui, et je suis un peu anxieuse!
AMINA Ah! Tu as le trac!
SANDRINE Un peu, oui. Toi, tu es toujours tellement chic, tu as confiance en toi, tu n'as peur de rien...

2

AMINA Mais Sandrine, la confiance en soi, c'est ici dans le cœur et ici dans la tête. J'ai une idée! Ce qui te donnerait du courage, c'est de porter une superbe robe.
SANDRINE Tu crois? Mais, je n'en ai pas...
AMINA Je m'en occupe. Quel style de robe est-ce que tu aimerais? Suis-moi!

3

Au marché...
AMINA Que penses-tu de ce tissu noir?
SANDRINE Oh! C'est ravissant!
AMINA Oui et ce serait parfait pour une robe du soir.
SANDRINE Bon, si tu le dis. Moi, si je faisais cette robe moi-même, elle finirait sans doute avec une manche courte et avec une manche longue!

6

STÉPHANE Attends. Forestier, Stéphane... Oh! Ce n'est pas possible!
ASTRID Quoi, qu'est-ce qu'il y a?
STÉPHANE Je dois repasser une partie de l'examen la semaine prochaine.
ASTRID Oh, ce n'est pas vrai! Il y a peut-être une erreur. Stéphane, attends!

7

Au P'tit Bistrot...
MICHÈLE Excusez-moi, Madame. Auriez-vous une petite minute?
VALÉRIE Oui, bien sûr!
MICHÈLE Voilà, ça fait deux ans que je travaille ici au P'tit Bistrot... Est-ce qu'il serait possible d'avoir une augmentation?

8

VALÉRIE Michèle, être serveuse, c'est un métier exigeant, mais les salaires sont modestes!
MICHÈLE Oui, je sais, Madame. Je ne vous demande pas un salaire très élevé, mais... c'est pour ma famille.
VALÉRIE Désolée, Michèle, j'aimerais bien le faire, mais, en ce moment, ce n'est pas possible. Peut-être dans quelques mois...

ACTIVITÉS

1 Vrai ou faux? **Indiquez si les affirmations suivantes sont vraies ou fausses.**

1. Sandrine a un peu peur avant son concert. Vrai.
2. Amina ne sait pas comment aider Sandrine. Faux.
3. Amina va faire une robe de velours noir. Faux.
4. Sandrine ne sait pas faire une robe. Vrai.
5. Pour la remercier (*To thank her*), Sandrine va préparer un dîner pour Amina. Faux.
6. Stéphane doit repasser tout le bac. Faux.
7. Astrid a reçu une très bonne note. Vrai.
8. Michèle travaille au P'tit Bistrot depuis deux ans. Vrai.
9. Valérie offre à Michèle une toute petite augmentation de salaire. Faux.
10. Michèle va retourner au P'tit Bistrot après ses vacances. Faux.

OPTIONS

Avant de regarder la vidéo Tell students to read the title and the scene setter. Then have them predict what might happen in this episode. Write their predictions on the board. After viewing the episode, have them confirm or correct their predictions.

Regarder la vidéo Show the video in four parts, pausing it before each location change. Have students describe what happens in each place. Write their observations on the board. Then show the entire episode again without pausing and have the class fill in any missing details to summarize the plot.

Valérie et Stéphane rencontrent de nouveaux problèmes.

4

5

AMINA Je pourrais en faire une comme ça, si tu veux.
SANDRINE Je préférerais une de tes créations. Si tu as besoin de quoi que ce soit un jour, dis-le-moi.
AMINA Oh, Sandrine, si je te fais une robe, c'est pour te faire plaisir.
SANDRINE Je pourrais te préparer un gâteau au chocolat?
AMINA Mmmm... Je ne dirais pas non.

Au lycée...
ASTRID Oh, Stéphane, c'est le grand jour! On va enfin connaître les résultats du bac! Je suis tellement nerveuse. Pas toi?
STÉPHANE Non, pas vraiment. Seulement si j'échoue, ma mère va m'étrangler. Eh! Félicitations, Astrid! Tu as réussi! Avec mention bien en plus!
ASTRID Et toi?

9

10

MICHÈLE Non, Madame! Dans quelques mois, je serai déjà partie. Je démissionne! Je prends le reste de mes vacances à partir d'aujourd'hui.
VALÉRIE Michèle, attendez! Mais Michèle! Ah, Stéphane, te voilà. Hé! Où vas-tu? Tu as eu les résultats du bac, non? Qu'est-ce qu'il y a?

STÉPHANE Maman, je suis désolé, mais je vais devoir repasser une partie de l'examen.
VALÉRIE Oh là là! Stéphane!
STÉPHANE Bon, écoute maman, voici ce que je vais faire: je vais étudier nuit et jour jusqu'à la semaine prochaine: pas de sports, pas de jeux vidéo, pas de télévision. J'irai à l'université, maman. Je te le promets.

Expressions utiles

Talking about hypothetical situations

- **Ce qui te donnerait du courage, c'est de porter une superbe robe.**
  Wearing a great dress would give you courage.
- **Ce serait parfait pour une robe du soir.**
  This would be perfect for an evening gown.
- **Si je faisais cette robe, elle finirait avec une manche courte et avec une manche longue!**
  If I made this dress, it would end up with one short sleeve and one long sleeve!
- **Je préférerais une de tes créations.**
  I would prefer one of your creations.
- **Je ne dirais pas non.**
  I wouldn't say no.
- **Si tu as besoin de quoi que ce soit un jour, dis-le-moi.**
  If you ever need anything someday, tell me.
- **Si j'échoue, ma mère va m'étrangler.**
  If I fail, my mother is going to strangle me.

Making polite requests and suggestions

- **Quel style de robe est-ce que tu aimerais? J'aimerais...**
  What kind of dress would you like? I would like...
- **Je pourrais en faire une comme ça, si tu veux.**
  I could make you one like this, if you would like.
- **Auriez-vous une petite minute?**
  Would you have a minute?
- **Est-ce qu'il serait possible d'avoir une augmentation?**
  Would it be possible to get a raise?

Additional vocabulary

- **le trac**
  stage fright
- **ravissant(e)**
  beautiful; delightful
- **faire plaisir à quelqu'un**
  to make someone happy

2 **Les mauvaises nouvelles** Stéphane, Valérie et Michèle ont été très déçus (*disappointed*) aujourd'hui pour des raisons différentes. Avec deux partenaires, décidez qui a passé la pire journée et pourquoi. Ensuite, discutez-en avec le reste de la classe.

3 **Écrivez** Pensez à un examen très important de votre vie et composez un paragraphe. Quel était l'examen? Qu'est-ce que vous avez fait pour le préparer? Comment était-ce? Comme l'histoire de Stéphane ou d'Astrid? Comment cet examen a-t-il affecté vos projets d'avenir?

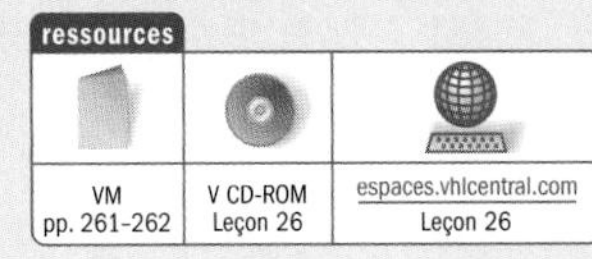

ressources
VM pp. 261-262
V CD-ROM Leçon 26
espaces.vhlcentral.com Leçon 26

ACTIVITÉS

Expressions utiles
- Model the pronunciation of the **Expressions utiles** and have students repeat them after you.
- As you work through the list, point out **le conditionnel** forms and **si** clauses. Tell students that these grammar points will be formally presented in the **Structures** section.
- Respond briefly to questions about **le conditionnel** and **si** clauses. Reinforce correct forms, but do not expect students to produce them consistently at this time.

1 Suggestion Have students correct the false statements.

1 Expansion For additional practice, give students these items. **11. Amina refuse le gâteau au chocolat parce qu'elle est au régime. (Faux.) 12. Astrid dit que la note de Stéphane est peut-être une erreur. (Vrai.) 13. Michèle veut une augmentation pour acheter une nouvelle voiture. (Faux.) 14. Stéphane promet d'étudier nuit et jour pour réussir au bac. (Vrai.)**

2 Suggestion If time is limited, this activity may be assigned as homework. Group students according to the person they believe had the worst day—Stéphane, Michèle, or Valérie. Have them prepare their arguments at home, then allow the groups time to work together before presenting their case to the class.

3 Expansion Have students exchange compositions for peer editing.

OPTIONS

Pairs Working in pairs, have students write a conversation between a boss and an employee, based on the conversation between Michèle and Valérie. In the conversation, the employee should negotiate something with the boss, such as extra vacation time, permission to come in late one day, or a day off. At first, the boss refuses, but eventually the two compromise and come to an agreement.

Extra Practice Write **j'aimerais** and **vous aimeriez** on the board. Ask students variations of the question: **Quel style de robe est-ce que vous aimeriez porter?** Tell them to respond with **J'aimerais...**. Examples: **1. Quelle profession est-ce que vous aimeriez avoir? 2. Quel salaire est-ce que vous aimeriez recevoir? 3. Quel film est-ce que vous aimeriez voir ce week-end?**

connections cultures
NATIONAL STANDARDS

Section Goals

In this section, students will:

- learn about unions and strikes in France
- learn some colloquial terms for talking about money
- learn about paid vacations and holidays in various francophone regions
- read about civil servants in France

Instructional Resources
espaces.vhlcentral.com: activities, downloads, reference tools

Culture à la loupe

Avant la lecture Have students look at the photo of the people protesting and describe what they see. Ask what they are protesting.

Lecture

- Point out the statistics chart. Ask students what information it shows. (the percentage of French people in favor of minimum service for the sectors listed) Then ask: **Pourquoi pensez-vous que tant de gens veulent un service minimum pour ces secteurs? Pourquoi ces services sont-ils très importants?**
- See **Unité 2 Panorama** on page 67 for more information on the SNCF.

Après la lecture Ask students: **Pourquoi fait-on la grève? Qu'espère-t-on obtenir quand on fait la grève?**

1 Suggestion Have volunteers write the answers to the questions on the board. Then go over the answers with the class.

CULTURE À LA LOUPE

Syndicats et grèves en France

Des passagers attendent un train pendant une grève de la SNCF.

Les gens se plaignent° souvent des grèves° en France, mais faire la grève est un droit. Ce sont les grandes grèves historiques qui ont apporté aux Français la majorité des avantages sociaux°: retraite, sécurité sociale, congés payés, instruction publique, etc. Les grèves en France sont accompagnées de manifestations ou de pétitions, et beaucoup d'entre elles ont lieu° en automne, après les vacances d'été. Des grèves peuvent avoir lieu dans tous les secteurs de l'économie, en particulier le secteur des transports. Une grève de la SNCF, par exemple, peut immobiliser tout le pays et causer des ennuis à des millions de voyageurs.

une manifestation de la CGT, un syndicat

Les syndicats organisent les trois quarts° de ces mouvements sociaux. La France est pourtant° le pays industrialisé le moins syndiqué° du monde. En 2000, seulement six à huit pour cent des salariés français étaient syndiqués contre 13% aux États-Unis ou 91% en Suède.

De plus en plus, des non-salariés, comme les médecins et les commerçants, font aussi la grève. Dans ce cas, ils cherchent surtout à faire changer les lois°.

En général, le public soutient° les grévistes, mais il demande aussi la création d'un service minimum obligatoire pour éviter la paralysie totale du pays. Ce service minimum obligerait° un petit nombre d'employés à travailler pendant chaque grève. La fréquence des grèves a diminué pendant les années 1970, 1980 et 1990, mais a vu° une certaine augmentation depuis l'année 2000.

Les Français favorables à un service minimum	
Dans le ramassage des ordures°	84%
Dans l'instruction publique	79%
Dans les transports aériens	77%
Dans les transports publics	74%

se plaignent *complain* **grèves** *strikes* **avantages sociaux** *benefits* **ont lieu** *take place* **trois quarts** *three quarters* **pourtant** *however* **syndiqué** *unionized* **faire changer les lois** *have the laws changed* **soutient** *supports* **obligerait** *would force* **a vu** *has seen* **ramassage des ordures** *trash collection*

ACTIVITÉS

1 Répondez Répondez aux questions d'après les textes.

1. Quel est un des droits des Français? Faire la grève est un des droits des Français.
2. Qu'est-ce que la grève a apporté aux Français? Elle leur a apporté des avantages sociaux.
3. Quand ont souvent lieu les grèves? Elles ont souvent lieu en automne.
4. Par qui la majorité des grèves sont-elles organisées? Elles sont organisées par les syndicats.
5. Les travailleurs français sont-ils très syndiqués? Non, la France est le pays industrialisé le moins syndiqué du monde.
6. Combien de travailleurs français étaient syndiqués en 2000? Entre six et huit pour cent des travailleurs étaient syndiqués en 2000.
7. Pourquoi les médecins et les commerçants font-ils la grève? Ils font la grève pour changer les lois.
8. Y a-t-il toujours eu un grand nombre de grèves en France? Non, la fréquence des grèves a diminué pendant les années 1970, 1980 et 1990.
9. Combien de Français sont favorables au service minimum dans l'instruction publique? 79% y sont favorables.
10. À quoi sont favorables 77% des Français? 77% des Français sont favorables à un service minimum dans les transports aériens.

OPTIONS

Les grèves During a strike, people in France march in large or small numbers, as is true in the United States. The media coverage of participants in a strike is also similar: unions consistently report a higher rate of participation than the police. In France, however, one might see police carrying body shields and using tear gas when large groups assemble to strike.

Small Groups Have students work in groups of three or four. Have them discuss the various options unions have for making their demands known: **la pétition, la grève, la manifestation,** and **le boycott**. Tell them to decide which means they think are the most and least effective and explain why.

LE FRANÇAIS QUOTIDIEN

L'argent

Voici d'autres noms familiers souvent utilisés pour parler de l'argent.

avoine (*f.*)	**oseille (*f.*)**
biffetons (*m.*)	**pépètes (*f.*)**
blé (*m.*)	**pèze (*m.*)**
cash (*m.*)	**pognon (*m.*)**
flouze (*m.*)	**radis (*m.*)**
fric (*m.*)	**ronds (*m.*)**
grisbi (*m.*)	**thune (*f.*)**

LE MONDE FRANCOPHONE

La durée des vacances et les jours fériés

Voici la durée des congés payés dans quelques pays francophones.

En Belgique 20 jours après une année de travail, plus 10 jours fériés par an

Au Luxembourg 25 jours et 12 jours fériés par an

Au Maroc 18 jours par an

Au Québec 10 jours et 8 jours fériés par an

Au Sénégal un minimum de 24 jours par an, plus pour les travailleurs avec ancienneté° et pour les mères de famille

En Suisse 20 jours pour les plus de 20 ans, 25 jours pour les moins de 20 ans

En Tunisie 12 jours par an pour les plus de 20 ans, 18 jours pour les 18-20 ans et 24 jours pour les moins de 18 ans

ancienneté *seniority*

PORTRAIT

Les fonctionnaires

Avec environ six millions de fonctionnaires° dans le pays, ou 21% de la population active°, la France bat des records°. Ces fonctionnaires travaillent pour l'État (dans le gouvernement, les universités, les lycées, les compagnies nationales), pour la fonction publique territoriale (le département, la région) ou pour la fonction publique hospitalière. Ils ont de nombreux avantages: des salaires compétitifs, une bonne retraite et une grande protection de l'emploi. Pour devenir fonctionnaire, il faut passer un concours°. Chaque année, près de 40.000 emplois sont ainsi° ouverts au public.

fonctionnaires *civil servants* **population active** *working population* **bat des records** *breaks records* **concours** *competitive examination* **ainsi** *thus*

SUR INTERNET

Quelle est la durée des congés payés de maternité et de paternité en France?

Go to **espaces.vhlcentral.com** to find more cultural information related to this **ESPACE CULTURE**.

ACTIVITÉS

2 Complétez Donnez une suite logique à chaque phrase.

1. La France bat des records avec... plus de six millions de fonctionnaires dans le pays.
2. Les fonctionnaires sont employés par... l'État.
3. Ils bénéficient de nombreux... avantages.
4. On peut devenir fonctionnaire après avoir passé... un concours.
5. Au Sénégal, on a des journées de vacances supplémentaires si on est... travailleur avec ancienneté ou mère de famille.
6. La durée des vacances dépend de l'âge en... Tunisie et en Suisse.

3 La grève Vous êtes journaliste et votre partenaire est un fonctionnaire en grève. Vous allez l'interviewer pour le journal télévisé de 20 heures. Préparez un dialogue où vous cherchez à comprendre pourquoi il ou elle est en grève et depuis combien de temps. Soyez prêts à jouer le dialogue devant la classe.

ressources

espaces.vhlcentral.com Leçon 26

Le français quotidien
- Model the pronunciation of each term and have students repeat it.
- Point out that **l'avoine** literally means *oats* and **le blé** means *wheat*.

Portrait
- Point out that the **concours** mentioned here is similar to a civil service exam in the United States.
- Ask students: **Quels sont les avantages des fonctionnaires en France? (des salaires compétitifs, une bonne retraite et une grande protection de l'emploi)**

Le monde francophone
- Explain that the number of days off refers to weekdays. To calculate the number of weeks of possible vacation, divide by five.
- Ask students: **Dans quel pays la durée des congés payés est-elle la plus longue? (au Luxembourg)**

2 Expansion Have students create three more items for this activity. Then tell them to exchange papers with a classmate and complete the sentences. Remind them to verify their answers.

3 Suggestion If time is limited, assign this activity as homework, so students can prepare their interview questions or responses. Then allow partners some time to work together during the next class before presenting their interviews.

OPTIONS

Extra Practice Tell students that federal civil service employees in the United States get ten paid holidays per year. Then ask these questions. **1. Quels pays ont le plus de jours fériés? (la Belgique et le Luxembourg) 2. Quelle région a le moins de jours fériés? (le Québec)**

Pairs Have students work in pairs to make a list of the sectors in which civil servants in France work. Also tell them to list some of the occupations these sectors include. Then have them get together with another pair and compare their lists.

Section Goals

In this section, students will learn:
- the conditional tense
- the use of the conditional for expressing polite requests and future actions in a past tense

Instructional Resources
WB/VM: Workbook, pp. 177-178
Lab Manual, p. 103
Lab MP3s
WB/VM/LM Answer Key
*IRCD-ROM: IRM (**Essayez!** and **Mise en pratique** answers; Lab Audioscript)*
espaces.vhlcentral.com: activities, downloads, reference tools

Suggestions
- Read the captions of the video stills and ask volunteers to indicate the verbs in the conditional.
- After going through the conjugations, check for understanding by asking volunteers to give different forms of verbs not listed: **finir, rendre, acheter**.
- Explain the concept of the conditional as *the future in the past*. Explain that the conditional is used to express some action that was yet to occur at some past time, and give more examples like this: **Je (ne) savais (pas) que je serais professeur de français.** Encourage students to make statements modeled on yours.
- Tell students to imagine they are shopping at the mall. Ask them what they would like to buy there. Example: **Que voudriez-vous acheter? (Je voudrais acheter ____.)** Tell students that **vouloir** in the conditional is a polite form. Emphasize how the conditional is used to make polite requests.

26.1 *Le conditionnel*

Point de départ The conditional expresses what you *would* do or what *would* happen under certain circumstances.

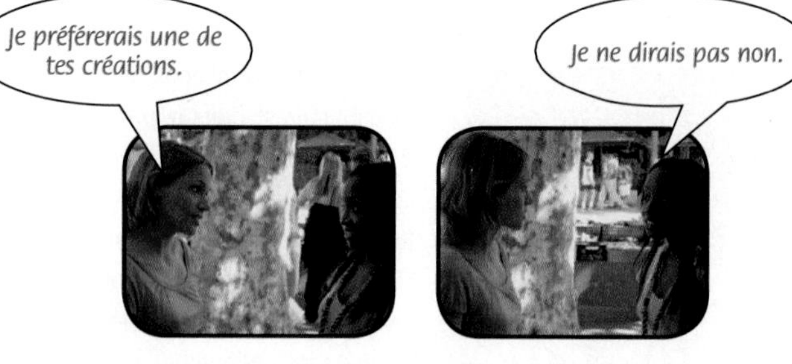

Je préférerais une de tes créations.
Je ne dirais pas non.

- The conditional uses the same verb stems as the future tense. The conditional endings are the same as those of the **imparfait**.

Conditional of regular verbs

	parler	réussir	attendre
je/j'	parlerais	réussirais	attendrais
tu	parlerais	réussirais	attendrais
il/elle	parlerait	réussirait	attendrait
nous	parlerions	réussirions	attendrions
vous	parleriez	réussiriez	attendriez
ils/elles	parleraient	réussiraient	attendraient

Au Québec, nous **parlerions** français.
In Quebec, we would speak French.

À ta place, je **lirais** les annonces.
In your place, I'd read the ads.

- The same patterns that you learned for forming the future tense of spelling-change **-er** verbs also apply to the conditional.

Vous m'**emmèneriez** à l'entretien?
Would you take me to the interview?

Tu **préférerais** être au chômage?
Would you prefer to be unemployed?

- The same irregular stems you learned for the future tense are used for the conditional.

J'**irais** chez toi, mais pas aujourd'hui.
I'd go to your house, but not today.

Elles **feraient** du vélo les week-ends.
They'd ride their bikes on weekends.

BOÎTE À OUTILS
See **Leçon 24** for the explanation of how to form the future tense of spelling-change verbs and for the list of verbs with irregular future stems.

MISE EN PRATIQUE

1 Changer de vie Alexandre parle à son ami de ce qu'il aimerait changer dans sa vie. Complétez ses phrases avec les formes correctes du conditionnel.

MODÈLE
Je n' <u>étudierais</u> (étudier) jamais le week-end.

1. Ma petite amie et moi <u>ferions</u> (faire) des études dans la même (*same*) ville.
2. Je <u>vendrais</u> (vendre) ma vieille voiture.
3. Nous <u>achèterions</u> (acheter) une Porsche.
4. Je <u>travaillerais</u> (travailler) à mi-temps.
5. Nos amis nous <u>rendraient</u> (rendre) souvent visite.
6. Quelqu'un <u>nettoierait</u> (nettoyer) la maison.

2 Les professeurs Que feraient ces personnes si elles étaient profs de français?

MODÈLE tu / donner / examen / difficile
Tu donnerais des examens difficiles.

1. Marc / donner / devoirs
Marc donnerait des devoirs.
2. vous / répondre / à / questions / étudiants
Vous répondriez aux questions des étudiants.
3. nous / permettre / à / étudiants / de / manger / en classe Nous permettrions aux étudiants de manger en classe.
4. tu / parler / français / tout le temps
Tu parlerais français tout le temps.
5. tes parents / boire / café / classe
Tes parents boiraient du café en classe.
6. nous / montrer / films / français
Nous montrerions des films français.

3 Sur une île Vous découvrez une île et vous y emmenez un groupe de différentes personnes et leurs familles. Assemblez les éléments des colonnes pour faire des phrases avec le conditionnel. Quels rôles joueraient ces personnes? Answers will vary.

MODÈLE
Le professeur enseignerait les mathématiques aux enfants.

A	B	C
agent de police	diriger	animaux
agriculteur/agricultrice	enseigner	disputes
chauffeur	éteindre	enfants
cuisinier/cuisinière	s'occuper de	fruits
électricien(ne)	organiser	nourriture
pompier/femme pompier	parler	problèmes
professeur	préparer	repas
psychologue	servir	réunions
vétérinaire	trouver	urgences
?	?	?

OPTIONS

Game To prepare for a relay race, line students up in teams of six several feet from the board. Write an infinitive on the board and call out **Commencez!** The first team members go to the board and write the **je** form of the verb in the conditional, then pass the chalk to the next team member, who writes the **tu** form, and so on. The team that finishes first and has all the forms correct wins the round.

Extra Practice Ask students what they would or would not do over the next six months if they could do anything they wanted and money and time were no object. Example: **Je ferais le tour du monde.** Call on volunteers to read their sentences, and then ask the class comprehension questions about what was said. Example: **Qu'est-ce que Paula ferait?**

COMMUNICATION

4 **Une grosse fortune** Avec un(e) partenaire, parlez de la façon dont (*the way in which*) vous dépenseriez l'argent si une vieille tante mourait et vous laissait une grosse fortune. Posez-vous ces questions à tour de rôle. Answers will vary.

1. Partirais-tu en voyage? Où irais-tu?
2. Quelle profession choisirais-tu?
3. Où habiterais-tu?
4. Qu'est-ce que tu achèterais? À tes amis? À ta famille?
5. Donnerais-tu de l'argent à des œuvres de charité (*charities*)? Auxquelles?
6. Qu'est-ce qui changerait dans ta vie quotidienne (*daily*)?

5 **Sans ça...** Par groupes de trois, dites ce qui (*what*) changerait dans le monde sans ces choses. Answers will vary.

MODÈLE sans devoirs?
Les étudiants s'amuseraient plus.

- sans voitures?
- sans télévisions?
- sans téléphones?
- sans ordinateurs?
- sans avions?
- ?

6 **Le tour de la France** Vous aimeriez faire le tour de la France avec un(e) partenaire. Regardez la carte et discutez de l'itinéraire. Où commenceriez-vous? Que visiteriez-vous? Utilisez ces idées et trouvez-en d'autres. Answers will vary.

MODÈLE
Nous commencerions à Paris.

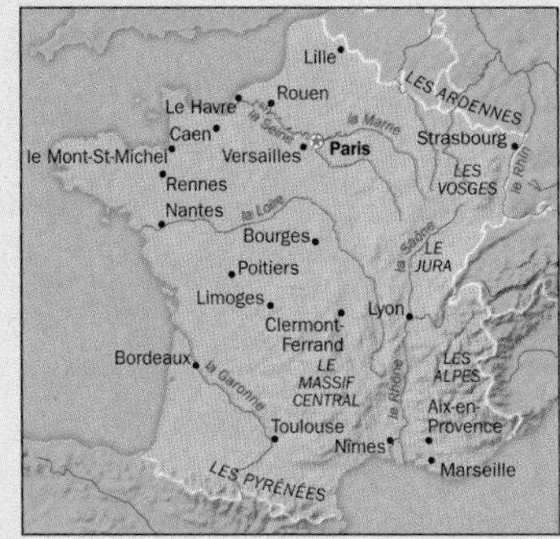

- les plages de la Côte d'Azur
- les randonnées dans le Centre
- le ski dans les Alpes
- les musées à Paris
- les châteaux (*castles*) de la Loire

- Use the conditional to make a polite request, soften a demand, or express what someone *could* or *should* do.

Je **voudrais** acheter une nouvelle imprimante.
I would like to buy a new printer.

Pourriez-vous nous dire où elles sont?
Could you tell us where they are?

Tu **devrais** dormir jusqu'à onze heures.
You should sleep until 11 o'clock.

Nous **aimerions** recevoir un salaire élevé.
We would like to receive a high salary.

Est-ce qu'il serait possible d'avoir une augmentation?

J'aimerais bien le faire, mais ce n'est pas possible.

- Use the conditional, along with a past-tense verb, to express what someone said or thought would happen in the future at a past moment in time.

Guillaume a dit qu'il **arriverait** vers midi.
Guillaume said that he would arrive around noon.

Nous pensions que tu **ferais** tes devoirs.
We thought that you would do your homework.

- The English *would* can also mean *used to*, in the sense of past habitual action. To express past habitual actions in French, use the **imparfait**.

Je **travaillais** pour une entreprise à Paris.
I would (used to) work for a company in Paris.

but

Je **travaillerais** seulement pour une entreprise à Paris.
I would work only for a company in Paris.

Essayez! **Indiquez la forme correcte du conditionnel de ces verbes.**

1. je (perdre, devoir, venir) *perdrais, devrais, viendrais*
2. tu (vouloir, aller, essayer) voudrais, irais, essaierais
3. Michel (dire, prendre, savoir) dirait, prendrait, saurait
4. nous (préférer, nettoyer, faire) préférerions, nettoierions, ferions
5. vous (être, pouvoir, avoir) seriez, pourriez, auriez
6. elles (dire, espérer, amener) diraient, espéreraient, amèneraient
7. je (boire, choisir, essuyer) boirais, choisirais, essuierais
8. il (tenir, se lever, envoyer) tiendrait, se lèverait, enverrait

Essayez! Have volunteers make up stories (two or three sentences long) using each of the items.

1 Suggestion Ask six volunteers to write the completed sentences on the board. Have other volunteers correct any errors.

2 Expansion Have students compose questions that would elicit the sentences from the activity as answers. Example: **Marc donnerait-il des devoirs?**

3 Suggestion Have students work in pairs on this activity.

4 Expansion Have volunteers use the third person to present their partner's responses to the questions.

5 Suggestion Before assigning the activity, have the class brainstorm other items similar to those in the activity. Ask a volunteer to write these items on the board.

6 Expansion Have pairs present their itinerary to the class. Ask volunteers to come up with questions for each pair.

OPTIONS

Pairs Have students take turns asking each other favors, using the conditional for courtesy. Partners respond by saying whether they will do the favor. If partners can't do it, they should make up an excuse. Example: **Pourrais-tu m'aider à faire mes devoirs ce soir? (Je suis désolé, je ne peux pas t'aider. Je dois aller chez mes parents ce soir.)**

Video Show the video again to give students more input on the use of the conditional. Stop the video where appropriate to discuss how and why the conditional was used.

NATIONAL STANDARDS comparisons

Section Goals

In this section, students will learn:

- the use of **si** clauses with the conditional
- **si** clauses with the present and **imparfait**

Instructional Resources
WB/VM: Workbook, pp. 179-180
Lab Manual, p. 104
Lab MP3s
WB/VM/LM Answer Key
*IRCD-ROM: IRM (**Essayez!** and **Mise en pratique** answers; Lab Audioscript)*
espaces.vhlcentral.com: activities, downloads, reference tools

Suggestions

- To help students sort out the possibilities with **si** clauses, make a chart with these headings: Condition, **Si** clause, Main clause. Under the first column, list the three types of **si** clauses introduced in this lesson: *contrary-to-fact, possible or likely,* and *suggestion or wish.* Under the second column, write these three items in order: **si** + *imperfect,* **si** + *present,* **si** + *imperfect.* Under the third column, write *imperfect, future or near future,* and *N/A.*
- Compare and contrast contrary-to-fact situations (which use the imperfect and the conditional) with events that are possible or likely to occur (which use the present and future) using the example sentences. Check understanding by providing main clauses and having volunteers finish the sentence with a **si** clause. Examples: **Je n'irais pas à Paris... (si je n'avais pas d'argent.) Elle travaillera comme professeur... (si elle obtient son doctorat.)**
- Ask volunteers to make a suggestion or express a wish using a **si** clause with the **imparfait.**
- Explain that a **si** clause in the past can also express something that is habitual in the past. Example: **Si mon amie m'invitait à une fête, j'y allais toujours.**

Essayez! Have students change the sentences from a contrary-to-fact situation to a possible or likely situation, and vice versa. Example: **1. Si on visite la Tunisie, on ira admirer les ruines.**

26.2 *Si* clauses

Point de départ **Si** (*If*) clauses describe a condition or event upon which another condition or event depends. Sentences with **si** clauses consist of a **si** clause and a main (or result) clause.

Si je faisais cette robe, elle serait laide.

- **Si** clauses can speculate or hypothesize about a current event or condition. They express what *would happen* if an event or condition *were to occur*. This is called a contrary-to-fact situation. In such instances, the verb in the **si** clause is in the **imparfait** while the verb in the main clause is in the conditional.

Si j'**étais** au chômage, je lui **enverrais** mon C.V.	Vous **partiriez** souvent en vacances si vous **aviez** de l'argent.
If I were unemployed, I'd send her my résumé.	*You would go on vacation often if you had money.*

- **Si** clauses can also express conditions or events that are possible or likely to occur. In such instances, the **si** clause is in the present while the main clause uses the **futur** or **futur proche**.

Si le patron me **renvoie**, je **trouverai** un emploi à mi-temps.	Si vous ne **signez** pas le contrat, vous **allez perdre** votre poste.
If the boss fires me, I'll find a part-time job.	*If you don't sign the contract, you're going to lose your job.*

- Use a **si** clause alone with the **imparfait** to make a suggestion or to express a wish.

Si nous **faisions** des projets pour le week-end?	Ah! Si elle **obtenait** un meilleur emploi!
What about making plans for the weekend?	*Oh! If only she got a better job!*

Essayez! **Complétez les phrases avec la forme correcte des verbes.**

1. Si on _visitait_ (visiter) la Tunisie, on irait admirer les ruines.
2. Vous _serez_ (être) plus heureux si vous faites vos devoirs.
3. Si tu _as_ (avoir) la grippe, tu devras aller chez le médecin.
4. Si elles _avaient_ (avoir) un million d'euros, que feraient-elles?
5. Mes parents me _rendront_ (rendre) visite ce week-end s'ils ont le temps.
6. J'_écrirais_ (écrire) au conseiller si j'avais son adresse.

MISE EN PRATIQUE

1 Questions Vous cherchez un emploi. Indiquez vos réponses aux questions du chef du personnel.

MODÈLE Quand est-ce que vous pourriez commencer? (vous / avoir besoin de moi / je / pouvoir commencer demain)
Si vous aviez besoin de moi, je pourrais commencer demain.

1. Est-ce que vous aimeriez travailler à plein temps? (vous / offrir un travail à plein temps / je / l'accepter) Si vous m'offriez un travail à plein temps, je l'accepterais.
2. Auriez-vous besoin d'assurance vie? (je / en avoir besoin / je / vous le dire) Si j'en avais besoin, je vous le dirais.
3. Quand prendriez-vous un congé? (mon/ma petite ami(e) / prendre un congé / nous / partir en mai) Si mon/ma petit(e) ami(e) prenait un congé, nous partirions en mai.
4. Voudriez-vous devenir cadre un jour? (vous / le permettre / je / devenir cadre dans deux ans) Si vous le permettiez, je deviendrais cadre dans deux ans.
5. Quand rentreriez-vous le soir? (nous / devoir travailler très tard / je / rentrer vers minuit) Si nous devions travailler très tard, je rentrerais vers minuit.

2 Et si... D'abord, complétez les questions. Ensuite, employez le conditionnel pour y répondre. Comparez vos réponses aux réponses d'un(e) partenaire. Some answers will vary.

MODÈLE Que ferais-tu si... tu / être malade?
Que ferais-tu si tu étais malade? Si j'étais malade, je dormirais toute la journée.

Situation 1: Que ferais-tu si...

1. tu / être fatigué(e)? ... si tu étais fatigué(e)?
2. il / pleuvoir? ... s'il pleuvait?
3. il / faire beau? ... s'il faisait beau?

Situation 2: Que feraient tes parents si...

1. tu / quitter l'université? ... si tu quittais l'université?
2. tu / choisir de devenir avocat(e)? ... si tu choisissais de devenir avocat(e)?
3. tu / partir habiter en France? ... si tu partais habiter en France?

3 Des réactions À tour de rôle avec un(e) partenaire, dites ce que (*what*) vous ferez dans ces circonstances. Answers will vary.

MODÈLE Vous trouvez votre petit(e) ami(e) avec un(e) autre garçon/fille.
Si je trouve mon petit ami..., je ne lui parlerai plus.

1. Vous n'avez pas de devoirs ce week-end.
2. Votre ami(e) organise une fête sans rien vous dire.
3. Vos parents ne vous téléphonent pas pendant un mois.
4. Le prof de français vous donne une mauvaise note.
5. Vous tombez malade.

OPTIONS

Video Replay the video episode, having students focus on **si** clauses. Ask students to write each one down as they hear it. Afterward, have them compare their notes in groups of four.

Extra Practice Ask each student to write a question that contains a **si** clause. Then have students walk around the room until you signal them to stop. On your cue, each student should turn to the nearest classmate. Give students three minutes to ask and answer one another's question before having them begin walking around the room again. Each time you say "stop," students should ask a new partner their question.

NATIONAL
communication
STANDARDS

COMMUNICATION

4 **L'imagination** Par groupes de trois, choisissez un de ces sujets et préparez un paragraphe par écrit. Ensuite, lisez votre paragraphe à la classe. Vos camarades décideront quel groupe est le gagnant (*winner*). Answers will vary.

- Si je pouvais devenir invisible,...
- Si j'étais un extraterrestre à New York,...
- Si j'inventais une machine,...
- Si j'étais une célébrité,...
- Si nous pouvions prendre des vacances sur Mars,...

5 **Le portefeuille** Vos camarades de classe trouvent un portefeuille (*wallet*) plein d'argent. Par groupes de quatre, parlez avec un(e) de vos camarades pour deviner ce que (*what*) feraient les deux autres. Ensuite, rejoignez-les pour comparer vos prédictions. Answers will vary.

MODÈLE

Étudiant(e) 1: *Si vous trouviez le portefeuille, vous le rendriez à la police.*
Étudiant(e) 2: *Oui, mais nous garderions l'argent pour aller dans un bon restaurant.*

6 **Interview** Par groupes de trois, préparez cinq questions pour un(e) candidat(e) à la présidence des États-Unis. Ensuite, jouez les rôles de l'interviewer et du/de la candidat(e). Alternez les rôles. Answers will vary.

MODÈLE

Étudiant(e) 1: *Que feriez-vous au sujet du sexisme dans l'armée?*
Étudiant(e) 2: *Alors, si j'étais président(e), nous...*

Le français vivant

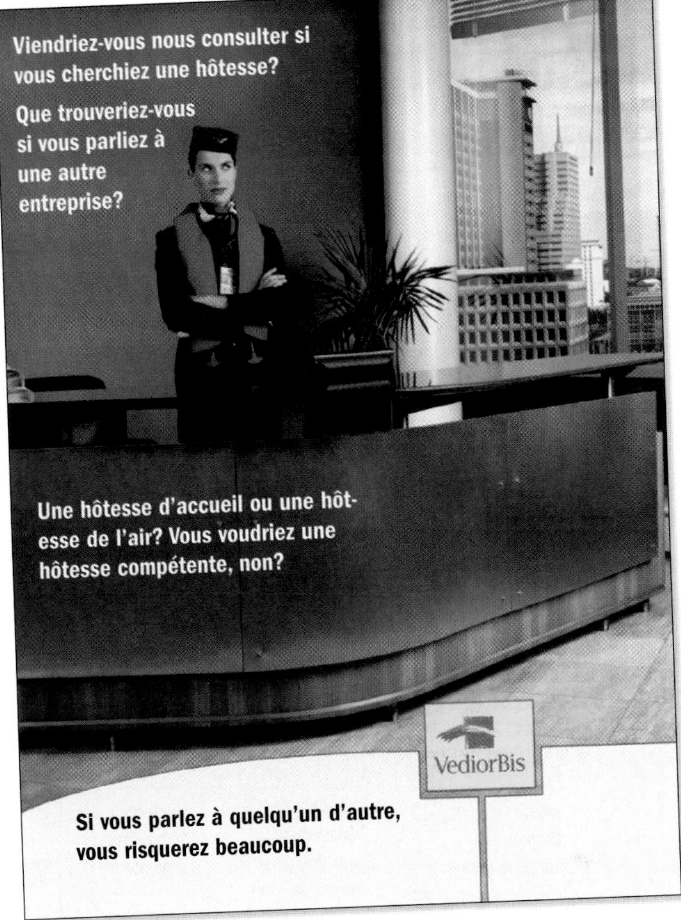
Viendriez-vous nous consulter si vous cherchiez une hôtesse?
Que trouveriez-vous si vous parliez à une autre entreprise?
Une hôtesse d'accueil ou une hôtesse de l'air? Vous voudriez une hôtesse compétente, non?
VediorBis
Si vous parlez à quelqu'un d'autre, vous risquerez beaucoup.

Identifiez Combien de phrases avec **si** trouvez-vous dans cette publicité (*ad*)? Lesquelles? Three: 1. Viendriez-vous nous consulter si vous cherchiez une hôtesse? 2. Que trouveriez-vous si vous parliez à une autre entreprise? 3. Si vous parlez à quelqu'un d'autre, vous risquerez beaucoup.

Questions À tour de rôle, avec un(e) partenaire, posez-vous ces questions. Answers will vary.

1. Pourquoi irait-on chez VediorBis?
2. Quelle erreur pourrait-on éviter?
3. Comment font les conseillers de VediorBis pour trouver l'emploi et l'employé(e) idéal(e) pour tous leurs clients?
4. Irais-tu consulter VediorBis si tu étais au chômage? Pourquoi?

1 Expansion Have students come up with three more questions for their **chef du personnel**. Then have students swap their questions with their classmates and answer their questions using **si** clauses.

2 Expansion Write more situations like those in the activity. Example: **Situation 3: Que feriez-vous si... 1. vous / gagner à la loterie? 2. le club de français / offre un voyage en France? 3. le professeur de français / être malade?**

3 Suggestion Organize the class into two groups: **si** + **le présent** and **si + l'imparfait**. Have each group complete the activity using the tenses according to their groups. Then discuss the different meanings of the sentences produced by each group.

4 Suggestion Before assigning this activity, write **Si nous pouvions prédire** (*predict*) **l'avenir...** on the board. Brainstorm possible main clauses with the whole class.

5 Expansion Have groups of four brainstorm other moral dilemmas using **Que feraient vos camarades de classe si...** Example: **...s'ils trouvaient les réponses de l'examen de français.**

6 Suggestions

- You may wish to have students pick a different prominent politician that interests them.
- Videotape the interviews and show parts during the next class or check out the tape to students for viewing out of class.

Le français vivant Call on a volunteer to read the ad aloud. Have students point out all the instances of the conditional.

OPTIONS

Pairs Ask students to reflect on their French study habits. Then assign them partners to write a list of eight complex sentences to express what they could do better. Example: **Si je lisais un journal français tous les jours, je pourrais mieux comprendre la langue.**

Small Groups Ask students to bring in the most outlandish news report they can find. In groups of four, have students write a list of statements that use **si** clauses about each report. Example: **Si les extraterrestres venaient à Washington, D.C. pour avoir un rendez-vous avec le président des États-Unis...**

Synthèse

Instructional Resources
IRCD-ROM: IRM (Info Gap Activities); Testing Program, pp. 101–104; Test Files; Testing Program MP3s; Test Generator espaces.vhlcentral.com: activities, downloads, reference tools

1 Suggestion Have volunteers share their list with the class.

2 Expansion Ask groups to choose a **métier** not listed in the activity. Then have them write a short paragraph describing what they would and would not do in that position. Have one volunteer from each group read the group's paragraph aloud.

3 Suggestion Point out that this activity elicits sentences that are contrary to fact. Remind students that their sentences should include the conditional tense in the main clause and the imperfect tense in the **si** clause.

4 Expansion Have partners continue the activity using magazine pictures and new sentences.

5 Suggestion Before assigning the activity, ask the class polite questions using **pouvoir** in the conditional tense. Examples: **Pourriez-vous me prêter votre livre? Pourrais-je vous poser une question? Pourriez-vous m'expliquer...?**

6 Suggestion Divide the class into pairs and distribute the Info Gap Handouts in the IRM on the IRCD-ROM for this activity. Give students ten minutes to complete the activity.

1 Du changement Avec un(e) partenaire, observez ces bureaux. Faites une liste d'au minimum huit changements que les employés feraient s'ils en avaient les moyens (*means*). Answers will vary.

MODÈLE

Étudiant(e) 1: *Si ces gens pouvaient changer quelque chose, ils achèteraient de nouveaux ordinateurs.*
Étudiant(e) 2: *Si les affaires allaient mieux, ils déménageraient.*

2 Si j'étais... Par groupes de quatre, discutez et faites votre propre (*own*) portrait à travers (*through*) ces métiers. Utilisez la phrase **Si j'étais...** Comparez vos réponses et présentez le portrait d'un(e) camarade à la classe. Answers will vary.

MODÈLE

Étudiant(e) 1: *Si j'étais cuisinier/cuisinière, je ne préparerais que des desserts.*
Étudiant(e) 2: *Si je travaillais comme chauffeur, je ne conduirais que sur l'autoroute.*

artiste	conseiller/ conseillère	médecin
chauffeur	cuisinier/cuisinière	patron(ne)
chef d'entreprise	femme au foyer	professeur
chercheur/chercheuse		

3 Je démissionnerais... Pour quelles raisons seriez-vous prêt(e)s à démissionner de votre travail? Par groupes de trois, donnez chacun(e) (*each one*) au minimum deux raisons positives et deux raisons négatives. Answers will vary.

MODÈLE

Étudiant(e) 1: *Je démissionnerais si je devais suivre ma famille et déménager loin.*
Étudiant(e) 2: *Moi, je démissionnerais tout de suite si je m'ennuyais dans mon travail.*

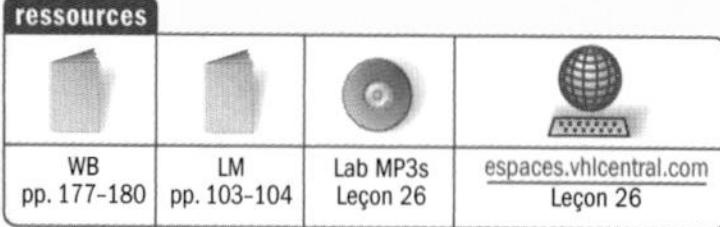

ressources
WB pp. 177–180
LM pp. 103–104
Lab MP3s Leçon 26
espaces.vhlcentral.com Leçon 26

4 Au travail Avec un(e) partenaire, observez ces personnes et écrivez une phrase avec **si** pour expliquer leur situation. Ensuite, comparez vos phrases aux phrases d'un autre groupe. Answers will vary.

MODÈLE

Si elle dort au travail, sa patronne la renverra.

1.

3.

2.

4.

5 Un(e) patron(ne) poli(e) Avec un(e) partenaire, inventez un dialogue entre un(e) patron(ne) et son/sa secrétaire. Le/La patron(ne) demande plusieurs services au/à la secrétaire, qui refuse. Le/La patron(ne) recommence alors ses demandes, mais plus poliment, et le/la secrétaire accepte. Answers will vary.

MODÈLE

Étudiant(e) 1: *Apportez-moi le téléphone!*
Étudiant(e) 2: *Si vous me parlez comme ça, je ne vous apporterai rien.*
Étudiant(e) 1: *Pourriez-vous m'apporter le téléphone, s'il vous plaît?*
Étudiant(e) 2: *Avec plaisir!*

6 Les emplois Votre professeur va vous donner, à vous et à votre partenaire, deux feuilles d'activités différentes sur les emplois. Attention! Ne regardez pas la feuille de votre partenaire. Answers will vary.

OPTIONS

Extra Practice Ask students to finish the following sentences logically: **1. S'il ne pleut pas demain... 2. Si j'avais assez d'argent... 3. Si mon/ma petit(e) ami(e) gagnait à la loterie... 4. Si j'étais psychologue... 5. S'il faisait beau...** Encourage them to be creative.

Pairs Have pairs write ten sentences about what they would do to improve their campus. First, ask them to list the problems they would change and how they would do so. Then have them form their sentences as contrary-to-fact statements. Example: **S'il y avait plus d'aide financière, les étudiants n'auraient pas de prêts étudiants** (*student loans*).

L'espace vert

UNITÉ 14

Pour commencer

- Où est le groupe d'amis?
  a. à la mer b. à la campagne c. en ville
- Qu'est-ce qu'ils vont faire?
  a. un pique-nique b. les courses c. du vélo
- Qu'est-ce qu'il y a derrière eux?
  a. une jungle b. une montagne c. un pont

Leçon 27

ESPACE **CONTEXTES**
pages 470–473
- Environmental concerns
- French and English spelling

ESPACE **ROMAN-PHOTO**
pages 474–475
- **Une idée de génie**

ESPACE **CULTURE**
pages 476–477
- The ecological movement in France

ESPACE **STRUCTURES**
pages 478–483
- Demonstrative pronouns
- The subjunctive (Part 1)
- **Synthèse**
- **Interlude**

Leçon 28

ESPACE **CONTEXTES**
pages 484–487
- Nature
- Homophones

ESPACE **ROMAN-PHOTO**
pages 488–489
- **La randonnée**

ESPACE **CULTURE**
pages 490–491
- National parks

ESPACE **STRUCTURES**
pages 492–497
- The subjunctive (Part 2)
- Comparatives and superlatives of nouns
- **Synthèse**
- **Le zapping**

Savoir-faire

pages 498–503

Panorama: L'Afrique de l'ouest et l'Afrique centrale

Lecture: Read an excerpt from a book.

À l'écoute: Listen to a speech about the environment.

Écriture: Write a letter or an article about an ecological concern.

Flash culture

Unit Goals

Leçon 27

In this lesson, students will learn:
- terms related to ecology and the environment
- common differences in French and English spelling
- about the ecological movement and nuclear energy in France
- the demonstrative pronouns **celui**, **celle**, **ceux**, and **celles**
- to form **le subjonctif**
- common impersonal expressions that take the subjunctive
- about singer Jacques Brel and painter Georges de Feure

Leçon 28

In this lesson, students will learn:
- terms to discuss nature and conservation
- about homophones
- about France's national park system and Madagascar
- about the subjunctive with verbs and expressions of will and emotion
- verbs with irregular subjunctive forms
- the comparative and superlative of nouns
- about Yves Rocher and the **Végétarium**

Savoir-faire

In this section, students will learn:
- cultural and historical information about the francophone countries of West and Central Africa
- to recognize chronological order in a text
- to listen for the gist and cognates
- to consider audience and purpose when writing
- more about the diverse geography of the francophone world through specially shot video footage

Pour commencer

- **b. à la campagne**
- **a. un pique-nique**
- **b. une montagne**

RESOURCES

Workbook/Video Manual: WB Activities, pp. 183–196
Laboratory Manual: Lab Activities, pp. 105–112
Workbook/Video Manual: Video Activities, pp. 263–266; pp. 297–298
WB/VM/LM Answer Key
Instructor's Resource CD-ROM [IRCD-ROM]: Instructor's Resource Manual [IRM] (Textbook Audioscript; Lab Audioscript; Videoscript; **Roman-photo** Translations; **Vocabulaire supplémentaire**; **Feuilles d'activités**; Info Gap Activities; **Le zapping** TV clip transcription; **Essayez!** and **Mise en pratique** answers); Transparencies #57, #58, #59; Testing Program, pp. 105–112; Test Files; Testing Program MP3s; Test Generator
Lab MP3s
Textbook MP3s
Video CD-ROM
Video on DVD
espaces.vhlcentral.com

Section Goals

In this section, students will learn and practice vocabulary related to:
- ecology
- the environment

Instructional Resources
*IRCD-ROM: Transparency #57; IRM (**Vocabulaire supplémentaire; Mise en pratique** answers; Textbook Audioscript; Lab Audioscript)*
Textbook MP3s
WB/VM: Workbook, pp. 183–184
Lab Manual, p. 105
Lab MP3s
WB/VM/LM Answer Key
espaces.vhlcentral.com: activities, downloads, reference tools

Suggestions
- Tell students to look over the new vocabulary and identify the cognates.
- Use **Transparency #57.** Point out people and things as you describe the illustration. Examples: **Elle recycle. Ils ont pollué. C'est une centrale nucléaire.**
- Point out the double consonants in the words **développer** and **environnement**.
- Point out the verb **interdire** and the sign next to it. Write on the board: **Il est interdit de....** Then have students finish the sentence with various things people might be forbidden to do, such as **gaspiller de l'énergie**.
- Ask students questions using the new vocabulary. Examples: **L'université a-t-elle un programme de recyclage? Quels objets recyclez-vous? Que faites-vous pour réduire la pollution? Quel est le plus gros problème écologique de notre région? L'énergie solaire est-elle mieux que l'énergie nucléaire? Pourquoi? Où y a-t-il souvent des glissements de terrain?**
- Additional vocabulary for this lesson can be found in the **Vocabulaire supplémentaire** in the IRM on the IRCD-ROM.

Leçon 27

You will learn how to...
- talk about pollution
- talk about what needs to be done

Sauvons la planète!

un nuage de pollution
la pluie acide
l'énergie nucléaire (*f.*)
l'énergie solaire (*f.*)
une centrale nucléaire
USINE AUTOMOBILE
la pollution
le covoiturage

Vocabulaire

abolir	*to abolish*
améliorer	*to improve*
développer	*to develop*
gaspiller	*to waste*
préserver	*to preserve*
prévenir l'incendie	*to prevent a fire*
proposer une solution	*to propose a solution*
sauver la planète	*to save the planet*
une catastrophe	*catastrophe*
un danger	*danger, threat*
des déchets toxiques (*m.*)	*toxic waste*
l'effet de serre (*m.*)	*greenhouse effect*
le gaspillage	*waste*
un glissement de terrain	*landslide*
une population croissante	*growing population*
le réchauffement de la Terre	*global warming*
la surpopulation	*overpopulation*
le trou dans la couche d'ozone	*hole in the ozone layer*
une usine	*factory*
l'écologie (*f.*)	*ecology*
un emballage en plastique	*plastic wrapping/packaging*
l'environnement (*m.*)	*environment*
un espace	*space*
un produit	*product*
la protection	*protection*
écologique	*ecological*
en plein air	*outdoor, open-air*
pur(e)	*pure*
un gouvernement	*government*
une loi	*law*

ressources
WB pp. 183–184 | LM p. 105 | Text MP3s Leçon 27 | Lab MP3s Leçon 27 | espaces.vhlcentral.com Leçon 27

OPTIONS

Extra Practice Whisper a vocabulary word in a student's ear. That student should draw a picture or a series of pictures that represent the word on the board. The class must guess the word, then spell it in French as a volunteer writes the word on the board.

Game Divide the class into two teams. Have a spelling bee using vocabulary words from **Contextes**. Pronounce each word, use it in a sentence, and then say the word again. Tell students that they must spell the words in French and include all diacritical marks.

Mise en pratique

1 Écoutez Écoutez l'annonce radio suivante. Ensuite, complétez les phrases avec le mot ou l'expression qui convient le mieux.

1. C'est l'annonce radio ______
   a. d'un groupe d'étudiants.
   b. d'une entreprise commerciale.
   (c.) d'une agence écologiste.
2. La protection de l'environnement, c'est l'affaire ______
   (a.) de tous.
   b. du gouvernement.
   c. des centres de recyclage.
3. L'annonce dit qu'on peut recycler ______
   (a.) les emballages en plastique et en papier.
   b. les boîtes de conserve.
   c. les bouteilles en plastique.
4. Pour les déchets toxiques, il y a ______
   a. le ramassage des ordures.
   (b.) le centre de recyclage.
   c. l'effet de serre.
5. Pour ne pas gaspiller l'eau, on peut ______
   a. acheter des produits écologiques.
   b. développer les incendies.
   (c.) prendre des douches plus courtes.

2 Composez Utilisez les éléments de chaque colonne pour former six phrases cohérentes au sujet de l'environnement. Vous pouvez composer des phrases affirmatives ou négatives. Answers will vary.

Les gens	Les actions	Les éléments
vous	développer	l'eau
on	gaspiller	le covoiturage
les gens	polluer	l'énergie solaire
le gouvernement	préserver	l'environnement
les entreprises	proposer	la planète
les centrales nucléaires	sauver	la Terre

3 Complétez Complétez les phrases suivantes avec le mot ou l'expression qui convient le mieux pour parler de l'environnement. N'oubliez pas les accords.

1. Nous avons trois poubelles différentes pour pouvoir ___recycler___.
2. ___L'effet de serre___ contribue au réchauffement de la Terre.
3. ___Les centrales nucléaires___ produisent près de 80% de l'énergie en France.
4. Les pluies ont provoqué ___un glissement de terrain___. À présent, la route est fermée.
5. Chez moi, ___le ramassage___ des ordures se fait tous les lundis.
6. L'accident à l'usine chimique a provoqué un ___nuage de pollution___.

1 Tapescript L'écologie, c'est l'affaire de tous! Aidez-nous à préserver et à améliorer l'environnement. Tout commence avec le ramassage des ordures: recyclez vos emballages en plastique et en papier! Ne polluez pas: votre centre de recyclage local est là pour s'occuper de vos déchets toxiques. Ne gaspillez pas l'eau, surtout en cette période de réchauffement de la Terre: comment? Prenez des douches plus courtes! Nous vous rappelons également qu'une loi interdit de laver sa voiture dans certaines régions de France quand il fait extrêmement chaud l'été. Ne gaspillez pas non plus l'énergie: faites attention à la consommation inutile d'énergie de vos appareils électriques. Enfin, évitez d'acheter des produits qui peuvent mettre l'environnement en danger: choisissez des produits écologiques. Ensemble, nous sommes plus forts! Nous développons et proposons des solutions simples. Alors, la prochaine fois que vous entendrez parler de pluies acides, de trou dans la couche d'ozone, de l'effet de serre, de pollution et de catastrophe écologique, vous pourrez être fier de dire que vous faites partie de la solution.

Ceci était un message de l'agence nationale pour la protection de l'environnement. *(On Textbook MP3s)*

1 Suggestion Go over the answers with the class. Ask volunteers to read the complete sentences.

2 Suggestion This activity can be done orally or in writing in pairs or groups.

3 Expansion For additional practice, give students these items. **7. Une nouvelle étude des Nations Unies confirme qu'il y a un risque de ____. (surpopulation) En 2050, il y aura neuf milliards (*billions*) de personnes sur Terre. 8. Le parti écologiste veut améliorer ____ de l'environnement. (la protection) 9. Le gouvernement vient de passer ____ sur le transport des déchets toxiques. (une loi) 10. Nous évitons de laisser ____ derrière nous quand nous mangeons dans le parc. (des ordures)**

OPTIONS

Game Play a game of **Dix questions**. Ask a volunteer to think of a word or expression from the new vocabulary. Other students get to ask one yes/no question, then they can guess what the word is. Limit attempts to ten questions per word. You may want to write some phrases on the board to cue students' questions.

Pairs Have students work in pairs. Write the following list of dangers facing our planet on the board. Tell students to rank them from the most serious to least serious and explain why. Dangers: **la surpopulation, le réchauffement de la Terre, les déchets toxiques, la pollution de l'environnement, la pluie acide, l'effet de serre, le risque d'accident dans une centrale nucléaire**, and **la crise de l'énergie**

4 Suggestion Tell students that their descriptions should include the weather, the time of day, and a possible location.

4 Expansion Bring in additional photos from magazines or the Internet that illustrate ecological problems and have students describe what they see.

5 Suggestion You may wish to assign groups specific situations so that all of them are covered.

6 Suggestion Ask a volunteer to read the **modèle** aloud. Then have students brainstorm a list of words and expressions that are used to inform, persuade, or register a complaint.

Communication

NATIONAL STANDARDS communication

4 Décrivez Avec un(e) partenaire, décrivez ces photos et donnez autant de détails et d'informations que possible. Soyez prêt(e)s à présenter vos descriptions à la classe. Answers will vary.

1.

3.

2.

4.

5 À vous de jouer Par petits groupes, préparez une conversation au sujet d'une des situations suivantes. Ensuite jouez la scène devant la classe. Answers will vary.

- Un(e) employé(e) du centre de recyclage local vient dans votre université pour expliquer aux étudiants un nouveau système de recyclage. De nombreux étudiants posent des questions.
- Un groupe d'écologistes rencontre le patron d'une entreprise accusée de polluer la rivière (*river*) locale.
- Le ministre de l'environnement donne une conférence de presse au sujet d'une nouvelle loi sur la protection de l'environnement.
- Votre colocataire oublie systématiquement de recycler les emballages. Vous avez une conversation animée avec lui/elle.

6 L'article Vous êtes journaliste et vous devez écrire un article pour le journal local au sujet de la pollution. Vous expliquez les causes et les conséquences sur l'environnement. Vous suggérez aussi des solutions pour améliorer la situation. Answers will vary.

MODÈLE

Les dangers de la pollution chimique

Les usines chimiques de notre région polluent! C'est une catastrophe pour notre environnement. Il faut leur interdire de fonctionner jusqu'à ce qu'elles améliorent leurs systèmes de recyclage…

OPTIONS

Pairs Write these expressions for circumlucution on the board: **C'est un endroit où…, Ça sert à…, C'est le contraire de…, C'est un synonyme de…, C'est quand on…**. Then have pairs of students write definitions for these vocabulary words. **1. améliorer 2. un incendie 3. le recyclage 4. le covoiturage 5. la pollution 6. une catastrophe 7. une loi 8. une usine 9. le réchauffement de la Terre**

Have pairs get together with another pair of students and take turns reading their definitions and guessing the word. Ask each group to choose their best definition and write it on the board for the whole class to guess.

COMMUNICATION

4 **La pollution** Que pensent vos camarades de la pollution? Posez ces questions à un(e) partenaire. Ensuite, présentez les réponses à la classe. Answers will vary.

1. Quelles voitures polluent le moins: les voitures hybrides ou les voitures de sport? Lesquelles préfères-tu?
2. Si tu devais choisir entre ces deux voitures, laquelle prendrais-tu: celle qui est la plus rapide ou celle qui pollue le moins? Pourquoi?
3. Connais-tu quelqu'un qui fait régulièrement du covoiturage? Qui? Pourquoi le fait-il/elle?
4. Les emballages en plastique polluent-ils plus que ceux en papier? Pourquoi?
5. Est-ce que ceux qui recyclent leurs déchets aident à préserver la nature? Pourquoi?
6. Parmi (*Among*) les pays industrialisés, lesquels polluent le plus? Lesquels polluent le moins?

5 **Définitions** Votre petit frère vous demande de lui expliquer ces expressions. Avec un(e) partenaire, alternez les rôles pour donner leurs définitions. Utilisez **celui qui, celle qui, ceux qui** et **celles qui.** Answers will vary.

MODÈLE

un pollueur
Étudiant(e) 1: *Qu'est-ce que c'est, un pollueur?*
Étudiant(e) 2: *C'est celui qui laisse des papiers sales dans la rue.*

- les déchets toxiques
- un(e) écologiste
- un écoproduit
- l'énergie solaire
- la pluie acide
- les voitures hybrides

6 **D'accord, pas d'accord** Par groupes de quatre, faites ce sondage (*survey*). Qui est d'accord ou qui n'est pas d'accord avec ces phrases? Justifiez vos réponses. Ensuite, comparez-les avec celles d'un autre groupe. Answers will vary.

	D'accord	Pas d'accord
1. Les déchets toxiques d'une centrale nucléaire sont plus dangereux que ceux d'une centrale électrique.	____	____
2. Les sacs en plastique sont aussi facilement recyclables que ceux en papier.	____	____
3. En ce qui concerne la voiture du futur, la voiture hybride est celle dont on parle le plus.	____	____
4. Les déchets qui polluent le plus sont ceux des centrales nucléaires.	____	____

Le français vivant

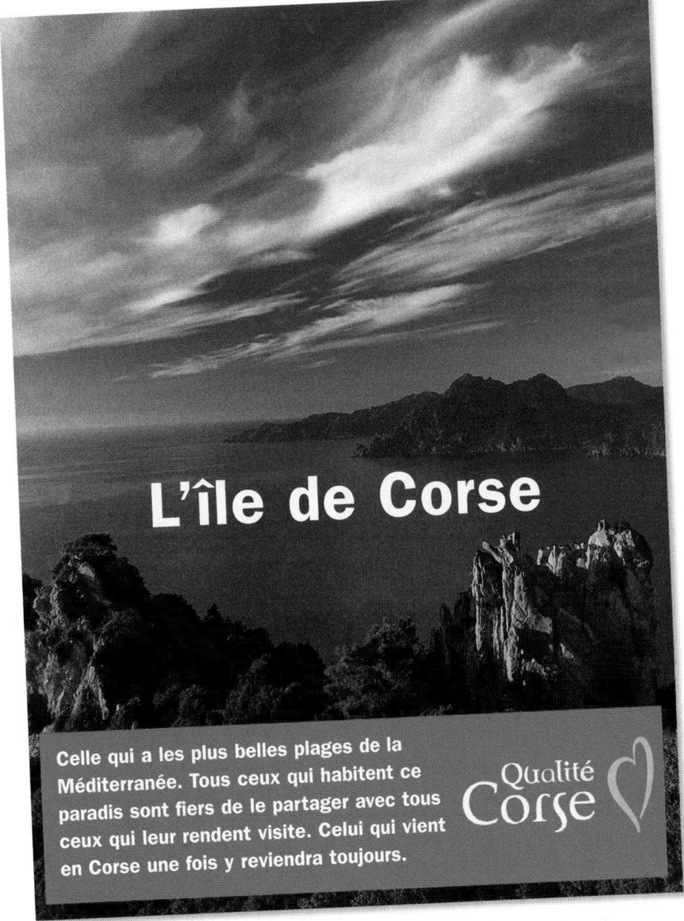

L'île de Corse
Celle qui a les plus belles plages de la Méditerranée. Tous ceux qui habitent ce paradis sont fiers de le partager avec tous ceux qui leur rendent visite. Celui qui vient en Corse une fois y reviendra toujours.
Qualité Corse

Identifiez Quels pronoms démonstratifs trouvez-vous dans la publicité (*ad*)? Celle, ceux, Celui

Questions À tour de rôle, avec un(e) partenaire, posez-vous ces questions. Employez des pronoms démonstratifs dans vos réponses, si possible. Answers will vary.

1. D'après (*According to*) la pub, quelles sont les plus belles plages de la Méditerranée? celles de la Corse
2. Qui est fier de partager la Corse? tous ceux qui y habitent
3. Que veut celui qui vient une fois en Corse? Celui qui vient en Corse veut y revenir.
4. Y a-t-il un endroit dans le monde qui a eu cet effet sur toi? Lequel?
5. Voudrais-tu visiter la Corse un jour? Pourquoi?

1 Suggestion You might want to have students complete items 1, 3, and 4 first. Then remind them of the suffixes **-ci** and **-là** before proceeding to items 2, 5, and 6.

2 Suggestion Remind students that French speakers usually refer to a near object with **-ci** before referring to a far object with **-là** in the same sentence.

3 Suggestion Have two volunteers read the **modèle** aloud to the class. Then review forms of the relative pronoun **lequel**. Make sure students understand the different ways **lequel** and **celui** are used.

4 Expansion Introduce students to a concept of personal responsibility from existentialism: **la mauvaise foi**. A person that acts in **mauvaise foi** behaves in a way that is inconsistent with his or her true beliefs. Ask the class to categorize certain behaviors as a **politique de bonne foi** or a **politique de mauvaise foi** for an environmentalist. Examples: **le covoiturage (bonne foi)** and **conduire une grosse voiture qui pollue l'air (mauvaise foi).**

5 Suggestion Have students draw pictures like those in children's books to accompany their definitions.

6 Expansion Have groups select a topic from the list and prepare a small debate. Regardless of their personal beliefs, one student should advocate **d'accord** and the other **pas d'accord**.

Le français vivant Hand out or have students copy the text in the advertisement. Tell them to underline the demonstrative pronouns. Then ask them what they think the antecedents are.

OPTIONS

Extra Practice Have small groups of students prepare a fashion outlook for the season. They should make collages with pictures from magazines or the Internet of the latest styles and tell the class what they think of them, using forms of the demonstrative pronoun **celui** whenever possible. Example: **Ce jean-ci est laid! J'aime mieux celui-là.**

Extra Practice Make a set of index cards, organized in pairs with two similar objects, one on each card. Then prompt students to evaluate the objects with questions using forms of **lequel** and **celui.** Example: (*two pictures of automobiles*) **Laquelle pollue moins, à votre avis? Celle-ci ou celle-là? (La voiture rouge!)**

Section Goals

In this section, students will learn:
- the present subjunctive of regular verbs
- to use the subjunctive after some impersonal expressions

Instructional Resources
WB/VM: Workbook, pp. 187–188
Lab Manual, p. 108
Lab MP3s
WB/VM/LM Answer Key
*IRCD-ROM: IRM (**Essayez!** and **Mise en pratique** answers; Lab Audioscript)*
espaces.vhlcentral.com: activities, downloads, reference tools

Suggestions
- Remind students that verbs ending in **-ier** have a double **i** in the **nous** and **vous** forms of the present subjunctive: **étudiiez, skiions**, etc. (They learned this in **Leçon 15** with the **imparfait**.)
- Tell the class that to negate impersonal expressions they should place the negative particles around the conjugated verb in the indicative not around the subjunctive verb that follows in the next clause. Example: **Il ne faut pas qu'elle mette ces ordures dans le bac à recyclage.**
- Point out to students that the expressions **il faut** and **il vaut mieux** can be followed by an infinitive. Example: **Il vaut mieux partager sa voiture de temps en temps.** You could also point out that the other expressions in the list can be followed by **de/d'** + *infinitive*. Example: **Il est nécessaire de partager sa voiture de temps en temps.**
- Read aloud a set of logical and illogical statements about environmentalism that make use of impersonal expressions and the subjunctive. Students should respond by saying **logique** or **illogique.** Example: **Pour éviter de gaspiller l'essence, il vaut mieux qu'on recycle le verre. (illogique)**

27.2 The subjunctive (Part 1)

Introduction, regular verbs, and impersonal expressions

Point de départ With the exception of commands and the conditional, the verb forms you have learned have been in the indicative mood. The indicative is used to state facts and to express actions or states that the speaker considers real and definite. In contrast, the subjunctive mood expresses the speaker's subjective attitudes toward events, as well as actions or states the speaker views as uncertain or hypothetical.

Present subjunctive of one-stem verbs

	parler	finir	attendre
que je/j'	parle	finisse	attende
que tu	parles	finisses	attendes
qu'il/elle	parle	finisse	attende
que nous	parlions	finissions	attendions
que vous	parliez	finissiez	attendiez
qu'ils/elles	parlent	finissent	attendent

- The present subjunctive endings are the same for all verb groups. For **je**, **tu**, **il/elle**, and **ils/elles**, add the endings to the stem of the **ils/elles** form of the present indicative.

INFINITIVE	PRESENT INDICATIVE OF ILS/ELLES	PRESENT SUBJUNCTIVE
parler	parlent	que je parle
finir	finissent	que je finisse
attendre	attendent	que j'attende

Il est nécessaire qu'on **évite** le gaspillage.
It is necessary that we avoid waste.

Il est important que tu **réfléchisses** aux dangers.
It is important that you think about the dangers.

- The **nous** and **vous** forms of the present subjunctive are the same as those of the **imparfait**.

Il vaut mieux que nous **préservions** l'environnement.
It is better that we preserve the environment.

Il est essentiel que vous **trouviez** un meilleur travail.
It is essential that you find a better job.

Il faut que nous **commencions**.
It is necessary that we start.

Il est bon que vous **réfléchissiez.**
It is good that you're thinking.

BOÎTE À OUTILS
English also uses the subjunctive. It used to be very common, but now survives mostly in expressions such as *if I were you* and *be that as it may*.

MISE EN PRATIQUE

1 Prévenir et améliorer Complétez ces phrases avec la forme correcte des verbes au présent du subjonctif.

1. Il est essentiel que je __recycle__ (recycler).
2. Il est important que nous __réduisions__ (réduire) la pollution.
3. Il faut que le gouvernement __interdise__ (interdire) les voitures polluantes (*polluting*).
4. Il vaut mieux que vous __amélioriez__ (améliorer) les transports en commun (*public transportation*).
5. Il est possible que les pays __prennent__ (prendre) des mesures pour réduire les déchets toxiques.
6. Il est indispensable que tu __boives__ (boire) de l'eau pure.

2 Sur le campus Quelles règles les étudiants qui habitent sur le campus doivent-ils suivre? Transformez ces phrases avec **il faut** et le présent du subjonctif.

MODÈLE Vous devez vous coucher avant minuit.
Il faut que vous vous couchiez avant minuit.

1. Le matin, vous devez vous lever à sept heures.
Le matin, il faut que vous vous leviez à sept heures.
2. Ils doivent fermer leur porte avant de partir.
Il faut qu'ils ferment leur porte avant de partir.
3. Tu dois prendre le bus au coin de la rue.
Il faut que tu prennes le bus au coin de la rue.
4. Je dois déjeuner au resto U à midi.
Il faut que je déjeune au resto U à midi.
5. Nous devons rentrer tôt pendant la semaine.
Il faut que nous rentrions tôt pendant la semaine.
6. Elle doit travailler pour payer ses études.
Il faut qu'elle travaille pour payer ses études.

3 Éviter une catastrophe Que devons-nous faire pour préserver notre planète? Avec un(e) partenaire, faites des phrases avec des expressions impersonnelles.
Answers will vary.

MODÈLE
Il est essentiel que tu évites le gaspillage.

A	B	C
je/j'	améliorer	les écoproduits
tu	développer	les emballages
on	éviter	le gaspillage
nous	préserver	les glissements de terrain
vous	prévenir	les industries propres
le président	recycler	la nature
les pays	sauver	la pollution
?	trouver	le ramassage des ordures

OPTIONS

Video Distribute copies of the script for the last scene of the video for **Leçon 27** and have students underline all the verbs. Ask them to identify the mood (indicative, imperative, or subjunctive) of each verb. When they realize that the subjunctive is used rarely, point out that native speakers often avoid the subjunctive because it can be tricky for them, too.

Extra Practice Have the class make up a list of ten environmental resolutions using some of the impersonal expressions listed on page 481. Help them when they need expressions such as *a recycling bin* (**un bac à recyclage**). Example: **Il est essentiel qu'on préserve la nature.**

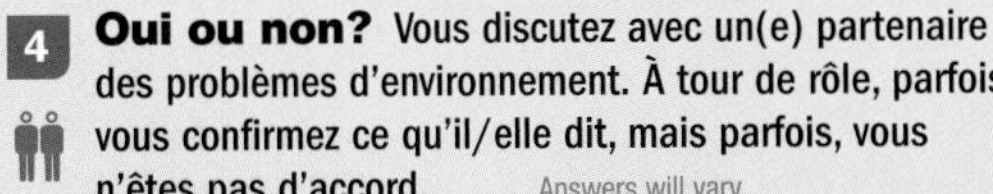

4 **Oui ou non?** Vous discutez avec un(e) partenaire des problèmes d'environnement. À tour de rôle, parfois, vous confirmez ce qu'il/elle dit, mais parfois, vous n'êtes pas d'accord. Answers will vary.

MODÈLE

Étudiant(e) 1: *Il faut que les pays industrialisés réduisent les émissions à effet de serre.*
Étudiant(e) 2: *C'est vrai, il faut qu'ils réduisent les émissions à effet de serre.*

1. Il est nécessaire que tu recycles les bouteilles.
2. Il est dommage que les étudiants prennent le bus pour aller à la fac.
3. Il est bon qu'on développe des énergies propres.
4. Il est essentiel qu'on signe le protocole de Kyoto.
5. Il est indispensable que nous évitions le gaspillage.
6. Il faut que les pays développent de nouvelles technologies pour réduire les émissions toxiques.

5 **Les opinions** Vous discutez avec un(e) partenaire des problèmes de pollution. À tour de rôle, répondez à ces questions. Justifiez vos réponses. Answers will vary.

MODÈLE

Étudiant(e) 1: *Faut-il que nous préservions l'environnement?*
Étudiant(e) 2: *Oui, il faut que nous préservions l'environnement pour éviter le réchauffement de la Terre.*

1. Est-il important qu'on s'intéresse à l'écologie?
2. Faut-il qu'on évite de gaspiller?
3. Est-il essentiel que nous construisions des centrales nucléaires?
4. Vaut-il mieux que j'utilise des bacs (*bins*) à recyclage pour le ramassage des ordures?
5. Est-il indispensable qu'on prévienne les incendies?
6. Est-il possible qu'on développe l'énergie solaire?

6 **L'écologie** Par groupes de quatre, regardez les deux photos et parlez des problèmes écologiques qu'elles évoquent. Ensuite, préparez par écrit une liste des solutions. Comparez votre liste avec celles de la classe. Answers will vary.

MODÈLE

Étudiant(e) 1: *Aujourd'hui, il y a trop d'ordures.*
Étudiant(e) 2: *Il faut qu'on développe le recyclage.*

- The verbs on the preceding page are called one-stem verbs because the same stem is used for all the endings. Two-stem verbs have a different stem for **nous** and **vous**, but the rule still applies: the forms are identical to those of the **imparfait**.

Present subjunctive of two-stem verbs

	acheter	venir	prendre	boire
que je/j'	achète	vienne	prenne	boive
que tu	achètes	viennes	prennes	boives
qu'il/elle	achète	vienne	prenne	boive
que nous	achetions	venions	prenions	buvions
que vous	achetiez	veniez	preniez	buviez
qu'ils/elles	achètent	viennent	prennent	boivent

- The subjunctive is usually used in complex sentences that consist of a main clause and a subordinate clause. The main clause contains a verb or expression that triggers the subjunctive. The word **que** connects the two clauses.

- These impersonal expressions of opinion are often followed by clauses in the subjunctive. They are followed by the infinitive, without **que**, if no person or thing is specified. Add **de** before the infinitive after expressions with **être**.

Il est bon que...	*It is good that...*	**Il est indispensable que...**	*It is essential that...*
Il est dommage que...	*It is a shame that...*	**Il est nécessaire que...**	*It is necessary that...*
Il est essentiel que...	*It is essential that...*	**Il est possible que...**	*It is possible that...*
Il est important que...	*It is important that...*	**Il faut que...**	*One must... / It is necessary that...*
		Il vaut mieux que...	*It is better that...*

Il est important qu'on **réduise** le gaspillage.
It is important that we reduce waste.

but

Il est important de réduire le gaspillage.
It is important to reduce waste.

Essayez! **Indiquez la forme correcte du présent du subjonctif de ces verbes.**

1. (améliorer, choisir, vendre) que je/j' *améliore, choisisse, vende*
2. (mettre, renvoyer, maigrir) que tu mettes, renvoies, maigrisses
3. (dire, partir, devenir) qu'elle dise, parte, devienne
4. (appeler, enlever, revenir) que nous appelions, enlevions, revenions
5. (démissionner, obtenir, apprendre) que vous démissionniez, obteniez, appreniez
6. (payer, répéter, lire) qu'ils paient, répètent, lisent

Essayez! Toss a tennis ball or a crumpled piece of paper to a student while saying a subject pronoun and the infinitive of a regular verb. He or she gives the present subjunctive form and tosses the object to another student while you call another pronoun and infinitive.

1 Expansion To ensure students' comprehension, ask them to categorize each statement as **une responsabilité gouvernementale, une responsabilité personnelle**, or **les deux**.

2 Expansion Have students reformulate each answer so that the subject is **je/j'**. Then ask them **C'est vrai?** to see if the statement is true for them personally. Example: **Le matin, il faut que je me lève à sept heures. (Ce n'est pas vrai! D'habitude, je me lève à neuf heures.)**

3 Suggestion Remind students to use each of the expressions in the columns at least once.

4 Expansion When students have completed this activity, suggest that they prepare a conversation between a passionate environmentalist and an environmentalism skeptic. Encourage them to use humor and to perform their conversation for the class.

5 Suggestion Have students develop two responses for each question, one that begins with **oui** and one that begins with **non**. They should summarize their arguments in writing when they've completed the activity and place a check next to the argument for each topic that they find most persuasive.

6 Expansion After completing the activity, write this statement on the board: **L'avenir de l'écologie, c'est les technologies**. Then ask students to find arguments that support or contradict it. You might suggest that they do Internet or library research to support their arguments.

OPTIONS

Extra Practice Have students complete the following sentences to practice the subjunctive with impersonal expressions.
1. Il ne faut pas qu'on ____ l'eau. (gaspille) 2. Pour prévenir les incendies, il vaut mieux que les visiteurs du camping ne ____ pas. (fument) 3. L'écologiste nous a dit qu'il fallait qu'on ____ la planète. (sauve)

Extra Practice Make a set of statements about the environment that use impersonal expressions and the subjunctive. Ask students to pretend that they are ecologists and to give a thumbs-up if they like what they hear or a thumbs-down if they don't. Example for thumbs-up: **Il faut qu'on réduise les déchets toxiques des usines.**

Synthèse

Instructional Resources
IRCD-ROM: IRM (Info Gap Activities); Testing Program, pp. 105–108; Test Files; Testing Program MP3s; Test Generator espaces.vhlcentral.com: activities, downloads, reference tools

1 Suggestion Tell students to complete this activity in phases. In the first phase, they describe the problem. In the second, they formulate a solution, using a sentence with the present subjunctive. In the third, they rewrite their solution using a form of **celui**.

2 Suggestion Explain to students that French speakers tend to write formal, respectful letters in these sorts of situations. Then supply them with a few of the formulas commonly used by native speakers in formal letters of complaint. Example: **Je vous prie d'agréer, Monsieur/Madame, l'expression de mes salutations respectueuses.**

3 Expansion For an extra challenge, suggest that students also give advice telling what *not* to do. Example for **votre camarade de chambre**: **Il ne faut pas que tu t'énerves quand tu lui expliques le problème.**

4 Suggestion This activity could also be completed by groups of three, so that each student comes up with a suggestion about how to address the situation. Tell students to rotate the order in which they give their suggestions.

5 Suggestion To make sure that students understand others' suggestions, ask the class to rate each suggestion on a scale of 1 (**C'est facile à faire!**) to 5 (**C'est très difficile à faire!**).

6 Suggestion Divide the class into pairs and distribute the Info Gap Handouts in the IRM on the IRCD-ROM for this activity. Give students ten minutes to complete the activity.

1 **Des solutions** Avec un(e) partenaire, décrivez ces problèmes et donnez des solutions. Utilisez le présent du subjonctif et un pronom démonstratif pour chaque photo. Présentez vos solutions à la classe. Answers will vary.

MODÈLE

Étudiant(e) 1: *Cette eau est sale.*
Étudiant(e) 2: *Il faut que celui qui a pollué cette eau paie une grosse amende.*

1.

3.

2.

4.

2 **Nettoyez** Avec un(e) partenaire, vous habitez un village où les autorités veulent construire un grand aéroport. Écrivez une lettre aux responsables où vous expliquez vos inquiétudes (*worries*). Utilisez des expressions impersonnelles, puis lisez la lettre à la classe. Answers will vary.

3 **Les plaintes** Par groupes de trois, interviewez vos camarades à tour de rôle. Que vous conseillent-ils de faire quand vous vous plaignez (*complain*) d'une de ces personnes? Écrivez leurs réponses, puis comparez-les à celles d'un autre groupe. Answers will vary.

MODÈLE

Il est important que tu écrives une lettre au gérant.

- vos parents
- votre professeur
- votre camarade de chambre
- un(e) serveur/serveuse
- un(e) patron(ne)
- un médecin

ressources

WB	LM	Lab MP3s	espaces.vhlcentral.com
pp. 185–188	pp. 107–108	Leçon 27	Leçon 27

4 **Si...** Avec un(e) partenaire, observez ces scènes et lisez les phrases. Pour chaque scène, faites trois phrases au présent du subjonctif, puis présentez-les à la classe. Answers will vary.

MODÈLE

Étudiant(e) 1: *Si l'eau est sale, il ne faut pas que les gens mangent les poissons.*
Étudiant(e) 2: *Oui, il faut qu'ils les achètent à la poissonnerie.*

1. Si l'eau est sale,...

3. S'il tombe une pluie acide,...

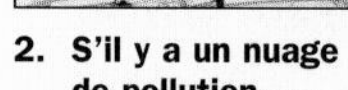
2. S'il y a un nuage de pollution,...

4. S'il y a un glissement de terrain,...

5 **Des propositions** Que peut-on faire pour préserver l'environnement? Avec un(e) partenaire, utilisez le présent du subjonctif et faites des propositions. Ensuite, comparez-les à celles d'un autre groupe. Answers will vary.

MODÈLE

Étudiant(e) 1: *Celui qui change l'huile de sa voiture? Il est essentiel qu'il recycle l'huile et qu'il l'apporte à un garagiste.*
Étudiant(e) 2: *Il ne faut pas qu'il change l'huile trop souvent ou qu'il utilise de l'huile de mauvaise qualité.*

6 **Non, Solange!** Votre professeur va vous donner, à vous et à votre partenaire, deux feuilles d'activités différentes sur les mauvaises habitudes de Solange. Attention! Ne regardez pas la feuille de votre partenaire. Answers will vary.

MODÈLE

Étudiant(e) 1: *Il est dommage que Solange conduise une voiture qui pollue.*
Étudiant(e) 2: *Il faut qu'elle conduise une voiture plus écologique.*

OPTIONS

TPR Read a list of admonishments that make use of the impersonal expressions on page 481 and the present subjunctive. Ask students to pantomime what you are asking them to do. Example: **Il faut que tu passes l'aspirateur dans ta chambre cet après-midi, Mike!**

Game Make two sets of cards, one labeled with **que/qu'** + *subject pronouns*, the other labeled with the infinitives of regular verbs. Students in small groups can "play" their hands by providing subjunctive verb forms suggested by pairs of cards. They should put down cards they've used and then draw more to collect as many as possible.

Interlude

communication cultures connections communities NATIONAL STANDARDS

Le plat pays

Pour le thème de la nature, la chanson, ***Le plat pays*** *(1962), est un hommage à la beauté et à la force de la Belgique, pays natal° du chanteur. Ce pays n'a pas de hautes montagnes. Il est plat°. Dans cette chanson, l'auteur parle des vents de l'est, de l'ouest, du nord et du sud qui évoquent les saisons. À chaque vent, il associe un caractère de son pays.*

JACQUES BREL (1929–1978) est né dans la banlieue de Bruxelles. Il enregistre son premier disque en 1955, mais ce n'est qu'en 1958 qu'il devient une vedette°. En 1966, il abandonne la chanson et commence une brillante carrière d'acteur. En 1975, il va habiter aux Marquises, îles de la Polynésie française (sa tombe est à côté de celle de Paul Gauguin). Brel est considéré comme un chanteur majeur du monde francophone, toujours très apprécié aujourd'hui.

Paysage acadien

GEORGES DE FEURE (1868–1928) était un créateur d'objets décoratifs et un peintre° français d'origine hollandaise°. Maître° du Symbolisme, il choisit de tourner sa carrière vers l'Art nouveau, mouvement artistique qui s'inspirait de la nature, thème qui occupait tous les esprits°. Dans le tableau°, ***Paysage° acadien****, on retrouve les couleurs flamboyantes et les formes qui sont une source d'inspiration pour ce mouvement.*

Activité

La chanson, *Le plat pays*, parle de la beauté et de la force de la nature. La Leçon 27 parle des problèmes de l'environnement. Quels sont les dangers qui menacent (*threaten*) le paysage de la peinture (*painting*), *Paysage acadien*? Écrivez un paragraphe pour décrire en quoi ce paysage est vulnérable face aux dangers de l'activité humaine. Vous devez couvrir les thèmes suivants dans votre paragraphe: Answers will vary.

- les déchets toxiques
- la pluie acide
- le réchauffement de la Terre
- la surpopulation
- les usines

SUR INTERNET

Go to **espaces.vhlcentral.com** for more information related to this **Interlude**.

natal *native* **plat** *flat* **vedette** *star* **peintre** *painter* **hollandaise** *Dutch* **Maître** *Master* **occupait tous les esprits** *was on everyone's mind* **tableau** *painting* **Paysage** *Landscape*

Section Goals

In this section, students will learn about:
- Jacques Brel
- Georges de Feure

Instructional Resources
espaces.vhlcentral.com: activities, downloads, reference tools

Le plat pays

- Point out that Jacques Brel was an international star. His music has influenced many singers and songwriters. Some of his songs were translated and recorded in English by such stars as Frank Sinatra, David Bowie, and Dionne Warwick. When the off-Broadway musical revue *Jacques Brel is Alive and Well and Living in Paris* debuted in 1968, it was a hit. In 1973, a movie was made of the show.
- To check comprehension, ask these questions.

1. Où Jacques Brel est-il né? (Bruxelles, Belgique)
2. Pourquoi l'année 1966 a-t-elle été une année importante pour lui? (parce qu'il a abandonné la chanson et qu'il a commencé une carrière d'acteur)
3. De quoi parle la chanson *Le plat pays*? (Elle parle de la beauté et de la force de la Belgique.)
4. Dans la chanson, avec quels éléments l'auteur associe-t-il chaque vent? (avec une saison et un caractère du pays)

Paysage acadien

- Have students brainstorm a list of words they associate with nature. Then have them use this list to describe the landscape in the painting.
- Mention that de Feure's painting depicts the region of Acadia, the first French colony in North America. It encompassed Nova Scotia, New Brunswick, and Prince Edward Island.

OPTIONS

Extra Practice Have students write a short poem or song about their country, using the song as a model. They may choose to write about specific features that are of particular interest to them (rivers, forests, animals, etc.).

Le symbolisme Symbolism was a literary and artistic movement of the late nineteenth century. It rejected reason and reality, and instead focused on sensitivity, mysticism, fantasy, and imagination. Gustave Moreau, Puvis de Chavannes, and Odile Redon are other famous symbolists.

Section Goals

In this section, students will learn and practice vocabulary related to:

- nature and conservation
- animals

Instructional Resources

*IRCD-ROM: Transparency #58; IRM (**Vocabulaire supplémentaire**; **Mise en pratique** answers; Textbook Audioscript; Lab Audioscript)*
Textbook MP3s
WB/VM: Workbook, pp. 189–190
Lab Manual, p. 109
Lab MP3s
WB/VM/LM Answer Key
espaces.vhlcentral.com: activities, downloads, reference tools

Suggestions

- Tell students to look over the new vocabulary and identify the cognates.
- Use **Transparency #58.** Point out people and things as you describe the illustration. Examples: **Ils voient une étoile. C'est une vache.**
- To practice the vocabulary, show drawings or magazine photos and ask students questions. Examples: **Qu'est-ce que c'est? C'est un lapin ou un écureuil? Y a-t-il un fleuve sur le dessin?**
- Additional vocabulary for this lesson can be found in the **Vocabulaire supplémentaire** in the IRM on the IRCD-ROM.

Leçon 28

You will learn how to...

- **discuss nature and the environment**
- **make comparisons**

En pleine nature

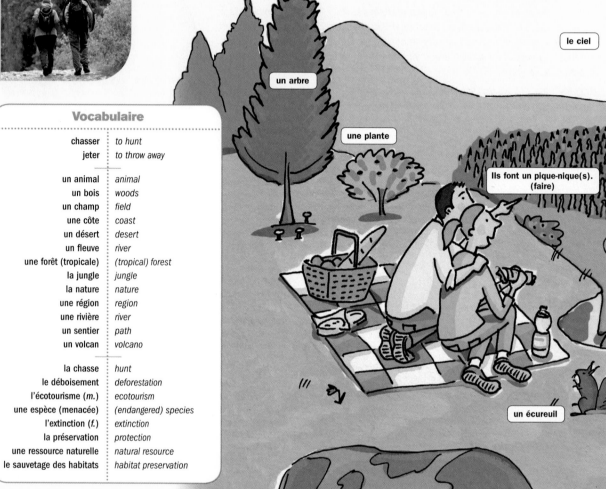

Vocabulaire	
chasser	*to hunt*
jeter	*to throw away*
un animal	*animal*
un bois	*woods*
un champ	*field*
une côte	*coast*
un désert	*desert*
un fleuve	*river*
une forêt (tropicale)	*(tropical) forest*
la jungle	*jungle*
la nature	*nature*
une région	*region*
une rivière	*river*
un sentier	*path*
un volcan	*volcano*
la chasse	*hunt*
le déboisement	*deforestation*
l'écotourisme (*m.*)	*ecotourism*
une espèce (menacée)	*(endangered) species*
l'extinction (*f.*)	*extinction*
la préservation	*protection*
une ressource naturelle	*natural resource*
le sauvetage des habitats	*habitat preservation*

un arbre
le ciel
une plante
Ils font un pique-nique(s). (faire)
un écureuil
une vache
l'herbe (*f.*)

ressources

WB pp. 189–190	LM p. 109	Text MP3s Leçon 28	Lab MP3s Leçon 28	espaces.vhlcentral.com Leçon 28

484 *quatre cent quatre-vingt-quatre*

OPTIONS

TPR Make a series of true/false statements related to the lesson theme using the new vocabulary. Tell students to remain seated if a statement is true and to stand if it is false. Examples: **Les lapins habitent dans les arbres.** (Students stand.) **On voit des étoiles dans le ciel.** (Students remain seated or sit down.)

Extra Practice Write these categories on the board: **Animaux** and **Éléments naturels** (*Natural features*). Dictate words from the vocabulary. Tell students to write the words under the correct heading on their papers. Examples: **serpent, île, désert, écureuil, volcan, falaise, vallée,** and **vache.**

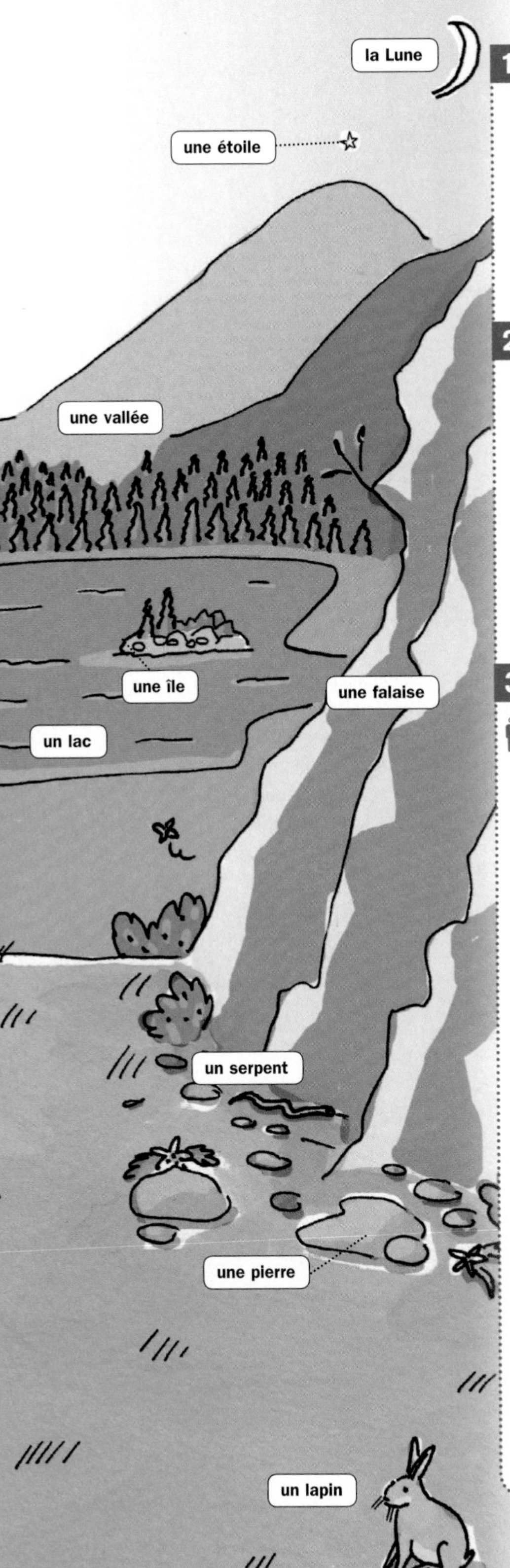

Mise en pratique

1 Écoutez Écoutez Armand parler de quelques-unes de ses expériences avec la nature. Après une deuxième écoute, écrivez les termes qui se réfèrent au ciel, à la terre et aux plantes. Some answers may vary.

Terre	Ciel	Plantes
nature	étoiles	forêt(s) tropicale(s)
forêt(s) tropicale(s)	Lune	arbres
sentiers		fleurs
campagne		nature

2 Par catégorie Faites correspondre les éléments de la colonne de gauche avec l'élément des colonnes de droite qui convient.

1. d la Seine
2. j la Martinique
3. h une vache
4. a l'Etna
5. i le pétrole
6. g le Sahara
7. e un arbre
8. c Érié

a. un volcan
b. une jungle
c. un lac
d. un fleuve
e. une plante
f. une forêt
g. un désert
h. un animal
i. une ressource naturelle
j. une île

3 La nature Choisissez le terme qui correspond à chaque définition. Ensuite choisissez trois autres termes dans la section **ESPACE CONTEXTES** et écrivez leur définition. Avec un partenaire, lisez vos définitions et devinez quels sont les termes que vous avez choisis.

le déboisement	une falaise	la préservation
l'écotourisme	une jungle	le sauvetage des habitats
l'environnement	une pierre	un sentier
l'extinction	un pique-nique	une vache

1. Là où l'homme vit l'environnement.
2. Sauver et protéger la préservation.
3. Lieu très chaud, très humide une jungle.
4. Chemin très étroit (*narrow*) un sentier.
5. Quand une espèce n'existe plus l'extinction.
6. Conséquence de la destruction des arbres le déboisement.
7. Action de sauver le lieu où vivent des animaux le sauvetage des habitats.
8. Vacances qui favorisent la protection de l'environnement l'écotourisme.
9. Un animal de taille importante qui mange de l'herbe une vache.
10. Quand on mange dans la nature un pique-nique.
11. Élément minéral solide, parfois gris une pierre.
12. Sur le dessin à gauche, c'est la masse rocheuse (*rocky*) à droite une falaise.

1 Tapescript ARMAND: Moi, j'adore la nature. Quand j'ai le temps, je quitte la vie en ville et je fais de l'écotourisme. C'est l'idéal pour profiter de la nature et protéger l'environnement en même temps. Je n'aime pas aller à la pêche parce qu'il y a déjà beaucoup de poissons qui sont en danger d'extinction. J'aime beaucoup les forêts tropicales. L'année dernière, je suis allé visiter la forêt tropicale du Cameroun. C'était magnifique! Il y avait des espèces d'arbres et de fleurs variées et j'ai marché des heures dans des sentiers très différents. Aussi, quand je peux, je vais rendre visite à mon grand-père pour me reposer. Il habite à la campagne. Le soir, on peut se coucher dans l'herbe et regarder les étoiles et la Lune. *(On Textbook MP3s)*

1 Suggestion Go over the answers with the class.

2 Expansion Ask students questions about the location of each item in this activity. Examples: **Dans quelle grande ville se trouve la Seine? (à Paris) Où trouve-t-on des vaches? (dans les vallées/ à la campagne)**

3 Suggestions
- Tell students to compare their answers with their partner's.
- Have students describe what they see in the photo.

OPTIONS

Game Have students fold a sheet of paper into 16 squares (four folds in half) and write a new vocabulary word in each square. Say definitions for words. If students have the defined word, they mark their paper. The first student to mark four words in a row (across, down or diagonally) calls out **«loto!»** To verify a win, the student should read the words in the row aloud.

Extra Practice To practice the new vocabulary, ask students these questions. **1. Préférez-vous la montagne ou la mer? 2. Êtes-vous déjà allé(e) dans le désert? dans une forêt tropicale? à la montagne? dans la jungle? 3. Quel est votre animal préféré? 4. Où préféreriez-vous faire un pique-nique? 5. Est-ce que vous chassez? Pourquoi ou pourquoi pas?**

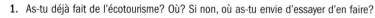

4 Expansion Have pairs get together with another pair of students and share what they learned about their partners.

5 Suggestion If time is limited, this activity may be assigned as homework. Then allow partners time to work together for peer editing in class.

6 Suggestion Encourage students to illustrate their brochures with drawings, magazine photos, or clip art.

7 Suggestion Have a volunteer read the **modèle**. You might suggest that students incorporate information from **Le monde francophone**, page 477, in their radio ads.

Communication

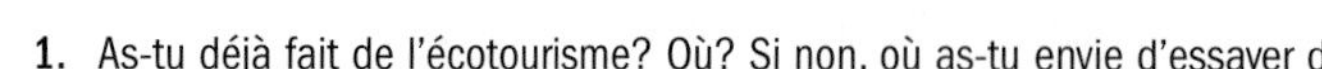

4 Conversez **Interviewez un(e) camarade de classe.** Answers will vary.

1. As-tu déjà fait de l'écotourisme? Où? Si non, où as-tu envie d'essayer d'en faire?
2. Aimes-tu les pique-niques? Quand en as-tu fait un pour la dernière fois? Avec qui?
3. Quelles activités aimes-tu pratiquer dans la nature?
4. As-tu déjà visité une forêt? Laquelle?
5. Connais-tu un lac? Quand y es-tu allé(e)? Quelles activités y as-tu pratiquées?
6. Es-tu déjà allé(e) dans un désert? Lequel?
7. Es-tu déjà allé(e) sur une île? Laquelle? Comment as-tu passé le temps?
8. Quelles sont les régions du monde que tu veux visiter? Pour quelle(s) raison(s)?
9. Si tu étais un animal, lequel serais-tu? Pourquoi?
10. Quand tu regardes le ciel, que trouves-tu de beau? Pourquoi?

5 La nature et moi **Écrivez un paragraphe dans lequel vous racontez votre expérience avec la nature. Ensuite, à tour de rôle, lisez votre description à votre partenaire et comparez vos paragraphes.** Answers will vary.

- Choisissez au minimum deux lieux naturels différents.
- Utilisez un minimum de huit mots de vocabulaire d'**ESPACE CONTEXTES.**
- Faites votre description avec le plus de détails possible.
- Expliquez ce que vous aimez ou ce que vous n'aimez pas à propos de chaque lieu.

6 Les écologistes **Vous faites partie d'un club d'écologistes à l'université. Avec deux camarades de classe et les informations suivantes, préparez une brochure pour informer les étudiants du campus d'un grave problème écologique. Présentez ensuite votre brochure au reste de la classe. Quel groupe a présenté le problème le plus sérieux? Quel groupe a proposé les solutions les plus originales?** Answers will vary.

- le nom de votre club
- la situation géographique du problème écologique
- la description du problème
- les causes du problème
- les conséquences du problème
- les solutions possibles au problème

7 À la radio **Vous travaillez pour le ministère du Tourisme d'un pays francophone et devez préparez un texte qui sera lu à la radio. L'objectif de ce message est de faire la promotion de ce pays pour son écotourisme. Décrivez la nature et les activités offertes. Utilisez les mots que vous avez appris dans la section ESPACE CONTEXTES.** Answers will vary.

MODÈLE

Venez découvrir la beauté de l'île de Madagascar. Chaque région vous offre des sentiers qui permettent d'admirer des plantes rares et des arbres magnifiques et de rencontrer des animaux extraordinaires… À Madagascar, la nature est unique, préservée. Le charme et l'exotisme sont ici!

OPTIONS

Game Play a game of **Dix questions**. Ask a volunteer to think of a word from the new vocabulary. Other students get one chance to ask one yes/no question, then they can guess what the word is. Limit attempts to ten questions per word. You may want to write some phrases on the board to cue students' questions.

Game Write vocabulary words related to animals and nature on index cards. On another set of cards, draw or paste pictures to match each term. Tape them face down on the board in random order. Divide the class into two teams. Play a game of Concentration in which students match words with pictures. When a player makes a match, that player's team collects those cards. The team with the most cards at the end of the game wins.

NATIONAL
comparisons
STANDARDS

Les sons et les lettres

Homophones

Many French words sound alike, but are spelled differently. As you have already learned, sometimes the only difference between two words is a diacritical mark. Other words that sound alike have more obvious differences in spelling.

a / à **ou / où** **sont / son** **en / an**

Several forms of a single verb may sound alike. To tell which form is being used, listen for the subject or words that indicate tense.

je parle	**tu** parles	**ils** parlent
vous parlez	**j'ai** parlé	**je vais** parler

Many words that sound alike are different parts of speech. Use context to tell them apart.

VERB	POSSESSIVE ADJECTIVE	PREPOSITION	NOUN
Ils sont belges.	**C'est son mari.**	**Tu vas en France?**	**Il a un an.**

You may encounter multiple spellings of words that sound alike. Again, context is the key to understanding which word is being used.

je peux *I can*	**elle peut** *she can*	**peu** *a little, few*
le foie *liver*	**la foi** *faith*	**une fois** *one time*
haut *high*	**l'eau** *water*	**au** *at, to, in the*

Prononcez Répétez les paires de mots suivants à voix haute.

1. ce se	4. foi fois	7. au eau	10. lis lit
2. leur leurs	5. ces ses	8. peut peu	11. quelle qu'elle
3. né nez	6. vert verre	9. où ou	12. c'est s'est

Choisissez Choisissez le mot qui convient à chaque phrase.

1. Je (lis / lit) le journal tous les jours.
2. Son chien est sous le (lis / lit).
3. Corinne est (née / nez) à Paris.
4. Elle a mal au (née / nez).

Jeux de mots Répétez les jeux de mots à voix haute.

Mon père est maire, mon frère est masseur.[2]
MAIRE DE PETITVILLE

Le ver vert va vers le verre.[1]

ressources

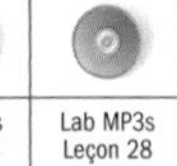

LM p. 110	Text MP3s Leçon 28	Lab MP3s Leçon 28	espaces.vhlcentral.com Leçon 28

[1] The green worm is going toward the glass.
[2] My father is a mayor, my brother is a masseur.

Section Goals

In this section, students will learn about homophones.

Instructional Resources
Textbook MP3s
Lab Manual, p. 110
Lab MP3s
WB/VM/LM Answer Key
IRCD-ROM: IRM (Textbook Audioscript; Lab Audioscript)
espaces.vhlcentral.com: activities, downloads, reference tools

Suggestions

- Model the pronunciation of the example words and have students repeat them after you.
- Point out these additional homophones: **là** (*there*) **/ la** (*the*); **ont** (*have*) **/ on** (*one*); **je vois** (*I see*) **/ il voit** (*he sees*) **/ une voie** (*a way*) **/ une voix** (*a voice*).
- Read each sentence in the **Choisissez** activity aloud. Then have students select the correct word to complete each one.
- Have students look in the end vocabulary or verb charts in **Appendice D** and identify other homophones.
- Dictate five sentences that contain familiar homophones, repeating each one at least two times. Then write them on the board or a transparency and have students check their spelling.

Dictons Make sure students understand the humor in the saying **«Mon père est maire, mon frère est masseur.»** Point out that it sounds like **«Mon père est mère, mon frère est ma sœur.»**

OPTIONS

Extra Practice Tell students to write six pairs of sentences using words in the **Prononcez** activity. Then have volunteers write their sentences on the board and go over them with the class.

Extra Practice Teach students this French tongue-twister that contains homophones. **Si six scies scient six cyprès, six cent six scies scient six cent six cyprès.**

Section Goals

In this section, students will learn functional phrases for expressing regrets, preferences, comparisons, and suggestions.

Instructional Resources
WB/VM: Video Manual, pp. 265–266
WB/VM/LM Answer Key
Video CD-ROM
Video on DVD
IRCD-ROM: IRM (Videoscript; ***Roman-photo*** *Translations)*
espaces.vhlcentral.com: activities, downloads, reference tools

Video Recap: Leçon 27
Before doing this **Roman-photo**, review the previous one with this activity.
1. Pourquoi Valérie est-elle de mauvaise humeur? (Michèle a démissionné. Stéphane n'a pas réussi son bac.)
2. Pourquoi Sandrine est-elle de mauvaise humeur? (Elle est/était anxieuse à cause de son concert/du départ de David.)
3. Quelle idée Rachid a-t-il eue? (d'aller à la montagne Sainte-Victoire)
4. Qui va aller à la montange Sainte-Victoire? (Rachid, Amina, David, Sandrine, Valérie et Stéphane)

Video Synopsis
At **la montagne Sainte-Victoire**, the group visits the **Maison Sainte-Victoire**, an eco-museum. The guide explains that the mountain is a nature preserve. After a picnic, Sandrine wants David to draw her portrait. Rachid and Amina share a romantic moment, until Stéphane interrupts them.

Suggestions
- Have students predict what the episode will be about based on the video stills.
- Tell students to scan the captions for vocabulary related to nature and conservation.
- After reading the **Roman-photo**, have students summarize the episode.

La randonnée

PERSONNAGES

Amina

David

Guide

Rachid

Sandrine

Stéphane

Valérie

1

À la montagne...
DAVID Que c'est beau!
VALÉRIE C'est la première fois que tu viens à la montagne Sainte-Victoire?
DAVID Non, en fait, je viens assez souvent pour dessiner, mais malheureusement c'est peut-être la dernière fois. C'est dommage que j'aie si peu de temps.

2

SANDRINE Je préférerais qu'on parle d'autre chose.
AMINA Elle a raison, nous sommes venus ici pour passer un bon moment.
STÉPHANE Tiens, et si on essayait de trouver des serpents?
AMINA Des serpents ici?
RACHID Ne t'inquiète pas, ma chérie. Par précaution, je suggère que tu restes près de moi.

3

RACHID Mais il ne faut pas que tu sois aussi anxieuse.
SANDRINE C'est romantique ici, n'est-ce pas?
DAVID Comment? Euh, oui, enfin...
VALÉRIE Avant de commencer notre randonnée, je propose qu'on visite la Maison Sainte-Victoire.
AMINA Bonne idée. Allons-y!

6

Après le pique-nique...
DAVID Mais tu avais faim, Sandrine!
SANDRINE Oui. Pourquoi?
DAVID Parce que tu as mangé autant que Stéphane!
SANDRINE C'est normal, on a beaucoup marché, ça ouvre l'appétit. En plus, ce fromage est délicieux!
DAVID Mais, tu peux manger autant de fromage que tu veux, ma chérie.

7

Stéphane laisse tomber une serviette...
VALÉRIE Stéphane! Mais qu'est-ce que tu jettes par terre? Il est essentiel qu'on laisse cet endroit propre!
STÉPHANE Oh, ne t'inquiète pas, maman. J'allais mettre ça à la poubelle plus tard.

8

SANDRINE David, j'aimerais que tu fasses un portrait de moi, ici, à la montagne. Ça te dit?
DAVID Peut-être un peu plus tard... Cette montagne est tellement belle!
VALÉRIE David, tu es comme Cézanne. Il venait ici tous les jours pour dessiner. La montagne Sainte-Victoire était un de ses sujets favoris.

ACTIVITÉS

1 Vrai ou faux? Indiquez si les affirmations suivantes sont vraies ou fausses.

1. David fait un portait de Sandrine sur-le-champ (*on the spot*). Faux.
2. C'est la première fois que Rachid visite la Maison Sainte-Victoire. Vrai.
3. Valérie traite la nature avec respect. Vrai.
4. Sandrine mange beaucoup au pique-nique. Vrai.
5. David et Sandrine passent un après-midi très romantique. Faux.
6. Le guide confirme qu'il y a des serpents sur la montagne Sainte-Victoire. Faux.
7. David est un peu triste de devoir bientôt retourner aux États-Unis. Vrai.
8. Valérie pense que David est un artiste sans talent. Faux.
9. Rachid est très romantique. Answers will vary.
10. Stéphane laisse Rachid et Amina tranquilles. Faux.

OPTIONS

Avant de regarder la vidéo Before viewing the video, have students work in pairs and brainstorm a list of words and expressions they expect to hear in an episode about a hike in the mountains.

Regarder la vidéo Show the video episode and tell students to check off the words or expressions on their lists when they hear them. Then show the episode again and have students give you a play-by-play description of the action. Write their descriptions on the board.

COMMUNICATION

3 **Enquête** Comparez vos idées sur la nature et l'environnement avec celles d'un(e) partenaire. Posez-vous ces questions. Answers will vary.

1. Que suggères-tu qu'on fasse pour protéger les forêts tropicales?
2. Vaut-il mieux qu'on ne chasse plus? Pourquoi?
3. Que recommandes-tu qu'on fasse pour arrêter la pollution?
4. Comment souhaites-tu que nous préservions nos ressources naturelles?
5. Quels produits recommandes-tu qu'on développe?
6. Quel problème écologique veux-tu qu'on traite tout de suite?

4 **Mme Quefège...** Mme Quefège donne des conseils à la radio. Pensez à une difficulté que vous avez et préparez par écrit un paragraphe que vous lui lirez. Elle va vous faire des recommandations. Avec un(e) partenaire, alternez les rôles pour jouer les scènes.

MODÈLE Answers will vary.

Étudiant(e) 1: *Ma petite amie fait constamment ses devoirs et elle ne quitte plus son appartement.*
Étudiant(e) 2: *Je suis désolée qu'elle n'arrête pas de travailler. Si elle ne quitte toujours pas l'appartement ce week-end, je suggère que vous écriviez à ses parents.*

5 **Les habitats naturels** Par groupes de trois, préparez le texte pour cette affiche où vous expliquez ce qu'on doit faire pour sauver les habitats naturels. Utilisez des verbes au présent du subjonctif. Answers will vary.

Verbs and expressions of emotion

aimer que...	*to like that...*	**être heureux / heureuse que...**	*to be happy that...*
avoir peur que...	*to be afraid that...*	**être surpris(e) que...**	*to be surprised that...*
être content(e) que...	*to be glad that...*	**être triste que...**	*to be sad that...*
être désolé(e) que...	*to be sorry that...*	**regretter que...**	*to regret that...*
être furieux / furieuse que...	*to be furious that...*		

- In English, the word *that* introducing the subordinate clause may be omitted. In French, never omit **que** between the two clauses.

Ils sont heureux **que** nous arrivions.
They're happy (that) we're arriving.

Elle préfère **que** tu partes avec elle.
She prefers (that) you leave with her.

- The infinitive is used with expressions of will and emotion if there is no change of subject. In the case of **avoir peur**, **regretter**, and expressions with **être**, add **de** before the infinitive.

Tu souhaites faire un pique-nique?
Do you wish to have a picnic?

Nous sommes tristes d'entendre la mauvaise nouvelle.
We're sad to hear the bad news.

- Some verbs have irregular subjunctive forms.

Present subjunctive of *avoir, être, faire*

	avoir	être	faire
que je/j'	aie	sois	fasse
que tu	aies	sois	fasses
qu'il/elle	ait	soit	fasse
que nous	ayons	soyons	fassions
que vous	ayez	soyez	fassiez
qu'ils/elles	aient	soient	fassent

Anne suggère que je **fasse** mes devoirs.
Anne suggests that I do my homework.

Tu es désolé que nous **soyons** au chômage.
You are sorry that we are unemployed.

Essayez! **Indiquez les formes correctes du présent du subjonctif des verbes.**

1. que je finisse (finir)
2. qu'il fasse (faire)
3. que vous soyez (être)
4. que leur enfant ait (avoir)
5. que nous prenions (prendre)
6. que nous fassions (faire)
7. qu'ils aient (avoir)
8. que tu attendes (attendre)

Essayez! Assign an infinitive to each row of students. They should take turns giving present subjunctive forms for their appointed verb. The first student should give the **que je/j'...** form, the second student the **que tu...** form, and so on. Example for one row of students: (*first student*) **que je fasse,** (*second student*) **que tu fasses,** etc.

1 Suggestion Encourage students to come up with creative suggestions for the people pictured and to share the most interesting suggestions with the class.

2 Suggestion Have one pair of students share their sentences with the class. Ask their classmates to say **d'accord** if they agree or **pas d'accord** if they don't agree with the statements.

3 Expansion Students could also answer these questions. **Avez-vous peur que des espèces soient menacées dans votre région? Que proposez-vous que l'on fasse pour éviter la destruction des habitats naturels autour des villes?**

4 Suggestion Ask students why they think the radio personality is named **Quefège.** (It sounds like the phrase **Que fais-je?**)

5 Expansion Have the class vote on the best text for the poster. Then have small groups create a television ad campaign in the same vein. They should produce a script modeled on the poster text and a storyboard that shows the visuals to appear on the screen. Remind the class that successful TV ads often use striking images and catchy slogans.

OPTIONS

Extra Practice Read aloud some sentence starters that refer to current events or celebrities. Each one should use an expression of emotion from page 493. Students should complete the sentences appropriately. Example: **Emeril Lagasse est furieux que... (qu'il n'y ait plus d'ail au supermarché.)**

Video As students watch the last scene of the video for **Leçon 28** again, pause periodically and ask them these questions. **Qu'est-ce que Valérie veut que Stéphane fasse? Qu'est-ce que Sandrine veut que David fasse? Qu'est-ce que Rachid veut qu'Amina fasse? Qu'est-ce que Rachid veut que Stéphane fasse?**

National Standards: comparisons

Section Goals

In this section, students will learn:

- comparatives with noun
- superlatives with nouns

Instructional Resources
WB/VM: Workbook, pp. 193–194
Lab Manual, p. 112
Lab MP3s
WB/VM/LM Answer Key
*IRCD-ROM: IRM (**Essayez!** and **Mise en pratique** answers; Lab Audioscript)*
espaces.vhlcentral.com: activities, downloads, reference tools

Suggestions

- Ask students what words are used in comparatives and superlatives for adjectives and adverbs. You might need to remind them by asking a few questions. Example: **Qui est le plus beau de la classe?** Once students have identified **plus/moins/aussi** + *adjective/adverb* + **que**, tell them that the words used to compare quantities for nouns are similar.
- Point out that **de** is used in all the examples of comparative noun constructions just as **que** is used with comparative adjectives and adverbs. You might copy the paradigms that appear under the photos on the board, adding **+ que**.
- Make statements about things in the classroom using comparatives and superlatives of nouns while students qualify them as **vrai** or **faux**. Example: **Sean a plus de livres que Jennifer.**
- Point out that native speakers distinguish **plus de** meaning *more of* from **plus de** meaning *anymore of* by pronouncing the **s** in the former. Example: **Je n'ai plus d'argent!** (**s** not pronounced) **J'ai plus d'argent que toi!** (**s** pronounced)

Essayez! Show a transparency with false statements and have students correct them. Examples: **Il y a plus d'habitants en France qu'aux États-Unis. Il y a autant d'ail dans un gâteau que dans une pizza. Le Grand Canyon est moins grand qu'un timbre postal.**

28.2 Comparatives and superlatives of nouns

Point de départ In **Leçon 18**, you learned how to compare nouns and verbs by using comparative and superlative forms of adjectives and adverbs. You will now learn how to compare nouns when talking about quantities.

Tu peux manger autant de fromage que tu veux.

Nous nous occupons de la forêt pour avoir moins d'incendies.

- To compare the amount of something, use these expressions:

plus de + [noun]	*more*
moins de + [noun]	*less; fewer*
autant de + [noun]	*as much; as many*

Elle fait **plus d'heures** que sa sœur.
She works more hours than her sister (does).

Il y a **moins d'arbres** dans le jardin que dans la forêt.
There are fewer trees in the garden than in the forest.

Vous recevez **autant de courrier** que vos amis.
You receive as much mail as your friends (do).

Il n'y a pas **autant d'animaux** dans la ville que dans la jungle.
There aren't as many animals in the city as (there are) in the jungle.

- To express the superlative quantity of a noun (*the most, the least/fewest*), add the definite article **le**: **le plus de, le moins de.**

Ce sont les forêts tropicales qui ont **le plus de plantes**.
Tropical rainforests have the most plants.

Ce sont les pays pauvres qui ont **le moins d'argent**.
Poor countries have the least money.

Essayez! **Complétez les phrases avec les comparatifs ou les superlatifs corrects.**

1. Mon ami n'a pas ___autant de___ (*as much*) travail que moi.
2. Qui a ___le moins de___ (*the fewest*) cousins?
3. La Corse a-t-elle ___autant de___ (*as many*) falaises que la Sicile?
4. Il y a ___moins de___ (*fewer*) déserts en Amérique du Nord qu'en Afrique.
5. Quel pays a ___le plus de___ (*the most*) rivières polluées?
6. Malheureusement, on a ___plus de___ (*more*) problèmes que de solutions.

MISE EN PRATIQUE

1 Avec qui sortir? Amaia compare deux garçons pour voir avec qui elle va accepter de sortir le week-end prochain. Assemblez ses phrases.

MODÈLE Kadir / avoir / plus / énergie / Jacques
Kadir a plus d'énergie que Jacques.

1. Kadir / avoir / moins / problèmes / Jacques
   Kadir a moins de problèmes que Jacques.
2. Jacques / avoir / plus / humour / Kadir
   Jacques a plus d'humour que Kadir.
3. Kadir / donner / plus / cadeaux / Jacques
   Kadir donne plus de cadeaux que Jacques.
4. Jacques / avoir / autant / amis / Kadir
   Jacques a autant d'amis que Kadir.
5. Kadir / avoir / moins / patience / Jacques
   Kadir a moins de patience que Jacques.
6. Jacques / avoir / plus / ambition / Kadir
   Jacques a plus d'ambition que Kadir.

2 À la campagne Lise parle de son séjour à la campagne et compare le nombre de choses qu'elle a observées dans la nature. Que dit-elle?

MODÈLE *J'ai observé autant de nuages blancs que de nuages gris.*

1. J'ai observé moins d'arbres que de fleurs./J'ai observé plus de fleurs que d'arbres.

2. J'ai observé moins d'écureuils que de lapins./J'ai observé plus de lapins que d'écureuils.

3. J'ai observé moins de chiens que de chats./J'ai observé plus de chats que de chiens.

4. J'ai observé moins de vaches que de serpents./J'ai observé plus de serpents que de vaches.

3 Combien de calories? Vous et votre partenaire êtes au régime. Faites au moins quatre comparaisons entre ces aliments. Dites à la classe quel aliment contient le plus de calories et lequel en contient le moins.
Answers will vary.

MODÈLE *Il y a autant de calories dans un café que dans un thé.*

banane	carotte	glace	poulet
biscuits	frites	pain	saucisses
bonbons	gâteau	porc	thon

OPTIONS

Extra Practice Ask students questions about themselves using comparative and superlative noun constructions. They should be able to answer each question by saying **Moi!** or remaining silent. Examples: **Qui a le plus de fichiers audio** (*audio files*) **de la classe? Qui a autant de stylos que Luan? Qui a moins de paires de chaussures que Nisha?**

Extra Practice Challenge students to formulate sentences that use comparatives and superlatives of nouns with the pronoun **en**. Ask them how they would substitute **en** for the nouns in the examples on this page. Example: **Elle fait plus d'heures que sa sœur. (Elle en fait plus que sa sœur.)**

COMMUNICATION

4 **Eh bien, moi...** Posez ces questions à un(e) partenaire, puis faites une comparaison. Answers will vary.

MODÈLE

Étudiant(e) 1: *Pendant combien d'heures par jour regardes-tu la télévision?*
Étudiant(e) 2: *Je regarde la télévision deux heures par jour.*
Étudiant(e) 1: *Je regarde plus d'heures de télévision que toi: Je la regarde trois heures par jour.*

1. Combien de frères (sœurs, cousins) as-tu?
2. Combien d'heures par jour étudies-tu?
3. Combien d'e-mails reçois-tu par jour?
4. Combien d'heures dors-tu chaque nuit?
5. Combien de cours as-tu ce semestre?
6. Combien de cafés prends-tu par jour?

5 **Où habiter?** Avec un(e) partenaire, comparez la vie dans une résidence universitaire à la vie dans un appartement. Décidez où vous préféreriez habiter si vous aviez le choix. Utilisez ce vocabulaire. Answers will vary.

MODÈLE

Étudiant(e) 1: *Dans un appartement, nous pouvons mettre plus d'affiches sur les murs.*
Étudiant(e) 2: *Oui, et dans une résidence, il y a moins d'espace.*

affiches	armoire	meuble	supervision
amis	espace	protection	télé
argent	fêtes	repas	?

6 **Un dialogue** Par groupes de trois, vous voulez voyager dans un pays francophone. Vous consultez une agence de voyages et vous posez des questions. Préparez un dialogue où vous utilisez **autant de, moins de** et **plus de** et alternez les rôles. Answers will vary.

MODÈLE

Étudiant(e) 1: *Où y a-t-il moins de pollution, au Cameroun ou à Paris?*
Étudiant(e) 2: *Il y a de la pollution aux deux endroits. Mais il y a plus de forêts tropicales au Cameroun.*
Étudiant(e) 3: *Où y a-t-il plus de sentiers? On voudrait faire des randonnées.*

Le français vivant

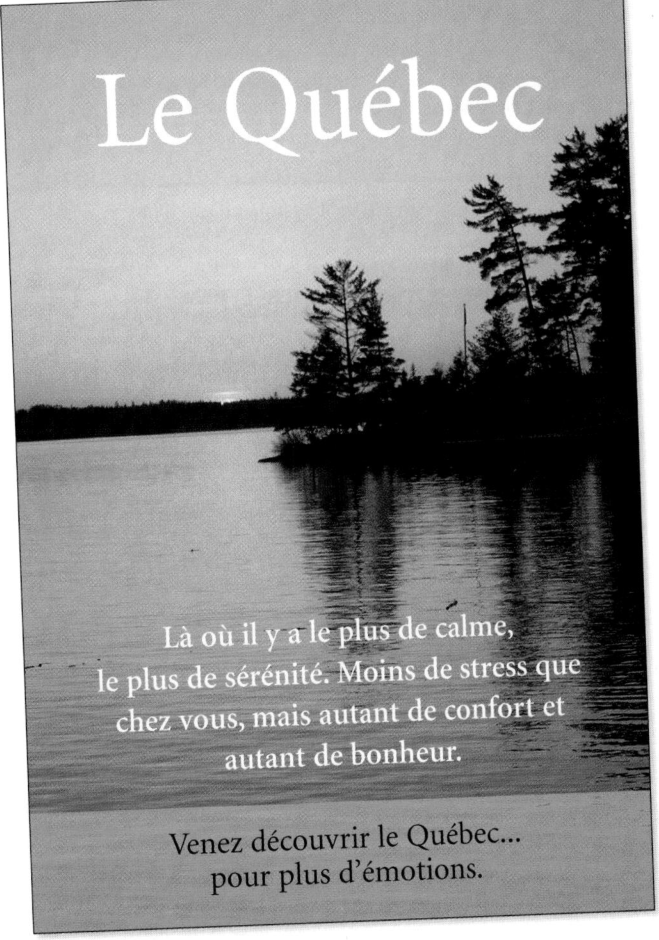

Le Québec
Là où il y a le plus de calme, le plus de sérénité. Moins de stress que chez vous, mais autant de confort et autant de bonheur.
Venez découvrir le Québec... pour plus d'émotions.

Identifiez Quels comparatifs et superlatifs trouvez-vous dans cette publicité (*ad*)? le plus de calme; le plus de sérénité; Moins de stress; autant de confort; autant de bonheur; plus d'émotions

Questions Posez ces questions à un(e) partenaire et répondez à tour de rôle. Employez des comparatifs et des superlatifs dans vos réponses, si possible. Answers will vary.

1. D'après (*According to*) cette pub, que cherche le touriste qui voudrait passer des vacances au Québec?
2. Quelle comparaison la pub fait-elle entre le Québec et l'endroit où habite le lecteur/la lectrice (*reader*)?
3. As-tu déjà passé des vacances au Québec? Voudrais-tu y aller un jour?
4. Si tu vas ou retournes au Québec un jour, voudras-tu y faire un séjour comme celui que la pub décrit? Pourquoi?

1 Expansion Tell students to write down six statements in which they compare themselves to a good friend or to a sibling.

2 Expansion Ask students to make similar observations about the campus by looking out the window or walking around outside.

3 Suggestion You can focus students' attention by grouping items from the list. Example: **gâteau / carotte (Il y a plus de calories dans un gâteau que dans une carotte.**)

4 Expansion When students have completed the activity, find out which student has the most of each item in the questions. Example: **1. Qui a le plus de frères de toute la classe?**

5 Suggestion Tally on the board how many students prefer apartments and dormitories. Then ask: **Y a-t-il plus d'étudiants qui préfèrent les appartements ou plus d'étudiants qui préfèrent les résidences universitaires?**

6 Expansion Ask students to take notes on their conversation for reference and then verify the travel agent's answers by doing some research on French-language Internet sites.

Le français vivant When students are working on question 3, ask them why the last statement might strike someone as contradicting the first two. Then ask them what you call a contradictory statement that may be true nonetheless (*a paradox*/ **un paradoxe**).

OPTIONS

Extra Practice Ask the class questions about objects around the classroom using comparative and superlative noun constructions. Example: **Qui a plus de crayons, Max ou Lina?** Students should answer in complete sentences.

Game Tell students to write three statements about themselves using comparatives or superlatives of nouns. Suggest that they mention characteristics that would allow their classmates to identify them. Example: **J'ai moins de cheveux que Jason.** Then collect the papers and read them aloud while students guess the identity of each writer. The student with the most correct guesses wins.

Synthèse

Instructional Resources
IRCD-ROM: IRM (Info Gap Activities); Testing Program, pp. 109–112; Test Files; Testing Program MP3s; Test Generator
espaces.vhlcentral.com: activities, downloads, reference tools

1 Expansion Write items like these on the board and ask students to say whether they would like more or fewer of them in town: **voitures, arrêts de bus, bars, musées, restaurants français, boutiques, prisons, commissariats de police, parcs, criminels, poubelles.** Example: **J'aimerais qu'il y ait moins de voitures dans notre ville.**

2 Suggestion Give students categories to help them think of tourist attractions to mention. Examples: restaurants, shopping, sports, museums, architecture, festivals, etc.

3 Suggestion Ask students to summarize what they said. Example: **C'est dommage qu'il n'y ait pas assez de poubelles sur le campus. Je souhaite qu'il y en ait plus à l'avenir.**

4 Suggestion Have the class identify the expressions listed on pages 481, 492, and 493 that would be useful in this activity. Examples: **Il faut que..., Je propose que... , Je regrette que...**, etc.

5 Expansion When students have finished, tell them to write a new conversation that includes a third speaker—an environmentalist hunter. Have them imagine what this person thinks about hunting while preserving animal species. (Environmental hunters tend to advocate strict controls that assure only overpopulated animal species are hunted, but not overhunted.)

6 Suggestion Divide the class into pairs and distribute the Info Gap Handouts in the IRM on the IRCD-ROM for this activity. Give students ten minutes to complete the activity.

1 Moins de déchets Avec un(e) partenaire, observez ces endroits. Dites à tour de rôle si vous aimeriez qu'il y ait **plus de** ou **moins de** certaines choses. Ensuite, comparez vos phrases à celles d'un autre groupe. Answers will vary.

MODÈLE

Étudiant(e) 1: *Je préférerais qu'il y ait plus d'eau dans cette rivière.*
Étudiant(e) 2: *J'aimerais mieux qu'il y ait plus d'herbe.*

1.

3.

2.

4.

2 Visite de votre région Interviewez vos camarades. Que recommandent-ils à des visiteurs qui ne connaissent pas votre région? Écrivez leurs réponses, puis comparez vos résultats à ceux d'un autre groupe. Utilisez ces expressions. Answers will vary.

MODÈLE

Étudiant(e) 1: *Que devraient faire les visiteurs de cette région?*
Étudiant(e) 2: *Je recommande qu'ils visitent les musées du centre-ville. Il serait bon qu'ils assistent aussi à un match de baseball.*

il est bon que	proposer que
il est indispensable que	recommander que
il faut que	suggérer que
?	?

3 Plus d'arbres Avec un(e) partenaire, pensez à votre environnement et dites si vous voulez qu'il y ait **plus de, moins de** ou **autant de** choses ou d'animaux. Quand vous n'êtes pas d'accord, justifiez vos réponses. Answers will vary.

MODÈLE

Étudiant(e) 1: *Je souhaite qu'il y ait plus d'arbres.*
Étudiant(e) 2: *Oui, il faut plus d'arbres sur le campus et en ville.*

4 Voyage en Afrique centrale Avec un(e) partenaire, vous voulez visiter ces endroits en Afrique centrale. Préparez un dialogue avec des verbes au présent du subjonctif et des comparatifs ou des superlatifs. Ensuite, échangez les rôles. Answers will vary.

MODÈLE

Étudiant(e) 1: *J'aimerais qu'on visite Kribi, au Cameroun. Il y a plus de plages.*
Étudiant(e) 2: *Il vaut mieux que nous visitions le marché, au Gabon.*

- la forêt de Dzanga-Sangha (République centrafricaine)
- le lac Kivu (Rwanda)
- les marchés (Gabon)
- le parc national de Lobéké (Cameroun)
- le parc national de l'Ivindo (Congo)
- les plages de Kribi (Cameroun)

5 Échange d'opinions Avec un(e) partenaire, imaginez une conversation entre un chasseur (*hunter*) et un défenseur de la nature. Préparez un dialogue où les deux se font des suggestions. Ensuite, jouez votre dialogue pour la classe. Answers will vary.

MODÈLE

Étudiant(e) 1: *Il est dommage que vous disiez que les chasseurs n'aiment pas la nature.*
Étudiant(e) 2: *Je souhaite que vous respectiez plus les animaux.*

6 La maman de Carine Votre professeur va vous donner, à vous et à votre partenaire, deux feuilles d'activités différentes sur Carine et sa mère. Attention! Ne regardez pas la feuille de votre partenaire. Answers will vary.

MODÈLE

Étudiant(e) 1: *Si Carine prend l'avion,...*
Étudiant(e) 2: *... sa mère veut qu'elle l'appelle de l'aéroport.*

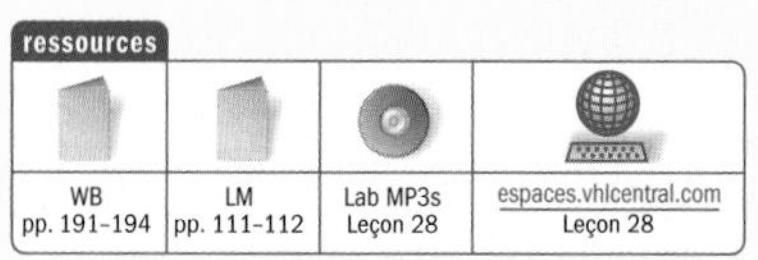

ressources
WB pp. 191–194
LM pp. 111–112
Lab MP3s Leçon 28
espaces.vhlcentral.com Leçon 28

OPTIONS

Game Ask small groups to write down three statements using comparative or superlative noun constructions. Two of the statements should be true; the third one should be false. Read the statements aloud. Groups identify the false statement in each set. The group with the most correct answers wins.

Extra Practice Put slips of paper, each with the names of two celebrities on it, in a bin. Have students draw slips, and then ask a question using a comparative or superlative that prompts them to identify one of the celebrities. Example: (1. Bill Cosby 2. Bill Gates) **C'est celui qui a le plus d'argent des deux.** (Bill Gates)

Le Végétarium, musée végétal

Yves Rocher est né à La Gacilly, en Bretagne. En 1958, ce village perdait ses habitants. Pour faire revivre° sa région et créer° des emplois, Yves Rocher a l'idée de fonder une entreprise tournée vers la nature et la beauté. Il commence à fabriquer° des produits cosmétiques à base de plantes. Aujourd'hui, La Gacilly est une petite ville vivante° et moderne qui respecte la nature.

En avril 1998, Yves Rocher crée le Végétarium. Situé dans un ancien moulin à eau°, c'est un musée qui fait découvrir le monde végétal à ses visiteurs.

—La Bretagne: son désert aride...

—Un lieu entièrement consacré au monde végétal...

Compréhension Répondez aux questions par des phrases complètes.

1. Où se trouve le musée? Il se trouve en Bretagne.
2. Pourquoi ce musée a-t-il été créé? Il a été créé pour mieux comprendre notre planète, mieux l'aimer et la protéger.
3. Est-ce un musée exceptionnel? Pourquoi? C'est le premier musée d'Europe entièrement consacré au monde végétal.
4. Quand le musée est-il ouvert? Il est ouvert tous les jours, de 10h00 à 18h45.

Discussion Par groupes de quatre, répondez ensemble aux questions. Answers will vary.

1. Connaissez-vous un musée comme le Végétarium? Où se trouve-t-il? Y êtes-vous déjà allé(e)? Si oui, qu'y avez-vous appris?
2. Est-ce une bonne idée d'avoir un musée végétal? Pourquoi?

SUR INTERNET

Go to **espaces.vhlcentral.com** to watch the TV clip featured in this **Le zapping**.

faire revivre *revive* **créer** *to create* **fabriquer** *to manufacture* **vivante** *lively* **moulin à eau** *water mill*

OPTIONS

La Gacilly Yves Rocher and his foundation developed a series of tourist attractions around the theme of the **Végétarium**. Museum visitors can wander through a unique botanical garden with more than 1,000 species of medieval and medicinal plants. From April to October, the **Végétarium** also has an exhibit of pictures of gardens from around the world in its large plant maze. Another tourist attraction at La Gacilly is the Yves Rocher industrial plant, where visitors can learn how the famous plant-based cosmetics are produced. Near La Gacilly, many other activities are available for nature lovers and families. At Saint-Just, for example, they can walk through the second largest field of prehistoric megaliths in France or climb the cliff above the pond of Val.

Section Goals

In this section, students will:

- read about Yves Rocher and the **Végétarium** museum
- watch a commercial for the museum
- answer questions about the museum and its commercial

Instructional Resources
*IRCD-ROM: IRM (**Le zapping** TV clip transcription)*
espaces.vhlcentral.com: activities, downloads, reference tools, TV clip

Introduction
To check comprehension, ask these questions.
1. Où est né Yves Rocher? (Il est né à La Gacilly, en Bretagne.)
2. Que fait-il en 1958 pour faire revivre sa région? (Il fonde une entreprise tournée vers la nature et la beauté et commence à fabriquer des produits cosmétiques à base de plantes.)
3. Le Végétarium, qu'est-ce que c'est? (C'est un musée dans un ancien moulin à eau qui fait découvrir le monde végétal à ses visiteurs.)

Avant de regarder la vidéo

- Have students look at the video stills, read the captions, and predict what is happening in the commercial for each visual.
- Before showing the video, explain that students do not need to understand every word they hear. Tell them to listen for cognates and museum-related vocabulary.

Compréhension Have students work in pairs or groups for this activity. Tell them to write their answers. Then show the video again so that they can check their answers and add any missing information.

Discussion

- Have volunteers report back to the class the results of their discussion.
- Take a quick class survey to find out students' opinions of this kind of museum.

Section Goals

In this section, students will learn historical and cultural information about West Africa and Central Africa.

Instructional Resources
IRCD-ROM: Transparency #59
WB/VM: Workbook, pp. 195–196
WB/VM/LM Answer Key
espaces.vhlcentral.com: activities; downloads; reference tools

Carte de l'Afrique de l'ouest et de l'Afrique centrale

- Have students look at the map or use **Transparency #59**. Ask volunteers to read the names of countries and major cities aloud. Model pronunciation as necessary.
- Point out the photos of Abidjan, the administrative and commercial center of **la Côte d'Ivoire**, and Kinshasa. Abidjan is a major port city, whereas Kinshasa is an inland city connected by rail to an Atlantic port city.

La région en chiffres

- For the countries of French-speaking West and Central Africa, French is the language of administration, education, and international communication. French is the official language and may share official status with English, Arabic, and other languages native to the country.
- Rwanda has three official languages, and Cameroon recognizes two official and 24 unofficial languages. The minimum number of recognized languages for any country in West or Central Africa is three.

Incroyable mais vrai! Today there is an estimated total of 250 mountain gorillas in Kahuzi-Biega National Park that the World Conservation Society is trying to protect.

Panorama

un marché en Afrique

L'Afrique de l'ouest

La région en chiffres

- **Bénin:** *(8.278.000 habitants), Porto Novo*
- **Burkina-Faso:** *(15.764.000), Ouagadougou*
- **Côte d'Ivoire:** *(19.625.000), Yamoussoukro*
- **Guinée:** *(9.996.000), Conakry*
- **Mali:** *(15.234.000), Bamako*
- **Mauritanie:** *(3.577.000), Nouakchott*
- **Niger:** *(15.550.000), Niamey*
- **Sénégal:** *(12.051.000), Dakar*
- **Togo:** *(5.826.000), Lomé*

SOURCE: Population Division, UN Secretariat

L'Afrique centrale

La région en chiffres

- **Burundi:** *(8.662.000), Bujumbura*
- **Cameroun:** *(18.347.000), Yaoundé*
- **Congo:** *(4.084.000), Brazzaville*
- **Gabon:** *(1.568.000), Libreville*
- **République centrafricaine:** *(4.430.000), Bangui*
- **République démocratique du Congo (R.D.C.):** *(71.272.000), Kinshasa*
- **Rwanda:** *(9.425.000), Kigali*
- **Tchad:** *(10.689.000), N'Djamena*

la ville d'Abidjan

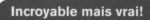

une femme à Kinshasa

Pays francophones

Personnages célèbres

- **Mory Kanté,** *Guinée et Mali, chanteur et musicien (1950–)*
- **Djimon Hounsou,** *Bénin, acteur (1964–)*
- **Françoise Mbango-Etone,** *Cameroun, athlète olympique (1976–)*

Incroyable mais vrai!

Progrès ou destruction? Dans le parc Kahuzi-Biega, à l'est de la R.D.C., habite une espèce menacée d'extinction: le gorille de montagne. Il est encore plus menacé, depuis ces dernières années, par l'exploitation d'un minerai, le coltan, utilisé dans la fabrication de portables. Aujourd'hui, le parc est sur la liste du patrimoine mondial en péril°.

liste du patrimoine mondial en péril *World Heritage in Danger List*

OPTIONS

Personnages célèbres **Mory Kanté** uses traditional African instruments and rhythms in his music. He plays the kora, which is a large harp-lute. Kanté is the first African musician to sell a million singles, and his music has topped European charts. **Djimon Hounsou** immigrated to France at the age of 13, where he was discovered and made a fashion model by Thierry Mugler. He has starred in major American and French films. He is also the first African male to be nominated for an Academy Award for his role in the movie *In America*. **Françoise Mbango-Etone** competes in the triple jump. She has won world championships, and she won an Olympic gold medal in 2004. She is the first Cameroonian athlete to win an Olympic medal.

Les gens

Léopold Sédar Senghor, le président poète (1906–2001)

Senghor, homme politique et poète sénégalais, était professeur de lettres en France avant de mener° le Sénégal à l'indépendance et de devenir le premier président du pays en 1960. Humaniste et homme de culture, il est un des pères fondateurs° de la Négritude, un mouvement littéraire d'Africains et d'Antillais noirs qui examinent et mettent en valeur leur identité culturelle. Il a aussi organisé le premier Festival mondial des arts nègres, à Dakar, en 1966. Senghor a produit une importante œuvre° littéraire dans laquelle il explore le métissage° des cultures africaines, européennes et américaines. Docteur honoris causa de nombreuses universités, dont Harvard et la Sorbonne, il a été élu° à l'Académie française en 1983.

La musique

Le reggae ivoirien

Alpha Blondy

La Côte d'Ivoire est un des pays d'Afrique où le reggae africain est le plus développé. Ce type de reggae se distingue du reggae jamaïcain par les instruments de musique utilisés et les thèmes abordés°. En fait, les artistes ivoiriens incorporent souvent des instruments traditionnels d'Afrique de l'ouest et les thèmes sont souvent très politiques. Alpha Blondy, par exemple, est le plus célèbre des chanteurs ivoiriens de reggae et fait souvent des commentaires sociopolitiques. Le chanteur Tiken Jah Fakoly critique la politique occidentale et les gouvernants africains, et Ismaël Isaac dénonce les ventes d'armes° dans le monde. Le reggae ivoirien est chanté en français, en anglais et dans les langues africaines.

Les lieux

Les parcs nationaux du Cameroun

Avec la forêt, la savane et la montagne dans ses réserves et parcs nationaux, le Cameroun présente une des faunes et flores les plus riches et variées d'Afrique. Deux cent quarante empreintes° de dinosaures sont fossilisées au site de dinosaures de Manangia, dans la province du Nord. Les différentes réserves du pays abritent°, entre autres, éléphants, gorilles, chimpanzés, antilopes et plusieurs centaines d'espèces de reptiles, d'oiseaux et de poissons. Le parc national Korup est une des plus anciennes forêts tropicales du monde. Il est connu surtout récemment pour une liane°, découverte là-bas, qui pourrait avoir un effet sur la guérison° de certains cancers et du VIH°.

Les arts

Le FESPACO

Le FESPACO (Festival Panafricain du Cinéma et de la télévision à Ouagadougou), créé en 1969 pour favoriser la promotion du cinéma africain, est le plus grand festival du cinéma africain du monde et le plus grand événement culturel d'Afrique qui revient régulièrement. Vingt films et vingt courts métrages° africains sont présentés en compétition officielle, tous les deux ans, à ce festival du Burkina-Faso. Le FESPACO est aussi une fête populaire avec une cérémonie d'ouverture à laquelle assistent 40.000 spectateurs et des stars de la musique africaine.

Qu'est-ce que vous avez appris? Répondez aux questions par des phrases complètes.

1. Qu'est-ce qui menace la vie des gorilles de montagne? L'exploitation du coltan menace la vie des gorilles.
2. Quelle est une des utilisations du coltan? Il est utilisé dans la fabrication de portables.
3. Pourquoi Senghor est-il important dans l'histoire du Sénégal? Il a mené le Sénégal à l'indépendance et a été le premier président du pays.
4. De quel mouvement Senghor était-il un des fondateurs? Il était un des fondateurs du mouvement de la Négritude.
5. Qu'est-ce qui fait la spécificité du son (*sound*) du reggae ivoirien? Les artistes utilisent des instruments traditionnels d'Afrique de l'ouest.
6. De quoi parlent souvent les chanteurs de reggae en Côte d'Ivoire? Ils parlent souvent de politique.
7. Qu'a-t-on trouvé sur le site de Manangia? On a trouvé des empreintes de dinosaures.
8. Pourquoi le parc national Korup est-il bien connu récemment? Il est connu pour la liane qu'on y a trouvée qui pourrait avoir des effets avantageux dans la guérison de cancers et du VIH.
9. Pourquoi le FESPACO a-t-il été créé? Le festival a été créé pour favoriser la promotion du cinéma africain.
10. Le FESPACO est-il un festival réservé aux professionnels du cinéma? Non, c'est aussi une fête populaire.

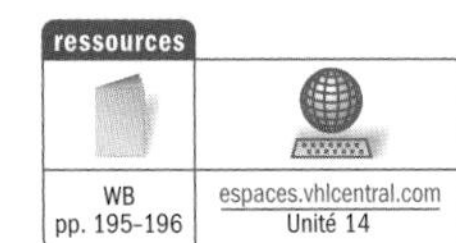

SUR INTERNET

Go to **espaces.vhlcentral.com** to find more cultural information related to this **PANORAMA**.

1. Trouvez des informations sur le mouvement de la Négritude. Qui en étaient les autres principaux fondateurs?
2. Écoutez des chansons de reggae ivoirien. De quoi parlent-elles?
3. Cherchez plus d'informations sur le gorille de montagne et le coltan. Quel est le statut (*status*) du gorille aujourd'hui?

mener *lead* **pères fondateurs** *founding fathers* **œuvre** *body of work* **métissage** *mixing* **élu** *elected* **abordés** *dealt with* **ventes d'armes** *weapons sales* **empreintes** *footprints* **abritent** *provide a habitat for, shelter* **liane** *vine* **guérison** *cure* **VIH** *HIV* **métrages** *films*

Léopold Sédar Senghor Senghor was president from 1960–1980. The concept of **la Négritude** is best exemplified in his ***Anthologie de la nouvelle poésie nègre et malgache*** (1948).

Le reggae ivoirien Some of the traditional African musical instruments are talking drums, djembe, balafone, kora, bolon, daro, and the gourd rattle. Many are made from natural materials such as seeds, grass, or wood.

Les parcs nationaux du Cameroun Cameroon's national parks are Waza, Boubandjidah, Bénoué, Kalamaloué, Faro, Mozogo-Gokoro, Korup, Dja, Boumba Bek, and Nki. Ask students: **Quelles espèces d'animaux peut-on voir dans les réserves du Cameroun? (éléphants, gorilles, chimpanzés, antilopes, reptiles, oiseaux et poissons)**

Le FESPACO

- One of the objectives of **FESPACO** is to contribute to the expansion and development of African films. The festival arranges free screenings of African films in rural areas and also offers monetary prizes to its winners.
- Have students locate Ouagadougou on the map on page 498.

OPTIONS

La Négritude **La Négritude** was a literary movement in the 1930s, 1940s, and 1950s. It began among French-speaking African and Caribbean writers living in Paris as a way to protest French colonial rule and forced assimilation into Western culture. A basic tenant of **Négritude** is to look to one's own cultural heritage, traditions, history, and beliefs with pride and to use them in the modern world. In literary works, the value and dignity of African traditions and peoples is manifested through the use of African subject matter and poetic traditions. For example, in poetry some of the traditional values are closeness to nature and constant contact with ancestors.

Section Goals

In this section, students will:
- learn to recognize chronological order
- read an excerpt from a French novel

Stratégie Tell students that understanding the order of events allows a reader to follow what is happening in the narrative.

Successful Language Learning Tell students to look for connecting words and transitions, because they are helpful in following a chain of events.

Examinez le texte
- Guide students to mention that geographers study the Earth's surface, its features, the distribution of life on the planet's surface, and the effect of climate and geography on human activity.
- Have volunteers describe the characters in the illustrations.

À propos de l'auteur
- Point out that ***Le Petit Prince*** is considered to be Saint-Exupéry's masterpiece.
- The wreckage from Saint-Exupéry's downed airplane was found in the Mediterranean seabed between Marseille and Cassis in April, 2004.
- The international airport in Lyon (**Aéroport Lyon-Saint-Exupéry**) is named after the famous writer and pilot.
- Ask these comprehesion questions. **1. Où est-ce qu'Antoine de Saint-Exupéry est né? (à Lyon) 2. Était-il seulement écrivain? (Non, il était aussi aviateur/pilote.) 3. Quels genres de littérature a-t-il écrits? (des romans) 4. Où est-ce que le Petit Prince a voyagé? (vers d'autres planètes)**

Lecture

Avant la lecture

STRATÉGIE

Recognizing chronological order

Recognizing the chronological order of events in a narrative is key to understanding the cause and effect relationship between them. When you are able to establish the chronological chain of events, you will easily be able to follow the plot. In order to be more aware of the order of events in a narrative, you may find it helpful to prepare a numbered list of the events as you read.

Examinez le texte

Dans l'extrait (*excerpt*) du *Petit Prince* que vous allez lire, le petit prince rencontre un géographe. Que fait un géographe? En quoi consiste son travail exactement? Est-ce un travail facile ou difficile, à votre avis? Regardez les illustrations et décrivez le géographe et le petit prince.

À propos de l'auteur
Antoine de Saint-Exupéry

Antoine de Saint-Exupéry est né à Lyon, en France, en 1900. C'est un écrivain français très apprécié dans le monde entier qui a aussi eu une carrière d'aviateur. En 1921, il entre dans l'armée, où il est formé comme pilote. Plus tard, en 1926, il devient pilote pour la compagnie Aéropostale et voyage entre la France, l'Afrique du Nord et l'Amérique du Sud. À cette époque, il écrit ses deux premiers romans°, *Courrier Sud* et *Vol de nuit*. De nouveau dans l'armée française, Saint-Exupéry écrit, en 1943, alors qu'il est en Afrique du Nord, son œuvre la plus célèbre, *Le Petit Prince*. Elle sera traduite en plus de 150 langues. Saint-Exupéry disparaît° en 1944 lors d'°une mission en avion.

Le Petit Prince raconte l'histoire d'un jeune garçon qui a quitté sa planète pour visiter d'autres planètes. Pendant son voyage, il rencontre des personnages et des animaux différents. Dans cet extrait, le petit prince arrive sur la sixième planète, où habite un vieux monsieur qui est géographe.

romans *novels* **disparaît** *disappears* **lors d'** *during*

Le Petit Prince

[...]

La sixième planète était une planète dix fois plus vaste. Elle était habitée par un vieux Monsieur qui écrivait d'énormes livres.

—Tiens! voilà un explorateur! s'écria-t-il°, quand il aperçut° le petit prince.

Le petit prince s'assit° sur la table et souffla° un peu. Il avait déjà tant° voyagé!

—D'où viens-tu? lui dit le vieux Monsieur.

—Quel est ce gros livre? dit le petit prince. Que faites-vous ici?

—Je suis géographe, dit le vieux Monsieur.

—Qu'est-ce qu'un géographe?

—C'est un savant° qui connaît où se trouvent les mers, les fleuves, les villes, les montagnes et les déserts.

—Ça, c'est intéressant, dit le petit prince. Ça, c'est enfin un véritable métier! Et il jeta un coup d'œil autour° de lui sur la planète du géographe. Il n'avait jamais vu encore une planète aussi majestueuse.

—Elle est bien belle, votre planète. Est-ce qu'il y a des océans?

—Je ne puis° pas le savoir, dit le géographe.

—Ah! (Le petit prince était déçu°.) Et des montagnes?

—Je ne puis pas le savoir, dit le géographe.

—Et des villes et des fleuves et des déserts?

—Je ne puis pas le savoir non plus, dit le géographe.

—Mais vous êtes géographe!

—C'est exact, dit le géographe, mais je ne suis pas explorateur. Je manque° absolument d'explorateurs. Ce n'est pas le géographe qui va faire le compte° des villes, des fleuves, des montagnes, des mers et des océans. Le géographe est trop important pour flâner°. Il ne quitte pas son bureau. Mais il reçoit les explorateurs. Il les interroge, et il prend note de leurs souvenirs°. Et si les souvenirs de l'un d'entre eux lui paraissent° intéressants, le géographe fait une enquête° sur la moralité de l'explorateur.

—Pourquoi ça?

—Parce qu'un explorateur qui mentirait° entraînerait° des catastrophes dans les livres de géographie. Et aussi un explorateur qui boirait° trop.

—Pourquoi ça? fit° le petit prince.

—Parce que les ivrognes° voient double. Alors le géographe noterait deux montagnes, là où il n'y en a qu'une seule.

—Je connais quelqu'un, dit le petit prince, qui serait mauvais explorateur.

OPTIONS

Extra Practice Have students research and write a summary about Saint-Exupéry's plane crash. They should find out what sort of a mission he was on, who found the plane's wreckage, and any other important or interesting details. Remind them to jot down notes of the events or details in chronological order.

Language Note Tell students that some verbs in this text are in the **passé simple**, which is the literary way of expressing the past tense in French. Have students give the **passé composé** form that corresponds to the **passé simple** form. Examples: **il fit (il a fait)**, **il dit (il a dit)**, **il s'assit (il s'est assis)**, and **il aperçut (il s'est aperçu)**.

—C'est possible. Donc, quand la moralité de l'explorateur paraît° bonne, on fait une enquête sur sa découverte°.

—On va voir?

—Non. C'est trop compliqué. Mais on exige qu'il en rapporte° de grosses pierres.

Le géographe soudain s'émut°.

—Mais toi, tu viens de loin! Tu es explorateur! Tu vas me décrire ta planète!

Et le géographe, ayant ouvert son registre°, tailla° son crayon. On note d'abord au crayon les récits des explorateurs. On attend, pour noter à l'encre°, que l'explorateur ait fourni des preuves°.

—Alors? interrogea le géographe.

—Oh! chez moi, dit le petit prince, ce n'est pas très intéressant, c'est tout petit. J'ai trois volcans. Deux volcans en activité, et un volcan éteint. [...]

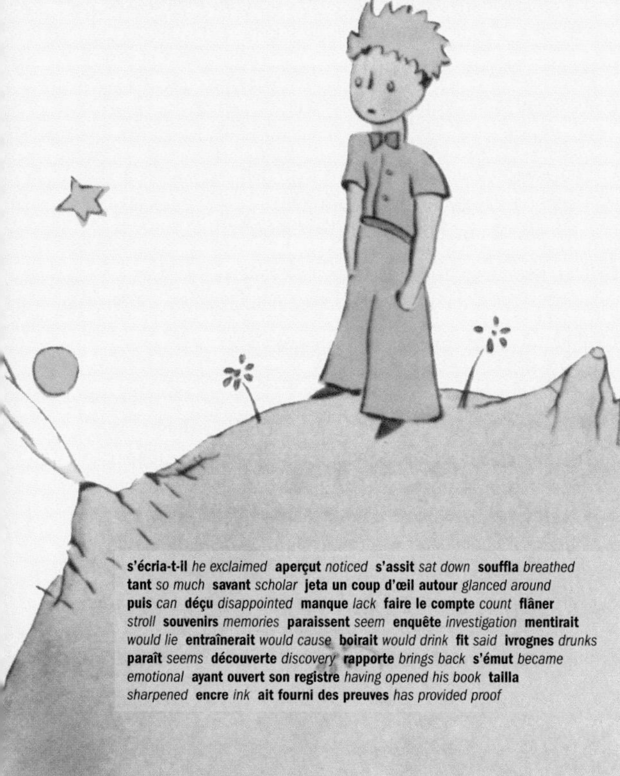

s'écria-t-il *he exclaimed* **aperçut** *noticed* **s'assit** *sat down* **souffla** *breathed* **tant** *so much* **savant** *scholar* **jeta un coup d'œil autour** *glanced around* **puis** *can* **déçu** *disappointed* **manque** *lack* **faire le compte** *count* **flâner** *stroll* **souvenirs** *memories* **paraissent** *seem* **enquête** *investigation* **mentirait** *would lie* **entraînerait** *would cause* **boirait** *would drink* **fit** *said* **ivrognes** *drunks* **paraît** *seems* **découverte** *discovery* **rapporte** *brings back* **s'émut** *became emotional* **ayant ouvert son registre** *having opened his book* **tailla** *sharpened* **encre** *ink* **ait fourni des preuves** *has provided proof*

Après la lecture

Le travail d'un géographe **Cherchez, dans le texte, les différentes étapes du travail du géographe et mettez-les dans l'ordre chronologique.**

1. __8__ Le géographe écrit la version du récit des explorateurs à l'encre.
2. __2__ Le géographe demande aux explorateurs de raconter leurs récits.
3. __3__ Le géographe note les découvertes des explorateurs au crayon.
4. __1__ Le géographe reçoit des explorateurs.
5. __7__ Les explorateurs donnent des preuves au géographe.
6. __5__ Le géographe fait une enquête sur les découvertes des explorateurs.
7. __4__ Le géographe fait une enquête sur la moralité des explorateurs.
8. __6__ Le géographe demande aux explorateurs de lui ramener (*bring back*) des pierres.

Répondez **Répondez aux questions par des phrases complètes.**

1. Où habite le géographe? Il habite sur la sixième planète.
2. Que faisait le géographe quand le petit prince est arrivé sur sa planète? Il écrivait d'énormes livres.
3. Pourquoi est-ce que le petit prince est fatigué quand il arrive chez le géographe? Il est fatigué parce qu'il a beaucoup voyagé.
4. D'après le géographe, quel est le métier du petit prince? Il pense que le petit prince est explorateur.
5. Pourquoi est-ce qu'un géographe n'explore jamais les endroits qu'il veut connaître? Il est trop important pour flâner.
6. Si un explorateur ment, quelles peuvent être les conséquences, d'après le géographe? Il peut y avoir des catastrophes dans les livres de géographie.
7. Qu'est-ce que le géographe demande au petit prince à la fin de l'extrait? Il lui demande de lui parler de sa planète.
8. Comment est la planète du petit prince? Elle est toute petite, avec deux volcans en activité et un volcan éteint.

Dans le futur **Nous sommes en 2650 et on peut voyager dans l'espace. Avez-vous envie de visiter les autres planètes, comme le petit prince? Expliquez. Comment sont les autres planètes, à votre avis? Sont-elles comme la Terre ou pas?**

Une lettre au géographe **Vous êtes un(e) des explorateurs/exploratrices qui travaillent pour le géographe. Aidez-le à mieux connaître la Terre. Écrivez-lui une lettre dans laquelle vous lui expliquez comment est votre région, votre pays ou un autre endroit dans le monde, si vous préférez.**

Le travail d'un géographe
If students have difficulty putting the events in order, have them refer to the text and mark the item number next to the corresponding line(s).

Répondez Go over the answers with the class.

Dans le futur This activity can be done in pairs or groups.

Une lettre au géographe
Have students exchange their letters for peer editing. Then tell them to ask questions about the letter's content as if they were **le géographe** in the story.

OPTIONS

Extra Practice Have the class discuss these topics. **1. *Le Petit Prince* est-il écrit pour les adultes ou pour les enfants?** Students should justify their opinions with examples from the reading. **2. Comment caractériseriez-vous** (*would you characterize*) **le géographe et le Petit Prince? 3. À votre avis, qu'est-ce que le géographe et le Petit Prince symbolisent** (*symbolize*)?

Extra Practice Have students research and compile a list of titles of Saint-Exupéry's literary works. Tell them to read a brief description of each title, choose a book that they would like to read, and explain why.

Section Goals

In this section, students will:

- learn to listen for the gist and for cognates
- listen to a paragraph and jot down the gist and some cognates
- listen to a speech at an environmental demonstration and complete several activities

Instructional Resources
Textbook MP3s
IRCD-ROM: IRM (Textbook Audioscript)
espaces.vhlcentral.com: downloads, reference tools

Stratégie

Script Les Français choisissent de plus en plus de passer des vacances «vertes», c'est-à-dire des vacances qui proposent des activités d'écotourisme. Ces voyages, qui sont souvent des voyages organisés, permettent à leurs participants de passer du temps dans la nature et de découvrir ce qu'ils peuvent faire pour contribuer plus activement à la protection de notre planète.

Préparation Have students look at the photo and describe what is happening. Then have them guess what the people might be saying.

À vous d'écouter

Script Bonjour à tous et merci beaucoup d'être venus participer à notre manifestation aujourd'hui. Si nous travaillons tous ensemble, nous pourrons trouver des solutions concrètes pour moins polluer notre environnement. Tout d'abord, il est essentiel que nous prenions tous l'habitude de trier nos déchets. Le verre et beaucoup d'autres emballages ménagers peuvent être recyclés. Il est aussi indispensable que vous achetiez des produits emballés dans des emballages recyclables. Ils aident à combattre la pollution de notre planète. Il est aussi nécessaire d'éviter le gaspillage. Ces suggestions sont un bon début, mais malheureusement, nous ne pouvons pas réussir seuls. Il faut absolument que notre gouvernement fasse plus d'efforts en ce qui concerne le recyclage et le ramassage des ordures. Il est également nécessaire que tous les gouvernements d'Europe ainsi que ceux des autres pays et continents fassent passer des lois beaucoup plus strictes en ce qui concerne les déchets toxiques. Nous ne voulons plus de déchets toxiques dans nos rivières ni dans nos océans! La pollution de l'eau, comme celle du reste de la Terre, est un véritable danger qu'il faut prendre très au sérieux. Trop d'espèces aussi sont en train de disparaître et je souhaite qu'aujourd'hui, nous promettions tous d'essayer de faire plus d'efforts pour favoriser l'écologie. Je propose en plus que nous écrivions tous au ministre de l'environnement pour demander des changements dès aujourd'hui!

À l'écoute

STRATÉGIE

Listening for the gist/Listening for cognates

Combining these two strategies is an easy way to get a good sense of what you hear. When you listen for the gist, you get the general idea of what you're hearing, which allows you to interpret cognates and other words in a meaningful context. Similarly, the cognates give you information about the details of the story that you might not have understood when listening for the gist.

 To practice these strategies, you will listen to a short paragraph. Write down the gist of what you hear and jot down a few cognates. What conclusions can you draw about what you heard?

Préparation

Regardez la photo. Que se passe-t-il à votre avis? Combien de personnes y a-t-il? Pour quelle cause ces personnes manifestent-elles (*demonstrate*)? De quoi vont-elles parler?

À vous d'écouter

Écoutez la personne qui a organisé la manifestation (*demonstration*) et encerclez les sujets mentionnés.

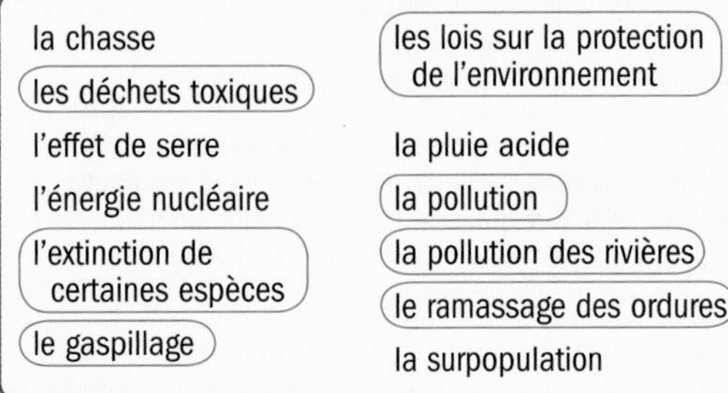

la chasse	(les lois sur la protection de l'environnement)
(les déchets toxiques)	la pluie acide
l'effet de serre	(la pollution)
l'énergie nucléaire	(la pollution des rivières)
(l'extinction de certaines espèces)	(le ramassage des ordures)
(le gaspillage)	la surpopulation

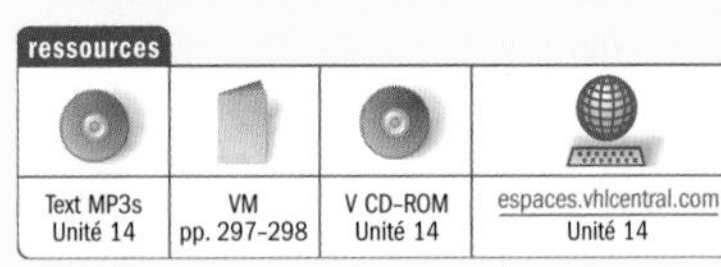

ressources
Text MP3s Unité 14 | VM pp. 297–298 | V CD-ROM Unité 14 | espaces.vhlcentral.com Unité 14

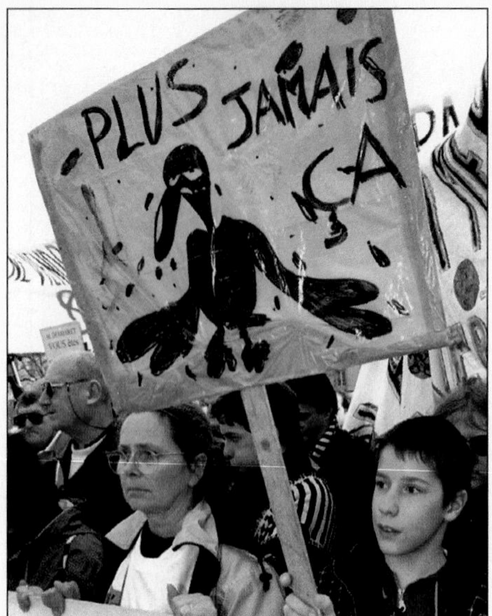

Compréhension

Complétez **Choisissez la bonne réponse pour terminer chaque phrase, d'après ce que vous venez d'entendre.**

1. On peut recycler __a__.
   a. le verre b. les déchets toxiques c. tous les déchets
2. Les emballages recyclables aident à __c__.
   a. éviter le ramassage des ordures b. trier (*to sort*) les déchets c. combattre la pollution de la Terre
3. Il faut __b__ le gaspillage.
   a. développer b. éviter c. polluer
4. Le gouvernement doit __a__.
   a. passer des lois plus strictes en ce qui concerne l'écologie b. éviter l'effet de serre c. réduire le trou dans la couche d'ozone
5. Il y a beaucoup de __a__ dans les rivières.
   a. déchets toxiques b. ressources naturelles c. verre
6. Trop __b__ sont en train de disparaître.
   a. d'écoproduits b. d'espèces c. d'océans

Les lois **Un(e) représentant(e) du Congrès vient à votre université pour discuter de l'environnement. Par petits groupes, choisissez un problème écologique qui est très important pour vous. Préparez des arguments à lui présenter. Vous voulez lui faire comprendre que le gouvernement doit faire plus dans le domaine que vous avez choisi. Soyez prêts à bien expliquer la situation actuelle (*today*) et les changements nécessaires pour l'améliorer. Pensez aussi à quelques nouvelles lois sur la protection de l'environnement que vous pourrez suggérer à votre représentant(e) du Congrès.**

Les arts

UNITÉ 15

Leçon 29

ESPACE CONTEXTES
pages 506–509
- Performance arts
- **Les liaisons obligatoires et les liaisons interdites**

ESPACE ROMAN-PHOTO
pages 510–511
- **Après le concert**

ESPACE CULTURE
pages 512–513
- Theater in France

ESPACE STRUCTURES
pages 514–519
- The verbs **voir** and **croire**
- The subjunctive (Part 3)
- **Synthèse**
- **Projet**

Leçon 30

ESPACE CONTEXTES
pages 520–523
- Literary arts
- TV and movies
- **Les abréviations et les sigles**

ESPACE ROMAN-PHOTO
pages 524–525
- **Au revoir, David!**

ESPACE CULTURE
pages 526–527
- Haitian painting

ESPACE STRUCTURES
pages 528–533
- The subjunctive (Part 4)
- Review of the subjunctive
- **Synthèse**
- **Interlude**

Pour commencer
- Où est David? Sur une falaise? Dans une classe? Dans un champ?
- Que dessine-t-il?
- Est-il nécessaire qu'il ait un modèle pour dessiner?
- Est-il possible qu'il soit déjà un artiste connu?

Savoir-faire
pages 534–539

Panorama: **Les Antilles** and **la Polynésie française**
Lecture: Read a poem.
À l'écoute: Listen to review of a play.
Écriture: Write a critique.
Flash culture

Unit Goals

Leçon 29
In this lesson, students will learn:
- terms related to the theater and performance arts
- rules for making liaisons and some exceptions
- about the theater in France and Molière
- the verbs **voir** and **croire**
- about the subjunctive with expressions of doubt, disbelief, and uncertainty
- some irregular forms of the subjunctive
- to write a report on the most famous artists of the French Antilles

Leçon 30
In this lesson, students will learn:
- terms for television and film
- terms for literature and fine arts
- about abbreviations and acronyms
- about Haitian painting and **le Cirque du Soleil**
- the subjunctive with conjunctions
- about singer France Gall and painter Paul Cézanne

Savoir-faire
In this section, students will learn:
- cultural, economic, and historical information about the Antilles and French Polynesia
- to make inferences and recognize metaphors
- to listen for key words and use context
- to write strong introductions and conclusions
- more about movie theaters and kiosks through specially shot video footage

Pour commencer
- **David est dans une classe.**
- **Il dessine des fruits.**
- Answers may vary.
- Answers may vary.

RESOURCES
Workbook/Video Manual: WB Activities, pp. 197–210
Laboratory Manual: Lab Activities, pp. 113–120
Workbook/Video Manual: Video Activities, pp. 267–270; pp. 299–300
WB/VM/LM Answer Key
Instructor's Resource CD-ROM [IRCD-ROM]: Instructor's Resource Manual [IRM] (Textbook Audioscript; Lab Audioscript; Videoscript; **Roman-photo** Translations; **Vocabulaire supplémentaire**; **Feuilles d'activités**; Info Gap Activities; **Le zapping** TV clip transcription; **Essayez!** and **Mise en pratique** answers); Transparencies #60, #61, #62; Testing Program, pp. 113–120, pp. 153–160, pp. 173–184; pp. 209–220; Test Files; Testing Program MP3s; Test Generator
Lab MP3s
Textbook MP3s
Video CD-ROM
Video on DVD
espaces.vhlcentral.com

Section Goals

In this section, students will learn and practice vocabulary related to:

- theater
- performance arts

Instructional Resources
*IRCD-ROM: Transparency #60; IRM (**Vocabulaire supplémentaire**; **Mise en pratique** answers; Textbook Audioscript; Lab Audioscript; Info Gap Activities)*
Textbook MP3s
WB/VM: Workbook, pp. 197–198
Lab Manual, p. 113
Lab MP3s
WB/VM/LM Answer Key
espaces.vhlcentral.com: activities, downloads, reference tools

Suggestions

- Tell students to look over the new vocabulary and identify the cognates.
- Use **Transparency #60**. Point out people and things as you describe the illustration. Examples: **Il joue du piano. C'est un opéra. La spectatrice applaudit.**
- Point out the differences in spelling between the French words **danse** and **membre** and the English words *dance* and *member*.
- Model the pronunciation of the word **début**, contrasting it with its English pronunciation.
- Point out the difference between **un personnage** and **une personne**.
- Tell students that **profiter de** does not necessarily have the negative connotation that *to take advantage of* does in English.
- Remind students to use **jouer à** with sports, but **jouer de** with musical instruments. Examples: **Il joue *au* tennis. Il joue *de* la guitare.**
- Ask students questions using the new vocabulary. Examples: **Quels réalisateurs célèbres connaissez-vous? Quelle est votre chanson préférée? Jouez-vous d'un instrument de musique? Si oui, lequel? Aimez-vous aller au théâtre? À l'opéra?**
- Additional vocabulary for this lesson can be found in the **Vocabulaire supplémentaire** in the IRM on the IRCD-ROM.

Leçon 29

You will learn how to...

- talk about performance arts
- express your feelings and opinions

Que le spectacle commence!

Vocabulaire

jouer un rôle	*to play a role*
présenter	*to present*
profiter de quelque chose	*to take advantage of/ to enjoy something*
un applaudissement	*applause*
une chanson	*song*
un chœur	*choir, chorus*
une comédie (musicale)	*comedy (musical)*
un compositeur	*composer*
un concert	*concert*
une danse	*dance*
un dramaturge	*playwright*
un entracte	*intermission*
un membre	*member*
un metteur en scène	*director (of a play, a show)*
un personnage (principal)	*(main) character*
une pièce de théâtre	*play*
un réalisateur/une réalisatrice	*director (of a movie)*
une séance	*show; screening*
une troupe	*company, troop*
le début	*beginning; debut*
la fin	*end*
un genre	*genre*
une sorte	*sort, kind*
célèbre	*famous*

ressources

WB pp. 197–198	LM p. 113	Text MP3s Leçon 29	Lab MP3s Leçon 29	espaces.vhlcentral.com Leçon 29

OPTIONS

Extra Practice Have students identify familiar artists, songs, films, plays, etc., by completing your statements with vocabulary from **Contextes**. Examples: **1. *Carmen* est ____ de Bizet. (un opéra) 2. *La Marseillaise* est ____. (une chanson) 3. *Giselle* est ____. (un ballet) 4. Steven Spielberg est ____. (un réalisateur)**

Extra Practice Write or have students write the names of well-known artists on sticky notes and put them on the backs of other students. Then tell them to walk around the room asking their classmates yes/no questions to determine their identity. Examples: **Est-ce que je suis dramaturge? Est-ce que j'écris des tragédies? Est-ce que je suis William Shakespeare?**

Mise en pratique

1 Écoutez  **Écoutez la conversation entre Hakim et Nadja pendant le spectacle de *Notre-Dame de Paris*, ensuite indiquez la bonne réponse.**

1. Hakim et Najda donnent leurs...
   a. places.
   (b.) billets.
   c. détails.
2. Leurs places sont situées...
   a. très loin de l'orchestre.
   b. au balcon.
   (c.) près de l'orchestre.
3. Le spectacle est...
   (a.) une comédie musicale.
   b. un concert.
   c. une tragédie.
4. Gilles Maheu est...
   a. un dramaturge.
   (b.) un metteur en scène.
   c. un personnage.
5. Hakim...
   a. n'a pas applaudi.
   b. a très peu applaudi.
   (c.) a beaucoup applaudi.
6. Nadja pense qu'Hakim...
   a. va devenir célèbre.
   (b.) n'est pas un bon danseur.
   c. est un bon compositeur.

2 Choisissez Choisissez la phrase de la colonne B qui complète le mieux les phrases de la colonne A. Notez que tous les éléments de la colonne B ne sont pas utilisés.

A

1. __a__ Pour entrer dans une salle de spectacle,
2. __g__ Georges Bizet a écrit **Carmen** en 1875;
3. __e__ Au milieu d'une pièce de théâtre
4. __d__ Un metteur en scène est chargé de
5. __h__ La tragédie **Hamlet** est une
6. __b__ Une comédie musicale est

B

a. il faut un billet.
b. un spectacle de musique et de danse.
c. un membre de la troupe.
d. guider les comédiens dans leur travail.
e. il y a souvent un entracte.
f. il faut danser à l'entracte.
g. c'est un des opéras français les plus célèbres.
h. des pièces de théâtre les plus connues de Shakespeare.

3 Associez Complétez les analogies suivantes par le mot ou l'expression de la section ESPACE CONTEXTES qui convient le mieux.

1. chanter ⟷ chanson = applaudir ⟷ __applaudissement__
2. heureux ⟷ comédie = triste ⟷ __tragédie__
3. théâtre ⟷ pièce = cinéma ⟷ __séance__
4. concert ⟷ orchestre = chanson ⟷ __chœur__
5. film ⟷ acteur = ballet ⟷ __danseur__
6. opéra ⟷ chanter = concert ⟷ __faire de la musique__
7. livre ⟷ écrivain = musique ⟷ __compositeur__
8. classe ⟷ étudiant = troupe ⟷ __membre__
9. film ⟷ réalisateur = pièce de théâtre ⟷ __metteur en scène__
10. danse ⟷ danseur = sculpture ⟷ __sculpteur__

1 Tapescript L'EMPLOYÉ: Soyez les bienvenus à *Notre-Dame de Paris*. Vos billets, s'il vous plaît.
NADJA: Oui, tenez.
E: Si vous voulez bien me suivre. Voici vos places.
HAKIM: C'est parfait. On n'est pas loin de l'orchestre. On pourra profiter de tous les détails du spectacle.
N: Ce soir, c'est la première de cette comédie musicale. C'est aussi les débuts de Julie Zenatti dans un des rôles principaux.
H: Tu sais qui est le metteur en scène?
N: Oui. C'est Gilles Maheu. Pourquoi?
H: Juste pour savoir. Oh, regarde! Le spectacle va commencer. On continuera de parler à l'entracte.
Un peu plus tard...
H: Tu ne m'avais pas dit qu'en plus de chansons, il y aurait de la danse.
N: Tu n'aimes pas ce genre de spectacle?
H: Si, j'adore. J'ai même mal aux mains tellement j'ai applaudi. Ça me donne envie de faire partie de la troupe. Je pourrais peut-être jouer un petit rôle, non?
N: Je ne suis pas sûre. Tu sais, il faut être très bon danseur. Et puis, en plus, tu ne fais pas de musique...
H: Ce n'est pas vrai. Je te rappelle que je joue de la guitare.
N: Ah, oui... Tu peux toujours te présenter à une audition, mais ne t'attends pas à beaucoup d'applaudissements.
H: Et bien, si c'est comme ça, tu n'auras pas de place pour mon premier concert!
(On Textbook MP3s)

1 Suggestion Go over the answers with the class.

2 Suggestion Write each of the phrases in column B on separate pieces of paper and distribute them. Have students read the items in column A aloud. Those with the correct ending finish the sentences.

3 Suggestion Have students explain the relationship between the first set of words, then give the answer.

OPTIONS

Game Write words for various types of artists on index cards. On another set of cards, write words for their works. Tape them face down on the board in random order. Divide the class into two teams. Play a game of Concentration in which students match artists with their works. Example: **dramaturge/pièce de théâtre**. When a player makes a match, that player's team collects those cards. The team with the most cards wins.

Notre-Dame de Paris Gilles Maheu (from Québec) is the actual director of the musical ***Notre-Dame de Paris***, which was adapted from Victor Hugo's novel (titled *The Hunchback of Notre Dame* in English). In addition, Julie Zenatti is the actress and singer who played Fleur-de-Lys in the 1999 movie version of the musical.

4 Suggestions

- Tell students to jot down notes during their interviews.
- Have students add two of their own questions to the interview.

5 Expansion Have pairs create two more illustrated sentences using the words from **Contextes**. Then tell them to exchange papers with another pair and complete the sentences.

6 Suggestion Divide the class into pairs and distribute the Info Gap Handouts in the IRM on the IRCD-ROM for this activity. Give students ten minutes to complete the activity.

7 Suggestions

- If time is limited, have students write their critiques as homework.
- Give students a set amount of time to write their comments before passing the papers on to the next student.

Communication

4 Répondez **Avec un(e) partenaire, posez-vous les questions suivantes et répondez-y à tour de rôle. Ensuite, comparez vos réponses avec celles d'un autre groupe.** Answers will vary.

1. Quelle sorte de chanson préfères-tu? Pour quelle(s) raison(s)?
2. Quel est le dernier concert auquel tu as assisté? Comment était-ce?
3. Quel est ton genre de spectacle favori? Pourquoi?
4. Quel réalisateur admires-tu le plus? Décris un de ses films.
5. Est-ce que tu fais de la musique? De quel genre?
6. Es-tu un(e) bon(ne) danseur/danseuse? Pour quelle(s) raison(s)?
7. Si tu pouvais jouer un rôle, lequel choisirais-tu? Pourquoi?
8. Est-ce que les arts sont importants pour toi? Lesquels? Pourquoi?

5 Le mot juste **Avec un(e) partenaire, remplissez les espaces par le mot qui est illustré. Faites les accords nécessaires.**

1. Ma petite sœur apprend à ___jouer de la batterie___. Ça fait beaucoup de bruit (*noise*) dans la maison. Elle prépare son premier ___concert___  qui sera en décembre.
2. Je dois me dépêcher de trouver ma ___place___  parce que la ___séance___ 

va bientôt commencer.
3. Marie-Claude Pietragalla a été ___danseuse___  étoile de l'Opéra de Paris. Je l'ai beaucoup aimée dans le ___rôle___  de Giselle.
4. Je sais ___jouer du piano___  et je voudrais apprendre à ___jouer du violon___ , mais je n'ai pas beaucoup de temps.

6 Les sorties **Votre professeur va vous donner, à vous et à votre partenaire, une feuille d'activités. Attention! Ne regardez pas la feuille de votre partenaire.** Answers will vary.

MODÈLE

Étudiant(e) 1: *Bonjour.*
Étudiant(e) 2: *Bonjour. J'aimerais voir quelques spectacles ce week-end. Pourriez-vous me dire quels sont les spectacles proposés?*
Étudiant(e) 1: *Bien sûr! Eh bien, vendredi soir...*

7 Le blog virtuel **Formez un petit groupe. Chaque membre du groupe choisit un film ou un spectacle différent.** Answers will vary.

- Écrivez une critique de ce film/spectacle.
- Passez-la à votre partenaire de gauche.
- Il/Elle écrit ensuite ses réactions.
- Continuez le processus pour faire un tour complet.
- Ensuite, discutez de tous vos commentaires.

OPTIONS

Game Have students stand. Toss a beanbag to a student at random and say the name of a famous artist or work. The player has four seconds to classify the work or artist. He or she then tosses the beanbag to another student and says a person or work. Example: *Macbeth* (**C'est une tragédie.**) Students who cannot classify the item in time or repeat one that has already been named are eliminated. The last person standing wins.

Pairs Have pairs of students create posters advertising performances or other types of artistic events on campus or in the community. To ensure variety, you might want to assign specific events. Tell students to use at least six vocabulary words in their posters. Then have students present them to the rest of the class.

Les sons et les lettres

Les liaisons obligatoires et les liaisons interdites

Rules for making liaisons are complex and have many exceptions. Generally, a liaison is made between pronouns, and between a pronoun and a verb that begins with a vowel or vowel sound.

vous en avez **nous habitons** **ils aiment** **elles arrivent**

Make liaisons between articles, numbers, or the verb **est** and a noun that begins with a vowel or a vowel sound.

un éléphant **les amis** **dix hommes** **Roger est enchanté.**

There is a liaison after many single-syllable adverbs, conjunctions, and prepositions.

très intéressant **chez eux** **quand elle** **quand on décidera**

Many expressions have obligatory liaisons that may or may not follow these rules.

C'est-à-dire... **Comment allez-vous?** **plus ou moins** **avant-hier**

Never make a liaison before or after the conjunction **et** or between a noun and a verb that follows it. Likewise, do not make a liaison between a singular noun and an adjective that follows it.

un garçon et une fille **Gilbert adore le football.** **un cours intéressant**

There is no liaison before **h aspiré** or before the word **oui** and before numbers.

un hamburger **les héros** **un oui et un non** **mes onze animaux**

Prononcez Répétez les mots suivants à voix haute.

1. les héros 2. mon petit ami 3. un pays africain 4. les onze étages

Articulez Répétez les phrases suivantes à voix haute.

1. Ils en veulent onze.
2. Vous vous êtes bien amusés hier soir?
3. Cristelle et Albert habitent en Angleterre.
4. Quand est-ce que Charles a acheté ces objets?

Dictons Répétez les dictons à voix haute.

Deux avis valent mieux qu'un.[1]

ressources: LM p. 114 | Text MP3s Leçon 29 | Lab MP3s Leçon 29 | espaces.vhlcentral.com Leçon 29

[1] Two heads are better than one. (lit. Two opinions are better than one.)
[2] The walls have ears.

Section Goals

In this section, students will learn about:

- obligatory liaisons
- exceptions to liaison rules

Instructional Resources
Textbook MP3s
Lab Manual, p. 114
Lab MP3s
WB/VM/LM Answer Key
IRCD-ROM: IRM (Textbook Audioscript; Lab Audioscript)
espaces.vhlcentral.com: activities, downloads, reference tools

Suggestions

- Model the pronunciation of the example phrases and have students repeat them after you.
- Tell students to avoid making liaisons with proper names.
- Point out that liaisons are optional in certain circumstances, such as after plural nouns or within compound verb phrases. Examples: **des enfants espagnols, tu es allé**.
- Ask students to provide additional examples of each type of liaison.
- Write the phrases in the **Prononcez** activity on the board or a transparency. Have students listen to the recording and tell you where they hear liaisons. Alternately, have students rewrite the phrases on their own paper and draw lines linking letters that form liaisons and crossing out silent final consonants.

OPTIONS

Extra Practice Write the following sentences on the board and have students copy them. Then read the sentences aloud. Tell students to mark the liaisons they hear and cross out silent letters. **1. Ils en veulent onze. 2. Vous vous êtes bien amusés hier soir? 3. Christelle et Albert habitent en Angleterre. 4. Quand Charles a-t-il acheté ces objets?**

Extra Practice Teach students this French tongue-twister that contains liaisons. **Un ange qui songeait à changer de visage se trouva soudain si changé que jamais plus ange ne songea à se changer.**

Section Goals

In this section, students will learn functional phrases for talking about a performance and for expressing certainty, doubt, necessities and desires.

Instructional Resources
WB/VM: Video Manual, pp. 267–268
WB/VM/LM Answer Key
Video CD-ROM
Video on DVD
*IRCD-ROM: IRM (Videoscript; **Roman-photo** Translations)*
espaces.vhlcentral.com: activities, downloads, reference tools

Video Recap: Leçon 28
Before doing this **Roman-photo**, review the previous one with this activity.

1. Le groupe a fait un pique-nique à ____. (la montagne Sainte-Victoire)
2. D'abord, ils ont visité ____. (la Maison Sainte-Victoire)
3. Sandrine voulait que David fasse ____, mais il préférait dessiner ____. (un portrait d'elle/la montagne)
4. Stéphane a essayé de prendre une photo de ____. (Rachid et Amina)

Video Synopsis
Rachid, Amina, and David discuss the musical comedy they just saw and Sandrine's performance in it. At **Le P'tit Bistrot**, Valérie wants to know about the show and Sandrine's performance. David says she's not a bad actress, but she can't sing very well. Sandrine overhears his comments and confronts him. They argue and Sandrine breaks up with him.

Suggestions
- Tell students to scan the captions for vocabulary related to shows and performances.
- After reading the **Roman-photo**, have students summarize the episode.

NATIONAL STANDARDS communication cultures

Après le concert

PERSONNAGES

Amina

David

Rachid

Sandrine

Valérie

Après le concert...
RACHID Bon... que pensez-vous du spectacle?
AMINA Euh... c'est ma comédie musicale préférée... Les danseurs étaient excellents.
DAVID Oui, et l'orchestre aussi!

RACHID Et les costumes, comment tu les as trouvés, Amina?
AMINA Très beaux!
RACHID Moi, je trouve que la robe que tu as faite pour Sandrine était le plus beau des costumes.
AMINA Vraiment?
DAVID Eh, voilà Sandrine.

SANDRINE Vous avez entendu ces applaudissements? Je n'arrive pas à croire que c'était pour moi... et toute la troupe, bien sûr!
DAVID Oui c'est vraiment incroyable!
SANDRINE Alors, vous avez aimé notre spectacle?
RACHID Oui! Amina vient de nous dire que c'était sa comédie musicale préférée.

VALÉRIE Et Sandrine?
DAVID Euh, comme ci, comme ça... À vrai dire, ce n'était pas terrible... C'est le moins que l'on puisse dire.
VALÉRIE Ah bon?
DAVID Comme actrice elle n'est pas mal. Elle a bien joué son rôle, mais il est évident qu'elle ne sait pas chanter.
VALÉRIE Tu ne lui as pas dit ça, j'espère!

DAVID Ben, non, mais... Je doute qu'elle devienne une chanteuse célèbre! C'est ça, son rêve. Croyez-vous que ce soit mieux qu'elle le sache?
SANDRINE Tu en as suffisamment dit...
DAVID Sandrine! Je ne savais pas que tu étais là.
SANDRINE De toute évidence! Il vaut mieux que je m'en aille.

À la terrasse...
DAVID Sandrine! Attends!
SANDRINE Pour quoi faire?
DAVID Je voudrais m'expliquer... Il est clair que...
SANDRINE Écoute, ce qui est clair, c'est que tu n'y connais rien en musique et que tu ne sais rien de moi!

ACTIVITÉS

1 Vrai ou faux? Indiquez si les affirmations suivantes sont vraies ou fausses.

1. Le spectacle est la comédie musicale préférée de Rachid. Faux.
2. Amina a beaucoup aimé les costumes. Vrai.
3. David a apporté des fleurs à Sandrine. Vrai.
4. David n'aime pas vraiment la robe de Sandrine. Faux.
5. Finalement, Sandrine a dû acheter sa robe elle-même. Faux.
6. Valérie est surprise d'apprendre que Sandrine n'est pas une très bonne chanteuse. Vrai.
7. Sandrine est furieuse quand elle découvre la véritable opinion de David. Vrai.
8. David a fait exprès (*on purpose*) de parler de Sandrine à voix haute. Il voulait être méchant avec elle. Faux.
9. Sandrine rompt (*breaks up*) avec David. Vrai.
10. David veut rompre avec Sandrine. Faux.

OPTIONS

Avant de regarder la vidéo Before viewing the video, have students work in pairs and brainstorm a list of things people might say after a concert or musical. What aspects of the show might they mention? What expressions might they use to praise or criticize a performance?

Regarder la vidéo Photocopy the videoscript from the IRM. Then white out words related to performance arts and other important vocabulary in order to create a master for a cloze activity. Distribute photocopies and tell students to fill in the missing information as they watch the video episode.

Les amis échangent leurs opinions.

SANDRINE C'est vrai? Je ne savais pas. (*Elle chante.*) J'adore cette chanson!
DAVID Euh... Sandrine, que tu es ravissante dans cette robe!
SANDRINE Merci, David. Elle me va super bien, non? Et toi, Amina, merci mille fois!

Au P'tit Bistrot...
VALÉRIE Alors c'était comment, la pièce de théâtre?
DAVID C'était une comédie musicale.
VALÉRIE Oh! Alors, c'était comment?
DAVID Pas mal. Les danseurs et l'orchestre étaient formidables.
VALÉRIE Et les chanteurs?
DAVID Mmmm... pas mal.

DAVID Sandrine, je suis désolé de t'avoir blessée, mais il faut bien que quelqu'un soit honnête avec toi.
SANDRINE À quel sujet?
DAVID Et bien..., la chanson... je doute que ce soit ta vocation.
SANDRINE Tu doutes? Et bien, moi, je suis certaine... certaine de ne plus jamais vouloir te revoir. C'est fini, David.

DAVID Mais, Sandrine, écoute-moi! C'est pour ton bien que je dis...
SANDRINE Oh ça suffit. Toi, tu m'écoutes... Je suis vraiment heureuse que tu repartes bientôt aux États-Unis. Dommage que ce ne soit pas demain!

Expressions utiles

Talking about a performance

- **Je n'arrive pas à croire que ces applaudissements étaient pour moi!**
  I can't believe all that applause was for me!
- **À vrai dire, ce n'était pas terrible... C'est le moins que l'on puisse dire.**
  To tell the truth, it wasn't great... That's the least that you can say.

Expressing doubts

- **Je doute qu'elle devienne une chanteuse célèbre!**
  I doubt that she will become a famous singer!
- **Croyez-vous que ce soit mieux qu'elle le sache?**
  Do you think it would be better if she knew it?
- **Je doute que ce soit ta vocation.**
  I doubt that it's your vocation/professional calling.

Expressing certainties

- **Il est évident qu'elle ne sait pas chanter.**
  It's obvious that she does not know how to sing.
- **Ce qui est clair, c'est que tu n'y connais rien en musique.**
  What's clear is that you don't know anything about music.
- **Il est clair que tu ne sais rien de moi.**
  It's clear that you know nothing about me.
- **Je suis certaine de ne plus jamais vouloir te revoir.**
  I'm certain that I never want to see you again.

Talking about necessities and desires

- **Il vaut mieux que je m'en aille.**
  It's better that I go.
- **Il faut bien que quelqu'un soit honnête avec toi.**
  It's really necessary that someone be honest with you.

ACTIVITÉS

2 **À vous!** David rentre chez lui et explique à Rachid qu'il s'est disputé avec Sandrine. Avec un(e) camarade de classe, préparez une conversation dans laquelle David dit ce qu'il a fait et explique la réaction de Sandrine. Rachid doit lui donner des conseils.

3 **Écrivez** Pauvre Sandrine! C'est vrai qu'elle ne chante pas bien, mais que son petit ami le dise, c'est blessant (*hurtful*). À votre avis, David a-t-il bien fait d'en parler? Pourquoi? Pour Sandrine, est-ce mieux de connaître ce que pense réellement David? Composez un paragraphe dans lequel vous expliquez votre point de vue.

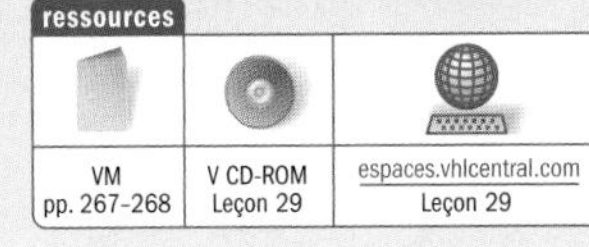

ressources
VM pp. 267–268
V CD-ROM Leçon 29
espaces.vhlcentral.com Leçon 29

Expressions utiles

- Model the pronunciation of the **Expressions utiles** and have students repeat them after you.
- As you work through the list, point out the use of the subjunctive with verbs of doubt, irregular forms of the subjunctive, and forms of **croire** and **revoir**. Tell students that these grammar points will be formally presented in the **Structures** section.
- Respond briefly to questions about the subjunctive, **croire**, and **revoir**. Reinforce correct forms, but do not expect students to produce them consistently at this time.
- Remind students that **terrible** often means *great* or *terrific*, not *terrible*. The phrase **pas terrible** (*not so great*) is an example of French understatement (**la litote**).
- Explain that **«Il vaut mieux que je m'en aille»** is a subjunctive version of **«Je m'en vais.»**

1 Suggestion Have students correct the false statements.

1 Expansion For additional practice, give students these items. **11. David pense que Sandrine est une bonne actrice. (Vrai.) 12. Amina n'aime pas les comédies musicales. (Faux.) 13. Selon Rachid, la robe de Sandrine est le plus beau des costumes. (Vrai.) 14. David repart aux États-Unis demain. (Faux.)**

2 Suggestion Remind students to use discourse connectors, such as **d'abord, puis**, and **après** in their conversations. Rachid should use a variety of structures when giving advice. Examples: **Dis-lui que...** and **À ta place je** (+ *conditional*)....

3 Expansion Have the class divide into two groups and debate whether or not David did the right thing by telling Sandrine what he thought of her singing.

OPTIONS

Pairs Have students work in pairs. Tell them to write predictions about what will happen in the final episode of the **Roman-photo**. Then have volunteers read their predictions aloud and ask the class if they agree or disagree.

Extra Practice Write a few expressions of doubt, certainty, and necessity from the **Roman-photo** on the board. Examples: **Je doute que..., Il est évident que...,** and **Il faut bien que....** Then have students create statements about the characters or their actions using these expressions. You might ask other students to react to their statements.

connections cultures NATIONAL STANDARDS

Section Goals

In this section, students will:
- learn about the theater in France
- learn some terms related to the theater
- learn about some famous francophone musicians
- read about Molière

Instructional Resources
espaces.vhlcentral.com: activities, downloads, reference tools

Culture à la loupe
Avant la lecture Have students describe the photo of the actors. Then ask: **Avez-vous déjà vu la représentation d'une pièce par une troupe professionnelle? Où? Quelle pièce de théâtre a-t-elle présentée?**

Lecture
- Point out the **Coup de main**. Ask: **Comment indique-t-on le début d'un spectacle aux États-Unis?**
- Explain that the word **amateur** is a cognate when it refers to a non-professional, such as an amateur actor, but it can also mean *lover of* (something), for example, **un amateur d'art** (*art lover*).
- Point out the statistics chart. Ask students what information it shows. (key statistics about theater performances in France during 2000–2003)

Après la lecture Ask students: **Comment savez-vous que le théâtre est populaire en France? Quelles parties du texte soutiennent cette idée?**

1 Suggestion Go over the answers with the class.

CULTURE À LA LOUPE

Le théâtre, un art vivant et populaire

la Comédie-Française

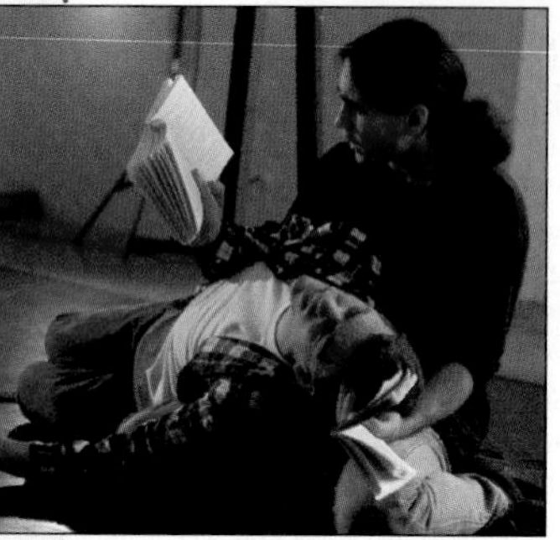

Les Français sont de plus en plus nombreux à fréquenter les théâtres: un Français sur trois voit° au moins une pièce par an. Ce public fréquente les théâtres privés, les théâtres municipaux et les cinq théâtres nationaux, dont le plus ancien est la Comédie-Française. Les spectacles d'amateurs sont aussi très appréciés. Les comédiens° de théâtre ont beaucoup de prestige et reçoivent des récompenses° professionnelles spéciales, les Molières. Le théâtre joue aussi un rôle social important, en particulier pour les jeunes.

Le théâtre français est né au XVIIe siècle. Le roi Louis XIV était un grand amateur° de spectacles et la cour° de Versailles offrait les divertissements° les plus extravagants°. Les œuvres° d'auteurs célèbres, comme Molière ou les tragédiens Pierre Corneille et Jean Racine, datent de cette époque. En 1680, Louis XIV crée l'institution théâtrale la plus prestigieuse de France, la Comédie-Française.

Aujourd'hui, elle s'appelle aussi «Maison de Molière» ou «Théâtre-Français» et elle est toujours le symbole de la tradition théâtrale française. Elle compte parfois jusqu'à 70 comédiens et elle est subventionnée par l'État. Elle a plus de 3.000 pièces à son répertoire et ses comédiens jouent dans près de 900 représentations° par an. Ils partent aussi en tournée° en province et à l'étranger et participent à des enregistrements° pour la radio et pour la télévision.

Pour assister à un de ces spectacles, il faut prendre une réservation et retirer des billets avant le début de la représentation. Au théâtre Richelieu, on peut admirer le fauteuil dans lequel Molière a joué° il y a plus de 300 ans!

Les chiffres clés du théâtre français sur trois saisons (2000–2003)
- 2.638 textes différents ont été joués
- 7.044 mises en scène° ont été programmées
- 31.884 représentations ont été données
- il y a eu entre 1 et 323 représentations par pièce

Coup de main
Les trois coups du lever de rideau°
A French tradition is to signal the beginning of a theater performance with three knocks. At the **Comédie-Française**, a six-knock signal is used instead.

voit *sees* **comédiens** *actors* **récompenses** *awards* **amateur** *lover* **cour** *royal court* **divertissements** *entertainment* **les plus extravagants** *wildest* **œuvres** *works* **représentations** *performances* **en tournée** *on tour* **enregistrements** *recordings* **a joué** *acted* **lever de rideau** *rise of the curtain* **mises en scène** *productions*

ACTIVITÉS

1 Complétez Complétez les phrases.

1. ___Un Français sur trois___ voit au moins une pièce par an.
2. Les comédiens de théâtre reçoivent ___des récompenses professionnelles spéciales, les Molières___.
3. ___Le théâtre français___ est né au XVIIe siècle.
4. Trois auteurs qui datent de cette époque sont ___Molière, Pierre Corneille et Jean Racine___.
5. ___La Comédie-Française___ a été créée par Louis XIV en 1680.
6. ___Maison de Molière et Théâtre-Français___ sont deux autres noms pour la Comédie-Française.
7. La Comédie-Française a un répertoire de plus de ___3.000 pièces___.
8. Ses comédiens partent aussi ___en tournée en province et à l'étranger___.
9. Au théâtre Richelieu se trouve ___le fauteuil dans lequel Molière a joué il y a plus de 300 ans___.
10. ___2.638 textes___ ont été joués en France sur trois saisons entre 2000 et 2003.

OPTIONS

Les dramaturges français Pierre Corneille (1606–1684) helped shape the French classic theatre and was a master at creating tragic protagonists of heroic dimension. ***Le Cid*** (1634) is one of his masterpieces.

Jean Racine (1639–1699) also exemplifies French classicism and replaced Corneille as France's leading tragic dramatist. His most memorable characters are the fierce and tender women of his tragedies. Early in his career Racine became friends with Molière, who produced his first two tragedies. ***Andromaque*** (1667), ***Bajazet*** (1672), ***Mithradate*** (1673), ***Iphigénie en Aulide*** (1674), and ***Phèdre*** (1677) are considered his greatest plays.

LE FRANÇAIS QUOTIDIEN

Les spectacles

billetterie (*f.*)	*box office*
jour (*m.*) de relâche	*day with no performances*
orchestre (*m.*)	*orchestra seats*
poulailler (*m.*)	*gallery*
rentrée (*f.*) théâtrale	*start of theatrical season*
reprise (f.)	*revival; rerun*
à l'affiche	*now playing*
incontournable	*must-see*

LE MONDE FRANCOPHONE

Des musiciens

Voici quelques musiciens francophones célèbres.

En Algérie Khaled, chanteur de raï, un mélange° de chanson arabe et d'influences occidentales

Aux Antilles le groupe Kassav, inventeur de la musique zouk

Au Cameroun Manu Dibango, célèbre joueur de saxophone

Au Mali Amadou et Mariam, couple de chanteurs aveugles°

À la Réunion Danyèl Waro, la voix° du maloya, musique typique de l'île

À Saint-Pierre et Miquelon Henri Lafitte, auteur, compositeur et interprète° de plus de 500 chansons

Au Sénégal Youssou N'Dour, compositeur et interprète de musique mbalax, un mélange de musique traditionnelle d'Afrique de l'ouest et de musique occidentale

mélange *mix* **aveugles** *blind* **voix** *voice* **interprète** *performer*

PORTRAIT

Molière (1622-1673)

LE THÉATRE A TRAVERS LES AGES
Molière et sa troupe.

Molière, dont le vrai nom est Jean-Baptiste Poquelin, est le génie de la Comédie-Française. D'origine bourgeoise, il choisit la vie difficile du théâtre. En 1659, il obtient le soutien° de Louis XIV et devient le premier acteur comique, auteur et metteur en scène de France. Molière est un innovateur: il écrit des satires et des farces quand la mode est aux tragédies néoclassiques. Avec le compositeur Lully, il invente la comédie-ballet. Après une vie riche en aventures, il meurt sur scène, dans le rôle du *Malade imaginaire*. Aujourd'hui, ses pièces sont toujours d'actualité° et Molière reste l'auteur le plus joué en France.

soutien *support* **d'actualité** *current*

SUR INTERNET

Qu'est-ce que le festival d'Avignon?

Go to **espaces.vhlcentral.com** to find more cultural information related to this **ESPACE CULTURE.**

ACTIVITÉS

2 Répondez Répondez aux questions par des phrases complètes.

1. Molière était-il d'origine populaire?
   Non, il était d'origine bourgeoise.
2. Que s'est-il passé dans la vie de Molière en 1659? Il obtient le soutien de Louis XIV et devient le premier acteur comique, auteur et metteur en scène de France.
3. Pourquoi Molière est-il un innovateur?
   Il écrit des satires et des farces quand la mode est aux tragédies néoclassiques.
4. Comment Molière est-il mort?
   Il est mort sur scène, dans le rôle du *Malade imaginaire.*
5. Qu'est-ce que le raï?
   C'est un mélange de chanson traditionnelle arabe et d'influences occidentales.
6. De quel instrument joue Manu Dibango?
   Il joue du saxophone.

3 Un festival Vous et un(e) partenaire allez organiser un festival de culture francophone. Faites des recherches sur des artistes francophones et choisissez qui vous allez inviter. Où vont-ils jouer? Indiquez les genres d'œuvres. Comparez ensuite votre programme avec celui d'un autre groupe.

ressources

espaces.vhlcentral.com
Leçon 29

Le français quotidien
- Model the pronunciation of each term and have students repeat it.
- Point out that **reprise** is a **faux ami** for the English word *reprise.*

Portrait Have students describe the theater poster. Then ask students: **Avez-vous déjà lu ou vu une comédie de Molière? Laquelle?**

Le monde francophone Have students write four true/false statements based on the information in this section. Then have them get together with a classmate and take turns reading their statements and responding.

2 Expansion For additional practice, give students these items. **7. Quel est le vrai nom de Molière? (Jean-Baptiste Poquelin) 8. Qu'a-t-il inventé avec le compositeur Lully? (la comédie-ballet) 9. Où a-t-on inventé la musique zouk? (aux Antilles)**

3 Suggestion Many festivals post their programs on the Internet. Provide students with a model of an actual program for a cultural festival to follow. Encourage them to be creative and use information they already know.

OPTIONS

Molière Sometimes referred to as the father of modern French comedy, Molière's plays often ridicule human vices and excesses, which are embodied in his characters. These characters encompass a broad spectrum and offer a wide view of seventeenth-century French society. ***L'École des femmes*** (1662), ***Le Tartuffe*** (1664), ***Don Juan*** (1665), ***Le Misanthrope*** (1666), ***Le Bourgeois gentilhomme*** (1670), and ***Les Femmes savantes*** (1672) are among his masterpieces.

Pairs Distribute a French theater schedule, including titles of plays, times of performances, and prices of seats. Then have students work in pairs, with one person playing the role of the theatergoer who wants to buy a ticket and the other person acting as the ticket seller.

Section Goals

In this section, students will learn the verbs **voir** and **croire**.

Instructional Resources

WB/VM: Workbook, pp. 199–200
Lab Manual, p. 115
Lab MP3s
WB/VM/LM Answer Key
*IRCD-ROM: IRM (**Essayez!** and **Mise en pratique** answers; Lab Audioscript; **Feuilles d'activités**)*
espaces.vhlcentral.com: activities, downloads, reference tools

Suggestions

- Point out the **-s**, **-s**, **-t**, **-ons**, **-ez**, **-ent** endings of both **voir** and **croire** seen before in irregular verbs. Then note that the **nous** and **vous** forms have irregular stems **voy-** and **croy-**.
- Go over the future and conditional tenses of both verbs, noting the irregular stems **verr-** and **croir-**. Test comprehension as you proceed by asking volunteers to supply the correct future or conditional verb form of the subjects you suggest. Example: **voir / tu**; future **(tu verras)**.
- Ask questions and give examples to practice **voir** and **croire** in the **passé composé**. Example: **Qui a vu la pièce de théâtre sur le campus? Moi, je l'ai vue la semaine dernière.**
- Have a volunteer write the paradigm of **revoir** on the board and model its pronunciation.
- Use pictures to elicit sentences with the verbs **voir** and **croire** in the present tense. Example: **Qu'est-ce que vous voyez? (Je vois une femme triste. Je crois qu'elle se dispute avec son petit ami.)** Continue until most students have had an opportunity to respond.

29.1 The verbs *voir* and *croire*

The verb *voir* (to see)

je vois	nous voyons
tu vois	vous voyez
il/elle voit	ils/elles voient

Demain, nous **voyons** une comédie musicale.
Tomorrow we're seeing a musical.

Tu **vois** les danseuses sur scène?
Do you see the dancers on stage?

Voyons… vous prenez cette rue-là et…

Écoute, je vois que tu n'y connais rien en musique.

- **Voir** takes **avoir** as an auxiliary verb in the **passé composé**, and its past participle is **vu**.

Tu **as vu** le nouveau spectacle?
Did you see the new show?

Ils **ont vu** *Un air de famille* en DVD.
They saw Un air de famille *on DVD.*

- The **futur simple** and **conditionnel** of **voir** are formed with the stem **verr-**.

Ils **verront** peut-être le film ce week-end.
Maybe they will see the film this weekend.

Elle **verrait** mieux si elle portait des lunettes.
She would see better if she wore glasses.

- The verb **revoir** (*to see again*) is derived from **voir** and is conjugated in the same way.

Au revoir!

On se **revoit** mercredi ou jeudi?
Will we see each other again Wednesday or Thursday?

On a **revu** *Les parapluies de Cherbourg*.
We saw Les parapluies de Cherbourg *again.*

MISE EN PRATIQUE

1 À la Martinique Alain et Chantal sont en vacances. Que disent-ils? Utilisez le présent de l'indicatif des verbes.

MODÈLE tu / voir / la plage et la mer
Tu vois la plage et la mer.

1. je / croire / que / l'île / être / merveilleux
Je crois que l'île est merveilleuse.
2. Chantal / voit / énorme / poisson
Chantal voit un énorme poisson.
3. ils / croire / que / marché aux fruits / fermer / tôt
Ils croient que le marché aux fruits ferme tôt.
4. nous / voir / le Carnaval / balcon de l'hôtel
Nous voyons le Carnaval du balcon de l'hôtel.
5. tu / croire / que / on / polluer / forêt tropicale
Tu crois qu'on pollue la forêt tropicale.
6. vous / voir / plantation de café / pendant / tour de l'île
Vous voyez une plantation de café pendant un tour de l'île.

2 Décidons Complétez la conversation entre Thomas et Rémi avec une forme des verbes **voir** ou **croire**. Faites attention aux temps (*tenses*)!

THOMAS Dis Rémi, tu (1) __vois/verras/verrais__ le film *Cyrano de Bergerac* avec moi ce soir?
RÉMI Je ne (2) __crois__ pas. Je l' (3) __ai vu__ hier.
THOMAS Tu (4) __crois__ que tu préférerais cette comédie musicale?
RÉMI Ça, c'est une bonne idée. (5) __Voyons__ plutôt ce spectacle. Tu penses que les acteurs sont bons?
THOMAS Je ne sais pas. On (6) __verra__!

3 Revoir Alain et Chantal ont beaucoup aimé leur séjour à la Martinique et ils disent à une amie qu'ils ont déjà vu ces endroits et qu'ils les reverraient volontiers.

MODÈLE
Nous avons vu la montagne Pelée et nous la reverrions volontiers.

la montagne Pelée (nous)

1. d'énormes poissons (tu)
Tu as vu d'énormes poissons et tu les reverrais volontiers.

3. le marché (Alain)
Alain a vu le marché et il le reverrait volontiers.

2. la forêt tropicale (je)
J'ai vu la forêt tropicale et je la reverrais volontiers.

4. les plages (vous)
Vous avez vu les plages et vous les reverriez volontiers.

OPTIONS

Extra Practice For oral practice, call out subject pronouns and have students respond with the correct form of **voir** or **croire**. Reverse the drill by starting with forms of **voir** or **croire** and asking students to give the corresponding subject pronouns.

Game Divide the class into teams of three. Each team has a piece of paper. Call out a subject, an infinitive, and a verb tense. Example: first person plural / **voir** / future. Each team composes a sentence with each person writing one part. The first team member writes the subject (**Nous**). The second writes the verb (**verrons**). The third gives a logical direct object (**la pièce de théâtre**). The first team to write a correct sentence wins. Team members should rotate positions each time a new verb is given.

COMMUNICATION

4 **Croire ou ne pas croire** Vous voulez mieux connaître votre partenaire. Posez-lui ces questions. Answers will vary.

1. Crois-tu à l'astrologie? Pourquoi?
2. Tu as cru au Père Noël jusqu'à quel âge?
3. Crois-tu aux extraterrestres? Pourquoi?
4. Quand tu étais petit(e), croyais-tu aux fantômes? Y crois-tu encore? Pourquoi?
5. Si tous les habitants du pays croyaient en l'importance des arts, que feraient-ils?
6. Si je te disais que tu vas gagner à la loterie le week-end prochain, me croirais-tu? Pourquoi?

5 **Enquête** Votre professeur va vous donner une feuille d'activités. Circulez dans la classe pour trouver un(e) camarade différent(e) qui donne une réponse affirmative à chaque question. Justifiez vos réponses. Answers will vary.

MODÈLE

Étudiant(e) 1: *Crois-tu qu'il faudra apprendre des langues étrangères à l'avenir?*
Étudiant(e) 2: *Oui, je crois qu'il faudra toujours apprendre des langues étrangères parce qu'il y aura toujours des cultures différentes.*

Activité	Nom
1. croire qu'il faudra apprendre des langues étrangères à l'avenir	Jacqueline
2. voir son/sa meilleur(e) ami(e) tous les jours	
3. croire qu'un jour il y aura la paix (peace) dans le monde	
4. voir parfois un prof au resto U	

6 **Au spectacle** Catherine et Jean-Yves, son petit ami, viennent de prendre leurs places au théâtre. Avec un(e) partenaire, suivez ces instructions et préparez la scène. Ensuite, présentez-la à la classe. Answers will vary.

Catherine	Jean-Yves
Demandez s'il croit que c'est une bonne troupe et pourquoi.	Dites ce que vous croyez et justifiez la réponse.
Expliquez que vous ne voyez pas bien la scène (stage) et dites pourquoi.	Dites si vous voyez bien ou mal la scène et proposez une solution.
Dites si vous croyez que c'est une bonne ou une mauvaise idée.	Décidez de changer de place ou pas.
Acceptez ou refusez la décision.	Expliquez comment vous éviterez ce problème la prochaine fois.

The verb *croire* (to believe)

je crois	nous croyons
tu crois	vous croyez
il/elle croit	ils/elles croient

Les personnages **croient** que quelqu'un envoie ces messages.
The characters believe that someone is sending those messages.

Tu **crois** que Madame Butterfly va retrouver son mari?
Do you think that Madame Butterfly is going to find her husband?

Je crois que les danseurs étaient excellents.

Alors, Stéphane, tu crois que tu vas gagner ton prochain match?

- **Croire** takes **avoir** as an auxiliary verb in the **passé composé**, and its past participle is **cru**.

J'**ai cru** que c'était la fin du spectacle.
I thought it was the end of the show.

Vous **avez cru** l'histoire de ce metteur en scène?
Did you believe that director's story?

- The **futur simple** and **conditionnel** of **croire** are formed with the stem **croir-**.

Nous le **croirons** si nous le voyons.
We will believe it if we see it.

On **croirait** que c'est une tragédie.
One would think it's a tragedy.

Essayez! Complétez les phrases avec les formes correctes du présent des verbes.

voir

1. La salle est trop sombre (*dark*). On ne ___voit___ rien.
2. Je ___vois___ très mal d'ici.
3. Ils ___voient___ le nouveau film de Jeunet.
4. Vous ___voyez___ pourquoi j'aime l'opéra?
5. Nous ___voyons___ parfois le prof de français au resto U.
6. Elle ___voit___ le problème.

croire

1. Nous ___croyons___ que le personnage principal est mort.
2. Tu ___crois___ qu'il va faire beau?
3. L'auteur ne ___croit___ pas en Dieu.
4. Vous ___croyez___ que cette interprétation est bonne.
5. Je ne ___crois___ pas son histoire sur l'accident.
6. Mes amis ___croient___ que j'ai tort.

Essayez! After assigning the activity, have pairs rewrite the sentences using different subjects.

1 Expansion Change the subjects of the dehydrated sentences in the activity and have students write or say the new sentences.

2 Expansion Have pairs rewrite the conversation to reflect a real exchange about a film or work of art they have recently seen. Have students perform the new conversation in front of the class.

3 Suggestions
- Model the activity by talking about a set of your own vacation photos.
- Remind students that the future form of **voir** and **revoir** is spelled with **rr**.

4 Expansion Have students use the third person to share their partner's responses with the class.

5 Suggestion Have two volunteers say the **modèle**, then distribute the **Feuilles d'activités** from the IRM on the IRCD-ROM.

5 Expansion Have students write five sentences using the information obtained through the **enquête**. Example: **On croit qu'il faudra apprendre les langues étrangères à l'avenir.**

6 Expansion Ask the class questions about their experiences at the theater using the vocabulary and all forms of the verbs from the lesson. Examples: **Avez-vous récemment vu une pièce de théâtre? Si vous aviez un rendez-vous au théâtre avec quelqu'un pour la première fois, verriez-vous une comédie ou une tragédie? Pourquoi?**

OPTIONS

Extra Practice Briefly show the class a picture or drawing with numerous objects displayed, for example, a photo of a messy or cluttered room. Ask students to study the objects they see in the photo. Then remove the picture from view and ask students what they remember seeing and what they did not see, using **croire** and/or the **passé composé** of **voir**. Examples: **J'ai vu un lit. Je crois que j'ai vu...**

Game Play a modified version of Charades. Create several cards with different actions or occupations written on them. Ask a volunteer to choose a card and act out the action or occupation for the class. Then the volunteer asks: **Que voyez-vous?** Have students guess what the card says by stating what they observe. Examples: **Je vois une femme qui joue de la guitare. Je crois que tu es quelqu'un qui joue de la guitare.**

Section Goals

In this section, students will learn:
- the subjunctive with expressions of doubt, disbelief, or uncertainty
- the subjunctive of irregular verbs **aller**, **pouvoir**, **savoir**, and **vouloir**

Instructional Resources
WB/VM: Workbook, pp. 201–202
Lab Manual, p. 116
Lab MP3s
WB/VM/LM Answer Key
*IRCD-ROM: IRM (**Essayez!** and **Mise en pratique** answers; Lab Audioscript)*
espaces.vhlcentral.com: activities, downloads, reference tools

Suggestions
- Review the subjunctive verb forms from **Structures 27.2**, pages 480–481 and **28.1**, pages 492–493.
- Explain that, although *that* is often optional in English, **que** is required in French. Example: *I doubt [that] the concert is good.* **Je doute que le concert soit bon.**
- Check for understanding by writing on the board main clauses ending in **que** that require a subjunctive in the subordinate clause. Invite volunteers to suggest several endings for each, using verbs they have just reviewed. Example: **Il est douteux que/qu'...(qu'il y ait un examen la semaine prochaine/que j'achète une nouvelle voiture/qu'on aille à Paris).**
- Point out that the subjunctive is used when there is a change of subject as well as an expression of doubt, disbelief, or uncertainty. If the subject does not change, the infinitive is used. Example: **Jacques n'est pas sûr de pouvoir aller à Paris cet été.**

29.2 The subjunctive (Part 3)

Verbs of doubt, disbelief, and uncertainty

- The subjunctive is used in a subordinate clause when there is a change of subject and the main clause implies doubt, disbelief, or uncertainty.

MAIN CLAUSE	CONNECTOR	SUBORDINATE CLAUSE
Je doute	**que**	le concert **soit** bon.
I doubt	*that*	*the concert is good.*

Je doute qu'elle devienne une chanteuse célèbre!

Je suis certaine que je ne veux plus jamais te revoir!

Expressions of doubt, disbelief, and uncertainty

douter que...	*to doubt that...*	**Il est impossible que...**	*It is impossible that...*
ne pas croire que...	*not to believe that...*	**Il n'est pas certain que...**	*It is uncertain that...*
ne pas penser que...	*not to think that...*	**Il n'est pas sûr que...**	*It is not sure that...*
Il est douteux que...	*It is doubtful that...*	**Il n'est pas vrai que...**	*It is untrue that...*

Il n'est pas sûr qu'il y **ait** un entracte.
It's not sure that there is an intermission.

Je ne crois pas qu'on **vende** les billets ici.
I don't believe that they sell the tickets here.

- The indicative is used in a subordinate clause when the main clause expresses certainty.

Expressions of certainty

croire que...	*to believe that...*	**Il est clair que...**	*It is clear that...*
penser que...	*to think that...*	**Il est évident que...**	*It is obvious that...*
savoir que...	*to know that...*	**Il est sûr que...**	*It is sure that...*
Il est certain que...	*It is certain that...*	**Il est vrai que...**	*It is true that...*

On **sait que** l'histoire **finit** mal.
We know the story ends badly.

Il est certain qu'elle **comprend**.
It is certain that she understands.

MISE EN PRATIQUE

1 Fort-de-France Vous discutez de vos projets avec votre ami(e) martiniquais(e). Complétez les phrases avec les formes correctes du présent de l'indicatif ou du subjonctif.

1. Je crois que Fort-de-France ___est___ (être) plus loin de Paris que de New York.
2. Il n'est pas certain que je ___vienne___ (venir) à Fort-de-France cet été.
3. Il est impossible que nous ___partions___ (partir) en croisière (*cruise*) ensemble.
4. Il est clair que nous ___ne partons pas___ (ne pas partir) sans toi.
5. Nous savons que ce voyage ___va___ (aller) te plaire.
6. Il est douteux que le ski alpin ___soit___ (être) un sport populaire ici.

2 Camarade pénible Vous faites une présentation sur la Martinique devant la classe. Un(e) camarade pénible commente toutes vos idées. Avec un(e) partenaire, jouez la scène. Answers will vary.

MODÈLE

Étudiant(e) 1: *Le carnaval martiniquais est populaire.*
Étudiant(e) 2: *Je doute qu'il soit populaire.*

1. Les Martiniquais sont très sympas.
2. Tout le monde va se promener dans la forêt.
3. Les Martiniquais savent parler français.
4. L'île a de belles plages.
5. Les enfants y font des randonnées.
6. On y boit des jus de fruits délicieux.

3 Le Tour de France Maxime veut participer un jour au Tour de France. Regardez les illustrations et faites des commentaires sur ses habitudes. Answers will vary.

MODÈLE

Je ne crois pas que tu dormes tous les jours jusqu'à midi!

1.

3.

2.

4.

OPTIONS

TPR Call out a series of sentences, using either an expression of certainty or an expression of doubt, disbelief, or uncertainty. Have students stand if they hear an expression of certainty or remain seated if they hear an expression of doubt. Example: **Il est impossible que j'apprenne une autre langue.** (Students remain seated.)

Pairs Have students write five absurd or strange sentences. Then have them switch sentences with a classmate. Students should write their reactions using a different expression of doubt, disbelief, or uncertainty. Example: **Toutes les femmes aiment bien faire le ménage. (Je ne crois pas que toutes les femmes aiment bien faire le ménage!)**

COMMUNICATION

4 Assemblez Imaginez que vous avez l'occasion de faire un séjour aux Antilles françaises. À tour de rôle avec un(e) partenaire, assemblez les éléments de chaque colonne pour parler de ces vacances. Answers will vary.

MODÈLE

Il n'est pas certain que nous allions visiter une plantation.

A	B	C
Il est certain que Il n'est pas certain que Il est évident que Il est impossible que Il est vrai que Il n'est pas vrai que Je doute que Je pense que Je sais que ?	je/j' tu mon copain ma sœur mon frère nous les touristes mes parents ?	être content(e)(s) faire des excursions faire beau temps faire du bateau jouer sur la plage pouvoir parler créole visiter une plantation ?

5 Comédie musicale Votre classe prépare une comédie musicale et vous organisez le spectacle. Votre partenaire voudrait y participer et il/elle postule pour un rôle. Alternez les rôles, puis présentez vos dialogues à la classe. Answers will vary.

MODÈLE

Étudiant(e) 1: *Est-il possible que je chante dans la chorale?*
Étudiant(e) 2: *Je doute qu'il soit possible que vous y chantiez. Il n'y a plus de place, mais je crois que...*

- acteur/actrice
- compositeur
- metteur en scène
- animateur/animatrice (*emcee*)
- chorale
- danseurs
- musiciens
- ouvreur/ouvreuse (*usher*)

6 Je doute, donc je suis? Votre partenaire veut mieux vous connaître. Préparez par écrit cinq phrases qui vous décrivent: quatre fausses et une vraie. Votre partenaire doit deviner laquelle est vraie et justifier sa réponse. Ensuite, alternez les rôles. Answers will vary.

MODÈLE

Étudiant(e) 1: *Je finis toujours mes devoirs avant de me coucher.*
Étudiant(e) 2: *Je doute que tu finisses tes devoirs avant de te coucher, parce que tu n'avais pas tes devoirs hier.*

- Sometimes a speaker may opt to use the subjunctive in a question to indicate that he or she feels doubtful or uncertain of an affirmative response.

Crois-tu que cet acteur **fasse** un bon Charles de Gaulle?
Do you believe that actor makes a good Charles de Gaulle?

Est-il vrai que vous **partiez** déjà en vacances?
Is it true that you're already leaving on vacation?

Croyez-vous que ce soit mieux qu'elle le sache?
Il vaut mieux que je m'en aille.

Present subjunctive of *aller, pouvoir, savoir, vouloir*

	aller	pouvoir	savoir	vouloir
que je/j'	aille	puisse	sache	veuille
que tu	ailles	puisses	saches	veuilles
qu'il/elle	aille	puisse	sache	veuille
que nous	allions	puissions	sachions	voulions
que vous	alliez	puissiez	sachiez	vouliez
qu'ils/elles	aillent	puissent	sachent	veuillent

Il faut qu'on **aille** au théâtre ce soir.
We have to go to the theater tonight.

Il vaut mieux que tu **saches** la nouvelle.
It's better that you know the news.

Je doute que la pièce **puisse** causer un effet comme celui-là.
I doubt that the play could cause an effect like that.

Est-il possible qu'il **veuille** apprendre à jouer du violon?
Is it possible that he wants to learn to play the violin?

Essayez! **Choisissez la forme correcte du verbe.**

1. Il est douteux que le metteur en scène (sait / sache) où est l'acteur.
2. Je sais que Carole Bouquet et Gérard Depardieu (sont / soient) mariés.
3. Il est impossible qu'il (est / soit) amoureux d'elle.
4. Ne crois-tu pas que l'histoire du Titanic (finit / finisse) bien?
5. Est-il vrai que les Français (font / fassent) uniquement des films intellectuels?
6. Je ne crois pas qu'il (peut / puisse) jouer le rôle du jeune prisonnier.
7. Tout le monde sait que le ballet (est / soit) d'origine française.
8. Il n'est pas certain qu'ils (peuvent / puissent) terminer le spectacle.

Essayez! Have students underline the main clauses in these sentences. Then have them create original sentences, using the indicative or subjunctive where appropriate.

1 Expansion Have pairs discuss why each subordinate clause is in the indicative or subjunctive. If the sentence is in the indicative, have pairs make the necessary changes in the main clause to elicit the subjunctive. Example: **1. Je ne crois pas que Fort-de-France soit plus loin de Paris que de New York.**

2 Expansion For emphasis, have **Étudiant(e) 1** counter the statement of doubt made by **Étudiant(e) 2** with another statement of certainty. Example: **Mais si! Il est sûr que le carnaval martiniquais est très populaire!**

3 Suggestion Before starting, have the class brainstorm what would be necessary for someone to do or be in order to participate successfully in the **Tour de France**. Examples: **Je sais qu'il faut être en pleine forme. Il est clair qu'on doit faire de l'exercice tous les jours avant d'y participer.**

4 Suggestion Have volunteers give sentences using elements from each of the three columns. Have other volunteers act as secretaries, writing examples on the board. Ask the class to help you correct the grammar and spelling.

5 Suggestion Ask two volunteers to read the **modèle** aloud. Correct any pronunciation errors.

6 Expansion Call on a student to read two statements about his or her partner, without revealing which one is true and which one is false. Have the class guess which statement is which, using expressions of doubt and certainty.

OPTIONS

Video Replay the video episode, having students focus on expressions of certainty, uncertainty, doubt, and disbelief. Stop the video where appropriate and ask students to repeat any construction that includes *main clause* + **que** + *subordinate clause* and explain why the indicative or subjunctive was used in each instance.

Extra Practice Have students write sentences about three things of which they are certain and three things they doubt or cannot believe. Students should use a different expression for each of their sentences. Have students share some of their sentences with the class.

Instructional Resources
IRCD-ROM: IRM (Info Gap Activities); Testing Program, pp. 113–116; Test Files; Testing Program MP3s; Test Generator
espaces.vhlcentral.com: activities, downloads, reference tools

1 Expansion Brainstorm other hobbies and occupations with the whole class. Then have pairs continue this activity using magazine pictures.

2 Expansion Give these additional items to the class.

- **Il n'y a pas de place pour les femmes dans les films d'action.**
- **La plupart des films américains sont violents.**
- **Les gens plus âgés n'aiment pas la musique rock.**

3 Suggestion Before students break into groups for this activity, ask a volunteer to explain the use of the indicative and subjunctive with **croire** and **penser**.

4 Expansion Have pairs create a new **annonce** for a **rôle principal**. Encourage students to be creative. Then have students exchange their **annonce** with another pair and repeat the activity.

5 Suggestion Ask a volunteer from each group to take notes on their conversations. After the groups have compared lists, have each volunteer write their group's selections on the board. Each group should take turns summarizing their selections and relating the expressions of doubt and certainty used in the activity.

6 Suggestion Divide the class into pairs and distribute the Info Gap Handouts in the IRM on the IRCD-ROM for this activity. Give students ten minutes to complete the activity.

Synthèse

1 Il est clair que... Observez ces personnages et imaginez leurs activités artistiques préférées. Avec un(e) partenaire, utilisez des expressions de doute et de certitude pour répondre aux questions et pour décrire chaque personnage. Answers will vary.

chanteur de chorale ou de comédie musicale?

danseur ou acteur?

chef d'orchestre ou metteur en scène?

compositeur d'opéra ou dramaturge?

2 Je ne pense pas Que pensent vos camarades de ces affirmations? Par groupes de quatre, trouvez au moins une personne qui soit d'accord avec chaque phrase et une qui ne soit pas d'accord. Utilisez des expressions de doute et de certitude. Ensuite, présentez vos arguments à la classe. Answers will vary.

MODÈLE La télévision fait du mal au cinéma.

Étudiant(e) 1: *Penses-tu que la télévision fasse du mal au cinéma?*
Étudiant(e) 2: *Non, je ne crois pas que ce soit vrai. Il est clair que les acteurs de cinéma sont plus célèbres que ceux de la télé.*

- Jimi Hendrix est le meilleur joueur de guitare.
- Mozart est le meilleur compositeur de musique classique.
- Personne n'aime les comédies musicales aujourd'hui.
- Un danseur est autant un sportif qu'un artiste.
- L'opéra est un genre trop ésotérique et ennuyeux.

3 Mes activités artistiques Faites la liste de quatre disciplines artistiques, une dans laquelle vous êtes bon(ne) et trois dans lesquelles vous n'êtes pas très bon(ne). Donnez les noms de ces disciplines à deux de vos camarades, qui devineront celle dans laquelle vous êtes bon(ne). Utilisez les verbes **croire** et **penser**. Ensuite, présentez vos discussions à la classe. Answers will vary.

4 C'est tout moi! Avec un(e) partenaire, vous voyez ces annonces dans le journal. Vous pensez qu'un de ces rôles est pour vous. Un(e) ami(e) n'est pas du tout d'accord, mais vous insistez. Utilisez des expressions de doute et de certitude dans votre dialogue. Answers will vary.

Cherchons jeune homme de 27-30 ans, sportif et musclé, avec permis moto et avion, pour rôle principal. Doit être un acteur expérimenté qui sache jouer du piano comme un professionnel et qui puisse monter à cheval. Doit avoir les yeux noirs, beaucoup de charme, de la présence et un look aventurier.

Cherchons jeune femme de 18-20 ans avec beaucoup de personnalité et qui ait une formation de chanteuse classique, pour rôle dans une comédie musicale en espagnol. Doit pouvoir danser le tango, la salsa et la rumba.
Venez rencontrer le compositeur et le metteur en scène, jeudi à 20 heures, au Théâtre de l'Arnaque.

5 Le meilleur Avec un(e) partenaire, observez cette liste et trouvez un exemple pour chaque catégorie. Ensuite, comparez votre liste avec celle d'un autre groupe et parlez de vos opinions. Utilisez des expressions de doute et de certitude. Answers will vary.

le/la meilleur(e) ... en ce moment

- film
- chanson à la radio
- danseuse
- chanteur
- actrice
- chanteuse
- acteur de comédie
- danseur

6 Les arts Votre professeur va vous donner, à vous et à votre partenaire, deux feuilles d'activités différentes sur les arts. Attention! Ne regardez pas la feuille de votre partenaire. Answers will vary.

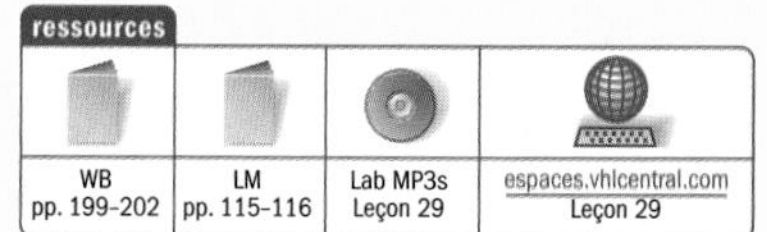

ressources
WB pp. 199-202
LM pp. 115-116
Lab MP3s Leçon 29
espaces.vhlcentral.com Leçon 29

OPTIONS

Extra Practice Have students imagine they are writing to a friend who is just about to start his or her freshman year of college. In their letter, students should give advice about the uncertainties of university life. Encourage students to use the expressions listed on page 516. You may want to collect students' papers and grade them.

Game Divide the class into two teams. One team writes sentences with expressions of certainty, while the other writes sentences with expressions of doubt, disbelief, or uncertainty. Put all the sentences in a hat. Students take turns drawing sentences for their team and stating the opposite of what the sentence says. The team with the most correct sentences wins.

Écrivez une dissertation

Vous écrivez une dissertation sur les artistes les plus connus des Antilles françaises.

Société des artistes antillais,
Germaine Casse

1 Faites un brouillon

Faites un brouillon° avant d'écrire votre dissertation. Pour vos recherches, servez-vous de° la boîte Sur Internet. Votre dissertation doit comprendre° ces éléments:

- une description du style de chaque artiste et les titres° de ses œuvres°
- des images d'œuvres de ces artistes
- une photo de chaque artiste, si possible
- les raisons pour lesquelles vous avez choisi ces artistes pour votre dissertation

2 Présentez votre travail

Faites un résumé° de votre dissertation devant la classe. Montrez les images que vous avez trouvées et demandez à vos camarades ce qu'ils pensent des œuvres d'art que vous avez sélectionnées.

brouillon *first draft* **servez-vous de** *use* **comprendre** *include* **titres** *titles, names* **œuvres** *works, pieces* **Faites un résumé** *Summarize*

SUR INTERNET

Go to **espaces.vhlcentral.com** for more information related to this **Projet**.

Section Goals

In this section, students will:

- use French as they research and interact with the wider world
- write a report on the most famous artists from the French Antilles

Instructional Resources
espaces.vhlcentral.com: activities, downloads, reference tools

Suggestion Students might need a week to complete the project, so at the beginning of that time period have them read through **Projet**. Explain that they are going to write a report about the most famous artists from the French Antilles and present a summary of their report to the class.

Faites un brouillon You may wish to have students work in small groups. Have them determine what artists they will include in their report and decide how to split up the work.

Présentez votre travail

- You may wish to set aside sufficient class time to do a few presentations at a time until all students have had a chance.
- Encourage students to ask questions about the artists' works.
- After completing the presentations, take a quick survey to find out who is their favorite artist.

EVALUATION

Criteria	Scale
Content	1 2 3 4
Organization	1 2 3 4
Grammatical accuracy	1 2 3 4
Use of visuals	1 2 3 4
Oral presentation	1 2 3 4

Scoring	
Excellent	18–20 points
Good	14–17 points
Satisfactory	10–13 points
Unsatisfactory	< 10 points

Section Goals

In this section, students will learn and practice vocabulary related to:

- fine arts
- films and television
- books

Instructional Resources
*IRCD-ROM: Transparency #61; IRM (***Vocabulaire supplémentaire; Mise en pratique*** answers; Textbook Audioscript; Lab Audioscript;* ***Feuilles d'activités****)*
Textbook MP3s
WB/VM: Workbook, pp. 203–204
Lab Manual, p. 117
Lab MP3s
WB/VM/LM Answer Key
espaces.vhlcentral.com: activities, downloads, reference tools

Suggestions

- Tell students to look over the new vocabulary and identify the cognates.
- Use **Transparency #61**. Point out people and things as you describe the illustration. Examples: **Elle fait de la peinture. C'est un film d'horreur.**
- Point out that the **f** in **chef-d'œuvre** and the **p** in **sculpture** are silent.
- Point out the difference in spelling between the French word **aventure** and the English word *adventure*.
- Explain that in France you say **une femme écrivain/auteur/peintre/sculpteur** or **elle est écrivain/auteur/peintre/sculpteur**. The terms **écrivaine** and **auteure** are used in Québec. Mention that the term **auteur** is more general than **écrivain**. **Auteur** can also mean *creator.*
- Explain that **les beaux-arts** (*fine arts*) is a term that refers collectively to a variety of artistic fields, particularly those concerned with the creation of beautiful things, such as painting and sculpture.
- Additional vocabulary for this lesson can be found in the **Vocabulaire supplémentaire** in the IRM on the IRCD-ROM.

Leçon 30

You will learn how to...

- **discuss films and television**
- **discuss books**

Au festival d'art

Vocabulaire

faire les musées	*to go to museums*
publier	*to publish*
les beaux-arts (*m.*)	*fine arts*
un chef-d'œuvre	*masterpiece*
un conte	*tale*
une critique	*review; criticism*
un dessin animé	*cartoon*
un documentaire	*documentary*
un drame psychologique	*psychological drama*
une émission (de télévision)	*(television) program*
un festival (festivals *pl.*)	*festival*
un feuilleton	*soap opera*
un film (d'aventures, policier)	*(adventure, crime) film*
une histoire	*story*
les informations (infos) (*f.*)	*news*
un jeu télévisé	*game show*
la météo	*weather*
les nouvelles (*f.*)	*news*
une œuvre	*artwork, piece of art*
un programme	*program*
une publicité (pub)	*advertisement*
les variétés (*f.*)	*popular music*
ancien(ne)	*ancient; old; former*
doué(e)	*talented, gifted*
gratuit(e)	*free*
littéraire	*literary*
récent(e)	*recent*
à la radio	*on the radio*
à la télé(vision)	*on television*

ressources

WB pp. 203-204	LM p. 117	Text MP3s Leçon 30	Lab MP3s Leçon 30	espaces.vhlcentral.com Leçon 30

OPTIONS

Game Write types of television shows or movies on index cards and place them in a box. Divide the class into two teams. Have students draw a card and describe the genre without saying the word, but they may use French titles as clues. Award points as follows: after one clue = 3 points, after two clues = 2 points, and after three clues = 1 point. If a team does not guess the answer after three tries, the other team has one chance to "steal" the point by guessing correctly.

Extra Practice Tell students that they have just returned from an arts festival. Ask them to describe what they did, saw, and heard. Example: **J'ai vu beaucoup de beaux tableaux et j'ai parlé à deux peintres.**

Interlude

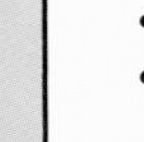

Cézanne peint

La chanson, ***Cézanne peint*** *(1984), rend hommage° au peintre Paul Cézanne, qui est né à Aix-en-Provence. C'est l'été. On entend les grillons°. Cézanne est dehors. Il peint la nature. Il révèle la beauté du monde.*

FRANCE GALL (1947–), qui rend hommage au peintre dans la chanson, ***Cézanne peint****, est née à Paris sous le nom d'Isabelle Gall. Elle commence sa carrière dans les années 60. En 1974, elle rencontre Michel Berger, chanteur et compositeur, qui deviendra son mari. Il va lui écrire toutes ses chansons, dont de nombreux tubes°. En 1992, Michel Berger meurt subitement°. Gall continue à chanter, mais en 1997, leur fille, Pauline, meurt aussi, à l'âge de 19 ans. France Gall, très affectée, quitte le monde du spectacle, mais elle est toujours une chanteuse très populaire.*

Pin à l'Estaque

PAUL CÉZANNE (1839–1906) était un peintre impressionniste français qui a passé la majorité de sa vie dans la région d'Aix-en-Provence. Son principal choix thématique était les paysages du sud de la France, comme ici ***Pin à l'Estaque****. Peintre autodidacte°, Cézanne avait un style bien particulier, s'écartant° finalement de celui de ses amis impressionnistes. Il est considéré aujourd'hui comme à l'origine des mouvements artistiques du vingtième siècle.*

Activité

Répondez à ces questions par des phrases complètes. Answers will vary.

1. Regardez la peinture, ***Pin à l'Estaque***. Aimez-vous le style de Paul Cézanne? Pourquoi?
2. Pourquoi France Gall choisirait-elle de rendre hommage à un peintre dans une de ses chansons?
3. Qui est votre peintre préféré(e)? Avez-vous vu une de ses œuvres dans un musée? En quoi son style diffère-t-il de celui de Paul Cézanne?

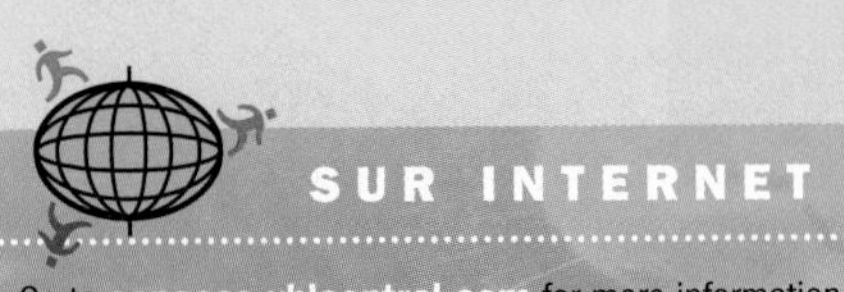

SUR INTERNET

Go to **espaces.vhlcentral.com** for more information related to this **Interlude**.

rend hommage *pays tribute* **grillons** *crickets* **tubes** *hits* **subitement** *suddenly* **autodidacte** *self-taught* **s'écartant** *breaking*

Section Goals

In this section, students will learn about:
- France Gall
- Paul Cézanne

Instructional Resources
espaces.vhlcentral.com: activities, downloads, reference tools

Cézanne peint
To check comprehension, ask these questions.
1. Où est Paul Cézanne dans la chanson? (Il est dehors.) Que fait-il? (Il peint la nature. / Il révèle la beauté du monde.)
2. Quand France Gall a-t-elle commencé sa carrière de chanteuse? (dans les années 60)
3. Qui a écrit beaucoup de chansons pour France Gall? (son mari Michel Berger)
4. Quelles sont les deux tragédies qui ont beaucoup affecté France Gall? (la mort de son mari et celle de sa fille)

Pin à l'Estaque
- Point out that **L'Estaque** is a coastal neighborhood located north of Marseilles. Cézanne painted mostly landscapes, still lifes, and portraits. Camille Pissarro, whom he met in 1861, influenced his development and introduced him to other impressionist painters. For information on Pissarro, see **Unité 9, Interlude**, page 317.
- Have students describe the painting. Then have them compare it to the painting on page 483. Ask them which landscape they prefer and have them explain why.

OPTIONS

France Gall France Gall's career took off in 1965 when she competed in **le Concours Eurovision de la Chanson**, an annual song contest featuring European singers. She won the contest for Luxembourg with ***Poupée de cire, poupée de son***, a song by Serge Gainsbourg. She was also part of **la génération yé-yé**.

Extra Practice As a summary, have students create a chart of the painters who appear in the **Interlude** sections (pages 51, 101, 159, 209, 267, 317, 425, 483, and 533). Tell them to list the artists' names and dates chronologically in the first column. In the second column, they should write the artistic movement that each represents and any important details about their styles or themes.

Section Goals

In this section, students will learn historical and cultural information about the Antilles and French Polynesia.

Instructional Resources
IRCD-ROM: Transparency #62
WB/VM: Workbook, pp. 209–210
WB/VM/LM Answer Key
espaces.vhlcentral.com: activities; downloads; reference tools

Carte des Antilles et de la Polynésie française
- Have students look at the map or use **Transparency #62**. Ask volunteers to read the names of countries and islands aloud.
- Point out the location of **la mer des Antilles** or **la mer des Caraïbes**.
- Give students a geographical description of a few locations and have them guess which francophone place you are describing.
- Mention that the tropical islands, which are mostly mountainous, have fertile soils that make for rich, abundant vegetation.

L'archipel en chiffres
- Have volunteers read the sections aloud. After each section, ask students questions about the content.
- Explain that an archipelago is a large group of islands. Point out that the **îles Gambier** and **îles de la Société** are composed of atolls.

Incroyable mais vrai! After the eruption, the accumulated ash and rock raised the summit of Mount Pelée from 5,000 feet to 6,000 feet. After a few more minor eruptions, the volcano now stands at 4,584 feet.

SAVOIR-FAIRE

Panorama

Les Antilles

L'archipel en chiffres

- **Guadeloupe:** *(460.000 habitants), Pointe-à-Pitre, Basse-Terre*
- **Haïti:** *(9.500.000), Port-au-Prince*
- **Martinique:** *(402.000), Fort-de-France*
- **Saint-Barthélémy:** *(6.858), Gustavia*
- **Saint-Martin:** *(en partie) (29.126), Marigot*

SOURCE: Population Division, UN Secretariat

Antillais célèbres

- **Aimé Césaire,** *la Martinique, poète (1913–)*
- **Raphaël Confiant,** *la Guadeloupe, écrivain (1951–)*
- **Garcelle Beauvais,** *Haïti, actrice (1966–)*
- **Wyclef Jean,** *Haïti, chanteur de rap (1972–)*

la ville de Gustavia, à Saint-Barthélémy

LES ÉTATS-UNIS
L'OCÉAN ATLANTIQUE
LES ANTILLES
CUBA
Porto Rico
Saint-Martin
Saint-Barthélémy
La Guadeloupe
La Martinique
LA JAMAÏQUE
HAÏTI
LE VENEZUELA
LE SURINAM
LA COLOMBIE
La Guyane française
LA GUYANA
L'OCÉAN PACIFIQUE
LE BRÉSIL
Régions francophones
0 1,000 milles
0 1,000 kilomètres

LA POLYNÉSIE FRANÇAISE
Les îles Marquises
L'OCÉAN PACIFIQUE
Les îles Tuamotu
Les îles de la Société
Tahiti
Les îles Gambier
Les îles Australes
0 500 milles
0 500 kilomètres

La Polynésie française

L'archipel en chiffres

- **Îles Australes:** *(6.386), Tubuai*
- **Îles de la Société:** *(214.445), Papeete*
- **Îles Gambier:** *(1.097), Mangareva*
- **Îles Marquises:** *(8.712), Nuku-Hiva*
- **Îles Tuamotu:** *(16.959), Fakarava, Rankiroa*

Polynésiens célèbres

- **Henri Hiro,** *Tahiti, îles de la Société, poète (1944–1990)*
- **Rodolphe Vinh Tung,** *Raiatea, îles de la Société, professionnel du wakeboard (1974–)*

les courses de pirogues° en Polynésie française

Incroyable mais vrai!

Jusqu'au vingtième siècle, Saint-Pierre était le port le plus actif des Antilles et la capitale de la Martinique. Mais en 1902, un volcan, la montagne Pelée, entre en éruption. Il n'y a eu que deux survivants°, dont un qui a été protégé par les murs de la prison où il était enfermé°. Certains historiens doutent de l'authenticité de l'histoire de cet homme.

survivants *survivors* **enfermé** *detained* **pirogues** *dugout canoes*

OPTIONS

Antillais et Polynésiens célèbres **Aimé Césaire** coined the term **«Négritude»**, which came from his poem **«Cahier d'un retour au pays natal»**. **Raphaël Confiant** has won many literary prizes for his works, which have been published in French, Creole, and English. He has championed Creole as a literary language and has been involved in social and political activities in Martinique. **Garcelle Beauvais** is a model and actress. She has appeared in American films and TV shows. **Wyclef Jean**'s music draws from his memories of his youth in Haiti and his multicultural experiences in a Creole environment after immigrating to the United States. **Henri Hiro** was responsible for a cultural resurgence of the traditional Polynesian customs in Tahitian theater, dance, music, and film.

Les arts

Les peintures de Gauguin

En 1891, le peintre Paul Gauguin (1848–1903) vend ses œuvres à Paris et déménage à Tahiti, dans les îles de la Société, pour échapper à° la vie moderne. Il y reste deux ans avant de rentrer en France et, en 1895, il retourne en Polynésie française pour y habiter jusqu'à sa mort en 1903. Inspirée par le nouvel environnement du peintre et la nature qui l'entoure°, l'œuvre «tahitienne» de Gauguin est célèbre pour sa représentation du peuple indigène et l'emploi° de couleurs vives°. Ses peintures de femmes font partie de ses meilleurs tableaux.

Les destinations

Haïti, première République noire

En 1791, un ancien esclave°, Toussaint Louverture, mène° une rébellion pour l'abolition de l'esclavage en Haïti, ancienne colonie française. Après avoir gagné le combat, Louverture se proclame gouverneur de l'île d'Hispaniola (Haïti et Saint-Domingue) et abolit l'esclavage. Il est plus tard capturé par l'armée française et renvoyé en France. Son successeur, Jean-Jacques Dessalines, lui-même ancien esclave, vainc° l'armée en 1803 et proclame l'indépendance d'Haïti en 1804. C'est la première République noire du monde et le premier pays du monde occidental à abolir l'esclavage.

L'économie

La perle noire

La Polynésie française est le principal producteur de perles° noires. Dans la nature, les perles sont très rares; on en trouve dans une huître° sur 15.000. Par contre°, aujourd'hui, la Polynésie française produit plusieurs tonnes de perles noires chaque année. Des milliers de Tahitiens vivent de° l'industrie perlière. Parce qu'elle s'est développée dans les lagons, la perliculture° a même aidé à repeupler° certaines îles et certains endroits ruraux, abandonnés par les gens partis en ville. Les perles sont très variées et présentent différentes formes et nuances de noir.

Les gens

Maryse Condé

Née en Guadeloupe, puis étudiante à la Sorbonne, à Paris, Maryse Condé a vécu° huit ans en Afrique (Ghana, Sénégal, Guinée, etc.). En 1973, elle enseigne dans les universités françaises et commence sa carrière d'écrivain. Elle sera ensuite professeur en Californie et à l'Université de Columbia. Ses nombreux romans, y compris° *Moi, Tituba Sorcière*, ont reçu de multiples récompenses°. Ses romans mêlent° souvent fiction et événements historiques pour montrer la complexité de la culture antillaise, culture liée° à celle de l'Europe et à celle de l'Afrique.

Qu'est-ce que vous avez appris? Répondez aux questions par des phrases complètes.

1. Que s'est-il passé en Martinique au début du vingtième siècle? La montagne Pelée est entrée en éruption.
2. L'éruption a-t-elle tué tous les habitants de Saint-Pierre? Non, deux habitants n'ont pas été tués.
3. Pour quelle raison Gauguin a-t-il déménagé à Tahiti? Il voulait échapper à la vie moderne.
4. Pour quelles raisons l'œuvre «tahitienne» de Gauguin est-elle célèbre? Elle est célèbre pour sa représentation du peuple indigène et pour l'emploi de couleurs vives.
5. Quelle est la principale particularité d'Haïti? C'est la première République noire du monde.
6. Qui a réussi à abolir l'esclavage en Haïti? Toussaint Louverture a réussi à abolir l'esclavage en Haïti.
7. D'où viennent la majorité des perles noires? Elles viennent de Polynésie française.
8. Comment la perliculture a-t-elle changé la population de la Polynésie? Elle a aidé à repeupler certaines îles et certains endroits ruraux.
9. Où Maryse Condé a-t-elle étudié? Où est-elle née? Elle a fait ses études à Paris. Elle est née en Guadeloupe.
10. Ses romans sont-ils entièrement des œuvres de fiction? Non, ils mêlent la fiction et l'histoire.

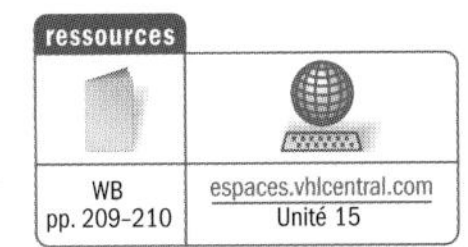

SUR INTERNET

Go to **espaces.vhlcentral.com** to find more cultural information related to this **PANORAMA**.

1. Cherchez des informations sur Aimé Césaire. Qu'a-t-il en commun avec Léopold Sédar Senghor, poète et homme politique mentionné dans **PANORAMA** de l'Unité 14?
2. Trouvez des informations sur la ville de Saint-Pierre. Comment est-elle aujourd'hui?
3. Cherchez des informations sur les courses de pirogues en Polynésie française. Quelle est leur signification?

échapper à *escape* **entoure** *surrounds* **emploi** *use* **vives** *bright* **esclave** *slave* **mène** *leads* **vainc** *defeats* **perles** *pearls* **huître** *oyster* **Par contre** *On the other hand* **vivent de** *make a living from* **perliculture** *pearl farming* **repeupler** *repopulate* **a vécu** *lived* **y compris** *including* **récompenses** *awards* **mêlent** *mix* **liée** *tied*

Les peintures de Gauguin

- Gauguin tried to capture authentic aspects of traditional Tahitian culture, emulated Oceanic traditions in his woodcuts, and often used the Tahitian language for titles of his works.
- Have students describe the painting. Ask: **Qui reconnait ce tableau? Devinez comment il s'appelle? (*Femmes de Tahiti [sur la plage]*) Savez-vous où le tableau original se trouve aujourd'hui? (Il est au musée d'Orsay à Paris.)**

Haïti, première République noire Haitian Creole and French are the two official languages of Haiti. The grammar of Haitian Creole is similar to languages of West Africa and other Caribbean creoles. Distribute examples of Haitian Creole and have students compare the language with French.

La perle noire Baby oysters are collected from the ocean and raised in pearl farms for three years. A small round piece of mother-of-pearl is inserted into the oyster, and the oyster begins the natural process of secreting nacre in layers onto the foreign substance which becomes a pearl after several years.

Maryse Condé In her historical novels, Maryse Condé has chronicled the migration and experience of the African people from West Africa to the United States and the Caribbean. Her books explore the clash of races and cultures using personal experiences of historical characters.

OPTIONS

Une tradition tahitienne The **Hawaiki Nui Va'a** is one of the world's premier outrigger canoe competitions, and it is an important celebration of Tahiti's traditional sports. Each year in late October or early November competitors paddle 80 miles between four islands over the span of three days.

Régions d'outre-mer Martinique and Guadeloupe are **départements** or **régions d'outre-mer (DOM/ROM)** of France. They have the same status and responsibilities as any other department of metropolitan France. French Polynesia is referred to as a **pays d'outre-mer** (previously **territoire d'outre-mer**) which is more independent, but still has some administrative ties to France.

Section Goals

In this section, students will:
- learn to make inferences and recognize metaphors
- read an African poem

Stratégie
- Tell students that poets do not generally spell out everything for their readers. They will need to look for clues in the poem to infer what is unstated and then draw conclusions in order to comprehend the poet's message.
- Review metaphors. Then write these sentences on the board. **Ses cheveux sont comme de la soie. Ses mots sont de la poésie.** Ask students which sentence is a metaphor. Then have students make up a metaphor in French and share it with the class.

Examinez le texte Students should mention that the text is a poem, the title is **«Note à mes lecteurs»**, and it is written in the first person. The illustrations indicate that the writer is a mother, she is writing outdoors under the starry night, and the people climbing the mountain are her readers.

À propos de l'auteur
- Mariama Mbengue Ndoye's hometown in Senegal is Rufisque. An old port city, Rufisque is now a distant suburb of Dakar.
- Ask students these comprehension questions. **1. Où est née Mariama Mbengue Ndoye? (Sénégal) 2. Où a-t-elle reçu son doctorat? (à l'Université de Dakar) 3. Qu'a-t-elle étudié à l'École du Louvre? (la muséologie) 4. Qu'avait-elle comme travail entre 1977–1986? (Elle était Conservateur du musée d'Art africain de l'Institut fondamental d'Afrique noire.) 5. Où habite-t-elle actuellement? (en Tunisie) 6. Quels thèmes trouve-t-on dans ses livres? (l'Afrique, la femme africaine et la vie dans les villages)**

Lecture

Avant la lecture

STRATÉGIE

Making inferences and recognizing metaphors

For dramatic effect and to achieve a smoother writing style, authors often do not explicitly supply the reader with all the details of a story or a poem. Clues (**indices**) in the text can help you infer (**déduire**) those things the writer chooses not to state in a direct manner. You simply "read between the lines" to fill in the missing information.

Metaphors (**Métaphores**) are figures of speech used in literature to make descriptions more vivid. They identify one thing with the attributes and qualities of another, as in *all the world's a stage*.

Examinez le texte

Regardez le texte. Est-ce un extrait de roman? Une nouvelle (*short story*)? Un poème? Quel en est le titre? Qu'indiquent le format et le titre à propos du genre du texte? Regardez aussi les illustrations. Qu'indiquent-elles sur le thème de la lecture?

À propos de l'auteur

Mariama Mbengue Ndoye

Mariama Mbengue Ndoye est née au Sénégal en 1953. Elle fait des études de lettres à l'Université de Dakar, où elle reçoit son doctorat en 1982. Elle obtient un certificat de muséologie de l'École du Louvre à Paris en 1977 et devient ensuite Conservateur du musée d'Art africain de l'Institut fondamental d'Afrique noire à Dakar. Après 15 ans passés en Côte d'Ivoire, elle habite maintenant en Tunisie, où elle écrit. Son œuvre comprend° plusieurs romans, dont *Soukeye* et *De vous à moi*, des recueils° de nouvelles et des livres pour enfants. Dans ses livres, elle parle de l'Afrique, de la femme africaine et de la vie dans les villages.

comprend *includes* **recueils** *collections*

Note À Mes

En forme de poème (1996)

Je m'appelle Mariama, Marie, Myriem, Marème,
Mouskeba, Maamou à votre aise°

Le O de mon nom Ndoye ouvre son gros œil sur
le monde

Je suis femme, je suis mère, je suis fille
porteuse de nichées d'espoirs°
lourde de hottes° de secrets
pourvoyeuse° de caresses et de claques°

OPTIONS

Pairs Remind students that they can appreciate the lyrical nature of poetry by reading a poem aloud. Have partners read **«Note à mes lecteurs»** to each other. Tell them to pay close attention to how the lines are punctuated and how the stanzas are arranged.

Extra Practice At the end of the poem the author says, **«Je "nous" écris, lisez-moi.»** Have students discuss why she makes that statement. What were her reasons? Then ask them if this poem makes them want to read more of her works. Have them justify their answers.

Lecteurs°

Je suis une nuit noire étoilée°
noire de la souffrance° des femmes en gésine°
noire du carbone d'où jaillit° le diamant
étoilée du sourire de mes sœurs d'Afrique

Je vais déambulant° dans les méandres de mon être et du temps
confiant° au papier blanc-ami les songes° fragiles de mon âme° d'enfant

Je gravis° ma colline° parfois je m'égratigne°

Je regarde mes compagnons de cordée°: Vous.

Je «nous» écris, lisez-moi.

Mariama Ndoye

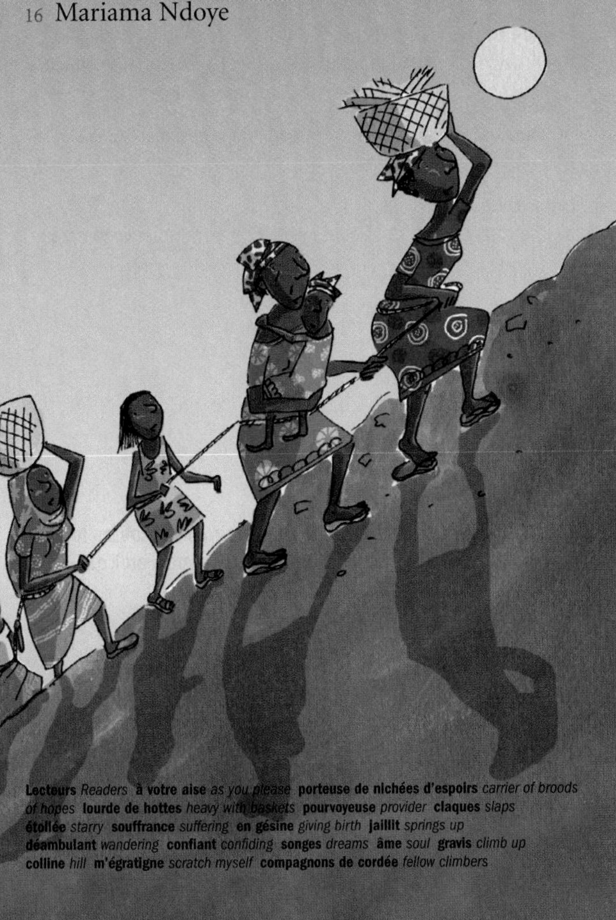

Lecteurs *Readers* **à votre aise** *as you please* **porteuse de nichées d'espoirs** *carrier of broods of hopes* **lourde de hottes** *heavy with baskets* **pourvoyeuse** *provider* **claques** *slaps* **étoilée** *starry* **souffrance** *suffering* **en gésine** *giving birth* **jaillit** *springs up* **déambulant** *wandering* **confiant** *confiding* **songes** *dreams* **âme** *soul* **gravis** *climb up* **colline** *hill* **m'égratigne** *scratch myself* **compagnons de cordée** *fellow climbers*

Après la lecture

Vrai ou faux? Indiquez si les phrases sont **vraies** ou **fausses**. Attention! Beaucoup de choses ne sont que suggérées dans le poème. Citez (*Quote*) le poème pour justifier votre réponse.

1. La femme du poème représente toutes les femmes.
   Vrai. «Je m'appelle Mariama, Marie, Myriem, Marème, Mouskeba, Maamou à votre aise»
2. Elle ne s'intéresse pas au monde.
   Faux. «Le O de mon nom Ndoye ouvre son gros œil sur le monde»
3. Elle n'a pas d'enfants.
   Faux. «je suis mère»
4. C'est une femme qui ne sait pas réprimander.
   Faux. «Je suis [...] pourvoyeuse de caresses et de claques»
5. Elle ressent (*feels*) le bonheur et la douleur des femmes.
   Vrai. «Je suis [...] noire de la souffrance des femmes en gésine [...] étoilée du sourire de mes sœurs d'Afrique»
6. Quand elle écrit, elle parle de ses rêves (*dreams*).
   Vrai. «confiant au papier blanc-ami les songes fragiles de mon âme d'enfant»
7. Elle trouve que c'est facile d'écrire.
   Faux. «Je gravis ma colline parfois je m'égratigne»
8. Quand elle parle de ses compagnons de cordée, elle fait référence à ses enfants.
   Faux. «Note à mes lecteurs [...] je regarde mes compagnons de cordée: Vous.»
9. Elle écrit seulement à propos d'elle-même et pour elle.
   Faux. «Je "nous" écris, lisez-moi.»
10. Ce poème a un ton plutôt pessimiste.
    Faux. «Je suis [...] porteuse de nichées d'espoir»

Métaphores Avez-vous trouvé des métaphores dans ce poème? Trouvez celles qui indiquent que l'auteur vient d'Afrique. Que signifient ces métaphores? L'auteur est-elle fière d'être Africaine?

Answers will vary. Suggested answers: «Je suis une nuit noire étoilée», «noire de la souffrance des femmes en gésine», etc. Les métaphores du poème illustrent la complexité de la vie des femmes africaines.

Escalader ensemble L'auteur compare ses lecteurs à des compagnons de cordée. Pourquoi à votre avis? Que doit-on faire quand on escalade (*climb*) une montagne? Avez-vous déjà escaladé une montagne ou une colline? Discutez en petit groupe.

Vrai ou faux? Go over the answers with the class.

Métaphores
- Have students work on this activity in pairs or have them compare their answers with a classmate.
- Ask students to think about conversations that they have had recently in which they used a metaphor. As a starting point, you might mention that the quote "All the world's a stage" from Shakespeare's *As You Like It* is an example of a metaphor.

Escalader ensemble Ask groups to share their opinions and ideas with the class.

Successful Language Learning Ask students if they approach reading in French or English differently after using the strategies presented in **ESPACES**.

OPTIONS

Extra Practice Have students write a short poem about themselves using this poem as a model. Encourage them to use metaphors. Ask volunteers to read their poems to the class.

Extra Practice Assign individual students one of the works by Mariama Mbengue Ndoye listed in the author biography or another work such as ***Des chemins pavoisés*, *Parfums d'enfance*, *La légende de Rufisque***, and ***Le sceptre de Justice***. Tell them to research and write a paragraph about the book that includes the themes, the main characters, and a brief plot summary.

Section Goals

In this section, students will:

- learn to listen for key words and use context
- listen to a letter sent to a job applicant and jot down key words
- listen to a radio advertisement for a play and complete several activities

Instructional Resources
Textbook MP3s
IRCD-ROM: IRM (Textbook Audioscript)
espaces.vhlcentral.com: downloads, reference tools

Stratégie
Script Monsieur, Nous vous remercions de votre lettre de candidature pour le poste d'ingénieur informatique et pour l'intérêt que vous portez à notre compagnie. Malheureusement, nous regrettons de vous informer que nous avons déjà retenu un candidat pour cet emploi. Nous vous prions d'agréer, Monsieur, l'expression de nos sentiments distingués.

Préparation Have students look at the photo and describe what they see. They should mention that the people are waiting in line at a box office of a theater.

À vous d'écouter
Script Les amateurs de Molière ne doivent surtout pas manquer *L'Avare* au Théâtre Monfort. Le metteur en scène, Yves Lemoîne, réinvente ce grand classique avec beaucoup de créativité. Avec dans le rôle d'Harpagon, le personnage principal qui a toujours peur qu'on lui prenne son argent, Julien Roche; un jeune comédien très talentueux qui a fait ses débuts il y a trois ans avec la troupe Comédia. *L'Avare* est une comédie très amusante et je suis certain que cette adaptation aura un grand succès. La première représentation a eu lieu hier soir et déjà les applaudissements étaient nombreux et enthousiastes. La pièce a aussi reçu une critique très positive dans le journal *Le Monde*. Si vous souhaitez voir *L'Avare* par Yves Lemoîne, les billets sont en vente au guichet du théâtre tous les jours de 10h00 à 18h00. Il y a deux représentations le vendredi et le samedi, à 19h00 et à 21h30 et une à 14h00 le dimanche.

À l'écoute

STRATÉGIE

Listening for key words/ Using the context

The comprehension of key words is vital to understanding spoken French. You can use your background knowledge of the subject to help you anticipate some key words. When you hear unfamiliar words, remember that you can use context to figure out their meaning.

To practice these strategies, you will listen to a paragraph from a letter sent to a job applicant. Jot down key words, as well as any other words you figured out from the context.

Préparation

Regardez et décrivez la photo. Où sont ces personnes? Que font-elles? Que vont-elles aller voir, à votre avis?

À vous d'écouter

Vous êtes en France et vous voulez inviter un(e) ami(e) à sortir ce week-end. Vous écoutez la radio et vous entendez une annonce pour un spectacle qui plaira peut-être à votre ami(e). Notez les informations principales pour pouvoir ensuite décrire ce spectacle à votre ami(e) et pour lui dire quand vous pourrez aller le voir. Answers will vary.

____

____

____

____

____

____

____

ressources

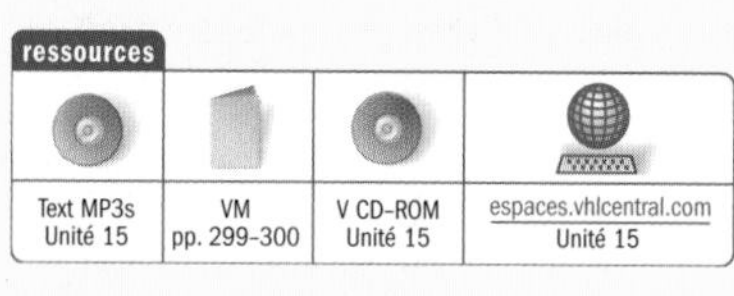

Text MP3s Unité 15
VM pp. 299-300
V CD-ROM Unité 15
espaces.vhlcentral.com Unité 15

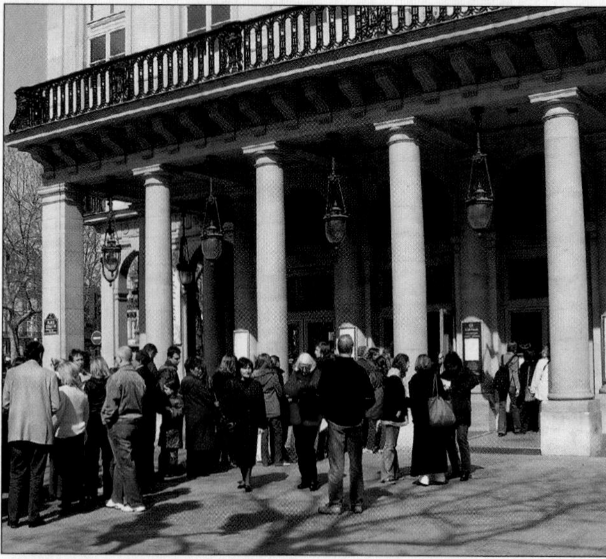

Compréhension

Complétez Complétez les phrases.

1. Molière est __a__ de *L'Avare*.
   a. l'auteur b. le metteur en scène c. le personnage principal
2. *L'Avare* est __c__.
   a. une exposition b. un jeune comédien très dynamique
   c. une pièce de théâtre
3. *L'Avare* est drôle. C'est __b__.
   a. une tragédie b. une comédie c. un drame psychologique
4. Yves Lemoîne est __c__ de *L'Avare*.
   a. l'auteur b. le journaliste qui a écrit la critique
   c. le metteur en scène
5. Harpagon est le nom du __a__.
   a. personnage principal b. spectacle c. poète
6. Dans le journal, il y avait __b__ positive de *L'Avare*.
   a. une pub b. une critique c. un applaudissement

Invitez votre ami(e)! Vous avez maintenant toutes les informations importantes nécessaires pour inviter votre ami(e) (un[e] camarade) à aller voir *L'Avare* ce weekend.

- Invitez-le/la au spectacle et dites-lui quand vous pourrez y allez.
- Il/Elle va vous poser quelques questions pour obtenir plus de détails sur le spectacle (histoire, personnages, acteurs, etc.).
- Ensuite, comme il/elle n'a pas très envie d'aller voir le spectacle, il/elle va faire plusieurs suggestions d'autres activités artistiques (films, concerts, expositions, etc.).
- Discuter de ces possibilités et choisissez-en une ensemble.

Successful Language Learning Ask students if they approach listening to French or English differently after using the strategies presented in **ESPACES**.

Écriture

STRATÉGIE

Writing strong introductions and conclusions

Introductions and conclusions serve a similar purpose: both are intended to focus the reader's attention on the topic being covered. The introduction presents a brief preview of the topic. In addition, it informs your reader of the important points that will be covered in the body of your writing. The conclusion reaffirms those points and concisely sums up the information that has been provided. A compelling fact or statistic, a humorous anecdote, or a question directed to the reader are all interesting ways to begin or end your writing.

For example, if you were writing a biographical report on Antoine de Saint-Exupéry, whom you learned about in **Unité 14 LECTURE**, you might start by noting that Saint-Exupéry's *Le Petit Prince* is considered to be one of the most widely read books ever. The rest of your introductory paragraph would outline the areas you would cover in the body of your paper, such as the author's life, his works, and the impact that *Le Petit Prince* has had on adult and children's literature. In your conclusion, you might sum up the most important information in the report and tie this information together in a way that would make your reader want to learn even more about the topic. You could write, for example, "Antoine de Saint-Exupéry, with his imagination and unique view on the world, has created one of the most well-known and enduring characters in world literature."

Watch the **FLASH CULTURE** segment on the **ESPACES** video for cultural footage related to this unit's theme.

Thème

Écrire la critique d'une œuvre artistique

Vous allez écrire la critique d'un film, d'une pièce de théâtre ou d'un spectacle de votre choix. Votre critique aura trois parties: l'introduction, le développement et la conclusion. Dans l'introduction, vous présenterez rapidement l'œuvre. Ensuite, dans le développement, vous la décrirez en détail. Enfin, dans la conclusion, vous donnerez votre opinion et expliquerez pourquoi vous recommandez ce spectacle ou non. Utilisez le plan suivant comme point de départ.

Introduction

- Donnez le titre de l'œuvre et le nom de son créateur.
- Décrivez le sujet et / ou le genre de l'œuvre.
- Dites quand et où vous l'avez vu.

Développement

- Faites un petit résumé de l'histoire.
- Donnez les noms des personnages ou des artistes.
- Décrivez les personnages, le(s) décor(s) et les costumes.

Conclusion

- Donnez votre opinion de l'œuvre.
- Expliquez pour quelles raisons vous la recommandez ou non.

Section Goals

In this section, students will:

- learn to write introductions and conclusions
- write a critique of a film, show, or theatrical work
- view authentic cultural footage of a movie theater and a kiosk

Instructional Resources
WB/VM: Video Manual, pp. 299–300
WB/VM/LM Answer Key
IRCD-ROM: IRM (Videoscript)
Video CD-ROM
Video on DVD
espaces.vhlcentral.com: activities, downloads, reference tools

Stratégie Explain that a strong introduction presents the topic and outlines the important points that will be addressed. Ask students why an introduction to a biography of Antoine de Saint-Exupéry that does not mention ***Le Petit Prince*** is not a strong introduction. Explain that a strong conclusion summarizes the information given. Ask students how this conclusion could be stronger: **Saint-Exupéry était un grand écrivain.**

Thème Tell students to follow the steps outlined here when writing their critique.

Proofreading Activity Have students correct these sentences. **1. Croyez-vous que ce soit meilleur qu'elle le sache? 2. Il est évidente qu'elle ne connaît pas chanter. 3. Il est clair que tu ne saches rien de moi.**

Flash culture Tell students that they will learn more about movie theaters and types of publications available at kiosks by watching a variety of real-life images narrated by Csilla. Show the video segment without sound and tell students to call out what they see. Then show the video segment again with sound. You can also use the activities in the video manual to reinforce this **Flash culture**.

EVALUATION

Criteria	Scale
Content	1 2 3 4 5
Use of vocabulary	1 2 3 4 5
Grammatical accuracy	1 2 3 4 5
Use of introductions/conclusions	1 2 3 4 5

Scoring	
Excellent	18–20 points
Good	14–17 points
Satisfactory	10–13 points
Unsatisfactory	< 10 points

Instructional Resources
Textbook MP3s
IRCD-ROM: IRM (Textbook Audioscript)
espaces.vhlcentral.com: downloads, reference tools

Aller au spectacle

applaudir	*to applaud*
présenter	*to present*
profiter de quelque chose	*to take advantage of/ to enjoy something*
un applaudissement	*applause*
une chanson	*song*
un chœur	*choir, chorus*
une comédie (musicale)	*comedy (musical)*
un concert	*concert*
une danse	*dance*
le début	*beginning; debut*
un entracte	*intermission*
un festival (festivals *pl.*)	*festival*
la fin	*end*
un genre	*genre*
un opéra	*opera*
une pièce de théâtre	*play*
une place	*seat*
une séance	*show; screening*
une sorte	*sort, kind*
un spectateur/ une spectatrice	*spectator*
une tragédie	*tragedy*
gratuit(e)	*free*

Le cinéma et la télévision

un dessin animé	*cartoon*
un documentaire	*documentary*
un drame psychologique	*psychological drama*
une émission (de télévision)	*(television) program*
un feuilleton	*soap opera*
un film (d'aventures, d'horreur, policier, de science-fiction)	*(adventure, horror, crime, science fiction) film*
une histoire	*story*
les informations (infos) (*f.*)	*news*
un jeu télévisé	*game show*
la météo	*weather*
les nouvelles (*f.*)	*news*
un programme	*program*
une publicité (pub)	*advertisement*
les variétés (*f.*)	*popular music*
à la radio	*on the radio*
à la télé(vision)	*on television*

ressources
Text MP3s Unité 15
espaces.vhlcentral.com Unité 15

Expressions de doute et de certitude

douter que...	*to doubt that...*
ne pas croire que...	*not to believe that...*
ne pas penser que...	*not to think that...*
Il est douteux que...	*It is doubtful that...*
Il est impossible que...	*It is impossible that...*
Il n'est pas certain que...	*It is uncertain that...*
Il n'est pas sûr que...	*It is not sure that...*
Il n'est pas vrai que...	*It is untrue that...*
croire que...	*to believe that...*
penser que...	*to think that...*
savoir que...	*to know that...*
Il est certain que...	*It is certain that...*
Il est clair que...	*It is clear that...*
Il est évident que...	*It is obvious that...*
Il est sûr que...	*It is sure that...*
Il est vrai que...	*It is true that...*

Les artistes

faire de la musique	*to play music*
faire de la peinture	*to paint*
jouer un rôle	*to play a role*
jouer de la batterie/ de la guitare/du piano/du violon	*to play the drums/ the guitar/the piano/ the violin*
un auteur/ une femme auteur	*author*
un compositeur	*composer*
un danseur/ une danseuse	*dancer*
un dramaturge	*playwright*
un écrivain/ une femme écrivain	*writer*
un membre	*member*
un metteur en scène	*director (of a play, a show)*
un orchestre	*orchestra*
un peintre/ une femme peintre	*painter*
un personnage (principal)	*(main) character*
un poète/ une poétesse	*poet*
un réalisateur/ une réalisatrice	*director (of a movie)*
un sculpteur/ une femme sculpteur	*sculptor*
une troupe	*company, troop*
célèbre	*famous*
doué(e)	*talented; gifted*

Les arts

faire les musées	*to go to museums*
publier	*to publish*
les beaux-arts (*m.*)	*fine arts*
un chef-d'œuvre	*masterpiece*
un conte	*tale*
une critique	*review; criticism*
une exposition	*exhibit*
un magazine	*magazine*
une œuvre	*artwork, piece of art*
une peinture	*painting*
un poème	*poem*
un roman	*novel*
une sculpture	*sculpture*
un tableau	*painting*
ancien(ne)	*ancient; old; former*
littéraire	*literary*
récent(e)	*recent*

Conjonctions suivies du subjonctif

à condition que...	*on the condition that..., provided that...*
à moins que...	*unless...*
avant que...	*before...*
jusqu'à ce que...	*until...*
pour que...	*so that...*
sans que...	*without...*

Expressions utiles	*See pp. 511 and 525.*
voir, croire, revoir	*See pp. 514–515.*

Le monde francophone

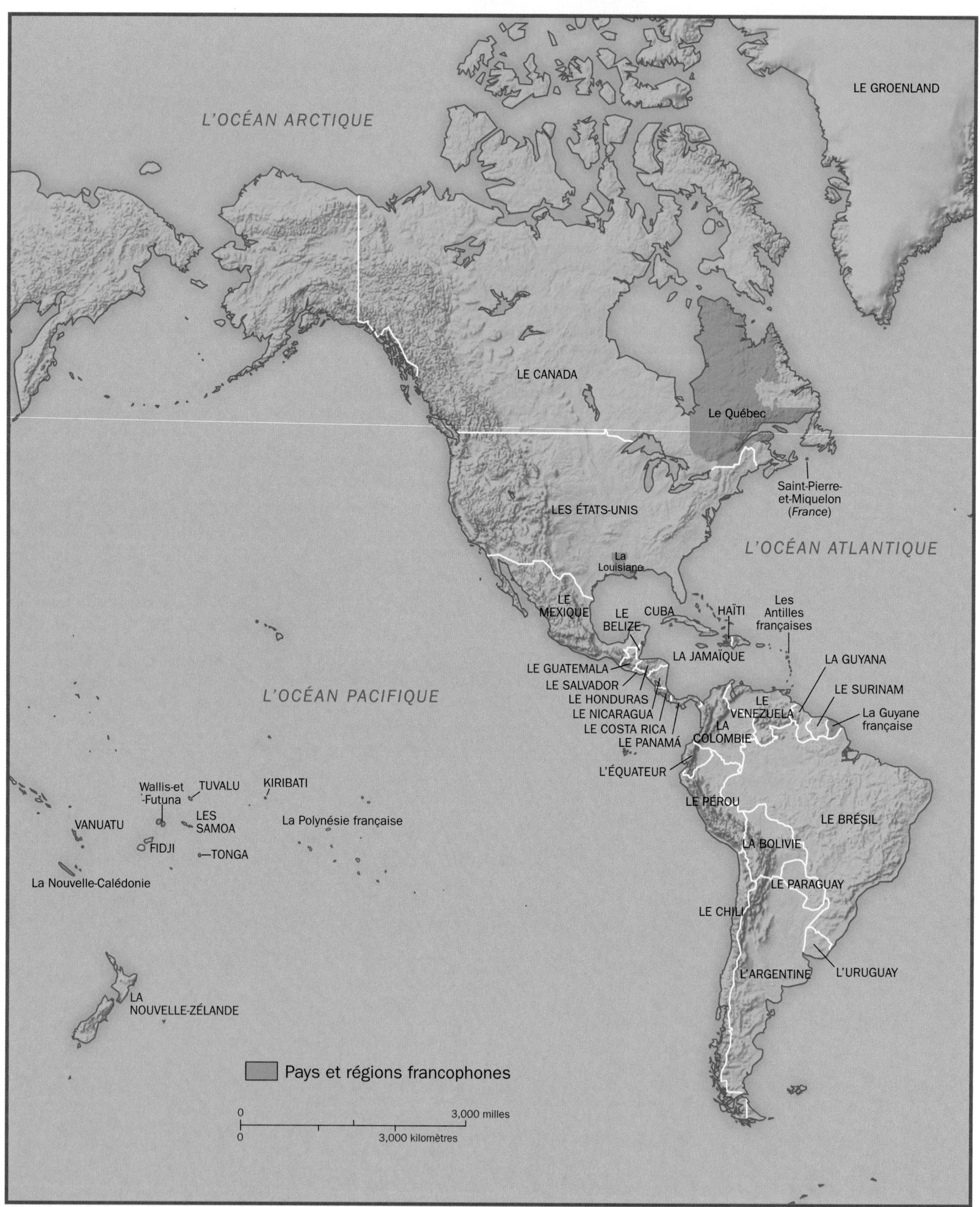
L'OCÉAN ARCTIQUE
LE GROENLAND
LE CANADA
Le Québec
Saint-Pierre-et-Miquelon (France)
LES ÉTATS-UNIS
L'OCÉAN ATLANTIQUE
La Louisiane
LE MEXIQUE
LE BELIZE
CUBA
HAÏTI
Les Antilles françaises
LA JAMAÏQUE
LE GUATEMALA
LE SALVADOR
LE HONDURAS
LE NICARAGUA
LE COSTA RICA
LE PANAMÁ
LA GUYANA
LE SURINAM
La Guyane française
LE VENEZUELA
LA COLOMBIE
L'ÉQUATEUR
LE PÉROU
LE BRÉSIL
LA BOLIVIE
LE PARAGUAY
LE CHILI
L'ARGENTINE
L'URUGUAY
L'OCÉAN PACIFIQUE
Wallis-et-Futuna
TUVALU
KIRIBATI
LES SAMOA
La Polynésie française
VANUATU
FIDJI
TONGA
La Nouvelle-Calédonie
LA NOUVELLE-ZÉLANDE
Pays et régions francophones
0
3,000 milles
0
3,000 kilomètres

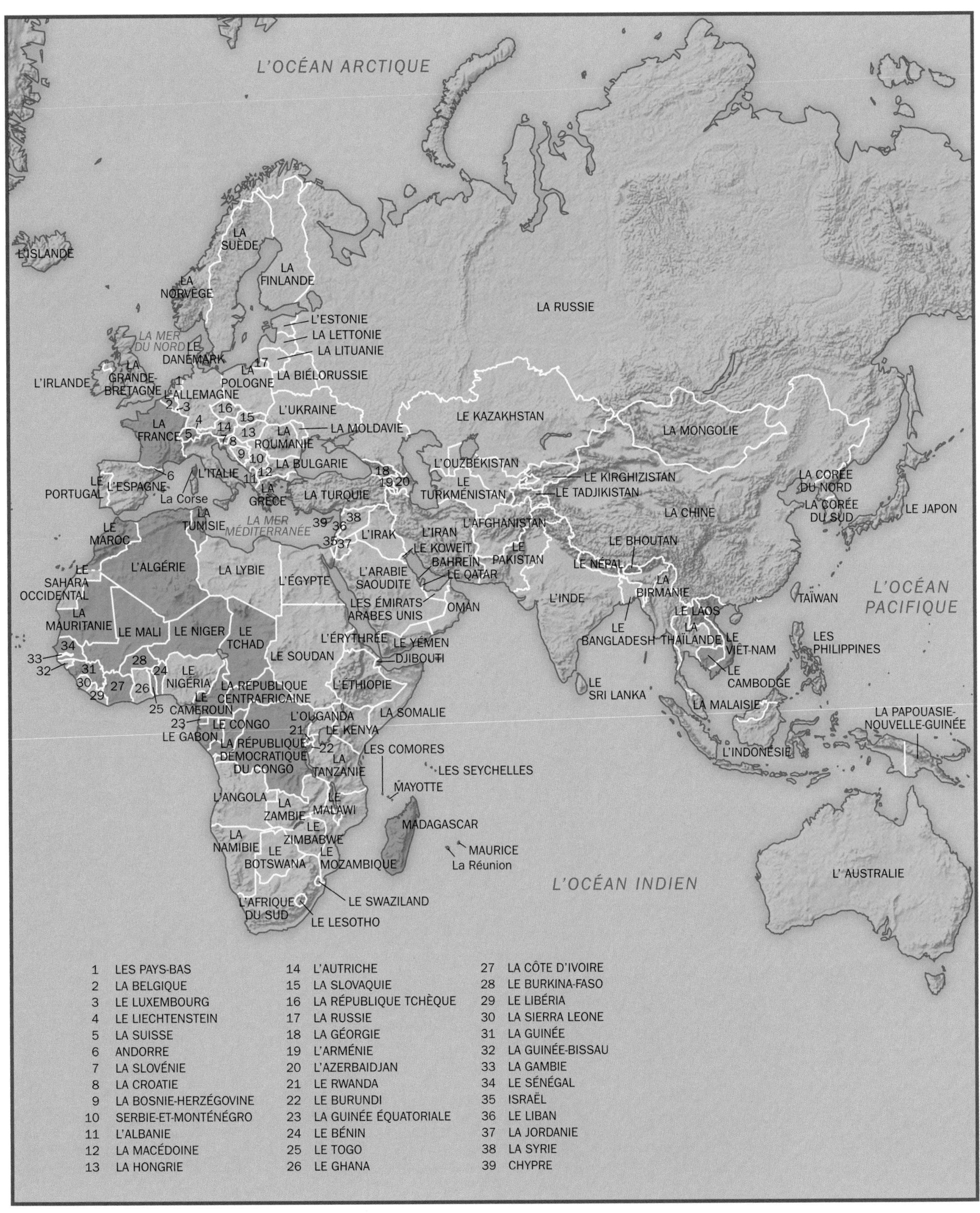
L'OCÉAN ARCTIQUE
L'ISLANDE
LA SUÈDE
LA FINLANDE
LA NORVÈGE
LA RUSSIE
L'ESTONIE
LA LETTONIE
LA LITUANIE
LA MER DU NORD
LE DANEMARK
L'IRLANDE
LA GRANDE-BRETAGNE
LA POLOGNE
LA BIÉLORUSSIE
L'ALLEMAGNE
L'UKRAINE
LA FRANCE
LA MOLDAVIE
LA ROUMANIE
LA BULGARIE
LE KAZAKHSTAN
LA MONGOLIE
L'OUZBÉKISTAN
LE KIRGHIZISTAN
LE TURKMÉNISTAN
LE TADJIKISTAN
LE PORTUGAL
L'ESPAGNE
L'ITALIE
La Corse
LA GRÈCE
LA TURQUIE
LA CORÉE DU NORD
LA CORÉE DU SUD
LE JAPON
LA CHINE
LA TUNISIE
LA MER MÉDITERRANÉE
L'IRAK
L'IRAN
L'AFGHANISTAN
LE MAROC
LE KOWEÏT
BAHREÏN
LE PAKISTAN
LE BHOUTAN
LE NÉPAL
L'ALGÉRIE
LA LYBIE
L'ÉGYPTE
L'ARABIE SAOUDITE
LE QATAR
LA BIRMANIE
LE SAHARA OCCIDENTAL
LES ÉMIRATS ARABES UNIS
OMAN
L'INDE
TAÏWAN
L'OCÉAN PACIFIQUE
LA MAURITANIE
LE MALI
LE NIGER
LE TCHAD
LE LAOS
L'ÉRYTHRÉE
LE YÉMEN
LE BANGLADESH
LA THAÏLANDE
LE VIÊT-NAM
LES PHILIPPINES
LE SOUDAN
DJIBOUTI
LE NIGÉRIA
LA RÉPUBLIQUE CENTRAFRICAINE
L'ÉTHIOPIE
LE CAMBODGE
LE SRI LANKA
LE CAMEROUN
LA SOMALIE
LA MALAISIE
L'OUGANDA
LE CONGO
LE KENYA
LE GABON
LA PAPOUASIE-NOUVELLE-GUINÉE
LA RÉPUBLIQUE DÉMOCRATIQUE DU CONGO
LES COMORES
L'INDONÉSIE
LA TANZANIE
LES SEYCHELLES
MAYOTTE
L'ANGOLA
LA ZAMBIE
LE MALAWI
MADAGASCAR
LE ZIMBABWE
LA NAMIBIE
LE BOTSWANA
LE MOZAMBIQUE
MAURICE
La Réunion
L'OCÉAN INDIEN
L'AUSTRALIE
L'AFRIQUE DU SUD
LE SWAZILAND
LE LESOTHO
1 LES PAYS-BAS
2 LA BELGIQUE
3 LE LUXEMBOURG
4 LE LIECHTENSTEIN
5 LA SUISSE
6 ANDORRE
7 LA SLOVÉNIE
8 LA CROATIE
9 LA BOSNIE-HERZÉGOVINE
10 SERBIE-ET-MONTÉNÉGRO
11 L'ALBANIE
12 LA MACÉDOINE
13 LA HONGRIE
14 L'AUTRICHE
15 LA SLOVAQUIE
16 LA RÉPUBLIQUE TCHÈQUE
17 LA RUSSIE
18 LA GÉORGIE
19 L'ARMÉNIE
20 L'AZERBAIDJAN
21 LE RWANDA
22 LE BURUNDI
23 LA GUINÉE ÉQUATORIALE
24 LE BÉNIN
25 LE TOGO
26 LE GHANA
27 LA CÔTE D'IVOIRE
28 LE BURKINA-FASO
29 LE LIBÉRIA
30 LA SIERRA LEONE
31 LA GUINÉE
32 LA GUINÉE-BISSAU
33 LA GAMBIE
34 LE SÉNÉGAL
35 ISRAËL
36 LE LIBAN
37 LA JORDANIE
38 LA SYRIE
39 CHYPRE

La France

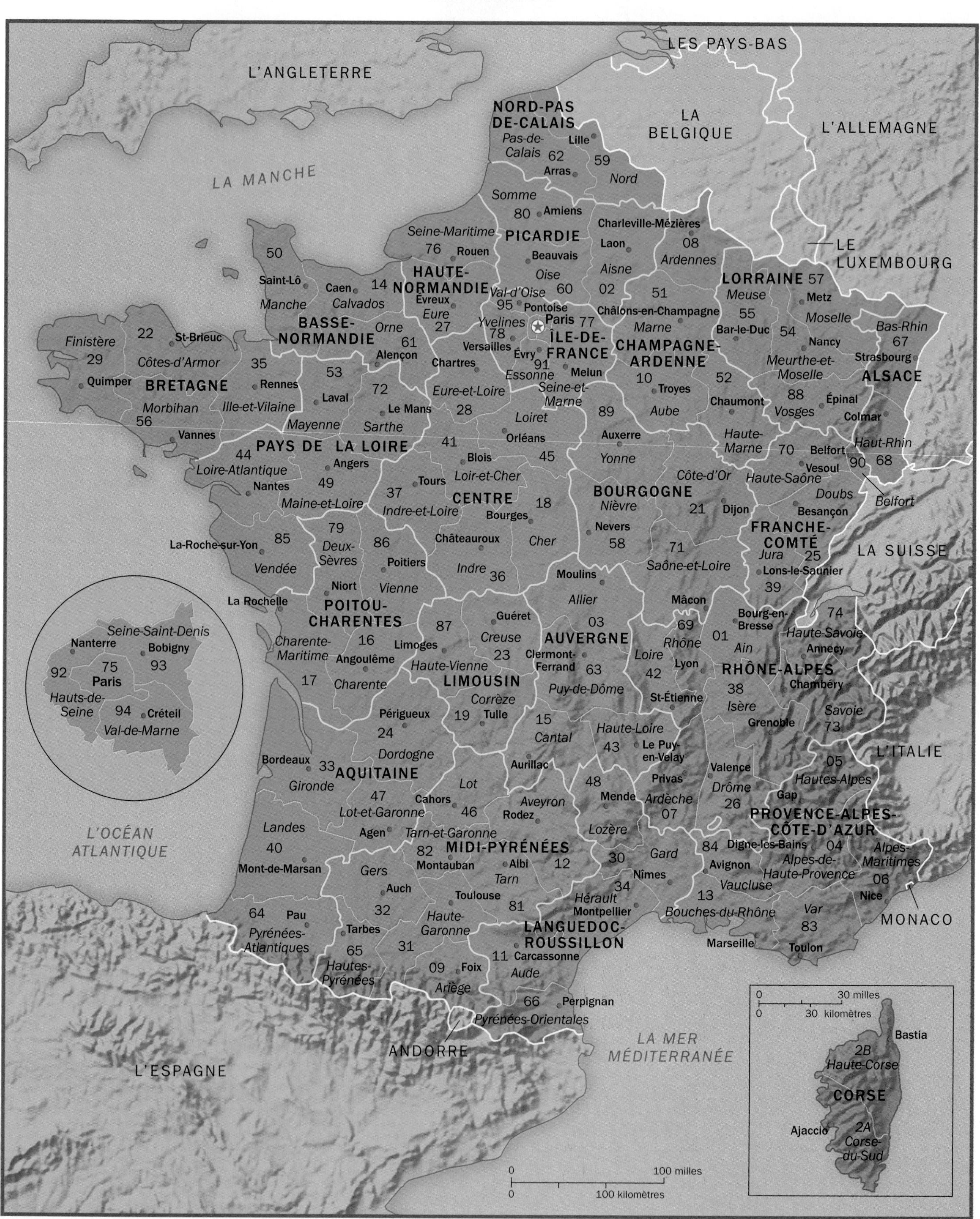
L'ANGLETERRE
LES PAYS-BAS
LA BELGIQUE
L'ALLEMAGNE
LE LUXEMBOURG
LA SUISSE
L'ITALIE
MONACO
ANDORRE
L'ESPAGNE
LA MANCHE
L'OCÉAN ATLANTIQUE
LA MER MÉDITERRANÉE
NORD-PAS DE-CALAIS
Pas-de-Calais 62
Lille
Arras
59 Nord
Somme 80
Amiens
PICARDIE
Seine-Maritime 76
Rouen
Beauvais
Oise 60
Charleville-Mézières
Laon
08 Ardennes
Aisne 02
HAUTE-NORMANDIE
Évreux
Eure 27
Val-d'Oise 95
Pontoise
Paris 77
Yvelines 78
Versailles
Évry
ÎLE-DE-FRANCE
Essonne 91
Melun
Seine-et-Marne
50
Saint-Lô
Manche
Caen
14 Calvados
BASSE-NORMANDIE
Orne 61
Alençon
Finistère 29
Quimper
22
St-Brieuc
Côtes-d'Armor
35
Rennes
BRETAGNE
Ille-et-Vilaine
Morbihan 56
Vannes
53
Laval
Mayenne
72
Le Mans
Sarthe
Chartres
Eure-et-Loire 28
44
PAYS DE LA LOIRE
Loire-Atlantique
Nantes
Angers
49
Maine-et-Loire
41
Blois
Loir-et-Cher
Orléans
Loiret
45
37
Tours
Indre-et-Loire
CENTRE
18
Bourges
Cher
Châteauroux
Indre 36
La-Roche-sur-Yon
85
Vendée
79
Deux-Sèvres
86
Poitiers
Niort
Vienne
La Rochelle
POITOU-CHARENTES
Charente-Maritime 17
16
Angoulême
Charente
Limoges
87
Haute-Vienne
Guéret
Creuse 23
LIMOUSIN
Corrèze
Tulle
19
Périgueux
24
Dordogne
Bordeaux
33
AQUITAINE
Gironde
47
Lot-et-Garonne
Agen
Landes 40
Mont-de-Marsan
64
Pau
Pyrénées-Atlantiques
Gers
Auch
32
Tarbes
65
Hautes-Pyrénées
Cahors
46
Lot
Tarn-et-Garonne
82
Montauban
MIDI-PYRÉNÉES
Albi
Tarn 81
Toulouse
Haute-Garonne 31
09
Foix
Ariège
12
Aveyron
Rodez
Aurillac
15
Cantal
LANGUEDOC-ROUSSILLON
11
Carcassonne
Aude
66
Perpignan
Pyrénées-Orientales
Hérault 34
Montpellier
Lozère 48
Mende
Gard 30
Nîmes
CHAMPAGNE-ARDENNE
51
Châlons-en-Champagne
Marne
10
Troyes
Aube
52
Chaumont
Haute-Marne
89
Auxerre
Yonne
BOURGOGNE
Nièvre
Nevers 58
Côte-d'Or 21
Dijon
71
Saône-et-Loire
Moulins
Allier 03
AUVERGNE
Clermont-Ferrand 63
Puy-de-Dôme
Haute-Loire 43
Le Puy-en-Velay
LORRAINE 57
Meuse 55
Metz
Moselle
Bar-le-Duc
54
Nancy
Meurthe-et-Moselle
88
Épinal
Vosges
Bas-Rhin 67
Strasbourg
ALSACE
Colmar
Haut-Rhin 68
Belfort 90
Belfort
70
Vesoul
Haute-Saône
Doubs
Besançon
FRANCHE-COMTÉ
Jura 25
Lons-le-Saunier 39
Mâcon
69
Rhône
Lyon
Loire 42
St-Étienne
01
Bourg-en-Bresse
Ain
74
Haute-Savoie
Annecy
RHÔNE-ALPES
38
Isère
Chambéry
Savoie 73
Grenoble
Valence
Drôme 26
Privas
Ardèche 07
05
Hautes-Alpes
Gap
PROVENCE-ALPES-CÔTE-D'AZUR
84
Digne-les-Bains
04
Alpes-de-Haute-Provence
Alpes-Maritimes 06
Nice
Avignon
Vaucluse
13
Bouches-du-Rhône
Marseille
Var 83
Toulon
Seine-Saint-Denis
Nanterre
Bobigny 93
92
75 Paris
Hauts-de-Seine
94
Créteil
Val-de-Marne
0 30 milles
0 30 kilomètres
Bastia
2B Haute-Corse
CORSE
Ajaccio
2A Corse-du-Sud
0 100 milles
0 100 kilomètres

L'Europe

0
500 milles
0
500 kilomètres
Pays francophones
LA MER DE BARENTS
LA MER DE NORVÈGE
L'ISLANDE
Reykjavik
LA SUÈDE
LA FINLANDE
LA NORVÈGE
Helsinki
LA RUSSIE
Tallinn
Oslo
Stockholm
L'ESTONIE
Moscou
LA MER BALTIQUE
Riga
LA LETTONIE
LA MER DU NORD
LE DANEMARK
LA LITUANIE
Copenhague
Vilnius
LA RUSSIE
Minsk
Dublin
LES PAYS-BAYS
LA BIÉLORUSSIE
L'IRLANDE
LA GRANDE BRETAGNE
Berlin
Varsovie
La Haye
Kiev
Londres
L'ALLEMAGNE
LA POLOGNE
Bruxelles
L'UKRAINE
LA BELGIQUE
Prague
L'OCÉAN ATLANTIQUE
Luxembourg
LA RÉPUBLIQUE TCHÈQUE
Paris
LA SLOVAQUIE
LE LIECHTENSTEIN
Bratislava
LA MOLDAVIE
LE LUXEMBOURG
Vienne
Chisinau
Budapest
Berne
L'AUTRICHE
LA HONGRIE
LA SUISSE
LA ROUMANIE
LA FRANCE
Ljubljana
Zagreb
LA MER NOIRE
Bucarest
LA SLOVÉNIE
Belgrade
LA CROATIE
LA BOSNIE-HERZÉGOVINE
SERBIE-ET-MONTÉNÉGRO
Monte Carlo
Sarajevo
LA BULGARIE
Andorre-la-Vieille
Sofia
L'ITALIE
Skopje
LE PORTUGAL
ANDORRE
MONACO
Tirana
LA MACÉDOINE
Rome
La Corse
Madrid
L'ALBANIE
LA TURQUIE
Lisbonne
L'ESPAGNE
LA GRÈCE
La Sardaigne
La Sicile
Athènes
Nicosie
CHYPRE
MALTE
La Valette
LA MER MÉDITERRANÉE
LE MAROC
LA TUNISIE
L'ALGÉRIE
L'ÉGYPTE
LA LYBIE

L'Afrique

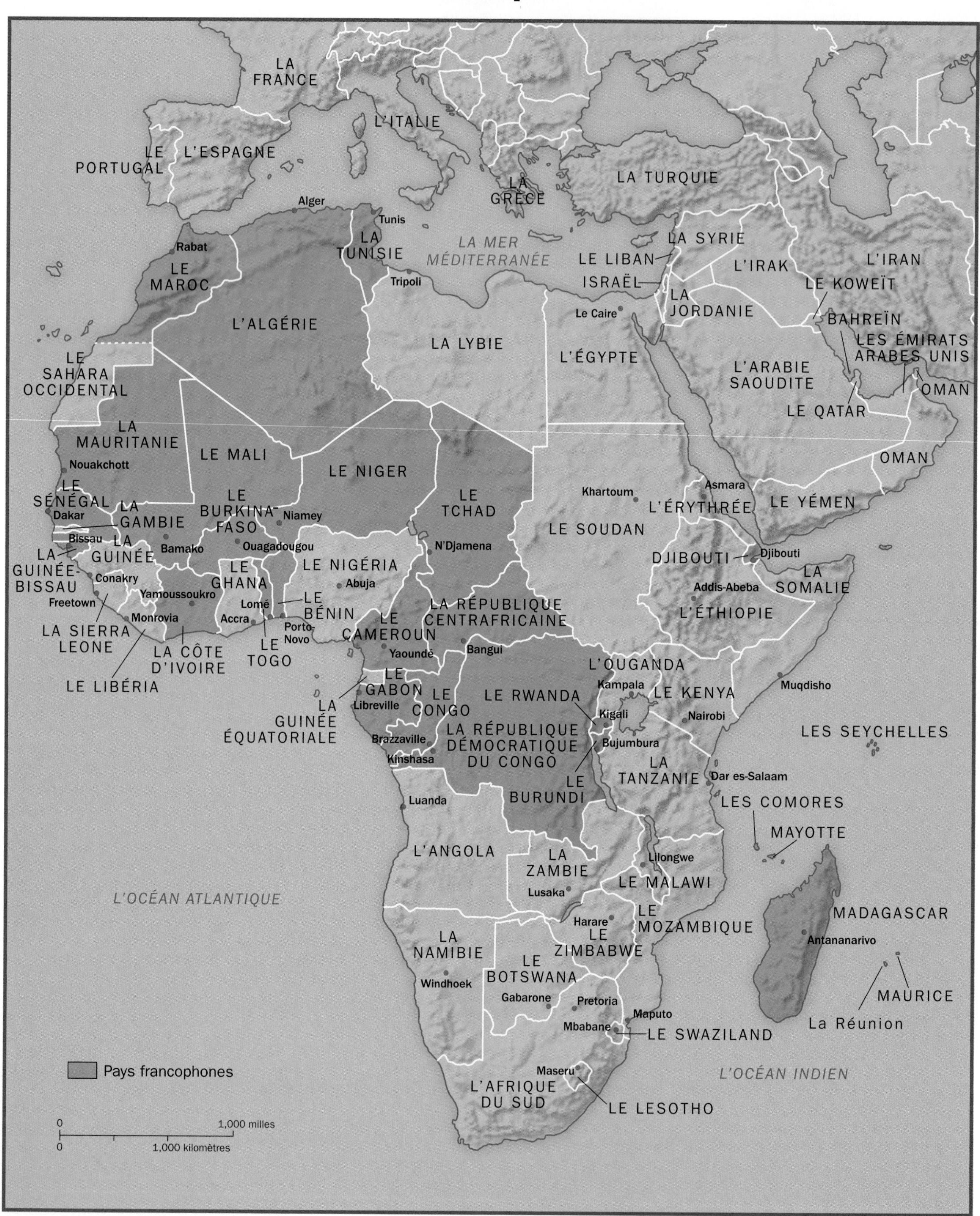
LA FRANCE
L'ITALIE
LE PORTUGAL
L'ESPAGNE
LA GRÈCE
LA TURQUIE
Alger
Tunis
LA TUNISIE
LA MER MÉDITERRANÉE
Rabat
LE MAROC
Tripoli
LE LIBAN
LA SYRIE
ISRAËL
L'IRAK
L'IRAN
LA JORDANIE
LE KOWEÏT
Le Caire
BAHREÏN
L'ALGÉRIE
LA LYBIE
L'ÉGYPTE
LES ÉMIRATS ARABES UNIS
L'ARABIE SAOUDITE
OMAN
LE QATAR
LE SAHARA OCCIDENTAL
LA MAURITANIE
LE MALI
LE NIGER
LE TCHAD
OMAN
Nouakchott
Asmara
Khartoum
LE SÉNÉGAL
Dakar
LA GAMBIE
LE BURKINA-FASO
Niamey
L'ÉRYTHRÉE
LE YÉMEN
LE SOUDAN
Bissau
LA GUINÉE
Bamako
Ouagadougou
N'Djamena
DJIBOUTI
Djibouti
LA GUINÉE-BISSAU
LE NIGÉRIA
Conakry
LE GHANA
Abuja
LA SOMALIE
Addis-Abeba
Freetown
Yamoussoukro
Lomé
LE BÉNIN
LA RÉPUBLIQUE CENTRAFRICAINE
L'ÉTHIOPIE
LA SIERRA LEONE
Monrovia
Accra
Porto-Novo
LE CAMEROUN
LA CÔTE D'IVOIRE
LE TOGO
Yaoundé
Bangui
LE LIBÉRIA
L'OUGANDA
LE GABON
Kampala
Muqdisho
LA GUINÉE ÉQUATORIALE
Libreville
LE CONGO
LE RWANDA
LE KENYA
Kigali
Nairobi
LA RÉPUBLIQUE DÉMOCRATIQUE DU CONGO
LES SEYCHELLES
Brazzaville
Bujumbura
Kinshasa
LA TANZANIE
Dar es-Salaam
LE BURUNDI
Luanda
LES COMORES
MAYOTTE
L'ANGOLA
LA ZAMBIE
Lilongwe
LE MALAWI
L'OCÉAN ATLANTIQUE
Lusaka
LE MOZAMBIQUE
MADAGASCAR
Harare
LA NAMIBIE
LE ZIMBABWE
Antananarivo
LE BOTSWANA
Windhoek
MAURICE
Gabarone
Pretoria
Maputo
La Réunion
Mbabane
LE SWAZILAND
Pays francophones
Maseru
L'OCÉAN INDIEN
L'AFRIQUE DU SUD
LE LESOTHO
0
1,000 milles
0
1,000 kilomètres

L'Amérique du Nord et du Sud

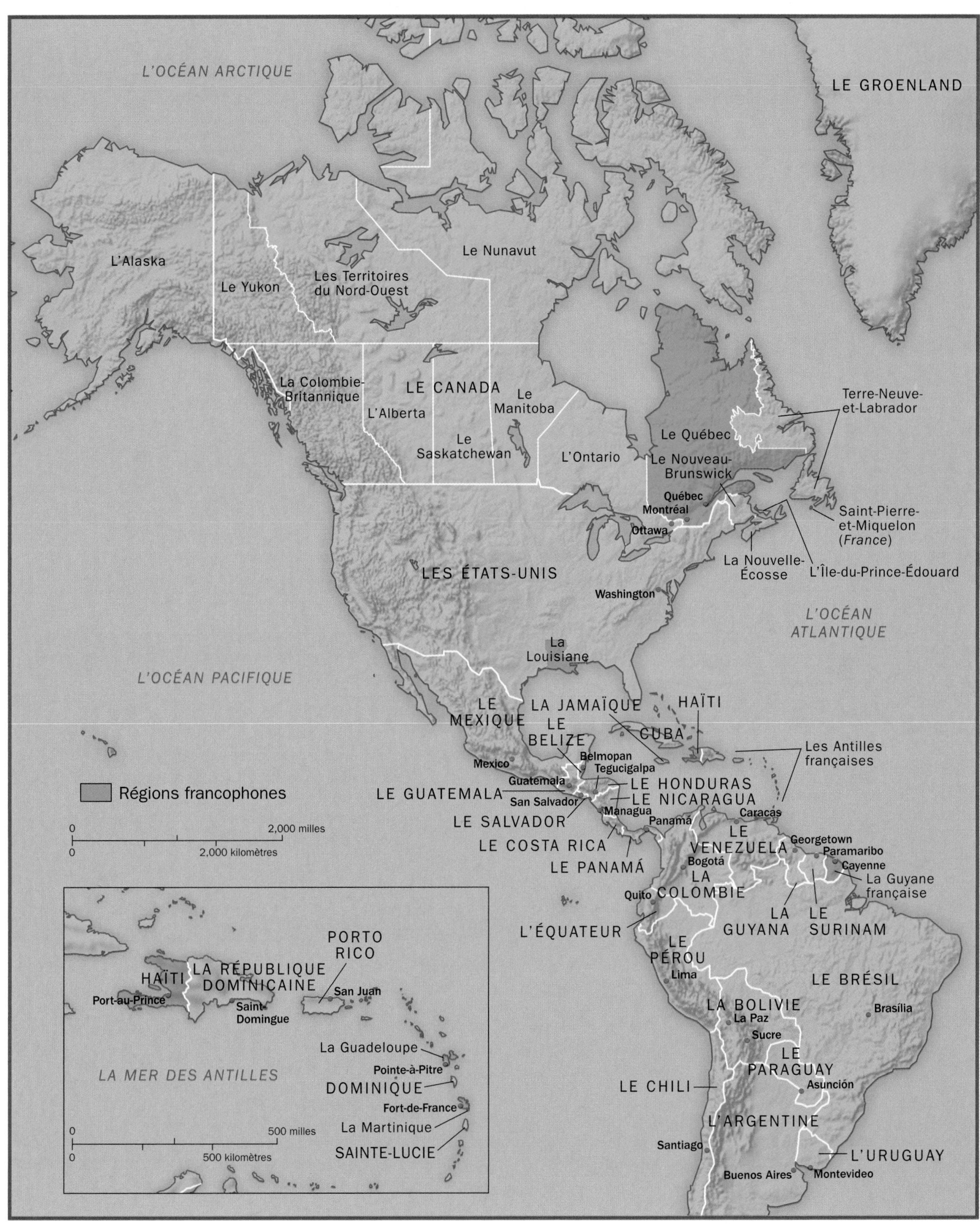
L'OCÉAN ARCTIQUE
LE GROENLAND
L'Alaska
Le Yukon
Les Territoires du Nord-Ouest
Le Nunavut
La Colombie-Britannique
LE CANADA
L'Alberta
Le Manitoba
Le Saskatchewan
L'Ontario
Le Québec
Terre-Neuve-et-Labrador
Le Nouveau-Brunswick
Québec
Montréal
Ottawa
Saint-Pierre-et-Miquelon (France)
La Nouvelle-Écosse
L'Île-du-Prince-Édouard
LES ÉTATS-UNIS
Washington
L'OCÉAN ATLANTIQUE
La Louisiane
L'OCÉAN PACIFIQUE
LE MEXIQUE
LA JAMAÏQUE
HAÏTI
CUBA
LE BELIZE
Belmopan
Tegucigalpa
Les Antilles françaises
Mexico
Guatemala
LE HONDURAS
Régions francophones
LE GUATEMALA
San Salvador
LE NICARAGUA
Managua
Caracas
Panamá
LE SALVADOR
0 2,000 milles
0 2,000 kilomètres
LE COSTA RICA
LE VENEZUELA
Georgetown
Paramaribo
Cayenne
LE PANAMÁ
Bogotá
LA COLOMBIE
La Guyane française
Quito
LA GUYANA
LE SURINAM
L'ÉQUATEUR
LE PÉROU
Lima
LE BRÉSIL
Brasília
LA BOLIVIE
La Paz
Sucre
LE PARAGUAY
Asunción
LE CHILI
L'ARGENTINE
Santiago
L'URUGUAY
Buenos Aires
Montevideo
PORTO RICO
HAÏTI
LA RÉPUBLIQUE DOMINICAINE
Port-au-Prince
Saint-Domingue
San Juan
La Guadeloupe
Pointe-à-Pitre
LA MER DES ANTILLES
DOMINIQUE
Fort-de-France
La Martinique
SAINTE-LUCIE
0 500 milles
0 500 kilomètres

French Terms for Direction Lines and Classroom Use

Mots utiles *Useful words*

une affirmation	*statement, sentence*
une brochure	*brochure*
un brouillon	*draft*
un but	*purpose, goal*
le contenu	*content*
une conversation	*conversation*
le début	*beginning*
le(s) devoir(s)	*homework*
une enquête	*survey*
une étape	*step*
un indice, une piste	*clue*
la lecture	*reading*
un nom	*name*
l'orthographe	*spelling*
un(e) partenaire	*partner*
un personnage	*a character*
la/les personne(s) décrite(s)	*person (people) described*
une phrase complète	*complete sentence*
un point de départ	*starting point*
le prochain examen	*next test*
une pub/publicité	*ad/advertisement; commercial*
une question	*question*
le rapport	*report*
les ressources	*resources*
un sondage	*opinion poll*
la suite	*ending*
le tableau	*blackboard*
un thème, un sujet	*topic*
dans lequel/laquelle/ lesquel(le)s	*in which*
par exemple	*for example*
avant	*before*
chaque	*each*
d'abord	*first*
dernier	*last*
efficace	*efficient*
ensemble	*together*
maintenant	*now*

Verbes utiles *Useful verbs*

ajouter	*to add*
combiner	*to combine*
converser	*to talk; to chat*
créer	*to create*
demander	*to ask*
deviner	*to guess*
dire	*to say*
discuter	*to talk; to discuss*
échanger	*to exchange*
écrire	*to write*
essayer	*to try*
inclure	*to include*
justifier	*to justify*
noter	*to jot down*
raconter	*to tell, to relate (a story)*
relier	*to link*
remplacer	*to replace*
souligner	*to underline*
suivre	*to follow*
traduire	*to translate*
utiliser	*to use*
vérifier	*to check*

Pour parler à vos camarades de classe *To talk with your classmates*

C'est ton tour./C'est mon tour.	*It's your/my turn.*
Épelez./Épelle.	*Spell.*
Je commence./Tu commences.	*I start./You start.*
Je suis d'accord/pas d'accord avec toi.	*I agree/disagree with you.*
Ne me dis pas la réponse.	*Don't tell me the answer.*
Veux-tu travailler avec moi?	*Do you want to work with me?*

Expressions utiles *Useful expressions*

Allez à la page 2.	*Go to page 2.*
Alternez les rôles.	*Switch roles.*
À tour de rôle...	*Take turns...*
À voix haute	*Aloud*
À votre/ton avis	*In your opinion*
Après une deuxième écoute...	*After a second listening...*
Articulez.	*Enunciate.; Pronounce carefully.*
Au sujet de, À propos de	*Regarding, about*
Avec un(e) partenaire/ un(e) camarade de classe	*With a partner/a classmate*
Avez-vous/As-tu des questions?	*Do you have any questions?*
Avez-vous/As-tu fini/terminé?	*Are you done?; Have you finished?*
Chassez l'intrus.	*Choose the item that doesn't belong.*
Choisissez le bon mot.	*Choose the right word.*
Circulez dans la classe.	*Walk around the classroom.*
Comment dit-on ____ en français?	*How do you say ____ in French?*
Comment écrit-on ____ en français?	*How do you spell ____ in French?*
Corrigez les phrases fausses.	*Correct the false statements.*
Créez/Formez des phrases...	*Create/Form sentences...*
D'après vous/Selon vous...	*According to you...*
Décrivez les images/dessins...	*Describe the images/ drawings...*
Désolé(e), j'ai oublié.	*I'm sorry, I forgot.*
Déterminez si...	*Decide whether...*
Dites si vous êtes/Dis si tu es d'accord ou non.	*Say if you agree or not.*
Écrivez une lettre/une phrase.	*Write a letter/a sentence.*
Employez les verbes de la liste.	*Use the verbs from the list.*
En utilisant...	*Using...*
Est-ce que vous pouvez/ tu peux choisir un(e) autre partenaire/ quelqu'un d'autre?	*Can you please choose another partner/ someone else?*
Êtes vous prêt(e)?/ Es-tu prêt(e)?	*Are you ready?*
Excusez-moi, je suis en retard.	*Excuse me for being late.*
Faites correspondre...	*Match...*
Faites les accords nécessaires.	*Make the necessary agreements.*
Félicitations!	*Congratulations!*
Indiquez le mot qui n'appartient pas.	*Indicate the word that doesn't belong.*
Indiquez qui a dit...	*Indicate who said...*
J'ai gagné!/Nous avons gagné!	*I won!/We won!*
Je n'ai pas/Nous n'avons pas encore fini.	*I/We have not finished yet.*
Je ne comprends pas.	*I don't understand.*
Je ne sais pas.	*I don't know.*
Je ne serai pas là demain.	*I won't be here tomorrow.*
Je peux continuer?	*May I continue?*
Jouez le rôle de.../la scène...	*Play the role of.../the scene...*
Lentement, s'il vous plaît.	*Slowly, please.*
Lisez...	*Read...*
Mettez dans l'ordre...	*Put in order...*
Ouvrez/Fermez votre livre.	*Open/Close your books.*
Par groupes de trois/quatre...	*In groups of three/four...*
Partagez vos résultats...	*Share your results...*
Posez-vous les questions suivantes.	*Ask each other the following questions.*
Pour demain, faites...	*For tomorrow, do...*
Pour demain, vous allez/ tu vas faire...	*Tomorrow you are going to do...*
Prononcez.	*Pronounce.*
Qu'est-ce que ____ veut dire?	*What does ____ mean?*
Que pensez-vous/penses-tu de...	*What do you think about...*
Qui a gagné?	*Who won?*
...qui convient le mieux.	*...that best completes/is the most appropriate.*
Rejoignez un autre groupe.	*Get together with another group.*
Remplissez les espaces.	*Fill in the blanks.*
Répondez aux questions suivantes.	*Answer the following questions.*
Soyez prêt(e)s à...	*Be ready to...*
Venez/Viens au tableau.	*Come to the board.*
Vous comprenez?/ Tu comprends?	*Do you understand?*
Vous pouvez expliquer encore une fois, s'il vous plaît?	*Could you explain again, please?*
Vous pouvez répéter, s'il vous plaît?	*Could you repeat that, please?*
Vrai ou faux?	*True or false?*

Glossary of Grammatical Terms

ADJECTIVE A word that modifies, or describes, a noun or pronoun.

des livres **amusants**
*some **funny** books*

un homme **grand**
*a **tall** man*

de **jolies** fleurs
*some **pretty** flowers*

Demonstrative adjective An adjective that specifies which noun a speaker is referring to.

cette chemise
***this** shirt*

ce placard
***this** closet*

cet hôtel
***this** hotel*

ces boîtes
***these** boxes*

Possessive adjective An adjective that indicates ownership or possession.

ma belle montre
***my** beautiful watch*

C'est **son** cousin.
*This is **his/her** cousin.*

tes crayons
***your** pencils*

Ce sont **leurs** tantes.
*Those are **their** aunts.*

ADVERB A word that modifies, or describes, a verb, adjective, or other adverb.

Michael parle **couramment** français.
*Michael speaks French **fluently**.*

Ces enfants sont **vraiment** intelligents.
*These children are **really** smart.*

Elle lui parle **très** franchement.
*She speaks to him **very** candidly.*

ARTICLE A word that points out a noun in either a specific or a non-specific way.

Definite article An article that points out a noun in a specific way.

le marché
***the** market*

la valise
***the** suitcase*

les dictionnaires
***the** dictionaries*

les mots
***the** words*

Indefinite article An article that points out a noun in a general, non-specific way.

un vélo
***a** bike*

une fille
***a** girl*

des oiseaux
***some** birds*

des affiches
***some** posters*

CLAUSE A group of words that contains both a conjugated verb and a subject, either expressed or implied.

Main (or Independent) clause A clause that can stand alone as a complete sentence.

J'ai un manteau vert.
I have a green coat.

Subordinate (or Dependent) clause A clause that does not express a complete thought and therefore cannot stand alone as a sentence.

Je travaille dans un restaurant **parce que j'ai besoin d'argent**.
*I work in a restaurant **because I need money.***

COMPARATIVE A construction used with an adjective or adverb to express a comparison between two people, places, or things.

Thomas est **plus petit** qu'Adrien.
*Thomas is **shorter than** Adrien.*

En Corse, il pleut **moins souvent qu'**en Alsace.
*In Corsica, it rains **less often than** in Alsace.*

Cette maison n'a pas **autant de fenêtres** que l'autre.
*This house does not have **as many windows as** the other one.*

CONJUGATION A set of the forms of a verb for a specific tense or mood, or the process by which these verb forms are presented.

Imparfait conjugation of **chanter**:

je chant**ais**	nous chant**ions**
tu chant**ais**	vous chant**iez**
il/elle chant**ait**	ils/elles chant**aient**

CONJUNCTION A word used to connect words, clauses, or phrases.

Suzanne **et** Pierre habitent en Suisse.
*Suzanne **and** Pierre live in Switzerland.*

Je ne dessine pas très bien, **mais** j'aime les cours de dessin.
*I don't draw very well, **but** I like art classes.*

CONTRACTION The joining of two words into one. In French, the contractions are **au**, **aux**, **du**, and **des**.

Ma sœur est allée **au** concert hier soir.
*My sister went **to a** concert last night.*

Il a parlé **aux** voisins cet après-midi.
*He talked **to the** neighbors this afternoon.*

Je retire de l'argent **du** distributeur automatique.
*I withdraw money **from the** ATM machine.*

Nous avons campé près **du** village.
*We camped **near the** village.*

DIRECT OBJECT A noun or pronoun that directly receives the action of the verb.

Thomas lit **un livre**.	Je **l'**ai vu hier.
*Thomas reads **a book**.*	*I saw **him** yesterday.*

GENDER The grammatical categorizing of certain kinds of words, such as nouns and pronouns, as masculine, feminine, or neuter.

Masculine
articles **le, un**
pronouns **il, lui, le, celui-ci, celui-là, lequel**
adjective **élégant**

Feminine
articles **la, une**
pronouns **elle, la, celle-ci, celle-là, laquelle**
adjective **élégante**

IMPERSONAL EXPRESSION A third-person expression with no expressed or specific subject.

Il pleut.	**C'est** très important.
***It's raining**.*	***It's** very important.*

INDIRECT OBJECT A noun or pronoun that receives the action of the verb indirectly; the object, often a living being, to or for whom an action is performed.

Éric donne un livre **à Linda**.
*Éric gave a book **to Linda**.*

Le professeur **m'**a donné une bonne note.
*The teacher gave **me** a good mark.*

INFINITIVE The basic form of a verb. Infinitives in French end in **-er**, **-ir**, **-oir**, or **-re**.

parler	**finir**	**savoir**	**prendre**
to speak	*to finish*	*to know*	*to take*

INTERROGATIVE An adjective or pronoun used to ask a question.

Qui parle?
***Who** is speaking?*

Combien de biscuits as-tu achetés?
***How many** cookies did you buy?*

Que penses-tu faire aujourd'hui?
***What** do you plan to do today?*

INVERSION Changing the word order of a sentence, often to form a question.

Statement: Elle a vendu sa voiture.

Inversion: A-t-elle vendu sa voiture?

MOOD A grammatical distinction of verbs that indicates whether the verb is intended to make a statement or command or to express a doubt, emotion, or condition contrary to fact.

Conditional mood Verb forms used to express what would be done or what would happen under certain circumstances, or to make a polite request, soften a demand, express what someone could or should do, or to state a contrary-to-fact situation.

Il irait se promener s'il avait le temps.
***He would go** for a walk if he had the time.*

Pourrais-tu éteindre la lumière, s'il te plaît?
***Would you** turn off the light, please?*

Je devrais lui parler gentiment.
***I should** talk to her nicely.*

Imperative mood Verb forms used to make commands or suggestions.

Parle lentement.	**Venez** avec moi.
***Speak** slowly.*	***Come** with me.*

Indicative mood Verb forms used to state facts, actions, and states considered to be real.

Je sais qu'**il a** un chat.
***I know** that **he has** a cat.*

Subjunctive mood Verb forms used principally in subordinate (dependent) clauses to express wishes, desires, emotions, doubts, and certain conditions, such as contrary-to-fact situations.

Il est important que **tu finisses** tes devoirs.
*It's important that **you finish** your homework.*

Je doute que **Louis ait** assez d'argent.
*I doubt that **Louis has** enough money.*

NOUN A word that identifies people, animals, places, things, and ideas.

homme *man*	**chat** *cat*
Belgique *Belgium*	**maison** *house*
amitié *friendship*	**livre** *book*

NUMBER A grammatical term that refers to singular or plural. Nouns in French and English have number. Other parts of a sentence, such as adjectives, articles, and verbs, can also have number.

Singular	**Plural**
une chose ***a*** *thing*	**des** choses ***some*** *things*
le professeur ***the*** *professor*	**les** professeurs ***the*** *professors*

NUMBERS Words that represent amounts.

Cardinal numbers Words that show specific amounts.

cinq minutes
five *minutes*

l'année **deux mille six**
the year ***2006***

Ordinal numbers Words that indicate the order of a noun in a series.

le **quatrième** joueur *the* ***fourth*** *player*	la **dixième** fois *the* ***tenth*** *time*

PAST PARTICIPLE A past form of the verb used in compound tenses. The past participle may also be used as an adjective, but it must then agree in number and gender with the word it modifies.

Ils ont beaucoup **marché**.
They have ***walked*** *a lot.*

Je n'ai pas **préparé** mon examen.
I haven't ***prepared*** *for my exam.*

Il y a une fenêtre **ouverte** dans le salon.
There is an ***open*** *window in the living room.*

PERSON The form of the verb or pronoun that indicates the speaker, the one spoken to, or the one spoken about. In French, as in English, there are three persons: first, second, and third.

Person	**Singular**	**Plural**
1st	**je** *I*	**nous** *we*
2nd	**tu** *you*	**vous** *you*
3rd	**il/elle** *he/she/it* **on** *one*	**ils/elles** *they*

PREPOSITION A word or words that describe(s) the relationship, most often in time or space, between two other words.

Annie habite **loin de** Paris.
Annie lives ***far from*** *Paris.*

Le blouson est **dans** la voiture.
The jacket is ***in*** *the car.*

Martine s'est coiffée **avant de** sortir.
Martine combed her hair ***before*** *going out.*

PRONOUN A word that takes the place of a noun or nouns.

Demonstrative pronoun A pronoun that takes the place of a specific noun.

Je veux **celui-ci**.
I want ***this one.***

Vas-tu acheter **celle-là**?
Are you going to buy ***that one?***

Marc préférait **ceux-là**.
Marc preferred ***those.***

Object pronoun A pronoun that functions as a direct or indirect object of the verb.

Elle **lui** donne un cadeau.
She gives ***him*** *a present.*

Frédéric **me l'**a apporté.
Frédéric brought ***it*** *to* ***me.***

Reflexive pronoun A pronoun that indicates that the action of a verb is performed by the subject on itself. These pronouns are often expressed in English with *-self*: *myself*, *yourself*, etc.

Je **me lave** avant de sortir.
I ***wash (myself)*** *before going out.*

Marie **s'est couchée** à onze heures et demie.
Marie ***went to bed*** *at eleven-thirty.*

Verbs with spelling changes

	Infinitive / Past participle	INDICATIVE					CONDITIONAL	SUBJUNCTIVE	IMPERATIVE
		Subject Pronouns	Present	Passé composé	Imperfect	Future	Present	Present	
7	acheter	j'	achète	ai acheté	achetais	achèterai	achèterais	achète	
	(to buy)	tu	achètes	as acheté	achetais	achèteras	achèterais	achètes	achète
		il/elle/on	achète	a acheté	achetait	achètera	achèterait	achète	
	acheté	nous	achetons	avons acheté	achetions	achèterons	achèterions	achetions	achetons
		vous	achetez	avez acheté	achetiez	achèterez	achèteriez	achetiez	achetez
		ils/elles	achètent	ont acheté	achetaient	achèteront	achèteraient	achètent	
8	appeler	j'	appelle	ai appelé	appelais	appellerai	appellerais	appelle	
	(to call)	tu	appelles	as appelé	appelais	appelleras	appellerais	appelles	appelle
		il/elle/on	appelle	a appelé	appelait	appellera	appellerait	appelle	
	appelé	nous	appelons	avons appelé	appelions	appellerons	appellerions	appelions	appelons
		vous	appelez	avez appelé	appeliez	appellerez	appelleriez	appeliez	appelez
		ils/elles	appellent	ont appelé	appelaient	appelleront	appelleraient	appellent	
9	commencer	je (j')	commence	ai commencé	commençais	commencerai	commencerais	commence	
	(to begin)	tu	commences	as commencé	commençais	commenceras	commencerais	commences	commence
		il/elle/on	commence	a commencé	commençait	commencera	commencerait	commence	
	commencé	nous	commençons	avons commencé	commencions	commencerons	commencerions	commencions	commençons
		vous	commencez	avez commencé	commenciez	commencerez	commenceriez	commenciez	commencez
		ils/elles	commencent	ont commencé	commençaient	commenceront	commenceraient	commencent	
10	essayer	j'	essaie	ai essayé	essayais	essaierai	essaierais	essaie	
	(to try)	tu	essaies	as essayé	essayais	essaieras	essaierais	essaies	essaie
		il/elle/on	essaie	a essayé	essayait	essaiera	essaierait	essaie	
	essayé	nous	essayons	avons essayé	essayions	essaierons	essaierions	essayions	essayons
		vous	essayez	avez essayé	essayiez	essaierez	essaieriez	essayiez	essayez
		ils/elles	essayent	ont essayé	essayaient	essaieront	essaieraient	essaient	
11	manger	je (j')	mange	ai mangé	mangeais	mangerai	mangerais	mange	
	(to eat)	tu	manges	as mangé	mangeais	mangeras	mangerais	manges	mange
		il/elle/on	mange	a mangé	mangeait	mangera	mangerait	mange	
	mangé	nous	mangeons	avons mangé	mangions	mangerons	mangerions	mangions	mangeons
		vous	mangez	avez mangé	mangiez	mangerez	mangeriez	mangiez	mangez
		ils/elles	mangent	ont mangé	mangeaient	mangeront	mangeraient	mangent	

	Infinitive / Past participle	INDICATIVE: Subject Pronouns	INDICATIVE: Present	INDICATIVE: Passé composé	INDICATIVE: Imperfect	INDICATIVE: Future	CONDITIONAL: Present	SUBJUNCTIVE: Present	IMPERATIVE
12	préférer	je (j')	préfère	ai préféré	préférais	préférerai	préférerais	préfère	
	(to prefer)	tu	préfères	as préféré	préférais	préféreras	préférerais	préfères	préfère
		il/elle/on	préfère	a préféré	préférait	préférera	préférerait	préfère	
	préféré	nous	préférons	avons préféré	préférions	préférerons	préférerions	préférions	préférons
		vous	préférez	avez préféré	préfériez	préférerez	préféreriez	préfériez	préférez
		ils/elles	préfèrent	ont préféré	préféraient	préféreront	préféreraient	préfèrent	

Irregular verbs

	Infinitive / Past participle	INDICATIVE: Subject Pronouns	INDICATIVE: Present	INDICATIVE: Passé composé	INDICATIVE: Imperfect	INDICATIVE: Future	CONDITIONAL: Present	SUBJUNCTIVE: Present	IMPERATIVE
13	aller	je (j')	vais	suis allé(e)	allais	irai	irais	aille	
	(to go)	tu	vas	es allé(e)	allais	iras	irais	ailles	va
		il/elle/on	va	est allé(e)	allait	ira	irait	aille	
	allé	nous	allons	sommes allé(e)s	allions	irons	irions	allions	allons
		vous	allez	êtes allé(e)s	alliez	irez	iriez	alliez	allez
		ils/elles	vont	sont allé(e)s	allaient	iront	iraient	aillent	
14	s'asseoir	je	m'assieds	me suis assis(e)	m'asseyais	m'assiérai	m'assiérais	m'asseye	
	(to sit down,	tu	t'assieds	t'es assis(e)	t'asseyais	t'assiéras	t'assiérais	t'asseyes	assieds-toi
	to be seated)	il/elle/on	s'assied	s'est assis(e)	s'asseyait	s'assiéra	s'assiérait	s'asseye	
		nous	nous asseyons	nous sommes assis(e)s	nous asseyions	nous assiérons	nous assiérions	nous asseyions	asseyons-nous
	assis	vous	vous asseyez	vous êtes assis(e)s	vous asseyiez	vous assiérez	vous assiériez	vous asseyiez	asseyez-vous
		ils/elles	s'asseyent	se sont assis(e)s	s'asseyaient	s'assiéront	s'assiéraient	s'asseyent	
15	boire	je (j')	bois	ai bu	buvais	boirai	boirais	boive	
	(to drink)	tu	bois	as bu	buvais	boiras	boirais	boives	bois
		il/elle/on	boit	a bu	buvait	boira	boirait	boive	
	bu	nous	buvons	avons bu	buvions	boirons	boirions	buvions	buvons
		vous	buvez	avez bu	buviez	boirez	boiriez	buviez	buvez
		ils/elles	boivent	ont bu	buvaient	boiront	boiraient	boivent	

	Infinitive / Past participle	INDICATIVE					CONDITIONAL	SUBJUNCTIVE	IMPERATIVE
		Subject Pronouns	Present	Passé composé	Imperfect	Future	Present	Present	
16	conduire	je (j')	conduis	ai conduit	conduisais	conduirai	conduirais	conduise	
	(to drive; to lead)	tu	conduis	as conduit	conduisais	conduiras	conduirais	conduises	conduis
		il/elle/on	conduit	a conduit	conduisait	conduira	conduirait	conduise	
	conduit	nous	conduisons	avons conduit	conduisions	conduirons	conduirions	conduisions	conduisons
		vous	conduisez	avez conduit	conduisiez	conduirez	conduiriez	conduisiez	conduisez
		ils/elles	conduisent	ont conduit	conduisaient	conduiront	conduiraient	conduisent	
17	connaître	je (j')	connais	ai connu	connaissais	connaîtrai	connaîtrais	connaisse	
	(to know, to be	tu	connais	as connu	connaissais	connaîtras	connaîtrais	connaisses	connais
	acquainted with)	il/elle/on	connaît	a connu	connaissait	connaîtra	connaîtrait	connaisse	
		nous	connaissons	avons connu	connaissions	connaîtrons	connaîtrions	connaissions	connaissons
	connu	vous	connaissez	avez connu	connaissiez	connaîtrez	connaîtriez	connaissiez	connaissez
		ils/elles	connaissent	ont connu	connaissaient	connaîtront	connaîtraient	connaissent	
18	courir	je (j')	cours	ai couru	courais	courrai	courrais	coure	
	(to run)	tu	cours	as couru	courais	courras	courrais	coures	cours
		il/elle/on	court	a couru	courait	courra	courrait	coure	
	couru	nous	courons	avons couru	courions	courrons	courrions	courions	courons
		vous	courez	avez couru	couriez	courrez	courriez	couriez	courez
		ils/elles	courent	ont couru	couraient	courront	courraient	courent	
19	croire	je (j')	crois	ai cru	croyais	croirai	croirais	croie	
	(to believe)	tu	crois	as cru	croyais	croiras	croirais	croies	crois
		il/elle/on	croit	a cru	croyait	croira	croirait	croie	
	cru	nous	croyons	avons cru	croyions	croirons	croirions	croyions	croyons
		vous	croyez	avez cru	croyiez	croirez	croiriez	croyiez	croyez
		ils/elles	croient	ont cru	croyaient	croiront	croiraient	croient	
20	devoir	je (j')	dois	ai dû	devais	devrai	devrais	doive	
	(to have to; to owe)	tu	dois	as dû	devais	devras	devrais	doives	dois
		il/elle/on	doit	a dû	devait	devra	devrait	doive	
	dû	nous	devons	avons dû	devions	devrons	devrions	devions	devons
		vous	devez	avez dû	deviez	devrez	devriez	deviez	devez
		ils/elles	doivent	ont dû	devaient	devront	devraient	doivent	

	Infinitive / Past participle	INDICATIVE						CONDITIONAL	SUBJUNCTIVE	IMPERATIVE
		Subject Pronouns	Present	Passé composé	Imperfect	Future		Present	Present	
21	dire	je (j')	dis	ai dit	disais	dirai		dirais	dise	
	(to say, to tell)	tu	dis	as dit	disais	diras		dirais	dises	dis
		il/elle/on	dit	a dit	disait	dira		dirait	dise	
	dit	nous	disons	avons dit	disions	dirons		dirions	disions	disons
		vous	dites	avez dit	disiez	direz		diriez	disiez	dites
		ils/elles	disent	ont dit	disaient	diront		diraient	disent	
22	écrire	j'	écris	ai écrit	écrivais	écrirai		écrirais	écrive	
	(to write)	tu	écris	as écrit	écrivais	écriras		écrirais	écrives	écris
		il/elle/on	écrit	a écrit	écrivait	écrira		écrirait	écrive	
	écrit	nous	écrivons	avons écrit	écrivions	écrirons		écririons	écrivions	écrivons
		vous	écrivez	avez écrit	écriviez	écrirez		écririez	écriviez	écrivez
		ils/elles	écrivent	ont écrit	écrivaient	écriront		écriraient	écrivent	
23	envoyer	j'	envoie	ai envoyé	envoyais	enverrai		enverrais	envoie	
	(to send)	tu	envoies	as envoyé	envoyais	enverras		enverrais	envoies	envoie
		il/elle/on	envoie	a envoyé	envoyait	enverra		enverrait	envoie	
	envoyé	nous	envoyons	avons envoyé	envoyions	enverrons		enverrions	envoyions	envoyons
		vous	envoyez	avez envoyé	envoyiez	enverrez		enverriez	envoyiez	envoyez
		ils/elles	envoient	ont envoyé	envoyaient	enverront		enverraient	envoient	
24	éteindre	j'	éteins	ai éteint	éteignais	éteindrai		éteindrais	éteigne	
	(to turn off)	tu	éteins	as éteint	éteignais	éteindras		éteindrais	éteignes	éteins
		il/elle/on	éteint	a éteint	éteignait	éteindra		éteindrait	éteigne	
	éteint	nous	éteignons	avons éteint	éteignions	éteindrons		éteindrions	éteignions	éteignons
		vous	éteignez	avez éteint	éteigniez	éteindrez		éteindriez	éteigniez	éteignez
		ils/elles	éteignent	ont éteint	éteignaient	éteindront		éteindraient	éteignent	
25	faire	je (j')	fais	ai fait	faisais	ferai		ferais	fasse	
	(to do; to make)	tu	fais	as fait	faisais	feras		ferais	fasses	fais
		il/elle/on	fait	a fait	faisait	fera		ferait	fasse	
	fait	nous	faisons	avons fait	faisions	ferons		ferions	fassions	faisons
		vous	faites	avez fait	faisiez	ferez		feriez	fassiez	faites
		ils/elles	font	ont fait	faisaient	feront		feraient	fassent	
26	falloir	il	faut	a fallu	fallait	faudra		faudrait	faille	
	(to be necessary)									
	fallu									

	Infinitive / Past participle	INDICATIVE						CONDITIONAL	SUBJUNCTIVE	IMPERATIVE
		Subject Pronouns	Present	Passé composé	Imperfect	Future		Present	Present	
27	lire	je (j')	lis	ai lu	lisais	lirai		lirais	lise	
	(to read)	tu	lis	as lu	lisais	liras		lirais	lises	lis
		il/elle/on	lit	a lu	lisait	lira		lirait	lise	
	lu	nous	lisons	avons lu	lisions	lirons		lirions	lisions	lisons
		vous	lisez	avez lu	lisiez	lirez		liriez	lisiez	lisez
		ils/elles	lisent	ont lu	lisaient	liront		liraient	lisent	
28	mettre	je (j')	mets	ai mis	mettais	mettrai		mettrais	mette	
	(to put)	tu	mets	as mis	mettais	mettras		mettrais	mettes	mets
		il/elle/on	met	a mis	mettait	mettra		mettrait	mette	
	mis	nous	mettons	avons mis	mettions	mettrons		mettrions	mettions	mettons
		vous	mettez	avez mis	mettiez	mettrez		mettriez	mettiez	mettez
		ils/elles	mettent	ont mis	mettaient	mettront		mettraient	mettent	
29	mourir	je	meurs	suis mort(e)	mourais	mourrai		mourrais	meure	
	(to die)	tu	meurs	es mort(e)	mourais	mourras		mourrais	meures	meurs
		il/elle/on	meurt	est mort(e)	mourait	mourra		mourrait	meure	
	mort	nous	mourons	sommes mort(e)s	mourions	mourrons		mourrions	mourions	mourons
		vous	mourez	êtes mort(e)s	mouriez	mourrez		mourriez	mouriez	mourez
		ils/elles	meurent	sont mort(e)s	mouraient	mourront		mourraient	meurent	
30	naître	je	nais	suis né(e)	naissais	naîtrai		naîtrais	naisse	
	(to be born)	tu	nais	es né(e)	naissais	naîtras		naîtrais	naisses	nais
		il/elle/on	naît	est né(e)	naissait	naîtra		naîtrait	naisse	
	né	nous	naissons	sommes né(e)s	naissions	naîtrons		naîtrions	naissions	naissons
		vous	naissez	êtes né(e)s	naissiez	naîtrez		naîtriez	naissiez	naissez
		ils/elles	naissent	sont né(e)s	naissaient	naîtront		naîtraient	naissent	
31	ouvrir	j'	ouvre	ai ouvert	ouvrais	ouvrirai		ouvrirais	ouvre	
	(to open)	tu	ouvres	as ouvert	ouvrais	ouvriras		ouvrirais	ouvres	ouvre
		il/elle/on	ouvre	a ouvert	ouvrait	ouvrira		ouvrirait	ouvre	
	ouvert	nous	ouvrons	avons ouvert	ouvrions	ouvrirons		ouvririons	ouvrions	ouvrons
		vous	ouvrez	avez ouvert	ouvriez	ouvrirez		ouvririez	ouvriez	ouvrez
		ils/elles	ouvrent	ont ouvert	ouvraient	ouvriront		ouvriraient	ouvrent	

	Infinitive / Past participle	INDICATIVE: Subject Pronouns	INDICATIVE: Present	INDICATIVE: Passé composé	INDICATIVE: Imperfect	INDICATIVE: Future	CONDITIONAL: Present	SUBJUNCTIVE: Present	IMPERATIVE
32	partir	je	pars	suis parti(e)	partais	partirai	partirais	parte	
	(to leave)	tu	pars	es parti(e)	partais	partiras	partirais	partes	pars
		il/elle/on	part	est parti(e)	partait	partira	partirait	parte	
	parti	nous	partons	sommes parti(e)s	partions	partirons	partirions	partions	partons
		vous	partez	êtes parti(e)(s)	partiez	partirez	partiriez	partiez	partez
		ils/elles	partent	sont parti(e)s	partaient	partiront	partiraient	partent	
33	pleuvoir	il	pleut	a plu	pleuvait	pleuvra	pleuvrait	pleuve	
	(to rain)								
	plu								
34	pouvoir	je (j')	peux	ai pu	pouvais	pourrai	pourrais	puisse	
	(to be able)	tu	peux	as pu	pouvais	pourras	pourrais	puisses	
		il/elle/on	peut	a pu	pouvait	pourra	pourrait	puisse	
	pu	nous	pouvons	avons pu	pouvions	pourrons	pourrions	puissions	
		vous	pouvez	avez pu	pouviez	pourrez	pourriez	puissiez	
		ils/elles	peuvent	ont pu	pouvaient	pourront	pourraient	puissent	
35	prendre	je (j')	prends	ai pris	prenais	prendrai	prendrais	prenne	
	(to take)	tu	prends	as pris	prenais	prendras	prendrais	prennes	prends
		il/elle/on	prend	a pris	prenait	prendra	prendrait	prenne	
	pris	nous	prenons	avons pris	prenions	prendrons	prendrions	prenions	prenons
		vous	prenez	avez pris	preniez	prendrez	prendriez	preniez	prenez
		ils/elles	prennent	ont pris	prenaient	prendront	prendraient	prennent	
36	recevoir	je (j')	reçois	ai reçu	recevais	recevrai	recevrais	reçoive	
	(to receive)	tu	reçois	as reçu	recevais	recevras	recevrais	reçoives	reçois
		il/elle/on	reçoit	a reçu	recevait	recevra	recevrait	reçoive	
	reçu	nous	recevons	avons reçu	recevions	recevrons	recevrions	recevions	recevons
		vous	recevez	avez reçu	receviez	recevrez	recevriez	receviez	recevez
		ils/elles	reçoivent	ont reçu	recevaient	recevront	recevraient	reçoivent	
37	rire	je (j')	ris	ai ri	riais	rirai	rirais	rie	
	(to laugh)	tu	ris	as ri	riais	riras	rirais	ries	ris
		il/elle/on	rit	a ri	riait	rira	rirait	rie	
	ri	nous	rions	avons ri	riions	rirons	ririons	riions	rions
		vous	riez	avez ri	riiez	rirez	ririez	riiez	riez
		ils/elles	rient	ont ri	riaient	riront	riraient	rient	

	Infinitive / Past participle	INDICATIVE: Subject Pronouns	INDICATIVE: Present	INDICATIVE: Passé composé	INDICATIVE: Imperfect	INDICATIVE: Future	CONDITIONAL: Present	SUBJUNCTIVE: Present	IMPERATIVE
38	savoir	je (j')	sais	ai su	savais	saurai	saurais	sache	
	(to know)	tu	sais	as su	savais	sauras	saurais	saches	sache
		il/elle/on	sait	a su	savait	saura	saurait	sache	
	su	nous	savons	avons su	savions	saurons	saurions	sachions	sachons
		vous	savez	avez su	saviez	saurez	sauriez	sachiez	sachez
		ils/elles	savent	ont su	savaient	sauront	sauraient	sachent	
39	suivre	je (j')	suis	ai suivi	suivais	suivrai	suivrais	suive	
	(to follow)	tu	suis	as suivi	suivais	suivras	suivrais	suives	suis
		il/elle/on	suit	a suivi	suivait	suivra	suivrait	suive	
	suivi	nous	suivons	avons suivi	suivions	suivrons	suivrions	suivions	suivons
		vous	suivez	avez suivi	suiviez	suivrez	suivriez	suiviez	suivez
		ils/elles	suivent	ont suivi	suivaient	suivront	suivraient	suivent	
40	tenir	je (j')	tiens	ai tenu	tenais	tiendrai	tiendrais	tienne	
	(to hold)	tu	tiens	as tenu	tenais	tiendras	tiendrais	tiennes	tiens
		il/elle/on	tient	a tenu	tenait	tiendra	tiendrait	tienne	
	tenu	nous	tenons	avons tenu	tenions	tiendrons	tiendrions	tenions	tenons
		vous	tenez	avez tenu	teniez	tiendrez	tiendriez	teniez	tenez
		ils/elles	tiennent	ont tenu	tenaient	tiendront	tiendraient	tiennent	
41	venir	je	viens	suis venu(e)	venais	viendrai	viendrais	vienne	
	(to come)	tu	viens	es venu(e)	venais	viendras	viendrais	viennes	viens
		il/elle/on	vient	est venu(e)	venait	viendra	viendrait	vienne	
	venu	nous	venons	sommes venu(e)s	venions	viendrons	viendrions	venions	venons
		vous	venez	êtes venu(e)(s)	veniez	viendrez	viendriez	veniez	venez
		ils/elles	viennent	sont venu(e)s	venaient	viendront	viendraient	viennent	
42	voir	je (j')	vois	ai vu	voyais	verrai	verrais	voie	
	(to see)	tu	vois	as vu	voyais	verras	verrais	voies	vois
		il/elle/on	voit	a vu	voyait	verra	verrait	voie	
	vu	nous	voyons	avons vu	voyions	verrons	verrions	voyions	voyons
		vous	voyez	avez vu	voyiez	verrez	verriez	voyiez	voyez
		ils/elles	voient	ont vu	voyaient	verront	verraient	voient	
43	vouloir	je (j')	veux	ai voulu	voulais	voudrai	voudrais	veuille	
	(to want, to wish)	tu	veux	as voulu	voulais	voudras	voudrais	veuilles	veuille
		il/elle/on	veut	a voulu	voulait	voudra	voudrait	veuille	
	voulu	nous	voulons	avons voulu	voulions	voudrons	voudrions	voulions	veuillons
		vous	voulez	avez voulu	vouliez	voudrez	voudriez	vouliez	veuillez
		ils/elles	veulent	ont voulu	voulaient	voudront	voudraient	veuillent	

Guide to Vocabulary

Abbreviations used in this glossary

adj.	adjective	*form.*	formal	*p.p.*	past participle
adv.	adverb	*imp.*	imperative	*pl.*	plural
art.	article	*indef.*	indefinite	*poss.*	possessive
comp.	comparative	*interj.*	interjection	*prep.*	preposition
conj.	conjunction	*interr.*	interrogative	*pron.*	pronoun
def.	definite	*inv.*	invariable	*refl.*	reflexive
dem.	demonstrative	*i.o.*	indirect object	*rel.*	relative
disj.	disjunctive	*m.*	masculine	*sing.*	singular
d.o.	direct object	*n.*	noun	*sub.*	subject
f.	feminine	*obj.*	object	*super.*	superlative
fam.	familiar	*part.*	partitive	*v.*	verb

French-English

A

à *prep.* at; in; to 4
À bientôt. See you soon. 1
à condition que on the condition that, provided that 15
à côté de *prep.* next to 3
À demain. See you tomorrow. 1
à droite (de) *prep.* to the right (of) 3
à gauche (de) *prep.* to the left (of) 3
à ... heure(s) at ... (o'clock) 4
à la radio on the radio 15
à la télé(vision) on television 15
à l'automne in the fall 5
à l'étranger abroad, overseas 7
à mi-temps half-time (*job*) 13
à moins que unless 15
à plein temps full-time (*job*) 13
À plus tard. See you later. 1
À quelle heure? What time?; When? 2
À qui? To whom? 4
À table! Let's eat! Food is on! 9
à temps partiel part-time (*job*) 13
À tout à l'heure. See you later. 1
au bout (de) *prep.* at the end (of) 12
au contraire on the contrary 15
au fait by the way 3
au printemps in the spring 5
Au revoir. Good-bye. 1
au secours help 11
au sujet de on the subject of, about 14
abolir *v.* to abolish 14
absolument *adv.* absolutely 8
accident *m.* accident 11
avoir un accident to have/to be in an accident 11
accompagner *v.* to accompany 12
acheter *v.* to buy 5
acteur *m.* actor 1
actif/active *adj.* active 3
activement *adv.* actively 8
actrice *f.* actress 1
addition *f.* check, bill 4
adieu farewell 14
adolescence *f.* adolescence 6
adorer *v.* to love 2
J'adore... I love... 2
adresse *f.* address 12
aérobic *m.* aerobics 5
faire de l'aérobic *v.* to do aerobics 5
aéroport *m.* airport 7
affaires *f., pl.* business 3
affiche *f.* poster 8
afficher *v.* to post 13
âge *m.* age 6
âge adulte *m.* adulthood 6
agence de voyages *f.* travel agency 7
agent *m.* officer; agent 11
agent de police *m.* police officer 11
agent de voyages *m.* travel agent 7
agent immobilier *m.* real estate agent 13
agréable *adj.* pleasant 1
agriculteur/agricultrice *m., f.* farmer 13
aider (à) *v.* to help (*to do something*) 5
aie (avoir) *imp. v.* have 7
ail *m.* garlic 9
aimer *v.* to like 2
aimer mieux to prefer 2
aimer que... to like that... 14
J'aime bien... I really like... 2
Je n'aime pas tellement... I don't like ... very much. 2
aîné(e) *adj.* elder 3
algérien(ne) *adj.* Algerian 1
aliment *m.* food; a food 9
Allemagne *f.* Germany 7
allemand(e) *adj.* German 1
aller *v.* to go 4
aller à la pêche to go fishing 5
aller aux urgences to go to the emergency room 10
aller avec to go with 6
aller-retour *adj.* round-trip 7
billet aller-retour *m.* round-trip ticket 7
Allons-y! Let's go! 2
Ça va? What's up?; How are things? 1
Comment allez-vous? *form.* How are you? 1
Comment vas-tu? *fam.* How are you? 1
Je m'en vais. I'm leaving. 8
Je vais bien/mal. I am doing well/badly. 1
J'y vais. I'm going/coming. 8
Nous y allons. We're going/coming. 9
allergie *f.* allergy 10
allô (*on the phone*) hello 1
allumer *v.* to turn on 11

alors *adv.* so, then; at that moment 2
améliorer *v.* to improve 13
amende *f.* fine 11
amener *v.* to bring (*someone*) 5
américain(e) *adj.* American 1
football américain *m.* football 5
ami(e) *m., f.* friend 1
petit(e) ami(e) *m., f.* boyfriend/girlfriend 1
amitié *f.* friendship 6
amour *m.* love 6
amoureux/amoureuse *adj.* in love 6
tomber amoureux/amoureuse *v.* to fall in love 6
amusant(e) *adj.* fun 1
an *m.* year 2
ancien(ne) *adj.* ancient, old; former 15
ange *m.* angel 1
anglais(e) *adj.* English 1
angle *m.* corner 12
Angleterre *f.* England 7
animal *m.* animal 14
année *f.* year 2
cette année this year 2
anniversaire *m.* birthday 5
C'est quand l'anniversaire de … ? When is …'s birthday? 5
C'est quand ton/votre anniversaire? When is your birthday? 5
annuler (une réservation) *v.* to cancel (a reservation) 7
anorak *m.* ski jacket, parka 6
antipathique *adj.* unpleasant 3
août *m.* August 5
apercevoir *v.* to see, to catch sight of 12
aperçu (apercevoir) *p.p.* seen, caught sight of 12
appareil *m.* (on the phone) telephone 13
appareil (électrique/ménager) *m.* (electrical/household) appliance 8
appareil photo (numérique) *m.* (digital) camera 11
C'est M./Mme/Mlle … à l'appareil. It's Mr./Mrs./Miss … on the phone. 13
Qui est à l'appareil? Who's calling, please? 13
appartement *m.* apartment 7
appeler *v.* to call 13
applaudir *v.* to applaud 15
applaudissement *m.* applause 15
apporter *v.* to bring (*something*) 4
apprendre (à) *v.* to teach; to learn (*to do something*) 4
appris (apprendre) *p.p., adj.* learned 6
après (que) *adv.* after 2
après-demain *adv.* day after tomorrow 2
après-midi *m.* afternoon 2
cet après-midi this afternoon 2
de l'après-midi in the afternoon 2
demain après-midi *adv.* tomorrow afternoon 2
hier après-midi *adv.* yesterday afternoon 7
arbre *m.* tree 14
architecte *m., f.* architect 3
architecture *f.* architecture 2
argent *m.* money 12
dépenser de l'argent *v.* to spend money 4
déposer de l'argent *v.* to deposit money 12
retirer de l'argent *v.* to withdraw money 12
armoire *f.* armoire, wardrobe 8
arrêt d'autobus (de bus) *m.* bus stop 7
arrêter (de faire quelque chose) *v.* to stop (doing something) 11
arrivée *f.* arrival 7
arriver (à) *v.* to arrive; to manage (*to do something*) 2
art *m.* art 2
beaux-arts *m., pl.* fine arts 15
artiste *m., f.* artist 3
ascenseur *m.* elevator 7
aspirateur *m.* vacuum cleaner 8
passer l'aspirateur to vacuum 8
aspirine *f.* aspirin 10
Asseyez-vous! (s'asseoir) *imp. v.* Have a seat! 10
assez *adv.* *(before adjective or adverb)* pretty; quite 8
assez (de) *(before noun)* enough (of) 4
pas assez (de) not enough (of) 4
assiette *f.* plate 9
assis (s'asseoir) *p.p., adj.* *(used as past participle)* sat down; (*used as adjective*) sitting, seated 10
assister *v.* to attend 2
assurance (maladie/vie) *f.* (health/life) insurance 13
athlète *m., f.* athlete 3
attacher *v.* to attach 11
attacher sa ceinture de sécurité to buckle one's seatbelt 11
attendre *v.* to wait 6
attention *f.* attention 5
faire attention (à) *v.* to pay attention (to) 5
au (à + le) *prep.* to/at the 4
auquel (à + lequel) *pron., m., sing.* which one 13
auberge de jeunesse *f.* youth hostel 7
aucun(e) *adj.* no; *pron.* none 10
ne… aucun(e) none, not any 12
augmentation (de salaire) *f.* raise (in salary) 13
aujourd'hui *adv.* today 2
aussi *adv.* too, as well; as 1
Moi aussi. Me too. 1
aussi … que *(used with an adjective)* as … as 9
autant de … que *adv.* *(used with noun to express quantity)* as much/as many … as 14
auteur/femme auteur *m., f.* author 15
autobus *m.* bus 7
arrêt d'autobus (de bus) *m.* bus stop 7
prendre un autobus to take a bus 7
automne *m.* fall 5
à l'automne in the fall 5
autoroute *f.* highway 11
autour (de) *prep.* around 12
autrefois *adv.* in the past 8
aux (à + les) to/at the 4
auxquelles (à + lesquelles) *pron., f., pl.* which ones 13
auxquels (à + lesquels) *pron., m., pl.* which ones 13
avance *f.* advance 2
en avance *adv.* early 2
avant (de/que) *adv.* before 7
avant-hier *adv.* day before yesterday 7
avec *prep.* with 1
Avec qui? With whom? 4
aventure *f.* adventure 15
film d'aventures *m.* adventure film 15
avenue *f.* avenue 12
avion *m.* airplane 7
prendre un avion *v.* to take a plane 7
avocat(e) *m., f.* lawyer 3
avoir *v.* to have 2
aie *imp. v.* have 7
avoir besoin (de) to need (*something*) 2
avoir chaud to be hot 2

avoir de la chance to be lucky 2
avoir envie (de) to feel like (*doing something*) 2
avoir faim to be hungry 4
avoir froid to be cold 2
avoir honte (de) to be ashamed (of) 2
avoir mal to have an ache 10
avoir mal au cœur to feel nauseated 10
avoir peur (de/que) to be afraid (of/that) 2
avoir raison to be right 2
avoir soif to be thirsty 4
avoir sommeil to be sleepy 2
avoir tort to be wrong 2
avoir un accident to have/to be in an accident 11
avoir un compte bancaire to have a bank account 12
en avoir marre to be fed up 3
avril *m.* April 5
ayez (avoir) *imp. v.* have 7
ayons (avoir) *imp. v.* let's have 7

B

bac(calauréat) *m.* an important exam taken by high-school students in France 2
baguette *f.* baguette 4
baignoire *f.* bathtub 8
bain *m.* bath 6
salle de bains *f.* bathroom 8
baladeur CD *m.* personal CD player 11
balai *m.* broom 8
balayer *v.* to sweep 8
balcon *m.* balcony 8
banane *f.* banana 9
banc *m.* bench 12
bancaire *adj.* banking 12
avoir un compte bancaire *v.* to have a bank account 12
bande dessinée (B.D.) *f.* comic strip 5
banlieue *f.* suburbs 4
banque *f.* bank 12
banquier/banquière *m., f.* banker 13
barbant *adj.*, **barbe** *f.* drag 3
baseball *m.* baseball 5
basket(-ball) *m.* basketball 5
baskets *f., pl.* tennis shoes 6
bateau *m.* boat 7
prendre un bateau *v.* to take a boat 7
bateau-mouche *m.* riverboat 7
bâtiment *m.* building 12
batterie *f.* drums 15
bavarder *v.* to chat 4
beau (belle) *adj.* handsome; beautiful 3
faire quelque chose de beau *v.* to be up to something interesting 12
Il fait beau. The weather is nice. 5
beaucoup (de) *adv.* a lot (of) 4
Merci (beaucoup). Thank you (very much). 1
beau-frère *m.* brother-in-law 3
beau-père *m.* father-in-law; stepfather 3
beaux-arts *m., pl.* fine arts 15
belge *adj.* Belgian 7
Belgique *f.* Belgium 7
belle *adj., f.* (*feminine form of* **beau**) beautiful 3
belle-mère *f.* mother-in-law; stepmother 3
belle-sœur *f.* sister-in-law 3
besoin *m.* need 2
avoir besoin (de) to need (*something*) 2
beurre *m.* butter 4
bibliothèque *f.* library 1
bien *adv.* well 7
bien sûr *adv.* of course 2
Je vais bien. I am doing well. 1
Très bien. Very well. 1
bientôt *adv.* soon 1
À bientôt. See you soon. 1
bienvenu(e) *adj.* welcome 1
bière *f.* beer 6
bijouterie *f.* jewelry store 12
billet *m.* (*travel*) ticket 7; (*money*) bills, notes 12
billet aller-retour *m.* round-trip ticket 7
biologie *f.* biology 2
biscuit *m.* cookie 6
blague *f.* joke 2
blanc(he) *adj.* white 6
blessure *f.* injury, wound 10
bleu(e) *adj.* blue 3
blond(e) *adj.* blonde 3
blouson *m.* jacket 6
bœuf *m.* beef 9
boire *v.* to drink 4
bois *m.* wood 14
boisson (gazeuse) *f.* (carbonated) drink/beverage 4
boîte *f.* box; can 9
boîte aux lettres *f.* mailbox 12
boîte de conserve *f.* can (of food) 9
boîte de nuit *f.* nightclub 4
bol *m.* bowl 9
bon(ne) *adj.* kind; good 3
bon marché *adj.* inexpensive 6
Il fait bon. The weather is good/warm. 5
bonbon *m.* candy 6
bonheur *m.* happiness 6
Bonjour. Good morning.; Hello. 1
Bonsoir. Good evening.; Hello. 1
bouche *f.* mouth 10
boucherie *f.* butcher's shop 9
boulangerie *f.* bread shop, bakery 9
boulevard *m.* boulevard 12
suivre un boulevard *v.* to follow a boulevard 12
bourse *f.* scholarship, grant 2
bout *m.* end 12
au bout (de) *prep.* at the end (of) 12
bouteille (de) *f.* bottle (of) 4
boutique *f.* boutique, store 12
bras *m.* arm 10
brasserie *f.* café; restaurant 12
Brésil *m.* Brazil 7
brésilien(ne) *adj.* Brazilian 7
bricoler *v.* to tinker; to do odd jobs 5
brillant(e) *adj.* bright 1
bronzer *v.* to tan 6
brosse (à cheveux/à dents) *f.* (hair/tooth)brush 10
brun(e) *adj.* (*hair*) dark 3
bu (boire) *p.p.* drunk 6
bureau *m.* desk; office 1
bureau de poste *m.* post office 12
bus *m.* bus 7
arrêt d'autobus (de bus) *m.* bus stop 7
prendre un bus *v.* to take a bus 7

C

ça *pron.* that; this; it 1
Ça dépend. It depends. 4
Ça ne nous regarde pas. That has nothing to do with us.; That is none of our business. 14
Ça suffit. That's enough. 5
Ça te dit? Does that appeal to you? 14
Ça va? What's up?; How are things? 1
ça veut dire that is to say 10
Comme ci, comme ça. So-so. 1
cabine téléphonique *f.* phone booth 12
cadeau *m.* gift 6
paquet cadeau wrapped gift 6
cadet(te) *adj.* younger 3
cadre/femme cadre *m., f.*

executive 13
café *m.* café; coffee 1
terrasse de café *f.* café terrace 4
cuillère à café *f.* teaspoon 9
cafetière *f.* coffeemaker 8
cahier *m.* notebook 1
calculatrice *f.* calculator 1
calme *adj.* calm 1; *m.* calm 1
camarade *m., f.* friend 1
camarade de chambre *m., f.* roommate 1
camarade de classe *m., f.* classmate 1
caméra vidéo *f.* camcorder 11
caméscope *m.* camcorder 11
campagne *f.* country(side) 7
pain de campagne *m.* country-style bread 4
pâté (de campagne) *m.* pâté, meat spread 9
camping *m.* camping 5
faire du camping *v.* to go camping 5
Canada *m.* Canada 7
canadien(ne) *adj.* Canadian 1
canapé *m.* couch 8
candidat(e) *m., f.* candidate; applicant 13
cantine *f.* cafeteria 9
capitale *f.* capital 7
capot *m.* hood 11
carafe (d'eau) *f.* pitcher (of water) 9
carotte *f.* carrot 9
carrefour *m.* intersection 12
carrière *f.* career 13
carte *f.* map 1; menu 9; card 12
payer avec une carte de crédit to pay with a credit card 12
carte postale *f.* postcard 12
cartes *f. pl.* (*playing*) cards 5
casquette *f.* (baseball) cap 6
catastrophe *f.* catastrophe 14
cave *f.* basement, cellar 8
CD *m.* CD(s) 11
CD-ROM *m.* CD-ROM(s) 11
ce *dem. adj., m., sing.* this; that 6
ce matin this morning 2
ce mois-ci this month 2
Ce n'est pas grave. It's no big deal. 6
ce soir this evening 2
ce sont... those are... 1
ce week-end this weekend 2
cédérom(s) *m.* CD-ROM(s) 11
ceinture *f.* belt 6
attacher sa ceinture de sécurité *v.* to buckle one's seatbelt 11
célèbre *adj.* famous 15
célébrer *v.* to celebrate 5
célibataire *adj.* single 3
celle *pron., f., sing.* this one; that one; the one 14
celles *pron., f., pl.* these; those; the ones 14
celui *pron., m., sing.* this one; that one; the one 14
cent *m.* one hundred 3
cent mille *m.* one hundred thousand 5
cent un *m.* one hundred one 5
cinq cents *m.* five hundred 5
centième *adj.* hundredth 7
centrale nucléaire *f.* nuclear plant 14
centre commercial *m.* shopping center, mall 4
centre-ville *m.* city/town center, downtown 4
certain(e) *adj.* certain 9
Il est certain que... It is certain that... 15
Il n'est pas certain que... It is uncertain that... 15
ces *dem. adj., m., f., pl.* these; those 6
c'est... it/that is... 1
C'est de la part de qui? On behalf of whom? 13
C'est le 1er (premier) octobre. It is October first. 5
C'est M./Mme/Mlle ... (à l'appareil). It's Mr./Mrs./Miss ... (on the phone). 13
C'est quand l'anniversaire de... ? When is ...'s birthday? 5
C'est quand ton/votre anniversaire? When is your birthday? 5
Qu'est-ce que c'est? What is it? 1
cet *dem. adj., m., sing.* this; that 6
cet après-midi this afternoon 2
cette *dem. adj., f., sing.* this; that 6
cette année this year 2
cette semaine this week 2
ceux *pron., m., pl.* these; those; the ones 14
chaîne (de télévision) *f.* (television) channel 11
chaîne stéréo *f.* stereo system 11
chaise *f.* chair 1
chambre *f.* bedroom 8
chambre (individuelle) *f.* (single) room 7
camarade de chambre *m., f.* roommate 1
champ *m.* field 14
champagne *m.* champagne 6
champignon *m.* mushroom 9
chance *f.* luck 2
avoir de la chance *v.* to be lucky 2
chanson *f.* song 15
chanter *v.* to sing 5
chanteur/chanteuse *m., f.* singer 1
chapeau *m.* hat 6
chaque *adj.* each 6
charcuterie *f.* delicatessen 9
charmant(e) *adj.* charming 1
chasse *f.* hunt 14
chasser *v.* to hunt 14
chat *m.* cat 3
châtain *adj.* (*hair*) brown 3
chaud *m.* heat 2
avoir chaud *v.* to be hot 2
Il fait chaud. (*weather*) It is hot. 5
chauffeur de taxi/de camion *m.* taxi/truck driver 13
chaussette *f.* sock 6
chaussure *f.* shoe 6
chef d'entreprise *m.* head of a company 13
chef-d'œuvre *m.* masterpiece 15
chemin *m.* path; way 12
suivre un chemin *v.* to follow a path 12
chemise (à manches courtes/longues) *f.* (short-/long-sleeved) shirt 6
chemisier *m.* blouse 6
chèque *m.* check 12
compte de chèques *m.* checking account 12
payer par chèque *v.* to pay by check 12
cher/chère *adj.* expensive 6
chercher *v.* to look for 2
chercher un/du travail to look for work 12
chercheur/chercheuse *m., f.* researcher 13
chéri(e) *adj.* dear, beloved, darling 2
cheval *m.* horse 5
faire du cheval *v.* to go horseback riding 5
cheveux *m., pl.* hair 9
brosse à cheveux *f.* hairbrush 10
cheveux blonds blond hair 3
cheveux châtains brown hair 3
se brosser les cheveux *v.* to brush one's hair 9
cheville *f.* ankle 10
se fouler la cheville *v.* to twist/sprain one's ankle 10
chez *prep.* at (*someone's*)

house 3, at (*a place*) 3
passer chez quelqu'un *v.* to stop by someone's house 4
chic *adj.* chic 4
chien *m.* dog 3
chimie *f.* chemistry 2
Chine *f.* China 7
chinois(e) *adj.* Chinese 7
chocolat (chaud) *m.* (hot) chocolate 4
chœur *m.* choir, chorus 15
choisir *v.* to choose 7
chômage *m.* unemployment 13
être au chômage *v.* to be unemployed 13
chômeur/chômeuse *m., f.* unemployed person 13
chose *f.* thing 1
quelque chose *m.* something; anything 4
chrysanthèmes *m., pl.* chrysanthemums 9
chut shh 15
-ci (*used with demonstrative adjective* **ce** *and noun or with demonstrative pronoun* **celui**) here 6
ce mois-ci this month 2
ciel *m.* sky 14
cinéma (ciné) *m.* movie theater, movies 4
cinq *m.* five 1
cinquante *m.* fifty 1
cinquième *adj.* fifth 7
circulation *f.* traffic 11
clair(e) *adj.* clear 15
Il est clair que... It is clear that... 15
classe *f.* (*group of students*) class 1
camarade de classe *m., f.* classmate 1
salle de classe *f.* classroom 1
clavier *m.* keyboard 11
clé *f.* key 7
client(e) *m., f.* client; guest 7
cœur *m.* heart
avoir mal au cœur to feel nauseated 10
coffre *m.* trunk 11
coiffeur/coiffeuse *m., f.* hairdresser 3
coin *m.* corner 12
colis *m.* package 12
colocataire *m., f.* roommate (*in an apartment*) 1
Combien (de)... ? *adv.* How much/many... ? 1
Combien coûte... ? How much is... ? 4
combiné *m.* receiver 13
comédie (musicale) *f.* comedy (musical) 15
commander *v.* to order 9
comme *adv.* how; like, as 2
Comme ci, comme ça. So-so. 1
commencer (à) *v.* to begin (*to do something*) 2
comment *adv.* how 4
Comment? *adv.* What? 4
Comment allez-vous?, *form.* How are you? 1
Comment t'appelles-tu? *fam.* What is your name? 1
Comment vas-tu? *fam.* How are you? 1
Comment vous appelez-vous? *form.* What is your name? 1
commerçant(e) *m., f.* shop-keeper 9
commissariat de police *m.* police station 12
commode *f.* dresser, chest of drawers 8
compact disque *m.* compact disc 11
complet (complète) *adj.* full (no vacancies) 7
composer (un numéro) *v.* to dial (a number) 11
compositeur *m.* composer 15
comprendre *v.* to understand 4
compris (comprendre) *p.p., adj.* understood; included 6
comptable *m., f.* accountant 13
compte *m.* account (*at a bank*) 12
avoir un compte bancaire *v.* to have a bank account 12
compte de chèques *m.* checking account 12
compte d'épargne *m.* savings account 12
se rendre compte *v.* to realize 10
compter sur quelqu'un *v.* to count on someone 8
concert *m.* concert 15
condition *f.* condition 15
à condition que on the condition that..., provided that... 15
conduire *v.* to drive 6
conduit (conduire) *p.p., adj.* driven 6
confiture *f.* jam 9
congé *m.* day off 7
jour de congé *m.* day off 7
prendre un congé *v.* to take time off 13
congélateur *m.* freezer 8
connaissance *f.* acquaintance 5
faire la connaissance de *v.* to meet (*someone*) 5
connaître *v.* to know, to be familiar with 8
connecté(e) *adj.* connected 11
être connecté(e) avec quelqu'un *v.* to be online with someone 7, 11
connu (connaître) *p.p., adj.* known; famous 8
conseil *m.* advice 13
conseiller/conseillère *m., f.* consultant; advisor 13
considérer *v.* to consider 5
constamment *adv.* constantly 8
construire *v.* to build, to construct 6
conte *m.* tale 15
content(e) *adj.* happy 13
être content(e) que... *v.* to be happy that... 14
continuer (à) *v.* to continue (*doing something*) 12
contraire *adj.* contrary 15
au contraire on the contrary 15
copain/copine *m., f.* friend 1
corbeille (à papier) *f.* wastebasket 1
corps *m.* body 10
costume *m.* (*man's*) suit 6
côte *f.* coast 14
coton *m.* cotton 12
cou *m.* neck 10
couche d'ozone *f.* ozone layer 14
trou dans la couche d'ozone *m.* hole in the ozone layer 14
couleur *f.* color 6
De quelle couleur... ? What color... ? 6
couloir *m.* hallway 8
couple *m.* couple 6
courage *m.* courage 13
courageux/courageuse *adj.* courageous, brave 3
couramment *adv.* fluently 8
courir *v.* to run 5
courrier *m.* mail 12
cours *m.* class, course 2
course *f.* errand 9
faire les courses *v.* to go (grocery) shopping 9
court(e) *adj.* short 3
chemise à manches courtes *f.* short-sleeved shirt 6
couru (courir) *p.p.* run 6
cousin(e) *m., f.* cousin 3
couteau *m.* knife 9
coûter *v.* to cost 4
Combien coûte... ? How much is... ? 4
couvert (couvrir) *p.p.* covered 11
couverture *f.* blanket 8
couvrir *v.* to cover 11
covoiturage *m.* carpooling 14
cravate *f.* tie 6

crayon *m.* pencil 1
crème *f.* cream 9
crème à raser *f.* shaving cream 10
crêpe *f.* crêpe 5
crevé(e) *adj.* deflated; blown up 11
pneu crevé *m.* flat tire 11
critique *f.* review; criticism 15
croire (que) *v.* to believe (that) 15
ne pas croire que... to not believe that... 15
croissant *m.* croissant 4
croissant(e) *adj.* growing 14
population croissante *f.* growing population 14
cru (croire) *p.p.* believed 15
cruel/cruelle *adj.* cruel 3
cuillère (à soupe/à café) *f.* (soup/tea)spoon 9
cuir *m.* leather 12
cuisine *f.* cooking; kitchen 5
faire la cuisine *v.* to cook 5
cuisiner *v.* to cook 9
cuisinier/cuisinière *m., f.* cook 13
cuisinière *f.* stove 8
curieux/curieuse *adj.* curious 3
curriculum vitæ (C.V.) *m.* résumé 13
cybercafé *m.* cybercafé 12

D

d'abord *adv.* first 7
d'accord *(tag question)* all right? 2; *(in statement)* okay 2
être d'accord to be in agreement 2
d'autres *m., f.* others 4
d'habitude *adv.* usually 8
danger *m.* danger, threat 14
dangereux/dangereuse *adj.* dangerous 11
dans *prep.* in 3
danse *f.* dance 15
danser *v.* to dance 4
danseur/danseuse *m., f.* dancer 15
date *f.* date 5
Quelle est la date? What is the date? 5
de/d' *prep.* of 3; from 1
de l'après-midi in the afternoon 2
de laquelle *pron., f., sing.* which one 13
De quelle couleur... ? What color... ? 6
De rien. You're welcome. 1
de taille moyenne of medium height 3
de temps en temps *adv.* from time to time 8
débarrasser la table *v.* to clear the table 8
déboisement *m.* deforestation 14
début *m.* beginning; debut 15
décembre *m.* December 5
déchets toxiques *m., pl.* toxic waste 14
décider (de) *v.* to decide *(to do something)* 11
découvert (découvrir) *p.p.* discovered 11
découvrir *v.* to discover 11
décrire *v.* to describe 7
décrocher *v.* to pick up 13
décrit (décrire) *p.p., adj.* described 7
degrés *m., pl.* *(temperature)* degrees 5
Il fait ... degrés. *(to describe weather)* It is ... degrees. 5
déjà *adv.* already 5
déjeuner *m.* lunch 9; *v.* to eat lunch 4
de l' *part. art., m., f., sing.* some 4
de la *part. art., f., sing.* some 4
délicieux/délicieuse delicious 8
demain *adv.* tomorrow 2
À demain. See you tomorrow. 1
après-demain *adv.* day after tomorrow 2
demain matin/après-midi/soir *adv.* tomorrow morning/afternoon/evening 2
demander (à) *v.* to ask *(someone)*, to make a request *(of someone)* 6
demander que... *v.* to ask that... 14
démarrer *v.* to start up 11
déménager *v.* to move out 8
demie half 2
et demie half past ... (o'clock) 2
demi-frère *m.* half-brother, stepbrother 3
demi-sœur *f.* half-sister, stepsister 3
démissionner *v.* to resign 13
dent *f.* tooth 9
brosse à dents *f.* toothbrush 10
se brosser les dents *v.* to brush one's teeth 9
dentifrice *m.* toothpaste 10
dentiste *m., f.* dentist 3
départ *m.* departure 7
dépasser *v.* to go over; to pass 11
dépense *f.* expenditure, expense 12
dépenser *v.* to spend 4
dépenser de l'argent *v.* to spend money 4
déposer de l'argent *v.* to deposit money 12
déprimé(e) *adj.* depressed 10
depuis *adv.* since; for 9
dernier/dernière *adj.* last 2
dernièrement *adv.* lastly, finally 8
derrière *prep.* behind 3
des *part. art., m., f., pl.* some 4
des (de + les) *m., f., pl.* of the 3
dès que *adv.* as soon as 13
désagréable *adj.* unpleasant 1
descendre *v.* to go down; to take down 6
désert *m.* desert 14
désirer (que) *v.* to want (that) 5
désolé(e) *adj.* sorry 6
être désolé(e) que... to be sorry that... 14
desquelles (de + lesquelles) *pron., f., pl.* which ones 13
desquels (de + lesquels) *pron., m., pl.* which ones 13
dessert *m.* dessert 6
dessin animé *m.* cartoon 15
dessiner *v.* to draw 2
détester *v.* to hate 2
Je déteste... I hate... 2
détruire *v.* to destroy 6
détruit (détruire) *p.p., adj.* destroyed 6
deux *m.* two 1
deuxième *adj.* second 7
devant *prep.* in front of 3
développer *v.* to develop 14
devenir *v.* to become 9
devoir *m.* homework 2; *v.* to have to, must 9
dictionnaire *m.* dictionary 1
différemment *adv.* differently 8
différence *f.* difference 1
différent(e) *adj.* different 1
difficile *adj.* difficult 1
dimanche *m.* Sunday 2
dîner *m.* dinner 9; *v.* to have dinner 2
diplôme *m.* diploma, degree 2
dire *v.* to say 7
Ça te dit? Does that appeal to you? 14
ça veut dire that is to say 10
veut dire *v.* means, signifies 9
diriger *v.* to manage 13
discret/discrète *adj.* discreet; unassuming 3
discuter *v.* discuss 6

disque *m.* disk 11
compact disque *m.* compact disc 11
disque dur *m.* hard drive 11
dissertation *f.* essay 11
distributeur automatique/de billets *m.* ATM 12
dit (dire) *p.p., adj.* said 7
divorce *m.* divorce 6
divorcé(e) *adj.* divorced 3
divorcer *v.* to divorce 3
dix *m.* ten 1
dix-huit *m.* eighteen 1
dixième *adj.* tenth 7
dix-neuf *m.* nineteen 1
dix-sept *m.* seventeen 1
documentaire *m.* documentary 15
doigt *m.* finger 10
doigt de pied *m.* toe 10
domaine *m.* field 13
dommage *m.* harm 14
Il est dommage que... It's a shame that... 14
donc *conj.* therefore 7
donner (à) *v.* to give (*to someone*) 2
dont *rel. pron.* of which; of whom; that 11
dormir *v.* to sleep 5
dos *m.* back 10
sac à dos *m.* backpack 1
douane *f.* customs 7
douche *f.* shower 8
prendre une douche *v.* to take a shower 10
doué(e) *adj.* talented, gifted 15
douleur *f.* pain 10
douter (que) *v.* to doubt (that) 15
douteux/douteuse *adj.* doubtful 15
Il est douteux que... It is doubtful that... 15
doux/douce *adj.* sweet; soft 3
douze *m.* twelve 1
dramaturge *m.* playwright 15
drame (psychologique) *m.* (psychological) drama 15
draps *m., pl.* sheets 8
droit *m.* law 2
droite *f.* the right (side) 3
à droite de *prep.* to the right of 3
drôle *adj.* funny 3
du *part. art., m., sing.* some 4
du (de + le) *m., sing.* of the 3
dû (devoir) *p.p., adj. (used with infinitive)* had to; *(used with noun)* due, owed 9
duquel (de + lequel) *pron., m., sing.* which one 13

E

eau (minérale) *f.* (mineral) water 4
carafe d'eau *f.* pitcher of water 9
écharpe *f.* scarf 6
échecs *m., pl.* chess 5
échouer *v.* to fail 2
éclair *m.* éclair 4
école *f.* school 2
écologie *f.* ecology 14
écologique *adj.* ecological 14
économie *f.* economics 2
écotourisme *m.* ecotourism 14
écouter *v.* to listen (to) 2
écran *m.* screen 11
écrire *v.* to write 7
écrivain/femme écrivain *m., f.* writer 15
écrit (écrire) *p.p., adj.* written 7
écureuil *m.* squirrel 14
éducation physique *f.* physical education 2
effacer *v.* to erase 11
effet de serre *m.* greenhouse effect 14
égaler *v.* to equal 3
église *f.* church 4
égoïste *adj.* selfish 1
Eh! *interj.* Hey! 2
électrique *adj.* electric 8
appareil électrique/ménager *m.* electrical/household appliance 8
électricien/électricienne *m., f.* electrician 13
élégant(e) *adj.* elegant 1
élevé *adj.* high 13
élève *m., f.* pupil, student 1
elle *pron., f.* she; it 1; her 3
elle est... she/it is... 1
elles *pron., f.* they 1; them 3
elles sont... they are... 1
e-mail *m.* e-mail 11
emballage (en plastique) *m.* (plastic) wrapping/packaging 14
embaucher *v.* to hire 13
embrayage *m.* (*automobile*) clutch 11
émission (de télévision) *f.* (television) program 15
emménager *v.* to move in 8
emmener *v.* to take (*someone*) 5
emploi *m.* job 13
emploi à mi-temps/à temps partiel *m.* part-time job 13
emploi à plein temps *m.* full-time job 13
employer *v.* to use 5
emprunter *v.* to borrow 12

en *prep.* in 3
en avance early 2
en avoir marre to be fed up 6
en effet indeed; in fact 14
en été in the summer 5
en face (de) *prep.* facing, across (from) 3
en fait in fact 7
en général *adv.* in general 8
en hiver in the winter 5
en plein air in fresh air 14
en retard late 2
en tout cas in any case 6
en vacances on vacation 7
être en ligne to be online 11
en *pron.* some of it/them; about it/them; of it/them; from it/them 10
Je vous en prie. *form.* Please.; You're welcome. 1
Qu'en penses-tu? What do you think about that? 14
enceinte *adj.* pregnant 10
Enchanté(e). Delighted. 1
encore *adv.* again; still 3
endroit *m.* place 4
énergie (nucléaire/solaire) *f.* (nuclear/solar) energy 14
enfance *f.* childhood 6
enfant *m., f.* child 3
enfin *adv.* finally, at last 7
enlever la poussière *v.* to dust 8
ennuyeux/ennuyeuse *adj.* boring 3
énorme *adj.* enormous, huge 2
enregistrer *v.* to record 11
enseigner *v.* to teach 2
ensemble *adv.* together 6
ensuite *adv.* then, next 7
entendre *v.* to hear 6
entracte *m.* intermission 15
entre *prep.* between 3
entrée *f.* appetizer, starter 9
entreprise *f.* firm, business 13
entrer *v.* to enter 7
entretien: passer un entretien *to have an interview* 13
enveloppe *f.* envelope 12
envie *f.* desire, envy 2
avoir envie (de) to feel like (*doing something*) 2
environnement *m.* environment 14
envoyer (à) *v.* to send (*to someone*) 5
épargne *f.* savings 12
compte d'épargne *m.* savings account 12
épicerie *f.* grocery store 4
épouser *v.* to marry 3

épouvantable *adj.* dreadful 5
Il fait un temps épouvantable. The weather is dreadful. 5
époux/épouse *m., f.* husband/wife 3
équipe *f.* team 5
escalier *m.* staircase 8
escargot *m.* escargot, snail 9
espace *m.* space 14
Espagne *f.* Spain 7
espagnol(e) *adj.* Spanish 1
espèce (menacée) *f.* (endangered) species 14
espérer *v.* to hope 5
essayer *v.* to try 5
essence *f.* gas 11
réservoir d'essence *m.* gas tank 11
voyant d'essence *m.* gas warning light 11
essentiel(le) *adj.* essential 14
Il est essentiel que... It is essential that... 14
essuie-glace *m.* **(essuie-glaces** *pl.***)** windshield wiper(s) 11
essuyer (la vaisselle/la table) *v.* to wipe (the dishes/the table) 8
est *m.* east 12
Est-ce que... ? *(used in forming questions)* 2
et *conj.* and 1
Et toi? *fam.* And you? 1
Et vous? *form.* And you? 1
étage *m.* floor 7
étagère *f.* shelf 8
étape *f.* stage 6
état civil *m.* marital status 6
États-Unis *m., pl.* United States 7
été *m.* summer 5
en été in the summer 5
été (être) *p.p.* been 6
éteindre *v.* to turn off 11
éternuer *v.* to sneeze 10
étoile *f.* star 14
étranger/étrangère *adj.* foreign 2
langues étrangères *f., pl.* foreign languages 2
étranger *m.* *(places that are)* abroad, overseas 7
à l'étranger abroad, overseas 7
étrangler *v.* to strangle 13
être *v.* to be 1
être bien/mal payé(e) to be well/badly paid 13
être connecté(e) avec quelqu'un to be online with someone 7, 11
être en ligne avec to be online with 11
être en pleine forme to be in good shape 10
études (supérieures) *f., pl.* studies; (higher) education 2
étudiant(e) *m., f.* student 1
étudier *v.* to study 2
eu (avoir) *p.p.* had 6
eux *disj. pron., m., pl.* they, them 3
évidemment *adv.* obviously, evidently; of course 8
évident(e) *adj.* evident, obvious 15
Il est évident que... It is evident that... 15
évier *m.* sink 8
éviter (de) *v.* to avoid *(doing something)* 10
exactement *adv.* exactly 9
examen *m.* exam; test 1
être reçu(e) à un examen *v.* to pass an exam 2
passer un examen *v.* to take an exam 2
Excuse-moi. *fam.* Excuse me. 1
Excusez-moi. *form.* Excuse me. 1
exercice *m.* exercise 10
faire de l'exercice *v.* to exercise 10
exigeant(e) *adj.* demanding 13
profession (exigeante) *f.* a (demanding) profession 13
exiger (que) *v.* to demand (that) 14
expérience (professionnelle) *f.* (professional) experience 13
expliquer *v.* to explain 2
explorer *v.* to explore 4
exposition *f.* exhibit 15
extinction *f.* extinction 14

F

facile *adj.* easy 2
facilement *adv.* easily 8
facteur *m.* mailman 12
faculté *f.* university; faculty 1
faible *adj.* weak 3
faim *f.* hunger 4
avoir faim *v.* to be hungry 4
faire *v.* to do; to make 5
faire attention (à) *v.* to pay attention (to) 5
faire quelque chose de beau *v.* to be up to something interesting 12
faire de l'aérobic *v.* to do aerobics 5
faire de la gym *v.* to work out 5
faire de la musique *v.* to play music 13
faire de la peinture *v.* to paint 15
faire de la planche à voile *v.* to go windsurfing 5
faire de l'exercice *v.* to exercise 10
faire des projets *v.* to make plans 13
faire du camping *v.* to go camping 5
faire du cheval *v.* to go horseback riding 5
faire du jogging *v.* to go jogging 5
faire du shopping *v.* to go shopping 7
faire du ski *v.* to go skiing 5
faire du sport *v.* to do sports 5
faire du vélo *v.* to go bike riding 5
faire la connaissance de *v.* to meet *(someone)* 5
faire la cuisine *v.* to cook 5
faire la fête *v.* to party 6
faire la lessive *v.* to do the laundry 8
faire la poussière *v.* to dust 8
faire la queue *v.* to wait in line 12
faire la vaisselle *v.* to do the dishes 8
faire le lit *v.* to make the bed 8
faire le ménage *v.* to do the housework 8
faire le plein *v.* to fill the tank 11
faire les courses *v.* to run errands 9
faire les musées *v.* to go to museums 15
faire les valises *v.* to pack one's bags 7
faire mal *v.* to hurt 10
faire plaisir à quelqu'un *v.* to please someone 13
faire sa toilette *v.* to wash up 10
faire une piqûre *v.* to give a shot 10
faire une promenade *v.* to go for a walk 5
faire une randonnée *v.* to go for a hike 5
faire un séjour *v.* to spend time *(somewhere)* 7
faire un tour (en voiture) *v.* to go for a walk (drive) 5
faire visiter *v.* to give a tour 8
fait (faire) *p.p., adj.* done; made 6
falaise *f.* cliff 14
faut (falloir) *v.* *(used with infinitive)* is necessary to... 5
Il a fallu... It was necessary

to… 6
Il fallait… One had to… 8
Il faut que… One must…/It is necessary that… 14
fallu (falloir) *p.p. (used with infinitive)* had to... 6
Il a fallu… It was necessary to… 6
famille *f.* family 3
fatigué(e) *adj.* tired 3
fauteuil *m.* armchair 8
favori/favorite *adj.* favorite 3
fax *m.* fax (machine) 11
félicitations congratulations 15
femme *f.* woman; wife 1
femme d'affaires business-woman 3
femme au foyer housewife 13
femme auteur author 15
femme cadre executive 13
femme écrivain writer 15
femme peintre painter 15
femme politique politician 13
femme pompier firefighter 13
femme sculpteur sculptor 15
fenêtre *f.* window 1
fer à repasser *m.* iron 8
férié(e) *adj.* holiday 6
jour férié *m.* holiday 6
fermé(e) *adj.* closed 12
fermer *v.* to close; to shut off 11
festival (festivals *pl.***)** *m.* festival 15
fête *f.* party 6; celebration 6
faire la fête *v.* to party 6
fêter *v.* to celebrate 6
feu de signalisation *m.* traffic light 12
feuille de papier *f.* sheet of paper 1
feuilleton *m.* soap opera 15
février *m.* February 5
fiancé(e) *adj.* engaged 3
fiancé(e) *m., f.* fiancé 6
fichier *m.* file 11
fier/fière *adj.* proud 3
fièvre *f.* fever 10
avoir de la fièvre *v.* to have a fever 10
fille *f.* girl; daughter 1
film (d'aventures, d'horreur, de science-fiction, policier) *m.* (adventure, horror, science-fiction, crime) film 15
fils *m.* son 3
fin *f.* end 15
finalement *adv.* finally 7
fini (finir) *p.p., adj.* finished, done, over 7
finir (de) *v.* to finish *(doing something)* 7
fleur *f.* flower 8
fleuve *m.* river 14
fois *f.* time 8
une fois *adv.* once 8
deux fois *adv.* twice 8
fonctionner *v.* to work, to function 11
fontaine *f.* fountain 12
foot(ball) *m.* soccer 5
football américain *m.* football 5
forêt (tropicale) *f.* (tropical) forest 14
formation *f.* education; training 13
forme *f.* shape; form 10
être en pleine forme *v.* to be in good shape 10
formidable *adj.* great 7
formulaire *m.* form 12
remplir un formulaire to fill out a form 12
fort(e) *adj.* strong 3
fou/folle *adj.* crazy 3
four (à micro-ondes) *m.* (microwave) oven 8
fourchette *f.* fork 9
frais/fraîche *adj.* fresh; cool 5
Il fait frais. *(weather)* It is cool. 5
fraise *f.* strawberry 9
français(e) *adj.* French 1
France *f.* France 7
franchement *adv.* frankly, honestly 8
freiner *v.* to brake 11
freins *m., pl.* brakes 11
fréquenter *v.* to frequent; to visit 4
frère *m.* brother 3
beau-frère *m.* brother-in-law 3
demi-frère *m.* half-brother, stepbrother 3
frigo *m.* refrigerator 8
frisé(e) *adj.* curly 3
frites *f., pl.* French fries 4
froid *m.* cold 2
avoir froid to be cold 2
Il fait froid. *(weather)* It is cold. 5
fromage *m.* cheese 4
fruit *m.* fruit 9
fruits de mer *m., pl.* seafood 9
fumer *v.* to smoke 10
funérailles *f., pl.* funeral 9
furieux/furieuse *adj.* furious 14
être furieux/furieuse que… *v.* to be furious that… 14

G

gagner *v.* to win 5; to earn 13
gant *m.* glove 6
garage *m.* garage 8
garanti(e) *adj.* guaranteed 5
garçon *m.* boy 1
garder la ligne *v.* to stay slim 10
gare (routière) *f.* train station (bus station) 7
gaspillage *m.* waste 14
gaspiller *v.* to waste 14
gâteau *m.* cake 6
gauche *f.* the left (side) 3
à gauche (de) *prep.* to the left (of) 3
gazeux/gazeuse *adj.* carbonated, fizzy 4
boisson gazeuse *f.* carbonated drink/beverage 4
généreux/généreuse *adj.* generous 3
génial(e) *adj.* great 3
genou *m.* knee 10
genre *m.* genre 15
gens *m., pl.* people 7
gentil/gentille *adj.* nice 3
gentiment *adv.* nicely 8
géographie *f.* geography 2
gérant(e) *m., f.* manager 13
gestion *f.* business administration 2
glace *f.* ice cream 6
glaçon *m.* ice cube 6
glissement de terrain *m.* landslide 14
golf *m.* golf 5
gonfler *v.* to swell 10
gorge *f.* throat 10
goûter *m.* afternoon snack 9; *v.* to taste 9
gouvernement *m.* government 14
grand(e) *adj.* big 3
grand magasin *m.* department store 4
grand-mère *f.* grandmother 3
grand-père *m.* grandfather 3
grands-parents *m., pl.* grandparents 3
gratin *m.* gratin 9
gratuit(e) *adj.* free 15
grave *adj.* serious 10
Ce n'est pas grave. It's okay.; No problem. 6
graver *v.* to record, to burn (CD, DVD) 11
grille-pain *m.* toaster 8
grippe *f.* flu 10
gris(e) *adj.* gray 6
gros(se) *adj.* fat 3
grossir *v.* to gain weight 7
guérir *v.* to get better 10
guitare *f.* guitar 15
gym *f.* exercise 5
faire de la gym *v.* to work out 5
gymnase *m.* gym 4

H

habitat *m.* habitat 14
sauvetage des habitats *m.* habitat preservation 14
habiter (à) *v.* to live (in/at) 2
haricots verts *m., pl.* green beans 9
Hein? *interj.* Huh?; Right? 3
herbe *f.* grass 14
hésiter (à) *v.* to hesitate (*to do something*) 11
heure(s) *f.* hour, o'clock; time 2
à ... heure(s) at ... (o'clock) 4
À quelle heure? What time?; When? 2
À tout à l'heure. See you later. 1
Quelle heure avez-vous? *form.* What time do you have? 2
Quelle heure est-il? What time is it? 2
heureusement *adv.* fortunately 8
heureux/heureuse *adj.* happy 3
être heureux/heureuse que... to be happy that... 14
hier (matin/après-midi/soir) *adv.* yesterday (morning/afternoon/evening) 7
avant-hier *adv.* day before yesterday 7
histoire *f.* history; story 2
hiver *m.* winter 5
en hiver in the winter 5
homme *m.* man 1
homme d'affaires *m.* businessman 3
homme politique *m.* politician 13
honnête *adj.* honest 15
honte *f.* shame 2
avoir honte (de) *v.* to be ashamed (of) 2
hôpital *m.* hospital 4
horloge *f.* clock 1
hors-d'œuvre *m.* hors d'œuvre, appetizer 9
hôte/hôtesse *m., f.* host 6
hôtel *m.* hotel 7
hôtelier/hôtelière *m., f.* hotel keeper 7
huile *f.* oil 9
huile *f.* (automobile) oil 11
huile d'olive *f.* olive oil 9
vérifier l'huile to check the oil 11
voyant d'huile *m.* oil warning light 11
huit *m.* eight 1
huitième *adj.* eighth 7
humeur *f.* mood 8
être de bonne/mauvaise humeur *v.* to be in a good/bad mood 8

I

ici *adv.* here 1
idée *f.* idea 3
il *sub. pron.* he; it 1
il est... he/it is... 1
Il n'y a pas de quoi. It's nothing.; You're welcome. 1
Il vaut mieux que... It is better that... 14
Il faut (falloir) *v.* (*used with infinitive*) It is necessary to... 6
Il a fallu... It was necessary to... 6
Il fallait... One had to... 8
Il faut (que)... One must.../ It is necessary that... 14
il y a there is/are 1
il y a eu there was/were 6
il y avait there was/were 8
Qu'est-ce qu'il y a? What is it?; What's wrong? 1
Y a-t-il... ? Is/Are there... ? 2
il y a... (*used with an expression of time*) ... ago 9
île *f.* island 14
ils *sub. pron., m., pl.* they 1
ils sont... they are... 1
immeuble *m.* building 8
impatient(e) *adj.* impatient 1
imperméable *m.* rain jacket 5
important(e) *adj.* important 1
Il est important que... It is important that... 14
impossible *adj.* impossible 15
Il est impossible que... It is impossible that... 15
imprimante *f.* printer 11
imprimer *v.* to print 11
incendie *m.* fire 14
prévenir l'incendie to prevent a fire 14
incroyable *adj.* incredible 11
indépendamment *adv.* independently 8
indépendant(e) *adj.* independent 1
indications *f.* directions 12
indiquer *v.* to indicate 5
indispensable *adj.* essential, indispensable 14
Il est indispensable que... It is essential that... 14
individuel(le) *adj.* single, individual 7
chambre individuelle *f.* single (hotel) room 7
infirmier/infirmière *m., f.* nurse 10
informations (infos) *f., pl.* news 15
informatique *f.* computer science 2
ingénieur *m.* engineer 3
inquiet/inquiète *adj.* worried 3
instrument *m.* instrument 1
intellectuel(le) *adj.* intellectual 3
intelligent(e) *adj.* intelligent 1
interdire *v.* to forbid, to prohibit 14
intéressant(e) *adj.* interesting 1
inutile *adj.* useless 2
invité(e) *m., f.* guest 6
inviter *v.* to invite 4
irlandais(e) *adj.* Irish 7
Irlande *f.* Ireland 7
Italie *f.* Italy 7
italien(ne) *adj.* Italian 1

J

jaloux/jalouse *adj.* jealous 3
jamais *adv.* never 5
ne... jamais never, not ever 12
jambe *f.* leg 10
jambon *m.* ham 4
janvier *m.* January 5
Japon *m.* Japan 7
japonais(e) *adj.* Japanese 1
jardin *m.* garden; yard 8
jaune *adj.* yellow 6
je/j' *sub. pron.* I 1
Je vous en prie. *form.* Please.; You're welcome. 1
jean *m., sing.* jeans 6
jeter *v.* to throw away 14
jeu *m.* game 5
jeu télévisé *m.* game show 15
jeu vidéo (des jeux vidéo) *m.* video game(s) 11
jeudi *m.* Thursday 2
jeune *adj.* young 3
jeunes mariés *m., pl.* newlyweds 6
jeunesse *f.* youth 6
auberge de jeunesse *f.* youth hostel 7
jogging *m.* jogging 5
faire du jogging *v.* to go jogging 5
joli(e) *adj.* handsome; beautiful 3
joue *f.* cheek 10
jouer (à/de) *v.* to play (*a sport/ a musical instrument*) 5
jouer un rôle *v.* to play a role 15
joueur/joueuse *m., f.* player 5
jour *m.* day 2
jour de congé *m.* day off 7
jour férié *m.* holiday 6

Quel jour sommes-nous? What day is it? 2
journal *m.* newspaper; journal 7
journaliste *m., f.* journalist 3
journée *f.* day 2
juillet *m.* July 5
juin *m.* June 5
jungle *f.* jungle 14
jupe *f.* skirt 6
jus (d'orange/de pomme) *m.* (orange/apple) juice 4
jusqu'à (ce que) *prep.* until 12
juste *adv.* just; right 3
juste à côté right next door 3

K

kilo(gramme) *m.* kilo(gram) 9
kiosque *m.* kiosk 4

L

l' *def. art., m., f. sing.* the 1; *d.o. pron., m., f. him; her; it* 7
la *def. art., f. sing.* the 1; *d.o. pron., f. her; it* 7
là(-bas) (over) there 1
-là *(used with demonstrative adjective* **ce** *and noun or with demonstrative pronoun* **celui***)* there 6
lac *m.* lake 14
laid(e) *adj.* ugly 3
laine *f.* wool 12
laisser *v.* to let, to allow 11
laisser tranquille *v.* to leave alone 10
laisser un message *v.* to leave a message 13
laisser un pourboire *v.* to leave a tip 4
lait *m.* milk 4
laitue *f.* lettuce 9
lampe *f.* lamp 8
langues (étrangères) *f., pl.* (foreign) languages 2
lapin *m.* rabbit 14
laquelle *pron., f., sing.* which one 13
à laquelle *pron., f., sing.* which one 13
de laquelle *pron., f., sing.* which one 13
large *adj.* loose; big 6
lavabo *m.* bathroom sink 8
lave-linge *m.* washing machine 8
laver *v.* to wash 8
laverie *f.* laundromat 12
lave-vaisselle *m.* dishwasher 8
le *def. art., m. sing.* the 1; *d.o. pron.* him; it 7
lecteur de CD/DVD *m.* CD/DVD player 11
légume *m.* vegetable 9
lent(e) *adj.* slow 3
lequel *pron., m., sing.* which one 13
auquel (à + lequel) *pron., m., sing.* which one 13
duquel (de + lequel) *pron., m., sing.* which one 13
les *def. art., m., f., pl.* the 1; *d.o. pron., m., f., pl.* them 7
lesquelles *pron., f., pl.* which ones 13
auxquelles (à + lesquelles) *pron., f., pl.* which ones 13
desquelles (de + lesquelles) *pron., f., pl.* which ones 13
lesquels *pron., m., pl.* which ones 13
auxquels (à + lesquels) *pron., m., pl.* which ones 13
desquels (de + lesquels) *pron., m., pl.* which ones 13
lessive *f.* laundry 8
faire la lessive *v.* to do the laundry 8
lettre *f.* letter 12
boîte aux lettres *f.* mailbox 12
lettre de motivation *f.* letter of application 13
lettre de recommandation *f.* letter of recommendation, reference letter 13
lettres *f., pl.* humanities 2
leur *i.o. pron., m., f., pl.* them 6
leur(s) *poss. adj., m., f.* their 3
librairie *f.* bookstore 1
libre *adj.* available 7
lieu *m.* place 4
ligne *f.* figure, shape 10
garder la ligne *v.* to stay slim 10
limitation de vitesse *f.* speed limit 11
limonade *f.* lemon soda 4
linge *m.* laundry 8
lave-linge *m.* washing machine 8
sèche-linge *m.* clothes dryer 8
liquide *m.* cash *(money)* 12
payer en liquide *v.* to pay in cash 12
lire *v.* to read 7
lit *m.* bed 7
faire le lit *v.* to make the bed 8
littéraire *adj.* literary 15
littérature *f.* literature 1
livre *m.* book 1
logement *m.* housing 8
logiciel *m.* software, program 11
loi *f.* law 14
loin de *prep.* far from 3
loisir *m.* leisure activity 5
long(ue) *adj.* long 3
chemise à manches longues *f.* long-sleeved shirt 6
longtemps *adv.* a long time 5
louer *v.* to rent 8
loyer *m.* rent 8
lu (lire) *p.p.* read 7
lui *pron., sing.* he 1; him 3; *i.o. pron. (attached to imperative)* to him/her 9
l'un(e) à l'autre to one another 11
l'un(e) l'autre one another 11
lundi *m.* Monday 2
Lune *f.* moon 14
lunettes (de soleil) *f., pl.* (sun)glasses 6
lycée *m.* high school 1
lycéen(ne) *m., f.* high school student 2

M

ma *poss. adj., f., sing.* my 3
Madame *f.* Ma'am; Mrs. 1
Mademoiselle *f.* Miss 1
magasin *m.* store 4
grand magasin *m.* department store 4
magazine *m.* magazine 15
magnétophone *m.* tape recorder 11
magnétoscope *m.* videocassette recorder (VCR) 11
mai *m.* May 5
maigrir *v.* to lose weight 7
maillot de bain *m.* swimsuit, bathing suit 6
main *f.* hand 5
sac à main *m.* purse, handbag 6
maintenant *adv.* now 5
maintenir *v.* to maintain 9
mairie *f.* town/city hall; mayor's office 12
mais *conj.* but 1
mais non (but) of course not; no 2
maison *f.* house 4
rentrer à la maison *v.* to return home 2
mal *adv.* badly 7
Je vais mal. I am doing badly. 1
le plus mal *super. adv.* the worst 9
se porter mal *v.* to be doing badly 10
mal *m.* illness; ache, pain 10
avoir mal *v.* to have an ache 10
avoir mal au cœur *v.* to feel nauseated 10
faire mal *v.* to hurt 10
malade *adj.* sick, ill 10
tomber malade *v.* to get sick 10
maladie *f.* illness 13

truc *m.* thing 7
tu *sub. pron., sing., fam.* you 1

U

un *m. (number)* one 1
un(e) *indef. art.* a; an 1
universitaire *adj. (related to the)* university 1
restaurant universitaire (resto U) *m.* university cafeteria 2
université *f.* university 1
urgences *f., pl.* emergency room 10
aller aux urgences *v.* to go to the emergency room 10
usine *f.* factory 14
utile *adj.* useful 2
utiliser (un plan) *v.* use (a map) 7

V

vacances *f., pl.* vacation 7
partir en vacances *v.* to go on vacation 7
vache *f.* cow 14
vaisselle *f.* dishes 8
faire la vaisselle *v.* to do the dishes 8
lave-vaisselle *m.* dishwasher 8
valise *f.* suitcase 7
faire les valises *v.* to pack one's bags 7
vallée *f.* valley 14
variétés *f., pl.* popular music 15
vaut (valloir) *v.*
Il vaut mieux que It is better that 14
vélo *m.* bicycle 5
faire du vélo *v.* to go bike riding 5
velours *m.* velvet 12
vendeur/vendeuse *m., f.* seller 6
vendre *v.* to sell 6
vendredi *m.* Friday 2
venir *v.* to come 9
venir de *v. (used with an infinitive)* to have just 9
vent *m.* wind 5
Il fait du vent. It is windy. 5
ventre *m.* stomach 10
vérifier (l'huile/la pression des pneus) *v.* to check (the oil/the tire pressure) 11
véritable *adj.* true, real 12
verre (de) *m.* glass (of) 4
vers *adv.* about 2
vert(e) *adj.* green 3
haricots verts *m., pl.* green beans 9
vêtements *m., pl.* clothing 6
sous-vêtement *m.* underwear 6
vétérinaire *m., f.* veterinarian 13
veuf/veuve *adj.* widowed 3
veut dire (vouloir dire) *v.* means, signifies 9
viande *f.* meat 9
vidéocassette *f.* videotape 11
vie *f.* life 6
assurance vie *f.* life insurance 13
vieille *adj., f. (feminine form of* **vieux***)* old 3
vieillesse *f.* old age 6
vietnamien(ne) *adj.* Vietnamese 1
vieux/vieille *adj.* old 3
ville *f.* city; town 4
vin *m.* wine 6
vingt *m.* twenty 1
vingtième *adj.* twentieth 7
violet(te) *adj.* purple; violet 6
violon *m.* violin 15
visage *m.* face 10
visite *f.* visit 6
rendre visite (à) *v.* to visit *(a person or people)* 6
visiter *v.* to visit *(a place)* 2
faire visiter *v.* to give a tour 8
vite *adv.* quickly 1; quick, hurry 4
vitesse *f.* speed 11
voici here is/are 1
voilà there is/are 1
voir *v.* to see 15
voisin(e) *m., f.* neighbor 3
voiture *f.* car 11
faire un tour en voiture *v.* to go for a drive 5
rouler en voiture *v.* to ride in a car 7
vol *m.* flight 7
volant *m.* steering wheel 11
volcan *m.* volcano 14
volley(-ball) *m.* volleyball 5
volontiers *adv.* willingly 10
vos *poss. adj., m., f., pl.* your 3
votre *poss. adj., m., f., sing.* your 3
vouloir *v.* to want; to mean *(with* **dire***)* 9
ça veut dire that is to say 20
veut dire *v.* means, signifies 9
vouloir (que) *v.* to want (that) 14
voulu (vouloir) *p.p., adj. (used with infinitive)* wanted to… ; *(used with noun)* planned to/ for 9
vous *pron., sing., pl., fam., form.* you 1; *d.o. pron.* you 7; your-self, yourselves 10
voyage *m.* trip 7
agence de voyages *f.* travel agency 7
agent de voyages *m.* travel agent 7
voyager *v.* to travel 2
voyant (d'essence/d'huile) *m.* (gas/oil) warning light 11
vrai(e) *adj.* true; real 3
Il est vrai que… It is true that… 15
Il n'est pas vrai que… It is untrue that… 15
vraiment *adv.* really, truly 5
vu (voir) *p.p.* seen 15

W

W.-C. *m., pl.* restroom(s)
week-end *m.* weekend 2
ce week-end this weekend 2

Y

y *pron.* there; at *(a place)* 10
j'y vais I'm going/coming 8
nous y allons we're going/ coming 9
on y va let's go 10
Y a-t-il… ? Is/Are there… ? 2
yaourt *m.* yogurt 9
yeux (œil) *m., pl.* eyes 3

Z

zéro *m.* zero 1
zut *interj.* darn 6

English-French

A

a **un(e)** *indef. art.* 1
able: to be able to **pouvoir** *v.* 9
abolish **abolir** *v.* 14
about **vers** *adv.* 2
abroad **à l'étranger** 7
absolutely **absolument** *adv.* 8; **tout à fait** *adv.* 6
accident **accident** *m.* 10
  to have/to be in an accident **avoir un accident** *v.* 11
accompany **accompagner** *v.* 12
account *(at a bank)* **compte** *m.* 12
  checking account **compte** *m.* **de chèques** 12
  to have a bank account **avoir un compte bancaire** *v.* 12
accountant **comptable** *m., f.* 13
acid rain **pluie acide** *f.* 14
across from **en face de** *prep.* 3
acquaintance **connaissance** *f.* 5
active **actif/active** *adj.* 3
actively **activement** *adv.* 8
actor **acteur/actrice** *m., f.* 1
address **adresse** *f.* 12
administration: business administration **gestion** *f.* 2
adolescence **adolescence** *f.* 6
adore **adorer** 2
  I love... **J'adore...** 2
  to adore one another **s'adorer** *v.* 11
adulthood **âge adulte** *m.* 6
adventure **aventure** *f.* 15
  adventure film **film** *m.* **d'aventures** 15
advertisement **publicité (pub)** *f.* 15
advice **conseil** *m.* 13
advisor **conseiller/conseillère** *m., f.* 13
aerobics **aérobic** *m.* 5
  to do aerobics **faire de l'aérobic** *v.* 5
afraid: to be afraid of/that **avoir peur de/que** *v.* 14
after **après (que)** *adv.* 7
afternoon **après-midi** *m.* 2
  ... (o'clock) in the afternoon **... heure(s) de l'après-midi** 2
afternoon snack **goûter** *m.* 9
again **encore** *adv.* 3
age **âge** *m.* 6
agent: travel agent **agent de voyages** *m.* 7
  real estate agent **agent immobilier** *m.* 13
ago *(with an expression of time)* **il y a...** 9
agree: to agree (with) **être d'accord (avec)** *v.* 2
airport **aéroport** *m.* 7
alarm clock **réveil** *m.* 10
Algerian **algérien(ne)** *adj.* 1
all **tout** *m., sing.* 4
  all of a sudden **soudain** *adv.* 8; **tout à coup** *adv.*; **tout d'un coup** *adv.* 7
all right? *(tag question)* **d'accord?** 2
allergy **allergie** *f.* 10
allow *(to do something)* **laisser** *v.* 11; **permettre (de)** *v.* 6
allowed **permis (permettre)** *p.p., adj.* 6
all the... *(agrees with noun that follows)* **tout le...** *m., sing;* **toute la...** *f., sing;* **tous les...** *m., pl.*; **toutes les...** *f., pl.* 4
almost **presque** *adv.* 5
a lot (of) **beaucoup (de)** *adv.* 4
alone: to leave alone **laisser tranquille** *v.* 10
already **déjà** *adv.* 3
always **toujours** *adv.* 8
American **américain(e)** *adj.* 1
an **un(e)** *indef. art.* 1
ancient *(placed after noun)* **ancien(ne)** *adj.* 15
and **et** *conj.* 1
  And you? **Et toi?,** *fam.*; **Et vous?** *form.* 1
angel **ange** *m.* 1
angry: to become angry **s'énerver** *v.* 10; **se mettre en colère** *v.* 10
animal **animal** *m.* 14
ankle **cheville** *f.* 10
answering machine **répondeur téléphonique** *m.* 11
apartment **appartement** *m.* 7
appetizer **entrée** *f.* 9; **hors-d'œuvre** *m.* 9
applaud **applaudir** *v.* 15
applause **applaudissement** *m.* 15
apple **pomme** *f.* 9
appliance **appareil** *m.* 8
  electrical/household appliance **appareil** *m.* **électrique/ménager** 8
applicant **candidat(e)** *m., f.* 13
apply **postuler** *v.* 13
appointment **rendez-vous** *m.* 13
  to make an appointment **prendre (un) rendez-vous** *v.* 13
April **avril** *m.* 5
architect **architecte** *m., f.* 3
architecture **architecture** *f.* 2
Are there... ? **Y a-t-il... ?** 2
area **quartier** *m.* 8
argue (with) **se disputer (avec)** *v.* 10
arm **bras** *m.* 10
armchair **fauteuil** *m.* 8
armoire **armoire** *f.* 8
around **autour (de)** *prep.* 12
arrival **arrivée** *f.* 7
arrive **arriver (à)** *v.* 2
art **art** *m.* 2
  artwork, piece of art **œuvre** *f.* 15
  fine arts **beaux-arts** *m., pl.* 15
artist **artiste** *m., f.* 3
as *(like)* **comme** *adv.* 6
  as ... as *(used with adjective to compare)* **aussi ... que** 9
  as much ... as *(used with noun to express comparative quantity)* **autant de ... que** 14
  as soon as **dès que** *adv.* 13
ashamed: to be ashamed of **avoir honte de** *v.* 2
ask **demander** *v.* 2
  to ask *(someone)* **demander (à)** *v.* 6
  to ask *(someone)* a question **poser une question (à)** *v.* 6
  to ask that... **demander que...** 14
aspirin **aspirine** *f.* 10
at **à** *prep.* 4
  at ... (o'clock) **à ... heure(s)** 4
  at the doctor's office **chez le médecin** *prep.* 2
  at (someone's) house **chez...** *prep.* 2
  at the end (of) **au bout (de)** *prep.* 12
  at last **enfin** *adv.* 11
athlete **athlète** *m., f.* 3
ATM **distributeur** *m.* **automatique/de billets** *m.* 12
attend **assister** *v.* 2
August **août** *m.* 5
aunt **tante** *f.* 3
author **auteur/femme auteur** *m., f.* 15
autumn **automne** *m.* 5
  in autumn **à l'automne** 5
available *(free)* **libre** *adj.* 7
avenue **avenue** *f.* 12
avoid **éviter de** *v.* 10

B

back **dos** *m.* 10
backpack **sac à dos** *m.* 1
bad **mauvais(e)** *adj.* 3

to be in a bad mood **être de mauvaise humeur** 8
to be in bad health **être en mauvaise santé** 10
badly **mal** *adv.* 7
I am doing badly. **Je vais mal.** 1
to be doing badly **se porter mal** *v.* 10
baguette **baguette** *f.* 4
bakery **boulangerie** *f.* 9
balcony **balcon** *m.* 8
banana **banane** *f.* 9
bank **banque** *f.* 12
to have a bank account **avoir un compte bancaire** *v.* 12
banker **banquier/banquière** *m., f.* 13
banking **bancaire** *adj.* 12
baseball **baseball** *m.* 5
baseball cap **casquette** *f.* 6
basement **sous-sol** *m.*; **cave** *f.* 8
basketball **basket(-ball)** *m.* 5
bath **bain** *m.* 6
bathing suit **maillot de bain** *m.* 6
bathroom **salle de bains** *f.* 8
bathtub **baignoire** *f.* 8
be **être** *v.* 1
sois (être) *imp. v.* 7; **soyez (être)** *imp. v.* 7
beach **plage** *f.* 7
beans **haricots** *m., pl.* 9
green beans **haricots verts** *m., pl.* 9
bearings: to get one's bearings **s'orienter** *v.* 12
beautiful **beau (belle)** *adj.* 3
beauty salon **salon** *m.* **de beauté** 12
because **parce que** *conj.* 2
become **devenir** *v.* 9
bed **lit** *m.* 7
to go to bed **se coucher** *v.* 10
bedroom **chambre** *f.* 8
beef **bœuf** *m.* 9
been **été (être)** *p.p.* 6
beer **bière** *f.* 6
before **avant (de/que)** *adv.* 7
before (*o'clock*) **moins** *adv.* 2
begin (*to do something*) **commencer (à)** *v.* 2; **se mettre à** *v.* 10
beginning **début** *m.* 15
behind **derrière** *prep.* 3
Belgian **belge** *adj.* 7
Belgium **Belgique** *f.* 7
believe (that) **croire (que)** *v.* 15
believed **cru (croire)** *p.p.* 15
belt **ceinture** *f.* 6
to buckle one's seatbelt **attacher sa ceinture de sécurité** *v.* 11
bench **banc** *m.* 12
best: the best **le mieux** *super. adv.* 9; **le/la meilleur(e)** *super. adj.* 9
better **meilleur(e)** *comp. adj.*; **mieux** *comp. adv.* 9
It is better that… **Il vaut mieux que/qu'…** 14
to be doing better **se porter mieux** *v.* 10
to get better (*from illness*) **guérir** *v.* 10
between **entre** *prep.* 3
beverage (carbonated) **boisson** *f.* **(gazeuse)** 4
bicycle **vélo** *m.* 5
to go bike riding **faire du vélo** *v.* 5
big **grand(e)** *adj.* 3; (*clothing*) **large** *adj.* 6
bill (*in a restaurant*) **addition** *f.* 4
bills (*money*) **billets** *m., pl.* 12
biology **biologie** *f.* 2
bird **oiseau** *m.* 3
birth **naissance** *f.* 6
birthday **anniversaire** *m.* 5
bit (of) **morceau (de)** *m.* 4
black **noir(e)** *adj.* 3
blackboard **tableau** *m.* 1
blanket **couverture** *f.* 8
blonde **blond(e)** *adj.* 3
blouse **chemisier** *m.* 6
blue **bleu(e)** *adj.* 3
boat **bateau** *m.* 7
body **corps** *m.* 10
book **livre** *m.* 1
bookstore **librairie** *f.* 1
bored: to get bored **s'ennuyer** *v.* 10
boring **ennuyeux/ennuyeuse** *adj.* 3
born: to be born **naître** *v.* 7; **né (naître)** *p.p., adj.* 7
borrow **emprunter** *v.* 12
bottle (of) **bouteille (de)** *f.* 4
boulevard **boulevard** *m.* 12
boutique **boutique** *f.* 12
bowl **bol** *m.* 9
box **boîte** *f.* 9
boy **garçon** *m.* 1
boyfriend **petit ami** *m.* 1
brake **freiner** *v.* 11
brakes **freins** *m., pl.* 11
brave **courageux/courageuse** *adj.* 3
Brazil **Brésil** *m.* 7
Brazilian **brésilien(ne)** *adj.* 7
bread **pain** *m.* 4
country-style bread **pain** *m.* **de campagne** 4
bread shop **boulangerie** *f.* 9
break **se casser** *v.* 10
breakdown **panne** *f.* 11
break down **tomber en panne** *v.* 11
break up (*to leave one another*) **se quitter** *v.* 11
breakfast **petit-déjeuner** *m.* 9
bridge **pont** *m.* 12
bright **brillant(e)** *adj.* 1
bring (*a person*) **amener** *v.* 5; (*a thing*) **apporter** *v.* 4
broom **balai** *m.* 8
brother **frère** *m.* 3
brother-in-law **beau-frère** *m.* 3
brown **marron** *adj., inv.* 3
brown (*hair*) **châtain** *adj.* 3
brush (hair/tooth) **brosse** *f.* **(à cheveux/à dents)** 10
to brush one's hair/teeth **se brosser les cheveux/les dents** *v.* 9
buckle: to buckle one's seatbelt **attacher sa ceinture de sécurité** *v.* 11
build **construire** *v.* 6
building **bâtiment** *m.* 12; **immeuble** *m.* 8
bumper **pare-chocs** *m.* 11
burn (CD/DVD) **graver** *v.* 11
bus **autobus** *m.* 7
bus stop **arrêt d'autobus (de bus)** *m.* 7
business (*profession*) **affaires** *f., pl.* 3; (*company*) **entreprise** *f.* 13
business administration **gestion** *f.* 2
businessman **homme d'affaires** *m.* 3
businesswoman **femme d'affaires** *f.* 3
busy **occupé(e)** *adj.* 1
but **mais** *conj.* 1
butcher's shop **boucherie** *f.* 9
butter **beurre** *m.* 4
buy **acheter** *v.* 5
by **par** *prep.* 3
Bye! **Salut!** *fam.* 1

C

cabinet **placard** *m.* 8
café **café** *m.* 1; **brasserie** *f.* 12
café terrace **terrasse** *f.* **de café** 4
cybercafé **cybercafé** *m.* 12
cafeteria **cantine** *f.* 9
cake **gâteau** *m.* 6
calculator **calculatrice** *f.* 1
call **appeler** *v.* 13
calm **calme** *adj.* 1; **calme** *m.* 1
camcorder **caméra vidéo** *f.* 11; **caméscope** *m.* 11
camera **appareil photo** *m.* 11
digital camera **appareil photo** *m.* **numérique** 11
camping **camping** *m.* 5

to go camping **faire du camping** *v.* 5
can (of food) **boîte (de conserve)** *f.* 9
Canada **Canada** *m.* 7
Canadian **canadien(ne)** *adj.* 1
cancel (a reservation) **annuler (une réservation)** *v.* 7
candidate **candidat(e)** *m., f.* 13
candy **bonbon** *m.* 6
cap: baseball cap **casquette** *f.* 6
capital **capitale** *f.* 7
car **voiture** *f.* 11
to ride in a car **rouler en voiture** *v.* 7
card *(letter)* **carte postale** *f.* 12;
credit card **carte** *f.* **de crédit** 12
to pay with a credit card **payer avec une carte de crédit** *v.* 12
cards *(playing)* **cartes** *f.* 5
carbonated drink/beverage **boisson** *f.* **gazeuse** 4
career **carrière** *f.* 13
carpooling **covoiturage** *m.* 14
carrot **carotte** *f.* 9
cartoon **dessin animé** *m.* 15
case: in any case **en tout cas** 6
cash **liquide** *m.* 12
to pay in cash **payer en liquide** *v.* 12
cat **chat** *m.* 3
catastrophe **catastrophe** *f.* 14
catch sight of **apercevoir** *v.* 12
CD(s) **CD** *m.* 11
CD/DVD player **lecteur de CD/DVD** *m.* 11
CD-ROM(s) **CD-ROM, cédérom(s)** *m.* 11
celebrate **célébrer** *v.* 5; **fêter** *v.* 6
celebration **fête** *f.* 6
cellar **cave** *f.* 8
cell(ular) phone **portable** *m.* 11
center: city/town center **centre-ville** *m.* 4
certain **certain(e)** *adj.* 9; **sûr(e)** *adj.* 15
It is certain that… **Il est certain que…** 15
It is uncertain that… **Il n'est pas certain que…** 15
chair **chaise** *f.* 1
champagne **champagne** *m.* 6
change *(coins)* **(pièces** *f. pl.* **de) monnaie** 12
channel (television) **chaîne** *f.* **(de télévision)** 11
character **personnage** *m.* 15
main character **personnage principal** *m.* 15
charming **charmant(e)** *adj.* 1
chat **bavarder** *v.* 4
check **chèque** *m.* 12; *(bill)* **addition** *f.* 4
to pay by check **payer par chèque** *v.* 12;
to check (the oil/the air pressure) **vérifier (l'huile/la pression des pneus)** *v.* 11
checking account **compte** *m.* **de chèques** 12
cheek **joue** *f.* 10
cheese **fromage** *m.* 4
chemistry **chimie** *f.* 2
chess **échecs** *m., pl.* 5
chest **poitrine** *f.* 10
chest of drawers **commode** *f.* 8
chic **chic** *adj.* 4
chicken **poulet** *m.* 9
child **enfant** *m., f.* 3
childhood **enfance** *f.* 6
China **Chine** *f.* 7
Chinese **chinois(e)** *adj.* 7
choir **chœur** *m.* 15
choose **choisir** *v.* 7
chorus **chœur** *m.* 15
chrysanthemums **chrysanthèmes** *m., pl.* 9
church **église** *f.* 4
city **ville** *f.* 4
city hall **mairie** *f.* 12
city/town center **centre-ville** *m.* 4
class *(group of students)* **classe** *f.* 1; *(course)* **cours** *m.* 2
classmate **camarade de classe** *m., f.* 1
classroom **salle** *f.* **de classe** 1
clean **nettoyer** *v.* 5; **propre** *adj.* 8
clear **clair(e)** *adj.* 15
It is clear that… **Il est clair que…** 15
to clear the table **débarrasser la table** 8
client **client(e)** *m., f.* 7
cliff **falaise** *f.* 14
clock **horloge** *f.* 1
alarm clock **réveil** *m.* 10
close (to) **près (de)** *prep.* 3
very close (to) **tout près (de)** 12
close **fermer** *v.* 11
closed **fermé(e)** *adj.* 12
closet **placard** *m.* 8
clothes dryer **sèche-linge** *m.* 8
clothing **vêtements** *m., pl.* 6
cloudy **nuageux/nuageuse** *adj.* 5
It is cloudy. **Le temps est nuageux.** 5
clutch **embrayage** *m.* 11
coast **côte** *f.* 14
coat **manteau** *m.* 6
coffee **café** *m.* 1
coffeemaker **cafetière** *f.* 8
coins **pièces** *f. pl.* **de monnaie** 12
cold **froid** *m.* 2
to be cold **avoir froid** *v.* 2
(weather) It is cold. **Il fait froid.** 5
cold **rhume** *m.* 10
color **couleur** *f.* 6
What color is… ? **De quelle couleur est… ?** 6
comb **peigne** *m.* 10
come **venir** *v.* 7
come back **revenir** *v.* 9
comedy **comédie** *f.* 15
comic strip **bande dessinée (B.D.)** *f.* 5
compact disc **compact disque** *m.* 11
company *(troop)* **troupe** *f.* 15
completely **tout à fait** *adv.* 6
composer **compositeur** *m.* 15
computer **ordinateur** *m.* 1
computer science **informatique** *f.* 2
concert **concert** *m.* 15
congratulations **félicitations** 15
consider **considérer** *v.* 5
constantly **constamment** *adv.* 8
construct **construire** *v.* 6
consultant **conseiller/conseillère** *m., f.* 13
continue *(doing something)* **continuer (à)** *v.* 12
cook **cuisiner** *v.* 9; **faire la cuisine** *v.* 5; **cuisinier/cuisinière** *m., f.* 13
cookie **biscuit** *m.* 6
cooking **cuisine** *f.* 5
cool: *(weather)* It is cool. **Il fait frais.** 5
corner **angle** *m.* 12; **coin** *m.* 12
cost **coûter** *v.* 4
cotton **coton** *m.* 6
couch **canapé** *m.* 8
cough **tousser** *v.* 10
count (on someone) **compter (sur quelqu'un)** *v.* 8
country **pays** *m.* 7
country(side) **campagne** *f.* 7
country-style **de campagne** *adj.* 4
couple **couple** *m.* 6
courage **courage** 13
courageous **courageux/courageuse** *adj.* 3
course **cours** *m.* 2
cousin **cousin(e)** *m., f.* 3
cover **couvrir** *v.* 11
covered **couvert (couvrir)** *p.p.* 11
cow **vache** *f.* 14
crazy **fou/folle** *adj.* 3
cream **crème** *f.* 9
credit card **carte** *f.* **de crédit** 12
to pay with a credit card **payer avec une carte de crédit** *v.* 12

crêpe **crêpe** *f.* 5
crime film **film policier** *m.* 15
croissant **croissant** *m.* 4
cross **traverser** *v.* 12
cruel **cruel/cruelle** *adj.* 3
cry **pleurer** *v.*
cup (of) **tasse (de)** *f.* 4
cupboard **placard** *m.* 8
curious **curieux/ curieuse** *adj.* 3
curly **frisé(e)** *adj.* 3
currency **monnaie** *f.* 12
curtain **rideau** *m.* 8
customs **douane** *f.* 7
cybercafé **cybercafé** *m.* 12

D

dance **danse** *f.* 15
  to dance **danser** *v.* 4
danger **danger** *m.* 14
dangerous **dangereux/ dangereuse** *adj.* 11
dark *(hair)* **brun(e)** *adj.* 3
darling **chéri(e)** *adj.* 2
darn **zut** 11
dash *(punctuation mark)* **tiret** *m.* 11
date *(day, month, year)* **date** *f.* 5; *(meeting)* **rendez-vous** *m.* 6
  to make a date **prendre (un) rendez-vous** *v.* 13
daughter **fille** *f.* 1
day **jour** *m.* 2; **journée** *f.* 2
  day after tomorrow **après-demain** *adv.* 2
  day before yesterday **avant-hier** *adv.* 7
  day off **congé** *m.*, **jour de congé** 7
dear **cher/chère** *adj.* 2
death **mort** *f.* 6
December **décembre** *m.* 5
decide *(to do something)* **décider (de)** *v.* 11
deforestation **déboisement** *m.* 14
degree **diplôme** *m.* 2
degrees *(temperature)* **degrés** *m., pl.* 5
  It is... degrees. **Il fait... degrés.** 5
delicatessen **charcuterie** *f.* 9
delicious **délicieux/délicieuse** *adj.* 4
Delighted. **Enchanté(e).** *p.p., adj.* 1
demand (that) **exiger (que)** *v.* 14
demanding **exigeant(e)** *adj.* 13
  demanding profession **profession** *f.* **exigeante** 13
dentist **dentiste** *m., f.* 3
department store **grand magasin** *m.* 4
departure **départ** *m.* 7
deposit: to deposit money **déposer de l'argent** *v.* 12
depressed **déprimé(e)** *adj.* 10
describe **décrire** *v.* 7
described **décrit (décrire)** *p.p., adj.* 7
desert **désert** *m.* 14
design (fashion) **stylisme (de mode)** *m.* 2
desire **envie** *f.* 2
desk **bureau** *m.* 1
dessert **dessert** *m.* 6
destroy **détruire** *v.* 6
destroyed **détruit (détruire)** *p.p., adj.* 6
detective film **film policier** *m.* 15
detest **détester** *v.* 2
  I hate... **Je déteste...** 2
develop **développer** *v.* 14
dial (a number) **composer (un numéro)** *v.* 11
dictionary **dictionnaire** *m.* 1
die **mourir** *v.* 7
died **mort (mourir)** *p.p., adj.* 7
diet **régime** *m.* 10
  to be on a diet **être au régime** 9
difference **différence** *f.* 1
different **différent(e)** *adj.* 1
differently **différemment** *adv.* 8
difficult **difficile** *adj.* 1
digital camera **appareil photo** *m.* **numérique** 11
dining room **salle à manger** *f.* 8
dinner **dîner** *m.* 9
  to have dinner **dîner** *v.* 2
diploma **diplôme** *m.* 2
directions **indications** *f.* 12
director *(movie)* **réalisateur/ réalisatrice** *m., f.*; *(play/show)* **metteur en scène** *m.* 15
dirty **sale** *adj.* 8
discover **découvrir** *v.* 11
discovered **découvert (découvrir)** *p.p.* 11
discreet **discret/discrète** *adj.* 3
discuss **discuter** *v.* 11
dish *(food)* **plat** *m.* 9
  to do the dishes **faire la vaisselle** *v.* 8
dishwasher **lave-vaisselle** *m.* 8
dismiss **renvoyer** *v.* 13
distinction **mention** *f.* 13
divorce **divorce** *m.* 6
  to divorce **divorcer** *v.* 3
divorced **divorcé(e)** *p.p., adj.* 3
do *(make)* **faire** *v.* 5
  to do odd jobs **bricoler** *v.* 5
doctor **médecin** *m.* 3
documentary **documentaire** *m.* 15
dog **chien** *m.* 3
done **fait (faire)** *p.p., adj.* 6
door *(building)* **porte** *f.* 1; *(automobile)* **portière** *f.* 11
doubt (that)... **douter (que)...** *v.* 15
doubtful **douteux/douteuse** *adj.* 15
  It is doubtful that... **Il est douteux que...** 15
download **télécharger** *v.* 11
downtown **centre-ville** *m.* 4
drag **barbant** *adj.* 3; **barbe** *f.* 3
drape **rideau** *m.* 8
draw **dessiner** *v.* 2
drawer **tiroir** *m.* 8
dreadful **épouvantable** *adj.* 5
dream (about) **rêver (de)** *v.* 11
dress **robe** *f.* 6
  to dress **s'habiller** *v.* 10
dresser **commode** *f.* 8
drink (carbonated) **boisson** *f.* **(gazeuse)** 4
  to drink **boire** *v.* 4
drive **conduire** *v.* 6
  to go for a drive **faire un tour en voiture** 5
driven **conduit (conduire)** *p.p.* 6
driver (taxi/truck) **chauffeur (de taxi/de camion)** *m.* 13
driver's license **permis** *m.* **de conduire** 11
drums **batterie** *f.* 15
drunk **bu (boire)** *p.p.* 6
dryer *(clothes)* **sèche-linge** *m.* 8
dry oneself **se sécher** *v.* 10
due **dû(e) (devoir)** *adj.* 9
during **pendant** *prep.* 7
dust **enlever/faire la poussière** *v.* 8

E

each **chaque** *adj.* 6
ear **oreille** *f.* 10
early **en avance** *adv.* 2; **tôt** *adv.* 2
earn **gagner** *v.* 13
Earth **Terre** *f.* 14
easily **facilement** *adv.* 8
east **est** *m.* 12
easy **facile** *adj.* 2
eat **manger** *v.* 2
  to eat lunch **déjeuner** *v.* 4
éclair **éclair** *m.* 4
ecological **écologique** *adj.* 14
ecology **écologie** *f.* 14
economics **économie** *f.* 2
ecotourism **écotourisme** *m.* 14
education **formation** *f.* 13
effect: in effect **en effet** 14
egg **œuf** *m.* 9

eight **huit** *m.* 1
eighteen **dix-huit** *m.* 1
eighth **huitième** *adj.* 7
eighty **quatre-vingts** *m.* 3
eighty-one **quatre-vingt-un** *m.* 3
elder **aîné(e)** *adj.* 3
electric **électrique** *adj.* 8
electrical appliance **appareil** *m.* **électrique** 8
electrician **électricien/électricienne** *m., f.* 13
elegant **élégant(e)** *adj.* 1
elevator **ascenseur** *m.* 7
eleven **onze** *m.* 1
eleventh **onzième** *adj.* 7
e-mail **e-mail** *m.* 11
emergency room **urgences** *f., pl.* 10
to go to the emergency room **aller aux urgences** *v.* 10
end **fin** *f.* 15
endangered **menacé(e)** *adj.* 14
endangered species **espèce** *f.* **menacée** 14
engaged **fiancé(e)** *adj.* 3
engine **moteur** *m.* 11
engineer **ingénieur** *m.* 3
England **Angleterre** *f.* 7
English **anglais(e)** *adj.* 1
enormous **énorme** *adj.* 2
enough (of) **assez (de)** *adv.* 4
not enough (of) **pas assez (de)** 4
enter **entrer** *v.* 7
envelope **enveloppe** *f.* 12
environment **environnement** *m.* 14
equal **égaler** *v.* 3
erase **effacer** *v.* 11
errand **course** *f.* 9
escargot **escargot** *m.* 9
especially **surtout** *adv.* 2
essay **dissertation** *f.* 11
essential **essentiel(le)** *adj.* 14
It is essential that… **Il est essentiel/indispensable que…** 14
even **même** *adv.* 5
evening **soir** *m.*; **soirée** *f.* 2
… (o'clock) in the evening **… heures du soir** 2
every day **tous les jours** *adv.* 8
everyone **tout le monde** *m.* 9
evident **évident(e)** *adj.* 15
It is evident that… **Il est évident que…** 15
evidently **évidemment** *adv.* 8
exactly **exactement** *adv.* 9
exam **examen** *m.* 1
Excuse me. **Excuse-moi.** *fam.* 1; **Excusez-moi.** *form.* 1
executive **cadre/femme cadre** *m., f.* 13
exercise **exercice** *m.* 10
to exercise **faire de l'exercice** *v.* 10
exhibit **exposition** *f.* 15
exit **sortie** *f.* 7
expenditure **dépense** *f.* 12
expensive **cher/chère** *adj.* 6
explain **expliquer** *v.* 2
explore **explorer** *v.* 4
extinction **extinction** *f.* 14
eye (eyes) **œil (yeux)** *m.* 10

F

face **visage** *m.* 10
facing **en face (de)** *prep.* 3
fact: in fact **en fait** 7
factory **usine** *f.* 14
fail **échouer** *v.* 2
fall **automne** *m.* 5
in the fall **à l'automne** 5
to fall **tomber** *v.* 7
to fall in love **tomber amoureux/amoureuse** *v.* 6
to fall asleep **s'endormir** *v.* 10
family **famille** *f.* 3
famous **célèbre** *adj.* 15; **connu (connaître)** *p.p., adj.* 8
far (from) **loin (de)** *prep.* 3
farewell **adieu** *m.* 14
farmer **agriculteur/agricultrice** *m., f.* 13
fashion **mode** *f.* 2
fashion design **stylisme de mode** *m.* 2
fast **rapide** *adj.* 3; **vite** *adv.* 8
fat **gros(se)** *adj.* 3
father **père** *m.* 3
father-in-law **beau-père** *m.* 3
favorite **favori/favorite** *adj.* 3; **préféré(e)** *adj.* 2
fax machine **fax** *m.* 11
fear **peur** *f.* 2
to fear that **avoir peur que** *v.* 14
February **février** *m.* 5
fed up: to be fed up **en avoir marre** *v.* 3
feel *(to sense)* **sentir** *v.* 5; *(state of being)* **se sentir** *v.* 10
to feel like *(doing something)* **avoir envie (de)** 2
to feel nauseated **avoir mal au cœur** 10
festival (festivals) **festival (festivals)** *m.* 15
fever **fièvre** *f.* 10
to have fever **avoir de la fièvre** *v.* 10
fiancé **fiancé(e)** *m., f.* 6
field *(terrain)* **champ** *m.* 14; *(of study)* **domaine** *m.* 13
fifteen **quinze** *m.* 1
fifth **cinquième** *adj.* 7
fifty **cinquante** *m.* 1
figure *(physique)* **ligne** *f.* 10
file **fichier** *m.* 11
fill: to fill out a form **remplir un formulaire** *v.* 12
to fill the tank **faire le plein** *v.* 11
film **film** *m.* 15
adventure/crime film **film** *m.* **d'aventures/policier** 15
finally **enfin** *adv.* 7; **finalement** *adv.* 7; **dernièrement** *adv.* 8
find (a job) **trouver (un/du travail)** *v.* 13
to find again **retrouver** *v.* 2
fine **amende** *f.* 11
fine arts **beaux-arts** *m., pl.* 15
finger **doigt** *m.* 10
finish *(doing something)* **finir (de)** *v.* 11
fire **incendie** *m.* 14
firefighter **pompier/femme pompier** *m., f.* 13
firm *(business)* **entreprise** *f.* 13;
first **d'abord** *adv.* 7; **premier/première** *adj.* 2; **premier** *m.* 5
It is October first. **C'est le 1er (premier) octobre.** 5
fish **poisson** *m.* 3
fishing **pêche** *f.* 5
to go fishing **aller à la pêche** *v.* 5
fish shop **poissonnerie** *f.* 9
five **cinq** *m.* 1
flat tire **pneu** *m.* **crevé** 11
flight *(air travel)* **vol** *m.* 7
floor **étage** *m.* 7
flower **fleur** *f.* 8
flu **grippe** *f.* 10
fluently **couramment** *adv.* 8
follow (a path/a street/a boulevard) **suivre (un chemin/une rue/un boulevard)** *v.* 12
food **aliment** *m.* 9; **nourriture** *f.* 9
foot **pied** *m.* 10
football **football américain** *m.* 5
for **pour** *prep.* 5; **pendant** *prep.* 9
For whom? **Pour qui?** 4
forbid **interdire** *v.* 14
foreign **étranger/étrangère** *adj.* 2
foreign languages **langues** *f., pl.* **étrangères** 2
forest **forêt** *f.* 14
tropical forest **forêt tropicale** *f.* 14
forget *(to do something)* **oublier (de)** *v.* 2
fork **fourchette** *f.* 9
form **formulaire** *m.* 12

former *(placed before noun)* **ancien(ne)** *adj.* 15
fortunately **heureusement** *adv.* 8
forty **quarante** *m.* 1
fountain **fontaine** *f.* 12
four **quatre** *m.* 1
fourteen **quatorze** *m.* 1
fourth **quatrième** *adj.* 7
France **France** *f.* 7
frankly **franchement** *adv.* 8
free *(at no cost)* **gratuit(e)** *adj.* 15
  free time **temps libre** *m.* 5
freezer **congélateur** *m.* 8
French **français(e)** *adj.* 1
French fries **frites** *f., pl.* 4
frequent *(to visit regularly)* **fréquenter** *v.* 4
fresh **frais/fraîche** *adj.* 5
Friday **vendredi** *m.* 2
friend **ami(e)** *m., f.* 1; **copain/copine** *m., f.* 1
friendship **amitié** *f.* 6
from **de/d'** *prep.* 1
  from time to time **de temps en temps** *adv.* 8
front: in front of **devant** *prep.* 3
fruit **fruit** *m.* 9
full *(no vacancies)* **complet (complète)** *adj.* 7
full-time job **emploi** *m.* **à plein temps** 13
fun **amusant(e)** *adj.* 1
  to have fun *(doing something)* **s'amuser (à)** *v.* 11
funeral **funérailles** *f., pl.* 9
funny **drôle** *adj.* 3
furious **furieux/furieuse** *adj.* 14
  to be furious that… **être furieux/furieuse que…** *v.* 14

G

gain: gain weight **grossir** *v.* 7
game *(amusement)* **jeu** *m.* 5; *(sports)* **match** *m.* 5
game show **jeu télévisé** *m.* 15
garage **garage** *m.* 8
garbage **ordures** *f., pl.* 14
garbage collection **ramassage** *m.* **des ordures** 14
garden **jardin** *m.* 8
garlic **ail** *m.* 9
gas **essence** *f.* 11
gas tank **réservoir d'essence** *m.* 11
gas warning light **voyant** *m.* **d'essence** 11
generally **en général** *adv.* 8
generous **généreux/généreuse** *adj.* 3
genre **genre** *m.* 15
gentle **doux/douce** *adj.* 3
geography **géographie** *f.* 2
German **allemand(e)** *adj.* 1
Germany **Allemagne** *f.* 7
get *(to obtain)* **obtenir** *v.* 13
get along well (with) **s'entendre bien (avec)** *v.* 10
get up **se lever** *v.* 10
  get up again **se relever** *v.* 10
gift **cadeau** *m.* 6
  wrapped gift **paquet cadeau** *m.* 6
gifted **doué(e)** *adj.* 15
girl **fille** *f.* 1
girlfriend **petite amie** *f.* 1
give *(to someone)* **donner (à)** *v.* 2
  to give a shot **faire une piqûre** *v.* 10
  to give a tour **faire visiter** *v.* 8
  to give back **rendre (à)** *v.* 6
  to give one another **se donner** *v.* 11
glass (of) **verre (de)** *m.* 4
glasses **lunettes** *f., pl.* 6
  sunglasses **lunettes de soleil** *f., pl.* 6
global warming **réchauffement** *m.* **de la Terre** 14
glove **gant** *m.* 6
go **aller** *v.* 4
  Let's go! **Allons-y!** 4; **On y va!** 10
  I'm going. **J'y vais.** 8
  to go back **repartir** *v.* 15
  to go down **descendre** *v.* 6
  to go out **sortir** *v.* 7
  to go over **dépasser** *v.* 11
  to go up **monter** *v.* 7
  to go with **aller avec** *v.* 6
golf **golf** *m.* 5
good **bon(ne)** *adj.* 3
  Good evening. **Bonsoir.** 1
  Good morning. **Bonjour.** 1
  to be good for nothing **ne servir à rien** *v.* 9
  to be in a good mood **être de bonne humeur** *v.* 8
  to be in good health **être en bonne santé** *v.* 10
  to be in good shape **être en pleine forme** *v.* 10
  to be up to something interesting **faire quelque chose de beau** *v.* 12
Good-bye. **Au revoir.** 1
government **gouvernement** *m.* 14
grade *(academics)* **note** *f.* 2
grandchildren **petits-enfants** *m., pl.* 3
granddaughter **petite-fille** *f.* 3
grandfather **grand-père** *m.* 3
grandmother **grand-mère** *f.* 3
grandparents **grands-parents** *m., pl.* 3
grandson **petit-fils** *m.* 3
grant **bourse** *f.* 2
grass **herbe** *f.* 14
gratin **gratin** *m.* 9
gray **gris(e)** *adj.* 6
great **formidable** *adj.* 7; **génial(e)** *adj.* 3
green **vert(e)** *adj.* 3
green beans **haricots verts** *m., pl.* 9
greenhouse **serre** *f.* 14
  greenhouse effect **effet de serre** *m.* 14
grocery store **épicerie** *f.* 4
groom: to groom oneself *(in the morning)* **faire sa toilette** *v.* 10
ground floor **rez-de-chaussée** *m.* 7
growing population **population** *f.* **croissante** 14
guaranteed **garanti(e)** *p.p., adj.* 5
guest **invité(e)** *m., f.* 6; **client(e)** *m., f.* 7
guitar **guitare** *f.* 15
guy **mec** *m.* 10
gym **gymnase** *m.* 4

H

habitat **habitat** *m.* 14
  habitat preservation **sauvetage des habitats** *m.* 14
had **eu (avoir)** *p.p.* 6
  had to **dû (devoir)** *p.p.* 9
hair **cheveux** *m., pl.* 9
  to brush one's hair **se brosser les cheveux** *v.* 9
  to do one's hair **se coiffer** *v.* 10
hairbrush **brosse** *f.* **à cheveux** 10
hairdresser **coiffeur/coiffeuse** *m., f.* 3
half **demie** *f.* 2
  half past … (o'clock) **… et demie** 2
half-brother **demi-frère** *m.* 3
half-sister **demi-sœur** *f.* 3
half-time job **emploi** *m.* **à mi-temps** 13
hallway **couloir** *m.* 8
ham **jambon** *m.* 4
hand **main** *f.* 5
handbag **sac à main** *m.* 6
handsome **beau** *adj.* 3
hang up **raccrocher** *v.* 13
happiness **bonheur** *m.* 6
happy **heureux/heureuse** *adj.*; **content(e)** 13
  to be happy that… **être content(e) que…** *v.* 14; **être heureux/heureuse que…** *v.* 14
hard drive **disque (dur)** *m.* 11

hard-working **travailleur/ travailleuse** *adj.* 3
hat **chapeau** *m.* 6
hate **détester** *v.* 2
I hate... **Je déteste...** 2
have **avoir** *v.* 2; **aie (avoir)** *imp., v.* 7; **ayez (avoir)** *imp. v.* 7; **prendre** *v.* 4
to have an ache **avoir mal** *v.* 10
to have to *(must)* **devoir** *v.* 9
he **il** *sub. pron.* 1
head *(body part)* **tête** *f.* 10; *(of a company)* **chef** *m.* **d'entreprise** 13
headache: to have a headache **avoir mal à la tête** *v.* 10
headlights **phares** *m., pl.* 11
health **santé** *f.* 10
to be in good health **être en bonne santé** *v.* 10
health insurance **assurance** *f.* **maladie** 13
healthy **sain(e)** *adj.* 10
hear **entendre** *v.* 6
heart **cœur** *m.* 10
heat **chaud** *m.* 2
hello *(on the phone)* **allô** 1; *(in the evening)* **Bonsoir.** 1; *(in the morning or afternoon)* **Bonjour.** 1
help **au secours** 11
to help *(to do something)* **aider (à)** *v.* 5
to help one another **s'aider** *v.* 11
her **la/l'** *d.o. pron.* 7; **lui** *i.o. pron.* 6; *(attached to an imperative)* **-lui** *i.o. pron.* 9
her **sa** *poss. adj., f., sing.* 3; **ses** *poss. adj., m., f., pl.* 3; **son** *poss. adj., m., sing.* 3
Here! **Tenez!** *form., imp. v.* 9; **Tiens!** *fam., imp., v.* 9
here **ici** *adv.* 1; *(used with demonstrative adjective* **ce** *and noun or with demonstrative pronoun* **celui***);* **-ci** 6;
Here is.... **Voici...** 1
heritage: I am of... heritage. **Je suis d'origine...** 1
herself *(used with reflexive verb)* **se/s'** *pron.* 10
hesitate *(to do something)* **hésiter (à)** *v.* 11
Hey! **Eh!** *interj.* 2
Hi! **Salut!** *fam.* 1
high **élevé(e)** *adj.* 13
high school **lycée** *m.* 1
high school student **lycéen(ne)** *m., f.* 2
higher education **études supérieures** *f., pl.* 2
highway **autoroute** *f.* 11
hike **randonnée** *f.* 5
to go for a hike **faire une randonnée** *v.* 5
him **lui** *i.o. pron.* 6; **le/l'** *d.o. pron.* 7; *(attached to imperative)* **-lui** *i.o. pron.* 9
himself *(used with reflexive verb)* **se/s'** *pron.* 10
hire **embaucher** *v.* 13
his **sa** *poss. adj., f., sing.* 3; **ses** *poss. adj., m., f., pl.* 3; **son** *poss. adj., m., sing.* 3
history **histoire** *f.* 2
hit **rentrer (dans)** *v.* 11
hold **tenir** *v.* 9
to be on hold **patienter** *v.* 13
hole in the ozone layer **trou dans la couche d'ozone** *m.* 14
holiday **jour férié** *m.* 6; **férié(e)** *adj.* 6
home *(house)* **maison** *f.* 4
at (someone's) home **chez...** *prep.* 4
home page **page d'accueil** *f.* 11
homework **devoir** *m.* 2
honest **honnête** *adj.* 15
honestly **franchement** *adv.* 8
hood **capot** *m.* 11
hope **espérer** *v.* 5
hors d'œuvre **hors-d'œuvre** *m.* 9
horse **cheval** *m.* 5
to go horseback riding **faire du cheval** *v.* 5
hospital **hôpital** *m.* 4
host **hôte/hôtesse** *m., f.* 6
hot **chaud** *m.* 2
It is hot (weather). **Il fait chaud.** 5
to be hot **avoir chaud** *v.* 2
hot chocolate **chocolat chaud** *m.* 4
hotel **hôtel** *m.* 7
(single) hotel room **chambre** *f.* **(individuelle)** 7
hotel keeper **hôtelier/ hôtelière** *m., f.* 7
hour **heure** *f.* 2
house **maison** *f.* 4
at (someone's) house **chez...** *prep.* 2
to leave the house **quitter la maison** *v.* 4
to stop by someone's house **passer chez quelqu'un** *v.* 4
household **ménager/ménagère** *adj.* 8
household appliance **appareil** *m.* **ménager** 8
household chore **tâche ménagère** *f.* 8
housewife **femme au foyer** *f.* 13
housework: to do the housework **faire le ménage** *v.* 8
housing **logement** *m.* 8
how **comme** *adv.* 2; **comment?** *interr. adv.* 4
How are you? **Comment allez-vous?** *form.* 1; **Comment vas-tu?** *fam.* 1
How many/How much (of)? **Combien (de)?** 1
How much is... ? **Combien coûte... ?** 4
huge **énorme** *adj.* 2
Huh? **Hein?** *interj.* 3
humanities **lettres** *f., pl.* 2
hundred: one hundred **cent** *m.* 5
five hundred **cinq cents** *m.* 5
one hundred one **cent un** *m.* 5
one hundred thousand **cent mille** *m.* 5
hundredth **centième** *adj.* 7
hunger **faim** *f.* 4
hungry: to be hungry **avoir faim** *v.* 4
hunt **chasse** *f.* 14
to hunt **chasser** *v.* 14
hurried **pressé(e)** *adj.* 9
hurry **se dépêcher** *v.* 10
hurt **faire mal** *v.* 10
to hurt oneself **se blesser** *v.* 10
husband **mari** *m.;* **époux** *m.* 3
hyphen *(punctuation mark)* **tiret** *m.* 11

I

I **je** *sub. pron.* 1; **moi** *disj. pron., sing.* 3
ice cream **glace** *f.* 6
ice cube **glaçon** *m.* 6
idea **idée** *f.* 3
if **si** *conj.* 13
ill: to become ill **tomber malade** *v.* 10
illness **maladie** *f.* 13
immediately **tout de suite** *adv.* 4
impatient **impatient(e)** *adj.* 1
important **important(e)** *adj.* 1
It is important that... **Il est important que...** 14
impossible **impossible** *adj.* 15
It is impossible that... **Il est impossible que...** 15
improve **améliorer** *v.* 13
in **dans** *prep.* 3; **en** *prep.* 3; **à** *prep.* 4
included **compris (comprendre)** *p.p., adj.* 6
incredible **incroyable** *adj.* 11
independent **indépendant(e)** *adj.* 1
independently **indépendamment** *adv.* 8

indicate **indiquer** *v.* 5
indispensable **indispensable** *adj.* 14
inexpensive **bon marché** *adj.* 6
injection **piqûre** *f.* 10
to give an injection **faire une piqûre** *v.* 10
injury **blessure** *f.* 10
instrument **instrument** *m.* 1
insurance (health/life) **assurance** *f.* **(maladie/vie)** 13
intellectual **intellectuel(le)** *adj.* 3
intelligent **intelligent(e)** *adj.* 1
interested: to be interested (in) **s'intéresser (à)** *v.* 10
interesting **intéressant(e)** *adj.* 1
intermission **entracte** *m.* 15
internship **stage** *m.* 13
intersection **carrefour** *m.* 12
interview: to have an interview **passer un entretien** 13
introduce **présenter** *v.* 1
I would like to introduce (*name*) to you. **Je te présente... ,** *fam.* 1
I would like to introduce (*name*) to you. **Je vous présente... ,** *form.* 1
invite **inviter** *v.* 4
Ireland **Irlande** *f.* 7
Irish **irlandais(e)** *adj.* 7
iron **fer à repasser** *m.* 8
to iron (the laundry) **repasser (le linge)** *v.* 8
isn't it? *(tag question)* **n'est-ce pas?** 2
island **île** *f.* 14
Italian **italien(ne)** *adj.* 1
Italy **Italie** *f.* 7
it: It depends. **Ça dépend.** 4
It is... **C'est...** 1
itself *(used with reflexive verb)* **se/s'** *pron.* 10

J

jacket **blouson** *m.* 6
jam **confiture** *f.* 9
January **janvier** *m.* 5
Japan **Japon** *m.* 7
Japanese **japonais(e)** *adj.* 1
jealous **jaloux/jalouse** *adj.* 3
jeans **jean** *m. sing.* 6
jewelry store **bijouterie** *f.* 12
jogging **jogging** *m.* 5
to go jogging **faire du jogging** *v.* 5
joke **blague** *f.* 2
journalist **journaliste** *m., f.* 3
juice (orange/apple) **jus** *m.* **(d'orange/de pomme)** 4
July **juillet** *m.* 5
June **juin** *m.* 5
jungle **jungle** *f.* 14
just *(barely)* **juste** *adv.* 3

K

keep **retenir** *v.* 9
key **clé** *f.* 7
keyboard **clavier** *m.* 11
kilo(gram) **kilo(gramme)** *m.* 9
kind **bon(ne)** *adj.* 3
kiosk **kiosque** *m.* 4
kiss one another **s'embrasser** *v.* 11
kitchen **cuisine** *f.* 8
knee **genou** *m.* 10
knife **couteau** *m.* 9
know *(as a fact)* **savoir** *v.* 8; *(to be familiar with)* **connaître** *v.* 8
to know one another **se connaître** *v.* 11
I don't know anything about it. **Je n'en sais rien.** 14
to know that... **savoir que...** 15
known *(as a fact)* **su (savoir)** *p.p.* 8; *(famous)* **connu (connaître)** *p.p., adj.* 8

L

laborer **ouvrier/ouvrière** *m., f.* 13
lake **lac** *m.* 14
lamp **lampe** *f.* 8
landlord **propriétaire** *m.* 3
landslide **glissement de terrain** *m.* 14
language **langue** *f.* 2
foreign languages **langues** *f., pl.* **étrangères** 2
last **dernier/dernière** *adj.* 2
lastly **dernièrement** *adv.* 8
late *(when something happens late)* **en retard** *adv.* 2; *(in the evening, etc.)* **tard** *adv.* 2
laugh **rire** *v.* 6
laughed **ri (rire)** *p.p.* 6
laundromat **laverie** *f.* 12
laundry: to do the laundry **faire la lessive** *v.* 8
law *(academic discipline)* **droit** *m.* 2; *(ordinance or rule)* **loi** *f.* 14
lawyer **avocat(e)** *m., f.* 3
lay off *(let go)* **renvoyer** *v.* 13
lazy **paresseux/paresseuse** *adj.* 3
learned **appris (apprendre)** *p.p.* 6
least **moins** 9
the least... *(used with adjective)* **le/la moins...** *super. adv.* 9
the least... , *(used with noun to express quantity)* **le moins de...** 14
the least... *(used with verb or adverb)* **le moins...** *super. adv.* 9
leather **cuir** *m.* 6
leave **partir** *v.* 5; **quitter** *v.* 4
to leave alone **laisser tranquille** *v.* 10
to leave one another **se quitter** *v.* 11
I'm leaving. **Je m'en vais.** 8
left: to the left (of) **à gauche (de)** *prep.* 3
leg **jambe** *f.* 10
leisure activity **loisir** *m.* 5
lemon soda **limonade** *f.* 4
lend *(to someone)* **prêter (à)** *v.* 6
less **moins** *adv.* 4
less of... *(used with noun to express quantity)* **moins de...** 4
less ... than *(used with noun to compare quantities)* **moins de... que** 14
less... than *(used with adjective to compare qualities)* **moins... que** 9
let **laisser** *v.* 11
to let go *(to fire or lay off)* **renvoyer** *v.* 13
Let's go! **Allons-y!** 4; **On y va!** 10
letter **lettre** *f.* 12
letter of application **lettre** *f.* **de motivation** 13
letter of recommendation/reference **lettre** *f.* **de recommandation** 13
lettuce **laitue** *f.* 9
level **niveau** *m.* 13
library **bibliothèque** *f.* 1
license: driver's license **permis** *m.* **de conduire** 11
life **vie** *f.* 6
life insurance **assurance** *f.* **vie** 13
light: warning light *(automobile)* **voyant** *m.* 11
oil/gas warning light **voyant** *m.* **d'huile/d'essence** 11
to light up **s'allumer** *v.* 11
like *(as)* **comme** *adv.* 6; to like **aimer** *v.* 2
I don't like ... very much. **Je n'aime pas tellement...** 2
I really like... **J'aime bien...** 2
to like one another **s'aimer bien** *v.* 11
to like that... **aimer que...** *v.* 14
line **queue** *f.* 12
to wait in line **faire la queue** *v.* 12

listen (to) **écouter** *v.* 2
literary **littéraire** *adj.* 15
literature **littérature** *f.* 1
little *(not much)* (of) **peu (de)** *adv.* 4
live (in) **habiter (à)** *v.* 2
living room *(informal room)* **salle de séjour** *f.* 8; *(formal room)* **salon** *m.* 8
located: to be located **se trouver** *v.* 10
long **long(ue)** *adj.* 3
a long time **longtemps** *adv.* 5
look *(at one another)* **se regarder** *v.* 11; *(at oneself)* **se regarder** *v.* 10
look for **chercher** *v.* 2
to look for work **chercher du/un travail** 12
loose *(clothing)* **large** *adj.* 6
lose: to lose (time) **perdre (son temps)** *v.* 6
to lose weight **maigrir** *v.* 7
lost: to be lost **être perdu(e)** *v.* 12
lot: a lot of **beaucoup de** *adv.* 4
love **amour** *m.* 6
to love **adorer** *v.* 2
I love... **J'adore...** 2
to love one another **s'aimer** *v.* 11
to be in love **être amoureux/amoureuse** *v.* 6
luck **chance** *f.* 2
to be lucky **avoir de la chance** *v.* 2
lunch **déjeuner** *m.* 9
to eat lunch **déjeuner** *v.* 4

M

ma'am **Madame.** *f.* 1
machine: answering machine **répondeur** *m.* 11
mad: to get mad **s'énerver** *v.* 10
made **fait (faire)** *p.p., adj.* 6
magazine **magazine** *m.* 15
mail **courrier** *m.* 12
mailbox **boîte** *f.* **aux lettres** 12
mailman **facteur** *m.* 12
main character **personnage principal** *m.* 15
main dish **plat (principal)** *m.* 9
maintain **maintenir** *v.* 9
make **faire** *v.* 5
makeup **maquillage** *m.* 10
to put on makeup **se maquiller** *v.* 10
make up **se réconcilier** *v.* 15
malfunction **panne** *f.* 11
man **homme** *m.* 1
manage *(in business)* **diriger** *v.* 13; *(to do something)* **arriver à** *v.* 2
manager **gérant(e)** *m., f.* 13
many (of) **beaucoup (de)** *adv.* 4
How many (of)? **Combien (de)?** 1
map *(of a city)* **plan** *m.* 7; *(of the world)* **carte** *f.* 1
March **mars** *m.* 5
marital status **état civil** *m.* 6
market **marché** *m.* 4
marriage **mariage** *m.* 6
married **marié(e)** *adj.* 3
married couple **mariés** *m., pl.* 6
marry **épouser** *v.* 3
Martinique: from Martinique **martiniquais(e)** *adj.* 1
masterpiece **chef-d'œuvre** *m.* 15
mathematics **mathématiques (maths)** *f., pl.* 2
May **mai** *m.* 5
maybe **peut-être** *adv.* 2
mayonnaise **mayonnaise** *f.* 9
mayor's office **mairie** *f.* 12
me **moi** *disj. pron., sing.* 3; *(attached to imperative)* **-moi** *pron.* 9; **me/m'** *i.o. pron.* 6; **me/m'** *d.o. pron.* 7
Me too. **Moi aussi.** 1
Me neither. **Moi non plus.** 2
meal **repas** *m.* 9
mean **méchant(e)** *adj.* 3
to mean (*with* **dire**) **vouloir** *v.* 9
means: that means **ça veut dire** *v.* 9
meat **viande** *f.* 9
mechanic **mécanicien/mécanicienne** *m., f.* 11
medication (against/for) **médicament (contre/pour)** *m., f.* 10
meet *(to encounter, to run into)* **rencontrer** *v.* 2; *(to make the acquaintance of)* **faire la connaissance de** *v.* 5, **se rencontrer** *v.* 11; *(planned encounter)* **se retrouver** *v.* 11
meeting **réunion** *f.* 13; **rendez-vous** *m.* 6
member **membre** *m.* 15
menu **menu** *m.* 9; **carte** *f.* 9
message **message** *m.* 13
to leave a message **laisser un message** *v.* 13
Mexican **mexicain(e)** *adj.* 1
Mexico **Mexique** *m.* 7
microwave oven **four à micro-ondes** *m.* 8
midnight **minuit** *m.* 2
milk **lait** *m.* 4
mineral water **eau** *f.* **minérale** 4
mirror **miroir** *m.* 8
Miss **Mademoiselle** *f.* 1
mistaken: to be mistaken *(about something)* **se tromper (de)** *v.* 10
modest **modeste** *adj.* 13
moment **moment** *m.* 1
Monday **lundi** *m.* 2
money **argent** *m.* 12; *(currency)* **monnaie** *f.* 12
to deposit money **déposer de l'argent** *v.* 12
monitor **moniteur** *m.* 11
month **mois** *m.* 2
this month **ce mois-ci** 2
moon **Lune** *f.* 14
more **plus** *adv.* 4
more of **plus de** 4
more ... than *(used with noun to compare quantities)* **plus de... que** 14
more ... than *(used with adjective to compare qualities)* **plus... que** 9
morning **matin** *m.* 2; **matinée** *f.* 2
this morning **ce matin** 2
Moroccan **marocain(e)** *adj.* 1
most **plus** 9
the most... *(used with adjective)* **le/la plus...** *super. adv.* 9
the most... *(used with noun to express quantity)* **le plus de...** 14
the most... *(used with verb or adverb)* **le plus...** *super. adv.* 9
mother **mère** *f.* 3
mother-in-law **belle-mère** *f.* 3
mountain **montagne** *f.* 4
mouse **souris** *f.* 11
mouth **bouche** *f.* 10
move *(to get around)* **se déplacer** *v.* 12
to move in **emménager** *v.* 8
to move out **déménager** *v.* 8
movie **film** *m.* 15
adventure/horror/science-fiction/crime movie **film** *m.* **d'aventures/d'horreur/de science-fiction/policier** 15
movie theater **cinéma (ciné)** *m.* 4
much (as much ... as) *(used with noun to express quantity)* **autant de ... que** *adv.* 14
How much (*of something*)? **Combien (de)?** 1
How much is... ? **Combien coûte... ?** 4
museum **musée** *m.* 4
to go to museums **faire les musées** *v.* 15
mushroom **champignon** *m.* 9
music: to play music **faire de la musique** 15
musical **comédie** *f.* **musicale** 15; **musical(e)** *adj.* 15

musician **musicien(ne)** *m., f.* 3
must *(to have to)* **devoir** *v.* 9
One must **Il faut...** 5
mustard **moutarde** *f.* 9
my **ma** *poss. adj., f., sing.* 3; **mes** *poss. adj., m., f., pl.* 3; **mon** *poss. adj., m., sing.* 3
myself **me/m'** *pron., sing.* 10; *(attached to an imperative)* **-moi** *pron.* 9

N

naïve **naïf (naïve)** *adj.* 3
name: My name is... **Je m'appelle...** 1
named: to be named **s'appeler** *v.* 10
napkin **serviette** *f.* 9
nationality **nationalité** *f.*
I am of ... nationality. **Je suis de nationalité...** 1
natural **naturel(le)** *adj.* 14
natural resource **ressource naturelle** *f.* 14
nature **nature** *f.* 14
nauseated: to feel nauseated **avoir mal au cœur** *v.* 10
near (to) **près (de)** *prep.* 3
very near (to) **tout près (de)** 12
necessary **nécessaire** *adj.* 14
It was necessary... *(followed by infinitive or subjunctive)* **Il a fallu...** 6
It is necessary.... *(followed by infinitive or subjunctive)* **Il faut que...** 5
It is necessary that... *(followed by subjunctive)* **Il est nécessaire que/qu'...** 14
neck **cou** *m.* 10
need **besoin** *m.* 2
to need **avoir besoin (de)** *v.* 2
neighbor **voisin(e)** *m., f.* 3
neighborhood **quartier** *m.* 8
neither... nor **ne... ni... ni...** *conj.* 12
nephew **neveu** *m.* 3
nervous **nerveux/nerveuse** *adj.* 3
nervously **nerveusement** *adv.* 8
never **jamais** *adv.* 5; **ne... jamais** *adv.* 12
new **nouveau/nouvelle** *adj.* 3
newlyweds **jeunes mariés** *m., pl.* 6
news **informations (infos)** *f., pl.* 15; **nouvelles** *f., pl.* 15
newspaper **journal** *m.* 7
newsstand **marchand de journaux** *m.* 12
next **ensuite** *adv.* 7; **prochain(e)** *adj.* 2
next to **à côté de** *prep.* 3
nice **gentil/gentille** *adj.* 3; **sympa(thique)** *adj.* 1
nicely **gentiment** *adv.* 8
niece **nièce** *f.* 3
night **nuit** *f.* 2
nightclub **boîte (de nuit)** *f.* 4
nine **neuf** *m.* 1
nine hundred **neuf cents** *m.* 5
nineteen **dix-neuf** *m.* 1
ninety **quatre-vingt-dix** *m.* 3
ninth **neuvième** *adj.* 7
no *(at beginning of statement to indicate disagreement)* **(mais) non** 2; **aucun(e)** *adj.* 10
no more **ne... plus** 12
no problem **pas de problème** 12
no reason **pour rien** 4
no, none **pas (de)** 12
nobody **ne... personne** 12
none (not any) **ne... aucun(e)** 12
noon **midi** *m.* 2
no one **personne** *pron.* 12
north **nord** *m.* 12
nose **nez** *m.* 10
not **nez ne... pas** 2
not at all **pas du tout** *adv.* 2
Not badly. **Pas mal.** 1
to not believe that **ne pas croire que** *v.* 15
to not think that **ne pas penser que** *v.* 15
not yet **pas encore** *adv.* 8
notebook **cahier** *m.* 1
notes **billets** *m., pl.* 11
nothing **rien** *indef. pron.* 12
It's nothing. **Il n'y a pas de quoi.** 1
notice **s'apercevoir** *v.* 12
novel **roman** *m.* 15
November **novembre** *m.* 5
now **maintenant** *adv.* 5
nuclear **nucléaire** *adj.* 14
nuclear energy **énergie nucléaire** *f.* 14
nuclear plant **centrale nucléaire** *f.* 14
nurse **infirmier/infirmière** *m., f.* 10

O

object **objet** *m.* 1
obtain **obtenir** *v.* 13
obvious **évident(e)** *adj.* 15
It is obvious that... **Il est évident que...** 15
obviously **évidemment** *adv.* 8
o'clock: It's... (o'clock). **Il est... heure(s).** 2
at ... (o'clock) **à ... heure(s)** 4
October **octobre** *m.* 5
of **de/d'** *prep.* 3
of medium height **de taille moyenne** *adj.* 3
of the **des (de + les)** 3
of the **du (de + le)** 3
of which, of whom **dont** *rel. pron.* 11
of course **bien sûr** *adv.;* **évidemment** *adv.* 2
of course not *(at beginning of statement to indicate disagreement)* **(mais) non** 2
offer **offrir** *v.* 11
offered **offert (offrir)** *p.p.* 11
office **bureau** *m.* 4
at the doctor's office **chez le médecin** *prep.* 2
often **souvent** *adv.* 5
oil **huile** *f.* 9
automobile oil **huile** *f.* 11
oil warning light **voyant** *m.* **d'huile** 11
olive oil **huile** *f.* **d'olive** 9
to check the oil **vérifier l'huile** *v.* 11
okay **d'accord** 2
old **vieux/vieille** *adj.; (placed after noun)* **ancien(ne)** *adj.* 3
old age **vieillesse** *f.* 6
olive **olive** *f.* 9
olive oil **huile** *f.* **d'olive** 9
omelette **omelette** *f.* 5
on **sur** *prep.* 3
On behalf of whom? **C'est de la part de qui?** 13
on the condition that... **à condition que** 15
on television **à la télé(vision)** 15
on the contrary **au contraire** 15
on the radio **à la radio** 15
on the subject of **au sujet de** 14
on vacation **en vacances** 7
once **une fois** *adv.* 8
one **un** *m.* 1
one **on** *sub. pron., sing.* 1
one another **l'un(e) à l'autre** 11
one another **l'un(e) l'autre** 11
one had to... **il fallait...** 8
One must... **Il faut que/qu'...** 14
One must... **Il faut...** *(followed by infinitive or subjunctive)* 5
one million **un million** *m.* 5
one million *(things)* **un million de...** 5
onion **oignon** *m.* 9

online **en ligne** 11
to be online **être en ligne** *v.* 11
to be online (with someone) **être connecté(e) (avec quelqu'un)** *v.* 7, 11
only **ne... que** 12; **seulement** *adv.* 8
open **ouvrir** *v.* 11; **ouvert(e)** *adj.* 11
opened **ouvert (ouvrir)** *p.p.* 11
opera **opéra** *m.* 15
optimistic **optimiste** *adj.* 1
or **ou** 3
orange **orange** *f.* 9; **orange** *inv. adj.* 6
orchestra **orchestre** *m.* 15
order **commander** *v.* 9
organize (a party) **organiser (une fête)** *v.* 6
orient oneself **s'orienter** *v.* 12
others **d'autres** 4
our **nos** *poss. adj., m., f., pl.* 3; **notre** *poss. adj., m., f., sing.* 3
outdoor *(open-air)* **plein air** 14
over **fini** *adj., p.p.* 7
overpopulation **surpopulation** *f.* 14
overseas **à l'étranger** *adv.* 7
over there **là-bas** *adv.* 1
owed **dû (devoir)** *p.p., adj.* 9
own **posséder** *v.* 5
owner **propriétaire** *m., f.* 3
ozone **ozone** *m.* 14
hole in the ozone layer **trou dans la couche d'ozone** *m.* 14

P

pack: to pack one's bags **faire les valises** 7
package **colis** *m.* 12
paid **payé (payer)** *p.p., adj.* 13
to be well/badly paid **être bien/mal payé(e)** 13
pain **douleur** *f.* 10
paint **faire de la peinture** *v.* 15
painter **peintre/femme peintre** *m., f.* 15
painting **peinture** *f.* 15; **tableau** *m.* 15
Palm Pilot **palm** *m.* 1
pants **pantalon** *m., sing.* 6
paper **papier** *m.* 1
Pardon (me). **Pardon.** 1
parents **parents** *m., pl.* 3
park **parc** *m.* 4
to park **se garer** *v.* 11
parka **anorak** *m.* 6
parking lot **parking** *m.* 11
part-time job **emploi** *m.* **à mi-temps/à temps partiel** *m.* 13
party **fête** *f.* 6
to party **faire la fête** *v.* 6
pass **dépasser** *v.* 11; **passer** *v.* 7
to pass an exam **être reçu(e) à un examen** *v.* 2
passenger **passager/passagère** *m., f.* 7
passport **passeport** *m.* 7
password **mot de passe** *m.* 11
past: in the past **autrefois** *adv.* 8
pasta **pâtes** *f., pl.* 9
pastime **passe-temps** *m.* 5
pastry shop **pâtisserie** *f.* 9
pâté **pâté (de campagne)** *m.* 9
path **sentier** *m.* 14; **chemin** *m.* 12
patient **patient(e)** *adj.* 1
patiently **patiemment** *adv.* 8
pay **payer** *v.* 5
to pay by check **payer par chèque** *v.* 12
to pay in cash **payer en liquide** *v.* 12
to pay with a credit card **payer avec une carte de crédit** *v.* 12
to pay attention (to) **faire attention (à)** *v.* 5
PDA **palm** *m.* 1
peach **pêche** *f.* 9
pear **poire** *f.* 9
peas **petits pois** *m., pl.* 9
pen **stylo** *m.* 1
pencil **crayon** *m.* 1
people **gens** *m., pl.* 7
pepper *(spice)* **poivre** *m.* 9; *(vegetable)* **poivron** *m.* 9
per day/week/month/year **par jour/semaine/mois/an** 5
perfect **parfait(e)** *adj.* 2
perhaps **peut-être** *adv.* 2
period *(punctuation mark)* **point** *m.* 11
permit **permis** *m.* 11
permitted **permis (permettre)** *p.p., adj.* 6
person **personne** *f.* 1
personal CD player **baladeur CD** *m.* 11
pessimistic **pessimiste** *adj.* 1
pharmacist **pharmacien(ne)** *m., f.* 10
pharmacy **pharmacie** *f.* 10
philosophy **philosophie** *f.* 2
phone booth **cabine téléphonique** *f.* 12
phone card **télécarte** *f.* 13
phone one another **se téléphoner** *v.* 11
photo(graph) **photo(graphie)** *f.* 3
physical education **éducation physique** *f.* 2
physics **physique** *f.* 2
piano **piano** *m.* 15
pick up **décrocher** *v.* 13
picnic **pique-nique** *m.* 14
picture **tableau** *m.* 1
pie **tarte** *f.* 9
piece (of) **morceau (de)** *m.* 4
piece of furniture **meuble** *m.* 8
pill **pilule** *f.* 10
pillow **oreiller** *m.* 8
pink **rose** *adj.* 6
pitcher (of water) **carafe (d'eau)** *f.* 9
place **endroit** *m.* 4; **lieu** *m.* 4
planet **planète** *f.* 14
plans: to make plans **faire des projets** *v.* 13
plant **plante** *f.* 14
plastic **plastique** *m.* 14
plastic wrapping **emballage en plastique** *m.* 14
plate **assiette** *f.* 9
play **pièce de théâtre** *f.* 15
play **s'amuser** *v.* 10; *(a sport/a musical instrument)* **jouer (à/de)** *v.* 5
to play sports **faire du sport** *v.* 5
to play a role **jouer un rôle** *v.* 15
player **joueur/joueuse** *m., f.* 5
playwright **dramaturge** *m.* 15
pleasant **agréable** *adj.* 1
please: to please someone **faire plaisir à quelqu'un** *v.* 13
Please. **S'il te plaît.** *fam.* 1
Please. **S'il vous plaît.** *form.* 1
Please. **Je vous en prie.** *form.* 1
Please hold. **Ne quittez pas.** 13
plumber **plombier** *m.* 13
poem **poème** *m.* 15
poet **poète/poétesse** *m., f.* 15
police **police** *f.* 11; **policier** *adj.* 15
police officer **agent de police** *m.* 11; **policier** *m.* 11; **policière** *f.* 11
police station **commissariat de police** *m.* 12
polite **poli(e)** *adj.* 1
politely **poliment** *adv.* 8
political science **sciences politiques (sciences po)** *f., pl.* 2
politician **homme/femme politique** *m., f.* 13
pollute **polluer** *v.* 14
pollution **pollution** *f.* 14
pollution cloud **nuage de pollution** *m.* 14
pool **piscine** *f.* 4

poor **pauvre** *adj.* 3
popular music **variétés** *f., pl.* 15
population **population** *f.* 14
growing population **population** *f.* **croissante** 14
pork **porc** *m.* 9
portrait **portrait** *m.* 5
position *(job)* **poste** *m.* 13
possess *(to own)* **posséder** *v.* 5
possible **possible** *adj.* 15
It is possible that… **Il est possible que…** 14
post **afficher** *v.* 13
post office **bureau de poste** *m.* 12
postal service **poste** *f.* 12
postcard **carte postale** *f.* 12
poster **affiche** *f.* 8
potato **pomme de terre** *f.* 9
practice **pratiquer** *v.* 5
prefer **aimer mieux** *v.* 2; **préférer (que)** *v.* 5
pregnant **enceinte** *adj.* 10
prepare (for) **préparer** *v.* 2
to prepare *(to do something)* **se préparer (à)** *v.* 10
prescription **ordonnance** *f.* 10
present **présenter** *v.* 15
preservation: habitat preservation **sauvetage des habitats** *m.* 14
preserve **préserver** *v.* 14
pressure **pression** *f.* 11
to check the tire pressure **vérifier la pression des pneus** *v.* 11
pretty **joli(e)** *adj.* 3; *(before an adjective or adverb)* **assez** *adv.* 8
prevent: to prevent a fire **prévenir l'incendie** *v.* 14
price **prix** *m.* 4
principal **principal(e)** *adj.* 12
print **imprimer** *v.* 11
printer **imprimante** *f.* 11
problem **problème** *m.* 1
produce **produire** *v.* 6
produced **produit (produire)** *p.p., adj.* 6
product **produit** *m.* 14
profession **métier** *m.* 13; **profession** *f.* 13
demanding profession **profession** *f.* **exigeante** 13
professional **professionnel(le)** *adj.* 13
professional experience **expérience professionnelle** *f.* 13
program **programme** *m.* 15; *(software)* **logiciel** *m.* 11; *(television)* **émission** *f.* **de télévision** 15
prohibit **interdire** *v.* 14
project **projet** *m.* 13
promise **promettre** *v.* 6
promised **promis (promettre)** *p.p., adj.* 6
promotion **promotion** *f.* 13
propose that… **proposer que…** *v.* 14
to propose a solution **proposer une solution** *v.* 14
protect **protéger** *v.* 5
protection **préservation** *f.* 14; **protection** *f.* 14
proud **fier/fière** *adj.* 3
psychological **psychologique** *adj.* 15
psychological drama **drame psychologique** *m.* 15
psychology **psychologie** *f.* 2
psychologist **psychologue** *m., f.* 13
publish **publier** *v.* 15
pure **pur(e)** *adj.* 14
purple **violet(te)** *adj.* 6
purse **sac à main** *m.* 6
put **mettre** *v.* 6
to put (on) (yourself) **se mettre** *v.* 10
to put away **ranger** *v.* 8
to put on makeup **se maquiller** *v.* 10
put **mis (mettre)** *p.p.* 6

Q

quarter **quart** *m.* 2
a quarter after … (o'clock) **… et quart** 2
Quebec: from Quebec **québécois(e)** *adj.* 1
question **question** *f.* 6
to ask *(someone)* a question **poser une question (à)** *v.* 6
quick **vite** *adv.* 4
quickly **vite** *adv.* 1
quite *(before an adjective or adverb)* **assez** *adv.* 8

R

rabbit **lapin** *m.* 14
rain **pleuvoir** *v.* 5
acid rain **pluie** *f.* **acide** 14
It is raining. **Il pleut.** 5
It was raining. **Il pleuvait.** 8
rain forest **forêt tropicale** *f.* 14
rain jacket **imperméable** *m.* 5
rained **plu (pleuvoir)** *p.p.* 6
raise (in salary) **augmentation (de salaire)** *f.* 13
rapidly **rapidement** *adv.* 8
rarely **rarement** *adv.* 5
rather **plutôt** *adv.* 1
ravishing **ravissant(e)** *adj.* 13
razor **rasoir** *m.* 10
read **lire** *v.* 7
read **lu (lire)** *p.p., adj.* 7
ready **prêt(e)** *adj.* 3
real *(true)* **vrai(e)** *adj.;* **véritable** *adj.* 3
real estate agent **agent immobilier** *m., f.* 13
realize **se rendre compte** *v.* 10
really **vraiment** *adv.* 5; *(before adjective or adverb)* **tout(e)** *adv.* 3; *(before adjective or adverb)* **très** *adv.* 8
really close by **tout près** 3
rear-view mirror **rétroviseur** *m.* 11
reason **raison** *f.* 2
receive **recevoir** *v.* 12
received **reçu (recevoir)** *p.p., adj.* 12
receiver **combiné** *m.* 13
recent **récent(e)** *adj.* 15
reception desk **réception** *f.* 7
recognize **reconnaître** *v.* 8
recognized **reconnu (reconnaître)** *p.p., adj.* 8
recommend that… **recommander que…** *v.* 14
recommendation **recommandation** *f.* 13
record **enregistrer** *v.* 11
(CD, DVD) **graver** *v.* 11
recycle **recycler** *v.* 14
recycling **recyclage** *m.* 14
red **rouge** *adj.* 6
redial **recomposer (un numéro)** *v.* 11
reduce **réduire** *v.* 6
reduced **réduit (réduire)** *p.p., adj.* 6
reference **référence** *f.* 13
reflect (on) **réfléchir (à)** *v.* 7
refrigerator **frigo** *m.* 8
refuse *(to do something)* **refuser (de)** *v.* 11
region **région** *f.* 14
regret that… **regretter que…** 14
relax **se détendre** *v.* 10
remember **se souvenir (de)** *v.* 10
remote control **télécommande** *f.* 11
rent **loyer** *m.* 8
to rent **louer** *v.* 8
repair **réparer** *v.* 11
repeat **répéter** *v.* 5
research **rechercher** *v.* 13
researcher **chercheur/chercheuse** *m., f.* 13
reservation **réservation** *f.* 7
to cancel a reservation **annuler une réservation** 7
reserve **réserver** *v.* 7
reserved **réservé(e)** *adj.* 1
residence **résidence** *f.* 8

resign **démissionner** *v.* 13
resort (ski) **station** *f.* **(de ski)** 7
respond **répondre (à)** *v.* 6
rest **se reposer** *v.* 10
restart **redémarrer** *v.* 11
restaurant **restaurant** *m.* 4
restroom(s) **toilettes** *f., pl.* 8; **W.-C.** *m., pl.*
result **résultat** *m.* 2
résumé **curriculum vitæ (C.V.)** *m.* 13
retake **repasser** *v.* 15
retire **prendre sa retraite** *v.* 6
retired person **retraité(e)** *m., f.* 13
retirement **retraite** *f.* 6
return **retourner** *v.* 7
  to return (home) **rentrer (à la maison)** *v.* 2
review (*criticism*) **critique** *f.* 15
rice **riz** *m.* 9
ride: to go horseback riding **faire du cheval** *v.* 5
  to ride in a car **rouler en voiture** *v.* 7
right **juste** *adv.* 3
  to the right (of) **à droite (de)** *prep.* 3
  to be right **avoir raison** 2
  right away **tout de suite** 7
  right next door **juste à côté** 3
ring **sonner** *v.* 11
river **fleuve** *m.* 14; **rivière** *f.* 14
riverboat **bateau-mouche** *m.* 7
role **rôle** *m.* 14
room **pièce** *f.* 8; **salle** *f.* 8
  bedroom **chambre** *f.* 7
  classroom **salle** *f.* **de classe** 1
  dining room **salle** *f.* **à manger** 8
  single hotel room **chambre** *f.* **individuelle** 7
roommate **camarade de chambre** *m., f.* 1
  (*in an apartment*) **colocataire** *m., f.* 1
round-trip **aller-retour** *adj.* 7
  round-trip ticket **billet** *m.* **aller-retour** 7
rug **tapis** *m.* 8
run **courir** *v.* 5; **couru (courir)** *p.p., adj.* 6
  to run into someone **tomber sur quelqu'un** *v.* 7

S

sad **triste** *adj.* 3
  to be sad that… **être triste que…** *v.* 14
safety **sécurité** *f.* 11
said **dit (dire)** *p.p., adj.* 7
salad **salade** *f.* 9
salary (a high, low) **salaire (élevé, modeste)** *m.* 13
sales **soldes** *f., pl.* 6
salon: beauty salon **salon** *m.* **de beauté** 12
salt **sel** *m.* 9
sandwich **sandwich** *m.* 4
sat (down) **assis (s'asseoir)** *p.p.* 10
Saturday **samedi** *m.* 2
sausage **saucisse** *f.* 9
save **sauvegarder** *v.* 11
  save the planet **sauver la planète** *v.* 14
savings **épargne** *f.* 12
savings account **compte d'épargne** *m.* 12
say **dire** *v.* 7
scarf **écharpe** *f.* 6
scholarship **bourse** *f.* 2
school **école** *f.* 2
science **sciences** *f., pl.* 2
  political science **sciences politiques (sciences po)** *f., pl.* 2
screen **écran** *m.* 11
screening **séance** *f.* 15
sculpture **sculpture** *f.* 15
sculptor **sculpteur/femme sculpteur** *m., f.* 15
sea **mer** *f.* 7
seafood **fruits de mer** *m., pl.* 9
search for **chercher** *v.* 2
  to search for work **chercher du travail** *v.* 12
season **saison** *f.* 5
seat **place** *f.* 15
seatbelt **ceinture de sécurité** *f.* 11
  to buckle one's seatbelt **attacher sa ceinture de sécurité** *v.* 11
seated **assis(e)** *p.p., adj.* 10
second **deuxième** *adj.* 7
security **sécurité** *f.* 11
see **voir** *v.* 15; (*catch sight of*) **apercevoir** *v.* 12
  to see again **revoir** *v.* 15
  See you later. **À plus tard.** 1
  See you later. **À tout à l'heure.** 1
  See you soon. **À bientôt.** 1
  See you tomorrow. **À demain.** 1
seen **aperçu (apercevoir)** *p.p.* 12; **vu (voir)** *p.p.* 15
  seen again **revu (revoir)** *p.p.* 15
self/-selves **même(s)** *pron.* 6
selfish **égoïste** *adj.* 1
sell **vendre** *v.* 6
seller **vendeur/vendeuse** *m., f.* 6
send **envoyer** *v.* 5
  to send (*to someone*) **envoyer (à)** *v.* 6
  to send a letter **poster une lettre** 12
Senegalese **sénégalais(e)** *adj.* 1
sense **sentir** *v.* 5
separated **séparé(e)** *adj.* 3
September **septembre** *m.* 5
serious **grave** *adj.* 10; **sérieux/sérieuse** *adj.* 3
serve **servir** *v.* 5
server **serveur/serveuse** *m., f.* 4
service station **station-service** *f.* 11
set the table **mettre la table** *v.* 8
seven **sept** *m.* 1
seven hundred **sept cents** *m.* 5
seventeen **dix-sept** *m.* 1
seventh **septième** *adj.* 7
seventy **soixante-dix** *m.* 3
several **plusieurs** *adj.* 4
shame **honte** *f.* 2
  It's a shame that… **Il est dommage que…** 14
shampoo **shampooing** *m.* 10
shape (*state of health*) **forme** *f.* 10
share **partager** *v.* 2
shave (oneself) **se raser** *v.* 10
shaving cream **crème à raser** *f.* 10
she **elle** *pron.* 1
sheet of paper **feuille de papier** *f.* 1
sheets **draps** *m., pl.* 8
shelf **étagère** *f.* 8
shh **chut** 15
shirt (short-/long-sleeved) **chemise (à manches courtes/longues)** *f.* 6
shoe **chaussure** *f.* 6
shopkeeper **commerçant(e)** *m., f.* 9
shopping **shopping** *m.* 7
  to go shopping **faire du shopping** *v.* 7
  to go (grocery) shopping **faire les courses** *v.* 9
shopping center **centre commercial** *m.* 4
short **court(e)** *adj.* 3; (*stature*) **petit(e)** 3
shorts **short** *m.* 6
shot (*injection*) **piqûre** *f.* 10
  to give a shot **faire une piqûre** *v.* 10
show **spectacle** *m.* 5; (*movie or theater*) **séance** *f.* 15
  to show (*to someone*) **montrer (à)** *v.* 6
shower **douche** *f.* 8
shut off **fermer** *v.* 11
shy **timide** *adj.* 1
sick: to get/be sick **tomber/être malade** *v.* 10
sign **signer** *v.* 12
silk **soie** 6

since **depuis** *adv.* 9
sincere **sincère** *adj.* 1
sing **chanter** *v.* 5
singer **chanteur/chanteuse** *m., f.* 1
single *(marital status)* **célibataire** *adj.* 3
single hotel room **chambre** *f.* **individuelle** 7
sink **évier** *m.* 8; *(bathroom)* **lavabo** *m.* 8
sir **Monsieur** *m.* 1
sister **sœur** *f.* 3
sister-in-law **belle-sœur** *f.* 3
sit down **s'asseoir** *v.* 10
sitting **assis(e)** *adj.* 10
six **six** *m.* 1
six hundred **six cents** *m.* 5
sixteen **seize** *m.* 1
sixth **sixième** *adj.* 7
sixty **soixante** *m.* 1
size **taille** *f.* 6
skate **patiner** *v.* 4
ski **skier** *v.* 5; **faire du ski** 5
skiing **ski** *m.* 5
ski jacket **anorak** *m.* 6
ski resort **station** *f.* **de ski** 7
skin **peau** *f.* 10
skirt **jupe** *f.* 6
sky **ciel** *m.* 14
sleep **sommeil** *m.* 2
to sleep **dormir** *v.* 5
to be sleepy **avoir sommeil** *v.* 2
sleeve **manche** *f.* 6
slice **tranche** *f.* 9
slipper **pantoufle** *f.* 10
slow **lent(e)** *adj.* 3
small **petit(e)** *adj.* 3
smell **sentir** *v.* 5
smile **sourire** *m.* 6
to smile **sourire** *v.* 6
smoke **fumer** *v.* 10
snack (afternoon) **goûter** *m.* 9
snake **serpent** *m.* 14
sneeze **éternuer** *v.* 10
snow **neiger** *v.* 5
It is snowing. **Il neige.** 5
It was snowing… **Il neigeait…** 8
so **si** 11; **alors** *adv.* 1
so that **pour que** 15
soap **savon** *m.* 10
soap opera **feuilleton** *m.* 15
soccer **foot(ball)** *m.* 5
sociable **sociable** *adj.* 1
sociology **sociologie** *f.* 1
sock **chaussette** *f.* 6
software **logiciel** *m.* 11
soil *(to make dirty)* **salir** *v.* 8
solar **solaire** *adj.* 14
solar energy **énergie solaire** *f.* 14
solution **solution** *f.* 14
some **de l'** *part. art., m., f., sing.* 4
some **de la** *part. art., f., sing.* 4
some **des** *part. art., m., f., pl.* 4
some **du** *part. art., m., sing.* 4
some **quelques** *adj.* 4
some (of it/them) **en** *pron.* 10
someone **quelqu'un** *pron.* 12
something **quelque chose** *m.* 4
Something's not right. **Quelque chose ne va pas.** 5
sometimes **parfois** *adv.* 5; **quelquefois** *adv.* 8
son **fils** *m.* 3
song **chanson** *f.* 15
sorry **désolé(e)** 11
to be sorry that… **être désolé(e) que…** *v.* 14
sort **sorte** *f.* 15
So-so. **Comme ci, comme ça.** 1
soup **soupe** *f.* 4
soupspoon **cuillère à soupe** *f.* 9
south **sud** *m.* 12
space **espace** *m.* 14
Spain **Espagne** *f.* 7
Spanish **espagnol(e)** *adj.* 1
speak (on the phone) **parler (au téléphone)** *v.* 2
to speak (to) **parler (à)** *v.* 6
to speak to one another **se parler** *v.* 11
specialist **spécialiste** *m., f.* 13
species **espèce** *f.* 14
endangered species **espèce** *f.* **menacée** 14
spectator **spectateur/spectatrice** *m., f.* 15
speed **vitesse** *f.* 11
speed limit **limitation de vitesse** *f.* 11
spend **dépenser** *v.* 4
to spend money **dépenser de l'argent** 4
to spend time **passer** *v.* 7
to spend time *(somewhere)* **faire un séjour** 7
spoon **cuillère** *f.* 9
sport(s) **sport** *m.* 5
to play sports **faire du sport** *v.* 5
sporty **sportif/sportive** *adj.* 3
sprain one's ankle **se fouler la cheville** 10
spring **printemps** *m.* 5
in the spring **au printemps** 5
square *(place)* **place** *f.* 4
squirrel **écureuil** *m.* 14
stadium **stade** *m.* 5
stage *(phase)* **étape** *f.* 6
stage fright **trac** 13
staircase **escalier** *m.* 8
stamp **timbre** *m.* 12
star **étoile** *f.* 14
starter **entrée** *f.* 9
start up **démarrer** *v.* 11
station **gare** *f.* 7; **station** *f.* 7
bus station **gare routière** *f.* 7
subway station **station** *f.* **de métro** 7
train station **gare** *f.* 7; **station** *f.* **de train** 7
stationery store **papeterie** *f.* 12
statue **statue** *f.* 12
stay **séjour** *m.* 7; **rester** *v.* 7
to stay slim **garder la ligne** *v.* 10
steak **steak** *m.* 9
steering wheel **volant** *m.* 11
stepbrother **demi-frère** *m.* 3
stepfather **beau-père** *m.* 3
stepmother **belle-mère** *f.* 3
stepsister **demi-sœur** *f.* 3
stereo system **chaîne stéréo** *f.* 11
still **encore** *adv.* 3
stomach **ventre** *m.* 10
to have a stomach ache **avoir mal au ventre** *v.* 10
stone **pierre** *f.* 14
stop (doing something) **arrêter (de faire quelque chose)** *v.*; *(to stop oneself)* **s'arrêter** *v.* 10
to stop by someone's house **passer chez quelqu'un** *v.* 4
bus stop **arrêt d'autobus (de bus)** *m.* 7
store **magasin** *m.*; **boutique** *f.* 12
grocery store **épicerie** *f.* 4
stormy **orageux/orageuse** *adj.* 5
It is stormy. **Le temps est orageux.** 5
story **histoire** *f.* 2
stove **cuisinière** *f.* 8
straight **raide** *adj.* 3
straight ahead **tout droit** *adv.* 12
strangle **étrangler** *v.* 13
strawberry **fraise** *f.* 9
street **rue** *f.* 11
to follow a street **suivre une rue** *v.* 12
strong **fort(e)** *adj.* 3
student **étudiant(e)** *m., f.* 1; **élève** *m., f.* 1
high school student **lycéen(ne)** *m., f.* 2
studies **études** *f.* 2
studio *(apartment)* **studio** *m.* 8
study **étudier** *v.* 2
suburbs **banlieue** *f.* 4
subway **métro** *m.* 7
subway station **station** *f.* **de métro** 7
succeed *(in doing something)* **réussir (à)** *v.* 7
success **réussite** *f.* 13

suddenly **soudain** *adv.* 8; **tout à coup** *adv.* 7.; **tout d'un coup** *adv.* 8
suffer **souffrir** *v.* 11
suffered **souffert (souffrir)** *p.p.* 11
sugar **sucre** *m.* 4
suggest (that) **suggérer (que)** *v.* 14
suit (*man's*) **costume** *m.* 6; (*woman's*) **tailleur** *m.* 6
suitcase **valise** *f.* 7
summer **été** *m.* 5
in the summer **en été** 5
sun **soleil** *m.* 5
It is sunny. **Il fait (du) soleil.** 5
Sunday **dimanche** *m.* 2
sunglasses **lunettes de soleil** *f., pl.* 6
supermarket **supermarché** *m.* 9
sure **sûr(e)** 9
It is sure that… **Il est sûr que…** 15
It is unsure that… **Il n'est pas sûr que…** 15
surf on the Internet **surfer sur Internet** 11
surprise (someone) **faire une surprise (à quelqu'un)** *v.* 6
surprised **surpris (surprendre)** *p.p., adj.* 6
to be surprised that… **être surpris(e) que…** *v.* 14
sweater **pull** *m.* 6
sweep **balayer** *v.* 8
swell **gonfler** *v.* 10
swim **nager** *v.* 4
swimsuit **maillot de bain** *m.* 6
Swiss **suisse** *adj.* 1
Switzerland **Suisse** *f.* 7
symptom **symptôme** *m.* 10

T

table **table** *f.* 1
to clear the table **débarrasser la table** *v.* 8
tablecloth **nappe** *f.* 9
take **prendre** *v.* 4
to take a shower **prendre une douche** 10
to take a train (plane, taxi, bus, boat) **prendre un train (un avion, un taxi, un autobus, un bateau)** *v.* 7
to take a walk **se promener** *v.* 10
to take advantage of **profiter de** *v.* 15
to take an exam **passer un examen** *v.* 2
to take care (of something) **s'occuper (de)** *v.* 10
to take out the trash **sortir la/les poubelle(s)** *v.* 8
to take time off **prendre un congé** *v.* 13
to take (*someone*) **emmener** *v.* 5
taken **pris (prendre)** *p.p., adj.* 6
tale **conte** *m.* 15
talented (*gifted*) **doué(e)** *adj.* 15
tan **bronzer** *v.* 6
tape recorder **magnétophone** *m.* 11
tart **tarte** *f.* 9
taste **goûter** *v.* 9
taxi **taxi** *m.* 7
tea **thé** *m.* 4
teach **enseigner** *v.* 2
to teach (*to do something*) **apprendre (à)** *v.* 4
teacher **professeur** *m.* 1
team **équipe** *f.* 5
teaspoon **cuillére à café** *f.* 9
tee shirt **tee-shirt** *m.* 6
teeth **dents** *f., pl.* 9
to brush one's teeth **se brosser les dents** *v.* 9
telephone (*receiver*) **appareil** *m.* 13
to telephone (*someone*) **téléphoner (à)** *v.* 2
It's Mr./Mrs./Miss … (on the phone.) **C'est M./Mme/Mlle … (à l'appareil.)** 13
television **télévision** *f.* 1
television channel **chaîne** *f.* **de télévision** 11
television program **émission** *f.* **de télévision** 15
television set **poste de télévision** *m.* 11
tell one another **se dire** *v.* 11
temperature **température** *f.* 5
ten **dix** *m.* 1
tennis **tennis** *m.* 5
tennis shoes **baskets** *f., pl.* 6
tenth **dixième** *adj.* 7
terrace (café) **terrasse** *f.* **de café** 4
test **examen** *m.* 1
than **que/qu'** *conj.* 9, 14
thank: Thank you (very much). **Merci (beaucoup).** 1
that **ce/c', ça** 1; **que** *rel. pron.* 11
Is that… ? **Est-ce… ?** 2
That's enough. **Ça suffit.** 5
That has nothing to do with us. That is none of our business. **Ça ne nous regarde pas.** 14
that is… **c'est…** 1
that is to say **ça veut dire** 10
theater **théâtre** *m.* 15
their **leur(s)** *poss. adj., m., f.* 3
them **les** *d.o. pron.* 7, **leur** *i.o. pron., m., f., pl.* 6
then **ensuite** *adv.* 7, **puis** *adv.* 7, **puis** 4; **alors** *adv.* 7
there **là** 1; **y** *pron.* 10
Is there… ? **Y a-t-il… ?** 2
over there **là-bas** *adv.* 1
(over) there (*used with demonstrative adjective* **ce** *and noun or with demonstrative pronoun* **celui**) **-là** 6
There is/There are… **Il y a…** 1
There is/There are.... **Voilà…** 1
There was… **Il y a eu…** 6; **Il y avait…** 8
therefore **donc** *conj.* 7
these/those **ces** *dem. adj., m., f., pl.* 6
these/those **celles** *pron., f., pl.* 14
these/those **ceux** *pron., m., pl.* 14
they **ils** *sub. pron., m.* 1; **elles** *sub.* and *disj. pron., f.* 1; **eux** *disj. pron., pl.* 3
thing **chose** *f.* 1, **truc** 7
think (about) **réfléchir (à)** *v.* 7
to think (that) **penser (que)** *v.* 2
third **troisième** *adj.* 7
thirst **soif** *f.* 4
to be thirsty **avoir soif** *v.* 4
thirteen **treize** *m.* 1
thirty **trente** *m.* 1
thirty-first **trente et unième** *adj.* 7
this/that **ce** *dem. adj., m., sing.* 6; **cet** *dem. adj., m., sing.* 6; **cette** *dem. adj., f., sing.* 6
this afternoon **cet après-midi** 2
this evening **ce soir** 2
this one/that one **celle** *pron., f., sing.* 14; **celui** *pron., m., sing.* 14
this week **cette semaine** 2
this weekend **ce week-end** 2
this year **cette année** 2
those are… **ce sont…** 1
thousand: one thousand **mille** *m.* 5
one hundred thousand **cent mille** *m.* 5
threat **danger** *m.* 14
three **trois** *m.* 1
three hundred **trois cents** *m.* 5
throat **gorge** *f.* 10
throw away **jeter** *v.* 14
Thursday **jeudi** *m.* 2
ticket **billet** *m.* 7
round-trip ticket **billet** *m.* **aller-retour** 7
bus/subway ticket **ticket de bus/de métro** *m.* 7
tie **cravate** *f.* 6

tight **serré(e)** *adj.* 6
time *(occurence)* **fois** *f.*; *(general sense)* **temps** *m., sing.* 5
a long time **longtemps** *adv.* 5
free time **temps libre** *m.* 5
from time to time **de temps en temps** *adv.* 8
to lose time **perdre son temps** *v.* 6
tinker **bricoler** *v.* 5
tip **pourboire** *m.* 4
to leave a tip **laisser un pourboire** *v.* 4
tire **pneu** *m.* 11
flat tire **pneu** *m.* **crevé** 11
(emergency) tire **roue (de secours)** *f.* 11
to check the tire pressure **vérifier la pression des pneus** *v.* 11
tired **fatigué(e)** *adj.* 3
tiresome **pénible** *adj.* 3
to **à** *prep.* 4; **au (à + le)** 4; **aux (à + les)** 4
toaster **grille-pain** *m.* 8
today **aujourd'hui** *adv.* 2
toe **orteil** *m.* 10; **doigt de pied** *m.* 10
together **ensemble** *adv.* 6
tomato **tomate** *f.* 9
tomorrow (morning, afternoon, evening) **demain (matin, après-midi, soir)** *adv.* 2
day after tomorrow **après-demain** *adv.* 2
too **aussi** *adv.* 1
too many/much (of) **trop (de)** 4
tooth **dent** *f.* 9
to brush one's teeth **se brosser les dents** *v.* 9
toothbrush **brosse** *f.* **à dents** 10
toothpaste **dentifrice** *m.* 10
tour **tour** *m.* 5
tourism **tourisme** *m.* 12
tourist office **office du tourisme** *m.* 12
towel (bath) **serviette (de bain)** *f.* 10
town **ville** *f.* 4
town hall **mairie** *f.* 12
toxic **toxique** *adj.* 14
toxic waste **déchets toxiques** *m., pl.* 14
traffic **circulation** *f.* 11
traffic light **feu de signalisation** *m.* 12
tragedy **tragédie** *f.* 15
train **train** *m.* 7
train station **gare** *f.* 7; **station** *f.* **de train** 7
training **formation** *f.* 13
translate **traduire** *v.* 6
translated **traduit (traduire)** *p.p., adj.* 6
trash **ordures** *f., pl.* 14
travel **voyager** *v.* 2
travel agency **agence de voyages** *f.* 7
travel agent **agent de voyages** *m.* 7
tree **arbre** *m.* 14
trip **voyage** *m.* 7
troop *(company)* **troupe** *f.* 15
tropical **tropical(e)** *adj.* 14
tropical forest **forêt tropicale** *f.* 14
true **vrai(e)** *adj.* 3; **véritable** *adj.* 6
It is true that… **Il est vrai que…** 15
It is untrue that… **Il n'est pas vrai que…** 15
trunk **coffre** *m.* 11
try **essayer** *v.* 5
Tuesday **mardi** *m.* 2
tuna **thon** *m.* 9
turn **tourner** *v.* 12
to turn off **éteindre** *v.* 11
to turn on **allumer** *v.* 11
to turn (oneself) around **se tourner** *v.* 10
twelve **douze** *m.* 1
twentieth **vingtième** *adj.* 7
twenty **vingt** *m.* 1
twenty-first **vingt et unième** *adj.* 7
twenty-second **vingt-deuxième** *adj.* 7
twice **deux fois** *adv.* 8
twist one's ankle **se fouler la cheville** *v.* 10
two **deux** *m.* 1
two hundred **deux cents** *m.* 5
two million **deux millions** *m.* 5
type **genre** *m.* 15

U

ugly **laid(e)** *adj.* 3
umbrella **parapluie** *m.* 5
uncle **oncle** *m.* 3
under **sous** *prep.* 3
understand **comprendre** *v.* 4
understood **compris (comprendre)** *p.p., adj.* 6
underwear **sous-vêtement** *m.* 6
undress **se déshabiller** *v.* 10
unemployed person **chômeur/chômeuse** *m., f.* 13
to be unemployed **être au chômage** *v.* 13
unemployment **chômage** *m.* 13
unfortunately **malheureusement** *adv.* 2
unhappy **malheureux/malheureuse** *adj.* 3
union **syndicat** *m.* 13
United States **États-Unis** *m., pl.* 7
university **faculté** *f.* 1; **université** *f.* 1
university cafeteria **restaurant universitaire (resto U)** *m.* 2
unless **à moins que** *conj.* 15
unpleasant **antipathique** *adj.* 3; **désagréable** *adj.* 1
until **jusqu'à** *prep.* 12; **jusqu'à ce que** *conj.* 15
upset: to become upset **s'énerver** *v.* 10
us **nous** *i.o. pron.* 6; **nous** *d.o. pron.* 7
use **employer** *v.* 5
to use a map **utiliser un plan** *v.* 7
useful **utile** *adj.* 2
useless **inutile** *adj.* 2; **nul(le)** *adj.* 2
usually **d'habitude** *adv.* 8

V

vacation **vacances** *f., pl.* 7
vacation day **jour de congé** *m.* 7
vacuum **aspirateur** *m.* 8
to vacuum **passer l'aspirateur** *v.* 8
valley **vallée** *f.* 14
vegetable **légume** *m.* 9
velvet **velours** 6
very *(before adjective)* **tout(e)** *adv.* 3; *(before adverb)* **très** *adv.* 8
Very well. **Très bien.** 1
veterinarian **vétérinaire** *m., f.* 13
videocassette recorder (VCR) **magnétoscope** *m.* 11
video game(s) **jeu vidéo (des jeux vidéo)** *m.* 11
videotape **vidéocassette** *f.* 11
Vietnamese **vietnamien(ne)** *adj.* 1
violet **violet(te)** *adj.* 6
violin **violon** *m.* 15
visit **visite** *f.* 6
to visit *(a place)* **visiter** *v.* 2; *(a person or people)* **rendre visite (à)** *v.* 6; *(to visit regularly)* **fréquenter** *v.* 4
voicemail **messagerie** *f.* 13
volcano **volcan** *m.* 14
volleyball **volley(-ball)** *m.* 5

W

waist **taille** *f.* 6
wait **attendre** *v.* 6
to wait *(on the phone)* **patienter**

v. 13
to wait in line **faire la queue** *v.* 12
wake up **se réveiller** *v.* 10
walk **promenade** *f.* 5; **marcher** *v.* 5
to go for a walk **faire une promenade** 5; **faire un tour** 5
wall **mur** *m.* 8
want **désirer** *v.* 5; **vouloir** *v.* 9
wardrobe **armoire** *f.* 8
warming: global warming **réchauffement de la Terre** *m.* 14
warning light (gas/oil) **voyant** *m.* **(d'essence/d'huile)** 11
wash **laver** *v.* 8
to wash oneself (one's hands) **se laver (les mains)** *v.* 10
to wash up (in the morning) **faire sa toilette** *v.* 10
washing machine **lave-linge** *m.* 8
waste **gaspillage** *m.* 14; **gaspiller** *v.* 14
wastebasket **corbeille (à papier)** *f.* 1
watch **montre** *f.* 1; **regarder** *v.* 2
water **eau** *f.* 4
mineral water **eau** *f.* **minérale** 4
way (*by the way*) **au fait** 3; (*path*) **chemin 12**
we **nous** *pron.* 1
weak **faible** *adj.* 3
wear **porter** *v.* 6
weather **temps** *m., sing.* 5; **météo** *f.* 15
The weather is bad. **Il fait mauvais.** 5
The weather is dreadful. **Il fait un temps épouvantable.** 5
The weather is good/warm. **Il fait bon.** 5
The weather is nice. **Il fait beau.** 5
web site **site Internet/web** *m.* 11
wedding **mariage** *m.* 6
Wednesday **mercredi** *m.* 2
weekend **week-end** *m.* 2
this weekend **ce week-end** *m.* 2
welcome **bienvenu(e)** *adj.* 1
You're welcome. **Il n'y a pas de quoi.** 1
well **bien** *adv.* 7
I am doing well/badly. **Je vais bien/mal.** 1
west **ouest** *m.* 12
What? **Comment?** *adv.* 4; **Pardon?** 4; **Quoi?** 1 *interr. pron.* 4
What day is it? **Quel jour sommes-nous?** 2
What is it? **Qu'est-ce que c'est?** *prep.* 1
What is the date? **Quelle est la date?** 5
What is the temperature? **Quelle température fait-il?** 5
What is the weather like? **Quel temps fait-il?** 5
What is your name? **Comment t'appelles-tu?** *fam.* 1
What is your name? **Comment vous appelez-vous?** *form.* 1
What is your nationality? **Quelle est ta nationalité?** *sing., fam.* 1
What is your nationality? **Quelle est votre nationalité?** *sing., pl., fam., form.* 1
What time do you have? **Quelle heure avez-vous?** *form.* 2
What time is it? **Quelle heure est-il?** 2
What time? **À quelle heure?** 2
What do you think about that? **Qu'en penses-tu?** 14
What's up? **Ça va?** 1
whatever it may be **quoi que ce soit** 13
What's wrong? **Qu'est-ce qu'il y a?** 1
when **quand** *adv.* 4
When is ...'s birthday? **C'est quand l'anniversaire de ...?** 5
When is your birthday? **C'est quand ton/votre anniversaire?** 5
where **où** *adv., rel. pron.* 4
which? **quel(le)(s)?** *adj.* 4
which one **à laquelle** *pron., f., sing.* 13
which one **auquel (à + lequel)** *pron., m., sing.* 13
which one **de laquelle** *pron., f., sing.* 13
which one **duquel (de + lequel)** *pron., m., sing.* 13
which one **laquelle** *pron., f., sing.* 13
which one **lequel** *pron., m., sing.* 13
which ones **auxquelles (à + lesquelles)** *pron., f., pl.* 13
which ones **auxquels (à + lesquels)** *pron., m., pl.* 13
which ones **desquelles (de + lesquelles)** *pron., f., pl.* 13
which ones **desquels (de + lesquels)** *pron., m., pl.* 13
which ones **lesquelles** *pron., f., pl.* 13
which ones **lesquels** *pron., m., pl.* 13
while **pendant que** *prep.* 7
white **blanc(he)** *adj.* 6
who? **qui?** *interr. pron.* 4; **qui** *rel. pron.* 11
Who is it? **Qui est-ce?** 1
Who's calling, please? **Qui est à l'appareil?** 13
whom? **qui?** *interr.* 4
For whom? **Pour qui?** 4
To whom? **À qui?** 4
why? **pourquoi?** *adv.* 2, 4
widowed **veuf/veuve** *adj.* 3
wife **femme** *f.* 1; **épouse** *f.* 3
willingly **volontiers** *adv.* 10
win **gagner** *v.* 5
wind **vent** *m.* 5
It is windy. **Il fait du vent.** 5
window **fenêtre** *f.* 1
windshield **pare-brise** *m.* 11
windshield wiper(s) **essuie-glace (essuie-glaces** *pl.***)** *m.* 11
windsurfing **planche à voile** *v.* 5
to go windsurfing **faire de la planche à voile** *v.* 5
wine **vin** *m.* 6
winter **hiver** *m.* 5
in the winter **en hiver** 5
wipe (the dishes/the table) **essuyer (la vaisselle/la table)** *v.* 8
wish that... **souhaiter que...** *v.* 14
with **avec** *prep.* 1
with whom? **avec qui?** 4
withdraw money **retirer de l'argent** *v.* 12
without **sans** *prep.* 8; **sans que** *conj.* 5
woman **femme** *f.* 1
wood **bois** *m.* 14
wool **laine** *f.* 6
work **travail** *m.* 12
to work **travailler** *v.* 2; **marcher** *v.* 11; **fonctionner** *v.* 11
work out **faire de la gym** *v.* 5
worker **ouvrier/ouvrière** *m., f.* 13
world **monde** *m.* 7
worried **inquiet/inquiète** *adj.* 3
worry **s'inquiéter** *v.* 10
worse **pire** *comp. adj.* 9; **plus mal** *comp. adv.* 9; **plus mauvais(e)** *comp. adj.* 9
worst: the worst **le plus mal** *super. adv.* 9; **le/la pire** *super. adj.* 9; **le/la plus mauvais(e)** *super. adj.* 9
wound **blessure** *f.* 10
wounded: to get wounded **se blesser** *v.* 10

write **écrire** *v.* 7
to write one another **s'écrire** *v.* 11
writer **écrivain/femme écrivain** *m., f.* 15
written **écrit (écrire)** *p.p., adj.* 7
wrong **tort** *m.* 2
to be wrong **avoir tort** *v.* 2

Y

yeah **ouais** 2
year **an** *m.* 2; **année** *f.* 2
yellow **jaune** *adj.* 6
yes **oui** 2; *(when making a contradiction)* **si** 2
yesterday (morning/afternoon evening) **hier (matin/après-midi/soir)** *adv.* 7
day before yesterday **avant-hier** *adv.* 7
yogurt **yaourt** *m.* 9
you **toi** *disj. pron., sing., fam.* 3; **tu** *sub. pron., sing., fam.* 1; **vous** *pron., sing., pl., fam., form.* 1
you neither **toi non plus** 2
You're welcome. **De rien.** 1
young **jeune** *adj.* 3
younger **cadet(te)** *adj.* 3
your **ta** *poss. adj., f., sing.* 3; **tes** *poss. adj., m., f., pl.* 3; **ton** *poss. adj., m., sing.* 3; **vos** *poss. adj., m., f., pl.* 3; **votre** *poss. adj., m., f., sing.* 3;
yourself **te/t'** *refl. pron., sing., fam.* 10; **toi** *refl. pron., sing., fam.* 10; **vous** *refl. pron., form.* 10
youth **jeunesse** *f.* 6
youth hostel **auberge de jeunesse** *f.* 7
Yum! **Miam!** *interj.* 5

Z

zero **zéro** *m.* 1

S

T

U

V

W

Y

Z

Text Credits

169 © Reprinted by permission of Nouveau Monde DDB and of Assessorat du Tourisme de la Vallée d'Aoste **241** © Reprinted by permission of Comité du tourisme des îles de Guadeloupe **373** © Reprinted by permission of BlackBerry® **392–393** © Reprinted by permission of Renée Lévy **407** © Reprinted by permission of Relais du Silence Silencehotel **445** © Reprinted by permission of BNP Paribas **459** © Reprinted by permission of Groupe Vedior France **500–501** © Excerpt from LE PETIT PRINCE by Antoine de Saint-Exupéry, copyright 1943 by Harcourt, Inc. and renewed 1971 by Consuelo de Saint-Exupéry, reprinted by permission of the publisher. **536–537** © Reprinted by permission of Mariama Ndoye Mbengue

Fine Art Credits

51 *Gbenonkpo* by Cyprien Tokoudagba. **66** *Joan of Arc Kissing the Sword of Deliverance* by Dante Gabriel Rossetti. **101** *Mother and Child* by Pierre-Auguste Renoir. **102** *Eldorado* Poster by Henri de Toulouse-Lautrec. **159** *Boulevard des Italiens in Paris, 1899* by Jean Béraud. **175** *Château d'Amboise* Poster by Constant Duval. **209** *Marcelle Lender Dancing the Bolero in "Chilperic"* by Henri de Toulouse-Lautrec. **211** Troubadour Plays Six Musical Instruments. **225** *Blue Dancers* by Edgar Degas. **267** *An Artist in His Studio* by Pascal-Adolphe-Jean Dagnan-Bouveret. **283** *Entry of Joan of Arc Into Orleans* by J.J. Scherrer. **354** *Zurich* Poster by Otto Baumberger. **355** *Portrait of Jean Jacques Rousseau* by Lacretelle. **375** *Amilcar* Poster by Paolo Garretto. **391** *The Son of Man* by René Magritte. **425** *After Lunch* by Berthe Morisot. **483** *An Acadian Landscape* by Georges de Feure. **533** *Pine in L'Estagne (Lanscape with Red Roof)* by Paul Cézanne. **535** *Tahitian Women on the Beach* by Paul Gauguin.

Illustration Credits

Sophie Casson: 2–3, 4, 16–17, 38–39, 40, 52–53, 74–75, 76, 88–89, 110–111, 124–125, 126, 146–147, 160–161, 182–183, 196–197, 198, 218–219, 220, 232–233, 254–255, 256, 268–269, 270, 290–291, 292, 304–305, 306, 326–327, 328, 340–341, 342, 362–363, 376–377, 378, 398–399, 412–413, 414, 434–435, 448–449, 470–471, 484–485, 506–507, 508, 520–521, 536–537.

Debra Spina Dixon: 472.

Hermann Mejía: 14, 18, 26, 46, 49, 50, 60, 83, 86, 87, 97, 98, 99, 100, 118, 132, 134, 136, 154, 157, 158, 169, 170, 172, 184, 190, 191, 192, 194, 206, 208, 226, 228, 242, 264, 265, 276, 298, 300, 301, 314, 334, 336, 348, 370, 372, 384, 406, 409, 492, 492, 494, 516, 531, 532.

Pere Virgili: 5, 8, 19, 41, 55, 77, 91, 113, 127, 149, 163, 178, 185, 199, 221, 230, 235, 244, 257, 266, 271, 293, 302, 307, 316, 329, 338, 343, 352, 365, 374, 379, 401, 410, 415, 424, 428–429, 437, 451, 460, 465, 473, 487, 509, 523.

Photography Credits

Alamy Images: cover (mmr) © Stockfolio, (br) © Jon Arnold Images. **9** (t) © Ian Dagnall. **28** (tml) © Bill Bachmann. **31** (tl) © Robert McGouey. **58** (r) © Directphoto.org. 67 (tl) © David Gregs. **68–69** Art Kowalsky. **102** (left panel, br) © Popperfoto. **138** (right panel, ml) © David Osborne, (right panel, mr) © Stockfolio. **139** (tl) © Pascal Quittemelle, (tr) © Jon Arnold Images, (bl) © Brian Harris. **175** (br) © Images-of-France. **202** © Frances Roberts. **211** (tl) © Foodfolio. **218** © Justin Kase. **260** (tr) © Michele Molinari. **268** © Directphoto.org. **275** (tl) © Ace Stock Limited. **318** (right panel, mr) © David Martyn Hughes. **354** (right panel, ml) © Andre Jenny. **355** (br) © Andre Jenny. **383** (m) © Glenn Harper. **390** (right panel, t) © Ray Roberts, (right panel, ml) © Chris McLennan, (right panel, mr) © Dallas & John Heaton. **391** © Danita Delimont. **395** © Robert Llewellyn. **411** © John Sylvester. **418** (bl) © Harald Theissen. **419** (t) © Justin Kase. **426** (mt) © Stephen Saks Photography. **427** (bl, br) © Rubens Abboud. **470** © David F. Frazier Photography, Inc.. **486** (r) © Jeremy Horner. **490** (l) © Vincent Lowe. **496** (right panel) © Nick Greaves. **513** (t) © Lebrecht Music & Arts 2. **514** (right panel, tr) © David Sanger, (right panel, mr) © Ray Roberts, (right panel, bl) © DanitaDelimont.com. **522** (l) © Jeff Morgan. **526** (l, tr) © DanitaDelimont.com. **532** (b) © Dallas & John Heaton. **534** (right panel, b) © David Sanger.

Martín Bernetti: 11 (tr, tml), **16, 25** (left panel, mmr), **27, 44** (tr), **54** (l), **68** (inset), **76, 82** (left panel, l), **84** (t, bml, br), **85** (t), **87** (tl), **89** (l), **90** (bl), **95** (b), **110, 112** (bl), **143, 148, 220, 234, 278** (mr, bl, br), **280** (right panel, t), **290, 291, 306, 315** (right panel, b), **349** (left panel), **436, 443** (tr), **461**.

Corbis: cover (tl) © Sandro Vannini, (ml) © Brian A. Vikander, (mml) © Paul A. Souders, (mr) © Paul Almasy. **4** (tr) © Jules Perrier. **24** (right panel, tl) © Rune Hellestad. **25** (left panel, tr) © Reuters/Shaun Best, (left panel, tl) © Frank Trapper, (left panel, bmr) © Reuters/Lucy Nicholson. **30** (left panel, t) © Hulton-Deutsch Collection, (left panel, tm) © Caroline Penn, (left panel, bm) © Jean-Pierre Amet/Bel Ombra, (left panel, b) © Eddy Lemaistre/For Pictures, (right panel, t) © Reuters/Carlos Barria, (right panel, b) © Eddy Lemaistre. **31** (tr) © Antoine Gyori, (bl) Owen Franken. **38** © Tom Stewart. **51** (t) © Eric Fougère, (b) © Christie's Images. **66** (left panel, t) © Christie's Images, (left panel, m) © Bettmann, (left panel, b) © Antoine Gyori, (right panel, ml) © Michael

S. Yamashita, (right panel, mr) © William Manning. **67** (tr) © Wolfgang Kaehler, (bl) © Stephane Cardinale. **81** (t) © Reuters/Pool, (m) © Pascal Le Segretain. **95** (tl) © Henri Tuillio, (tr) © Patrick Roncen, (mr) © Pascal Ito. **97** (br) © R. Holz. **101** (t) © Sunset Boulevard, (b) © The Barnes Foundation, Merion Station, Pennsylvania. **102** (left panel, t) © Hulton-Deutsch Collection, (left panel, bl) © Rufus F. Folkks, (right panel, t) © Macduff Everton, (right panel, ml) © Peter Harholdt, (right panel, b) © Robert Holmes. **103** (bl) © Keren Su. **117** (t) © Inge Yspeert, (m) © France Soir/PH.Cabaret. **122** (t) © Kelly-Mooney Photography, (b) © Jon Hicks. **131** © Gail Mooney. **138** (left panel, t) © Chris Hellier, (left panel, b) © Hulton-Deutsch Collection, (right panel, t) © Chris Lisle, (right panel, b) © Robert Estall. **152** (l) © Philippe Lauernson, (r) © Stephane Reix. **153** (t) © Victor Fraile, (m) © Reuters/Arko Datta. **159** (t) © Alain Keler. **162** © Dave Bartruff. **167** (m) © Reuters/Stefano Rellandini, (b) © Corbis TempSport. **174** (left panel, t) © Bettmann, (left panel, b) © Hulton-Deutsch Collection, (right panel, t) © Dean Conger, (right panel, ml) © Reuters/Daniel Joubert, (right panel, mr) © Yann Arthus-Bertrand, (right panel, b) © Charles & Josette Lenars. **175** (tl) © Swin Ink 2, LLC, (bl) © Reuters/ Daniel Joubert. **188** (l) © Eric Gaillard, (r) © Earl & Nazima Kowall. **189** (t) © Reuters/Mal Langsdon, (m) © Reuters/Mal Langsdon. **202** (l) © Philippe Wojazer. **203** (t) © Hulton-Deutsch Collection, (m) © Corbis Sugma/Pierre Vauthey, (b) © Corbis Sygma/Tierry Orban. **209** (t) © Bettmann, (b) © Francis G. Mayer. **210** (left panel, t, b) © Bettmann, (right panel, t) © Frederik Astier, (right panel, ml) © Yves Forestier, (right panel, mr) © Charles & Josette Lenars, (right panel, b) © Bettmann. **211** (tr) © Chris Bland; Eye Ubiquitous, (bl) © Owen Franken, (mr) © Historical Picture Archive. **224** (t) © Stephen Frink/zefa, (b) © Douglas Peebles. **225** (t) © Christine Osborne, (mr) © Archivo Iconografico, S.A.. **229** © Randy Faris. **238** (l) © Hubert Stadler. **239** (t) © Cees Van Leeuwen. **246** (left panel, t) © Patric Forestier (Special), (left panel, bl) © Bettmann, (left panel, br) © Stefano Bianchetti, (right panel, t) © Picimpact/John Norris, (right panel, ml) © Dave G. Houser, (right panel, mr) © Larry Dale Gordon/zefa, (right panel, b) © Tom Brakefield. **247** (tl) © Frederic Pitchal, (tr) © Reuters/John Schults, (br) © Bryn Colton/Assignments Photographers. **248–249** © L. Janicek/zefa. **261** (t) © Nik Wheeler. **267** (tr) © Christophe Russeil, (l) © Fine Art Photographic Library. **275** (mr) © Robert Holmes, (b) © Massimo Listri. **282** (left panel, t) © Bettmann, (left panel, b) © Stephane Cardinale, ((right panel, t) © Richard Klune, (right panel, ml) © Adam Woolfitt, (right panel, b) © Patrick Ward. **283** (tr) © Dianni Dagli Orti, (bl) © Thierry Tronnel, (br) © Annie Griffiths Belt. **284** © Jan Butchofsky-Houser. **284–285** (t) Adam Woolfitt. **285** (inset) © Adam Woolfitt. **287** © John Heseltine. **311** (tl) © Sergio Pitamitz. **317** (t) © Corbis SYGMA, (b) © Philadelphia Museum of Art. **318** (left panel, t, m) © Bettmann, (left panel, b) © Paris Claude, (right panel, t) © Chris Lisle, (right panel, ml) © Adam Woolfitt. **319** (br) © Corbis. **333** (tr) © Philippe Giraud. **346** (br) © Gilles Fonlupt. **347** (t) © Stefano Bianchetti. **353** © Steve Smith. **354** (left panel, t) © Bettmann, (left panel, b) © Pierre Vauthey, (right panel, t) © Swim Ink 2, LLC, (right panel, mr) © Peter Guttman, (right panel, b) © Carl & Ann Purcell. **355** (tr) © Archivo Iconografico. **356** (t) © Pete Saloutos. **357** © Jose Luis Pelaez. **369** t) © Alain Nogues, (b) © Philippe Eranian. **375** (t) © Stephane Cardinale, (b) © Swin Ink 2, LLC. **382** (l) © David Cooper/Toronto Star/ZUMA. **383** (t) © Bettmann, (b) © Matthias Kulka. **385** (l) © Bernard Annebicque. **388** © Philippe Eranian. **390** (left panel, t) © Corbis KIPA, (left panel, bl) © Robert Galbraith, (left panel, br) © Stephane Cardinale, **391** (tl) © E. Streichan/zefa, (bl) © Dave Bartruff, (br) © Christie's Images. **398** © Tatiana Markow. **405** (t) © Reuters/Matt Dunham. **419** (m) © Jean-Marc Charles, (b) © Ric Ergenbright. **421** (right panel, b) © Richard T. Norwitz. **425** (t) © Reuters/Jacky Naegelen, (b) © Kimbell Art Museum. **426** (left panel, t) © Sophie Bassouls, (left panel, ml) © Stephane Cardinale, (left panel, b) © Reuters/Jason Cohn, (right panel, t) © W. Perry Conway, (right panel, mb) © Yann Arthus-Bertrand, (right panel, b) © Richard T Nowitz. **427** (tl) © Reuters/Mike Blake. **441** (T) © Anna Clopet, (b) © Reuters/Philippe Wojazer. **454** (tr) © Owen Franken, (bl) © Peter Turnley. **462** (left panel) © Mike King, (right panel, t) © Patrick Ward, (right panel, ml) © Paul A. Souders, (right panel, mr) © Nik Wheeler, (right panel, b) © Frans Lemmens/zefa. **463** (tl) Nik Wheeler, (tr) © Sophie Bassouls, (bl) © Lawrence Manning, (br) © Jonny Le Fortune/zefa. **464** © Annebicque/Corbis Sygma. **472** (tl) © Stephane Ruet/Corbis Sygma, (bl) © Morton Beebe, (br) © Stephanie Maze. **476** (l) © Bernard Bisson, (tr) © Michael Busselle. **477** (t) © Yann Arthus-Bertrand, (m) © Bernard Bisson, (b) © Manfred Vollmer. **483** (tr) © Corbis KIPA, (bl) © Christie's Images. **485** © Paul A. Souders. **486** (l) © Stephanie Maze. **490** (r) © Philip Gould. **491** (t) © Gallo Images/Martin Harvey, (m) © Arne Hodalic, (b) © Christophe Russeil. **498** (left panel, t) © Reuters/Shaun Best, (left panel, b) © Reuters/Kai Pfaffenbach, (right panel, t) © Charles & Josette Lenars, (right panel, ml) © Albrecht G. Schaefer, (right panel, b) © Gallo Images/Martin Harvey. **499** (tl) © Sophie Bassouls, (tr) © Eric Fougere/ VIP Images, (bl) © David A. Northcott. **500** © Bettmann. **502** © Reuters/Daniel Joubert. **503** Kevin Flemming. **506** © Eric Robert. **512** (l) © Tom Stewart. **513** (b) © Jacques Morell. **514** (right panel, br) © Richard Klune. **519** © Swim Ink 2, LLC. **526** (br) © Kelly/ Mooney Photography. **527** (tl) © Robbie Jack, (m) © Rune Hellestad, (b) © Kin Cheung. **533** (t) © Collection Corbis KIPA, (b) © Archivo Iconografico. **534** (left panel, t) © Sophie Bassouls, (left panel, b) © Lori Conn, (right panel, t) © Dave Bartruff, (right panel, m) © Owen Franken. **535** (tl) © Bettmann, (tr) © Richard Bickel, (bl) © Louie Psihoyos, (br) © Philippe Giraud.

Getty Images: 24 (tr) © Ghislain & Marie David de Lossy. **30** © Lonely Planet Images/Ariadne Van Zandbergen. **359** © Ebby May.

Index Stock Imagery: iii © HIRB. **59** (b) © HIRB. **282** (right panel, mr) © Diaphor Agency. **299** (r) © ThinkStock LLC. **303** © David Burch. **333** (m) © Thomas Craig. **446** © Bill Lai. **472** HIRB. **482** (left panel, bl) © Hoa Qui. **496** (left panel, tr) © Jeff Greengerg, (bl) © Travel Ink Photo Library.

Rossy Llano: 4 (br), **18, 28** (bml), **29, 52, 58** (l), **83, 85** (br), **176** (b), **412, 430, 431.**

Library and Archives Canada: 428.

Lonely Planet Images: 427 © Richard Cummins. **498** (right panel, mr) © Leanne Logan.

Anne Loubet: 2, 8, 9 (b), **11** (br), **13** (right panel, bl, br), **22, 24** (left panel), **25** (left panel, bml), **28** (tl, bl, tr, tmr, bmr, br), **35, 45** (b), **61, 66** (right panel, t, b), **70, 74, 80, 81** (b), **84** (bmr), **87** (bl, br), **88, 89** (m, r), **90** (t, mml, mmr, br), **94, 100, 103** (br), **356** (b), **105, 106, 107, 112** (t), **116** (l), **126, 141, 142, 146 166, 167** (t), **179, 196, 205, 207, 214, 215, 232, 250, 260** (l), **261** (b), **269, 270, 274** (l), **279** (l), **280** (l, br), **286, 296** (r), **304, 310, 313** (mr), **315** (left panel, tl, br), **346** (t), **358, 362, 364, 376, 378, 382** (r), **394, 400** (tl, tr, bm, br), **422** (ml), **238** (tr), **443** (br), **449, 450, 455** (t), **459, 466, 467, 520.**

Pascal Pernix: iii, 13 (left panel), **34, 44** (l), **45** (t), **59** (t), **69** (inset), **71** (t), **102** (right panel, mr), **116** (t), **124, 125, 130, 131** (t, m), **182, 247** (bl), **250, 274** (r), **296** (l), **332, 355** (tl), **368** (r), **400** (tm, bl), **404** (r), **405** (b), **418** (br), **422** (mr), **440, 514** (left panel, b), **522** (r), **532** (t), **539.**

Photononstop: 390 (b) © A.J. Cassaigne.

23: (t) exerpt from: *Superdupont – Tome* 1 © LOB/Gotlib/Alexis/Fluide Glacial.
31: (br) published with the kind authorization of the *Service de communication pour la Francophonie-Conception et création Cyclope Interactive Production – mars 2005.*
175: (tr) © Reprinted by permission of *Le Printemps de Bourges* © graphisme: Lola Duval/photo: Dietmar Busse (Courtesy of Clamp Art, New York City).
279: (l) photo location: Sofitel Vieux Port-Marseille.
499: *FESPACO 2005* Poster; Design: Nur Eldine.

Video Credits

Production Company: Klic Video Productions, Inc.
Lead Photographer: Pascal Pernix
Photographer, Assistant Director: Barbara Ryan Malcolm
Photography Assistant: Pierre Halart

Le zapping Credits

15 Moulinex La triplette © Cinémathèque JM Boursicot
65 Clairefontaine © Cinémathèque JM Boursicot
123 Baguépi © Cinémathèque JM Boursicot
173 La météo © France Télévision
231 Air Afrique © Cinémathèque JM Boursicot
281 Monsieur Propre © Cinémathèque JM Boursicot
339 Diadermine © Cinémathèque JM Boursicot
389 Renault © Cinémathèque JM Boursicot
447 DHL © Cinémathèque JM Boursicot
497 Le Végétarium © Cinémathèque JM Boursicot

About the Authors

Cherie Mitschke received her Ph.D. in Foreign Language Education with specializations in French and English as a Second Language from the University of Texas at Austin in 1996. She has taught French at Southwest Texas State University, Austin Community College, and, since 2001, she is Assistant Professor of French at Southwestern University in Georgetown, Texas. Dr. Mitschke is also an experienced writer and editor of French educational materials who has worked with several major educational publishing houses.

Cheryl Tano received her M.A. in Spanish and French from Boston College and has also completed all course work toward a Ph.D. in Applied Linguistics with a concentration in Second Language Acquisition at Boston University. She is currently teaching French at Emmanuel College and Spanish at Tufts University.

Valérie Thiers-Thiam received her Ph.D. from New York University. She also holds a **Maîtrise** in Applied Languages & Communication from **Université Blaise Pascal**, Clermont-Ferrand, France. She has taught French at the University of Iowa, New York University, and Oklahoma University. Since 2003, she is Assistant Professor of French at Borough of Manhattan Community College in New York City.

About the Illustrators

A French Canadian living in the province of Quebec, **Sophie Casson** has been a professional illustrator for the past ten years. Her illustrations have appeared in local and national magazines throughout Canada, as well as in children's books.

Born in Caracas, Venezuela, **Hermann Mejía** studied illustration at the **Instituto de Diseño de Caracas**. Hermann currently lives and works in the United States.

Pere Virgili lives and works in Barcelona, Spain. His illustrations have appeared in textbooks, newspapers, and magazines throughout Spain and Europe.